D1130543

A Compendious Dictionary of the English Language

Noah Webster

A facsimile of the first (1806) edition

A Compendious Dictionary of the English Language

A facsimile of the first (1806) edition

Noah Webster

with an Introduction by PHILIP B. GOVE
Editor in Chief

Webster's Third New International Dictionary

Bounty Books A DIVISION OF CROWN PUBLISHERS, INC.

© 1970 by Crown Publishers, Inc.
Library of Congress Catalog Card Number: 70-122578
Printed in the United States of America
Published simultaneously in Canada by General Publishing Company Limited

INTRODUCTION

In Noah Webster's words, "every man of common reading knows that a living language must necessarily suffer gradual changes in its current words, in the significations of many words, and in pronunciation" (p. vi). If this is true, and it is except for what the word *suffer* implies, then why would anyone today be interested in a book of definitions brought together more than a century and a half ago? There are several answers.

To the browser this facsimile reproduction (enlarged for easier reading) of *A Compendious Dictionary of the English Language* should be a delight. According to Noah Webster, *corps* is an ill word, *difficultly* a harsh word, and *bamboozle* a low word. A *mizzy* is a bog or quagmire, and a *staffish* person is a harsh or firm one. Other obsolete words, so labeled, are *extradictionary* "real," *accend* "to start a fire," *minish* "to make less," and *ingeny* "wit." A milliner is "one who makes women's caps," horsemeat is "meat for horses," and nepotism refers to "fondness or affection for nephews." Here one can read that the word *tongue* is "more correctly *tung*" and the word *leather* "more correctly *lether*." Other curious spellings are *doctrin, insted,* and *porpess.* On every page occurs the old-fashioned long *s*. (The letter *f* has a brief horizontal crossline at the base of the ascender; the long *s* only a tick to the left at the same place.) One who is not used to it may be led to believe momentarily that a quiver is a café for arrows instead of a case. But these are merely oddities.

Thousands upon thousands of the definitions in this *Compendious* could be used unchanged in a modern dictionary limited to a vocabulary of the same size. A column-by-column comparison between it and, for example, *Webster's New Ideal Dictionary*, recently edited for much the same body of users, will confirm the soundness of Noah Webster's definitions. He has long been known as "a born definer."

A *Compendious Dictionary of the English Language* was not, however, an inflated spelling book for schoolchildren. It was a serious work for adults, a contribution to the development of lexicography. It was not only a book for the merchant, the student, and the traveler, as stated on the title page, but "a convenient portable work for gentlemen [which then included lawyers, statesmen, and physicians], and for the higher seminaries of learning" (p. xxiv), *seminary* being at the time a generic word for a college or school more often for young men than for young women. To Webster the word *compendious* meant "concise." His vocabulary of 37,000 words was intended to surpass in size and in correctness of definition those dictionaries available in London. (Two earlier American dictionaries were slight and relatively unimportant.) He added such technical-scientific terms as *vaccination, platina* (early name of platinum), *aeriform* and *electrometer;* such Americanisms as *skunk, tomahawk, snowshoe,* and *selectman;* such legal-political terms as *docket, political, presidency, constitutionality,* and *congressional* (an inclusion condemned by Webster's critics, along with *applicant, advocate, lengthy,* and *departmental*); such commercial terms as *dutiable, cent, dime,* and *dollar* (these last three also Americanisms).

The idea of making a dictionary had been in the back of Webster's mind for over two decades when he settled down at the beginning of the nineteenth century to produce his *Compendious.* He was then in his forties and had been pedagogically interested in American English from his early days as a schoolteacher. He had already written a spelling book that was to become an all-time best seller—over seventy million copies—and a grammar. The fact that he had already determined upon a two-volume lifework dictionary—although he probably did not guess then that it was twenty-two more years away—made the *Compendious* a better concise dictionary than it might have been as an end in itself. From this situation stems the historical importance of the preface, for much of the matter discussed there applies more to the big dictionary than the little one. In fact the whole preface leads up to Webster's announcement of a plan for a dictionary "which shall exhibit a far more correct state of the language than any work of this kind" (p. xxiii). He promised to "prosecute the work with diligence, and execute it with a fidelity suited to its importance." He kept his promise faithfully. The two-volume folio *American Dictionary of the English Language* appeared in 1828. Its importance rests "not merely in itself," as Robert K. Leavitt writes in *Noah's Ark, New England Yankees, and the Endless Quest* (1947, p. 23), a short history of the original Webster dictionaries, with particular reference to their first hundred years as publications of G. & C. Merriam Company. The *American Dictionary* is important, Leavitt goes on, "as the direct ancestor of that series of great revisions begun by Webster himself in his *Corrected and Enlarged* edition of 1841, carried on after his death by a succession of direct literary heirs of the great lexicographer and continued without a break of editorial succession through the famous unabridged editions to today's" Merriam-Webster *Third New International Dictionary*.

> Philip B. Gove
> Editor in Chief
> *Webster's Third New International Dictionary*

CHRONOLOGY

A *chronology of major dictionaries*
edited by Noah Webster and Merriam-Webster

A COMPENDIOUS DICTIONARY OF THE ENGLISH LANGUAGE	*1806*
AN AMERICAN DICTIONARY OF THE ENGLISH LANGUAGE	*1828*
AN AMERICAN DICTIONARY OF THE ENGLISH LANGUAGE *Second Edition*	*1840*
AN AMERICAN DICTIONARY OF THE ENGLISH LANGUAGE *New Revised Edition*	*1847**
AN AMERICAN DICTIONARY OF THE ENGLISH LANGUAGE *Royal Quarto Edition, Unabridged*	*1864*
WEBSTER'S INTERNATIONAL DICTIONARY	*1890*
WEBSTER'S NEW INTERNATIONAL DICTIONARY	*1909*
WEBSTER'S NEW INTERNATIONAL DICTIONARY *Second Edition*	*1934*
WEBSTER'S THIRD NEW INTERNATIONAL DICTIONARY	*1961*

*Following Noah Webster's death in 1841, George and Charles Merriam obtained exclusive publishing rights to Webster's American Dictionary copyrighted in 1840, which was Webster's last and most comprehensive work, together with exclusive rights to publish revisions and abridgments. They published the first Merriam-Webster dictionary in 1847.

A Compendious Dictionary
of the English Language

Noah Webster

A facsimile of the first (1806) edition

A

Compendious Dictionary

OF THE

English Language.

In which FIVE THOUSAND Words are added
to the number found in the BEST ENGLISH COMPENDS ;

The ORTHOGRAPHY is, in some instances, corrected ;

The PRONUNCIATION marked by an Accent or other suitable Direction ;

And the DEFINITIONS of many Words amended and improved.

TO WHICH ARE ADDED FOR THE BENEFIT OF THE

MERCHANT, the STUDENT and the TRAVELLER,

I.——TABLES of the MONEYS of most of the commercial Nations in the world, with the value expressed in Sterling and Cents.

II.——TABLES of WEIGHTS and MEASURES, ancient and modern, with the proportion between the several weights used in the principal cities of Europe.

III.——The DIVISIONS of TIME among the Jews, Greeks and Romans, with a Table exhibiting the Roman manner of dating.

IV.——An official List of the POST-OFFICES in the UNITED STATES, with the States and Counties in which they are respectively situated and the distance of each from the seat of Government.

V.——The NUMBER of INHABITANTS in the United States, with the amount of EXPORTS.

IV.——New and interesting CHRONOLOGICAL TABLES of remarkable Events and Discoveries.

By NOAH WEBSTER, Esq.

From Sidney's Press,
FOR HUDSON & GOODWIN, BOOK-SELLERS, HARTFORD, AND INCREASE COOKE & CO.

BOOK-SELLERS, NEW-HAVEN.

1806.

PREFACE.

ON the firſt publication of my Inſtitutes of the Engliſh Language, more than twenty years ago, that eminent claſſical ſcholar and divine, the late Dr. Goodrich of Durham, recommended to me to complete a ſyſtem of elementary principles, for the inſtruction of youth in the Engliſh language, by compiling and publiſhing a dictionary. Whatever reſpect I was inclined to pay to that gentleman's opinion, I could not, at that time, believe myſelf qualified for ſuch an undertaking; and various private conſiderations afterwards interpoſed to retard its execution. My ſtudies however have occaſionally had reference to an ultimate accompliſhment of ſuch a work; and for a few years paſt, they have been directed immediately to that object. As I have advanced in my inveſtigations, I have been, at every ſtep, more and more impreſſed with the importance of this work; and an acquaintance with the Saxon language, the mother tongue of the Engliſh, has convinced me, that a careful reviſion of our preſent dictionaries is abſolutely neceſſary to a correct knowledge of the language.

To men who have been accuſtomed to repoſe almoſt implicit confidence in the authors of our principal dictionaries and grammars, it may appear at firſt incredible, that ſuch writers as Johnſon and Lowth, ſhould have miſtaken many of the fundamental principles of the language. But that ſuch is the fact, will appear certain to any man who will read a few pages in a Saxon author. For example, thoſe diſtinguiſhed ſcholars, following the opinion of Wallis, ſuppoſe *own*, to be a participle of the verb to *owe*; when a moderate acquaintance with the Saxon will ſhow that it has not the remoteſt connection with that verb. Indeed a man, well verſed in etymology, will at once ſee the improbability, not to ſay, impoſſibility, that two words of ſuch diſtinct ſignifications, as to *be indebted* and to *poſſeſs*, can have ſprung from a common root. *Own*, in Saxon *agen*, *agenan*, *agenne*, is derived from the verb *agan*, to poſſeſs †; the g being in Saxon a mere guttural aſpirate, ſuppreſſed in the progreſs of civilization, as in *nagel*, nail, *ſtagen*, ſtay, *agen*, own. " Each, ſays Johnſon, denotes, 1ſt. Either of two. 2d. Every one of any number. *This ſenſe is rare except in poetry.*" To prove the laſt remark to be an error, we need not reſort to the Saxon, for every book we read, and every converſation we hear, demonſtrates the fact. " The princes of Iſrael, being twelve men, *each* one was for the houſe of his fathers."—Numb. i. 44. This is the true original import of the word; it has no appropriate reference to *two*, more than to ten thouſand. " Thyder man ne mihte geſeglian on anum monthe, gyf man on nyht wicode and *ælce dæge* hæfde amberne wind." " Thither a man could not ſail in a month, if he ſhould watch at night and *each day* ſhould have a fair wind." Alfred's Oroſius, Ch. 1. See alſo page 61, 63, 79, 219. Lond. 1773. and Sax. Ch. by Gibſon, page 185, 186. The ſecond definition of Johnſon is therefore the only true one; but not well expreſſed.

" *Either*, ſays Lowth, is often uſed improperly for *each*; *each* ſignifies both taken ſeparately; *either* properly ſignifies *only the one or the other*, taken disjunctively." In purſuance of this falſe rule, he condemns ſuch paſſages as this. " They crucified two others with him, on *either* ſide one and Jeſus in the midſt." But the ſenſe in which the word is here uſed in the true primitive one, and ſtill uſed by the beſt writers. " Mycell wæl thær on *ægthere* hand gefeoll." " There was great ſlaughter on *either* hand." Sax. Ch. 134. " Thet *ægther* hiora on other hawede," " That *either* of them might ſee the other," p. 133. " Swithe mycel here *ægther* ge land-here ge ſcip-here of Swatheode." " A very great army, *either* land army, and ſhip-army from Sweden." That is *both*. p. 153. So far is Lowth's rule from the truth, that *either*, in our primitive writers, was rarely or never uſed in a disjunctive ſenſe. In reading conſiderable volumes of the beſt Saxon writings, I have not found a ſingle inſtance. Its disjunctive uſe is modern; but its original ſenſe is ſtill in uſe and perfectly proper.

" There full in view, to *either* hoſt diſplayed." Hoole's Taſſo, 22. 602.
The paſſages in ſcripture, the language of which Lowth condemns, are preciſely correct.
Says Lowth, " the prepoſitions *to* and *for* are often underſtood, chiefly before the pronoun, as give

† *See Saxon Chronicle, by Gibſon, page 149, 176, &c.*

me the book; get *me* fome paper, " that is, *to me, for me.*" But in truth thefe expreffions contain the true dative cafe of the Saxon; *me* is in the dative, like the latin *mihi*, and no prepofition was ever ufed before the pronoun in thefe and the like phrafes.

Says Lowth, " the prepofition *in* or *on* is often underftood before nouns expreffing time; as this day, next month, laft year; that is, on this day, &c." It is a little ftrange that fo excellent a claffical fcholar as Dr. Lowth fhould have made this miftake. The Saxons, like the Greeks, ufed nouns of time without preceding prepofitions. Thus they ufed, *dæges*, and *nihtes*, day and night, in the genitive, like the Greeks—and continuance of time was marked by the accufative, as in the latin language—*thuy dages*, three days. This conftruction is of the higheft antiquity; the Greek, Latin and Saxon languages all having a common origin, the idiom in queftion is to be confidered as primitive; no prepofition, in thefe cafes, having been ever ufed and none being underftood.

Leffer, fays Johnfon, is a barbarous corruption of *lefs*, formed by the vulgar from the habit of terminating comparatives in *er*. He denounces *worfer* in the fame ftyle; and Lowth and all other grammarians repeat the fentence of profcription. Had thefe authors ever read a Saxon book with attention, they muft have perceived their error. *Leffer* and *worfer* are not *double* comparatives, but mere corruptions of *læffe, læffu; wyrfe, wyrfa*, which were *fimple* comparatives in the Saxon. *Worfer* is now obfolete; but *leffer* maintains its ground as the equivalent of *lefs*. See Sax. Ch. p. 171. Alf. Oros. page 16, 17.

" He is miftaken, tho *never* fo wife," Johnfon thinks to be juftly accufed of folicifm. But this is the true original Saxon idiom—" Nan man ne dorfte flean otherne man, neefde he *næfre fwa mocel* yfel gedon with thone otherne. " No man durft flay another, let him have done to him *never fo much evil.*" Sax. Ch. 190. The true refolution of the phrafe is, let him have done fo much evil to him as *never* before—or as never was done before—a very forcible manner of expreffing the idea. " If I make my hands *never* fo clean"—" Charm he *never* fo wifely"—" Afk me *never* fo much dowry and gift"—are legitimate Englifh phrafes, which our beft writers have ufed; which are preferved in popular practice, and which the grammarian has no right to profcribe——How would the elegant Addifon, that pre-eminent writer of unadulterated Englifh, fmile, were he to rife from the grave, and fee this genuine idiom in the Spectator, ftigmatized, by a hypercritical Editor, as bad grammar, and printed in Italics!

" The neuter pronoun *it*, fays Murray, on the authority of Campbell, is fometimes omitted and underftood—thus we fay, " *as appears*" " *as follows*," for, " as *it* appears," " as *it* follows." This remark is a grofs and mifchievous error, arifing from the author's not underftanding the word *as*, which has moft abfurdly been claffed with conjunctions. The truth is, *as* is a relative pronoun, equivalent to *who, which* or *that*; as may be feen in the German, the elder fifter of the Englifh. There is fcarcely a page of any Eng'ifh book in which we do not obferve it, both in the nominative and objective cafes, reprefenting either perfons or things. In the phrafes mentioned, *as appears*, *as* is the nominative to the verb—being only another word for *which*—*which* appears—*which* follows—and by inferting *it*, " which it follows," we convert the phrafes into palpable nonfenfe.

" *That*," fays Lowth, " is ufed indifferently both of perfons and things; but *perhaps* would be more properly confined to the latter." Campbell, in his Philofophy of Rhetoric, remarks upon this obfervation of Lowth, that " there are cafes wherein we cannot conveniently difpenfe with this relative as applied to perfons:" as in this fentence, " Who *that* has any fenfe of religion would have argued thus?" Murray remarks, that, " *that* as a relative, is often ufed to prevent the too frequent repetition of *who* and *which*," and in another place, copying from Campbell, that we cannot conveniently difpenfe with this relative as applied to perfons."

The fmalleft acquaintance with our mother tongue, would fhow that thefe writers have inverted the true ftate of the fact, and that inftead of ufurping the province of *who* and *which*, *that*, is the primitive relative whofe place is ufurped by *who* and *which*.

In the Saxon, *who* was never a fimple relative. In the volumes I have read, it does not occur in that character, in a fingle inftance. It occurs very rarely, perhaps not ten times in an octavo volume, and then only as an interrogative, or in the fenfe of *whoever*, or *any perfon*, equivalent to the Latin *quifpiam* or *quifquis* at the beginning of fentences. From the fragments of the Roman laws of the firft kings and of the twelve tables which are ftill extant, there is reafon to believe that this was the primitive fenfe of *qui*, or *who*. The Saxons ufed for a relative, *the* and *that*, which we have blended into one word, *that*. This is our true primitive relative; and any perfon who will examin the prefent tranflation of the bible, or the cuftomary language of converfation, will find that it maintains its place as the principal relative in the language. It ftill holds a primary, and not a fubordinate place.

Thefe examples are fufficient to demonftrate the importance of inveftigating the original of the

English Language; and how much mischief has been done by men who have compiled elementary books, without qualifying themselves by such previous investigation.*

More formidable objections than these may be made to our present grammars; but the limits of this preface will not permit a full discussion of this subject which is reserved for another work. It is proper to confine my observations, in this place, to the more immediate objects of this publication.

Of the numerous dictionaries of the English Language which are used in the United States, Bailey's and Johnson's are those which are considered as containing the most original materials; and Johnson's in particular is the fund from which modern compilers have selected the substance of their works. On Bailey's orthography, etymologies and definition of mathematical terms, Johnson has made little improvement. The excellence of Johnson's work consists chiefly in presenting to the reader the various different significations of words distinctly arranged and exemplified. On this part of the work, the author has bestowed uncommon pains, and has usually displayed critical discernment aided by extensive and various reading. Yet even in this part of his dictionary, many errors escaped his pen, and some of them are so obvious that it is not easy to number them with the effects of ordinary negligence.

Thus according to Johnson's definition, an administratrix is a woman "who administers in consequence of a will"; and obvious as the error is, we find it copied into Sheridan, Walker, Jones. &c.

Misnomer, says Johnson, is "an indictment or any other act vacated by a wrong name"; an incorrect definition, copied into Sheridan, Walker, Perry, Entick, Jones, Ash, &c.

Obligee Johnson defines to be " one bound by a legal and written contract"—the true definition of *obligor*; and this obvious blunder is transcribed into Sheridan, Walker, Entick, Perry, Ash and Jones.

Such mistakes are the more surprising, because the compiler had Jacob and Cowel before him, and usually copied the definition of law terms from one or the other of those authorities. These errors are corrected by Mason; but others have escaped his notice. For example, Johnson's definition of *murder* is not technically correct, as it would answer equally well for *man-slaughter*; yet Mason has not noticed the inaccuracy. *Specially* Johnson defines by *particularity*; and what is singular, cites for exemplification a passage from Hale, in which the word has its technical sense of a bond or instrument under seal. Yet this palpable error has escaped the observation of Mason, and been transcribed by other compilers into their dictionaries.

Boll is defined by Johnson "a round stalk or stem;" the verb *to boll*, "to rise in a stalk," "the flax was *bolled*." Ex. 9, 31. I have ever supposed the most unlettered reader of the bible to have a correct understanding of this passage; and the mistake of the lexicographer has always appeared to me a remarkable instance of negligence. Yet it may be accounted for. *Boll*, is the Saxon *bolla*, was the ancient correct orthography of *bowl*, and probably is derived from the Hebrew gebōl, the word used in this passage. The translaters unquestionably used this old orthography of *bowl*, which Johnson mistook for *bole*, a stem, and without examining the original, explained it in conformity with that idea. But the real sense of the passage is, that the seed vessel of the flax, the pericarp or capsule, was formed. The Seventy translate the Hebrew by *spermatizon*, *seeded*, or *seeding*, and this sense is rendered certain by the corresponding term used to denote the state of the barley, *abib*, *eared* or *being in the ear*.

This error of Johnson, however obvious, has been transcribed by most or all later compilers of English dictionaries. It is received also into the Latin dictionaries of Ainsworth and Entick; into the Dutch dictionary of Willcocks, the German of Fahrenkruger, by N. Bailey; the French of Boyer and the Italian of Montucci.

This fact is a remarkable proof of the indolence of authors, of their confidence in the opinions of a great man, and their willingness to live upon the labors of others. It shows us also the extensive mischiefs resulting from the mistakes of an eminent author, and the danger of taking his opinions upon trust.

Johnson's mistake in the definition of *clout* is the more remarkable, as it proves him to have misinterpreted his favorite author, Shakespear, as well as Milton. The *clouted* brogues and *clouted* shoon of those poets were shoes with soles studded with nails; such shoes as our country people have worn within my memory, and I am told, still wear, in some parts of America. Johnson supposed the word

---

* From the censure implied in this remark, I am not myself wholly free, having relied too much on certain modern authorities of eminent literary attainments. Since I have explored the more remote sources of our language, so many mistakes in our present systems of grammar have been detected, that I have declined to alienate the copy right of my own grammar, and shall not consent to a republication of it, until revised and amended.——The grammars of our language, now taught in our seminaries of learning, are rapidly banishing from books, some of its best established and most legitimate idioms.

A 2

clouted to fignify *patched* or *mended coarfely*—an error which the paffage cited from Shakefpear readily detects, for the "clouted brogues" were put off, to prevent the nails from making too much noife.

But the inflances in which Johnfon has wholly miftaken the fenfe of words, are far lefs numerous than thofe in which he has failed to explain the appropriate fenfes of words apparently fynonymous. Thus *abdicate* and *refign* may, by negligent writers, be ufed in nearly the fame fenfe. But in ftrict- nefs, each has a diftinct appropriate and technical fenfe—*abdication* denoting the abandonment of an office or truft without formality, and *refignation*, the voluntary furrender of a commiffion or office to the conftituent.

Alleviate, fays Johnfon, is to "*make light*, to *eafe*, to *foften*." True; but what is its appropriate fenfe? to what objects does it apply? a fhip is *made light* by unloading, and a guinea is *made light* by clipping; but neither of them is *alleviated*. A metal is *foftened* by fufion, tho it is not *alleviated*. The appropriate fenfe of the word is to make lighter or diminifh an *evil*, or *burden*, as pain, grief, cares and the like; and a principal ufe of dictionaries is to mark this particular application of words.

To exemplify this word, Johnfon cites from Harvey the following paffage. "The pains taken in the fpeculative will much *alleviate me* in defcribing the practical part." Here *alleviate* is ufed for *relieve*; or the words *my tafk* ought to have been ufed inftead *of me*. To *alleviate me*, is hardly Eng- lifh; and this is one of a multitude of inflances, in which Johnfon has cited as an authority what he fhould have condemned as an error.

Acquire, fays Johnfon, is "to gain by one's *own labor*, what is *not received from nature, or tranf- mitted by inheritance*." Yet Blackftone writes with accuracy that "an heir *acquires an eftate by de- fcent*," B. 2. Ch. 14; And a plant *acquires* a green color from the folar rays, which is the work of nature and not of its own labor. Johnfon has therefore wholly miftaken the appropriate fenfe of the word, in deducing it from the *manner* of obtaining, rather than from the *nature* of the thing obtain- ed. *Acquire* is to get or obtain fomething which becomes *permanent* or *inherent* in the poffeffor. We *acquire* titles to property, rights, qualities, &c. but the chemift who *obtains* fpirit by diftillation does not *acquire* it; nor do we *acquire* a book which we borrow.

This fpecies of imperfection is one of the principal defects in all our dictionaries; it occurs in almoft every page, defeating, in a great degree, the object of fuch works, and contributing to a want of precifion which is a blemifh in our beft authors.

ORTHOGRAPHY.

The orthography of our language is extremely irregular; and many fruitlefs attempts have been made to reform it. The utility and expedience of fuch reform have been controverted, and both fides of the queftion have been maintained with no inconfiderable zeal.

On this fubject, as on moft others which divide the opinions of men, parties feem to have erred by running into extremes. The friends of a reform maintain that our alphabet fhould be rendered per- fectly regular, by rejecting fuperfluous characters, and introducing new ones to fupply defects; fo that every found may be reprefented by a diftinct letter, and no letter have more founds than one. This fcheme is impracticable, and not at all neceffary.*

The oppofers of a reform, on the other hand, contend that no alterations fhould be made in or- thography, as they would not only occafion inconvenience, but tend to render old books ufelefs, and obfcure etymology. It is fortunate for the language and for thofe who ufe it, that this doctrin did not prevail in the reign of Henry the fourth; for it was as juft then as it is now; and had all changes in fpelling ceafed at that period, what a fpectacle of deformity would our language now exhibit! The doctrin is as mifchievous in its confequences, as the reafons on which it is founded are falfe. Every man of common reading knows that a living language muft neceffarily fuffer gradual changes in its current words, in the fignifications of many words, and in pronunciation. The unavoidable confequence then of fixing the orthography of a living language, is to deftroy the ufe of the alphabet. This effect has, in a degree, already taken place in our language; and letters, the moft ufeful in- vention that ever bleffed mankind, have loft and continue to lofe a part of their value, by no longer being the reprefentatives of the founds originally annexed to them. Strange as it may feem, the fact is undeniable, that the prefent doctrin that no change muft be made in writing words, is deftroy- ing the benefits of an alphabet, and reducing our language to the barbarifm of Chinefe characters inftead of letters. What is ftill ftranger, this doctrin is pertinacioufly maintained by the men who

* *In the year* 1786, *Dr. Franklin propofed to me to profecute his fcheme of a Reformed Alphabet, and offered me his types for the purpofe. I declined accepting his offer, on a full conviction of the utter imprac- ticability, as well as inutility of the fcheme. The orthography of our language might be rendered fufficient- ly regular, without a fingle new character, by means of a few trifling alterations of the prefent characters, and retrenching a few fuperfluous letters, the ufe of which are corruptions of the original words.*

make pretenses to exquisit taste and refinement in polite literature. And if any thing can add to the contradictions which such a principle involves, it is that the same men, who object to the minutest alterations of orthography, are the most active in effecting changes of pronunciation; thus aiding to destroy the use of letters, by creating new differences between the written and spoken language.

The correct principle respecting changes in orthography seems to lie between these extremes of opinion. No great changes should ever be made at once, nor should any change be made which violates established principles, creates great inconvenience, or obliterates the radicals of the language. But gradual changes to accommodate the written to the spoken language, when they occasion none of these evils, and especially when they purify words from corruptions, improve the regular analogies of a language and illustrate etymology, are not only proper, but indispensable.

On this general principle have all learned and civilized nations proceeded in refining their languages and preserving the use of alphabetical writing. Hence we observe as great a difference between the orthography in the laws of Romulus, Servius Tullius and the Decemvirs, and that of Cicero and Livy, as between the orthography of Chaucer and that of Addison. This principle also prevailed universally in the English nation, from the revival of letters to the last century, when certain eminent authors adopted an idea, as absurd as incompatible with improvement, that a living language can be fixed beyond the possibility of change; and to the prevalence of this error, we may ascribe many of the irregularities of our present orthography.

From this error, or perhaps from a total inattention to the history of our language, has originated another mistake which now governs public opinion on this subject; this is, that the present state of our orthography exhibits the true etymology of words, and that every alteration would tend to obscure it. There are some classes of words of which this is true; but let it be noted that no small part of the anomalies in the spelling of words, are egregious corruptions of the primitive orthography. Thus the present orthography of leather, feather, weather, stead, wealth, mould, son, ton, wonder, worship, thirst, &c. is corrupt; having been vitiated during the dark ages of English literature, under the Norman princes. The true orthography from the first Saxon writings to the 12th century, was lether, fether, wether, sted or stede, welga, mold, suna, tunna, wundor, wurthscipe, thurst.

Broad, was written brade, brede, and braed. We have preserved the first in the adjective broad, but the pronunciation of the noun bredth we take from the second, and the orthograhy most absurdly from the last.*

Tongue, was in Saxon written tung, tonge or tunga, which we pronounce correctly tung, omitting the last letter as in other Saxon words, and yet we write the word most barbarously tongue. Launch from lance, is a corruption introduced at a very early period, with daunce for dance, auncient for ancient, maister for master, plaister for plaster, and numerous similar corruptions which mark the barbarism which succeeded the Norman conquest.

Heinous from the French haine, which is correctly pronounced hainous as it was formerly written, is such a palpable error that no lexicographer can be justified in giving it his sanction.

Though is also a vitious orthography; tho being much nearer to the original word.

Drought and height are corruptions of drugothe, heatho; which the Saxons formed from dryg and heh or heah, dry and high, by adding the termination th as in length from leng; strength from streng, and as we form truth from true, width from wide, warmth from warm. The Saxon termination th is universally preserved in the popular pronunciation of this country; and so far is it from being an error or corruption, that it is the very essence of the nouns, drouth and highth. Men therefore who use this pronunciation, tho chargeable with "a zeal for analogy," as Johnson observes of Milton, and tho they may not imitate Garrick as Walker does, will still have the honor to be correct, and to preserve the purity of the original orthography. They will further have the honor of conforming to what is in fact the national pronunciation, and has been, from the earliest records of our language. Height is an innovation comparatively modern; and drought is the Belgic dialect of the Teutonic; but neither of these words existed in the Saxon, the parent of our language.

The use of k at the end of words after c, deserves notice, as it affords a remarkable proof of the corruption of language by means of heedless writers. Johnson remarks that c, having no determinate sound, according to English orthography never ends a word. Had this eminent critic examined ancient authorities with more care, he would have found the reverse of his affirmation to be the truth. The practice, in his time, of closing all words with k after c, on which he founded his observation, was a Norman innovation.

The history of these letters is shortly this. The Romans used c as an equivalent for the Greek k, as

---

* Chaucer wrote brede; and bredth the true orthography is preserved in the first Charter of Massachusetts. Haz, Col. Vol. 1, p, 240, 241, 243, as it is in many old authors.

appears by the tranflations of Greek into Latin, and of Latin into Greek, made while both were living languages. The Roman *c* is the Hebrew caph inverted and rounded at the angles, and the Greek kappa was probably formed from the fame character. The Greek alphabet did not recognize *c*, nor the Roman alphabet *k*. When therefore the Romans borrowed and naturalized Greek words containing a *k*, they ufed for it their own equivalent letter *c*.

Hence the Greek *keler*, fwift, was written in Latin *celer; kentauros*, a centaur, *centaurus; keros*, wax, *cera; kio*, to move, *cieo; kinnabaris*, cinnabar; *kinnamon*, cinnamum; *moufikos, muficus*; leaving not a particle of doubt that *c* and *k* were letters of precifely the fame power.

The Saxons had probably no knowledge of letters, till they fettled in England; and in that country, no letters were known, but thofe of the Roman alphabet, a knowledge of which had been left there by the Romans. The Saxons therefore adopted the Roman characters, with a few variations, which were required by particular founds in their language. Hence, till after the conqueft, *c* was ufed to exprefs the power of *k*, as in the Latin language; and infted of not terminating any Englifh word, as Johnfon alleges, it terminated *every* word, where the power of *k* occured; as in boc, book; folc, folk; wic, wick; ric, rick. In a volume of Saxon hiftory, written in the twelfth century, the letter *k* is not found in ten words.

The Norman conqueft however effected a change in the power of *c*, and eftablifhed it as the equivalent of *s* before *e, i* and *y*. This, like moft innovations, introduced confufion, and rendered it convenient or neceffary to ufe *k* in all words in which the power of *k* was wanted before thofe vowels. Thus the Saxon cepan, to keep; liccian, to lick; licean, to like; locian, to look, were converted into the prefent English words; and in many words, *k* ufurped the place of *c* without a like neceffity, as book from boc. Hence we find that in moft of our Saxon words, *k* is written at the end, after *c* or in lieu of it; and we cannot, without it, form the paft time and participle of verbs; for *licked, locked* would lead to a falfe pronunciation.

Such is the hiftory of the introduction of *k* into our language. But *c* at the end of words retains its place and power, particularly in all words formed from Greek and Latin adjectives in *kos* and *cus*, and confequently in all words not from the fame originals, but formed according to that analogy; as mufic, public, republic, nitric, camphoric, majeftic. To add *k* after *c* in fuch words is beyond meafure abfurd, for both have the fame power, having been formed from the fame original character. If any thing can add to the impropriety, it is that *k* is always omitted in the derivatives, mufical, publication, republican. Uniformity is a prime excellence in the rules of language, and furely no perfon will contend for the propriety of mufickal, publickation and republickan. Fortunately, moft modern writers have rejected the *k* from words in which it is ufelefs; and it is defirable that dictionaries fhould add their authority to the practice.

We have a few words of another clafs which remain as outlaws in orthography. Thefe are fuch as end in *re*, as *fceptre, theatre, metre, mitre, nitre, luftre, fepulchre, fpectre*, and a few others. Moft of thefe have found their way into our language from the Greek and Roman, through the channel of the French. This termination is common in the Saxon as well as the French, and probably the final *e* was pronounced after the confonant. However this may have been, Englifh writers have unanimoufly formed a different analogy by tranfpofing the letters, fo that the *re* in *fceptre* can not be confidered as an Englifh termination. And it is among the inconfiftences which meet our obfervation in every part of orthography, that the French *nombre, chambre, difaftre, difordre, diametre, tigre, chartre, arbitre, tendre, fievre, entre, monftre*, and the Saxon *hongre*, and hundreds of other words fhould be converted into *number, chamber, difafter, diforder*, &c. conformable to the pronunciation, and that *luftre, fceptre, metre*, and a few others fhould be permitted to wear their foreign livery. This is the more furprifing, as the moft diftinguifhed writers of the laft and preceding centuries, Newton, Shaftfbury, Dryden, Prideaux, Hook, Whifton, Bolingbroke, Middleton, &c. wrote thefe words in the regular Englifh manner.

"Having the imperial fcepter."—Newton chron. 308.

"The fcepter of Babylon was broken."—Prideaux con. 1, 2.

See Boling, let. 8. Hook. Rom. hift. 1. 79. Whifton, Jofephus, 2. 14. Hift. of California, 1. 91, &c. And this orthography gives *fceptered*, as written by Milton, Pope and other poets, which cannot be regularly formed from the French *fceptre*.

"The powers of earth, and fcepter'd fons of jove."—Pope Iliad, B. 1.

The prefent practice is not only contrary to the general uniformity obfervable in words of this clafs, but is inconfiftent with itfelf; for *Peter*, a proper name, is always written in the Englifh manner; while in falt *petre*, the word, derived from the fame original, is written in the French manner. *Metre* alfo retains its French fpelling, while the fame word in compofition, as in diameter, barometer, and thermometer, is conformed to the Englifh orthography. Such palpable inconfiftencies and prepofterous anomalies do no honor to English literature, but very much perplex the student, and offend the man of taste.

A like inconsistency is observable in another class of words which we receive from the French language. Musquet, masque, risque, paquet, picquet, chequer, relique, &c. have received a regular English orthography—musket, mask, risk, packet, picket, checker, relic, &c. while burlesque, grotesque, picturesque, pique and oblique retain their French livery. *Opaque* is now written *opake*, by most authors; and it is presumed that the few outlaws which remain, will soon be subjected to the laws of English orthography.

A similar inconsistency prevails in the pronunciation of the words of Greek original, beginning with *arch*, in which *ch*, receive their English sound before a consonant, as in archbishop, and the sound of *k* before a vowel, as in a *architect*. But *arch*, being established in its English pronunciation, becomes the root from which every word of this class is considered as derived, and will naturally control the pronunciation of the whole. Nor ought this principle of uniformity to be violated; for uniformity in the classes of words is the most convenient principle in the structure of language, and whatever arbitrary rules the learned may frame, the greatest part of men will be governed by habits of uniformity. To these habits we are indebted for all the regularity which is found in our own language or in any other.

For this reason, rather than from a rigid adherence to the originals, we ought to write defense, pretense, offense, recompense, &c. with *s* instead of *c*; for we always use that letter in the derivatives, defensive, offensive, pretension, recompensing.

For a like reason, as well as to purify our orthography from corruptions and restore to words their genuine spelling, we ought to reject *u* from honor, favor, candor, error, and others of this class. Under the Norman princes, when every effort of royal authority was exerted to crush the Saxons and obliterate their language, the Norman French was the only language of the English courts and legal proceedings, and the Latin words which, at that period, were introduced into use in England, came clothed with the French livery. At the same time, to preserve a trace of their originals, the *o* of the Latin *honor*, as well as the *u* of the French *honeur* was retained in the terminating syllable. Hence for some centuries, our language was disfigured with a class of mongrels, splendour, inferiour, superiour, authour, and the like, which are neither Latin nor French, nor calculated to exhibit the English pronunciation. Johnson, in reverence to usage, retained this vitious orthography, without regarding the palpable absurdity of inserting *u* in primitive words, when it must be omitted in the derivatives, *superiority*, *inferiority* and the like; for no person ever wrote *superiourity*, *inferiourity*. A sense of propriety however, has nearly triumphed over these errors; and our best writers have almost unanimously rejected the *u* from this whole class of words, except perhaps ten or twelve. From these also Ash has very consistently rejected *u*, restoring the purity of the original orthography.

Johnson often committed errors, but seldom gave his sanction to innovations, unauthorized by any good principle. Yet in a few instances he has departed from his usual caution. An instance occurs in his change of *sceptic* to *skeptic*. This innovation had some countenance in the pronunciation which had been corrupted by the Universities; for Greek scholars had discovered that the original was *skeptikos*, from *skeptomai*. The mischiefs which proceed from such *partial views* of subjects are incalculable. It is a thing of no consequence whether we pronounce vowels and consonants as the Greeks and Romans pronounced them—but it is of immense practical importance, that when we have analogies established in our own language, we should, on no account, violate them by introducing unnecessary exceptions.

By immemorial usage, the English nation had established the Latin orthography of words of this class, as *scene*, from *skene*; *scepter*, from *skeptron*; *sciamachy*, from *skiamachia*; in which, contrary to the original founds of the *k* and the *c*, *sc* had been pronounced as *s*. To change *one* word of this class, without the others, was to innovate without reason, or the prospect of utility; to deform our orthography with anomaly and embarrass the student with needless difficulties. The same reason would authorize *skience* for *science*; *skiolist* from *sciolus*, and *skintillation* from *scintillatio*; nay, *civil* must be written and pronounced *kivil*; *celebrate*, *kelebrate*, and *circle*, *kircle*; for in all words, *c* in Latin had the found of *k*. Such are the mischiefs of innovation! Fortunately, the corrupt pronunciation of *sceptic*, has made little progress in this country? and in this, as in many other words, if we can be permitted to think and reason for ourselves, we may still preserve the purity of our language.

We have some classes of words received from the Latin through the French, to which a final *e* was anciently affixed, either for the purpose of forming a syllable or to soften a preceding vowel, in conformity with the established pronunciation of the French. Such are *determine*, *examine*, *doctrine*, *discipline*, *medicine*, and others with a different terminating syllable. This practice of ending words with *e* was doubtless warranted by the pronunciation, during the ages which followed the Norman conquest in England. In many cases of Saxon words ending in *a*, which formed a distinct syllable,

I find the Normans changed the *a* into *e*, and the flight evanescent found of this vowel being finally omitted in pronunciation, the vowel was at last retrenched. In other words, the French influence introduced a final *e*, in words of Saxon original, to which the Saxons affixed no vowel. But whatever reasons might once exist for the use of final *e* in *poete*, *lande*, *behinde*, *businesse*, and a multitude of other words, none furely can be assigned for annexing it to the words before mentioned. The letter does not belong to the originals, *determino*, *examino*, *doctrina*, &c. it has no use in modifying the preceding vowel; and it is never used in the derivative words, *determination*, *examination*, *doctrinal*, *disciplinarian*, *medicinal*; while in some classes of words, it leads to a false pronunciation. It is a relic of barbarism which ought not to be tolerated in the language. It ought to be retrenched, as it has been from *origin* and *deposit*.

In some words we observe most singular corruptions. *Doubt*, is the French doute, with a *b* inferted out of complafance to its Latin original *dubito*. *Debt* and *indebted* stand nearly on the same footing.

Redoubt, is the French *redoute*, corrupted perhaps by a fuppofed alliance of the word with *doubt*, with which it has not the least connection.

Pincers holds a place in books, tho rarely heard in pronunciation. This word is a remarkable proof of the inveteracy of cuftom, even when obvioufly wrong ; for tho the verb *pinch* is formed immediately from the French *pincer*, yet the noun used in conversation is *pinchers*, the correct and regular derivative of the English verb, *pinch*.

The introduction of *e* into *vineyard* is a modern corruption; the word not being compounded of *vine* and *yard*, but of the primitive [win] *vin* and *yard*, the correct pronunciation of which we retain. It is precifely analogous to *wisdom*, which is compounded of the ancient *wis* [not the modern *wife*] and *dom*. We might just as well write *wisdom* as *vineyard*. In this as in almost every other inftance of anomaly, the pronunciation has been preferved correct by cuftom, while the orthography has been corrupted by authors.

It is fingularly unfortunate, that English tranflators of foreign languages, have not uniformly tranflated *letters* as well as *words*. The practice of receiving foreign words into our language, in a foreign orthography, is one of the most ferious and growing evils which the friends of an elegant and regular language have to combat. The powers of many of the letters are very different in different languages. When therefore a French, or a German word is introduced into English, the letters fhould be tranflated—and the true founds of the foreign words expreffed in English characters of correspondent powers. Thus *foup* in French, when the letters are tranflated, becomes *foop* in English—*tour* becomes *toor*—fchiftus in German, is fhiftus in English—*pacha*, *bedouin*, in French are pafha, or bafhaw and bedoween in English—Wolga in German is Volga in English ; Michigan, Chenango in French are Mifhigan, Shenango in English. The great body of a nation cannot poffibly know the powers of letters in a foreign language; and the practice of introducing foreign words in a foreign orthography, generates numerous diverfities of pronunciation, and perplexes the mafs of a nation. And the practice is, I believe, peculiar to the English. The Romans gave to all foreign words, their own letters, terminations and inflections; and a fimilar practice obtains among the modern nations on the Continent of Europe.

There are other corruptions of English orthography, which may be mentioned ; but thefe examples are fufficient to fhow, firft, the extreme negligence of authors, whofe bufinefs it is to purify and refine orthography, no lefs than to enrich the language with new terms and improve its general ftructure. Secondly, the utter miftake entertained by fuperficial obfervers, in fuppofing our prefent orthography to be correctly deduced from the originals.

A few of these errors may ftill be corrected, as the emendations will require trifling changes, which can occafion no perceptible inconvenience; while they will purify the orthography, illuftrate etymology and relieve the learner from embarraffment.

But it would be ufelefs to attempt any change, even if practicable, in thofe anomalies which form whole claffes of words, and in which, change would rather perplex than eafe the learner. That *h* is pronounced before *w* in *when*, tho written after it ; and that *tion* are pronounced *fhon* or *fhun*, are things of no great inconvenience; for thefe irregularities, occurring uniformly in many words, which conftitute claffes, form the anomalies into general rules, which are as eafily learnt as any other general principles.

PRONUNCIATION.

The pronunciation of words is a fubject which prefents even greater difficulties than the orthography ; and difficulties which multiply in proportion to the efforts made to furmount them. The friends of refinement have entertained fanguine expectations, that men of letters might agree upon fome ftandard by which pronunciation might be regulated, and reduced to a good degree of uniformity. My own hopes of fuch an event are very much abated by the ill fuccefs of the ingenious compilers of *standards* in Great Britain; and the more I reflect upon the subject, the more I am convinced that a living language admits of no fixed state, nor of any certain standard of pronunciation by which even the learned in general will consent to be governed. Elphinstone adopted the visionary idea of a perfect alphabet and fell into disrepute. Kenrick did not reach the point of refinement demanded by the Court and Stage, and was neglected. Sheridan carried his refinements and his fashionable peculiarities so far, that the nation almost unanimously rejected a great part of his scheme. Walker succeeded, condemned one half of Sheridan's court pronunciation, and for a short period, enjoyed a tide of popularity. Nares, whose work I have not seen, but whose reputation stands high even with Walker and his other competitors, condemns Walker in some particulars; and Jones, the latest compiler of distinction and popularity, sweeps a large part of Walker's peculiarities of prounciation, into the lumber-room of corruptions. Who is to succeed and condemn them all, is yet uncertain; but it is not to be doubted that the next period of twenty years will produce as many *standard authors,* as the last, no two of which will agree in their scheme of pronunciation.

That a complete standard, to which all the polite and learned of a nation will conform, is, in its own nature, impracticable, may be satisfactorily proved from the structure of the human mind; from the various modes in which different men view the same subject; the different effect of the same degrees of evidence on different minds; the different impressions made by education, which become the ground-work of uncontrollable prejudices; and the extreme reluctance which men feel in relinquishing their peculiar notions, and yielding to the opinions of others. The same consequence may be deduced from the variableness of pronunciation among the leading characters of a nation. So far is the present pronunciation of the court and stage in England from being fixed, that no two writers are yet agreed what it is; and if the case were otherwise, there is no probability that it would remain the same for any considerable time. Any man who will read Sheridan, Walker and Jones, will be satisfied not only that there is no uniformity in what is called the *best* pronunciation, but that such attempts as have hitherto been made to ascertain and establish a standard, render it impossible there ever should be one; and that every succeeding compiler only multiplies the obstacles to the accomplishment of his own wishes. Every compiler has some peculiarities in his scheme; some local practices to which he is accustomed, and which he mistakes for the *best* pronunciaton. Both Sheridan and Walker abound with such local usages. The more books are made, the more local usages will be exalted into a standard of correctness, each of which will have adherents, and the more the honest inquirer will be perplexed and confounded with various usages and discordant principles.

To satisfy my readers that I do not exagerate the difficulties of this subject and the contradictions between the most respectable standard authors, I will here exhibit a few examples, in which the pronunciation of each author is given, not in his own letters and figures, for these might not be understood by persons unacquainted with his works; but in letters of known powers, and which the most ordinary reader cannot mistake.

SHERIDAN.	WALKER.	JONES.
Ab'bey, abby	Ab'bee	Ab'by
Abbrévyate	Abbréveeate	Abbrévyate
Abbrévyature	Abbréveeachure	Abbrévyature
Ab'dicate	Ab'deecate	Ab'dicate
Abdic'ativ	Ab'dicativ	Ab'dicativ
Abdom'inal	Abdom'eenal	Abdom'inal
Aberun'cate	Abeeruncate	Aberun'cate
Abee'ance	Abáyanee	Abáyance
Ab'jectly	Ab'jectlee	Ab'jectly
Abil'ity	Abil'eetee	Abil'ity
Ab'lepfy	Ab'lepfee	Ab'lepfy
Ab'negate	Ab'neegate	Abnegate
Abominátion	Abomeenátion	Abominátion
Abor'tively	Abor'tivelee	Abortively
Abrupt'ly	Abrupt'lee	Abruptly
Abscis'fion	Abcizhon	Abfcizhon
Abfin'thyated	Abfintheeated	Abfinthyated
Abftémyus	Abftémeeus	Abftéemyus
Abftémyusly	Abftémeeufly	Abftéemyusly
Abftémyusnefs	Abftémeeufnefs	Abftéemyusnefs
Ab'ftinence	Ab'fteenence	Ab'ftinence
Ab'ftinent	Ab'fteenent	Ab'ftinent
Abftract'edly	Abftract'edlee	Abftract'edly

These twenty three words, in the pronunciation of which the three authors are not agreed, are found in the four firſt pages of my edition of Walker. If the differences are as numerous in the whole work, which is not to be queſtioned, the words differently pronounced amount to *five thouſand two hundred and ninety.*

It will be obſerved that the principal difference in the foregoing table, is in the ſound of *i* and *y,* in unaccented ſyllables; Walker directing the ſound to be uttered as the long *e* in *me, ſee.* Thus according to his ſcheme, *ability, vanity* are to be pronounced abileetee, vaneetee; which, as Jones has juſtly obſerved, is no "trivial error." Indeed this error is ſo material, as to render his book a very improper guide to pronunciation. It is utterly repugnant to the genius of our language—and if followed, would totally deſtroy the harmony of our metrical compoſition. Let theſe lines be read with Walker's pronunciation.

" The proper ſtudee of mankind is man"—
" A being darklee wiſe and rudelee great"—

We ſee at once the pernicious effects of this ſcheme of pronunciation, in the confuſion of poetic feet and loſs of melody.＊

This miſtake of Walker's, extends to a greater number of words, than any other—It extends literally to thouſands. Sheridan and Jones have avoided it, and given to the *i* and *y* unaccented, the ſhort ſound of *e,* which correſponds with the practice in the United States.

Let the differences of pronunciation be noted alſo in the following words.

	SHERIDAN.	WALKER.	JONES.
Bench, &c.	Bentſh	Benſh	Bentſh
	Beltſh	Belſh	Beltſh
	Filtſh	Filſh	Filtſh
	Brantſh	Branſh	Brantſh
	Intſh	Inſh	Intſh
	Pintſh	Pinſh	Pintſh
	Buntſh	Bunſh	Buntſh

In this claſs of words, Sheridan and Jones are unqueſtionably right; and with them correſponds the practice of this country. Where Walker learnt to give the French ſound of *ch,* to ſuch words, I cannot conceive.

Let the following examples of variance be noted.

SHERIDAN.	WALKER.	JONES.
Accentuation	Accenchuation	Accentuation
Gratulation	Grachulation	Gratulation
Habitual	Habichual	Habitual
Furnichur	Furneeture	Furniture
Multichood	Multeetude	Multitude
Protrood	Protrude	Protrude
Prochooberant	Protuberant	Protuberant
Shooperb	Superb	Superb
Chooter	Tutor	Tutor
Choomult	Tumult	Tumult

Theſe examples are ſelected from whole claſſes of words, conſiſting of many hundreds, in which each author has preſcribed to himſelf ſome rule which he deems ſo clearly correct, as to admit of no doubt or controverſy. And how is the honeſt inquirer to know which is right, or whether either of them is entitled to be a ſtandard authority? Do not ſuch pointed differences, among authors of diſtinction, prove that there is no uniformity of pronunciation among the higher ranks of ſociety in Great Britain; and conſequently, that no ſtandard can be found in their practice? This unqueſtionably is a fair inference from the facts.

Sheridan, the firſt author whoſe work engaged public attention, took the liberty to omit, in his ſcheme, the Italian ſound of *a,* which we hear in *aſk, demand, father;* which letter he has marked in theſe words as having its ſhort ſound in *hat.* Outrageous as this innovation was, extending perhaps to thouſands of words, whoſe pronunciation was thus perverted, it was followed in ſome parts of this country, producing that mincing, affected pronunciation of *dance, pſalm, aſk, father,* &c. which is obſerved by ſtrangers among the people of the middle States.

＊ *Palpable as this error is, we find Murray has introduced it, with other miſtakes of Walker, into his Spelling Book; giving a whole table of ſuch words as daily, ſafely, holy, nobly, &c. with directions to pronounce "both the ſyllables long."*

Sheridan's book enjoyed unrivalled popularity for ten or fifteen years; and after having corrupted the pronunciation of millions of people, it was succeeded by Walker, who now informs us that Sheridan is not a correct standard; and that he has grossly mistaken the true pronunciation in a great number of particulars.—This author has restored the Italian *a*, in most words—has restored the found of *t* in tshooter, or tutor, and in that whole class of words—the found of *s* in shooperfede, and that class of words—which Sheridan had perverted, and has corrected many other faults of his predecessor.

But no man is destined to arrive at the point of excellence to which his efforts are directed. While Walker was doing his country much service in arresting the progress of Sheridans popularity, he fell into such palpable mistakes, in his own scheme, as utterly to defeat his object. His perversion of the short *i* and *y*, which has been the subject of preceding remarks, is alone sufficient to impeach his authority. His rule, that *t* before *u* not accented, has the found of *tsh* or *ch*; as in *future, perpetual,* pronounced fuchure, perpechual; but when *u* is under the accent, *t* retains its proper found, as in *futurity, perpetuity*—has no foundation, except in his own imagination. Nor is it true, that *u* has the found of *eu* or *yu*, as he alleges, except in a few words, as measure, union, &c. in which the found is changed, for the fake of easy utterance.

Equally erroneous appears to be the decision of Walker and Jones in such words as partiality, ingratiate, officiate, which they pronounce parsheality, ingratheate, offisheate, contrary to ancient usage, and the opinion of Sheridan. This pronunciation also involves an inconsistency; for in primitives, they all agree to give to *ti* and *ci* the found of *sh*, as parshal, offishal.

The source of the mistake is, that they consider the consonant *t*, *s* and *c* before the vowels *e* and *i*, as sliding into the found of *sh*. The fact is not so—It is the rapid transition of the voice from the consonant to the vowel following, or rather the rapid passage of the voice over the vowel, which blends the *two* founds into that of *sh*. The vowel therefore, in these combinations, *ti, ci, ce, si*, is incorporated into the found of *sh*—it forms an essential ingredient in the composition; and is not to be repeated after the *sh*; for this is to use it both in the composition of *sh*, and in its separate capacity. Sheridan, in words of this class, is right, in giving to these combinations the same found in the primitive and derivative—parshal—parshality—substanshal—substanshate—offishal—offishate, &c. Had the true reason of this change of found been well understood, and the early practice of the nation, investigated, Walker could not have given countenance to such a mistake. The principle which decides this point, is of great antiquity—The Saxon *sceal, scearp, sceam, sceaft, scead, ceuf, ceale*, are now written and pronounced shall, sharp, shame, shaft, shade, chaff, chalk; not sheal, shearp, sheame, sheaft, sheade, cheaf, chealk—the found of the vowel being blended and lost in the *sh* and *ch*. It is true that *se* in some Saxon words have formed the modern *sh*; and *c* alone been converted into *ch* or *k*; but in these cases, the found of a single succeeding vowel alone is preserved, as in *cheap* from *ceapian*, and sheath from *sceath*. The pronunciation of *cia, tia*, &c. as two syllables, is a violation of principle, and long established usage. Hence the present spelling of *fashion* is grossly incorrect. The *ci* of the old French *facion*, [Lat. facies] from which we receive the word, blend and coalesce to form the *sh*; and therefore to write *i* after *sh* is a palpable absurdity.*

Another mistake of Walker, which is noticed and censured by Jones; is, his making no distinction in the vowel founds of took and tool, and in several other words of this class. In this part of his work, his scheme also is imperfect, and tends to mislead a learner; for he markes the found of single *o* in move, as the second found of *o*; that is *oo*; then places the same figure over both the vowels when two of them occur in the same word; as in stoop. According to his own scheme then this found of *o* in such words is to be repeated—and stoop must be pronounced stoo oop. This inaccuracy runs through his whole work.

A like inaccuracy is observable in his marking the found of *y* and *u*. To *u* he assigns the found of *ew*; cubic, he says, is to be pronounced kewbic. Rule 171. In Rule, 53 he informs us that *y* consonant is equivalent to *ee*, and to express the pronunciation of *use, usage, volume*, he writes the words yuse, yuzidje, volyume. Upon his own principles then these words are to be pronounced eeewse, eewzidje voleeewme! Such are the mischiefs of excessive refinement, on subjects which require no rules at all, or in which the ear in common practice is a much surer guide than rules and nice distinctions. Excessive refinement itself greatly increases the difficulty of acquiring a good pronunciation—the five hundred and forty five rules of Walker are more difficult to learn than the language itself; but the contradictory rules of authors of equal reputation preclude the possibility of knowing from them what is right or wrong.

The inattention of these authors has introduced also an improper distinction in the found of *u* long. In pure, purify, cube, blue, the English writers give the long found of *u* proper; but in *prune, prude,*

---

* How would Walker and Jones read this line of Pope? "Expatiate free o'er all this scene of man."

rude, they change the *u* into *oo*. This error, which runs through all the standard books, proceeds from a slight modification of the sound of *u* by the preceding consonant. It is a modification observable in other vowels, which proceeds from the transition of the organs from the position in which they are placed to pronounce the preceding consonants, to that which utters the following vowel. But it is an egregious mistake to suppose that this unavoidable modification of the vowel changes the sound of it to that of another letter.

Much less ought this modification of sound to be considered as a new vocal sound. It is this blunder which has introduced the sound of *e* before *i* and *y* in *sky, kind, disguise*, &c. *skey, keind, disgyise*. The consonants *g* and *k* bring the organs to a position, in passing from which to the following vowel, they are apt to form a slight sound of *e*; but good speakers should be careful not to fall into this error. *Skey* and *kyind* are precisely the faults which distinguishes the vulgar of New-England, in *keow, geown*; and the fault in both cases proceeds from the same cause. It is carelessly pronouncing an *e*, after the *same* consonants before a *different* vowel. But whether in the vulgar of N. England or in the court and stage of England, it is, as Nares, in a passage cited by Walker, declares, a "monster of pronunciation."*

In the accentuation of some words, the English practice is so palpably wrong, that no consideration can justify us in adopting it. From the great attention paid to the Greek and Latin languages, and from the influence of other causes, the best English speakers seem to have sought for rules of accentuation in the terminating syllable, in the Greek and Roman radicals, in the practice of poets, every where but in the words themselves, in which alone they are to be found. Hence they have wholly overlooked or considered as of secondary importance, the primary and almost only principles which regulate accent in every language—the *ease of pronunciation* and the *melody of sounds*. That mode of articulating the syllables of a word, which is most easy to the speaker, and most agreeable to the hearer, constitutes the supreme rule of accentuation; a rule which has insensibly established the accent of those words in which all men agree. To prove that rules derived from foreign languages, and from arbitrary opinions of great men, have had no influence in adjusting the accent of most of our words, but that the effect has been entirely produced by the preference of sounds, let any man attempt to vary the customary accentuation of the following words; *construction, termination, probability, supremacy, principle, rapidity, correspondent, denote, devise, invent.* The trial will evince that the accent upon the syllable which has been preferred, gives to all parts of the word a full distinct articulation, with the least effort of the organs. But vary the accent, and the words are pronounced with more difficulty, while the articulation is less distinct.

This principle decides the accent of such words as *accept'able, accept'ableness, confes'sor, commend'able, refrac'tory, irrefra'gable.* The English accentuation of the first syllable of the first five and the second syllable of the last, is harsh, unnatural, contrary to analogy, and on the first two words, absolutely impracticable. No authority of poets or lexicographers can ever give it general reception.

The same reason operates to preserve the accent in ordinary practice, on the first syllable of *horizon* and *asylum*. The poets regulate their accentuation of these words most pedantically by the Greek accent—a circumstance which has nothing to do in adjusting the accent of English words. They ought, by the same rule, to accent *orátor* and *senátor* upon the second syllable. The natural English accent of *horizon* and *asylum* on the first syllable, renders the pronunciation easy, bold and melodious. With the Greek accent, the pronunciation is harsh, unnatural; and in poetry, with an elision of *h, horizon* is usually preceded by a most disgusting hiatus.

This is the reason why the rules of of lexicographers and the practice of poets are utterly disregarded by the bulk of the nation; who regulate and will forever regulate, their practice by a decided preference of sounds—that is, by what may be termed the *natural accent.* To oppose this popular preference of a natural, easy, English accent, is as fruitless, as it is destructive of the uniformity of pronunciation and the beauties of speaking.

There is another circumstance in adjusting accent which has been overlooked or disregarded; which is, the effect of an augmentation of syllables upon the articulation of words. Thus we customarily accent the same syllable of a participle, as of the verb from which it is formed, and this circumstance should be considered in adjusting the accent of the verb. For example, we find no difficulty in laying an accent upon the second syllable of *demon'strate, compens'ate*; but when the

---

* *To accelerate the progress of errors, we have Spelling Books compiled to teach the contradictory schemes of Sheridan and Walker. In one part of the United States, our youth are to be initiated in Sheridan's pronunciation, in another part, in Walker's; tho the authority of both is called in question in Great Britain, and will be in a great degree, superseded by Jones. Who is to succeed and condemn them all, is yet to be determined.*

number of fyllables is augmented, the accent upon that fyllable leaves the two laft fyllables of *demon'ftrating, demon'ftrated, compens'ating, compens'ated,* wholly unaccented, with terminating confonants fomewhat harfh. and of difficult articulation in a rapid utterance. Hence proceeds the common practice of accenting the firft fyllable of the verbs, dem'onftrate, com'penfate, which enables the fpeaker in pronouncing the participles, to lay a fecondary accent upon the third fyllable, dem'onftrating, which relieves him from the difficulty, and renders the articulation eafy, and the pronunciation flowing and melodious. The unnatural accent here defcribed in this line of Pope's.

"Each feeming want conpenf'ated of courfe"—renders it one of the moft feeble and unmafical that is to be found in his works.

Lexicographers, in my opinion, err very much in oppofing artificial rules to this popular practice; for whatever the pride of learning may fuggeft, a ftrong general inclination or tendency to a particular pronunciation always proceeds from fome intrinfic reafons of preference, which all men may not be able to explain, but which their fenfes recognize as fatisfactory and conclufive, and which in fact, are the bafis of all accentuation. On this fubject, it is proper to notice another miftake of Walker, who, in affigning a reafon for the different accentuation of certain nouns and verbs which have the fame orthography, remarks that "This feems an inftinctive effort in the language to compenfate in fome meafure, for the want of different terminations."

This remark is wholly unworthy of the critical difcernment of the author, and the artificial reafon he affigns for the difference of accent, has had not the fmalleft influence in determining the place of the accent. The difference is wholly owing to the neceffity of fhifting the accent of the nouns, to enable the fpeaker to utter the participles and inflections of the verbs. It will be obferved that the words of this clafs are diffylables, which readily admit the accent upon the firft; and were all the inflections of the verbs to confift of two fyllables only, the accent of the noun and the verb, would reft upon the fame fyllable. But thefe words are fo formed, that when the number of fyllables is augmented, the pronunciation, with the accent of the noun, becomes harfh or difficult. Thus the verbs *conduct, abftract, infult,* are as eafily accented upon the firft fyllable as the nouns; but the participles and inflections, conducted, abftracting, infulted, cannot be eafily and diftinctly pronounced without removing the accent to the fecond fyllable. This change of accent is not the work of reafoning; it is the natural and infenfible effect of an effort to articulate the feveral fyllables with the leaft exertion of the organs. This is and ought to be the governing principle of accent in all words.

The diftinction of ranks in England feems to have had no inconfiderable influence in regulating the pronunciation of words. Who could believe, without pofitive evidence, that a compiler of Walker's character, fhould utter the following fentiment. "The accent on the fecond fyllable of this word, (commendable) is grown vulgar, and *there needs no other reafon for banifhing it from polite pronunciation*" Are we then reduced to this condition of fociety, that the polite and the vulgar muft have diftinct languages! What! the commonnefs of pronunciation, the very reafon why it ought to be preferred, is made the ground of its profcription! The eafe of fpeaking, the beauties of the language, its eftablifhed analogies, muft be facrificed to artificial refinements and a fashionable averfion to every thing common! Reafons like this may be well received in Great Britain; but to men who confider language as the inftrument of common intercourfe in fociety, and equally the property of every clafs of men, and who value uniformity and regular analogies as the prime excellencies of a language, will reprobate fuch reafons as falfe and dangerous, or receive them with coldnefs and difguft.

In a number of words, the Englifh pronunciation is anomalous, where the American is re ular or divided. Thus *deaf,* in Englifh *def,* is more correctly pronounced in this country *deef,* like leaf and fheaf. *Angel, ancient,* the Englifh pronounce *anegel, anecient,* contrary to every good principle. Indeed fuch a departure from analogy, from the original founds of the vowel, and from uniformity, feems not eafily explained; there being no fhadow of reafon why *a* in *angel, ancient,* fhould have a different found from that in *angelic, an'iquity, angle, anguifh.* In thefe and many other words, the pronunciation in this country is more correct than that of the Englifh; and it would be reprehenfible fervility in us to relinquifh a correct practice and adopt an Englifh corruption.

In the northern ftates, it has been cuftomary for gentlemen of education to follow the rule laid down by the great Dr. Johnfon, "That thofe are the moft elegant fpeakers, who deviate leaft from the written language." Notwithftanding what Walker has remarked upon this obfervation, I muft confider it as preeminently the beft rule to direct the national practice of pronunciation, that was ever offered, and the only correct ftandard by which ufage can be gene.ally regulated.

Neither this rule, nor any other can reach every cafe. Differences between the orthography and pronunciation exift, which are too inveterate to be removed. But this rule furnifhes the moft effectual barrier which can be erected againft the rage of innovation—it offers a ftandard, in moft words, fuperior to the authority of local ufages, and lefs invidious than the opinions of individuals. It is further recommended by this fupreme excellence, that it correfponds with the original defign of alphabetical writing, and preferves the benefits of that invention—benefits which local ufages tend to deftroy, but which no authority of court and ftage, nor of compilers claiming to be ftandards of propriety, fhould induce us ever to relinquifh.

This reafoning is juftified by a remarkable fact. Before the publication of Sheridan's Dictionary, the pronunciation of words in the northern ftates was fo uniform, that it is doubtful whether the gentlemen of education differed in fifty words; and this uniformity ftill exifts, among thofe who have made no ufe of any ftandard author. Yet the ftandard authors themfelves and thofe who follow them, differ in fome thoufands of words. It is further to be remarked that the common unadulterated pronunciation of the New England gentlemen, is almoft uniformly the pronunciation which prevailed in England, anterior to Sheridan's time, and which, I am affured by Englifh gentlemen, is ftill the pronunciation of the body of the Britifh nation : the pronunciation recommended by Sheridan and Walker being there called the London dialect, and confidered as a corruption. However this may be, I know from careful examination, that the old pronunciation is eftablifhed on the authority of a thoufand years practice; that it accords with the above recited rule of Johnfon, correfponding beft with the written language, preferving the natural founds of the letters and the eftablifhed principles of analogy. To thefe principles, men of tafte fhould bow, with the reverence which is infpired by antiquity, and fupported by a love of truth. The Englifh authors who aim to fix a ftandard, refine too much upon founds; for exceffive refinement in language, like metaphyfical fubtleties in ethics and theology, inftead of producing the defired conformity of opinions, tend to awaken doubts, diftract opinions, and generate endlefs controverfy and confufion.

Real improvements fhould never be checked; but the changes which are made by the fafhionable part of a nation, who are fometimes ignorant and often capricious and proud of fingularity, prove not unfrequently to be grofs improprieties, which, like modes of drefs, have a temporary currency, and are then condemned to neglect and oblivion. Hence from the practice of the gay and fafhionable world, there is always an appeal to a higher tribunal; the great body of literary and well informed men in a nation, whofe opinion of propriety is not to be feduced, nor their judgment perverted by the influence of names and of fafhion. Hence the eftablifhed popular ufages of a nation are rarely changed, but by a conqueft or great revolution among the inhabitants of a country. Cuftom among a whole people erects an impregnable bulwark againft the affaults of innovation; and we are indebted to popular ufage for the prefervation of many Englifh idioms, which writers and critics, from an affectation of refinement, have moft injudicioufly attempted to banifh. It is a curious fact, which I fhall, in another work, demonftrate, that the principal corruptions of our language, within the laft five hundred years, are the work, not of the vulgar, as is commonly fuppofed, but of authors and writers, pretending to purify and refine the language.

Real improvements in pronunciation arife from a popular tendency to abridge words which are of difficult pronunciation; to foften or reject harfh letters and fyllables; and to give to letters and fyllables fuch founds, and to words fuch a difpofition of accent, as beft fuit the organs of utterance and of hearing. Any alteration in pronunciation which is not recommended by thefe advantages, will never become general.

Men who offer their court and ftage refinements for adoption, fhould contemplate the infuperable difficulty of changing eftablifhed national practice. Two inftances, of a multitude which are within my knowledge, will exhibit this difficulty in its true light.—The Saxon preterit tenfe of the verb *come*, was the fame as the prefent tenfe, *come*. Came is a modern word, introduced long after the conqueft, but for fome centuries, has been conftantly ufed in books. Yet this manner of writing the word, and even its ufe in the vulgar tranflation of the bible, which our people read or hear every week or every day, have never brought the word into common ufe, nor made the leaft impreffion on popular practice. Nineteen twentieths of our nation ftill ufe the primitive word *come*, as the preterit of the verb, pronouncing the word as it was written and pronounced in the days of Alfred. And where is the critic who can impeach the practice?

Another fact is witneffed in the word *afk*, which our common people pronounce *aks*. The latter is the true pronunciation of the original word; the Saxon verb being written *acfian* or *axian*. The tranfpofition of letters which gives the prefent orthography and pronunciation is a modern innovation of writers; but it has not changed the primitive pronunciation among the body of our people, and it is doubtful whether a complete change can ever be effected.

. Facts of this fort refute the idle vifions of the theorift, and fhould appall the courage of the innovator.*

* A more ftriking example will be found hereafter in the word women.

ETYMOLOGY.

Thefe animadverfions, already extended to too great a length, fhall be clofed with fome remarks on etymology—a fubject which moft men difregard as of little ufe, but which my refearches have exalted to a high degree of importance in my own eftimation.

Mafon in the preface to his fupplement to Johnfon's Dictionary, remarks, that "that Lexicographer's etymologies are defervedly reckoned the moft erroneous part of his Dictionary." To apologize for not undertaking to revife that part of Johnfon's work, he mentions his want of fufficient knowledge of the early languages—and fays "learning of fuch kind is rather matter of curiofity than of common utility." In the latter fentiment I cannot agree with him—but it is true, that imperfect etymologies or thofe which throw no light on the hiftory of language and of ideas, are of little ufe; and to the wretched ftate of etymological learning we are probably to afcribe the common miftake refpecting its utility. In truth, few men have obtained knowledge enough of the fubject to appreciate its value. This feems to have been the cafe with Swift, whofe ridicule had a mifchievous effect in bringing the ftudy of etymology into difrepute.

Johnfon, who, when correctnefs depended folely on the exertions of his vaft intellectual powers, feldom made a miftake, was often betrayed into errors, by his natural indolence, which led him to write often without inveftigation, or he muft have been preffed by difeafe and poverty, to fend his papers to the prefs in an unfinifhed ftate. Whatever reafons may be affigned for the fact, it is not to be queftioned that his Dictionary was left very imperfect, and efpecially in the etymologies. In this part of his work he informs us, that he relied chiefly on Skinner and Junius, who fometimes mifled him—certain it is, he neglected to confult fome of the beft authorities on the fubject.

I have not finifhed the inveftigation of this part of his work; but as far as I have proceeded, I find a multitude of palpable errors; and a ftill greater number of etymologies imperfectly ftated. His miftake in the etymology of *comptroller* has had a mifchievous effect, and it is the more furprizing, as he deferted Skinner, Junius, Bailey, and I believe, every other authority, and gave a falfe orthography, without deducing it from any originals.

It is evident that Johnfon fuppofed *comptroller*, to have a different original from *control*; than which nothing can be more falfe. It is fimply a combination of two French words *contre*, and *rolle*—which are from the Latin *contra-rotula*. The ancients *rolled* their parchments into the form of a wheel; hence a regifter or record, obtained, in the middle ages, the name of *rotula*, a little wheel, which the French foftened into *rolle*. Hence *controll*, that is, *contre-rolle*, is to *counter check*—to check or govern by a *counter regifter*—and the officer who does this is a *controller*, formerly called in barbarous Latin, *contra-rotulator*, and in French *controllleur*. This derivation gives the precife fignification of the word. But *comptroller*, deduced from *compter*, to count, from *computo*, gives for fignification, a *counter of the records* or *computer of the rolls*—which is nonfenfe. That fuch a blunder fhould ever have been made by a man of letters, is not eafily accounted for; but that it fhould ftill hold its place in dictionaries and in practice, would be incredible, if our laws, records and conftant practice were not evidences of the fact.

Johnfon gives for the etymology of *ifland*, the Latin *infula*, the Italian *ifola*, and *ealand*, which he calls *Erfe*. Now the two firft have nothing to do with the word, and the latter, tho it may be Erfe, is alfo a Saxon word which the Englifh dictionaries do not explain. The Saxons wrote the word *igland*, *ealond*, and *ieland*, which, with a ftrong guttural afpirate, are not very different in found. It is a compound of *ea* water, ftill preferved in the French *eau*, and *land*,—*ealand*, water land, land in water, a very fignificant word. The etymology however was loft, and the word corrupted by the French, into *ifland*, which the Englifh fervilely adopted, with the confonant *s*, which no more belongs to the word, than any other letter in the alphabet. Our pronunciation preferves the Saxon *ieland*, with a trifling difference of found; and it was formerly written by good authors, iland *

For the original of *acre*, Johnfon gives the Saxon *æcre*; which, by the way, is a miftake, for, in every inftance, in which I have found it in Saxon books, the order of the letters is *acer*, *æcere*. Of what ufe is it that the author has given this word for the original of *acre*, without further information ? The hiftory of the word is this. *Agros* in Greek, and *ager* in Latin fignified an open field of indeterminate limits. Our Teutonic anceftors wrote the word *acker*, converting the g into the clofe confonant k, which is ftill the German orthography; but the word was not reftricted to a particular quantity of

The word Stamford has been recently corrupted in Connecticut. The original word in England was Stanford, that is Stoneford. The name was correctly written by our anceftors. The legal name of the town is Stanford, and was always fo fpelt in our laws for half a century, or a century, after the town was fettled. The correct pronunciation is not yet loft among common men, who are the laft to yield to innovation.

land, until the reign of Edward 1. and then the quantity was afcertained by ftatute. In the German and Dutch, the word retains its orthography acker, akker, and its primitive fenfe of field.

Before the Norman conqueft and for fome time after, the word was correctly written in Englifh acer, the c, in Saxon, always having the power of k—acer was therefore aker. In the confufion of tongues which followed the conqueft in England, when c was foftened before e and i, the order of the letters was changed, and the word written in the aukward Norman manner acre—which barbarous orthography we are careful to preferve—for fear, as our critics tell us, of obfcuring the etymology!!!

But the hiftory of our language exhibits blunders, even more extraordinary than this; an inftance of which we have in the plural noun women, which we pronounce wimmen. Thefe are two diftinct words, the firft fyllables of which are from different radicals. In the Saxon, wimman and wimmen are the only words ufed; being compounded of wif-man, wife-man; the f, being changed into m, the letter that begins the following word, in accordance with eftablifhed analogy in like cafes, as alligation for adligation; appofition, for adpofition. No other word than wimmen was ufed by our ancestors, till after the conqueft. In the Babyonifh confufion of tongues which followed the conqueft, woman and women were introduced into books—The firft in the fingular number, we continue to ufe in pronunciation; the laft is continued in books, but never pronounced; the ancient plural wimmen, being the only word known in fpeaking. Thus we write one word and pronounce another, juft as if we fhould write fhip and pronounce it veffel; or houfe and call it edifice. In this example, the learned have changed the written language—the people have retained the original oral language—another beacon to warn innovators of their folly, and an illuftrious proof how much language is governed by ufage, and how little by books and rules!

Errors of this kind which have corrupted the orthography or perverted the definitions of words, are numerous; but far lefs fo, than imperfect etymologies, or fuch as throw no light upon the origin of words, nor give any hiftory of ideas. Thus when Johnfon and Baily give the Saxon freond for the original of friend, they inform us only of a trifling change in the orthography. Of what ufe is this? If they had traced the word to its root, they would have informed us that freond is the participle of the prefent tenfe of the Saxon verb freon, to love; and we fhould be led to the radical idea of the word. When they refer the word again, to the Saxon agen, they give us no ufeful information refpecting its origin, and they are inaccurate in giving the leaft ufual fpelling of the Saxon. Again, is only a different orthography of againft, and from the fame radical, ongean, which was fometimes written togeanes, agen, &c. for the Saxon orthography was, in fome degree, unfettled, as might be expected among a people who had neither dictionaries nor printing preffes. The true fpelling was ongean. This is a compound of on and gean, equivalent to the Latin contra, and not improbably gean and contra may have a common radical. The fenfe of the word is contrary, or in oppofition to, which we retain in the word againft. The primitive fenfe of again, is contrary; the word being firft applied to moving in an oppofit direction. To come again, is to come contrary, that is, contrary to the firft courfe; and from this fenfe, the tranfition was eafy to that of return or fecond going; and hence from vifible action in a fecond going, the word came to fignify the abftract idea of repetition.

Johnfon refers our word obey to the French obeir. He might, with equal truth, have inverted the derivation and deduced the French obeir from the Englifh obey. Both words have a like meaning, and both are from the fame original. Had the author been more careful and more inquifitive, he would have found the root in the Saxon abugan, from bugan to bend, which alfo is the root of bow.*

In numerous particulars Johnfon's etymologies are erroneous or imperfect. In fome inftances, he refers a word to a Saxon original, which he fhould have traced back to the Hebrew, as earth, which is certainly of Hebrew origin. In many cafes he refers words to the Latin which are of Greek or Arabic original; as cinnabar, cinnamon, amomum; and what is worfe, he fome times refers us to a word which never exifted; as accommodable to a Latin word accommodabilis; adverfative, to adverfativus; effluxion to affluxio, which are certainly not found in the Latin language.†

* This is the direct derivation, deducing the idea of obedience from that of bending. So the Latin obedio is from the Hebrew obid, to work, labor or ferve, to till, cultivate or fubdue the earth. Poffibly obey and obedio may have a common root.

† Altho, in a revifion of the Englifh dictionaries, my duty impofes upon me the tafk of expofing the obvious errors of Dr. Johnfon, yet it is my intention to treat that author with the utmoft refpect. Nor can I omit this opportunity of expreffing my difapprobation of the difrefpectful manner in which Mr. Mafon has mentioned him in his fupplement. The charges of "ftupidity" and "wilful impofition," are contradicted by the whole courfe of Dr. Johnfon's life and character; and the contemptuous expreffion, "poor Johnfon," is utterly incompatible with the candor and civility, due from one author to another. Every man is liable to err; and who is equal to the tafk of tracing to its original

PREFACE. xix

Thefe are a few examples only of the miftakes and imperfections found in the beft dictionary of the Englifh language. Etymology judicioufly traced and difplayed, exhibits not merely the origin of words, but the hiftory of the progrefs of ideas and of the human intellect. Indeed the etymology of the languages of Europe will throw no inconfiderable light on the origin and hiftory of the feveral nations who people it, and confirm in no fmall degree, the fcripture account of the difperfion of men. But I have feen no work on this fubject which is well executed. From an examination of the Hebrew, Saxon and Gothic radicals, I can affirm, that the etymologies of Baily and Johnfon are fo defective, that they ought not to be republifhed without a careful revifion, with numerous emendations.

When to this confideration is added the neceffity of fupplying the new terms with which common ufage and various difcoveries and improvements, fince the publication of Johnfon's work, have augmented the catalogue of Englifh words; it is prefumed that the merit of this undertaking will be duly appreciated. Words, as Horace and Quintilian obferve, are like the leaves of trees; fome falling into difufe, and others growing into practice. "Nedum fermonum ftet honos et gratia vivax "* A living language, like a vaft river, moves with a flow but irrefiftible current. Even the genius of a Bacon, or a Shakefpear could not prevent words which they ufed from fliding infenfibly into neglect; and many of the terms, which, in their time, were familiar to an Englifh ear, cannot now be underftood without a gloffary.

The following work is an enlargement and improvement of Entick's fpelling dictionary, which public opinion, both in Great Britain and the United States, has pronounced the beft compilation of the kind. His felection of words, his orthography, pronunciation and definitions, undoubtedly juftify this preference. To his lift of words which is the moft complete, I have added about *five thoufand* others, which have been moftly collected from the beft writers, during a courfe of feveral years

and defining correctly every word in a copious language? The imperfections of man demand the mutual exercife of more candor; and a real fcholar cannot fpeak of Johnfon with contempt.

Dr. Johnfon was certainly one of the brighteft luminaries of Englifh literature; and whenever correctnefs depended on his own mind, as in ethics, for example, he feldom made a miftake. But technical precifion of terms, is to be learnt only by a knowledge of the fciences to which they belong; and with fome of the fciences, he had very little or no acquaintance. Thus in law and natural hiftory, he chofe generally to copy his definitions from Hill, Woodward and Cowel; and when he did fo, his explanations are generally correct. But in fome inftances, he evidently neglected this precaution and fell into miftakes. And it may be affirmed with fafety, that no original work of high reputation in our language, in which fo much is well executed, contains fo many errors and imperfections, as his dictionary.

To affign the caufes of thefe defects, is by no means difficult. We are told in the accounts given of Johnfon's life, that he was almoft always depreffed by difeafe and poverty; that he was naturally indolent, and feldom wrote until he was urged by want, or the neceffity of fulfilling his engagements with his bookfeller. Hence it happened, that he often received the money for his writings before his manufcripts were prepared. Then, when called upon for copy, he was compelled to prepare his manufcripts in hafte; and it may be reafonably fuppofed, that, in fome inftances, they were fent to the prefs in an unfinifhed ftate. We may indeed collect thefe facts from his own declarations in the preface to his dictionary, in which he tells us, that "it is the fate of thofe who toil at the lower employments of life, to be rather driven by the fear of evil, than attracted by the profpect of good." —"In making this collection, I trufted more to memory, than, in a ftate of difquiet and embarraffment, memory can contain, and purpofed to fupply at the review, what was left incomplete in the firft tranfcription."—"I foon found that it is too late to look for inftruments, when the work calls for execution, &c."—"I then contracted my defign, determining to *confide in myfelf*, and no longer to folicit auxiliaries, which produced more incumbrance than affiftance."

Thefe facts, while they may account for, by no means excufe the multitude of errors in his dictionary. A work, intended to furnifh to a nation an explanation of the terms of language, which is the key to fcience, fhould not be undertaken as a drudgery and toil, nor executed without the ufe of all poffible "inftruments and auxiliaries."

Yet how can Mafon be excufed for the afperity with which he treats Dr. Johnfon, whofe "palpable errors" he profeffes to rectify, and whofe "material omiffions" he profeffed to fupply, when his own work contains fcarcely a new term in all the various branches of natural hiftory, in which moft of the improvements of our language have been made? Even the common words, expenditure, ftatement, developement, difmemberment, poftponement, refpectability, prefcriptive, inadmiffible, &c. are in vain fought for in his fupplement.

* Hor. D. Art. Poet. l. 69. Quint. lib. 10.

reading. The purchasers of this compend will therefore find the lift of words by far the moft com-plete of any vocabulary extant.

I have made no material alterations in the orthography of words, except to correct moft palpable errors. In a few inftances, I have preferred the orthography of Newton, Prideaux, Hook, Dryden, Whifton, &c. to that of Johnfon, as being more analogical and purely Englifh, as in *fcepter*, *fepulcher*. In omitting *u* in *honor* and a few words of that clafs, I have purfued a common practice in this coun-try, authorized by the principle of uniformity and by etymology, as well as by Afh's dictionary. In omitting *k* after *c*, I have unequivocal propriety, and the prefent ufage for my authorities. In a few words, modern writers are gradually purifying the orthography from its corruptions. Thus Ed-wards in his hiftory of the Weft-Indies, and Gregory in his Economy of Nature, Pope, Hoole, &c. reftore *mold* to its true fpelling; and it would be no fmall convenience to revive the etymological fpelling of *aker*. Cullen in his tranflation of Clavigero, follows Bacon and Davenant in the true Sax-on orthography of *drouth*, and the elegant Blackftone has corrected the orthography of *nufance* and *duchy*.

The dipthongs in words borrowed from the Latin language, have gradually been finking into de-fuetude for a century; the few which remain, I have expunged.

Many words ufed in the reign of Elizabeth and James I. and found in authors who are ftill read, are really obfolete ; but as long as the books in which they occur, are in common ufe, it is proper and even neceffary to infert them in common dictionaries. Such of thefe words as are no longer ufed in the current language of the prefent age, are noted as obfolete. In executing this part of my plan, I may have fometimes erred ; for it is not eafy, nor perhaps poffible, to decide in every cafe, when a word has ceafed to be ufed.

The new nomenclature of chemiftry, has been inferted in this work from Lavoifier, Fourcroy, Chaptal, Black and Thompfon, with the few terms of the old chemiftry of Prieftley, Scheele and Stahl. In mineralogy, I have chiefly relied upon Kirwan's lateft treatife ; confulting however Cron-ftedt, and the various fyftems exhibited in Fourcroy and the Encyclopedia.

As the writers on thefe fubjects are not perfectly agreed upon the orthography of all the new terms, I have taken the liberty to attempt to reduce it to a fyftem, correfponding with Englifh analogies. For inftance, the new term for the acidifying principle, is written by fome authors, *oxygene*, by oth-ers, *oxygen*, and by others, *oxigene*. If authors would attend to analogy, they could not thus differ. The Englifh, in words of Greek original, have copied the Roman manner of tranflating the Greek *u* into *y* ; as in fynonymous, etymology, analyze. This eftablifhed rule ought not to be violated, for *uniformity* is the firft excellence in the conftruction of a language—it relieves the mind of the learner ; affifts his memory, and facilitates the acquifition of terms, and confequently, of knowledge. This and other new chemical terms from like radicals, ought therefore to be fpelt with *y*. To determin what ought to be the true found of *g* in this word and in hydrogene, we fhould advert to eftablifhed practice in like cafes. Is there an inftance of a word borrowed from the Greek or Latin, in which *g* followed by *e* has its hard found as in *get?* I do not advert to one inftance. In genius, genial, hete-rogeneous, geography, geometry, general, genefis, &c. *g* has its foft found as *j*. This rule therefore decides its true found in oxygene and hydrogene ; and to prevent a falfe pronunciation, the words fhould end with *e*. The orthography of Thompfon therefore, oxygen, is highly to be reprobated, and for an additional reafon : if *g* has its hard found as in *get*, in the primitive words, it muft retain it in the derivatives, oxygenous, oxygenate, hydrogenous, which would be monftrous ; and to give it a different found, in the primitive and in derivatives, would be a total departure from all the eftablifhed rules of our language.

Oxyd, fome writers have ufed as a verb ; but the participles of this word, oxyded, oxyding, offer to the ear fuch ungrateful founds, that I have not admitted it as a verb ; preferring *oxydate*, which is ufed by the beft chemical writers, and whofe derivatives oxydated, oxydation, are well formed and more agreeable to the ear.*

In the terms ufed to exprefs a combination of an acid with a bafe of earth, alkali, or metal, there is a difference of orthography ; fome authors clofe the words with *ate* and others with *at*, as fulphate and fulphat. The difference is not very effential ; but in fome words, the termination *at* appears to be unpleafingly abrupt, and the more general practice of adding *e* to lengthen and foften the cloting found of the word, feems worthy of preference.

* *Since this work was put to prefs, I have feen, in the new Difpenfatory, oxydize, which is well form-ed, according to Englifh analogy. Which word will ultimately prevail, is uncertain ; but uniformity is very defirable, and it is to be regretted, that an attempt is made to introduce a diverfity of terms expreffing the fame idea.*

Among the new words introduced into this work, are many terms of botany, collected from the Linnean school. In this part of our language, much improvement is wanted. The difficulty which the English reader encounters, in learning the technical language of botany, proves no inconsiderable obstacle to the study of that agreeable science. I cannot but hope that, notwithstanding the little attention now devoted in America, to the study of natural history, the time is coming and not far distant, when it will be disreputable for persons of property, to be unacquainted with the general principles of chemistry, botany, zoology and mineralogy. It will however be very difficult to make young people, and especially young ladies, relish the study of botany, unless the terms can be stripped of technical obscurity. One of the first improvements should be, to reduce the terms to an English form, with English terminations. This work is begun by some late writers, but it ought to be prosecuted with less timidity. *

How easy would it be to call a plant a monander, a pentander, a monogyn, or a pentagyn ; thus denoting the class or order by a single term ; then to form regular adjectives from these words, and express the class and order in two words, as, a pentandrian monogyn, a syngenesian monecian, a monegynian icosander, a trigynian decander. The nouns would thus admit of a plural termination, and instead of the circumlocution, *the plants belonging to the class decandria*, we should write simply, *the decanders*. I have not ventured to form and insert such words in this Vocabulary ; but have gone as far as my authorities warrant, in giving to Latin words an English termination. In a few instances, I have taken a greater licence, and ventured to give English terminations to words, without any authority, but obvious propriety. How can authors be so inattentive to convenience and regularity, as to write *barytes*, *pyrites*, *stalactites*, in the singular number, with the Greek termination ? We have occasion to use these words in both numbers ; the singular therefore should be *baryte*, *pyrite*, *stalactite* ; the addition of *s* would then form the plural, without adding a syllable in pronunciation ; and the derivatives would be regularly formed, barytical or barytic, pyritical or pyritaceous, stalactical. †

Adjectives, formed from names of places and persons, I have ventured to introduce, without the authority of any precedent ; for I see no good reason why they should be omitted. *Newtonian, Athenian, Libyan, Parisian*, are words in constant use ; and even when the name is foreign, the adjective is formed according to English analogies, and is really an English word. Besides, many words of this sort, really require explanation, as in cases where the original name is no longer used or generally known—instances of which we have in *Balearic, Adriatic, Belgic, Belgian*, and *Ligurian*. In all cases, the orthography and pronunciation require that they should have a place in dictionaries, for the use of those who are learning the language.

In the alphabetical arrangement of words, I have separated the letter *J* from *I*, and *V* from *U*, placing first in order the primitive characters *I* and *U*. More than a century has elapsed, since *J* and *V* have been used as characters with powers distinct from *I* and *U*; and no man who ever consulted a lexicon, can have been insensible to the inconvenience and perplexity which are created by an intermixture of words beginning with different letters. Yet one compiler after another proceeds in the customary mode, and apparently for no reason, but because it is easier to *transcribe* than to *reform* ‡

In a Compend of this kind, it is not possible to exhibit complete definitions of all the words inserted. At the same time, the definitions of a great number of words are, in Entick, left so very brief or imperfect, as to give no just idea of their true import. I have therefore judged it expedient to alter, or enlarge the definitions of a multitude of words, with a view to render this cheap volume more extensively useful. Examples of these alterations may be seen after the words, abate, abatement, abdicate, acceptance, access, action, actionable, adapt, advance, age, agent, annoy, appetence, affinity, appeal, animal, arraign, arrest, arbitration, argument, assassin, assault, atone, audit, avenge, averment, au-

---

* *See Martyn's Language of Botany—the translations of the works of Linneus by the Lichfield Society—and Barton's Elements of Botany. I had ventured to give English terminations to many botanical terms, without any precedent, and put this work to press before I received the European works mentioned. In comparing these with the same words in Martyn, and the Lichfield translations, I am happy to find an almost exact correspondence.*

† *The latter noun should rather be formed from the Greek, stalacty, plural, stalacties, and the adjective stalactic, or stalactical.*

‡ *Anderson in his History of Commerce charges his countrymen with being very slow in making or receiving improvements. There is some justness in the observation, tho it is not true as a general one. In purifying and regulating the orthography of their language, the English are indeed behind the nations on the Continent ; and it is remarkable that the reformation of the Julian Calendar, by Pope Gregory in 1581, was not adopted in England till 1751. Such is the almost invincible power of custom, even when wrong and vexatiously troublesome.*

thority, alkali, amber, bail, bank, bankrupt, burglary, bar, brafs, bronze, beauty, convoy, crime, calx, chalk, cifalpine, coal, combuftion, cryftal, default, depofition, element, enamel, efcheat, farm, farmer, gas, government, life, herb, houfe, hope, honor, fublimation, fpeculation, impoft, &c. With thefe improvements this work may be a good fubftitute for an octavo Dictionary.

Some change of definitions is rendered neceffary by new difcoveries. Thus *coral* was formerly fuppofed to be, and is defined, a marine *plant ;* but late inquiries prove it to be an *animal* production. Gold is called, in our dictionaries, the heavieft of the metals, which defcription, fince the difcovery of platina is become incorrect.

Some words are either new in the United States, or what is more ufual, Englifh words have received a new fenfe. Words of thefe kinds, when in general ufe in a ftate or number of ftates, or fanctioned by public authority in laws and judicial procedings, are admitted into this work. When the ufe is local, that circumftance is noted. Thus the fyftem of taxation in Connecticut has converted *fourfold* into a verb, as have the laws of New York and Pennfylvania, the word *docket,* and the practice of courts in many ftates, the word *default.* The fyftem of ecclefiaftical polity in fome ftates, has given a new meaning to *affociation and confociation*—the courfe of commercial tranfactions and the fyftem of finance have originated new terms, as *dutiable, cuftomable, irred:emable.* The farmer *girdles* his trees, the planter *gins* his cotton, or ftocks up the *rattoons* of his fugar cane ; altho the language of England furnifhes him with no words with meanings fuited to his ideas. The merchant imports his *rom als, humhums, baftas,* and *gurrahs ;* new fpecies of cloths in this country ; fome perhaps deftined to be of durable ufe, with their foreign names; others, with their names, to flide into difufe and oblivion. *Lots* and *locations* of land, with *located* and *unlocated rights,* form, in this country, a new language, to which the Britifh people are ftrangers.

In every country where the Englifh language is ufed, improvements will continually demand the ufe of new terms. The artift invents his *telegraph,* the chemift, his *pyrometer* and *gazometer,* and the philofopher difcovers *galvanifm ;* while the phyfician introduces *vaccination* to reftrain the ravages of difeafe, and mitigate the evils of human life. The chemift and mineralogift, by decompofing the materials of the atmofphere and the globe, difcover new fubftances, combinations and properties, which require new names ; the navigator explores the diftant parts of the earth, and returns with animals, plants and marine productions before unknown ; while a new fyftem of civil polity in the weftern world, originates new ideas, and brings into queftion the *conftitutionality* of powers, the *irrepealability* of laws, and the *removability* of men from office.

Thus the Englifh, like every living language, is in a ftate of progreffion, as rapid now as at any former period ; even more rapid, than before the great Dr. Johnfon " flattered himfelf that he might fix the language and put a ftop to alterations"—an idea as chimerical as that of Sheridan and Walker, who have attempted to make the mouthing enunciation of the ftage, a fixed ftandard of national pronunciation. It is fruitlefs to attempt to fix that which is in its nature, changeable, and to fix which beyond the power of alteration, would be the greateft evil that could happen to a living language. " If the language of theology, fays Johnfon, were extracted from Hooker, and the tranflation of the bible ; the terms of natural knowledge from Bacon ; the phrafes of policy, war and navigation from Raliegh ; the dialect of poetry and fiction, from Spenfer and Sidney ; and the diction of common life from Shakefpear, few ideas would be loft to mankind for want of Englifh words in which they might be expreffed." How fhortfighted was that learned man ! Many words found in all the authors mentioned are no longer ufed ; and two of thefe writers cannot be read without a gloffary. Scarcely was this lexicographer in his grave, when new difcoveries in natural hiftory originated a language almoft entirely new, in fome of its branches, and changed the whole face of the fcience. From the changes in civil policy, manners, arts of life and other circumftances attending the fettlement of Englifh colonies in America ; moft of the language of heraldry, hawking, hunting, and efpecially that of the old feudal and hierarchal eftablifhments of England, will become utterly extinct in this country —much of it already forms a part of the neglected rubbifh of antiquity.

The Hebrew, Greek and Latin languages, with the Teutonic and all its branches, the German, Dutch, Swifs, Swedifh, Danifh, Englifh and Icelandic, proceeded from one parent ftock ; the identity of their origin being difcoverable in the radicals of many words common to them all. The Englifh as a main branch of that ftock, now becomes the parent ftock of the languages of the countries colonized by Britifh fubjects. The defcendants of the fettlers in the Indies, in America, in New Holland, in the South Seas, will continue forever to fpeak the Englifh language, but with numerous variations, arifing from difference of climate, plants, animals, arts, manufactures, manners and policy.

In each of the countries peopled by Englifhmen, a diftinct dialect of the language will gradually be formed ; the principal of which will be that of the United States. In fifty years from this time, the *American-Englifh* will be fpoken by more people, than all the other dialects of the language, and in eas hundred and thirty years, by more people than any other language on the globe, not excepting the Chinese. Thofe words which exprefs ideas common to the feveral nations will remain fo nearly the fame in all the dialects, as to render mutual intercourfe eafy—a circumftance for which the citizens of each country will be much indebted to the art of printing, which will retard the progrefs of variations. But thofe terms in Great Britain, which exprefs local ideas only, will be loft in the dialects of India and America, while local circumftances among the defcendants of the Englifh in their new fettlements, will originate new words, or give to old words new fignifications, which will never be generally received or known in Great Britain.

With thefe extenfive views of this fubject, have I entered upon the plan of compiling, for my fellow citizens, a dictionary, which fhall exhibit a far more correct ftate of the language than any work of this kind. In the mean time, this compend is offered to the public, as a convenient manual. No perfon acquainted with the difficulties attending fuch a compilation, will flatter himfelf or the public, that any thing like perfection is within the compafs of one man's abilities. Nothing like this is here promifed. All that I have attempted, and all that I can believe to be executed, is a dictionary with confiderable improvements; a work required by the advanced and advancing ftate of fcience and arts. The dictionaries of a living language muft be revifed every half century, or muft neceffarily be erroneous and imperfect.

I am not unapprized of the objections which have been made to this defign, even by good men and fincere patriots. But it will readily occur to a candid mind, that a perfon, who has never turned his attention to this fubject, may entertain views of it very different from thofe of a man who has directed his inveftigations to it for fome years, and not fatisfied with modern criticifms, has mounted to higher fources of knowledge. Candid men however will not differ much on the fubject, when they have the advantage of the fame evidence; and that the great body of my fellow-citizens are of this character, is beyond a queftion.

From a different clafs of men, if fuch are to be found, whofe criticifms would fink the literature of this country, even lower than the diftorted reprefentations of foreign reviewers; whofe veneration for trans-atlantic authors leads them to hold American writers in unmerited contempt; from fuch men I neither expect nor folicit favor. Men who take pains to find and to exhibit to the world, proofs of our national inferiority in talents and acquirements, are certainly not deftined to decide the ultimate fate of this performance.

However arduous the tafk, and however feeble my powers of body and mind, a thorough conviction of the neceffity and importance of the undertaking, has overcome my fears and objections, and determined me to make one effort to diffolve the charm of veneration for foreign authorities which facinates the mind of men in this country, and holds them in the chains of illufion. In the invefti gation of this fubject, great labor is to be fuftained, and numerous difficulties encountered; but with a humble dependence on Divine favor, for the prefervation of my life and health, I fhall profecute this work with diligence, and execute it with a fidelity fuited to its importance.

New-Haven, Jan. 1806.

ABBREVIATIONS EXPLAINED.

a.	ſtands for adjective or attribute.	*v.*	for verb, when the verb may be uſed	
ad.	for adverb.		tranſitively or intranſitively.	
n.	for noun or name.	*v. t.*	for verb tranſitive.	
pr.	for prepoſition.	*v. i.*	for verb intranſitive.	
pret.	for preterit.	*conj.*	for conjunction.	
pron.	for pronoun.	*exclam.*	for exclamation.	
pa.	for participle.	*ob.*	for obſolete.	

Local uſages are noted by the firſt letters in the names of the ſtates, where they prevail; as *Maſſ.* for Maſſachuſetts, *Con.* for Connecticut, *Penn.* for Pennſylvania, &c.

DIRECTIONS FOR THE PRONUNCIATION OF WORDS.

When a vowel has the accent over it, its ſound is long, as in vócal, relàte, redúce, bríghten.

When the accent is placed after a conſonant, the preceding vowel is ſhort, as in habît, cus'tom, amend', abhor'rence, abrupt', cyl'inder.

When the accented ſyllable contains a digraph or a dipthongal ſound, the ſound being indicated with ſufficient clearneſs by the letters, the accent is placed at the end of the ſyllable, as in renew', rejoice', deſtroy', devour', withdraw'. The accent has the ſame poſition when *a* has its fourth ſound as in *aſk*, thus, countermand', diſarm'.

When the pronunciation of a word is very different from that which the letters naturally indicate, it is expreſſed by a different orthography.

Ch have their Engliſh ſound, as in *church*, unleſs a different pronunciation is noted.

The ſound of *g* before *e* and *i* being reducible to no general rule, it is to be remarked that *g* retains its ſoft ſound like *j*, as in *general*, unleſs the contrary is noted.

Whenever a direction is given concerning the pronunciation of a radical word, let the direction be conſidered as extending to all the derivatives. Thus *g* being hard in *get* and *give*, remains ſo in *forget*, *forgive*, &c. The learner being directed to pronounce *rough*, *ruff*, will extend the rule to *rough'y* and *roughneſs*.

Italic letters are ſilent, as in br*ea*d, *ea*rth.

A double accent thus, lo''gic, ma''gic, a''cid, denotes that the ſound of the ſucceeding conſonant belongs to the firſt ſyllable, *c* and *g* in ſuch caſes being ſoft, as loj :, majjic, aſſid. Poſi''tion is pronounced *poſiſhun*.

It is needleſs to give very minute directions for pronunciation; for in regular words, which are nine tenths of the whole number, the accent alone is ſufficient to teach the pronunciation. The accent being laid on the right ſyllable and letter, and the accented vowel correctly pronounced, the pronunciation of the unaccented vowels is extremely eaſy; ſo eaſy indeed, that it is more difficult to be wrong than right.

In my ſpelling book, the words of irregular pronunciation are claſſed in tables, with directions how they are to be pronounced. The tables and directions are few and ſimple; and if children are fully inſtructed in them, as they ought to be, they will have overcome the chief difficulties which occur in learning the pronunciation.

This work, being intended for a convenient portable book for gentlemen, and for the higher ſeminaries of learning, an abridgement will be publiſhed for the uſe of common Engliſh ſchools, and ſold at a reduced price.

A

COMPENDIOUS

DICTIONARY

Of the English Language.

A or An *a*. one, denoting a fingle perfon or thing

Aback', *ad.* back, backward, behind

Ab'acot, *n.* a kind of old double crown

Ab'acus, *n.* an old kind of defk or table, the higheft member of a column

Abad'don, *n.* a name given to the devil or fatan

Abaft', *ad.* towards the ftern from a fhip's head

Aba'ifance, *n.* a bow of refpect or humility, *ob.*

Abálienate, *v. t.* to transfer to another perfon

Aban'don, *v. t.* to forfake wholly, defert, quit

Aban'doned, *pa.* forfaken, deferted, wicked

Aban'doning, *pa.* forfaking wholly, renouncing

Aban'donment, *n.* entire defertion, renunciation

Abáfe, *v. t.* to bring low, humble, caft down

Abáfed, *pa.* brought low, humbled, difgraced

Abáfement, *n.* the act of humbling, a low eftate

Abafh', *v.t.* to put to the blufh, confound, perplex

Abafh'ed, *pa.* put out of countenance, confufed

Abafh'ment, *n.* aftonifhment, confufion, fhame

Abáte, *v.* to decreafe, leffen, pull down, fail as a writ; remit as a tax (Con.)

Abátable, *a.* that may be abated, defeated, remit-

Abáted, *pa.* leffened, lowered, taken off [ted

Abátement, *n.* a fum abated, an allowance, decreafe, a remitting as of a tax, failure as of a writ, the removing of a nufance

Abátor, *n.* one who abates, or enters on an eftate before the heir

Ab'attis, *n.* rubbifh, branches of trees fharpened

Abb, *n.* the yarn of a weaver's fhoot, a wool

Ab'ba, *n.* father, a fcriptural word for father

Ab'bacy, *n.* the rights and poffeffions of an abbot

Ab'befs, *n.* the governefs of a nunnery [of monks

Ab'bey, or Ab'by, *n.* the refidence of an abbot or

Ab'bot, *n.* the head of a fociety of monks

Abbré'viate, *v. a.* to fhorten, abridge, cut off

Abbreviátion, *n.* the act or art of fhortening

Abbré'viator, *n.* one who fhortens or abridges

Abbré'viature, *n.* abridgement, a letter for a word

Ab'deft, *n.* a Mahometan purification by wafhing

Ab'dicate, *v. t.* to abandon an office or power,

without a formal refignation [office

Abdicátion, *n.* the deferting of a public truft or

Ab'ditive, *a.* hiding, that has the power of hiding

Ab'domen, *n.* the lower or big part of the belly

Abdom'inal, *a.* belonging to the lower belly

Abdom'inals, *n.* a clafs of fifh with ventral fins behind the pectoral

Abdom'inous, *a.* paunchbellied, unwieldy, large

Abdúce, *v. t.* to feparate, draw away, pull back

Abdúcent, *a.* drawing or pulling back or away

Abduc'tion, *n.* the act of drawing back or away

Abduc'tor, *n.* a mufcle, any mufcle that contracts

Abecedárian, *n.* one who teaches or is learning the alphabet

Abéle, *n.* the white poplar [the alphabet

Abed', *ad.* in bed, on the bed

Ab'erdavin, *n.* the fifkin, an elegant fong bird

Aber'rance, *n.* a wandering from, a deviation

Aber'rant or Aber'ring, *a.* going wrong or aftray

Aberrátion, *n.* the act of wandering, a deviation

Abet', *v. t.* to encourage, help, fupport, fet on

Abet'ment, *n.* encouragement, aid, help, fupport

Abet'tor, *n.* one who aids or encourages another

Abey'ance, [ey as ay] *n.* a ftate of expectancy, as in cafe of an eftate not vefted

Abhor', *v. t.* to deteft, hate, loathe, diflike muck

Abhor'red, *pa.* detefted, hated very much

Abhor'rence, *n.* deteftation, averfion, great hatred

Abhor'rent, *a.* inconfiftent with, detefting, odious

Abhor'rer, *n.* one who abhors, a hater, a detefter

A'bib, *n.* the firft month of the Jewifh year

Abíde, *v.* abode, *pret.* abiding *pa.* to ftay in a place, dwell, bear, fupport

Abíding, *pa.* continuing; *n.* continuance, ftay

Ab'ject, *a.* mean, worthlefs, funk very low, vile

Abjec'tion, Ab'jectnefs, *n.* a meannefs, a low ftate

Ab'jectly, *ad.* meanly, wretchedly, bafely

Abil'ity, *n.* power, capacity, fkill, means [a will

Abinteft'ate, *a.* inheriting to one who died without

Abjurátion, *n.* the act of abjuring, a forfwearing

Abjúre, *v. t.* to reject upon oath, to quit religion

Ablactátion, *n.* a weaning a child, a kind of grafting

Ablaq'ueate, *v. t.* to lay bare the roots of trees

Ablátion, n. the act of taking away, a removal

Ab'lative, a. taking away, as the ablative case in Latin, the sixth case of nouns

A'ble, a. having power, capable of doing, strong

Ablebod'ied, a. strong of body, powerful, robust

A'bleness, n. force, power, strength, sufficiency

A'bler, a. having more power, skill, or learning

Ab'luent, a. washing off, from or away, cleansing

Ablútion, n. the act of cleansing or washing

Ab'negate, v. t. to deny, disown, refuse

Abnegátion, n. a positive denial, a renunciation

Abnodátion, n. a cutting excrescences from trees

Abnor'mity, n. deformity, irregularity

Abnor'mous, a. out of rule or order, irregular

Aboard, ad. in a ship, safe, secure, at ease

Abóde, n. a habitation, stay, continuance, delay

Abóde, v. t. to prognosticate, foreshow, ob.

Abódement, n. a secret anticipation, a presage, ob.

Abol'ish, v. t. to destroy, repeal, make void

Abol'ishable, a. that may be destroyed

Abol'isher, n. a person that abolishes or destroys

Abol'ishment, Aboli''tion, n. the act of repealing

Abom'inable, a. detestable, very hateful, abhorred

Abom'inableness, n. extreme odiousness

Abom'inably, ad. very hatefully, odiously

Abom'inate, v. t. to hate, loathe, abhor, detest

Abominátion, n. an object of hatred, a pollution

Abori''ginal, a. first or primitive

Abori''ginals, n. pl. first or primitive inhabitants

Abor'tion, Abort'ment, n. a miscarriage in women

Abor'tive, a. untimely, unsuccessful; n. a vellum

Abor'tiveness, n. the state of being abortive

Abound', v. i. to have in plenty, or be in plenty

Abcund'ing, pa. plentiful, increasing [ry way

About', pr. near to, concerning; ad. around, eve-

Above', [abuv] pr. higher, more; ad. overhead

Above''board, ad. without reserve or artifice

Abovecited, a. cited before, mentioned before

Above'ground, ad. alive, living, not in the grave

Above'mentioned, a. mentioned above or before

Abráde, v. t. to rub or scrape off, to grate

Abrásion, n. a rubbing, wearing or scraping off

Abreast', ad. side by side, on a line with, opposite

Abridge', v. t. to contract, shorten, deprive

Abridg'ed, pa. shortened, deprived of

Abridg'er, n. a person that shortens or contracts

Abridg'ment, n. a work abridged or shortened

Abroach', ad. in readiness to run or come out

Abroad, [abrawd] ad. out, out of doors, in anoth-er country

Ab'rogate, v. t. to repeal, annul, abolish

Abrogátion, n. the act of repealing [nected

Abrupt', a. sudden, hasty, broken, rough, uncon-

Abrup'tion, n. a violent and sudden separation

Abrupt'ly, ad. suddenly, unseasonably, roughly

Abrupt'ness, n. great haste, suddenness, roughness

Ab'scess, n. a swelling or cavity containing matter

Abscind', v. t. to cut off, pare off, rend off or away

Abscis''sion, n. the act of cutting or rending off

Abscond', v. i. to hide one's self, go off, disappear

Absconding, pa. withdrawing from public view

Ab'sence, n. a being absent, distance, inattention

Ab'sent, a. not present, lost in thought, from home

Absent', v. i. to keep away, keep off, withdraw

Absentée or Absent'er, n. a person who absents himself, or does not attend

Abfist', v. i. to stand or leave off, quit, remove

Absolve', v. t. to pardon, forgive, acquit, finish

Absolv'ed, pa. pardoned, forgiven, acquitted

Ab'solute, a. not limited, arbitrary, complete

Ab'solutely, ad. positively, arbitrarily, completely

Ab'soluteness, n. positiveness, arbitrary power, per-

Absolútion, n. forgiveness, a pardoning [fection

Ab'solutory, a. tending to absolve or acquit

Ab'sonant, Ab'sonous, a. absurd, foolish, harsh

Absorb', v. t. absorbed, pret. absorbed, absorpt, pa. to suck up, swallow up, waste

Absorbabil'ity, n. capacity of being absorbed

Absorb'able, a. that may be imbibed or absorbed

Absorb'ent, a. sucking up, drying up, imbibing

Absorb'ent, n. a vessel or substance which absorbs

Absorp'tion, n. the act of swallowing up, a waste

Absorp'tive, a. absorbing, tending to imbibe

Abstáin, v. i. to forbear, refrain, deny one's self

Abstémious, a. temperate in diet

Abstémiously, ad. temperately

Abstémiousness, n. temperance in diet

Absterge' or Absterse', v. t. to cleanse, to wipe off

Abster'gent or Abster'sive, a. cleansing, scouring

Abster'sion, n. the act of cleansing or wiping

Ab'stinence, n. a refraining from, temperance

Ab'stinent, a. refraining from, temperate

Abstract', v. t. to separate, remove, shorten, take

Ab'stract, n. an abridgement, a summary

Ab'stract, a. abstracted, separated, pure

Abstract'ed, pa. separated, abstruse, absent

Abstract'edly, Ab'stractly, ad. simply, by itself

Abstract'edness, n. an abstracted state

Abstrac'tion, n. a drawing from, a separating of ideas, withdrawing from the world

Abstrúse, a. difficult to be understood, obscure

Abstrúsely, ad. obscurely, not plainly, darkly

Abstrúseness, n. obscurity of meaning

Absurd', a. contrary to reason, foolish, inconsistent

Absurd'ity, n. unreasonableness, inconsistency

Absurd'ly, ad. unreasonably, inconsistently

Absurd'ness, n. absurdity, inconsistency

Abun'dance, n. great plenty, great numbers, &c.

Abun'dant, a. plentiful, abounding with or in

Abun'dantly, ad. plentifully, perfectly, fully

Abúse, v. t. [abuze] v. t. to treat ill, revile, impose on

Abúse, n. the ill use of any thing, injury, affront

Abúsed, pa. used ill, treated roughly, reviled

Abúser, n. one that uses another person &c. ill

Abúsive, a. conveying abuse, offensive, rude

Abúsively, ad. in an abusive manner, rudely

Abúsiveness, n. ill usage, bad language, rudeness

Abut', v. i. to border upon, join, terminate

Abut'ment, *n.* that which joins to another thing, as the folid part of a bridge next the land

Abut'tals, *n. pl.* boundaries, limits

Abyfm' or Abyfs', *n.* a bottomlefs pit, a gulf, hell

Abyffin'ian, *n.* a native of Abyffinia

Abyffin'ian, *a.* pertaining to Abyffinia

Aca'cia, *n.* a plant, the Egyptian thorn

Acadèmian, Academ'ic, Academi''cian, Acad'e-mift, *n.* a ftudent at, or member of, an academy

Academ'ic, Academ'ical, *a.* pertaining to an Academ'ic, *n.* a Platonic philofopher [academy

Acad'emy, *n.* a fchool of liberal arts and fciences

Acal'tapon, *n.* a Mexican lizard

Acanácious, *a.* prickly, fharp, pointed, rough

Acan'thias, *n.* a fifh whofe fkin is ufed for polifhing

Acanth'ine, *a.* pertaining to Acanthus

Acanth'us, *n.* the herb bear's foot, the figure of its leaves in building

Ac'arus, *n.* an infect infefting animal bodies

Acatalec'tic, *n.* a verfe with complete fyllables

Acatalep'tic, *a.* very myfterious, incomprehenfible

Accéde, *v. i.* to come near to, join, agree, com-

Accel'erate, *v. t.* to haften or quicken [ply with

Accel'erated, *pa.* haftened, increafed in motion

Acceleràtion, *n.* a haftening or quickening, hafte

Accend', *v. t.* to light, kindle, fet on fire, *ob.*

Accen'fion, *n.* the act of kindling or firing, flame

Ac'cent, *n.* a mark on a word, a modulation of the

Accent', *v. t.* to note the accent, to mark [voice

Accent'ual, *a.* relating to accent

Accentuàtion, *n.* a placing or marking of accent

Accept', *v. t.* to take, admit, receive favorably

Accept'able, *a.* agreeable, received with pleafure

Accept'ably, *ad.* pleafingly, agreeably

Accept'ance, *n.* approbation, the receiving of a bill of exchange fo as to bind the acceptor

Acceptàtion, Accep'tion, *n.* acceptance, the mean.

Accept'er, *n.* one who accepts [ing of a word

Accefs', *n.* admiffion, approach, addition, means of approach, invafion of difeafe or paroxifm

Accefs'ary, *a.* contributing, adding

Accefs'ible, *a.* that may be come at, to, or near

Acceffibil'ity, *n.* the ftate of being approachable

Acces''fion, *n.* the act of arriving at, an addition

Ac'ceffory, *n.* one who aids in or gives countenance

Ac'cidence, *n.* a book of firft rudiments [to a crime

Ac'cident, *n.* a property of a thing, that which comes to pafs without being forefeen

Accident'al, *a.* cafual, happening by chance

Accident'ally, *ad.* by chance, unexpectedly, oddly

Ac'cipenfers, *n.* a genus of amphibious fifh as the fturgeon, ruthen and hufo

Accip'iters, *n.* an order of fowls with hooked bills

Accláim, Acclamàtion, *n.* a fhout of applaufe, ap-

Accliv'ity, *n.* the afcent of a hill, &c. [probation

Accloy', *v. t.* to cloy, furfeit, fatiate, *ob.*

Accom'modable, *a.* that may be fitted or applied

Accom'modate, *v. t.* to fuit, fit, apply, reconcile

Accom'modate, *a.* fuited, fitted, adapted

Accom'modated, *pa.* fuited, fupplied, made up

Accommodàtion, *n.* an adjufting, a convenience

Accommodations, *n. pl.* conveniences, lodgings

Accom'panied, *pa.* attended by, attended with

Accom'paniment, *n.* an addition by way of orna-ment, the act of accompanying

Accom'pany, *v. t.* to join with, to go along with

Accom'plice, *n.* a partaker, an affociate in a crime

Accom'plifh *v. t.* to finifh, effect, fulfil, adorn

Accom'plifhed, *pa.* completed, effected, elegant

Accom'plifher, *n.* one who completes or adorns

Accom'plifhment, *n.* a completion, an acquire-ment which adds worth, ornament or dignity

Accompt, *n.* falfe orthography, *fee account*

Accord', *n.* agreement, confent, harmony, union

Accord', *v.* to fuit with, agree, unite, tune

Accord'ance, *n.* agreement, conformity, harmony

Accord'ant, *a.* willing, agreeable, confenting

According, *pa.* agreeable to, in compliance with

Accord'ingly, *ad.* confequently, in purfuance of

Accoft, *v. t.* to addrefs, fpeak firft to, falute

Accoft'able, *a.* eafy of accefs, free

Account', *v. t.* to reckon, compute, efteem, think

Account', *n.* a regard, rank, narrative, fum ftated, value, fake; explanation

Account'able, *a.* fubject to an account, anfwerable

Account'ablenefs, Accountabil'ity, *n.* a being fub-ject to anfwer, or account for [accounts

Account'ant, *n.* one who keeps or is fkilled in

Account'ed, *pa.* reckoned, valued, efteemed, in-

Accou''ple, *v. t.* to join or link together [puted

Accòuter or Accòoter, *v. t.* to equip, drefs, furnifh

Accòuterments, *n. pl.* equipage, drefs, trappings

Accred'it, *v. t.* to give credit to, to authorife in a public character

Accred'ited, *pa.* authorifed in a public character of allowed reputation

Accre''tion, *n.* a growing to another, an increafe

Accre'tive, *a.* growing to, adding to

Accre'ted, *a.* added by natural growth

Accrùe, *v. i.* to arife, come, be added [meaſ

Accubàtion, *n.* the ancient pofture of leaning at

Accumb'ent, *a.* lying, reclining

Accùmulate, *v. t.* to heap together, pile up, add

Accùmulated, *pa.* heaped up, increafed, added

Accumulàtion, *n.* an heaping up, heap, increafe

Accùmulative, *a.* that heaps up, increafes or adds

Accùmulator, *n.* one that accumulates [care

Ac'curacy, Ac'curatenefs, *n.* exactnefs, nicety,

Ac'curate, *a.* exact, curious, nice, nicely done

Ac'curately, *ad.* exactly, nicely, correctly, well

Accur'fe, *v. t.* to doom to mifery, devote, curfe

Accur'fed, *pa. a.* curfed, excommunicated

Accùfable, *a.* blamable, that may be cenfured

Accufàtion, *n.* a complaint, charge of fome crime

Accùfative, *a.* the fourth cafe ufed in grammar

Accùfatory, *a.* containing a charge, blaming

Accùfe, *v. t.* to cenfure, charge, impeach, blame

Accùfed, *pa.* charged with a crime, cenfured

Accuſer, n. one who brings a charge, indicts, &c.
Accus'tom, v.t. to uſe one's ſelf to a thing, to uſe
Accus'tomably, Accus'tomarily, ad. uſually, ob.
Accus'tomary, a. cuſtomary, uſual. common, ob.
Accus'tomed, pa. uſual, uſed, frequented
Ace. n. a unit on cards or dice, ſpot, mere trifle
Aceph'alous, a. wanting a head, poor, low
A'cerb, a. bitter, ſharp, ſour, rough, harſh, ſevere
Acerb'ity, n. roughneſs, ſourneſs, ſharpneſs
A''cerous or A''ceröſe, a. like chaff, chaffy, linear
Aces'cent, a. tending to ſourneſs, ſharp
Aces'cency, n. a tendency to ſourneſs
A''cetate, n. a neutral ſalt formed by acetic acid and any baſe ſaturated, as acetate of lime
A''cetated, a. combined with acetic acid
Acet'ic, a. fully ſaturated with oxygene the principle of acidity
A''cetite, n. a neutral ſalt formed by acetous acid with any baſe, not ſaturated
Acétous, a. partially acidified, ſour
Ache or Ake, [ch as k] v. to be in pain
Ache or Ake, n. a continued pain in any part, pain
Achéan, a. pertaining to Achaia in Greece
Achéan, n. a native of Achaia
Achiéve, v.t. to do, perform, act, obtain, finiſh
Achiéved, pa. done, performed, completed, ended
Achiévement, n. a deed, performance, eſcutcheon
Achiéver, n. one who achieves, does or performs
Acic'ular, a. like need'es, conſiſting of needles
Acic'ularly, ad. in the form of needles
Achromat'ic, [ch as k] a. without color, colorleſs
A''cid, a. ſour, ſharp, like vinegar
A''cid, n. a ſalt giving the ſenſation of ſourneſs, formed by oxygene and ſome baſe
Acid'ify, v. to make or become acid, to convert into an acid by combination with oxygene
Acid'ifiable, a. that may be acidified
Acid'ification, n. the act of acidifying
Acid'ity, A''cidneſs, n. ſharpneſs, ſourneſs
Acid'ulate, v.t. to tinge with acids, to make ſour
Acid'ulous, a. ſlightly acid
A''cinaciform, a. ſhaped like a cimetar
A''cinöſe, a. full of kernels or grains
Acknow/ledge, v.t. to confeſs, own, grant, requite
Acknow/ledged, pa. owned, believed, declared
Acknowl'edging, pa. confeſſing, grateful for
Acknowl'edgment, n. a confeſſion, owing, return
Ac'me, n. the height or top of a thing, head, criſis
Ac'olin, n. a bird of the partridge kind
Acol'othiſt, n. a ſervitor to a maſs-prieſt, a deacon
Ac'onite, n. wolf's bane, a poiſonous herb, poiſon
Acon'tias, n. the jaculus or dart ſnake
A'corn, n. the ſeed or fruit of an oak, a ſhell [lobes
Acotyle'don, n. a plant whoſe ſeeds have no ſide
Acotyled'onous, a. without a cotyledon or lobe
Acous'tics, n. pl. the ſcience or theory of ſounds, medicines or inſtruments uſed to help hearing
Acquáint, v.t. to inform, make known, declare
Acquáintance, n. familiarity, knowledge, fellow

ſhip, a friend, a perſon with whom we converſe
Acquáinted, pa. informed, familiar, verſed
Acqueſt' or Acquiſt', n. acquiſition, a thing gained
Acquies'ce, v.i. to ſubmit to what is not moſt agreeable, to yield or aſſent to
Acquies'cence, n. conſent, compliance, ſubmiſſion
Acquirable, a. that may be acquired
Acquire, v.t. to gain ſomething permanent
Acquired, pa. gained, gotten, attained to
Acquirement, Acquiſi''tion, n. attainment, gain
Acquirer, n. one who acquires
Acquis'itive, a. that is acquired or gained
Acquit', v.t. to diſcharge, free from, clear
Acquit'ment, n. the act of acquitting or freeing
Acquit'tal, n. a deliverance, diſcharge, releaſe
Acquit'tance, n. a receipt in full for debt
A'cre or A'ker, n. a piece of land containing 4 perches long and 4 broad, or 4840 ſquare yards
Ac'rid, a. of a hot biting taſte, ſharp, pungent
Ac'ridneſs, n. a bitter quality, pungency
Acrim onious, a. ſharp, corroſive, tart, auſtere
Ac'rimony, n. ſharpneſs, tartneſs, illnature
Ac'ritude, n. an acrid taſte, &c. auſterity
Acroamat'ical, a. belonging to deep learning
Acron'ical, a. riſing or ſetting at ſunſet
Acroſs, ad. or prep. croſswiſe, athwart, over, upon
Acros'tic, n. a kind of poem whoſe initial letters form the name of ſome perſon or thing
Act, v.t. to do, perform, imitate, move, play; int. to conduct or behave
Act, n. a deed, exploit, decree, diviſion of a play
Act'ed, pa. done, performed, repreſented
Actin'ia, n. a genus of ſea-animals
Ac'tinolite, n. a ſpecies of magneſian ſtone
Ac'tion, n. a thing done, deed, battle, ſuit at law, geſture, exerciſe, operation
Ac'tionable, a. for which a ſuit may be ſuſtained
Ac'tionary, Ac'tioniſt, n. a holder of public ſtock
Ac'tions, n. pl. behaviour, ſtocks in the funds
Act'ive, a. that acts, quick, nimble, lively, briſk
Act'ively, ad. nimbly, in a nimble manner
Act'iveneſs, Activ'ity, n. quickneſs, nimbleneſs
Act'or, n. a man that acts on a ſtage, doer, agent
Act'reſs, n. a woman who acts or does, an agent
Act'ual, a. really in act, real, certain, poſitive
Act'ually, ad. really, verily, truly, certainly, indeed
Act'uary, n. a regiſter or clerk of a court [excite
Act'uate, v.t. to put into action, ſtir up, move,
Act'uated, pa. moved, driven on, excited
Actuátion, n. effectual operation or act
Ac'uate, v.t. to make ſharp, ſharpen, point
Ac'uleate, a. prickly, having a ſting or ſharp point
Ac'umen, n. ſharpneſs, quickneſs of intellects
Acu'minate, v.t. to ſharpen at the point, to point
Acu'minate, a. ſharp-pointed [point
Acumination, n. the ending in a point, a ſharp
Acúte, n. an accent in grammar, marked thus (´), to ſhow when the voice ought to fall with force on a letter

Acútely, *ad.* sharply, keenly, shrewdly

Acúteness, *n.* sharpness, subtleness, quickness

Ad'age, *n.* a proverb, an old or common saying

Adágio, *n.* a mark or sign of slow time ; *a.* slow

Ad'am, *n.* the first man created

Ad'amant, *n.* a diamond, very hard stone, loadstone

Adamant'ean, *a.* extremely hard, impenetrable

Adamant'ine, *a.* made of or like adamant, hard

Ad'amites, *n. pl.* heretics who assembled naked

Adapt', *v.t.* to suit, make fit, adjust, apply, join

Adaptátion, *n.* the act of fitting or suiting

Adapt'er, *n.* a chemical vessel with two necks, called also Aludel

Adapt'nefs, *n.* fitness, suitableness, adjustment

Add, *v.t.* to join or put to, increase, number up

Adde"cimate, *v.t.* to take tithes, to value tithes

Ad'der, *n.* a serpent, a kind of poisonous serpent

Ad'dible, *a.* that may be added, joined or increased

Addict', *v.t.* to devote, dedicate, give up, apply

Addict'ed, *pa.* given up to, devoted, fond of

Addict'edness, Addic'tion, *n.* devotedness

Addit'ament, *n.* a thing added, an addition made

Addi"tion, *n.* an adding to, act of adding, an increase, advantage, rule for adding sums together

Addi"tional, *a.* that is or may be added, further

Ad'dle, *v.t.* to make barren, corrupt, grow

Ad'dle, *a.* rotten, bad, barren, empty ; *n.* dry lees

Ad'dlepated, *a.* empty-headed, weak, silly, stupid

Addrefs', *v.t.* to speak or write to, pray, direct to, make love, consign

Addrefs', *n.* a speech, prayer, dexterity, direction, manner of speaking

Addrefs'es, *n. pl.* attentions of a lover, courtship

Addrefs'er, *n.* one who speaks or writes to others

Addúce, *v.t.* to draw to, bring in, allege, assign

Addúcent, *a.* drawing together, as muscles

Adduct'or, *n.* a muscle which draws a joint inwards

Ademp'tion, *n.* the act of taking away or revoking

Adenog'raphy, Adenol'ogy, *n.* a description of the glands in the body

Adept', *n.* a person well skilled in an art, an artist

Adept', *a.* completely skilled, skilful, well versed

Ad'equate, *a.* sufficient, equal, even, just

Ad'equately, *ad.* in proportion, justly, fitly, duly

Ad'equateness, *n.* fitness, propriety, proportion

Adfect'ed, *a.* consisting of different powers

Adhére, *v.i.* to stick close, to take part with

Adhérence, *n.* attachment, sticking to, union

Adhérent, *a.* united with or to, sticking close to

Adhérent or Adhérer, *n.* a follower, a favorer

Adhésion, *n.* the act of sticking or cleaving to

Adhésive, *a.* sticking to, tenacious, clammy

Adhésiveness, *n.* an adhesive quality

Adhib'it, *v.t.* to apply, make use of, admit, take

Adiaph'orous, *a.* neutral, indifferent, similar

Adiaph'ory, *n.* neutrality, equality, likeness

Adieú, *ad.* farewell ; for *a Dieu je vous commende*

Adipóse, *a.* fat, greasy, unctuous. oily

Ad'it, *n.* an entrance into a pit or mine, access

Adjácency, *n.* that which is adjacent, a nearness

Adjácent, *a.* lying close to, near, bordering upon

Adjec'tion, *n.* the act of adding, a thing added

Ad'jective, *a.* that is added, a word added to a noun to denote some property of it

Ad'jectively, *ad.* in the manner of an adjective

Adjóin, *v.* to join to, bear or lie near, add to

Adjoin'ing, *pa.* lying close to, adding

Adjourn', *v.t.* to put off, postpone, defer

Adjourn'ment, *n.* a putting off for a time, a delay

Adjud'ge, *v.t.* to judge, decree, pass sentence

Adjudg'ed, *pa.* determined, decreed, sentenced

Adjudg'ment, *n.* the act of adjudging or awarding

Adjúdicate, *v.t.* to determin by law, to adjudge

Adjudicátion, *n.* judicial trial or sentence

Ad'junct, *n.* something joined to another thing

Adjunc'tion, *n.* the act of joining, the thing joined

Adjurátion, *n.* the tendering or taking of an oath

Adjúre, *v.t.* to tender an oath, charge in God's name strictly and earnestly, command, enjoin

Adjust', *v.t.* to fit, adapt, settle, set right

Adjust'er, *n.* he or that which regulates

Adjust'ing, Adjust'ment, *n.* a regulation, a setting in order, a setting right, disposition, order

Ad'jutant, *n.* a military officer who aids in the execution of orders

Ad'jutancy, *n.* the office of an adjutant

Adjútor, *n.* a helper, assistant, promoter, advancer

Ad'jutory, *a.* helping, assisting, advancing

Adlegátion, *n.* a joint embassage

Admeas'ure, *v t.* to take the dimensions [mensions

Admeas'urement, *n.* a measuring or taking of dimension

Admin'ister, *v.* to give, conduce, supply, execute, enforce, dispense, settle an intestate estate

Administérial, Administra'tive, *a.* pertaining to the executive branch of government, or to administration

Administrátion, *n.* the act of administering, rule

Administrátor, *n.* a man that administers or rules

Administ'ratorship, *n.* the office of an administrator

Administrátrix, *n.* a woman that administers [ble

Ad'mirable, *a.* to be admired, rare, wonderful, noble

Ad'mirableness, *n.* a quality raising admiration

Ad'mirably, *n.* wonderfully, excellently, very

Ad'miral, *n.* a principal sea-officer, a shell

Ad'miralship, *n.* the office or duty of an admiral

Ad'miralty, *n.* the supreme naval power or office for settling maritime affairs

Admirátion, *n.* astonishment, wonder, esteem

Admíre, *v.t.* to regard, wonder at, esteem, value

Admíred, *pa.* regarded, esteemed, valued, loved

Admírer, *n.* one that admires or regards, a lover

Admifs'ible, *a.* that may be admitted, suitable

Admissibil'ity, *n.* the state of being admissible

Admifs'ion, *n.* leave to enter, access, a concession

Admit', *v.* to allow, suffer, grant, let in, receive

Admit'table, *a.* that may be admitted, proper

Admit'tance, *n.* the act or power of entering

Admit'ted, *pa.* allowed, granted, let in, received

Admix', v.t. to mix or mingle together, ob.
Admix'ture, n. a mixing, that which is mixed
Admon'ish, v.t. to warn, reprove, advise, remind
Admon'ished, pa. warned, reproved, advised, ex-
Admon'isher, n. a reprover, an adviser [horted
Admoni''tion, n. counsel, advice, direction, hint
Admon'itor, n. one who admonishes or advises
Admon'itory, a. that admonishes, warning
Adnas'cent, a. growing on something else
Ad'nate, a. pressing close to the stem
Ad'noun, n. a word joined to a noun, an adjective
Adó, [adoo] n. trouble, difficulty, bustle, stir
Adoles'cence, n. the state of a person growing, youth
Ado'nis, n. a charmer, a small gold colored fish
Adopt', v.t. to take as one's own what is another's,
to copy, select and take
Adopt'edly, ad. by way of adoption or choice
Adopt'er, n. one who adopts or makes choice
Adop'tion, n. the act of adopting, a free choice
Adopt'ive, a. adopted by or adopting another
Adórable, a. worthy of adoration, divine, noble
Adórableness, n. a quality exciting adoration
Adórably, ad. with adoration or worship, nobly
Adorátion, n. divine worship, homage, respect
Adóre, v.t. to worship, reverence, love greatly
Adóred, pa. worshipped, very highly esteemed
Adórer, n. one that adores, a worshipper, a lover
Adorn', v.t. to deck, dress, embellish (ment
Adorn'ing, Adorn'ment, n. embellishment, orna-
Ados'culation, n. the impregnation of plants by
the farin which falls on the pistils
Adown, ad. down, downward, towards the ground
Adriatic, a. belonging to the gulf of Venice; used
also as a noun for that gulf
Adrift', a. floating at random, at large
Adroit', a. active, skilful, dexterous, ingenious
Adroit'ly, ad. nimbly, dexterously, skilfully
Adroit'ness, n. quickness, readiness, dexterity, skill
Adry', a. thirsty, desirous of drinking
Adsciti''tious, a. assumed, borrowed, counterfeit
Adstric'tion, a. the act of binding together
Adulátion, n. fawning behavior, flattery, praise
Ad'ulator, n. a fawning person, flatterer, parasite
Ad'ulatory, a. fawning, flattering, complimental
Adult', n. a person grown up to maturity, a man
Adult', a. grown up, past the age of infancy
Adult'erate, v.t. to debase, corrupt, mix
Adult'erate, Adult'erated, pa. polluted, debased,
corrupted, mixed, counterfeited, false
Adulterátion, n. a corruption by base mixtures
Adul'terer, n. a man that is guilty of adultery
Adult'eress, n. a woman that commits adultery
Adul'terine, a. proceeding from adultery
Adult'ery, n. a defilement of the marriage bed
Adult'erous, a. guilty of adultery, idolatrous
Ad'umbrate, v.t. to shadow out, typify, resemble
Adumbrátion, n. a faint sketch, a shadowing out
Adun'city, n. crookedness, a bend inwards
Adunc'ous, Adúnque, a. crooked, bending in

Adust', Adust'ed pa. burnt or dried up, scorched
Adust'ible, a. that may be burnt up or scorched
Adust'ion, n. the act of burning up
Advan'ce, n. a progression, promotion, increase,
profit, first offer or hint, payment beforehand
Advan'ce, v. to proceed, improve, move forward,
raise or rise, promote, offer, supply on credit
Advan'ced, pa. preferred, improved, asserted, mov-
ed forward, in front, old
Advance'ment, n. promotion, improvement, pro-
Advan'cer, n. a promoter, a forwarder (gression
Advan'cive, a. tending to promote
Advant'age, v.t. to benefit, promote, improve
Advant'age, n. superiority, benefit, over-measure
Advant'aged, pa. having advantages, profited
Advantágeous, a. profitable, convenient, useful
Advantágeously, ad. profitably, conveniently
Advantágeousness, n. convenience, usefulness, use
Advéne, v. to come to or be added
Adve'nient, a. coming to, added externally
Ad'vent, n. four weeks before Christmas, a coming
Adventi''tious, a. accidental, casual, not natural,
additional, added
Advent'ual, a. belonging to advent, accidental
Advent'ure, n. accident, chance, enterprise, trial
Advent'ure, v.t. to try the chance, dare, hazard
Advent'urer, n. one that hazards or tries (ring
Advent'urous, Advent'uresome, a. hazardous, da-
Advent'urously, ad. boldly, daringly, hazardously
Ad'verb, n. a word which modifies the action of a
verb, or the quality of other words
Adverb'ial, a. relating to or like an adverb
Adverb'ially, ad. in manner or form of an adverb
Ad'versary, n. an opponent, enemy, foe, competitor
Ad'versary, a. having an opposing party
Advers'ative, a. denoting opposition
Advers'ative, n. that which denotes opposition
Ad'verse, a. contrary, calamitous, unfortunate
Ad'versely, ad. unfortunately, oppositely, crossly
Advers'ity, n. affliction, calamity, misery, distress
Advert', v. to turn, attend, regard, observe, heed
Advert'ence or Advert'ency, n. attention, heed
Advertise, v.t. to warn, inform, tell, publish
Advertised, pa. published in a newspaper, told
Advert'isement, n. information, a public notice
Advertiser, n. one who, or what, gives information
Advertising, pa. giving notice, informing
Advíce, n. instruction, information, notice, hint
Advísable, a. prudent, fit to be done, fit, proper
Advísableness, n. fitness, meetness, propriety
Advíse, v. to give advice, consult, give notice
Advísed, pa. counseled, informed, prudent
Advísedly, ad, prudently, wisely, purposely
Advíser, n. one who gives advice, a counsellor
Advísory, a. containing advice
Advísement, n. counsel, caution, advice
Ad'vocacy, n. intercession, plea
Ad'vocate, n. one who defends or pleads for another
Ad'vocate, v.t. to defend, plead in favor of

Advow'fon, *n.* the right of prefenting a prieft to a benefice

Adz, *n.* a cutting tool with an arching edge

A'erate, *v.t.* to impregnate or faturate with carbonic acid or fixed air

A'erated, *pa.* containing air, faturated with air

A'eriform, *a.* having the form of air, as gas

A'erify, *v.t.* to combine with air

Aerificâtion, *n.* the act of uniting with air, or being combined with it

Aérial, *a.* belonging to the air, lofty, flighty

Aerol'ogy, *n.* the doctrin or theory of the air

Aerom'etry, *n.* the art of meafuring air, its preffure, elafticity and rarefaction

A'eromancy, *n.* a divination by figns in the air

A'eronaut, *n.* an aerial failor in a balloon   (igation

Aeronaut'ic, *a.* pertaining to balloons or aerial navAcroftat'ic, *a.* belonging to aeroftation, light

Aeros'copy, *n.* an obfervation of the air   (loons

Aeroftâtion, *n.* a paffing through the air in balA'ery, *n.* a neft of eagles or any birds of prey

Afar', *ad.* at, to or from, a great diftance, remotely

Aféard, *a.* afraid, affected with fear

Affabil'ity, *n.* civility, readinefs to converfe

Af'fable, *a.* civil, eafy of converfation

Af'fablenefs, *n.* civility, a readinefs to converfe

Af'fably, *ad.* civilly, courteoufly, kindly, mildly

Affáir, *n.* a bufinefs, matter, concern, intrigue

Affairs, *n. pl.* bufinefs in general, ftate of property

Affect', *n.* affection, paffion, *ob.*

Affect', *v.* to move the paffions, aim, try, affume

Affectâtion, *n.* conceit, formality, pretenfe

Affect'ed, *pa.* moved, conceited, afflicted

Affect'edly, *ad.* hypocritically, conceitedly, vainly

Affect'ednefs, *n.* affectation, conceit, pride, vanity

Affect'ing, *pa.* moving, aiming at, imitating

Affec'tion, *n.* love, fondnefs, zeal, quality, habit

Affec'tionate, *a.* fond, tender, kind, good, zealous

Affec'tionately, *ad.* lovingly, tenderly, kindly

Affec'tioned, *a.* inclined, difpofed, affected

Affect'ive, *a.* that affects, moving, tender

Affeér, *v.t.* to afcertain an amercement

Affeéror, *n.* one who fixes or affeffes a fine

Affeérment, *n.* afcertainment of a fine

Affi'ance, *n.* confidence, truft, hope, a contract

Affi'ance, *v.t.* to truft in, hope, betroth, contract

Affidâvit, *n.* a declaration or depofition upon oath

Affied, Affi'anced, *pa.* joined by contract, be- [trothed

Affil'iated, *a.* affociated as in a family

Affiliâtion, *n.* the adoption of a fon

Affi'ned, *a.* related to another, related, *ob.*

Affin'ity, *n.* kindred, relation by marriage, likenefs, tendency to combine or unite

Affirm', *v.t.* to declare, avouch, confirm

Affirm'able, *a.* that may be affirmed, true, certain

Affirm'ance, *n.* confirmation

Affirm'ative, *a.* that affirms or declares

Affirm'ative, *n.* that which affirms, oppofed to negative

Affirm'atively, *ad.* pofitively, abfolutely, in favor of confirming

Affirmâtion, *n.* a folemn or pofitive declaration

Affirm'ed, *pa.* pofitively declared, confirmed

Affirm'er, *n.* one who affirms, affures or declares

Affix', *v.t.* to fubjoin, add, faften to the end

Af'fix, *n.* a particle, a particle joined to a word

Affix'ed, *pa.* joined to, added, fet or put after

Afflâtion, *n.* the act of breathing upon, a blaft

Afflict', *v.t.* to give pain, trouble, vex, affect

Afflict'ed, *pa.* troubled, diftreffed, grieved

Afflic'tion, *n.* diftrefs, mifery, grief, forrow, pain

Afflict'ive, *a.* diftreffing, painful, grievous

Af'fluence, *n.* plenty, wealth, riches, great ftore

Af'fluent, *a.* wealthy, plentiful, abundant   [flows

Afflux', Afflux'ion, *n.* the act of flowing, what

Afförd, *v.* to fet a price, to yield or grant, to be able to fell

Affran'chife, *v.t.* to make free, give freedom

Affráy, *v.t.* to affright, *ob.*

Affráy, *n.* a quarrel with violence and blows

Affric'tion, *n.* friction, the act of rubbing, *ob.*

Affright, *v.t.* to fright, terrify, fcare, alarm, confound

Affright, Affrightment, *n.* terror, great fear   [fufe

Affrightful, *a.* frightful, terrible, dreadful, *ob.*

Affront', [affrunt] *n.* an infult, wrong, difgrace

Affront', *v.t.* to provoke, infult, offend

Affront'ed, *pa.* offended, infulted, ufed ill

Affront'er, *n.* one who affronts, one who infults

Affront'ing, *pa.* caufing affront, provoking

Affûfe, [affuze] *v.t.* to pour one thing on another,

Affûfion, *n.* a pouring upon   ob.

Affy', *v.t.* to betroth, promife, engage, put truft, *ob.*

Afiéld, *ad.* to or in the field, abroad, out of doors

Afloat, *a.* unfixed, fwimming, moving

Afoot', *ad.* on foot, in action, in defign or intent

Afóre, *prep.* and *ad.* before, in front, in time paft

Aforegoing, *a.* going before

Aforehand, *ad.* beforehand, before

Aforenamed, Aforefaid, *a.* named, or faid, before

Aforetime, *ad.* in time paft, formerly, of old

Afráid, *a.* fearful, in fear, apprehenfive

Afrefh', *ad.* anew, again, over again, once more

Af'rica, *n.* a quarter of the globe

Af'rican, *a.* pertaining to Africa

Af'rican, *n.* a native of Africa

Aft, *ad.* or *a.* the ftern or towards the ftern

Aft'er, *pr.* later in time, behind, in purfuit of, according to

Aft'er, *a.* later, latter, belonging to the ftern

Aft'erages, *n.pl.* pofterity, times following

Aft'er-all, *ad.* at laft, at length, in fhort, in brief

Aft'erbirth, *n.* the membrane inclofing the young

Aft'erclap, *n.* an unexpected demand afterwards

Aft'eréye, *v.* to follow in view, to look after ora-

Aft'ermath, Aft'ercrop, *n.* the fecond crop   [gain

Aft'ermoft, *a.* neareft the ftern

Aft'ernoon, *n.* the time from noon to the evening

Aft'erpains, *n. pl.* a woman's pains after childbirth

Aft'erthought, *n.* thought after any thing is done

Aft'erwards, *ad.* in time to come, next in order

Aft'erwit, *n.* wit or thought that comes too late

Agá, *n.* a high or chief Turkiſh military officer

Agáin, *ad.* once more, beſides, in return

Againſt, *prep.* in oppoſition to, contrary to, oppo-ſite in place, in proviſion for

Agápe, *ad.* with ſtaring eagerneſs, with ſurpriſe

Ag'aric, *n.* a ſpecies of fungus, a drug [red

Ag'aric mineral, *n.* a calcareous ſtone of a whitiſh

Agázed, or Aghaſt', *n.* amazed, aſtoniſhed, frighted

Ag'ate, *n.* a claſs of gems, of many varieties

Age, *n.* the life of an animal or other being, a part of life, the latter part of life, the period when a perſon may act for himſelf, a generation, a cen-'ury

A'ged, *a.* advanced in age or years, old, ancient

A'gency, *n.* buſineſs performed by an agent, action, operation, inſtrumentality

A'gent, *n.* a ſubſtitute or dealer for another, any active power or cauſe

Aggeneration, *n.* a growing together, *ob.*

Agglom'erate, *v.t.* to gather into a ball, to grow

Agglomeration, *n.* a gathering into a ball

Agglútinate, *v.t.* to glue or unite together

Agglutination, *n.* a union, the act of uniting

Agglútinative, *a.* having the quality of glue

Aggrand'íze, *v.a.* to make great, advance, exalt

Aggrand'ized, *pa.* made great, preferred, exalted

Aggrand'ízement, *n.* a being aggrandized or raiſed

Ag'gravate, *v.t.* to make worſe, or more ſevere, *uſed of evils only*

Ag'gravated, *pa.* made worſe, increaſed

Aggravátion, *n.* a making worſe, that which in-creaſes an evil

Ag'gregate, *v.t.* to collect, add or heap together

Ag'gregate, *a.* in an aſſemblage, total

Ag'gregate, *n.* the whole of ſeveral particulars

Ag'gregately, *ad.* in a maſs, the whole together

Aggregátion, *n.* the act of gathering into one maſs, the whole maſs, the union of like bodies

Ag'gregative, *a.* tending to unite in a maſs

Aggreſs', *v.t.* to begin violence, ſet upon, attack

Aggreſ"ſion, *n.* a ſetting upon with violence, an

Aggreſs'or, *n.* an aſſaulter, firſt invader [attack

Aggriévance, *n.* an injury, oppreſſion

Aggriéve, *v.t.* to injure, hurt, oppreſs

Aggróup, [aggroop] *v.t.* to bring into one figure

A"gile, *a.* active, nimble, light, quick, ready, briſk

Agil'ity, *n.* activity, nimbleneſs, readineſs, ſpeed

A'gio, *n.* the difference of exchange between bank-notes or bank-bills and current money

Agiſt', *v.t.* to take in cattle to feed by the week

Agiſt'age, Agiſt'ment, *n.* the taking of cattle to feed, or the price paid in lieu of it

A"gitate, *v.t.* to move, ſhake, examin, debate

A"gitated, *pa.* toſt, ſhaken, diſturbed, debated

Agitátion, *n.* a motion, diſturbance, debate

A"gitator, *n.* a diſturber of the peace

Ag'let, *n.* the repreſentation of ſome animal, a tag

Agnat'ic, *a.* pertaining to the male line of anceſt-

Agnátion, *n.* kindred by the father's ſide [orſ

Agni"tion, *n.* an owning, an acknowledgment

Agníze, *v.t.* to own, acknowledge, confeſs *ob.*

Agó, Agóne, *ad.* paſt, in time paſt, ſince

Agóg', *ad.* in a ſtate of deſire, very deſirous

Agóing, *ad.* in action, going, moving, ſtriking off

Ag'oniſt or Agoniſt'es, *n.* a Grecian prize-fighter

Agoniſt'ic, *a.* relating to prize-fighting

Ag'onize, *v.* to be in or feel very great pain, to writhe with pain

Ag'ony, pain that cauſes ſtruggles, anguiſh

Ag'oty, *n.* an American animal like a hare

Agrárian, *a.* relating to an equal diviſion of lands

Agrée, *v.* to be of one mind, to be conſiſtent, to conſent, ſtrike a bargain, reconcile

Agree'able, *a.* ſuitable, pleaſing, according to

Agree'ableneſs, *n.* pleaſantneſs, conformity

Agree'ably, *ad.* conſiſtently, pleaſingly, fitly

Agréed, *pa.* ſettled by conſent, fixed [blance

Agree'ment, *n.* love, harmony, bargain, reſem-

Agres'tic, *a.* rural, unpoliſhed, ruſtic

Ag'riculture, *n.* huſbandry, the act of tillage

Agricult'ural, *a.* of or relating to agriculture

Agricult'uriſt, *n.* a huſbandman, farmer, tiller of

Ag'ricultor, *n.* a huſbandman, a farmer [land

Ag'rimony, *n.* the plant liverwort

A'griot, *n.* a kind of very ſour cherry

Aground', *a.* run on the ground, ſtranded, ſtopt

A'gue, *n.* a chilly fit, an intermitting fever

A'gueſix, *n.* the fit of an ague, the time of the fit

A'guiſh, *a.* like an ague, ſhivering, cold [tempt

Ah, *ex.* denoting diſlike, compaſſion and con-

Ahá, *n.* an unexpected ſtop or impediment, a ſtop

Ahá, *ex.* denoting pleaſure, triumph or ſurpriſe

Ahéad, *ad.* headlong, raſhly, before, further on

Aid, *v.t.* to help, aſſiſt, ſuccor, ſupport, relieve

Aid, Aídance, *n.* help, ſupport, ſubſidy, a helper

A'iding, *pa.* helping, aſſiſting, ſupporting

A'iddecamp, *n.* an officer attendant on a general

A'ider, *n.* one who aids, a helper, aſſiſtant, ally

A'idleſs, *a.* helpleſs, unſupported, friendleſs

A'igulet, *n.* a point with tags to it, points of gold

Ail, A'ilment, *n.* diſorder, indiſpoſition, pain

Ail, *v.* to be ſick, diſordered, or troubled

A'iling, *pa.* ſickly, unhealthy, diſordered

A'ilment, *n.* illneſs, diſeaſe [pointed at

Aim, *n.* an endeavor, direction, deſign, object

Aim, *v.t.* to take ſight, level, direct, deſign

A'imed, *pa.* levelled, directed, deſigned

Air, *n.* the element in which we breathe, a tune, a geſture, appearance, affected manner

Airs, *n. pl.* lofty or diſdainful carriage

Air *v.t.* to give or take air, warm a little, dry

A'irbladder, *n.* a bladder filled with air, a bubble

A'irbuilt, *a.* built in the air, fanciful, light

A'irgun, *n.* a gun to be charged or loaded with air

A'irhole, *n.* a hole made to let in or out the air

A'irily, *ad.* gayly, brifkly, merrily, fprightfully
A'irinefs, *n.* gayety, levity, an expofure to the air
A'iring, *n.* a fhort tour abroad ; *pa.* warming
A'irlefs, *a.* void of air, clofe, confined, warm, hot
A'irpump, *n.* a machine to draw air out of veffels
A'irfhaft, *n.* the paffage for frefh air into mines
A'iry, *a.* light as air, open to the air, gay, brifk (choir
Aifle or Aile, *n.* a walk in a church, the wing of a
Ajútage, *n.* a tube or pipe in the mouth of a veffel
Ake, *v. i.* to be in continued pain
Akin', *a.* related, allied by blood, like
A'king, *pa.* feeling pain, diftreffed
Ak'ochy, *n.* an animal like a rabbit
Al'abatter, *n.* a foft white marble ; *a.* very white
Alac'rity, *n.* cheerfulnefs, livelinefs, readinefs
Alamóde, *ad.* in the fafhion ; *n.* a thin black filk
Alarm', *n.* a notice of danger, a clock (turb
Alarm', *v.t.* to give notice of danger, furprife, dif-
Alarm'ing, *pa.* giving alarm, exciting fear
Alas', Alack', *ex.* betokening forrow or pity
Alâte, *a.* winged, fpread like wings
Al'batros, *n.* a water fowl of the fize of a goofe
Albéit, *ad.* altho, though, notwithftanding
Al'bemofk, *n.* a fpecies of Syrian mallow
Al'bion, *n.* the ancient name of Great Britain
Al'bumen, *n.* the white part of the blood, an egg,
Albúmenous, *a.* like albumen (or fœd
Alcáic, *n.* a kind of verfe (of a city in Spain
Alcáid, *n.* a governor of a caftle in Barbary, a judge
Al'catras, *n.* a fpecies of pelican in Mexico
Alcavála, *n.* a cuftom-houfe duty paid in Spain
Alchem'ical, *a.* relating to alchemy, myfterious
Al'chemift, *n.* a ftudier or profeffor of alchemy
Al'chemy, *n.* fublime chemiftry, a mixed metal
Al'co, *n.* a quadruped of South America like a dog
Al'cohol, *n.* rectified fpirit compofed of oxygene,
carbon and hydrogene, an impalpable powder
Alcohol'ic, *a.* like or pertaining to alcohol
Al'coran, *n.* the Turkifh bible, *fee* Koran (pofe
Al'cove, *n.* an apartment for books, a recefs of re-
Al'der, *n.* a common tree of feveral varieties
Al'derman, [oldèrman] *n.* a city magiftrate and
Al'dermanly, *a.* becoming an alderman (judge
Al'dern, *a.* made of alder
Ale, *n.* a liquor made by infufing malt and hops
in boiling water, and then fermenting them
A'leconner, *n.* an officer to examin ale pots, &c.
Al'ecoft, *n.* a fpecies of tanfy
Al'egar, *n.* four ale, an acid made of or from ale
A'lehoof, *n.* a kind of root, groundivy, gill
A'lehoufe, *n.* a place where ale is fold
Alem'bic, *n.* a chemical veffel, a kind of ftill
A'lemeafure, *n.* a meafure by which ale is fold
Alert', *a.* quick, nimble, brifk, lively
Alert'ly, *ad.* quickly, nimbly, brifkly
A'lewife, *n.* a woman who keeps an alehoufe, a fifh
Alexan'drian, *a.* pertaining to Alexandria
Alexan'drine, *n.* an Englifh verfe of 12 fyllables

Alexiphar'mic, Alexiter'ic, *a.* what expels poifon
Al'gebra, *n.* literal and univerfal arithmetic
Algebrãic, Algebrãical, *a.* pertaining to algebra
Algebrãically, *ad.* by means of algebra
Al'gebraift, *n.* one who is fkilled in algebra
Algeri'ne, [algerêne] *a.* pertaining to Algiers
Algeri'ne, *n.* a native of Algiers
Al'gid, *a.* extremely cold, very cold, *not ufed*
Al'gous, *a.* pertaining to flags
A'lias, *ad.* otherwife, or elfe ; *n.* a fecond writ
Al'ibi, *n.* a plea of being elfewhere
A'lien, *a.* foreign ; *n.* a foreigner, a ftranger
Aliéns, *v.t.* to eftrange, fell, transfer title
A'lienable, *a.* that may be transferred to another
A'lienate, *v. t.* to transfer, eftrange, withdraw
A'lienate, *a.* withdrawn from, ftrange to, averfe
Alienátion, *n.* a making over, a felling, a change
Alight, *v. i.* to fall upon, defcend, get off a horfe
Alike, *ad.* in the fame manner or form ; *a.* equal
Al'iment, *n.* food, nourifhment, fupport
Aliment'al, Aliment'ary *a.* pertaining to food,
Al'imony, *n.* a feparate maintenance (nourifhing
Al'iquant, *a.* that does not meafure or divide ex-
Al'iquot, *a.* that meafures exactly (actly
A'lifh, *a.* refembling or like ale, tafting like ale
Alive, *a.* not dead, active, fufceptible, in full force,
regenerated
A.'kali, *n.* a falt of an acrid, or cauftic tafte of, three
kinds ; vegetable fixed alkali, as potafh ; mine-
ral fixed alkali, as foda ; and volatile alkali,
as ammoniac
Al'kaline, *a.* having the qualities of alkali
Alkal'ízate, *v.t.* to reduce or bring to an alkali
Alkales'cent, *a.* tending to an alkali
Alkales'cency, *n.* a tendency to become alkaline
Al'kalize, *v.t.* to make alkaline
Al'kalify, *v.* to form or become alkaline
Alkali"genous, *a.* producing alkali
Alkalizátion, *n.* the act of uniting with alkali
Al'kanet, *n.* a plant, a fpecies of gromwell
All *a.* every one ; *n.* the whole ; *ad.* wholly
Alláy, *v.t.* to abate, pacify, quiet
Alláy, *fee* alloy
Alláyed, *pa.* eafed, leffened, abated, fuppreffed
Alláyer, *n.* who or what allays, eafes or leffens
Alláyment, *n.* mitigation
Al'legany, *n.* the main or higheft ridge of moun-
tains in the middle and fouthern ftates of Amer-
Allegánean, *a.* pertaining to the allegany (ica
Allege', *v.t.* to affirm, declare, fay, affign, plead
Allege'able, *a.* that may be alleged or pleaded
Alleg'ed, *pa.* affirmed, given, affigned, pleaded
Allegátion, *n.* affirmation, plea, reafon, excufe
Allégiance, *n.* the duty of fubjects to princes, or to
the ftate in which they live
Allégiant, *a.* loyal, dutiful, obedient *ob.* (legory
Allegor'ic, Allegor'ical, *a.* pertaining to an al-
Allegor'ically, *ad.* in an allegorical manner
Al'legorize, *v.t.* to form or ufe allegories

Al'legory, n. a figurative or allusive speech, allusion

Al'legro, n. a sprightly motion in music ; a. brisk

Allelújah, n. praise to the Lord, praise to God

Allemand', n. a grave and slow piece of music, a figure in dancing

Alléviate, v.t. to ease, lessen, allay ; used of evils

Alleviátion, n. the act of making more light

Al'ley, n. a narrow passage, narrow walk, place

Allfóurs, n. pl. the name of a game at cards

Allháil, ex. all health be to you, be well, &c.

Allhal'lowtide, n. the term near all saints' day

Alliáceous, a. pertaining to garlic, onions, &c.

Alliance, n. an union by treaty or marriage

Alli"ciency, n. the power of attracting, not used

Allíed, pa. united, related, confederated (metic

Alli·átion, n. a tying together, a rule of arith-

Alligátor, n. a large crocodile, a kind of pear

Alli'sion, n. a striking one thing against another

Alliterátion, n. the beginning of two or more words with the same letter

Allit'erative, a. pertaining to alliteration (mision

Allocátion, n. a putting to or near, allowance, ad-

Allocútion, n. a speech to another, an address

Allódial, a. independent, not held of a superior

Allon'ge, n. a pass or thrust made at an enemy

Allot', v.t. to share out, distribute, assign, grant

Allot'ment, n. a part or share allotted, a division

Allow', v.t. to permit, grant, pay to, abate, approve

Allow'able, a. that may be allowed, lawful

Allow'ableness, n. lawfulness, fitness, propriety

Allow'ance, v.t. to put upon allowance (ment

Allow'ance, n. a salary, share, approbation, abate-

Alloy', n. a baser metal mixed with a finer; or the mixture of different metals; evil mixed with good (bate by mixture

Alloy', v.t. to reduce a fine metal by a baser ; to a-

Alloy'age, n. the act of reducing a metal ; mixture

All'spice, n. the berry of the pimento [of metals

Allúde, v.t. to refer indirectly, hint at

Allúre, v.t. to tempt by some good, or apparent good, to entice

Allúre, Allúrement, n. enticement, temptation

Allúrer, n. one who allures, entices or tempts

Allúring, pa. engaging, pleasing, enticing

Allúringly, ad. in an alluring manner, pleasingly

Allúsion, n. a hint, indirect reference

Allúsive, a. hinting at, refering to indirectly

Allúsively, ad. in an allusive manner, remotely

Allúvial, a. washed to land, added by water

Allúvion, n. the washing of water against land, by which the bank is enlarged ; the increase of land so made (er tie

Ally', v.t. to unite by compact, marriage, or eth-

Ally', n. a friend, confederate, relation

Al'manack, n. a calendar of months, days, high water, rising and setting of the sun and moon, the moons changes, fasts, &c.

Almightiness, n. a power over or to do all things

Almighty, a. all-powerful; n. GOD, the Divine Being

Alm'ond, n. the nut of a tree, a fruit

Alm'onds of the throat, n. pl. two round glands

Alm'oner, n. a distributer of alms, an officer

Alm'onry, Am'bry, n. a place for giving victuals

Almóst, ad. nearly, near, well nigh (away

Alms, n. sing. or pl. a gift to the poor, charity

Alms'deed, n. charitable gift or bequest, charity

Alms'giver, n. one that gives alms or bestows cha-

Alms'house, n. a house set apart for the poor (rity

Alms'man, n. one who lives upon alms or charity

Aln'age, n. ell-measure, a measuring by the ell

Al'oe, n. a kind of trees of several species, the inspissated juce of which is used as a medicin, and called aloes

Aloet'ic, Aloet'ical, a. consisting of aloes, bitter

Aloft', ad. on high, in the air, above ; pr. above

Alóne, a. without company, single, lonely

Along', ad. onward, forward, lengthwise

Al'opex, n. a species of dog called field fox

Aloof', ad. at a distance, unconnected

Alóse, n. a fish of passage, the shad

Aloud', ad. loudly, with a great or strong noise

Al'pha, n. the Greek A or a ; a. the first

Al'phabet, n. the letters in any language ranged in customary order

Al'phabet, v.t. to make an alphabet

Alphabet'ical, a. of or according to the alphabet

Alphabet'ically, ad. according to the alphabet

Al'pine, a. pertaining to the Alps, or to high mountains, very lofty

Already, ad. before this time, at a time mentioned

Al'so, ad. likewise, in like manner, and (nion

Al'tar, n. a place for divine offerings or commu-

Alt'er, v. to make or suffer a partial change, to vary

Alt'erable, a. changeable, that may be changed

Alt'erability, n. susceptibility of change

Alt'erably, ad. in an alterable manner, changeably

Alt'erant, a. producing or causing a change (ing

Alterátion, n. a change made, the act of chang-

Al'terative, a. altering, varying

Alt'erative, n. a medicine that changes the humors of the body without sensible evacuation

Alt'ercate, v.i. to dispute with heat or slight anger

Altercátion, n. a dispute with anger, a wrangle

Alt'ered, pa. changed, varied, made different

Alt'erer, n. one who alters, one who changes

Alt'ern, Altern'ate, a. by turns, in succession

Al'ternate, v.t. to change or perform by turns

Altern'ately, ad. mutually, by turns (succession

Alternátion, Altern'ity, n. a mutual change or

Altern'ative, n. a choice of one of two things

Althe'a, a. a shrub, a species of Syrian Mallow

Altho' or Although, a verb in the imperative mode undeclined, grant, allow, admit

Altim'eter, n. an instrument for measuring altitude

Altim'etry, n. the art of measuring hights

Alt'itude, n. the highth of a place

Alt'o, n. the upper or counter tenor ; a. high

Altogeth'er, *ad.* completely, wholly, entirely

Al'udel, *n.* a chemical veffel, wideft in the middle and open at the ends

Al'um, *n.* the fulphate of alumin and potafh, a falt compofed of fulphuric acid, alumin, and potafh

Al'umin, *n.* argil, or pure clay, the bafe of alum

Alumin'iform, *a.* like alumin

Alúminous, *a.* containing or like alum or alumin

Al'veolar, *a.* containing fockets or cells

Al'veolate, *a.* deeply pitted, like a honey comb

Al'vine, *a.* belonging to the inteftinal canal

Al'way or Al'ways, *ad.* for ever, ever, continually

Am, the firft perfon of the verb, *to be ;* which fee. The prefent tenfe runs thus : *I am, thou art,* or *you are, he is, we are,* &c.

Amabil'ity, *n.* lovelinefs, a power of pleafing

Amáin, *ad.* with all power, violently

Amal'gam, *n.* a mixture of quickfilver with other metal ; a well mixed compound

Amal'gamate, *v.t.* to mix metals with quickfilver

Amalgamátion, *n.* the act of mixing quickfilver with other metal ; a mixing

Amanuen'fis, *n.* a writer of another's words or works

Am'aranth, *n.* a plant, a durable flower

Amaranth'ine, *a.* relating to amaranths, lafting

Amar'itude, *n.* bitternefs, feverity

Amafs'ment, *n.* a heap, collection, pile or piling up

Amafs', *v.t.* to heap up, collect together, gather

Amateúr, *n.* a virtuofo, a lover of the fine arts

Am'atory, *a.* relating to or caufed by love

Amato'rial, *a.* relating to or induced by love

Amatórially, *ad.* in the manner of love

Amáze, *v.t.* to confound with furprife, aftonifh

Amáze, Amázement, *n.* aftonifhment, great fear

Amázed, *pa.* furprifed, confufed, perplexed

Amázing, *pa.* aftonifhing, wonderful

Amázingly, *ad.* in a manner to aftonifh

Am'azon, *n.* a virago, a mafculine or bold woman

Amazónian, *a.* pertaining to Amazons, bold

Ambáges, *n.* a circumlocution, tedioufnefs, round

Ambas'fador, *n.* a minifter of the higheft rank, *better written* Embaffador, which fee

Ambas'fage, *ob.* fee Embaffy

Am'ber, *n.* a hard, femi-pellucid fubftance, white or yellow, found in the earth, or thrown on fhore by the fea

Am'bergris, *n.* a hard, opake, refinous fubftance, formed in the fpermaceti whale

Ambidex'ter, *n.* one that ufes both hands equally well, a double-dealer (with equal eafe

Ambidex'trous, *a.* double dealing, ufing both hands

Am'bidexterity, Ambidex'troufnefs, *n.* the power of ufing both hands with equal eafe ; double dealing

Am'bient, *a.* compaffing, furrounding, invefting

Ambigúity, *n.* a double meaning occafioning doubt

Ambig'uous, *a.* doubtful, myfterious, hidden, dark

Ambig'uoufly, *ad.* in a doubtful manner

Ambig'uoufnefs, *n.* doubtfulnefs, obfcurity

Am'bit, *n.* a compafs, a circumference

Ambi"tion, *n.* an earneft defire or wifh, pride

Ambi"tious, *a.* defirous, fond, afpiring, proud, vain

Ambi"tioufly, *ad.* in an ambitious manner

Am'ble, *v.i.* to move with an amble

Am'ble, Am'bling, *n.* a pace in which a horfe moves the two legs on one fide at the fame time

Am'bler, *n.* a horfe or perfon that ambles, a pacer

Ambrófia, *n.* a plant, the feigned food of the gods

Ambrófial or Ambrófian, *z.* delicious, fragrant

Ambulátion, *n.* the act of walking

Am'bulatory, *a.* walking, moving (cealed

Am'bufcade, *n.* a place of furprife, the troops con-

Am'bufcade, *v.t.* to lie in wait, attack by furprife

Am'bufh, *n.* a private ftation for troops to lie in wait in, the act of furprifing, the ftate of lying in wait, the perfons lying in wait

Am'bufh, *v.t.* to lie in wait, to fall on by furprize

Am'bufhed, *pa.* placed or lying in ambufh

Am'bufhment, *n.* an ambufh, a fecret poft

Amen', fo be it, verily, fo may it be ; *n.* truth

Aménable, *a.* refponfible, anfwerable, fubject

Amend', *v.* to correct, grow better, reform, mend

Amend'able, *a.* that may be amended

Amend'atory, *a.* containing an amendment

Amend'ment, *n.* a change for the better, a correc-

Amends', *n.pl.* a recompence, a fatisfaction (tion

Aménity, *n.* pleafantnefs of fituation, pleafure

Am'ent, *n.* a catkin, a calyx confifting of a flender

Amentáceous, *a.* having or being like a catkin (axis

Amerce', *v.t.* to punifh with or lay a fine, to fine

Amerce'ment, *n.* an arbitrary fine

Amer'ica, *n.* a continent between the Atlantic and Pacific oceans

Amer'ican, *n.* a native of America

Amer'ican, *a.* pertaining to America

Amer'icanifm, *n.* love of America and preference of her intereft

Amer'icanize, *v.t.* to render American

Am'ethyft, *n.* a precious ftone of a violet blue, white, gray or green

Amethys'tine, *a.* like an amethyft

A'miable, *a.* lovely, pleafing, charming

A'miablenefs, *n.* lovelinefs, agreeablenefs

Am'ianth, *n.* a mineral fubftance, like afbeftos

Amianth'inite, *n.* a fpecies of amianth

Am'icable, *a.* friendly, kind, obliging, courteous

Am'icablenefs, *n.* friendlinefs, kindnefs

Am'icably, *ad.* in a friendly way, obligingly

Am'ice, *n.* a Romifh prieft's fhoulder-cloth, worn under his furplice or alb, a cap

Amid', Amidft', *pr.* in the middle, amongft, in

Am'ilot, *n.* a white fifh in Mexican lakes

Amifs', *a.* or *ad.* wrong, in an ill fenfe, improperly

Am'ity, *n.* friendfhip, love, agreement, harmony

Am'mony or Ammóniac, *n.* a gummy refinous fubftance, alfo a volatile alkali very pungent

Ammóniac, *a.* pertaining to ammony

Am'modyte, *n.* a venomous ferpent, the fand-eel
Ammuni'tion, *n.* all forts of military ftores, fhot
Am'nefty, *n.* a general pardon, an act of oblivion
Among', Amongft', *pr.* in a mingled ftate, amidft
Am'oriit, Am'orofo, *n.* a gallant, lover, admirer
Am'orous, *a.* fond, loving, inclined to love
Am'oroufly, *ad.* lovingly, fondly, very kindly
Am'oroufnefs, *n.* lovingnefs, love, fondnefs
Amorph'ous, *a.* not having a determinate form
Amotion, *n.* the act of putting away, a removal
Amove, *v.t.* to remove, difplace, alter, move
Amount', *v.i.* to rife in value, come, increafe
Amount', *n.* the fum total, whole, refult, upfhot
Amour, [amoor] *n.* a love-intrigue, gallantry
Am'pelite, *n.* cannel coal, which fee
Amphib'ia, *n.pl.* a clafs of animals, living on land and a long time under water
Amphib'ious, *a.* living in two different elements
Amphibol'ogy, *n.* a double fpeech, an ambiguity
Amphib'ioufnefs, *n.* the faculty of living on land or in water, (council of Greece
Amphyc'tions, *n. pl.* members of the Supreme
Amphictyon'ic, *a.* relating to the high court of Greece
Amphitheater, *n.* a round or oval playhoufe
Am'ple, *a.* large, extended, wide, copious, liberal
Am'plenefs, *n.* largenefs, extent, width, liberality
Amplex'icaul, *a.* embracing the ftem
Ampliation, Amplification, *n.* a diffufe defcription or difcourfe
Amp'lifier, *n.* one who enlarges or exaggerates
Amp'lify, *v.t.* to enlarge, exaggerate, expound
Amp'litude, *n.* extent, an arch of the horizon
Amp'ly, *ad.* largely, liberally, gencroufly, fully
Amp'utate, *v.t.* to cut off a limb, cut off, lop off
Amputation, *n.* the act of cutting off limbs, &c.
Am'ulet, *n.* an appendant medicine, charm, fpell
Amufe, *v.t.* to entertain, pleafe, deceive, detail
Amufement, *n.* a paftime, toy, entertainment, diAmufing, *pa.* entertaining, pleafing (verfion
Amufive, *a.* that has the power to amufe, pleafing
Amygdaloid', *n.* a ftone with an argillaceous bafis containing ftones of other kinds
Amyg'daline, *a.* pertaining to almonds
Amyla'ceous, *a.* partaking of the nature of ftarch, or the farinaceous part of corn
Amyz'lin, *n.* the fea lion, found in the Pacific, on the American coaft
Anabap'tift, *n.* one who holds adult baptifm
Anacam'tic, *a.* reflected, turned back
Anach'ronifn, *n.* an error in the account of time
Anacreon'tic, *a.* pertaining to Anacreon, a Greek poet
An'agram, *n.* a tranfpofing the letters of a name, as, *W, i, l, l, l, i, a, m N, o, y—I moyl in law*
A'nal, *a.* pertaining to the anus
Analem'ma, *n.* a projection made on the meridian
Analep'tic, *a.* comforting, ftrengthening
Analo'gical, *a.* pertaining to analogy, fimilar

Analo'gically, *ad.* by way of analogy or likenefs
Anal'ogous, *a.* having an analogy, proportional
Anal'ogy, *n.* a refemblance, relation, proportion
Anal'yfis, *n.* a feparation of the parts, a refolution
An'alyft, *n.* one who analyzes
Analyt'ical, *a.* of or belonging to analyfis (parts
Analyt'ically, *ad.* by feparating or refolving the
An'alyze, *v.t.* to refolve into firft principles
Ananas, *n.* a fine kind of plant, the pine-apple
An'apeft, *n.* a poetic foot of three fyllables, the two firft fhort, the third long
Anapeft'ic, *a.* pertaining to the anapeft
An'arch, [ch as k] *n.* an author of confufion
Anarch'ial, *a.* without rule, confufed, irregular
An'archy, *n.* a want of government, confufion,
Anafarc'a, *n.* a kind of dropfy (diforder
Anafarc'ous, *a.* dropfical
Anas'tomofe, *v.i.* to inofculate, or unite as the mouths of two veffels
Anaftom'ofy, *n.* the opening of one veffel into another, as the veins and arteries
Anas'trophy, *n.* an inverfion of the order of words
Anath'ema, *n.* a curfe, excommunication, cenfure
Anath'ematize, *v.t.* to curfe, to excommunicate
Anatom'ical, *a.* belonging to anatomy, diffected
Anatom'ically, *ad.* by way of diffection, in parts
Anat'omift, *n.* one who anatomizes (open
Anat'omize, *v.t.* to diffect an animal, divide, lay
Anat'omy, *n.* the art, &c. of diffection, a fkeleton
An'ceftor, *n.* one from whom we defcend
An'ceftrel, *a.* claimed from anceftors, ancient, old
An'ceftry, *n.* a pedigree, birth, defcent, lineage
Anch'or, [ch as k] *n.* an iron inftrument for holding fhips at reft, any firm fupport
Anch'or, *v.* to caft an anchor, ftop at, reft on
Anch'orage, *n.* ground or duty for anchoring
Anch'ored, *pa.* come to anchor, held at anchor
Anch'oret, Anch'orite, *n.* a hermit, a reclufe
Anch'orfmith, *n.* a perfon who makes anchors
An'chovy, *n.* a very little feafifh ufed for fauce
An'cient, *a.* old, belonging to former times
An'ciently, *ad.* in old times, formerly, long ago
An'cientnefs, *n.* great age, oldnefs, antiquity
An'cientry, *n.* ancient lineage, dignity of birth
An'cients, *n. pl.* thofe who lived in old times
An'cillary, *a.* relating to a female fervant
An'cony, *n.* an iron bar, or bloomery
And, *conj.* joining fentences and words
Andant'e, *ad.* diftinctly, regularly, flow
And'iron, *n.* an iron utenfil to hold wood, or a fpit
Andro'ginal, Andro'ginous, *a.* partaking of both
An'ecdote, *n.* a piece of fecret hiftory (fexes
Anecdot'ical, *a.* relating to anecdotes
Anemog'raphy, *n.* defcription of the winds
Anemom'eter, *n.* an inftrument to afcertain the force and velocity of the wind
Anem'ony, *n.* a plant, the windflower
Anem'ofcope, *n.* an inftrument to fhow the direction of the wind.

An'eurifm, *n.* a tumor from the burfting of an ar-
An'eurif'mal, *a.* belonging to aneurifm (tery
Anew', *ad.* afrefh, over again, newly, repeatedly
An'gel, *n.* a heavenly or divine meffenger, beau-
tiful perfon, old gold coin worth about 10s. ffer.
Angel'ica, *n.* the name of a plant (above human
Angel'ical, Angel'ic, An'gel, *a.* refembling angels,
An''ger, *n.* paffion excited by injury, inflammation
An''ger, *v.t.* to provoke, vex, difpleafe, heat, fret
Angiol'ogy, *n.* the doctrine of the veffels in the body
Angiofperm'ous, *a.* having feeds inclofed or cover-
Angiot'omy, *n.* the opening of a blood veffel (ed
An''gle, *n.* a corner, a point where two lines meet
An''gle, *v. n.* to fifh, to fifh with a rod and hook
Ang'ler, *n.* one who fifhes with a rod and hook
Ang'ler, *n.* a large ill fhaped fifh
An'glicize, *v.t.* to render Englifh
Ang'licifm, *n.* an Englifh idiom or expreffion
Ang'ling, *n.* the art of fifhing with a rod
Anglofax'on, *a.* pertaining to the Saxons who fet-
tled in England; *n.* their language
An''grily, An''gerly; *ad.* in an angry manner
An''gry, *a.* moved with anger, inflamed, vext
Anguil'liform, *a.* refembling an eel
An''guifh, *n.* exceffive pain, pain, very great grief
An''guifhed, *a.* exceffively pained, very anxious
An''gular, An''gulous, *a.* having corners, hooked
An'gularly, *ad.* in an angular form
An''gulate, *a.* formed with angles, bent, pointed
Anguftation, *n.* the act of making narrow, ftrait-
Anhelation, *n.* the act or ftate of panting (nefs
Anights, *ad.* night after night, at or in the night
Animadver'fion, *n.* cenfure, reproof, criticifm
Animadvert', *v.i.* to cenfure, criticife, attend, pun-
Animadvert'er, *n.* a cenfurer, critic, judge (ifh
An'imal, *n.* a being with an organized body, en-
dowed with life, fenfation, and fpontaneous mo-
An'imal, *a.* pertaining to an animal, grofs (tion
An'imalflower, *n.* the fea nettle, or fea anemony
An'imalize, *v.t.* to form into an animal
Animaliz ätien, *n.* the endowing with the nature
of animals
Animal'cule, *n.* a fmall or little animal, an infect
Animal'ity, *n.* the ftate of animal exiftence, life
An'imate, *v.t.* to give life, ftir up, incite, enliven
An'imate, *a.* alive, living, poffeffing animal life
An'imated *pa.* enlivened, moved, fpirited, lively
Animation, *n.* the act of animating, life, fpirit
An'imator, *n.* one who or that which gives life
Animos'ity, *n.* extreme hatred, averfion, rage
An'ife, *n.* a plant, an aromatic fpecies of parfley
Ank'er, *n.* a veffel containing nine or ten gallons
An''kle, *n.* the joint between the foot and the leg
An'nalift, *n.* a writer, former or difpofer of annals
An'nals, *n. pl.* hiftories digefted into years
An'nates or An'nats, *n.* firft-fruits, maffes for a year
Anneal', *v.t.* to temper glafs, feafon, heat, bake
An'nex, *n.* a thing annexed, a thing fubjoined
Annex', *v.t.* to join, add, connect, fubjoin, unite

Annexátion, Annex'ion, *n.* an addition, an union
Annex'ed, *pa.* joined, added, connected, united
Annihilable, *a.* capable of being annihilated
Annihilate, *v.t.* to reduce to nothing, to deftroy
the fpecific form of a thing
Annihilátion, *n.* an abolifhing, deftruction, ruin
Anniverf'ary, *n.* a yearly commemoration or feaft
Anniverf'ary, *a.* yearly, returning with the year
An'no Dom'ini, *n.* in the year of our Lord
Anno'na, *n.* cuftard apple, a genus of plants (ment
Annotátion, *n.* an explication, note, remark, com-
An'notator, *n.* a commentator, a writer of notes
Annot'to or Arnot'to, *n.* a plant, an elegant red
color, and the fubftance which forms it
Announce', *v.t.* to publifh, declare, proclaim, tell
Announ'ced, *pa.* declared, made known, told
Announce'ment, *n.* public notice, introduction
Annoy', *v.t.* to incommode, injure by continued
or repeated acts
Annoy', Annoy'ance, *n.* injury, hurt, moleftation
Annoy'er, *n.* one who annoys, one who injures
An'nual, *a.* yearly, lafting only a year
Annual', *n.* a plant whofe root dies yearly
An'nually, *ad.* yearly, year by year
Annúitant, *n.* a perfon who has an annuity
Annúity, *n.* a yearly allowance or fet payment
Annul', *v.t.* to make void, abolifh, repeal
An'nular, *a.* in form of or like a ring, round
An'nulate, *a.* having rings or belts
An'nulet, *n.* a little ring, a mark in heraldry
Annúmerate, *v.t.* to add, reckon up, *not ufed*
Annumerátion, *n.* the act of adding, *not ufed*
Annun'ciate, *v.t.* to bring tidings, *not ufed*
Annunciátion-day, *n.* the day on which an angel
appeared to the virgin Mary, to declare our
Saviour's birth, the twenty-fifth day of March
An'odyne, *n.* a medicine to affuage pain and dif-
An'odyne, *a.* mitigating pain, eafing (pofe to fleep
Anoint', *v.t.* to rub with oil, &c. to confecrate
Anoint'ed, *pa.* rubbed with oil, &c. confecrated
Anoint'ing, *n.* an unction, a confecration
Anóle, *n.* a fpecies of lizard in the W. Indies
Anom'alous, *a.* irregular, out of rule, deviating
Anom'aloufly, *ad.* irregularly, unequally (from
Anom'aly, *n.* irregularity, deviation, unlikenefs
Anon', *ad.* foon, quickly, fhortly, in a fhort time
Anon'ymous, *a.* wanting a name, namelefs
Anon'ymoufly, *ad.* without a name
An'orexy, *n.* want of appetite
Anoth'er, [anuther] *a.* fome other, a fecond
An'fers, *n. pl.* an order of fowls, as ducks and geefe
An'fwer, *v.* to reply, folve, fulfil, fucceed, fuit,
witnefs for, be accountable
An'fwer, *n.* a reply, return, confutation, folution
An'fwerable, *a.* fuitable, accountable, like
An'fwerably, *ad.* fuitably, agreeably, fitly
An'fwerer, *n.* one who anfwers or replies
An'fwering, *pa.* replying, vindicating, agreeing
Ant, *n.* a fmall induftrious infect, a pifmire

C

Antag'onift, n. an opponent, adverfary, mufcle
Antag'onift, a. oppofing, counteracting
Antarc'tic, a. of or relating to the fouthern pole
Ant'bear, n. a quadruped feeding on ants
Ant'eater, n. a quadruped fubfifting on ants
Antecéde, v. t. to precede, to go before in time
Antecédent, n. what goes before as a noun
Antecédent, a. going before, foregoing, prior
Antecédently, ad. before in time, previoufly   [er
An'techamber, n. an outer room leading to anoth-
An'tedate, v. t. to date a thing before the time
Antedilúvian, a. exifting or done before the flood
Antedilúvian, n. one who lived before the flood
Ant'elope, n. a kind of goat with curled horns
Antemerid'ian, a. relating to the forenoon
Antemund'ane, a. being before the world, eternal
Ant'epaft, n. a foretafte, anticipation, luncheon
Antepenult', n. the laft fyllable but two in words
Antepenult'imate, a. of the laft fyllable but two
Antérior, a. former, going before, previous, prior
An'teroom, n. a room before another room
Anterior'ity, n. priority in time, &c. precedence
Anthelmint'ic, n. a remedy for worms
Anthelmint'ic, a. good againft worms
Anth'er, n. the top of the flamen of a flower, con-
taining the fecundating duft
Antherif'erous, a. producing an anther or anthers
Ant'hill, n. a hilloc raifed by ants
An'them, n. a holy or divine fong, a kind of hymn
Anthol'ogy, n. a collection of poems or flowers
An'thrax, n. a carbuncle, a dangerous fore
Anthropog'raphy, n. defcription of human bodies
Anthrop'olite, n. a petrified human body
Anthropol'ogy, n. a difcourfe on human nature
Anthropoph'agi, n. pl. eaters of men, cannibals
Anthropoph'agy, n. the act of eating human flefh
Antia'cid, a. correcting acids, abforbent
Antia''cid, n. that which corrects acidity
Antibafil'ican, a. oppofed to royal ftate, or mag-
nificence
Ant'ic, n. a buffoon; a. odd, ridiculoufly w'ld, &c.
An'tichrift, n. one who oppofes Chrift
Antichris'tian, a. againft Chrift or Chriftianity
Anti''cipate, v. t. to take before, foretafte, pre-
Anticipátion, n. a foretafte, prevention   [vent
Anticlimax, n. a fentence in which the laft part
is lower than the firft, a finking or depreffion
Anticonta'gious, a. oppofing contagion
Anticonvuls'ive, a. good againft convulfions
Anticourt'ier, n. a man that oppofes the court
Ant'idotal, a. expelling, efficacious againft
Ant'idote, n. a remedy for poifon or evil
Antiemet'ic, a. checking, vomiting
Antifébrile, a. expelling or good againft fevers
Antiminifte'rial, a. oppofed to adminiftration
Antimonarch'ical, a. that is againft monarchy
Antimónial, a. made of or relating to antimony
Ant'imony, n. a brittle heavy metal ufed in med-
icine and the arts

Antimónic, a. denoting antimony and oxygene
Antinómians, n. a fect who prefer faith to practice
An'tinomy, n. a contradiction in laws
Antinómian, a. of thofe who condemn works
Antip'athy, n. a natural averfion, diflike, hate
Antipeftilen'tial, a. good againft infection
Antiphlogis'tian, n. an oppofer of the theory of
phlogifton
Antiphlogis'tic, a. reducing inflammation
Antiph'ony, n. finging by way of refponfe
An'tipode, n. one who lives on the oppofite fide of
Antip'odal, a. relating to the antipodes [the globe
Ant'ipope, n. a perfon who ufurps the popedom
Ant'iquary, n. one ftudious of antiquities
Antiqua'rian, a. relating to antiquity
Ant'iquate, v. t. to make obfolete, to make void
Ant'iquated, pa. grown old or out of fafhion
Antíque, [antéke] a. ancient, old
Antíque, n. a remnant of antiquity, an old relic
Antíquenefs, n. antiquity, ancientnefs, an old ftate
Anti''quity, n. old times, great age, ancientnefs
An'tirevolu'tionary, a. oppofing revolution
Antirevolu'tionift, n. an oppofer of a revolution
Antifcorbútic, a. good for or againft the fcurvy
Antifcep'tic, n. a medicine to prevent putrefaction
Antifplenet'ic, a. good againft the fpleen   [ode
Antis'trophy, n. fecond ftanza of every three in an
Antiftrumat'ic, a. good againft the king's evil
Antith'efis, n. an oppofition of words and thoughts
Antithet'ical, a. relating to antithefis
Antitrinitárian, n. a man who denies the Trinity
Ant'itype, n. that which is formed according to a
type, as the Pafchal lamb was the type, and
Chrift the antitype
Antivenéreal, a. good againft the venereal difeafe
Ant'ler, n. a branch, a branch of a ftag's horn
An'vil, n. an iron block for fmith's work
Anxíety, Anx'ioufnefs, n. uneafinefs, folicitude
Anx'ious, a. much concerned, very eager, uneafy
Anx'ioufly, ad. with great defire, very carefully
A''ny, a. every, whoever, whatever, either, one
A'nywife, ad. in any manner
A'orift, a. indeterminate with refpect to time
Aorif'tic, indefinite in time
Aor'tal, a. pertaining to the aorta or great artery
which carries the blood from the heart
Apáce, ad. quickly, haftily, fpeedily, faft
Apago''gical, a. that proves any thing by fhowing
the abfurdity of denying it, indirect
Apalach'ian, a. pertaining to the mountains in
Georgia   [afide
Apart', ad. feparately, diftinctly, at a diftance,
Apart'ment, n. a part of a houfe, a diftinct room
Ap'athy, n. a want of paffion or feeling, indolence
Ape, n. a kind of monkey, mimic, fimpleton, fool
Ape, v. t. to imitate as an ape, imitate, mimic
Apep'fy, n. a want of regular digeftion
Apérient, a. gently purgative, opening, purging
Aper'itive, a. that has the power of opening or

Aper'tion, *n.* a paffage, gap, opening, [purging

Ap'erture, *n.* an open place, opening, hole, paffage

Apet'alous, *a.* having no petal or flower leaf

A'pex, *n.* the top or angular part of a thing

Aphélion, *n.* the greateft diftance from the fun

Aphidiv'orous, *a.* eating or devouring the aphis

A'phis, *n.* the infect called puceron, vine fretter

Aph'orifm, *n.* a maxim, precept, general rule

Aph'rodite, *n.* a genus of fea infects, the fea moufe

Aphoris'tic, *a.* in the form of aphorifms

Aphyl'lous, *a.* deftitute of leaves

A'piary, *n.* a place where bees are kept [rately

Apiéce, *ad.* to each one's fhare, for each, fepa-

A'pifh, *a.* fimple, filly, foppifh, affected, wanton

A'pifhly, *ad.* in an apifh manner, foolifhly, drolly

A'pifhnefs, *n.* buffoonery, foolery, folly, foppery

Apoc'alypfe; *n.* the book of Revelation

Apocalyp'tical, *a.* containing revelation

Apoc'opy, *n.* a cutting off the laft fyllable

Apoc'rypha, *n. pl.* books of doubtful authority

Apoc'ryphal, *a.* not canonical, uncertain, fecret

Apodic'tical, *a.* demonftrative, *not ufed*

Ap'odes, *n. pl.* fifh having no ventral fins

Ap'odal, *a.* without feet, or ventral fins

Ap'ogee, *n.* the point of the fun's &c. orbit fartheft

Apol'lo, *n.* the God of arts, the fun [from the earth

Apol'lyon, *n.* the deftroyer

Apologet'ical, *a.* defending, excufing, leffening

Apol'ogift, *n.* one who makes an apology or plea

Apol'ogize, *v. i.* to plead for, defend, excufe

Ap'ologue, *n.* a fable or tale teaching moral truths

Apol'ogy, *n.* a defence, excufe, juftification, plea

Ap'ophthegm, *n.* a remarkable faying, a maxim

Apoplec'tic, *a.* belonging to an apoplexy

Ap'oplexy, *n.* a diforder that affects the brain

Apos'tafy, *n.* a falling from one's former profeffion

Apos'tate *n.* one that forfakes his religion or party

Apos'tatize, *v. i.* to forfake one's religion or party

Apos'temate, *v. t.* to corrupt or form into matter

Apos'teme, *n.* a hallow and purulent fwelling

Apos'tle, *n.* a meffenger fent to preach the gofpel

Apos'tlefhip, *n.* the office, ftate, &c. of an apoftle

Apos'tolate, *n.* the office of an apoftle

Apoftol'ic, Apoftol'ical, *a.* delivered by the apoftles

Apoftol'ically, *ad.* in the manner of the apoftles

Apos'trophy, *n.* in rhetoric, a turning the courfe of fpeech, contraction of words by (') mark

Apos'trophic *a.* pertaining to an apoftrophy

Apos'trophize, *v. t.* to addrefs by an apoftrophy

Apoth'ecary, *n.* a compounder, &c. of medicines

Apotheóns, *n.* the making a god, a confecration

Ap'ozem; *n.* a medical decoction of herbs, &c.

Appall', *v. t.* to fright fo as to difpirit, to difmay

Appal'led, *pa.* ftruck with fear, terrified

Ap'panage, *n.* lands for younger children of princes

Apparátus, *n.* tools, things, furniture, equipage

Appar'el, *n.* clothing, cloaths, raiment, drefs

Appar'el, *v. t.* to drefs, deck, adorn, fet off

Apparent, *a.* vifible, evident, plain, open, certain

Apparently, *ad.* vifibly, in appearance only

Appari'tion, *n.* an appearance, ghoft, vifion, view

Appar'itor, *n.* a low officer in ecclefiaftical courts

Appay', *v. t.* to content, *ob.*

Appéach, *v. t.* to accufe, impeach, *ob.*

Appéal, *n.* removal of a caufe from a lower to a higher court, reference to a witnefs, accufation

Appéal, *v. t.* to remove from a lower to a higher court, call to witnefs, accufe

Appéar, *v. i.* to be in fight, feem, look, anfwer

Appéarance, *n.* a refemblance, likelihood, fhow,

Appéafe, *v. t.* to quiet, pacify, calm [entrance

Appéafement, *n.* act of quieting, reconciliation

Appel'lant, *n.* a perfon who appeals, a challenger

Appel'late, *a.* belonging to appeals

Appellátion, *n.* a name, title, term, addrefs

Appel'lative, *a.* common to many or all, general

Appel'lative, *n.* the name of a whole fpecies

Appellor', *n.* the plaintiff in appeal, he who appeals

Appellee', *n.* the defendant in appeal, he who is appealed

Append', *v. t.* to hang or join to, hang on, add

Append'age, Append'ant, *n.* an addition

Append'ant, Append'ed, *a.* hanging or joined to

Append'icate, *v. t.* to add, append, annex, *ob.*

Append'icle, *n.* a fmall appendage

Append'ix, *n.* an addition, a fupplement

Ap'penine, *a.* relating to the Appenines, mountains in Italy

Appertáin, *v. i.* to belong, relate, depend upon

Appertáining, *pa.* belonging, relating, depending

Appert'ment, *a.* belonging or relating to

Ap'petence or Ap'petency, *n.* fenfual defire, a tendency in organized matter to unite with or felect particles of matter

Appetibil'ity, *n.* a defirable ftate or quality, defire

Ap'petible, *a.* defirable, pleafing, engaging

Ap'petite, *n.* a ftomach, defire of food, or other fenfual gratification

Ap'pian, *a.* relating to Appius, as Appian way

Applaud', *v. t.* to praife, commend, extol, cry up

Applaud'er, *n.* one who praifes, one who commends

Applaufe', *n.* public praife, commendation, credit

Ap'ple, *n.* a common fruit, the pupil of the eye

Apply', *v. t.* to put to certain ufe, ftudy, attend

Ap'pliable or Ap'plicable, *a.* fuitable, proper, fit

Ap'plicablenefs, *n.* a fitnefs to be applied

Applicabil'ity, *n.* the ftate of being applicable

Ap'plicant, *n.* one who makes requeft [daiiry

Applicátion, *n.* the act of applying, clofe ftu ly, in-

Ap'plicative, Ap'plicatory, *a.* that applies, proper

Applier, *n.* one who applies, a ftudent

Appoint', *v. t.* to fix upon, determin, fettle, name and commiffion to an office

Appoint'able, *a.* that may be appointed

Appoint'ed, *pa.* fixed on, fet, chofen, equipped

Appoint'ment, *n.* an order, falary, poft, defignation to office

Apport', *v. t.* to carry, bring, convey, tranfier, *ob.*

Apportion, v. t. to divide or part out, to affign
Ap'posit, a. proper, fit, fuitable, well adapted to
Ap'positly, ad. properly, fitly, fuitably, timely
Ap'positness, n. propriety, fitness, fuitableness
Appofi'tion, n. a putting to or near, an addition
Appraife, v. t. to value goods by authority, to
set a price on, fee apprife, a more correct fpelling
Appraifement, n. the act of appraifing
Appraifer, n. an authorifed perfon who values
Appre'ciate, v. to value, ettimate, rife in value
Appreciation, n. a due ettimate, a rifing in value
Appre'ciable, a. capable of being eftimated
Apprehend', v. t. to feize, take, underftand, fear
Apprehend'ed, pa. caught, conceived, feared
Apprehend'er, n. a conceiver, a thinker
Apprehens'ible, a. that may or can be apprehended
Apprehen'fion, n. conception, fufpicion, fear
Apprehens'ive, a. fearful, fenfible, [henfive
Apprehen'fivencfs, n. the quality of being appre-
Apprent'ice, n. one covenanted to learn a trade
Apprent'ice, v. t. to bind out as an apprentice
Apprent'icefhip, n. the time an apprentice ferves
Appreft', a. preffed clofe, lying near the ftem
Apprife, a. to value by authority, to fet a price on
Apprifement, n. a valuation under authority
Appri'fer, n. one appointed to value
Apprize, v. t. to inform, to acquaint
Apprized, pa. informed, told, inftructed
Approach, v. to draw or bring near, to come up to
Approach, n. the act of drawing near, an advance
Approachable, a. that may be approached
Approbation, n. the approving of a thing
Appropriate, v.t. to fet apart for a certain purpofe,
or for one's felf
Appropriate, a. peculiar, fet, apart, affigned, put
Appropriable, a. that may be appropriated [able
Appropriatenefs, n. the quality of being very fuit-
Appropriation, n. an application to fome particu-
lar ufe or meaning, an alienation [benefice
Appropriator, n. one who has an appropriated
Approve, [approov] v. t. to like or allow of, ren-
der one's felf worthy, juftify, prove, fhow
Approvable, a. worthy of approbation [bation
Approval, Approvance, Approve'ment, n. appro-
Approved, pa. liked, proved, tried, examined
Approver, n. one who approves, a felon who
turns informer [plice
Approve'ment, n. an informing againft an accom-
Approx'imate, a. near or joining to, ob. [near
Approx'imate, v. i. to come near, approach, bring
Approximation, n. a near approach to any thing
Appulfe', n. the act of ftriking againft
Appul'fion, n. a ftriking againft by a moving body
Appul'five, a. ftriking againft by a moving body
Appurt'enance, n. that which belongs or relates to
fomething elfe, or the principal thing
Appur'tenant, a. belonging to by right
A'pricot, n. a fine kind of ftone fruit
A'pril, n. a month, the fourth month of the year

A'pron, n. a part of drefs worn before, a cover
A'proned, a. wearing or having an apron
Apt, a. fit, ready, qualified, inclined, tending
Apt'itude, n. aptnefs, fitnefs, tendency, difpofition
Apt'ly, ad. properly, fitly, duly, readily, wittily
Apt'nefs, n. fitnefs, quicknefs of apprehenfion
Apt'ote, n. a noun that has but one termination
Ap'ters, n. pl. infects without wings
Apy'rous, a. refifting fire, incombuftible
Aquafor'tis, n. liquor made of nitrous acid, with a
fmall portion of fulphuric acid
Aquarius, n. one of the 12 figns of the zodiac, the
rainy fign
Aquat'ic, a. growing or living in water, watery
Aq'ueduct, n. a conveyance for water, canal, pipe
A'queous, a. watery, confifting of water
A'queoufnefs, n. a watery quality
Aq''uiline, a. like an eagle or its beak, hooked
Ar'abic, n. the language fpoken by the Arabians
Arabian, a. pertaining to Arabia in Afia; n. a na-
tive of the country
Ar'able, a. fit for tillage or plowing, plowed
Araneous, a. like a cobweb, or fpider
Ar'balat, Ar'balift, n. a crofbow, ob.
Ar'biter, n. an umpire, one who controls
Arbit'rament, n. will, determination, award
Ar'bitrarily, ad. without control, abfolutely
Ar'bitrarinefs, n. wilfulnefs, tyranny, defpotifm
Ar'bitrary, a. abfolute, defpotic, governed or dic-
tated by will only
Ar'bitrate, v. to hear and judge as an arbitrator
Arbitration, n. reference of a controverfy to per-
fons chofen by the parties, a hearing before
arbitrators, award
Ar'bitrator, n. a perfon chofen by a party to de-
cide a controverfy, one who has the fovereign
right to judge and control
Ar'bitrefs, n. a female arbiter
Arboreous, Ar'borous, a. belonging to trees
Arbores'cence, n. the refemblance of trees in mof-
fes and minerals, the habits of a tree [of trees
Arbores'cent, a. having the habits or refemblance
Arborization, n. the appearance of trees in mine-
Ar'boret, n. a fmall tree, a fhrub [rals
Ar'borift, n. a naturalift in or judge of trees
Ar'bor, n. a bower, a feat fhaded with trees, &c.
Ar'bute, n. a kind of plant, the ftrawberry-tree
Arc, n. part of a circle or bridge
Arcade, n. a continuation of arches, a long arch
Arcadian, n. a native of Arcadia in Greece
Arcadian, a. relating to Arcadia
Arcanum, n. a fecret, myftery, noftrum
Ar'chi', n. a fpecies of lichen, or mofs
Arch, a. chief, notorious, waggith
Arch, n. a curve line, or part of a circle, any work
in that form, or covered by an arch
Arch, v.t. to form an arch
Arch'aifm, [ch as k] n. an ancient or obfolete
phrafe, &c.

Archan'gel, *n.* a chief angel, a plant, dead-nettle
Archangel'ic, *a.* belonging to or like archangels
Archapos'tate, *n.* the chief apostate
Archbish'op, *n.* a chief bishop, a leading bishop
Archbish'opric, *n.* the power, &c. of an archbishop
Archdéacon, *n.* a chief deacon, a bishop's deputy
Archdéaconry, Archdéaconship, *n.* the office of an
Archduch'efs, *n.* a grand duchefs [archdeacon
Archdúke, *n.* a grand duke, a chief or head prince
Archdúcal, *a.* pertaining to an archduke
Arch'ed, *pa.* bent in form of an arch, vaulted
Arch'er, *n.* one who shoots or fights with a bow
Arch'ery, *n.* the art, &c. of shooting with a bow
Arch'etypal, *a.* belonging to the original
Arch'etype, *n.* the original, a pattern, a model
Archidiac'onal, *a.* belonging to an archdeacon
Archiepifc'opal, *a.* belonging to an archbishop
Arch'itect, *n.* a chief builder, furveyor, planner
Architect'ive, *a.* belonging to architecture
Architecton'ic, *a.* of or relating to an architect
Arch'itecture *n.* the fcience or act of building
Architec'tural, *a.* pertaining to the art of building
Arch'itrave, *n.* principal beam, the part of a column next above the capital
Arch'ives, *n. pl.* records, a place ufed for records
Arch'ivift, *n.* the keeper of archives
Arch'on, [ch as k]*n.* a chief magiftrate of Athens
Arch'onship, *n.* the office of an Archon
Archprel'ate, *n.* a chief prelate
Archpres'byter, *n.* a chief prefbyter
Archprieft, *n.* a chief prieft
Archtreas'urer, *n.* a chief treafurer
Arch'wife, *ad.* in the form of an arch, crookedly
Arc'tic, *a.* northern, lying in or towards the north
Arc'uate, *v. t.* to make or bend like an arch
Arcuátion, *n.* an arching, crookednefs [heat
Ar'dency, Ar'dentnefs, *n.* eagernefs, zeal, paffion,
Ar'dent, *a.* hot, fierce, keen, zealous, affectionate
Ar'dently, *ad.* eagerly, zealoufly, affectionately
Ar'dor, *n.* heat, warmth, zeal, fervency, affection
Ar'duous, *a.* difficult, hard to attain, laborious
Ar'duoufnefs, *n.* difficulty and laborioufnefs
A'rea, *n.* the fuperficial contents of a thing
A'real, *a.* pertaining to an area
Aréad or Aréed, *v. t.* to advife, direct, guefs, *ob.*
Ar'efy, *v. t.* to dry, *not ufed*
Arefac'tion, *n.* the ftate or act of drying, drynefs
Arenáceous, Arenófe, *a.* fandy, or of full of fand
Arena'tion, *n.* the ufing of a fand bath
Areop'agus, *n.* the fupreme court of ancient Athens
Areop'agite, *n.* a member of the court of Athens
Areom'eter, *n.* an inftrument to afcertain the fpecific gravity of liquids
Ar'gent, *a.* filvercolored, white, fhining, bright
Ar'gentate, *n.* a combination of the oxyd of filver with another fubftance
Argentátion, *n.* an overlaying with filver
Argentiferous, *a.* producing filver
Ar'gentine, *a.* like filver, confifting of it

Ar'gentine, *n.* pyritaceous limeftone
Argent'ic a"cid, a faturated combination of filver
Ar'gill, *n.* fat foft earth, pure clay [and oxygene
Argilláceous, Argil'lous, *a.* clayifh, confifting of clay
Argilliferous, *a.* producing or abounding with clay
Ar'gillite, *n.* flate, a fpecies of fhiftus [and iron
Argillit'ic, *a.* pertaining to argillite
Argillocal'cite, *n.* clay and calcareous earth
Argillomu'rite, *n.* magnefia combined with clay
Ar'gonaut, *n.* one who attended Jafon in his voyage after the golden fleece
Argonaut'ic, *a.* relating to the voyage of Jafon
Ar'gofy, *n.* a large veffel ufed for merchandife, *ob.*
Ar'gue, *v.* to reafon, to draw inferences from
A'rguer, *n.* a difputer, debater, reafoner [premifes
Ar'gument, *n.* reafon alleged to induce belief, feries of inferences, fubject of difcourfe, debate, a fummary of contents
Argument'al, *a.* belonging to argument
Argumentátion, *n.* the act, art, &c. of reafoning
Argument'ative, *a.* containing argument
Argúte, *a.* fharp, fhrill, fubtle, keen, witty
A'rian, *n.* a follower or difciple of Arius
A'rianifm. *n.* a denial of the real divinity of Chrift
Ar'id, *a.* dry, parched up with heat
Arid'ity, Ar'idnefs, *n.* drynefs, drouth
A'ries, *n.* one of the 12 figns, the ram
Arietátion, *n.* the act of butting, a pufh, a conflict
Ariet'ta, *n.* a little fhort fong, air or tune
Aright, *ad.* in order, without miftake, rightly, du'y
Ar'il, *n.* the outer coat of a feed
Ariolátion or Hariolátion, *n.* foothfaying
Arife, *v. i.* arofe, *pr.* arifen, *pa.* to rife, get or mount up, appear, take place, be active
Ariftoc'racy, *n.* a government by nobles or peers
Aris'tocrat, *n.* one who favors ariftocracy
Ariftocrat'ic, *a.* of or relating to an ariftocracy
Arith'metic, *n.* the act or fcience of computation
Arithmet'ical, *a.* of or according to arithmetic
Arithmet'ically, *ad.* by means of arithmetic
Arithmeti"cian, *n.* a perfon fkilled in arithmetic
Ark, *n.* a lumber veffel or fhip, veffel, cheft, arch
Arm, *n.* a limb of the body, branch, inlet, ftrength
Arm, *v.* to furnifh with or take up arms, to aid
Armáda, *n.* a large and ftrong fleet of fhips of war
Armadil'lo, *n.* a fmall quadruped of America, having a fnout, and covered with a fhell compofed of movable belts or fcales [war
Arm'ament, *n.* a land or naval force equipped for
Arm'ature, *n.* armor, defence, fkill in arms
Arm'ed, *pa.* furnifhed with arms, defended
Arme'nian, *a.* pertaining to Armenia in Afia
Arm'gaunt, *a.* flender, weak through want, *ob.*
Armi"gerous, *a.* bearing arms
Arm'illary, *a.* of or refembling a bracelet, circular
Armin'ian, *n.* one who denies predeftination, and holds to free will, and univerfal redemption
Armin'ianifm, *n.* the tenets of Arminians
Armip'otent, *a.* powerful in arms, warlike, brave

Arm'iftic, *n.* a ceſſation of arms, a ſhort truce
Arm'let, *n.* a ſmall arm of the ſea, &c. a bracelet
Arm'or, *n.* defenſive arms for the body
Arm'orer, *n.* a perſon that makes or ſells arms
Armórial, *a.* belonging to family-arms, armor
Armor'ic, *a.* pertaining to Brittanny in France,
  n. the language of the country
Arm'ory, *n.* a repoſitory or place of arms, armor
Arm'or-bearer, *n.* one who carries another's arms
Arm'pit, *n.* the hallow place under the ſhoulder
Arms, *n. pl.* the enſigns of a family, weapons, war
Arms-énd, *ad.* at a due diſtance, far off
Arm'y, *n.* a body of armed men, a great number
Ar'nuts, *n.* tall oat graſs   [their fragrance
Ar'oma, *n.* the quality of plants which conſtitutes
Aromat'ic, Aromat'ical, *a.* ſpicy, fragrant, ſweet
Aromat'ics, *n. pl.* all kinds of ſpices or perfumes
Ar'omatize, *v. t.* to impregnate with aroma, to
Aroma'tous, *a.* containing aroma   [ſcent
Around', *ad.* and *prep.* in a round or circle, about
Arouſe', *v. t.* to awaken from ſleep ſuddenly, to
Aroynt', *v.* begone, go away, depart, *ob.* [excite
Ar'pent, *n.* a French acre, or 100 ſquare rods
Ar'quebuſe, *n.* a large handgun
Arrac', *n.* the ſpirit of the cocoa-nut, a plant
Arráign, *v. t.* to call to anſwer in court, to accuſe
Arráigned, *pa.* accuſed, called to appear & anſwer
Arráignment, *n.* the act of arraigning, a charge
Arrange', *v. t.* to ſet in order, to put in due place
Arrange'ment, *n.* the ſtate of being put in order
Ar'rant, *a.* very bad, vile, notorious, wicked
Ar'rantly, *ad.* ſhamefully, corruptly, wickedly
Ar'ras, *n.* tapeſtry, hangings of tapeſtry
Arráy, *n.* order of men for battle, dreſs, the im-
  pannelling of a jury, or the jury
Arráy, *v. t.* to put in order, dreſs, impannel
Arráyed, *pa.* dreſſed, clothed, in.pannelled
Arréar, Arréarage, *n.* the part of a debt unpaid
Arreſt', *v. t.* to ſeize by warrant, ſtop, hinder
Arreſt', *n.* a ſeizure by warrant, ſtop, hindrance,
  ſtay of judgement after verdict
Arreſta'tion, *n.* reſtraint, ſeizure, hindrance
Arreſt'ed, *pa.* ſeized for debt, ſtopped, hindered
Arret', *n.* an edict of a ſovereign court, a writ
Arríval, *n.* the act of coming to a place   [rival
Arrívance, *n.* a company arriving or coming, ar-
Arrive, *v. i.* to come to or reach a place, to gain
Ar'rogance, *n.* haughtineſs, pride, preſumption
Ar'rogant, *a.* haughty, very proud, ſelf-conceited
Ar'rogantly, *ad.* haughtily, very proudly, ſaucily.
Ar'rogate, *v. t.* to claim unjuſtly, aſſume, take
Arron'diſment, *n.* a diſtrict, circuit of juriſdiction
Ar'row, *n.* a pointed weapon to be ſhot from a bow
Ar'rowhead, *n.* a genus of plants with arrow ſha-
  ped leaves   [yields a ſtarch very nutritive
Ar'rowroot, *n.* a genus of plants, one of which
Ar'rowy, *a.* conſiſting of or having arrows
Ars'enal, *n.* a repoſitory for arms, &c. a magazine
Ar'ſenic, *n.* a metal, opake, heavy, friable, brilliant

and poiſonous
Arſen'ical, *a.* containing arſenic, or pertaining to it
Arſéniac a'cid, arſenic combined with oxygene
Arſe'niate, *n.* a neutral ſalt, formed by arſeniac acid
  with a baſe
Arſen'icated, *a.* impregnated with arſenic
Ar'ſon, *n.* the malicious burning of a building by
  which life is endangered
Art, *n.* cunning, device, ſkill, ſcience, trade
Artérial, *a.* belonging to or like an artery
Ar'tery, *n.* a veſſel, conveying blood from the heart
Arteriot'omy, *n.* the opening of an artery
Art'ful, *a.* cunning, crafty, dexterous
Art'fully, *ad.* cunningly, dexterouſly, ſkilfully
Art'fulneſs, *n.* art, cunning, ſlineſs, dexterity, ſkill
Arthrit'ic, *a.* gouty, belonging to the joints
Art'ichoke, *n.* a garden vegetable, a ſunflower
Art'icle, *n.* a term, condition, part of ſpeech, part
  of a diſcourſe, a clauſe or item, a diſtinct but
  undefined thing
Art'icle, *v. i.* to covenant, agree, make terms
Artic'ular, *a.* of or belonging to articles or joints
Artic'ulate, *v. t.* to pronounce diſtinctly
Artic'ulate, *a.* diſtinct in ſpeech, clear, expreſs
Artic'ulate, Artic'ulated, *a.* having joints
Artic'ulately, *ad.* diſtinctly, clearly, plainly
Articulátion, *n.* connection by joints, diſtinct utter-
Art'ifice, *n.* a trick, device, ſtratagem   [ance
Artif'icer, *n.* an artiſt, manuſacturer, contriver
Artifi''cial, *a.* made by art, fictitious
Artifi''cialneſs, *n.* the ſtate of being artificial
Artifi''cially, *ad.* by art, not naturally
Artil'lery, *n.* weapons for war, chiefly cannon, mor-
  tars and their appendages, the men who man-
Art'iſan, *n.* an artiſt, a profeſſor of an art [age them
Art'iſt, *n.* a perſon profeſſing or ſkilled in an art
Art'leſs, *a.* without art or deſign, ſimple, honeſt
Art'leſsneſs, *n.* ſimplicity of heart, ſincerity
Art'leſsly, *ad.* without art, naturally, ſincerely
Arundélian marbles, marble tables found in
  Greece containing ancient chronology
Arundin'eous, *a.* abounding with or like reeds
Arus'pice, *n.* a divination from the entrails of beaſts
As, *pron. that, who, which,* in like manner or de-
  gree, like, while
Aſafet'ida, *n.* a ſtrong ſcented gum reſin
Aſbeſt'ine, *a.* that cannot be burnt or conſumed
Aſbeſ'tinite, *n.* a ſpecies of magneſian earth
Aſbes'tus, *n.* a ſpecies of magneſian ſtone or earth,
  which is incombuſtible
Aſbeſt'oid, *n.* a ſpecies of aſbeſtus
Aſcend', *v.* to go up, riſe, recur back in time
Aſcend'ant, *n.* highth, influence, ſuperiority, rule
Aſcend'ant, *a.* higher, ſuperior, overpowering
Aſcend'ency, *n.* ſuperiority, influence, power
Aſcen'ſion, *n.* the act of aſcending or riſing, riſe
Aſcen'ſion-day, *n.* the day on which our Savior
  aſcended or went into heaven, holy Thurſday
Aſcent', *n.* an eminence, riſe, the riſing of a hill

Afcertåin, *v. t.* to make certain, gain certain knowledge

Afcertåined, *pa.* made certain, learnt to a certainty

Afcertåinment, *n.* a making certain, gaining certainty

Afcertåinable, *a.* that may be certainly known

Afcet'ic, *n.* a retired and devout perfon, a hermit

Afcet'ic, *a.* employed in devotion, ftrict, auftere

Afcit'ic, *a.* dropfical, hydropic

Afciti"tious, *a.* fupplemental, additional

Afcríbe, *v. t.* to attribute, impute, affign

Afcríbable, *a.* that may be afcribed or imputed

Afcrip'tion, *n.* the act of afcribing

Afh, *n.* the name of a well-known tree   [bafhed

Afhåmed, *a.* covered with fhame, confufed, a-

Afh'colored, *a.* of the color of afhes or the afh

Afh'en, *a.* made or formed of afh-wood, like afh

Afh'es, *n. pl.* the remains of what is burnt, the duft or remains of a dead body, a dead body

Afh'lar, *n.* freeftone as rough out of the quarry

Afhöre, *ad.* at or on fhore, on the land, in fafety

Afh-Wedn'efday, *n.* the firft day of Lent

Afh'y, *a.* afhcolored, like afhes

Afia, *n.* a great divifion of the earth

Afiat'ic, *a.* pertaining to Afia

Afiat'ic, *n.* a native of Afia

Afíde, *ad.* on one fide, apart, out of the right way

As'inine, *a.* belonging to an afs, ftupid

Afk, *v.* to make requeft, petition, feek, inquire, fet a price on

Afkáunce or Afkáunt, *ad.* fideways, obliquely

Afk'er, *n.* an inquirer, water-newt, eft

Afkew', *ad.* fideways, contemptuoufly, proudly

Aflant', *ad.* on one fide, aflope, obliquely, awry

Afléep, *a.* at reft, in or into fleep, in a fleeping ftate

Aflòpe, *ad.* awry, in a flanting manner

Afp or As'pic, *n.* a fmall venomous ferpent, whofe poifon is faid to kill like an opiate

Afpar'agus, *n.* a grafs, fpeerage or fparrow grafs

As'pect, *n.* a look, air, appearance, pofition, view

Afpect'able, *a.* that may be feen, vifible, *ob.*

Afpec'tion, *n.* the act of beholding, a view, *ob.*

Afp'en, *n.* a tree, the poplar, or a fpecies of it

Afp'en, *a.* of or belonging to the afpen

Afp'er, *n.* a Turkifh coin, near 2 cents; *a.* rough

Afp'erate, *v. t.* to make rough or uneven   [leaves

Afperifo'liate, Afperifo'lious, *a.* having rough

Afper'ity, *n.* roughnefs of objects, or of temper

Afp'erous, *a.* rough, uneven, irregular, harfh

Afperfe', *v. t.* to fprinkle, attack with flander

Afper'fion, *n.* a fprinkling, flander   (phaltis

Afphalt'ic, *a.* bituminous, pertaining to lake Af-

Afphalt', *n.* a black bituminous fubftance, found on the lake Afphaltis, &c.

As'phodel, *n.* a kind of plant, the day-lily

As'pirate, *v. t.* to pronounce with a full emiffion of breath   [breath in pronunciation

As'pirate, *n.* a letter or mark of an emiffion of

As'pirated, *pa.* pronounced very full or ftrong

Afpirätion, *n.* an ardent wifh, a full pronunciation

Afpíre, *v. i.* to defire eagerly, pant after, aim at what is lofty or difficult

Afportåtion, *n.* a carrying away, removal   (fhut

Afquint', *ad.* afkaunt, on one fide, with one eye

Afs, *n.* an animal of burden, a dull ftupid perfon

Affáil, *v. t.* to affault, attack, fet upon

Affáilable, *a.* that may be attacked or fet upon

Affáilant, *a.* attacking, invading, fetting upon

Affáilant, Affáiler, *n.* one who attacks or invades

Affafs'in, Affafs'inator, *n.* one who kills or attempts to kill by treachery, or fecret affault

Affafs'inate, *v. t.* to murder by fecret affault

Affaffinätion, *n.* the act of affaffinating

Affault', *n.* violent attack, ftorm of a fort, a blow or attempt to ftrike

Affault', *v. t.* to attack, fet or fall upon, ftorm

Affault'er, *n.* one who affaults or ftorms

Affáy, *v.* to try, prove, examin, attempt

Affáy, *n.* a trial, proof, examination, firft effort

Affay'er, *n.* one who affays or tries metals, &c.

Affecůtion, *n.* an attaining, an attendance, *ob.*

Affem'blage, *n.* a collection or joining of things

Affem'ble, *v.* to bring, call or meet together, to

Affem'bled, *pa.* met together   (collect

Affem'bly, *n.* a company affembled or met, a ball, a legiflature or a branch of it

Affent', *v. t.* to agree, confent, yield, admit

Affent', Affent'ment, *n.* the act of agreeing, confent

Affent'er, *n.* one who affents

Affert', *v. t.* to affirm, maintain, claim, vindicate

Affer'tion, *n.* the act of afferting, an affirmation

Affert'ive, *a.* pofitive, implying affertion

Affert'or, *n.* an affirmer, a maintainer   (taxing

Affefs', *v. t.* to tax, to value for the purpofe of

Affefs'ment, *n.* the act of affeffing, a cefs, a tax

Affefs'or, *n.* one that lays taxes or values, an affiftant judge

Afs'ets, *n. pl.* effects left by one dead to pay debts

Affeverätion, *n.* a folemn or pofitive affirmation

Affidúity, *n.* diligence, continued application

Affid'uous, *a.* diligent, conftant in application

Affid'uoufly, *ad.* diligently, clofely, continually

Affient'o, *n.* a contract with Spain to fupply flaves

Affi'gn, *v. t.* to appoint, fix, transfer, allege

Affi'gnable, *a.* that may be transferred or alleged

Affignätion, *n.* an appointment of time and place

Affignée, *n.* one who is appointed or entrufted

Affi'gner, *n.* one who affigns or appoints

Affi'gnment, *n.* an appointment, a making over

Affim'ilate *v. t.* to make or grow like

Affimilátion, *n.* the act of making or growing like

Affift', *v. t.* to help, fuccor, relieve, ftand by

Affift'ance, *n.* help, aid, fuccor, relief, fupport

Affift'ant, *n.* one who affifteth ; *a.* helping

Affi'ze, *n.* a meafure, rate, court of juftice, jury

Affi'ze, *v. t.* to fix meafures or rates, fix, fettle

Affi'zer, *n.* one who fixes weights and meafures

Affóciate, *v. t.* to keep company, to unite

Affóciate, *n.* a companion, partner, partaker, fha-
Affóciate or Affóciated, *pa.* joined in league   (rer
Affóciable, *a.* that may be joined or united
Affóciate, *a.* connected, influenced one by another
Affociabil'ity *n.* the faculty of being affected by
    fympathy, or connection
Affociátion, *n.* a convention of clergymen, (N. E.)
Affociátion, *n.* an union, confederacy, partnerfhip
Affoil', *v. t.* to difcharge, releafe, acquit, *ob.*
Affort', *v. t.* to range in claffes, arrange, fort
Affort'ment, *n.* a ranging, variety, proportion
Affuáge, *v.t.* to foften, eafe, abate, leffen, pacify
Affuágement, *n.* an abatement, mitigation, eafe
Affuáger, *n.* one that affuages, leffens or pacifies
Affuáfive, *a.* mitigating, foftening, eafing
Affuefac'tion, *n.* the being accuftomed to, cuftom
Affuétude, *n.* cuftom, habitual ufe
Affúme, *v. t.* to take what is not juft or natural,
    or without proof, to undertake or promife
Affúmed, *pa.* taken, taken for granted
Affúmer, *n.* an affuming, bufy or arrogant perfon
Affúming, *pa.* taking, haughty, impertinent
Affump'fit, *n.* a promife or action founded on one
Affump'tion, *n.* a taking, fuppofition, undertaking
Affump'tive, *a.* poffible or fit to be affumed
Affúre, *v. t.* to make fecure or confident, to tell
Affúrance, *n.* confidence, want of modefty, cer-
    tain knowledge, certainty, fecurity againft lofs,
    poffitive declaration
Affúred, *pa.* perfuaded, certain, infured
Affúredly, *ad.* certainly, without doubt, really
Affúrer, *n.* one that affures, one that engages
Affyr'ian, *n.* a native of Affyria on the Euphrates
Affyr'ian, *a.* pertaining to Affyria
As'terifk, *n.* the mark (*) in printing or writing
As'terifm, *n.* a fet or conftellation of fixed ftars
Aften'ic, *a.* without tone or ftrength
Aftern', *ad.* in the hinder part of a fhip, behind
Afth'ma, *n.* a difficulty of breathing   (afthma
Afthmat'ic, Afthmat'ical, *a.* troubled with an
Afton'ifh, Aftound', *v.t.* to amaze, to confound
Afton'ifhed, *pa.* amazed, ftruck dumb with furprife
Afton'ifhingly, *ad.* in an aftonifhing manner
Afton'ifhment, *n.* amazement, furprife, confufion
Aftrad'dle, *ad.* with legs acrofs or open, aftride
As'tragal, *n.* a molding on a pillar or cannon, the
    upper bone of the foot
As'tral, *a.* belonging to the ftars, ftarry
Aftráy, *ad.* out of or from the right way, wrong
Aftrict', *v. t.* to contract by application, bind, tie
Aftric'tion, *n.* the act or art of contracting parts
Aftrict'ive, *a.* having a binding quality, bracing
Aftríde, *ad.* acrofs, with legs open as upon a horfe
Aftringe', *v. t.* to draw together, bind, brace, ftop
Aftrin'gency, *n.* the power of contracting
Aftrin'gent, *a.* binding, contracting, bracing
Aftrin'gent, *n.* a medicin which, ufed internally,
    contracts and ftrengthens
Aftrog'raphy, *n.* defcription of the ftars

As'trolabe, *n.* an armillary fphere
Aftrol'ogy, *n.* the art of foretelling by the ftars
Aftrol'oger, Aftrológian, *n.* one who foretels by the
Aftrolo''gical, *a.* relating to aftrology   (ftars
Aftrolo''gically, *ad.* after the way of aftrologers
Aftron'omer, *n.* one who ftudies the heavenly bo-
Aftronom'ical, *a.* belonging to aftronomy   [dies
Aftronom'ically, *ad.* in the manner of aftronomy
Aftron'omy, *n.* the fcience or ftudy of the ftars
Afun'der, *ad.* apart, feparately, into two parts
As'ylum or Afy'lum, *n.* a refuge, fanctuary, retreat
Afym'metry, *n.* a want of juft proportion, *ob.*
At, *pr.* in, by, near by, towards
Ataba'l, *n.* a kind of drum among the Moors
At'araxy, *n.* eafe, quiet, a freedom from pain, &c.
Atax'y, *n.* a want of order, diforder, irregularity
Ate, *pret.* of *to eat*
Athana'fian, *a.* relating to the creed of Athanafius
A'theifm, *n.* a difbelief of the being of a God
A'theift, *n.* one who denies a God, an infidel
Atheift'ical, *a.* denying a God, impious
Atheift'ically, *ad.* in an atheiftical manner
Athe'nian, *n.* a native of Athens
Athe'nian, *a.* pertaining to Athens
Athirft', *a.* thirfty, dry, in want of drink, eager
Athlet'ic, *a.* belonging to wreftling, ftrong, bony
Athwart', *ad.* and *pr.* acrofs, through, wrong
At'las, *n.* a collection of maps, joint, rich filk
Atlan'tic, *n.* the ocean between Europe, Africa,
    and America   (Atlantic
Atlan'tic, Atlante'an, *a.* pertaining to Atlas or the
At'mofphere, *n.* the furrounding air and vapors
Atmofpher'ic, *a.* belonging to the atmofphere
At'om or At'omy, *n.* an extreme fmall particle
Atom'ical, *a.* confifting of or relating to atoms
At'omift, *n.* an advocate for or holder of atoms
Atóne, *v.* to expiate by facrifices, make fatisfac-
    tion, or be equivalent   [tion
Atónement, *n.* fatisfaction, expiation, reconcilia-
Atop', *ad.* at or on the top, above
Atrabilárian, Atrabilárious, *a.* affected with bile
Atrament'al, Atrament'ous, *a.* inky, very black
Atrip', *ad.* as far as poffible, perpendicularly
Atrócious, *a.* hainous, outrageoufly wicked
Atrócioufly, *ad.* outrageoufly, enormoufly
Atrócioufnefs, Atro''city, *n.* extreme hainoufnefs
At'rophy, *n.* a want of due nourifhment, a languor
Attach', *v. t.* to take by legal procefs, arreft, win
Attach'ment, *n.* a feizure, regard, a writ
Attaek', *v. t.* to affault, fall upon, or to, invade
Attack', *n.* an affault, onfet, charge, brunt
Attack'ed, *pa.* affaulted, fet upon, charged
At'tagen, *n.* a beautiful bird like a pheafant
Attáin, *v.* to come to, reach, or gain by an effort
Attáinable, *a.* that may be attained or come at
Attáinablenefs, *n.* the quality of being attainable
Attáinder, *n.* the act of attainting in law, a taint
Attáinment, *n.* a thing attained, acquifition
Attáint, *v. t.* to taint, corrupt, ftain, condemn

Attâint, *n.* a ftain, fpot, reproach, hurt

Attâint, *n.* a writ againſt a jury for falſe verdict

Attemp'er, Attemp'erate, *v. t.* to reduce or qualify by mixture, foften, fit, proportion, regulate

Attemp'ered, *pa.* qualified by mixture, fuited

Attempt', *n.* a trial, endeavor, effort, aim, attack

Attempt', *v. t.* to try, endeavor, aim, eſſay, attack

Attempt'able, *a.* that may be attempted

Attempt'er, *n.* one who attempts, one who attacks

Attend', *v.* to wait, liften, accompany

Attend'ance, *n.* the act of waiting, duty, a train

Attend'ant, *a.* waiting on, connected with, joined

Attend'ant, *n.* one that attends, one that waits on

Attend'ed, *pa.* waited on, accompanied

Attent', *a.* intent, attentive, regardful, *ob.*

Atten'tion, *n.* the act of attending or minding

Attent'ive, *a.* heedful, regardful, careful, intent

Attent'ively, *ad.* carefully, diligently, clofely, in-

Attent'iveneſs, *n.* attention, carefulneſs [tenfely

Atten'uant, *a.* making lefs vifcid, making flender

Atten'uant, *n.* that which makes lefs vifcid

Atten'uate, *v. t.* to thin, dilute, make lefs vifcid

Atten'uate, Attenuáted, *pa.* thinned, diluted

Attenuátion, *n.* a making thin or flender

Atteft', *v. t.* to bear or call to witnefs, affirm, fay

Atteft', Atteftátion, *n.* teftimony, official teftimony

Atteft'ed, *pa.* witneffed, proved, fupported

At'tic, *a.* elegant, delicate, like the Athenians

At'tic, *n.* an order of fquare pillars on the roof

At'tic ftory, the upper ftory

At'ticifm, *n.* delicate wit, as that of Athenians

Attíre, *v. t.* to drefs, habit, array, deck, fet off

Attíre, *n.* clothes, apparel, the horns of a buck

At'titude, *n.* a pofture, gefture, action, fixed ftate

Attol'lent, *a.* raifing, drawing up, lifting

Attor'ney, *n.* one who acts for another in law, a

Attor'ney, *v. i.* to ufe or do by a proxy, *ob.* [proxy

Attor'neyfhip, *n.* the office of an attorney

Attract', *v. t.* to allure, invite, draw, engage

Attrac'tion, *n.* the power or act of drawing, allure-

Attract'ible, *a.* that may be attracted [ment

Attract'ive, *n.* what draws, engages or incites

Attract'ive, *a.* alluring, enticing, inviting

Attract'iveneſs, *n.* the quality which draws

Attract'or, *n.* one who attracts, one who draws

At'tribute or Attrib'ute *v. t.* to fuppofe to belong to, afcribe, impute

Attrib'utable, *a.* that may be afcribed, imputable

At'tribute, *n.* a property, inherent quality, mark

Attribútion, *n.* the act of afcribing, qualities afcri-

Attrib'utive, *a.* relating to an attribute [bed

Attrib'utive, *n.* a word which denotes quality

Attríte, *a.* ground, fretted, worn by rubbing

Attri"tion, *n.* the act of rubbing, forrow for fin

Attúne, *v. t.* to put in tune, to make mufical

Atwéen, Atwíxt, *ad.* in the middle of, between

Aúburn, *a.* brown, of a tan or dark color

Auc'tion, *n.* a public fale to the higheft bidder

Auc'tionary, *a.* fold at or belonging to auctions

Auctionéer, *n.* the manager of an auction or fale

Audácious, *a.* very daring, contemning reſtraint,

Audácioufly, *ad.* boldly, impudently, (impudent

Audácioufneſs, Audácity, *n.* boldneſs, fpirit, raſh-

Aud'ible, *a.* that may be heard [neſs

Aud'ibly, *ad.* in a manner to be heard

Aud'ience, *n.* hearers, auditory, hearing, interview

Aud'it, *n.* an examination of accounts under authority [fons authorized

Aud'it, *v. t.* to examin and adjuft accounts by per-

Aud'itor, *n.* a hearer, an examiner of accounts

Aud'itory, *n.* an affembly of hearers; *a.* able to

Aud'itreſs, *n.* a woman that hears [hear

Aug'er, *n.* a carpenter's tool to bore holes with

Aught, *n.* any thing [ger

Augment', *v. t.* to increaſe, make or become lar-

Aug'ment, *n.* an increaſe, ſtate of increaſe, prefix

Augmentátion, *n.* the act or ſtate of increaſing

Aug'ur, *n.* a diviner by the flight of birds [gueſs

Aug'ur, Aug'urate, *v. i.* to judge by augury, to

Augurátion, *n.* the act or practice of augury

Augúrial, *a.* of or relating to augury

Aug'urous, *a.* foreboding, portending by figns

Aug'ury, *n.* an omen, a divination by birds, &c.

Aug'uft, *n.* a month, the 8th month of the year

Auguft', *a.* grand, magnificent, impreffing venera-

Auguft'neſs, *n.* dignity, majefty, grandeur [tion

Auk, *n.* a genus of water fowls, anfers

Aul'ic, *a.* belonging to a prince's court, royal

Auln or Alne, *n.* a meafure of length, an ell

Auln, *n.* a liquid meafure of 40 gallons

Aúrate, *n.* a combination of the oxyd of gold with another fubftance

Aúra, *n.* an airy exhalation [oxygene

Aúric acid, a faturated combination of gold and

Aurélia, *n.* the firft change of a maggot or form from which an infect is hatched

Aurélian, *a.* like or belonging to the aurelia

Aúricle, *n.* the external ear, a part of the heart

Auric'ula, *n.* a beautiful kind of rofe

Auric'ular, *a.* of or fpoken in the ear, private

Auric'ularly, *ad.* in the ear, in a fecret manner

Auric'ulate, *a* fhaped like the ear

Aurif'erous *a.* bearing or producing gold

Aurigátion, *n.* a driving of chariots, &c.

Aúrift, *n.* one who cures diforders of the ear

Auróra, *n.* the dawning light, the morning, goddefs of the morning

Auróra-boreális, *n.* the northern lights

Aus'pice, Aus'pices, *n.* omens, favor, patronage

Aufpícious, *a.* profperous, lucky, favorable

Aufpícioufly, *ad.* profperoufly, happily, kindly

Auftére, *a.* fevere, rigid, harfh, four, rough, ftern

Auftérely, *ad.* feverely, rigidly, harfhly, fternly

Auftéreneſs, *n.* feverity, ftrictnefs, roughnefs

Aufter'ity, *n.* feverity, cruelty, a mortified life

Aus'tral, *a.* of or tending to the fouth, fouthern

Aus'trian, *n.* a native of Auftria in Germany

Aus'trian, *a.* pertaining to Auſtria

Authent'ic, Authent'ical, *a.* genuine, original

Authent'ically, *ad.* with marks of credibility

Authent'icalneſs, Authenti"city, *n.* genuineneſs,

Authent'icate, *v. t.* to eſtabliſh by proof [authority

Auth'or, *n.* one who makes or cauſes, a writer

Auth'oreſs, *n.* a female author, a female writer

Author'ity, *n.* legal power, warrant, teſtimony, rule, precedent, influence derived from offiſe or character, credit, credibility ; in Con. the Magiſtracy or body of juſtices

Author'itative, *a.* having authority, poſitive

Author'itatively, *ad.* with authority, poſitively

Authorizátion, *n.* an eſtabliſhment by authority

Auth'orize, *v. t.* to give authority, juſtify, make

Aútocrat, *n.* an abſolute ſovereign [legal

Autoc'racy, *n.* independence, abſolute ſovereignty

Aútograph, *n.* an original writing, exact copy

Autograph'ical, *a.* relating to one's own writing

Automat'ical, Autom'atous, *a.* having a power of ſelf-motion

Autom'aton, *n.* an engine that moves of itſelf

Autop'ſy, *n.* ocular inſpection, *ob.*

Autop'tical, *a.* ſeen with one's own eyes, *ob.*

Autop'tically, *ad.* by means of one's own eyes, *ob.*

Aútumn, *n.* the third ſeaſon of the year, fall

Autum'nal, *a.* of or belonging to autumn

Auxil'iar, *n.* that which aids, a helper

Auxil'iaries, *n. pl.* troops aſſiſting another nation

Auxil'iary, *a.* helping, aſſiſtant ; *n.* a helper

Avǎil, *n.* advantage, profit, uſe, effect [Con.

Avǎils, *n. pl.* proceeds of property ſold, produce

Avǎil, *v. t.* to profit, aſſiſt, promote, do

Available, *a.* profitable, able to effect the object

Availableneſs, *n.* the power of promoting

Availably, *ad.* with ſucceſs or effect

Avant'guard, *n.* the front of an army, the van

Av'arice, *n.* covetouſneſs, exceſſive love of money

Avari"cious, *a.* covetous, greedy after wealth

Avari"ciouſly, *ad.* covetouſly, greedily, meanly

Avari"ciouſneſs, *n.* covetouſneſs, undue love of

Avaſt', *ex.* ceaſe, hold, ſtop [money

Avaunt', *ex.* get away, be gone

A've-Máry, *n.* a prayer to the Virgin Mary

Avenáceous, *a.* like oats

Avenge', *v. t.* to take juſt ſatisfaction, vindicate, defend, puniſh [puniſhment, vindication

Avenge'ance, Avenge'ment, *n.* vengeance, juſt

Aven'ged, *pa.* vindicated, having received ſatisfac-

Aven'ger, *n.* a puniſher, vindicator [tion

Aven'turine, *n.* a variety of the quartz

Av'enue, *n.* an entrance to any place, way, walk

Aver', *v. t.* to declare poſitively, affirm, aſſert

Av'erage, *n.* a mean proportion, a medium

Av'erage, *a.* relating to a mean or medium

Av'erage, *v. t.* to reduce to a mean

Aver'ment, *n.* poſitive aſſertion, aſſertion in law with an offer to verify

Aver'red, *pa.* aſſerted poſitively, avouched, ſaid

Averrunc'ate, *v. t.* to root up, *not uſed*

Averſátion, *n.* hatred, great diſlike, abhorrence

Averſe', *a.* unfavorable, contrary, hating, diſin-

Averſe'ly, *ad.* unwillingly, backwardly [clined

Averſe'neſs, *n.* unwillingneſs, backwardneſs

Aver'ſion, *n.* hatred, diſlike, diſapprobation

Avert', *v. t.* to turn aſide or away, to keep off

A'viary, *n.* a place for keeping birds in, a decoy

Avid'ity, *n.* greedineſs, eagerneſs, intenſeneſs

Avocádo, *n.* the alligator pear

Avocátion, *n.* the act of calling away, hinderance

Avoid', *v.* to ſhun, eſcape, quit, make void

Avoid'able, *a.* that may be avoided or ſhunned

Avoid'ance, *n.* the act of avoiding, or becoming

Avoid'ed, *pa.* ſhunned, eſcaped, left [vacant

Avoid'er, *n.* one who avoids, one who ſhuns

Avordupois', *n.* a weight of 16 ounces to the lb.

Avolátion, the act of flying away, *not uſed*

Av'oſet, *n.* a water fowl of the grallic order

Avouch', *v. t.* to vouch, affirm, aſſert, ſay, juſtify

Avouch', *n.* confirmation, declaration, *ob.*

Avouch'er, *n.* one who avouches, one who affirms

Avow', *v. t.* to juſtify, own, acknowledge

Avow'able, *a.* that is capable of being juſtified

Avow'al, *n.* a juſtifying, frank declaration

Avow'ant, *n.* the defendant in replevin

Avow'edly, *ad.* in an avowed manner, openly

Avow'er, *n.* one who avows, juſtifies or affirms

Avow'ry, *n.* declaration of one who diſtrains

Avul'ſion, *n.* a pulling one thing from another

Awǎit, *v. i.* to wait for, expect, attend, be due to

Awǎke, *a.* not ſleeping, ready, lively, heedful

Awǎke, *v.* awaked, awoke, *pret.* awaked, *pa.* to ceaſe to ſleep, rouſe up, riſe from the dead

Awǎken, *v.* to awake, to rouſe up, put in action

Award', *v. t.* to adjudge, to aſſign by ſentence

Award', *n.* a ſentence, a determination [mines

Award'er, *n.* one who affigns, judges or deter-

Awáre, *a.* foreſeeing, apprized before, watchful

Awáre, *v. i.* to beware, be cautious, take care

Awáy, *ad.* at a diſtance, begone, let us go

Awe, *n.* fear mingled with reverence, dread

Awe, *v. t.* to ſtrike with awe, reverence or fear

Aw'ful, *a.* ſtriking awe, terrible, hateful

Aw'fully, *ad.* in an awful manner, ſolemnly

Aw'fulneſs, *n.* the quality of ſtriking with awe

Awhile, *ad.* for ſome ſpace of time [unpolite

Awk'ward, *a.* clumfy, unhandy, ungraceful,

Awk'wardly, *a.* clumfily, roughly, ungracefully

Awk'wardneſs, *n.* clumfineſs, ungracefulneſs

Awl, *n.* a pointed inſtrument to bore holes with

Aw'leſs, *a.* without fear, or power to excite awe

Awl'wort, *n.* a plant, the rough leaved alyſſon

Awme, *n.* a liquid meaſure of 36 gallons Engliſh

Awn, *n.* the beard of corn or graſs

Awn'ing, *n.* a covering from the ſun, &c. cano-

Awn'leſs, *a.* without awn [py, fail

Awn'y, *a.* containing awn

Awǒke, *pret.* of to awake

Awork'ing, *ad.* at or on work, bufy

Awry', *ad.* or *a.* afquint, unevenly, uneven, afide

Ax, *n.* an iron tool to cut or hew wood

Ax'il, *n.* the angle between the ftem and leaf, or the trunk and a branch

Ax'illary, *a.* belonging to the armpit, or axil

Ax'iom, *n.* a felfevident propofition or truth

Ax'is, *n.* the line on which any thing revolves

Ax'le, Ax'letree, *n.* a fhaft on which carriage wheels turn

Ax'olot, *n.* a Mexican fifh with feet like a lizard

Ax'ual, *a.* pertaining to an axis or axletree

Ay, *ad.* yes, ufed to affirm or affent

Aye, *ad.* always, ever, again, once more

Azaróle, *n.* a fpecies of thorn

Az'erit, *n.* a fpecies of a plum or prunus [imal life

Azóte, *n.* a gas, or kind of air which deftroys an-

Azot'ic, *a.* pertaining to azote, noxious to life

Az'ure, *a.* blue, faint or light blue, fky-colored

Az'ure, *n.* a fine light-blue color, the fky

B

BA'A, *v. i.* to cry like a fheep, to bleat

Báal, *n.* the name of a Canaanitifh idol

Bab'ble, *v. i.* to talk idly or much, to tell fecrets

Bab'ble, Bab'blement, Bab'bling, *n.* idle talk, chat

Bab'bler, *n.* an idle or great talker, a telltale

Babe, *n.* an infant child of either fex, baby

Bábery, *n.* finery to pleafe or amufe a child with

Babiro'fa, *n.* an indian quadruped of the hog kind

Bábifh, *a.* childifh, foolifh, trifling, whimfical, pet-

Baboon', *n.* a large fpecies of monkey (tifh

Báby, *n.* a child, infant, girl's doll, little image

Bábyhood, *n.* the ftate of being a baby, childhood

Babylo'nian, Babylo'nifh, *a.* pertaining to Babylon, anciently a city in Affyria

Baccalau'reate, *n.* the degree of a bachelor of arts

Bacchanálian, [ch as k] *n.* a drunkard, riotous perfon

Bacchana'lian, *a.* pertaining to reveling

Bac'chanals, *n. pl.* drunken feafts, mad revels

Baccif'erous, *a.* bearing or producing berries

Bacciv'orous, *a.* eating or fubfifting on berries

Bach'elor, *n.* a man who has not been married, one who takes his firft degree in any profeffion, a low knight

Bach'elorfhip, *n.* the ftate of a bachelor

Back, *n.* the hinder part, rear, thick part, outfide

Back, *ad.* backward, behind, on things paft

Back, *v. t.* to mount, fecond, fupport, put back

Back'bite, *v. t.* backbit, *pret.* backbit, backbitten, *pa.* to flander an abfent perfon

Back'biter, *n.* one who flanders any one fecretly

Back'biting, *n.* reproach caft on an abfent perfon·

Back'board, *n.* a board put to fupport the back

Back'bone, *n.* the bone in the middle of the back

Back'door, *n.* a door placed behind a houfe

Backgam'mon, *n.* a game with dice and tables

Backhand'ed, *a.* with the hand turned backward

Back'houfe, *n.* a building behind the houfe

Back'room, *n.* a room behind another

Back'piece, *n.* a piece of armor made for the back

Back'fide, *n.* the hinder part of any thing or place

Backflide, *v. i.* backflide, *pret.* backflidden, *pa.* to fall off, depart from, apoftatize

Backflider, *n.* one who falls off or goes back

Backfliding, *n.* a falling back, off or away, a revolt

Back'ftairs, *n.* ftairs in the back part of a houfe

Back'ftays, *n. pl.* ropes to fteady a maft

Back'fword, *n.* a ftrong fword with one fharp edge

Back'ward, *a.* unwilling, dull, flow, fluggifh

Back'ward or Back'wards, *ad.* back, in time paft

Back'wardly, *ad.* unwillingly, flowly, perverfely

Back'wardnefs, *n.* a want of will, fluggifhnefs

Bácon, *n.* hog's flefh cured with falt and dried

Bad, *a.* ill, fick, wicked, hurtful, poor, imperfect

Bad or Bade, *pret.* of *to bid*

Badge, *n.* a mark of diftinction; *v. t.* to mark

Badg'er, *n.* a quadruped of the fize of a hog, a ped-

Bad'ly, *ad.* in a bad manner, not well (lar

Bad'nefs, *n.* a bad ftate, a want of good qualities

Baf'fle, *v. t.* to deceive, elude, confound, defeat

Baf'fler, *n.* one who confounds, one who defeats

Baf'tas, *n.* plain india muflins from 7 8ths. to 9 8ths. wide

Bag, *n.* a fack, pouch, purfe, ornament, udder

Bag, *v.* to put into a bag, pocket, fwell, puff up

Bagatell'e, *n.* a trifle, a thing of no importance

Bag'gage, *n.* a worthlefs woman, utenfils of an ar- my, clothing, &c. carried on a journey or voy-

Bag'ging, *n.* cloth for bags (age

Bagn'io, *n.* a hot bath, a houfe of ill fame

Bag'pipe, *n.* a common Scotch mufical inftrument

Bag'piper, *n.* a perfon who plays on a bagpipe [ikal

Báikalite, *n.* a magnefian ftone from the Lake Ba-

Bail, *n.* a furety for another, releafe from cuftody on giving fecurity, handle, hoop

Bail, *v.* to give bail or fecurity, to admit to bail, releafe upon bail, deliver goods in charge, lade water with a bucket, &c.

Báilable, *a.* that may be bailed, admitting bail

Báiliff, *n.* an officer that arrefts, fteward, overfeer

Báiliwick, *n.* the jurifdiction of a bailiff

Báiler, *n.* one who delivers goods in truft

Báilee, *n.* one who receives goods in truft

Báilment, *n.* a delivery of goods in truft

Báilbond, *n.* the bond given by bail (of bail

Báilpiece, *n.* a paper containing the recognizance

Bait, *v.* to put on a bait, give or take refrefhment fet dogs upon, clap

Bait, *n.* a temptation, meat to allure, refrefhment

Báited, *pa.* having a bait, fed, attacked, fet on

Baize, *n.* a fort of rough or nappy woolen cloth

Bake, *v.* baked, *pret.* baked, baken, *pa.* to heat or harden by fire, be baked, drefs

Bákehoufe, *n.* a place for baking bread, &c. in

Báker, *n.* a perfon that bakes for a livelihood

Bal'an, *n.* a fifh of a beautiful yellow

Bal'ance, *n.* a pair of fcales, part of a watch, con- ftellation, difference of accounts, power

Bal'ance, v. to make equal, settle, hefitate
Bal'ancer, n. a member of an infect for balancing
Bal'ancemafter,n.one fkilled in the art of balancing
Bal'cony, n. a gallery on the outfide of an houfe
Bald, a. without hair on the top and back part of the head, bare, plain, inelegant
Bal'derdafh, n. an odd mixture, confufed difcourfe
Bald'ly, ad. nakedly, meanly, poorly, inelegantly
Bald'nefs, n. a want of hair, meannefs of writing
Bale, n. a pack of goods, mifery, calamity, forrow
Bale, v. to put into bales (in the Mideterranean
Balear'ic, a. pertaining to Majorca and Minorca,
Báleful, a. forrowful, fad, full of mifchief or ruin
Balk, n. a rafter, beam, ridge, difappointment
Balk, v. t. to difappoint, mifs of, refufe
Ball, n. any round thing, an entertainment of dan-
Bal'lad, n. a fong, a trifling fong (cing
Bal'ladfinger, n. a perfon who fings ballads
Bal'laft, n. weight ufed to fteady a fhip, &c. with
Bal'laft, v. to load with ballaft, to keep fteady
Bal'let, n. an hiftorical dance (fel for ærial failing
Balloon', n. a kind of ball, a large veffel, a filk vef-
Bal'lot, n. a little ball, little ticket, chance, lot
Bal'lot, v. t. to choofe or vote by ballot
Bal'loting, n. the act of giving ballots (anoint
Balm, n. the name of a plant; v. t. to footh, to
Balm'y, a. of or like balm, fweet, fragrant, foft
Bal'neary, n. a bathing-room, bath, bagnio, ftove
Balneation, n. a bathing, the act of bathing
Bal'fam, n. an oily, aromatic fubftance flowing from trees, that which gives eafe
Balfam'ic, a. healing, mitigating, unctuous, foft
Balfam'ic, n. a healing foftening medicine
Bal'famin, n. the immortal eagle flower
Bal'tic, n. a fea in the north of Europe
Bal'tic, a. pertaining to the Baltic fea
Bal'utter, n. a rail, a fmall pillar or column
Bal'uftrade, n. a row or fet of little pillars
Bamboo, n. a plant of the reed kind in India
Bamboozle, v. t. to trick, a low word
Ban, n. a public notice, curfe, cenfure, interdict
Ban, v. t. to curfe, doom, excommunicate, ob.
Banána, n. [accented a as in afk] a fpecies of plaintain
Band, n. a tie, bandage, linen ornament, company
Band, v. t. to tie or join together, unite, confpire
Band'age, n. fomething bound over, fillet, roller
Band'box, n. a flight or thin kind of box (bers
Bandit'ti, n. pl. men outlawed, highwaymen, rob-
Ban'dle, n. an Irifh meafure of two feet in length
Bandoléers, n. fmall cafes for charges of powder
Band'y, v. to beat or tofs about, debate, contend
Band'y, a. crooked, n. a crooked ftick, club, play
Band'ylegged, a. having crooked legs (poifon
Bane, n. mifchief, ruin, poifon; v. t. to hurt, to
Báneful, a. hurtful, deftructive, poifonous
Bánefulnefs, n. a deftructive nature or quality
Bang, v. t. to beat, thump, ufe or treat roughly
Bang, n. a blow, thump, knock, ftroke, rap
Ban'ifh, v. t. to drive or force away, to exile

Ban'ifher, n. one who drives others away
Ban'ifhment, n. an expulfion from one's own coun-
  try by authority, exile, a voluntary abandon-
  ment of one's country
Ban'nifter, n. the fame as balluſter
Bank, v. t. to raife a mound, inclofe with a bank
Bank, n. a ridge of earth, fide of a ftream, bench
  of rowers, a joint fund for difcounting notes,
  and iffuing bills, a banking company, or their
  edifice
Bank'bill, n. a note for money in or on the bank
Bank'able, a. that may be difcounted by a bank
Bank'er, n. one who deals in money, or difcounts notes
Bank'rupt, n. a trader who fails to make payment
  when due, flops bufinefs, or does any act to de-
  fraud creditors
Bank'rupt, a. broke for debt, unable to pay (debts
Bank'rupt, v. t. to break, to render unable to pay
Bank'ruptcy, n. a failure in trade
Ban'ner, n. a flag, military ftandard, ftreamer
Ban'neret, n. a knight made in the field of battle
Ban'nerol, Band'roll, n. a little flag or ftreamer
Ban'noc or Jan'noc, n. a loaf made of oatmeal
Banoy', n. a fpecies of hawk
Ban"quet, n. a feaft, grand entertainment, treat
Ban"quet, v. to give a feaft, feaft, fare very well
Bant'er, n. rallery, flight fatire, ridicule, joke
Bant'er, v. t. to play, to run upon, rally, ridicule
Bant'erer, n. one who ridicules or rallies, a droll
Bant'ling, n. a very little or young child, an infant
Bap'tifm, n. a wafhing or fprinkling with water, a
  holy ordinance and fign of admiffion into
  Chrift's Church
Baptis'mal, a. pertaining to baptifm
Bap'tift, n. one who holds to baptifm by immerfion
Bap'tift, Baptizer, n. one who chriftens or dips
Bap'tiftery, n. the place for baptizing at, a font
Baptize, v. t. to chriften, plunge, apply water as a
  fign of admiffion into the church
Bar, n. a bolt, ftop, crofs beam for fecurity, inclo-
  fure in an inn or court room, divifion in mufic,
  bank of fand in a river, body of lawyers, an ex-
  ception in pleading, &c.
Bar, v. t. to faften, fecure, hinder, fhut out, ftop
Barb, v. t. to furnifh horfes with armor, to fhave
Barb, n. a barbary horfe, arrow point, beard
Barb'acan, n. an outward fortification, watchtower
Barb'acue, n. a hog dreffed whole with fpices
Barbarefk', n. the afh colored fquirrel of Barbary
Barbárian, n. a man uncivilized or brutal, a favage
Barbárian, a. favage, cruel, wild, rude, uncivilized
Barbar'ic, a. foreign, outlandifh, rude
Barb'arifm, n. favagenefs, ignorance, impropriety
  of fpeech, an uncivilized ftate
Barbar'ity, n. a favage ftate, cruelty
Barb'arize, v. t. to make or render barbarous
Barb'arous, a. cruel, rude, uncivilized, improper
Barb'aroufly, ad. cruelly, inhumanely, ill, rudely

Barb'aroufnefs, n. cruelty, impropriety of fpeech
Barb'atel, n. a bat with hairy lips (Africa
Barb'ary, n. and a. the name of the north coaft of
Barb'ate, a. bearded, having hairs in tufts
Barb'ed, pa. jagged with hooks, bearded, fhaved
Barb'el, n. the name of a large but coarfe fifh
Barb'er, n. one that fhaves beards, &c. v.t. to drefs
Barb'erry, n. a prickly fhrub, and its berry
Barb'et, n. a bird of Ceylon of two fpecies
Bard, n. a poet, an ancient Britifh or Gaulifh poet
Bare, a. naked, plain, fimple, poor, lean, mere
Bare, v.t. to make bare or naked, ftrip, uncover
Bárefaced, a. fhamelefs, impertinent, unmafked
Bárefacedly, ad. fhamefully, openly, impudently
Bárefacednefs, n. impudence, boldnefs, affurance
Bárefoot, a. without fhoes or ftockings, unfhod
Báreheaded, a. with the head uncovered
Bárely, ad. merely, only, nakedly, openly
Bárenefs, n. nakednefs, leannefs, poverty, want
Bar'gain, n. a contract, agreement, purchafe, fale
Bar'gain, v.i. to make a contract, agree, buy, fell
Bar'gainer, Bargainor', n. one who fells, or agrees
Bargaineé, n. one who buys or agrees [to fell
  to take a thing to be transferred
Barge, n. a row-boat for landing or pleafure
Barge'man, Bar'ger, n. one who manages a barge
Baril'la, n. a plant which furnifhes an alkali for
  making glafs and foap; alfo the alkali
Bark, n. the rind or coat of a tree, a fmall fhip
Bark, v. to make a noife, clamor, ftrip trees
Bark'bared, a. ftripped or divefted of the bark
Bark'er, n. one that barks or coughs, a fnarler
Bark'ing, n. the noife of dogs, the act of coughing
Bark'y, a. having or confifting of bark, like bark
Bar'ley, n. a fort of grain that malt is made of
Bar'leycorn, n. a grain of barley, the third part of
Barm, n. yeaft, fcum of malt-liquor [an inch
Barm'y, a. containing or like barm, frothy (&c.
Barn, n. a ftorehoufe ufed for corn, hay, ftabling,
Barn'acle, n. a large bird like a goofe, a fhellfifh
Barn'acles, n. pl. irons on horfes' nofes, fpectacles
Bar'olite, n. baryte combined with fixed air (acid
Barofel'enite, n. baryte combined with fulphuric
Barom'eter, n. an inftrument to fhow the weight
  of the atmofphere
Baromet'rical, a. relating to a barometer
Bar'on, n. a degree of nobility next to a vifcount
Bar'onage, n. the dignity of a baron, whole body
Bar'onefs, n. a baron's lady, or wife (of barons
Bar'onet, n. a title, a knight of the firft degree
Baro'nial, a. belonging to a barony
Bar'ony, n. a lordfhip that gives title to a baron
Bar'rack, n. a building to lodge foldiers in, a hut
Bar'rator, n. a wrangler, an encourager of law-fuits
Bar'ratry, n. foul practice in law, any fraud of a
  fhipmafter
Bar'rel, n. a wooden veffel, part of a gun, cylinder
Bar'rel, v.t. to put into a barrel
Bar'ren, a. unfruitful, fcanty, dull, unmeaning

Bar'ren, n. an unfertile tract of land
Bar'renly, ad. unfruitfully, unprofitably, dully
Bar'rennefs, n. unfruitfulnefs, a want of matter
Barricáde, v.t. to ftop up, faften, fortify, fecure
Barricáde or Barricádo, n. an obftruction, bar,
  ftop, impediment, hinderance, defenfe, fafety
Bar'rier, n. a boundary, limit, ftoppage, defenfe
Bar'rifter, n. a pleader at the bar, a lawyer
Bar'row, n. a hand carriage, a gelt fwine, a hilloc
  raifed over the dead
Bar'fhot, n. two balls joined by a bar
Bar'ter, v.t. to exchange, truck, fwop, trade
Bar'ter or Bar'tery, n. traffick by exchange or truck
Bar'terer, n. one who trafficks by exchange
Bary'te, n. a very heavy earth or ftone
Baryt'ic, a. pertaining to baryte
Bafalt', n. a hard ftone black or green, confifting
  of prifmatic cryftals, in upright blocks
Bafalt'ic, a. refembling or pertaining to bafalt
Bas'anite, n. black jafper, a filiceous ftone
Bafalt'iform, a. in the form of bafalt
Bafalt'ine, n. a column of bafalt
Bafe, n. the bottom, foundation, pedeftal, fupport,
  the graveft part in mufic, in chemiftry, the
  chief ingredient, or that which fixes another
Bafe, a. mean, vile, worthlefs, cowardly, low
Báfeborn, a. born out of wedlock, baftard
Báfelefs, a. without fupport, chimerical
Báfely, ad. meanly, dishonorably, vilely, cowardly
Báfement, n. the lower ftory, fupporting pillars
Báfenefs, n. meannefs, vilenefs, baftardy, deepnefs
Báfeviol, n. an inftrument, a fiddle for the bafe
Bafhaw', n. a Turkifh viceroy, a very lordly perfon
Bafh'ful, a. wanting due confidence, modeft
Bafh'fully, ad. timoroufly, fheepifhly, modefily
Bafh'fulnefs, n. want of confidence, extreme
  modefty, diffidence
Bas'il, n. the floping of a tool, or angle at the edge
Bas'il, v.t. to grind a tool to an angle
Bas'il, n. a genus of aromatic plants (the head
Bas'ilar, a. noting an artery and feveral bones of
Bafil'icon, n. a kind of falve or ointment
Bas'ilifk, n. a cockatrice-ferpent, a kind of cannon
Bátin or Báfon, n. a veffel, pond, bay, dock
Báfis, pl. bafes, n. foundation, fupport, chief in-
  gredient, &c.
Bafk, v. i. to lie expofed to the heat, to warm
Bafk'et, n. a veffel made of rufhes, willows, &c.
Bafs, n. a mat to kneel on, rufh, a fifh
Bafs'et, n. the name of a game at cards
Baffoon', n. a mufical wind inftrument
Bafs-relief', n. fculpture whofe figures do not
  ftand out from their ground in full proportion
Bas'tard, n. a fpurious child or thing, a. fpurious
Bas'tardize, v.t. to determin one a baftard
Bas'tardy, n. a fpurious or unlawful ftate of birth
Bafte, v.t. to beat, few flightly, drip butter, &c.
Bas'til, n. a jail, formerly the ftate-prifon of France
Baftonáde, v.t. to beat the feet, knock, cudgel

D

Baſtonáde, n. a beating on the feet, a cudgelling
Bas'tion, n. a bulwark, fortreſs, very great maſs
Bas'to, n. a name of the ace of clubs at quadrille
Bat, n. a ſtick uſed at cricket, an animal
Batávia, n. the ancient name of Holland
Batávian, n. a native of Holland
Batávian, a. pertaining to Holland, Dutch
Batch, n. a quantity of any thing, a ſmall coin
Bate, v. to take leſs, abate, ſink, cut off
Báteful, a. contentious, quarrelſome, ob. (gallons
Bath, n. a place to bathe in, a meaſure of 7 1-2
Bathe, v. t. to waſh in water, ſoak, ſoften, ſupple
Báting, pa. abating, deducting
Bat'let, n. an inſtrument to beat linen with
Batoon', n. a club, truncheon, ſtaff, part of a bend
Bat'tailous, a. warlike, in order of battle, ob
Battal'ia, n. pl. the order of battle, battle-array
Battal'ion, n. a body of foot from 500 to 800 men
Bat'tement, n. a ſtriking, percuſſion
Bat'ten, v. to fatten, indulge, form with battens
Bat'ten, n. a narrow piece of board, a ſcantling
Bat'ter, n. a mixture of flour, water, eggs and ſalt
Bat'ter, v. to bruiſe by beating, wear down
Bat'teringram, n. an engine for beating down walls
Bat'tery, n. act of battering, line of cannon, parapet, in law, a layinghands on, a vat to beat indigo in
Bat'tle, n. a combat, engagement, main body
Bat'tle, v. to contend in fight, diſpute warmly
Bat'tle-arráy, n. an array, form or order of battle
Bat'tle-ax, n. a weapon uſed in battle, a long bill
Bat'tledoor, n. an inſtrument to ſtrike ſhuttlecocks
Bat'tlement, n. a wall indented on the tops of buildings
Battóe, n. a long flat boat, broad in the middle
Bav'aroy, n. a kind of cloak, not uſed
Baulm, n. the name of ſeveral plants
Baubée, n. a Scotch halfpenny
Bavárian, n. a native of Bavaria in Germany
Bavárian, a. pertaining to Bavaria
Bav'in, n. a bundle of ſmall wood, a faggot, ob.
Baw'ble, n. a gewgaw, trifle, trifling thing
Bawb'ling, a. trifling, contemptible, ob.
Bawd or Baud, n. a procureſs of lewd women
Bawd, v. i. to act the bawd, to procure
Bawd'ily, ad. obſcenely, lewdly, offenſively
Bawd'ineſs, n. ribaldry, obſcenity
Bawd'ry, n. the employment of a bawd, filthy talk
Bawd'y, a. unchaſte, filthy, foul, obſcene
Bawd'yhouſe, n. a houſe of ill fame, bagnio, ſtew
Bawl, v. to ſpeak very loud, call out, cry aloud
Bawl'ing, n. great noiſe, loud talking or crying
Bay, v. to bark as a dog, hem in, ſurround, dam
Bay, a. inclining to a cheſnut brown
Bay, n. a receſs or arm of the ſea, an incloſure in a barn, a ſtate of being hemmed in, land covered with the bay tree, (Carol.)
Bay, n. the bay tree or laurel, a numerous genus
Bay'berry, n. a ſhrub with oily berries

Bay'ſalt, n. ſalt formed in baſons by evaporation
Báyonet, n. a broad dagger fixt at the end of a gun
Báyonet, v. t. to ſtab with a bayonet
Bays, n. pl. an honorary crown or garland, a prize
Bazar', Bezes'tin, n. in Turkey a market place
Bdel'lium, n. the name of a ſweet ſmelling gum
Be, v. i. and auxiliary, paſt, was, pa. been, to exiſt, or have a certain ſtate   (ſtate
Been, [bin] pa. having exiſted or had a certain
Beach, n. a ſandy ſhore, ſtrand
Béacon, n. any object to give notice of danger, but chiefly a light to direct ſeamen
Béadle, n. a cryer, meſſenger, petty officer of a court, pariſh, college, &c.
Béadroll, n. a liſt of perſons who are prayed for
Bead, n. a ſmall ball or drop, a globule, a moiding
Béagle, n. a ſmall hound, a kind of hunting dog
Beak, n. the bill of a bird, a promontory, a point
Béaked, a. having a beak, hooked, pointed
Béaker, n. a cup with a ſpout like a bird's beak
Beam, n. a main timber, balance of ſcales, ray of the ſun, &c. yoke of a chariot, horn of a ſtag
Beam, v. i. to throw out rays, dart, glitter, ſhine
Béamleſs, a. without rays of light
Béamy, a, ſhining, bright, radiant, having horns
Bean, n. the name of many kinds of vetches or pulſe, &c.   (preſs, convey, ſupply, produce
Bear, v. t. bore, pret. borne, pa. to carry, endure,
Bear, v. i. bore, pret. born, pa. to bring forth a child
Bear, n. an animal, rude man, conſtellation
Beard, n. hair on the chin, &c. a jag, point, wool
Beard, v. t. to pull by the beard, oppoſe, take off
Beard'ed, pa. having a beard, jagged, pointed
Beard'leſs, a. without a beard, ſmooth, youthful
Béarer, n. a carrier of any thing, ſupporter, poſt
Beárgarden, n. any place of noiſe and confuſion
Bearing, n. the poſition of a place with reſpect to another
Beaſt, n. an irrational animal, brute, brutiſh man
Béaſtlineſs, n. brutality, naſtineſs, filthineſs, dir-
Béaſtly, a. brutiſh, naſty, filthy, obſcene   (tineſs
Beat, v. beat, pret. beat, beaten, pa. to ſtrike, throb, outdo, conquer, rouſe, thraſh, pound, meaſure time in ſinging, fail in a zigzag form
Beat, n. the ſound of a drum, a ſtroke, a motion
Béater, n. one who beats or ſtrikes, what beats
Beatif'ic, a. making happy, heavenly, bliſsful
Beatif'ically, ad. in a very happy manner
Beatificátion, n. an admiſſion to heavenly honors
Beat'ify, v. t. to bleſs, to make happy or bleſſed
Béating, n. a correction by blows; pa. ſtriking
Beat'itude, n. happineſs, bleſſedneſs, bliſs, glory
Beau [bo, pl. boes] n. a man of dreſs, coxcomb,
Beaúiſh [bóiſh] a. gay, foppiſh, gallant   (fop
Beaumon'de[bomond']n.gay or faſhionable people
Béaver, n. an animal, hat of beaver-fur, covering
Béavered, a. covered with or having a beaver
Beaúteous, Beaútiful, a. fair, charming, pleaſing
Beaúteouſly, ad. in a beauteous manner, finely

Beaúteoufnefs, *n.* handfomenefs, beauty, grace

Beaútifully *ad.* in a beautiful manner, finely (off

Beaútify, Beaúty, *v. t.* to adorn, grace, deck, fet

Beaúty,*n.* whatever pleafes the eye, as fymmetry, grace, handfomenefs of perfon, elegance of building; affemblage of ornaments; a very handfome perfon

Becafi'co, *n.* a fine fmall bird, figpecker, figeater

Becálm, *v. t.* to quiet, appeafe, make eafy, ftill

Becalm'ed,*pa.* in a quiet ftate, having no wind

Becaufe', *conj.* for this reafon, on this account, for

Bechance', *v.i.* to happen, befall, fall out, *ob.*

Beck, *n.* a fign with the hand or head, a brook

Beck, Beck'on, *v. t.* to make a fign, to hint

Becóme [becum] *v. i.* became,*pret.* become,*pa.* to fit, befit, fit gracefully, be made or done

Becom'ing, *pa. a.* fuitable to, pleafing, graceful

Becom'ingly, *ad.* in a becoming manner, fitly

Becom'ingnefs, *n.* fuitablenefs, propriety, grace

Becúne, *n.* the fea pike of the W. Indies

Bed, *n.* a place to fleep on, lodging, channel of a river, plat in a garden, bank of earth

Bed, *v.* to put to or into bed, lie, fleep, fow

Bedafh', *v. t.* to bemire, befpatter, wet,*ob.*

Bedawb', *v. t.* to daub or cover over, befmear, foil

Bed'chamber, *n.* a room or place ufed to fleep in

Bed'cloaths,*n.* the blankets and quilts,&c. on a bed

Bed'ding, *n.* all the materials belonging to a bed

Bedeck', *v. t.* to deck, trim, adorn, drefs up,

Bedew', *v. t.* to moiften gently, to wet with dew

Bed'fellow, Bed'mate, *n.* one lying in the fame bed

Bedight, Bediz'en, *v.t.* to adorn, deck, drefs up

Bedim', *v. t.* to make dim, darken, obfcure

Bed'lam, *a.* a mad houfe, confufed houfe, hofpital

Bed'lamite, *n.* a madman, a noify perfon (rooms

Bed'maker, *n.* one who makes beds and cleans

Bed'poft,*n.* the poft placed at the corner of a bed

Bed'preffer, *n.* a lazy perfon, fluggard, *ob.*

Bedrag'gle, or Bedag'gle, *v. t.* to dirty the clothes

Bed'rid, Bed'ridden, *a.* confined to the bed

Bed'room,*n.* an apartment for a bed

Bedrop,' *v. t.* to befprinkle, to fpeckle with drops

Bed'fted, *n.* the frame that fupports or holds a bed

Bed'time, *n.* the hour of going to reft, fleeping time

Bee, *n.* a genus of infects, of which there are more than fifty fpecies,one of which is kept for honey

Beebread, *n.* a wax collected by bees as food for

Bee-eater, *n.*a bird which eats bees [their young

Beech, *n.* the name of a large tree, a timber-tree

Beech'en,*a.* made of, like or belonging to beech

Beef, *n.* the flefh of an ox, cow, or bull; *a.* of beef

Beef-eater, *n.* a yeoman of the guards, (Eng.) a grofs perfon

Beegarden, *n.* a place ufed to fet hives of bees in

Beehive, *n.* the cafe in which bees are preferved

Beer, *n.* a liquor made of malt and hops, porter,

Beet, *n.* the name of a garden root (19 threads

Beetle, *n.* a large heavy mallet, rammer, infect

Beetle, *v. t.* to jut out, hang over, project, fwell

Beetlebrowed, *a.* prominent in the forehead

Beetlehead, *a.* dull, ftupid, heavy, blockifh

Beeves, *n. pl.* oxen, cattle for flaughter

Befall', *v.i.* befell,*pret.* befallen,*pa.* to happen to, come to pafs, fall out

Befit', *v. i.* to become, fuit, be fuitable, adorn

Befool', *v. t.* to make a fool, to deceive, *ob.*

Before, *pr.* in front, fooner, in prefence of, fuperi-

Before, *ad.* fooner, in time previous (or fo

Beforehand, *ad.* before in thing, time or place

Beforehand, *a.* well provided with means

Beforetime, *ad.* formerly, of old, of old time

Befoul', *v. t.* to make foul, foul, daub, dirty, foil

Befriend', *v. t.* to favor, ufe kindly, ferve, ailt

Befringe', *v. t.* to adorn with fringe, *ob.*

Beg, *v. t.* to afk earneftly, take for granted

Beget', *v. t.* begat, begot, *pret.* begot, begotten, *pa.* to generate, produce, caufe

Beget'ter, *n.* one who begets or produces, a father

Beg'gar, *n.* one who lives by begging, a petitioner

Beg'gar, *v.t.* to bring to beggary or want, to ruin,

Beg'garlinefs, *n.* poverty, meannefs, ftinginefs

Beg'garly, *a.* very poor, mean, ftingy; *ad.* meanly

Beg'gary,*n.* great want, indigence, poverty

Begin, *v.* began, begun, *pret.* begun, *pa.* to take rife, enter upon, try, do the firft act

Begin'ner, *n.* one who begins, a firft attempter

Begin'ning, *n.* the firft part of time, original, firft caufe, act or ftate, commencement

Begird', *v. t.* begirt, *pret.* begirded, begirt, *pa.* to gird, bind round, furround, inclofe

Beg'lerbeg, *n.* the governor of a Turkifh province

Begrim', *v. t.* to make dirty or footy, daub, ob.

Beguile, *v. t.* to deceive, amufe, cheat, cozen,

Begun', *pret* and *pa.* of *to begin* (impofe upon

Behalf', *n.* favor, caufe, fupport,intereft, account

Behave, *v.* to carry, demean, conduct, act

Behávior, *n.* conduct, carriage, a courfe of life

Behead', *v. t.* to cut off the head, decapitate

Behemoth,*n.* the river-horfe, or hippopotamy

Beheft', *n.* a command, order, meffage, promife

Behight,*pa.* called, named, promifed,*ob.*

Behind, *pr.* or *ad.* at the back, in the rear, out of fight, remaining, inferior to

Behindhand, *ad.* behind in any thing, in arrears

Behold, *v. t.* beheld, *pret.* beheld, *pa.* to look at,

Beholden, *a.* obliged, indebted (view, fee, obferve

Beholder, *n.* one who beholds, a fpectator

Behoof', *n.* what behoves, profit, advantage, ufe

Behoov'able, Behoove'ful, *a.* fit, becoming, proper fuitable, ufeful, profitable, ferviceable (come

Behoove', or Behóve, *v. i.* to be fit, be meet, be-

Béing, *n.* exiftence, a perfon or thing that exifts

Being, *pa.* exifting

Belábor, *v.t.* to thump, thump hard, beat foundly

Belated, *a.* late in time, benighted, too late

Beláy, *v. t.* to waylay, lie in wait, faften

Belch, *v. i.* to throw out wind from the ftomach

Belch, *n.* the act of belching, malt liquor (lady

Bel'dam, *n.* a hag, old or scolding woman, fine
Beleaguer, *v. t.* to befiege, block up, perplex
Bel'founder, *n.* a cafter or maker of bells
Bel'fry, *n.* a place where bells hang and are rung
Bel'gium, *n.* the ancient name of Flanders
Bel'gian, *n.* a native of Flanders, a Fleming
Bel'gic, *a.* pertaining to Belgium, or Flanders
Bélial, *n.* fatan, the devil, wickednefs, vice
Belíe, *v. t.* to flander, fpeak falfely of, feign
Belíef, *n.* credit given to evidence, ftrong or full
   perfuafion of mind, opinion, creed   (true
Believe, *v.* to truft in, credit, have faith, think
Believable, *a.* deferving credit, credible
Believingly, *ad.* with full credit, or faith
Believer, *n.* one that believes, one that credits
Belike, *ad.* probably, perhaps, peradventure, *ob*
Bell, *n.* a hollow founding veffel made of metal
Bell, *v. i.* to grow like a bell in fhape, to fwell
Belle, *n.* a handfome, gay, young lady, a fine lady
Belles-let'tres, *n. pl.* all kinds of polite literature
Bell'founder, *n.* one whofe bufinefs is to caft bells
Bell'foundery, *n.* a place for cafting bells
Bell'flower, *n.* a flower in fhape of a bell, a genus
   of plants of more than forty fpecies
Bell'fhaped, *a.* having the fhape of a bell
Belli"gerent, *a.* carrying on war, engaged in war
Belli"gerent, *n.* a party engaged in war
Bell'man, *n.* a cryer of goods, &c. a common crier
Bell'metal, *n.* a compofition of copper, tin, zink
   and antimony
Bel'low, *v. i.* to roar like a bull or the fea, to roar
Bel'lowing, *n.* a roaring, a great noife
Bel'lows, *n. fing.* or *pl.* an inftrument to blow a fire
Be'luine, *a.* beaftly, brutal, favage, untamed
Bel'ly, *n.* the part of the body containing the en-
   trails, that which refembles it
Bel'ly, *v. i.* to bulge or hang out, project, fwell
Belong, *v. i.* to be the property of, to appertain
Beloved, *a.* loved by, dear to, valued much
Below, *pr.* and *ad.* under, lower, inferior, unbe-
  coming, on earth, or in hell, as oppofed to heaven
Belt, *n.* a lethern girdle, fafh, zone, ftrait
Beluga, *n.* fifh of the fturgeon kind
Belvidére, *n.* a pavilion, eminence, fine view
Bel'wether, *n.* the fheep which leads the flock
Bemire, Bemoil, *v. t.* to daub with mire, to foil
Bemoan, *v. t.* to make a moan, lament, bewail
Bemoaner, *n.* one who bemoans, one who laments
Bemons'ter, *v. t.* to make monftrous, *ob.*
Bemufed, *a.* overcome with mufic   [&c. fitting
Bench, *n.* a feat to fit on, a judge's feat, juftices,
Bench, *v. t.* to furnifh with benches, fix on feats
Bench'er, *n.* a fenior member in the inns of court
Bend, *v.* bended, bent, *pret.* bended, bent, *pa.* to
   crook, bow, fubmit, apply, fubduc, fatten
Bend, *n.* a part bent, turn, curve, knot, band
Bend'er, *n.* who or what bends, or makes to bend
Beneath, *pr.* and *ad.* under, below, unworthy of
Benedic'tine, *n.* a monk of St. Benedict's order

Benedic'tion, *n.* a bleffing, an acknowledgement
Benefac'tion, *n.* a charitable gift, benefit, favor
Benefac'tor, *n.* one who beftows charity, or favors
Benefac'trefs, *n.* a woman who confers benefits
Ben'efice, *n.* a church-living, benefit, kindnefs
Ben'eficed, *a.* poffeffed of a benefice, preferred
Benef'icence, *n.* generofity, bounty, goodnefs
Benef'icent, *a.* kind, delighting in good works
Benefi"cial, *a.* advantageous, profitable, ufeful
Benefi"cially, *ad.* advantageoufly, ufefully
Benefi"cialnefs, *n.* profitablenefs, ufefulnefs, ufe
Benefi"ciary, *n.* one who has or holds a benefice
Ben'efit, *n.* kindnefs, favor, advantage, profit, ufe
Ben'efit, *v.* to do or receive good, profit, favor
Benev'olence, *n.* good-will, kindnefs, a free gift
Benev'olent, *a.* kind, good, affectionate, generous
Bengal', *n.* a flight Indian cotton-ftuff
Benight, *v. i.* to involve in night, to darken
Benighted, *pa.* overtaken by the night, involved
   in darknefs or ignorance
Benign, *a.* kind, generous, liberal, wholefome
Benignity, *n.* kindnefs, gracioufnefs, liberality
Benignly, *ad.* kindly, gracioufly, favorably
Ben'ifon, *n.* a bleffing, benediction, reward, gift
Ben'net, *n.* a fifh of the African feas
Bent, *n.* a curve, tendency, inclination, grafs
Bent, *pa.* crooked, inclined, difpofed
Benum', *v. t.* to make numb or torpid, to ftupify
Ben'zoin, *n.* a balfam which exudes from the
   ftyrax, a tree in Afia
Ben'zoic, *a.* belonging to benzoin
Ben'zoate, *n.* a falt formed by a faturated combi-
   nation of the benzoic acid, with a bafe
Beotian, *n.* a native of Beotia in Greece
Beotian, *a.* pertaining to Beotia
Bepinch', *v. t.* to pinch, *ob.*
Beplume, *v. t.* to adorn with plumes, *ob.*
Bequeath, *v. t.* to leave, to leave or give by will
Bequeft', *n.* a legacy, a gift by will
Berat'tle, *v. t.* to rattle off, fcold, chide
Berb, *n.* an animal of the weafel kind, the foffane
Bereave, *v. t.* bereaved, bereft, *pret.* bereaved,
   bereft, *pa.* to deprive, ftrip, rob
Bereavement, *n.* lofs, deprivation   (perfume
Ber'gamot, or Bur'gamot, *n.* a pear, fine fnuff,
Berhyme, *v. t.* to celebrate in doggerel rhyme
Ber'lin, *n.* a kind of coach contrived at Berlin
Berob', *v. t.* to rob, plunder, pillage, rob
Ber'oe, *n.* a fea animal of an oval form
Ber'ry, *n.* a fmall fruit; *v. i.* to bear berries
Ber'ried, *a.* furnifhed with berries
Ber'yl, *n.* a pellucid gem, of a grayifh green
Ber'yline, *a.* like a beryl, greenifh, light-green
Befeech, *v. t.* to befought, *pret.* befought, *pa.* to en-
   treat, pray, beg, afk with earneftnefs
Befeem, *v. i.* to become, befit, fit neatly, *ob.*
Befet, *v. t.* befet, *pret.* befet, *pa.* to hem in, way-
   lay, perplex, harafs
Befhrew', *v.* to curfe, rail at, happen ill to, *ob.*

Besíde, or Besídes, *pr.* near to, over and above, off
Besiége, *v. t.* to lay fiege to, befet, attack clofely
Besiéger, *n.* one who befieges, one who befets
Befméar, Befmirch', *v. t.* to daub, foil, foul, fully
Befmóke, *v. t.* to foul with or dry in fmoke
Befmut', *v. t.* to fmut over, to blacken,
Béfom, *n.* a common tool to fweep with, a broom
Befort', *v. t.* to fuit, fit, become, *ob.*
Befot', *v. t.* to ftupify, to make ftupid, or foolifh
Befought, *pret.* and *pa.* from *befeech*
Befpan''gle, *v.* to adorn with fpangles, to deck
Befpat'ter, *v. t.* to fprinkle with dirt, to flander
Befpawl', *v. t.* to fpit upon, daub with fpittle, *ob.*
Befpéak, *v. t.* befpoke, *pret.* befpoken, *pa.* to fpeak to, entreat, order, forebode
Befpéaker, *n.* one who befpeaks, one who orders
Befpot', *v. t.* to mark with fpots, variegate, *ob.*
Befpread', *v. t.* befpread, *pret.* befpread, *pa.* to fpread over, cover over, ftrew
Befprènt', *a.* befprinkled, moiftened, wetted, *ob.*
Befprin''kle, *v. t.* to fprinkle over, moiften, wet
Befput'ter, *v. t.* to daub by fputtering upon, *ob.*
Beft, *a.* moft good, moft choice, moft preferable
Beftead', *v. t.* beftead, *pret.* beftead, befteaded, *pa.* to profit, ferve, befriend, treat, *ob.*
Béftial, *a.* like a beaft, beaftly, brutal, filthy
Beftial'ity, *n.* the quality of a beaft, degeneracy from human nature
Beftir', *v. t.* to move quickly or much, to haften
Eeftów, *v. t.* to give, lay out or up, place, apply
Beftówer, *n.* one who beftows, a giver, a difpofer
Beftówment, *n.* the act of conferring
Beftraught', *a.* diftracted, mad, enraged, *ob.*
Beftrew', *v. t.* to fcatter, to fprinkle over, *ob.*
Beftríde, *v. t.* beftride, beftrid, *pret.* beftridden, *pa.* to ftride over, to crofs
Beftud', *v. t.* to ftud, to adorn with ftuds, *ob.*
Bet, *n.* a wager, ftake, name, *abbrev.* for *Beity*
Bet, *v. t.* to lay a bet or wager, ftake a wager
Betáke, *v. i.* betook, *pret.* betaken, *pa.* to have recourfe, apply, go (nefe
Be'tel, *n.* a fpecies of pepper chewed by the Chi-
Bethink', *v. i.* bethought, *pret.* bethought, *pa.* to recollect, reflect, confider
Bethral', *v. t.* to enflave, fubdue, perplex, *ob.*
Betíde, *v. i.* betid, betided, *pret.* betid, betided, *pa.* to befal', happen to, become
Betíme, or betimes, *ad.* early, foon, feafonably
Betóken, *v. t.* to fignify, forefhow, denote, mark
Bet'ony, *n.* a genus of plants bitter and ftimulant
Betoók, *pret.* from *to betake*
Betráy, *v. t.* to violate a truft, deliver up treach-eroufly, difclofe in violation of duty or truft, expofe what is meant to be concealed
Betráyer, *n.* one who betrays, or tells, a traitor
Betrim', *v. t.* to trim, drefs up, deck, *ob.*
Betroth', *v. t.* to give or receive a marriage-pro-mife, contract, name to a benefice
Betroth'ment, *n.* mutual contract of marriage

Betruft', *v. t.* to intruft, put into power, believe
Betruft'ment, *n.* act of entrufting, thing entrufted
Bet'ter, *a.* more good or choice; *v.* an advantage
Bet'ter, *v. t.* to improve, mend, advance, exceed
Bet'ters, *n. pl.* fuperiors in age or qualities
Bet'tor, *n.* one that lays bets or wagers
Bet'ty, *n.* an inftrument to break open doors with
Betwéen, Betwixt, *pr.* in the middle, common
Bev'el, *n.* a kind of fquare rule [to two or more
Bev'el, *v. t.* to form to an angle (drink
Bev'erage, *n.* drink, liquor in general, a treat in
Bev'y, *n.* flock of birds, brood, company
Bewáil, *v. t.* to lament, grieve for, bemoan, mourn
Bewáre, *v. i.* to be cautious, take care of, avoid
Bewéep, *v. i.* bewept, *pret.* bewept, *pa.* to weep over or for, to bedew with tears, *ob.*
Bewil'der, *v. t.* to puzzle, perplex, miflead, lofe
Bewitch', *v. t.* to charm, pleafe very much, injure
Bewitch'ment, *n.* the act or power of charming
Bewráy, *v. t.* to betray, difclofe perfidioufly
Bewrayer, *n.* a betrayer, a difcoverer
Bey [bay, alfo beg] a Turkifh governor or viceroy
Beyond', *pr.* over, out of reach, before, further
Bezóar, *n.* a ftone-like fubftance found in the ftomach of goats, anti-poifonous
Bezóardic, *n.* compound with or like bezoar
Bezóla, *n.* a fifh of a dufky blue color
Bías, *n.* an inclination, bent, weight on one fide
Bias, *v. t.* to incline partially, prepoffefs, move
Bib, *n.* a cloth under the chins of infants, a fifh
Bib, *v. i.* to tipple, fip or drink often, tope
Biang'ular, Biang'ulous, *a.* having two angles
Bibácious, *a.* fond of, or addicted to drinking
Biba''city, *n.* the act or quality of drinking much
Bib'ler, *n.* a drinker, tippler, drunkard, toper, foc
Bible, *n.* the books of the old and new teftament
Bib'lical, *a.* of or relating to the bible or divinity
Bibliothe'cal, *a.* relating to a library
Bib'ulous, *a.* fpongy, foft, that drinks up moifter
Bicapfular, *a.* having two capfules, or feed cafes
Bicau'da, *n.* a fifh of the fword fifh kind
Bice, *n.* a pale blue color ufed in painting
Bicip'ital or Bicip'itous, *a.* having two heads
Bick'er, *v. i.* to difpute about trifles, quiver
Bick'erer, *n.* one who wrangles or fkirmifhes
Bick'ering, Bick'erment, *n.* a difpute, wranling, (ftrife
Bicorn, Bicornous, *a.* having two horns
Bicufpidate, *a.* terminated by two points
Bid, *v. t.* bad, bade, bid, *pret.* bid, bidden, *pa.* to offer a price, command, order, invite
Bid'der, *n.* one who bids, one who offers a price
Bid'ding, *n.* a command, order, charge, publifhing
Bide, *v.* to abide, continue, live, endure, *ob.*
Bedent'al', *a.* having or containing two teeth
Bidet', *n.* a fmall borfe, or nag
Biding, *n.* refidence, habitation, ftop, ftay, *ob.*
Bien'nial, *a.* containing or living two years
Bien'nial, *n.* a plant whofe root lives but two years
Bier, *n.* a wooden hand-carriage ufed for the dead

Biéftings, *n.* the firft milk of a cow after calving

Bifa'rious, *a.* growing only on the oppofite fide

Bifo'd, *a.* twofold, double, doubtful (of a ftem

Bifid, Bifidate, *a.* divided into two parts, cleft

Biflo'rous, *a.* bearing two flowers

Bifurc'ate, *a.* fhooting into two heads or forks

Bifurcation, *n.* a forking, dividing into two parts

Big, *a.* large, fwelled, proud, haughty, pregnant

Big'amift, *n.* he who has two wives at one time

Big'amy, *n.* the crime of having two wives at once

Bigem'inous, Bigem'inate, *a.* bearing double pairs, as when a petiole is divided and each part bears feveral leaflets

Big'gel, *n.* an E. India quadruped, like a deer

Big'gin, *n.* a kind of cap or coif ufed for a child

Bight or Bite, *n.* one round of a rope or cable

Big'ly, *ad.* hugely, haughtily, proudly

Big'nefs, *n.* fize, bulk, greatnefs of quantity

Big'ot, *n.* one unduly devoted to a party, or creed

Big'oted, *a.* unduly devoted, prejudiced

Big'otry, *n.* blind zeal, prejudice, fuperftition

Big'fwoln, *a.* greatly fwelled, lofty, haughty

Bijugous, *a.* double paired, as two pair of leaflets on a fingle petiole

Bilábiate, *a.* divided as two lips

Bilam'ellate, *a.* having two thin plates

Bilat'eral, *a.* having two fides

Bil'berry, *n.* a fhrub and its berry

Bilander, *n.* a fmall veffel, a kind of hoy

Bil'bo, *n.* a rapier, fword, fine or choice fword

Bil'boes, *n. pl.* a fort of ftocks ufed on board a fhip

Bile, *n.* a thick bitter liquor, an angry fwelling

Bile'duct, *n.* a veffel to convey bile

Bile'ftone, *n.* a concretion of vifcid bile

Bilge, *n.* the whole breadth of a fhip's bottom

Bilge, *v.* to fracture a fhip's bottom

Bilge'water, *n.* water lying in the bilge of a fhip

Bil'ingfgate, *n.* a fifh market, foul language, fcold

Bil'ious, Bil'iary, *a.* confifting of bile, choleric

Bilk, *v. t.* to defraud, cheat, overreach, deceive

Bill, *n.* the beak of a fowl, a hooked inftrument for cutting, an account or ftatement of particulars, as goods &c. a note, draft of a law not enacted, exhibition of charges, &c.

Bill, *v.* to kifs, carefs, fondle, publifh, mark

Bill'et, *v. t.* to quarter foldiers, fettle, fix upon

Bill'et, *n.* a fmall letter, ticket, fmall log of wood,

Bil'etdoux, *n.* a fhort love-letter, a card (ingot

Bil'liards, *n. pl.* a game with balls and fticks

Bil'lions, *n. pl.* two or twice millions

Bil'low, *v. i* to fwell or roll like waves, to fwell

Bil'low, *n.* a large roaring wave

Bil'lowy, *a.* fwelling or rolling like a wave

Bilóbed, Bilóbate, *a.* having two lobes, like a bean

Biloc'ular, *a.* having two cells for feeds

Bin, *n.* a repofitory for corn or wine, cheft, box

Bin'acle, *n.* a box on the deck of a veffel to cover the compaffes and lights

Binarious, Binary, *a.* double, two and two, of two

Bi'nate, *a.* bearing two oppofite leaflets on the top of a fimple petiole

Bind, *v. i.* to become clofe or hard as dry clay

Bind, *v. t.* bound, *pret.* bound, *pa.* to gird, faften, oblige, ratify, make coftive

Bind, *n.* a fpecies of hops, band, quantity of eels

Binder, *n.* one who covers books, or binds fheaves

Bin'ding, *n.* a cover, bandage, faftening, feizing on

Binoc'ular, *a.* having or containing two eyes

Binómial, *a.* having two parts, terms or members

Biog'rapher, *n.* a writer of perfon's lives (biography

Biograph'ical, *a.* relating to biography, containing

Biog'raphy, *n.* a hiftory of lives, a writing of lives

Bip'arous, *a.* producing two at a birth

Bipart'ible, Bip'artile, *a.* divifible into two

Bip'artite, *a.* divided, cut or cleft, into two parts

Biped, *n.* an animal having only two feet, a human

Bip'edal, *a.* having two feet (man being

Bipen'nate, *a.* having two wings

Bipet'alous, *a.* containing two leaves

Biquad'rate, *n.* or *a.* the fquare of a fquare or fourth power in mathematics

Biquadrat'ic, *a.* relating to the fourth power

Birch, *n.* the name of a tree, a rod made of birch

Birch, Birch'en, *a.* made of birch

Bird, *n.* a feathered animal, fowl

Bird'cage, *n.* a cage to keep birds in

Bird'catcher, *n.* one that catches birds, a fowler

Birds'eye, *n.* cloth with figures like bird's-eyes

Bird'lime, *n.* a glutinous fubftance to catch birds

Birth, *n.* the act of coming into life, regeneration, lineage, origin, convenient room, place to lodge in (or the anniverfary of it

Birth'day, *n.* the day on which any one is born

Birth'place, *n.* the place of any one's birth

Birth'right, *n.* right or privilege by birth

Birth'wort, *n.* a genus of plants of many fpecies

Bis'cuit, *n.* a kind of hard flat bread, cake

Bifect', *v. t.* to divide or cut into two equal parts

Bifec'tion, *n.* a divifion into two equal parts

Bifh'op, *n.* a fpiritual head of a diocefe, a liquor

Bifh'op, *v. t.* to confirm in the church

Bifh'opric, *n.* the jurifdiction of a bifhop, a diocefe

Bifk, *n.* foup, broth made of feveral forts of flefh

Bis'muth, *n.* a femi metal of a reddifh or yellowifh white, heavy, brittle and eafily melted

Bis'muthic, *a.* pertaining to bifmuth

Bis'on, *n.* a quadruped of the cow kind

Biffex'tile, *n.* leap-year, every fourth year

Bis'ter, *n.* a paint of a deep brown color

Biftort', *n.* knot-grafs of many fpecies

Bifulc'eous, *a.* clovenfooted, cleft or cut in the foot

Bit, *n.* the iron of a bridle, a morfel, a coin

Bit, *v. t.* to put a bit in the mouth, to check

Bitch, *n.* the female of canine animals

Bite, *n.* a piece feized with the teeth, trick, cheat

Bite, *v. t.* bit, *pret.* bitten, *pa.* to feize or break with the teeth, caufe to fmart, cheat

Bite, *n.* act of biting, thing bitten off, coil of a

rope, a bay or inlet, a trick

Biter, n. one that bites, a sharper, a trickster

Biter'nate, a. having three ternated leaves on a petiole

Bit'ter, a. sharp, cruel, severe, keen, afflictive

Bit'ter, n. a thing that is bitter, a coil or turn

Bit'terish, a. somewhat bitter

Bit'terishnefs, n. a small degree of bitternefs

Bit'terly, ad. sharply, cruelly, severely, keenly

Bit'tern, n. the name of a seawater-fowl, a brine

Bit'ternefs, n. a bitter tafte, malice, forrow, grief

Bit'ters, n. bitter vegetables or an infufion of them

Bit'umen, n. a fat giutinous foffil fubftance

Bitu'minous, a. containing or like bitumen

Bivalv'ular, or Bi'valve, a. having two valves

Bizant'ine, n. a piece of gold worth about 15l. fter.

Blab, v. to tell or let out, tell a fecret, tattle

Blab, Blab'ber, n. a telltale, a thoughtlefs babbler

Black, a. dark, cloudy, mournful, difmal, wicked

Black, n. a blackamoor, darkeft color, mourning

Black, v. t. to make black, blacken, darken, foil

Black'berry, n. the fruit of the bramble, the plant

Black'bird, n. in England a finging bird, in Ameri-

Black'cap, n. a fmall fong bird   [ca the grackle

Black'en, v. t. to make black, darken, defame

Black'guard, n. a perfon of foul fcurrilous language

Black'ifh, a. fomewhat black, rather dirty, mean

Black'lead, n. plumbago, or iron and carbon

Black'moore, or Black'amoor, n. a negro, a black

Black'nefs, n. darknefs, a dark color   (perfon

Black'fmith, n. a perfon who works on iron

Black'thorn, n. the floe, a fhrub ufed for hedges

Blad'der, n. a veffel containing fome liquid in the body as urine, bile, &c.

Blad'dery, a. containing or like bladders

Blade, n. a fpire of grafs, cutting part of a fword, &c. fierce or gay perfon, flat part of an oar

Blades, n. pl. leaves of maiz ufed for fodder, (Southern ftates)

Bláded, a. having blades or fpires pointed out

Blain, n. a boil, blifter, blotch, ulcer, diforder

Blámable, a. deferving of blame, guilty, faulty

Blame, v. t. to cenfure, find fault with

Blame, n. fault, guilt, expreffion of difapprobation

Blámelefs, a. innocent, guiltlefs, inoffenfive, up-

Blámelefsly, ad. innocently, harmlefsly   [right

Blámelefsnefs, n. innocence, harmlefsnefs, purity

Blámer, n. one that cenfures or finds fault with

Blámeworthy, a. deferving of blame or reproach

Blanch, v. to whiten, fkin almonds, evade

Blanch'er, n. one who blanches, one who whitens

Bland, a. courteous, foft, mild, gentle, kind

Bland'ifh, v. t. to fmooth, foften, wheedle, flatter

Bland'ifhment, n. kind words, fondnefs, flattery

Blank, a. white, pale, unwritten, dejected, dull

Blank, n. a void fpace, unwritten paper, difappoint-ment, aim, v. t. to caft down, damp, annul

Blank'et, n. a woollen covering for a bed

Blank'et, v. t. to cover with, or tofs in, a blanket

Blank'ly, ad. in a blank manner, palely, fillily

Blank'nefs, n. palenefs, wannefs, confufion, fhame

Blafphéme, v. t. to fpeak wickedly, curfe, revile

Blafphémer, n. a perfon who reviles God, a curfer

Blas'phemous, a. full of blafphemy, very prophane

Blafphémoufly, ad. in a blafphemous manner

Blas'phemy, n. a horrid iadignity offered to God

Blaft, n. a guft of wind, found, blight, explofion of powder, one fmelting of ore

Blaft, v. t. to caufe to wither, blow up, difappoint

Blátant, a. bellowing as a calf, noify, ob.

Blat'ta, n. a genus of infects with inclined heads, membranaceous wings and feet formed for run-

Blat'ter, v. i. to roar, bellow, babble, ob.   [ning

Blaze, v. to flame, flare, burn, publifh abroad, tell

Blaze, n. a flame, the light of a flame, a report

Blázer, n. a fpreader or publifher of reports

Blázon, v. t. to explain, adorn, difplay, tell, blaze

Blázon, Blázonry, n. the act of heraldry, a difplay

Bleach, v. to whiten, to make or grow white

Bléaching, n. the act or art of whitening

Bleak, a. cold, chill, pale, wan, n. a fmall fifh

Bléaknefs, n. coldnefs, chilnefs, palenefs, wannefs

Bléaky, a. bleak, cold, coldifh, chilly, pale, wan

Blear, a. watery, dim, weak, fore, bloody

Blear, v. t. to make the eyes watery, dim or fore

Bléarednefs, n. dimnefs through water or blood

Bléareyed, a. having watery or red eyes

Bleat, v. i. to cry like a fheep

Bleat, Bléating, n. the cry of a fheep or goat

Bleb, n. a fmall cavity in a fubftance

Bleed, v. bled, pret. bled, pa. to lofe or let blood, perifh by bleeding, lofe fap, feel keen diftrefs

Bléeding, n. an iffue of blood, a letting of blood

Blem'ifh, v. t. to deform, mark, hurt, defame

Blem'ifh, n. a deformity, difgrace, fault, ftain, fpot

Blench, v. i. to fhrink, ftart back, hinder, ob.

Blend, v. t. to mix, mingle, confound in a mafs

Blend, n. a mineral compofed of zink, fulphur, iron and arfenic

Blend'ed, Blent, pa. mixed together, confufed

Blendófe, a. pertaining to blend

Blen'ny, n. a tribe of fifh, of many varieties

Blefs, v. t. to give fuccefs, make happy, pronounce a wifh of happinefs, confecrate by prayer, praife or glorify

Blefs'ed, Bleft, pa. very happy or eafy, profpered

Blefs'ednefs, n. happinefs, content, joy, holinefs

Blefs'ing, n. a good wifh, divine favor, gift, enjoy-ment   [terranean fprings by fenfation

Blétonifm, n. the faculty or art of perceiving fub-

Blétonift, n. one who can perceive fubterranean

Blew, pret. of to blow   [fprings

Blight, n. mildew, a difappointment; v. t. to blaft

Blind, a. diftitute of fight, dark, weak, unfeen

Blind, v. t. to darken, ftop the fight, cover

Blind, n. any thing that intercepts the fight, a cover

Blínded, pa. made blind, deprived of fight

Blindfold, v. t. to cover the eyes, to hoodwink

Blindfold, a. having the eyes covered, dark, weak
Blindly, ad. tamely, fimply, without judgment
Blindnefs, n. a want of fight or fenfe, ignorance
Blindfide, n. a weaknefs, foible, defeft, failing
Blindworm, n. a fmall kind of venomous viper
Blink, v. i. to wink, fhut, clofe, fee darkly
Blink'ard, n. a perfon that has bad weak eyes
Blifs, n. happinefs, blefsednefs, great gladnefs, joy
Blifs'ful, a. very happy, bleffed, full of joy
Blis'ter, n. a watery rifing in the fkin, a plafter
Blis'ter, v. to rife in or raife blifters, to fwell
Blite, n. a plant, the ftrawberry fpinage
Blithe, Blithefome, a. gay, airy, merry, fprightly
Bloat, v. to fwell, puff up, grow puffy, enlarge
Bloatednefs, n. a bloated or fwelled ftate [drance
Block, n. a heavy piece of wood, &c. pulley, hin-
Block, v. t. to fhut or ftop up, inclofe, hinder
Blockáde, n. the military fhutting up of a place
Blockáde, v. t. to fhut up or in, furround, inclofe
Block'head, n. a ftupid or dull perfon, dunce, dolt
Block'headed, Block'ifh, a. ftupid, dull, heavy
Block'houfe, n. a fortrefs built to command a pafs
Blood, [blud] n. a fluid which circulates in ani-
mals, a family, race, life, death, rake, guilt, pun-
ifhment for fhedding blood, carnal part oppo-
fed to fpiritual, vegetable fap
Blood, v. t. to ftain with or let blood, to bleed
Bloodguilt'inefs, n. the guilt of murder, murder
Blood'hound, n. a large hunting dog
Blood'ily, ad. cruelly, malicioufly, very wickedly
Blood'inefs, n. a bloody ftate, cruelty
Blood'lefs, a. deftitute of blood, dead, innocent
Blood'fhed, n. lofs of blood, murder flaughter
Blood'fhedder, n. a murderer, deftroyer, ravager
Blood'fhedding, n. the aft or crime of fhedding
Blood'fhot, a. filled with blood, red [olood
Blood'fucker, n. one who thirfts after blood, a leech
Blood'thirfty, a. defirous of fhedding blood, cruel
Blood'veffel, n. any veffel in which the blood moves
Blood'y, a. ftained with blood, murderous, cruel
Blood'yminded, a. cruel, barbarous, horrid
Blood'wort, n. a plant
Bloom, n. the bloffom or flower of a tree, &c. a fine
native color, perfection, fquare iron bar
Bloom, v. i. to yield bloffoms, be young, flourifh
Bloom'ing, Bloom'y, a. full of bloffoms, youthful
Bloom'ary, n. iron once hammered in bars
Blofs'om, n. the flowers of trees or plants, prime
Blofs'om, v. i. to put forth bloffoms, to bloom
Blot, v. t. to blur, ftain, efface, difgrace, darken
Blot, n. a blur, fpot, ftain, mark, crime, difgrace
Blotch, n. a fpot or puftule on the fkin, a pimple
Blote, v. t. to fmoke, dry with fmoke, fwell
Blow, n. a ftroke, misfortune, gale of wind, egg
of a fly
Blow, v. blew, pret. blowed, blown, pa. to make
a current of air, impel by wind, move as air,
pant, found with wind, bloffom, fwell, depofit
an egg as a fly

Blower, n. one who or what blows, a whale
Blowpipe, n. a tube or machine to fufe metals by
a fmall current of air
Blowth, n. a bloom, bloffom in general
Blowze, n. a ruddy fat wench, a flattern
Blowz'y, a. funburnt, ruddy
Blub'ber, n. whale-oil not boiled, a fort of feafifh
Blub'ber, v. t. to fwell the cheeks with weeping
Bluebird, n. a fmall bird, the upper part blue
Blub'bered, pa. fwelled with weeping, bloated
Bludgeon, n. a fhort thick ftick, a weapon
Blue, a. fkycolored, blank, dejected; n. a fkycolor
Bluebottle, n. the name of a flower, a large fly
Blueeyed, a. having blue eyes, bewitching
Bluely, ad. with a blue color, palely, wanly
Bluenefs, n. the quality of being blue, wannefs
Bluff, a. big, large, fwelled, furly, bluftering
Bluff, n. a fteep bank or high bold fhore
Bluing, n. the art of giving a blue color
Bluefifh, n. a fpecies of fifh in America
Bluifh, a. inclined to bluenefs, rather blue
Blun'der, v. i. to miftake grofsly, err, ftumble
Blun'der, n. a miftake, falfe ftep, grofs overfight
Blun'derbufs, n. a fhort wide gun, a blunderer
Blun'derer, Blun'derhead, n. a ftupid fellow
Blunt, a. dull, rough, unpolite, plain, hard
Blunt, v. t. to dull the edge or point, to weaken
Bluntly, ad. rudely, roughly, plainly
Bluntnefs, n. a want of edge, rudenefs, roughnefs
Blur, n. a blot, fpot, ftain, miftake, imperfection
Blur, v. to blot, fpot, ftain, efface, hurt
Blurt, v. t. to blab out, to fpeak inconfiderately
Blufh, v. i. to redden in the face
Blufh, n. a reddifh color excited by fhame, &c.
Blufhing, pa. reddening, modeft
Blufh'lefs, a. paft blufhing, impudent
Blufh'y, a. having the color of a blufh
Blus'ter, v. i. to roar, bully, hector, puff, fwagger
Blus'ter, n. a roar, noife, tumult, great ftir, boaft
Blus'terer, n. a noify roaring perfon a fwaggerer
Blus'trous, a. noify, tumultuous, rough, harfh
Bóa, n. a genus of amphibious ferpents
Boar, n. the male of fwine [victuals
Board, n. a piece of wood, table, deck, court held,
Board, v. to lay or fence with boards, enter a
fhip by force, attack, give or receive diet
Bóarder, n. one who pays to live with another
Bóardingfchool, n. a fchool where the pupils are
lodged and fed by the inftructor
Boardwages, n. pl. an allowance made for victuals
Bóarifh, a. rude, hoggifh, brutal, rough
Boaft, v. to brag, fpeak highly, glory in, exult
Boaft, n. a proud fpeech, brag, caufe of boafting
Bóafter, n. one who boafts, a braggart, a puffer
Bóaftful, Bóaftive, a. vain, proud, haughty, lofty
Bóafting, n. the act or caufe of boafting, a boaft
Bóaftingly, ad. in a boafting or proud manner
Boat, n. a fmall veffel ufually moved by oars
Boat, v. t. to convey in a boat

Bóatable, a. navigable with boats
Bóathook, n. a pole armed with a hook and point to pufh or pull a boat [tranfporting in boats
Bóating, pa. and n. conveying, or the practice of
Bóatbill, n. a genus of birds with a bill like a boat
Bóatman, n. a manager of a boat [ging
Bóatfwain, n. one who has the care of a fhip's rig-
Bob, v. to dangle, play about, dodge, cheat, drub
Bob, n. any thing that hangs loofe, a blow, a wig
Bob'bin, n. a fmall piece of wood with a notch, a
Bóbo, n. an excellent table fifh in Mexico [cord
Bob'tailed, a. having the tail made or cut fhort
Bocáke, n. an animal like a rabbit
Bode, v. t. to prefage, forefhow, portend
Bódement, n. a foreboding, omen, fign, ob.
Bod'ice, n. a fort of ftays for women
Bod'ilefs, a. void of body, fpiritual, pure, refined
Bod'ily, a. of or relating to the body, real, actual
Bod'kin, n. a long inftrument, large needle
Bod'y, n. the whole trunk of an animal or tree, a
  ' perfon, matter oppofed to fpirit, main part,
  mafs, fpirit in liquors, folid figure, a fyftem, a
  number of troops, a corporation, reality, the flefh
Bod'y, v. t. to produce in fome form, to imbody
Bog, n. a marfh, fen, morafs, foft or wet ground
Bog'bane, n. the marfh trefoil
Bog'berry, n. a plant, the bogwort
Bog'gle, Bodge, v. t. to ftart, doubt, waver, fear
Bog'gler, n. one that doubts, a timorous perfon
Bog'gling, pa. ftarting back; n. hefitation, delay
Bog'gy, a. marfhy, fwampy, fenny, watery, foft
Bog'houfe, n. a houfe of office, a neceffary houfe
Boguácu, n. a ferpent of the largeft kind
Bohéa, n. a coarfe tea of inferior quality
Bohémian, n. a native of Bohemia
Bohémian, a. pertaining to Bohemia
Boióbi, n. a green fnake an ell long
Boita'po, n. a venomous ferpent of eight feet length
Boil, v. t. to bubble through heat, to drefs meat
Boil'ed, pa. dreffed in boiling water, much heated
Boil'er, n. a veffel for boiling of water, &c.
Boil'ery, n. a place for and apparatus of boiling
Boil'ing, n. the act or ftate of boiling
Bois'terous, a. violent, furious, ftormy, unwieldly
Bois'teroufly, ad. violently, furioufly, very loudly
Bó'ar, a. pertaining to bole, a kind of earth
Bold, a. brave, ftout, daring, impudent, full
Bólden, v. t. to make bold or confident, not ufed
Bóldface, n. an impudent faucy perfon, faucinefs
Bóldfaced, a. impudent, faucy, impertinent, bold
Bóldly, ad. in a bold manner, bravely, impudently
Bóldnefs, n. courage, liberty, affurance
Bóle, n. a meafure of fix bufhels, ftem of a tree, an
  earth, vifcid, foft, friable and flightly aftringent
Boll, n. two bufhels, a pericarp or feed veffel, a
  capfule
Boll, v. i. to feed or form into a feed veffel
Bólfter, n. a large pillow, long cufhion, pad, quilt
Bólfter, v. t. to pad, fupport, prop, hold up

Bólftered, pa. fupported or held up by a bolfter
Bolt, n. a bar of a door, dart, arrow, ring, light-
  ning, a piece of canvas of 28 ells or 38 yards
Bolt, v. i. to fhut, faften, fift, fally or rufh out
Bólter, n. a fieve to feparate flour from bran
Bóltingmill, n. a mill where meal is fifted [faftened
Bóltrope, n. a rope to which the edges of fails are
Bólus, n. a large pill, gobbet, dofe, kind of earth
Bom, n. a large harmlefs ferpent [from a mortar
Bomb, n. a fhell to be filled with powder, and fent
Bomb, v. to attack with bombs, not ufed
Bombard', n. a cannon, not ufed
Bombard', v. t. to throw or attack with bombs
Bombardiér, n. an officer, a bomb-engineer
Bombard'ment, n. an attack made with bombs
Bombafiné, n. a flight black ftuff mixed with filk
Boin'baft, Bombaft'ic, a. high-founding, fulfome
Bom'baft, n. fuftian, big empty words
Bombilátion, n. a great found, buzzing noife, ob.
Bomb'cheft, n. a cheft for containing bombs
Bom'bic, a. pertaining to the filk worm
Bom'biate, n. a falt formed by bombic acid and a
  bafe faturated
Bomb'ketch, n. a ftrong fhip for bearing bombs
Bomby"cinous, a. pertaining to filk, or the filk
  worm [long main and fhort horns
Bonáfus, n. a quadruped of the cow kind with a
Bond, n. any thing that binds, an obligation, union
Bond, a. in a fervile ftate, enflaved, bound
Bond'age, n. flavery, captivity, imprifonment
Bond'maid, Bond'man, n. a woman or man flave
Bond'fervant, Bond'flave, n. an abfolute flave
Bond'fervice, n. a ftate of abfolute flavery
Bonds'man, n. one bound for another, a furety
Bone, n. the moft folid part of the body, a die
Bone, v. t. to take out, or put in bones
Bónelace, n. a coarfe kind of lace, a flaxen lace
Bónelefs, a. void of bones, foft, tender
Bónefetter, n. a man that fets bones, a furgeon
Bonet'ta, n. a fifh
Bon'fire, n. a rejoicing fire, a fire for triumph
Bon'ito, n. a fifh with a greenifh back
Bon'net, n. a covering for the head of very varia-
  ble form, a fmall fail
Bon'nily, ad. prettily, finely, gaily
Bon'ten, n. a narrow woollen ftuff
Bónus, n. a premium on a loan
Bon'ny, a. handfome, beautiful, fine, merry, gay
Bon'nyclabber, n. a name for four buttermilk
Bo'ny, a. full of bones, ftrong, ftout, large
Bon'zes, n. priefts in China, Japan, &c.
Boob'y, n. a dull empty fellow, dunce, large bird
Book, n. a volume in which we read or write
Book, v. t. to enter in a book, note down, regifter
Book'binder, n. one who binds books
Book'ifh, a. much given to reading, ftudious
Book'ifhnefs, n. fondnefs for reading, ftudy
Book'keeper, n. one that keeps another's accounts
Book'keeping, n. the art or act of keeping accounts

Book'learned, *a*. learned in books, well read
Book'learning, *n*. an acquaintance with books
Book'lefs, *a*. ignorant, unlettered, unlearned
Book'mate, *n*. a fchoolfellow, a play fellow
Book'feller, *n*. a feller of or dealer in books
Book'worm, Book'man, *n*. a clofe ftudent, a mite
Boom, *n*. a fpar to extend a fail, a chain or cable acrofs a river
Boom, *v. i*. to rufh with violence, to fail very faft
Boon, *a*. gay, merry, pleafant, cheerful, good, kind
Boon, *n*. a gift, prefent, favor, prayer, bone
Boops, *n*. a Mediterranean fifh with large eyes
Boor, *n*. a clown, lout, countryfellow, rude man
Boor'ifh, *a*. clownifh, ruftic, countryfied, rough
Boor'ifhnefs, *n*. clownifhnefs, rufticity, rudenefs
Boofe, *v. i*. to drink to excefs *n*. a ftall
Bo'fy, *a*. t'pfy, drunk, *vulgar*
Boot, *v*. to profit, gain advantage, put on bouts
Boot, *n*. profit, gain, advantage, booty, a covering for the legs, part of a coach, kind of rack
Boot'catcher, *n*. a perfon who pulls off boots, &c.
Boot'ed, *pa*. in boots, equipped, ready
Bootee, *n*. a fhort boot
Booth, *n*. a place of entertainment, a ftall in a fair
Boot'lefs, *a*. ufelefs, unavailing, unprofitable, vain
Boot'tree, *n*. a piece of wood to fhape a boot
Boot'y, *n*. pillage, plunder, fpoil, prey, unfair play
Bórable, *a*. that may or can be bored
Boráchio, *n*. a drunkard, a leathern bottle
Bor'age, *n*. the name of a plant, buglofs [foda
Bórax, *n*. an artificial falt formed by an acid with
Bo'racite, *n*. a magnefian earth combined with bo racic acid
Bo'racited, *a*. combined with boracic acid
Bora''cic, *a*. pertaining to borax, fully acidified
Bórate, *n*. a falt formed by boracic acid and a faturated bafe [oxygene
Borácous acid is borax, partially faturated with
Bord'er, *n* an edge or edging, hem, boundary, bed
Bord'er, *v*. to make a border, join to, touch upon
Bord'erer, *n*. an inhabitant near or on the borders
Bore, *v*. to make a hole, to pufh forward or out
Bore, *n*. a hole made by boring, the fize of a hole
Bore, *pret*. of to bear
Bóreal, *a*. northern, tending towards the north
Bóreas, *n*. a cold wind, the north wind
Borée, *n*. a dance of three fteps in two motions
Bórer, *n*. one who bores, a piercer, a gimblet
Born, *pa*. brought into the world or life
Borne, *pa*. carried, brought, fupported, paid
Borne, *n*. limit, boundary
Bor'ough, *n*. a corporation-town, a company
Bor'row, *v. t*. to take by confent to ufe and return the fame, or an equivalent in kind, to copy
Bor'rower, *n*. one who borrows of another perfon
Bors'holder, *n*. a headborough, a petty conftable
Bofc'age, *n*. woods, woodlands, maft, *ob*.
Bofk'y, *a*. woody, rough, fwelled, fat, *ob*.
Bófom, *n*. the breaft, heart, tender affections, love

Bófom, *v. t* to put or conceal in the bofom
Bófom, *a*. confidential, trufty, intimate
Bofs, *n*. a ftud, knob, raifed work, clufter, knot
Bos'ton. *n*. the chief town in Maffachufetts
Bostónian, *n*. an inhabitant of Bofton
Botan'ic, Botan'ical, *a*. of or relating to plants
Bot'anift, *n*. a perfon fkilled in plants and herbs
Bot'any, *n*. the knowledge or defcription of plants
Botanol'ogy, *n*. a difcourfe on plants
Bot'anize, *v. i*. to inveftigate plants
Botch, *v. t*. to mend chumfily, mend, patch, fpot
Botch, *n*. a bile, ulcer, fore, fwelling, patchwork
Botch'er, *n*. a mender of old clothes, a bungling
Botch'ing, *n*. the mending of old clothes [fewer
Botch'y, *a*. marked with or full of botches
Botet'to, *n*. a Mexican fifh fwelling when touched, and its liver poifonous
Both, *a*. the two, of two, as well, likewife
Both'er, *v. t*. to vex, teafe, [*vulgar, from pother*]
Boto'toe, *n*. a bird of the parrot kind
Bot'ryoid, *a*. refembling or like a bunch of grapes
Bots, *n. pl*. fmall worms in the entrails of horfes
Bot'tle, *n*. a veffel for liquor, viol, quart, bundle
Bot'tle, *v. t*. to put up into bottles, to keep clofe
Bot'tlefcrew, *n*. a fcrew to draw corks
Bot'tom, *n*. the loweft part, a foundation, a valley, ball, fhip, dregs
Bot'tom, *v*. to put a bottom, to reft or fix upon
Bot'tomlefs, *a*. having no bottom, unfathomable
Bot'tomry, *n*. a borrowing of money, and pledging a fhip to fecure the repayment
Bouge, *v. i*. to fwell, fwell or bulge out, projeft
Bough, *n*. an arm of a tree, branch, large fhoot
Bought, *pret*. and *pa*. of to buy; *n*. a knot, a bend
Bought'en [bawten] purchafed, foreign-made
Bougié, *n*. a thin wax-candle, an inftrument
Bounce, *v. i*. to leap, fpring, crack, boaft, bully
Bounce, *n*. a leap, kick, fudden noife or blow, boaft
Boun'cer, *n*. one who bounces, a boafter, a bully
Boun'cing, *n*. a great or fudden noife, a crack
Bound, *v*. to limit, end, fpring, fly back, rebound
Bound, *pa. paff*. of to bind; *a*. deftined, going to
Bound, *n*. limit, mark of divifion, a leap, fpring
Bound'ary, *n*. a limit, mark, reftraint, end
Bound'en, *a*. required, neceffary, obliged to
Bound'lefs, *a*. unconfined, unlimited, infinite
Bound'leffnefs, *n*. ftate of being without limit
Bound'ftone, *n*. ftone to play with, a landmark
Boun'ty, *n*. free gift, generofity, a premium
Boun'teous, Boun'tiful, *a*. liberal, generous, kind
Boun'teoufly, Boun'tifully, ad. liberally, freely
Boun'teoufnefs, Boun'tifulnefs, *n*. liberality, gen erofity, kindnefs, goodnefs
Bout, *n*. a turn, trial, effay, attempt
Bóvine, *a*. pertaining to cattle, or the cow kind
Bow, *v. t*. to bend down, ftoop, crufh, fink under
Bow, *n*. a bending in token of civility or reverence, the rounding part of a fhip's fide forward
Bow, *n*. an inftrument to fhoot arrows and another

er to play on a violin, rainbow, part of a yoke, of a knot, &c.

Bowbent, a. bent like a bow, arched, crooked

Bowel, v. to pierce or take out of the bowels

Bowellefs, a. cruel, mercilefs, unfeeling, unkind

Bow'els, n. pl. parts within the body, feeling

Bow'er, n. an arbor made in a garden, an anchor

Bow'ery, a. full of bowers, fhady, retired, cool

Bowl, n. the hallow of a cup or glafs, a veffel ufed

Bowl, n. a ball ufed in playing bowls [for punch

Bowl, v. t. to play at or cast bowls, trundle, roll

Bowlegged, a. having crooked legs

Bowl'er, n. one who bowls, one who plays at bowls

Bowl'in, Bow'ling, n. the name of a fhip's rope

Bowl'inggreen, n. a level green kept for bowlers

Bowl'ingknot, a fort of knot that will not flip

Bow'man, n. one who fhoots with bows, an archer

Bowfe, v. to pull or haul

Bowfprit, n. a large fpar at a fhip's head, fupporting the forward fails

Bowftring, n. a ftring ufed for a bow

Bowyer, n. an archer, bowman, maker of bows

Box, n. a tree, a cafe or coffer, feat in a playhoufe or court room, a blow on the ear, a cylinder for an axletree, quantity in a box

Box, v. t. to put in a box, to ftrike with the fift

Box'en, a. made of box, refembling or like box

Box'er, n. one who boxes or fights with the fift

Box'ing, n. the act of fighting with the fift

Boy, n. a male child, lad, youth, word of contempt

Boy, v. i. to act or treat like a boy, not ufed

Boy'hood, n. the age, ftate or condition, of a boy

Boy'ifh, a. like a boy, childifh, trifling, fimple

Boy'ifhly, ad. childifhly, foolifhly, fimply, idly

Boy'ifhnefs, Boy'ifm, n. childifhnefs, folly, play

Boyúna, n. a flender ferpent of America

Boyupecan'ga, n. a thick ferpent very venomous

Brab'ble, n. a noify conteft; v. i. to clamor, ob.

Brace, v. t. to bind, tie, faften, ftrain up, tighten

Brace, n. a bandage, tightnefs, pair, couple, line

Bracelet, n. an ornament on the wrifts, a hound

Bracer, n. a bandage, any thing that tightens

Brach'ial, [ch as k] a. belonging to the arm

Brach'iate,[ch as k] a. having pairs at right angles

Brach'man, [ch as k] n. a philofopher in India

Brach'ygraphy, [ch as k] n. fhort-hand writing

Brack, n. a breach, crack, flit, rent; a. falt

Brack'et, n. a fmall fupport of wood, &c. a cramp

Brack'ifh, a. faltifh, falt, like feawater

Brack'ifhnefs, n. a faltifh tafte, ftate or quality

Brac'te, or Brac'ty, n. a prop or floral leaf

Brac'teate, a. having floral leaves

Brad, n. a thin nail with a flat head

Brag, v. i. to boaft, fwagger, puff, make a parade

Brag, n. a boaft, parade, name of a game at cards

Braggadócio, n. a bragger, vain boafter, fwaggerer

Brag'gart, a. boafting, boaftful, vainglorious, vain

Brag'gart, Brag'ger, n. a boafter, a puffing fellow

Braid, v. t. to weave together, plat, fold

Braid, n. a weaving, knot, lace, edging

Brail, v. t. to haul up or furl

Brails, n. pl. ropes to furl the fails with

Brain, n. a foft fubftance within the fkull, the feat of fenfation and intellect

Brains, n. fenfe, underftanding

Brain, v. to knock or take out the brains, ob.

Bráinifh, a. hotheaded, hot, furious, violent, ob.

Bráinlefs, a. deftitute of thought, filly, foolifh

Bráinpan, n. the fkull, containing the brains

Bráinfick, a. difeafed in the underftanding, giddy,

Brake, pret. of to break, ob. (weak

Brake, n. a thicket of brambles or fhrubs, inftrument for dreffing flax, kneadingtrough, bit, handle of a pump

Bráky, a. prickly, rough, thorny

Bram'a, or Brum'ma, n. the chief Deity in India

Bram'ble, n. a very prickly or thorny fhrub

Bram'bling, n. the mountain-finch or fea lark

Bram'in, n. a follower of Brama a Gentoo prieft

Bran, n. the hufks of ground corn

Branch, n. a fmall bough, any thing that fhoots from a ftock, a fmall ftream entering a larger, offspring, divifion of a fubject, &c.

Branch, v. to fpread into branches, extend, adorn

Branch'lefs, a. having no branches, naked, barren

Branch'let, n. the divifion of a branch

Branch'y, a. full of or having branches (to burn

Brand, v. t. to mark with a brand or infamy,

Brand, n. a burnt or burning piece of wood, fword, an iron to burn the figure of letters, the mark burnt, a ftigma

Brand'ed, pa. burnt with an iron, marked, difgraced

Brand'ifh, v. t. to wave, fhake, flourifh

Brand'ling, n. the name of a fmall worm (fruit, &c.

Brand'y, n. a fpirit diftilled from wine, cider or

Bran"gle, v. i. to fquabble, wrangle, difpute, ob.

Bran"gle, n. a quarrel, fquabble, conteft, ob.

Brank, n. a fort of grain, buck-wheat

Bran'lin, n. a fifh of the falmon kind

Bran'ny, a. confifting of or like bran, foul

Bráfier, n. one who works, &c. in brafs, a pan

Brafil', n. part of South America belonging to

Brafil'ian, n. a native of Brafil (Portugal

Brafil', or Brafilian, a. pertaining to Brafil

Brafil'wood, n. a wood ufed in dying

Brafs, n. a fubftance, compofed of copper, zink and calamin; effrontery, impudence, ftrength durability

Brafs, a. made of brafs, brazen, yellow, impudent

Brafs'y, a. hard as brafs, made of brafs, very bold

Brafs'inefs, n. a braffy nature or appearance

Brat, n. a child, by way of contempt, an offspring

Bravádo, n. a brag, boaft, threat, boafting fellow

Brave, a. courageous, gallant, noble, excellent

Brave, n. a hector, bully, fwaggerer, bravo, boaft

Brave, v. t. to defy, dare, encounter with firmnefs

Brávely, ad. gallantly, nobly, finely, generoufly

Brávery, n. courage, heroifm, gallantry; in the

fenfe of fhow, ob.

Brávo, n. one who murders for hire, an affaffin

Brawl, v. i. to make a great noife, fcold, quarrel

Brawl, n. a quarrel, fquabble, great noife, dance

Brawl'er, n. a wrangler, a noify perfon (quarrel

Brawling, pa. making a great noife; n. a noify

Brawn, n. a boar's flefh, a thick mufcular part

Brawn'inefs, n. great ftrength, firmnefs, hardnefs

Brawn'y, a. flefhy, bulky, ftrong, firm, mufcular

Bray, n. a noife as of an afs, great found, harfh cry

Bray, v. to beat in a mortar, mix, cry like an afs

Bráyer, n. one that brays, an inftrument to ftir up

Braze, v. t. to cover or folder with brafs (ink

Brázen, a. made of brafs, impudent, bold, daring

Brázen, v. i. to bully, be impudent, ftand out

Brázenface, n. a bold impudent wretch, a bold girl

Brázenfaced, a. impudent, fhamelefs, very bold

Brázennefs, n. a brazen quality, great boldnefs

Breach, n. an opening, gap, difference, quarrel, violation, invafion, bruife, affliction by a lofs

Bread, n. food made of flour or meal, provifions in general

Bread'corn, n. any corn of which bread is made

Bread'lefs, a. deftitute of bread, or food

Bread'tree, n. a tropical tree, whofe fruit is food

Breadth or Bredth, n. meafure from fide to fide

Break, v. brake, broke, pret. broken, broke, pa. to part by force, dafh to pieces, tame, become a bankrupt, ruin, fall out, violate, dawn as the day, cafhier, decline in ftrength

Break, n. an opening, breach, failure, paufe, line

Breákage, n. a breaking or allowance for things broke

Break'er, n. one that breaks, a large wave, a rock

Break'faft, v. i. to eat the morning's meal

Break'faft, n. the firft meal in the day

Bream, n. a kind of coarfe fifh

Bream, v. t. to cleanfe a fhip's bottom by fire

Breaft, n. a part of the body, confcience, the heart

Breafthigh, a. high as or reaching up to the breaft

Breaft'knot, n. a knot of ribands worn on the breaft

Breaft'plate, n. armor for the breaft (breaft

Breaft'plow, n. a fmall plough driven by the

Breaft'work, n. a parapet as high as the breaft

Breath, n. life, air refpired, a breeze, refpit, reft, eafe, fingle moment, inftant

Breathe, v. to refpire, live, take breath or reft, move as air, exhale, give vent, utter filently, make to found

Bréathing, n. a drawing breath, prayer, refpit, run

Breath'lefs, a. out of breath, hurried, dead

Brec'cia, n. a ftone confifting of fragments agglutinated together

Brede, n. a knot, complication, bredth, ob.

Breech, [brich] n. the hind part, back of a gun

Breech, v. to put into breeches, to fit with a

Breech'es, n. pl. a garment for men (breech

Breed, v. bred, pret. bred, p. t. to hatch, contrive, raife, bring up, feed, multiply (her

Breed, n. a caft, kind, fort, race, offspring, number

Breéder, n. one that breeds, raifes or brings up

Breéding, n. education, manners; pa. with young

Breeze, n. a gentle wind, a ftinging fly

Breézelefs, a. having no breezes, quite calm

Breézy, a. fanned or fanning with gales, cooling

Bréhon, n. an Irifh judge or lawyer

Breth'ren, n. pl. of brother

Breve, n. a note in mufic, kind of writ, fummons

Brevet', n. a commiffion giving rank without pay or without command, a warrant

Bréviary, n. a Romifh prieft's office-book

Bréviat, n. a compendium, fhort copy, extract

Breviér, n. a fmall fort of printing letter

Brev'ity, n. fhortnefs, concifenefs, difpatch

Brew, v. to make liquors, plot, contrive, hatch

Brew'er, n. one who brews, one who contrives

Brew'ery, n. a houfe and apparatus for brewing

Brew'houfe, n. a houfe or place for brewing in

Brew'ing, n. the act of making malt liquors, the liquor brewed, a plotting

Briárean, a. like Briáreus the giant, huge

Bribe, n. a gift to pervert the judgment, &c.

Bribe, v. t. to gain or corrupt by gifts, to hire

Bríber, n. one that gives bribes, hires or corrupts

Bríbery, n. the act or crime of bribing, hire

Brick, n. clay with fand and water, fhaped in a mold, a loaf like a brick

Brick, v. t. to lay, form, or wall up, with bricks

Brick, a. made or built of brick

Brick'bat, n. a broken piece or part of a brick

Brick'duft, n. duft made by pounding, &c. bricks

Brick'kiln, n. imitation of a brick wall on plafter

Brick'kiln, n. a kiln ufed for burning bricks in

Brick'layer, n. a mafon, a worker in bricks

Brick'maker, n. one who makes or deals in bricks

Brick'y, a. like a brick

Brídal, n. a marriage-feaft; a. belonging to marriage

Bride, n. a new-married woman, a book (riage

Brídebed, n. a marriage-bed,

Brídecake, n. cake given to guefts at a wedding

Brídegroom, n. the name of a new-married man

Brídemaid, n. a woman who attends a bride at marriage

Brídewell, n. a houfe of correction, a petty prifon

Bridge, n. a building to pafs over water on, paffage, part of the nofe or of a violin

Bridge, v. t. to form a bridge over [horfe, a check

Brídle, n. an inftrument to guide and reftrain a

Brídle, v. to put on a bridle, reftrain, hold up

Brídlehand, n. the left or better hand, a fupport

Brief, n. fhort extract or inftructions, letters patent

Brief, a. fhort, concife, narrow, common, rife

Briefly, ad. fhortly, concifely, in few words

Brief'nefs, n. fhortnefs, concifenefs

Brier or Briar, n. a very prickly fhrub

Briery, n. full of briers, rough, prickly, fharp

Brig or Brig'antine, n. a veffel with two mafts fquare rigged

Brigáde, n. a divifion of troops under a Brigadier, confifting of feveral regiments or battalions

Brigadíer, n. an officer commanding a brigade

Brigand', n. a robber, plunderer, freebooter, thief

Brig'andine, n. anciently a coat of mail

Bright, a. fhining, clear, evident, famous, witty

Bríghten, v. to make bright, polifh, clear up, mend

Brightly, ad. in a bright manner, clearly; wittily

Brightnefs, n. lufter, fplendor, acutenefs

Bril'liancy, n. fparkling lufter, dazzling excellence

Bril'liant, a. fhining, fparkling; n. a fine diamond

Brim, n. the edge, lip, top, fide, bank

Brim, v. to fill or be full to the top

Brimful, a. full to the brim or top, overloaded

Brim'mer, n. a bumper, a bowl full to the brim

Brim'ftone, n. a kind of yellow mineral, fulphur

Brin'ded or Brin'dled, a. ftreaked, fpotted, tabby

Brine, n. water impregnated with falt, the fea

Brine'lefs, a. deftitute of falt or brine, frefh

Bring, v. t. brought, pret. brought, pa. to bear to or nearer, fetch, bear in perfon, reduce to any ftate, induce, conduct or drive, produce, as fruit

Bring'er, n. one who brings, a guide, an inftructor

Brínifh, Bríny, a. having the tafte of brine, faltifh

Brink, n. the edge, fide, verge, border

Brifk, a. quick, lively, gay, jovial, bright, ftrong

Brifk'et, n. the part of the breaft next the ribs

Brifk'ly, ad. in an active or gay manner, nimbly

Brifk'nefs, n. activenefs, quicknefs, livelinefs, life

Bris''tle, n. a part of fwine's hair, very ftrong hair

Bris''tle, v. to raife up the briftles, to grow angry

Bris''tly, a. fet thick with briftles, rough

Bris'tol-ftone, n. a kind of foft trifling diamond

Brit'ain, n. England and Scotland united

Britan'nic, a. pertaining to Britain, but prefixed only or chiefly to the word Majefty

Brit'ifh, a. belonging to or made in Britain

Bri'ton, n. a native or fubject of Britain

Brit'tle, a. apt to break, fhort, weak, frail, tender

Brit'tlenefs, n. an aptnefs to break, tendernefs

Broach, n. a fpit, excrefcence, kind of inftrument

Broach, v. t. to tap, fpit, give out, utter

Broacher, n. an opener or teller of a thing, a fpit

Broad, [brawd] a. wide extended, open, plain, coarfe [bandry

Broad'caft, n. a fcattering of feed widely, in huf-

Broad'cloth, n. a very fine kind of woollen cloth

Broad'en, v. to grow or make broad, to widen

Broad'ly, ad. in a broad manner, plainly, grofsly

Broad'nefs, n. width, coarfenefs of meaning

Broad'fhouldered, a. broad over the fhoulders

Broad'fide, n. a fide of a fhip, volley, large fheet

Broad'fword, n. a fharp fword with a broad blade

Brocáde or Brocádo, n. a kind of fine flowered filk

Brocáded, q. woven as, or dreffed in brocade

Brócage, n. the trade or dealing in old things

Broc'coli, n. a fpecies of cabbage with colored leaves

Brock, n. the name of an animal, a badger

Brock or Brock'et, n. a red deer two years old

Brogue, n. a kind of fhoe, a corrupt or bad fpeech

Broid'er, v. t. to adorn with curious needlework

Broid'ery, n. embroidery, variegated needlework

Broil, n. a tumult, quarrel, difturbance, trouble

Broil, v. to drefs over coals, be very hot, fweat

Brókage, n. the trade of, or allowance to a broker

Broke or Bróken, pa. paff. of to break

Brokenheart'ed, a. very uneafy, quite caft down

Brókenmeat, n. pieces of meat cut and left

Bróker, n. one who does bufinefs for other perfons

Brókerage, n. an allowance to a broker, brokage

Bronch'ial, [ch as k] a. belonging to the throat

Bronch'ocele, n. a tumor on the throat, the goiter

Bronchot'omy, n. an incifion of the windpipe

Bronze, n. a compound of copper and tin, and fometimes zink, a figure of bronze

Bronze, a. made of bronze, or having its color

Bronze, v. t. to imitate or overlay with bronze

Brooch, n. a jewel; v. t. to adorn with jewels

Brood, n. an offspring, production, hatch, breed

Brood, v. to fit upon eggs, fit over, hatch, mufe

Brook, n. a little river, rivulet, trifling current

Brook, v. to endure, bear, be contented to fuffer

Broom, n. a kind of fhrub, a befom to fweep with

Broom'ftick, n. the handle or ftick of a broom

Broom'y, a. full of or having broom, like broom

Broth, n. the liquor in which flefh, &c. is boiled

Broth'el, n. a houfe of ill fame, ftew

Broth'er, n. a male born of the fame parents, or of one of them, an affociate, one of the fame race

Broth'erhood, n. union, a fociety, clafs, order

Broth'erly, a. like brother, loving, fond, kind

Broth'erly, ad. in a very loving friendly manner

Brought, pret. and pa. paff. of to bring

Brow, n. the forehead, the edge or fide

Brow'beat, v. t. browbeat, pret. browbeat, browbeaten, pa. to bear down, humble, deprefs

Brown, n. the name of a reddifh color; a. reddifh

Brown'ifh, a. inclined to a brown color, reddifh

Brown'nefs, n. a brown color or ftate, reddifhnefs

Brown'ift, n. a follower of Brown, a rigid puritan

Brown'ftout, n. a fpecies of ftrong porter

Brownftud'y, n. very deep meditation or thought

Browse, n. the young fprouts of trees, underwood

Browfe, v. to feed upon or eat browfe, to feed

Bruife, v. t. to hurt with blows, hurt, beat, crufh

Bruife, n. a hurt in the flefh, wound, mark, fpot

Brúifing, n. the act or art of boxing, a crufhing

Bruit, n. a report, a noife; v. t. to noife abroad, ob.

Brúmal, a. of or belonging to winter, cold

Brunette', n. a woman of a brown complexion

Brunónian, a. pertaining to Brown and his Elements of Medicin

Brunónian, n. a believer in Brown's Syftem

Brunt, n. a fhock, ftroke, attack, onfet, violence

Brufh, n. a hairy inftrument, brifk attack, tail, fhrubs, lopped branches of trees

Brufh, v. to rub with a brufh, ftrike flightly, fkim

Brufh'ed, pa. cleaned with a brufh, repaired

E

Bruth'wood, *n.* low or fmall wood, underwood
Bruth'y, *a.* like a brufh, rough, fhaggy, very thick
Brus"tle, *v.* to crackle, ruftle, hector, bully, boaft
Brutal, *a.* favage, cruel, inhuman, vile, fenfelefs
Brutal'ity, *n.* favagenefs, inhumanity, beaftlinefs
Brutalize, *v.* to grow or make brutal or cruel
Brutally, *ad.* cruelly, inhumanly, favagely, rudely
Brute, *n.* a creature without reafon, a rude perfon
Brute, *a.* fenfelefs, favage, wild, rude, rough
Brutify, *v. t,* to make brutifh
Brutifh, *a.* refembling a beaft, rude, ignorant
Brutifhly, *ad.* in a brutifh manner, rudely, favagely
Brutifhnefs, *n.* brutality, beaftlinefs, rudenefs
Bry'ony, *n.* a genus of plants, with acid juice
Bub, *n.* ftrong beer, ftrong malt-liquor
Bub'ble, *n.* a bladder, or veffel of fluid filled with air, any thing wanting folidity, empty project, one cheated   [gurgling noife
Bub'ble, *v.* to rife in bubbles, cheat, run with a
Bub'bler, *n.* a cheat, knave
Bubo, *n.* a fwelling tumor, fore, owl
Bubonocéle, *n.* an inguinal rupture
Bubul'ca, *n.* a flat circular fifh of a filvery color
Bubulus, *n.* an animal like a cow and goat
Bucaó, *n.* a fcreech owl of beautiful plumage
Buceph'alus, *n.* a quadruped of the gazell tribe
Buccaneer, *n.* a pirate, a free-booter
Buccinator, *n.* a mufcle which contracts the mouth as in blowing   [deer, &c.
Buck, *n.* water to wafh clothes, the male of rabbits,
Buck, *v.* to wafh or fteep clothes in lye
Buckeé, *n.* a plant, a fpecies of diofma
Buck'et, *n.* a veffel to draw or carry water in
Buc"kle, *n.* a faftening, ornament, curl of hair
Buc"kle, *v.* to faften with a buckle, curl, bend, bow, condefcend, apply, prepare for, engage
Buck'ler, *n. a* fhield; *v. t.* to defend, to fupport
Buck'ram, *n.* a coarfe cloth ftiffened with glue
Buck'fkin, *n.* the fkin or leather of a buck
Buck'thorn, *n.* a kind of thorn, a prickly bufh
Buck'wheat, *n.* a plant and its berry, ufed for food
Bucol'ic, *a.* relating to fhepherds, paftoral
Bucol'ics, *n. pl.* paftoral fongs or poems, paftorals
Bud, *n.* the firft fhoot of a tree, &c. a rife
Bud, *v.* to put forth buds, fhoot, inoculate, graft
Bud'lefs, *a.* without buds
Bud'let, *n.* a fmall bud
Budge, *v. i.* to ftir, go, move, move off the place
Budge, *n.* the fkin of lambs dreffed, a mean thief
Budge, *a.* ftiff, formal, four, brifk, *ob.*
Budg'et, *n.* a bag, pouch, ftock, ftore, propofal
Buff, *n.* a fort of lether dreffed with oil
Buff'colored, *a.* of the color of buff, yellow
Buff, Buff'et, *v. t.* to box, beat, ftrike, exercife
Buffalo, *n.* an animal, a kind of wild ox or bull
Buff'colored, *a.* of the color of buff, yellow
Buff'et, *n.* a blow with the fift, box on the ear, ftroke, kind of cupboard for plate or china
Buffle, *v. t.* to puzzle, confound, perplex, *ob.*

Buf'fleheaded, *a.* having a very large head, ftupid
Buffoon', *n.* an arch fellow, droll, merry-andrew
Buffoon'ery, *n.* very low jefts, mimicry, drollery
Bug, *n.* a genus of infects of more than a hundred fpecies
Bug'bear, *n.* a frightful object, falfe dread, terror
Bugeé, *n.* a fpecies of monkey in India
Bug'gery, *n.* beftiality, unnatural union
Bug'gy, *a.* full of or having bugs
Bugle, *n.* a fmall piece of glafs, bead, plant, bull
Buglehorn, *n.* a kind of huntinghorn
Buglofs', *n.* the name of feveral kinds of plants
Build, *v.* built, *pret.* builded, built, *pa.* to raife a building, depend, reft, place, conftruct
Build'er, *n.* one who builds houfes, &c. a former
Build'ing, *n.* a houfe, &c. built or raifed
Built, *n.* peculiar form of ftructure
Built, *pret.* and *pa.* of *to build*   [round beard
Bulb, *n.* a round root, as of tulips, onions, &c. a
Bulbiferous, *a.* producing bulbs
Bulb'ous, *a.* having round roots or heads, large
Bulgarian, *n.* a native of Bulgaria in Turkey
Bulgarian, *a.* pertaining to Bulgaria
Bulge, *v.* to fwell in the middle, to bilge
Bulimy, *n.* a difeafe, a moft ravenous apetite
Bulk, *n.* fize, quantity, a chief part, ftall, cargo
Bulkhead', *n.* a part of a fhip, a partition of boards
Bulk'inefs, *n.* largenefs of fize, heavinefs, weight
Bulk'y, *a.* lufty, big, large, grofs, heavy [blunder
Bull, *n.* the male of the bovine genus, pope's edict, a
Bull'ace, Bull'is, *n.* a kind of wild plum
Bull'late, *a.* bladdery, full of blifters
Bull'baiting, *n.* a fight of large dogs with a bull
Bull'dog, *n.* a large dog remarkable for courage
Bull'etin, *n.* a record, certificate, official notice
Bull'et, *n.* a ball of lead or iron ufed for fhooting
Bull'eyed, *a.* having very large eyes
Bull'finch, *n.* the name of a fmall finging bird
Bull'frog, *n.* a very large fpecies of frog
Bull'head, *n.* a ftupid heavy perfon, a kind of fifh
Bull'ion, *n.* gold and filver in the lump or mafs, a
Bulli"tion, *n.* the act or ftate of boiling [plate
Bull'ock, *n.* an ox, a young bull
Bull'y, *n.* a noify quarrelfome fellow, a hector
Bull'y, *v.* to overbear, hector, daunt, be very noify
Bul'rufh, *n.* a large rufh growing near rivers
Bul'wark, *n.* a fortification, fort, fecurity, defenfe
Bul'wark, *v. t.* to fortify, fecure, *ob.*
Bumbailiff, *n.* an under bailiff
Bump, *n.* a fwelling, blow, ftroke
Bump, *v.* to make a loud noife, beat, thump, fwell
Bump'er, *n.* a glafs filled with liquor to the brim
Bump'kin, *n.* a very aukward perfon, clown, lout
Bump'kinly, *ad.* in a clownifh aukward manner
Bun, *n.* a fmall kind of cake or fweet bread
Bunch, *n.* a clufter, knot, hard lump, fwelling
Bunch, *v.* to grow in knobs, clufter, fwell out
Bunch'y, *a.* growing in or full of bunches, large
Bun'dle, *n.* a parcel of things bound up together

Bun'dle, *v. t.* to tie, put or throw up in a bundle
Bung, *n.* a stopper for the mouth of a barrel
Bung, *v. t.* to stop close, close or fasten up, secure
Bun"gle, *v.* to do clumsily or badly, to botch
Bun"gle, *n.* a botch, bad work, clumsiness
Bun"gler, *n.* a bad, clumsy or aukward workman
Bun"glingly, *ad.* clumsily, roughly, aukwardly
Bun'fing, *n.* a quadruped of the Cape of Good Hope
Bunt'ing, *n.* thin linen cloth, a lark
Buoy, *n.* a floating cask or light piece of wood fastened over an anchor or shoal water for a direction, or to bear a cable
Buoy, *v.* to keep afloat, float, support, uphold
Buoy'ancy, *n.* the quality of floating, lightness
Buoy'ant, *a.* that will not sink, floating, light [ring
Bur, *n.* the prickly head of a plant, as of burdoc, a
Bur'bot, *n.* a voracious fish like an eel
Bur'den, *v. t.* to load, encumber, lay upon, oppress
Bur'den, *n.* a load, weight, birth, capacity of a ship
Bur'dener, *n.* one who lays on burdens or oppresses
Bur'denous, *a.* grievous, oppressive, hard, *ob.*
Bur'densome, *a.* grievous, troublesome, heavy
Bur'densomeness, *n.* oppressiveness
Bur'doc, *n.* a genus of plants
Bureau, [búro] *n.* a kind of small chest of drawers
Bur'gage, *n.* a tenure proper to cities and towns
Bur'gamot, *n.* a kind of pear
Bur'ganet, *n.* a kind of old helmet or head-piece
Burgaû, *n.* a species of sea snail
Burgee, *n.* a flag like a broad pennant
Burgeois' [burjois'] *n.* a kind of printing letter
Burg'ermaster, *n.* a voracious waterfowl
Bur'gess, *n.* a citizen, freeman, representative
Burgh, *n.* a borough-town, a corporation[freeman
Bur'gher, *n.* an inhabitant of a borough or city, a
Bur'glar, Burglárian, *n.* one guilty of burglary
Burglárious, *a.* of or relating to housebreaking
Burglárioufly, *ad.* in a burglarious manner
Bur'glary, *n.* the crime of housebreaking by night, with intent to commit felony
Bur'gomafter, *n.* a principal citizen in Holland
Bur'grave, *n.* a German count, a chief governor
Bur'gundy, *n.* a wine produced in Burgundy
Bur'ial, [ber'rial] *n.* a funeral, the act of burying
Búrine, *n.* a kind of graving-tool, a graver
Burlefque', *v. t.* to ridicule, rally, lampoon, traduce
Burlefque', *n.* that fpecies of language which excites laughter or ridicule by ludicrous images
Burlefque', *a.* merry, jocular, ridiculing, droll
Burlet'ta, *n.* a musical entertainment, farce, play
Bur'ly, *a.* large, great, big, bulky, *ob.*
Burn, *v.* burned, burnt, *pret.* burned, burnt, *pa.* to consume by fire, to be hot or in a passion, to scorch, be inflamed, or on fire, to rage
Burn, *n.* a hurt or wound caused by fire
Burn'cow, *n.* a genus of insects pernicious to cattle
Burn'er, *n.* one who burns, one who fets on fire
Burn'et, *n.* the name of a plant or coarse grass
Burn'ing, *n.* a consuming by fire, fire, heat

Burn'ingglafs, *n.* a glass that collects the fun's rays
Burn'ifh, *v.* to polish, brighten, grow bright
Burn'ifher, *n.* a person or tool that burnishes
Burr, *n.* the lobe or lap of the ear, a knob, a plant
Bur'rel, *n.* a kind of pear, infect, stinging fly
Bur'relfhot, *n.* nails, stones, &c. shot from cannon
Bur'row, *v. i.* to make holes or lodge in the earth
Bur'row, *n.* a rabbit-hole, corporate town in Eng.
Burs'al, *a.* pertaining to a purse or sack
Burs'ar, *n.* the treasurer of a college, &c. a butler
Burfe, *n.* an exchange for merchants, a shop, *ob.*
Burft, *v.* burft, *pret.* burft, burften, *pa.* to break asunder, fly open or out, spring, issue suddenly
Burft, *n.* a sudden breaking or rent, an eruption
Burft, Burft'en, *pa.* broken, having a rupture
Bur'then, *see* Burden   bury, &c.
Bur'y, [berry] *n.* a dwelling-place; as Alderman-
Bur'y, *v. t.* to inter, as in a grave, to hide or lose in surrounding matter, to retire to solitude
Bufh, *n.* a thick shrub, bough, tail of a fox, a cylender in a block
Bufh, *v.* to grow bufhy, furnifh with a bufh
Bufh'el, *n.* a dry meafure of four pecks, a ftrike
Bufh'iness, *n.* fulness, thickness, largeness
Bufh'ment, *n.* a clufter or heap of bufhes, *ob.*
Bufh'y, *a.* full of bufhes, thick, large full
Bus'ily [bizzily] *ad.* with conftant attention
Bus'iness, *n.* an employment, trade, affair (ftays
Bufk, *n.* whalebone or fteel to keep down women's
Bufk'in, *n.* a fhort or half boot worn on the ftage
Bufk'ined, *a.* dressed in or wearing bufkins
Bufs, *n.* a kifs, veffel, fifhing-boat; *v. t.* to kifs
Buft, *n.* a half ftatue, pile, ancient funeral pile
Buft'ard, *n.* a bird, a kind of wild turky
Bus"tle, [bufsle] *v. i.* to be bufy, hurry, ftir
Bus"tle, *n.* a tumult, hurry, confufion, ftir
Bus"tler, *n.* an active ftirring person, a bufy body
Buft'o, *n.* a buft, a half ftatue or figure
Bus'y, [bizzy] *v. t.* to make bufy, to employ
Bus'y, *a.* conftantly occupied, meddling, active
Bus'yboddy, *n.* a meddling or officious person
But *an old verb or pr.* except, be out, without, take away, only
But, *conj.* more, further, noting addition
But, *n.* a boundary, bound, limit, end, *ob.*
Butch'er, *n.* a person who kills animals to fell
Butch'er, *v. t.* to kill, to flay inhumanly
Butch'erbird, *n.* the fhrike, a bird of prey
Butch'erly, *a.* cruel, barbarous, bloody, inhuman
Butch'ery, *n.* murder cruelty, a place of killing
But'end, *n.* the larger or thicker end of a thing
But'ler, *n.* one who has the care of liquors & plate
But'lerage, *n.* money paid or given to a butler, a
But'ment, *n.* the support of an arch   (duty
Butt, *n.* a mark, object of ridicule, cafk, blow or ftroke, end of a fhip's plank, a hinge
Butt, *v. t.* to ftrike with the head like a ram, &c.
But'ter, *n.* a food or fubftance made from cream
But'ter, *v. t.* to cover or moiften with butter

But'terflower, n. a bright yellow flower of May

But'terfly, n. a genus of insects of a variety of species with four wings, a spiral tongue and hairy body, a gay fellow

But'teris, n. a farrier's or smith's tool to pare with

But'termilk, n. the whey of churned cream

But'ternut, n. an American tree with an oblong nut, alfo the nut (with

But'terprint, n. a piece of wood to mark butter

But'tertooth, n. one of the great broad fore teeth

But'tery, n. the place where provifions are kept

But'tery, a. fmeared with or like butter, oily

But'tock, n. the thick part of the thigh, the rump

But'ton, n. a part of apparel, knob, bud, urchin

But'ton, v. t. to faften with or by buttons, to drefs

But'tenhole, n. a hole made to faften a button by

But'trefs, n. a prop, fhore, fupport; v. t. to prop

But'treffed, pa. propt or held up by a buttrefs

Butyra'ceous, But'yrous, a. having the qualities of butter

Bux'om, a. lively, brifk, gay, wanton, obedient

Bux'omly, ad. brifkly, airily, wantonly, loofely

Bux'omnefs, n. airinefs, wantonnefs, amoroufnefs

Buy, v. bought, pret. bought, pa. to obtain by a price, purchafe, bribe, to redeem

Buyer, n. one who buys, one who purchafes

Buzz, n. a humming, low talk or noife, whifper

Buzz, v. to make a noife like bees, hum, whifper

Buzz'ard, n. a fpecies of hawk, a blockhead

Buzz'er, n. a whifperer, telltale, blabber, babbler

Buzz'ing, n. a humming noife, whifper, low talk

By, pr. denoting the agent, caufe, way or means

By-and-by, ad. in a fhort time, fhortly

By'-bag, n. a bag for letters betwixt country places

By'-end, n. private advantage, intereft (a dwelling

Bye, n. not the direct object of regard; by the bye;

By'-law, n. a private rule made for or by a fociety

By'-path, By'-walk, n. a private path or road

By-refpect, n. a private end, a private view or aim

By'-room, n. a private or retired room

By'ftander, n. a looker on, a perfon unconcerned

By'-ftreet, By-way, n. a private ftreet, a back way

By'-word, n. a cant word, tauat, fcoff, jeft, proverb

C

CAB, n. Jewifh meafure of about three pints

Cabal', n. a private junto of men, an intrigue

Cabal', v. to intrigue privately, plot, unite, join

Cabal', Cab'ala, n. the Jewifh traditions

Cab'alift, n. one fkilled in Jewifh traditions, a fac-

Cabalift'ic, Cabalift'ical, a. myfterious, fecret (tor

Cabal'ler, n. an intriguer, plotter, contriver

Cab'bage, n. a genus of plants of twelve fpecies

Cab'bage, v. to fteal in cutting clothes, to head

Cab'bagetree, n. a tropical tree affording a head like a cabbage, ufed as food

Cab'in, n. a part of a fhip, cottage, hut, tent, room

Cab'in, v. to live or confine in a cabin

Cab'ined, pa. belonging to, or fhut in, a cabin

Cab'inet, n. a fet of drawers, a place for counfel,

the executive counfel of a ftate

Cab'inetmaker, n. one who makes nice things in

Cable, n. a thick rope for an anchor (wood

Caboofe', n. a fhip's movable fire place for cooking

Cabure, n. a bird of Brazil of the owl kind

Cach'alot, n. the phyfeter or fperm whale

Cachec''tical, a. that has a bad habit of body

Cach'et, n. a feal, a fealed or private letter of ftate

Cachex'y, [ch as k] n. a difordered habit of body

Cach'olong, n. white calcedony

Cac''kle, n. the noife of a goofe or fowl, laughter

Cack'ler, n. a perfon who or that which cackles

Cac'ochymy, [ch as k] n. a bad ftate of blood

Cacoon', n. a climbing and fpreading plant

Cada''erous, a. relating to a dead body, death-like

Cad'dis, n. a kind of tape or ftuff, a worm or grub

Cad'dy, n. a fmall box for tea

Cade, a. tame, foft, delicate, tender; n. a cafk

Cadence, n. a fall of the voice, found, decline, ftep

Cadent, a. falling, finking, falling gently

Cadet', n. a volunteer, a younger brother

Cadme'an, a. pertaining to Cadmus, who intro-duced letters into Greece

Cadi, n. a chief magiftrate amongft the Turks

Caducous, a. falling at the firft opening of the flower, or before the end of fummer

Caf'tan, n. a kind of habit, a Perfian garment

Cag, n. a little barrel or cafk

Cage, n. a place of confinement; v. t. to confine

Ca''git, n. a beautiful green parrot

Caiffon', or Caiffoon', n. a cheft of bombs or powder

Caitiff, a. mean, bafe, forry, defpicable, knavifh

Caitiff, n. a bafe fellow, villain, knave, wretch

Caj'eput, n. an oil from the Eaft Indies

Cajole, v. t. to flatter, coax, footh, deceive, be-

Cajoler, n. a wheedler, flatterer, deceiver (guile

Cajoling, pa. coaxing, wheedling; n. flattery

Cajo'ta, n. a Mexican animal like a wolf and dog

Cake, n. a fmall loaf, a compofition of flour, butter, &c, fweetened, a concretion in flefh

Cake, v. i. to form into a lump or concretion

Cal'abafh, n. a tree, a veffel made of the fruit of the tree, or of a gourd fhell

Calamanc'o, n. a kind of woollen ftuff

Cal'amin, n. the ore or oxyd of zink

Cal'amint, n. a fpecies of baum, catmint (flictive

Calam'itous, a. unfortunate, diftreffing, very af-

Calam'ity, n. misfortune, caufe of diftrefs, mifery

Cal'amus, n. a kind of reed or fweetfcented wood

Cal'ander, n. a mifchievous infect of the beetle kind

Calan'dra, n. an American finging bird

Calafh', n. a fort of open carriage, a headdrefs

Cal'carate, a. furnifhed with or like a fpur

Calcareous, a. of the nature of lime, as chalk

Calcaval'la, n. a fweet wine from Portugal

Cal'ceated, a. fhod, furnifhed with fhoes (gray

Cal'cedony, n. a fpecies of filiceous ftone ufually

Cal'ciform, a. in the form or ftate of calx or oxyd

Calcimu'rite, n. an earth compofed of magnefia,

lime and iron

Calcinátion, *n.* the act, &c. of pulverizing by fire

Cal'cine, *v. t.* to burn to a powder or hard cinder

Cal'cinable, *a.* that may be reduced to a pulverable state by fire (juft

Cal'culate, *v. t.* to compute, reckon, caft up, ad-

Calculátion, Cal'cule, *n.* a computation, a reckon-

Cal'culator, *n.* a computer, reckoner, teller (ing

Cal'culous, *a.* ftony, gravelly, gritty, rough, hard

Cal'dron, *n.* a very large kettle, pot, boiler (land

Caledónian, *n.* a native of Scotland; *a.* of Scot-

Calefac'tion, *n.* the act of warming or heating

Calefac'tory, *a.* tending to warm, heating

Calefa'cient, *a.* warming; *n.* that which warms

Cal'efy, *v.* to grow or make hot, to be heated

Cal'endar, *n.* an almanac, a regifter of the year

Cal'ender, *v. t.* to give linen a glofs, to fmooth

Cal'ender, *n.* an engine to calender, a hot-prefs

Cal'ends, *n. pl.* the firft day of every month

Cal'enture, *n.* a fun-fever, frequent in hot climates

Calf, *pl.* calves, the young of a cow, thick part of the leg

Cal'iber, *n.* the bore of fire arms, diameter

Cal'id, *a.* hot, very hot, burning, fcorching

Calid'ity, Cal'idnefs, *n.* great or burning heat

Cal'iduct, *n.* a conductor of heat

Caligátion, *n.* darknefs, cloudinefs, dimnefs, obfcurity

Cali"ginous, *a.* dark, dufky, dim, obfcure (fcurity

Calig'raphy, *n.* fair, fine or beautiful, writing

Cal'iner, *n.* a kind of gun, handgun, mufket, fufee

Cáliph, *n.* the high or chief prieft of the Saracens

Ca'liphate, *n.* the office and dignity of a Caliph

Calk, or Caulk, *v. t.* to ftop the feams of a fhip

Calk'er, *n.* one who calks, one who ftops feams

Call, *v. t.* to name, invite, publifh, fummon, read

Call, *n.* a demand, claim, addrefs, fummons, pipe

Cal'lico, *n.* printed cotton cloth

Callid'ity, Cal'lidnefs, *n.* craftinefs, cunning, art

Call'ing, *n.* an employment, profeffion, trade, clafs

Cal'lipers, *n. pl.* compaffes having bowed fhanks

Callos'ity, or Cal'lus, *n.* a hard fwelling, hardnefs

Cal'lous, *a.* hard, thick, hardened, infenfible

Cal'loufnefs, *n.* hardnefs, thicknefs, infenfibility

Cal'low, *a.* wanting fethers, unfledged, naked

Calm, *v. t.* to pacify, appeafe, ftill, quiet, compofe

Calm, *n.* repofe, ftillnefs, quiet, reft, eafe, peace

Calm, or Calm'y, *a.* ftill, quiet, undifturbed, eafy

Calm'er, *n.* one who gives quiet or appeafes

Calm'ly, *ad.* quietly, coolly, without paffion

Calm'nefs, *n.* mildnefs, ftillnefs, quiet, reft, peace

Cal'omel, *n.* dulcified fublimate of mercury

Calor'ic, *n.* the matter or fimple element of heat

Calor'ic, *a.* pertaining to the matter of heat

Calorif'ic, *a.* heating, caufing or producing heat

Calorim'eter, *n.* an apparatus to meafure relative quantities of heat, or the fpecific caloric of bodies (ity

Calótte, *n.* a cap worn by cardinals, a round cav-

Cal'trop, *n.* an inftrument of three fpikes, a plant

Cal'umet, *n.* the pipe of peace among the Indians

Cal'umny, *n.* flander, afperfion, a falfe charge

Calum'niate, *v. t.* to accufe falfely, flander, revile

Calumniátion, *n.* a falfe reprefentation, flander

Calumniátor, *n.* a falfe accufer, a flanderer

Calum'nious, *a.* flanderous, reproachful, bafe, vile

Cal'vary, *n.* the place of a fkull and of execution

Calve, *v. i.* to bear or bring forth a calf

Cal'vinifm, *n.* the doctrins held by Calvin

Cal'vinift, *n.* a follower, &c. of Calvin

Calvinit'ic, Calvinift'ical, *a.* relating to Calvinifm

Calx, *pl.* Calx'es, *n.* a fubftance deprived by heat of its cementing principle, as lime from calcined ftone or fea fhells

Ca'lyx, *n.* the cover or outer leaves of a flower

Calyc'ulate, *a.* having a calyx furrounded at the bafe with a leffer one

Cal'ycin, *a.* pertaining to a calyx

Cal'ycle, *n.* a row of leaflets at the bafe of a calyx

Cam'bering, Cam'bing, *a.* rifing like an arch

Câmbric, *n.* a kind of fine linen from Flanders

Came, *pret.* of *to come*

Cam'el, *n.* a large quadruped, a machine for bearing fhips over bars

Camellep'ard, *n.* the giraff, a fpotted animal of Africa with a long neck

Caméo, *n.* a picture of only one color

Cam'era-obfcura, *n.* a philofophical apparatus and optical machine ufed to exhibit images by

Camifáde, *n.* an attack made by night in fhirts

Cam'let, or Cam'blet, *n.* a ftuff made of wool

Cam'moc, *n.* a plant, petty whin (and fills

Cam'omile, *n.* a genus of plants ufed medicinally

Camoys', *a.* flat nofed, bent upwards, *ob.*

Camp, the place where troops lodge, order of tents or huts, troops in order of encampment

Camp, *v. t.* to encamp

Campáign, *n.* a large open level country, the time that an army keeps the field in one year

Campaigner, *n.* one who has ferved feveral campaigns, an old experienced foldier, a veteran

Campan'iform, Campan'ulate, *a.* bell fhaped

Campes'tral, *a.* growing in the fields, open, wild

Cam'phire, Cam'phor, the concrete juice of a fpecies of laurel in E. Indies, a bitter aromatic and ftimulant

Cam'phorate, *a.* pertaining to camphor

Cam'phorated, *a.* impregnated with camphor

Cam'phorate, *n.* a falt formed by camphoric acid

Camphor'ic, *a.* pertaining to camphor (and a bafe

Cam'pion, *n.* a plant of feveral kinds

Can, *v. i.* could, *pret.* to be able, to have power

Can, *n.* a veffel for liquids, a kind of cup

Can'ada, *n.* a province north of the U. States

Cana'dian, *n.* a native of Canada; *a.* of Canada

Canáil, *n.* the loweft of the people, refufe flows

Canal', *n.* a bafon or courfe of water, a duct

Can'nelcoal, *n.* a fine kind of coal

Canalic'ulate, *a.* channelled, furrowed

Canáry, n. a kind of wine, a finging bird
Can'cel, v. t. to blot out, make void, deftroy
Can'cellated, a. crofsbarred, croffed by lines
Cancella'tion, n. the act of cancelling
Can'celled, pa. blotted out, erafed, made void
Caa'cer, n. a crabfifh, fign, virulent fore or ulcer
Can'cerate, v. i. to grow or become cancerous
Cancera'tion, n. the formation of a cancer
Can'cerous, a. inclining to or like a cancer
Can'dent, a. hot, burning, fiery, glowing, fhining
Can'did, a. white, fair, frank, honeft, kind
Can'didate, n. one who fues or is propofed for an
Can'didly, ad. uprightly, fairly, honeftly (office
Can'didnefs, n. uprightnefs, opennefs, fairnefs,
Can'dle, n. light made of tallow, wax, &c. (candor
Can'dlelight, n. the light that is given by a candle
Can'dlemas, n. the feaft of the purif. of B. V. M.
Can'dleftick, n. an inftrument that holds candles
Can'dor, n. opennefs, honefty, fincerity
Can'dy, v. t. to conferve with fugar, to congeal
Cane, n. a reed, a walking-ftick; v. t. to cudgel
Canebrake, n. a thicket of canes
Canef'cent, a. growing white or old, white, hoary
Canic'ular, a. of or belonging to the dogftar
Canine, a. belonging to or like a dog, fnappifh
Caning, n. a beating with a cane
Can'ifter, n. a box for holding tea, a fmall bafket
Cank'er, n. a difeafe in plants, an eating fore
Cank'er, v. to grow corrupt, ruft, corrode, pollute
Cank'erworm, n. a worm very deftructive to fruit
Can'nibal, n. a man-eater, a moft cruel wretch
Can'nibalifm, n. practice of eating human flefh
Can'non, n. a great gun, the largeft fort of types
Cannonáde, v. t. to difcharge or fire cannon at
Cannonáde, n. difcharge of or attack with cannon
Cannonball', Cannonbul'let, n. a ball for a cannon
Cannoniér, n. one who manages cannon in war
Cannonfhot', n. a cannonball or the range it makes
Cannot, of can and not   [or a hollowed tree
Canoe', or Canoo, n. a fmall boat made of bark,
Can'on, n. a rule, law, dignitary of the Church
Can'onefs, n. a woman living like a canon
Canon'ical, a. regular, fcriptural, ecclefiaftical
Canon'ically, ad. agreeable to the canons, orderly
Canon'icals, n. the drefs of the eftablifhed clergy
Canon'icate, Can'onry, Can'nonfhip, n. a benefice
   in a cathedral church, or allowance from its
   revenues
Can'onift, n. a profeffor or doctor of canon-law
Canonizátion, n. the act of making any one a faint
Can'onize, v. t. to make a faint, to examin duly
Can'opied, a. covered with or having a canopy
Can'opy, n. a cloth of ftate for the head, a tefter
Can'opy, v. t. to cover or adorn with a canopy
Canórous, a. mufical, harmonious, tuneful, loud
Cant, n. corrupt or whining talk, a turn
Cant, v. to flatter, whine, turn quick; tofs, caft
Cantáta, n. a fong, tune, air, grave piece of mufic
Can'teleup, n. a fpecies of mufkmelon

Cant'er, v. t. to go as a horfe; n. a pace, a hypocrite
Canthar'ides, n. pl. Spanifh flies ufed for blifters
Cant'icles, n. pl. the fong of Solomon, pious fongs
Cant'ing, pa. a. talking in a canting manner, de-
Can'tle, v. t. to cut into pieces, ob.   (ceitful
Can'tle, Cant'let, n. a piece, part, fragment, ob.
Cant'o, n. a part of a poem, fection, divifion, fong
Can'ton, n. the divifion of a country, a part, a clan
Can'ton, Can'tonize, v. t. to divide or part land
Can'ton, v. t. to diftribute an army in tents or huts
Can'tonment, n. a diftribution of troops in camp,
Can'tonal, a. pertaining to cantons (encampment
Can'vas, n. a coarfe ftiffcloth, a fail
Can'vafs, v. t. to examin, fift, fue for honor
Can'vafs, n. a fifting or examining
Can'vafser, n. one who folicits votes, an examiner
Cány, a. abounding with or like canes
Canzonet', n. a little fong, a fhort fong or air
Cap, n. a covering for the head, top, a thick block
Cap, v. t. to cover the top or head, puzzle
Cap-a-pié, ad. from head to foot, all over, wholly
Capabil'ity, n. a capacity, capable ftate, fitnefs
Cápable, a. fufficient, able to receive, qualified
Capácious, a. wide, large, extended, vaft
Capácioufnefs, n. largenefs, width, extent, fpace
Capa''citate, v. t. to qualify, make fit, fit, enable
Capa''city, n. ability, fenfe, ftate, fpace, contents
Capar'ifon, n. a fine or pompous drefs for a horfe
Capar'ifon, v. t. to drefs pompoufly, adorn, fet off
Cape, n. a headland, neckpiece to a coat, &c.
Cáper, n. a kind of berry, pickle, leap, fkip, frolic
Cáper, v. i. to fkip, dance, frifk, jump, leap
Cáperer, n. a fkipper, dancer, leaper
Cápias, n. a writ for appearance or of execution
Cap'ibar, n. an animal partaking of the form of a
Capilláir, n. a firrup   (hog and a rabbit
Cap'illary, a. fmall as or like a hair, minute
Cap'illary, n. a minute veffel in animals
Cap'illament, n. the filament of a flower, nerve, &c.
Capil'liform, a. in the fhape of a hair or hairs
Cap'ital, n. principal fum, ftock, large letter, up-
   per part of a pillar or column, chief city
Cap'ital, a. principal, fine, deferving death, large
Cap'itally, ad. in a capital manner, finely
Cap'itate, a. growing in a head
Capitátion, n. a numeration of heads, a poll-tax
Cap'itol, n. a fplendid caftle and temple at Rome,
   a government houfe in the U. States
Capit'ular, n. ftatute, or a member of a chapter
Capit'ulate, v. i. to yield up on capitulation
Capitulátion, n. a furrender on terms, conditions
Cápon, n. a gelded cock, eunuch, mean wretch
Capot', v. t. to win all the tricks at piquet; n. a
Capóuch, n. a monk's or friar's hood   (flant
Cappadócian, n. a native of Cappadocia in Afia
Cap'reolate, a. having tendrils as vines
Cap'rice, n. a whim, fancy, freak, humor
Capri''cious, a. whimfical, fanciful, humorous
Capri''cioufly, ad. whimfically, fancifully

Capri″cioufaefs, n. whimficalnefs, oddnefs, fancy
Cap'ricorn, n. a fign of the zodiac, the goat, a fly
Caprificátion, n. the practice of ripening figs by expofing them to be pricked by infects
Cap'riped, a. having feet like thofe of a goat
Capsize, v. t. to upfet, overturn [fea phrafe]
Cap'ftan, n. an engine to draw up great weights
Cap'fule, n. a feed veffel of plants, a hollow pericarp with cells for feeds
Cap'fular or Cap'fulary, a. hollow like a cheft
Cap'fulate, a. inclofed in a capfule, inclofed
Cap'tain, n. the commander of a fhip or troop
Cap'taincy, n. the rank or commiffion of a captain
Cap'tainfhip, n. the rank or poft of a captain
Captátion, n. the practice or art of catching favor
Cap'tion, n. a taking, figning of a commiffion, preamble
Cap'tious, a. apt to find fault, peevifh, enfnaring
Cap'tioufly, ad. in a fnarling manner, crofsly
Cap'tioufnefs, n. peevifhnefs, ill-nature, crofsnefs
Cap'tivate, v. t. to fubdue by charms, take captive
Cap'tive, n. one taken in war, a prifoner, a flave
Cap'tive, a. made prifoner, enflaved, fubject
Captiv'ity, n. bondage, flavery, fubjection, thrall
Cap'tor, n. a perfon who takes prizes or prifoners
Cap'ture, n. the act of taking any thing, a prize
Cap'ture, v. t. to take as a prize in war
Capuchin', n. a friar, kind of woman's cloak, cowl
Cap'ucin, n. the fagoo, a fpecies of monkey
Cap'ulin, n. the Mexican cherry
Cap'ward, n. an amphibious animal of Brazil
Cáracal', n. an E. Indian quadruped of the feline
Car, n. a cart, a chariot, a conftellation [kind
Car'ac, n. a Spanifh galleon, a large fhip of burden
Car'at, n. a weight of four grains, the 24th part of gold or filver coin [or pilgrims
Car'avan, n. a large carriage, a body of merchants
Caravan'fary, n. an inn for travellers in the Eaft
Car'avel or Car'vel, n. a fmall veffel ufed in the herring fifhery
Car'away, n. a plant with pungent aromatic feed
Carbiniér or Carabiniér, n. a fhort gun
Carbiniér or Carabiniér, n. a light horfeman
Carbonáde, v. t. to fcore and broil, ob.
Car'bon, n. a pure charcoal
Car'bonate, n. a falt formed by carbonic acid and
Car'bonated, a. combined with carbon [a bafe
Carbon'ic, Carbonáceous, a. pertaining to carbon
Carbon'ic acid, a faturated combination of carbon and oxygene [gene
Car'bonous acid, carbon not faturated with oxy-
Car'buret, n. a combination of carbon with a metal, earth or alkali [drogene
Carbonohy'drous, a. compofed of carbon and hy-
Car'buncle, n. a precious ftone, red fpot, pimple
Car'buncled, a. fet with carbuncles, fpotted, red
Carbun'cular, a. like a carbuncle [animal
Car'cajo, n. the glutton, a voracious, carnivorous
Car'cafs, n. a dead body, body, fhell

Card, n. a complimentary, &c. note, inftrument, painted paper, part of a compafs, chart, map
Card, v. to comb or work wool
Card'er, n. one who cards, one who plays at cards
Card'iac, a. cordial, ftrengthening, cheering
Card'inal, a. principal, chief, leading, eminent
Card'inal, n. a dignitary of the Romifh church, American bird, a kind of woman's cloak
Card'inal-points, n. the eaft, weft, north and fouth
Card'inal-vir'tues, n. the four virtues, prudence, temperance, juftice and fortitude
Cardoon', n. a plant refembling the artichoke
Care, n. uneafinefs, charge, regard, caution, atten-
Care, v. i. to be folicitous, regard, heed, mind [tion
Caréen, v. to heave a fhip on one fide for calking, &c. to incline to one fide
Caréer, n. a courfe, race, motion; v. t. to run faft
Cáreful, a. full of cares, cautious, diligent, faving
Cárefully, ad. with care, with heed, with caution
Cárefulnefs, n. great care, watchfulnefs, caution
Cárelefs, a. heedlefs, unconcerned, giddy, gay
Cárelefsly, ad. without care, heedlefsly, giddily
Cárelefsnefs, n. heedleffnefs, inattention
Carefs', v. t. to embrace with affection, fondle
Carefs', n. fond embrace, act of endearment
Carefs'ed, pa. fondled, treated with kindnefs
Cáret, n. this mark (ʌ) noting an omiffion
Car'go, n. a fhip's lading, freight, load
Caribó, n. a quadruped of the ftag kind
Car'icature, n. a figure or defcription in which beauties are concealed, and blemifhes exaggerated
Car'icature, v. t. to exhibit worfe than the life
Car'icous, a. relating to or like figs, fwelled up
Cáries, Carios'ity, n. rottennefs of the bones
Car'inate, a. like a fhip's keel
Cárious, a. rotten, fpungy, putrefied, decayed
Cark, v. t. to be careful, n. great care, ob.
Cark'ing, pa. diftreffing, perplexing, preying, ob.
Carl or Carle, n. a mean rude man, clown, ob.
Car'man, n. one who drives a cart
Car'melite, n. a kind of begging friar, a pear
Carmin', n. a powder of a beautiful crimfon color
Carmin'ative, n. a medicin that expels wind
Carmin'ative, a. expelling wind
Carn'age, n. flaughter, havoc, devaftation, flefh
Carn'al, a. flefhly, luftful, fenfual, lewd, loofe
Carnal'ity, n. flefhly luft, fenfuality, lewdnefs
Carn'ally, ad. according to the flefh, lewdly
Carnátion, n. flefh-color, a kind of fine flower
Carnélian, n. a filicious ftone, red, yellow, or white
Carn'eous or Carn'ous, a. flefhy, plump, fat, large
Car'nival, n. fhrovetide, a time of mirth, a feaft
Carniv'orous, a. eating or feeding upon flefh
Carnos'ity, n. a flefhly excrefcence, flefhinefs
Car'ol, n. a fong of joy, devotion or praife
Car'ol, v. to fing, warble, praife, extol, magnify
Caroli'na, n. the name of two American States
Carolin'ian, n. a native of Carolina

Carolin'ian, a. pertaining to Carolina [to the head

Carot'id, a. noting the arteries which convey blood

Carous'al, n. a festival, feast, hard drinking-bout

Carouse', v. to drink hard or freely, to quaff

Carouse', n. a hard drinking-match, much liquor

Carous'er, n. a toper, hard drinker, drunkard

Carp, v. to censure peevishly, n. a fish

Carp'ed, pa. censured, blamed, found fault with

Carp'enter, n. a worker in wood, a builder [gary

Carpathian, mountains between Poland and Hungary

Carp'er, n. a caviller

Carp'et, n. a covering for a floor or table

Carp'et, v. t. to cover or spread with carpets

Carp'ing, pa. censuring, censorious, captious

Carrabô, n. an animal of the deer kind in S. Am.

Car'riage, n. what is carried, a vehicle, expense of thing carried, conveyance, conduct, behavior

Car'rier, n. one who carries, a porter, messenger

Car'rion, n. bad meat, a worthless woman

Carronáde, n. a short piece of ordnance

Car'rot, n. the name of a garden root

Car'roty, a. like a carrot, redhaired, red

Car'ry, v. to bear, convey, behave, manage, imply

Cart, n. a carriage of two wheels used for burden

Cart, v. t. to carry or expose in a cart, to convey

Carte-Blânche, n. a blank paper to be filled up

Cartel', n. an agreement made between enemies

Cart'er, n. a person who drives a cart

Cartésian, n. a follower of Des Cartes, who taught the doctrin of vortexes round the sun and planets

Cartésian, a. pertaining to Des Cartes

Carthagin'ian, n. a native of ancient Carthage

Carthagin'ian, a. pertaining to Carthage

Carthúsians, n. an order of austere monks

Cart'horse, n. a horse used to draw in a cart

Cart'ilage, n. a kind of tough substance, a gristle

Cartila"ginous, a. having or like gristles, gristly

Cart'load, n. the quantity that will load a cart

Carton' or Cartoon', n. a painting on large paper

Cartouch', n. a case for balls, a kind of ornament

Cart'ridge, n. a paper-case for gunpowder or ball

Cart'ridgebox, n. a box to contain cartridges

Cart'rut, n. a cut or mark made by a cartwheel

Cart'way, n. a road that a waggon or cart may pass

Cart'wright n. a maker or seller of carts

Carve, v. t. to cut wood, stone or meat, to choose

Carv'er, n. one who carves, one who chooses

Carv'ing, n. a cutting, sculpture, figure carved

Car'uncle, n. a fleshy excrescence or tumor

Carun'culate, Carun'culated, a. having a fleshy substance like a cock's comb

Cafcáde, n. a waterfall, a jet or steep fall of water

Cafcáde, v. t. to throw or cast up or out

Cafe, n. a covering, sheath, outer part of a thing, box, state, condition, variation of nouns

Cafe, v. t. to cover with or put in a case

Cafehar'den, v. t. to make hard the outside

Cáfeknife, n. a kitchen or table knife

Cáfemate, n. an arch in the flank of a bastion

Cáfement, n. a part of a window having hinges

Cáfeshot, n. balls inclosed in a case

Ca'feous, a. pertaining to cheese

Cas'ern, n. a lodge for soldiers near ramparts

Cáfeworm, n. a worm that makes itself a case

Cash, n. any money, but properly ready money

Cash'book, n. a book to keep an account of cash in

Cashiér, n. a cashkeeper; v. t. to dismiss, to discard

Cash'keeper, n. a person entrusted with cash

Cashoô, n. the juice or gum of an East-Indian tree

Cask, n. a barrel or wooden vessel used for liquor

Cask, Cafque, n. a helmet, a headpiece [put up

Cask'et, n. a small box, a chest for jewels; v. t. to

Cas'pian, a. denoting a sea of that name in Asia

Cas'fada, n. a genus of plants, some of whose roots yield a bread, and one, the India rubber

Cafs, Cafs'ate, v. t. to make void, annul, abolish

Caffátion, n. a repealing, making void

Cas'fia, n. a genus of plants of thirty species

Cas'fidony, n. French lavender

Cafs'oc, n. the long under-garment of a clergyman

Cas'fowary, n. a large fowl with small useless wings

Cast, n. a throw, motion, squint, turn, form, shade

Cast, v. cast, pret. cast, pa. to throw, fling, shed, contrive, form, grow crooked, overcome

Cast'anet, n. small shells of ivory or hard wood

Cast'away, n. an abandoned person; a. useless, reprobate

Cast'ellany, n. the lordship, &c. of a castle [fuse

Cast'ellet, n. a small castle or weak fortress

Cast'er, n. a thrower or calculator, a walled town

Cast'igate, v. t. to chastise, punish, correct, beat

Castigátion, n. punishment, correction, reproof

Castil'ian, n. a native of Castile in Spain

Castil'ian, a. pertaining to Castile

Cast'ing, n. a vessel or other thing cast

Cast'ingnet, n. a net thrown by the hand

Cast'ingvote, n. the vote that decides when the others are equally divided [chefs

Cas"tle, n. a house of defence, &c. project, term at

Cas"tled, a. furnished with castles, well defended

Cas'tor, n. the name of a star, an animal, a beaver

Caftrametátion, n. the laying out of a camp

Caftren'fian, a. pertaining to a camp

Cas'trate, v. t. to geld, make imperfect, lop away

Caftrátion, Cas'trature, n. a gelding, a curtailing

Gas'ual, a. accidental, not certain, uncertain

Cas'ually, ad. accidentally, by chance, oddly

Cas'ualty, n. an accident, chance, fortune

Cas'uift, n. a nice resolver of cases of conscience

Cafuift'ical, a. relating to cases of conscience

Cas'uiftry, n. the science or skill of a casuist

Cat, n. a domestic animal, kind of ship, whip, fish

Cat'achresis, [ch ask] n. the abuse of a trope

Catachres'tical, a. forced, farfetched, abused

Cat'acombs, n. pl. burial-places, vaults, caverns

Catacous'tic, a. of or relating to reflected sounds

Cat'alepsy, n. a sudden loss of sensation & motion

Catalep'tic, a. relating to catalepsy

Cat'alogue, n. a list or register of names or things

Cat'alogue, v. t. to put into a catalogue

Catal'pa, n. a beautiful tree in the S. States

Cat'amite, n. a boy that is kept for vile purpofes

Cat'amount, n. a quadruped of the panther kind

Cat'aphract, n. a horfeman in complete armor

Cat'aplafm, n. a kind of poultice, a foft plafter

Catapult', n. an engine to throw ftones, darts, &c.

Cat'aract, n. a water fall, a diforder in the eyes

Catarrh', n. a difeafe of the head, &c. a defluxion

Catarrh'al, Catarrh'ous, a. relating to a catarrh

Catas'trophy, n. a final event, a difafter (plays

Cat'cal, n. a fqueaking inftrument to condemn

Catch, v. catched, caught, pret. catched, caught
pa. to ftop, feize, enfnare, charm, kindle

Catch, n. the act or pofture of feizing, what catches, a prize, kind of fong, fmall fhip, taint

Catch'er, n. one who or that which catches

Catch'ing, pa. feizing, apt to catch, infectious

Catch'poll, n. a fergeant, bumbailiff, low bailiff

Catch'word, n. the laft word occurring in a page

Catechet'ical, [ch as k] a. in queftions and anfwers

Catechet'ically, ad. with queftions and anfwers

Cat'echife, v. t. to inftruct by or afk queftions

Cat'echifer, n. one who catechifes or inftructs

Cat'echifm, n. a form of inftruction in religion

Cat'echift, n. one that teaches the catechifm, &c.

Catechumen, [ch as k] n. a perfon inftructed

Categor'ical, a. abfolute, pofitive, exprefs

Categor'ically, ad. abfolutely, exprefsly, fully

Cat'egory, n. a clafs, rank, order of ideas

Cat'enate, v. t. to connect by a feries of links

Catenárian, a. relating or belonging to a chain

Catenátion, n. a regular connexion, chain, link

Caten'ulate, a. confifting of little chains

Cáter, v. i. to provide food, to lay in victuals

Cáter, Cáterer, n. a provider of food or victuals

Cáterefs, n. a woman that provides victuals

Cat'erpillar, n. the general name of winged infects
in their reptile or worm ftate; the varieties are
numerous; a plant

Cat'erwaul, v. i. to cry or make a noife like a cat

Cates, n. pl. cakes, dainties, ob.

Cat'fifh, n. a fifh of the fhark kind, &c.

Cat'gut, n. a kind of canvas, a gut for fiddleftrings

Cathar'tic, n. a purgative medicine

Cathar'tic, Cathar'tical, a. purging, cleanfing

Cathédral, n. the head church of a diocefe

Cathédral, a. epifcopal, antique, venerable

Cath'olic, a. univerfal, very general, liberal

Cathol'icifm, n. univerfality, liberality

Cathol'icon, n. an univerfal or prime medicin

Cat'kin, n. the calyx of certain plants like a thong

Cat'mint, n. a plant, calamint, catnip

Catop'trical, a. of or relating to reflected vifion

Cat'fup, n. a kind of nice pickle from mufhrooms

Cat'tle, n. pl. beafts of pafture that are not wild,
but moftly ufed for animals of the bovine kind

Cauca'fean, a. pertaining to mount Caucafus in Afia

Cau'cus, n. a cant name of fecret meetings for

electioneering purpofes

Caud'al, a. pertaining to the tail

Cau'dex, pl. Caudexes, n. the part of a plant
which connects the roots with the leaves

Cau'dle, n. child-bed food; v. i. to make caudle

Cauf, n. a cheft with holes for keeping fifh in the
Caught, pret. and pa. from to catch (water

Cauk, n. a coarfe kind of fpar found in mines

Caul, n. a membrane covering the lower part of
the bowels, a fmall net

Caules'cent, a. having a ftem different from that
which produces the flower

Caulif'erous, a. having a ftem

Cau'liform, a. like a ftem or ftalk

Cau'line, a. growing on a ftem

Caul'iflower, n. a fine or admired fort of cabbage

Caus'al, a. relating to or implying caufes, prime

Caufal'ity, Caufation, n. the power, act or quality,
of caufing, the agency of a caufe, agency

Caus'ative, a. expreffive of fome caufe or reafon

Caus'able, a. that may be produced by a caufe

Caufe, n. a reafon, motive, party, fource, fake

Caufe, v. to effect, produce, occafion, debate

Caufe'lefs, a. having no juft reafon, original

Caus'er, n. one who caufes or produces, an agent

Caus'fey, or Caufe'way, n. a raifed or paved way

Caus'tic, a. burning, hot; n. a burning application

Causti"city, n. the quality of burning or corroding

Caut'elous, a. cautious, cunning, crafty, wily, fly

Caut'eloufly, ad. cautioufly, cunningly, craftily

Cauterization, n. the act of burning with irons

Caut'erize, v. t. to burn with hot irons, to fear

Caut'ery, n. an iron for or the act of burning
animal flefh

Cau'tion, n. prudence, forefight, care, a warning

Cau'tion, v. t. to warn, give notice, advife, tell

Cau'tionary, a. giving fecurity, given in pledge

Cau'tious, a. wary, fcrupulous, watchful, prudent

Cau'tioufly, ad. in a cautious manner, prudently

Cau'tioufnefs, n. watchfulnefs, prudence, care

Cav'alcade, n. a proceffion on horfeback, a fhow

Cavaliér, n. a partifan, knight, royalift, a mound

Cavaliér, a. gay, brave, warlike, haughty, proud

Cavaliérly, ad. haughtily, arrogantly, proudly

Cav'alry, n. horfe-troops, horfe-foldiers

Cave, n. a den, a hallow; v. i. to live in a cave

Cáveat, n. a law term to prevent farther proceedings, bill, caution, hint, admonition, warning

Cav'ern, n. a cave, den, hole, hollow place

Cav'erned, Cav'ernous, a. full of caverns, hollow

Cavet'to, n. a concave molding in a cornifh

Caviáre, n. the fpawn of fturgeon, &c. pickled

Cav'il, n. a captious or frivolous objection

Cav'il, v. i. to raife objections, wrangle, quarrel

Cav'iller, n. one who cavils, a captious difputant

Cav'illous, a. full of objections, wrangling

Cav'ity, n. hollownefs, a hollow place, a cavern

Cav'y, n. the name of a large tribe of quadrupeds
fomewhat like a rabbit and a pig

Caw, v. i. to cry as a rook, raven or crow
Cayenn'e, n. a ftimulating pepper
Cáyman, n. a fpeeies of crocodile or alligator
Cazique', or Caz'ic, n. an Indian Chief (ed body
Cear'ment, n. the bandage put round an enbalm-
Ceafe, v. to leave off, ftop, be extinct or at an end, fail, put an end to; n. an extinction, a failure
Céafelefs, a. never ceafing, inceffant, perpetual
Ce'cias, n. the north eaft wind
Ce''city, n. blindnefs, a want or lofs of fight, ob.
Cédar, n. a genus of trees, evergreens, and very durable timber
Cede, v. t. to yield or give up, furrender, refign
Cédrine, a. of or belonging to cedar, like cedar
Ceil, v. t. to make a ceiling, roof, overlay, cover
Céiling, n. the inner roof, the upper part of a room
Cel'andine, n. prickly poppy, a tree
Cel'ebrate, v. t. to praife, extol, folemnize
Celebrát:on, n. a folemn performance, an extolling
Celébrious, a. famous, famed, renowned, noted
Celeb'rity, n. fame, renown, celebration, folemnity
Cele'riac, n. the opium or parfley
Celer'ity, n. fwiftnefs, fpeed, hafte
Cel'ery, n. the name of a well-known falad-herb
Celes'tial, n. an inhabitant of heaven; a. heavenly
Celes'tially, ad. in a tranfporting manner
Ce'liac, a. relating to the lower belly
Celib'acy, n. a fingle life or ftate
Cell, n. a fmall clofe room, cave, hut, hole, partition in plants, bag of fluids in animals
Cell'ar, Cell'arage, n. a ground-floor for liquors
Cellaret', n. a cafe of cabinet work for liquors
Cellif'erous, a. producing cells
Cell'ular, a. made up of cells or cavities, hollow
Celt'ic, a. pertaining to the ancient people of Eu-
Celt'ic, n. the language of the Celts (rope
Celtibe'rians, n. Celts on the Iberus in Spain
Cem'ent, n. that which joins bodies together
Cement', v. t. to unite, join together, folder
Cementátion, n. the uniting by an intermediate fubftance, a change of metals by a cement
Cement'atory, Cementi'tious, a. cementing, tending to unite or to change metals
Cem'etery, n. a burial-place, church yard, tomb
Cenat'ical, Cen'atory, a. of or belonging to fupper
Cenobit'ic, Cenobit'ical, a. living in community
Cénotaph, n. an empty tomb in honor of the dead
Cenfe, n. public rates; v. t. to perfume, ob.
Cens'er, n. an incenfe-pan, a pan ufed for incenfe
Cens'or, n. a Roman magiftrate who taxed eftates and infpected the manners of citizens
Cenfórian, Cenfórial, a. belonging to a cenfor
Cenfórious, a. fevere, full of invectives, railing
Cenfórioufly, ad. in a cenforious manner (demn
Cenfórioufnefs, n. a difpofition to reproach or con-
Ceus'orfhip, n. the office or dignity of a cenfor
Cens'ual, a. rated, liable to be rated, relating to a cenfus
Cens'urable, a. deferving of cenfure or blame

Cens'ure, n. blame, reproach, judgment, opinion
Cens'ure, v. t. to blame, condemn, revile, judge
Cens'urer, n. one who blames or condemns, a critic
Cens'us, n. an enumeration of inhabitants, a regifter of people, &c. (hundredth part of a dollar
Cent, n. a copper coin of the U. States, value one
Cent n. an abbreviation of a hundred, as 1 per ct.
Cent'aur, n. a poetical being half man half horfe, monfter, fign, the archer in the zodiac
Cen'taury, n. a plant of feveral kinds
Cent'enary, a. relating to a hundred; n. a hundred
Cent'er, n. the middle of a place or object
Cen'ter, v. to place on a center, meet, reft, end
Centes'imal, a. the hundredth
Centefimátion, n. felecting every hundredth perfon for punifhment
Centif'idous, a. divided into a hundred parts
Centifo'lious a. having a hundred leaves
Cent'iped, n. a noxious infect of many feet
Cent'ner, n. the hundred ufed in affaying metals, or a certain weight divifible into a hundred
Cent'o, n. a collection of many fcraps (parts, &c.
Cent'ral, a. of or belonging to the center, middle
Cent'rally, ad. in or with regard to the center
Cent'ric, a. placed in the center, fet in the middle
Centrifúgal, a. flying off from the center or axis
Centripétal, a. tending to or towards the center
Cen'tumvir, n. one of the hundred judges in Rome
Cen'tuple, a. hundred fold, manifold
Centúrion, n. a military officer over 100 men
Cent'ury, n. the fpace of an hundred years, 100
Cephal'ic, a. belonging to or eafing the head
Cépheus, n. a northern conftellation of 17 ftars
Céphus, n. a bird of the duck kind, a monkey
Cerafeé, n. the male balfam apple
Ceras'tes, n. a kind of ferpent, a horned ferpent
Cérate, n. a foft kind of falve made of wax and oil
Cérated, a. covered with cerate or wax
Cercopith'ecan, a. belonging to monkeys
Cere, v. t. to cover or fmear over with wax, to wax
Cere'cloth, n. a cloth dipped in melted wax, &c.
Ceremónial, n. the outward form, a book of rites
Ceremónial, Ceremónious, a. civil to a fault, formal
Ceremónioufly, ad. in a formal manner (mal
Ceremónioufnefs, n. formality, fondnefs for ceremony, ceremony, affectation of politenefs
Cer'emony, n. an outward rite, a formal civility
Céres, n. a pagan goddefs, the inventor of corn, a newly difcovered planet
Cerif'erous, a. producing wax
Cern'uous, a. hanging down, looking to the ground
Ceroon', n. a fquare bale or bag
Cer'tain, a. fure, undoubted, fixed, regular, fome
Cer'tainly, Cer'tes, ad. furely, without fail, yes
Cer'tainty, Cer'titude, n. a fulnefs of affurance
Certif'icate, n. a teftimony given in writing
Cer'tified, pa. affured, made certain, informed
Cer'tify, v. t. to give certain notice, affure, tell
Certiorári, n. a kind of writ iffued in chancery

Cerúlean, Cerúleous, *a.* fkycolored, blue, light-blue
Cerulif'ic, *a.* producing or caufing a blue color
Cer'ufe, *n.* whitelead, white oxyd of lead
Cerv'ical, *a.* belonging to the neck
Cerv'ine, *a.* pertaining to the deer
Cefs, *n.* a tax, a rate ; *v. t.* to tax, affefs, *ob.*
Cefs'pool, *n.* a receiver of filth in a drain
Ceffátion, *n.* a ftop, reft, paufe, refpite, interval
Ceffibil'ity, *n.* the quality or ftate of giving way
Cefs'ible, *a.* liable or eafy to give way, *ob.*
Ces''fion, *n.* a giving way, yielding up, refignation
Cefs'ment, *n.* an affeffment, tax, levy, rate, *ob.*
Ces'tus, *n.* a kind of girdle, the girdle of Venus
Céfure, *n.* a paufe in a poetic verfe
Ces'ural, *a.* pertaining to a paufe
Cetáceous, *a.* of or belonging to the whale-kind
Cet'arach, *n.* fpleenwort, a fmall plant
Chace, *fee* Chafe
Chafe, *v.* to fret, fume, rage, warm, vex, rub
Chafe, *n.* a heat, fume, rage, fury, paffion
Chaff, *n.* the hufks of corn, any worthlefs thing
Chaff'er, *v.* to haggle, bargain, *n.* a beetle
Chaff'erer, *n.* a hard bargainer, buyer, dealer
Chaff'ery, *n.* the act of buying and felling, traffic
Chaff'inch, *n.* the name of a fmall common bird
Chaff'lefs, *a.* deftitute of chaff
Chaff'y, *a.* like or full of chaff, foul, light
Cháfingdifh, *n.* a kind of difh to put hot coals in
'Chagrin', *n.* ill-humor, vexation, fretfulnefs
Chagrin', *v. t.* to vex, hurt, teafe, put out of hu-
Chagrin'ed, *pa.* vexed, provoked, fretted (mor
Chain, *n.* a line of links, bond, continuation, feries
Chain, *v. t.* to faften with a chain, join, enflave
Cháinfhot, *n.* two bullets faftened by a chain
Chair, *n.* a moveable feat, a fedan (ries a chair
Cháirman, *n.* a prefident of a fociety, one who car-
Chaife, [ch as fh] *n.* a riding carriage (in brafs
Chalcog'raphy, [ch as k] *n.* the art of engraving
Chaldáic, [ch as k] *a.* pertaining to ancient Chaldea
on the Euphrates in Afia, called Shinar
Chaldéan, *n.* a native of Chaldea
Chal'dee, *n.* the language of Chaldea
Chal'dron, *n.* a meafure of coals of 36 bufhels
Chal'ice, [ch as k] *n.* a cup ftanding on a foot
Chalk, *n.* carbonic acid and lime, or carbonate of
lime, a neutral falt, powerfully abforbent
Chalk, *v. t.* to mark or manure with chalk, to
point out
Chalk'pit, *n.* a pit or place where chalk is dug
Chalk'y, *a.* containing or like chalk, white
Chalk'inefs, *n.* a ftate of being chalky
Chal'lenge, *v. t.* to claim, accufe, call to fight, ob-
ject to a juror or jury
Chal'lenge, *n.* a fummons to fight, a demand, an
exception to a juror or jury
Chal'lenger, *n.* one who gives a challenge [or fteel
Chaiyb'eate, [ch as k] *a.* impregnated with iron
Cham or Chan, [ch as k] *n.* the fovereign prince
of Tartary

Chamáde, [ch as fh] *n.* the beat of drum for a parley
Cham'ber, *v. i.* to riot, revel, intrigue, keep clofe
Cham'ber, *n.* a part of a houfe, gun or mine, a cav-
Cham'berer, *n.* a man of intrigue or luxury (ity
Cham'bering, *n.* debauchery, riot, intrigue
Cham'berlain, *n.* one who takes care of chambers,
the fixth officer of the crown, a fteward
Cham'berlainfhip, *n.* the office of chamberlain
Cham'bermaid, *n.* a fervant who has the care of
rooms, or dreffes a lady
Chaméleon, [ch as k] *n.* an animal of the lizard
kind, whofe color changes with his pofition to
the light
Cham'fer, *v. t.* to form grooves, channel, flope off
Cham'ois, [ch as fh] *n.* an animal of the goat kind
Champ, *v. t.* to bite, chew, gnaw, eat, devour
Champáign, *n.* a flat open country, a kind of wine
Cham'perty, *n.* the offenfe of maintenance in law
Champign'on, *n.* a fmall kind of nice mufhroom
Cham'pion, *n.* a fingle combatant, a hero ; *v. t.* to
Chance, *v. i.* to happen, to fall out - (challenge
Chance, *n.* fortune, accident, hazard, an event
Chance, Chance'able, *a.* accidental, cafual
Chan'cel, *n.* the part of a church between the al-
tar, and the railing inclofing it
Chan'cellor, *n.* a great officer of ftate, a judge
Chan'cellorfhip, *n.* the office of chancellor
Chancemed'ley, *n.* the killing of a perfon by chance
Chan'cery, *n.* a court of equity, and confcience
Chan''cre, [ch as fh] *n.* a kind of venereal ulcer
Chandeliér, [ch as fh] *n.* a branch for candles
Chand'ler, *n.* a perfon who deals in candles
Change, *v. t.* to alter, mend, exchange, barter
Change, *n.* an alteration, novelty, fmall money
Changeable, Chángeful, *a.* fickle, inconftant, va-
Chángeablenefs, *n.* ficklenefs, inconftancy [riable
Chángeling, *n.* a fickle or unfteady perfon, idiot,
fool, filly fellow, child changed for another
Chánger, *n.* one who changes money, &c.
Chan'na, *n.* a Mediterranean fifh
Chan'nel, *n.* the courfe for a ftream of water, a
groove, gutter, ftrait, means
Chan'nel, *v. t.* to cut into channels, to hollow
Chan'nelled, *pa.* having a longitudinal groove
Chant, *n.* a fong, tune, melody, chathedral fervice
Chant, *v. t.* to fing, to fing cathedral fervice
Chant'er, *n.* a finger in cathedrals, &c. a fongfter
Chant'icleer, *n.* the cock, a clear finger (finger
Chant'refs, *n.* a woman that chants or fings, a fine
Chant'ry, *n.* a chapel for priefts to fing mafs in
Cháos, [ch as k] *n.* an indigefted heap, confufion
Chaot'ic, *n.* indigefted, confufed, mixed
Chap, *n.* a cleft, chink, opening, crack, jaw, beak
Chap, *v. t.* to open, gape, crack, cleave, divide
Chape, *n.* a thin plate at the point of a fcabbard,
catch of a buckle
Chap'el, *n.* a place of worfhip, a kind of church
Chap'elry, *n.* the diftrict or bounds of a chapel
Chaperon', a cap worn by knights of the garter

Chap'faln, a. having the mouth fhrunk, dejected
Chap'iter, n. the capital or top of a pillar
Chap'lain, n. the minifter of a fhip, regiment, &c.
Chap'lainfhip, the office, or ftate of a chaplain
Chap'lefs, a. having no flefh about the mouth
Chap'let, n. a garland wreath, firing of beads
Chap'man, n. one who cheapens or deals in goods
Chap'ped, Chapt, pa. cracked, cleft, divided
Chap'ter, n. a divifion of a book, place, whole body of clergymen in a cathedral and church
Chap'trel, n. a capitol fupporting an arch
Char, n. work done by the day, a fifh, fedge
Char, v. to burn wood to charcoal or carbon
Char'acter, [ch as k] n. a mark, letter, reputation, peculiar qualities, dignity, a perfon (preffive
Characteris'tic, a. diftinguifhing, peculiar to, ex-
Characteris'tic, n. a mark, fign, token, quality
Characteris'ticalnefs, n. a characteriftic quality
Char'acterize, v. t. to give a character, to mark
Char'coal, n. a coal made by burning wood under cover, and expelling all volatile matter
Charáde, [ch as fh] n. a compofition in which a word and each fyllable of it contains an enigma
Charge, v. t. to enjoin, exhort, entruft, impute, load, accufe, attack
Charge, n. care, command, expence, coft, load
Charge'able, a. expeafive, coftly, heavy, accufable
Charge'ably, ad. expenfively, at or with coft
Char'ger, n. a large kind of difh or plate
Chárinefs, n. caution, care, nicety, frugality, ob.
Char'iot, n. a half coach; v. t. to carry in a chariot
Chariotéer, n. a driver of a chariot, a coachman
Char'ioting, pa. driving or going in a chariot
Char'itable, a. kind, bountiful, loving, candid
Char'itably, ad. kindly, bountifully, lovingly (dor
Char'ity, n. love, affection, tendernefs, alms, can-
Chark, v. t. to burn to a black cinder, ob.
Char'latan, [ch as fh] a quack, mountebank
Charlatan'ical, a. quackifh, ignorant, pretended
Charl'atanry, n. the practices of a quack
Char'lock, n. a plant growing among grain
Charm, v. t. to bewitch, delight, allay
Charm, n. a fpell or enchantment
Charm'a, n. a fifh refembling the fea wolf
Charm'er, n. one who charms
Charm'ing, pa. very pleafing, delightful, fine
Charm'ingly, ad. very pleafingly, delightfully
Charm'ingnefs, n. the power of pleafing, beauty
Char'nelhoufe, n. a place for the bones of the dead
Charr, n. a fifh about a foot in length
Chart, n. a delineation of coafts, iflands, &c.
Chart'er, n. a patent, deed, grant, privilege
Chart'er, v. t. to hire or let a fhip
Chart'ered, a. privileged, endowed, contracted
Chart'erpar'ty, n. a writing containing an agreement for the hire of a veffel
Char'woman, n. a woman hired by the day only
Cháry, a. cautious, careful, frugal, diligent, ob.
Chafe, v. t. to hunt, purfue, drive, enchafe, cut

Chafe, n. a hunting, hunt, purfuit, whole length of a gun, ftation for beafts larger than a park, a veffel purfued, a printer's frame
Cháfed, pa. purfued, driven, adorned, enchafed
Cháfer, n. a hunter, purfuer, driver, remover
Chafm, [ch as k] n. a cleft, gap, opening, blank
Chafte, a. undefiled, pure, true, honeft, unmixed
Cháftely or Cháftly, ad. in a chafte manner
Chaft'en, Chaftife, v. t. to correct, punifh, beat
Chas'tifement or Chafti'sement, n. correction
Chaftifer, n. one who corrects or punifhes
Chas'tity, Cháftenefs, n. purity of body, &c.
Chat, v. i. to prate, prattle, talk, converfe
Chat, n. prate, talk, converfation, a twig, feed
Chat'ellany, n. the diftrict under a caftle
Chatoy'ant, a. changing colors
Chat'tel, n. any moveable property or poffeffion
Chat'ter, v. i. to make a noife like birds or with the teeth, prate, jabber, talk idly or much
Chat'ter, n. the noife of birds, &c. prate, talk
Chat'terer, n. a great talker, a bird
Chav'ender, Chev'en, Chev'in, n. a fifh, the chub
Cheap, a. of a low price compared with its value, eafy to be obtained, low, common
Chéapen, v. t. to afk the price, leffen, degrade
Chéaply, ad. at a low price or rate, meanly
Chéapnefs, n. lownefs of price or value
Chear, Chear'ful, fee Cheer, Cheerful
Cheat, n. a trickfter, deceiver, fraud, trick fham
Cheat, v. t. to defraud in a bargain, to deceive for the purpofe of gaining an advantage
Chéated, pa. defrauded, impofed on, deceived
Chéater, n. one who cheats or practices fraud
Check, v. to reprove, chide, curb, ftop, clafh
Check, n. a reftraint, ftop, order on a bank, checkered cloth
Check'ed, Checkt, pa. reproved, curbed, ftopped
Check'er, v. t. to diverfify, vary, mix
Check'ers, n. pl. a game
Cheek, n. the fide of the face, or a machine, &c.
Chéekbone, n. the high bone within the cheek
Chéektooth, n. a hind large tooth, a hinder tufk
Cheer, n. entertainment, food, jolity, huzza
Cheer, v. to encourage, comfort, grow gay, face
Cheérer, n. a perfon or thing that cheers
Cheérful, a. merry, full of mirth and life, gay
Cheérfully, Cheer'ly, ad. merrily, gaily, readily
Cheérfulnefs, n. mirth, gaity, pleafure, readinefs
Cheérlefs, a. comfortlefs, fad, gloomy, difmal
Cheérly or Cheery a. merry, gay, fprightly, lively
Cheefe, n. a fort of food made from milk-curds
Cheéfecake, n. a cake of curds, fugar and butter
Cheefe'monger, n. one who deals in or fells cheefe
Chees'y, a. like cheefe, tafting of cheefe, containing cheefe
Chegóe, n. a tropical infect which enters the fkin
Chel'idon, n. a brown fly with filvery wings
Chély, n. the claw of a fhellfifh
Chem'iftry, [ch as k] n. modern and falfe orthog-

rophy,)the fcience which teaches the properties of bodies by decompofition and combination

Chem'ical, *a.* pertaining to chemiftry

Chem'ically, *ad.* on chemical principles

Chem'ift, *n.* one verfed in chemiftry

Chequer, *fee* checker

Chériff, *n.* the high prieft of the Moors

Cher'ifh, *v. t.* to nurfe, nourifh, comfort, fupport

Cher'ifher, *n.* a comforter, fupporter, encourager

Cher'ry, *n.* a fruit ; *a.* ruddy, blooming, healthy

Cher'rycheeked, *a.* having red cheeks, blooming

Cherfonéfe, [ch as k] *n.* a peninfula

Chert, *n.* a kind of flint, flints lying in thin ftrata

Cher'ub, *n.* a kind of angel, a high celeftial fpirit

Cherúbic, Cherubim'ical, *a.* angelical, divine

Cher'up, *v. t.* to chirup, to ufe a cheerful voice

Cherv'il, *n.* a plant, the cow weed

Ches'nut, *n.* a tree, valuable as timber, and its nut

Ches'opeak, *n.* a large bay in Virginia and Mary-

Chefs, *n.* a difficult kind of game, a plant   (land

Chefs'board, *n.* a kind of board to play chefs upon

Chefs'man, *n.* a puppet ufed at the game of chefs

Cheft, *n.* a large box, the breaft ; *v. t.* to lay up

Chevaliér, [ch as fh]*n.* a knight, motion of a horfe

Chevaux-de-frife, *n.* a military fence, a trimming

Chev'eril, *n.* a kid, leather made of a kid's fkin

Chev'ifance, *n.* a bargain, unlawful agreement

Chevrotáin, *n.* the fmalleft of the antelope kind

Chew, *v.* to grind with the teeth, to meditate on

Chía, *n.* a beautiful Mexican plant

Chicáne, Chicánery, [ch as fh] *n.* fophiftry, cunning

Chicáner, *n.* a wrangler, caviller, quibbler

Chick, Chick'en, *n.* the young of hens, a darling

Chick'enhearted, *a.* fearful, timorous, cowardly

Chick'enpox, *n.* a mild eruptive difeafe of children

Chick'lingpea, *n.* a genus of plants of feveral fpecies

Chick'weed, *n.* a genus of plants ufed as food

Chide, *v.* chid, *pret.* chidden, *pa.* to fcold, brawl, reprove, rebuke, blame

Chíder, *n.* one who reproves or clamors

Chíding, *pa.* fcolding ; *n.* the act of reproving

Chief, *a.* principal, eminent, capital; *n.* a leader

Chiéflefs, *a.* deftitute of a head or leader

Chiéfly, *ad.* principally, eminently, above all

Chiéftain, *n.* a leader, commander, head, chief

Chil'blain, *n.* a fore made by cold or froft (fpecies

Child, *n.* a male or female offspring of the human

Childbearing, *n.* the act of bearing children

Childbed, Childbirth, *n.* the ftate of being in labor

Childhood, *n.* the ftate of a child, infancy

Childifh, *a.* like a child, fimple, trifling, ignorant

Childifhly, *ad.* fimply, ignorantly, weakly, idly

Childifhnefs, *n.* fimplenefs, ignorance, weaknefs

Childlefs, *a.* having no children, barren, lonely

Childlike, *a.* like or becoming a child

Chil'dren, *n. pl.* of child, defcendants

Chil'iad, [ch as k] *n.* the fum of a thoufand   (fides

Chilihédron, [ch as k] *n.* a figure of a 1000 equal

Chil'iarch, (ch as k)*n.* a commander of a 1000 men

Chill, *a.* moderately cold, cold with fhivering, forbidding, dull, dejected

Chill, *n.* moderate cold, or with dampnefs and fhivering, the fit which precedes fever

Chill, *v. t.* to make cold, deject, deprefs, blaft

Chill'inefs, Chill'nefs, *n.* a fhivering, a coldnefs

Chill'y, *a.* fomewhat cold, very fenfible of cold

Chil'li, *n.* great pepper, much ufed by the Mexicans

Chime, *n.* a found of bells, agreement, concord

Chime, *v. i.* to gingle, found together, join, agree

Chiméra, [ch as k] *n.* a wild or odd fancy, a feigned monfter

Chimer'ical, *a.* imaginary, fancied, whimfical

Chimer'ically, *ad.* vainly, wildly, fancifully, oddly

Chim'ney, *n.* a paffage made for fmoke, a fireplace

Chimneycórner, *n.* the firefide, the place of idlers

Chim'neypiece, *n.* an ornament about a fireplace

Chim'neyfweeper, *n.* one who fweeps chimneys

Chin, *n.* the loweft part or end of the human face

Chína, *n.* a fine earthern ware, a country

Chinch, *n.* a genus of fmall infects

Chinéfe, *n. fing.* or *plu.* a native or natives of China

Chinéfe, *a.* pertaining to China

Chin'cough, *n.* a very violent cough of children

Chine, *n.* the back bone; *v. t.* to cut into chines

Chink, *n.* a fmall opening; *v. t.* to found like money

Chink'y, *a.* full of chinks, gaping, open

Chink'opin, *n.* an American tree, a fpecies of fagus

Chinfe, *v. t.* to ftop a feam with oakum

Chintz, *n. pl.* Indian cottons, fine printed calico

Chip, *v. t.* to cut into fmall pieces, hack, leffen

Chip, Chip'ping, *n.* a piece cut off, a fragment

Chip'ped, Chipt, *pa.* cut into pieces, cut, hewed

Chirk, *a.* in a comfortable ftate, cheerful, N. E.

Chirog'rapher, [ch as k] *n.* an officer in the Common-Pleas who engroffes fines in that court, Eng.

Chirog'raphy, *n.* a writing with one's own hand

Chiromancy, [ch as k] *n.* a divination made by the hand

Chirp, *v. i.* to imitate the noife of birds, &c. make a noife, make or become cheerful

Chirp'er, *n.* one who chirps, one who is cheerful

Chirp'ing, *n.* the noife made by birds or infects

Chirur'geon, a furgeon, but with its derivitives, *ob.*

Chirur'gery, *n.* a manual operation, furgery, *ob.*

Chirur'gic, Chirur'gical, *a.* belonging to furgery, *ob.*

Chis'el, *n.* a carpenter's tool to pare with, bran

Chis'el, *v. t.* to cut, make or form with a chifel

Chit, *v. i.* to fprout; *n.* a baby, child, fprout

Chit'chat, *n.* prattle, common talk; *a.* prattling

Chiv'alry, [ch as fh] *n.* knighthood, military exploits

Chives, *n. pl.* a kind of onions, threads in flowers

Chlórite, [klorite] *n.* a fpecies of muriatic earth mixed with iron

Choc'olate, *n.* a nice liquor made of the cocoa-nut

Choice, *n.* a thing chofen, the power of choofing

Choice, *a.* felect, of great value, frugal, careful

Choice'ly, *ad.* curioufly, valuably, carefully, well

Choice'nefs, *n.* nicety, a particular value, worth

Choir,[ch as k]*n*.a part of a church, body of fingers
Choke, *v. t.* to ftop the windpipe, block up, hin-
Choke, *n.* part of an artichoke   (der, overpower
Chókepear, *n.* a pear that contracts the mouth
Chóky, *a.* tending to choke
Chol'er, [ch as k] *n*, the bile, gall, anger, rage
Chol'eric, *a.* full of choler, angry, paffionate
Choofe, Chufe, *v.* chofe,*pret.* chofen, chofe,*pa.* to
    make choice, pick out, felect
Choos'er, *n.* one who choofes, one who felects
Chop, *v.* to cut with a blow, cut, mince, devour,
    come quickly upon, change, crack, gape, open
Chop, *n.* a fmall piece of meat, crack, cleft, jaw
Chop'houfe, *n.* a houfe to eat provifions at
Chop'in,*n.* a Scotch quart in wine-meafure, a pint
Chop'ping, *a.* large, lufty, ftout, plump, healthy
Chop'ping, *n.* a cutting, a fort of high-heel'd fhoe
Chop'pingblock, *n.* a block to chop meat on
Chop'pingknife, *n.* a knife to cut or mince meat
Chop'py, *a.* full of holes or cracks, gaping
Chóral, [ch as k] *a.* of, belonging to, a choir
Chord, [ch as k] *n.* a ftring of a mufical inftru-
    ment, a line
Chord, *v. t.* to furnifh or faften with ftrings, to
Chore,*n.* a fmall job, domeftic work   (agree
Chor'iſter, [ch as k] *n.* a finger in cathedrals
Chorog'rapher, [ch as k]*n.* a defcriber of countries
Chorograph'ical, [ch as k] *a.* belonging to chorog-
    raphy
Chorog'raphy, [ch as k] *n.* a defcription of places
Chórus, [ch as k] *n.* a number of fingers, concert,
Chofe, *pret. tenfe* of *to choofe*   (choir
Chófen, *pa.* made choice of, taken out, felected
Cheugh, [chuff] *n.* a kind of fea-bird
Chouſe, *v. t.* to cheat, to trick ; *n.* a trick, a fool
Chow'der, *n.* a difh of fifh boiled with bifcuit, &c.
Chow'der, *v. t.* to make a chowder
Chrifm, [ch as k] *n.* a holy unguent or oil, unction
Chris'om, [ch as k] *n.* a child that dies within a
    month, a cloth
Chrift, [ch as k] *n.* the Anointed one, our Saviour
Chris'ten, *v. t.* to baptize, to name   (tians
Chris''tendom, *n.* the body or general ftate of chrif-
Chris'tening, *n.* the act of baptizing, a baptifm
Chris'tian, *n.* a follower or difciple of Chrift
Chris'tian, *a.* of or belonging to Chriftianity, &c.
Chriftian'ity, *n.* the religion taught by Jefus Chrift
Chris'tianize, *v. t.* to make or render Chriftian
Chris'tianly, *ad.* in a Chriftian manner or ftate
Chris'tian-name, *n.* the name given at baptifm
Chrift'mas, *n.* the feaft of the nativity of Chrift
Chromat'ic, [ch as k] *a.* relating to colors   (time
Chron'ic, Chron'ical, [ch as k] *a.* continued a long
Chro'mum or Chrome, [ch as k] *n.* a metal, very
    hard, gray and brittle
Chro'mic, *a.* pertaining to chrome
Chron'icle, *n.* a kind of hiftory, a regifter of events
Chron'icle, *v. t.* to record in hiftory, to regifter
Chron'icler, *n.* an hiftorian   (letters fhow its date

Chron'ogram, *n.* a kind of verfe, whofe figurative
Chronogram'matift,*n.* a writer of chronograms
Chronol'oger, Chronol'ogift, [ch as k] *n.* an ex-
    plainer of paft time
Chrono'lo''gical, *a.* relating to chronology
Chronolo''gically, *ad.* in the exact courfe of time
Chronol'ogy,*n.* the fcience of computing time
Chronom'eter, (ch as k) *n.* an inftrument to mea-
    fure time   (a maggot
Chrys'alis, (ch as k) *n.* the firft apparent change of
Chrysober'yl, (ch as k) *n.* a fpecies of filiceous ftone
Chrys'olite, (ch as k) *n.* a fpecies of filiceous ftone
    of a yellowifh green   (green color
Chrys'oprafe, (ch as k) *n.* a fpecies of topaz, of a
Chub, *n.* the name of a fifh, a dunce
Chub'bed, *a.* bigheaded, bluff, ftupid   (gently
Chuck, *v.* to make a noife like a hen, to ftrike
Chuck, *n.* the noife of a hen, ftroke, game
Chuc''kle, *v.* to laugh much, fondle, call as a hen
Chuff, *n.* a blunt clownifh perfon; *a.* blunt, furly
Chuff'ily, *ad.* in a furly manner, morofely
Chum, *n.* a chambermate, meffmate
Chump or Chunk, *n.* a fhort piece of wood, a log
Church, *n.* a place of divine worfhip, affembly or
    body of chriftians, congregation
Church, *v. t.* to return thanks after childbirth
Church'ing, *n.* the act of giving thanks in the
    church after childbirth, fervice in the church
Church'man, *n.* a member of the church of Eng.
Church'warden, *n.* a church-officer chofe annual-
    ly by the minifter and parifhoners of a place
Church'yard,*n.* a ground where the dead are buried
Churl, *n.* a ruftic, rude man, niggard, mifer
Churl'ifh, *a.* rude, furly, niggardly, felfifh
Churl'ifhly, *ad.* rudely, brutally, furlily, felfifhly
Churl'ifhnefs, *n.* rudenefs, furlinefs, meannefs
Churm or Churme,*n.* a confufed noife or found
Churn, *v. t.* to make butter, to fhake very much
Churn, *n.* a kind of veffel to churn cream in
Churn'ing, *n.* the act of making butter in a churn
Chyláceous, Chy'lous, [ch as k] *a.* of or belonging
    to chyle
Chyle, *n.* a white juice formed in the ftomach
Chylifac'tion, *n.* the act of making chyle
Chylifac'tive, *a.* forming chyle
Chylopoet'ic, *a.* forming or producing chyle
Chym'ical, (ch as k) *a.* made by, or relating to
    chymiftry
Chym'ically, *ad.* in a chymical manner
Chym'ift, *n.* a man who practifes chymiftry
Chym'iſtry, *n.* the fcience of determining the pro-
    perties of bodies by decompofing and combining
Cibárious, *a.* pertaining to food   (their elements
Cib'ol, *n.* a fmall or degenerate fort of onion
Cica'da,*n.* a genus of infects of the cricket kind
Cic'atrice, *n.* a fcar or mark left after a wound
Cic'atricle, *n.* a little mark as in vegetable feeds
Cicatrizátion, *n.* the act of healing a wound
Cic'atrize, *v. t.* to fkin over a fore, heal, clofe up

Cic'atrizant, *n.* that which caufes to form a fcar
Cic'atrifive, *a.* tending to form a fcar
Cic'atrized, *pa.* fkinned over, healed over or up
Cicerónian, *a.* like Cicero, elegant, forcible
Ci''cely, *n.* a plant, the wild myrrh
Cicifbéo, *n.* a gallant, at attendant upon a lady
Cic'urate, *v. t.* to make tame or mild, *ob.*
Cicurátion, *n.* the act of taming or fubduing, *ob.*
Cíder, *n.* a liquor made from the juice of apples
Cigar', *n.* a fmall roll of tobacco for fmoaking
Cil'iary, *a.* belonging to the eyelids
Cil'iate, Cil'iated, *a.* having briftles like the eye-
Cili''cian, *n.* a native of Cilicia in Afia   (lafhes
Cili''cious, *a.* made of hair, hairy, rough   (fword
Cim'eter, *n.* a Turkifh hanger, a fhort crooked
Cim'bric, *a.* relating to the Cimbri, an ancient people of Denmark
Cimmérian, *a.* relating to the Crimea on the north of the Euxine, formerly thought to be perpetually dark
Cinc'ture, *n.* a belt, fafh, girdle, ring, inclofure
Cin'der, *n.* fmall particles or coals of an ignited body
Cinerátion, *n.* a reducing to afhes
Cinéreous, *a.* of the color of wood afhes
Cineri''tious, *a.* having the form or ftate of afhes
Cin''gle, *n.* a girth, a girth ufed for a horfe
Cin'nabar, *n.* vermilion, quickfilver combined with fulphur and called red fulphuret of mercury
Cin'namon, *n.* the inner bark of two fpecies of bay tree or laurel
Cinque, *a.* five; *n.* five, the number five on dice
Cinque'foil, *n.* a grafs, a kind of five-leaved clover
Cíon, *n.* a fprout, fhoot of a plant, valve
Cípher, *v.* to caft accounts, to write obfcurely
Cípher, *n.* the figure or mark (o) in numbers, the initial letters of a perfon's name interwoven
Cíphering, *n.* the act or art of cafting accounts
Circas'ian, *n.* a native of Circafia, between the Euxine and Cafpian
Circéan, *a.* pertaining to or like Circe, bewitching
Circen'fian, *a.* pertaining to the games of the Circus in Rome
Cir'cinal, *a.* rolled fpirally from top to bottom
Cir''cle, *n.* a round body, curve, company, feries
Cir''cle, *v. t.* to move round, inclofe, confine
Circ'led, *pa.* furrounded, formed like a circle, round
Circ'let, *n.* a fmall or little circle
Circ'ling, *pa.* circular, roundifh
Cir'cuit, *n.* a fpace, act of moving round, journeys of the judges to hold affizes
Cir'cuit, *v. i.* to move in a circle, to go round
Circuiteer, *n.* one who travels or goes a circuit
Circui''tion, *n.* the act of going round or about
Cir'cuitous, *a.* going round in a circuit, tedious
Circ'ular, *a.* like a circle, round, fucceffive
Circular'ity, Circ'ularnefs, *n.* a circular form
Circ'ularly, *ad.* in a circular manner, round
Circ'ulate, *v.* to put or pafs about, to move round
Circ'ulating, *pa.* moving round, returning back

Circulátion, *n.* a circular motion, courfe, return
Cir'culatory, *a.* circulating
Cir'culatory, *n.* a chemical veffel receiving vapors, &c. which circulate
Circumam'biency, *n.* the act of encompaffing
Circumam'bient, *a.* furrounding, encompaffing
Circumam'bulate, *v.* to walk or pafs round about
Circ'umcife, *v. t.* to cut off the forefkin, to cut a-
Circumci''fion, *n.* the act of circumcifing   (bout
Circumduct', *v. t.* to make void, to carry about
Circum'ference, *n.* a compafs, circle, periphery
Circum'ference, *v. t.* to inclofe in a round fpace
Circumferen'tial, *a.* pertaining to circumference
Circumferent'or, *n.* an inftrument ufed in furveying
Circ'umflex, *n.* an accent over a fyllable to make it found long, marked thus (ˆ); *a.* bent round
Circ'umflex, *v. t.* to put or fix a circumflex over
Circum'fluent, *a.* flowing round about
Circum'fluous, *a.* flowing or running round
Circumfúfe, *v. t.* to pour or fpread round, to dif-
Circumfúfile, *a.* that may be poured round   (fufe
Circumfúfion, *n.* the act or art of pouring round
Circum'gyrate, *v. t.* to roll, turn or wheel round
Circumgyrátion, *n.* a whirling about
Circumjácent, *a.* lying round about, bordering
Circumlocútion, *n.* the ufe of indirect words
Circumloc'utory, *a.* pertaining to circumlocution
Circummúred, *a.* walled or fenced round
Circumnav'igate, *v. t.* to fail around
Circumnavigátion, *n.* the act of failing round
Circumnav'igable, *a.* that may be failed round
Circumnav'igator, *n.* one who fails round the world
Circumpólar, *a.* about or near a pole
Circumpofi''tion, *n.* a placing of things circularly
Circumrotátion, *n.* the act of whirling round
Circumrótatory, *a.* turning or whirling round
Circumfcríbe, *v. t.* to inclofe, limit, confine, fix
Circumfcrip'tion, *n.* a limitation, a confinement
Circumfcrip'tive, *a.* inclofing, limiting
Circ'umfpect, *a.* cautious, wary, watchful, wife
Circumfpec'tion, Circ'umfpectnefs, *n.* caution, watchfulnefs, care, heed, attention, prudence
Circumfpect'ive, *a.* cautious, watchful, attentive
Circ'umfpectly, *ad.* cautioufly, warily, prudently
Circ'umftance, *n.* a condition, event, incident, fact
Circ'umftanced, *a.* placed, fituated, fet, attended
Cir'cumftances, *n. pl.* condition with refpect to property
Circumftan'tial, *a.* particular, minute, accidental
Circumftan'tially, *ad.* minutely, exactly, really
Circumvallátion, *n.* a furrounding with walls or trenches boarded with breaftwork, a trench
Circumvent', *v. t.* to deceive, cheat, gull, overreach
Circumven'tion, *n.* fraud, impofture, prevention
Circumveft', *v. t.* to cover, put or garnifh, round
Circumvolve', *v. t.* to roll round or about
Circumvolútion, *n.* a turning round or about, a turn
Cir'cus, Cirque, *n.* a place of fports, or fhows
Cirl, *n.* an Italian bird of the fize of a fparrow

Cirrif'erous, a. producing tendrils or clafpers
Cir'rus, n. a tendril or clafper
Cir'rous, Cirros'e, a. terminating in a clafper
Cifalp'ine, a. lying on the hither fide of the Alps, with regard to Rome, that is, the fouth fide
Cifs, v. i. to hifs, as water on hot metal *corruption*
Cift, n. a cafe, coat, covering, bag, tumor (*of hifs*
Cift'ed, a. contained in a cift or bag, fwelled up
Cift'ern, n. a veffel to catch or hold water, a pit
Cift'us, n. the rock rofe, a genus of evergreen and flowering fhrubs
Cit, n. a cant term for citizen, a pert townfman
Cit'adel, n. a fortrefs, caftle, place of or for arms
Cital, Citátion, n. a fummons, quotation, recital
Citatory, a. having the form or power of citing
Cite, v. t. to fummon, quote, enjoin, anfwer, re-
Citer, n. one who cites, one who quotes (cite
Cit'efs, n. a woman inhabiting a city
Cith'ern, n. a harp, a kind of ancient harp
Cit'izen, n. one inhabiting a city, a freeman
Cit'rate, n. a neutral falt formed by the citric acid
Cit'ric, a. belonging to lemons (and a bafe
Cit'ril, n. a beautiful fong bird of Italy
Cit'rine, a. like a citron, of a lemon color, yellow
Cit'rine, n. a fpecies of very fine cryftal
Cit'ron, n. a fruit fomething like a lemon (citron
Cit'ron-water, n. *aqua-vitæ* diftilled with rind of
Cit'y, n. a walled or a large town, an incorporated town, the inhabitants of fuch a town
Cit'y, a. pertaining to a city
Civ'et, n. an animal of the weafel genus, the perfume which the animal yields
Cives or Chives, n. a plant, allium
Civ'ic, a. relating to civil honors and practices
Civ'il, a. pertaining to fociety, and oppofed to *criminal, military*, and *eclefiaftical*, as a *civil* fuit, *civil* magiftrate, &c. civilized, kind, obliging, polite
Civil'ian, n. a doctor or profeffor of civil law
Civil'ity, n. freedom, kindnefs, politenefs
Civilizátion, n. the act of civilizing, a civilized ftate, refinement, improvement, politenefs
Civ'ilize, v. t. to make civil, polifh, reclaim
Civ'ilized, pa. polifhed, improved, polite, civil
Civ'illy, ad. kindly, politely, well, with refpect
Civ'ifm, n. patriotifm, attachment to the public
Clack, n. a part of a mill, the tongue (welfare
Clack, v. i. to make repeated noifes
Clad, *pret.* and *pa.* of *to clothe* (right
Claim, n. a demand, a title; v. t. to demand of
Cláimable, a. that may be claimed or demanded
Cláimant, n. one who demands, one who owns
Cláimed, pa. demanded, required, owned, taken
Clam, n. a genus of bivalvular fhell fifh
Clam'ming, n. the taking of clams
Clámant, a. crying, calling to or upon, begging
Clam'ber, v. i. to climb, to climb with difficulty
Clamm, v. t. to clog, ftop up, ftick, glue, ftarve
Clam'med, pa. clogged up with matter, ftarved

Clam'minefs, n. ropinefs, toughnefs, ftickinefs
Clam'my, a. ropy, like glue, tough, fticky, moift
Clam'or, n. a great noife, cry, outcry
Clam'or, v. i. to complain, make a noife, cry out
Clam'orous, a. noify, troublefome, importunate
Clamp, n. a thick piece of wood faftened to another, an iron to confine guns to the carriages
Clamp, v. t. to faften with a clamp
Clan, n. a family, race, fect, fet, defpicable body
Clan'ifh, a. difpofed to unite in clans
Clan'ifhnefs, n. a difpofition to affociate in clans
Clan'fhip, n. a ftate of union in tribes
Clanc'ular, a. clandeftine, fecret, private, *ob.*
Clandes'tine, a. fecret, hidden, fly, done craftily
Clandes'tinely, ad. fecretly, privately, craftily
Clang, Clan''gor, Clank, n. a fharp or fhrill noife
Clang or Clank, v. to clatter, to ftrike together
Clan''gous, a. making a very fharp or fhrill noife
Clap, v. to ftrike together, hit gently, move or do haftily, applaud, approve of, add, infect
Clap, n. a loud noife with hands in praife, blow fudden act or motion, venereal complaint (ings
Clap'board, n. a narrow board ufed to cover building
Clap'per, n. one who claps, the tongue of a bell
Clap'perclaw, v. i. to fcold, chide, abufe, revile
Clarenciéux, n. the fecond king at arms, a herald
Clare-obfcúre, n. light and fhade in painting
Clar'et, n. an admired red French wine
Clarificátion, n. the act or art of making clear
Clar'ified, pa. made clear, freed from fediment
Clar'ifier, n. that which fines liquor, a veffel for the purpofe
Clar'ify, v. t. to make clear or bright, to purify
Clar'ion, n. a martial inftrument, a trumpet
Clar'itude, Clarity, n. brightnefs, clearnefs, *ob.*
Cla'ry, n. a plant of feveral fpecies
Clafh, n. oppofition, a noife made by two bodies
Clafh, v. to contradict, oppofe, dafh againft, meet
Clafh'ing, pa. ftriking againft; n. oppofition
Clafp, v. t. to embrace, hug, hold faft, clofe, faften
Clafp, n. a kind of hook, holdfaft, clofe embrace
Clafp'er n. one who clafps, a thread of plants
Clafp'ered, a. furnifhed with tendrils
Clafs, v. t. to range or fet in claffes, to regulate
Clafs, Clafs'is, n. a rank, order, degree, fet, form
Clafs'ic, n. an author or writer of the firft rank
Clafs'ical, a. relating to ftandard-authors of the firft rank
Clafs'ically, ad. in order of claffes, elegantly
Clafs'ify, v. t. to form into claffes
Claffif'ic, a. conftituting a clafs
Claffificátion, n. the act of arranging or ftate of being arranged in a clafs
Clafs'ifier, n. one who forms claffes
Clat'ter, n. a confufed noife or found
Clat'ter, v. to make a confufed noife, ftrike, jar
Clat'tered, pa. ftruck fo as to make a clatter
Clat'tering, n. a loud noife or talk
Claufe, n. a fentence, article, condition, provifo

Claus'tral, *a.* relating or belonging to a cloifter
Claus'ure, *n.* a fhutting up, confinement, hedge
Clav'ate, Clav'ated, *a.* club-fhaped
Clave, *pret.* of *cleave*
Clav'iary, *n.* fcale of lines and fpaces in mufic
Clav'icle, *n.* the collar bone
Claw, *n.* a hooked nail of beaft, bird, or fifh, a hand
Claw, *v.* to tear with claws, fcratch, tickle, fcold
Clawed, *pa.* armed with claws, fcratched, torn
Clay, *n.* a fimple earth, adhefive and ufed to form veffels; the earth, frailty
Clay, *v. t.* to cover with clay, to purify, as fugar
Cláyed, *pa.* purified with clay, &c.
Cláycold, *a.* cold as the earth, lifelefs, dead
Clayey, Clayifh, *a.* containing or like clay
Cláymarl, *n.* a marly clay, a kind of chalky clay
Clean, *a.* free from dirt, &c. neat, innocent, pure
Clean, *v. t.* to get out of the dirt, &c. purify, refine
Clean, *ad.* quite, fully, perfectly, entirely
Clean'linefs, Cléannefs, *n.* neatnefs, purity
Clean'ly, *a.* free from dirt and mire, neat, pure
Clean'ly, *ad.* elegantly, nicely, well
Cleanfe, *v. t.* to make clean, fcour, purify, clear
Cleans'ed *pa.* cleaned, purified, freed, cleared
Cleans'er, *n.* one who or that which cleanfes
Clear, *ad.* clean, quite, completely, entirely
Clear, *v.* to free, make pure, brighten, acquit, exonerate, make profit, render manifeft, &c.
Clear, *a.* free from mixture, tranfparent, pure, innocent, obvious, acute, loud, &c.
Clearance, *n.* the act of clearing, an acquittal
Cléarer, *n.* one that makes clear, bright or plain
Cléarly, *ad.* brightly, plainly, evidently, eafily
Cléarnefs, *n.* brightnefs, plainnefs, fairnefs
Cléarfighted, *a.* judicious, difcerning, quick, keen
Cléarftarch, *v. t.* to ftiffen any thing with ftarch
Cléarftarcher, *n.* one that wafhes fine linen
Cleat, *n.* a piece of wood for faftening ropes
Cleave, *v.* clave, clove, *pret.* cleft, cloven, *pa.* to ftick, join, hold, fplit, divide
Cléaver, *n.* one that cleaves, a butcher's inftrument
Clef or Cliff, *n.* a mark in mufic, the key in mufic,
Cleft, *n.* a crack, crevice, opening, piece of wood
Cleft'graft, *v. t.* to graft by cleaving a tree
Clem'ency, *n.* kindnefs, mercy, humanity, ten-
Clem'ent, *a.* kind, merciful, courteous (dernefs
Clepe, *v. t.* to call, name, denominate, *ob.*
Cler'gy, *n.* the whole order, fet or body, of divines
Cler'gyable, *a.* admitting the benefit of clergy, which is an exemption from certain punifhments
Cler'gyman, *n.* a perfon in holy orders, a minifter
Cler'ical, *a.* of or relating to the clergy
Clerk, *n.* a clergyman, fcholar, writer, officer
Clerk'fhip, *n.* the office, &c. of a clerk, fcholarfhip
Clev'er, *a.* fkilful, dexterous, fmart, fenfible
Clev'erly, *ad.* fkilfully, dexteroufly, fitly, well
Clev'ernefs, *n.* fkill, knowledge, dexterity, art
Clew, *n.* a ball of thread, &c. guide, corner of a fail

Clew, *v. t.* to raife the fails, to draw up
Click, *v. i.* to make a fharp and fucceffive noife
Click'er, *n.* a caller-in at a fhop, fervant, clerk
Click'et, *n.* the knocker of a door, clapper, clack
Client, *n.* an employer of an attorney, a dependant
Cliented, *a.* fupplied with or having clients
Clientéle, C'fentfhip, *n.* the condition of a client
Cliff or Clift, *n.* a rock, fteep hill, precipice, clef
Climac'ter, *n.* every feventh or ninth year
Climac'teric, *a.* fucceeding, critical, dangerous
Climac'teric, *n.* a critical year of a perfon's life
Climate, Clime, *n.* a tract of land, country, air
Climax, *n.* a rhetorical figure, gradation, afcent
Climb, *v.* climbed, climbed, *pa.* to mount by the hands as well as feet, to afcend with labor
Climber, *n.* one that climbs, a plant, an herb
Clinch, *v. t.* to hold faft, confirm, bend, faften
Clinch, *n.* a pun, witty faying, part of a cable
Clinch'er, *n.* a holdfaft, cramp, full anfwer, veffel
Cling, *v.* clung, *pret.* clung, *pa.* to twine round, ftick, hold (dry up, confume *ob.*)
Clin'ic, *n.* a fick perfon confined to his bed
Clin'ical, *a.* keeping bed, by the bed-fide
Clink, *v. t.* to found like metal; *n.* a fharp noife
Clink'er, *n.* a kind of paving brick, bad cinders
Clinoid', *a.* refembling a bed
Clin'quant, *n.* embroidery, fpangles, falfe glitter
Clip, *v.* to cut fhort, cut, embrace, confine, tara
Clip'per, *n.* one who clips, a money-cutter
Clip'ping, *n.* a part cut off; *pa.* cutting off
Clipt, *pa.* cut off with fciffors, cut, fhortened
Cliv'ers, *n.* goofegrafs or hairiff
Cloak, fee Cloke
Cloath, fee Clothe
Clock, *n.* an inftrument to fhow time, beetle, large infect, ornament, part of a ftocking
Clock'maker, *n.* one who makes or fells clocks
Clock'work, *n.* movements by weights or fprings
Clod, *n.* a lump of dirt or clay, clown, dunce, dolt
Clod, *v.* to harden into a lump
Clod'dy, *a.* full of clods, rough, hard, mean
Clod'pate, Clod'poll, *n.* a heavy or ftupid fellow
Clod'pated, *a.* ftupid, dull, heavy, thoughtlefs
Clog, *v.* to load, burden, encumber, hinder, ftick
Clog, *n.* a load, weight, obftruction, fort of fhoe
Clog'ged, *pa.* having a clog, loaded, hindered
Clog'gy, *a.* apt to clog, heavy, miry, dirty, filthy
Clois'ter, *n.* a place of religious retirement, monaf-tery, nunnery, kind of fquare with piazzas
Clois'ter, *v. t.* to fhut up in a cloifter, to confine
Clois'teral, Clois'tered, *a.* retired, folitary, lonely
Cloke, *n.* an outer garment, cover, blind
Cloke, *v. t.* to cover, hide, difguife
Clos'trefs, *n.* a nun, religious reclufe, female devo-
Cloomb, *pret.* of *to climb, ob.* (tee
Cloa'ic, *a.* relating to motion or agitation
Cloom, *v. t.* to clofe with a glutinous matter, *ob.*
Clofe, [cloze] *v.* to fhut, finifh, join, comply, inclofe
Clofe, [cloze] *n.* a fmall inclofed field, end, iffue

Clofe, a. fhut faft, private, concife, confined, near, referved, conftant, hot, full

Clófehanded, a. a. clofe fifted, covetous, niggardly

Clofehaul'ed, a. brought clofe up to the wind

Clófely, Clofe, ad. conftantly, nearly, greedily

Clófenefs, n. nearnefs, privacy, heat, a want of air

Clófer, n. a finifher, a concluder ; a. more clofe

Clos'et, n. a fmall private room, or apartment

Clos'et, v.t. to take into a clofet, to fhut up clofe

Clófure, n. an inclofure, end, conclufion, period

Clot, n. any thing clotted or curdled, a hard lump

Clot, Clot'ter, v.t. to curdle, to hang together

Cloth, n. a thing woven, linen covering, canvas

Clothe, v. t. clad, clothed, pret. clad, clothed, pa. to find clothes, drefs, cover, inveft

Clóthier, n. one who fulls and fcours cloths; In England, a maker of cloths

Clóthing, Clothes, n. a garment, drefs

Cloth'fhearer, n. one who trims or dreffes cloth

Clot'ty, a. full of clots, hard, lumpy, heavy, foul

Cloud, n. a body of vapors or duft in the air, gloom a multitude in a body, difcoloration

Cloud, v.t. to darken with clouds, to variegate

Cloud'capt, a. topped with clouds, very high, lofty

Cloudcompel'ling, pa. raifing up clouds

Cloud'ed, pa. darkened with clouds, fpots, &c.

Cloud'ily, ad. darkly, gloomily, heavily, fullenly

Cloud'inefs, n. darknefs, dulnefs, heavinefs, care

Cloud'lefs, a. free from clouds, clear, bright, pure

Cloud'y, a. dark, obfcure, gloomy, heavy, fpotted

Clove, pret. of to cleave, ob.

Clove, n. a kind of fpice, a grain or root of garlic

Clovegil'liflower, n. carnation, pinks

Clóven, pa. cleft, fplit, flit, feparated, divided

Clóvenfooted, a. having the feet cleft or divided

Clóver, n. an excellent fort of grafs, trefoil-grafs

Clóvered, a. having, fown or covered with, clover

Clough, n. a cliff, defcent, allowance in weight

Clout, n. a piece of cloth for cleanlinefs, a plate of iron on an axletree, a flender nail, a blow

Clout, v.t. to cover with a clout or cloth, to infert nails, ftrike (clout, ftruck

Clout'ed, pa. ftudded with nails, covered with a

Clown, n. a countryman, ill-bred man, churl

Clown'ifh, a. uncivil, ill-bred, rude, clumfy

Clown'ifhly, ad. rudely, clumfily, aukwardly

Clown'ifhnefs, n. rudenefs, ill-breeding

Cloy, v. t. to furfeit, glut, (fpike, nail up, ob.)

Cloy'ed, pa. furfeited, glutted, fpiked, pricked

Cloy'lefs, a. that cannot furfeit or glut, lafting

Cloy'ment, n. a cloyed ftate, fatiety, glut, fulnefs

Club, n. a heavy ftick, fhot, fociety, fuit of cards

Club, v.i. to join, to join in common expence

Club'headed, a. having a thick or large head

Club'law, n. a fighting, force, anarchy

Club'room, n. a room kept for a club to meet in

Cluck, v.i. to call together or cry like a hen

Clue, fee Clew

Clump, n. a clufter, fhapelefs piece

Clum'fily, ad. aukwardly, badly, clownifhly

Clum'finefs, n. aukwardnefs, heavinefs, thicknefs

Clum'fy, a. aukward unhandy, thick, heavy,

Clung, pret. and part. of to cling

Clus'ter, n. a bunch, heap, herd, body, collection

Clus'ter, v. to grow in bunches, collect, crowd

Clus'tered, pa. gathered into a clufter, fwelled

Clutch, n. a grafp, gripe, hand, fift, claw, talon

Clutch, v.t. to hold faft, gripe, clinch, double

Clut'ter, n. a noife, buftle, hurry, clamor; v. i. to

Clys'ter, n. an injection, a glyfter (hurry)

Coa''cervate, a. heaped up or together, added

Coacervátion, n. the act or art of heaping up

Coach, n. a kind of carriage for ftate or pleafure

Coach, v.t. to carry in or take a coach

Coacheé, n. a kind of coach open in front

Cóachhire, n. money paid for the ufe of a coach

Cóachhorfe, n. a horfe that draws a coach

Cóachhoufe, n. a houfe to put a coach in

Cóachmaker, n. a man who makes coaches, &c.

Cóachman, n. a perfon who drives a coach

Coac'tion, n. compulfion, force, reftraint, union

Coact'ive, a. having the power of forcing, aiding

Coad'jutant, Coadjútor, n. an affiftant, helper, ally

Coadjúvancy, n. united or joint help, fupport

Coad'unate, a. having more than two united

Coagment', v.t. to heap together, join, cement

Coagmentátion, n. the act of heaping together

Coag'ulate, v.t. to run into clots, curdle, congeal

Coag'ulable, a. capable of concreting (curdling

Coagulátion, n. the act of, or the body formed by

Coag'ulative, a. having power to coagulate

Coagulátor, n. that which caufes to curdle

Coag'ulum, n. runnet

Coak, n. foffil coal charred, or burnt

Coal, n. wood &c. burnt or burning, any combuftible from which the volatile parts have been expelled by fire, an inflammable foffil

Coal, v.t. to burn wood to charcoal, to fketch out

Coalblack, a. very or extremely black, horrid

Cóalery, n. the land or place where coals are dug

Coalefce', v.i. to unite, join, grow together, clofe

Coalef'cence, n. the act of uniting together, union

Coali''tion, n. an union in one mafs, junction

Cóalmine, Cóalpit, n. a place for digging coals

Cóalftone, n. a very fine coal, a kind of canal-coal

Cóaly, a. like coal, containing coal (other

Coaptátion, n. the adjuftment of parts to each

Coarct', v.t. to ftraiten, confine, contract

Coarc'tate, a. clofe or preffed together

Coarctátion, n. confinement, reftraint, contraction

Coarfe, a. not fine, rough, rude, grofs, large

Cóarfely, ad. roughly, rudely, inelegantly, badly

Cóarfenefs, n. roughnefs, rudenefs, meannefs

Coaft, n. an edge of the land, fide, fhore, border

Coaft, v. i. to fail along the coaft, to fail near to

Cóafter, n. a perfon who fails or trades coaftwife, a veffel in the coafting trade

Cóafting, n. a failing near land, or from port to

port in the fame dominions

Cóat, *n.* a man's upper garment, the upper covering of animals, any covering or integument

Coat, *v.t.* to cover with a coat or layer

Co'ati, *n.* a fpecies of weafel in America

Coax, *v.t.* to wheedle, flatter, fawn upon, entice

Cóaxer, *n.* a wheedler, flatterer, fawner, fondler

Cob, *n.* a head, the fpike of ears of maiz

Cobalt', *n.* a metal of a reddifh white, ufed to give a blue color to glafs, enamel, porcelain, &c.

Cobalt'ic, *a.* pertaining to cobalt

Cobaltic acid is a faturated combination of cobalt

Cob'ble, *n.* a fmall roundifh ftone (and oxygene

Cob'ble, *v.t.* to mend coarfely or clumfily, mend

Cob'bler, *n.* a mender of fhoes, botcher, bungler

Cob'cal, *n.* a fandal worn by ladies in the eaft

Cob'iron, *n.* an iron with a knob at one end of it

Cob'nut, *n.* a kind of nut or hazel, a boy's game

Cob'fwan, *n.* the head or leading fwan

Cob'web, *n.* a fpider's web, a trap; *a.* trifling, weak

Cocci'ferous, *a.* producing berries

Co'chenil, *n.* a blood red color

Cochinéal, *n.* a fly or infect ufed to die fcarlet

Coch'leary, Coch'leate,-[ch as k] *a.* formed like a

Cochóte, *n.* the green parrot of Mexico (fcrew

Cock, *v.t.* to fet upright, fet up the hat, fix, train

Cock. *n.* the male of birds, form of a hat, part of a gun, fpout, fmall heap of hay, matter

Cockáde, *n.* a ribbon worn on a hat

Cockatoo', *n.* a fpecies of beautiful parrots

Cock'atrice, *n.* a poifonous ferpent or viper

Cock'boat, *n.* a fmall boat belonging to a fhip

Cock'broth, *n.* broth made from boiling a cock

Cock'chaffer, *n.* the dor-beetle

Cock'crowing, *n.* the break of day, early time

Cock'er, *v.t.* to fondle, carefs, indulge, pamper

Cock'er, *n.* a perfon who handles or fights cocks

Cock'erel, *n.* a young cock, a fmall or little cock

Cock'et, *n.* a ticket from the cuftom-houfe, a feal

Cock'horfe, *a.* riding on horfeback, triumphant

Cock'ing, Cock'fight, *n.* a fight or match of cocks

Coc'kle, *n.* a genus of fhellfifh, the weed cornrofe

Coc'kle, *v.t.* to run into wrinkles, to fhrink up

Cock'led, *pa.* wrinkled up, contracted, fhelled

Coc'kleftairs, *n.* ftairs that wind and turn much

Cock'loft, *n.* the room that is over the garret

Cock'match, *n.* a battle of cocks made for money

Cock'ney, *n.* a Londoner, mean citizen, foundling

Cock'pit, *n.* place where cocks fight, part of a man of war

Cocks'comb, *n.* part of a cock's head, a plant

Cock'roach, *n.* a genus of troublefome infects

Cock'fure, *a.* quite fure or certain, very confident

Cócoa, *n.* a nut, and the tree producing it

Cocóon, *n.* an oblong ball in which the filk worm involves itfelf, formed by threads which com-

Coc'tion, *n.* the act of boiling, digeftion (pofe filk

Cod, *n.* a feafifh, the bag or hufks of feeds

Cod, *v.i.* to inclofe in or produce cods

Cod'dle, *v.t.* to parboil or foften in water

Code, *n.* a book or volume of the civil law, a book

Cod''ger, *n.* a laborer, a ruftic

Cod'icil, *n.* an addition or fupplement to a will

Codille', *n.* a term at ombre, a winning of a game

Cod'lin, *n.* a fort of early apple

Cod'line, *n.* line or cord for taking codfifh

Cod'ling, *n.* a young codfifh

Coef'ficacy, Coeffi''ciency, *n.* a joint power

Coeffi'cient, *a.* working together, contributing

Coemp'tion, *n.* the act buying up the whole

Coéqual, *a.* equal with, being in the fame ftate

Coequal'ity, Coéqualnefs, *n.* an equal or like ftate

Coéqualed, *a.* reduced to a mean or equality

Coerce', *v.t.* to reftrain by force, compel, check

Coer'cible, *a.* that is capable of being reftrained

Coer'cion, *n.* force, reftraint, check, limitation

Coer'cive, *a.* ferving to reftrain or check, forcible

Coer'civenefs, *n.* a coercive ftate, forciblenefs

Coeffen'tial, *a.* that partakes of the fame effence

Coeffential'ity, *n.* a partaking of the fame effence

Coetáneous, *a.* being of the fame age or time

Coeter'nal, *a.* equally eternal with another

Coeternity, *n.* equal exiftence from eternity

Coéval, *a.* a cotemporary, one of the fame age

Coéval, Coévous, *a.* being of the fame age, equal

Coexift', *v.i.* to exift together or at one time

Coexift'ence, *n.* exiftence at the fame time

Coexift'ent, *a.* exifting at one or the fame time

Coextend', *v.t.* to extend to the fame fpace or time

Coexten'fion, *n.* an equal extenfion

Coextens'ive, *a.* equally extenfive

Coextens'ivenefs, *n.* equal extenfion

Coffee, *n.* the name of a berry and liquor

Cof'feehoufe, *n.* a houfe where coffee, &c. is fold

Cof'feemill, *n.* a mill to grind coffee by

Cof'feepot, *n.* a pot for making coffee in

Cof'fer, *n.* a cheft, a treafure; *v.t.* to treafure up

Cof'ferer, *n.* a principal court officer, a treafurer

Cof'fin, *n.* a cheft for dead bodies, mold, hoof

Cof'fin, *v.t.* to fhut into a coffin, fhut up, mold

Cof'fined, *pa.* put into or inclofed in a coffin

Cog, *v.* to play unfairly, lie, wheedle, fix cogs

Cog, *n.* the tooth of a wheel, a kind of boat

Coguar', *n.* a carnivorous quadruped of America

Cógency, *n.* force, ftrength, power of conviction

Cógent, *a.* forcible, ftrong, powerful, convincing

Cógently, *ad.* forcibly, ftrongly, with power

Cog'ger, *n.* one who cogs, a flatterer, *not ufed*

Cogitation, *n.* thought, meditation, care, purpofe

Co''gitative, *a.* given to thought or meditation

Cog'nate, *a.* born together, like, related, allied

Cognátion, *n.* kindred, relationfhip, defcent

Cogni''tion, *n.* knowledge, conviction, trial

Cog'nitive, *a.* having the power of knowing

Cog'nizable, *a.* proper to be tried (diction

Cog'nizance, *n.* judicial notice, knowledge, jurif-

Cognizor', *n.* one who paffes a fine to another perfon

Cognizée, *n.* one to whom a fine is acknowledged

Cognom'inal, *a.* being ofthe fame name, cognizee, &c.

Cognos'cible, *a.* that may be known or found out

Cohab'it, *v.i.* to live together as man and wife

Cohab'itant, *n.* a perfon living in the fame place

Cohabitátion, *n.* the act of living together

Cohéir, (coáre) *n.* a joint heir with another

Coheir'efs, *n.* a woman that is a joint heirefs

Cohére, *v.i.* to ftick together, agree, fuit, fit

Cohérence or Cohérency, *n.* connexion, fitnefs

Cohérent, *a.* fticking together, confiftent, fuited

Cohéfion, *n.* a ftate of union, a clofe connexion

Cohéfive, *a.* having a fticking quality, fticky

Cohéfivenefs, *n.* quality of cohering

Cohib'it, *v.t.* to reftrain, hinder, hold in, curb

Cóhobate, *v.t.* to diftil again or a fecond time

Cohobátion, *n.* a repeated or fecond diftillation

Cohóes, *n.* a fall of water, cateract

Cóhort, *n.* a troop of Roman foldiers about 500

Coif, *n.* a woman's headdrefs, cap, ferjeant's cap

Coif'ed, *a.* wearing a cap, made a ferjeant at law

Coif'fure, *n.* a headdrefs, a cap

Coil, *v.t.* to roll up a rope, to wind up in a ring

Coil, *n.* a circular form of a rope (tumult, *ob.*)

Coin, *n.* a corner, money ftamped, cafh, payment

Coin, *v.t.* to make money, ftamp, forge, invent

Coin'age, *n.* coining, money coined, a forgery

Coincíde, *v.i.* to agree, concur, meet, fuit, fit

Coin'cidence, *n.* agreement, concurrence, union

Coin'cident, *a.* agreeing with, confiftent, united

Coin'ed, *pa.* made into money, forged, invented

Coin'er, *n.* a maker of money, inventor, devifer

Coin'ing, *n.* the act or art of making money

Cois'tril, *n.* a cowardly cock, coward, *ob.*

Coi''tion, *n.* a copulation, meeting, union, junction

Co'jamet, *n.* the pecar, a tropical animal like a boar

Cojopol'lin, *n.* a Mexican animal like a moufe and pig   (wolf

Cojóte, *n.* a Mexican quadruped like a dog and

Cojoin', *v.t.* to unite in the fame thing

Col'bertine, *n.* a kind of lace for women

Cold, *a.* not hot, not hafty, chafte, coy, referved

Cold, *n.* cold weather, coldnefs, chilnefs, a diforder

Cóldfinch, *n.* a bird feen in the weft of England

Cóldifh, *a.* rather cold, fhy, referved, coy

Cóldly, *ad.* indifferently, carelefsly, coyly, oddly

Cóldnefs, *n.* a want of heat, indifference, chaftity

Cóldfhort, *a.* brittle when cold, as fome metals

Cóleperch, *n.* a fmall fifh, lefs than a perch

Cólewort, *n.* a fort of cabbage

Col'ic, *n.* a diftemper affecting the bowels

Col'in, *n.* an American bird of the partridge kind

Collapfe', *v.i.* to fall clofe or together

Collapfe', *n.* a clofing, as the fides of a blood veffel

Col'lar, *n.* fomething put around the neck, a band

Col'lar, *v.t.* to feize by the collar, to roll hard up

Colláte, *v.t.* to compare, examin, prefer, raife

Collat'eral, *a.* fet fide by fide, concurrent, like

Collat'erally, *ad.* in a collatteral manner, clofely

Collátion, *n.* repaft, treat, gift, comparifon

Col'lative, *a.* that may be conferred by a bifhop in his own right

Collátor, *n.* one who compares, raifes or prefers

Col'league, *n.* a partner; *v.i.* to unite with or in

Collect', *v.t.* to gather, get, recover, infer

Col'lect, *n.* a fhort comprehenfive prayer

Collect'ed, *pa.* gathered, inferred, cool, firm

Collect'ednefs, *n.* coolnefs of mind, felf-poffeffion

Colláneous, *a.* collected, compiled from various authors

Collect'ible, *a.* that may be gathered or deduced

Collec'tion, *n.* the act of collecting, money or things collected, an affembly, an inference

Collect'itious, *a.* collected, gathered, gleaned

Collect'ive, *a.* apt to gather or infer, whole, full

Collect'ively, *ad.* in a body, together, wholly

Collect'or, *n.* a gatherer, a receiver of taxes or du-

Col'lege, *n.* a houfe of learning, a fociety   (ties

Collégial, *æ.* of or belonging to a college

Collégian, Collégiate, *n.* a member of a college

Collégiate, *a.* having a college, in or like a college

Col'let, *n.* that part of a ring where a ftone is fet

Collíde, *v.t.* to dafh or ftrike together, *ob.*

Col'lier, *n.* a digger of or dealer in coals, a coalfhip

Col'liery, *n.* a place where coals are dug

Colligátion, *n.* the act or art of binding together

Col'liquate, *v.t.* to melt, diffolve, liquify, foften

Col'liquable, *a.* that may be rendered liquid

Colliquátion, *n.* the act of melting

Colliquative, *a.* tending to melt or diffolve

Colliquefac'tion, *n.* the act of melting together

Colli''fion, *n.* a ftriking together, clafh, ftroke

Col'locate, *v.t.* to place, fet in order, ftation

Col'locate, *a.* put into fome place or ftation, fet

Collocátion, *n.* the act or art of placing together

Col'lop, *n.* a fmall cut or flice of meat, a child

Collóquial, *a.* relating to converfation, familiar

Col'loquy, *n.* a conference, converfation, talk

Col'low, Col'ly, *n.* the black grime of coals, foot

Colluctátion, *n.* a conteft, oppofition, ftruggle

Collúfion, *n.* a fecret agreement to defraud

Collúfive, *a.* fraudulent, deceitful, combined

Collúfively, *ad.* in a collufive manner, falfely

Col'ly, *v.t.* to grime with coal, black, fmut

Coloc'olo, *n.* the water raven, an Indian bird

Cólon, *n.* the point (:), the great gut, a member

Col'onel, (curnel) *n.* commander of a regiment

Co'lonelfhip, *n.* the office or rank of a colonel

Co'lonelcy, *n.* the office or grade of a colonel

Colónial, *a.* belonging to, or living in, a colony

Colonizátion, *n.* the act of fettling a new colony

Col'onize, *v.t.* to plant or fettle with inhabitants

Colonnáde, *n.* a row or fet of pillars

Col'ony, *n.* a plantation from the mother country

Col'ophony, *n.* rofin, grofs turpentine, pitch

Co'oquin'tida, *n.* the bitter apple

Col'or, (culler) *n.* a green, red, blue, &c. a pretence

Col'or, *v.t.* to dye, tinge, ftain, blufh, cloak, excufe

Col'orable, a. plaufible, fpecious, probable, likely
Col'orably, ad. in a fpecious manner, probably
Col'orate, a. colored, dyed, tinged, ftained, marked
Col'ored, pa. painted, tinged, ftreaked, palliated
Colorif'ic, a. that is able to produce color or tint
Col'oring, n. an art in painting, color, art, excufe
Col'orift, n. one who excels in coloring pictures
Color'lefs, a. having no color, quite pale, clear
Col'ors, n. a banner, flag, ftreamer, victory, honor
Colos'fian, n. a native of Coloffus in Afia
Colofs'us, n. a very large ftatue, a giant
Colofséan, Colofs'al, a. gigantic, very large, huge
Côlt, n. a young horfe, a man without experience ;
Côltifh, a. wanton, frifky, gay   (v. t. to befool
Côlter, n. the fore iron in a plow
Col'uber, n. a genus of ferpents with fcaly tails
Colum'bary, n. a dovehoufe, a pigeonhoufe
Col'umbine, a. of, like or belonging to a pigeon,
a genus of plants
Colum'bo, n. a plant whofe root is ufed as medicinal
Col'umn, n. a round pillar, part of a page or troops
Colum'nar, a. formed in or like columns
Co'lures, n. two great circles, interfecting at the
folftices
Comart', n. an agreement, compact, bargain, ob.
Comâte, n. a companion, affociate, ob.   (hairy
Co'mate, a. furrounded by a bufhy appearance,
Comatôfe, a. much given to fleep, drowfy, heavy
Comb, n. an inftrument, creft, part, dry meafure
Comb, v. t. to divide, drefs, trim, clean, fmooth
Comb'lefs, a. deftitute of a comb or caruncle
Com'bat, n. a battle, fight, duel, conteft, difpute
Com'bat, v. to fight, engage, conteft, oppofe, refift
Com'batant, n. one who fights, a champion
Com'binate, a. betrothed, fettled, promifed, ob.
Combinâtion, n. an affociation, confpiracy, plot
Combíne, v. t. to unite, agree, link, join
Combínable, a. capable of being combined
Combíned, pa. joined or united together, varied
Cómbbird, n. a gallinaceous bird of Africa
Com'bear, n. a long flender fifh with a red back
Combus'tible, a. that will eafily take fire or burn
Combuftibil'ity, Combus'tiblenefs, n. the quality
of taking fire and burning
Combus'tion, n. a burning, or the union of a com-
buftible body with oxygene, attended with
light and heat—alfo hurry, confufion
Some, (cum) v. i. came, come ; pret. come ; pa. to
draw near, move, be quick, proceed, happen
Comédian, n. an actor or writer of comedies
Com'edy, n. a laughable or droll dramatic piece
Come'linefs, n. grace, beauty, decency, fitnefs
Come'ly, a. graceful, decent, handfome, proper
Come'ly, ad. gracefully, handfomely, properly
Com'er, n. one that comes, one that draws near
Com'et, n. a kind of ftar, a blazing-ftar
Com'fit, (cumfit) n. a fweatmeat, or preferve
Com'fit, v. t. to preferve fruit and dry it
Com'fort, (cumfort) v. t. to eafe, cheer, revive

Com'fort, n. fupport, affiftance, eafe, pleafure, joy
Com'fortable, a. giving comfort, pleafing
Com'fortably, ad. with comfort, pleafingly
Com'forter, n. one who comforts, one who fupports
Com'fortlefs, a. being without comfort, forlorn
Com'frey, (cumfrey) n. a genus of plants
Com'ic, a. relating to comedy, raifing mirth
Com'ical, a. diverting, merry, droll, queer, odd
Com'ically, ad. in a comical, droll, or odd manner
Com'ing, a. an arrival, the act of drawing near
Com'ing, pa. advancing, future, fond, forward
Comi'tial, a. relating to Roman affembl es
Com'ma, n. the point (,) implying a little paufe
Command', v. t. to order, direct, govern, overlook
Command', n. the right of commanding, an order
Command'able, a. that may be commanded
Commandant', n. a temporary commander
Command'er, n. a chief, leader, mallet   (jeftic
Command'ing, pa. ordering, governing, ma-
Command'ment, n. a command, order, law, power
Command'refs, n. a woman of chief power or rule
Commatérial, a. confifting of the fame matter
Commem'orable, a. worthy to be commemorated
Commem'orate, v. to preferve the memory, to ce-
Commemorátion, n. a public celebration (lebrate
Commem'orative, a. preferving a remembrance
Commence', v. t. to begin, affume, take
Commence'ment, n. a beginning, date, meeting
Commend', v. t. to recommend, praife, intruft
Commend'able, a. deferving praife, worthy, good
Commend'ably, ad. in a praifeworthy manner
Commend'am, n. a void or doubl e benefice
Commendátion, n. recommendation, praife
Commend'atory, a. tending to recommend
Commend'er, n. one who commends, a praifer
Commenfal'ity, n. a fellowfhip of table. ob.   (fure
Commens'urable, a. having fome common mea-
Commenfurabil'ity, Commens'urablenefs, n. a ca-
pacity of being compared with another in
meafure, equal proportion
Commens'urate, a. reducible to a meafure, equal,
proportionable, commenfurable
Commenfurátion, n. a reduction to fome meafure.
Com'ment, v. i. to explain, glofs, write notes
Com'ment, Com'mentary, n. an explanation, notes
Commentátor, Com'menter, n. one who explains
Commenti'tious, a. imaginary, feigned, forged
Com'merce, v. i. to hold a correfpondence, ob.
Com'merce, n. trade, traffic, connexion, a game
Commer'cial, a. relating to trade, trading
Com'mercing, pa. holding intercourfe, dealing
Com'migrate, v. i. to remove or go away in a body
Commigrátion, n. the act of removing in a body
Commination, n. a threatening of punifhment
Commin'gle, v. t. to mix, blend or join together
Commin''gling, pa. mixing, uniting in one mafs
Comminúte, v. t. to grind, to reduce to powder
Comminútion, n. the act of reducing to fmall parts
Commis'erable, a. deferving pity, wretched, mean

Commis'erate, v. t. to pity, to take or have pity on
Commiferátion, n. compaſſion, pity, fympathy,
Com'miſſary, n. a delegate, deputy, officer (feeling
Commiſſárial, a. pertaining to a commiſſary
Commis'ſion, n. a truſt, warrant of office, order
Commis'ſion, Commis'ſionate, v. t. to empower,
authorize, intruſt, appoint, depute, delegate
Commis'ſioner, n. one who is empowered to act
Commiſs'ure, n. a joint, feam, future, pore
Commit', v. t. to impriſon, ſend, do, intruſt, to
pledge by ſome act (ting
Commit'ment, n. the act of, or order for, commit-
Commit'tee, n. a ſelect number of men chofen to
confider, examin or manage, any matter
Commit'ter, n. one who commits or impriſons
Commit'tible, a. that is liable to be committed
Commix', v. t. to mingle together, blend, unite
Commix'ion, Commix'ture, n. a mixture, a com-
Commóde, n. a woman's headdreſs (pound
Commódious, a. convenient, fuitable, ufeful, fit
Commódiouſly, ad. conveniently, fitly, properly
Commódiouſneſs, n. convenience, advantage, ufe
Commod'ity, n. any article of traffic, goods, wares,
produce; in the fenſe of intereſt, profit, ufe, ob.
Com'modore, n. the commander of a fquadron
Com'mon, a. equal, public, ufual, vulgar, mean
Com'mon, Com'mons, n. land belonging to a num-
ber and not divided or feparated by fences
Com'mon, v. i. to have a right of common, to
diet in common
Com'monable, a. held in common, public
Com'monage, n. a right to feed on a common
Com'monalty, n. the bulk or body of the people
Com'moner, n. one of the people not ennobled
Com'monly, Com'mon, ad. frequently, ufually
Com'monneſs, n. frequency, an equal ſhare
Com'monplace, a. often ufed, trite, frequent
Commonpláce, v. t. to reduce to general heads
Commonpláce-book, n. a book for general heads
Com'mons, n. pl. the commonalty, parliament-
men, food on equal pay, food, proportion, ſhare
Com'monweal, n. public good or welfare
Commonwealth', n. a government in which the
people bear the chief rule, a republic, the public
Com'morance, n. a dwelling, refidence, abode
Com'morant, a. dwelling, refiding, abiding
Commótion, n. a tumult, difturbance, uneafineſs
Commóve, v. t. to difturb, unfettle, ob.
Commúne, v. i. to converfe, confer, examine
Commúne, n. a territorial diftrict in France
Communal, a. pertaining to a commune
Commúnicable, a. that may be communicated
Communicant, n. one who receives the commun-
ion of the Lord's ſupper (Lord's ſupper
Commúnicate, v. to impart, reveal, receive the
Communication, n. the act of imparting or ex-
changing, a converfation, boundary, paſſage
Commúnicative, a. free, ready, to impart, open,
Commúnicativeneſs, n. freeneſs, openneſs (kind

Commúnion, n. a taking of the Lord's ſupper,
union in faith, union, fellowſhip, intercourfe
Commúnity, n. a fociety, a common poſſeſſion
Commutabil'ity, n. a commutable quality, change
Commútable, a. that may be exchanged or put off
Commutátion, n. a change of one thing for another
Commútative, a. relating to exchange or barter
Commúte, v. t. to exchange, atone, buy off
Commútual, a. mutual, reciprocal, alternate, like
Com'pact, n. a contract, bargain, fet agreement
Compact', v. t. to join together, to league with
Compact', a. firm, clofe, folid, ftout, brief, exact
Compact'ile, a. that may be eafily compacted
Compact'ly, ad. firmly, clofely, neatly (neſs
Compact'neſs, Compact'edneſs, n. firmneſs, clofe-
Compact'ure, Compaginátion, n. ftructure, ob.
Compan'ion, n. a partner, comrade, aſſociate, the
porch or cover of the entrance into a cabin
Compan'ionable, a. fit for a companion
Com'pany, (company) n. aſſembly of perfons,
fellowſhip, firm or partnerſhip, a ſhip's crew, a
military band
Com'pany, v. to aſſociate with, to attend, ob.
Com'parable, a. of equal regard or value, like
Compar'ative, a. that is capable of comparifon
Compar'atively, ad. by or by way of comparifon
Compáre, v. t. to liken, examin to find agree-
ment or difagreement; in the fenfe of procure ob.
Compáre, n. a comparifon, likeneſs, illuſtration
Compar'ifon, n. a fimile, likeneſs, juſt eftimate
Compart', v. t. to divide, arrange, mark out, part
Compart'iment, n. a divifion of a picture or defign
Comparti'tion, n. the act of dividing, a divifion
Com'paſs, (cum'paſs) v. t. to furround, grafp, ob-
tain, effect, accomplifh
Com'paſs, n. a circle, fpace, limits, moderation
Com'paſſes, n. pl. an inſtrument to make circles
Compaſſ'ion, n. pity, mercy, feeling; v. t. to pity
Compaſſ'ionate, a. merciful, tender; v. t. to pity
Compaſſ'ionately, ad. mercifully, tenderly, kindly
Compatibil'ity, Compat'ibleneſs, n. fuitableneſs
Compat'ible, a. confiſtent, agreeable, fit
Compat'ibly, ad. confiftently, agreeably
Compat'riot, n. a perfon of the fame country
Compéer, n. an equal, peer, companion, colleague
Compéer, v. to be equal with or to, match, fuit
Compel', v. t. to force, oblige, conſtrain, drive
Compellátion, n. the ſtyle of addreſs, an addreſs
Compel'ler, n. one who compels, one who forces
Compend'ious, a. ſhort, brief, concife, ſummary
Compend'iouſly, ad. ſhortly, briefly, concifely
Compend'iouſneſs, n. ſhortneſs, concifeneſs, brev-
Compend'ium, Com'pend, n. an abridgement (ity
Com'penſate, v. t. to make amends, counter-
Com'penſated, pa. requited, paid (balance
Compenſátion, n. a recompence, amends, return
Compenſ'ative, a. making amends
Com'petence, Com'petency, n. fufficiency, power
Com'petent, ad. fit, fuitable, qualified, fufficient

Com'petently, _ad._ properly, fitly, reasonably
Competibil'ity, _n._ fuitableneſs, fitneſs, _ob._
Compet'ible, _a._ fuitable to, confiſtent with, _ob._
Competi''tion,_n._ conteſt, rivalſhip, ſtrife, diſpute
Compet'itor, _n._ a rival, opponent, claimant
Compilátion, _n._ a collection of matter, a robbing
Compíle, _v. t._ to collect and write from authors
Compílement, _n._ the act or art of compiling (ers
Compíler, _n._ a writer of books collected from oth-
Complácency, _n._ gratification of mind, approba-
tion, calm pleaſure; in the ſenſe of civility, _ob._
Complácent, _a._ cheerful, civil, affable, ſoft, kind
Compláin, _v._ to murmur, lament, bewail, accuſe
Compláinant, _n._ a plaintiff in a ſuit, complainer
Compláiner, _n._ one who complains or laments
Compláint, _n._ a lamentation, accuſation, diſeaſe
Com'plaiſance, _n._ civility, an obliging behavior
Com'plaiſant, _a._ civil, courteous, obliging, kind
Com'plaiſantly, _ad._ in a civil or obliging manner
Complánate, Compláne,_v.t._to level,to ſmooth,_ob._
Com'plement, _n._ the full number, perfection
Complement'al, _a._ filling up, completing, adding
Compléte,_a._ perfect, full, finiſhed
Compléte, _v. t._ to perfect, to finiſh
Complétely, _ad._ fully, perfectly, entirely, wholly
Complétement, _n._ the act of completing, fulneſs
Compléteneſs, _n._ perfection, a perfect ſtate
Complétion, _n._ fulfilling, perfect ſtate, end
Complétive, _a._ denoting completion
Com'plex, _a._ compounded of many parts (lection
Com'plex, Complex'edneſs,_n._ a compound, a col-
Complex'neſs, Complex'ity, _n._ complex ſtate
Complex'ion, _n._ the color of the face, conſtitution
Complex'ional, _v._ belonging to the complexion
Complex'ly, _ad._ intricately, obſcurely, darkly
Complíance, _n._ the act of yelding, ſubmiſſion
Complíant, _a._ yelding, bending, civil, kind
Com'plicate, _v. t._ to entangle, fold together, unite
Com'plicate, _a._ compounded of many parts, dark
Com'plicated _pa._ entangled, intricate, dark
Com'plicateneſs, _n._ difficulty, intricacy, darkneſs
Complicátion, _n._ an interweaving, a fold
Com'plice, _n._ a partner in an ill action, _ob._
Complíſed, _pa._ ſubmitted or agreed to, granted
Complíer, _n._ a perſon who is of an eaſy temper
Com'pliment, _n._ an act of civility, obliging, words
Com'pliment, _v. t._ to uſe compliments, to flatter
Compliment'al, _a._ expreſſive of reſpect, polite
Compliment'ally, _ad._ civilly, obligingly, kindly
Compliment'ary, _a._ complimental, obliging, kind
Com'pline,_n._ evening-ſervice, laſt prayers or devo-
Com'plot, _n._ a plot, combination, conſpiracy (tion
Complot', _v. t._ to plot, conſpire, join, unite
Complot'ter, _n._ a joint plotter, a joint conſpirator
Comply', _v. i._ to yield or ſubmit to, grant, ſuit
Com'ponent, _a._ conſtituent, forming, compoſing
Compórt, _v._ to bear, endure, agree, ſuit, behave
Compórt, Compórtment, _n._ behavior, conduct
Compórtable, _a._ conſiſtent, ſuitable, proper, fit

Compóſe, _v. t._ to quiet, ſettle, put together, form
Compóſed, _pa._ formed, calm, ſedate, ſerious
Compóſedly, _ad._ calmly, ſedately, ſeriouſly
Compóſedneſs,_n._ calmneſs, ſedateneſs, eaſe
Compóſer, _n._ an author, writer, former, uniter
Com'poſit, _a._ the laſt of the orders of columns
Compoſi''tion, _n._ a mixture, invention, agreement
to accept leſs than a debt, work, book
Compos'itor, _n._ one who ſets types in printing
Com'poſt, _n._ a mixture of ſubſtances for manure
Compóſt, _v. t._ to lay on manure, to enrich earth
Compóſure, _n._ calmneſs, order, form, diſpoſition
Compotátion, _n._ a drinking match
Compound', _v._ to mingle, mix, come to terms
Com'pound, _n._ a maſs of ingredients, a mixture
Compóund'able, _a._ that may be compounded
Compound'ed, _pa._ mixed, compoſed, formed
Compound'er,_n._ one who brings to terms or mixes
Comprehend', _v.t._to include, conceive, underſtand
Comprehen'ſible, _a._ intelligible, conceivable
Comprehen'ſion, _n._ knowledge, capacity, epitome
Comprehen'ſive, _a._ capacious, full, extenſive
Comprehen'ſively, _ad._ in an extenſive manner
Comprehen'ſiveneſs, _n._ the quality of containing
much in few words or a narrow compaſs
Compreſs', _v. t._ to ſqueeze cloſe, embrace, reduce
Com'preſs,_n._ a bolſter of linen rags, a bandage
Compreſs'ible, _a._ capable of being compreſſed
Compreſſibil'ity, Compreſs'ibleneſs, _n._ the quality
of being compreſſible
Compreſ''ſion, _n._ the act of bringing parts near
Compreſs'or, _n._ a muſcle which compreſſes
Compreſs'ure, _n._ the act of preſſing hard againſt
Comprint', _v. i._ to print another perſon's copy
Compríſe, _v. t._ to contain, include, hold, take in
Comprobátion, _n._ a full proof, a joint atteſtation
Com'promiſe,_n._ an agreement, a bargain
Com'promiſe, _v._ to compound, adjuſt, make up
Com'promiſed, _pa._ ſettled, adjuſted, made up
Com'promit, _v. t._ to commit, pledge, engage
Compt'ible,_a._ accountable, reſponſible, _ob._
Comptrol'ler, _n._ a palpable blunder, ſee controller
Compuls'atory,_a._ compelling, obliging, forcing
Compul'ſion, _n._ the act of compelling, force
Compuls'ive, Compuls'ory, _a._ obliging, forcing
Compuls'ively, Compuls'orily, _ad._ by violence
Compunc'tion, _n._ a pricking, remorſe, ſorrow
Compunc'tious, Compunc'tive, _a._ cauſing remorſe
Compurgátion, _n._ a vouching for another by oath
Compurgátor, _n._ one who vouches for another
Compútable, _a._ that may be numbered up
Computátion, _n._ a calculation, the ſum computed
Compúte, _v. t._ to calculate, count, reckon, think
Compúte, _n._ a computation, calculation, reſult
Compúted, _pa._ calculated, counted, reckoned
Compúter, Com'putiſt, _n._ a calculator, a reckoner
Com'rade, _n._ a companion, intimate partner, aſſo-
ciate   (contra, againſt
Con, prefix denoting _with_ or _joint_, or uſed for

Con, v. t. to study, know, give, render, fix
Concam'erate, v. t. to arch over, to vault, ob.
Concat'enate, v. t. to link or join together
Concatenátion, n. an uniting, union, series of links
Con'cave, a. hollow in the inside, arched
Concav'ity, n. inside, hollowness of a round body
Concávous, a. regularly hollowed, concave
Concávously, ad. in a concave or hollow manner
Conceál, v. t. to hide, keep secret or close, cover
Conceálable, a. that may be concealed or hidden
Conceáler, n. one who conceals, one who hides
Conceálment, n. the act of hiding, secrecy, shelter
Concéde, v. t. to admit, grant, yield, give up
Conceit, n. a fancy, idea, opinion, fondness, pride
Conceit, v. t. to imagin, fancy, believe, suppose
Concéited, pa. imagined, proud, vain, affected
Conceitedly, ad. proudly, whimsically, fancifully
Conceitedness, n. pride, fantasticalness, conceit
Conceitless, a. thoughtless, stupid, dull, ob.
Concéivable, a. that may be conceived (able
Conceivableness, n. the quality of being conceiv-
Concéivably, ad. intelligibly (think
Concéive, v. to become with child, understand,
Concéiver, n. one who conceives or understands
Concent', n. harmony, agreement, consistency ob.
Concent'rate, v. t. to bring into a narrow compass
Concentra'tion, n. the act of drawing to a center
or point
Concen''ter, v. to come or bring to one point
Concent'ric, a. having one and the same center
Concent'ring, pa. tending to one point, uniting
Concep'tacle, n. what contains any thing, a seed
vessel with one valve and loose seeds
Concep'tible, a. that may be conceived, ob.
Concep'tion, n. a formation in the womb, a notion
Concep'tive, a. capable of conceiving, forming
Concern', v. t. to affect, move, trouble, belong to
Concern', n. an affair, importance, care, trouble
Concern'ed, pa. engaged, affected, troubled
Concern'ing, pa. relating to, regarding
Concern'ment, n. a concern, affair, business, care
Concert', v. t. to contrive, to settle privately
Con'cert, n. a piece of music in several parts, har-
Concert'o, n. music made for a concert (mony
Conces''sion, n. a thing yielded, grant, permission
Conces'sionary, a. yielded by indulgence
Conces's'ive, a. yielded by way of concession
Conces's'ively, ad. by way of concession or grant
Conch, (ch as k) n. a shellfish or the shell
Conchoid', n. a curve approaching a line without
touching it. (a shell
Conchoid'al, a. pertaining to or like a conchoid or
Conchyol'ogy, n. the science of shellfish
Concil'iate, v. t. to gain, get, procure, reconcile
Concil'iating, pa. gaining, reconciling, healing
Conciliátion, n. the act of reconciling, an union
Conciliátor, n. a reconciler, peacemaker, friend
Concil'iatory, a. tending to reconcile, healing
Concin'nity, n. neatness, fitness, good connexion

Concin'nous, a. neat, fit, becoming, proper
Con'cio, n. a meeting of clergymen
Concíse, a. short, brief, contracted, trifling
Concísely, ad. shortly, briefly, in few words
Concíseness, n. shortness, briefness, brevity, force
Conci''sion, n. a cutting off or short, an excision
Concitátion, n. a stirring up or disturbing, noise
Conclamátion, n. an exclamation, shout, noise
Con'clave, n. an assembly of cardinals (infer
Conclúde, v. t. to finish, close, determin, settle,
Conclúdency, n. a consequence, a regular proof, ob.
Conclúdent, a. decisive, convincing, forcible, ob.
Conclúder, n. one who concludes, ends or infers
Conclúsible, a. determinable, admitting of proof, ob.
Conclúsion, n. a close, end, decision, consequence
Conclúsive, a. decisive, convincing, full, strong
Conclúsively, ad. decisively, fully, satisfactorily
Conclúsiveness, n. the power of determining
Concoag'ulate, v. t. to congeal together, ob.
Concoct', v. t. to digest in the stomach, to purify
Concoc'tion, n. digestion in the stomach, a boiling
Concol'or, a. of the same color, like, similar, ob.
Concom'itance, n. the act of subsisting together
Concom'itant, a. accompanying, joined with or to
Concom'itant, n. a companion, a close attendant
Concom'itate, v. t. to be joined with any thing, ob.
Con'cord, n. agreement, union, harmony, consent
Concord'ance, n. an index to the scriptures
Concord'ant, a. agreeable, agreeing, suitable
Concord'at, n. a compact, covenant, agreement
Concor'porate, v. t. to mix in one mass, ob.
Con'course, n. persons assembled, resort, meeting
Concres'cence, n. a joining of different particles
Concres'cible, a. that may concrete together
Concréte, v. t. to unite or form into one mass
Con'crete, a. composed of different matters
Concrétely, ad. in a concrete manner
Concréteness, n. a state of being concrete
Concréte, n. a mass or body formed by concretion
Concre''tion, n. an union of various parts, a mass
Concrétive, a. of or causing concretion, uniting
Concúbinage, n. the keeping of a mistress, forni-
Conc'ubine, n. a kept mistress (cation
Concúpiscence, n. an irregular desire, lust, sense
Concúpiscent, a. lustful, lewd, sensual, fond
Concupis'cible, a. impressing desire, very desirable
Concupis'cibleness, n. a concupscible quality
Concur', v. i. to agree, join, unite, meet, help
Concur'rence, n. union, joint claim, help
Concur'rent, a. acting in conjunction, uniting
Concus''sion, n. a shaking, shock of an earthquake
Concus'sionary, a. causing a concussion, shaking
Concus's'ive, a. able or tending to shake
Condemn', v. t. to pass sentence upon, to blame
Condemn'able, a. blameable, improper, wrong
Condemn'ableness, n. a condemnable quality
Condemnátion, n. a sentence to punishment
Condem'natory, a. passing condemnation, fatal
Condem'ned, pa. found guilty, blamed, censured

Condem'ner, *n.* one who condemns or blames
Condens'able, *a.* that may or can be condensed
Condens'ate, *v.* to make or grow thick or dark
Condens'ate, *a.* made thick or dark, thickened
Condensâtion, *n.* the act of thickening a body
Condenfe', *v.* to make or grow thicker
Condenfe', *a.* thick, clofe, denfe, contracted
Condens'er, *n.* a veffel for condenfing air
Condefcend', *v. i.* to yield, fubmit, confent
Condefcend'ing, *pa,* fubmitting, obliging
Condefcend'ingly, *ad.* obligingly, civilly, kindly
Condefcen'fion, *n.* fubmiffion, compliance, cour-
Condign, *a.* deferved, fuitable, due, juft (tefy
Condîgnly, *ad.* fitly, properly, juftly, worthily
Condîgnnefs, *n.* fuitablenefs, juftnefs
Con'diment, *n.* a feafoning, fauce, pickle, zeft
Con'dite, *v. t.* to feafon, pickle, *ob.*
Condi''tion, *n.* a term of agreement, article, pro-
perty, difpofition, temper, quality, rank, ftate
Condi''tion, Condi''tionate, *v. i.* to make terms
Condi''tional, *a.* implying conditions or terms
Condi''tionally, *ad.* with limitation, upon terms
Condi''tionary, *a.* agreed upon, ftipulated, *ob,*
Condi''tionate, *a.* fettled on terms, conditional, *ob.*
Condi''tioned, *a.* having qualities, or ftipulations
Condôle, *v.* to lament, mourn, grieve with others
Condôlement, *n.* grief, forrow, mutual diftrefs
Condôlence, *n,* grief for another's lofs, fympathy
Con'doma, *n.* a quadruped of the goat kind
Con'dor, *n.* a fowl of S, America, the largeft known
Coadúce, *v.* to help, promote, ferve, lead, conduct
Condúcible, *a.* having the power of conducing
Condúcive, *a.* promoting, contributing
Condúcivenefs, *n.* a conducive or helping quality
Con'duct, *n.* behavior, management, direction
Conduct', *v.t.* to lead, guide, manage, direct, behave
Conducti''tious, *a.* hired, employed, engaged
Conduct'or, *n.* a leader, director, general, chief
Con'duit, *n.* a waterpipe, pipe, canal, duct, cock
Condúplicate, *a.* doubled together
Conduplicâtion, *n.* a doubling or folding over
Con'dyl, *n.* a protuberance on a bone (er jaw
Condyloid', *n.* end of the pofterior part of the low-
Con'epate, *n.* an animal of the weafel kind
Cone, *n.* a folid body in the form of a fugarloaf
Confab'ulate, *v. i.* to talk together, converfe, *not ufed*
Confabulâtion, *n.* eafy converfation, chat, talk
Confab'ulatory, *a.* relating to converfation (ther
Confarriâtion, *n.* marriage by eating bread toge-
Con'fect, Confec'tion, *n.* a fweetmeat, a mixture
Confec'tionary, *n.* a place to put fweetmeats in
Confec'tioner, *n.* one who fells fweetmeats
Confed'eracy, *n.* a league, bond, union, engagment
Confed'erate, *v. t.* to league, unite, ally, combine
Confed'erate, *a.* united in league, combined
Confed'erate, *n.* an accomplice, companion, ally
Confederâtion, *n.* a clofe alliance, league, union
Confed'erative, *a.* conftituting a federal compact
Confer', *v.* to difcourfe, beftow, compare

Con'ference, *n.* a difcourfe, parley, meeting for
Confert', *a.* thick or clofe fet (religious converfe
Confefs', *v. t.* to acknowledge, grant, own, fhow
Confefs'ed, *pa.* owned, declared, told, allowed
Confefs'edly, *ad.* avowedly, on purpofe, actually
Confes''fion, *n.* an acknowledgment, a profeffion
Confes''fional, Confes''fionary, *n.* a confeffor's feat
Confefs'or, *n.* one who hears confeffion, a martyr
Confeft', *ufed* for confeffed
Confidant', *n.* one trufted with a fecret
Confîde, *v. i.* to truft fully in, to rely upon
Con'fidence, *n.* truft, firmnefs, boldnefs, affurance
Con'fident, *a.* pofitive, bold, daring, impudent
Confiden'tial, *a.* admitted to confidence, trufty
Confiden'tially, *ad.* in full confidence of fecrecy
Con'fidently, *ad,* without doubt, pofitively
Configurâtion, *n.* the act of forming or fafhioning
Config'ure, *v. t.* to difpofe into form, to fafhion
Con'fine, *n.* a limit, border, boundary, fide, edge
Confi'ne, *v.* to border, bound, fix, tie up, keep
Con'finelefs, *a.* unbounded, unlimited, *ob.*
Confi'nement, *n.* a reftraint, an imprifonment
Confi'ner, *n.* one who confines, a near neighbor
Confin'ity, *n.* a great nearnefs, neighborhood
Confirm', *v. t.* to make certain, fix, eftablifh, ad-
minifter the church-rite of confirmation
Confirm'able, *a.* that is capable of being proved
Confirmâtion, *n.* proof, rite by which baptized
perfons are confirmed in the faith, an eftab-
lifhing
Confirmâtor, Confirm'er, *n.* one who confirms
Confirm'atory, *a.* that confirms or ftrengthens
Confirm'ednefs, *n.* a fixed or fettled ftate, fafety
Confif'cable, *a.* that is fubject to confifcation
Con'fifcate, *v. t.* to fieze, for the ufe of the public
or ftate, the property of one guilty of a high
Con'fifcated, *pa.* forfeited to a ftate or king (crime
Confifcâtion, *n.* the feizing of private property
Con'fitent, *a.* confeffing ; *n.* one confeffing, *ob.*
Con'fiture, *n.* a fweetmeat ; *a.* relating to a con-
Confix', *v. t.* to fix or faften down (fection
Conflâgrant, *a.* burning together, confuming all
Conflagrâtion, *n.* a general fire or burning, fire
Conflâtion, *n.* a blowing together, an union
Conflict', *v. t.* to fight, conteft, ftruggle, ftrive
Con'flict, *n.* a conteft, ftruggle, combat, agony
Con'fluence, *n.* a flowing together, a multitude
Con'fluent, *a.* running into one channel or body,
united at the bafe, growing in tufts
Con'flux, *n.* a junction of currents, a crowd
Confluxibil'ity, Conflux'iblenefs, *n.* an aptnefs or
tendency to flow together
Conform', *a.* conformable, agreeable, fimilar
Conform', *v.* to comply, yield, adapt, fuit
Conform'able, *a.* agreeable, fuitable, like, fimilar
Conform'ably, *ad.* agreeably, fuitably (of ftrength
Conformâtion, *n.* a good difpofition of parts, trial
Conform'ed, *pa.* made like, adapted, fuited
Conform'ift, *n.* one who complies with the rites of

G

the eftablifhed church   (likenefs
Conform'ity, *n.* a compliance with, refemblance,
Confortátion, *n.* the aét or árt of ftrengthening, *ob.*
Confound', *v. t.* to mix, perplex, deftroy, amaze
Confound'ed, *pa.* aftonifhed, hateful, hurtful
Confound'edly, *ad.* hatefully, fhamefully, very
Confound'er, *n.* one who perplexes or deftroys
Cònfrater'nity, *n.* a religious brotherhood, a body
Confricátion, *n.* a rubbing together, friétion
Confront', [confrunt]*v. t.* to face, oppofe, compare
Confrontátion, *n.* the aét of bringing face to face
Confront'ed, *pa.* brought face to face, oppofed
Confúfe, *v. t.* to confound, perplex, hurry, mix
Confúfedly, *ad.* haftily, indireétly, in a lump
Confúfednefs, *n.* a want of diftinétnefs, confufion
Confúfion, *n.* diforder, hurry, aftonifhment, ruin
Confútable, *a.* that may be difproved, falfe
Confutátion, *n.* the aét of confuting, a difproof
Confúte, *v. t.* to difprove, conviét, baffle, crufh
Con'ge, *n.* a mold feparating two members of a
Congeé, *n.* a bow, reverence, leave   (column
Congeé, *v. i.* to take leave of, bow, retire, go off
Conge'able, *a.* done with leave or permiffion
Congéal, *v.* to freeze, harden, grow ftiff, thicken
Congéalable, *a.* that may be congealed or frozen
Congéalment, *n.* a mafs formed by froft, ftiffnefs
Conge-d'Ífre, *n.* leave given to choofe a bifhop
Congelátion, *n.* the aét of congealing, ftiffnefs
Congenerátion, *n.* the aét of giving birth together
Con'gener, *n.* a thing of the fame nature
Con'gener, Congen'erous, *a.* of the fame kind
Congénial, *a.* partaking of the fame nature, like
Congenial'ity, *n.* a famenefs, a likenefs
Con'genite, *a.* being of the fame birth or kind, *ob.*
Con''ger, *n.* a fine kind of large eel, the fea-eel
Congéries, *n.* a mafs of fmall bodies, heap, pile
Congeft', *v. t.* to heap or lay up, amafs, colleét
Congeft'ible, *a.* that may be heaped or colleéted
Conges'tion, *n.* a colleétion of matter or humors
Con'giary, *n.* a Roman meafure of corn, a bounty
Congláciate, *v. t.* to turn into ice, freeze, harden
Conglóbate, Conglóbe, *v. t.* to gather in a hard
Conglóbated, *pa.* formed into a hard ball (ball
Conglobátion, *n.* a conglobing, a round hard body
Conglom'erate, *a.* crowded together irregularly
Conglom'erate, *v. t.* to make round, to wind up
Conglom'erated, *pa.* colleéted, twifted round
Conglomerátion, *n.* a colleétion, mixture, heap
Conglútinate, *v. t.* to glue or cement together
Conglutinátion, *n.* a gluing together, a healing
Con''go, *n.* a kind of tea of a middle quality
Congrat'ulant, *a.* rejoicing in participation with
Congrat'ulate, *v.* to wifh joy to, to compliment
Congratulátion, *n.* a giving or wifhing of joy
Congrat'ulatory, *a.* expreffing joy, complimentary
Congrée, *v. i.* to agree, unite, join, *ob.*
Congréet, *v. i.* to falute mutually or by turns
Con''gregate, *a.* colleéted, hardened, firm, clofe
Con''gregate, *v.* to colleét, affemble, meet, unite

Congregátion, *n.* a colleétion, affembly, mafs, pile
Congregátional, *a.* relating to a congregation, and
    to a church government by confent and eleétion
Congregátionalifm, *n.* church government by the
    members of the church and congregation
Congregátionalift, *n.* an adherent to the congrega-
    tional form of church government
Con''grefs, *n.* a meeting, affembly, combat, the
    legiflature of the United States of America
Congrefs'ive, *a.* meeting, encountering, ftruck
Congres'fional, *a.* pertaining to the Congrefs of
    the United States
Congrúe, *v. i.* to agree, fit, fuit, conform, *ob.*
Con''gruence, Con''grument, *n.* agreement, fitnefs
Con''gruent, *a.* agreeing, correfpondent, fit, fuita-
Congrúity, *n.* fitnefs, confiftency, reafon   (ble
Con''gruous, *a.* fit, fuitable, meet, proper, like (ly
Con''gruoufly, *ad.* fuitably, confiftently, pertinent-
Cóniac or Cog'niac, *n.* a kind of brandy from France
Con'ic, Con'ical, *a.* in form of or like a cone
Con'ics, *n. pl.* the doétrin of conic feétions
Con'ically, *ad.* the ftate of being conical
Conif'erous, *a.* producing conical feed veffels
Conjéc'tor, *n.* a gueffer, a diviner, *ob.*
Conjéc'tural, *a.* depending on conjeéture
Conjéc'turally, *ad.* by conjeéture or guefs
Conjéc'ture, *n.* a guefs, notion, idea, fuppofition
Conjéc'ture, *v. t.* to guefs, judge by guefs, fuppofe
Conjéc'turer, *n.* one who conjeétures or gueffes
Conjoin', *v.* to conneét, league, unite, faften, join
Conjoin'ed, *pa.* conneéted, united, linked
Conjoint', *a.* conneéted, united, joint, mutual
Conjoint'ly, *ad.* in union, together, jointly with
Con'jugal, *a.* belonging to marriage or union
Con'jugate, *a.* that fprings from one original, hav-
    ing leaflets in pairs
Con'jugate, *v. t.* to join, unite, infleét verbs
Conjugátion, *n.* the form of infleéting verbs
Conjuné', *a.* conjoined, conneéted, united
Conjunc'tion, *n.* a meeting together, union, league,
    affociation, bond, the fixth part of fpeech
Conjunét'ive, *a.* clofely united, the mode of a verb
Conjunét'ively, Conjunét'ly, *ad.* jointly, together
Conjunét'ivenefs, *n.* a conjunét ftate or quality
Conjunét'ure, *n.* a critical time, a combination
Conjurátion, *n.* a plot, form, enchantment, magic
Con'jure, *v.* to raife or lay fpirits, to play tricks
Conjúre, *v.* to enjoin folemnly, adjure, confpire
Conjúred, *pa.* bound by an oath   (man
Con'jurer, *n.* an enchanter, fortuneteller, cunning
Con'jurement, *n.* a ferious injunétion or order
Connas'cence, *n.* common birth, *ob.*
Connáte, *a.* born at the fame time with another,
    having oppofite leaves united at the bafe
Connat'ural, *a.* fuitable to nature, like   (ture
Connatural'ity, Connat'uralnefs, *n.* the fame na-
Connat'urally, *ad.* by the aét of nature, originally
Conneét', *v. t.* to join, unite, link, tie, faften, knit
Conneét'ed, *pa.* joined, united, linked, tied

Connec'ticut, n. a river and one of the U. States

Connec'tive, a. connecting, joining, regular

Connec'tive, n. that which joins together (ther

Connec'tively, ad. in conjunction, in union, toge-

Connec'tion, n. a linking together, relation, union

Connex', v. t. to link together, unite, ob.

Connex'ion, Connex'ity, n. fee connection

Connex'ive, a. having the force of connection

Connivance, n. a winking, voluntary blindness

Connive, v. i. to wink at a fault, pass by, forbear

Connoisseur, n. a critic, a judge of letters or arts

Con'notate, Connóte, v. t. to denote, to imply, ob.

Connotation, n. the act of implying something, ob.

Connûbial, a. of or relating to marriage, conjugal

Connutri"tious, a. nourished with or together

Con'oid, n. a figure partaking of or like a cone

Conoid'ic, a. relating to a conoid

Conquals'ate, v. t. to shake, move, dash, ob.

Con"quer, v. to overcome, subdue, win, beat

Con"querable, a. that may be overcome or beaten

Con"queror, n. one who overcomes or subdues

Con"quest, n. victory, a thing gained or gotten

Confanguin'eous, a. near of kin, related by birth

Confanguin'ity, n. a relationship by blood or birth

Con'science, n. natural knowledge, simple reason

Confcien'tious, a. fcrupulous, exact, just, honest

Confcien'tiously, ad. with confcience, honestly

Confcien'tioufnefs, n. exact justice, real honesty

Con'fcionable, a. reafonable, just, proper (priety

Con'fcionablenefs, n. reafonablenefs, justice, pro-

Con'fcionably, ad. reafonably, justly, fitly

Con'fcious, a. inwardly perfuaded, privy

Con'fcioufly, ad. with inward or real perfuafion

Con'fcioufnefs, n. perception of what paffes in the mind, attended with certainty

Confcribed, a. formed round, circumfcribed

Con'fcript, a. written, regiftered, enrolled

Con'fcript, n. an enrolled militia man

Confcrip'tion, n. an enrollment, a regiftering

Con'fecrate, v. t. to dedicate, devote, hallow

Con'fecrated, pa. dedicated, made facred

Con'fecrater, n. one who confecrates or devotes

Confecration, n. the act of making facred or holy

Confectáneous, Confect'ary, a. following of courfe

Confect'ary, n. a corollary, inference, deduction

Confecútion, n. a train of confequences, fucceffion

Confec'utive, a. following in order, fucceffive

Confeffion, Confent', n. agreement, concord

Con'fent', v. i. to be of one mind, agree, fubmit

Confentáneous, a. agreeable to, confiftent with

Confentáneoufnefs, n. agreement

Confentáneoufly, ad. agreeably, confiftently

Confent'er, n. one who gives his confent

Confen'tient, a. agreeing, uniting in opinion

Con'fequence, n. an effect, inference, importance

Con'fequent, a. following naturally or regularly

Con'fequent, n. what naturally follows, an effect

Confequen'tial, a. conclufive, important, very big

Confequen'tially, ad. by confequence, in courfe

Con'fequently, ad. of or by confequence, therefore

Con'fequentnefs, n. a regular connexion (Thames

Conferv'ancy, n. a prefervation of the fifhery in the

Confervátion, n. the act of preferving, prefervation

Conferv'ative, a. having power to prefeve

Confervátor, n. a preferver, keeper, defender

Conferv'atory, a. having the quality of preferving

Conferv'atory, n. a place where any thing is kept

Con'ferve, n. a fweetmeat, preferved fruits

Conferve', v. t. to preferve or candy fruits

Conferv'er, n. one who preferves, faves or lays by

Conferv'ing, pa. candying, preferving, faving

Confid'er, v. to think, examin, requite, regard

Confid'erable, a. worthy of regard, great, valuable

Confid'erablenefs, n. importance, value, merit

Confid'erably, ad. importantly, very much, toler-

Confid'erance, n. confideration, reflection (ably

Confid'erate, a. thoughtful, prudent, moderate

Confid'erately, ad. calmly, coolly, prudently

Confid'eratenefs, n. thoughtfulnefs, prudence, care

Confiderátion, n. ferious thought, regard, pru-

dence, reafon, account, motive, recompence

Confid'ered, pa. thought on, examined, regarded

Confid'erer, n. a perfon of reflection or thought

Confign, v. t. to make or fend over, to intruft

Confignátion, n. the act of configning

Confignée, n. one to whom any thing is configned

Confignment, n. a deed to make things over, goods or things configned to any one

Confignor', n. one who configns or entrufts goods to another

Confimil'ity, n. a common or joint likenefs

Confift', v. i. to be made up of, fubfift, agree

Confift'ence, n. natural ftate of bodies, agreement

Confift'ent, a. conformable, probable, firm, folid

Confift'ently, ad. agreeably, fuitably, properly

Confiftórial, a. relating to a confiftory or court

Confift'ory, n. a fpiritual court, affembly, tribunal

Confóciate, n. an accomplice, partner, ally

Confóciate, v. t. to unite, hold together, join

Confociátion, n. an alliance, union, confederacy, a convention of paftors and meffengers of churches

Confociátional, a. pertaining to a confociation

Confólable, a. admitting or taking comfort

Confolátion, n. comfort, an alleviation of mifery

Confol'atory, n. a fpeech containing comfort

Confol'atory, a. tending to give comfort or eafe

Confóle, v. t. to comfort, cheer, revive

Confóler, n. one that gives comfort (arch

Con'fole, n. an ornament cut upon the key of an

Confol'idate, v. to harden, become one body, join

Confolidátion, n. the making of two bodies one

Con'fonance, n. an accord of found, agreement

Con'fonant, a. agreeable, confiftent, fuitable

Con'fonant, n. a letter not founded by itfelf only

Con'fonantly, ad. agreeably, confiftently, fitly

Confopiátion, n. the act of laying to fleep, not ufed

Con'fort, n. a hufband or wife, companion

Confort', v. i. to affociate, join, mix, marry
Confort'able, a. fit to rank with, fuitable, ob.
Confort'ed, pa. joined in company or marriage
Con'found, n. the name of feveral fpecies of plants
Confpectúity, n. the fenfe of feeing, fight, ob.
Confpicúity, n. brightnefs, clearnefs, ob.
Confpic'uous, a. eafy to be feen, clear, eminent
Confpic'uoufly, ad. plainly, remarkably, eminent-
Confpic'uoufnefs, n. clearnefs, fame, renown (ly
Confpir'acy, n. a plot, combination, union
Confpirant, a. engaged in a confpiracy, uniting
Confpirátion, n. a confpiracy, a combination
Confpir'ator, Confpirer, n. a plotter, a contriver
Confpíre, v. i. to plot, agree, concert, conduce
Confpíring, pa. plotting, agreeing, tending
Con'ftable, in Eu. a governor or commander, in
   Am. a town officer of the peace, with the pow-
   ers of an under fheriff
Con'ftablefhip, n. the office or poft of conftable
Con'ftablewick, n. the jurifdiction of a conftable
Con'ftancy, n. firmnefs, refolutenefs, continuance
Con'ftant, a. firm, unchangeable, certain, fixed
Con'ftantly, ad. invariably, fteadily, always, ever
Conftantinopol'itan, a. of Conftantinople
Conftel'late, v. i. to fhine with one general light
Conftellátion, n. a clufter of fixed ftars, a body
Confternátion, n. fear, wonder, aftonifhment, fur-
Con'ftipate, v. to crowd, thicken, ftop, bind (prife
Conftipátion, n. the act of crowding, a ftoppage
Conftit'uent, a. effential, real, compofing, forming
Conftit'uent, n. a perfon who deputes, an elector
Con'ftitute, v. t. to make, appoint, depute, fet up
Con'ftitutor, n. a perfon who ordains or appoints
Conftitútion, n. the frame of body or mind, a law,
   decree, form of government
Conftitútional, a. legal, according to the original
   eftablifhed government, eftablifhed, fixed
Con'ftitu'tionality, n. the ftate of being agreeable
   to the conftitution, or of affecting the conftitu-
   tion
Conftitútionalift, n. an adherent to the conftitution
Con'ftitutive, a. effential, able or fit to eftablifh
Conftráin, v. t. to compel, force, confine, prefs
Conftráinable, a. liable to conftraint, not free
Conftráint, n. compulfion, force, confinement
Conftric'tion, n. contraction, compreffion, force
Conftringe', v. t. to contract, comprefs, bind
Conftrin'gent, a. binding, of a binding quality
Conftruct', v. t. to build, form, compile (ing, order
Conftruc'tion, n. a building or making, a mea-
Conftruct'ive, a. arifing from conftruction (tion
Conftruct'ively, ad. by conftruction, or interpreta-
Conftruct'ure, n. a pile, building, edifice, ob.
Con'ftrue, v. t. to tranflate, interpret, explain
Confluprátion, n. a deflouring, violation, rape
Confubftan'tial, a. of the fame fubftance or kind
Confubftantiality, n. two bodies in one fubftance
Confubftan'tiate, v. t. to unite into one fubftance
Confubftantiátion, n. two bodies in one fubftance

Confúetude, n. cuftom, ufage, ufe, habit
Con'ful, n. a chief officer at Rome, a chief mana-
   ger of trade for his nation in foreign parts
Con'fular, a. relating or belonging to a conful
Con'fulate, Con'fulfhip, n. the office of a conful
Confult', v. to afk advice of, debate, examin
Con'fult, Confultátion, n. the act of confulting
Confult'er, n. one who confults or afks advice
Confúmable, a. that may be confumed or fpent
Confúme, v. to fpend, deftroy, wafte, leffen, pine
Confúmed, pa. fpent, deftroyed, wafted away
Confúmer, n. one who fpends, deftroys or waftes
Con'fummate, v. t. to complete, fulfil, perfect
Confum'mate, a. complete, perfect, accomplifhed
Confummátion, n. a completion, an end
Confump'tion, n. the act of confuming, a difeafe
Confump'tive, a. deftructive, inclined to the con-
   fumption
Confump'tivenefs, n. a tendency to a confumption
Con'tact, n. a touch, juncture, very clofe union
Contac'tion, n. the act of touching, a juncture
Contágion, n. fecreted matter from a difeafed bo-
   dy capable of communicating the difeafe to a
   body in health, tendency to fpread by example,
   morbid exhalations
Contágionift, n. a believer in the propagation of
   certain difeafes by contagion
Contágious, a. infectious, catching, tainting
Contágioufly, ad. in a contagious manner
Contágioufnefs, n. an infectious quality (ftrain
Contáin, v. t. to hold, comprife, keep chafte, re-
Contáinable, a. that may be contained or held
Contam'inate, v. t. to defile, pollute, corrupt
Contam'inate, a. defiled, polluted, corrupted
Contaminátion, n. a defilement, pollution, taint
Contemn', v. t. to defpife, fcorn, neglect, defy
Contem'ner, n. a defpifer, fcorner, fcoffer, defier
Contemp'er, Contemp'erate, v. t. to moderate
Contemp'erament, n. the degree of any quality
Contemperátion, n. the act of tempering, propor-
Con'template, v. to mufe, meditate, ftudy (tion
Contemplátion, n. meditation, ftudy, thought
Contemp'lative, a. ftudious, thoughtful, ferious
Contemp'latively, ad. thoughtfully, attentively
Contemp'lativenefs, n. a contemplative ftate
Con'templator, n. one employed in ftudy, a ftudent
Contemp'orary, n. one who lives in the fame age
Contemp'orary, Contemporáneous, a. exifting at
   the fame time, better written cotemporary
Contemp'orife, v. t. to place in the fame age, ob.
Contempt', n. hatred of a mean object, without
   anger, envy or fear
Contempt'ible, a. deferving contempt, pitiful
Contempt'iblenefs, n. meannefs, lownefs, vilenefs
Contempt'ibly, ad. meanly, pittifully, wretchedly
Contempt'uous, a. fcornful, proud, haughty
Contempt'uoufly, ad. with fcorn, haughtily
Contempt'uoufnefs, n. fcornfulnefs, haughtinefs
Contend', v. to ftrive, vie, conteft, difpute.

Contend'ed, pa. ftriven, contefted, difputed
Contend'ent, n. an antagonift, opponent, ob.
Contend'er, n. a combatant, champion, hero
Content', a. fatisfied, pleafed, eafy, willing, ready
Content', v. t. to fatisfy, pleafe, gratify, pacify
Content', n. fatisfaction, eafe, contentment
Contentátion, n. fatisfaction, content, ob.
Content'ed, pa. fatisfied, pleafed, quiet, eafy
Content'edly, ad. in a contented manner, quietly
Conten'tion, n. ftrife, quarrel, debate, zeal, eagernefs
Conten'tious, a. quarrelfome, perverfe, crofs
Conten'tioufly, ad. in a quarrelfome manner
Conten'tioufnefs, n. a difpofition to quarrelling
Content'lefs, a. uneafy, diffatisfied, difcontented
Content'ment, n. fatisfaction, gratification, eafe
Con'tents, n. pl. the heads of a book, an index, what is contained, an amount, capacity
Conterm'inous, a. bordering upon, touching, near
Conterráneous, a. relating to the fame country.
Con'teft, n. a difpute, debate, difference, quarrel
Conteft', v. to difpute, wrangle, ftrive, vie with
Conteft'able, a. difputable, doubtful, uncertain
Conteftátion, n. act of contefting, difpute, ftrife
Contex', v. t. to weave together, knit, unite, ob.
Context', a. knit together, united, firm, clofe
Con'text, n. the feries or order of a difcourfe
Context'ure, n. an interweaving, fyftem, texture
Contignátion, n. a frame, &c. of beams or boards ob.
Contigúity, n. a clofe fituation, actual contact
Contig'uous, a. adjoining, touching, clofe
Contig'uoufly, ad. without intermediate fpace
Con'tinence, Con'tinency, n. chaftity, moderation
Con'tinent, n. land not feparated by the fea
Con'tinent, a. chafte, temperate, fober, connected
Continent'al, a. pertaining to a continent, or a whole country
Con'tinently, ad. chaftely, moderately, foberly
Contin'gence, Contin'gency, n. accident, cafualty
Contin'gent, a. accidental, cafual, uncertain
Contin'gent, n. a chance, proportion, quota, part
Contin'gently, ad. accidentally, by chance only
Contin'ual, a. inceffant, uninterupted, conftant
Contin'ually, ad. without ceafing, always, ever
Contin'uance, n. duration, perfeverence, abode
Contin'uate, a. continual, uninterrupted, united
Continuátion, n. a conftant fucceffion, perfever-
Contin'uative, a. denoting continuance (ance
Continuátor, n. one who continues a thing
Contin'ue, v. to remain in the fame ftate, perfevere, ftay, repeat, protract, carry on, unite
Contin'ually, ad. without interruption, jointly
Contin'uer, n. one who continues or perfeveres
Contin'uing, pa. remaining, abiding, repeating
Continúity, n. uninterrupted connection, cohefion
Contin'uous, a. joined together, clofely united
Contort', v. t. to twift, turn, writhe, wreft, torture
Contort', a. twifted, fpiral
Contor'fion, n. a twift, ftrain, wry or odd motion

Con'tour, n. the outline of a figure, a bending
Con'tra, ad. on the other fide or part
Con'traband, a. unlawful, illegal, forbidden by
Con'tract, n. an agreement, bargain, deed (law
Contract', v. t. to fhrink up, fhorten, bargain, get
Contract', Contract'ed, pa. fhortened, abridged, bargained, covenanted, betrothed, narrow, low
Contract'ible, a. that is capable of contraction
Contractibil'ity, n. the quality of being capable of
Contract'ile, a. able to contract itfelf (contraction
Contractil'ity, n. the power of contracting itfelf
Contrac'tion, n. an abbreviation, the act of fhortening or fhrinking
Contract'or, n. one who makes bargains or agrees
Contract'ure, n. a rigidity of joints, a leffening
Contradict', v. t. to oppofe, be contrary to, deny
Contradict'er, n. an oppofer, gainfayer, denier
Contradic'tion, n. oppofition, cavil, inconfiftency
Contradic'tious, a. oppofite, crofs, inconfiftent
Contradic'tioufnefs, n. oppofition, inconfiftency
Contradict'orily, ad. contrarily, inconfiftently
Contradict'ory, a. contrary, inconfiftent
Contradiftinc'tion, n. a diftinction by oppofits
Contradiftin"guifh, v. t. to diftinguifh by oppofits
Contradiftinct'ive, a. diftinguifhing by oppofition
Contrapofi"tion, n. the act of placing againft
Contraregular'ity, n. a difference from fome rule
Contráriant, a. contradictory, crofs, inconfiftent
Con'traries, n. pl. propofitions that oppofe or deny
Contraríety, n. oppofition, inconfiftency (ftroy
Con'trarily, ad. in a different manner, crofsly
Contrárious, a. contrary, repugnant, oppofite
Contrárioufly, Con'trariwife, ad. on the contrary
Con'trary, a. oppofite, difagreeing; v. t. to oppofe
Con'trait, n. an oppofition in things of a like kind
Contraft', v. i. to place in oppofition, to confront
Contraft'ed, pa. fet in oppofition, compared
Contravallátion, n. an oppofite fortification
Contravéne, v. t. to oppofe, obftruct, hinder
Contraven'tion, n. oppofition, violation
Contrayerv'a, n. a plant of feveral fpecies (fon
Contrib'utary, a. paying tribute to the fame perCon'tribute, or Contrib'ute, v. to give, beftow, conduce
Contrib'uting, pa. giving, conducing, promoting
Contribútion, n. the act of contributing, a gift
Contrib'utive, a. tending to promote or advance
Contrib'utor, n. one who bears or gives a part
Contrib'utory, a. advancing, promoting, helping
Contris'tate, v. t. to make fad or forrowfully, ob.
Contriftátion, n. the act of making fad or heavy, ob.
Con'trite, a. truly penitent, very forrowful, worn
Con'tritely, ad. in a penitent manner
Con'tritenefs, n. contrition, real repentance, grief
Contri'tion, n. real forrow for fin, a grinding
Contrívable, a. poffible, to be contrived or planned
Contrivance, n. a fcheme, conceit, plot, plan, art
Contríve, v. t. to plan, invent, project, devife
Contríver, n. an inventor, plotter, fchemer

Contról, *n.* power, authority, a check, a reſtraint
Contról, *v. t.* to govern, check, reſtrain, ſtop
Contróllable, *a.* ſubject to control, governable
Contróller, *n.* one who controls, an officer who checks other officers by a counter regiſter of accounts
Contróllerſhip, *n.* the office or poſt of controller
Contrólment, *n.* reſtraint, oppoſition, refutation
Controver'ſial, *a.* relating to diſputes, unſettled
Controver'ſialiſt,*n.* one who is fond of controverſy
Con'troverſy, *n.* a diſpute, quarrel, enmity (poſe
Con'trovert, *v. t.* to debate, diſpute, quarrel, op-
Controvert'ible, *a.* diſputable, uncertain, dubious
Con'trovertiſt, *n.* a diſputer, wrangler, reaſoner
Contumácious, *a.* obſtinate, ſtubborn, perverſe
Contumáciouſly, *ad.* obſtinately, perverſely
Contumáciouſneſs, Con'tumacy, *n.* obſtinacy, ſtubbornneſs, perverſeneſs, haughtineſs, pride
Contumélious, *a.* reproachful, abuſive, rude
Contuméliouſly, *ad.* reproachfully, rudely
Contuméliouſneſs, *n.* reproach, rudeneſs
Con'tumely, *n.* reproach, bad language abuſe
Contúfe, *v. t.* to bruiſe, cruſh, beat together, *ob.*
Contúſion, *n.* the act of bruiſing, a bruiſe, a hurt
Conun'drum, *n.* a low jeſt or conceit
Con'uſance, *n.* knowledge, notice
Con'uſant, *a.* knowing, having notice of
Convaleſ'cence, *n.* a renewal or return of health
Convaleſ'cent, *n.* a perſon recovering his health
Convénable, *a.* conſiſtent with, agreeable to, *ob.*
Convéne, *v. t.* to call together, aſſemble, collect
Convéned, *pa.* called or met together
Convénience, *n.* fitneſs, accommodation, uſe
Convénient, *a.* fit, ſuitable, proper, handy
Convéniently, *ad.* fitly, ſuitably, commodiouſly
Con'vent, *n.* a religious houſe, nunnery, monaſtery
Convent', *v. t.* to call before a judge, to ſummon
Convent'ed, *pa.* ſummoned before a court, cited
Convent'icle, *n.* a meetinghouſe, a ſecret aſſembly
Convent'icler, *n.* one who belongs to a conventicle
Conven'tion, *n.* an aſſembly, meeting, temporary treaty, an aſſembly of repreſentatives to form a conſtitution
Conven'tional, *a.* agreed on or done by contract
Conven'tionary, *a.* acting or ſettled by contract
Conven'tioner, *n.* one who belongs to a convention
Conven'tual, *a.* belonging to a convent, monaſtic
Conven'tual, *n.* a monk, nun, recluſe
Convergé, *v. i.* to tend or incline to one point
Conver'gence, *n.* the tending to a point (nearer
Conver'gent, *a.* tending to a point, approaching
Conver'ging, *pa.* tending to one point, bending
Convers'able, *a.* fit for converſation, ſociable
Con'verſant, *a.* acquainted with, experienced in
Converſátion, *n.* familiar diſcourſe, behavior
Convers'ative, *a.* of or relating to public life
Converſe', *v. i.* to diſcourſe, talk, live, cohabit
Con'verſe, *n.* converſation, acquaintance
Con'verſe, *a.* contrary, directly oppoſite

Con'verſely, *ad.* by a change of order or place
Conver'ſion, *n.* a change from one ſtate to another
Convers'ive, *a.* converſable, communicative
Con'vert, *n.* one who changes his opinion or religion
Convert', *v.* to change, turn, apply, appropriate
Convert'er, *n.* one who turns or makes converts
Convert'ible, *a.* that may be changed, reciprocal
Convertibil'ity, *n.* the quality of being convertible
Convert'ibly, *ad.* reciprocally, mutually, by turns
Con'vex, *a.* riſing like the outſide of a globe
Con'vex, *n.* a convex or ſpherical body
Con'vexed, *a.* convex, riſing in a circular form
Convex'edly, Con'vexly, *ad.* in a convex form
Convex'ity, Con'vexneſs, *n.* a ſpherical form
Convéy, [convây] *v. t.* to carry, make over
Convey'able, *a.* that may be conveyed
Convey'ance, *n.* the act and means of conveying
Convey'ancer, *n.* one uſed to convey property
Convey'ancing, *n.* the act or buſineſs of drawing deeds, leaſes, &c.
Convey'ed, *pa.* ſent, ſent or carried elſewhere
Convey'er, *n.* one who conveys or carries
Con'vict, *n.* a perſon convicted, caſt or detected
Convict', *v. t.* to prove guilty, caſt, detect, confute
Convict'ed, *pa.* found guilty, caſt, confuted
Convic'tion, *n.* a full proof, detection, ſenſe
Convict'ive, *a.* able or tending to convince, full
Convince', *v. t.* to make one ſenſible of, to prove
Convince'ment, *n.* conviction, ſatisfaction, proof
Convin'cible, *a.* capable of being convinced
Convin'cingly, *ad.* without room to doubt, fully
Convíve, *v. i.* to entertain, feaſt, revel, *ob.*
Conviv'ial, *a.* feſtive, ſocial, jovial, gay
Convivial'ity, *n.* mirth excited by feaſting
Con'vocate, *v. t.* to call or ſummon together
Convocátion, *n.* an aſſembly, eccleſiaſtical ſenate
Convóke, *v. t.* to ſummon, call together, collect
Convolve', *v. t.* to roll up or together, wind, turn
Con'volute, *a.* having the margins rolled together
Convolv'ulus, *n.* bindweed, a genus of plants
Convolútion, *n.* a rolling or twiſting together
Con'voy, *v. t.* to accompany for defenſe
Con'voy, *n.* an attendance for defenſe, protection, the thing protected
Convulſe', *v. t.* to give violent motion, tear, rend
Convul'ſion, *n.* an irregular and violent motion
Convulſ'ive, *a.* given to or cauſing convulſions
Con'y, or Co''ney, *n.* a kind of animal, a rabbit
Con'ycatch, *v. t.* to cheat, trick, bite, *ob.*
Coo, *v. i.* to cry like a dove or pigeon
Coo'ing, *n.* the noiſe made by a pigeon
Cook, *n.* a man or woman who dreſſes victuals
Cook, *v. t.* to dreſs victuals, prepare, manage
Cook'ery, *n.* the art or act of dreſſing victuals
Cook'maid, *n.* a maid that dreſſes victuals, a cook
Cookt, *pa.* dreſſed, prepared for table, ordered
Cool, *v.* to make or grow cool, moderate, allay
Cool, *a.* ſomewhat cold, coldiſh, indifferent

Cool, *n.* a freedom from heat, temperature, fhade
Cool'er, *n.* what cools the body, a brewing veffel
Cool'ly, *ad.* without paffion or regard, flightly
Cool'nefs, *n.* moderate cold, indifference
Coom, *n.* foot, greafe for wheels, duft, refufe of ap-
Coomb, *n.* a corn-meafure of four bufhels   (ples
Coop, *n.* a wooden cage for poultry, barrel, cart
Coop, *v. t.* to cage, fhut up, confine, imprifon
Coopeé, *n.* a ftep in dancing
Coop'er, *n.* a maker of barrels, &c.
Coop'erage, *n.* a place or price for cooper's work
Co-op'erate, *v.* to work, labor or act with
Co-operátion, *n.* a joint labor for one end   (end
Co-op'erative, *a.* tending to the fame purpofe or
Co-op'erátor, *n.* a perfon who jointly endeavors
Co-optátion, *n.* an election, affumption, choice
Co-or'dinate, *a.* holding the fame rank, equal
Co-or'dinately, *ad.* with equal rank
Co-ordinátion, *n.* a ftate of holding the fame rank
Coot, *n.* a genus of black water-fowls
Copai'ba or Capi'vi, *n.* a tree and its juice which
     is a tranfparent refin
Co'pal, *n.* the Mexican name of refins and gums,
     but chiefly a refin ufed in varnifhing   (eftate
Copar'cenary, Copar'ceny, *n.* an equal fhare in an
Copart'ner, *n.* a joint partner in any bufinefs
Copart'nerfhip, *n.* the having of an equal fhare, a
     joint concern in bufinefs
Cope, *n.* a prieft's cloak, hood, concave arch, hill
Cope, *v.* to contend, ftrive, oppofe, point, cover
Coper'nican, *a.* pertaining to Copernicus and the
     folar fyftem which he revived
Cópefmate, *n.* a companion, friend, partner, *ob.*
Co'pied, *pa.* taken from or off, tranfcribed
Cop'ier, *n.* a perfon who copies, imitates or fteals
Cóping, *n.* the covering or upper part of a wall
Cópious, *a.* plentiful, abundant, full, large, long
Cópioufly, *ad.* plentifully, diffufively, at large
Cópioufnefs, *n.* plenty, abundance, profufenefs
Cópift, Cop'yift, *n.* one who copies or tranfcribes
Cop'ped, Cop'pled, *a.* rifing to a top or head, fharp
Cop'per, *n.* a metal of a reddifh color, a large boiler
Cop'peras, *n.* a folution of iron in fulphuric acid
Cop'pernofe, *n.* a dark red nofe   (copper
Cop'perplate, *n.* an impreffion from a figure on
Cop'perfmith, *n.* one who works in or fells copper
Cop'pery, *a.* tafting of, like or mixed with copper
Cop'pice, Copfe, *n.* a wood of fmall or low trees
Cop'pleduft, *n.* a powder ufed to purify metals
Copfe, *v. t.* to preferve or keep for underwoods
Cop'tic, *a.* pertaining to the Copts, the chriftians
     in Egypt
Cop'tic, *n.* the language of the ancient Egyptians
Cop'ulate, *v.* to couple, join, unite, mix   (union
Copulátion, *n.* the joining of fexes together, an
Cop'ulative, *a.* joining or mixing together
Cop'y, *n.* a manufcript, imitation, pattern to
     write after, duplicate of an original writing,
     picture

Cop'y, *v.* to tranfcribe, write from or out, imitate
Cop'ybook, *n.* a book to write copies in
Cop'yhold, *n.* a tenure under the lord of a manor
     by copy of court roll or record
Cop'yholder, *n.* one who has land, &c, in copyhold
Cop'yright, *n.* fole right to print a book or work
Cop'yrighted, *a.* the fole right being fecured
Coqual'lin, *n.* the black fquirrel
Coquet', *v.* to act the lover, dally, jilt
Cóquetry, *n.* deceit in love, affectation, vanity
Coquet', *n.* a jilting airy girl, a vain woman
Cor'al, *n.* a genus of animals and their fhells,
     growing in the fea, a child's ornament
Cor'alline, *a.* made of or like coral
Coral'form or Coral'liform, *a.* like coral
Cor'alline, *n.* the fubftance formed by corals
Coralloid', *n.* certain fpecies of corallines
Cor'altree, *n.* a genus of flowering fhrubs
Corant', *n.* a nimble or fprightly kind of dance
Corb, *n.* a kind of bafket ufed in coaleries
Corb'an, *n.* a gift, alms, almfbafket, box, facrifice
Cor'bel, *n.* reprefentation of a bafket in building
Cor'bil, *n.* a projection in building
Cor'cle, *n.* the heart or germ of a plant
Cord, *n.* a fmall rope, line, finew, meafure of wood
     of 128 fquare feet
Cord, *v. t.* to tie or faften with cords, pile wood
Cord'age, *n.* a parcel of ropes, the ropes of a fhip
Cord'ate, *a.* heart-fhaped
Cord'ed, *pa.* tied, bound or faftened with cords
Cordeliér, *n.* a Francifcan friar, a gray friar
Cor'dial, *n.* a cherifhing draft, what comforts
Cor'dial, *a.* reviving, hearty, fincere, friendly
Cordial'ity, *n.* fincerity, affection, efteem, love
Cor'dially, *ad.* heartily, fincerely, honeftly, truly
Cor'diform, *a.* in form of a heart
Cor'diner, Cord'wainer, *n.* a fhoemaker
Cord'on, *n.* a row of ftones, line, twift of ropes
Corduroy', *n.* thick cotton ftuff, ribbed
Cord'wain, *n.* a kind of Spanifh lether
Cord'wood, *n.* wood piled or fold by the cord
Core, *n.* the heart or inner part of a thing, a body
Córed, *a.* rolled in falt and prepared for drying
Coriáceous, *a.* confifting of or like lether
Corian'der, *n.* the name of a plant or hot feed
Cor'inth, *n.* the fruit ufually called currant
Corinth'ian, *a.* relating to Corinth or an order of
     architecture   (on a horfe fhoe
Cork, *n.* a tree, bark, bottle-ftopple, a fharp point
Cork, *v. t.* to ftop with a cork, to form fharp points,
     or fhoe with points
Cork'ed, *pa.* ftopped or fecured with a cork
Cork'ingpin, *n.* a large kind of pin
Cork'y, *a.* like cork, confifting or made of cork
Cor'morant, *n.* a bird of prey, glutton, mifer
Corn, *n.* grain, a hard lump in the flefh
Corn, *v. t.* to fprinkle with falt, to form into grains
Corn'blades, *n.* leaves of maiz   (*S. States*)
Corn'chandler, *n.* a retailer or feller of corn

Corn'crake, n. a bird living among corn
Corn'cutter, n. a perſon who cuts or eaſes corns
Cor'nel, n. a kind of tree, the cornelian-cherry
Cornel', n. coarſe meal (N. York)
Cornélian, n. a precious ſtone of a fleſh-color
Corn'eous, a. horny, like horn, hard, tough
Corn'er, n. an angle, extremity, ſecret place, end
Corn'erwiſe, ad. with the corner before, acroſs
Corn'et, n. a muſical inſtrument, an officer of horſe
Cor'netcy, n. the office or rank of a cornet
Corn'eter, n. one who blows or plays on a cornet
Corn'ice, Corn'iſh, n. the top of a wall or column,
Corn'icle, n. a little or ſmall horn (a molding
Cornic'ulate, a. having ſharp horny points
Corni"gerous, a. bearing or having horns, horned
Corn'land, n. land for corn
Corn'maſter, n. a perſon who raiſes corn for ſale
Corn'mill, n. a mill for grinding corn
Corn'pipe, n. the joint of a green ſtalk of corn ſlit
Corn'ſtalk, n. a ſtalk or ſtem of maiz
Cornucópia, n. the horn of plenty, abundance
Cornúte, v. to give a man horns, to cuckold
Cornúted, pa. having horns, cuckolded, fierce
Cornúto or Cornúte, n. a man horned, a cuckold
Corn'y, a. hard like horn, producing horn, tough
Cor'ody, n. an allowance out of the revenues of a
  biſhopric
Cor'ol, n. the flower leaves, or petals of a plant
Corolláceous, a. pertaining to a corol
Cor'ollary, n. an inference, deduction, ſurplus
Cor'ollate, a. having flowers in form of a crown
Corollúle, Corollet', n. a little corol, or that of a
Cor'onal, n. a crown, chaplet, garland (floret
Cor'onal, a. of or relating to the top of the head
Cor'onary, a. of, relating to, or placed as, a crown
Coronátion, n. the ſolemnity or act of crowning
Cor'oner, n. an officer who inquires into the cauſe
  of ſudden and accidental death
Cor'onet, n. a nobleman's crown, a little crown
Coróniform, a. in ſhape of a crown
Coronúle, n. a little crown, or downy tuft on a ſeed
Coronoid', a. noting the upper proceſs of the end
  of the lower jaw
Cor'poral, n. an inferior or loweſt military officer
Cor'poral or Corpóreal, a. bodily, material, groſs
Corporál'ity, n. the quality of being imbodied
Cor'porally, ad. bodily, in a body or lump
Cor'porate, a. united into a body or community
Corporátion, n. a body corporate, a body politic
Corporéity, n. a bodily ſubſtance, materiality
Corpórify, v. t. to imbody, ob.
Corps, n. a body of ſoldiers [an ill word]
Corpſe, n. the dead body of a human being
Cor'pulence, n. fleſhineſs, exceſſive fatneſs
Cor'pulent, a. big, groſs, heavy, fleſhy, fat
Cor'puscle, n. a very ſmall part or body, an atom
Corpus'cular, a. of or relating to bodies or atoms
Corrádiation, n. an union of different rays
Correct', v. t. to puniſh, mend faults, temper

Correct', a. exact, reviſed with exactneſs
Correct'ed, pa. puniſhed, reproved, ſet right
Correc'tion, n. puniſhment, reproof, amendment
Correc'tional, a. pertaining to correction
Correc'tioner, n. a jailbird, priſoner, not uſed
Correct'ive, n. what has the power of correcting
Correct'ive, a. able to correct, able to alter
Correct'ly, ad. accurately, exactly, juſtly, neat
Correct'neſs, n. accuracy, exactneſs, nicety, care
Correct'or, n. one who or what corrects
Corrégidor, n. a high or chief magiſtrate in Spain
Cor'relate, n. what ſtands in an oppoſite relation
Correl'ative, a. having a reciprocal relation, like
Correp'tion, n. reproof, chiding, rebuke, ob.
Correp'tory, a. reproving, rebuking, blaming, ob.
Correſpond', v. i. to ſuit, anſwer, agree, write to
Correſpond'ence, n. agreement, fitneſs, intercourſe
Correſpond'ent, a. ſuitable, anſwerable, proper
Correſpond'ent, n. one who holds correſpondence
Correſpons'ive, a. adapted, ſuited (by letters
Corridór, n. a gallery round a houſe, a covered way
Cor'rigible, a. puniſhable, that may be mended
Corrob'orant, a. ſtrengthening, confirming
Corrob'orant, n. a medicin which gives ſtrength
Corrob'orate, v. t. to ſtrengthen, confirm, ratify
Corrob'orate, a. confirmed, made ſtrong or ſure
Corroborátion, n. the act of ſtrengthening
Corrob'orative, a. able or tending to ſtrengthen
Corróde, v. t. to eat away by degrees, to gnaw
Corródible, a. that may be corroded
Corróſion, n. the act of eating or wearing away
Corróſive, n. a corroding medicin, a hot quality
Corróſive, Corródent, a. able to corrode, eating
Corróſively, ad. in a corroding manner (away
Corróſiveneſs, n. the quality of being corroſive
Cor'rugate, v. t. to wrinkle, purſe up, contract
Corrugátor, n. a muſcle which contracts the ſkin
  of the eye brows
Corrupt', v. to ſpoil, defile, grow rotten, bribe
Corrupt', a. rotten, debauched, wicked, vile
Corrupt'ed, pa. debauched, led aſtray, rotten
Corrupt'er, n. one who corrupts, one who taints
Corruptibil'ity, n. a corruptible ſtate or quality
Corrupt'ible, a. that may or can be corrupted
Corrupt'ibly, ad. in a corruptible manner or ſtate
Corrup'tion, n. wickedneſs, rottenneſs, matter,
Corrupt'ive, a. able to corrupt, able to taint (taint
Corrupt'ly, ad. wickedly, improperly, badly
Corrupt'neſs, n. badneſs of morals, ſpeech, &c.
Cor'ſair, n. a pirate, a plunderer
Corſe, n. a dead or putrid body, carcaſs, offering
Cor'ſelet or Cor'ſlet, n. a light armor for the breaſt
Cor'ſican, n. a native of Corſica
Cor'ſican, a. pertaining to Corſica
Cort'es, n. the aſſembly of the ſtates at Madrid
Cor'tical, a. barky, belonging to or like bark
Cor'ticated, a. infuſed with or reſembling bark
Cor'ticoſe, Cor'ticous, a. full of bark, barky
Cor'vet, Corvet'to, n. a curvet, leap, frolic

Corvet', *n.* an advice boat.

Corus'cant, *a.* flashing, glittering, shining, bright

Coruscátion, *n.* a flashing of light, glare, glitter

Cor'ymb, *n.* a cluster of flowers proceeding from partial flower stalks, rising to an equal highth

Corymbif'erous, *a.* bearing a corymb

Corym'bous, *a.* like or pertaining to a corymb

Cofmet'ic, *a.* beautifying, promoting beauty

Cofmet'ic, *n.* a kind of wash to improve the skin

Cos'mical, *a.* rising or setting with the sun

Cos'mically, *ad.* together with the sun (the world

Cofmog'ony, *n.* the science of the formation of

Cofmog'onist, *n.* one who gives an account of the origin of the world

Cofmol'ogy, *n.* an account of the world

Cofmog'rapher, *n.* a describer of the world

Cofmograph'ical, *a.* pertaining to cofmography

Cofmog'raphy, *n.* a defcription of the visible world

Cofmol'atory, *n.* worship paid to the univerfe or

Cofmop'olite, *n.* a citizen of the world (its parts

Cofs'acs, *n. pl.* a certain kind of foldiers

Cos'fas, *n.* plain India muslins of various qualities from 7 to 10-8ths wide

Cofs'et, *n.* a lamb brought up by the hand

Coft, *n.* price paid, charge, expence, hurt, lofs

Coft, *v. i.* coft, *pret.* coft, *pa.* to be bought or pro-

Coft'al, *a.* of or belonging to the ribs (cured for

Coft'ard, *n.* a head, blockhead, kind of large apple

Coft'ive, *a.* bound in the body, clofe-binding, hard

Coft'iveness, *n.* a coftive ftate, a hardnefs

Coft'linefs, *n.* expenfivenefs, extravagance, coft

Coft'ly, *a.* expenfive, of great price, dear, high

Coft'mary, *n.* a plant, the alecoft

Coft'ume, *n.* a juft proportion of parts

Cot, Cot'tage, *n.* a hut, a very fmall or little houfe

Cote, *v. t.* to leave behind ; *n.* a pen, fold, cot

Cotem'orary, *a.* living or being at the fame time with another

Cotem'porary, *n.* one living at the fame time

Coterie', *n.* an affembly, meeting, club, fociety

Cotic'ular, *a.* in form of a whetftone

Cotil'lion, *n.* a kind of light French dance (decks

Cott, *n.* a bedframe or box fufpended between

Cot'tager, *n.* a perfon who lives in a cottage

Cot'ton, *n.* a kind of plant, wool, ftuff made of it

Cot'ton, *a.* made of cotton

Cot'ton, *v. i.* to rife with a nap, unite, *ob.*

Cotylédon, *n.* a fide lobe of vegetable feed, a plant

Cotyled'onous, *a.* having or pertaining to co-tyledons

Couch, *v.* to fquat or lie down, hide, fix, take off,

Couch, *n.* a feat for eafe, bed, layer (contain

Couch'ant, *a.* fquatting, lying down, refting on

Couch'ed, *pa.* cleared, comprehended, expreffed

Cough, [cauf] *n.* a diforder or effort of the lungs

Cough, *v. i.* to try to throw off matter by the

Cough'er, *n.* a perfon that coughs (lungs

Cough'ing, *n.* a throwing off matter by the lungs

Could, [cood] *imperf. tenfe* of *can*

Coul'ter or Col'ter, *n.* a fharp iron of a plough

Coun'cil, *n.* an affembly met for confultation

Coun'cillor, *n.* a member of a council

Coun'fel, *n.* advice, art, a defign, fcheme, pleader

Coun'fel, *v. t.* to give advice, advife, direct

Coun'felable, *a.* willing to take advice, *ob.*

Coun'felled, *pa.* advifed, inftructed, defired, told

Coun'fellor, *n.* one who gives advice, a friend

Count, *v.* to reckon, tell, efteem, depend

Count, *n.* a foreign title, tale, number, declaration

Count'ed, *pa.* reckoned, fuppofed, imputed

Count'enance, *n.* a face, look, fupport, pretenfe

Count'enance, *v. t.* to fupport, defend, favor

Count'enancer, *n.* one who gives countenance to

Count'er, *n.* fomething to keep reckoning, a fhop-table, room, prifon

Count'er, *ad.* contrary to, in a wrong way

Counteract', *v. t.* to act contrary to, hinder, ftop

Counterac'tion, *n.* oppofit action, defeat

Counterbal'ance, *n.* an oppofit weight of power

Counterbal'ance, *v. t.* to make amends, to equal

Count'erbuff, *n.* a ftroke producing a recoil, *ob.*

Counterbuff', *v. t.* to ftrike back, to repel, *ob.*

Count'ercafter, *n.* a bookkeeper, clerk, *ob.*

Count'erchange, *n.* an exchange, *ab.*

Count'ercharm, *n.* that which diffolves a charm

Countercharm', *v. t.* to deftroy an enchantment

Count'ercheck, *n.* a ftop, rebuke, cenfure, reproof

Count'erevidence *n.* oppofit evidence or proof

Count'erfeit, *a.* forged, deceitful ; *n.* an impofture

Count'erfeit, *v. t.* to forge, feign, imitate, copy

Coun'terfeiter, *n.* one who counterfeits, a forger

Count'erfeitly, *ad.* with forgery, feignedly, falfely

Count'erferment, *n.* ferment oppofed to ferment

Count'ermand, *n.* a contrary order, repeal, ftop

Countermand', *v. t.* to contradict an order (duet

Count'ermarch, *n.* a march back, a change of con-

Countermarch', *v. t.* to march or go back again

Count'ermine, *n.* a fubterraneous paffage oppofed to another

Countermine, *v. t.* to defeat fecretly, to prevent

Count'ermotion, *n.* a contrary motion or march

Counternat'ural, *a.* contrary to nature, unnatural

Count'erpace, *n.* a contrary meafure, oppofition

Count'erpane, *n.* a fine upper covering of a bed

Count'erpart, *n.* a correfpondent or fecond part

Count'erplea, *n.* a replication in law, a reply

Counterpléad, *v. t.* to contradict, deny, oppofe

Count'erplot, *n.* a plot oppofed againft a plot

Count'erpoife, *n.* equal weight, a balance

Counterpoife', *v. t.* to equal, to balance

Coun'terpoifon, *n.* poifon to defeat poifon

Counterprefs'ure, *n.* an oppofit preffure or force

Count'erproject, *n.* a correfpondent part of a fcheme

Counterrevolútion, *n.* a revolution oppofing an other, and reftoring a former ftate of things

Counterrevolûtionary, *a.* pertaining to a coun-terrevolution

Counterrevolútioniſt, *n.* one engaged in a counterrevolution

Count'erſcarp, *n.* a ditch or ſlope next the camp

Counterſign, *v. t.* to underſign, confirm, ſettle

Coun'terſign, *n.* a military watch word

Counterten'or, *n.* one of the middle parts of muſic

Count'ertide, *n.* a contrary tide or fluctuation

Count'ertime, *n.* defenſe, oppoſition, reſiſtance, *ob.*

Count'erturn, *n.* the height or turn of a play

Countervail, *v. t.* to have equal power, to requite

Count'erview, *n.* an oppoſition, contraſt, defenſe

Counterwork', *v. t.* to counteract, hinder, oppoſe

Count'eſs, *n.* the lady of a count, an earl's lady

Count'inghouſe, *n.* a room where accounts are kept

Count'leſs, *a.* numberleſs, infinite, very large, vaſt

Coun'trified, aukward, plain, ignorant, ſimple

Coun'try, *n.* a tract of land, region, native place

Coun'try, *a.* belonging to the country, ruſtic

Coun'tryman, *n.* one of the ſame country, a ruſtic

Count'y, *n.* a ſhire, portion of a country, court

Count'y, *a.* relating to a county or ſhire

Cou"ple, [cupple] *n.* a brace, pair, chain, rafter

Cou"ple, *v. t.* to join together, chain, link, marry

Coup'let, *n.* two verſes, a pair of rhymes, a pair

Cour'age, *n.* bravery, valor, boldneſs, ſpirit, activity

Courágeous, *a.* brave, bold, ſpirited, daring

Courágeouſly, *ad.* bravely, boldly, daringly, nobly

Courágeouſneſs, *n.* courage, bravery, boldneſs

Courant', *n.* a kind of quick dance, a newſpaper

Courb, *v. t.* to bend, bow, ſtoop ; *a.* crooked, *ob.*

Cour'ier, *n.* a meſſenger ſent in haſte, a runner

Courſe, *n.* a race, place of running, paſſage, progreſs, way, order of ſucceſſion, ſervice of meat

Courſe, *v.* to hunt, run, purſue, rove about

Cóurſer, *n.* a racehorſe, horſeracer, hunter, diſputer

Cóurſes, *n.* the principal ſails of a veſſel

Cóurſing, *n.* the purſuit of hares with grayhounds

Court, *n.* the reſidence of a prince, a ſeat of juſtice

Court, *v. t.* to woo, make love to, ſeek, flatter

Courtchap'lain, *n.* a chaplain to a king or queen

Cóurtday, *n.* a day for adminiſtering juſtice, a high

Cóurtdreſſer, *n.* a flatterer, fawner, *ob.* (day

Court'eous, *a.* civil, complaſant, well-bred, kind

Court'eouſly, *ad.* civilly, complaſantly, kindly

Court'eouſneſs, *n.* civility, complaſance, kindneſs

Cour'teſan or Cour'tezan, *n.* a proſtitute, a harlot

Court'eſy, *n.* civility, kindneſs, female act of reſpect

Court'eſy, *v. i.* to do an act of reverence

Cóurtfavor, *n.* a favor or love beſtowed by princes

Cóurthand, *n.* a kind of hand uſed for records

Cóurtier, *n.* an attendant of or on a court, a lover

Cóurtlady, *n.* a lady well known at court

Courtléet, *n.* the court of the lord of a manor

Cóurtlike, *a.* polite, well-bred, civil, obliging

Cóurtlineſs, *n.* civility, complaſance, form

Cóurtly, *a.* polite, flattering, elegant, ſpruce, ſoft

Cóurtly, *ad.* in the manner of courts, politely

Cóurtmar'tial, *n.* a court to try military offenſes

Cóurtſhip, *n.* the making of love to a woman, love

Couſ'in, *n.* a relation at a diſtance, eſpecially the child of an uncle or aunt

Cove, *n.* a ſmall creek, ſhelter, hole, arch (ment

Cov'enant, [o as u] *n.* a bargain, contract, agree-

Cov'enant, *v. i.* to bargain, contract, agree

Covenantée, *n.* one who enters into a covenant

Cov'enanter, *n.* a perſon who makes a covenant

Cov'er, [o as u] *v. t.* to overſpread, hide, ſave

Cov'er, *n.* concealment, ſcreen, ſhelter, pretence

Cov'ering, *n.* any thing that covers, dreſs, clothes

Cov'erlet, Cov'erlid, *n.* an upper bed-covering

Cov'ert, *a.* covered, hid, ſheltered, ſecret, married

Cov'ert, *n.* a ſhelter, thicket, defenſe, married wo-

Cov'ertly, *ad.* ſecretly, privately, cloſely (man

Cov'erture, *n.* a cover, ſhelter, the ſtate of a wife

Cov'et, [o as u] *v. t.* to deſire earneſtly, to luſt for

Cov'etable, *a.* that may be deſired or wiſhed for

Cov'etous, *a.* very deſirous of ſaving, greedy, near

Cov'etouſly, *ad.* greedily, niggardly, eagerly

Cov'etouſneſs, *n.* eager deſire, greedineſs

Cov'ey, *n.* a brood of birds, hatch, company, ſet

Cov'in, *n.* a deceitful agreement, colluſion, deceit

Cov'inous, *a.* colluſive, fraudulent

Co'ving, *n.* an arch or projection

Cow, *n.* the female of the ox kind

Cow, *v. t.* to diſpirit, depreſs

Cow'ard, *n.* one who wants courage, a poltroon

Cow'ardice, Cow'ardineſs, *n.* a want of courage

Cow'ardly, *ad.* in manner of a coward, meanly

Cow'ardly, Cow'ardous, *a.* fearful, timorous, mean

Cow'ardſhip, *n.* a cowardly character, meanneſs, *ob.*

Cow'er, *v. i.* to ſink by bending the knees, ſhrink,

Cow'hage, *n.* a kind of kidney beans (ſtoop

Cow'herd, *n.* one who tends or keeps cows

Cow'houſe, *n.* a houſe to keep cows in

Cow'itch, *n.* a plant which cauſes an itching

Cow'iſh, *a.* cowardly, fearful, fainthearted

Cowl, *n.* a monk's hood, veſſel for water, tub

Cow'leech, *v. i.* to profeſs the cure of cows

Cowl'ſtaff, *n.* a ſtaff for two to bear a veſſel

Cow'pen, *n.* an incloſure for cows or cattle

Cow'pox, *n.* a diſeaſe from cows, like ſmall pox, the vaccine diſeaſe

Cow'ſlip, *n.* the name of an early yellow flower

Cox'comb, *n.* a cock's topping or caruncle, a fop

Coxcom'ical, *a.* conceited, foppiſh, pert (ſerve

Coy, *a.* reſerved, modeſt; *v. i.* to behave with re-

Çoy'iſh, *a.* rather reſerved or ſhy, modeſt, chaſte

Coy'ly, *ad.* with reſerve, ſhily, modeſtly, chaſtely

Coy'neſs, *n.* reſerve, ſhineſs, modeſty, chaſteneſs

Coz'en, [o as u] *v. t.* to cheat, trick, defraud,

Coz'enage, *n.* cheating, fraud, impoſition, deceit

Coz'ener, *n.* a cheater, knave, villain, deceiver

Crab, *n.* a fiſh, wild apple, peeviſh perſon, *a.* ſour

Crab'bed, *a.* peeviſh, ſour, difficult, perplexed

Crab'bedly, *ad.* peeviſhly, ſourly, moroſely

Crab'bedneſs, *n.* ſourneſs, croſſneſs, a difficulty

Crack, *n.* a ſudden noiſe, chink, boaſter

Crack, v.t. to break into chinks, fplit, craze, boaſt
Crack'brained, a. crazy, maddiſh, whimſical
Crack'er, n. a firework, a boaſter, hard biſket
Crack'hemp, n. one who is fated to the gallows, ob.
Crac''kle, v. i. to make flight cracks, to bounce
Crack'ling, n. a noiſe made by flight cracks
Crack'nel, n. a kind of hard brittle cake, ob.
Cradle, n. a moveable bed, frame, caſe, infancy, a machine uſed in cutting and laying grain
Cradle, v. t. to lay or rock in a cradle, to eaſe, to cut and lay grain in a ſwath
Cradleclothes, n. pl. clothes belonging to a cradle
Craft, n. cunning, trade, a ſmall ſhip
Craft'ily, ad. cunningly, artfully, ſlily
Craft'ineſs, n. craft, cunning, fraud, a ſtratagem
Crafts'man, n. an artificer, workman, mechanic
Crafts'maſter, n. one who is ſkilled in his trade
Craft'y, a. cunning, ſubtle, artful, ſly, deceitful
Crag, n. a rough ſteep rock, the nape of the neck
Crag'ged, Crag'gy, a. rough with rocks, rugged
Crag'gedneſs, Crag'gineſs, n. roughneſs, ſteepneſs
Crake, n. a migratory bird of the rail kind
Cram, v. to ſtuff, force down, eat greedily
Cram'bo, n. a rhyme, a play where one perſon gives a word and another is to find a rhyme
Cramp, n. a contraction of the limbs, confinement, bent piece of iron to keep things faſt by
Cramp, v. t. to confine, hinder, ſtop, bind, pain
Cramp'ed, pa. faſtened, confined, hindered, held
Cramp'fiſh, n. the torpedo or electric ray
Cran'berry, n. a plant and its berry uſed as a ſauce
Crane, n. a bird, engine, machine, crooked pipe
Crane's-bill, n. a kind of plant, a pair of pinchers
Cranefly, n. an inſect called father-long-legs
Crank, n. the end of an iron axis, beam, conceit
Crank, a. healthy, luſty, ſprightly, eaſy to overſet
Cran''kle, v. to run in and out, to break into angles
Cran'nied, a. full of or having chinks
Cran'ny, n. a chink, cleft, crevice, little crack
Crape, n. a thin kind of ſtuff uſed in mourning
Crap'nel, n. a drag, a hook uſed to drag up with
Craſh, v. to make a noiſe, break, bruiſe, cruſh
Craſh, n. a loud mixed noiſe made by a fall
Craſh'ing, pa. making a ſudden noiſe, breaking
Craſis, n. a temperature, mixture, conſtitution
Crafs, a. groſs, coarſe, thick, fat, ob.
Craſ'sament, n. the red thick part of blood (vineſs
Craſs'itude, n. groſſneſs, coarſeneſs, thickneſs, hea-
Cratch, n. a kind of rack for hay or ſtraw, ob.
Crate, n. a kind of hamper to pack earthenware in
Craunch, v. t. to craſh with the teeth
Cravat', n. an ornament for the neck, a neckcloth
Crave, v. to aſk earneſtly, beg, beſeech (cow, ob.
Craven, n. a conquered cock, a coward; v. t. to
Craver, n. one who craves, a mean weak perſon
Craw, n. the crop or firſt ſtomach of birds
Craw'fiſh or Crayfiſh, n. a fiſh, the river lobſter
Crawl, v. i. to creep, move ſlowly, cringe, fawn
Crawl'er, n. a creeper, drone, very ſluggiſh perſon

Crayfiſh, n. a ſpecies of crab, like a lobſter
Crayon, n. a paſte, pencil, roll, picture, drawing
Craze, v. t. to break, crack the brain, powder
Crazedneſs, n. a broken ſtate, weakneſs, defect
Crazineſs, n. a crazy ſtate, weakneſs, feebleneſs
Crazy, a. broken, weak, feeble, ſickly, maddiſh
Creak, v. i. to make a harſh, grating noiſe
Creaking, pa. making a harſh noiſe, grating
Cream, n. the oily part of milk, the very beſt part
Cream, v. i. to yield or take off cream
Creamfaced, a. paleface, pale, cowardly
Creamy, a. full of cream, luſcious, rich, nice
Creaſe, n. a plait or fold; v. t. to mark by folding
Create, v. t. to form, make, cauſe, produce, beget
Created, pa. formed out of nothing, made, ſet up
Creation, n. the act of creating, univerſe, world
Creative, a. able or having the power to create,
Creator, n. one who gives exiſtence, GOD (fertile
Creature, n. a thing created, word of contempt, and tenderneſs, man, animal, one dependent, a
Credence, n. belief, aſſent, credit, reputation (tool
Creden'da, n. pl. articles of faith or belief
Credent, a. eaſy of belief, having credit, certain
Creden'tials, n. pl. a teſtimonial (bability
Credibil'ity, Cred'ibleneſs, n. a claim to credit, pro-
Cred'ible, a. worthy of credit, probable, likely
Cred'ibly, ad. in a credible manner, probably
Cred'it, n. belief, reputation, eſteem, influence, truſt or time given for payment on a ſale
Credit, v. to believe, admit, truſt, ſet off, honor
Cred'itable, a. that may be believed, reputable
Cred'itableneſs, n. credit, reputation, eſtimation y
Cred'itably, ad. with credit, with truſt, reputabl
Cred'itor, n. one who gives credit, or to whom another is indebted
Credulity, Cred'uloufneſs, n. eaſineſs of belief
Cred'ulous, a. apt to believe, eaſily deceived, fond
Creed, n. a form or confeſſion of faith, a belief
Creek, n. a ſmall bay, alley, nook, corner, turn
Creek'y, a. full of or having creeks, winding
Creep, v. i. crept, pret. creeped, crept, pa. to move ſlowly, loiter, fawn, bend
Creeper, n. one who creeps, a plant, an inſtrument
Creephole, n. a hole or way of eſcape, an excuſe
Creepingly, ad. ſlowly, in a dull manner, ſlily,
Cremation, n. a burning, the act of burning (ſoftly
Cremor, n. a creamy or milky ſubſtance
Crenate, a. notched, indented, jagged
Creole, n. a native of the Weſt Indies or Spaniſh America, deſcended from European anceſtors
Crepitation, n. a low crackling or rattling noiſe
Crept, pret. and pa. from to creep
Crepus''cle, n. a very doubtful light, the twilight
Crepus'culous, Crepus'cular, a. pertaining to twilight, glimmering, dim
Creſcent, n. an increaſing moon, a half moon
Creſ'cent, Creſ'cive, a. increaſing, growing
Crefs, n. the name of a water-herb
Creſ'set, n. a light ſet on a beacon, &c. ob.

Creſt, n. a plume of fethers, comb, pride, ſpirit
Creſt'ed, Creſt'ate, a. wearing a creſt or comb
Creſt'fallen, a. dejected, low, ſpiritleſs, cowed
Creſt'leſs, a. without armor, &c. mean, low
Cretáceous, Crétous, a. chalky, having chalk
Crétan, n. a native of Crete, now Candia
Crétan, a. pertaining to Crete
Crev'ice, n. a crack, cleft, fiſh (pret. of to crow
Crew, n. a ſhip's company, ſet, mean aſſembly;
Crew'el, n. worſted, a ball of worſted, yarn or ſilk
Crib, n. a manger, rack, ſtall, cottage, pouch, bag
Crib, v. t. to ſteal, cage, ſhut up, confine
Crib'bage, n. the name of a game at cards
Crib'bed, pa. ſtolen, pent up, ſhut up, confined
Cribrátion, n. the act of ſifting or cleanſing
Crib'riform, a. reſembling a ſieve
Cricétus, n. the hamſter or large rat of Germany
Crick, n. the noiſe of a hinge, a pain in the neck
Crick'et, n. a ſmall inſect, game, low ſeat, ſtool
Crier, n. one who cries goods for ſale or proclaims
Crime, n. a violation of law to the injury of the
    public, a public offenſe, ſin
Crimeful, a. criminal, guilty, faulty, wicked, ob.
Crimeleſs, a. innocent, free from guilt, ob.
Crim'inal, a. a perſon accuſed or guilty
Crim'inal, Crim'inous, a. guilty, faulty, not civil
Crim'inally, Crim'inouſly, ad. wickedly, badly
Criminal'ity, n. guilt, the quality of being criminal
Criminátion, n. an accuſation, charge, cenſure
Crim'inatory, a. tending to accuſe, cenſorious
Crim'inouſneſs, n. crime, guilt, ob.
Crim'oſin, n. a ſpecies of red color, crimſon, ob.
Crimp, a. eaſily crumbled, brittle, criſp
Crimp, n. an agent for coals or ſhipping, one hir-
    ed to procure ſeamen, Eng.
Crimp, v. t. to procure ſeamen for a premium
Crimp'age, n. premium paid for hiring ſeamen
Crim"ple, v. t. to lay in plaits, curl up, contract
Crimp'ling, pa. curling, contracting, lamiſh
Crim'ſon, n. a very deep red color; v. t. to die red
Crinc'um, n. a whim, cramp, contradiction
Cringe, n. a low bow, mean reverence, ſervility
Cringe, v. to bow, fawn, flatter, contract, ſhrink
Crini"gerous, Crinoſe, a. hairy, very rough
Crin'gle, n. a hole on a bolt rope, formed by a
    twiſted ſtrand, a hank or open ring on a ſtay
Cri'nite, a. having hairs or filaments like hairs
Crink, Crin"kle, n. a wrinkle, a winding, a fold
Crin"kle, v. i. to run in wrinkles or folds, to wind
Crinos'ity, n. hairineſs, ſhaggineſs, roughneſs
Crip'ple, n. a very lame perſon; v. t. to make lame
Criſe, Criſis, n. a critical time or turn, a ſentence
Criſp, v. t. to curl, twiſt, indent, make brittle
Criſp, Criſp'y, a. curled, brittle, ſhort
Criſpātion, n. the act of curling, a curled ſtate
Cris'pature, n. a curling
Criſp'ingpin, n. a kind of iron, a curling-iron
Criſp'itude, Criſp'neſs, n. a criſpy ſtate, ſhortneſs
Cris'tate, a. having a tufted creſt, tufted

Critérion, n. a mark whereby to judge, a ſtandard
Crit'ic, n. one ſkilled in criticiſm, a nice cenſurer
Crit'ic, Crit'ical, a. nice, judicious, keen, exact,
    indicating the criſis of a diſeaſe
Crit'iciſe, v. t. to judge and remark with nice
    diſcernment, to cenſure
Crit'iciſm, n. the act or art of judging accurately,
    diſcriminating remarks, cenſure
Crit'ically, ad. exactly, curiouſly, judiciouſly
Crit'icalneſs, n. exactneſs, nicety, accuracy, care
Critíque, n. the act of criticiſing, a criticiſm
Criz'zle, v. i. to contract roughneſs as glaſs
Croak, n. the cry of a frog, raven or crow (growl
Croak, v. i. to cry like a frog, raven or crow, to
Cróaking, pa. making a hoarſe continued noiſe
Cróceous, a. like or having ſaffron, yellow
Croch'es n. pl. knobs on the top of a deer's horn
Crock, n. an earthen pot, pan, black of a pot
Crock, v. t. to blacken with foul matter
Crock'ery, n. all kinds of earthen or china ware
Croc'odile, n. an amphibious voracious animal
Crócus, n. a flower, ſaffron, yellow powder
Croft, n. a ſmall field near a houſe, a little cloſe
Croiſáde or Croiſádo, ſee cruſade
Crone or Croan, n. an old ewe, a very old woman
Cróny, n. an old acquaintance, companion, friend
Crook, n. a hooked ſtick; v. t. to bend, to pervert
Crook'backed, a. having round or bent ſhoulders
Crook'ed, pa. bent, winding, perverſe, croſs
Crook'edly, ad. not ſtraitly, untowardly
Crook'edneſs, n. a crooked ſtate, deformity of body
Croop, n. a diſeaſe in the windpipe
Crop, n. a produce, thing cut off, bird's ſtomach
Crop, v. to lop, cut off or ſhort, reap, ſow, yield
Crop'ful, a. quite full, crammed, glutted, ſatisfied
Crop'ſick, a. ſick, ſick through exceſs in eating
Cropt, pa. cut, cut off at the end, reaped, ſown
Cróſier, n. a biſhop's ſtaff with a croſs upon it, paſ-
    toral ſtaff, inſtrument
Croſs'let, n. a ſmall croſs, frontlet, headcloth
Croſs, n. a gibbet, misfortune, oppoſition, trial
Croſs, a. athwart, oppoſit, peeviſh, difficult
Croſs, v. t. to lay athwart, paſs over, oppoſe, vex,
    ſign, cancel, put out; ad. over, from ſide to ſide
Croſs'bill, n. a bird with croſſing mandibles of the bill
Croſs'bite, n. a cheat, a deception; v. t. to cheat
Croſs'bow, n. a weapon uſed for ſhooting
Croſſexam'in, v. t. to examin by different parties
Croſs'grained, a. troubleſome, illnatured, croſs
Croſs'ly, ad. peeviſhly, perverſely, unfortunately
Croſs'neſs, n. peeviſhneſs, perverſeneſs, oddneſs
Croſs way, n. a path that runs acroſs a wider road,
    a raiſed way over wet ground
Croſs'wind, n. a wind blowing from right to left
Croſs'wiſe, ad. in the form of a croſs, acroſs
Croſs'wort, n. a plant of ſeveral ſpecies
Crotch, n. a kind of hook, the forked part of a tree
Crotch'et, n. a mark uſed in muſic or printing,
    hook, odd fancy, whim, ſtrange conceit, tooth

Crouch, v. to ftoop low, bend, cringe, crofs
Croup, [croop] n. the rump, a difeafe
Croupáde, n. a high leap, a dreffed loin of mutton
Crow, n. a bird, cock's voice, iron lever, iron bar
Crow, v. i. crowed or crew, pret. crowed, pa. to make the noife of a cock, boaft, hector, exult
Crowd or Croud, n. a multitude, mob, fiddle
Crowd, v. to prefs or fet clofe, fwarm, encumber
Crowd'er, n. a fiddler
Crówfoot, n. a plant with a yellow flower, ranun-
Crów-filk, n. a water vegetable, conferva (culus
Crown, n. top of the head, money, ornament, garland, regal power, a kind of paper
Crown, v. t. to inveft with a crown, reward, finifh
Crównet, n. a net for taking wild fowls
Crown'glafs, n. the fineft fort of window-glafs
Crown'office, n. an office of the King's bench
Crúcial, a. tranfverfe, running acrofs, croffed
Crúcian, n. a fhort, thick, broad fifh
Crúciate, v. t. to torture, torment, pain, ob.
Crúcible, n. a chymift's pot to melt metals in
Crucif'erous, a. carrying or having a crofs
Crúcified, pa. put to death or fixed on a crofs
Crúcifix, n. a figure of Chrift upon the crofs
Crucifix'ion, n. the act of nailing to or on a crofs
Crúcify, v. t. to hang to or faften on a crofs
Crúciform, a. in fhape of a crofs
Crude, a. raw, unripe, undigefted, chill
Crúdely, ad. rawly, unripely, not duly digefted
Crúdenefs, Crúdity, n. want of ripenefs, indigeftion
Cru''dle, v. to curdle, turn to curds, fee curdle
Crúel, a. hardhearted, inhuman, bloody, fierce
Crúelly, ad. barbaroufly, inhumanly feverely
Crúelnefs, Crúelty, n. barbarity, inhumanity
Cruent'ate, a. fmeared or covered with blood, ob.
Cruent'ous, a. bloody, ftained with blood, ob.
Crúet, n. a kind of large vial for vinegar or oil
Crúife, n. a voyage made for plunder
Cruize, v. i. to fail, to fail in queft of an enemy
Crúizer, n. a fhip, one that feeks a prey
Crum, n. a fragment of bread (the foft part, ob.)
Crum, Crum'ble, v. to break or fall into pieces
Crum'my, a. full of crums, fmall, foft, plump
Crump, a. crooked in the back, bowed, bent
Crum''ple, v. t. to make wrinkly, ruffle, diforder
Crump'ling, n. a very rough apple, a green codlin
Crunk, Crun''kle, v. i. to cry like a crane
Crup'per, [u as oo] n. a lether to keep a faddle
Crup'per, v. t. to put on a crupper (back
Crúral, a. belonging or relating to the leg
Crufáde, n. a Portugal coin, a holy war
Crufáder, a. a perfon engaged in a crufade
Crúfe, n. a fmall veffel
Crúfet, n. a goldfmith's melting pot
Crufh, v. to fqueeze, bruife, difpirit, fubdue, ruin
Crufh, n. a crafh, a falling down, violence, force
Crufh'ed, pa. preffed clofe, fqueezed, overcome
Cruft, n. a hard covering, cafe, piece of bread
Cruft, v. to cover with or contract a hard cafe

Cruftáceous, a. fhelly, having foft fhells in feveral pieces, as a lobfter
Cruft'ily, ad. fnappifhly, peevifhly, furlily
Cruft'inefs, n. peevifhnefs, morofenefs, furlinefs
Cruft'y, a. fnappifh, crofs, morofe, fturdy (port
Crutch, n. a fuppart ufed by cripples; v. t. to fup-
Cry, v. to weep, call, fquall, yell, proclaim, blame
Cry, n. a weeping, a fhrieking, outcry, yell, found
Cryp'tic, Cryp'tical, a. fecret, hidden, private
Cryptogam'ia, n. concealed fructification, a clafs of plants fo called
Cryptogam'ian, a. pertaining to fecret fecundation
Cryptog'raphy, n. a fecret kind of writing, cyphers
Cryptol'ogy, n. a very doubtful language, a whifper
Crys'tal, n. a tranfparent ftone, a regular form of falt or other fubftance made from a folution by evaporation
Crys'tal, Crys'taline, a. tranfparent, clear, bright
Cryftalizátion, n. a congelation into cryftals
Crys'talize, v. to form or be formed into a regular figure, like a cryftal, as falt from a folution
Crys'talized, pa. formed or frozen into cryftals
Crys'talizable, a. that may be cryftalized
Crys'talform, a. in the fhape of cryftals
Cryftallog'raphy, n. the fcience of cryftalization
Cub, n. the young of a fox, &c. a whelp
Cub, v. t. to bring forth cubs, to whelp
Cúbature, n. the folid contents of a body (root
Cube, n. a fquare folid body, die, third power of a
Cube, v. t. to multiply twice into itfelf
Cúbebs, n. a plant, a fpecies of pepper
Cúbic, Cúbical, a. formed like a cube, folid
Cúbit, n. a meafure of about 18 inches, a bone
Cúbital, a. as long as or belonging to a cubit
Cuck'old, n. the hufband of an adultrefs (lute
Cuck'old, v. t. to make a man a cuckold, to pol-
Cuck'oldly, a. poor, low, mean, defpicable
Cuck'oldom, n. the act or ftate of adultery, infamy
Cuck'oo, [u as oo] n. a genus of birds (hood
Cúcullate, a. hooded, rolled in form of a cone or
Cúcumber, n. the name of a plant and its fruit
Cucur'bit, n. a chymical veffel like a gourd
Cucurbitáceous, a. pertaining to or like a gourd
Cud, n. food once digefted, food to be chewed over
Cud'dy, n. a clown, a cabin or cook room
Cud'dle, v. to lie low or clofe, fquat, hug
Cudg'el, n. a thick ftick, a fighting-ftick
Cudg'el, v. i. to beat with a cudgel, beat, bang
Cudg'elproof, a. able to bear or refift a cudgel
Cud'weed, n. a plant, cotton weed
Cue, n. the end or tail of a thing, a hint, humor
Cuer'po, n. the body in fhort clothes or real fhape
Cuff, n. a box, blow, ftroke, part of a fleeve
Cuff, v. to ftrike with the fift, beat, knock, fight
Cuirafs, n. a breaft plate made of lether or fteel
Cuiraffíer, n. a foldier in armor, one in arms
Cuifh, n. armor to cover or fhield the thighs
Cúlinary, a. belonging to the kitchen or cookery
Cull, v. t. to felect from others, pick out, choofe

H

Cull'ender, n. a draining veffel, a colander
Cull'ion, n. a fcoundrel, mean perfon, a plant
Cull'y, n. a man deceived or jilted by a woman
Cull'y, v. t. to befool, cheat, trick, impofe upon
Culm, n. a kind of fmall coal, foot, fmoke, ftalk
Culmiferous, a. having a culm or ftalk
Culm'inate, v. i. to be or come on the meridian, to come to the higheft point or degree
Culmination, n. a coming to the meridian or the higheft point
Cul'pable, a. guilty, criminal, faulty, blamable
Cul'pablenefs, Culpabil'ity, n. guilt, fault, blame
Cal'pably, ad. with blame, with guilt, criminally
Cul'prit, n. one who is arraigned before a judge
Cul'tivable, a. capable of cultivation
Cul'tivate, v. t. to till, manure, improve, refine
Cultivation, n. a manuring, tilling, improvement
Cul'tivator, n. one who cultivates or improves
Cul trate, a. fmooth like the edge of a knife
Cul'ture, n. the act of cultivation; v. t. to culti-
Cul'ver, n. a fort of pigeon, a woodpigeon (vate
Cul'verin, n. a fpecies of ordnance, a cannon
Culv'ert, n. an open paffage or channel
Cum'ber, v. t. to clog, burden, embarrafs, diftract
Cum'ber, n. vexation, embarrafsment, obftruction
Cumberland, n. a river and a mountain in Ten-
neffee, &c.
Cum'berfome, a. troublefome, unmanageable
Cum'berfomely, Cum'bronfly, ad. troublefomely
Cum'brance, n. an encumbrance, burden, load
Cum'brous, a. troublefome, heavy, oppreffive
Cum'in, n. a genus of aromatic plants
Cúmulate, v. t. to heap or pile up, amafs, not ufed
Cúmulation, n. the act of heaping up, not ufed
Cunctation, n. a delay, procraftination, ftop, not ufed
Cúneal, a. like or belonging to a wedge
Cúneate, a. made or fhaped like a wedge
Cuniform, a. in fhape of a wedge
Cun'ning, a. artful, fly, knowing, fkilful, expert
Cun'ning, Cun'ningnefs, n. artifice, flinefs, fkill
Cun'ningly, ad. artfully, flily, craftily, fharply
Cunningman, n. a fortuneteller, a conjurer, ob.
Cup, n. a drinking veffel, part of a flower, liquor
Cup, v. t. to bleed by fcarification, to fupply cups
Cup'bearer, n. an officer of a king's houfhold
Cup'board, n. a place for cups, glaffes, &c. v. t.
to hoard (tals, to abforb the drofs
Cup'pel or Cup'el, n. a veffel ufed in refining me-
Cup'pel, v. t. to refine in a cuppel
Cuppellation, n. the refining of metals in a cuppel
Cupid'ity, n. luft, exceffive or fenfual defire
Cupola, n. a dome, arched roof, turret, bowl
Cup'per, n. one who cups, one who fcarifies
Cupreous, a. coppery, containing or like copper
Cupric..''cid, a facurated comb'nation of copper and
oxygene (with another fubftance
Cúprate, n. a combination of the oxyd of copper
Cupriferous, a. producing copper
Cups, n. pl. a drunken fit, drunkennefs, liquor

Cur, n. a dog, bad or mean man, fnappifh perfon
Cúrable, a. that may be cured, healed or remedied
Cúracy, n. the employment of a curate
Curas'so, n. an American bird large as a fmall turky
Cúrate, n. an officiating minifter under the incum-
Cúrative, a. relating to the cure of difeafes (bent
Cúrator, n. one who manages or directs
Curb, v. t. to reftrain, check, ftop, manage, bridle
Curb, n. a part of a bridle, oppofition, reftraint,
box round a well
Curd, n. a coagulation of milk or of any liquid
Curd, Cur''dle, v. to turn or fhoot into curds
Curd'y, a. curdled, full of or having curds, clotty
Cure, n. a remedy, the employment of a curate
Cure, v. t. to heal, reftore to health, falt, feafon
Cúred, pa. healed, reftored, preferved, falted,
Cúrelefs, a. having no remedy, incurable (weaned
Cúrer, n. one who cures, a healer, a phyfician
Cur'few, n. eight o'clock bell, a cover for a fire
Cúriality, n. privilege or ftate of a court, ob.
Curios'ity, n. an inquifitivenefs, nicenefs, rarity
Cúrious, a. inquifitive, nice, neat, exact, rare
Cúrioufly, ad. inquifitively, neatly, exactly, well
Curl, n. a ringlet or ornament of hair, a wave
Curl, v. to turn into ringlets, turn, twift, wave
Cur'lew, n. a kind of water and land fowl
Curmud''geon, n. a mifer, niggard, griper, churl
Curmud''geonly, a. covetous, niggardly, churlifh, ob
Cur'rant, n. the name of a fhrub and fruit
Cur'rency, n. a circulation, currentnefs, paper paf-
fing for, and eftablifhed as, current money
Cur'rent, a. circulatory, fafhionable, common
Cur'rent, n. a ftream, courfe, great crowd or body
Cur'rently, ad. generally, without oppofition
Cur'rentnefs, n. circulation, fluency (horfes
Cur'ricle, n. a chaife of two wheels drawn by two
Cur'ried, pa. dreffed, cleaned, beaten, drubbed
Cur'rier, n. a dreffer of lether already tanned
Cur'rifh, a. like a dog, fnappifh, quarrelfome
Cur'ry, v. t. to drefs lether, rub, drub, flatter
Cur'rycomb, n. an iron comb to drefs horfes with
Curfe, n. a bad wifh or name, vexation, torment
Curfe, v. t. to wifh evil to, torment, afflict, load
Curs'ed pa. a. under a curfe, vexatious, hateful
Curs'edly, ad. miferably, fhamefully, badly, very
Curs'ednefs, n. a curfed ftate or quality, badnefs
Cur'fhip, n. croffnefs, illnature, meannefs
Curs'itor, n. an officer or clerk in chancery
Curs'ory, a. hafty, quick, carelefs, flight
Curs'orily, ad. haftily, without care, flightly
Curs'orinefs, n. flight attention, careleffnefs
Curft, pa. curfed, peevifh, crofs, malicious
Curft'hefs, n. peevifhnefs, crofsnefs, illnature, ob.
Curtáil, v. t. to cut fhort, fhorten, abridge
Cur'tain, n. part of a bed, window or fortification
Cur'tain, v. t. to inclofe, fix, &c. with curtains
Cur'tain-lec'ture, n. a bed-lecture from a wife
Curtána, n. a blunt fword borne at coronations
Curtátion, n. a diftance of a ftar from the ecliptic

Curv'ated, *a.* curved, bent, bowed, crooked

Curvâtion, *n.* the act of bending, a being bent

Curv'ature, *n.* a crookednefs, a bend, a winding

Curve,*a.* crooked, bent ; *v. t.* to bend, to crook

Curve, *n.* any thing that is bent, crookednefs

Curv'et, *n.* a leap, bound, frolic, prank

Curvet, *v. i.* to leap, fkip, bound, frifk, prance

Curvilin'eal, *a.* compofed of crooked lines, curve

Curvilinear'ity, *n.* a confifting of a curving line

Curv'ity, *n.* crookednefs, a bent or bowed ftate

Cur'ule, *a.* fenatorian, triumphal, magnificent

Cufhew'bird, *n.* a bird like the Curaffo

Cufh'ion, [u as oo] *n.* a foft feat for a chair, a pillow

Cufh'ion, *v. t.* to place on or fupport by cufhions

Cus'kin, *n.* a kind of ivory cup

Cufp, *n.* the horns of the moon, &c. a point

Cufp'idate, *a.* ending in a point, like a fpear

Cus'fion, *n.* a plant, the fea pink

Cus'tard, *n.* a fort of fweet food of eggs, milk, &c.

Cus'tody, *n.* imprifonment, prifon, care, fecurity

Cus'tom, *n.* a habit, fafhion, practice, ufage; ufe, way, duties on imports and exports

Cus'tomable, *a.* fubject to duties, *(L. of Mafs.)*

Cus'tomably, *ad.* according to cuftom, commonly

Cus'tomarilv, *ad.* ufually, commonly, chiefly

Cus'tomary Cus'tomed, *a.* ufual, common, general

Cus'tomer, *n.* one who buys any thing

Cus'tomhoufe, *n.* a houfe where duties are received on imports and exports

Cut, *v. t.* cut, *pret.* cut, *pa.* to carve, hew, lop, fhape, crofs, divide, part

Cut, *pa.* prepared for ufe, hewed, lopped, hurt

Cut, *n.* a cleft or wound with an edged tool, flice of meat, &c. lop, canal, picture, impreffion, fool

Cutáneous, *a.* relating to the fkin

Cúticle, *n.* outer or thin fkin, the fcarffkin

Cutic'ular, *a.* lying no deeper than the outfide

Cut'lafh or Cut'lafs, *n.* a broad cutting fword

Cut'ler, *n.* one who makes or fells knives, &c.

Cut'purfe, *n.* a pickpocket, thief, footpad, rogue

Cut'ter, *n.* one who cuts, a fwift-failing veffel

Cut'throat, *n.* a murderer, affaffin, ruffian, villain

Cut'throat, *a.* cruel, inhuman, bloody, vile

Cut'ting, *pa.* dividing with a knife, fevere, keen

Cut'ting, *n.* a piece cut off, chop, branch, fprig

Cut'tle, *n.* a kind of fifh, a foulmouthed fellow

Cut'water,*n.* the fore part of a veffel's prow, a bird

Cyath'iform, *a.* fhaped like a cup

Cy"cle, *n.* a circle, round of time, revolution

Cycloid', *n.* a figure of the circular kind (tionary

Cyclopédia, *n.* a body or circle of fciences, a dic-

Cyclop'ian, *n.* relating to the Cyclops, fabled giants with but one eye and that in the forehead

Cyg'net, *n.* a young or little fwan (hollow

Cyl'inder, *n.* a long round body, roller, plafter,

Cylindráceous, Cylin'drical, *a.* like a cylinder

Cymar', *n.* a kind of flight covering, fcarf, fimar

Cym'bal, *n.* a mufical inftrument

Cym'biform, *a.* fhaped like a boat

Cym'ling, *n.* a name of the fquafh, [Virginia]

Cyme, *n.* an aggregate flower with florets on peduncles from the fame point, but with faftigiate and irregular pedicels

Cy'mous, *a.* containing or in form of a cyme

Cyn'ic, *n.* a fnarling philofopher, fnarler, brute

Cyn'ic, Cyn'ical, *a.* fatirical, fnarling, churlifh

Cyn'ically, *ad.* in a cynical manner

Cyn'icalnefs, *n.* morofenefs, churlifhnefs

Cy'nofure, *n.* the north-ftar, what attracts the eye

Cy'prefs, *n.* a tree, an emblem of mourning

Cyp'rin, *a.* denoting a kind of toothlefs fifh, with gills of three rays

Cy'prus, *n.* a very thin ftuff or filky gauze, a rufh

Cyp'riot, *n.* a native of Cyprus

Cyrénian, *n.* a native of Cyrene in Africa

Cyft, *n.* a bag, bag of morbid matter, bladder

Cys'tic, *a.* pertaining to a cyft

Cyftot'omy, *n.* the act of cutting tumors

Czar, *n.* the ufual title of the emperor of Ruffia

Czarína, *n.* the title of the emprefs of Ruffia

Czar'ifh, *a.* pertaining to the Czar of Ruffia

D

DAB, *v. t.* to ftrike or hit gently, to moiften

Dab, *n.* a gentle blow, flat fifh, artift

Dab'ble, *v.* to play in water, wet, fmear, meddle

Dab'bler, *n.* one who dabbles, one who meddles

Dab'chick, *n.* a very young chicken, a waterfowl

Dacápo, *n.* a repetition of the firft part of a tune

Dace, *n.* a kind of fifh refembling a roach

Dac'tyl, *n.* a poetical foot or meafure, confifting of one long fyllable and two fhort ones, a fifh

Dac'tylic, *a.* pertaining to or confifting of dactyls

Dad or Dad'dy, *n.* a term for father

De'dal, Dedálian, *a.* cunning, expert, intricate

Daffe, *v. t.* to daunt, dafh, put afide ; *n.* a coward

Daf'fodil, *n.* narciffus, a plant

Daft, *v. t.* to tofs or throw afide, *ob.*

Dag, *v. t.* to daggle, dirty daub, trim

Dag, Dag'ger, *n.* a kind of fhort fword (quarrel

Dag'gerfdrawing, *n.* a near approach to force, a

Dag'ges, *n. pl.* lethern latchets, the ends of wool

Dag'gle, *v.* to trail or be in dirt, dirty, fprinkle

Dágon, *n.* an idol worfhipped in Canaan

Dagy'fa, *n.* a fmall angular fifh

Dáily or Dáyly, *a.* and *ad.* day by day, every day

Dáintily, *ad.* elegantly, delicioufly, nicely, foftly

Dáintinefs, *n.* delicacy, fqueamifhnefs, nicenefs

Dáinty, *a.* delicate, curious, nice, fqueamifh

Dáinty, *n.* a delicacy, nice thing, titbit

Dáiry, *n.* a milk farm, houfe or room, pafturage for

Dáirymaid, *n.* a maid that attends the dairy (cows

Dáified, *a.* full of or adorned with daifies

Dáify, *n.* a fmall common fpring-flower

Dákerhen, *n.* a gallinaceous bird like a quail

Dale, *n.* a vale, valley, fpace between two hills

Dal'liance, *n.* fondnefs, love, paftime, delay

Dal'lier, *n.* one who dallies, a fondler, a trifler

Dal'ly, *v.* to delay, toy, trifle

Dalmátian, a. pertaining to Dalmatia, on the Gulf of Venice

Dam, n. a mother of brutes, bank to ftop water

Dam, v. t. to ftop or fhut up, confine, obftruct

Dam'age, n. mifchief, hurt, lofs, injury,

Dam'age, v. t. to injure, hurt, mar, impair, fpoil

Dam'ageable, a. that may be hurt, mifchievous

Dam'aged, pa. injured, hurt, impaired, fpoiled

Dam'afk, n. filk, woolien, &c. woven into flowers

Dam'afk, v. t. to weave into flowers, &c. to warm

Damafkéen, v. t. to inlay with gold or filver

Dame, n. a lady, a woman in general

Damn, v. t. to curfe, condemn, doom, hifs down

Damnability, Dam'nablenefs, n. a damnable ftate

Dam'nable, a. deftructive, moft wicked, odious

Dam'nably, ad. deftructively, wickedly, odioufly

Damnátion, n. the punifhment of the damned

Dam'natory, a. tending to condemn

Dam'ned, pa. curfed, doomed, exploded, ruined

Dam'nify, v. t. to injure, damage, hurt, impair

Dam'aingnefs, n. a tendency to damnation or ruin

Damp, a. moift, wet, foggy, dejected, funk (nefs

Damp, n. a moifture, fog, dejection, heavinefs, low-

Damp, v. t. to wet, caft down, difpirit, weaken

Damp'er, n. a valve in a furnace to ftop or leffen the quantity of air admitted

Damp'ifh, a. rather damp, moift, wettifh

Damp'ifhnefs, Damp'nefs, n. moiftnefs, fogginefs

Damp, n. the popular name for deadly vapors in pits, wells, &c. chiefly for carbonic acid gas, or hydrogenous gas

Damp'y, a. forrowful, caft down, gloomy, heavy

Dam'fel, n. a young maiden or girl, a country lafs

Dam'fon, Dam'afcene, n. a fmall black plum

Dance, v. to move by mufic, wait upon, put into motion

Dance, n. a mufical motion, caper, hurry, purfuit

Dan'cer, n. one who dances, one who cuts capers

Dan'cing, n. a motion of the feet by art or to mufic

Dan'cingmafter, n. a perfon who teaches to dance

Dandelion, n. the name of a plant or herb (lay

Dan'dle, v. t. to fondle, fhake gently, dance, de-

Dan'dler, n. one who dandles, a fondler, a trifler

Dan'der or Dan'druff, n. fcurf formed on the head

Dane, n. a native of Denmark

Dánegelt, n. a tax paid by the Englifh, formerly for every hide of land to the Danes

Dánewort, n. a kind of plant, dwarf-elder

Dan'ger, n. rifk, hazard, a duty; v. t. to endanger

Dan'gerlefs, a. free from danger or rifk, very fafe

Dan'gerous, a. full of danger, hazardous, unfafe

Dan'geroufly, ad. with or in danger, unfafely

Dan'geroufnefs, n. danger, hazard, rifk, peril

Dan"gle, v. t. to hang loofe or about, to follow

Dang'ler, n. one who hangs about women, a trifler

Dánifh, a. pertaining to Denmark or the Danes

Dánifh, n. the language of the Danes

Dank, a. damp, moift, wet; n. moifture, water

Dank'ifh, a. fomewhat damp or moift, wettifh

Dank'ifhnefs, n. a trifling moifture or wetnefs

Dap, v. t. to drop or let fall gently into water

Dap'per, a. little and active, lively, neat, tight

Dap'ple, a. of various colors, ftreaked; v. t. to ftreak

Dare, v. dared, durft, pret. dared, pa. to defy, challenge, have courage, ftare

Dare, n. a defiance, challenge, fifh, pain, harm

Dar'ic, n. an ancient gold coin of Darius the Mede, value about 25s. fter. or 556 cents

Dáring, a. bold, adventurous, fearlefs, impudent

Dáringly, ad. boldly, courageoufly, faucily, pertly

Dáringnefs, n. boldnefs, impudence, faucinefs

Dark, n. darknefs, obfcurity, ignorance, perplexity

Dark, a. void of light, blind, obfcure

Dark'en, v. to make or grow dark, fully, perplex

Dark'ifh, a. rather dark, dufky, dull, obfcure

Dark'ling, a. being in the dark, void of light, dull

Dark'ly, ad. in the dark, blindly, obfcurely

Dark'nefs, n. want of light, obfcurity, wickednefs

Dark'fome, a. wanting light, gloomy, obfcure

Dar'ling, n. a favorite, a delight; a. dear, beloved

Darn, v. t. to mend holes or rents

Darn'el, n. a common field-weed, Colium

Dar'rain, v. t. to range troops for battle, ob.

Dárt, n. a weapon thrown by the hand

Dart, v. to pafs, as a dart, to throw offenfively

Dart'ing, pa. throwing, fhooting, painful

Dart'ingly, ad. in manner of a dart, very fwiftly

Dafh, v. t. to ftrike againft, rufh, blot out, mix

Dafh, n. a ftroke, blow, mixture, this mark (—)

Das'tard, n. a coward, fainthearted fellow, poltroon

Das'tard, Das'tardize, v. t. to terrify, to frighten

Das'tardly, a. cowardly, timorous, mean, bafe

Date, v. t. to give, mark or note the precife time

Date, n. a point of time, fruit of the palm tree

Dáted, pa. marked with the true or exact time

Dátelefs, a. having no date mentioned, not dated

Dátive, a. the third of the fix cafes in grammar, ufed in actions of giving and reftoring

Dav'it, n. a beam to hoift the flukes of anchors

Daub, v. t. to fmear, trim gaudily, flatter, bribe

Daub'er, n. a coarfe low painter

Daub'ry, n. bad or coarfe painting, art, flattery

Daub'y, a. fticky, glutinous, ropy, tough

Daugh'ter, n. a female child, a female penitent

Daunt, v. to difcourage, difpirit, frighten, dafh

Daunt'ed, pa. difpirited, frightened, terrified

Daunt'lefs, a. fearlefs, not dejected, bold, ftout

Dauph'in, n. the eldeft fon of the king of France

Dauph'inefs, n. the wife or lady of the dauphin

Daw, n. the name of a black bird, the jackdaw

Dawk, v. t. to mark with a cut, to chip; n. a cut

Dawn, v. i. to grow light, glimmer, open, appear

Dawn, n. the firft rife, beginning, break of day

Day, n. time from funrife to its fetting, 24 hours

Dáybed, n. a bed ufed for idlenefs or indulgence

Dáybreak, n. the firft dawn or appearance of day

Dáylaborer, n. a man who works only by the day

Dáylight, n. the light that is afforded by the day

Dáyfpring, n. the beginning or firft dawn of day
Dáyftar, n. the morning-ftar, the laft ftar, Venus
Dáytime, n. the time whilft the day lafts
Dáywork, n. work done by the day only
Daze, Daz'zle, v. t. to overpower with light
Dázied, a. befpangled with or having dafies
Déacon, n. a church-officer, an overfeer
Déaconefs, n. a female deacon, attendant, helper
Déaconry, n. the dignity or office of a deacon
Dead, a. deprived of life, cold, dull, taftelefs, loft
Dead, n. ftillnefs, quietnefs, filence, gloom, depth
Dead, Dead'en, v. t. to weaken, to make taftelefs
Dead'doing, a. deftructive, wafteful, mifchievous
Dead'eye, n. a block pierced with three holes for
a laniard, to extend fhrouds, &c.
Dead'lift, n. a hopelefs diftrefs, extremity, pinch
Dead'light, n. a wooden port to fecure a cabin
window, form of a window
Dead'ly, a. deftructive, mortal, dangerous, cruel
Dead'ly, ad. mortally, irreconcileably, very
Dead'nefs, n. faintnefs, a want of warmth
Deadreck'oning, n. a reckoning independent of ob-
fervation (a fhip's ftern as fhe fails
Dead'water, n. the water that whirls in eddies at
Deaf, a. wanting the fenfe of hearing
Deaf, Déafen, v. t. to make deaf, ftupify, confound
Déafifh, a. fomewhat deaf, dull of hearing, dull
Déafly, ad. obfcurely, to the ear, flatly, badly
Déafnefs, n. the want of proper hearing, dulnefs
Deal, n. a quantity, portion, part, firwood
Deal, v. dealt, pret. dealt, pa. to diftribute, give,
divide, trade, treat, contend
Déaler, n. one who deals, one who trades
Déaling, n. practice, bufinefs, concern, treatment
Dealt, pa. given to or out, ufed, treated, handled
Dean, n. a confiderable dignitary in the church
Deanry, n. the office, revenue or houfe of a dean
Dear, a. beloved, coftly, high, fcarce, fad, grievous
Dear, n. a word of endearment, a perfon beloved
Déarbought, a. purchafed at too high a price
Déarly, ad. with great fondnefs, at a high price
Déarnefs, n. fondnefs, a high price, coft, fcarcity
Dearth, n. a great fcarcity, want, barrennefs (tion
Death, n. an extinction of life, mortality, damna-
Death'bed, n. the bed of a dying perfon, laft bed
Death'lefs, a. never dying, immortal, perpetual
Death'like, a. refembling death, ftill, motionlefs
Debar', v. t. to exclude, fhut out, hinder, deprive
Debark', v. to land, difembark, to ftrip of bark
Debáfe, v. t. to leffen, degrade, fink, adulterate
Debáfement, n. the act of debafing or leffening
Debáfer, n. one who debafes, one who pollutes
Debátable, a. difputable, uncertain, not clear
Debate, v. t. to confider, argue, difpute, conteft
Debáte, Debátement, n. a difpute, conteft, quar-
Debáted, pa. argued, difputed, deliberated (rel
Debáter, n. one who debates, one who wrangles
Debauch', n. a drunken bout, excefs, lewdnefs
Debauch', v. to feduce, corrupt, fpoil, ruin, rake

Debauchée, n. a drunkard, rake, very loofe man
Debauch'er, n. a man who debauches or corrupts
Debauch'ery, n. lewdnefs, intemperance, excefs
Debauch'ment, n. the act of debauching, ob.
Debel', Debel'late, v. t. to conquer by war, ob.
Debellátion, n. the act of fubduing by war, ob.
Debent'ure, n. a writ by which a debt is claimed
Deb'ile, a. weak, feeble, infirm, crazy, faint, ob.
Debil'itate, v. t. to weaken, enfeeble, make faint
Debilitátion, n. a weakening, weaknefs, decay
Debil'ity, n. weaknefs, feeblenefs, faintnefs, decay
Deb'it, n. debt, the debtor fide of an account
Deb'it, v. t. to charge with debt in an account
Debonáir, a. elegant, well-bred, gay, airy, brifk
Debt, n. what is another's juft due, a fort of writ
Debt'ed, a. indebted, obliged to or by another
Debtee', n. a creditor, one to whom a debt is due
Debt'or, n. one who is in debt; a. owing, due
Dec'ade, n. the fum or number of ten, a term of
ten days in the new French calendar
Decagyn'ia, n. an order of plants with ten ftyles
Dec'agon, n. a figure having ten equal fides
Decahe'dron, n. a figure of ten fides
Decahe'dral, a. having ten fides
Dec'alogue, n. the ten commandments or laws
Decamp', v. to fhift a camp, to move or run off
Decamp'ment, n. the act of decamping or fhifting
Decant', v. t. to pour off or out, to tilt
Decan'gular, a. having ten angles or corners
Decan'dria, n. a clafs of plants with ten ftamens
Decanta'tion, n. the act of decanting
Decant'er, n. a glafs veffel ufed for holding liquor
Decap'itate, v. to behead, to cut or lop off the top
Decapitátion, n. the act of beheading
Decaphyl'lous, a. having ten leaves
Decáy, n. a falling away or off, decline, lofs
Decáy, v. to confume, decline, wither, rot, fall
Decáyer, n. that which caufes decay or lofs
Decéafe, n. a departure from life, death, demife
Decéafe, v. i. to depart from or quit life, to die
Decéafed, pa. departed from life, dead, gone
Decédent, n. one dead (Law of N. J. & Penn.)
Deceit', n. treachery, artifice, pretence
Deceit'ful, a. full of deceit, treacherous, falfe, bafe
Deceit'fully, ad. in a deceitful manner, falfely
Deceit'fulnefs, n. a tendency to deceive, deceit
Deceivable, a. that may be deceived, deceitful
Deceivablenefs, n. the ftate of being deceivable
Deceive', v. t. to miflead, mock, cheat, impofe on
Deceived, pa. miftaken, cheated, impofed on
Deceiver, n. one who deceives, an impoftor, a
December, n. the laft month in the year (cheat
Decemden'tate, a. having ten points or teeth
De''cemfid, a. divided into ten parts
Decemloc'ular, a. having ten cells for feeds
De''cemvir, n. one of the Roman council of ten
Decem'viral, a. pertaining to the decemvirs
Decem'virate, n. a government by ten rulers
Décency, n. fitnefs, propriety, modefty, cleanlinefs

H 2

De''cennary, *n.* a term of ten years
Decen'nial, *a.* of, containing or lasting ten years
Decen'noval, Decen'novary, *a.* of or relating to 19
Décent, *a.* becoming, fit, suitable, proper, modest
Décently, *ad.* in a fit or proper manner, fitly, well
Decep'tible, *a.* that may be deceived or cheated
Decep'tion, *n.* a deceiving, deceit, cheat
Decep'tious, *a.* deceitful, false, treacherous, base
Decep'tive, *a.* able to deceive, deceitful, false
Decerp'tion, *n.* the act of pulling or rending off
Decharm', *v. t.* to counteract a charm, *ob.*
Decíde, *v. t.* to determin, finish, conclude, settle
Decídedly, *ad.* absolutely, positively, really, fully
De''cidence, *n.* the act of falling off or away, *ob.*
Decíder, *n.* a person who determins quarrels, &c.
Decíd'uous, *a.* falling off, fading, not continual
De''cimal, *a.* numbered by tens; *n.* a tenth part
De''cimally, *ad.* by means of decimals or tens
De''cimate, *v. t.* to take the tenth, to tithe
Decimátion, *n.* the act of taking the tenth
Decípher, *v. t.* to unfold, unravel, explain, mark
Decípherer, *n.* one who explains characters
Decí''sion, *n.* the determination of a difference
Decísive, *a.* settling a matter, determining, final
Decísively, *ad.* conclusively, positively, fully
Decísiveness, *n.* a decisive state, power or quality
Decísory, *a.* able or tending to decide, full, final
Deck, *v. t.* to dress, adorn, trim, set off, cover
Deck, *n.* the floor of a ship, a large pile of cards
Deck'er, *n.* a person who dresses or adorns
Decláim, *v. i.* to harangue, speak, inveigh
Decláimer, Declamátor, *n.* a man who declaims
Declamátion, *n.* a discourse, harangue, speech
Declam'atory, *a.* of or belonging to declamation
Declárable, *a.* capable of declaration or proof
Declarátion, *n.* an affirmation, publication, order
Declar'ative, *a.* explanatory, proclaiming
Declar'atorily, *ad.* by way of declaration
Declar'atory, *a.* affirmative, expressive, clear, full
Declàre, *v.* to say, affirm, tell, publish, proclaim
Declen'sion, *n.* a variation of nouns, corruption of
  morals, decay, decline, diminution, change
Declínable, *a.* that may be declined
Declinabil'ity, *n.* capacity of being declined
Declínate, *a.* bending towards the earth
Declinátion, *n.* a bending, declension, decay
Declinátor, *n.* an instrument used in dialing
Declíne, *v.* to lean, bend, decay, shun, vary words
Declíne, *n.* a decay, tendency to worse, change
Declínatory, *a.* tending to shun, avoiding
Decliv'ity, *n.* inclination downwards, descent, slope
Declívous, *a.* descending or sloping gently
Decoct', *v. t.* to boil, seeth, digest, strengthen
Decoct'ible, *a.* that may be boiled or digested
Decoc'tion, *n.* a preparation by boiling, digestion
Decoct'ive, *a.* that may be easily decocted
Decoct'ure, *n.* what is drawn off by decoction
Decollátion, *n.* the act of beheading or cutting off
Decomplex', *a.* composed of several complex

Decompóse, *v. t.* to separate parts combined by
  affinity (ly combined
Decomposi'tion, *n.* a separation of parts chemical-
Decompós'able, *a.* that may be decompofed
Decompound', *v. t.* to compound a second time
Decompound', Decom'posit, *a.* compounded again
Decompound'able, *a.* that may be decompounded
Decompound'leaves are when a divided petiole
  connects many leaflets
Dec'orate, *v. t.* to adorn, embellish, beautify, trim
Decorátion, *n.* ornament, dress
Decórous, *a.* decent, becoming, seemly, suitable
Docor'ticate, *v. t.* to strip off the bark, to peel
Decorticátion, *n.* a stripping off bark
Decórum, *n.* decency, fitness, order, good grace
Decou''ple, *a.* uncoupled, parted, separated
Decoy', *v. t.* to allure, mislead, insnare, entrap
Decoy', *n.* a place to catch wild fowl in, a lure
Decoy'-duck, *n.* a duck that decoys or lures others
Decréase, *v.* to grow or make less, lessen, decline
Decréase, *n.* a growing less, a decay
Decréased, *pa.* lessened, diminished, impaired
Decrée, *v. t.* to appoint, order, sentence, doom
Decrée, *n.* an edict, law, determination, rule
Dec'rement, *n.* decrease, diminution
Decrep'it, *a.* wasted and worn away by age, weak
Decrep'itate, *v.* to crackle, to roast salt, &c.
Decrepitátion, *n.* a crackling noise, as from salt
Decrep'itness, Decrep'itude, *n.* craziness, weakness
Decres'cent, *a.* growing less, decreasing, waning
Decrétal, *a.* of, belonging to or having, a decree
Decrétal, *n.* a book of decrees, a pope's letter
Décretory, *a.* judicial, definitive, final, critical
Decry', *v. t.* to cry down, lessen, censure, blame
Decum'bence, *n.* the act of lying down or low
Decum'bent, *a.* lying on the ground, lying low
Decúple, *a.* tenfold, repeated or taken ten times
Decúrion, *n.* a commander or officer of ten men
Decur'rent, *a.* running down along the stem
Decur'sion, *n.* the act of running, or running down
Decurs'ive, *a.* extending down the sides of a petiole
Decurs'ively, *a.* in a decursive manner
Decus'sate, *a.* growing in opposit pairs alternately
Decurtátion, *n.* the act of shortening or cutting
Décussate, *v. t.* to cut or cross at unequal angles
Decussátion, *n.* a crossing like threds in net work
Ded'alous, *a.* with variegated margins
Dedálian or De'dal, *a.* various, variegated
Dedenti'tion, *n.* a loss or shedding of teeth
Ded'icate, *v. t.* to consecrate, appropriate, inscribe
Ded'icate, Ded'icated, *pa.* consecrated, inscribed
Dedicátion, *n.* the act of dedicating, a consecration
Ded'icator, *n.* one who dedicates, one who inscribes
Ded'icatory, *a.* composing a dedication, flattering
Dedi''tion, *n.* the act of yielding up, a surrender
Dedúce, *v. t.* to gather, infer, draw, lay down
Dedúcement, *n.* a thing deduced, an inference
Dudúcible, *a.* that may be deduced or inferred
Deduct', *v. t.* to subtract, take away, separate

Deduc'tion, *n.* an abatement, conclufion, inference
Deduct'ive, *a.* that may be deduced, deducible
Deduct'ively, *ad.* by deduction, by confequence
Deed, *n.* an action, exploit, agency, fact, writing
Deed, *v. t.* to give or transfer by deed
Deedlefs, *a.* inactive, idle, indolent, fluggifh
Deem, *n.* a judgment, opinion, belief, *ob.*
Deem, *v. t.* to judge, conclude, think
Deep, *a.* far to the bottom, knowing, affecting, dark
Deep, *n.* the fea, a folemn or ftill part, depth
Deep, Deeply, *ad.* in a high degree, forrowfully
Deepen, *v. t.* to make deep or fad, darken, cloud
Deepmouthed, *a.* making a hoarfe and loud voice
Deepmufing, *a.* loft in thought, penfive, fad
Deepnefs, *n.* a deep ftate or quality, depth, fkill
Deer, *n.* a fine foreft-animal hunted for venifon
Deerftealing, *n.* the act or crime of ftealing deer
Deface, *v. t.* to disfigure, deftroy, erafe, blot out
Defacement, *n.* a disfiguring, violation, injury
Defacer, *n.* a disfigurer, deftroyer, abolifher
Defailance, *n.* a failure, mifcarriage, defect, *ob.*
Defalc'ate, *v. t.* to cut or lop off, prune, abridge
Defalcation, *n.* a cutting off, a diminution
Defamation, *n.* flander, reproach, cenfure, blame
Defam'atory, *a.* flanderous, fcandalizing, falfe ·
Defame, *v. t.* to cenfure falfely, fcandalize, revile
Defamer, *n.* one who defames, one who flanders
Defat'igate, *v. t.* to tire, weary, fatigue, *ob.*
Default', *n.* an omiffion, non-appearance of a de-
fendant in court when called, defect, fault, flaw
Default', *v. t.* to call a defendant in court and de-
clare him in default for non-appearance
Default'er, *n.* one who fails in payment, a debtor
Defeafance, *n.* the act of annulling, a defeat
Defeafible, *a.* that may be annulled or revoked
Defeat, *v. t.* to overthrow, rout, deftroy, difappoint
Defeat, *n.* an overthrow, deprivation, deftruction
Defeated, *pa.* overthrown, routed, difappointed
Defeature, *n.* a change of the features, *ob.*
Def'ecate, *v. t.* to cleanfe, clear, purify, brighten
Def'ecate or Def'ecated, *pa.* purged from lees
Defecation, *n.* the act of cleanfing, a purification
Defect, *n.* an error, fault, blemifh, want
Defect, *v. i.* to be deficient, to fail, *ob.*
Defectibil'ity, *n.* a deficiency, an imperfection, *ob.*
Defect'ible, *a.* deficient, imperfect, wanting, *ob.*
Defec'tion, *n.* a falling off or away, failure, revolt
Defect'ive, *a.* deficient, imperfect, blamable
Defect'ivenefs, *n.* defect, imperfection, faultinefs
Defenfe', *n.* a guard, refiftance, vindication, reply
Defenfe'lefs, *a.* left naked, unguarded, unarmed
Defend', *v.* to guard, protect, fupport, vindicate
Defend'ant, *n.* one who defends in law, combat, &c.
Defend'ant, *a.* defenfive, fit to ufe for defence
Defend'er, *n.* a champion, afferter, advocate, pro-
Defens'ative, *n.* a defenfe, guard, bandage (tector
Defens'ible, *a.* that may be defended, juftifiable ·
Defens'ive, *a.* proper for defenfe, defending
Defens'ive, *n.* a fafeguard, guard, ftate of defenfe

Defer', *v.* to put off, delay, refer, fubmit, yield
Def'erence, *n.* regard, refpect, fubmiffion
Deferen'tial, *a.* expreffing deference
Defer'ent, *n.* what carries or conveys, a circle, *ob.*
Defer'ent, *a.* carrying up and down, conveying, *ob.*
Defi'ance, *n.* a challenge, a ftate of refiftance
Defi'ciency, *n.* a defect, imperfection, want, fail-
Defi'cient, *a.* defective, wanting, failing   (ure
Defi'er or Defy'er, *n.* one who defies or challenges
Defile, *n.* a narrow paffage or pafs, a narrow lane
Defile, *v. t.* to pollute, corrupt, taint, file off
Defil'ed, *pa.* polluted, corrupted, ravifhed
Defile'ment, *n.* pollution, corruption, bafenefs
Defil'er, *n.* one who defiles, a corrupter, a polluter
Defi'nable, *a.* that may be afcertained or fixed
Define, *v.* to explain, limit, mark out, fix, decide
Defi'ner, *n.* one who defines, one who defcribes
Def'inite, *more correctly* Def'init, *a.* certain, limi-
ted, bounded, precife
Def'inite, *n.* a thing defined or explained
Def'initely, *ad.* in a definite manner, clearly
Def'initenefs, *n.* a definite ftate, a fixed quality
Defini'tion, *n.* a full defcription, a determination
Defin'itive, *a.* determinate, exprefs, pofitive, real
Defin'itively, *ad.* exprefsly, pofitively, decifively
Deflagrabil'ity, *n.* an aptnefs to burn or take fire
Deflagrable, *a.* wafting or confuming by fire
Def'lagrate, *v. t.* to burn, to confume
Deflagration, *n.* a burning, a confuming by fire
Deflect', *v. i.* to turn afide or away, to deviate
Deflec'tion, *n.* a turning afide or from, a deviation
Deflex'ure, *n.* a bending down, reflection, turn
Def'lorate, *a.* having caft its farin or pollen
Defloration, *n.* a felection of what is beft, a rape
Deflour', *v. t.* to ravifh, ruin, take away beauty
Deflour'er, *n.* one who deflours, a ravifher
Defluxion, *n.* a falling down of humors, a flow
Defedation, *n.* the act of making filthy, *ob.*
Defoliation, *n.* the fhedding or time of cafting
leaves in autumn
Deforce', *v. t.* to withhold or drive out by force
Deforciant, *n.* one who keeps another out of the
poffeffion of an eftate
Deform', *v. t.* to disfigure, mar, difhonor, difgrace
Deform', Deform'ed, *a.* disfigured, ugly, crooked
Deform'ity, *n.* uglinefs, crookednefs, irregularity
Defraud', *v. t.* to injure by withholding or de-
priving of right, to cheat
Defraud'ed, *pa.* cheated, deceived, deprived
Defraud'er, *n.* one who defrauds, one who cheats
Defray', *v. t.* to bear charges or expences, to pay
Defrayer, *n.* one who defrays, one who expends
Deft, *a.* neat, trim, fpruce, dexterous, *ob.*
Deft'ly, *ad.* neatly, fprucely, dexteroufly, *ob.*
Defunct', *a.* deceafed, dead; *n.* a perfon dead
Defunc'tion, *n.* a deceafe, extinction, death, *ob.*
Defy', *v. t.* to challenge, dare, outbrave, defpife.
Defy', *n.* a challenge, defiance, contempt
Degar'nifh, *v. t.* to ftrip of furniture or apparatus

Degar'nifhment, n. the ftripping of furniture

Degen'eracy, n. departure from virtue, &c. vice

Degen'erate, a. unlike anceftors, unworthy, bafe

Degen'erate, v. i. to decay in virtue or kind

Degen'eratenefs, n. a degenerate ftate

Degenerátion, n. the act or ftate of degenerating

Degen'erous, a. degenerated, vile, bafe, ob.

Degen'eroufly, ad. meanly, bafely, unworthily,ob.

Deglútinate, v. to unglue, undo, loofen, flacken

Degluti''tion, n. the act of fwallowing, a fwallow

Degradátion, n. a degeneracy, removal, fhade

Degráde, v. to leffen, place lower, difgrace, turn out

Degrée, n. a quality, clafs, ftation, proportion, the 360th part of a circle, on the earth 60 miles

Dehis'cence, n. a gaping, the opening of capfules, or the feafon for it

Dehort', v. t. to diffuade, difcourage, damp, ob.

Dehortátion, n. diffuafion, advice to the contrary

Dehort'atory, a. tending or aiming to diffuade, ob.

Déicide, n. the death of our Savior, a murderer, ob.

Deject', v. t. to caft down, grieve, afflict, crufh

Deject'edly, ad. in a dejected manner, heavily

Deject'ednefs, n. dejection, a lownefs of fpirits

Dejec'tion, n. melancholy, lownefs, weaknefs, a

Deject'ure, n. excrements, a ftool, refufe (ftool

Deificátion, n. a deifying, the making of a god

Déify, v. t. to make a god, adore, praife much

Deign, [dane] v. i. to vouchfafe, grant, allow

Déifm, n. a denial or rejection of all revelation

Déift, n. one who adheres to deifm, a difbeliever

Déiftical, a. belonging or tending to deifm

Déity, n. a divinity, God, the nature of God

Delaps'ed, a. falling or bearing down, fallen

Delāte, v. t. to carry, convey, bear, accufe, ob.

Delátion, n. the act of conveying, an accufation, ob.

Delátor, n. an accufer, informer, telltale, ob.

Del'aware, n. a river, and a ftate upon its bank

Deláy, v. to defer, put off, ftop, hinder, detain

Deláy, n. a deferring, ftop, ftay, hinderance

Deláyer, n. one who delays, one who hinders

Dele, v. blot out, efface, obliterate

Delec'table, a. pleafing, delightful, charming

Delec'tably, ad. pleafingly, delightfully, finely

Delectátion, n. pleafure, delight, tranfport, ob.

Del'egate, v. t. to fend away, appoint, intruft, de-

Del'egate, n. a deputy, commiffioner, truftee (pute

Del'egate, Del'egated, pa. appointed, deputed

Del'egates, n. pl. a court of appeal in chancery

Delegátion, n. a fending away, commiffion, truft

Deletérious, Delétery, a. deadly, deftructive

Delétion, n. the act of blotting out, deftruction

Delf, Delph, n. a mine, quarry, fine earthen ware

De'lian, a. pertaining to Delos a Grecian ifle

Delib'erate, v. t. to debate, think, mufe, hefitate

Delib'erate, a. circumfpect, wary, advifed, flow

Delib'erately, ad. circumfpectly, advifedly, coolly

Deliberátion, n. the act of deliberating, confulta-

Delib'eratenefs, n. circumfpection, thought (tion

Delib'erative, a. pertaining to deliberation

Del'icacy, n. daintinefs, nicety, foftnefs, politenefs

Del'icate, a. dainty, nice, foft, neat, fine, polite

Del'icately, ad. choicely, daintily, foftly, politely

Del'icatenefs, n. tendernefs, foftnefs, effeminacy

Del'icates, n. pl. dainties, niceties, rarities

Deli''cious, a. fweet, pleafant, very nice or fine

Deli''cioufly, ad. fweetly, delightfully, nicely

Deli''cioufnefs, n. great fweetnefs, delight

Deligátion, n. the act of tying or binding up

Delight, n. joy, great pleafure, content,

Delight, v. to give or receive great pleafure,

Delightful, a. pleafant, very pleafing, charming

Delightfully, ad. with delight, charmingly, very

Delightfulnefs, n. pleafantnefs, comfort, delight

Delightlefs, a. affording no delight

Delightfome, a. pleafant, pleafing, delightful

Delin'eate, v. t. to draw, paint, defcribe, fketch

Delineátion, n. the outlines of a picture, a fketch

Delin''quency, n. a fault, offenfe, failure in duty

Delin''quent, n. an offender, criminal, defaulter

Del'iquate, v. t. to melt, diffolve, clarify

Del'iquated, pa. melted, diffolved, clarified

Deliquátion, n. the act of melting or diffolving

Deliquefce', v. i. to diffolve or foften in air

Deliques'cible, a. that will melt in air

Deliques'cence, n. a diffolving in air

Deliques'cent, a. melting or growing liquid in air

Deli''quium, n. a diftillation by fire, a fwooning

Delir'ious, a. lightheaded, raving, mad, doting

Delir'ium, n. an alienation of the mind, dotage

Deliv'er, v. t. to give, offer, free, fave, relate

Deliv'erable, a. that may or ought to be delivered

Deliv'erance, n. freedom, refcue, utterance

Deliv'ered, pa. given, prefented, freed, faved

Deliv'erer, n. a preferver, favior, relater

Deliv'ery, n. a releafe, utterance, childbirth, fur-

Dell, n. a valley, pit, hollow, hole (render

Delph'ine, a. pertaining to the dolphin and a gen- us of fifh (Greece and the oracle of that place

Delph'ic, Delph'ian, a. relating to Delphi in

Del'toid, a. of the fhape of the Greek delta, tri- angular

Delúdable, a. that may be deluded or deceived

Delúde, v. t. to deceive, gull, difappoint, debauch

Delúder, n. a beguiler, deceiver, impoftor, cheat

Delve, v. i. to dig, open, fift, fathom, examin

Delve, n. a ditch, pit, den, cave, hole, quantity

Delv'er, n. one who digs or opens with a fpade

Delúfive, Delufory, a. apt or tending to deceive

Delúfion, n. cheat, guile, deception, falfhood

Del'uge, v. t. to drown, overwhelm, overrun, cover

Del'uge, n. a great overflow of water, &c. a flood

Dem'agogue, n. a ringleader of a rabble or faction

Demáin, n. eftate in the hands of the lord, or ad- joining to the manfion

Demand', n. a claim, queftion, inquiry, call (ity

Demand', v. t. to claim, afk, afk for with author-

Demand'able, that may be demanded or afked

Demand'ant, n. the plaintiff in an action at law

Demand'er, *n.* one who demands, one who afks
Demarcátion, *n.* a boundary or divifional line afcertained
Deméan, *v.* to behave, carry, debafe, undervalue
Deméan, Deméanor, *n.* carriage, behavior
Demeph'itize, *v. t.* to purify from foul air
Demephitizátion, *n.* a cleanfing from foul air
Demer'it, *n.* an ill-deferving, crime, guilt, defert
Demer'it, *v. t.* to deferve punifhment, *not ufed*
Demers'ed, *a.* drowned, plunged, funk, put under
Demer'fion, *n.* the act of drowning or plunging
Demefne, fee demain
Dem'i, *a.* half; *n.* a half fellow at Oxford
Demibrigáde, *n.* a half brigade
Dem'igod, *n.* half a god, a worthy, a great hero
Dem'ilance, *n.* a light or fmall lance, a fpear
Dem'irep, *n.* a woman of fufpicious character
Demífable, *a.* that may be bequeathed
Demífe, *n.* death, deceafe, departure, will, leafe
Demífe, *v. t.* to bequeath at one's death, to let
Demis''fion, *n.* a degradation, diminution, *ob.*
Demit', *v. t.* to let fall, degrade, deprefs, *ob.*
Democ'racy, *n.* a popular form of government
Dem'ocrat, *n.* an adherent to gov. by the people
Democrat'ical, *a.* of or belonging to a democracy
Demol'ifh, *v. t.* to deftroy, raze, overthrow, ruin
Demol'ifher, *n.* one who demolifhes or deftroys
Demoli''tion, *n.* the act of demolifhing, ruin, havoc
Démon, *n.* an evil fpirit or angel, a fpirit
Demóniac, *n.* one who is poffeffed with a demon
Demon'ical, Demónian, *a.* devilifh, infernal
Demol'ogy, *n.* a treatife upon evil fpirits
Demons'trable, *a.* that admits of certain proof
Demons'trably, *ad.* certainly, clearly, plainly
Dem'onftrate, *v. t.* to prove with certainty
Dem'onftrated, *pa.* proved beyond difpute, proved
Demonftrátion, *n.* indubitable or real proof
Demons'trative, *a.* conclufive, certain, evident
Demons'tratively, *ad.* certainly, clearly, plainly
Dem'onftrator, *n.* one who demonftrates or fhows
Demor'alize, *v. t.* to corrupt, undermine or deftroy moral principles
Demoralizátion, *n.* the deftruction of morality
Demul'cent, *a.* foftening, eafing, affuaging
Demur', *v.* to doubt, hefitate, delay, put off, ftop
Demur', *n.* a doubt, hefitation, objection, delay
Demúre, *v. i.* to put on an affected modefty, *ob.*
Demúre, *a.* very grave, affectedly modeft, prim
Demúrely, *ad.* gravely, very modeftly, formally
Demúrenefs, *n.* gravity, affected modeft, purity
Demúring, *pa.* putting on an affected look
Demur'rage, *n.* an expenfe for delaying a fhip
Demur'rer, *n.* one who demurs, a ftop in a lawfuit
Demy', *n.* paper of a certain fize
Den, *n.* a cavern, cave for beafts, hole, valley
Dénary, *a.* of or relating to ten, containing ten
Denáy, *n.* a denial, refufal, rejection, *ob.* (plant
Den'drite, *n.* a ftone with the figure of a tree, or
Dendrit'ical, *a* having the form of a tree or plant

Den'droid, *a.* refembling a fhrub (plants
Den'drolite, *n.* petrified fhrubs, plants, or parts of
Dendrom'eter, *n.* an inftrument to meafure the highth and diameter of trees
Deníable, *a.* that may be denied or difbelieved
Denial, *n.* a denying, refufal, rebuff, objection
Deníer, *n.* one who denies
Deniér, *n.* a fmall French coin 1-12 of a fol.
Denígrate, *v. t.* to blacken, make black, *ob.*
Denigrátion, Denfgrature, *n.* a blackening, *ob.*
Denizátion, *n.* the act of making a man free
Den'izen, *n.* a citiven, a freeman; *v. t.* to make
Denom'inate, *v. t.* to name, to give name to (free
Denominátion, *n.* a name, name given, a title
Denom'inative, *a.* giving or conferring a name
Denom'inator, *n.* the giver of a name, a number
Denotátion, *n.* the act of denoting or marking
Denóte, *v. t.* to mark, fhow, betoken, point out
Denounce', *v. t.* to threaten, to declare
Denounce'ment, *n.* the declaration of a threat
Denoun'cer, *n.* one who threatens or declares
Denfe, *a.* clofe, compact, almoft folid, hard, thick
Denfe'nefs, Dens'ity, *n.* clofenefs, thicknefs
Dent, *v. t.* to indent, notch, mark with notches
Dent'al, *a.* belonging to the teeth; *n.* a fhellfifh
Dentil'li, *n. pl.* modillions in architecture, props
Den'ticle, *n.* a point like a fmall tooth
Dentic'ulate, Dent'ate, *a.* fet with fmall teeth
Denticulátion, *n.* the act of fetting with teeth
Den'tiform, *a.* in fhape of a tooth
Denti''tion, *n.* the cutting or breeding of teeth
Dent'rifice, *n.* a powder for cleaning the teeth
Den'udate, Denúde, *v. t.* to ftrip, to make naked
Denundátion, *n.* the act of ftripping or laying bare
Denunciátion, *n.* a public threat or declaration
Denunciátor, *n.* one who threatens or proclaims
Deny', *v. t.* to difown, refufe, contradict, gainfay
Deobftruct', *v. t.* to remove impediments, to clear
Deob'ftruent, *a.* opening or removing obftructions
Déodand, *n.* a forfeiture in law made to GOD
Deop'pilative, *a.* removing obftructions, clearing
Deofculátion, *n.* a kiffing, the act of kiffing, *ob.*
Deox'ydate, *v. t.* to deprive of oxygene
Deoxydátion, *n.* a depriving of oxygene
Depáint, *v. t.* to picture, defcribe, depict, *ob.*
Depart', *v.* to go away, quit, leave, defift, die, part
Depart', Depart'ure, *n.* a going off or away, death
Depart'ment, *n.* a feparate office, province, duty
Department'al, *a.* pertaining to a department
Depaup'erate, *v. t.* to make poor, confume, *ob.*
Depec'tible, *a.* tough, clammy, fticky, *ob.*
Depend', *v. t.* to hang from, rely on, truft to, reft
Depend'ence, *n.* connection, reliance
Depend'ant, *n.* one who relies on another for fupport or favor
Depend'eat, *a.* hanging down or from, loofe
Deperdi''tion, *n.* lofs, wafte, deftruction, havoc
Dephleg'mate, Dephlegm', *v. t.* to purify from phlegm or aqueous matter

Dephlegmátion, *n.* a clearing of phlegm, &c.
Dephlegm'ednefs, *n.* a ftate cleared from phlegm
Dephlogis'ticate, *v.* to deprive of phlogifton
Dephlogis'ticated, *n.* deprived of phlogifton
Depict', Depict'ure, *v. t.* to paint, defcribe, relate
Depict'ed, *pa.* painted, defcribed, told, fhown
Depil'atory, *n.* a means ufed to take away hair
Depilous, *a.* deprived of hair, quite fmooth, *ob.*
Deplétion, *n.* the act of emptying out
Deplórable, *a.* lamentable, miferable, difmal, fad
Deplórablenefs, *n.* a deplorable ftate
Deplórably, *ad.* miferably, lamentably, fadly, very
Deplóre, *v. t.* to lament, bewail, bemoan, pity
Deplórer, *n.* one who deplores or laments
Deplúmated, Deplúmed, *a.* ftripped of feathers, *ob.*
Deplumátion, *n.* a fore fwelling with fall of hair
Dep'onent, *a.* laying down, noting a kind of verbs
Depóne, *v. t.* to pledge, rifk, lay down, fwear
Depónent or Dep'onent, *n.* one who gives written teftimony upon oath, a witnefs
Depop'ulate, *v. t.* to lay wafte, deftroy, unpeople
Depopulátion, *n.* havoc, wafte, deftruction, ruin
Depopulátor, *n.* a deftroyer or wafter of mankind
Depórt, *v. i.* to carry, demean, conduct, *ob.*
Depórt, Depórtment, *n.* conduct, behavior
Deporta'tion, *n.* tranfportation, banifhment, exile
Depófe, *v.* to witnefs, atteft, lay down, degrade
Depófed, *pa.* attefted, laid down, degraded
Depos'itory, *n.* a perfon who has a thing in truft
Depos'it, *v. t.* to truft in the hands of another, to
Depos'it, *n.* a pledge, pawn, wager (caft down
Depofi'tion, *n.* an affidavit, or attefted written teftimony, the act of degrading from office, or cafting to the bottom
Depos'itory, *n.* a place where things are lodged
Depravátion, *n.* depravity, corruption, degeneracy
Depráve, *v. t.* to corrupt, vitiate, taint, fpoil
Deprávednefs, Deprávement, Deprav'ity, *n.* corrup
Depráver, *n.* one who depraves or corrupts (tion
Dep'recate, *v. i.* to pray earneftly or againft
Deprecátion, *n.* a prayer againft evil, an entreaty
Dep'recatory, *a.* ferving to deprecate or entreat
Depréciate, *v. i.* to leffen, cry down, undervalue
Depreciátion, *n.* a falling in value
Dep'redate, *v.* to rob, plunder, fpoil, devour
Depredátion, *n.* a robbing, a fpoiling, wafte (fter
Depredátor, *n.* a robber, plunderer, devourer, wa-
Deprehend', *v. t.* to take unawares, to find out, *ob.*
Deprefs', *v. t.* to humble, deject, caft or let down
Depref'fion, *n.* dejection, lownefs, humiliation
Deprefs'ive, *a.* able to caft or let down, ftrong
Deprefs'or, *n.* a mufcle which draws downwards
Deprivátion, *n.* the act of depriving, lofs, difgrace
Deprive, *v. t.* to take from, debar, put out, free
Depth, *n.* deepnefs, a deep place, highth, fkill
Depul'fory, *a.* putting away, removing, averting
Dep'urate, *a.* cleanfed, purified, free from dregs
Dep'urate, Depúre, *v. t.* to cleanfe, purify, purge
Depurátion, *n.* a cleanfing or purifying

Depúratory, *a.* tending to cleanfe, purify or free
Deputátion, *n.* the act of deputing, a commiffion
Depúte, *v. t.* to fend, appoint, empower (ther
Dep'uty, *n.* one who officiates in the name of ano-
Dep'utize, *v. t.* to empower to act as a deputy, [Con.]
Dera"cinate, *v. t.* to root or tear up, to root out
Deráign or Deráin, *v. t.* to prove, juftify, turn
Derange', *v.* to put out of order, embarrafs
Derangément, *n.* ftate of diforder, embarraffment
Der'elict, *a.* abandoned, *n.* a thing abandoned
Derelic'tion, *n.* an utter forfaking or leaving, want
Deríde, *v. t.* to laugh at, ridicule, mock, fcorn
Derider, *n.* a laugher, mocker, fcoffer, buffoon
Deri"fion, *n.* a laughingftock, jeft, fcorn, contempt
Derifive, Derifor, *a.* jefting, ridiculing, mocking
Derivable, *a.* coming by derivation, arifing
Derivátion, *n.* a tracing from fome original
Deriv'ative, *a.* derived or deduced from another
Deriv'ative, *n.* a word derived from another
Deríve, *v.* to trace, deduce, take or defcend from
Derived, *pa.* drawn, deduced, fpread abroad
Deríver, *n.* one who derives, one who draws from
Der'nier, *a.* the laft, the only one, only remaining
Der'ogate, *v.* to detract, leffen, take from, injure
Der'ogate, *a.* leffened, damaged, injured
Der'ogated, *pa.* controlled, leffened, weakened
Derogátion, *n.* a difparagement, injury
Derog'ative, Derog'atory, *a.* degrading, leffening
Der'vis or Der'vife, *n.* a Turkifh prieft or monk
Def'cant, *n.* a fong, tune, air, difcourfe, difputation
Defcant', *v. i.* to fing, difcourfe, enlarge
Defcend', *v. i.* to come down or from, fpring, fink
Defcend'able, *a.* that may or can defcend
Defcend'ant, *n.* the offspring or race of an anceftor
Defcend'ant, *a.* proceeding from another, falling
Defcen'fion, *n.* a defcent, a declenfion
Defcent', *n.* a flope, invafion, family, birth, ftep
Defcríbe, *v. t.* to reprefent by words or figures
Defcríbable, *a.* that may be defcribed (out
Defcríber, *n.* one who defcribes, one who marks
Defcrier, *n.* a perfon who difcovers or finds out
Defcrip'tion, *n.* the act of defcribing, reprefentation
Defcrip'tive, *a.* containing defcription (cover
Defcry', *n.* a difcovery; *v. t.* to fpy out, to dif-
Des'ecrate, *v. t.* to pollute things facred, *ob.*
Defecrátion, *n.* a pollution of things facred, *ob.*
Defert', *n.* merit, worth, a claim to reward, a reward
Defert', *v.* to forfake, leave, quit, run off or away
Des'ert, *n.* a wildernefs, wafte, wafte country
Des'ert, *a.* wild, folitary, wafte, untilled, rough
Defer'ter, *n.* one who deferts, one who forfakes
Defer'tion, *n.* the act of deferting or forfaking
Defert'lefs, *a.* void of merit, worthiefs, vile
Deferve', *v. t.* to be worthy, to merit good or bad
Deferv'edly, *ad.* worthily, juftly, properly, fitly
Deferv'er, *n.* one who is deferving of reward
Deferv'ing, *pa.* worthy of, worthy; *n.* defert
Defic'cant, *n.* a drier up of humors in medicia

Defic'cate, v. t. to dry up, to exhale moifture
Deficcátion, n. the act of drying or making dry
Defic'cative, a. able or tending to dry, drying
Defid'erate, v. t. to defire, wifh for, want, ob.
Defid'erated, pa. defired, wifhed for, miffed
Defiderátum, n. fomething wanted, the point aimed
Design, v. t. to purpofe, intend, plan, devote
Design, n. a purpofe, intention, plan, fcheme, aim
Designable, a. that is capable of being defigned
Defignátion, n. an appointment, meaning, intention
Designedly, ad. purpofely, intentionally
Designer, n. a contriver, framer, drawer, architect
Designing, pa. intending, deceitful, artful
Defignment, n. a fcheme, plot, intention, fketch, ob.
Defip'ient, a. trifling, foolifh, playful
Desirable, a. worthy of defire, pleafing, good, fine
Desire, n. a paffion excited by the love of an object, or love excited into action, a wifh to obtain
Desire, v. t. to wifh, long for, afk, beg, entreat
Desirer, n. a perfon who is eager after any thing
Desirous, a. full of defire, longing after, eager for
Defist', v. t. to ceafe, give over or up, ftop
Defist'ance, n. the act of defifting or ceafing
Des'itive, a. ending, concluding, finifhing, ob.
Defk, n. an inclined table, a pulpit
Des'olate, v. t. to lay or make wafte, to deprive of
Des'olate, a. laid wafte, left, folitary, uninhabited
Des'olatenefs, n. a defolate ftate or condition
Defolátion, n. deftruction, fadnefs, gloominefs
Defpair, n. extreme grief without hope, a deftitution of hope or expectation
Defpáir, v i. to be without hope of relief
Defpáirer, n. one who defpairs, one who mourns
Defpáirful, a. hopelefs, loft, defperate, very bad
Defpáiringly, ad. in a defpairing or very low way
Defpatch', v. t. to fend away, finifh, execute, kill
Defpatch', n. hafte, fpeed, an exprefs, management
Defpatch'ful, a. bent on hafte, quite in a hurry, ob.
Defpec'tion, n. the act of looking downward (man
Defperádo, n. a defperate or furious perfon, a mad-
Des'perate, a. having no hope, rafh, furious, mad
Des'perately, ad. rafhly, haftily, furioufly, mad
Des'peratenefs, n. rafhnefs, folly, fury, madnefs
Defperátion, n. hopeleffnefs, defpair, rafhnefs, fury
Des'picable, a. contemptible, worthlefs, vile, low
Des'picablenefs, n. meannefs, vilenefs, bafenefs
Des'picably, ad. meanly, fordidly, fcandaloufly
Defpífable, a. defpicable, contemptible, mean
Defpífe, v. t. to fcorn, difdain, flight, overlook
Defpífer, n. one who defpifes, one who flights
Defpíte, n. malice, anger, defiance, hate, contempt
Defpíte, v. t. to fpite, affront, provoke, diftrefs
Defpíteful, a. malicious, full of fpleen
Defpítefully, ad. malicioufly, malignantly
Defpítefulnefs, n. malice, malignity, hatred, hate
Defpoil', v. t. to fpoil, rob, plunder, ftrip, deprive
Defpoil'ed, pa. robbed, ftript, deprived, bereft
Defpond', v. i. to defpair, lofe hope, faint, ficken
Defpond'ency, n. defpair, hopeleffnefs, lownefs

Defpond'ent, a. defpairing, hopelefs, dejected
Defpond'ently, ad. with or in defpair, without hope
Defpons'ate, v. t. to efpoufe, betroth, unite
Des'pot, n. an abfolute prince, a tyrant
Defpot'ic, a. abfolute, arbitrary, lofty, unlimited
Defpot'ically, ad. abfolutely, arbitrarily   (pride
Def'potifm, n. abfolute power, tyranny, cruelty,
Defpumátion, n. a foaming, fcum, frothinefs
Defquámation, n. the act of fcaling off, as fkin after fever
Deffert', n. the laft courfe ferved at a feaft, fruit
Deftinátion, n. a purpofe intended, defign, courfe
Des'tine, v. t. to doom, devote, fix, appoint, order
Des'tiny, n. fate, doom, an unalterable ftate, death
Des'titute, a. forfaken, in want, wretched, poor
Deftitútion, n. a forfaken ftate, want, poverty
Deftroy', v. t. to lay wafte, kill, put an end to, ruin
Deftroy'er, Deftruc'tor, n. a perfon who deftroys
Deftruc'tible, a. that may be deftroyed
Deftruc'tion, n. ruin, havoc, maffacre, death eternal
Deftruc'tive, a. that deftroys, wafteful, ruinous
Deftruc'tively, ad. ruinoufly, mifchievoufly
Deftruc'tivenefs, n. a deftructive quality
Defudátion, n. an immoderate fweating   (difufe
Defúetude, n. the difcontinuence of a cuftom,
Defulph'urate, v. t. to free from fulphur
Defulphurátion, n. a purifying from fulphur
Des'ultorily, ad. in a defultory manner, loofely
Des'ultorinefs, n. inconftancy, unconnectednefs
Des'ultory, a. unfettled, inconftant, unconnected
Defult'ure, n. a fkip, a leap from horfe to horfe
Defúme, v. t. to take from any thing, to borrow, ob.
Detach', v. t. to feparate, divide, fend off a party
Detach'ed, pa. feparated, drawn or fent off
Detach'ment, n. a party fent off   (cularly
Detáil, n. a minute relation ; v. t. to relate parti-
Detáin, v. t. to hold in cuftody, ftop, keep back
Detáinder, n. a writ to detain or keep in cuftody
Detáiner, n. one who detains, one who keeps back
Detect', v. t. to difcover, find out, lay open, reveal
Detect'er, n. one who detects, one who difcovers
Detec'tion, n. a difcovery, the act of finding out
Deten'tion, n. the act of detaining, a reftraint
Deter', v. to difcourage, difhearten, frighten, ftop
Deterge', v. t. to cleanfe, clean, wipe or rub off
Deter'gent, a. cleanfing, wiping or rubbing off
Deter'gent, n. a medicin which cleanfes
Dete'riorate, v. to make or grow worfe
Deteriorátion, n. a making or growing worfe
Deter'ment, n. the act or caufe of difcouragement
Determ'inable, a. that may be decided or fettled
Determ'inate, v. t. to limit, fix, decide, fettle, ob.
Determ'inate, a. decifive, limited, fettled, refolved
Determ'inately, ad. decifively, refolutely, really
Determinátion, n. a decifion, refolution, conclufion
Determ'inative, a. decifive, conclufive, limiting
Determ'inator, n. one who determins or decides
Determ'in, v. t. to refolve, decide, fettle, conclude
Determ'ined, pa. refolved, fixed, decided, fettled

Deterrátion, _n._ a difcovery by removing earth,_ob._
Deter'fion, _n._ the act of cleanfing or wiping clean
Deters'ive, _a._ able to cleanfe, able to wipe off
Deteſt', _v. t._ to hate, diflike greatly, abhor,loathe
Deteſt'able, _a._ hateful,odious, abominable, vile
Deteſt'ably, _ad._ hatefully, abominably, vilely
Deteſtátion, _n._ hatred, abomination, abhorrence
Deteſt'er, _n._ one who deteſts, one who abhors
Dethróne, _v. t._ to diveſt of royalty, to depofe
Dethrónement,_n._ the act of dethroning or depofing
Det'onate, _v. i._ to explode, to burn with fudden
    report
Detonátion, _n._ a thundering, a very great noife
Det'onize,_v. t._ to calcine with detonation or noife
Detonizátion,_n._ the act of exploding
Detort', _v. t._ to wreſt from the original meaning
Detract', _v._ to leffen, flander, fcandaiize, defame
Detract'er, _n._ one who detracts, one who flanders
Detrac'tion, _n._ flander, fcandal, defamation, cen-
Detract'ive, _a._ apt or tending to detract   (fure
Detract'ory, _a._ defamatory, fcandalous, bafe, vile
Det'riment, _n._ a lofs, hurt,damage,weaknefs,duty
Detriment'al, _a._ caufing lofs, hurtful, injurious
Detrúde, _v. t._ to thruſt down or lower, to caſt
Detrúfion, _n._ the act of thruſting down or lower
Devaſtátion, _n._ havoc,waſte, deſtruction, ruin
Deuce, _n._ the two on cards or dice, the devil
Devel'ope, _v. t._ to unfold, detect, unravel, clear
Devel'opement, _n._ an unfolding, difclofure
Deveſt', _v. t._ to ſtrip, take off,or away, free from
Déviate,_v. i._ to wander, go aſtray, err, offend
Deviátion, _n._ a fwerving, error, offenfe, fault
Device, _n._ a contrivance, fcheme, emblem, ſtory
Devil', _n._ a fallen angel, a very wicked perfon
Devililh, _a._ like a devil, very wicked
Devilifhly, _ad._ in a wicked manner, very badly
Dévious, _a._ going aſtray, erring, lonely
Devife, _n._ a contrivance, the act of giving by will
Devife, _v. t._ to contrive, plan, confider, bequeath
Devifed,_pa._ contrived, given or left by will
Devifee,_n._ a perfon to whom a thing is devifed
Devifer, _n._ one who divifes, one who bequeathes
Devoid', _a._ void, empty, vacant, free, deſtitute
Devoir', _n._ fervice, duty, an act of civility, a tax
Devolve', _v._ to fall by fucceffion, fall, roll down
Devolútion, _n._ the act of devolving,a removal
Devóte, _v. t._ to dedicate, vow, give up, curfe
Devótednefs, _n._ a devoted ſtate, devotion
Devotée, _n._ a bigot, a fuperſtitious perfon
Devótion, _n._ piety, worſhip, zeal, difpofal, power
Devótional, _a._ pertaining to devotion, pious, holy
Devótioniſt, _n._ one who is much given to piety
Devour', _v. t._ to eat ravenoufly, confume, waſte
Devourer, _n._ one who or that which devours
Devout', _a._ pious, religious, godly, holy, fincere
Devoutly, _ad._ pioufly, religioufly, go lily, much
Devout'nefs, _n._ devotion, piety, zeal, ferioufnefs
Deut'erofcopy, _n._ a fecond intention or view
Deuteron'omy, _n._ a fecond book of the law

Dew, _n._ a thin cold vapor; _v. t._ to wet, to moiſten
Dew'berry, _n._ a kind of fruit, a blackberry (dewy
Dewbefprent', _a._ fprinkled or covered with dew
Dew'drop,_n._ a drop of dew, a fpangle of dew
Dew'lap,_n._ the fleſh hanging from an ox's throat
Dew'worm,_n._ a genus of worms, annulated
Dew'y, _a._ refembling or wet with dew, moiſt
Dexter'ity, _n._ activity,readinefs, expertnefs, art
Dex'terous, _a._ active,ready, expert, cunning,keen
Dex'teroufly, _ad._ actively, expertly, artfully, well
Dex'tral, Dex'ter, _a._ fet on the right hand or fide
Dextral'ity, _n._ a beginning on the right fide
Dey, _n._ the title of a Mooriſh governor or prince
Diabétes,_n._ an involuntary difcharge of urine
Diabet'ic, _a._ pertaining to the diabetes
Diabol'ic, Diabol'ical, _a._ devililh, very wicked
Diabol'ically, _ad._ in a diabolical manner
Diacódion or Diacódium, _n._ firup of poppies
Diadel'phia, _n._ a clafs of plants with ſtamens united
    in two fets
Diadem, _n._ a crown, wreath, mark of royalty
Diademed, _a._ adorned with a diadem, crowned
Diadrom,_n._ the time of performing any motion
Diagnos'tic, _a._ diſtinguiſhing, characteriſtic
Diag'onal, _n._ a line drawn from angle to angle
Diag'onal, _a._ drawn acrofs from angle to angle
Diag'onally, _ad._ in a diagonal direction
Diagram, _n._ a mathematical,fcheme, figure, plan
Diagraph, _n._ a difcription, reprefentation, plan
Dial, _n._ a plate where the hand fhows the hour
Dialect, _n._ a language,fpeech, particular fpeech
Dialect'ical, _a._ logical,argumentative, probable
Dialect'ics, _n. pl._ logic, the art of good reafoning
Dialing, _n._ the act or fcience of making dials
Dialiſt, _n._ a maker of dials, one ſkilled in dialling
Dialogue, _n._ a converfation between two or more
Dialogue, _v. i._ to difcourfe together, to converfe
Diam'eter, _n._ a line of a circle or other figure, divi-
    ding it into two equal parts
Diam'etral, _a._ pertaining to a diameter   (acrofs
Diam'etrally, _ad._ in the direction of a diameter,
Diamet'rical, _a._ defcribing or like a diameter
Diamet'rically, _ad._ directly, over againſt, quite
Diamond,_n._ a moſt valuable gem, a fort of letter
Dian'dria, _n._ a clafs of plants with two ſtamens in
    hermaphrodite flowers
Diapáfon, _n._ an octave in mufic, concord, unifon
Diaper, _n._ a fort of fine flowered linen, a napkin
Diaper, _v. t._ to variegate, flower, draw flowers
Diaphanéity,_n._ tranfparency, great clearnefs,_ob._
Diaphan'ic, Diaph'anous, _a._ tranfparent, very clear
Diaphoret'ic, _a._ exciting perfpiration, fudorific
Diaphragm or Diaphram, _n._ the midriff, a mufcular
    fubſtance which feparates the parts of the ſtom-
    ach from the abdomen
Diarrhéa, _n._ a flux of the belly, flux, loofenefs
Diarrhet'ic, _a._ purgative, purging, opening (a day
Diary, _n._ a daily account, a journal; _a._ daily, of
Dias'tole, Dias'toly, _n._ the making a ſhort fyllable

long, the dilatation of the heart, adivifion
Dib'ble, n. a tool, gardener's planting tool, fpade
Dib'ftone, n. a play, a ftone thrown at another
Dice, n. pl. of die ; v. i. to game at or with dice
Dicebox, n. a box to throw dice from
Dicer, n. a player or gamefter with dice, ob.
Dichot'omous, [ch as k] a. forked, divided into
Dichot'omy, n. a divifion into two parts (two parts
Dichot'omize, v. t. to divide or cut into two parts
Dick'er, n. the quantity or number of ten hides
Dicoc'cous, a. having two feeds in cells
Dicotylédon, n. a plant whofe feeds have two lobes
Dicotyled'onous, a. having feeds with two lobes
Dic'tate, v. t. to tell what to write, to inftruct
Dic'tate, n. a rule, maxim, hint, fuggeftion, order
Dictátor, n. a chief ruler, an abfolute magiftrate
Dictatórial, a. authoritative, dogmatical, proud
Dictátorfhip, n. the office of a dictator, infolence
Dic'tion, n. a ftyle, language, fpeech, expreffion
Dic'tionary, n. a book of words explained in al-
Did, pret. of to do   (phabetical order
Didac'tic, a. preceptive, doctrinal
Didac'tically, ad. in a didactic manner, orderly
Didas'calic, a. giving rules, ob.
Did'ymous, a. double, in pairs
Didynam'ia, n. a clafs of plants with two ftamens
longer than the others   (dye
Die, v. to lofe life, expire ; in the fenfe of color, fee
Die, n. a fmall cube to play with, ftamp ufed in
coinage ; color, hue, fee dye
Diécia or Dioécia, n. a clafs of plants having the
ftamens and piftils on different individuals
Dier, n. one who colors, &c. fee dyer
Diet n. food, a regimen, an affembly of princes
Diet, v. to board, fupply with food, eat by rule
Dietdrink, n. a drink made of feveral herbs, &c.
Dieted, pa. boarded, confined to a certain food
Dietet'ic, Dietet'ical, a. relating to diet or food
Di'etine, n. a fubordinate or local diet, or affembly
Dif'fer, v. i. to be unlike, vary, difagree, contend
Dif'ference, n. unlikenefs, difa'—ement, difpute
Dif'ference, v. t. to make or cau' to be different
Dif'ferent, a. unlike, diftinct, contrary, various
Differen'tial, n. an infinitely fmall part or portion
Dif'ferently, ad. in a different manner, varioufly
Diffi''cil, a. difficult, hard, fcrupulous, ob.
Diffi''cilnefs, n. a difficulty to be perfuaded, ob.
Dif'ficult, a. hard, troublefome, crabbed, crofs
Dif'ficultly, ad. with difficulty, [a harfh word]
Dif'ficulty, n. hardnefs, trouble, labor, diftrefs, cavil
Diffi'de, v. i. to diftruft, to have no confidence in, ob.
Dif'fidence, n. diftruft, doubt, want of confidence
Dif'fident, a. diftruftful, fufpicious, bafhful
Dif'fluence, n. the act or quality of flowing, ob.
Dif'fluent, Dif'fluous, a. flowing every way, ob
Difform', a. not uniform, irregular, uneven, unlike
Differm'ity, n. diffimilitude, irregularity in form
Diffranch'ifement, n. the taking away a privilege
Diffúfe, [diffuzed] v. t. to pour out, fcatter, difperfe

Diffúfe, a. copious, full, widely fpread
Diffúfed, [diffuzed] pa. difperfed, fpread abroad
Diffúfely, Diffúfively, ad. widely, copioufly, full
Diffúfible, a. that may be fpread or difperfed
Diffúfibil'ity, n. the quality of being capable of
diffufion
Diffúfion, Diffúfivenefs, n. difperfion, copioufnefs
Diffúfive, a. difperfed, fpreading far, copious, full
Dig, v. digged, dug, pret. digged, dug, pa. to turn
up with a fpade, make fearch, obt..in
Digas'tric, a. having a double belly
Digeft, n. a volume or collection of laws, a fyftem
Digeft', v. to diffolve, fet in order, arrange, cleanfe
Digeft'er, n. a perfon who or that which digefts,
a veffel to confine elaftic vapors
Digeft'ible, a. that may be digefted or concocted
Digeftibil'ity, n. the ftate of being capable of
digeftion
Diges''tion, n. a diffolving of food in the ftomach
Digeft'ive, a. caufing digeftion, methodifing
Dig'ger, n. one who digs or turns up the ground
Dight, v. t. to drefs, deck, adorn, trim, ob.
Dighted, pa. dreffed, adorned, tricked out
Di'git, n. three-fourths of an inch, a twelfth part
of the diameter of the fun or moon, any num-
ber expreffed by a fingle figure, a figure
Di''gital, a. of or relating to a digit or the fingers
Di''gitate, a. divided like fingers
Digladiátion, n. a combat with fwords, ob.
Dignificátion, n. exaltation, promotion, dignity
Dig'nified, pa. invefted with honors, exalted
Dig'nify, v. t. to advance, raife, exalt, prefer hon-
Dig'nitary, n. a dignified or exalted clergyman (or
Dig'nity, n. grandeur, rank, honor, merit, a poft
Dig'onous, a. having two angles
Dignótion, n. diftinction, a mark of diftinction, ob.
Di'graph, n. a combination of two letters of which
one only is pronounced
Digrefs', v. i. to turn from a fubject, deviate, err
Digres''fion, n. a deviation from the fubject
Digyn'ia, n. an order of plants with two ftyles
Dihe'dron, n. a figure with two fides, or furfaces
Dihe'dral, a. having two fides
Dike, n. a ditch, channel, bank, mound, fence
Dila''cerate, v. t. to tear, rend, force in two, fpoil
Dilacerátion, n. a tearing or rending in pieces
Dilániate, v. t. to tear in pieces, mangle, deftroy
Dilap'idate, v. t. to ruin, to throw or pull down
Dilapidátion, n. a deftroying of buildings, a decay
Dilatibil'ity, n. the quality of admitting extenfion
Dilátable, a. capable of extenfion, elaftic
Dilatátion, n. the act or ftate of extenfion, width
Diláte, v. to extend, widen, enlarge, fwell
Dilátor, n. what extends or widens, a mufcle
Dil'atorially, ad. in a dilatory manner, flowly, idly
Dil'atorinefs n. flownefs, flothfulnefs, idlenefs
Dil'atory, a. flow, flothful, idle, backward, long
Dilec'tion, n. the act of loving, love, kindnefs, ob.
Dilem'ma, n. a vexatious alternative, a difficulty

I

Dil'igence, n. industry, activity, readiness, care
Dil'igent, a. industrious, persevering, attentive
Dil'igently, ad. with industry, with perseverance
Dill, n. a plant with aromatic seeds
Dilúcidate, v. t. to make clear, explain, ob.
Dilucidátion, n. a making clear to be understood, ob
Dil'uent, Dilúter, n. what dilutes, what thins
Dilúte, v. t. to thin, to weaken with water
Dilúted, pa. made thin, weakened, softened
Dilútion, n. the act of diluting or making thin
Dilúvian, a. relating or belonging to the deluge
Dim, a. dark, not clear in fight or apprehenfion
Dim, v. t. to cloud, darken, obfcure, overcaft
Dime, n. a filver coin of the U. S. of ten cents
Dimen'fion, n. the folid bulk, bulk, capacity, fize
Dimen'fionlefs, a. without dimenfions or bounds
Dimens'ive, a. marking out limits, bounding, ob.
Dimid'iate, a. halved, divided in two
Dimin'ish, v. to leffen, decreafe, decay, degrade
Dimin'ifhingly, ad. in a vilifying or bad manner
Diminútion, n. the act of leffening, lofs, difcredit
Dimin'utive, a. fmall, little, contemptible, mean
Dimin'utively, ad. in a diminutive manner
Dimin'utivenefs, n. a diminutive flate, fmallnefs
Dim'ifh, a. fomewhat dim, fomewhat dark or dull
Dim'iffory, a. fent from bifhop to bifhop
Dim'ity, n. a kind of white fuftian, a fine fuftian
Dim'ly, ad. not with clear fight, darkly, obfcurely
Dim'nefs, n. a defect of fight, ftupidity, dulnefs
Dim''ple, n. a fmall hollow in the cheek or chin
Dim''ple, v. i. to form dimples, to fink into holes
Dimp'led, pa. fet with or having dimples
Dimp'ly, a. full of or like dimples, hollow
Din, n. a noife, clatter, continued found
Din, v. t. to ftun with noife, bawl, rattle
Dine, v. i. to eat or give a dinner; n. a dinner
Dinet'ical, a whirling or turning round, rotary, ob.
Ding, v. to dafh, fling, caft, blufter, huff, bounce
Dingdong, ad. like a bell, very faft or hard
Din''gle, n. a hollow between two hills, dale, vale
Din'gy, a. dark, dirty, foul, foiled, fullied
Diningroom, n. a room to dine in, or for company
Din'ner, n. our chief or principal meal
Din'nertime, n. the ufual time of dining, noon
Dint, n. a blow, ftroke, force, power, mark, hole
Dint, v. t. to make a cavity or hollow, to mark
Diocéfan, n. a bishop; a. blonging to a diocefe
Diocefs or Diocefe, n. the jurifdiction of a bifhop
Dio'don, n. a genus of fifh of a fingular form
Diomede, n. an aquatic bird of the fize of a duck
Diop'trics, n. the fcience of refracted vifion
Diop'trical, a. pertaining to dioptrics
Dip, v. to put, fink, plunge, engage, pierce, look
Dipet'alous, a. having two flower leaves
Dip'fas, n. a ferpent whofe bite caufes thirft
Diphyl'lous, c. having two leaves
Diplóma, n. a deed of fome privilege or degree
Diplomat'ic, a. pertaining to diplomas, privilege, relating to public minifters

Diplomat'ics, n. the fcience of ancient literary documents, as charters, &c.
Dip'per n. one who dips, a veffel to dip with
Dip'tote, n. a fubftantive that has only two cafes
Dip'thong, n. two vowels fet or founded together
Dip'tych, n. a regifter of martyrs or bifhops
Dire, Direful, a. dreadful, difmal, horrible
Direct', a. ftrait, right, open, exprefs, plain, full
Direct'. v. t. to order, rule, regulate. inform, aim
Direct'ed, pa. ordered, fhown, pointed, aimed
Direc'tion, n. an order, rule, aim, fuperfcription
Direct'ive, a. able to inform, fhowing the way
Direct'ly, ad. immediately, foon, in a ftrait line
Direct'nefs, n. ftraitnefs, a nearnefs of way
Direct'or, n. a fuperintendant, guide, ruler, rule
Direct'ory, n. a rule or book to direct, a prayer
Direct'ory, a. enjoining, commanding
Direct'refs, n. a female who directs
Directórial, a. containing direction or command
Direnefs, n. dreadfulnefs, difmalnefs, horror
Direp'tion, n. the act of plundering, robbery
Dirge, n. a mournful or funeral ditty, a fervice
Dirk, n. a kind of dagger, v. t. to fpoil, to ruin
Dirt, [durt] n. earth, filth, meannefs
Dirt, v. t. to foul, to ftain, make filthy
Dirt'ily, ad. naftily, fhamefully, meanly
Dirt'inefs, n. filthinefs, bafenefs, meannefs, dirt
Dirt'y, a. foul, filthy, nafty, fullied, bafe, mean
Dirt'y, v. t. to foul, foil, dirt, fcandalize, difgrace
Dirup'tion, n. the act or ftate of burfting, a rent
Difabil'ity, n. want of power or right, weaknefs
Difáble, v. t. to render unable or incapable, to
Difabúfe, v. t. to fet right, to undeceive (lame
Difacquaintance, n. difufe of familiarity, ob.
Difadvant'age, n. lofs, prejudice; v. t. to injure
Difadvantágeous, a. prejudicial, hurtful
Difadvantágeoufly, ad. with lofs or inconvenience
Difadvantágeoufnefs, n. lofs, inconvenience
Difaffect', v. t. to fill with difcontent or diflike
Difaffect'ed, pa. not wifhing well to, hating, averfe
Difaffect'edly, ad. in a difaffected manner
Difaffec'tion, n. want of affection, difloyalty
Difaffirm', v. t. to deny, difprove, contradict
Difaffirm'ance, n. a confutation, difproof, denial
Difaffor'eft, v. t. to throw open, to make public
Difagrée, v. i. to differ, clafh, quarrel, not agree
Difagreéable, a. unfuitable, unpleafant, odious
Difagreéablenefs, n. contrariety, offenfivenefs
Difagreé'ably, ad. in a difagreeable manner
Difagreément, n. a difference, an unfuitablenefs
Difallow', v. t. to deny, reject, cenfure, condemn
Difallow'able, a. not allowable, improper, unfit
Difallow'ance, n. a forbidding, rejection, diflike
Difan'imate, v. t. to difcourage, to kill ob.
Difanimátion, n. a privation of life, death, ob.
Difannul', v. t. to annul, make void, abolifh
Difappéar, v. i. to vanifh, be loft, fly off or away
Difappoint', v. t. to defeat of expectation, to balk
Difappoint'ment, n. a defeat of hopes, a balk

Difapprobátion, *n.* cenfure, blame, diflike, hate

Difappropriate, *v. t.* to divert from an appropriation

Difapprove', *v. t.* to cenfure, blame, diflike, hate

Difarm', *v. t.* to take way arms, confound, foil

Difarm'ed, *pa.* deprived of arms, ftript, confuted

Difarrangé, *v. t.* to put out of order, to diforder

Difarrangément, *n.* a putting out of order, diforder

Difarráy, *n.* diforder, confufion, hurry, undrefs

Difas'ter, *v. t.* to blaft, afflict, injure, hurt, *ob.*

Difas'ter, *n.* a misfortune, calamity, blaft

Difas'trous, *a.* unlucky, miferable, gloomy, difmal

Difas'troufly, *ad.* unluckily, in a difmal manner

Difavouch', Difavow', *v. t.* to difown, deny, reject

Difavow'al, Difavow'ment, *n.* a denial, a refufal

Difauth'orize, *v. t.* to deprive of power or credit,

Difband', *v. t.* to difmifs, break up, feparate (*ob.*

Difbark', *v. t.* to land from a fhip, land, unload, ftrip bark from a tree

Difbeliéf, *n.* a refufal of belief, doubt, difcredit

Difbeliéve, *v. t.* not to believe or credit, to deny

Difbeliéver, *n.* one who does not believe

Difbench', *v. t.* to drive from a bench or feat, *ob.*

Difbranch', *v. t.* to feparate, lop, break off, *ob.*

Difbur'den, *v. t.* to unload, difcharge, eafe, put off

Difburfe', *v. t.* to expend or lay out money

Difburfe'ment, *n.* a laying out money, expenfe

Difburs'er, *n.* a perfon who difburfes or expends

Difcal'ceate, *v. t.* to take off or deprive of fhoes, *ob.*

Difcalceátion, *n.* the act of pulling off the fhoes, *ob.*

Difcan'dy, *v. t.* to diffolve, melt, foften, *ob.*

Difcard', *v. t.* to difmifs, caft off, lay out cards

Difcard'ed, *pa.* difmiffed, difgraced, caft off

Difcarn'ate, *a.* ftripped of the flefh, flayed, *ob.*

Difcáfe, *v. t.* to ftrip, undrefs, flay, take off

Difceptátion, *n.* the act of difputing, a difpute

Difcern', *v. t.* to fee, perceive, diftinguifh, judge

Difcern'er, *n.* one who difcerns, one who defcries

Difcern'ible, *a.* difcoverable, diftinguifhable, vifible

Difcern'ibly, *ad.* apparently, vifibly, plainly

Difcern'ing, *pa. a.* feeing, judicious, knowing

Difcern'ingly, *ad.* judicioufly, fkilfully, acutely

Difcern'ment, *n.* the faculty of difcerning, fkill

Difcerp'ible, *a.* that may be torn or rent in pieces

Difcerpibil'ity, *n.* the quality of being difcerpible

Difcerp'tion, *n.* the act of tearing in pieces, a rent

Difcharge', *v. t.* to difmifs, pay, clear, unload, fire

Difcharge', *n.* a difmiffion, acquittance, explofion

Difcharg'er, *n.* a perfon who difcharges or pays

Difcind', *v. t.* to divide, to cut in pieces (correct

Difcíple, *n.* a fcholar, learner, follower; *v. t.* to

Difcíplefhip, *n.* the ftate, duty, &c. of a difciple

Dis'ciplin, *n.* rule, order, regulation, punifhment

Dis'ciplin, *v. t.* to educate, regulate, punifh, beat

Dis'ciplinable, *a.* capable of inftruction, gentle

Dis'ciplinablenefs, *n.* an aptnefs to improve

Difciplinárian, *n.* one who keeps ftrict difciplin

Difciplinárian, Dis'ciplinary, *a.* relating or belonging to difciplin, fharp, ftrict

Difclaim, *v. t.* to difown, deny, renounce, quit

Difcláimer, *n.* a perfon who difclaims or difowns

Difclófe, *v. t.* to tell, reveal, difcover, open, bud

Difclófer, *n.* one who difclofes, one who reveals

Difclófure, *n.* the revealing of fecrets, a difcovery

Difcol'or, *v. t.* to change the color, ftain, tinge

Difcolorátion, *n.* a change of color, ftain, die

Difcom'fit, *v. t.* to defeat, overthrow, vanquifh

Difcom'fit, Difcom'fiture, *n.* a defeat, an overthrow

Difcom'fort, *v. t.* to grieve, afflict, deject, *ob.*

Difcom'fort, *n.* uneafinefs, forrow, melancholy, *ob.*

Difcom'fortable, *a.* caufing fadnefs, melancholy, *ob.*

Difcommend', *v. t.* to blame, cenfure, difpraife

Difcommend'able, *a.* blamable, cenfurable

Difcommendátion, *n.* blame, cenfure, reproach

Difcommóde, *v. t.* to put to an inconvenience

Difcommódious, *a.* inconvenient, troublefome

Difcommod'ity, *n.* inconvenience, trouble, hurt

Difcompófe, *v. t.* to diforder, fret, vex, difturb

Difcompófed, *pa.* ruffled, unfettled, fretted, hurt

Difcompófure, *n.* diforder, trouble, difturbance

Difconcert', *v. t.* to unfettle, difappoint, thwart

Difconform'ity, *n.* a want of agreement, unlikenefs

Difcongrúity, *n.* difagreement, inconfiftency, *ob.*

Difconnect', *v. t.* to feparate, difunite

Difconnect'ed, *pa.* freed from a connection

Difconnec'tion, *n.* a ftate of being feparated

Difcons'olate, *a.* fad, dejected, melancholy

Difcons'olately, *ad.* in a difconfolate manner

Difcons'olatenefs, *n.* a difconfolate ftate, fadnefs

Difcontent', *n.* a want of content, forrow, trouble

Difcontent', *v. t.* to make uneafy, to difpleafe

Difcontent', Difcontent'ed, *a.* uneafy, diffatisfied

Difcontent'edly, *ad.* in a difcontented manner

Difcontent'ednefs, *n.* uneafinefs, diffatisfaction

Difcontent'ment, *n.* difcontent, uneafinefs

Difcontin'uance, Difcontinuátion, *n.* a breaking off, breach, feparation, want of union of parts

Difcontin'ue, *v.* to drop, leave or break off, ceafe

Difcontinúity, *n.* a difunity of parts, a feparation

Difcontin'uous, *a.* difcontinued, broken off

Difconvénience, *n.* difagreement, inconfiftency, *ob.*

Dis'cord, *n.* a difagreement, oppofition, anger, ftrife

Difcord', *v. i.* to difagree, differ, not fuit, *ob.*

Difcord'ance, *n.* difagreement, an inconfiftency

Difcord'ant, *a.* difagreeing, inconfiftent, oppofite

Difcord'antly, *ad.* inconfiftently, contradictorily

Difcov'er, *v. t.* to difclofe, fhow, find out, efpy

Difcov'erable, *a.* that may be found out, apparent

Difcov'ered, *pa.* found out, revealed, betrayed

Difcov'erer, *n.* one who difcovers or finds out

Difcov'ery, *n.* the act of difcovering, an invention

Difcov'erture, *n.* a ftate of being teleafed from the coverture of a hufband

Difcoun'fel, *v. t.* to diffuade, to advife againft, *ob.*

Dis'count, *v. t.* to draw or pay back, to deduct, to lend the amount of, deducting the intereft at the time

Difcount'able, *a.* that may be difcounted

Dis'count-day, n. the day on which a bank discounts notes or bills

Dis'count, n. a drawback, allowance, abatement

Difcount'enance, v. t. to difcourage, check, abafh

Difcount'enance, n. cold treatment, coolnefs

Difcount'enancer, n. one who difcountenances

Difcour'age, v. t. to dishearten, deter, diffuade

Difcour'agement, n. what difcourages, caufe of fear

Difcour'ager, n. one who difcourages or diffuades

Difcourfe, n. converfation, talk, fpeech, treatife

Difcourfe, v. i. to talk, reafon, preach, treat upon

Difcourfer, n. a talker, fpeaker, writer (farly

Difcourfive, a. containing dialogue, paffing regu-

Difcourt'eous, a. uncivil, unpolite, rude, rough

Difcourt'eoufly, ad. uncivilly, rudely, roughly

Difcourt'efy, n. incivility, rudenefs, difrefpect

Difc'ous, a. broad, wide, round, flat like a difh

Difcred'it, n. a want of credit, difgrace, reproach

Difcred'it, v. t. not to believe, to difgrace, to hurt

Difcred'itable, a. injurious to reputation

Difcreet, a. prudent, wife, cautious, modeft, fober

Difcreetly, ad. prudently, properly, cautioufly

Difcreetnefs, n. difcretion, prudence, fitnefs, care

Dis'crepance, n. a difference, a contrariety, ob.

Difcrete, a. diftinct, feparated, diftinguifhed

Difcre"tion, n. prudence, caution, liberty to act

Difcre"tional, a. fubject to difcretion only, not

Difcre"tionally, ad. at difcretion, (limited

Difcre"tionary, a. left at large, unlimited, full

Difcretive, a. disjunctive, fit or able to feparate

Difcrim'inate, v. t. to diftinguifh, to feparate

Difcrimination, n. a diftinction, feparation, mark

Difcrim'inative, a. diftinctive, characteriftical

Difcrim'inous, a. dangerous, hazardous, ob.

Difcubitory, a. fitted to a leaning pofture, ob.

Difcul'pate, v. t. to excufe, free from blame

Difcum'bency, n. the act of leaning at meat, reft

Difcum'ber, v. t. to unburden, free, difengage

Difcur'fion, n. the act of running to and fro

Difcurs'ive, a. roving, irregular, progreffive

Difcurs'ively, ad. in a roving or irregular manner

Difcurs'ory, a. argumentative, rational, irregular

Dife'us, n. a quoit, a round iron ufed to play with

Difcufs', v. t. to examin, fift, try, argue, difperfe

Difcuf'fion, n. debate, invefligation

Difcufs'ive, a. able to difcufs, able to difperfe

Difcu'tient, n. a repelling medicine; a. repelling

Difdain, n. fcorn, haughtinefs, pride, indignation

Difdain, v. t. to fcorn, defpife, flight, reject, hate

Difdainful, a. fcornful, haughty, lofty, proud

Difdainfully, ad. with haughty fcorn, proudly

Difdainfulnefs, n. haughty fcorn, contempt, pride

Difeafe, n. a diftemper, ficknefs, uneafinefs, pain

Difeafe, v. t. to afflict, vex, torment, pain, infect

Difeafed, pa. afflicted with a diftemper, pained

Difeafednefs, n. ficknefs, crazinefs, badnefs, pain

Difedg'ed, a. blunted, made blunt, dulled, ob.

Difembark', v. t. to put men or goods on fhore, to

Difembar'rafs, v. t. to extricate, free, clear up (land

Difembit'ter, v. t. to fweeten, to make fweet

Difembod'ied, a. divefted of body, fpiritual, pure

Difembogue, v. to difcharge, run, flow, vent

Difembow'elled, a. taken out of the bowels

Difembroil', v. t. to clear up, free, difentangle

Difennable, v. t. to deprive of power, to difable

Difenchant', v. t. to free from enchantment

Difencum'ber, v. t. to free from encumbrance

Difencum'brance, n. a deliverance from trouble

Difengage, v. t. to extricate, rid, free, draw off

Difengaged, pa. being at leifure, cleared, free

Difengagement, n. a releafe, a freedom

Difentan"gle, v. t. to unravel, loofe, clear, free

Difentan"gled, pa. loofed, cleared, difengaged

Difenthrall', v. t. to fet free, free, refcue, deliver

Difenthrone, v. t. to depofe a king or fovereign

Difentrance', v. t. to awaken from a trance

Difefpoufe', v. t. to divorce, feparate, break off

Difefpous'ed, pa. feparated after promife, left

Difefteem, n. flight diflike; v. t. to flight

Disfavor, n. difcountenance, diflike, an ill turn

Disfavor, v. t. to difcountenance, diflike, hate

Disfiguration, n. the act of disfiguring or hurting

Disfig'ure, v. t. to deform, mangle, maim, deface

Disfig'urement, n. defacement, a deformity

Disfig'urer, n. one who disfigures, one who mangles

Disfran'chife, v. t. to deprive of chartered rights

Disfran'chifement, n. a depriving of free privilege

Disfur'nifh, v. t. to deprive, ftrip, take away

Difgar'nifh, v. t. to ftrip, diveft, take off or away

Difglorify, v. t. to deprive of glory, abafe, ob.

Difgorge', v. t. to vomit, to pour out with force

Difgrace, v. t. to difhonor, difmifs, turn out, de-

Difgrace, n. difhonor, fhame, a lofs of favor (grade

Difgraceful, a. fhameful, infamous, bafe, mean

Difgracefully, ad. dishonorably, fhamefully, ill

Difgracefulnefs, n. dishonor, infamy, reproach

Difgracer, n. a perfon that expofes to fhame

Difgracious, a. unkind, uncivil, unfavorable

Difguife, n. a drefs to deceive, pretenfe; cloke

Difguife, v. t. to conceal, hide, disfigure, deform

Difguifed, pa. concealed, disfigured, overcome

Difguifement, n. a drefs of concealment, ob.

Difguifer, n. one who difguifes, one who conceals

Difguft', n. averfion, diflike, offenfe conceived

Difguft', v. t. to give a diflike, offend, provoke

Difguft'ful, a. naufeous, unpleafant, diftafteful

Difh, n. a veffel to ferve up meat in, meat ferved

Difh, v. t. to put or ferve up in a difh

Dis'habille, n. an undrefs, a loofe or bad drefs

Dis'habille, a. undreffed, very negligently dreffed

Dishab'it, v. t. to throw out of place, to expel, ob.

Dishab'ited, pa. driven away from a habitation

Disheart'en, v. t. to difcourage, caft down, terrify

Dish'ed, pa. put into a difh, ferved up in a difh

Disher'it, v. t. to cut off from inheritance

Dishev'el, v. to put the hair in diforder, to diforder

Dishev'elled, pa. difordered, dangling, loofe

Dish'ing, a. ferving up, refembling a difh, hollow

Dishoa'eft, a. knavifh, bafe, faithlefs, unchafte

Dishon'eftly, ad. knavifhly, wickedly, bafely

Dishon'efty, n. knavery, bafenefs, deceit, lewdnefs

Dishon'or, n. reproach, difgrace, cenfure, blame

Dishon'or, v. t. to difgrace, hurt, violate, deflour

Dishon'orable, a. fhameful, bafe, vile, ungenerous

Dishon'orably, ad. in an unbecoming manner

Dishon'orer, n. one who treats another perfon ill

Dishôrn, v. t. to ftrip of horns, ob.

D.shûmor, n. ill-humor, peevifhnefs, croffnefs

Dilincar'cerate, v. t. to fet at liberty, to fet free

Difinclinátion, n. diflike, hate, want of affection

Difincline, v. t. to excite or produce a diflike

Difincor'porate, v. t. to feparate, diffolve, deftroy

Difinfect', v. t. to cleanfe from infection (ter

Difinfec'tion, n. a purification from infecting mat-

Difingen'uous, a. illiberal, unfair, mean, bafe, fly

Difingen'uoufnefs, n. mean fubtility, low craft, art

Difinher'ifon, n. a debarring from inheritance

Difisher'it, v. t. to deprive of inheritance, to cut off

Difintégrable, a. that may be feparated into parts, or fall to pieces

Difintégrate, v. i. to feparate or fall to pieces

Difintegrátion, n. a feparation into parts, a falling

Difinter', v. t. to take out of a grave (to pieces

Difinter'ment, n. a taking out of the grave

Difin'tereft, Difin'tereftednefs, n. a difregard to private intereft

Difin'tereffed, Difin'terefted, a. void of felf-intereft

Difin'tereftedly, ad. in a difintereted manner

Disjoin', v. to feparate, difunite, divide

Disjoin'ed, pa. feparated, divided

Disjoint', v. t. to part or feparate joints

Disjoint'ed, pa. feparated, not coherent

Disjudicátion, n. the act of determining, ob.

Disjunct', a. feparated, divided, disjoined

Disjunc'tion, n. a parting, feparation, difunion

Disjunct'ive, a. making oppofition or feparation

Disjunct'ively, ad. diftinctly, feparately, afunder

Difk, n. a quoit, the face of the fun, moon, &c.

Difkindnefs, n. an injury, a want of affection

Diflike, n. averfion, difapprobation, difagreement

Diflike, v. t. to hate, difapprove, flight, condemn

Diflik'en, v. t. to make or render unlike, ob.

Diflikenefs, n. unlikenefs, difference, variety

Diflik'er, n. a perfon who diflikes or difapproves

Diflimn, v. t. to ftrike or put out of a picture, ob.

Dis'locate, v. t. to disjoint, difplace, put out, flip

Diflocátion, n. the act of difplacing, a joint put out

Diflodge', v. t. to drive out, remove, go away

Difloy'al, a. not true to allegiance, treacherous

Difloy'ally, ad. in a difloyal manner

Difloy'alty, n. a want of allegiance, inconftancy

Dis'mal, a. terrible, dark, gloomy, forrowful

Dis'malnefs, n. a difmal or dark ftate

Dis'mally, ad. horribly, gloomily, forrowfully

Difman'tle, v. t. to ftrip, overthrow, deftroy, loofe

Difmafk', v. t. to put off or by, uncover, diveft

Difmaft', v. t. to deprive of mafts

Difmáy, v. t. to affright, terrify, dafh, difcourage

Difmáy, n. a fall of courage, fright, terror, fear

Difmáyednefs, n. a want of courage, a dejection

Difme, n. a tenth part or portion, the tithe, ob.

Difmem'ber, v. t. to cut off a limb or in pieces

Difmem'berment, n. the cutting off of a member or a part, the partition of a ftate

Difmifs', v. t. to fend or put away, difcard, depofe

Difmifs'al, n. a difmiffing, removal from office

Difmifs'ed, pa. fent away, put out, difcharged

Difmis'fion, n. a fending off or away, a difcharge

Difmort'gage, v. t. to redeem from mortgage

Difmount', v. to alight or throw from a horfe, &c.

Difnátured, a. wanting natural affection, ob.

Difobédience, n. a breach of duty, frowardnefs

Difobédient, a. breaking lawful commands, undu-

Difobédiently, ad. in an undutiful manner (tiful

Difobey', v. t. to tranfgrefs, neglect, not to do

Difobligátion, n. an offenfe, a caufe of difguft, ob.

Difoblige, v. t. to offend, provoke, vex, difguft

Difobliging, pa. difpleafing offenfive, difgufting

Difobligingly, ad. in a difobliging manner, amifs

Diforb'ed, a. thrown or put out of proper place

Difor'der, n. confufion, ficknefs, difcompofure

Difor'der, v. t. to difturb, ruffle, make fick

Difor'dered, pa. confufed, irregular, loofe, ill

Difor'derly, a. confufed, irregular, lawlefs, loofe

Difor'derly, ad. confufedly, irregularly, ill

Difor'dinate, a. living irregularly, loofe, ob.

Difor'ganize, v. t. to feparate organized parts

Diforganizátion, n. the act of deftroying organic ftructure or connected fyftem

Difor'ganizer, n. one who deftroys or attempts to deftroy, a regular ftructure

Difôwn, v. t. not to own, to deny, to renounce

Difoxy'genate, v. t. to free from oxygene

Difoxygenátion, n. the depriving of oxygene

Difpar'age, v. t. to undervalue, leffen, degrade

Difpar'agement, n. a difgrace, dishonor, reproach

Dis'parate, a. unlike, different, oppofit, o'.

Difpar'ity, n. inequality, unlikenefs, difference

Difpark', v. t. to throw open a park, to lay open

Difpark'ed, pa. laid open, made common land

Difpart', v. to part, divide, feparate, fplit

Difpas'fion, n. coolnefs of temper, compofure

Difpas'fionate, a. cool, calm, compofed, moderate

Difpas'fionately, ad. coolly, compofedly, fairly,

Difpátch, fee Defpatch (fuftly

Difpel', v. t. to drive off or away, banifh, difperfe

Difpend', v. t. to fpend, lay out, confume, ob.

Difpens'ary, n. a place for difpenfing medicines to the fick and needy

Difpensátion, n. a diftribution, exemption, leave

Difpensátor, n. one who deals out or diftributes

Difpens'atory, n. the directory for making medi-

Difpenfe', v. to diftribute, exempt, excufe (cines

Difpenfe', n. a difpenfation, exemption, difcharge

Difpens'er, n. one who difpenfes, one who excufes

Difpéople, v. t. to depopulate, lay wafte, deftroy

Difpéopler, *n.* one who depopulates or lays wafte
Difperge', *v. t.* to fprinkle, fcatter, *ob.*
Difperm'ous, *a.* having two feeds together
Difperfe', *v.* to feparate, go or drive away, fcatter
Dïfpers'edly, *ad.* in a difperfed manner, confufedly
Difpers'ednefs, *n.* a difperfed itate, thinnefs
Difpers'er, *n.* one who difperfes, one who fpreads
Difpers'ive, *a.* having a tendency to fcatter
Difper'fion, *n.* a fpreading or fcattering abroad
Difpir'it, *v. t.* to difcourage, damp, dejeĉt, opprefs
Difpir'ited, *pa.* disheartened, caft down (der
Difplâce, *v. t.* to put out of place, remove, difor-
Difplâcement, *n.* the act of difplacing
Difplácency, *n.* incivility, difguft, offenfe, *ob.*
Difplant', *v. t.* to remove, to drive out or away, *ob.*
Difplantátion, *n.* a removal of plants or people, *ob.*
Difpláy, *v. t.* to fpread, fhow, exhibit, defcribe
Dïf láy, *n.* a fetting to view, exhibition, pomp
Difpleas'ant, *a.* unpleafant, offenfive, odious
Difpléafe, *v. t.* to offend, vex, provoke, difguft
Difpléafingnefs, *n.* an offenfive quality
Difpleas'ure, *v. t.* to difpleafe, offend, provoke
Difpleas'ure, *n.* offenfe, anger, hate, uneafinefs
Difplóde, *v. i.* to vent or burft with violence
Difplófion, *n.* a burfting with noife, an explofion
Difpórt, *n.* fport, play, paftime, merriment, mirth
Difpórt, *v.* to fport, play, wanton, divert, pleafe
Difpófable, *a.* that may be difpofed of, at command
Difpófal, *n.* management, regulation, command
Difpófe, *v.* to place, prepare, incline, give, fell,
Difpófe, *n.* a difpofal, will, difpofition, *ob.* (bargain
Difpófed, *p r.* ranged, placed, fet, inclined, fold
Difpófer, *n.* one who difpofes, one who fets in order
Difpofi''tion, *n.* a method, tendency, temper, ftate
Difpos'itive, *a.* implying difpofal, fetting, *ob.*
Difpos'itively, *ad.* diftributively, in order, *ob.*
Difpoffefs', *v. t.* to deprive of, difplace, diffeize
Difpoffes'fion, *n.* the act of putting out or from
Difpófture, *n.* a difpofal, pofture, ftate, condition
Difpráife, *n.* blame, cenfure, reproach, difgrace
Difpráife, *v.* to blame, cenfure, condemn, leffen
Difpráifingly, *ad.* with blame or cenfure, ill
Difpread', *v. t.* to difpread, *pret.* difpread, *pa.* to
    fpread or flow different ways
Difproof', *n.* a confutation, a refutation of error
Difpropórtion, *v. t.* to mifmatch (nefs
Difpropórtion, *n.* a want of proportion, unfuitable-
Difpropórtionable, Difpropórtional Difpropórtion-
    ate, *a.* unequal, unfuitable, unfit
Difpropórtionably, Difpropórtionally, Difpropór-
    tionately, *ad.* unequally, unfuitably
Difprópriate, Difapprópriate, *v. t.* to deftroy ap-
    propriation or make common
Difprove', *v. t.* to confute, refute, convict of error
Difpun'ihable, *a.* free from penal reftraint
Difpurfe', *v. t.* to difburfe, lay out, fpend, expend
Difpútable, *a.* liable to be contefted, uncertain
Dis'putant, *n.* a difputer, reafoner, controvertift
Difputátion, *n.* the fkill or act of controverfy

Dirputátious, Difpútative, *a.* inclined to difpute
Difpúte, *v. t.* to contend, debate, wrangle, oppofe
Difpúte, *n.* a conteft, controverfy, debate
Difpútelefs, *a.* undifputed, undeniable, *ob.*
Difpúter, *n.* one given to difputing
Difqualificátion, *n.* any thing which difqualifies
Difqual'ify, *v. t.* to make unfit, difable, deprive
Difquant'ity, *v. t.* to leffen, to diminifh, *ob.*
Difquiet, *v. t.* to difturb, trouble, vex, fret, ruffle
Difquiet, Difquietnefs, Difquietude, *n.* uneafinefs
Difquieter, *n.* one who difquiets, one who difturbs
Difquietly, *ad.* without reft, uneafily, anxioufly
Difquifi''tion, *n.* examination, fearch, inquiry
Difregard', *n.* a flight notice, neglect, contempt
Difregard', *v. t.* to flight, neglect, defpife, fcorn
Difregard'ful, *a.* negligent, heedlefs, carelefs
Difrel'ifh, *n.* a bad tafte, naufeous, diflike, hatred
Difrel'ifh, *v. t.* to make naufeous, to diflike
Difrep'utable, *a.* difgraceful, unbecoming, mean
Difreputátion, Difrepúte, *n.* difgrace, dishonor
Difrefpect', *n.* a want of refpect, incivility
Difrefpect'ful, *a.* uncivil, irreverent, rude
Difrefpect'fully, *ad.* uncivilly, irreverently, ill
Difróbe, *v. t.* to undrefs, uncover, ftrip
Difroot', *v. t.* to extirpate, remove the roots
Difrupt', *a.* rent, torn, broken, broken in pieces
Difrup'tion, *n.* a breaking afunder, breach, rent
Diffatisfac'tion, *n.* difcontent, diflike, difguft
Diffatisfac'tory, *a.* not giving content, defective
Diffat'isfied, *pa.* difcontented, difpleafed
Diffat'isfy, *v. t.* to difpleafe, difoblige, offend, vex
Diffect', *v. t.* to cut in pieces, divide, anatomize
Diffec'tion, *n.* the act of diffecting, anatomy
Diffeifée, *n.* a perfon that is put out of his lands
Diffeifin, *n.* an unlawful ejectment from right
Diffeifor, *n.* one who difpoffeffes or ejects
Diffeize, *v. t.* to difpoffefs, eject, deprive of right
Diffem'ble, *v.* to play the hypocrit, to pretend
Diffem'bled, *pa.* made to diffemble, pretended
Diffem'bler, *n.* a hypocrit, pretender, cheat
Diffem'blingly, *ad.* hypocritically, falfely, bafely
Diffem'inate, *v. t.* to fow, difperfe, propagate
Diffeminátion, *n.* the act of fcattering feed, &c.
Diffem'inator, *n.* one who fcatters or difperfes
Diffen'fion, *n.* contention, difcord, difagreement
Diffen'fious, *a.* contentious, quarrelfome, crofs
Diffent', *v. i.* to difagree, to differ in opinion
Diffent', *n.* difagreement, difference in opinion
Diffent'er, *n.* one who diffents, or does not comply
    with the difciplin of an eftablifhed church
Diffep'iment, *n.* a partition between the cells in a
    pericarp or feed veffel
Differtátion, *n.* a difcourfe, effay, treatife, fpeech
Differve', *v. t.* to injure, do harm or damage to
Differv'ice, Differv'iceablenefs, *n.* injury, harm
Differv'iceable, *a.* injurious, hurtful, pernicious
Diffev'er, *v. t.* to part in two, part, divide, disjoin
Diffev'ering, *pa.* parting in two; *n.* a feparation
Dis'fident, *n.* a diffenter from an eftablifhed religion

Diffil'ient, a. burfting with elafticity, as pods

Diffili''tion, n. the act of burfting or flying back

Diffim'ilar, a. unlike, different, difagreeing with

Diffimilar'ity, Diffimil'itude, n. unlikenefs

Diffimulátion, n. a diffembling, hypocrify, guile

Difs'ipable, a. eafily fcattered or difperfed

Difs'ipate, v. t. to difperfe, fquander, fpend

Diffipátion, n. a difperfing, extravagance, wafte

Diffóciate, v. t. to feparate, part, difunite

Diffociátion, n. feparation, difunion

Diffolv'able, Difs'oluble, a. that may be diffolved

Diffolve', v. t. to melt, feparate, break up, deltroy

Diffolv'ed, pa. melted, broken up, deftroyed, end-

Diffolv'ent, a. having the power of melting (ed

Diffolv'ent, Diffolv'er, n. one who or what diffolves

Difs'olute, a. loofe, lewd, debauched, luxurious

Difs'olutely, ad. in a diffolute manner, lewdly

Difs'olutenefs, n. loofenefs, lewdnefs, debauchery

Diffolútion, n. a diffolving, ruin, end, death

Difs'onance, n. difcord, difagreement, harfhnefs

Difs'onant, a. difcordant, contrary, harfh, jarring

Diffuáde, v. t. to advife to the contrary, to divert

Diffuáder, n. one who diffuades or difcourages

Diffuáfion, n. an endeavor to diffuade

Diffuáfive, n. an argument tending to diffuade

Diffuáfive, a. tending, apt or proper to diffuade

Diffyl'lable, n. a word that has two fyllables

Diffyllab'ic, a. confifting of two fyllables

Dis'taff, n. a ftaff ufed in fpinning, a woman

Diftáin, v. t. to ftain, tinge, blot, defame, defile

Dis'tance, n. a fpace, refpect, referve, coolnefs

Dis'tance, v. t. to leave behind, to caft out or off

Dis'tanced, pa. left behind, caft out of a race

Dis'tant, a. remote in time or place, farfetched, fhy

Dis'tantly, ad. in a diftant manner, far off, coolly

Diftáfte, n. a diflike, averfion, difguft, hatred

Diftáfte, v. t. to diflike, loathe, difguft, vex, four

Diftáfteful, a. naufeous, offenfive, malevolent

Diftemp'er, v. t. to diforder, difeafe, affect, difturb

Diftemp'er, n. a diforder, difeafe, ficknefs, uneafinefs

Diftemp'erate, a. intemperate, immoderàte, ob.

Diftemp'erature, n. intemperance, confufion, noife

Diftemp'ered, pa. difeafed, afflicted, difturbed

Diftend', v. t. to ftretch out in breadth, to fwell

Diftend'ed, Diftent', pa. widened, fwelled

Diftens'ible, a. that may be diftended (deftention

Diftenfibil'ity, n. the quality of being capable of

Diftent', n. the fpace or length of extenfion, extent

Diften'tion, n. a ftretching or enlarging, breadth

Dis'tich, [ch as k] n. a couple of verfes, a complet

Dis'tichate, a. in two rows on the fides of branches

Diftil', v. to drop, flow or run gently, ufe a ftill

Diftillátion, n. the act of diftilling or dropping

Diftil'latory, a. belonging to diftillation, dropping

Diftil'ler, n. one whofe trade is to diftil fpirits

Diftil'ment, n. what is drawn off by diftillation, ob.

Diftinct', a. clear, plain, full, different, marked out

Diftinc'tion, n. a difference, note, difcernment

Diftinct'ive, a. able to diftinguifh, particular

Diftinct'ively, Diftinct'ly, ad. plainly, feparately

Diftinct'nefs, n. clearnefs, plainnefs, difference

Diftin''guifh, v. to make a diftinction, make eminent, note, difcern, perceive

Diftin''guifhable, a. able to be diftinguifhed

Diftin''guifhed, pa. a. noted, eminent, extraordi-

Diftin''guifher, n. one who diftinguifhes (nary

Diftin''guifhingly, ad. with diftinction, keenly

Diftort', v. t. to twift, writhe, wreft, mifreprefent

Diftor'tion, n. a grimace, turn, mifreprefentation

Diftract', v. t. to make mad, perplex, vex, divide

Diftract'ed, pa. a. mad, wild, confufed, divided

Diftract'edly, ad. madly, wildly, confufedly, very

Diftract'ible, a. that may be drawn off or afide

Diftrac'tion, n. madnefs, confufion, feparation

Diftráin, v. t. to feize, to feize goods for debt

Diftráinable, a. fubject to be feized for debt

Diftráint, n. a feizure of goods for debt

Diftráught, pa. diftracted, mad, ob.

Diftréam, v. i. to run or flow out, to run down

Diftrefs', v. t. to harafs, perplex, afflict, feize

Diftrefs', n. the act of diftraining, mifery, want

Diftrefs'ed, pa. perplexed, afflicted, in diftrefs

Dis'tribute or Diftrib'ute, v. t. to divide among a
number, to allot, fhare, fcatter

Dis'tributed or Diftrib'uted, pa. divided, allotted

Diftribútion, n. the act of diftributing, a divifion

Diftrib'utive, a. that ferves to diftribute or give

Diftrib'utively, ad. with or by diftribution, fingly

Dis'trict, n. a circuit, region, country, part, power

Dis'trict, v. t. to divide into circuits, or parts

Diftruft', v. t. to fufpect, difbelieve, fear

Diftruft', n. fufpicion, a lofs of confidence

Diftruft'ful, a. fufpicious, timorous, modeft, fhy

Diftruft'fulnefs, n. a diftruftful ftate or temper

Diftruft'lefs, a. free from diftruft or fufpicion

Difturb', v. t. to difquiet, confound, hinder, turn

Difturb'ance, n. perplexity, confufion, tumult

Difturb'ed, pa. perplexed, interrupted, uneafy

Difturb'er, n. one who difturbs, one who difquiets

Difturn', v. t. to turn off or afide, turn, ob.

Difûnion, n. a feparation, a breach of agreement

Difunîte, v. to divide, disjoin, part, feparate

Difûnity, n. a ftate of actual feparation

Difûfage, Difûfe, n. a want of practice, neglect

Difûfe, [difyúze] v. t. to drop a cuftom, leave off

Difvaluátion, n. a difgrace, a lofs of credit, ob.

Difval'ue, v. t. to undervalue, flight, difregard, ob.

Difvouch', v. t. to contradict, deny, ob.

Difwit'ted, a. mad, diftracted, ob.

Ditch, v. i. to make a ditch or ditches

Ditch, n. a long trench, cut, moat in fortification

Ditch'er, n. a man who makes or cleans ditches

Dithyram'bic, n. a fort of mad or licentious verfe

Di''tion, n. rule, power, government dominion

Dittan'der, n. a plant, pepperwort

Dit'tany, n. a plant of feveral kinds

Dit'tied, a. fung, fitted or adapted to mufic

Dit'to, n. the aforefaid, the fame thing repeated

Dit'ty, Hit, *n.* a fonnet, fong, fhort mufical poem
Diuret'ic, Diuret'ical, *a.* good to provoke urin
Diur'nal, *a.* daily, performed or done in a day
Diur'nal, *n.* a daybook, journal, daily account
Diur'nally, *ad.* daily, every day, day by day
Diuturn'ity, *n.* length of time, continuance
Divan', *n.* the Ottoman grand council, a hall, a
Divar'icate, *v.* to divide, feparate (court
Divar'icate, *a.* ftanding wide apart
Divarication, *n.* a divifion, a ftanding apart
Dive, *v. i.* to fwim or go under water, to go deep
Divel'lent, *a.* drawing afunder, feparating
Diver, *n.* one who dives, a water-fowl, a didapper
Diverberation, *n.* the act of beating through
Diverge', *v. i.* to bend or depart from one point
Diver'gence, *n.* a feparating or going farther apart
Diver'gent, *a.* going farther afunder, departing
Diverg'ing, *pa.* feparating at a greater diftance
Diverg'ingiy, *ad.* in a diverging manner
Divers, *a.* feveral, fundry, many
Diverfe, *a.* different, unlike, contrary, oppofit
Diverfification, *n.* a change, alteration, variety
Divers'ify, *v. t.* to variegate, vary, alter, diftinguifh
Diver'fion, *n.* a turning afide, fport, paftime, game
Divers'ity, *n.* a difference, unlikenefs, variety
Diverfly, *ad.* differently, varioufly, contrarily
Divert', *v. t.* to turn afide, entertain, pleafe, ruin
Divert'er, *n.* one who or a thing that diverts
Divert'ing, *pa. a.* turning, pleafing, agreeable
Divert'ingly, *ad.* in an entertaining manner
Divertife, *v. t.* to divert, amufe, pleafe, ob.
Divert'ifement, *n.* diverfion, pleafure, recreation,
Divert'ive, *a.* diverting, amufing, pleafing (ob.
Diveft', *v. t.* to ftrip, make naked, difpoffefs
Diveft'ure, *n.* the act of ftripping or putting off
Dividable, Dividant, *a.* divifible, feparate, ob.
Divide, *v. t.* to part, feparate, diftribute, give
Divided, *pa.* parted, feparated, fhared out, given
Dividend', *n.* a fhare, part, number to be divided
Divider, *n.* one who divides, one who diftributes
Divi'ders, *n. pl* a pair of mathematical compaffes
Divid'ual, *a.* divided, parted, fhared out, pointed, ob.
Divination, *n.* a prediction, a foretelling of things
Divine, *v. t.* to foretel, foreknow, forefee, guefs
Divine, *a.* heavenly, godiike, very fine, prefcient
Divine, *n.* a clergyman, a minifter of the gofpel
Divinely, *ad.* heavenly, in a godlike manner, very
Divinenefs, *n.* divinity, excellence, fublimity
Divi'ner, *n.* a foothfayer, fortuneteller, gueffer
Divinerefs, *n.* a prophetefs, a forcerefs, ob.
Divinip'otent, *a.* divinely powerful
Divin'ity, *n.* the Deity, the fcience of divine things
Divifibil'ity, *n.* the quality of admitting divifion
Divis'ible, *a.* that may be divided, cut or parted
Divi'fion, *n.* a dividing, variance, part of a difcourfe,
Divis'ional, *a.* dividing, feparating (juft time
Divi'fionary, *a.* pertaining to a divifion
Divi'for, *n.* a number that divides
Divorce, *v. t.* to feparate married perfons by law

Divorce, Hivorcement, *n.* a feparation in marriage
Divorcer, *n.* a perfon who or that which divorces
Divulge', *v. t.* to publifh, proclaim, tell, difclofe
Divul'ger, *n.* one who divulges or proclaims
Divul'fion, *n.* the act of plucking off or away
Dizen, *v. t.* to deck, drefs, trim, fet off, ob.
Diz'zinefs, *n.* giddinefs, great thoughtleffnefs
Diz'zy, *a.* giddy, thoughtlefs; *v. t.* to make giddy
Do, *v.* did, *pret.* done, *pa.* to perform, to act,
deal with, fucceed, anfwer the purpofe
Do, *n.* buftle, ftir, hurry, noife, confufion
Do"cible, Do"cile, *a.* eafy to be taught, tractable
Do"ciblenefs, Docil'ity, *n.* an aptnefs to be taught
Docimas'tic, *a.* pertaining to the effaying of metals
Dock, *n.* a place for fhips, cut tail, chine, herb
Dock, *v. t.* to lay a fhip in a dock, to cut fhort
Dock'ed, *pa.* having or laid in a dock, cut fhort
Dock'et, *n.* a direction tied upon goods, a fummary,
a lift of cafes in court
Dock'et, *v. t.* to place in or mark with a docket
Dock'yard, *n.* a yard for holding naval ftores, &c.
Doc'tor, *n.* a title in divinity, law, &c. a teacher
Doc'tor, *v. t.* to phyfic, cure, heal, take care of
Doc'torate, *n.* the degree of doctor granted by a
college or univerfity
Doc'torally, *ad.* in the manner of a doctor, wifely
Doc'torfhip, *n.* the higheft academical degree
Doc'trefs, *n.* a woman fkilled in phyfic
Doc'trin, *n.* a precept, principle, act of teaching
Doc'trinal, *a.* containing or relating to doctrin
Doc'trinally, *ad.* by way of doctrin, pofitively
Doc'ument, *n.* an inftruction, direction, proof
Doc'ument, *v. t.* to furnifh with written proofs or
inftructions
Document'al, *d.* relating to inftruction or proof
Dod'der, *n.* a kind of bad winding plant or weed
Dod'dered, *a.* overgrown with or having dodder
Dodec'agon, *n.* a figure of twelve equal fides
Dodecahedron, *n.* a folid having twelve equal ba-
Dodecahedral, *a.* having twelve fides (fes
Dodecan'dria, *n.* a clafs of plants having from
twelve to nineteen ftamens in hermaphrodite
flowers
Dodge, *v.* to fly from, follow artfully, quibble
Dod'kin, *n.* a very fmall coin, a mere trifle
Do'do, *n.* a fowl of the gallinaceous order
Dodonian, *a.* relating to Dodona, in which was an
oracle of Jupiter
Doe, *n.* a fhe-deer, the female of a buck, a feat
Doer, *a.* a perfon who does or performs a thing
Doff, *v. t.* to put off drefs, ftrip, fhift off, delay
Dog, *n.* a domeftic animal, lump of iron, wretch
Dog, *v. t.* to follow flily and continually, to hunt
Dog'days, *n. pl.* days named from the dogftar
Doge, *n.* the chief magiftrate of Venice or Genoa
Dog'fifh, *n.* a variety of the fhark
Dog'fly, *n.* a fpecies of troublefome woodfly
Dog'ged, *a.* four, morofe, fullen, crofs, followed
Dog'gedly, *ad.* peevifhly, fourly, fullenly, crofsly

Dog'gednefs, n. fournefs, morofenefs, fullennefs
Dog'ger, n. a fmall fithing-veffel of one maft
Dog'gerel, n. vile mean verfes; a. mean, wretched
Dog'german, n. a failor belonging to a dogger
Dog'gith, a. currifh, fnappifh, churlifh, brutal
Dog'hearted, a. cruel, mercilefs, brutal, malicious
Dog'hole, n. a vile hole or place, a mean houfe
Dog'kennel, n. a kennel or hut for dogs
Dog'ma, n. an eftablifhed principle, tenet, notion
Dogmat'ical, a. magifterial, pofitive, obftinate
Dogmat'ically, ad. magifterially, pofitively
Dogmat'icalnefs, n. pofitivenefs, confidence
Dog'matifm, n. magifterial affertion   (affertor
Dog'matift, Dog'matizer, n. a pofitive teacher or
Dog'matize, v. i. to affert or teach magifterially
Dog'fleep, n. a falfe or pretended fleep
Dogs'meat, n. very bad or coarfe meat, refufe, offal
Dog'ftar, n. a ftar that gives name to the dogdays
Dog'tooth, n. a tooth next the grinders
Dog'trick, n. an ill turn, brutal or bad treatment
Dog'trot, n. a gentle eafy trot like that of a dog
Dog'weary, a. quite tired, very much fatigued
Dog'wood, n. a tree of hard wood
Doil'y, n. a kind of linen; a. coarfe, homely, ob.
Doings, n. pl. actions, conduct, ftir, merriment
Doit, n. a fmall piece of Dutch money, a trifler
Dolab'riform, a. refembling an ax
Dole, n. a fhare, part, gift, forrow, moan, mifery
Dole, v. to diftribute alms, give, grieve, lament
Doleful, a. forrowful, piteous, woful, difmal, fad
Dolefully, ad. in a doleful manner, wofully, ill
Dolefulnefs, n. a difmal or fad ftate, melancholy
Doll, n. abbrev. for Dorothy, a puppet or baby
Dol'lar, a filver coin of the U. S. value 100 cents,
  but in Europe the name is given to coins of
  different values
Dol'omite, n. a calcareous earth or lime ftone con-
  taining an unufual quantity of fixed air
Dolor, n. grief, forrow, lamentation, heavinefs, pain
Dolorific, a. caufing grief or pain
Dol'orous, a. forrowful, doleful, difmal, painful
Dol'oroufly, ad. mournfully, fadly, painfully
Dol'phin, n. a kind of beautiful feafifh
Dolt, n. a heavy ftupid perfon, blockhead dunce
Doltifh, a. ftupid, blockifh, dull, heavy, mean
Doltifhnefs, n. ftupidity, dulnefs, weaknefs
Domain, n. a poffeffion, eftate, dominion, power
Dome, n. an arched roof, cupola, building, houfe
Domes'tic, a. belonging to a houfe, private, tame
Domes'tic, n. a fervant in the houfe, a dependant
Domes'ticate, v. t. to make domeftic or tame
Domestication, n. the act of taming, ftate of being
  tamed
Dom'icil, n. a manfion-houfe, permanent refidence
Dom'iciled, Domicil'iated, a. having permanent
  refidence
Domicil'iary, a. pertaining to private manfions
Dom'inant, a. ruling, prevailing, governing
Dom'inate, v. t. to prevail, rule over, govern

Domination, n. power, dominion, tyranny, rule
Domineer, v. t. to hector, to behave with infolence
Domin'ical, a. denoting the Lord's day
Dominicans, n. an order of monks or friars
Domin'ion, n. fovereign authority, a territory
Dom'ino, n. a kind of hood, a kind of long drefs
Don, n. a Spanifh title for a gentleman
Don, v. t. to put on, inveft with, drefs, ob.
Donation, n. a gift, prefent, bounty, grant
Do'natifm, n. the doctrins of the donatifts, who held
  all baptifm null, unlefs adminiftered in their
  churches
Do'natift, n. an adherent to donatifm
Donative, n. a gift, dole, benefice, kind of living
Done, pa. paff. of the verb to do, [pron, dun]
Done, v. ufed to confirm a wager, let it be done
Donée, n. a perfon to whom lands, &c. are given
Donor, n. a giver, beftower, benefactor, friend
Doo'dle, n. a trifler, idler, fimple fellow, fool
Doom, v. t. to fentence, condemn, deftine, judge
Doom, n. a fentence, judgment, fate, deftruction
Doom'age, n. fine or penalty.   Law of N. H.
Doom'ed, pa. condemned, deftined, fated, fixed
Dooms'day, n. the day of judgment, the laft day
Dooms'day-book, n. a book for regiftering eftates
Door, [dore] n. the gate of a houfe, an opening for
  entrance, means of admittance
Door'keeper, n. one who keeps a door, a porter
Dor, an infect, the hedge chafer
Dora'do, n. a large fifh like the dolphin
Doree', n. a fifh, oval and depreffed on the fides
Dor'ic, a. relating to an order of architecture
Dor'mant, a. fleeping, lying, neglected, concealed
Dor'mitory, n. a place to fleep in, a burial place
Dor'moufe, n. a tribe of fmall animals which re-
  pofe during winter
Doron, n. a gift, prefent, meafure of three inches
Dor'fal, a. pertaining to the back
Dorfiferous, Dorfip'arous, a. producing feed on
  the back as fern leaves
Dor'ture, n. a dormitory, a chamber, ob.
Dofe, n. enough at one time, a fhare, a medicin
Dofe, v. t. to give a dofe, to proportion
Dofs'el or Dofs'il, n. a pledget, lump of lint, tent
Dot, n. a fmall fpot or point ufed in writing or
Dot, v. t. to make dots thus, ...   (printing
Dot'age, n. a lofs of underftanding, over-fondnefs
Dotal, a. relating to a portion or dowery
Dotard, Doter, n. a doting fellow, one foolifhly fond
Dotation, n. endowment, act of endowing
Dote, v. i. to grow filly or dull, to love extremely
Doted, a. endowed with, gifted, poffeffed
Dotingly, ad. very fondly, with great fondnefs
Dot'tard, n. a tree that is kept low by cutting
Dot'terel, n. a bird, called alfo morinel
Double, a. twofold, twice as much, deceitful
Double, v. to make double, fold, pafs round, in-
  creafe, play tricks, wind in running, repeat
Double, n. twice the quantity or number, a turn

Doub'lebiting, a. cutting with both the sides
Doublebut'toned, a. having two rows of buttons
Doubledéaler, n. a deceitful mean perfon, a knave
Doubledéaling, n. diffimulation, low cunning, art
Doubledy'e, v. t. to dye twice
Doublehand'ed, a. having two hands, deceitful
Doubielock', v. t. to lock twice, to make fecure
Doublemínded, a. deceitful, treacherous, falfe, fly
Doub'ler, n. one who doubles, one who folds up
Doubiefhíning, a. fhining with double lufter
Doub'let, n. a pair, waiftcoat, patent, falfe ftone
Doubleton'gued, a. deceitful, falfe, hollow, bafe
Doub'ling, n. the act of doubling, a fold, a plait
Doubloon', n. a Spanifh gold coin of two piftoles
Doub'ly, ad. with twice the quantity, twice
Doubt, v. to queftion, fcruple, fufpect, diftruft
Doubt, n. fufpenfe, fufpicion, fcruple, difficulty
Doubt'er, n. one who doubts, one who fufpects
Doubt'ful, a. uncertain, not determined or fixed
Doubt'fully, Doubt'ingly, ad. uncertainly
Doubt'fulnefs, n. uncertainty, fufpenfe, diftrefs
Doubt'ing, n. doubt, hefitation, fufpenfe
Doubt'lefs, a. and ad. without doubt, without fear
Douceur, n. a bribe, gift, prefent
Dove, [duv] n. a pigeon, a kind of wild pigeon
Dove'cot, Dove'houfe, n. a houfe to keep pigeons in
Dove'like, a. meek, gentle, harmlefs, innocent
Dove'tail, n. a joint in form of a dove's tail
Dove'tail, v. t. to unite, with a dovetail joint
Dough, n. unbaked pafte, kneaded flour
Dough'ty, a. brave, illuftrious, noble, eminent
Dough'y, a. foft, not quite baked, unhealthy, pale
Doufe, v. to plunge into water, to lower
Dow'able, a. that may or ought to be endowed
Dow'ager, n. a widow with a dowery or jointure
Dow'dy, n. an aukward and ill-dreffed woman
Dow'er or Dow'ery, n. a jointure, wife's portion
Dow'ered, a. portioned, having a jointure (gift
Dower'lefs, a. being without a fortune, poor
Dow'las, n. a kind of coarfe ftrong linen
Down, n. a large open plain, very foft fethers, &c.
Down, prep. along a defcent; ad. on the ground
Down, v. to fubdue, bring low, deftroy, go down
Down'caft, a. bent down, uneafy, dejected, dull
Down'fall, n. a fall, ruin, calamity, fudden change
Down'fallen, a. fallen down, caft down, ruined
Down'gyred, a. let down in round wrinkles, ob.
Down'haul, n. a rope to haul down a fail
Down'hill, a. defcending, floping; n. a defcent
Down'looking, a. downcaft, gloomy, fullen
Down'right, a. open, undifguifed, plain, honeft
Down'right, ad. plainly, honeftly, completely
Downs, n. a hilly open country, the fea near Deal
Down'fitting, n. a fitting down, reft, repofe, eafe
Down'ward, a. bending down, dejected, uneafy
Down'ward, Down'wards, ad. from higher to lower
Down'y, a. covered with or like down, foft, eafy
Doxol'ogy, n. a fhort form of giving glory to God
Dox'y, n. a foldier's trull, loofe wench

Doze, v. to flumber, ftupify, dull; n. a flumber
Doz'en, [duzn] n. twelve; a. relating to twelve
Dózinefs, n. a flumbering, drowfinefs, heavinefs
Dózy, a. fleepy, drowfy, heavy, ftupid, dull, flow
Drab, n. a dirty woman, a thick woollen cloth
Drach'ma [drakma] or Dram, n. the eighth of an
ounce, a Grecian coin, value 14 cents
Draff, n. refufe, any thing caft away, fwill, wafh
Draft, n. a bill drawn on any perfon for money,
quantity drank, a drawing, that which is drawn,
delineation, fketch, detachment, depth
Draft, v. t. to draw, felect from a number, detach
Draft, a. ufed for or in drawing
Drafts, n. a game played on checkers
Drag, v. to pull or carry by force, draw, trail
Drag, n. a hook, net, harrow, hand-cart, tail
Drag'gle, v. t. to make dirty to draw on the
Drag'gled, pa. made dirty by walking (ground
Drag'net, n. a large net drawn along the bottom
Drag'on, n. a ferpent, devil, conftellation, plant
Drag'onet, n. a fifh with a flender round body
Drag'onfifh, n. a fpecies of fifh, the weever
Drag'onfly, n. a genus of large flying infects
Drag'onifh, Drag'onlike, a. furious, fiery, fierce
Dragoon', n. a kind of horfe foldier, bravo, bully
Dragoon', v. t. to enflave with folders, to force
Drain, n. a channel to carry off water, a fink
Drain, v. t. to empty, exhauft, make dry
Drain'age, n. a drawing off
Drake, n. the male of a duck, a kind of cannon
Dram, n. a glafs of any fpirit, the eighth of an
ounce, a coin
Dram, v. i. to drink drams or fpiritous liquors
Dráma, n. the action of a play, a play, a poem
Dramat'ic, a. reprefented by action, theatrical
Dramat'ically, ad. by reprefentation, theatrically
Dram'atift, n. an author or writer of plays
Drank, pret. and pa. of to drink
Drape, v. i. to make cloth, ob.
Dráper, n. a perfon who fells or deals in cloth
Drápery, n. clothwork, the drefs of a picture or
Drápet, n. a cloth, table cloth, coverlet, ob. (ftatue
Dras'tic, a. powerful, efficacious, ftrong
Drave, pret. of to drive, ob.
Draught, n. the act of drinking, fee draft
Draught'houfe, n. a place for filth
Draw, v. drew, pret. drawn, pa. to pull, take out,
unfheath, allure, attract, fuck, defcribe
Draw'back, n. money paid back on exportation
Draw'bridge, n. a bridge that can be drawn up
Draw'er, n. one who draws a bill of exchange or
note, a fliding box in a cheft
Drawee, n. one on whom a bill is drawn
Draw'ers, n. pl. a kind of light or thin breeches
Draw'ing, n. a delineation, reprefentation, fketch
Draw'ingroom, n. a room for receiving company
Drawl, v. i. to fpeak in a flow and drivelling way
Drawn, pa. pulled, unfheathed, defcribed
Draw'-well, n. a deep well to draw water from

Dray, n. a kind of cart ufed by brewers, a neſt
Dráyhorſe, n. a horſe ufed to draw in a dray
Dráyman, n. a man that attends a dray
Draz'el, n. a mean low wretch, dirty woman, drab
Dread, n. great fear, terror, awe, a caufe of awe
Dread, v. to be in great fear, fear, ſtand in awe
Dread, a. great, mighty, high, awful, terrible
Dread'er, n. one who lives in continual fear
Dread'ful, a. terrible, frightful, alarming, horrid
Dread'fully, ad. terribly, frightfully, piteoufly
Dread'fulneſs, n. terriblenefs, frightfulnefs, horror
Dread'lefs, a. fearlefs, undaunted, very bold, daring
Dread'leſſneſs, n. fearleſſneſs, courage, boldnefs
Dream, n. thought in ſleep, an idle fancy, a whim
Dream, v. i. dreamed, dreampt, pret. dreamed,
    dreampt, pa. to think in ſleep, imagin, fancy,
    have idle notions, to be ſluggiſh
Dréamer, n. one who dreams, a mope, a ſluggard
Dréamleſs, a. having no dreams, quite awake
Drear or Dréary, a. mournful, diſmal, gloomy, fad
Dréarinefs, ʻn. gloominefs, heavinefs, dulnefs
Dredge, n. an oyſter-net, oats and barley mixed
Dredge, v. t. to fprinkle flour on roaſting meat
Dredg'ingbox, n. a box ufed for dredging meat
Dreen, n. a drain, a channel for carrying off water
Dreen, v. to draw off water, to exhauſt entirely
Dreg'ginefs, n. fulnefs of dregs, foulnefs, muddi-
Dreg'gy, a. containing dregs, foul, muddy   (nefs
Dregs, n. fediments of liquor, lees, refufe, drofs
Drench, v. t. to foak, ſteep, fill with drink, waſh
Drench, n. a horſe's phyſical draught, ſwill, waſh
Drench'ed, pa. foaked, filled, waſhed, cleanſed
Dreſs, n. clothes, ornament, finery, ſkill in dreſſing
Dreſs, v. t. to clothe, deck, adorn, prepare, cook,
    cover a wound, trim, rub, curry, beat
Dreſs'er, n. a perfon who dreſſes, a kitchen-table
Dreſs'ing, n. the act of clothing, falve, a trimming,
    a covering of manure
Dreſs'ingroom, n. a place made ufe of to dreſs in
Dreſs'y, a. dreſſing much, ſhowy in drefs
Drib'ble, v. i. to drop or fall ſlowly, ſlaver, drivel
Drib'let, n. a ſmall part of a large fum, a portion
Drier, n. what fucks up moiſture; a. more dry
Drift, n. a defign, ſcope, float, heap, ſtorm, ſhaft
Drift, v. to throw on heaps, float, drive along
Drill, v. t. to bore, cut, delay, drag ſlowly, range
Drill, n. a ſharp inſtrument, ſmall furrow, baboon
Drink, n. liquor to be drank, any liquor, beer, &c.
Drink, v. drank, pret. drank, pa. to ſwallow, li-
quors, to fuck up or in, to practice drinking to
    excefs
Drink'able, a. fuch as may be drank, tolerable
Drink'er, n. one who drinks, a drunkard, a fot
Drink'ing, n. the act of ſwallowing liquors
Drip, v. i. to drop down; n. what falls in drops
Drip'ping, n. the fat that drops from roaſt meat
Drip'pingpan, n. a pan for the fat of roaſt meat
Drip'ple, a. weak, rare, unuſual, uncommon
Drive, v. drove, pret. driven, pa. to force, knock,

ruſh, go, urge, aim
Driv'el, v. i. to ſlaver, drop, dote, be foolifh
Driv'el, n. ſlaver, fpittle, a fool, idiot, driveller
Driv'eller, n. a fool, idiot, oaf, ſimpleton, dotard
Driv'en, pa. of to drive   (on
Dri'ver, n. one who drives, one who forces or urges
Driz'zle, v. i. to come or fall in ſmall drops
Driz'zly, a. raining in ſmall drops, wettiſh, miſty
Drock, n. an upright piece of wood in a plow
Droll, v. i. to work lazily, n. a drone, ob.
Droll, n. a jeſter, odd or arch fellow, buffoon, farce
Droll, v. i. to play the buffoon, jeſt, be merry, ob.
Droll, a. comical, farcical, humorous, odd, merry
Droll'ery, n. buffoonery, archnefs, mirth
Drom'edary, n. a very ſwift fort of camel
Dromo, n. a ſwift-failing veſſel, a very ſwift fiſh
Drone, n. the male bee, ſluggard, idler, hum in mu-
Drone, v. i. to live in idleneſs, to dream on   (ſic
Dróneſly, n. an infect with a ſhort thick body
Dróniſh, a. idle, ſluggiſh, ſlow, dull, heavy, ſtupid
Droop, v. i. to pine away, languiſh, faint, ſiak
Droop'ing, pa. languiſhing, fainting, ſinking
Drop, n. a ſmall quantity of a liquid, an earring
Drop, v. to fall in drops, fall, let fall, utter ſlight-
ly, quit, come, vaniſh, ſink into ſilence, die
Drop'let, n. a little drop, a ſmall earring, ob.   (ing
Drop'ping, n. that which falls down in drops, a fall-
Drop'ſical, Drop'ſied, a. troubled with a dropfy,
Drop'ſicalnefs, n. a tendency to a dropfy   (watery
Drop'ſy, n. a bad watery diſeaſe, a watery humor
Drop'ſtone, n. ſpar in the form of drops
Drop'wort, n. a plant of feveral ſpecies
Drofs, n. the ſcum of metals, ruſt, refufe, dregs
Drofs'ineſs, n. a droſſy ſtate or quality, foulnefs
Drofs'y, a. full of drofs, foul, worthlefs, mean
Drove, n. a herd of cattle, crowd of people, num-
Dróver, n. one who drives cattle to market   (ber
Drought, Drouth, n. dry weather, drynefs, thirſt
Drought'y, Drouth'y, a. wanting rain, thirſty, dry
Drown, v. t. to choke with water, overflow, loſe
Drowſe, v. to make heavy with ſleep, to ſlumber
Drowſ'ily, ad. ſleepily, heavily, dully, lazily
Drows'ineſs, n. ſleepinefs, heavinefs with ſleep
Drows'y, a. ſleepy, heavy, dull, ſluggiſh, ſtupid
Drub, v. a thump, knock, blow, bang, ſtroke, cuff
Drub, v. t. to thraſh, to bang or beat with a ſtick
Drub'bing, n. a beating, chaſtifement, correction
Drudge, v. i. to labor in mean offices, labor, toil
Drudge, Drudg'er, n. a mean laborious ſervant, a
Drudg'ery, n. hard and mean labor, ſlavery (ſlave
Drudg'ingly, ad. laboriouſly, toilfomely, cloſely
Drug, n. a medical ſimple, a thing of little worth
Drug, v. t. to feafon with drugs, to make offenſive
Drug'ged, pa. having drugs, made offenſive
Dsug'get, n. a ſlight kind of woollen ſtuff
Drug'giſt, Drug'ſter, n. a perfon who fells drugs
Drúid, n. an ancient Britiſh prieſt, poet, &c.
Drúideſs, n. a female druid
Druid'ical, a. of or relating to the Druids

Drúidifm, *n.* the religion of the Druids

Drum, *n.* a military inftrument, a part of the ear

Drum, *v. i.* to beat a drum, beat, knock, lay on

Drum'ble, *v. i.* to be idle or fluggifh, loiter, *ob.*

Drum-májor, *n.* the chief or firft drummer

Drum'maker, *n.* one who makes or fells drums

Drum'mer, *n.* one who drums, one who lays on

Drum'ftick, *n.* a ftick to beat a drum with

Drunk, Drunk'en, *a.* having too much liquor

Drunk'ard, *n.* one given to too much drink, a fot

Drunk'enly, *ad.* in a drunken manner or ftate, fot-

Drunk'ennefs, *n.* a drunken ftate or habit   (tifhly

Drupe, *n.* a pericarp of pulp, inclofing a ftone as a

Drupáceous, *a.* containing drupes   (peach

Drufy, *a.* abounding with very minute cryftals

Dry, *a.* having no moifture, thirfty, flat, droll

Dry'ad, *n.* à wood nymph

Dry, *v. t.* to free from moifture, drain, wipe

Dry'er, *n.* what dries or fucks up moifture

Dry'eyed, *a.* void of tears, hard, unfeeling

Dry'ly, *ad.* coldly, feverely, barrenly, flily

Dry'nefs, *n.* a want of moifture, fap or affeftion

Dry'nurfe, *n.* one who brings up without the breaft

Dry'nurfe, *v. t.* to bring up without the breaft

Dry'fhod, *a.* having the feet dry; *ad.* with the feet

Dúal, *a.* expreffing the number 2, fecond   (dry

Dub, *v. t.* to confer a title of dignity; *n.* a blow

Dub'bed, *pa.* made, formed, invefted with honor

Dubios'ity, Dúbioufnefs, *n.* doubtfulnefs, doubt

Dúbious, Dúbitable, *a.* doubtful, uncertain

Dúbioufly, *ad.* uncertainly, doubtfully, in doubt

Dubitátion, *n.* the aft of doubting, a doubt, miftruft

Dúcal, *a.* pertaining or relating to a duke

Ducápe, *n.* a kind of filk worn by women

Duc'at, *n.* a foreign coin of different values

Duch'efs, *n.* the wife of a Duke, or female owner of a Duchy

Duch'y, *n.* the territory and jurifdiftion of a Duke

Ducatoon', *n.* an Italian coin value about 195 cents

Duck, *n.* a fowl, word of fondnefs, caft, ftoop, a fpecies of fine canvas

Duck, *v.* to dive or put under water, dip, ftoop

Duck'er, *n.* a perfon who ducks, a diver, a loon

Duck'ing, *n.* the aft of putting under water

Duck'ingftool, *n.* a ftool to duck fcolds in

Duck'legged, *a.* having fhort thick legs, ftumpy

Duck'ling, *n.* a young or little duck, a darling

Duft, *n.* a paffage, channel, guidance, direftion

Duft'ile, *a.* traftable, pliable, eafy to be drawn

Duft'ilenefs, Dufti/ity, *n.* flexibility, compliance

Dud'geon, *n.* a fmall dagger, ill-will, malice

Due, *a.* owing, proper, fit, exaft; *v. t.* to pay off

Due, *n.* a debt, right, title, claim, tribute, cuftom

Dúel *n.* a fight between two perfons, a conteft

Dúel *v.* to fight a fingle combat, attack fingly,

Dúeller, Dúelhft, *n.* one who fights a duel   (fight

Duel'lo, *n.* a duel the rules or terms of duelling

Dúenefs, *n.* a due or fit quality, propriety, fitnefs

Duen'na, *n.* an old governance to a lady, an old ma-

Duet', Duet'to, *n.* a fong or air in two parts (tron

Dug *pret.* of *to dig*; *n.* the pap or teat of a beaft

Duke *n.* a title, the next dignity below a prince

Dúkedom, *n.* the poffeffions or title of a duke

Dul'brained, *a.* dull, ftupid, heavy, thick, foolifh

Dul'cet, *a.* fweet, harmonious, lufcious, rich

Dulcificátion, Dulcorátion, *n.* the aft of fweetning

Dul'cify, Dul'corate, *v. t.* to fweeten, purify

Dul'cimer, *n.* an old kind of mufical inftrument

Dul'head, Dull'ard, *n.* a blockhead, a ftupid perfon

Dúlia, *n.* a lower kind of adoration or worfhip, *ob.*

Dull, *a.* ftupid, flow, blunt, dejefted, gloomy, fad

Dull, *v. t.* to ftupify, blunt, clog, damp, fadden

Dull'y, *ad.* ftupidly, flowly, fluggifhly, heavily

Dull'nefs or Dul'nefs, *n.* ftupidity, fluggifhnefs, hea-

    vinefs, dimnefs, bluntnefs

Duloc'racy, *n.* a predominance of, or rule by, flaves

Dulfe or Dilfe *n.* a palmated feaweed

Dúly, *ad.* properly, fitly, exaftly, regularly, juftly

Dúmal, Dúmous, *a.* full of bufhes, briery, rough

Dumb, *a.* unable to fpeak, fpeechlefs, filent, mute

Dumb'found, *v. t.* to ftrike dumb, *ob.* and *vulgar*

Dumb'ly, *ad.* without ufing words, filently   (fence

Dumb'nefs, *n.* a dumb ftate, inability to fpeak, fi-

Dump'ifh, *a.* fomewhat four or fad, melancholy

Dump'ling, *n.* a fort of boiled pudding; *a.* thick

Dumps, *n. pl.* fullennefs, heavinefs, melancholy

Dun, *n.* between brown and black, dark, gloomy

Dun, *n.* a troublefome clamorous creditor, a color

Dun, *v. t.* to prefs hard or afk often for a debt

Dunce, *n.* a dullard, blockhead, thickfcull (dung

Dung, *n.* foil, excrement; *v. t.* to manure with

Dun'geon, *n.* a very dark prifon made under ground

Dung'fork, *n.* a fork ufed to throw out dung

Dung'hil, *n.* a heap of dung, a mean or low man

Dung'hill, *a.* mean, low, vile, worthlefs, defpicable

Dung'y, *a.* full of dung, dirty, mean, low, vile

Dun'nage, *n.* faggots or boughs laid on fhips to keep   goods from the bottom

Dun'ner, *n.* one who is employed to get in debts

Dun'ning, *pa.* preffing often or much for a debt

Duodecahédron, *n.* a body with twelve fides

Duodecahédral, *a.* having twelve fides

Duode''cemfid, *a.* divided into twelve parts

Duode'cimo, *a.* having twelve leaves to a fheet

Dupe, *v. t.* to cheat, trick, deceive, impofe on

Dupe, *n.* a credulous perfon, one eafily tricked

Dúplicate, *v. t.* to fold together, fold up, double

Dúplicate, *n.* a copy, an exaft copy of any thing

Dúplicate, *a.* containing fquares, double

Duplicátion, *n.* the aft of doubling, a fold, a turn

Dúplicature, *n.* a fold, any thing that is doubled

Dupli''city, *n.* doubledealing, deceit, treachery

Dúrable, *a.* lafting, continuing long, ftrong, firm

Dúrablenefs, Durabil'ity, *n.* power of lafting

Dúrably *ad.* in a lafting or ftrong manner

Dúrance, *n.* imprifonment, cuftody, continuance

Durant', *n.* a glazed woollen ftuff

Durátion, *n.* continuance, time, length of time

Dure, *v. i.* to laft, continue, remain, endure, *ob.*
Dúreleſs, *a.* not continuing, fading, frail, *ob.*
Dureſs', *n.* conftraint by confinement or menaces
Dúring, *pa.* for, in, for the time of continuance
Dúrity, *n.* hardneſs, firmneſs, cruelty
Durft, *pret.* of *to dare*
Duſk, *a.* tending to darkneſs, rather dark, dark
Duſk, *n.* a tendency to darkneſs or blackneſs
Duſk'ily, Duſk'iſhly, *ad.* darkly, cloudily, dimly
Duſk'iſh, Duſk'y, *a.* inclining to darkneſs, heavy
Duſk'ineſs, *n.* flight obfcurity
Duft, *n.* earth dried to powder, the grave
Duft *v.* to throw duft upon, free from duft, beat
Duft'ineſs, *n.* a dufty ftate or condition
Duft'man, *n.* one who takes or carries away duft
Duft'y, *a.* clouded or covered with duft, filthy
Dutch'eſs, *n.* falfe orthography, fee duchefs
Dutch, *a.* pertaining to the inhabitants of Holland
Dutch, *n.* the language of Holland or the people
Dúteous, Dútiful, *a.* obedient, fubmiffive, kind
Dútiable, *a.* fubject to duties or impoft
Dútifully, *ad.* obediently, refpectfully, kindly
Dútifulneſs, *n.* obedience, fubmiffion, refpect, duty
Dúty, *n.* obedience, obligation, a tax, cuftom
Du'ty, *v. t.* to impofe a duty or cuftoms
Dúumvir, *n.* one of two officers in Rome
Duum'viral, *a.* pertaining to a duumvirate
Duum'virate, *n.* a government held by two perfons
Dwale, *n.* a name for night ſhade
Dwarf, *n.* a man, &c. below the ufual fize
Dwarf, *v. t.* to hinder or keep from growing
Dwarf, *a.* that is below natural fize, fmall, low
Dwarf'ed, *pa.* ftopped in the growth, ftunted
Dwarf'iſh, *a.* below the common fize, very ſhort
Dwell, *v. i.* dwelled, dwelt, *pret.* dwelt, *pa.* to
live, inhabit, refide, continue, ftay
Dwell'er, *n.* a perfon that dwells, an inhabitant
Dwell'ing, *n.* a habitation, abode, ftate of life
Dwell'ing-place, *n.* a place of refidence
Dwin'dle, *v. i.* to ſhrink, fall away, grow feeble
Dye, *v. t.* to tinge, color, give a different color
Dye, *n.* coloring matter, tinge, color
Dy'eing, *a.* coloring; *n.* the art of coloring
Dy'ing, *pa.* expiring, finking, withering
Dynam'ical, *a.* pertaining to power
Dynaft'ic, *n.* a fovereign, governor, ruler, prince
Dy'nafty, *n.* fovereignty, government
Dys'cracy, *n.* a diftemper in the blood or juices
Dys'entery, *n.* a loofeneſs, a flux, the bloody flux
Dysenter'ic, *a.* pertaining to or having dyfentery
Dys'orexy, *n.* an impaired or depraved appetite
Dyfpep'fy, *n.* indigeftion, depraved ftate of the
Dyfpep'tic, *a.* troubled with indigeftion (ftomach
Dyſpnéa, *n.* difficult refpiration
Dys'ury, *n.* a difficulty or heat in making urine

E

EACH, *a.* or *pron.* every one of a number feparately confidered
E'ager, *a.* zealous, keen, hot, quick, four

E'agerly, *ad.* zealoufly, keenly, hotly, ſharply
E'agerneſs, *n.* earneftneſs, keenneſs, violence, hot-
E'agle, *n.* a large and furious bird of prey (neſs
E'agle-eyed, *a.* quickfighted, ſharpfighted
E'aglefpeed, *n.* a fwiftneſs like that of an eagle
E'aglet, *n.* a young eagle, a fmall or little eagle
E'ager, *n.* one tide fwelling above another
Eam or Eme, *n.* an uncle, a friend (*local*)
Ear *n.* the organ of hearing, handle, fpike of corn
Ear, *v.* to ſhoot out into ears, plow, till
E'ared, *pa.* having ears, plowed, ear-ſhaped
E'aring, *n.* a ſhooting into ears, tillage
Earl, *n.* a noble title next to that of a marquis
Earl'dom, *n.* the feigniory or dignity of an earl
E'arleſs, *a.* having no ears, void of ears
Ear'ly, *ad.* foon, betimes; *a.* coming foon (ripeneſs
Ear'lineſs, *n.* the ftate of being early or foon, early
Earlmarſh'al, *n.* a manager of military folemnities
Earn, *v. t.* to gain or deferve by fervices
Earn'ed, *pa.* gained or merited by fervices
Earn'ings, *n.* the reward of or due for, fervices
Earn'eft, *a.* eager, hot, diligent, important, feriouſ
Earn'eft, *n.* money advanced, a pledge, ferioufneſs
Earn'eftly, *ad.* eagerly, warmly, affectionately
Earn'eftneſs, *n.* eagerneſs, zeal, warmth, great care
E'arring, *n.* a ring with jewels to put in the ear
E'arſhot, *n.* the hearing of the ear, fpace heard in
Earth, *n.* the globe we live on, land, mold
Earth, *v.* to cover with mold, to get under ground
Earth'born, *a.* born of the earth, meanly born
Earth'en, *a.* made of earth, made of clay, brittle
Earth'lineſs, *a.* an earthly quality, groffneſs
Earth'ling, *n.* a poor frail creature, mortal, man
Earth'ly, *a.* of this world, vile, mean, fordid, low
Earth'pike, *n.* a fpecies of lizard in the W. Indies
Earth'quake, *n.* a tremor or ſhaking of the earth
Earth'ſhaking *a.* that caufeth an earthquake
Earth'worm, *n.* a worm, a poor or mean wretch
Earth'y, *a.* confifting of or like earth, groſs, foul
E'arwax, *n.* wax that gathers in the ear
E'arwig, *n.* a harmleſs infect, a whifperer
E'arwitneſs, *n.* one who attefts a thing as heard
Eaſe, *n.* freedom from labor, &c. quiet, comfort
Eaſe, *v. t.* to relieve, affuage, leffen, flacken, free
E'aſel, *n.* a painter's frame to put his canvas on
E'aſement, *n.* eafe, relief, refreſhment, a fervice
E'aſily, *ad.* gently, readily, without trouble
E'aſineſs, *n.* eafe, reft, quiet, readineſs, freedom
Eaft, *n.* the quarter where the fun rifes (paffover
E'after, *n.* the feaft of Chrift's refurrection or the
E'afterly, *a.* and *ad.* towards or from the eaft
E'aftern, *a.* of or belonging to the eaft
E'aftward, *ad.* to or towards the eaft
E'aſy, *a.* placed at eafe, quiet, credulous, not hard
Eat, *v.* ate, eat, *pret.* eaten, *pa.* to take food,
fwallow, devour, feed upon, corrode
E'atable, *a.* that may be eaten, fit to eat, not bad
E'aten, *pa.* fwallowed, devoured, confumed
E'ater, *n.* one who or what eats, a corrofive

Eath, a. eafy, very practicable ; ad. eafily, ob.

E'atinghoufe, n. a public houfe or place to eat at

Eaves, n. pl. the edges of the roof of a building

E'avefdrop, v. i. to liften, hearken, lurk, catch

E'avefdropper, n. one who liftens under windows

Ebb, v. i. to flow back, vary, wafte, decline,decay

Ebb, n. a flowing back, return, turn, wafte, decay

Ebbtíde, n. the reflux or falling of tide water

Eb'on, or Eb'ony, n. a hard black wood ; a. black

Ebrac'tate, a. without bracties or floral leaves

Ebríety, Ebrios'ity, n. habitual drunkennefs

Ebul'liate, v. i. to boil or bubble out. to work

Ebulli'tion, n. the act of boiling or bubbling up

Ecaúdate, a. without a tail or fpur

Eccen'tric, a. deviating from the center, irregular

Eccentri''city, n. a deviation from the center

Ecclefiaft'ic, n. a clergyman, minifter,prieft,divine

Ecclefiaft'ical, a. of or relating to the church

Ech'inate, [ch as k] a. fet with prickles, briftled

Ech'inite, n. petrified fhells with prickles

Ech'o, [ch as k] n. a found returned

Ech'o, v. to give back or reflect found

Ecláircife, v. t. to clear up, to explain

Ecláirciffement, n. a full or clear explanation

Eclát, n. fplendor, lufter, glory, honor, renown

Eclec'tic, a. felecting, picking, choofing at will

Eclec'tics, n. philofophers who felected their fyftem from various others

Eclec'tically, ad. by way of felection

Eclipfe, n. an obfcuration of a luminary, darknefs

Eclipfe, v. t. to darken, cloud, put out, difgrace

Eclips'ed, pa. darkened, clouded, difgraced, loft

Eclip'tic, n. a line on the fphere of the world, which the fun defcribes in its annual revolution.

Ec'logue, n. a paftoral poem, a kind of rural poem

Econ'omy, n. management, frugality in expendi-

Econ'omift, n. one who is frugal in expenfes (tures

Econ'omize, v. to be frugal in expenfes

Econom'ical, a. faving, frugal, prudent

Econom'ically, ad. frugally (delighted

Ecs'tafied, a. ravifhed, enraptured, tranfported,

Ecs'tafy or Ecs'tacy, n. rapture, tranfport, diftrac-tion, enthufiafm, excefs

Ecftat'ic, a. ravifhing, enrapturing, tranfporting,

Ec'type, n. a copy, draught, reprefentation (noble

Ecumen'ical, a. general, univerfal

Eda''city, n. voracity, ravenoufnefs, greedinefs

Ed'der, n. wood on the tops of fences; v. t. to bind

Ed'dy, n. a circular motion of wind or water

Ed'dy, a. whirling, moving round or circularly

Ed'elite, n. a filiceous ftone of a light gray color

Edem'atous, a. fwelling, full of humors, dropfical

Edge, n. the fharp part of an inftrument, a brink

Edge, v. to fharpen, provoke, border, move

Edg'ed, pa. fharpened, fet, provoked, bordered

Edge'lefs, a. void of edge, blunt, unable to cut

Edge'tool, n. a fharp or cutting inftrument

Edge'wife, ad. by or in full direction of the edge

Edg'ing, n. a kind of narrow lace, a border

Ed'ible, a. eatable, fit to be eaten, tolerable

E'dict, n. an ordinance, decree, proclamation, law

Edification, n. a building up in faith, inftruction

Ed'ifice, n. a building, ftructure, fabric, houfe

Ed'ifier, n. one who edifies, one who improves

Ed'ify, v. t. to build up, inftruct, improve, profit

Ed'ifying, pa. building up, inftructing, profiting

Edi''tion, n. the impreffion or print of a book

E'dile, n. a Roman magiftrate, furveyor, juftice

E'dilefhip, n. the office of an Edile

Ed'it, v. t. to publifh, to fuperintend a publication

Ed'itor, n. one who prepares a book for the prefs

Editórial, a. pertaining to or written by an editor

Ed'ucate, v. t. to bring up, breed, inftruct

Education, n. the inftruction of children, fkiil

Ed'ucator, n. one who educates or brings up

Edúce, v. t. to bring or draw out, extract, fhow

Educ'tion, n. the act of drawing out or fhowing

Educt', v. t. to lead or draw forth

Educt', n. that which is drawn forth or extracted

Educt'or, n. he or that which draws forth

Edul'corate, v. t. to render more fweet, mild or pure

Edulcorátion, n. the act of making more mild or

Eel, n. a kind of creeping flimy fifh, a rich fifh (pure

Ee'lpout, n. the burbot, a thick kind of eel

Ef'fable, a. expreffible, utterable, fit to be told

Efface, v. t. to deftroy, deface, blot or ftrike out

Effect', n. a thing produced, end, iffue, confequence

Effect' v. t. to bring to pafs, produce, perform

Effect'ible, a. that may be effected, practicable

Effec'tion, n. a deduced conftruction, a problem

Effect'ive, a. able to produce, ufeful, ferviceable

Effect'ive, n. an able man, a foldier fit for duty

Effect'ively, ad. with effect, powerfully, really

Effect'ivenefs, n. an effective quality, power

Effect'lefs, a. having no effect, ufelefs, very weak

Effect'or, n. one who effects or produces, a maker

Effects, n. pl. goods, moveables, furniture, eftate

Effect'ual, a. efficacious, powerful, real, true

Effect'ually, ad. powerfully, to good purpofe, fully

Effect'uate, v. t. to bring to pafs, to fulfil

Effem'inacy, n. exceffive delicacy, loofe pleafure

Effem'inate, a. womanifh, tender, voluptuous

Effem'inate, v. t. to make womanifh, to foften

Effem'inately, ad. in an effeminate manner

Effervefce', v. i. to be agitated as bodies which diffolve each other and throw out air with a hiffing

Effervef'cence, n. a boiling up, heat of paffion

Effervef'cent, a. boiling up, fermenting

Effervef'cible, a. capable of effervefcing

Efféte, a. barren, worn out with age, very weak

Efficácious, a. productive of effect, powerful

Efficácioufly, ad. effectually, powerfully, ftrongly

Effi'cacy, n. ability or power to effect, ftrength

Effi''ciency, n. a producing of effects, agency, act

Effi''cient, a. caufing or producing effects, acting

Ef'figy, n. an image, reprefentation, likenefs

Efflorefce, v. i. to form fine white powder or

threads on the furface
Efflores'cence, *y.* the white matter like powder on falts, &c. the red fpots in fever, the flowering of plants
Efflores'cent, *a.* fhooting out in form of flowers
Efflores'cible, *a.* capable of efflorefcence
Ef'fluence, *n.* what iffues from another principle
Ef'fluent, *a.* flowing from or out, running out
Efflúvium, *n.* an emanation, vapor, fmell
Ef'flux, *n.* the act of flowing out, an effufion
Efflux', *v. i.* to flow out or from, to run out
Efflux'ed, *pa.* run out or from, difcharged
Effluxion, *n.* a flowing out or from, an effluvium
Efförce, *v. t.* to force, break in or through, *ob.*
Efform', *v. t.* to form, fafhion, fhape, make, *ob.*
Efformátion, *n.* the act of forming or fhaping, *ob.*
Ef'fort, *n.* a ftruggle, ftrong endeavor, attempt
Effos'fion, *n.* the act of digging out of the earth
Effráiable, *a.* dreadful, frightful, terrible, *ob.*
Effront'ery, *n.* affurance, impudence, faucinefs
Efful'gence, *n.* lufter, brightnefs, great light
Efful'gent, *a.* fhining out, bright, luminous, clear
Efful'ging, *a.* fending forth light
Effúfe, [effuze] *v. t.* to pour out, fpill, fhed
Effúfe, *a.* very great, lavifh, wafteful, *ob.*
Effúfe, Effúfion, *n.* a pouring out, wafte, liberality
Effúfive, *a.* pouring out, difperfing largely, kind
Eft, *n.* a poifonous animal; *ad.* foon, quickly
Eftfoons', *ad.* foon afterwards, frequently, often
Egeft, *v. t.* to difcharge food, throw out, *ob.*
Egéan, *a.* denominating the fea between Greece and Afia
Eges'tion, *n.* the difcharging digefted food, *ob.*
Egg, *n.* the production or feed of fowls and infects
Egg, *v. t.* to incite, fpur on, [*ob. edge* is ufed for it]
Egland'ulous, *a.* deftitute of glands
Eg'antine, *n.* a fpecies of the rofe, a fweet brier
E'gotifm, *n.* felf-commendation, felf-fufficiency
E'gotift, *n.* one who commends or talks of himfelf
E'gotize, *v. i.* to talk of or praife one's felf
Egrégious, *a.* eminent, remarkable, notorious
Egrégioufly, *ad.* eminently, notably, fhamefully
E'grefs, Egres'fion, *n.* the act of going out, departure
E'gret, *n.* a flower for the head, a tuft or down on feeds, the lefs or white heron
E'griot, *n.* a kind of four cherry
Egyp'tian, *n.* a native of Egypt
Egyp'tian, *a.* pertaining to Egypt
Ejac'ulate, *v. t.* to throw or fhoot out, dart, utter
Ejaculátion, *n.* a fhooting out, prayer, fpeech
Ejac'ulatory, *a.* fudden, hafty, fervent, darted out
Eject', *v. t.* to caft or throw out, turn out, reject
Eject'ed, *pa.* caft, fent or turned out, rejected
Ejec'tion, *n.* the act of cafting out, expulfion
Eject'ment, *n.* a writ to caft out of poffeffion, ejec-
Eigh, *ex.* expreffing fudden pleafure (tion
Eight, [ate] *a.* the number, twice four
Eight'een, *a.* ten and eight united together
Eight'fold, *a.* taken or repeated eight times

Eight'ly, *ad.* in the eighth place, order or clafs
Eight'fcore, *a.* twenty taken or added eight times
Eight'y, *a.* ten taken eight times, fourfcore
E'ither, *pron.* or *a.* one or the other of two, both
Eju'lation, *n.* a lamentation, moan, great outcry
Eke or Eek, *v. t.* to increafe, add, fill up, fpin out
Eke, *ad.* alfo, likewife, befide, moreover, further
E'king, *pa.* adding; *n.* the act of fupplying
Elab'orate, *v. t.* to produce with labor, to improve
Elab'orate, *a.* finifhed with exactnefs, ftudied
Elab'orately, *ad.* very laborioufly, with great labor
E'aborátion, *n.* an improvement by great pains
E'land, *n.* a fpecies of antelope in Africa
Elance', *v. t.* to throw or dart out, let fly, *ob.*
E'lapidation, *n.* the act of clearing from ftones
E'lapfe', *v. i.* to pafs away, run out, lofe a right
Elaft'ic, *a* fpringing back, recovering
Elas'tically, *ad.* with a fpring (power
Elafti''city, Elaft'icnefs, *n.* a fpring in bodies, a
E'láte, *a.* flufhed with fuccefs, lofty, haughty, high
E'áte, *v. t.* to puffup, fwell, exalt, make proud
Elátion, *n.* haughtinefs, arrogance, pride
El'bow, *n.* the bend of the arm, a corner, an angle
El'bow, *v.* to pufh with the elbow, jut out, bend
El'bowchair, *n.* a large chair that has arms to it
El'bowroom, *n.* room to place or move the elbows
Eld, *n.* old people, old times, old age, oldnefs, *ob.*
Eld'er, *a. (compar.* of *old)* having more years, firft
Eld'er, *n.* the name of a tree, a foft kind of wood
Eld'erly, *a.* growing fomewhat in years, rather old
Eld'ers, *n. pl.* ancient rulers, officers, anceftors
Eld'erfhip, *n.* feniority, prefbytery, dignity, rule
Eld'eft, *a. (fuperl.* of *old)* the oldeft or firft-born
E'ecampáne, *n.* a kind of herb, ftarwort
Elect', *v. t.* to choofe, felect for favor, prefer
Elect, Elect'ed, *pa.* chofen, felected, preferred
Elec'tion, *n.* the act or power of choofing, choice
Electioneer', *v. i.* to make intereft for a candidate
Electioneering, *pa.* making efforts or ufing arts to carry an election (tions
Electioneering. *n.* the ufe of arts or efforts in elec-
Elect'ive, *a.* relating to or excercifing choice
Elect'ively, *ad.* by choice, with or in preference
Elect'or, *n.* one who elects, a title of fome princes
Elect'oral, *a.* belonging or relating to an elector
Elect'orate, *n.* the territory or ftate of an elector
Elec'tor, *n.* amber, a kind of mixed metal, *ob.*
Elec'trat, *n.* a combination of electricity with a metallic fubftance
Elec'tric, *n.* any fubftance in which electricity can be excited by rubbing, and which will not tranfmit the fluid
Electri'cal, *a.* of or relating to electricity
Electri'cian, *n.* one verfed in electricity
Elec'trically, *ad.* in the manner of electricity
Electri''city, *n.* a particular kind of attraction and repulfion, or the caufe of it
Elec'trify, *v.* to communicate to or affect by the electrical fluid, to become electric

Elec'trize, v. t. to affect by electricity

Elec'trifiable, a. that may receive electricity or become electric

Elec'tron, n. a name given to the fun, the fuppo- fed center and fource of electricity

Electrom'eter, n. an inftrument to meafure the quantity of electricity

Elect'uary, n. a form of medicine, a compound

Eleemos'ynary, a. living on charity, charitable

El'egance, n. beauty without grandeur, neatnefs

El'egant, a. beautiful, pleafing, fine, nice, neat

El'egantly, ad. in a pleafing manner, finely, well

Elégiac, a. ufed in eligies, mournful, difmal, fad

El'egy, n. a funeral poem, a plaintive fong

El'ement, n. a fimple body, or body which human art cannot divide, as caloric, oxygene, pure metal, fulphur, clay, &c. In popular language, fire, air, earth and water are called elements, a conftituent or firft principle

El'ement, v. t. to compound of elements, ob.

Element'al, a. produced by elements, fimple, pure

Element'arinefs, n. the real fimplicity of nature

Element'ary, a. not compounded, fimple, prime

Elench', n. an argument, fophifm, confutation, ob.

El'ephant, n. the largeft of all beafts, ivory

Elephant'ine, a. pertaining to an elephant, huge

Eleufin'ian, a. relating to a great feftival and the myfteries of Ceres celebrated at Eleufis in Greece

El'evate, v. t. to exalt, raife, lift up, elate

El'evate, El'evated, pa. exalted, raifed up or aloft

Elevation, n. a raifing up, exaltation.highth, angle

Elevátor, n. a mufcle which draws upwards

Elev'en, a. ten and one, ten and one added together

Elf n. a fairy, a devil; [v. t. to entangle hair, ob.]

Elf'lock, n. hair fuppofed to be twifted by elves, ob.

Eli''cit, v. t. to ftrike out, fetch out, draw out

Eli''cit, pa. brought into act, drawn out

Elicitátion, n. the will deduced or lured into act

Elíde, v. t. to break or dafh in pieces, to deftroy

Elíded, pa. dafhed or cut in pieces, deftroyed

El'igibie, a. fit to be chofen, preferable, defirable

El'igiblenefs, Eligibil'ity, n. fitnefs to be chofen

El'igibly, ad. pleafingly, advantageoufly

Eliguri''tion, n. the act of devouring, gluttony, ob.

Elim'inate, v. t. to expel or fet at liberty

Elimination, n. a forcing out or expelling

Elin''guid, a. tonguetied, dumb, fpeechlefs. ob.

Eliquátion, n. the act of feparating by melting

Eli''fion, n. a cutting off, feparation, dafh

Elifor, n. a fheriff's fubftitute to return a jury when he and the coroner are interefted

Elixátion, n. the act of boiling out or extracting

Elix'ir, n. the quinteffence, a medicine, a cordial

Elk, n. a very large wild beaft of the ftag-kind

Ell, n. a meafure of one yard and a quarter, three

Ellips'is, n. an oval figure, figure, defect (quarters

Ellip'tical, a. oval, roundifh, defective, wanting

Elm, n. a tree for fhade or timber

Elocútion, n. utterance, delivery, fluency, fpeech

Eloin', v. t. to convey away, remove

Eloin'ment, n. removal to a diftance

Elon'gate, v. to draw out, protract, depart, go off

Elongátion, a. the act of lengthening, departure

Elópe, v. i. to run off or away, to efcape privately

Elópement, n. a departure from juft reftraint, a

E'lops, n. a kind of fifh, the fea ferpent (flight

El'oquence, n. elegant fpeaking or writing, fluen- cy of fpeech, power of fpeaking with pathos, oratory

El'oquent, a. having the power of oratory, fluent

El'oquently, ad. in an eloquent manner, fluently

Elfe, pron. other, one befide; ad. otherwife, befide

Efewhére, ad. in fome other or a different place

Elúcidate, v. t. to explain, to clear up (lution

Elucidátion, n. an explanation, a clearing up, a fo-

Elúcidator, n. an explainer, expofitor, clearer up

Elúde, v. t. to efcape or avoid by artifice, to fhun

Elúdible, a. that may be eluded or defeated

Elv'ifh, a. relating to elves or wandering fpirits

Elúfion, n. artifice, art, fraud, efcape, evafion

Elúfive, Elúfory, a. tending to elude, evafive

Elúte, v. t. to wafh off or clean, cleanfe, clear

Elútriate, v. t. to decant, to pour or ftrain off

Elutriátion, n. a purification of fubftances by wafh- ing and pouring off the lighter parts

Elux'ate, v. t. to ftrain, wrench, put out of joint

Elys''ian, a. exceedingly delightful, very pleafant

Elys''ium, n. the reputed heaven of the heathens

Emáciate, v. to lofe flefh, wafte, pine away, decay

Emáciated, pa. grown thin or lean, wafted

Em'anant, a. iffuing or proceeding from, flowing

Em'anate, v. i. to proceed from or flow out of

Emanátion, n. the act of iffuing or flowing out

Em'anative, a. flowing or tending to flow from

Eman'cipate, v. t. to fet at liberty, free, deliver

Emancipátion, n. a deliverance from flavery, free- dom (margin

Emar'ginate, a. notched, having notches in the

Emafc'ulate, v. t. to caftrate, to effeminate

Emafculátion, n. a caftration, mean effeminacy

Emath'ian, a. pertaining to Macedonia & Theffaly

Embále, v. t. to make up into bales, to inclofe

Embáling, pa. forming into a bundle or heap

Emball', v. t. to make into a ball, to make round

Embalm', v. t. to take out the inteftines of a body and fill it with aromatics to preferve it

Embalm'er, n. one who embalms bodies

Embar', v. t. to fhut in, block up, hinder, ob.

Embar'go, n. a prohibition to prevent veffels from leaving a port, or commodities from be- ing exported (exportation of fhips

Embar'go, v. t. to prohibit the failing of fhips or

Embark', v. to put or go on fhipboard, to engage

Embarkátion, n. a putting or going on fhipboard

Embar'rafs, v. t. to perplex, entangle, clog, diftrefs

Embar'raffment, n. perplexity, diftrefs, trouble

Embáfe, v. t. to impair, degrade, ob. (a meffenger

Embafs'ador, n. a public minifter of the firft rank,

Em'baſſage, Em'baſſy, *n.* a public meſſage or truſt

Embat'tle, *v. t.* to ſet or range in order of battle

Embáy, *v. t.* to incloſe in a bay, waſh, bathe

Embel'liſh, *v. t.* to adorn, trim, beautify, ſet off

Embel'liſhment, *n.* ornament, decoration, grace

Em'bers, *n. pl.* hot cinders, aſhes not yet dead

Embez'zle, *v. t.* to defraud by appropriating to *one's own uſe,* what is entruſted to one's care,

Embez'zlement, *n.* fraud by uſing anothers prop-erty for one's own benefit

Emblázon, *v. t.* to blazon, adorn, paint, deſcribe

Em'blem, *n.* a moral device, repreſentation, token

Em'blem, *v. t.* to repreſent or deſcribe alluſively

Emblemat'ical, *a.* uſing emblems, alluſive

Emblemat'ically, *ad.* alluſively, with alluſion

Emblem'atiſt, *n.* a writer or inventor of emblems

Em'blements, *n. pl.* the produce from ſown land

Em'boliſm, *n.* an intercalation, a time inſerted

Emboſs', *v. t.* to adorn with riſing work, to incloſe

Emboſs'ing, *n.* the art of making figures in relievo

Emboſs'ment, *n.* relief, riſing work, a ſculpture

Embot'tle, *v. t.* to include in bottles, to bottle up

Embow'el, *v. t.* to take out the entrails, to gut

Embráce, *v. t.* to ſqueeze, take, compriſe

Embráce, Embrácement, *n.* a claſp, hug, cruſh

Embrácery, *n.* an attempt to influence a jury cor-ruptly   (a jury

Embrácing, *n.* the crime of attempting to corrupt

Embraſúre, *n.* a battlement, an opening in a wall

Em'brocate, *v. t.* to foment or rub a part diſeaſed

Embrocátion, *n.* fomentation, rubbing, lotion

Embroid'er, *v. t.* to adorn with figure-work

Embroid'erer, *n.* a perſon who works embroidery

Embroid'ery, *n.* a ſort of variegated needlework

Embroil', *v. t.* to diſturb, confuſe, involve, broil

Embroth'el, *v. t.* to ſhut in a brothel, *ob.*

Embrúted, *a.* reduced to brutality, very depraved

Em'bryo, Em'bryon, *n.* the rudiments of an ani-mal or plant, before the parts are diſtinctly formed, the beginning

Em'bryon, *a.* pertaining to firſt rudiments

Emendátion, *n.* a correction, alteration, change

Em'erald, *n.* a gem, a kind of green precious ſtone

Emerge', *v. i.* to iſſue, to riſe out of, from or up

Emer'gency, *n.* a riſing out of, preſſing neceſſity

Emer'gent, *a.* coming out or into fight, ſudden

Em'erods, *n.* the piles

Emer'ſion, *n.* the act of riſing out of water, a riſe

Em'ertis, *n.* plain India muſlins, thin and of infe-rior quality, about 7 8ths in width

Em'ery, *n.* a kind of iron ore, a glazier's diamond

Emet'ic, *a.* that provokes vomiting ; *n.* a vomit

Emicátion, *n.* the act of ſparkling or glittering

Emic'tion, *n.* urine, the making of urine   [away

Em'igrant, *a.* going from place to place, moving

Em'igrant, *n.* a perſon who quits his own country to reſide in another

Em'igrate, *v. i.* to remove from place to place

Emigrátion, *n.* a change of habitation or place

Em'inence, *n.* height, honor, top, a cardinal's title

Em'inent, *a.* high, lofty, remarkable, celebrated

Em'inently, *ad.* conſpicuouſly, in a high degree

E'mir, *n.* a Turkiſh prince, Vizer or Baſhaw

Em'iſſary, *n.* a ſecret agent, agent, ſpy, ſcout

Emiſ'ſion, *n.* a throwing out, a vent, a ſhooting

Emit', *v.* to dart, let fly, ſend out, iſſue out, diſ-

Em'met, *n.* a kind of infect, ant, piſmire   (charge

Emmew', *v. t.* to mew, ſhut or coop up, *ob.*

Emmóve, *v. t.* to move, ſtir or rouſe up, *ob.*

Emolles'cence, *n.* ſoftneſs, or the loweſt degree of fuſibility in bodies

Emol'lient, *a.* ſoftening, ſuppling, moiſtening

Emol'lient, *n.* a medicin which ſoftens

Emolli'tion, *n.* the act of ſoftening or relaxing

Emol'ument, *n.* profit, gain, advantage, benefit

Emolument'al, *a.* uſeful, producing emolument

Emótion, *n.* a ſudden motion, diſturbance of mind

Empále, *v. t.* to incloſe, fortify, fence in, put on a ſtake   (flower

Empálement, *n.* a fixing on a ſtake, the calyx of a

Empéople, *v.* to form into a community, *ob.*

Em'peror, *n.* a monarch, a title ſuperior to king

Em'phaſis, *n.* a remarkable ſtreſs laid on a word

Em'phaſize, *v. t.* to pronounce with a ſtreſs of voice

Emphat'ical, *a.* ſtrong, forcible, ſtriking, eager

Emphat'ically, *ad.* ſtrongly, forcibly, ſtrikingly

Emphyſem'atous, *a.* bloated, ſwelled, puffed up

Emp'ire, [Emp'ery,] *n.* imperial power, command,

Emp'iric, *n.* a pretended phyſician, a quack (rule

Empir'ical, *a.* experimental, practiced by rote

Empir'ically, *ad.* experimentally, pretendedly

Empir'iciſm, *n.* the practice or profeſſion of quacks

Emplaſt'er, *v. t.* to cover with a plaſter

Emplaſt'ic, *a.* viſcous, glutinous, clammy, tough

Employ', *v. t.* to keep at work, exerciſe, uſe, ſpend

Employ', Employ'ment, *n.* buſineſs, a public office

Employ'able, *a.* fit to be employed or uſed

Employ'er, *n.* one who employs or ſets to work

Empois'on, *v. t.* to poiſon, to deſtroy by poiſon

Empois'oner, *n.* one who poiſons another perſon

Empórium, *n.* a ſeat of merchandiſe, a mart

Empov'eriſh, *ſee* Impoveriſh

Empow'er, *v. t.* to authoriſe, to enable   (dignity

Emp'reſs or Emp'ereſs, *n.* a woman having imperial

Empríſe, *n.* an attempt of danger, enterpriſe, *ob.*

Emp'tier, *n.* one who empties, one who makes void

Emp'tineſs, *n.* a void ſpace, vanity, ignorance

Emp'tion, *n.* the act of buying, a purchaſe

Emp'ty, *a.* void, unfurniſhed, ignorant, fooliſh

Emp'ty, *v. t.* to exhauſt, make void, deprive

Empur'ple, *v. t.* to make or dye of a purple color

Empuz'zle, *v. t.* to puzzle, perplex, confound, *ob.*

Empyr'cal, *a.* refined, beyond aerial, heavenly

Empyréan, *n.* the higheſt heaven

Empyr'eum, *n.* the very higheſt heaven or region

Empyreumat'ical, *a.* reſembling burnt ſubſtances

Empyróſis, *n.* a general fire, a conflagration

Em'u, *n.* a very large bird of S. America, ſix feet

high, with fmall ufelefs wings
Em'ulate, v. t. to rival, ftrive to equal or excel
Emulation, n. rivalry, contention, ftrife, envy
Em'ulative, a. inclined or tending to emulate
Em'ulator, n. a rival, competitor, opponent
Emul'gent, a. milking or draining out
Em'ulous, a. rivaling, defirous to excel, eager
Em'uloufly, ad. with a defire of excelling, hotly
Emul'fion, n. a kind of liquid foftening medicin
Emuls'ive, a. foftening, yielding a foft fubftance
Enáble, v. t. to make able, give power, authorize
Enact', v. t. to order, decree, pafs, perform, effect
Enact'ed, pa. decreed, eftablifhed, performed
Enact'or, n. one who enacts, one who paffes a law
Enal'lage, n. a figure, change of things, inverfion
Enam'bufh, v. t. to hide in ambufh, to conceal
Enam'el, v. t. to cover or paint with enamel
Enam'el, n. a fubftance imperfectly vitrified, or
having a glaffy furface without tranfparency
Enam'ellar, a. like enamel, fmooth, gloffy
Enam'eller, n. one who enamels or inlays colors
Enam'or, v. t. to inflame with love or defire
Enam'ored, pa. inflamed, captivated
Enarrátion, n. a declaration, account, recital, re-
Encáge, v. t. to coop up, to confine (lation
Encamp', v. to reft in tents, to pitch or fix tents
Encamp'ment, n. tents pitched in order, a camp
Encáve, v. t. to fhut up, hide or conceal in a cave
Encaus'tice, n. the art of enamelling or painting
with burnt wax (with burnt wax
Encauft'ic, a. relating to enamelling, or painting
Encháfe, v. t. to enrage, provoke, fret, chafe
Enchain, v. t. to fatten with a chain, bind, tie
Enchant', v. t. to bewitch, charm, delight highly
Enchant'er, n. a forcerer, magician, wizard, conjurer
Enchant'ingly, ad. in an enchanting manner
Enchant'ment, n. magical charms, high delight
Enchant'refs, n. a forcerefs, an extreme beauty
Encháfe, v. t. to fet in gold, filver, &c. to adorn
Enchirid'ion, [ch as k] n. a fmall volume, a manual
Encir'cle, v. t. to inclofe in a circle or ring, to fur-
Encirc'let, n. a circle, fmall circle, ring (round
Enclit'ic, a. leaning, inclining
Enclit'ics, n. the art of conjugating and declining,
Enclófe, fee Inclofe (words inclining upon others
Encómiaft, n. a panegyrift, praifer, commender
Encómium, n. a panegyric, praife, commendation
Encom'pafs, v. t. to fhut or hem in, to furround
Encomp'affment, n. the act of fhutting in, a cir-
Encóre, ad. again, once more (cumlocution
Encóre, v. t. to cry out encore, to defire to repeat
Encount'er, n. a duel, battle, hot attack, accident
Encount'er, v. to fight, engage, attack, oppofe, meet
Encour'age, v. t. to embolden, to give fpirits to
Encour'agement, n. incitement, fupport, reward
Encour'ager, n. one who encourages or incites
Encróach, v. i. to invade, intrude, advance
Encróacher, n. one who encroaches or invades
Encroachment, n. an unlawful intrufion on right

Encum'ber, fee Incumber
Encyc'lical, a. circular, fent round about
Encyclopédia, n. the whole circle of fcience
Encyclopédift, n. a compiler of an Encyclopedia
Encyft'ed, a. inclofed in a bag or bladder
End, n. a defign, point, conclufion, event, death
End, v. to come to a conclufion, conclude, finifh
Endam'age, v. t. to hurt, harm, injure, prejudice
Endan'ger, v. t. to bring into danger, to hazard
Endéar, v. t. to render dear, make beloved, recom-
Endéarment, n. the caufe and ftate of love (mend
Endeav'or, n. an effort, exertion, attempt
Endeav'or, v. to ftrive, attempt, try, labor, work
Endeav'orer, n. one who endeavors or labors
Endeíctic, a. fhowing, giving a view
Endémial, Endem'ic, a. peculiar to a country or
Enden'ize, v. t. to naturalize, ob. (place
Endew', v. t. to difgorge, throw up, cleanfe, ob.
Endict, Endite, v. t. to charge with fome crime
Endictment, n. an accufation, a declaration
End'ing, pa. concluding, finifhing; n. the end
End'ive, n. a common falad-herb, fuccory
End'lefs, a. that has no end, infinite, continual
End'lefsly, ad. inceffantly, continually, for ever
End'leffnefs, n. an endlefs ftate or quality, round-
End'long, ad. in a ftraight line, directly on (nefs
Endorfe', fee Indorfe
Endow', v. t. to give a portion, enrich, endue
Endow'ed, pa. portioned, gifted, poffeffed of
Endow'ment, n. wealth given, a gift of nature
Endúe, v. t. to fupply with graces, &c. to inveft
Endúrance, n. fufferance, continuance, ob.
Endúre, v. to continue, laft, undergo, fuffer, bear
End'wife, ad. on end, with the end upward or firft
En'ecate, v. t. to kill, deftroy, not ufed
En'emy, n. a foe, public or private
Energet'ic, a. forcible, ftrong, vigorous, active
Energet'ically, ad. forcibly, powerfully, ftrongly
Energet'ically, ad. forcibly, powerfully, ftrongly
En'ergy, n. force, power, vigor, influence, faculty
En'ergize, v. t. to give ftrength or vigor
En'ergizer, n. that which gives energy
En'ervate, Enervé, v. t. to weaken, reduce, crufh
En'ervate, En'ervated, pa. weakened, enfeebled
Enerv'ous, a. having no nerves
Enervátion, n. the act of weakening or crufhing
Enféeble, v. t. to weaken, to deprive of ftrength
Enfeoff', v. t. to inveft, to put into poffeffion
Enfeoff'ment, n. the act or deed of enfeoffing
Enfet'ter, v. t. to put in chains, bind faft, ob.
Enfet'tered, pa. put into chains, bound, ob.
Enfiláde, n. a narrow paffage, a row
Enfiláde, v. t. to pierce or rake in a line
Enfórce, v. to force, ftrengthen, urge, prove, fhow
Enfórce, n. force, power, ftrength, violence, ob.
Enfórcedly, ad. by force or compulfion, ob.
Enfórcement, n. compulfion, exigence, neceffity
Enfórcer, n. one who enforces, one who compels
Enfran'chife, v. t. to make free of a corporation

Enfran'chifement, *n.* the act of making free
Engáge, *v.* to oppofe, fight, enter upon, embark,
   win over, attach, employ, bind, make liable
Engágement, *n.* a battle, obligation, bond, bufinefs
Engaól, *v. t.* to put into prifon, to confine, *ob.*
Engar'rifon, *v.* to defend by or put a garrifon, *ob.*
Engen'der, *v. t.* to beget, caufe, excite, bring forth
En'gine, *n.* a machine, inftrument, agent
Engineer, *n.* one who directs engines or artillery
Enginéer, *v. i.* to manage engines
En'ginery, *n.* artillery, the management of artillery
Engird', *v. t.* engirded, engirt, *pret.* engirded, en-
   girt, *pa.* to furround, encompafs, hem in
Eng'lifh, *n.* the people or language of England
Eng'lifh, *a.* belonging or relating to England, &c.
Eng'lifh, *v. t.* to tranflate or turn into Englifh
Englut', *v. t.* to glut, fwallow up, pamper, *ob.*
Engorge', *v. t.* to gorge, fwallow, devour, riot
Engráil, *v. t.* to indent in curve lines, *ob.*
Engráin, *v. t.* to die in grain, to die deep or full
Engrap'ple, *v. i.* to clofe or contend with
Engráve, *v. t.* engraved, *pret.* engraved, engra-
   ven, *pa.* to cut out figures, to imprint
Engráver, *n.* a man who engraves in copper, &c.
Engráving, *n.* a picture or mark engraved
Engrófs, *v. t.* to monopolize, to write a fair copy
Engróffer, *n.* one who engroffes, a monopolizer
Engróffment, *n.* the act of engroffing
Enguard', *v. t.* to protect, defend, keep, *ob.*
Enhance', *v. t.* to advance, increafe, raife
Enhance'ment, *n.* an increafe, aggravation, rife
Enharmon'ic, *a.* in mufic, the eighth of a tone, is
   called an enharmonic interval
Enig'ma, *n.* a riddle, a dark or obfcure queftion
Enigmat'ical, *a.* dark, obfcure, hidden, doubtful
Enigmat'ically, *ad.* darkly, obfcurely, doubtfully
Enig'matift, *n.* one who deals in obfcurities, &c.
Enjoin', *v. t.* to prefcribe, to command
Enjoin'ment, *n.* a direction, command, order, rule
Enjoy', *v. t.* to feel with pleafure, to have poffeffion
Enjoy'ment, *n.* the quality of enjoying, happinefs
Enkin'dle, *v. t.* to fet on fire, fire, incite, raife up
Enlarge', *v.* to increafe, fwell, expatiate, releafe
Enlarge'ment, *n.* an increafe, copioufnefs, releafe
Enlíght, Enlíghten, *v. t.* to give light, to inftruct
Enlíghtener, *n.* one who illuminates or teaches
Enlink', *v. t.* to link, chain or faften together, *ob.*
Enlíven, *v. t.* to give life to, animate, cheer
Enlívener, *n.* one who or that which enlivens
Enmefh', *v. t.* to net, entangle, entrap, inclofe
En'mity, *n.* ill-will, malice, hatred, oppofition
Ennean'dria, *n.* a clafs of plants with hermaphrodite
   flowers of nine ftamens
Enneapet'alous, *a.* having nine petals
Ennóble, *v. t.* to make noble, elevate, dignify
Ennóbled, *pa.* raifed high, exalted, dignified
Ennóblement, *n.* an ennobling, exaltation, honor
Enóde, *a.* without knots or joints
Enodátian, *n.* the folution of a difficulty or knot

Enorm'ity, *n.* very great wickednefs or corruption
Enorm'ous, *a.* very great or wicked, irregular
Enorm'oufly, *ad.* beyond meafure, out of rule, very
Enough', [enuff]a. fufficient; *n.* fufficiency, plenty
Enow', *pl.* of *enough*, fufficient, *ob.*
Enráge, *v. t.* to provoke, to make furious
Enrange', Enrank', *v. t.* to place in ranks, *ob.*
Enrap'ture, *v. t.* to tranfport with pleafure
Enrav'ifh, *v. t.* to fill with rapture, to tranfport
Enrav'ifhment, *n.* an ecftacy of delight or joy
Enrich', *v. t.* to make rich or fruitful, ftock, ftore
Enrich'ment, *n.* an increafe of wealth or ftore
Enridge', *v. t.* to form in ridges, *ob.*
Enring', *v. t.* enrung, *pret.* enringed, enrung, *pa.*
   to bind or put round, to encircle, *ob.*
Enrípen, *v.* to ripen, grow or become ripe, *ob.*
Enróbe, *v. t.* to drefs, clothe, cover, inveft, adorn
Enról, *v. t.* to regifter, record, enter, inwrap
Enróller, *n.* one who enrols, one who regifters
Enról'ment, *n.* a regifter, writing of record, record
Enroot', *v. t.* to fix by the root, to implant, *ob.*
Enround', *v. t.* to furround, inclofe, *ob.*   (plify
Enfam'ple, *n.* an example, a pattern; *v. t.* to exem-
Enfan'guine, *v. t.* to fmear with gore
Enfan'guined, *pa.* ftained with blood or gore
En'fate, *a.* having fword-fhaped leaves
Enfched'ule, *v. t.* to infert in a fchedule, *ob.*
Enfconce', *v. t.* to cover as with a fort, to fecure, *ob.*
Enféam, *v. t.* to fow, clofe up, *ob.*
Enféar, *v. t.* to ftop by fire or heat, to ftaunch, *ob.*
Enfhiéld, *v. t.* to fhield, cover, defend, *ob.*
Enfhríne, *v. t.* to preferve as a holy relic, to lay up
Enfíf'erous, *a.* bearing or carrying a fword
En'fiform, *a.* in fhape of a fword   (it
En'fign, *n.* a flag or ftandard, an officer that carries
En'fignbearer, *n.* he that carries a flag, an enfign
En'figncy, *n.* the rank or commiffion of an enfign
Enfky', *v. t.* to place in the fkies, to deify, *ob.*
Enfláve, *v. t.* to deprive of liberty, to fubject
Enflávement, *n.* an enflaving, ftate of flavery, bond-
Enfláver, *n.* one who enflaves other perfons   (age
Enftamp', *v. t.* to imprefs with a ftamp, or deeply
Enftéep, *v. t.* to fteep, put under water, *ob.*
Enfúe, *v.* to follow, purfue, fucceed, arife
Enfúrance, *fee* Infure
Entab'lature, *n.* that part of a column which is over
   the capital, comprehending the architrave, frize
   and cornifh
Entáil, *n.* an eftate fettled on certain conditions
Entáil, *v. t.* to fix or fettle an eftate unalienably
Entáme, *v. t.* to tame, fubdue, make gentle
Entan'gle, *v. t.* to twift, confufe, puzzle, infnare
Entan'glement, *n.* an entangled ftate, perplexity
Entan'gler, *n.* a perfon who entangles or perplexes
Ent'er, *v.* to go or come in, write down, engage in,
   lodge manifeft of goods, &c. at a cuftom houfe
Enterdéal, *n.* mutual tranfactions, *ob.*
Ent'ering, *n.* a paffage into a place, an entrance
Ent'erprife, *n.* an undertaking, attempt, project

Ent'erprise, v. t. to take in hand, attempt, receive
Ent'erpriser, n. an adventurer, fchemer, plotter
En'terprifing, pa. bold and active in new under-
takings
Entertáin, v. t. to talk with, treat, keep, amufe
Entertáining, pa. a. treating, keeping, pleafing
Entertáinment, n. a reception, welcome, treat, fare,
diverfion, amufement, kind of lower comedy
Entertiſ"ſued, a. interwoven, intermixed, ob.
Enthróne, v. t. to place upon a throne, to exalt
Enthúfiafm, n. a heat of the imagination or fancy
Enthúfiaſt, n. one of a hot credulous imaginatioń
Enthufiaſt'ic, a. very zealous or hot in any thing
En'thymeme, n. an imperfect fyllogifm, an idea
Entíce, v. t. to invite or tempt to evil, allure
Entícement, n. an enticing, allurement, lure, bait
Entícer, n. one who enticcs, one who allures
Entícingly, ad. in an enticing or artful manner
Eatíre, a. whole, undivided, complete, hearty
Entírely, ad. wholly, completely, fully, firmly
Entírenefs, Entírety, n. completenefs, fulnefs
Entítle, v. t. to give a title or right, call, name
Entítled, pa. having a right or claim, named
Ent'ity, n. being, real being, real exiftence
Entoil', v. t. to infnare, entangle, perplex, ob.
Entomb', [entoom] v. t. to put or lay in a tomb
Entomol'ogy, n. the fcience of infects   (fects
Entomolo"gical, a. pertaining to the fcience of in-
Ent'rails, n. pl. the bowels or guts, inward parts
Ent'rance, n. a going in, paffage, admiffion
Entrance', v. t. to throw into a trance or ecftacy
Entrap', v. t. to trap, infnare, entangle
Entréat, v. to beg, beg earneftly, requeft, treat
Entréaty, n. a requeft, an earneft prayer
Ent'ry, n. an entrance, act of entering, paffage,
giving an account of a cargo to the officer of the
cuftoms
Enúbilous, a. free from or void of clouds, fair
Enúmerate, v. t. to number up, count over, recite
Enumerátion, n. a numbering or counting over
Enun"ciate, v. t. to declare, proclaim, exprefs
Enunciátion, n. a plain declaration, intelligence
Enun"ciative, a. declarative, expreffive, full
Envel'op, v. t. to wrap, fold, cover, furround, hide
Envel'ope, n. a wrapper, fold, outward eafe, work
Envel'opement, n. a wrapping up, or inclofing
Enven'om, v. t. to poifon, enrage, make hateful
En'viable, a. deferving envy, exciting envy
En'vier, n. one who envies another perfon
En'vious, a. infected with envy, malicious, greedy
En'vioufly, ad. with envy, with ill-will or malice
Environ, v. t. to furround, hem in, inveft, befet
Environs, n. pl. places adjacent, neighborhood
En'voy, n. a public minifter fent to foreign ftates
En'vy, v. to wifh for, to grieve at another's good
En'vy, n. vexation or pain at another's profperity
Enwhéel, v. t. to encompafs, furround, ob.
Enwómb, v. t. to make fruitful, hide, ob.
Eóliań, a. pertaining to Eolia in Afia, or to Eolus

the god of the winds   (fpoken in Eolia
Eol'ic, a. denominating that dialect of the Greek,
Eol'ipile, n. a hollow globe of metal to be filled
with water, and heated to fhow the force of
fteam
E'pact, n. 11 days of the folar above the lunar year,
a Hebrew meafure of about three pecks
Epainet'ic, a. praifing, commending, extolling, ob.
Ep'aulet, n. a fhoulderknot, knot of lace, ornament
Epkem'eral, a. daily, lafting a day   (motions
Ephem'eris, n. a daily account of the planetary
Ephem'erift, n. a man who ftudies aftrology, &c.
Ephem'era, n. an infect whofe life is one day only,
or very fhort
Ephéfian, n. an inhabitant of Ephefus in Afia
Ephéfian, a. pertaining to Ephefus
Eph'od, n. a linen girdle worn by Jewifh priefts
Ep'ic, a. containing narrative, heroic, noble
Epicédium, n. an elegy, funeral poem, ob.
Ep'icene, a. common to both the fexes
Ep'icure, n. one addicted to luxury, an epicurean
Epicúrean, n. a follower of Epicurus; a. luxurious
Epicúreanifm, n. love of pleafure, fenfuality
Ep'icurifm, n. luxury, grofs or fenfual pleafure
Ep'icurize, v. i. to live or think like an epicure
Epidem'ic, a. general, affecting numbers
Epidem'ic, n. a popular or general difeafe
Epiderm'is, n. the outer thin fkin, the cuticle
Epiderm'ic, Epiderm'idal, a. belonging to the
fcarf fkin   (bowels
Epigas'tric, a. pertaining to the upper part of the
Ep'igram, n. a kind of fhort pointed poem
Epigrammat'ic, a. dealing in epigrams, pointed
Epigram'matift, n. a writer or judge of epigrams
Ep'ilepfy, n. a convulfion with the lofs of fenfe
Epilep'tic, a. affected with epilepfy, convulfed
Ep'ilogue, n. a fpeech made at the end of a play
Epiph'any, n. a manifeftation, the twelfth day
Epiphon'ema, n. an exclamation, a moral reflection
Epiploon', n. the caul or omentum
Epiplóic, a. pertaining to the caul
Epifc'opacy, n. a church-government by bifhops
Epifc'opal, a. belonging or relating to bifhops, or
a church governed by bifhops   (Church
Epifcopálian, n. an adherent to the Epifcopal
Epifc'opate, n. the ftate or dignity of a bifhop
Ep'ifode, n. a digreffion, or feparate ftory or action,
connected with the main plot of a poem
Epifod'ic, Epifod'ical, a. contained in an epifode
Epifpaft'ic, a. drawing, bliftering; n, a blifter
Epis'tle, n. a letter, a meffage fent under cover
Epis'tolary, a. relating to or tranfacted by letters
Epis'trophy, n. a conclufion with the fame word
Ep'itaph, n. an infcription upon a tombftone
Epithalámium, n. a nuptial fong or poem
Ep'ithet, n. an adjective denoting a quality, &c.
Epit'ome, better written Epit'omy, n. an abridg-
ment, an abftract, the heads
Epit'omife, v. t. to abridge, fhorten, abftract, reduce

Epit'omifer, Epit'omift, n. one who abridges
E'poch or Ep'ocha, [ch as k] n. a point of time to date from (ode
Ep'ode, n. a ftanza following the ftrophe, poem,
Ep'opy or E'pos, n. an epic poem or its fubject
Ep'ulary, a. relating or belonging to a feaft, jolly
Epulation, n. a feaft, a banquet, jollity, joy
Epulot'ic, a. healing, cicatrizing, drying up fores
Equabil'ity, n. equality, evennefs, uniformity
E'quable, a. equal to itfelf, even, uniform, alike
E'quably, ad. equally, evenly, uniformly, fteadily
E'qual, a. like another, even, uniform, fame, juft
E'qual, n. one who is of the fame rank and age
E'qual, E'qualize, v. t. to make or become equal, portion out, compare, recompenfe (nefs
Equal'ity, n. likenefs, evennefs, uniformity, fame-
E'qually, ad. of or on the fame degree, impartially
Equanim'ity, n. evennefs of mind, compofure
Equan'imous, a. even, calm, cool, compofed
Equátion, n. a bringing of things to an equality
Equátor, n. a line dividing the globe into 2 equal
Equatórial, a. pertaining to the equator (parts
E'querry, n. one who has care of horfes, a ftable
Equeft'rian, a. appearing on horfeback, noble
Equian"gular, a. having equal or like angles
Equicrúral, a. having equal legs or fides, ifofceles
Equidis'tant, a. fet or being at the fame diftance
Equidis'tantly, ad. at the fame diftance
Equiform'ity, n. uniformity, equality, likenefs
Equilat'eral, a. having the fides equal
Equilíbrate, v. t. to balance equally (equipoife
Equilibrátion, Equilib'rium, n. equality of weight,
Equimult'iple, a. multiplied by the fame number
E'quine, a. pertaining to the horfe kind
Equine"ceffary, a. equally neceffary, proper or fit
Equinoc'tial, n. a line that anfwers to the equator
Equinoc'tial, a. pertaining to or near the equinox
E'quinox, n. the time when the day and night are
Equinúmerant, a. having the fame number (equal
Equip', v. t. to drefs or fit out, provide, furnifh
E'quipage, n. attendance, horfes and carriage, furniture, a woman's watch and trinkets, ftate
Equip'ment, n. the act of equipping or fitting out
E'quipoife, n. an equality of weight or force
Equipol'lent, a. having equal force or power, like
Equipond'erant, Equipond'ious, a. of equal weight
Equipond'erate, v. i. to weigh equally with
E'quitable, a. juft, right, fit, impartial, equal
E'quitablenefs, n. the ftate of being juft, equity
E'quitably, ad. juftly, reafonably, impartially, duly
E'quitant, a. riding, denoting leaves of a plant whofe fides approach, fo that the outer embrace the inner
E'quity, n. juftice, right, honefty (to equal
Equiv'alence, n. equality of worth or power; v. t.
Equiv'alent, a. equal in value, force or meaning
Equiv'alent, n. a thing that is of the fame value
Equiv'ocal, a. uncertain, doubtful, ambiguous
Equiv'ocally, ad. uncertainly, doubtfully, doubly

Equiv'ocalnefs, Equiv'ocal, n. a double meaning
Equiv'ocate, v. i. to fpeak doubly, fhuffle, waver
Equivocátion, n. a fhuffling, delufive words
Equiv'ocator, n. one who equivocates or fhuffles
E"quivoke, n. an equivocal faying
E'ra, n. an epoch, an account or date of time
Eradiátion, n. a fending out of rays or brightnefs
Erad'icate, v. t. to root up or out, deftroy, cut off
Eradicátion, n. the act of rooting or pulling up
Eráfe, v. t. to rub or fcrape out, root up, deftroy
Eráfable, a. that may be erafed
Eráfed, pa. expunged, fcratched out, torn away
Eráfement, n. expunction, abolition, deftruction
Eráfure, n. a blotting out, expunging
Ere, ad. before, fooner than, ever, always
Er'ebus, n. a place of darknefs, lower regions
Erect', v. to build or fet up, raife, exalt, rife upright
Erect', a. raifed, upright, confident, vigorous
Erec'tion, n. the act of building or raifing up
Erect'nefs, n. an erect ftate, an upright pofture
Erelong', ad. before a long time paffes, fhortly, foon
Er'emit, n. a hermit, reclufe, very retired perfon
Eremit'ical, a. folitary, retired, religious, devout.
Erenow' ad. before now, before this time
Erewhíle, ad. fome time ago, heretofore, formerly
Erin"go, n. a kind of plant, the fea holly
Er'melin, Er'min, n. a fmall animal with delicate white fur, the fkin or fur
Er'mined, a. clothed in or covered with ermin
Eróde, v. t. to canker, eat away, corrode, confume
Eróse, a. notched as if bitten
Eróſion, n. the act of eating away, corrofion, wafte
Erot'ic, a. belonging to love (amifs
Err, v. i. to go out of the way, ftray, miftake, do
Err'able, a. liable to err or miftake, fallible
Err'and, n. a meffage, a thing any one is fent about
Err'ant, a. wandering, roving, notorious, arrant
Err'antnefs, Err'antry, a. a wandering ftate
Errátum, pl. errata, n. miftake, error in printing
Errat'ic, a. wandering, irregular, uncertain, loofe
Errat'ically, ad. without rule, order or method
Er'rhine, a. occafioning fneezing, purging the head
Er'rhine, n. that which promotes fneezing
Errôneous, a. fubject to or full of errors, falfe
Errôneoufly, ad. by, from or with, miftake, falfely
Errôneoufnefs, n. error, miftake, fault, falshood
Err'or, n. a miftake, blunder, fin, crime, offenfe
Erft, ad. when time was, at firft, formerly, once
Erubes'cence, n. rednefs, a blufhing, a blufh (ward
Eructátion, n. a belch, a fudden burft of wind up-
Er'udite, a. inftructed, taught, learned, fkilled
Erudi"tion, n. inftruction, learning, knowledge
Erúginous, a. coppery, rufty, foul, nafty, brown
Erupt', v. t. to burft forth or eject with force
Erup'tion, n. a breaking out, burft, puftule, fpot
Erup'tive, a. burfting forth, tending to burft, foul
Eryfip'elas, n. an acrid eruption on the fkin
Eryfipelátous, a. eruptive, like eryfipelas
Efcaláde, n. the act of fcaling the walls of a place

Efcal'op, n. a fhellfifh, oyfters broiled or roafted

Efeápe, v. to get out of danger, avoid, fhun, fly

Efcápe, n. a getting clear, flight, overfight, error

Efcáped, pa. got out of danger or confinement

Efcar'gatoire, n. a nurfery or neft of fnails

Efchalót,n. a kind of fmall fine onion, a fhalote

Efch'ar or Efc'ar, n. a fcar, mark, wound healed

Efcharot'ic, [ch as k] a. burning, fearing, cauftic

Efchéat, n. the falling of lands to the owner, or to the ftate by forfeiture or failure of heirs, the lands fo falling

Efchéat, v. i. to fall to the owner or the ftate

Efchéator, n. an officer who has the care of efcheats

Efchew', v.-t. to fly, avoid, fhun, refift, oppofe

Efcutch'eon, n. a coat of arms

Efcort', n. a convoy, a guard by land

Efcort', v.t. to convoy, to guard to or from a place

Efcout', n. a fcout, fpy, liftener, ob.

Efcritóir, n. a kind of defk on a cheft of drawers

Ef'crow, n. deed delivered to a third perfon to be delivered to the grantee on his performing certain conditions   (phyfic

Efculápian, a. pertaining to Efculapius, the god of

Efc'ulent, a. eatable, good for food; n. any food

Efcúrial, n. the palace of the King of Spain

Efot'eric, a. private, not open or public

Efpal'ier, n. a row of drawf-trees planted in rails

Efpe"cial, a. principal, chief, leading, particular

Efpe"cially, ad. principally, chiefly, particularly

Efpíal, n. a fpy, fcout, ob.

Es'pionage, n. the art or practice of fpies (ed way

Efplar áde, n. the floping of the parapet of a cover-

Efpous'al, a. relating to efpoufals or betrothing

Efpou-'als, n. pl. the act of betrothing, marriage

Efpoufe', v. t. to betroth, engage for marriage, marry, adopt, take upon, maintain, defend

Efpy', v. t. to fee at a diftance, watch, look at, fpy

Efquíre, n. a title below a knight, the title of mag-iftrates and public officers

Efquíre or Squíre, v. t. to attend or wait on

Eífáy, v. t. to attempt, endeavor, try, examin

Efs'ay,n. an attempt, endeavor, trial, experiment

Efsáyift, n. a writer or publifher of effays

Efs'ence, n. the nature, fubftance or being of any thing, exiftence, a perfume, fmell, fcent, odor

Efs'ence, v. t. to perfume, fcent, fprinkle

Effen'tial, a. neceffary, very important, pure

Effen'tial, n. exiftence, a chief point or thing

Effen'tially, ad. abfolutely, neceffarily, truly

Effential'ity, n. the quality of being effential

Effenes, n. a fect among the Jews who lived re-clufe, they admitted a future ftate, but denied a refurrection

Effoin', n. an excufe for non-appearance

Eftab'lifh, v. t. to fettle, fix, confirm, found

Eftab'lifhed, pa. fettled, fixed, confirmed, built

Eftab'lifhment, n. a fettlement, a ftated falary

Eftáte, n. property, plantation, farm, rank

Eftáte, v. t. to fettle an eftate on

Eftéem, v. t. to value, think well of, prize, reckon

Eftéem, n. high value in opinion, regard, refpect

Efteémable, a. worthy of efteem

Eftéemer, n. one who values or refpects

Es'timable, a. worthy of efteem, valuable, good

Es'timate, v. t. to rate, compute, fet a value upon

Es'timate, n. a calculation, valuation, account

Eftimátion, n. valuing, efteem, honor, opinion

Es'timative, a. having the power of comparing

Es'timator, n. one who eftimates, rates or values

Es'tival, a. relating to the fummer, ob.

Eftivátion, n. the act of pafling the fummer, the ftate of the petals in a bud or germ, (own act

Eftop'pel, n. a bar in law, arifing from a man's

Eftránge, v. t. to keep at a diftance, to alienate

Eftrángement,n.dift • ance,a diftant removal,referve

Eftráy, n. a beaft which wanders from his owner

Eftréat, n. a copy of an original writing

Es'tuary, n. an arm or mouth of the fea, a frith

Eftuátion, n. a boiling, a fwelling

Es'ture, n. violence, commotion, great heat, ob.

Efúrine, a. corroding, eating, confuming, ob.

Etc. or &c. contrac. for et cætera, and fo forth

Etch, v. t. to mark out prints with aquafortis

Eter'nal, a. perpetual, endlefs, conftant; n. GOD

Eter'nize, v. t. to immortalize, make endlefs

Eter'nally, ad. perpetually, always, forever

Eter'nity, n. duration without end, perpetuity

Etéfian, a. denoting durable winds like the mon-foons, fometimes northern winds

E'ther, n. highly rectified fpirit, confifting of al-cohol, hydrogene and oxygene, a pure thin element

Ethéreal, Ethéreous, a. heavenly, refined, pure

E'therize, v. t. to convert into ether

Eth'ic, Eth'ical, a. moral, of or relating to morals

Eth'ically, ad. by or according to morality, purely

Eth'ics n. pl. the doctrine of morality, morals

Ethiópian, n. a native of Ethiopia, now Abyffinia

Ethiópian, a. pertaining to Ethiopia, black

Eth'nic, a. heathen, pagan; n. a heathen, a pagan

Etio'lation, n. a making or growing white

E'tiolate, v. t. to blanch, bleach or whiten

Etiol'ogy, n. an account of the caufes of difeafes

Eth'moid, a. refembling a fieve, cribriform

Etiquet', n. forms of civility or ceremony

E'tite, n. eagle ftone, a bog iron   (Greece

Etólian, n. a native of Etolia, in the center of

Etólian, a. pertaining to Etolia

Et'nean, a. pertaining to Etna, a volcanic moun-tain in Sicily

Et'weecafe, n. a cafe ufed for pocket inftruments

Etymolo"gical,a. relative to etymology,derivative

Etymol'ogy, n. the true derivation of words

Et'ymon, n. an original root or primitive word

Eudiom'eter, n. an inftrument to determin the purity of air

Eudiomet'rical, a. belonging to an Eudiometer

Eúcharift, [ch as k] n. the Lord's fupper

Eucharift'ical, relating to the Lord's fupper (body
Eúchrafy, [ch as k] *n.* good temperature of the
Eúchymy, [ch as k] *n.* a good habit of the body
Fúlogy, *n.* praife, encomium, a public difcourfe
Eúlogift, *n.* one who praifes (by way of panegyric
Eúlogize, *v. t.* to praife, commend
Eúnomy, *n.* a conftitution or fet of valuable laws
Eúnuch, [ch as k] *n.* a caftrated perfon (culate
Eúnuchate, *v. t.* to make an eunuch, geld, emaf-
Eúnuchifm, *n.* the ftate of being emafculated
Eu'pepfy, *n.* a good concoction or digeftion
Eúphrafy, *n.* the herb eyebright
Euroc'lydon, *n.* a tempeftuous N. E. wind
European, *a.* of or belonging to Europe
European, *n.* a native or inhabitant of Europe
Euthan'afy, *n.* a gentle eafy death
Eúxine, *n.* the fea in Afia, called alfo Black Sea
Eúxine, *a.* denoting the Black Sea
Evac'uate, *v. t.* to make void, empty, quit
Evacuátion, *n.* an emptying, difcharge, abolition
Evac'uant, *n.* a medicin which evacuates
Eváde, *v.* to avoid, efcape, fhift off, baffle
Evagátion, *n.* the act of wandering, a ramble
Evaginátion, *n.* the act of unfheathing or drawing
Evanes'cence, *n.* the act or ftate of vanifhing
Evanes'cent, *a.* vanifhing, fmall, imperceptible
Evangel'ical, *a.* agreeable to the gofpel, divine
Evan'gelifm, *n.* the promulgation of the gofpel
Evan'gelift, *n.* a writer or preacher of the gofpel
Evangelift'ery, *n.* a manufcript-copy of the gofpels
Evan'gelize, *v. i.* to preach the gofpel, to preach
Evan'id, *a.* faint, weak, vanifhing, decaying, *ob.*
Evan'ifh, *v. i.* to vanifh, difappear
Evan'ifhment, *n.* a vanifhing, difappearance
Evap'orable, *a.* that may be refolved into vapors
Evap'orate, *v.* to refolve into vapors, vent, fly off
Evaporátion, *n.* the act of flying away in fames
Eváfion, *n.* an efcape, excufe, equivocation, fhift
Eváfive, *a.* elufive, equivocating, fhuffling, fly
Eváfively, *ad.* in an evafive or fly manner
Eve, *n.* the clofe of the day, the faft of a holiday
E'ven, *a.* level, parallel, calm, uniform; *ad.* verily
E'ven, *v. t.* to equal, level, balance an account
E'venhanded, *a.* impartial, juft, equitable, fair
E'vening or E'ven, *n.* the clofe or end of the day
E'venly, *ad.* equally, uniformly, impartially
E'vennefs, *n.* levelnefs, calmnefs, regularity, fame-
E'venfong, *n.* evening-worfhip, the evening (nefs
Event', *n.* an end, conclufion, iffue, confequence
Event'erate, *v. t.* to rip up or open the belly, *ob.*
Event'ful, *a.* full of incidents or changes
E'ventide, *n.* the time of the evening, even
Event'ilate, *v. t.* to winnow, fan, fift out, difcufs
Event'ual, *a.* confequential, refulting, accidental
Event'ually, *ad.* in the laft refult, in the end
Event'uate, *v. i.* to iffue, come to an end
Ev'er, *ad.* at any time, eternally, always, ftill
Everbub'bling, *a.* always boiling or rifing up
Everburn'ing, *a.* unextinguifhed, never put out

Everdúring, *a.* lafting always, eternal, endlefs
Ev'ergreen, *n.* a fhrub that is green all the year
Everhon'ored, *a.* always honored or refpected
Everlaft'ing, *n.* a plant of feveral fpecies
Everlaft'ing, *a.* perpetual, having no end, endlefs
Everlaft'ing, Everlaft'ingnefs, *n.* eternity, perpetuity
Everlaft'ingly, *ad.* eternally, without end
Everliv'ing, *a.* living ever or always, immortal
Evermóre, *ad.* eternally, without end, for ever
Everfe', Evert', *v. t.* to overthrow, fubvert, *ob.*
Ever'fion, *n.* the act of overthrowing, deftruction
Ev'ery, *a.* each, each one of all, belonging to all
Ev'erywhere, *ad.* in every place, in all places
Evict', *v. t.* to difpoffefs, take away, prove, fhow
Evict'ed, *pa.* taken away, proved, evinced, fhown
Evic'tion, *n.* ejection, proof, evidence, conviction
Ev'idence, *n.* a proof, teftimony, witnefs (fhow
Ev'idence, *v. t.* to prove, give teftimony, evince,
Ev'ident, *a.* plain, clear, apparent, notorious
Ev'idently, *ad.* plainly, clearly, certainly
E'vil, *a.* wicked, mifchievous, bad, ill, miferable
E'vil, E'vilnefs, *n.* wickednefs, calamity, difeafe
Evilaffect'ed, *a.* ill difpofed, malicious
Evildóer, *n.* one who does evil, a wicked perfon
Evilfavored, *a.* ill-countenanced, very ugly
Evilminded, *a.* malicious, mifchievous, vile
Evilfpeaking, *n.* defamation, flander, fcandal,
Evilwifh'ing, *a.* wifhing evil or harm (abufe
Evilwork'er, *n.* one who works wickednefs or ill
Evince', *v. t.* to prove, fhow, make plain, convict
Evin'cive, *a.* tending to prove, making plain
Evin'cible, *a.* demonftrable, capable of proof
Evis'cerate, *v. t.* to gut, embowel, fearch the bowels
Ev'itable, *a.* that may be avoided or efcaped
Ev'itate, *v. t.* to avoid, fhun, efcape, get off, *ob.*
Evocátion, *n.* the act of calling out, off or from
Evóke, *v. t.* to call out or upon, invoke, fummon
Evolátion, *n.* the act of flying out or away
Evolve', *v. t.* to unfold, difentangle, open, difclofe
Evolútion, *n.* a difplay, motion, extraction
Evul'fion, *n.* the act of plucking out or away
Ewe, *n.* a fhe-fheep, a female fheep
Ew'er, *n.* a jug to hold water to wafh with
Exacerbátion, *n.* the highth of a difeafe, a taunt
Exacerbes'cence, *n.* increafe of difeafe or fever fit
Exact', *a.* nice, accurate, methodical, punctual
Exact', *v. t.* to demand, require, extort, enjoin
Exact'ed, *pa.* demanded, extorted, impofed
Exact'er, *n.* a perfon who exacts, an extortioner
Exac'tion, *n.* a demand, extortion, fevere tax
Exact'ly, *ad.* nicely, fitly, accurately, punctually
Exact'nefs, *n.* nicety, accuracy, regularity, care
Exa"ggerate, *v. t.* to heap up, aggravate, enlarge
Exaggerátion, *n.* the act of heaping up, the act of
  enlarging, aggravation, addition, increafe
Exag'geratory, *a.* containing exaggeration
Exa"gitate, *v. t.* to ftir up, fhake, difquiet, purfue
Exalbúminous, *a.* without albumen or the white
Exalt', *v. t.* to lift up, raife, extol, magnify (part

Exaltátion, n. the act of raifing up, an elevation

Exam'in, v. t. to afk queitions, confider, try, look

Examinátion, n. difquifition, inquiry (over,fearch

Exam'inate, n. a perfon that is examined, ob.

Exam'inator, Exam'iner, n. one who examins

Examp'lary, a. ferving for example, ob.

Exam"ple, n. a pattern, copy, model, inftance

Exan"guious or Exan"guous, a. void of blood

Exan'imate, a. dead, lifelefs, fpiritlefs, dejected

Exanimátion, n. a deprivation of life or fenfe

Exanthem'atous, a. eruptive, efflorefcent

Exant'late, v. t. to draw out, exhauft, wafte, ob.

Exafp'erate, v.t. to vex, provoke, enrage, increafe

Exafperátion, n. a provocation, an exaggeration

Exauc'torate, v. t. to difmifs, to difcharge, ob.

Exauctorátion, n. a difmiffion, a degradation, ob.

Excal"ceated, a. deprived of fhoes, barefoot

Excandes'cence, n. heat, warmth, growing anger

Excantátion, n. difenchantment by countercharm

Ex'cavate, v. t. to hollow, to cut into hollows

Excavátion, n. a hollow made by art or force

Excéed, v. to furpafs, pafs or go beyond, excel

Excéeding, pa. a. furpaffing, exceffive, great

Excéeding, Exceed'ingly, ad. to a great degree

Excel', v. t. to furpafs, exceed, outdo, beat

Ex'cellence, n. fuperior greatnefs or goodnefs

Ex'cellency, n. great value, a title of honor given
    to public minifters, governors, &c.   (fine

Ex'cellent, a. eminent, having great value, very

Ex'cellently, ad. in a high degree, very well

Except', v. to leave or take out, exempt, object

Except'ing, pa. taking away, excluding

Excep'tion, n. an exclufion, objection, diflike, bar

Excep'tionable, a. liable to fome objection

Excep'tious, a. froward, peevifh, illnatured, crofs

Except'ive, a. including or having an exception

Except'lefs, a. neglecting exceptions, ob.

Except'or, n. one who excepts, one who objects

Excern', v.t. to ftrain out or from, fift, feparate

Excerpt', a. plucked off, cropt, picked, gathered

Excerp'tion, n. the act of gleaning, a felection

Excefs', n. fuperfluity, intemperance, violence

Excefs'ive, a. exceeding juft bounds, vehement

Excefs'ively, ad. exceedingly, eminently, vaftly

Exchange', v. t. to give one thing for another

Exchange', n. the act of bartering, a place of meet-
    ing for merchants, &c. a balance of money

Exchange'able, a. fit or proper to be exchanged

Exchangeabil'ity, n. the quality of being exchange-
    able

Exchang'er, n. a perfon who practifes or exchanges

Exche"quer, n. the place for the king's money, En.

Excife, n. a duty on goods paid by the merchant,
    manufacturer or retailer, or duty on the con-
    fumption

Excife, v. t. to fubject to the excife-duty, to levy

Excifeable, a. fit or liable to be excifed

Excifeman, n. a man who infpects excifed goods

Exci"fion, n. extirpation, deftruction, utter ruin

Excitátion, n. the act of ftirring up or moving

Excíte, v.t. to roufe; awaken, ftir up, move

Excítable, a. capable of being excited or ftimulated

Excitabil'ity, n. the quality of being fufceptible of
    excitement or ftimulation

Excítement, n. a motive to excite, a ftate of action

Excítant, n. that which promotes action

Excíter, n. one who or what excites

Excláim, v. i. to cry out or aloud, to rail againft

Excláim, Exclamátion, n. an outcry, clamor, mark

Excláimer, n. a perfon who exclaims or cries out

Exclam'atory, a. relating to exclamation   (hinder

Exclúde, v. t. to fhut out, debar, except againft

Exclúfion, n. a rejection, exception, difmiffion, bar

Exclúfive, a. independent, debarring, excepting

Exclúfively, ad. feparately, without taking in

Exclúfory, a. able to exclude or fhut out

Excoct', v.t. to boil up or much, to make by boiling

Exco"gitate, v. t. to invent, ftrike out, hit off

Excogitátion, n. a thought, device, invention, hit

Excom'miffary, n. a commiffary who is out of office

Excommúnicate, v. t. to exclude, put out, expel

Excommúnicate, a. put out of communion

Excommunicátion, n. an ecclefiaftical cenfure

Excóriate, v. t. to flay, ftrip off the fkin, bark

Excoriátion, n. a flaying, the lofs of fkin, plunder

Excorticátion, n. the act of pulling off the bark

Ex'crement, n. ufelefs matter difcharged from an-
    imal bodies

Excrement'al, a. voided as excrement, filthy

Excrementi"tious, a. confifting of excrement

Excres'cence, n. an irregular growth or tumor

Excres'cent, a. growing out irregularly

Excréte, v. t. to difcharge from the body by the
    pores or other paffages

Excre'tion, n. a difcharge by the paffages of the
    body, the matter difcharged

Ex'cretive, a. able or tending to eject excrements

Ex'cretory, a. able to throw off fuperfluous parts

Excrúciate, v. t. to torture, torment, pain, hurt

Excrúciate, Excrúciated, pa. tormented, hurt

Excrúciating, pa. torturing, very painful

Excubátion, n. the act of watching all night

Excul'pate, v. t. to excufe, clear, free, juftify

Exculpátion, n. excufe, juftification

Excul'patory, a. excufing, juftifying

Excur'fion, n. a digreffion, ramble, walk, journey

Excurs'ive, a. deviating, rambling, wandering, ro-

Excúfable, a. fit to be excufed, pardonable   (ving

Excúfablenefs, n. a pardonable ftate or quality

Excúfably, ad. in a manner to be excufed

Excúfatory, a. pleading or making an excufe

Excúfe, [f as z] v. t. to forgive, remit, free, leffen

Excúfe, Excufátion, n. a pardon, apology, plea

Excúfelefs, a. having no excufe, inexcufable

Excúfer, n. one who forgives, one who pleads for

Excufs', v.t. to feize by law, detain property, ob.

Excus"fion, n. the act of feizing or detaining, ob.

Exdirect'or, n. one who has been director

Ex'ecrable, a. curfed, abominable, vile, odious

Ex'ecrably, ad. curfedly, abominably, horridly

Ex'ecrate, v. t. to curfe, wifh ill to, abhor, deteft

Execrátion, n. a curfe, an imprecation of fome evil

Exect', v. t. to cut out, off or away, ob.

Ex'ecute, v. t. to perform, do, effect, put to death

Exec'utor, n. one who executes, one who is appointed by will to fettle an eftate

Execútion, n. a performance, feizure, death, writ

Execútioner, n. a man who puts the law in force

Exec'utive, a. having a power or tending to act

Exec'utive, n. executive power, or the perfon or council adminiftering a government

Exec'utor, n. one who performs the will of another

Exec'utorfhip, n. the office or ftate of an executor

Exec'utory, a. to be carried into effect in future

Exec'utrix, n. a female executor, a female truftee

Exeget'ical, a. explanatory, expofitory, clear, full

Exemp'lar, n. a copy, pattern, model, plan, example

Exemp'larily, ad. by way of example or terror

Exemp'lary, a. worthy of imitation or notice

Exemplificátion, n. a copy, example, illuftration

Exemp'lifier, n. one who exemplifies or fhows

Exemp'lify, v. t. to copy, illuftrate, fhow

Ex'empt, v. t. to privilege, to free

Exempt', a. free, not liable to

Exempt', n. one who is not fubject

Exemp'tion, n. a privilege, a freedom from

Ex'equies, n. pl. funeral rites, funeral folemnities

Exer'cent, a. exercifing, practifing, following

Ex'ercife, v. to employ, practice, ufe, labor, train

Ex'ercife, Exercitátion, n. employment, ufe, a tafk

Exer'gue, n. the fpace near the edge of a medal

Exert', v. t. to enforce, ftrive, ufe, employ, fhow

Exer'tion, n. an effort, ftruggle, ufe, act of exerting

Exéfion, n. the act of eating through, from or out

Exeftuátion, n. a boiling up, great heat

Exfóliate, v. to fhell, peel off, fcale off as a bone

Exfoliátion, n. a feparation of bad or carious bones

Exfóliative, a. caufing or tending to an exfoliation

Exhalátion, n. an evaporation, vapor, fume

Exhále, v. to draw or fend out, emit, breathe out

Exhálement, n. matter exhaled, a vapor, a fume

Exhauft', v. t. to drain, draw quite off, wafte, fpend

Exhauft'ible, a. that may be exhaufted or drained

Exhauft'ion, n. the act of exhaufting or draining

Exhauft'lefs, a. inexhauftible, endlefs

Exhib'it, n. a paper produced in evidence, a voucher

Exhib'it, v. t. to difplay, fhow, prefent, produce

Exhib'ited, pa. difplayed, fhown, produced, held

Exhib'iter, n. one who exhibits, one who fhows

Exhibi'tion, n. a fetting forth, difplay, allowance

Exhil'arate, v. t. to make cheerful, to gladden

Exhilarátion, n. the act of making glad or merry

Exhort', v. t. to advife, perfuade, incite, caution

Exhortátion, n. a perfuafive or cheering argument

Exhort'ative, Exhort'atory, a. tending to exhort

Exhort'er, n. one who exhorts, one who advifes

Exhumátion, n. a digging out of the earth what

has been buried

Ex'igence, n. neceffity, want, occafion, caufe

Ex'igent, n. a preffing bufinefs, occafion, end, writ

Ex'igible, a. demandable, requirable

Exigúity, n. fmallnefs, littlenefs, diminutivenefs

Exig'uous, a. fmall, little, diminutive

Ex'ile, Exílement, n. banifhment, a perfon banifhed

Ex'ile, v. t. to banifh, drive out or away, tranfport

Ex'ile, a. fmall, flender, thin, fine

Exilí'tion, n. a fpringing out, flendernefs

Exil'ity, n. flendernefs, finenefs, thinnefs

Eximani'tion, n. an emptying out, privation, ob.

Exift', v. i. to be, have a being, live, remain, ftay

Exift'ence, or Exift'ency, n. a ftate of being, life

Exift'ent, a. having or poffeffed of being (death

Ex'it, n. a going away or off, paffage, departure,

Ex'legiflátor, n. one lately a legiflator

Ex'odus, n. a departure from a place, the act of going out, title of the fecond book in the Bible

Exon'erate, v. t. to unload, difburden, difcharge from refponfibility

Exonerátion, n. a difburdening or unloading, eafe

Ex'orable, a. that may be moved by entreaty

Exor'bitance, n. extravagance, an exceffive wrong

Exor'bitant, exceffive, extravagant, unreafonable

Exor'bitate, v. i. to deviate, to go out of the way

Ex'orcife, v. t. to caft out evil fpirits, to adjure

Ex'orcifm, n. the act of exorcifing, conjuration

Ex'orcift, n. a cafter out of evil fpirits, a conjurer

Exor'dium, n. an introduction, a preamble

Exornátion, n. an ornament, an embelifhment

Exor'tive, a. relating to the eaft, rifing

Exofs'eous, a. bonelefs, wanting bones, foft, weak

Exot'eric, a. public, tranfacted abroad

Exot'ic, a. foreign; n. a foreign plant, fhrub or tree

Expand', v. to fpread, open, extend, diffufe

Expanfe', n. a wide extent or fpace, heaven

Expanfibil'ity, n. a capacity of being expanded

Expans'ible, a. that is capable of expanfion

Expans'ile, a. capable of expanding (fpace

Expan''fion, n. a fpreading out, extent, furface,

Expans'ive, a. able or tending to expand, wide

Expátiate, v. i. to enlarge upon, range at large, rove (country

Expat'riate, v. t. banifhed, withdrawn from one's

Expat'riate, v. t. to quit one's native country with a view of fettling in another, to banifh

Expat'riated, a. banifhed, living from one's home

Expatriátion, n. the act of leaving one's country for perpetuity

Expect', v. to look for, hope, wait for, ftay, attend

Expect'able, a. that may be expected or hoped

Expect'ancy, n. fomething that is expected, hope

Expect'ant, a. waiting in expectation or hope of

Expect'ant, Expect'er, n. one who expects or waits

Expectátion, n. a looking or waiting for, hope

Expect'orate, v. to caft from the breaft, to fpit up

Expectorátion, n. a difcharge by coughing, &c.

Expect'orant, n. that which promotes difcharges

L

from the breast

Expect'orative, a. promoting expectoration, easing

Expédience, n. fitnefs, propriety, difpatch, hafte

Expédient, a. fit, proper, fuitable, quick, ready

Expédient, n. a way, means, temporary advice, art

Expédiently, ad. fitly, fuitably, quickly, foon

Exped'itate, v. t. to cut out the balls of the foot

Ex'pedite, v. t. to facilitate, haften, difpatch, free

Ex'pedite, a. active, quick, ready, light-armed

Ex'peditely, ad. with quicknefs or readinefs, foon

Expedi'tion, n. fpeed, hafte, a warlike enterprife

Expedi'tious, a. quick, ready, active, alert, nimble

Expedi'tioufly, ad. quickly, foon, with difpatch

Expel', v. t. to drive out, force away, banifh, eject

Expel'lable, a. that may be expelled or driven out

Expend', v. t. to fpend, lay out, confume, wafte

Expend'iture, n. the act of expending, fum expended (wafte

Expenfe', n. money expended, charge, coft, lofs,

Expenfe'ful, a. expenfive, coftly, chargeable

Expenfe'lefs, a. free from expenfe, coft or charge

Expens'ive, a. given to expenfe, coftly, dear, lavifh

Expens'ively, ad. with or at great expenfe, lavifhly

Expens'ivenefs, n. coftlinefs, extravagance, wafte

Expérience, n. practice, knowledge by practice

Expérience, v. t. to know by practice, try, receive

Expérienced, pa. wife by long practice (trials

Expériencer, Exper'imenter, n. one who makes

Exper'iment, v. t. to try, to fearch out by trial

Experiment, n. the trial of any thing, effay, proof

Experiment'al, a. founded upon experiment, real

Experiment'alift, n. one who makes experiments

Experiment'ally, ad. by experience, by trial, really

Expert', a. fkilful, intelligent, ready, dexterous

Expert'ly, ad. fkilfully, readily, with dexterity

Expert'nefs, n. fkill, art, readinefs, dexterity

Ex'piable, that may be atoned for or fatisfied

Ex'piate, v. t. to atone for a crime, fatisfy, avert

Expiátion, n. an atonement, a fatisfaction

Ex'piatory, a. capable of expiating or atoning for

Expirátion, n. the act of breathing, an end, death

Expíre, v. to breathe out, exhale, die, end, clofe

Expláin, v. t. to illuftrate, clear up, fhow, expound

Expláinable, a. that is capable, of explanation

Expláiner, n. one who explains, one who clears up

Explanátion, n. illuftration, interpretation

Explan'atory, a. containing explanation, clearing

Ex'pletive, n. an occafional fyllable or word (up

Ex'plicable, a. that is poffible to be explained

Ex'plicate, v. t. to unfold, explain, clear up, fhow

Explicátion, n. a difplay, an explanation

Ex'plicative, a. tending to explain or clear up

Expli'cit, a. unfolded, plain, clear, open, exprefs

Expli'citly, ad. plainly, clearly, openly, directly

Explóde, v. t. to decry, hifs, reject, make a report

Exploit', n. a feat, an action; v. t. to perform

Explórate, Explóre, v. t. to fearch, examin, try

Explorátion, n. a clofe fearch, examination, trial

Explóratory, a. fearching out, examining, trying

Explórement, n. an exploration, fearch, trial, teft

Explófion, n. a difcharge of gunpowder, &c. noife

Explófive, a. driving out with great noife

Expórt, v. t. to carry or fend out of a country

Ex'port, n. any thing carried or fent out in traffic

Expórtable, a. that may be exported

Exportátion, n. the act of fending goods abroad

Expórter, n. one who fends goods abroad in trade

Expófe, v. t. to lay open or bare, caft out, fubject

Expofi'tion, n. an explanation, fituation, place

Expos'itor, n. an expounder, interpreter, clearer

Expos'tulate, v. i. to reafon, argue, debate, difpute

Expoftulátion, n. a reafoning with, debate, charge

Expos'tulatory, a. of or containing expoftulation

Expófure, n. a laying open, an expofed ftate

Expound', v. t. to interpret, explain, clear up, lay

Expound'er, n. an interpreter, an explainer (open

Expréfect, n. a prefect out of office

Exprefs', v. t. to declare, reprefent, fqueeze

Exprefs', a. plain, downright, full, clear, copied

Exprefs', n. a meffenger fent on a fpecial occafion, a fpecial meffage

Exprefs'ible, a. that may be uttered or fqueezed

Expres'fion, n. a preffing out, a form of fpeech

Exprefs'ive, a. proper to exprefs, full, ftrong, clear

Exprefs'ively, ad. in a full or ftrong manner, fully

Exprefs'ivenefs, n. the power of expreffing

Exprefs'ly, ad. in direct terms, plainly, clearly

Expres'fure, n. expreffion, utterance, form, ob.

Ex'probate, v. t. to upbraid, cenfure, blame, charge

Exprobrátion, n. reproach, cenfure, blame, charge

Exprópriate, v. t. to part with, give up a claim, ob.

Expugnátion, n. a taking by affault, a conqueft

Expulfe', v. t. to drive out, force away, expel, ob.

Expul'fion, n. an expelling or driving out, force

Expuls'ive, a. having power or tending to expel

Expunge', v. t. to blot or crofs out, erafe, efface

Expurgátion, n. the act of cleanfing, a purification

Expur'gatory, a. ufed in cleanfing or purifying

Ex'quifite, a. excellent, curious, choice, complete

Ex'quifitely, ad. nicely, perfectly, completely

Ex'quifitenefs, n. nicety, choicenefs, perfection

Exrep'refentative, n. one lately a reprefentative

Exfanguin'eous, Exfan'guious, a. bloodlefs or deftitute of red blood

Exfec'retary, n. one lately a fecretary

Exfec'tion, n. a feparation by cutting off or out

Exfert', a. ftanding forth, as ftamens above a corol

Exfen'ator, n. one who has been fenator

Exfibilátion, n. the act of hiffing off the ftage

Exfic'cant or Exic'cant, a. drying up, able to dry

Exfic'cate, v. t. to dry, to dry up or off

Exficcátion, n. a drying up, drynefs

Exfpui'tion, n. a fpitting, a difcharge by fpitting

Exftip'ulate, a. without ftipules

Exfuc'tion, n. the act of fucking out, off or from

Exfuffiátion, n. a blaft working up or under, ob.

Exfuf'folate, v. t. to whifper, buzz in the ear, ob.

Extacy or Ex'tafy, fee Ecftacy

Ex'tancy, n. a rifing, parts rifing above the reft
Ex'tant, a. now in being, ftanding in view
Extemp'oral, Extemporáneous, Extemp'orary, a.
　fudden, unpremeditated, without ftudy
Extemp'ore, ad. readily, without premeditation
Extemp'orize, v. i. to fpeak extempore or at once
Extend', v. t. to ftretch out, enlarge, increafe
Extend'er, n. one who or that which extends
Extend'ible or Extens'ible, a. capable of extenfion
Extenfibil'ity, n. capacity of being extended
Extens'ile, a. capacity of being extended
Exten'fion, n. the act of extending, enlargement
Extens'ive, a. extended far, wide, large, general
Extens'ively, ad. widely, largely, greatly, much
Extens'ivenefs, n. extent, widenefs, largenefs
Extent', n. a compafs, length, degree, execution
Exten'uate, v. t. to leffen, palliate, degrade, make
Extenuátion, n. a mitigation, a paliation　(thin
Extérior, a. outward, eEternal, foreign
Extérior, n. the outfide, that which appears (away
Exterm'inate, Exterm'in, v. t. to root out, to drive
Exterm'inatory, a. tending to exterminate
Extermination, n. a rooting out, deftruction, ruin
Exterm'ined, pa. rooted or caft out, deftroyed
Extern', Extern'al, a. outward, only in appearance
Extern'ally, ad. outwardly, in fhow
Exterráneous, a. foreign, coming from abroad
Exter'fion, n. the act of wiping or rubbing off
Extil', v. i. to drop out or from, to diftil from
Extillátion, n. the act of falling from in drops
Extim'ulate, v. t. to prick on, excite, ftir up, urge
Extimulátion, n. the power of raifing fenfation
Extinct', a. extinguifhed, abolifhed, at an end,
Extinc'tion, n. abolition, deftruction　(dead
Extin"guifh, v. to quench, put out, deftroy, obfcure
Extin"guifhable, a. that may be quenched or de-
Extin"guifher, n. a thing to put out candles (ftroyed
Extin"guifhment, n. an extinction, an abolition
Extirp', Ex'tirpate, v. t. to root up or out, to deftroy
Extirpátion, n. the act of rooting out, deftruction
Extirpátor, n. one who extirpates or roots out
Extifpi"cious, a. relating to entrails, augurial, ob.
Extol', v. t. to praife, cry up, magnify, exalt, raife
Extor'five, a. getting from by force, compulfive
Extort', v. to get by force, wreft, take too much
Extort'er, n. one who opprefles, an extortioner
Extor'tion, n. an unlawful exaction, oppreffion
Extor'tioner, n. one who practifes extortion
Ex'tract, n. a fubftance extracted, an abftract
Extract', v. t. to draw out of, felect, take, feparate
Extract'ed, Extraught', pa. taken from or out
Extrac'tion, n. a drawing out, lineage, defcent
Extract'ive, a. that may be extracted
Extradic'tionary, a. not verbal only, real, ob.
Extrafoliáceous, a. on the outfide of a leaf
Extragéneous, a. of or belonging to another kind
Extrajudi"cial, a. done out of the courfe of law
Extramis"fion, n. the act of fending outwards
Extramundáne, a. beyond the bounds of the world

Extráneous, a. foreign, ftrange, outward, unlike
Extraor'dinarily, Extraor'dinary, ad. uncommonly
Extraor'dinarinefs, n. remarkablenefs, eminence
Extraor'dinary, a. more than common, remarkable
Extraparóchial, [ch as k] a. not in a parifh
Extraprofes'fional, a. foreign from ones profeffion
Extrareg'ular, a. not fubject to rule　(rage
Extrav'agance, n. wafte, fuperfluous expenfe, out-
Extrav'agant, a. wafteful, lavifh, expenfive, wild
Extrav'agantly, ad. in an extravagant manner
Extrav'agantnefs, n. extravagance, excefs, wafte
Extrav'afated, a. forced out of the proper veffels
Extravafátion, n. the act of being let out of veffels
Extravéaate, a. let out of or from the veins, ob.
Extraver'fion, n. the act of throwing out, ob.
Extréme, a. greateft, moft, utmoft, higheft, laft
Extréme, n. the utmoft point, an extremity
Extrémely, ad. in the utmoft degree, greatly, very
Extrémeft, a. the moft extreme, utmoft, higheft
Extrém'ity, n. the utmoft part, excefs, mifery
Ex'tricate, v. t. to difentangle, fet free, deliver
Extricátion, n. the act of difentangling or freeing
Extrins'ic, a. outward, external, foreign, ftrange
Extrins'ically, ad. outwardly, from without
Extruct', v. t. to build, raife, erect, form, make
Extrúde, v. t. to pufh or thruft off to drive out
Extrúfion, n. the act of thrufting out, off or from
Extúberance, n. a protuberant part, knob, knot
Extumes'cence, n. a fwelling on the body, a knob
Exúberance, n. an overgrowth, luxuriance, plenty
Exúberant, a. fuperfluous, abundant, plenteous
Exúberantly, ad. abundantly, plentifully, fully
Exúberate, v. i. to abound greatly, to overflow
Ex'udate, Exúde, v. i. to fweat out, to difcharge
Exudátion, n. a fweating out, fweat
Exul'cerate, v. t. to make fore, earage, fret
Exulcerátion, n. the act of making fore, forenefs
Exult', v. i. to rejoice above meafure, to triumph
Exult'ance, Exultátion, n. joy, tranfport, triumph
Exundátion, n. an overflow, great abundance, ob.
Exúperance, n. an overbalance, ob.
Exúviæ, n. pl. caft fkins, fpoils from an enemy
Ey'as, n. a young hawk juft taken from its neft
Eye, n. the organ of fight, view, face, a hole, a bud
Eye, v. to watch, obferve, view, appear, fhow
Eyeball, n. the ball or apple of the eye
Eyebright, n. a fpecies of plant, euphrafia
Eyebrow, n. the hair that grows juft over the eye
Eyedrop, n. what drops from the eye, a tear
Eyeglafs, n. a glafs ufed to help the fight, in tel-
　efcopes, the glafs next to the eye
Eyelafh, n. the hair upon the edge of the eyelid
Eyelefs, a. having no eyes, not feeing, blind
Eyelet-hole, n. a fmall hole for light or lace
Eyelid, n. that which clofes or fhuts up the eye
Eyefhot, n. a fight, glance, tranfient view
Eyefight, n. the fight of the eye, the fenfe of feeing
Eyefore, n. fomething offenfive to the fight
Eyeftring, n. the ftring or tendon, of the eye

Eyetooth, n. the tooth next to the grinders
Eyewink, n. a wink made as a hint, sign or token
Eyewitness, n. one who saw what he attests
Eyre, n. the court going on the circuits, a circuit
Eyry, n. a place where birds build nests, a nest

F

FABIAN, a. in imitation of Fabius, delaying
Fable, n. an instructive fiction, story, tale, lie
Fable, v. to feign, invent, devise, frame, lie
Fabled, pa. told in fables, feigned (form
Fabric, n. a building, a system; v. t. to build, to
Fabricate, v. t. to build, construct, forge, devise
Fabrication, n. the act of framing or forging
Fabulist, n. a person who writes or invents fables
Fabulous, a. feigned, invented, forged, false
Fabulously, ad. in fiction, feignedly, falsely
Face, n. a visage, front, appearance, boldness, surface
Face, v. t. to oppose, to meet or cover in front
Facepainting, n. the art of drawing portraits
Facet, n. a small surface or face
Facetious, a. affable, gay, cheerful, merry, witty
Facetiously, ad. affably, merrily, wittily (lery
Facetiousness, n. affability, cheerfulness, wit, drol-
Facial, a. pertaining to a band and a pair of nerves
Facile, a. easy to be done, flexible, pliant
Facilitate, v. t. to make easy, lessen, clear
Facilitation, n. the act of making easy
Facility, n. easiness, ease, readiness, quickness
Facilities, n. pl. means to promote or render easy
Facinerious, Facinorous, a. wicked, very bad, vile
Facing, pa. fronting, set over against, opposit to
Facing, n. an ornamental covering in front
Fact, n. an act, action, deed, reality, truth, product
Faction, n. a party, tumult, sedition, discord
Factionary, n. a factious person, a partyman, ob.
Factious, a. given to faction, seditious, loud, noisy
Factiously, ad. in a factious manner, seditiously
Factitious, a. made by art, artificial, counterfeit
Factor, n. an agent for another, deputy, substitute
Factory, n. a body, or place of merchant-agents, a manufactory
Faculty, n. ability, power, talent, privilege, body
Facundity, n. eloquence, readiness of speech
Faddle, v. i. to trifle, idle, toy, play the fool
Fade, v. to wither, decay, grow weak, lose color
Fadge, v. i. to agree, fit, suit, become, succeed
Fady, a. tending to fade or decay, pale, weak
Fag, v. to labor, toil, work, tire, beat
Fag, Fag'end, n. the worst part or loose end
Fagot, n. a bundle of wood, nominal soldier, mark
Fagot, v. t. to make fagots, tie up, bind, bundle
Fagout, v. i. to become loose or untwisted
Fail, v. to break in business, be deficient or short, miss, perish, die, desert, neglect
Failing, Failure, n. a becoming insolvent, deficiency, defect, omission, fault
Fain, a. glad, merry, obliged; ad. gladly, fondly
Faint, v. to swoon, sink, grow feeble, deject
Faint or Fainty, a. languid, low, weak, cowardly

Fainthearted, Faintling, a. cowardly, timorous
Faintheartedly, ad. timorously, dejectedly
Fainting, n. a short loss of animal motion
Faintish, a. rather faint or low, ready to faint
Faintishness, n. a slight weakness, a lowness
Faintly, ad. feebly, imperfectly, without color
Faintness, n. feebleness, a want of spirit or life
Faints, n. grofs and fetid oil [W. Indies]
Fair, a. beautiful, white, clear, not cloudy, just
Fair, ad. gently, civilly, happily, on good terms
Fair, n. the female sex, a free market, honesty
Fairing, n. a gift or present made at a fair
Fairly, ad. honestly, justly, openly, duly, clearly
Fairness, n. beauty, whiteness, honesty, candor
Fairspoken, a. courteous, in speech, civil
Fairy, n. a very small phantom, elf, enchantress
Fairy, a. given by fairies, belonging to fairies
Faith, n. belief, fidelity, honesty, truth, promise
Faithbreach, n. a breach of faith, treachery, deceit
Faithed, Faithful, a. firm to the truth, trusty, loyal
Faithfully, ad. honestly, sincerely, truly, steadily
Faithfulness, n. honesty, sincerity, loyalty, truth
Faithless, a. unbelieving, false, base, vile, disloyal
Faithlessness, n. unbelief, treachery, deceit, fraud
Fake, n. a coil of a rope, a single turn of a cable
Fakir, [a as in ask] n. a monk in India, very austere
Falcate, a. hooked, crooked, bent like a sythe
Falcation, n. crookedness, a cutting or mowing
Falchion or Fau'chion, n. a short crooked sword
Falcon, n. a large kind of hawk, a sort of cannon
Falconer, n. one who breeds or trains up hawks
Falconer, n. a small falcon or cannon
Falconry, n. a training up or fowling with hawks
Fall, v. fell, pret. fallen, pa. to tumble, drop, cut down, sink, decrease, revolt
Fall, n. the act of falling, descent, disgrace, ruin
Fallacious, a. deceitful, producing a mistake
Fallaciously, ad. deceitfully, treacherously, craftily
Fallaciousness, n. a tendency to deceive or cheat
Fallacy, n. deceit, fraud, guile, sophistry
Fallibility, n. a liableness to be deceived or err
Fallible, a. liable to error or mistake, frail
Falling, n. a sinking, fall, error, sin
Falling-sickness, n. a kind of disease, the epilepsy
Fallow, v. i. to plow in order to plow again (rest
Fallow, a. uncultivated, unoccupied; n. ground at
Fallowness, n. a fallow state, rest, barrenness
False, [a as o] a. untrue, deceitful, dishonest, base
Falsehearted, a. treacherous, deceitful, false, base
Falsely, ad. erroneously, treacherously, basely
Falseness, n. falsehood, deceit, mistake, baseness
Falsehood, Falsity, n. a lie, cheat, want of truth
Falsific, a. making false, dealing falsely, base
Falsification, n. the act of falsifying, a confutation
Falsifier, n. a person who falsifies or forges, a liar
Falsify, v. to counterfeit, forge, lie, break
Falter, [a as o] v. i. to stammer, hesitate, fail
Faltering, pa. stammering, hesitating, failing
Falteringly, ad. with hesitation or difficulty, badly

Fame, *n.* reputation, renown, glory, report, talk
Famed, *a.* renowned, noted, much talked of
Famelefs, *a.* having no fame, obfcure, unknown
Famil'iar, *a.* intimate, affable, free, common
Famil'iar, *n.* an intimate acquaintance, a demon
Familiar'ity, *n.* intimacy, eafy intercourfe
Famil'iarize, *v.* to habituate, to accuftom
Famil'iarly, *ad.* intimately, without formality
Fam'ilift, *n.* one of the fect named family of love
Fam'ily, *n.* a houfehold, lineage, tribe, race, clafs
Fam'ine or Fam'in, *n.* a dearth, a want of fufficient food for the inhabitants of a country
Fam'ifh, *v.* to ftarve, to kill or die with hunger
Fam'ifhment, *n.* a want of food, hunger, thirft
Famous, *a.* renowned, noted, diftinguifhed, great
Famoufly, *ad.* with great renown, cleverly, well
Fan, *n.* an inftrument ufed by the ladies to cool themfelves, an inftrument to winnow corn
Fan, *v. t.* to blow or winnow with a fan, to cool
Fanat'ic, *n.* an enthufiaft, one very ftrongly bigoted
Fanat'ic, Fanat'ical, *a.* enthufiaftic, frantic
Fanat'icifm, *n.* enthufiafm, religious frenzy
Fan'ciful, *a.* imaginative, whimfical, ftrange, odd
Fan'cifully, *ad.* in a fanciful manner, ftrangely
Fan'cifulnefs, *n.* a fanciful difpofition or temper
Fan'cy, *n.* imagination, whim, inclination, mind
Fan'cy, *v. t.* to imagin, fuppofe, think, long for
Fan'cymonger, *n.* a dealer in tricks of imagination
Fan'cyfick, *a.* difordered in the imagination
Fane, *n.* a temple, a church, *ufed in poetry*
Fanfaronáde, *n.* a bluster, parade, *not ufed*
Fang, *n.* a long tufk, talon, nail; *v. t.* to feize
Fang'ed, *pa.* furnifhed with or having fangs
Fan''gle, *n.* a foolifh attempt, a trifling fcheme
Fan''gled, *a.* vainly fond of novelty, dreffed up
Fang'lefs, *a.* toothlefs, having no teeth, very old
Fan'nel, *n.* a fort of fcarf worn on a prieft's arm
Fan'ner, *n.* one who fans, one who plays a fan
Fant'afied, *a.* filled with fancies, very whimfical
Fant'afm, *n.* an idle conceit, whim, fantom
Fantas'tic, Fantas'tical, *a.* whimfical, fanciful
Fantas'tically, *ad.* whimfically, capricioufly, oddly
Fantas'ticalnefs, *n.* whimficalnefs, oddnefs
Fant'afy, *n.* fancy, conceit, humor, inclination
Fant'om, *n.* a fpecter, a ghoft, fomething imagin-
Fap, *a.* fuddled, drunk, *ob.* (ary
Far, *a.* a great way off, diftant; *ad.* afar, from afar
Far, *n.* a diftant place, a litter of pigs
Farce, *n.* a mock-comedy; *v. t.* to ftuff, to paint
Far'cical, *a.* belonging to a farce, foolifh, droll
Farc'tate, *a.* ftuffed, full, crouded
Far'cy, *n.* a kind of infectious leprofy in horfes
Fard, *n.* a kind of paint; *v. t.* to paint, to adorn
Fard'el, *n.* a little pack or bundle, a packfaddle
Fare, *n.* provifions, food, diet, the hire of carriage
Fare, *v. i.* to be in a ftate good or bad, to live
Barewel, *ad.* adieu; *n.* a parting compliment, leave
Far'fetch, *n.* a farfetched thought, wile, fhift, art
Far'fetched, *a.* forced, brought from afar, dear

Far'in, *n.* the meal of grain, the pollen of anther
Farináceous, *a.* mealy, refembling or like meal
Farm, *n.* land occupied by a farmer; in *America,* a tract of land cultivated by one man, or containing what is fuitable for cultivation, as arable, pafture, &c. whether freehold or under leafe
Farm, *v. t.* to leafe or rent, to let for a price
Farm'er, *n.* one who takes land on leafe, the owner who cultivates land, one who takes other things on rent
Farm'ing, *n.* the act of cultivating lands
Far'moft, *a.* moft diftant or remote, laft of all
Far'nefs, *n.* diftance, remotenefs, fpace, way, extent
Far'piercing, *a.* piercing deep or a great way
Farra''ginous, *a.* formed of very different materials
Farrágo, *n.* a confufed heap, medley, hodgepodge
Far'rier, *n.* a man who fhoes horfes, a horfedoctor
Far'riery, *n.* the art of fhoeing or curing horfes
Far'row, *n.* a litter of pigs; *v. t.* to bring forth pigs
Far'row, *a.* barren, not bearing young, [a corruption of *fallow*]
Far'ther, *a.* being at a greater diftance, longer
Far'ther, *ad.* and *conj.* more remotely, moreover
Far'ther, *v. t.* to promote, fee *furthr*
Far'therance, *n.* advancement, encouragement, *ob.*
Far'thermore, *ad.* befides, moreover, likewife, *ob.*
Far'theft, *a.* at or to the greateft diftance, the laft
Far'thing, *n.* the fourth part of a penny
Far'thingale, *n.* an old kind of hoop, a kind of ruff
Far'thingfworth, *n.* what is fold for a farthing
Fas'ces, *n. pl.* rods carried before confuls, &c.
Fas'cial, *a.* belonging to the fafces
Fas'ciate, *a.* bundled, growing in a bundle
Fafciátion, *n.* the act or art of tying up, a bandage
Fas'cicle, *n.* a little bundle
Fafcic'ular, *a.* of or relating to a bundle
Fafcic'ularly, *ad.* in form of a bundle
Fafcic'ulate, *a.* growing in bundles
Fas'cinate, *v. t.* to bewitch, enchant, charm
Fafcinátion, *n.* a bewitching, an enchantment
Fafcíne or Fafcéne, *n.* a bundle of faggots
Fas'cinous, *a.* acting or done by witchcraft
Fafh'ion, *more correctly* Fafh'on, *n.* form, cuftom, mode, tafte, fort, rank
Fafh'ion, *v. t.* to form, mo'd, figure, caft, adapt
Fafh'ionable, *a.* being in the fafhion or mode, fine
Fafh'ionablenefs, *n.* a modifh elegance, fmartnefs
Fafh'ionably, *ad.* agreeably to the mode, finartly
Fafh'ioned, *pa.* formed, made, adapted, fitted
Fafh'ioner, *n.* one that fafhions or forms, a fop
Fas'fet, *n.* a tap for drawing liquors
Faft, [a as in afk] *v. i.* to abftain from all food
Faft, *n.* an abftinence from all food, a day fet apart for fatting, that which faftens
Faft, *a.* firm, fixed, fure, fpeedy; *ad.* firmly, foon
Faft'en, *v.* to make faft, fecure, fix, link, join
Faft'ener, *n.* one who faftens or fixes
Faft'ening, *pa.* making faft; *n.* what faftens or fe-
Faft'er, *n.* one who abftains from all food (cures

Fail'handed, a. covetous, niggardly, mean, close

Faitid'ioufnefs, n. haughtinefs, fqueamifhnefs

Faitid'ious, a. fqueamifh, nice, difdainful, proud

Faftid'ioufly, ad. fqueamifhly, nicely, difdainfully

Faiti"giate, a. proportioned in length fo as to form an even furface, as the footftalks of a flower

Faft'ingday, Faft'day, n. a day of fafting, a faft

Faft'nefs, n. a firmnefs, fecurity, ftrong place, hold

Fat, n. the oily part of flefh, fometimes ufed for vat. In Britain, a certain meafure

Fat, v. to make or grow fat, fatten, feed, increafe

Fat, Fat'ty, a. plump, flefhy, grofs, greafy, rich

Fatal, a. deadly, mortal, deftructive, neceffary

Fatalifin, n. the doctrin of fate or neceffity

Fatalift, n. one who holds a fatality or neceffity

Fatal'ity, n. a decree of fate, a tendency to danger

Fatally, ad. mortally, deftructive, neceffarily

Fate, n. deftiny, deftruction, death, event, caufe

Fated, a. decreed by fate, deftined, doomed, fet

Fath'er, [a as in afk] n. one who begets a child, a parent, an old man, a protector

Fath'er, v. t. to adopt a child, affign, afcribe

Fath'erhood, n. the character or ftate of a father

Fatherlafh'er, n. a fifh with a large head, armed with fpines

Fath'erlefs, a. having no father, deftitute, lonely

Fath'erlinefs, n. the tendernefs of a father

Fath'er'ly, a. like a father, tender, kind, careful

Fath'erly, ad. in the manner of a father

Fath'om, n. fix feet, compafs, penetration, reach

Fath'om, v. t. to compafs, found, try, penetrate

Fath'omlefs, a. bottomlefs, impenetrable, fecret

Fatid'ic. Fatid'ical, a. prophetical, foretelling

Fatigue, [fatégue] n. wearinefs, labor, toil, work

Fatigue, Fat'igate, v. t. to tire, weary, perplex

Fatis'cence, n. a gaping open, a ftate of being chinky

Fatkid'neyed, a. fat, grofs, plump, large, heavy

Fat'ling, n. a lamb or kid that is fed for facrifice

Fat'ner, n. one who or that which gives increafe

Fat'nefs, n. plumpnefs, fat, greafe, fruitfulnefs

Fat'ten, v. to make or grow fat, plump, enrich

Fatuity, n. foolifhnefs, weaknefs, ftupidity

Fat'uous, a. weak, ftupid, foolifh, filly, impotent

Fat'witted, a. dull, heavy, ftupid, grofs, thick

Fau'cet or Fas'set, n. a tap to put into a barrel

Fault, [foit] n. a crime, offenfe, miftake, blemifh

Fault'er, n. one who commits a fault, an offender

Fault'ily, ad. in a faulty or improper manner

Fault'inefs, n. badnefs, wickednefs, evil, defect

Fault'lefs, a. having no fault, perfect, complete

Fault'y, a. guilty of a fault, bad, wrong, defective

Faun'ic, a. wild, ruftic, rude, artlefs, plain

Favil'lous, a. confifting of or refembling afhes

Favor, v. t. to countenance, fupport, affift, befriend, fpare, eafe, refemble

Favor, n. countenance, fupport, kindnefs, refemblance, a knot of ribands upon a hat, &c.

Favorable, a. propitious, kind, gracious, tender

Favorablenefs, n. a favorable ftate or quality, favor

Favorably, ad. in a favorable or kind manner

Favored, pa. helped, fpared, regarded, featured

Favorer, Faut'or, n. one who favors or regards

Favorite, n. one particularly loved, a near friend

Favoritifm, n. a difpofition to aid friends to the prejudice of others having equal claims, partiality, the act of favoring

Fawn, v. i. to footh, to flatter; n. a young deer

Fawn'er, n. one who fawns, one who flatters

Fawn'ing, pa. cringing, flattering, fondling

Fawn'ingly, ad. in a cringing manner, meanly

Fax'ed, a. hairy, rough, coarfe, frightful, ob.

Fay, n. a fairy, an elf, [faith, ob.]

Fay, v. i. to fit or join clofely

Fayence', n. potters ware called delf

Féa'ty, n. homage, fubmiffion, fidelity, loyalty

Fear, n. the expectation of evil, apprehenfion, reverence, anxiety, folicitude

Fear, v. to expect evil, apprehend, ftand in awe of

Féarful, a. timorous, afraid, awful, terrible

Féarfully, ad. timorously, dreadfully, awfully

Féarfulnefs, n. timoroufnefs, fear, dread, terror

Féarlefs, a. free from fear, undaunted, very bold

Féarlefsly, ad. in a fearlefs manner, very boldly

Feafibil'ity, n. practicability, poffibility

Féafible, a. practicable, performable, poffible

Feaft, n. a fumptuous meal, treat or entertainment

Feaft, v. to eat or entertain fumptuoufly, to pamper

Féafter, n. one who feeds delicioufly, an epicure

Féaftful, a. luxurious, feftive, gay, joyful, riotous

Féaftrite, n. the cuftom obferved at a feaft, ob.

Feat, n. an action, exploit, trick; a. nice, dexterous

Féater, a. neater, nicer, prettier, quicker, readier

Feath'er or Feth'er, n. a plume, covering of birds, ornament or badge of honor

Feath'er, v. t. to cover with plumes or plumage

Feath'erdriver, n. a perfon who cleans feathers

Feath'ered, Feath'ery, a. covered with feathers

Feath'eredged, a. made thin or floped on one fide

Feath'erlefs, a. having no feathers, naked, bare

Féatly, ad. neatly, nimbly, dexteroufly, ob.

Féature, n. the caft, &c. of the face; v. t. to be like

Febrifácient, a. caufing fever

Febrifácient, n. any thing producing fever

Feb'rifuge, n. a medicin ferving to cure a fever

Fébrile, a. relating or belonging to a fever, hot

Feb'ruary, n. the fecond month in the year

Februátion, n. a facrifice or prayer for the dead

Féces, n. dregs, lees, excrement

Fécal, a. containing or belonging to dregs

Fec'ulence, n. muddinefs, foulnefs, fediment, lees

Fec'ulent, a. muddy, foul, dreggy, full of dregs

Fec'ulum, n. a dry, dufty, taftelefs fubftance obtained from plants

Fécund, a. fruitful, plentiful, abundant, rich

Fécundate, v. t. to make fruitful or prolific

Fecundátion, n. the act of making fruitful or rich

Fecund'ity, n. fruitfulnefs, abundance, fluency

Fed, pret. and pa. of to feed

Fed'ary, Fed'erary, *n.* a confederate, partner, dependant

Fed'eral, *a.* of or relating to a league or compact

Fed'eral, Fed'eralift, *n.* a friend to the Conftitution of the U. States

Fed'erate, *a.* confederate, leagued, united, joined

Federátion, *n.* the act of uniting in a league

Fed'erative, *a.* uniting in a confederacy

Fee, *n.* a reward, perquifite, perpetual right, claim

Fee, *v. t.* to retain, engage, bribe, pay, hire, fan

Fee'ble, *a.* weak, fickly, infirm; *v. t.* to weaken

Fee'bled, *pa.* enfeebled, made weak or infirm

Fee'blenefs, *n.* weaknefs, infirmity, helpleffnefs

Fee'bly ,*ad.* weakly, faintly, without ftrength

Feed, *v.* fed, *pret.* fed, *pa.* to fupply with food, nourifh, fatten, eat, live

Feed, *n.* food, food for cattle, meat, pafture

Féeder, *n.* one who gives food, eats or encourages

Feel, *v.* felt, *pret.* felt, *pa.* to perceive by the touch, handle, try, grope, know

Feel, *n.* the fenfe or act of feeling, the touch

Féeler, *n.* a perfon who feels, the horn of an infect

Féeling, *pa. a.* handling, groping, humane

Féeling, *n.* fenfibility, humanity, tendernefs, love

Féelingly, *ad.* with great fenfibility, tenderly

Feet, *n. pl.* of foot

Féetlefs, *a.* void or deftitute of feet, helplefs

Feign, [fane] *v.* to pretend, devife, invent, make

Feign'ed, *pa.* pretended, devifed, diffembled, falfe

Feign'edly, *ad.* in fiction, with or by diffimulation

Feign'er, *n.* a diffembler, inventor, contriver, forger

Feint, [faint] *n.* a falfe fhow, pretenfe

Fell'citate, *v. t.* to congratulate, to make happy

Felicitátion, *n.* a congratulation, a good wifh, joy

Feli'city, *n.* happinefs, bleffednefs, joy, profperity

Féline, *a.* pertaining to cats, and their kind

Fell, *a.* fierce, cruel, favage, bloody,; *n.* a fkin

Fell, *v. t.* to knock or beat down, to cut down

Fell, *pret.* of *to fall*

Fel'ler, *n.* one who fells, one who cuts down

Fell'monger, *n.* a dealer in the fkins of fheep

Fell'ow, *n.* an affociate, equal, mean man, rafcal

Fell'ow, *v. t.* to match, pair, fuit, agree, fit

Fellowcréature, *n.* a creature of like nature

Fellowféeling, *n.* fympathy, care, joint intereft

Fellowhéir, *n.* a joint or common heir

Fellowlaborer, *n.* one laboring for the fame end

Fell'owlike, *a.* like a companion or friend, kind

Fellowferv'ant, *n.* one having the fame mafter

Fell'owfhip, *n.* fociety, intercourfe, connexion, partnerfhip, a ftation in a college

Fellowfóldier, *n.* one having the fame commander

Fellowftúdent, *n.* one who ftudies with another

Fellowfuf'ferer, *n* one fharing in the fame evils

Fell'y, *ad.* fiercely, cruelly, favagely, brutally

Fell'y, *n.* the rim of a wheel

Fel'o-de-fé, *n.* a felf-murderer, one who kills himfelf

Fel'on, *n.* one who is guilty of felony (felf

Fel'on, Felónious, *a.* villanous, wicked, vile, cruel

Felónioufly, *ad.* in a felonious or bafe manner

Fel'ony, *n.* a capital crime, a very hainous offenfe

Fel'fite, *n.* compact felfpar, a filiceous ftone

Fel'fpar *n.* a fpecies of filiceous ftone of a flefh red, gray or whitifh color, or brownifh yellow

Felt, *pret.* and *pa.* of *to feel*

Felt, *v. t.* to unite or join wool, &c. by fulling

Felt, *n.* a kind of ftuff made by fulling wool, or wool and fur, a hat fo made

Fel'ter, *v. t.* to clot together like felt, *ob.*

Feluc'ca, *n.* a fmall veffel with lateen fails and oars

Fel'wort, *n.* a fpecies of plant, gentian

Fémale, *n.* the fex which bears young

Fémale, Fem'inine, *a.* belonging to the female, effeminate, kind, tender, foft, delicate, weak

Feminal'ity, *n.* female nature, a female ftate, *ob.*

Fem'oral, *a.* belonging or relating to the thigh

Fen, *n.* a marfh, morafs, bog, flat and moift land

Fence, *n.* a guard, fecurity, inclofure, hedge

Fence, *v.* to practice fencing, guard, defend, inclofe

Fence'lefs, *a.* void of inclofure, open, expofed

Fen'cer, *n.* one who teaches or practices fencing

Fen'cible, *a.* capable of defenfe, able to defend

Fen'cibles, *n.* foldiers fo called

Fen'cing, *n.* the art or act of defenfe by weapons

Fen'cingmafter, *n.* a perfon who teaches fencing

Fend, *v.* to keep off, fhut out, fhift off, difpute

Fend'er, *n.* a fecurity againft cinders, &c.

Fenerátion, *n.* ufury, increafe by ufury, intereft, *ob.*

Fen'nel, *n.* a plant of feveral kinds

Fen'ny, *a.* marfhy, boggy, inhabiting a marfh

Fen'ugreek, *n.* a plant, trigonella

Féodal, *a.* held from another, *fee* feudal

Feoff, *v. t.* to inveft with the fee of lands

Fcoffée, *n.* one who is vefted with the fee of land

Feoff'er, *n.* one who gives a fee to another

Feoff'ment, *n.* a granting or giving of a fee

Ferácious, *a.* fruitful, plentiful, abundant

Fera''city, *n.* fruitfulnefs, plenty, abundance

Féral, *a.* gloomy, difmal, fad, deadly, mortal

Feriátion, *n.* the act of keeping holyday, *ob.*

Férine, *a.* wild, favage, barbarous, cruel, bafe

Ferinenefs, Fer'ity, *n.* wildnefs, barbarity, cruelty

Fer'ment, *n.* an inward motion, tumult, riot

Ferment', *v.* to work as leaven on beer, to rife

Ferment'able, *a.* fufceptible of fermentation

Ferment'al, Ferment'ative, *a.* caufing to ferment

Fermentátion, *n.* a fwelling or working, heat

Fern, *n.* a genus of plants very numerous

Fern'y, *a.* overgrown with or having fern

Feró'cious, *a.* favage, fierce, ravenous, rapacious

Feróciounefs, *n.* favage fiercenefs and cruelty

Fero''city, *n.* favagenefs, cruelty, fiercenefs, fury

Fer'reous, *a.* made of or like iron (drive out

Fer'ret, *n.* a fmall animal, a filk tape; *v. t.* to

Fer'ric acid is the acid of iron faturated with oxygene

Fer'riage, *n.* the fare or toll for paffing a ferry

Ferrical'cite, *n.* a calcareous earth combined with

Fer'rilite, *n.* a variety of trap, containing iron (iron

Ferrúginous, *a.* partaking of or like iron, rusty

Fer'rule, *n.* a ring put at the end of a stick, &c.

Fer'ry, *n.* a place for passing a river or lake,[a boat, *but in this sense not used with us*]

Fer'ry, *v. t.* to convey over water in a boat

Fer'ryman, *n.* one who keeps or plies at a ferry

Fer'tile, *a.* fruitful, abundant, plenteous, rich

Fer'tilize, *v. t.* to make fruitful, to enrich

Fertil'ity, *n.* fruitfulness, abundance, plenty

Fer'vency, *n.* heat, warmth, ardor, eagerness, zeal

Fer'vent, *a.* hot, ardent, vehement, eager, zealous

Fer'vently, *ad.* hotly, warmly, vehemently, eagerly

Ferves'cent, *a.* growing hot or warm, warm

Fer'vid, *a.* hot, vehement, eager, zealous, boiling

Fer'vidness, Fer'vor, *n.* heat, passion, spirit, zeal

Ferulâceous, *a.* like or pertaining to reed or cane

Fer'ule, *n.* a wooden slapper used in schools

Fes'cue, *n.* a thing used to point out letters

Fes'tal, *a.* relating to feasts, joyous, gay

Fés'ter, *v. i.* to corrupt, rot, suppurate, rankle

Fes'tinate, *a.* hasty, rash, hurried, *ob.*

Fes'tinately, *ad.* hastily, speedily, *ob.* (day

Fes'tival, *n.* a feast, solemn day, anniversary, holy-

Fes'tival, Fes'tive, *a.* pertaining to feasts, joyous

Festiv'ity, *n.* joyfulness, mirth, gaiety, a festival

Festoon', *n.* a garland, wreath, border of flowers

Fest'ucous, *a.* formed of or resembling straw, *ob.*

Fet, *n.* a piece, bit, part, portion, quantity, *ob.*

Fetch, *v. t.* to go and bring a thing, to reach

Fetch, *n.* a stratagem, artifice, art, trick, pretense

Fet'id, *a.* rank, strong, offensive to the smell

Fet'idness, *n.* a fetid quality, an offensive smell

Fetif'erous, *a.* producing young, bearing fruit

Fétor, *n.* a stink, offensive or bad smell, nastiness

Fet'ter, *v. t.* to chain, shackle, bind, tie, fasten

Fet'ter, *n.* a chain for the feet of felons, &c.

Fet'tle, *v. i.* to trifle, idle, loiter, do idly, *ob.*

Fétus, *pl.* fetuses, *n.* an animal from the time its parts are distinctly formed to its birth

Feud, *n.* a quarrel, contention, hatred, broil

Feud or Feod, *n.* land or right held of a superior on condition of rendering to him military service or other duty

Feúdal, *a.* held from a lord ; *n.* dependance, fee

Feúdalism, *n.* the system of feudal tenures

Feúdatory, *n.* one who holds from a lord

Féver, *n.* a disease, heat ; *v. t.* to put into a fever

Féverfew, *n.* a plant, wild wormwood

Féverish, Féverous, Fé'very, *a.* tending to or troubled with a fever, burning, hot, too hot

Feúillage, *n.* a bunch or row of leaves in carving

Few, *a.* not many, belonging to a small number

Few'el, *see* Fuel

Few'ness, *n.* smallness or defect of number

Fib, *n.* a lie, falsehood, story, untruth

Fib, *v. i.* to tell a lie, to utter a falsehood

Fib'ber, *n.* a teller of lies, liar, storyteller

Fiber, Fibril, *n.* a small thread, a very small root

Fíbrin, *n.* the fibrous substance of plants

Fibrous, *a.* composed of or having fibres, thin

Fic''kle, *a.* changeable, unsteady, wavering, light

Fic''kleness, *n.* inconstancy, unsteadiness, caprice

Fick'ly, *ad.* without certainty, unsteadily, oddly

Fico, *n.* an act of contempt shown by the fingers

Fic'tile, *a.* made by a potter or of earth, *ob.*

Fic'tion, *n.* a story invented, tale, device, lie, false-

Fic'tious, Ficti''tious, *a.* counterfeit, false (hood

Ficti''tiously, *ad.* counterfeitly, falsely, untruly

Ficti''tiousness, *n.* a counterfeit or fabulous state

Fid or Fidd, *n.* a pointed iron used by sailors, a de-

Fid'dle, *n.* a kind of musical instrument (sense

Fid'dle, *v.* to play on a fiddle, trifle, do little, idle

Fid'dler, *n.* one who plays upon a fiddle, a trifler

Fid'dlestick, *n.* a bow to play on a fiddle with

Fid'dlestring, *n.* a string used for a fiddle

Fidel'ity, *n.* faithfulness, honesty, justice, loyalty

Fidge or Fidg'et, *v. i.* to move nimbly or by fits

Fid'get, *n.* constant motion, restlessness

Fidg'eting, Fidg'ety, *a.* restless, uneasy

Fidúcial, Fidúciary, *a.* confident, certain, steady

Fidúciary, *n.* one who holds in trust, one who de-

Fie, *exclam.* denoting dislike (pends on faith only

Fief, *n.* a fee, manor, tenure, dependance, homage

Field, *n.* a piece of inclosed ground, extent, blank space, place of battle, course for races

Fieldbook, *n.* a book used by surveyors

Fieldduck, *n.* a species of bustard

Fielded, *a.* being in the field of battle, encamped,

Fieldfare, *n.* a bird of the thrush-kind (pitched

Fieldpiece, *n.* a small cannon to be used in battle

Fiend, *n.* a devil, infernal being, fury, enemy, foe

Fierce, *a.* violent, furious, forcible, savage, wild

Fierce'ly, *ad.* violently, furiously, passionately

Fierceness, *n.* violence, fury, rage, heat, savageness

Fierily, *ad.* in a fiery or passionate manner, hotly

Fieriness, *n.* hotness, passion, warmth of temper

Fiery, *a.* hot, passionate, warm, vehement, fierce

Fife, *n.* a small pipe or wind instrument of music

Fife, *v.* to play on a fife

Fifer, *n.* one who plays upon or makes use of a fife

Fif'teen, *a.* five and ten united, five added to ten

Fifth, *a.* next above the fourth

Fifth'ly, *ad.* in the fifth place

Fif'tieth, *a.* noting the number fifty

Fif'ty, *a.* five tens, ten taken five times

Fig, *n.* a tree and its fruit, mark of contempt, disease

Fig, *v.* to insult with ficos, to give useless advice

Fig'leaf, *n.* the leaf of a figtree, thin covering

Fig'tree, *n.* the tree which bears figs

Fight, *v.* fought, *pret.* fought, *pa.* to contend in battle, war, engage, resist

Fight, *n.* a battle, combat, duel, contest, dispute

Fighter, *n.* a warrior, combatant, hero, disputant

Fighting, *pa.* fit for or employed in war, brave

Fig'ment, *n.* an invention, fiction, device, tale, lie

Fig'ulate, *a.* made of earth or potter's clay

Fig'urable, *a.* that is capable of being formed

Figurabil'ity, *n*. a being capable of a form

Fig'ural, Fig'urate, *a*. reduced to form or fhape

Fig'urative, *a*. typical, metaphorical, allufive

Fig'uratively, *ad*. of, by or in, a figure, by allufion

Fig'ure, *n*. a number, fhape, image, type, perfon

Fig'ure, *v. t.* to form into fhape, to reprefent

Fig'ured, *pa*. formed, caft, reprefented, adorned

Fig'wort, *n*. the plant, fcrop'ularia

Filáceous, *a*. confifting of threads or wires

Fil'acer, *n*. an officer in the Common Pleas

Fil'ament, *n*. a flender or fmall thread, fiber, ray

Filament'ous, *a*. like a filament

Fil'bert, *n*. a fine kind of hazel-nut

Filch, *v. t.* to fteal, pilfer, rob, deprive of, cheat

Filch'er, *n*. one who filches, a thief, rogue, cheat

File, *n*. a fmith's tool, wire for or bundle of papers, row of foldiers

File, *v*. to cut with a file, to march in file, to place papers in order in a bundle, &c. with a minute of the contents

Fil'emot, *n*. a brown color, a yellow-brown, *ob*.

Fil'ial, *a*. belonging to, like or becoming, a fon

Filiátion, *n*. the relation a fon bears to a father

Fil'iform, *a*. in fhape of a thred or filament

Fil'igree, *n*. curious work in gold or filver reprefenting threds, grains or leaves

Filings, *n. pl*. fmall particles rubbed off by a file

Fill, *v*. to make full, fatisfy, glut, furfeit, pour

Fill, *n*. fulnefs, plenty, content, part of a carriage

Fill'er, *n*. a perfon who or thing that fills, a horfe

Fil'et, *n*. a joint of veal, a headband ; *v. t.* to bind

Fill'ip, *v. t.* to ftrike or hit with the finger

Fill'ip, *n*. a fudden ftroke or tofs with the finger

Fill'y, *n*. a young mare, colt, wild young girl

Film, *n*. a thin fkin ; *v. t.* to cover with a thin fkin

Film'y, *a*. compofed of films, having thin fkins

Filt'er, *v. t.* to ftrain, to pour clear off; *n*. a ftrainer

Filth, *n*. dirt, foil, naftinefs, corruption, foul play

Filth'ily, *ad*. dirtily, naftily, obfcenely, meanly

Filth'inefs, *n*. dirtinefs, dirt, naftinefs, corruption

Filth'y, *a*. dirty, nafty, foul, polluted, obfcene

Fil'trate, *v. t.* to filter, ftrain, percolate

Filtration, *n*. the act or art of filtering, a refining

Fim'briate, *a*. bordered, edged, fringed

Fin, *n*. a fifh's membrane, fupported by bony rays for fwimming, &c.

Fin, *v. t.* to carve or cut up a chub

Finable, *a*. that may be fined, fubject to a fine

Final, *a*. laft, ending, clofing, conclufive, mortal

Finally, *ad*. laftly, at laft, beyond all recovery

Finance', *n*. a revenue, income, profit, treafure, fine

Finan'cial, *a*. of or relating to matters of finance

Financiér, *n*. one fkilled in matters of revenue, an officer who has the care of revenues

Finch, *n*. a genus of birds with fharp conical bills

Find, *v. t.* found, *pret*. found, *pa*. to difcover, meet with, get, allow, feel, learn

Finder, *n*. one who difcovers what is loft or not known to be in that place

Fin'dy, *a*. plump, weighty, folid, firm, hard, *ob*.

Fine, *a*. fhowy, nice, handfome, pure, clear

Fine, *n*. a penalty, forfeiture, advance-money, end

Fine, *v*. to inflict a penalty, refine, purify, adorn

Finely, *ad*. beautifully, gaily, neatly, keenly, well

Finenefs, *n*. elegance, fhow, purity, artfulnefs

Finer, *n*. one who purifies metals ; *a*. more fine

Finery, *n*. fine drefs, fhow, a fplendid appearance

Finefs', *n*. artifice, art, ftratagem, wile, device

Finefs', *v. i.* to ufe ftratagem or artifice

Fin'fifh, *n*. a fpecies of flender whale

Fin''ger, *n*. a part of the hand, hand, meafure, art

Fin''ger, *v. t.* to handle, touch, pilfer, fteal, thieve

Fin'ical, *a*. nice, fpruce, gay, foppifh, affected, vain

Fin'ically, *ad*. in a finical manner, gayly, foppifhly

Finingpot, *n*. a pot or veffel for refining metals

Finis, *n*. an end, conclufion, determination

Fin'ifh, *v. t.* to perfect, complete, end, fettle

Fin'ifher, *n*. one who accomplifhes or completes

Fin'ifhing, *pa*, ending ; *n*. the laft ftroke, &c.

Fi'nite, *a*. bounded, limited, fixed

Fi'nitelefs, *a*. unbounded, unlimited, infinite, *ob*.

Fi'nitely, *ad*. within certain bounds or limits

Fi'nitenefs, Fin'itude, *n*. limitation, confinement

Fin'lefs, *a*. having no fins, deftitute of fins

Fin'like, *a*. like or formed in the manner of fins

Fin'ned, *a*. made like fins, having broad edges

Fin'nikin, *n*. a fpecies of pigeon with a creft

Fin'ny, *a*. furnifhed with or having fins, like fins

Fip'ple, *n*. a ftopper, a thing to ftop up with, *ob*.

Fir, *n*. the name of a tree or its wood (eruption

Fire, *n*. what burns, heat, paffion, courage, love,

Fire, *v*. to take or fet on fire, kindle, difcharge

Firearms, *n. pl*. guns, &c. (firearms

Fireball, *n*. a meteor, a grenade

Firebrand, *n*, a piece of wood on fire, an incendiary

Firebrufh, *n*. a brufh to fweep the hearth with

Firedrake, *n*. a firework, a fiery ferpent or meteor

Fireengine, *n*. an engine to extinguifh fire

Firefly, *n*. an infect which exhibits light at night

Fireflare, *n*. a fifh with a barbed fpine in the tail

Firelock, *n*. a gun, foldier's gun, mufket

Fireman, *n*. a man employed to extinguifh fires

Firenew, *a*. new from the forge, quite new

Fireoffice, *n*. an office of infurance againft fire

Firepan, *n*. a pan to hold or carry fire in

Fireplace, *n*. a hearth or place for fire

Firer, *n*. one who fets on fire, one who ftirs up

Firefhip, *n*. a fhip that carries combuftibles, to fet fire to enemy's fhips

Firefide, *n*. a hearth, chimney, family (metal

Fireftone, *n*. pyrite, a compound of fulphur and a

Firewarden, *n*. an officer who directs at fires

Firework, *n*. a fine fhow of fire from gunpowder

Firing, *n*. fomething ufed for the fire, fuel

Firk, *v*. to whip, beat, correct, chaftife, *ob*.

Firk'in, *n*. a fmall veffel, a veffel of nine gallons

Firm, *a*. ftrong, conftant, unfhaken, fteady

Firm, *v. t.* to confirm, eftablifh, fix, fettle

Firm *n.* the name or names under which the bufinefs of any houfe is carried on or fettled
Firm'ament, *n.* the fky, heaven, atmofphere, air
Firmament'al, *a.* belonging to the firmament
Firm'an, *n.* a permiffion, or paffport to trade
Firm'ly, *ad.* ftrongly, immoveable, fteadily, fafely
Firm'nefs, *n.* a firm ftate, folidity, conftancy
Firft, *a.* one, chief, earlieft ; *ad.* in the firft place
Firft'begotten, Firft'born, *a.* the firft or eldeft
Firft'fruits, *n. pl.* the firft produce of any thing
Firft'ling, *n.* the young of cattle firft produced
Fifc, Fifc'al, *n.* an exchequer, treafury, reveaue
Fifc'al, *a.* pertaining to a treafury or revenue
Fifh, *n.* a clafs of animals living in water, a timber to ftrengthen a maft or fpar, a machine to hoift the flukes of an anchor
Fifh, *v.* to catch fifhes, catch by art, fift, faften
Fifh'er, Fifh'erman, *n.* one who catches fifhes
Fifh'ery, *n.* the place or bufinefs of catching fifh
Fifh'ful, *a.* full of, abounding with or having, fifh
Fifh'hook, *n.* a barbed hook to catch fifh with
Fifh'ing, *n.* the art or practice of catching fifh, &c.
Fifh'kettle, *n.* a kettle ufed to boil fifh in
Fifh'meal, *n.* a meal on fifh only, flender or low diet
Fifh'monger, *n.* a dealer in or feller of fifh
Fifh'pond, *n.* a pond in which fifh are kept
Fifh'y, *a.* like fifh, fmelling of fifh, ftrong
Fiffile, *a.* that may be cleft, fplit or divided
Fiffil'ity, *n.* capacity of being fplit or cleft
Fif'fure, *n.* a cleft, a chafm ; *v. t.* to cleave, to gape
Fif'fured, *a.* divided or notched with even margins
Fift, *n.* the hand, the hand in a clinched ftate
Fift, *v. t.* to beat, ftrike or hold faft, with the fift
Fift'icuffs, *n. pl.* a battle or conteft with fifts
Fift'ula, *n.* a pipe, fore difeafe, winding ulcer
Fift'ular, Fift'ulous, *a.* like a hollow pipe
Fit, *n.* a paroxyfm, complaint, motion
Fit, *a.* proper, right, meet, convenient, qualified
Fit, *v.* to fuit, adapt, adjuft, qualify, fix, equip
Fitch'et, *n.* the polecat or fomart, a wild pea
Fit'ful, *a.* full of or having fits, varied by fits
Fit'lier, *a.* more fit, more proper or fuitable
Fit'lieft, *a.* moft fit, moft proper or fuitable
Fit'ly, *ad.* properly, juftly, meetly, conveniently
Fit'ment, *n.* fomething that is fitted, *ob.* (venience
Fit'nefs, *n.* propriety, fuitablenefs, juftnefs, con-
Fitz'ler, *n.* an animal of the weafel kind, the ratel
Fivefold, *a.* taken or repeated five times
Fives, *n. pl.* a game with a ball, a difeafe in horfes
Fix, *v.* to faften, ftick, place, fettle, determin
Fixable, *a.* that may be fixed
Fixa'tion, Fix'ednefs, *n.* fteadinefs, abode, confine-
Fix'ed, *pa.* faftened, fettled, determined (ment
Fix'edly, *ad.* firmly, invariably, certainly, truly
Fixid'ity, Fix'ity, *n.* a firm coherence of parts
Fixt'ure, *n.* any furniture fixed to the premifes
Fiz'gig, *n.* a kind of fpear to ftrike fifh with
Flab'binefs, *n.* a flabby ftate or quality, foftnefs
Flab'by, *a.* foft, loofe, eafily moved

Flab'ellate, *a.* fhaped like a fan
Flac'cid, *a.* lax, weak, limber, withered, drooping
Flaccid'ity, *n.* laxnefs, weaknefs, limbernefs
Flag, *v.* to grow weak or feeble, droop, decline, tire, lay. with flags or flat ftones
Flag, *n.* a plant, a large flat ftone, colors
Flagellátion, *n.* the act of fcourging or lafhing
Fla''gelet, *n.* a kind of fmall flute
Flag'gy, *a.* full of flags, weak, limber, foft
Flagi''tious, *a.* very wicked, villanous, vile, bafe
Flagi''tioufnefs, *n.* moft atrocious wickednefs
Flag'officer, *n.* the commander of a fquadron
Flag'on, *n.* a veffel, a two-quart meafure of wine
Flágrancy, *n.* burning heat, fire, great eagernefs
Flágrant, *a.* burning, very hot, notorious, vile
Flag'fhip, *n.* the head-fhip of a fquadron
Flag'ftaff, *n.* a ftaff to fupport a flag
Flail, *n.* an inftrument to thrafh with
Flake, *n.* a fcale of iron, flock of fnow or fire, layer, a fcaffold made of hurdles for drying codfifh
Flake *v.* to break into flakes, to part into fcales
Flâky, *a.* hanging loofely together, eafily broken
Flam, *n.* a pretence, lie, falfehood, idle ftory, *ob.*
Flam, *v. t.* to deceive, impofe upon, gull, *ob.*
Flam'beau, [flam'boe] *n.* a lighted torch (love
Flame, *n.* light given by fire, a blaze, heat, paffion,
Flame, *v. i.* to fhine or burn as fire, to blaze
Flámecolored, *a.* having a bright yellow color
Flámen, *n.* a prieft, an ancient heathen prieft
Fláming, *pa. a.* burning, hot, inflaming, fine
Flamin''go, *n.* a red bird with black wing feathers, and webbed feet, found in warm climates
Flamin'ian, *a.* made or pertaining to Flaminius
Flammabil'ity, *n.* an aptnefs to take fire or burn
Flammátion, *n.* the act or ftate of burning, heat
Flam'meous, *a.* confifting of or like flame, hot
Flámy, *a.* like fire, fiery, flaming, burning, hot
Flank, *n.* the fide ; *v. t.* to attack or hit on the fide
Flan'nel, *n.* a kind of foft woollen cloth
Flap, *n.* a blow, difeafe, thing pulled up or down
Flap, *v.* to beat, hit, move with noife, fall in flaps
Flap'dragon, *v. t.* to fwallow, to devour ; *n.* a game
Flap'eared, *a.* having loofe and broad ears
Flare, *v. i.* to burn with unfteady light, te glitter
Fláring, *pa.* burning unfteadily, fhowy, glittering
Flafh, *n.* a fudden and fhort blaze, dafh, fpurt
Flafh, *v.* to blaze out fuddenly, dafh, throw up
Flafh'y, *a.* fhowy, gaudy, fine, gay, empty, infipid
Flafk, *n.* a kind of bottle, powderhorn, mark, bed
Flafk'et, *n.* a fort of large bafket, a kind of tray
Flat, *n.* a level, even ground, fhallow, dulnefs, a broad boat, a mark of depreffion in mufic
Flat, *a.* level, even, fmooth, null, infipid, pofitive
Flat, *v.* to make or grow flat, level, hinder, draw
Flat'long, Flat'wife, *ad.* with the flat part down
Flat'ly, *ad.* evenly, dully, without fpirit, downright
Flat'nefs, *n.* evennefs, lownefs, dulnefs, deadnefs
Flat'ten, *v.* to make flat, beat down, difpirit, fall
Flat'ter *v. t.* to footh, praife, give falfe hopes

Flat'terer, *n.* a wheedler, fawner, coaxer, praiser
Flat'tering, Flat'tery, *n.* falfe or empty praife
Flat'tifh, *a.* rather flat, rather low or dull
Flat'ulency, Flatuos'ity, *n.* windinefs, vanity
Flat'ulent, Flat'uous, *a.* windy, puffy, empty, vain
Flaunt, *v. i.* to ftrut about dreffed, fly about, walk
Flaunt, *n.* any thing that hangs loofely and airily
Flavor, *n.* a tafte, relifh, fcent, fmell
Flavor, *v. t.* to give a pleafant tafte or fmell
Flavorous, *a.* palatable, nice, fweet-fmelling
Flaw, *v. t.* to crack, break, violate, injure, hurt
Flaw, *n.* a crack, breach, defect, fault, blaft, guft
Flaw'lefs, *a.* void of flaw, crack or defect, found
Flaw'y, *a.* having flaws, cracked, defective, faulty
Flax, *n.* the plant from which linen is made
Flax'en, *a.* made of or like flax, fair, yellowifh
Flay, *v. t.* to take or ftrip off the fkin   (fleas
Flea, *n.* a troublefome infect; *v. t.* to clean from
Fléabane, *n.* a plant of feveral fpecies
Fléabite, *n.* a mark from the bite of a flea, a trifle
Fléabitten, *a.* bitten or ftung by fleas, mean
Fleak, *n.* a fmall lock of any thing, thread, twift
Fleam, *n.* an inftrument ufed to bleed cattle with
Fleck, Fleck'er, *v. t.* to fpot, mark, ftreak, *ob.*
Fledge, *v. t.* to furnifh with fethers or wings
Fledge, Fledg'ed, *pa. a.* full fethered
Flee, *v.* fled, *pret.* fled, *pa.* to run, fhun, avoid
Fleece, *n.* wool fheared from a fheep at one time
Fleece, *v. t.* to ftrip a perfon of his fubftance, to clip
Flee'ced, *pa.* ftripped of fubftance, plundered
Flee'cy, *a.* covered with or like wool, woolly, foft
Fleer, *v. i.* to mock, fneer, leer, grin with fcorn
Fleer, *n.* mockery, a deceitful or faucy kind of grin
Fleet, *a.* fwift, quick, faft, nimble, active, ready
Fleet, *n.* a number of fhips in company, a navy,
   [creek, bay, *local*]
Fleet, *v.* to fly or pafs fwiftly, flit, fkim
Fleet'ing, *pa.* paffing fwiftly, fkimming, fading
Fleet'nefs, *n.* fwiftnefs, quicknefs, fpeed
Flem'ing, *n.* a native of Flanders, or Belgium
Flem'ifh, *a.* pertaining to Flanders; *n.* the language
Flefh, *n.* a part of the animal body, luft, worldlinefs
Flefh, *v. t.* to initiate, eftablifh, harden, glut, fill
Flefh'brufh, *n.* a brufh to rub the flefh
Flefh'color, *n.* the color or likenefs of flefh
Flefh'fly, *n.* a large blue fly that feeds upon flefh
Flefh'hook, *n.* a hook to take up meat with
Flefh'inefs, *n.* plumpnefs, fatnefs, fleeknefs (grofs
Flefh'lieft, *a.* the moft flefhly, the moft carnal or
Flefh'linefs, *n.* flefhly defire, carnal appetite, luft
Flefh'ly, *a.* carnal, grofs, human, bodily, lovely, dear
Flefh'meat, *n.* the flefh of beafts and birds
Flefh'ment, *n.* eagernefs from a good beginning, *ob.*
Flefh'monger, *n.* a dealer in flefh, a pimp or bawd
Flefh'pot, *n.* a veffel ufed to put or cook flefh in
Flefh'quake, *n.* a trembling of the flefh, *ob.*
Flefh'y, *a.* full of flefh, plump, fat, large, jucy
Fletch'er, *n.* one who makes bows and arrows
Flew, *pret.* of *to fly*

Flew'ed, *a.* chapped, mouthed, deepmouthed
Flexibil'ity, Flex'iblenefs, *n.* pliancy, compliance
Flex'ible, Flex'ile, *a.* pliant, compliant, eafily bent
Flex'ion, *n.* the act of bending, a caft, turn, joint
Flex'or, *n.* the contracting mufcle of a joint
Flex'uous, *a.* winding, bent, crooked, unfteady
Flex'ure, *n.* a part bent, bend, act of bending, joint
Flick'er, *v.* to flutter, play the wings, laugh, *ob.*
Flier, *n.* a runaway, the flying part of a machine
Flight, *n.* a running away, efcape, fally, flock
Flighty, *a.* wild, odd, full of imagination, fwift
Flim'fy, *a.* thin, flight, limber, weak, mean, poor
Flinch, *v. i.* to fhrink or draw back, to fail
Flinch'er, *n.* one who fhrinks back or fails
Fling, *v.* flung, *pret.* flung, *pa.* to throw, caft,
   flounce, baffle, overreach
Fling, *n.* a throw, caft, infinuation, fneer, gibe, jeer
Flint, *n.* a very hard kind of ftone, a cruel wretch
Flint'y, *a.* made of flint, ftrong, hardhearted, cruel
Flip, *n.* a drink made with beer, fpirits and fugar
Flip'pant, *a.* of rapid fpeech, pert, talkative
Flip'pantly, *ad.* in a flippant or pert manner
Flip'pantnefs, *n.* pertnefs, talkativenefs
Flirt, [flurt] *v.* to jeer, run about, kick, flutter
Flirt, *n.* a pert huffy, fudden trick or motion, caft
Flirtátion, *n.* a quick or fprightly motion, a flirt
Flit, *v. i.* to flutter, fly, move, pafs, go
Flitch, *n.* a fide of bacon, the fide of a dried hog
Flit'ter, *n.* a rag, tatter, loofe piece, pancake
Flit'ting, *n.* a fluttering, [offenfe, fault, *ob.*]
Flix, *n.* down, foft hair, fur, the fur of hares, *ob.*
Float, *n.* any thing fwimming on the water, a raft
Float, *v.* to fwim on the furface, to deluge
Flóatage, *n.* floating or things floated
Flóaty, *a.* fwimming on the top or furface, light
Floc'culent, *n.* a ftate of being in flocks or flakes
Floc'culence, *a.* in the form of flocks or flakes
Flock, *n.* a company of fheep, &c. crowd, lock
Flock, *v. i.* to gather in crowds, affemble, collect
Flock'bed, *n.* a bed filled only with locks of wool
Flog, *v. t.* to whip, lafh, beat, chaftife, correct
Flog'ging, *n.* a whipping or beating, correction
Flood, [flud] *n.* flow of tide, inundation
Flood, *v. t.* to overflow, deluge, cover with water
Flood'gate, *n.* a gate to ftop or let out water
Flood'mark, *n.* the mark that is left by the flood
Floor, [flore] *v. t.* to lay a bottom to a room
Floor, Floor'ing, *n.* the bottom of a room, a ftory
Flop, *v. t.* to clap the wings with noife, beat, flap
Flóral, *a.* relating or belonging to flowers
Flor'entine, *n.* a native of Florence in Italy, a fpe-
   cies of filk cloth
Flor'entine, *a.* pertaining to Florence
Flores'cence, *n.* the act of flowering in plants
Flóret, *n.* a fmall flower making part of a com-
Flos'cule, *n.* a little flower or floret (pound flower
Flos'culous *a.* confifting of tubulous florets
Flor'id, *a.* flufhed with red, red, rhetorical
Flor'idnefs, Florid'ity, *n.* a very frefh color, elegance

Florif'erous, a. producing flowers
Flor'in, n. a foreign coin of different values
Flórist, n. one who cultivates or is fond of flowers
Flóta, n. the Spanish annual rich West-India fleet
Flotil'la, n. a fleet of small vessels or boats
Flot'son, n. goods swimming on the sea
Flounce, v. to plunge, kick, roll, deck with flounces
Flounce, n. a loose trimming on women's apparel
Floun'der, v.i. to flounce, to have irregular motion
Floun'der, n. the name of a small flat-fish (sifted
Flour, n. the fine part of grain when ground and
Flour, v.t. to sprinkle with flour, to grind and bolt
Flour'ish, v. to thrive, boast, brag, adorn, cut, play
Flour'ish, n. a boast, bravado, ornament, shake
Flour'isher, n. one who is in prime or prosperity
Flout, n. mockery, insult; v.t. to mock, to insult
Flow, v. to pour in as water, run, overflow, melt
Flow, n. a rise of water, run, plenty, sudden plenty
Flow'er, n. the blossom of a plant, the prime
Flow'er, v. to be in flower, bloom, froth, adorn
Flow'ery, a. adorned with flowers, fine, florid
Flo'wingly, ad. with volubility, with abundance
Flown, pa. of to fly; gone off or away, cracked
Fluc'tuant, a. floating, wavering, uncertain
Fluc'tuate, v.i. to float, waver, be in suspense
Fluctuá'tion, n. uncertainty, motion, change
Flud'der, n. an aquatic diving fowl
Flue, n. soft down or fur, the pipe of a chimney
Fluel'lin, n. the plant speedwell
Flúency, n. eloquence, readiness, ease, abundance
Flúent, a. eloquent, flowing, copious; n. a stream
Flúently, ad. flowingly, quickly, readily, fast
Flúid, n. any thing that runs, any animal juice
Flúid, a. flowing, running as water, melted, soft
Fluíd'ity, Flúidness, n. a fluid state or quality
Fluke; n. the broad part of an anchor, a flounder
Flume, n. a channel or passage for water
Flum'mery, n. a spoonmeat made of milk and flour
Flung, pret. and pa. of to fling
Flúor, n. a fluid state or quality, a mineral called
spar, consisting of calcareous earth and an acid
Flúate, n. salt formed by fluoric acid and a base
Fluor'ic acid is the acid of fluor, the radical of which
is unknown
Flúorous acid is the acid of fluor in the first degree
of oxygenation
Flúorated, a. combined with fluoric acid
Flur'ry, n. a hurry, surprise, flutter of spirits, gust
Flur'ry, v.t. to put in a flurry, confuse, frighten
Flush, a. fresh, full of vigor, abounding, level
Flush, n. a violent flow, impulse, cards of a suit
Flush, v. to come in haste, redden, heat, elate, rise
Flush'ed, pa. reddened, heated, puffed up, elated
Flush'er, n. the lesser butcher bird
Flus'ter, v.t. to disorder, confuse, heat, swell
Flute, n. a musical pipe, furrow in columns, boat
Flute, v. to cut hollows in pillars, &c. to play on a
Flú'ting, n. fluted work on a pillar (flute
Flut'ter, v. to fly hither y, hurry, confuse, disorder

Flut'ter, n. a motion, hurry, confusion, fright
Flut'tering, n. the act of moving, agitation
Fluviat'ic, a. belonging to rivers
Flux, n. the act of flowing, a purging, a concourse
Flux, v.t. to melt, to salivate; a. inconstant, flow-
Flux'ible, a. capable of being made fluid (ing
Fluxibil'ity, n. capacity of being fused
Flux'ility, n. an easiness of separating parts
Flux'ion, n. a flowing of humors, &c. a melting
Fly, v. flew, pret. flown, pa. to move with wings
run away, shun, burst
Fly, n. a kind of insect, the upper part of a jack
Fly'bane, n. a plant called catch fly
Fly'blow, n. the egg of a fly
Fly'blow, v.t. to fill with maggots, to taint
Fly'boat, n. a large flat bottomed Dutch vessel
Fly'catcher, n. one who catches flies, a genus of
birds of various species
Fly'er, n. one who flies or runs away, a stair, a fly
Fly'fish, v.i. to angle with a fly made on a hook
Fly'fishing, n. the act or art of angling with a fly
Fly'ing, n. the act of moving upon wings
Fly'ingfish, n. a small fish which uses its pectoral
fins for flight (tive plant
Fly'trap, n. a trap to catch flies, a species of sensi-
Foal, v.i. to breed or bring forth a foal
Foal, n. the offspring of a mare, a young mare
Foam, v.i. to froth, gather froth, be in a rage
Foam, n. froth, great passion, fury, rage
Fóamy, a. covered with foam, frothy, empty
Fob, n. a small breeches-pocket
Fob, v.t. to cheat, trick, defraud, put off
Fócal, a. belonging to a focus or point
Fócus, pl. focuses, n. a place where rays meet, point
Fod'der, n. food for cattle; v.t. to feed cattle
Fódient, a. digging, turning or throwing up
Foe, n. an enemy, opponent, persecutor
Fog, n. a thick mist, misty state, vapor, aftergrass
Fog'giness, n. a foggy state, mistiness, darkness
Fog'gy, a. misty, thick, dull, heavy, dark
Foi'ble, n. a weak or blind side, failing, fault, defect
Foil, v. to defeat, overcome, push, set off
Foil, n. a defeat, deception, thrust, sword, gilding
Foin, v.i. to push in fencing
Fois'on or Foiz'on, n. plenty, abundance, ob.
Foist, v.t. to insert by forgery, to put or cram in
Foist'iness, n. fustiness, moldiness, ob.
Foist'y, a. fusty, mouldy, smelling badly, ob.
Fold, n. a double or plait, pen for sheep, flock
Fold, v.t. to double up, put sheep into a fold, con-
Fóldage, n. the liberty of penning up sheep (fine
Fólder, n. a flat instrument to fold sheets of paper
Foliáceous, a. consisting of leaves or thin scales,
growing on leaves
Fóliage, n. leaves, tufts of trees, branched work
Fóliar, a. pertaining to or growing from a leaf
Fóliate, a. leafy, furnished with leaves
Fóliate, n. a certain curve of the second order
Fóliate, v.t. to beat into thin plates or leaves

Foliâtion, *n.* the act of beating into thin plates, the folded state of leaves while in the bud

Fo'iſerous, *a.* producing leaves

Fólio, *n.* a book of two leaves to a ſheet, a mark

Folióſe, *a.* having leaves interſperſed with flowers

Fóliole, *n.* a ſmall leaf of a compound leaf

Fo'k, Fo'ks, *n.* people, mankind, mortals, nations

Fólkmote, *n.* a council or aſſembly of the people

Fol'licle *n.* a cavity or bag, a feed veſſel of a fingle valve, opening lengthwiſe and feeds not faſtened

Follic'ulous, *a.* producing follicles

Fol'low, *v.* to go or come after, purſue, imitate

Fol'lower, *n.* one who follows, a dependant, a copier

Fol'ly, *n.* a want of underſtanding, imprudence

Fomart', *n.* a name of the polecat or fitchet

Foment', *v. t.* to encourage, abet, cheriſh, bathe

Fomentâtion, *n.* a bathing with any thing, a lotion

Foment'ed, *pa.* promoted, cheriſhed, bathed

Foment'er. *n.* an encourager, abettor, ſupporter

Fond, *a.* much pleaſed with, tender, fooliſh, vain

Fond, Fon''dle, *v.* to be fond of, doat on, careſs, try

Fond'ler, *n.* one who fondles, one who careſſes

Fond'ling, *n.* one much cockered or doated on

Fond'ly, *ad.* with fondneſs, fooliſhly, weakly

Fond'neſs, *n.* exceſs of love, liking, tenderneſs

Font, *n.* the baptiſmal baſon, a complete ſet of letters

Font'anel, *n.* a place of diſcharge, an iſſue (ters

Fontangé, *n.* a knot of ribands worn on the head

Fonti''genous, *a.* growing or breeding near wells

Food, *n.* victuals, meat, proviſion for the mouth

Food'ful, *a.* full of or affording food, fruitful

Food'y, *a.* fit or proper for food, eatable

Fool, *n.* a fooliſh perſon, oaf, buffoon, wicked man

Fool, *v.* to trifle, toy, diſappoint, defeat, cheat

Fool'born, *a.* born of a fool, fooliſh from the birth

Fool'ed, *pa.* treated as a fool, cheated, deceived

Fool'ery, *n.* folly, habitual folly, mere nonſenſe

Fool'hardineſs, *n.* fooliſh raſhneſs

Fool'hardy, *a.* madly adventurous, raſh (wicked

Fool'iſh, *a.* weak in underſtanding, imprudent,

Fool'iſhly, *ad.* weakly, imprudently, idly, wickedly

Fool'iſhneſs, *n.* folly, a want of underſtanding

Fools'cap, *n.* paper of a ſmall ſize

Fool'trap, *n.* a trap or ſnare laid to catch fools

Foot, *n.* that on which a thing ſtands, a ſtep, meaſure of 12 inches, a meaſure in poetry, infantry

Foot, *v.* to dance, walk, tread, ſpurn, ſettle

Foot'ball, *n.* a bladder in a leathern caſe, a game

Foot'boy, *n.* a boy in livery, a ſervant

Foot'bridge, *n.* a narrow bridge for paſſengers

Foot'ed, *a.* ſhaped in the foot, danced, walked, trod

Foot'ing, *n.* foundation, dance, tread, road, entrance,

Foot'lieker, *n.* a ſlave, a flatterer (ſettlement, lace

Foot'man, *n.* a man-ſervant in livery, runner, ſtand

Foot'manſhip, *n.* the act of a footman or runner

Foot'pace, *n.* a ſlow walk, part of a ſtaircaſe, cloth

Foot'pad, *n.* a perſon who robs on foot

Foot'path, *n.* a narrow way for foot-paſſengers

Foot'poſt, *n.* a poſt or meſſenger that travels on foot

Foot'ſoldier, *n.* a ſoldier that ſerves on foot (ſign

Foot'ſtep, *n.* a mark of a foot, track, trace, token,

Foot'ſtool, *n.* a place to put the feet on, a ſupport

Fop, *n.* a coxcomb, effeminate beau, ſaucy man

Fop'pery, *n.* affectation, ſhow, folly, impertinence

Fop'piſh, *a.* gaudy, vain, ſilly, fooliſh, ſaucy, rude

Fop'piſhly, *ad.* in a foppiſh manner, gaudily, vainly

Fop'piſhneſs, *n.* foppiſh behavior, vanity, folly

For, *pr.* or *conj.* becauſe of, conducive to, in hope of, in place of, in favor of, on this account

For'age, *n.* proviſion, food, a ſearch for proviſions

For'age, *v.* to go in ſearch of proviſions, to ſtrip

Foram'inous, *a.* full of holes, pierced, bored (that

Foraſmuch', *conj.* ſince, ſeeing, becauſe, becauſe

Forbeâr, *v.* forbare, forbore, *pret.* forborn, *pa.* to ceaſe, ſtop, abſtain, decline, ſpare

Forbeârance, *n.* act of forbearing, delay, mildneſs

Forbeârer, *n.* one who forbears, one who hinders

Forbid', *v.* forbad, forbade, forbid, *pret.* forbid, forbidden, *pa.* to order not to do, hinder, oppoſe, put a ſtop to, blaſt, curſe

Forbid'dance, *n.* the act of forbidding, a reſtraint

Forbid'denly, *ad.* in an unlawful manner

Forbid'der, *n.* one who forbids or ſtops (diſlike

Forbid'ding, *pa.* hindering, hateful, cauſing

Force, *n.* violence, ſtrength, armed power, fate

Force, *v.* to oblige, overpower, ſtorm, raviſh, cut

Fórcedly, *ad.* with or by force, violently

Fórceful, *a.* violent, hot, vehemently, ſtrong

For'ceps, *n.* nippers to extract any thing

Fórcible, *a.* violent, ſtrong, powerful, binding

Fórciblenefs, *n.* force, violence, ſtrength

Fórcibly, *ad.* by force, ſtrongly, powerfully, fully

For'cipate, *a.* formed like pinchers

Ford, *n.* a place where a river is croſſed by wading

Ford, *v. t.* to paſs a river on foot or by wading

Fórdable, *a.* paſſable on the bottom by wading

Fórded, *pa.* paſſed over by wading

Fore, *a.* coming firſt or before; *ad.* before

Foreappoint', *v. t.* to appoint beforehand

Forearm', *v. t.* to appoint beforehand for reſiſtance

Forebóde, *v. i.* to foretel, foreknow, gueſs, divine

Forecaſt', *v. t.* forecaſt, *pret.* forecaſt, *pa.* to ſcheme or plan beforehand, to foreſee

Fórecaſt, *n.* contrivance beforehand, foreſight

Fórecaſtle *n.* the part where the foremaſt ſtands

Fórecited, *a.* quoted before or above

Foreclóſe, *v. t.* to ſhut up, preclude, prevent, ſtop

Foreclóſure, *n.* a prevention, a ſtop

Fóredeck, *n.* the deck upon the forepart of a ſhip

Foredeſign, *v. t.* to ſcheme or plan beforehand

Foredó, *v. t.* foredid, *pret.* foredone, *pa.* to ruin, ob.

Foredoom', *v. t.* to predeſtinate, to fix or determin

Fóre-end, *n.* the nearer end, the forepart (before

Fórefather, Fóregoer, *n.* an anceſtor, founder, head

Forefend', *v. t.* to hinder, keep off or away, ſecure

Fórefinger, *n.* the finger next the thumb

Fórefoot, *n.* one of the feet before, a crofs courfe
Fórefront, *n.* the front, forehead, very hottest part
Foregó, *v. t.* forewent, *pret.* foregone, *pa.* to go
  before, quit, give up, refign, lofe
Fóreground, *n.* the part that lies before the figures
Fórehand, *n.* the part of a horfe before the rider
Fórchand, *a.* done beforehand or too foon
For'ehead,*n.* the upper part of the face,impudence
Fóreholding, *n.* a foreboding, prediction, *ob.*
For'eign,[forun] *a.* belonging to another country,
  diftant, not connected with   (an alien
For'eigner, *n.* a ftranger, one of another country,
For'eignnefs,*n.* remotenefs, inconfiftency
Foreina''gin, *v.t.* to conceive before proof is had,
Forejudgé, *v. t.* to judge beforehand or too haftily
Foreknów, *v. t.* foreknew,*pret.* foreknown, *pa.*
  to know beforehand, to forefee
Foreknowl'edge,*n.* knowledge of future events
Fóreland, *n.* a headland, promontory, cape,fpace
Foreláy, *v. t.* forelaid, forelayed, *pret.* forelaid,
  forelayed,*pa.* lay wait for
Fórelock, *n.* a lock of hair on the forehead, a flat
Fóreman, *n.* a chief man in a fhop, &c.   (wedge
Fóremaft, *n.* the firft maft towards a fhip's head
Fórementioned, Fórenamed, *a.* mentioned or na-
Fóremoft, *a.* firft in place   (med before
Fórenotice, *n.* information given beforehand
Forens'ic, *a.* of or relating to courts of judicature
Foreordáin, *v. t.* to determin or fet beforehand
Fórepart,*n.* a part before, a main or principal part
Fórepoffeffed, *a.* prepoffeffed, preengaged, *ob.*
Fórerank, *n.* the firft or leading rank,the forefront
Forereách, *v. i.* to fail fafter, to get or go firft
Forerun', *v.* foreran, *pret.* forerun, *pa.* to come
  or get before, to precede   (fign
Forerun'ner, *n.* one fent before, a prognoftic, a
Forefáy,*v. t.* forefaid, *pret.* forefaid, *pa.* to fay
  beforehand, foretel, prophefy, predict, *ob.*
Forefée, *v. t.* forefaw, *pret.* forefeen, *pa.* to fee
  beforehand, foreknow, divine
Forefháme, *v. t.* to fhame, to bring reproach upon
Forefhor'ten, *v. t.* to fhorten the forefingers(part
Forefhor'tening, *n.* the act of fhortening the fore-
Forefhów,*v. t.* forefhowed,*pret.* forefhowed,fore-
  fhown, *pa.* to fhow beforehand, to foretel
Fórefight,*n.* the feeing a thing before,penetration
Foresíghtful, *a.* feeing beforehand, cautious, *ob.*
Forefig'nify, *v. t.* to forefhow, point out, typify
Fórefkin, *n.* the prepuce
Fórefkirt, *n.* the part of the fkirt that lies before
Forefslów, *v.* to loiter, delay, hinder, neglect, *ob.*
Forefpur'rer, *n.* a perfon who rides before, *ob.*
For'eft, *n.* wafte ground, a natural wood   (or up
Foreftall', *v. t.* to anticipate, prevent, buy before
Foreftall'er, *n.* one who anticipates a market
For'eftborn, *a.* born in a foreft, born in a wild, *ob.*
For'etter, *n.* an officer or inhabitant of a foreft
Foretáfte,*v. t.* to tafte or take before,to anticipate
Fóretafte, *n.* a tafte taken beforehand, a fpecimen

Foretel', *v. t.* foretold, *pret.* foretold, *pa.* to tell
  beforehand, prophefy, predict
Foretel'ler, *n.* a perfon who foretels or prophefies
Forethink', *v. t.* forethought, *pret.* forethought,
  pa. to think or contrive beforehand   (cience
Fórethought, *n.* provident care, caution, pref-
Forctóken,*v.t.* to forefhow; *n.*a token,fign,omen
Fóreftay,*n.* the ftay which reaches from the fore-
  maft head to the bowfprit end, a prop to fup-
  port the carriage of a printing prefs
Fóretop, *n.* the hair on the top of the head before,
  top of a foremaft
Forevouch'ed, *a.* affirmed or declared before, *ob.*
Fóreward, *n.* the van, the front, a bargain
Forewarn', *v. t.* to admonith, caution, advife, tell
Forewarn'ing, *n.* warning or caution beforehand
Forewifh', *v. t.* to wifh beforehand, *ob.*
Forewórn, *a.* worn out, wafted by time or ufe
For'feit, *v. t.* to lofe by fome offenfe, to become
  liable to lofe or have feized
For'feit, *a.* forfeited, liable to feizure
For'feit, *n.* that which is loft by an offenfe
For'feitable, *a.* that may be forfeited
For'feiture, *n.* a thing forfeited, feizure, fine
Forfend', *v. t.* to prevent, hinder, ftop, forbid
Forge, *n.* a place where iron is beaten into form
Forge,*v. t.* to form by hammering or craft, coun-
For'ged, *pa.* made, formed, counterfeited (terfeit
For'ger, *n.* one who makes, one who counterfeits
For'gery, *n.* the crime of falfification, a falfity
Forget', *v. t.* forgat, forgot, *pret.* forgot, forgot-
  ten,*pa.* not to think of, to neglect, to flight
Forget'ful, *a.* not remembering, carelefs, heedlefs
Forget'fulnefs, *n.* inattention, careleffnefs
Forgive', *v. t.* forgave, *pret.* forgiven, *pq.* to
  pardon, excufe, pafs by or over, remit, give up
Forgive'nefs,*n.* the act of forgiving,pardon,excufe
Forgot', Forgot'ten,*pa.* not remembered,dropped
Fork, *v. i.* to fhoot out into blades or branches
Fork, *n.* an inftrument with two or three prongs
Fork'ed, Fork'y, *a.* opening into two or more parts
Fork'ednefs, Fork'inefs,*n.* a forked ftate or quality
Forlorn', *a.* forfaken, loft, wretched, defpicable
Forlorn'nefs, *n.* a forlorn ftate, wretchednefs
Form,*n.* a method, fhape, feat, bench, ceremony
Form,*v. t.* to model,make,plan,contrive,arrange
Form'al, *a.* ceremonious, ftiff, regular, outward
Form'alift,*n.* a lover or great obferver of formality
Formal'ity, *n.* form, ceremony, order, robe
Form'ally, *ad.* according to rule, ceremonioufly
Form'ate, *n.* a neutral falt compofed of the formic
  acid and a bafe
Formátion, *n.* the act or manner of forming
Form'ative, *a.* having power or tending to form
Form'er, *n.* a maker, creator, contriver
Form'er, *a.* the firft of two, the firft in place, paft
Form'erly,*ad.* in time paft, of old, heretofore,once
Form'ic, *a.* pertaining to ants   (creeping of ants
Formicátion, *n.* a tingling like that made by the

Form'idable, a. terrible, dreadful, frightful, great
Form'idableness, n. a formidable state or quality
Form'idably, ad. in a terrible or dreadful manner
Form'lefs, a. having no form or shape, irregular
Form'ula, n. a prescribed or general form
Form'ularity, Form'ulary, n. a book of fet forms
Forn'icate, n. vaulted, arched like an oven
For'nicate, v. i. to lie with an unmarried person
Fornication, n. incontinence of unmarried persons, lewdnefs, idolatry
For'nicator, n. a single person guilty of incontinence, an idolator, any lewd person
Forfake, v. t. forfook, pret. forfaken, pa. to leave, go away from, quit, defert, flight
Forfooth', ad. certainly, verily, truly, to be sure
Forfwear, v. i. forfware, forfwore, pret. forfworn, pa. to fwear falfely, perjure, deny on oath
Fort, n. a fortified place, fortification, castle
Forted, a. having or guarded by a fort (out of
Forth, ad. forward, on, out, out of doors; pr.
Forthcom'ing, a. ready, or willing to appear
Forthis'fuing, a. coming out, or from a cover
Forthright, ad. ftrait forward or on, ob.
Forthright, n. a direct path, way or course, ob.
Forthwith', ad. immediately, directly, very foon
For'tieth, a. the tenth taken four times
Fortification, n. a place built for defenfe, defenfe
For'tifier, n. one who fortifies, fences or fupports
For'tify, v. t. to ftrengthen, fecure, confirm, prepare
Fortilage, Fortin, n. a fmall or little fort, ob.
For'titude, n. ftrength or firmnefs of mind, bravery
Fort'night, n. the fpace of two complete weeks
For'trefs, n. a fortified place, ftrong hold, defenfe
Fortuitous, a. accidental, cafual, uncertain, vague
Fortuitously, ad. accidentally, cafually, by chance
For'tunate, a. lucky, fuccefsful, thriving, happy
For'tunately, ad. luckily, fuccefsfully, happily, well
For'tunatenefs, n. luckinefs, good luck, profperity
For'tune, n. chance, luck, portion, riches, eftate
For'tune, v. to fall out, befal, happen, portion
For'tunehunter, n. a hunter of women of fortune
For'tunetell, v. t. to tell any one's fortune, ob.
For'tuneteller, n. one who pretends to tell fortunes
For'ty, a. ten repeated four times
Forum, n. a market-place in Rome, a court of justice, a tribunal (part
For'ward, a. ready, confident, bold, in the fore
For'ward, v. t. to haften, quicken, advance, promote (on
For'ward, For'wards, ad. in front, progreffively,
For'wardly, ad. eagerly, haftily, readily, boldly
For'wardnefs, n. eagernefs, readinefs, boldnefs
Fofs, n. a ditch, moat, intrenchment, cavity
Foffane, n. an animal of the weafel kind, the herb
Fofs'il, n. any thing dug from the earth; a. dug
Fofs'ilift, n. one fkilled in foffils (up
Foffil'ogy, n. a difcourfe or treatife on foffils
Fofs'road, Fofs'way, n. a Roman high road or way
Fos'ter, v. t. to nurfe, feed, cherifh, pamper, fupport

Fos'terage, n. the charge or care of nurfing a child
Fos'terchild, n. a child not nurfed by its parents
Fos'terdam, Fos'terer, Fos'ternurfe, n. a nurfe
Fos'tered, pa. nurfed, nourifhed, fed, cherifhed
Fought, Foughten, [fawt] pa. of to fight
Foul, a. unclean, dirty, not bright, entangled
Foul, ad. with great force or violence
Foul, v. t. to daub, dirty, bemire, pollute, fully
Foul'faced, a. having an ugly face, ugly, rough
Foul'ly, ad. naftily, dirtily, filthily, hatefully, ill
Foul'mouthed, a. ufing ill language, fcurrilous
Foul'nefs, n. naftinefs, filthinefs, uglinefs, dishon-
Found, pret. and pa. of to find (efty
Found, v. t. to lay a foundation, place, build, fettle, fix, eftablifh, caft metals
Foundation, n. a bottom, rife, eftablifhment, caufa
Found'er, n. a builder, former, cafter, benefactor
Found'er, v. to grow or make lame; fink, fail
Found'ery, n. a place to caft veffels of metals
Found'ling, n. a deferted or expofed infant
Fount, Fount'ain, n. a well, fpring, fpout of water
Fount'ful, a. full of or having many fprings
Fourfold, a. four times as much or many
Fourfold, n. a quadruple affeffment for neglect to make return of taxable eftate (Con.)
Fourfold, v. t. to affefs in a fourfold ratio
Fourfooted, a. having or going on four feet
Fourfcore, a. twenty added or repeated four times
Fourfquare, a. having four equal fides and angles
Fourteen, a. four and ten united, four added to ten
Fourwheeled, a. having four wheels to run upon
Fovil'la, n. a fine fubftance emitted by the pollen of a flower
Fowl, n. a winged animal, a bird; v. i. to catch
Fowl'er, n. a fportsman for birds, a cannon (birds
Fowl'ing, n. the act of catching or killing birds
Fowl'ingpiece, n. a gun for fhooting birds with
Fox, n. a wild animal of the canine kind, a fly or
Fox'cafe, n. the fkin of a fox (knavifh person
Fox'chafe, n. the purfuit of a fox with hounds
Fox'glove, n. a plant of feveral fpecies
Fox'hunter, n. one who is fond of hunting foxes
Fox'trap, n. a gin or fnare to catch foxes with
Fract, v. t. to break, violate, infringe, not ufed
Frac'tion, n. the act of breaking, part of an integral
Frac'tional, a. of, relating to or having, a fraction
Frac'tious, a. crofs, peevifh, quarrelfome, ftrange
Frac'tioufnefs, n. crofsnefs, peevifhnefs
Fract'ure, v. t. to break a bone, to break or crack
Fract'ure, n. a breach or feparation of folid parts, the manner of breaking
Fra''gile, a. brittle, fhort, weak, frail
Fragil'ity, n. brittlenefs, weaknefs, frailty, defect
Frag'ment, n. a broken or imperfect piece, a part
Frag'mentary, a. compofed of fragments, fmall
Fragor, n. a harfh noife, violent crafh
Fragrance or Fragrancy, n. a fweetnefs of fmell
Fragrant, a. fweet-fmelling, nice, agreeable

Frágrantly, ad. with a fweet or pleafant fmell
Fráicheur, n. frefhnefs,coolnefs,fhadinefs,not ufed
Frail, a. weak, liable to error; n. a bafket, a rufh
Fráilnefs, Fráilty, n. weaknefs, a fin of infirmity
Frame,v. t. to put in a frame,make,devife,invent
Frame, n. a cafe, fhape, fupport,difpofition,order
Frámer, n. one who frames, a maker, a contriver
Fran'chife, v. t. to make free; n. a privilege, a
  freedom   (St. Francis
Francis'cans, n. an order of Monks inftituted by
Franc'olin, n. a bird of the patridge kind
Fran'gible, a. that is eafily broken, brittle
Frank, a. liberal, generous, open, fincere, free
Frank, n. a free letter, French filver coin of 18 1-2
  cents value [a hogfty, ob.]
Frank, v. t. to make free, exempt, pay for,fatten
Frankin'cenfe, n. a ftrong odoriferous gum
Franklin'ian, a. pertaining to Dr. Franklin
Frank'ly, ad. liberally, freely, without referve
Frank'nefs,n. plainnefs,opennefs,candor,freedom
Frank'pledge, n. a pledge or furety for freedom
Frant'ic, a. mad, crazy, tranfported with paffion
Frant'icly, ad. madly, furioufly, outrageoufly
Frater'nal, a. brotherly, pertaining to brothers
Frater'nity, n. a brotherhood, fociety, company
Frat'ricide,n. the murder or murderer of a brother
Fraud, n. deception or breach of truft with a view
  to impair the rights of another, a trick or dif-
  honeft tranfaction, an attempt to gain an ad-
  vantage by immoral means
Fraud'ulence or Fraud'ulency, n. deceitfulnefs,art
Fraud'ulent, Fraud'ful,a. deceitful,fubtle,trickifh
Fraud'ulently, ad. by fraud, deceitfully
Fraught, v. t. to load, to crowd, ob.
Fraught,a. full, loaded, replete
Fraught and Fraughtage, for freight, ob.
Fraxinel', n. the plant white dittany
Fray,n. a quarrel, a fright ; v.t. to frighten,to rub
Fráyed,pa. frightened, rubbed, worn by rubbing
Freak, n. a whim, a fudden fancy; v.t. to varie-
Freakifh, a. whimfical, capricious, odd   (gate
Freakifhnefs, n. whimficalnefs, caprioufnefs
Freck'kle, n. a fpot in the fkin; v. t. to get fpots
Freck'led, pa. full of freckles, fpotted, marked
Freck'ly, a. marked with or full of freckles
Free, a. fet at liberty,open,friendly,innocent,void
Free, v. t. to fet at liberty, deliver, rid, unlock
Free'booter, n. a robber, plunderer, pillager,pirate
Free'born, a. born free, inheriting freedom
Free'cott, n. a freedom from all expenfe or charges
Freedman, n. a man made free from flavery
Free'dom,n. liberty, unreftraint,privilege,civility,
Free'footed, a. not confined in walking,loofe(eafe
Free'hearted, a. liberal generous, kind, civil, free
Free'hold, n. land held in or by perpetual right
Free'holder, n. a perfon poffeffed of a freehold
Free'ly, ad. at liberty, liberally, kindly, plainly
Free'man, n. one at liberty or free of a corporation
Freemafon, n. one of the fraternity of Mafons

Free'minded, a. unreftrained, devoid of care,eafy
Free'nefs, n. opennefs, unrefervednefs, generofity
Freefchool, n. a fchool open to all without pay
Free'fpoken, a. fpeaking without referve, civil
Free'ftone, n. a kind of grit or fand ftone
Free'thinker, n. a defpifer of revelation,an infidel
Free'will, n. the power of acting at will or pleafure
Freeze, v. froze, pret. frozen, pa. to kill or be
  congealed by cold
Freight, [frate] n. the lading of a fhip, carriage,
  price of tranfportation by water
Freight, v. t. to load a veffel, to load
French, a. made in or belonging to France
French,n. the language of the French
French'ified, a. addicted to or like the French
Frenet'ic,a. that hath a frenzy, diftracted, mad
Fren'zy, n. diftraction of mind, madnefs, folly
Fréquence, n. a crowd, mob, concourfe, affembly
Fréquency, n. a common occurrence, a concourfe
Fréquent, a. often done or feen, common, ufual
Frequent',v. t. to vifit often,refort to,haunt,keep
Frequent'able, a. converfable, fociable,ob.
Frequentátion, n. the act of frequenting
Frequent'ative, a. repeating frequently or often
Frequent'ed, pa. vifited often, well accuftomed
Frequent'er,n. one who goes frequently to a place
Fréquently, ad. often, commonly, repeatedly
Frefc'o, n. coolnefs, fhade, dufkinefs, paint
Frefh, a. not falt, cool, new, brifk, ruddy, fweet
Frefh, n. a fall of land water into a river, a flood
Frefh'es, n. the mingling of frefh water with the
  falt in rivers and bays, the place of their meet-
  ing, or the increafed current of an ebb tide
  from land floods, a flood
Frefh'en, v. to make or grow frefh,refrefh,revive
Frefh'et, n. a flood in rivers from rain or melted
  fnow, [a ftream or pool of frefh water, ob.]
Frefh'ly, ad. coolly, newly,lately, brifkly
Frefh'nefs, n. coolnefs, newnefs, ruddinefs,bloom
Frefh'water, a. raw, unexperienced, unfkilled
Fret, n. an agitation of liquor or mind, fume,work
  rifing in protuberances, ornament, flop, frith
Fret, v. to vex, be angry or uneafy,rub,wear,eat
Fret'ful, a. peevifh,angry, uneafy, diffatisfied
Fret'fulnefs, n. peevifhnefs, crofsnefs, uneafinefs
Fret'work, n. a kind of raifed work in mafonry
Friabil'ity, n. a capacity of being eafily powdered
Friable, a. that may be powdered or crumbled to
Friar n. a religious brother of fome order (pieces
Friarlike, Friarly, Friary, a. like or refembling a
  friar, unfkilled in the world, retired, reclufe
Friary, n. a place where friars live, a monaftery
Frib'ble, n. a fop of the loweft kind ; v.i. to trifle
Frib'bler, n. one who trifles, a trifler, a mere idler
Frib'blifh, a. like a fribble, foppifh, trifling, idle
Fricafée, n. cut meat, &c. dreffed with a rich fauce
Fricátion, Fric'tion, n. the act of rubbing together
Friday, n. the fixth day of the week
Friend, n. a familiar companion; v. t. to befriend

Friend'ed, *pa.* befriended, helped, fupported
Friend'lefs, *a.* deftitute of friends, helplefs
Friend'linefs, *n.* kindnefs, a difpofition to friendfhip
Friend'ly, *a.* kind, favorable, fociable
Friend'ly, *ad.* kindly, obligingly, civilly, tenderly
Friend'fhip, *n.* kindnefs, favor, regard, conformity
Frieze, Freeze, *n.* the flat part of a column between the architrave and cornifh, a coarfe cloth
Friézelike, *a.* like frieze, refembling a frieze
Frig'at or Frig'ate, *n.* a fmall fwift fhip of war
Fright, *n.* fudden terror or fear, panic, fcarecrow
Fright, Frighten, *v. t.* to terrify, daunt, difcourage
Frightful, *a.* terrible, dreadful, horrid, unpleafing
Frightfully, *ad.* dreadfully, horridly (feeling
Fri"gid, *a.* cold, impotent, dull, unmoved, un-
Frigid'ity, *n.* coolnefs, want of heat or zeal, dulnefs
Fri"gidly, *ad.* coolly, dully, unfeelingly, weakly,
Frigorif'ic, *a.* caufing or producing cold, cool
Frill, *v. i.* to quake, to fhake; *n.* a kind of ruffle
Fringe, *n.* a kind of trimming; *v. t.* to trim
Frin,gy, *a.* having or adorned with fringes, fhaggy
Frip'pery, *n.* a place where botchers of old clothes dwell, *ob.* old clothes, mean words
Frifk, *v. i.* to leap, fkip, dance, be frolicfome or gay
Frifk'er, *n.* one who is frifky, one who is wanton
Frifk'et, *n.* a frame ufed to confine fheets of paper in printing
Frifk'inefs, *n.* livelinefs, life, gaiety, wantonnefs
Frifk'y, *a.* frolicfome, lively, gay, airy, wanton
Frit, *n.* fand and alkali baked and calcined for making glafs, but not melted
Frith, *n.* a narrow part of the fea, net, wood
Frit'illary, *n.* a fpecies of plant
Frit'ter, *n.* a kind of pancake, fmall piece, fhred.
Frit'ter, *v. t.* to confume by piecemeal, break, cut
Frit'tered, *pa.* divided or cut into fmall pieces
Frivol'ity, Frivoloufnefs, *n.* triflingnefs, meannefs
Friv'olous, *a.* flight, trifling, unimportant
Friv'eloufly, *ad.* in a frivolous manner, fimply, idly
Friz, *v. t.* to form nap into fmall burs
Friz'zle, *v. t.* to curl in fhort curls, curl, crifp
Fro, *ad.* from, backward, back, in a returning ftate
Frock, *n.* a drefs, outward garment, kind of coat
Frog, *n.* a fmall amphibious animal, part of a hoof
Frog'fifh, *n.* an animal which changes from the fhape of a frog to that of a fifh
Frol'ick, *n.* a prank, a whim; *v. i.* to play pranks
Frol'ick, Frol'ickfome, *a.* full of pranks or tricks, gay
From, *pr.* away, out of, becaufe of, fince, ever fince
From'ward or From'wards, *ad.* away or back, *ob.*
Frond, *n.* a ftem and leaf united, as in fern
Frondófe, *a.* having the leaf and ftem in one body
Frondes'cence, *n.* the putting forth of leaves, or the time when plants firft put forth their leaves
Front, [frunt] *n.* the face, forepart, van, boldnefs, impudence, the part oppofed to the face
Front, *v.* to put in front, ftand oppofit to, oppofe
Front'al, *a.* belonging to the front (dow
Front'al, *n.* a pediment over a fmall door or win-

Front'al or Front'let, *n.* a band with infcriptions worn in Jewifh ceremonies
Front'ed, *pa.* made with or having a front, oppofed
Frontiér, *n.* a limit, boundary, border on another country, furtheft fettlements
Frontiér, *a.* placed on the frontiers, bordering
Frontigniác, *n.* a very lufcious French white wine
Front'ifpiece, *n.* a picture fet facing a titlepage
Front'lefs, *a.* fhamelefs, impudent, faucy, very bold
Front'let, *n.* a bandage worn upon the forehead
Frore, Frorne, *a.* frozen, congealed, *ob.*
Froft, *n.* the act or power of congelation, ice
Froft, *v. t.* to cover with fomething like hoarfroft
Froft'bitten, *a.* nipped or withered by the froft
Froft'ed, *a.* laid on like hoarfroft, prepared for the
Froft'ily, *ad.* coldly, without affection (froft
Froft'inefs. *n.* freezing coldnefs, coldnefs
Froft'y, *a.* like froft, hoary, very cold, freezing
Froth, *n.* foam, emptinefs, vain words; *v. i.* to foam
Froth'inefs, *n.* a frothy ftate, lightnefs, vanity
Froth'y, *a.* full of froth, vain, empty, trifling, foft
Frounce, *v. t.* to curl the hair; *n.* a diforder, a wart
Frouz'y or Frow'zy, *a.* fmelling ftrong, mufty, nafty
Frow'ard, *a.* peevifh, fretful, angry, ungovernable
Frow'ardly, *ad.* peevifhly, crofsly, perverfely
Frow'ardnefs, *n.* peevifhnefs, perverfenefs, whim
Frow'er, *n.* a fharpedged tool to cleave laths
Frown, *n.* a wrinkled or four look, a look of d flike
Frown, *v. i.* to fhow diflike by frowns, to look crofs
Frown'ingly, *ad.* fternly, with difpleafure
Frózen, *pa.* from *to freeze*
Fructes'cence, *n.* the cafting of ripe fruit, or the time when plants caft their feeds
Fructif'erous, Frugif'erous, *a.* bearing fruit
Fructificátion, *n.* the act of bearing, fruitfulnefs, the part of plants appropriated to generation
Fruc'tify, *v.* to make or render fruitful, to bear fruit
Fruc'tuous, *a.* bearing fruit, fruitful, fertile, ufeful
Frúgal, *a.* thrifty, fparing careful, faving of expenfe without meannefs
Frugal'ity, Frúgalnefs, *n.* good hufbandry, thrift
Frúgally, *ad.* thriftily, fparingly, carefully, nearly
Frugiv'orous, *a.* eating or fubfifting on fruits
Fruit, *n.* the produce of trees, &c. profit, effect
Frúitage, *n.* fruit, fruit collectively or in general
Frúitbearing, *a.* producing or having fruit
Frúiterer, *n.* a perfon who fells or deals in fruit
Frúitery, *n.* a fruitloft, fruitage, fruit itfelf
Frúitful, *a.* bearing fruit, plenteous, childbearing
Frúitfully, *ad.* plenteoufly, abundantly, richly
Frúitfulnefs, *n.* plenty, abundance, richnefs
Frúitgrove, *n.* a clofe plantation of fruit-trees
Frui"tion, *n.* enjoyment, poffeffion, pleafure
Frúitive, *a.* enjoying, poffeffing, *not ufed*
Frúitlefs, *a.* void of fruit, barren, unprofitable, vain
Frúitlefsly, *ad.* idly, unprofitably, vainly, in vain
Frúitloft, *n.* a loft to put or preferve fruit in
Frúittree, *n.* a tree that bears or produces fruit
Frumentárious, *a.* of or belonging to corn

M 2

Frumentáceous,*a*. refembling wheat (the Romans

Frumentátion, *n*. a gift or largefs of corn among

Frufh, *v. t.* to break, bruife, crufh ; *n*. a horn, *ob*.

Fruftráneous,*a*. vain; ufelefs, unprofitable, empty

Fruit'rate, *a*. vain, ineffectual, ufelefs, void

Fruft'rate, *v. t.* to difappoint, baik, defeat, make

Fruftrátion, *n*. a difappointment, defeat,lofs (null

Fruft'rative, Fruft'ratory, *a*. making void, ufelefs

Frus'tum, *n*. a part cut off from a figure

Frutes'cent, *a*. full of fmall fhoots, fhrubby

Fruticófe, *a*. fhrubby, perennial with woody ftems

Fry, *n*. a thing fried, fifh juft fpawned, child, fieve

Fry, *v*. to drefs in a fryingpan, broil, melt, fume

Fry'ingpan, *n*. an iron pan to fry things in

Fub, *v. t.* to fob, put off, cheat, trick ; *n*. a fatboy

Fúcus, *n. pl.* fucufes, paint or dye, a genus of fea-
   weeds

Fud'dle, *v*. to make or get drunk, to drink hard

Fúel, *n*. matter for the fire; *v. t.* to feed the fire

Fuga''city, *n*. the act of flying away, unfteadinefs

Fugh, *exclam.*expreffing diflike,hatred or averfion

Fúgitive, *n*. a runaway,deferter,vagabond,vagrant

Fúgitive,*a*. flying, wandering, unftable, volatile

Fúgitivenefs, *n*.inconftancy,uncertainty,giddinefs

Fúgue, *n*. a chafe in mufic, or fucceffion in the parts

Ful'ciment,*n*. a prop, fupport, ftay, point,*not ufed*

Ful'crate, *a*. having props or fupports

Ful'crum, *n. pl.* fulcrums, the prop or fupport of
   a lever, or of a plant,&c.

Fulfil', *v. t.* to perform, complete, anfwer, fill up

Fulfill'ing, Fulfil'ment, *n*. a completion

Fulfráught, *a*. fully ftored, completely loaded, *ob*.

Ful'gent, Ful'gid, *a*. fhining, dazzling, very bright

Ful'gor, *n*. a great or dazzling brightnefs, fplendor

Fuli''ginous, *a*. like foot, footy, fmoky, black

Fuli''ginoufly, *ad*. by being footy

Full, *a*. filled, crowded, plump, fatisfied, entire

Full, *n*. a complete meafure or ftate, the whole

Full, *ad*. fully, quite, without abatement, plump

Full, *v. t.* to cleanfe and fcour cloth, and render
   it more compact

Full'blown, Full'fpread, *a*. fpread to the utmoft

Full'bottomed,*a*. having a full or large bottom

Full'eared, *a*. having the head full of grain, large

Full'er, *n*. one who fulls cloth

Fuller's-earth, *n*. a kind of clay ufed by fullers

Full'eyed, *a*. having large and prominent eyes

Fullfed', *a*. quite or very fat, plump, fattened

Full'-laden, *a*. deeply or very heavily laden

Full'nefs, Ful'nefs, *n*. a full ftate, plenty, extent

Full'orbed, *a*. round, like the full moon

Full'fummed, *a*. complete, perfect, entire, whole

Full'y, *ad*. to the full, completely, perfectly, quite

Ful'mer, *n*. a bird which fpouts oil from its bill a-
   gainft its foe

Ful'minant, *a*. thundering, making a loud noife

Ful'minate, *v. i.* to make a noife like thunder, to

Fulminátion, *n*. a thundering, ban, cenfure   (roar

Ful'minatory, *a*. thundering, relating to thunder

Ful'fome, *a*. naufeous, rank, offenfive, obfcene

Ful'fomenefs, *n*. naufeoufnefs, obfcenity

Fulv'ous, *a*. yellow, like faffron

Fumádo, *n*. a fmoked or dried fifh, *ob*.

Fúmatory, *n*. a fpecies of plant

Fun'ble,*v*.to do or handle awkwardly,puzzle,play

Fum'bler,*n*.an awkward,bungling or clumfy perfon

Fum'blingly, *ad*. in an awkward manner, badly

Fume, *n*. fmoke, vapor, ftew, heat, rage, paffion

Fume, *v*. to fmoke, be in a rage or paffion, rave

Fúmid, *a*. fmoaky, full of or like fmoke, vaporous

Fúmigate, *v. t.* to fmoke, fume, perfume   (fion

Fumigátion,*n*. a fcent or vapor raifed by fire, ero-

Fúmingly, *ad*. in a fume, in a rage or heat, angrily

Fúmitory, *n*. a genus of plants

Fúmous, Fúmy, *a*. producing fume, full of vapor

Fun, *n*. a joke, frolic, fport, merriment, mirth

Funambulátion,*n*.rope-dancing,walking on a rope

Func'tion, *n*. an office, employment,charge,power

Func'tionary, *n*. one who holds a public office

Fund, *n*. a ftock,ftock or bank of money,capital

Fund,*v. t.* to appropriate a fund or revenue to the
   regular payment of intereft

Funds,*n. pl.*funded debts evidenced by certificates

Fund'ament, *n*. the hinder part

Fundament'al, *a*. original, chief, principal, prime

Fundament'ally, *ad*. originally, effentially, chiefly

Fúneral, *n*. a burial, the folemnization of a burial

Fúneral, *a*. ufed for or relating to a burial

Funéreal, *a*. dark, difmal, mournful, funeral

Fun''gous, *a*. fpongy, foft, porous, excrefcent

Fun''gus, *n. pl.* Fun''gufes, mufhroom, a genus of
   plants, an excrefcence

Fun'giform, *a*. in the form of a mufhroom

Funic'ular, *a*. having fmall cords or fibers, fibrous

Funk, *n*. offenfive fmell, great fright, panic

Fun'nel, *n*. a kind of pipe,part of a chimney,paffage

Fun'ny, *a*. odd, droll, laughable, whimfical, merry

Fur, *n*. the fine foft hair of wild beafts, fkins containing fur, matter on the tongue

Fur, *v. t.* to line or cover with fur

Fur'below, *n*. fur or fringe fewed on petticoats

Fur'below, *v. t.* to adorn with plaits of fur, &c.

Fur'bifh, *v. t.* to polifh,clean,rub up,put into order

Fur'bifher, *n*. one who polifhes or cleans up, a bur-

Fur'cate, *a*. forked, branching as a fork   (nifher

Furcátion, *n*. a forked ftate, a forkinefs

Fúrfuráceous, *a*. like dander, fcaly, fcurfy

Fúrious, *a*. mad, frantic, raging, violent, fierce

Fúrioufly, *ad*. madly, frantioly, hotly, violently

Fúrioufnefs, *n*. fury, madnefs, paffion, heat, force

Furl, *v. t.* to draw up,wrap up, fold, contract,bind

Fur'long,*n*.the eighth part of a mile, a ridge of land

Fur'lough, *n*. leave given for abfence from duty

Fur'lough, *v. t.* to furnifh with a furlough

Fur'menty or Frúmenty, *n*. wheat boiled in milk

Fur'nace, *n*. an inclofed fireplace, a large veffel

Fur'nace, *v*. to throw out fparks, &c. heat, melt

Fur'nifh,*v,t.*to fupply,provide,equip,fit out,adorn

Fur'niture, *n.* moveables, goods, utenfils, decorations

Fur'rier, *n.* a dealer in or dreffer of furs (tions

Fur'row, *n.* a long trench or hollow, drain, wrinkle

Fur'row, *v. t.* to cut into furrows or hollows, to

Fur'ry, *a.* covered with or made of fur (wrinkle

Fur'ther, *ad.* at a diftance, beyond this, moreover

Fur'ther, *v. t.* to affift, forward, promote, advance

Fur'therance, *n.* affiftance, help, advancement

Fur'therer, *n.* a helper, promoter, advancer

Fur'thermore, *ad.* yet further, moreover, befides

Fur'thermoft, *a.* the moft diftant, the fartheft

Fur'tive, *a.* ftolen, gotten by ftealth, fecret

Fur'uncle, *n.* a large bile, an angry fpot or fwelling

Fur'wrought, *a.* wrought or adorned with fur

Fu'ry, *n.* madnefs, rage, frenzy, violent paffion

Furze, *n.* a very prickly fhrub, gorfe

Furze'bufh, *n.* a bufh or quantity of furze

Furz'y, *a.* full of, overgrown with or having furze

Fufe, [füze] *v.* to melt, liquefy, foften, be melted

Fufee, *n.* a firelock, part of a watch, match, track

Fufibil'ity. *n.* a melted or melting quality

Fü̃ble, Fúfile, *a.* capable of being melted

Fúfiform, *a.* in the fhape of a fpindle

Fufilee'r, *n.* a footfoldier armed with a fufee

Fúfion, *n.* the act of melting, melted ftate, foftnefs

Fufs, *n.* a ftir, buftle, tumult, noife

Fuft'ian, *n.* a cotton-cloth, fwelling ftyle, bombaft

Fuft'ian, *a.* made of fuftian, high-fwelling, lofty

Fus'tic, *n.* a Weft-India wood for dying yellow

Fuftilárian, *n.* a mean fellow, wretch, *ob.*

Fuft'inefs, *n.* a fufty ftate or quality, moldinefs

Fuft'y, *a.* ill-fmelling, rank, ftrong, nafty, moldy

Fútile, *a.* trifling, worthlefs, filly, fimple, talkative

Futil'ity, *n.* a want of folidity, vanity, talkativenefs

Fut'tocks, *n.* the middle timbers of a fhip

Fúture, *a.* that is to come, happen or be, hereafter

Fúture, Futúrity, *n.* a future ftate or being, the

Fúturely, *ad.* in time to come, *ob.* (time to come

Futuri"tion, *n.* future exiftence, futurity, *ob.*

Puzz, *v. i.* to fly or run out in fmall particles

Fuzz'ball, *n.* a kind of mufhroom full of duft, a puff

Fy ! *exclam.* expreffing diflike, hate or abhorrence

G

G AB'ARDINE, *n.* a coarfe frock, *ob.*

Gab, Gab'ble, *v. i.* to prate, to chatter

Gab'ble, *n.* loud talk without meaning, prate

Gab'bler, *n.* a prating or chattering perfon, prater

Gábel, *n.* a kind of excife, cuftom, tax on falt

Gábion, *n.* a wicker bafket ufed in fortifications

Gáble, *n.* the floping end of a building

Gad, *n.* a wedge of fteel, club, graver, perch

Gad, *v. i.* to rove or ramble about idly

Gad'der, *n.* one who runs about from place to place

Gad'fly, *n.* a fly that ftings cattle, the breeze-flye

Gádus, *n.* a fifh with an oblong body

Gaff, *n.* a hook, harpoon, a fmall boom

Gaf'fer, *n.* mafter, father, friend, old fir, *ob.*

Gaf'fle, *n.* an artificial fpur to put upon cocks

Gag, *v. t.* to ftop the mouth fo as to hinder fpeech

Gag, *n.* fomething ufed to hinder the fpeech

Gage, *v.* to lay, give, meafure ; *n.* a pledge, ftandard,

Gag'gle, *v. i.* to make a noife like a goofe (depth

Gáily, *ad.* fplendidly, *fee* gayly

Gain, *n.* profit, benefit, intereft, a bevelling fhoulder or lapping of timber

Gain, *v.* to get, obtain, procure, win, draw, attain

Gáiner, *n.* one who gains or receives advantage

Gáinful, *a.* profitable, advantageous, lucrative

Gáinfully, *ad.* profitably, with gain

Gáingiving, *a.* mifgiving, giving againft, *ob.*

Gáinlefs, *a.* unprofitable, without gain

Gáinleffnefs, *n.* unprofitablenefs, ufeleffnefs

Gáinly. *ad.* handily, dexteroufly, quickly, readily

Gainsáy, *v. t.* gainfaid, *prt.* gainfaid, *pa.* to contradict, oppofe, thwart, deny

Gainsáyer, *n.* an opponent, adverfary, denier

Gainsáying, *n.* contradiction, oppofition

Gáinftand, *v.* to withftand, oppofe, object to, *ob.*

Gáirifh, *a.* gaudy, fhowy, very fine, beautifh, flighty

Gáirifhnefs, *n.* gaudinefs, finery, extravagant joy

Gait, *n.* a manner of walking, walk, marsh, ftep

Gáiters, *n.* coverings for the legs

Gal'a, *n.* a grand or high feftivity, a grand proceffion

Galátian, *n.* a native of Galatia, now Amafia on the fouth fhore of the Euxine

Galan'gal, *n.* a plant having a knotty root

Gal'axy, *n.* a broad circle in the fky, the milky way

Gal'banum, *n.* a refinous gummy fubftance

Gale, *n.* a blaft of wind ; *v.* to bawl, flout, fail faft

Gáleas, *n.* a kind of heavy low-built veffel

Gal'eated, Gal'eated, *a.* covered with a helmet

Galecto, *n.* a fifh of a greenifh color

Galéna, *n.* fulphuret of lead, or fulphur and lead

Galen'ic, *a.* pertaining to Galena, relating to Galen the phyfician

Gal'enift, *n.* a follower of Galen

Gal'iot, *n.* a little galley, a kind of brigantine

Gall, *n.* bile, rancor, great anger, wrath, a fore, a nut

Gall, *v. t.* to hurt the fkin, hurt, fret, vex, harafs

Gallant', *n.* a wooer, fuiter, lover, attendant

Gallant', *a.* civil, polite, attentive

Gal'lant, *a.* brave, bold, noble, fine, gay, fhowy

Gal'lantly, *ad.* bravely, nobly, generoufly (intrigue

Gal'lantry, *n.* bravery, generofity, fhow, courtfhip,

Gall'ed, *pt.* hurt, fretted, injured, vexed, grieved

Gal'leon, *n.* a large fhip having four or five decks

Gal'lery, *n.* a long narrow apartment, a balcony

Gal'ley, *n.* a veffel flat built and long, navigated with fails and oars, a fhips cook room

Gal'leyflave, *a.* one condemned to row the galleys

Gal'leytile, *n.* a kind of tile, an earthen ware

Gal'liard, *a.* a gay brifk man, lively dance, *ob.*

Gal'liardife, *n.* gaity, merriment, mirth, joy, *ob.*

Gal'lic, *a.* pertaining to Gaul, now France

Gall'ic, *a.* belonging to galls, or oak apples

Gall'ate, *n.* a neutral falt formed by the gallic acid with a bafe

Gal'lican, *a.* relating to France or the French

Gallicifm, n. a peculiarity of the French tongue

Galligafk'ins, n. pl, flops, a kind of large open hofe

Galliléans, n. a fect of Jews who refufed tribute to the Romans

Gallimauf'ry, n. a medley, a hotchpotch, ob.

Gallináceous, a. denoting or pertaining to, domeftic fowls, or the gallinæ

Gallinúle, n. a tribe of fowls

Gal'lipot, n. a fmall pot painted and glazed

Gal'lon, n. a meafure containing four quarts (ing

Galloon', n. a kind of lace, a kind of riband or bind-

Gal'lop, v. i. to ride faft, move fait, drive on

Gal'lop, n. the full fpeed or fwifteft pace of a horfe

Gal'loper, n. a horfe or perfon that gallops

Gal'low, v. t. to terrify, frighten, daunt, ob.

Gal'lowy, n. a horfe under fourteen hands high

Gal'lowglaffes, n. pl. a long coat of mail, foldiers

Gal'lows, n. pl. a tree of execution, gibbet, frame

Gal'lowsfree, a. delivered by fate from hanging

Gal'lowftree, n. a tree or place of execution

Gal'ly, n. a printers cafe to receive types from the compofing ftick

Gal'lyworm, n. an infect of the centiped kind

Gal'vanifm, n. the name given to effects refembling electricity, produced by metallic fubftances

Galvan'ic, a. pertaining to galvanifm

Gal'vanize, v. t. to affect with the galvanic fluid

Gal'vanift, n. one verfed in or believing in the doctrins of galvanifm

Gambáde or Gambádo, n. fpatterdafhes for riding

Gam'ble, v. i. to play for money, to game

Gam'bler, n. a cheating gamefter, fharper, knave

Gam'boge, or Cam'boge, n. a tree and its gum

Gam'bet, n. a bird refembling the red fhank

Gam'bol, n. a fkip, leap, frolic, prank, trick, fport

Gam'bol, v. i. to frifk, dance, fkip, leap, frolic, (play

Gam'brel, n. one of the hind legs of a horfe (play

Game, n. a play, fport, jeft, animals purfued

Game, v. i. to play extravagantly, fport, deride

Gámecock, n. a cock bred to fight battles

Gámekeeper, n. one who looks after the game

Gámefome, a. frolicfome, gay, fportive, lively

Gámefter, n. one addicted to gaming, a gambler

Gáming, n. play, the act of playing deep

Gam'mer, n. miftrefs, mother, neighbor, ob.

Gam'mon, n. a buttock of a hog falted and dried

Gam'ut, n. the fcale of mufical notes, the firft note

Ganch, v. i. to throw down and punifh upon hooks

Gan'der, n. the male of the goofe, the leading goofe

Gang, n. a company, crew, fet; v. i. to go

Gang'lion, n. a hard tumor, a knot of nerves (rot

Gan''grene, n. a mortification; v. t. to mortify, to

Gangrénous, a. mortified, corrupted, rotten

Gan''gue, n. ftony fubftances united with metals

Gang'way, n. a paffage in or to a building, a plat-

Gan'il, n. a kind of brittle limeftone (form in fhips

Gan'net, n. the Soland goofe

Gant'let, n. a military form of punifhment, a box-

Gan'za, n. a kind of wild goofe (ing-glove

Gaol, n. a prifon, place of confinement, jail

Gaóler, n. the keeper or mafter of a prifon, a jailor

Gap, n. an opening, breach, paffage, hole, defect

Gape, [a as in afk] v. i. to open the mouth, yawn,

Gáper, n. one who gapes and ftares about (ftare

Gáping, n. the act of gaping, a yawning

Gap'toothed, a. having fpaces between the teeth

Garb, n. clothes, drefs, appearance, tafte, fheaf

Garagáy, n. a rapacious bird of Mexico

Garb'age, n. offals, bowels, entrails, guts

Gar''ble, v. t. to fift, feparate, part, cull, pick

Garb'ler, n. one who feparates, one who picks

Gar'boil, n. a diforder, tumult, uproar, ob.

Gar'den, v. i. to cultivate or make a garden

Gar'den, n. a place to raife kitchen plants, flowers and fruits, a well cultivated fpot

Gar'dener, n. a perfon who cultivates a garden

Gar'dening, n. the act or art of cultivating gardens

Gar'denftuff, n. things grown in a garden

Gard'on, n. a fifh of the roach kind

Gar'garifm, Gar''gle, n. a medicin for the throat

Garg'et, n. a fwelling in the throat of cattle

Garg'il, n. a difeafe in geefe

Gar''gle, v. t. to wafh the throat with a medicin

Gar'gol, n. a diftemper common to hogs

Gar'land, n. a wreath of flowers, collar, net

Gar'lic, n. a plant, a kind of ftrong onion

Gar'licky, a. abounding with or like garlic

Gar'ment, n. a covering for the body, drefs, clothes

Gar'ner, n. a granary, place to put threfhed grain in

Gar'ner, v. t. to ftore or lay up in a place of fafety

Gar'net, n. a red gem, precious ftone, fmall tackle

Gar'nifh, v. to adorn, decorate, fet off, fetter, warn

Garnifheé, n. one in whofe hands property of an abfconding debtor is attached

Gar'nifh, Gar'nifhment, Gar'niture, n. ornament, a

Gárous, a. like pickle made of fifh, briny, falt (fee

Gar'ran, n. a ftrong fmall horfe, a galloway

Gar'ret, n. the uppermoft room, [rotten wood, ob.]

Garretéer, n. one that lives in a garret

Gar'rifon, n. a fort, or foldiers to defend it

Gar'rifon, v. to fecure by or put in foidiers

Garrúlity, n. loquacity, talkativenefs, babbling

Gar'rulous, a. prating, chattering, talkative, noify

Gar'ter, v. i. to tie up, bind or faften with a garter

Gar'ter, n. a band to tie up the ftockings, a riband

Gar'terfifh, n. a fifh with a long flattifh body

Gas, n. an aeriform fluid, or a fluid which is invifible, in diftinction from vapor which is vifible

Gas'eous, a. in the form of gas, invifible

Gas'ify, v. t. to convert into gas

Gafification, n. a converting into gas

Gafconáde, n. a boaft, brag, bravado; v. i. to brag

Gafh, n. a deep and long cut; v. t. to hack, to cut

Gafk'et, n. a plaited cord to tie fails to yards

Gafk'ins, n. pl. very wide hofe or breeches

Gafp, v. to endeavor or gape for breath, to long for

Gafp, n. a fhort or convulfive catch of the breath

Gas'tric, a. belonging to the ftomach

Gaftrot'omy, *n*. a cutting open the belly

Gate, *n*. a large door, frame of wood, entrance, way

Gat'fifh, *n*. a fifh of a beautiful yellow color

Gath'er, *v*. to bring or draw together, affemble, pick or take up, crop, pluck, get, thicken, fwell

Gath'erer, *n*. one who gathers, a collector

Gath'ering, *n*. a collection, fwelling, tumor

Gath'ers, *n. pl.* plaits, folds, a plaiting of cloth

Gaude, *v. i.* to rejoice greatly, exult, *ob.*

Gaude, Gaud'ery, *n*. an ornament, finery, *ob.*

Gaud'ily, *ad*. with gaudinefs, fhowily, finely, gaily

Gaud'inefs, *n.* fhowinefs, a tinfel appearance, finery

Gaud'y, *a*. fhowy, oftentatioufly fine ; *n*. a feaft

Gauge, *v. t.* to meafure the contents of a veffel

Gauge, *n.* a meafure, ftandard, rod, guefs, fkill, art

Gauger, *n*. a man who gauges or meafures veffels

Gauging, *n*. the act or art of meafuring veffels

Gaul'ifh, *a*. pertaining to Gaul or France

Gaunt, *a*. lean, meager, fpare, thin, flender

Gauntlet, *n*. an iron glove, cock's fpur, gantlet

Gauze, *n*. a very thin filk or linen

Gau'zy, *a*. like gauze, thin as gauze

Gave, *pret*. of *to give*   (the fons

Gav'elkind, *n*. an equal divifion of lands among all

Gáveloc, *n*. a kind of long iron bar, a pick-javelin

Gávelocs, *n. pl.* javelins, warlike inftruments

Gav'ilan, *n*. a fpecies of hawk in the Philippine ifles

Gav'iot, *n*. an aquatic fowl of Brazil

Gav'ot, *n*. a brifk dance, a lively air or tune

Gay, *a*. airy, merry, fine, fhowy ; *n*. an ornament

Gáyety or Gáiety, *n*. airinefs, cheerfulnefs, finery

Gáyly or Gáily, *ad*. airily, merrily, fhowily, finely

Gaze, *v. i.* to look hard or earneftly ; *n.* a fixed look

Gázehound, *n*. a hound that purfues by the eyes

Gazell', *n*. an African animal like a goat and deer

Gázer, *n*. one who gazes or looks very hard

Gazett'e *n*. a kind of newfpaper or public print

Gazettéer, *n*. a writer of news, newfpaper, book ,

Gazet'to, *n*. a fifh with a thick broad body

Gázingftock, *n*. one gazed at with fcorn, &c.

Gazom'eter, *n*. an inftrument to meafure gas, or to afford it in a uniform current

Gazom'etry, *n*. the art or practice of determining and regulating the volume of gas in experiments

Gaz'on, *n*. a piece of turf to line a breaft-work

Gear, [g hard] *n*. accouterments, drefs, traces, ftuff, goods

Gear, *v. t.* to drefs, deck, put harnefs on horfes

Geck, [g hard] *n*. one eafily impofed on; *v. t.* to

Geefe, [g hard] *n. pl.* of *goofe*   (cheat, *ob.*

Gel'atin, *n*. jelly, a fubftance like jelly

Gelat'inate, *v. t.* to form or become jelly

Gelatinátion, *n*. the ftate of being turned into jelly

Gelat'inous, *a*. formed into a jelly, ftiff

Geld, [g hard] *v. t.* gelded, gelt, *pret*. gelded, gelt, *pa*. to caftrate, emafculate, *n*. a tax

Geld'er, *n*. one who gelds cattle of any kind

Geld'ing, *n*. a horfe that has been gelded

Gel'id, *a*. extremely or very cold, cold as ice

Gel'ly, *n*. a liquor of meat boiled to a confiftence

Gelt, [g hard] *n*. a gelded animal, gelding, tinfel

Gem, *n*. a jewel, the firft bud of a tree

Gem, *v*. to adorn with jewels, to bud

Gem'inate, *a*. double, growing in pairs

Geminátion, *n*. a repetition, a doubling, a fold

Gem'ini, *n. pl.* twins, a pair, brace, couple, fign

Gem'inous, *a*. double, twofold, fimilar, equal

Gemmátion, *n*. the ftate or form of the gem or bud of a plant

Gem'mery, Gem'meous, *a*. pertaining to jewels

Gemmip'arous, *a*. producing buds or gems

Gem'my, *a*. bright, fhining, glittering, fparkling

Gen'der, *n*. a fex, breed, race, fort, kind, difference

Gen'der, *v*. to beget, produce, copulate, engender

Genealo'gical, *a*. pertaining to genealogy

Geneal'ogift, *n*. one fkilled in genealogy

Geneal'ogy, *n*. the hiftory of family-defcendants

Gen'eral, *a*. common, ufual, public, extenfive, large

Gen'eral, *n*. a whole, great military officer, director

Generalifs'imo, *n*. a commander in chief, a title

General'ity, *n*. a general ftate, moft part, bulk

Gen'eralize, *v. t.* to make or render general

Generalizátion, *n*. the act of making general

Gen'erally, *ad*. in general, commonly, ufually

Gen'eralnefs, *n*. a wide extent, commonnefs

Gen'eralfhip, *n*. the fkill or office of a general

Gen'erant, Gen'erator, *n*. what begets or produces

Gen'erate, *v. t.* to beget, produce, propagate, caufe

Generátion, *n*. an age, race, family, production

Gen'erative, *a*. able to produce, fruitful

Gener'ic, *a*. comprehending the genus, large

Gener'ically, *ad*. with regard to the genus

Generos'ity, Gen'eroufnefs, *n*. liberality, bounty

Gen'erous, *a*. liberal, openhearted, noble, ftrong

Gen'eroufly, *ad*. in a generous or noble manner

Gen'efis, *n*. the firft book of Mofes, generation

Gen'et, *n*. a fmall Spanifh horfe, a quadruped of the weafel kind and its fur

Genéva, or Gin, *n*. a fpirit diftilled from grain, fometimes flavored with juniper berries or oil

Gene'van, *n*. a native of Geneva (of turpentine

Gene'van, *a*. belonging to Geneva

Génial, *a*. contributing to propagation or mirth,

Génially, *ad*. cheerfully, gaily, naturally (native

Genic'ulate, *a*. bent like the knee at the joints

Génii, *n. pl.* fpirits, demons

Génio, *n*. a perfon of fome particular turn of mind

Gen'itals, *n. pl.* the parts of generation,

Gen'iting, *n*. the name of an early apple

Gen'itive, *a*. the fecond cafe of nouns

Génius, *n*. a nature, difpofition, bent, wit, fpirit

Genoéfe, *n*. a native of Genoa, in Italy

Genoéfe, *a*. pertaining to Genoa

Gentéel, *a*. polite, civil, kind, elegant, graceful

Gentéeily, *ad*. politely, kindly, gracefully, well

Gentéelnefs, Gentil'ity, *n*. politenefs, gracefulnefs

Gen'tian, *n*. a plant, fellwort

Gen'tile, *n*. a heathen ; *a*. heathen, pagan

Gentiléffe, *n.* politenefs, complaifance, *ob.*

Gent'alifm, *n.* heathenifm, paganifm, ignorance

Gentilli'tious, *a.* peculiar to a nation, hereditary

Gen'tle, *a.* tame, foft, meek, peaceable; *v. t.* to

Gen'tle, *n.* a kind of worm ufed in fifhing (tame

Gen'tleman, *n.* a term of complaifance (man

Gen'tlemanlike, Gen'tlemanly, *a.* like a gentle-

Gen'tlenefs, *n.* tamenefs, meeknefs, tendernefs

Gen'tlefhip, *n.* the carriage of a gentleman, *ob.*

Gen'tlewoman, *n.* a woman of genteel behavior

Gent'ly, *ad.* foftly, flowly, with care, tenderly

Gen'too, *n.* a native of India or Indoftan

Gen'too, *a.* pertaining to the Gentoos

Gent'ry, *n.* perfons of a ftate above the vulgar

Genóo, [g hard] *n.* an African animal whofe form

   partakes of the horfe, the ox and the deer

Genuflec'tion, *n.* an act of religiouskneeling (true

Gen'uine, *a.* original, free from adulteration, real,

Gen'uinely, *ad.* naturally, originally, really, truly

Gen'uinenefs, *n.* a genuine quality

Génus, *n.* in fcience, a clafs of beings, kind, mode

Geocent'ric, *a.* having the fame center as the earth

Géod, *n.* a fmall rounded lump of agate, filled with

   cryftals   (earth

Geognos'tic, *a.* relating to the knowledge of the

Geog'rapher, *n.* a perfon converfant in geography

Geograph'ical, *a.* of or relating to geography

Geog'raphy, *n.* a defcription of the earth

Geol'ogy, *n.* the fcience of the earth and its conftit-

   uent parts

Geol'ogift, *n.* one verfed in a knowledge of the earth

Geolo'gical, *n.* pertaining to geology

Géomancer, *n.* a diviner by lines on the ground

Géomancy, *n.* divination by lines on the earth-

Geomant'ic, *a.* pertaining to geomancy   (metry

Geom'eter, Geometri'cian, *n.* one verfed in geo-

Geomet'rical, *a.* pertaining to or done by geometry

Geomet'rically, *ad.* in a geometrical manner, very

Geom'etrize, *v. t.* to perform or do geometrically

Geom'etry, *n.* the fcience of quantity, extenfion

   or magnitude, abftractedly confidered

Geopon'ical, *a.* relating to agriculture, *ob.* (a loaf

George, *n.* a figure worn by knights of the garter,

Geor'gia, *n.* the mott fouthern of the U. States

Geor'gian, *n.* a native of Georgia

Geor'gic, *n.* a rural poem; *a.* relating to agriculture

Gerànium, *n.* cranes bill, a genus of plants

Ger'man, *n.* a relation; *a.* related, akin

German'ic, Ger'man, *a.* belonging to Germany

German'der, *n.* a fpecies of plant

Germ, Germ'en, *n.* a fprout, fhoot, bud

Germ'inate, *v. i.* to fprout, fhoot, bud, put forth

Germinátion, *n.* the act of fprouting, a growth,

   the time in which feeds germinate

Ger'und, *n.* a kind of verbal noun in grammar

Geft, *n.* a lift of ftages in travelling, fhow, ftory, *ob.*

Geftátion, *n.* the act of carrying young in the belly

Geft'ic, *a.* relating to gefture or tricks, antic, droll

Geftic'ulate, *v. i.* to ufe geftures, to play odd tricks

Gefticulátion, *n.* various poftures of the body

Geft'ure, *n.* an action, motion, pofture, trick

Geft'ure, *v.* to accompany with or ufe action

Get, [g hard] *v.* gat, got, gotten, *pa.* to procure,

   gain, win, learn, arrive, induce

Get'ting, *n.* the act of getting, gain, profit (fhowy

Gew'gaw, [g hard] *n.* a trifle, toy, bawble; *a.*

Ghaft'linefs, *n.* horror of countenance, palenefs

Ghaft'ly, *a.* horrid, fhocking, frightful, like a ghoft

Ghaft'nefs, *n.* ghaftlinefs, horror, dreadfulnefs

Gherk'in, *n.* a fmall cucumber for pickling

Ghoft, *v.* to haunt, die, give up the ghoft, *ob.*

Ghoft, *n.* the foul of a perfon deceafed, foul, fpirit

Ghóftly, *a.* of or relating to the foul, fpiritual

Giant, *n.* a man unnaturally tall or large

Giantefs, *n.* a woman uncommonly tall

Giantlike, Giantly, *a.* very tall or large, huge

Giaróla, [g hard] *n.* a bird of the lark kind

Giarólo, [g hard] *n.* a bird of the fnipe kind

Gib'ber, [g hard] *v. i.* to talk unintelligibly, *ob.*

Gib'berifh, *n.* cant words, nonfenfe

Gib'bet, *n.* a gallows to expofe criminals

Gib'bet, *v. t.* to hang and expofe on a gallows

Gib'bier, *n.* any kind of wild fowl, game

Gibbos'ity, Gib'boufnefs, *n.* convexity

Gib'bon, [g hard] *n.* the long armed ape

Gib'bous, [g hard] *a.* protuberant, fwelled (back

Gib'boufifh, *n.* a fifh with a protuberance on its

Gib'cat, *n.* an old worn-out cat, and old woman

Gibe, *v.* to fneer, taunt, reproach

Gibe or Gybe, *n.* a fneer, fcoff, taunt, reproach

Gibe, *n.* a fneerer, fcoffer, taunter, reproacher

Gibingly, *ad.* fcornfully, contemptuoufly

Gib'lets, *n. pl.* parts of a goofe or duck

Gid'dily, [g hard] *ad.* heedlefly, ufteadily, idly

Gid'dinefs, *n.* carelefnefs, a fwimming in the head

Gid'dy, *a.* heedlefs, thoughtlefs, carelefs, light, rafh

Gid'dybrained, Gid'dyheaded, *a.* thoughtlefs, wild

Gid'dypaced, *a.* moving irregularly, very unfteady

Gift, [g hard] *n.* a thing given, bribe, faculty

Gift'ed, *a.* endowed, invefted, given

Gig, [g hard] *n.* a thing that whirls round, top,

Gigant'ic, *a.* like a giant, huge, vaft,   (chaife

Gig'gle, [g hard] *v. i.* to laugh, laugh idly, titter

Gig'gler, *n.* a foolifh or idle laugher, a titterer

Gig'let, *n.* a wanton lacivious girl; *a.* wanton

Gild, [g hard] *v. t.* gilded, gilt, *pret.* gilded, gilt,

   pa. to wafh over with gold, &c. adorn, fet off

Gild'er, *n.* one who gilds, a kind of fmall coin

Gild'ing, *n.* gold or filver laid on for ornament

Gill, *n.* meafure, liquor, herb, mifs

Gill, [g hard] *n.* the membranes and opening near

   the heads of fifh which admit air to the blood

   and let out water taken in at the mouth

Gill'houfe, *n.* a houfe where gill is fold

Gill iflower, *n.* a very fine flower   (perfons

Gil'lotin, [g hard] *n.* an engine for beheading

Gil'lotin, *v. t.* to cut off heads with a gillotin

Gilt, [g hard] *n.* any thing gilt or fine, *ob.*

Gilt'head, *n.* a fish with a golden crescent be-
Gim, Gim'my,*a,* neat, spruce, gay (tween its eyes
Gim'bal, [g hard] *n.* a kind of double ring
Gimb'let, [g hard] *n.* a borer for nails
Gim'crack, *n.* a little pretty thing or device, a toy
Gim'mer,[g hard]*n.*a movement,machinery,ewe
Gimp, [g hard] *n.* a silk twist or lace, edging, trimming   (machine to clean cotton
Gin, *n.* a snare, trap, engine, pump, geneva, a
Gin, *v. t.* to clean cotton of its seeds by a gin
Gin'ger, *n.* a hot spice root, a plant
Gin'gerbread,*n.* a bread made of flour, ginger and treacle, a kind of sweet spicy bread
Gin'gerly, *ad.* cautiously, tenderly, softly, *ob.*
Ging''ham, [g hard] *n.* a cloth of cotton and linen striped and glazed
Gin'gival, *a.* belonging to the gums
Gin''gle,*v.* to make or cause a sharp noise,to tinkle
Gin''gle, *n.* a found, a shrill resounding noise
Ginseng',*n.*ninzin, a genus of plants of five species
Gip'sy,*n.* a pretended fortuneteller, a beggar
Giraff', [g hard] *n.* the camel leopard, an animal of Africa with a long neck like the camel, and a body spotted like the leopard (proach, sneer
Girafole, *n.* the herb turnfol, the opal stone
Gird, [g hard] *n.* a pang, twitch, sharp pain, re-
Gird, *v.* girded, girt, *pret.* girded, girt, *pa.* to bind or tie round, dress, reproach, sneer
Gird'er, *n.* the largest timber in a floor
Gir''dle, [g hard] *n.* a thing tied round the waist
Gir''dle, *v. t.* to bind with a girdle, *in America,* to cut a ring through the bark and sap of trees to kill them
Girl, [g hard] *n.* a female child, a young woman
Girl'ish, *a.* acting like a girl, childish, giddy
Girl'ishness, *n.* a girlish state or behavior
Gir'roc,*n.* the lacertus, a fish of the gar-fish kind
Girt, [g hard] *n.* a bandage for a saddle, &c.
    v. t. to gird   (a girt
Girth, [g hard] *n.* the compass made by a string,
Gift, *n.* in law the main point
Give, [g hard] *v.* gave, *pret.* given,*pa.* to bestow, deliver, pay, grant, yield, resign, apply
Giv'en, *pa.* bestowed, granted, yielded, addicted
Giv'er,*n.* one who gives,one who bestows or grants
Giz'zard, [g hard] *n.* the hard stomach of a fowl
Glabrous, *a.* smooth, having an even surface
Glacial, *a.* relating to or like ice, icy, frozen
Glaciation, *n.* the act of freezing, ice formed
Glacier,*n.* a perennial body of ice
Glacis, *n.* a sloping bank in fortifications
Glad, *a.* cheerful, merry, pleased, pleasing,bright
Glad, Glad'den, *v. t.* to make glad, delight,cheer
Glad'der *n.* one who makes glad, one who revives
Glade *n.* an opening in a wood or in ice
Gladiate, *a.* shaped like a sword
Gladiator,*n.* a sword player, a kind of prizefighter
Gladiatorial, *a.* of or relating to gladiators,bloody
Gladiole, *n.* a plant of several species

Glad'ly,*ad.* cheerfully,joyfully,readily,commonly
Glad'ness,*n.* cheerfulness,joy, delight, pleasure
Glad'some, *a.* cheering, causing joy, pleasing, gay
Glad'win, *n.* a strong smelling plant
Glair, *n.* the white of an egg, a kind of halbert
Glair, *v. t.* to smear with the white of eggs
Glance,*n.* a quick view,the dart of a beam of light
Glance, *v.* to view obliquely, shoot, strike, allude
Glanc'ingly, *ad.* obliquely, transiently, shortly
Gland, *n.* a secreting vessel in animals or plants, a nut   (nose
Gland'ers, *n. pl.* a disease, the running of a horse's
Glandif'erous, *a.* bearing or having acorns
Gland'iform, *a.* in form of a gland
Gland'ule, *n.* a small gland or grain
Glandulation, *n.* the system of glands in a plant
Glandulif'erous, *a.* bearing glandules
Glandulos'ity, *n.* a collection or set of glands
Gland'ulous, *a.* like or pertaining to the glands
Glare, *n.* an overpowering brightness, luster, flash
Glare, *v.* to shine so as to dazzle the eyes, to dart
Glaring, *pa. a.* shining, shocking, barefaced
Glafs, *n.* transparent substance made of sand and
Glafs, *a.*made of or resembling glass (alkaline salts
Glafs, *v. t.* to behold or view as in a glass, to glaze
Glafs'ed, Glast, *pa.* covered with glass, glazed
Glafs'furnace, *n.* a place for melting glass in
Glafs'gazing, *a.* finical, foppish, affected, vain
Glafs'grinder, *n.* one who grinds or polishes glass
Glafs'house, *n.* a house or place where glass is made
Glafs'man, *n.* one who deals in or sells glass
Glafs'metal, *n.* glass when in a state of fution
Glafs'work, *n.* a making or manufactory of glass
Glafs'wort, *n.* the kali, a plant
Glafs'y, *a.* resembling glass, clear, smooth, brittle
Glauc'ous,*a.* having a light-green color, greenish
Glaucus, *n.* a genus of fishes of three species
Glave, Glavie, *n.* a broad sword, a large bill, *ob.*
Glav'er, *v. t.* to flatter, wheedle, coax, *ob.* (glass
Glaze, *v. t.* to put in or cover with glass, to set a
Glaze, *n.* a polish or composition for covering earthen ware
Glazier, *n.* a man who sets glass in windows, &c,
Glead or Glede, *n.* a kite, a buzzard   (suddenly
Gleam, *n.* a sudden shoot of light; *v. i.* to shine
Gleaming,*pa.* shining, flashing; *n.* a gleam
Gleamy, *a.* flashing, shooting sudden light, bright
Glean,*v. t.* to gather the remains, pick up, select
Glean, *n.* a collection made slowly and laboriously
Gleaner, *n.* one who gleans, one who selects
Gleaning, *n.* the act of gleaning, a thing gleaned
Glebe, *n.* a church-estate, turf, soil, sulphur
Glebos'ity, *n.* a glebous state or quality
Glebous, Gleby, *a.* turfy, cloddy, full of clods
Glee, *n.* joy, mirth, merriment, pleasure, gaity
Gleeful, *a.* merry, cheerful, laughing, gay
Gleek, *n.* music, a musician; *v. i.* to sneer, *ob.*
Gleek'ing,*pa.* sneering, acting the droll, *ob.*
Gleen, *v. i.* to shine from heat or polish, *ob.*

Gleet, *n.* a venereal complaint; *v. t.* to run flowly
Glen, *n.* a valley, vale, fpace between two hills
Glib, *a.* fmooth, flippery, quick, ready
Glib, *v. t.* to geld, to caftrate, *ob.*
Glib'ly, *ad.* fmoothly, quickly, readily, eafy, faft
Glib'nefs, *n.* fmoothnefs, flipperinefs, eafe (pafs
Glide, *v. i.* to flow gently, filently and fwiftly, to
Glide, *n.* the act and manner of pafsing fmoothly
Glide, *n.* a fneer, fcoff, flout; *v. t.* to jeer, *ob.*
Glim'mer, *v. i.* to fhine faintly; *n.* a foffil
Glim'mering, *n.* a weak or faint light, a fhort view
Glimpfe, *n.* a fhort appearance or view, a faint light
Glis'fa, *n.* a fifh of the tunny kind without fcales
Glis'ten or Glis'ter, *v. i.* to fhine, fparkle, glitter
Glit'ter, *v. i.* to fhine brightly, glare, gleam, fparkle
Glit'ter, Glit'tering, *n.* lufter, brightnefs, fhow
Gloat, *v. i.* to look wantonly or afquint, *ob.*
Globate, Glóbed, *a.* formed like a globe, round
Globe, *n.* a round body, fphere, ball, body of men
Globófe, Glóbous, *a.* fpherical, round
Globos'ity, Glóboufnefs, *n.* a roundnefs of form
Glob'ular, Glob'ulous, *a.* like a globe, round
Glob'ule, *n.* a very fmall globe, round particle, drop
Glome, *n.* a roundifh head of flowers
Glom'erate, *v. t.* to gather, roll or form into, a ball
Glom'erate, *a.* crowded together, clofe
Glom'erule, *n.* a fmall glome
Gloom, *n.* darknefs, cloudinefs, heavinefs
Gloom'ily, *ad.* dimly, darkly, heavily, fullenly
Gloom'inefs, *n.* want of light, cloudinefs of look
Gloom'y, *a.* dark, cloudy, difmal, fullen, dejected
Gloried, *a.* illuftrious, noble, honorable, honored
Glorificátion, *n.* the act of giving glory, praife, glory
Glórify, *v. t.* to make glorious, praife, extol
Glórious, *a.* illuftrious, noble, excellent, haughty
Glórioufly, *ad.* illuftrioufly, nobly, bravely, finely
Glóry, *n.* honor, praife, fame, happinefs, circle
Glóry, *v. i.* to boaft, be proud of, rejoice (of rays
Glórying, *pa.* boafting, *n.* the act of boafting
Glofs, *n.* a fcholium, comment, brightnefs
Glofs, *v. t.* to explain, palliate, cover, adorn
Glofs'ary, *n.* a dictionary of old or obfcure words
Gloffog'raphy, *n.* the writing of comments
Gloffator, Gloffog'rapher, *n.* a commentator (glofs
Glofs'inefs, *n.* a fmooth polifh, fuperficial lufter,
Glofs'ing, *n.* an explanation by gloffes or notes
Glofs'y, *a.* fhining, fhowy, fmoothly polifhed, foft
Glove, [gluv] *n.* a cover for the hand and arm
Glove, *v. t.* to cover with gloves
Glov'er, *n.* one who makes or fells gloves
Glout or Glowt, *v. i.* to pout, to look fullen, *ob.*
Glow, *v.* to burn, grow or be hot, redden, fhine
Glow, *n.* a heat, warmth, paffion, brightnefs
Glowworm, *n.* a fpecies of fire fly
Glaze, *n.* flattery, falfe infinuation, a glofs, *ob.*
Glaze, *v. i.* to flatter, wheedle, comment, *ob.*
Glúcin, *n.* a foft white earth obtained from beryl
and emerald
Glue, *n.* a ftrong cement ufed to join fubftances

Glue, *v. t.* to join together with glue, unite, flick
Glum, *a.* fullen, four, gloomy, grave, ftubborn
Glume, *n.* hufk or chaff on the feeds of plants
Glumófe, *a.* having a hufk at the bafe
Glut, *v.* to devour, cloy, difguft, overload, cram,
Glut, *n.* a great plenty, more than is enough (fill
Glúten, *n.* glue, the principle of glue in grain
Glútinous, Glúey, *a.* like glue, ropy, fticky, tough
Glútinoufnefs, *n.* a ftate of being vifcous
Glut'ton, *n.* one who eats to excefs, an animal
Glut'tonous, *a.* given to exceffive feeding, greedy
Glut'tonoufly, *ad.* in a gluttonous manner
Glut'tony, *n.* excefs in eating, great luxury
Gly ph, *n.* an ornamented cavity in building
Gnar or Gnarl, *v. i.* to growl, fnarl, *ob.*
Gnarl'ed, *a.* knotted, knotty, rough
Gnafh, *v.* to grind the teeth in a rage, to clafh
Gnafh'ing, *n.* the act of grinding the teeth, anguifh
Gnat, *n.* a fmall winged ftinging infect
Gnaw, *v. t.* to bite, tear with the teeth, wafte, fret
Gnéifs, *n.* a compound ftone of a fibrous texture
Gnome, *n.* a fuppofed being in the earth guarding
mines, &c. (dial
Gnómen, *n.* an index, the ftyle, hand or pin of a
Gnomol'ogic, *a.* pertaining to maxims or proverbs
Gnomon'ic, *a.* pertaining to a gnomon
Gnomon'ics, *n. pl.* the art or fcience of dialing
Gnos'fian, *a.* pertaining to Gnoffus in Crete, and
to Ariadne, who was born there, alfo to a crown
of 7 ftars which fhe received from Bacchus,
which was made a conftellation
Gnos'tics, *n.* heretics who corrupted chriftianity
by eaftern philofophy, and the doctrin of cons
emanating from GOD
Gnos'ticifm, *n.* the fyftem of the Gnoftics
Go, *v. i.* went, *pret.* gone, *pa.* to walk, travel,
move, proceed, reach, decay
Goad, *n.* a fharp inftrument ufed to drive oxen
Goad, *v. t.* to prick with a goad, drive, urge, vex
Goal, *n.* a ftarting-poft, prifon, point, final purpofe,
Goat, *n.* an animal between a deer and fheep (end
Góatherd, *n.* one who tends or takes care of goats
Góatifh, *a.* rank or luftful as a goat, ftrong, filthy
Góatfucker, *n.* a bird of the fwallow kind
Gob, Gob'bet, *n.* a mouthful, piece, fmall quantity
Gob'bet, *v. t.* to eat or fwallow at a mouthful
Gob'ble, *v. t.* to fwallow haftily and with noife
Gob'let, *n.* a kind of bowl, a kind of large cup
Gob'lin, *n.* an evil fpirit, apparition, elf, hobgoblin
Góby, *n.* a delufion, artifice, cheat, evafion, efcape
Gócart, *n.* a thing ufed to teach children to walk
God, *n.* the fupreme being, a ruler, an idol
God, *v. t.* to make a god, deify, adore
God'defs, *n.* a female deity, a heavenly woman
God'defshood, *n.* the ftate of a goddefs, divinity
God'defslike, *a.* divine, charming, beautiful
God'father, *n.* a male fponfor in baptifm
God'head, *n.* the divine nature, godfhip, deity, god
God'lefs, *a.* irreligious, profane, very wicked, vile

God'like,a.divine,heavenly,holy,pious,excellent
God'linefs,n. piety to God, real or true religion
God'ly, a. pious, religious, righteous; ad. piously,
God'mother,n. a female fponfor in baptifim (holily
God'fhip,n.the character of God,godhead,divinity
God'fon, n. a boy for whom one has been fponfor
God'ward, ad. towards or with refpect to God
God'wit, n. a bird with a long bill and legs
Göer, n. one who goes, a runner, walker,traveller
Goff, n. a fort of play with a flick and ball
Gog'gle, v. i. to look afquint or afide, roll, move
Gog'gles,n. glaffes to cure fquinting, or defend
   the eyes
Gog'gleeyed,a. having large roling eyes,fquinting
Göing, n. the act of walking, a departure, a preg-
Goi'ter, n. the bronchocele or fwelled neck (nancy
Gold, n. the moft precious of all metals
Göldbeater, n. one who beats gold into fine leaves
Göldbound, a. bound or furrounded with gold
Gölden, a. made of or like gold, valuable, happy
Göldenly, ad. fplendidly, delightfully, very finely
Göldfinch, n. a fmall beautiful finging bird
Göldfifh, n. a fifh having a gloffy gold color
Göldlaced, a. trimmed with lace made of gold
Göldleaf, n. a very thin plate of gold for gilding
Göldfinny, n. a fmall fifh like the wraff
Göldylocks, n. a plant of feveral kinds
Göldfmith, n. one who works in gold, a banker
Gome, n. the black oily greafe of a cartwheel
Gon'dola, n. a long flat boat chiefly ufed at Venice
Gondoliér, n. a boatman or waterman at Venice
Gone, pa. of to go [pron. gawn]
Gon'falon or Gon'fanon, n. a ftandard or enfign,ob.
Goniom'etry, n. the meafuring of angles
Goniomet'rical, a. pertaining to the meafuring
   of angles
Gonorrhéa, n. a morbid flux, the venereal difeafe
Good, n. that which affords real happinefs or
   pleafure, or the means of obtaining it
Good, a. having defirable qualities, fit; ad. well
Good'linefs, n. beauty, grace,elegance,fhow,tafte
Good'ly, a. beautiful,graceful, comely,fine,happy
Good'man, n. gaffer, mafter, neighbor,friend (lity
Goodnáture,n. an obliging temper, kindnefs,civi-
Goodnátured, a. obliging, kind, civil, gentle, eafy
Good'nefs, n. all defirable qualities, virtue, piety
Good'now,exclam,denoting wonder,love or efteem
Goods,n. pl. furniture,wares,merchandize,move-
Good'y, n. a low term of civility, miftrefs (ables
Goo'gings, n. iron clamps to fupport a rudder
Goofan'der, n. the merganfer, a water fowl
Goofe, n. a large fowl, taylor's iron, fimpleton
Goofe'berry, n. the name of a bufh and its fruit
Goofeberryfoöl, n. a difh made of goofeberries,
   milk and fugar, mixed together
Gord, n. an inftrument of gaming,whirlpool,eddy
Gor'dian, a. inextricable, very intricate or cramp
Gor'dianknot, n. an inextricable difficulty
Gore, n. clotted or corrupt blood, a flip, a piece

Gore, v. t. to wound with horns,ftab,pierce,pufh
Gorge, n. the fwallow or throat, a molding,a line
Gorge, v. t. to fwallow, to fill up to the throat
Gor'geous, a. fine, fhowy, glittering, fumptuous
Gor'geoufly, ad. finely, fplendidly, richly, ftately
Gor'gerin, n. a little frize between the aftragal
   and annulets of a capital
Gor'get, n. armor for the throat, a part of drefs
Gor'gon, n. a monfter, any thing horrid; a. ugly
Gor'mandize, v. i. to devour or eat ravenoufly
Gor'mandizer, n. a voracious eater, a glutton
Gor'mandizing, pa. eating greedily, ravenous
Gorfe, n. a very prickly fhrub ufed for firing,furze
Góry, a. covered with or like gore, bloody
Gos'hawk, n. a hawk of a large kind or breed
Gos'ling, n. a young goofe, a fort of excrefcence
Gos'pel,n. GOD'S word through CHRIST
Gos'pel, v. t. to inftruct in the gofpel
Gos'pelled, pa. inftructed in chriftianity
Gos'peller, n. a follower or admirer of Wickliff
Gofs'amer, n. the down of plants, a long cobweb
Gofs'ip, n. a fponfor in baptifim, tattler, prater
Gofs'ip, v. i. to chat, prate, fpend time idly
Got, Got'ten, pa. paff. of to get
Goth'ic, a. pertaining to Goths, rude, ancient
Goth'icifm, n. roughnefs, rudenefs, barbarity
Gouge, n. a kind of chifel having a round edge
Gourd, n. a plant refembling a melon, a bottle
Góurd'y, a. fwelled in the legs, large, thick,greafy
Gout, n. a moft painful diforder, [goo, fte]
Gout'y, a. afflicted with or liable to the gout,
Gout'wort,n. a plant, wild angelica
Gov'ern, [guv'ern] v. t. to rule, regulate,reftrain
Gov'ernable, a. fubject to rule, manageable, mild
Gov'ernance, n. rule, management, control,care
Governant',n. a lady who tutors young girls
Gov'ernefs, n. an inftructrefs, tutorefs, miftrefs
Gov'ernment, n. general fyftem of polity for reg-
   ulating a fociety, a ftate or body politic, ad-
   miniftration or executive power, direction or
   control
Gov'ernor, n. a chief executive magiftrate, a
   commander,one who has high authority,a tutor
Gov'ernorfhip, n. the office of governor
Gown, n. a long upper garment, loofe habit,drefs
Gown'ed, a. dreffed in or having a gown
Gowns'man, n. one promoting peace, a ftudent
Grab'ble, v. to grope, feel, fprawl on the ground
Grace, n. favor, privilege, virtue, ornament, a ti-
   tle, the act of craving a bleffing on our meat
Grace, v. t. to favor, adorn, dignify, exalt, raife
Grácecup, n. the cup of health drank after grace
Gráced, pa. a. favored, adorned, dignified, chafte
Gráceful, a. comely, beautiful, ftriking, pleafing
Grácefully, ad. in a graceful or comely manner
Grácefulnefs, n. comelinefs, elegance, dignity
Grácelefs, a. void of grace, abandoned, wicked
Grácious, a. merciful, kind, good,civil, graceful
Grácioufly, ad. kindly, with condefcenfion

N

Gráciousnefs, n. a kind of civil condefcenfion
Gradátion, n. a regular progrefs, degree, order
Grad'atory, n. a flight of fteps, a fhort ftaircafe
Grade, n. a ftep, a degree of rank or dignity
Grádient, a. walking, proceeding, advancing, ob.
Grad'ual, a. ftep by ftep, regular; n. a fet of fteps
Graduátion, n. a regular progreffion, the act of graduating
Grad'ually, ad. by fteps or degrees (to improve
Grad'uate, v. t. to honor or mark with degrees,
Grad'uate, n. one admitted to academical degrees
Graft, n. a young cion inferted in another tree, a
Graft, v. t. to to infert a cion or branch (ditch
Graft'er, n. one who grafts, one who inferts
Grain, n, corn, one feed of corn or fruit, a fmall particle, weight, color, temper, make
Grain, v. t. to form into grains, to granulate
Gráined, a. rough, uneven, irregular, varied
Gráining, n. a fifh of the dace kind
Grains, n. pl. the remains of malt after brewing
Gral'lic, a. ftilted, belonging to the Grallæ or order of fowls called waders
Gramin'eal, Gramin'eous, a. having grafs, grafly
Graminiv'orous, a. eating or living upon grafs
Gram'mar, n. the fcience of writing correctly
Grammárian, n. one who is fkilled in grammar
Grammat'ical, a. belonging to grammar, exact
Grammat'ically, ad. according to grammar
Grammaticaft'er, n. a low grammarian, a pedant
Gramp'us, n. a cetaceous fifh of the Dolphin genus
Granadil'la, n. a plant
Gran'ary, n. a ftorehoufe to put thrafhed grain in
Gran'ate or Gran'it, n. a fine marble, a gem
Grand, a. very great, fplendid, noble, lofty
Grand'child, n. the child of a fon or daughter
Grand'daughter, n. a fon's or daughter's daughter
Grandée, n. a man of great rank or power
Grand'eur, n. ftate, magnificence, fhow
Grand'father, n. a father's or mother's father
Grandil'oquous, a. ufing a haughty or lofty ftyle
Grandju'ror, n. one of a grand jury, in Con. a peace officer
Grandjúry, n. a jury to decide on bills of indictment
Grand'mother, n. a father's or mother's mother
Grand'fire, n. a grandfather, anceftor, head, origin
Grand'fon, the fon of a fon or daughter
Grange, n. a farm, a very retired place
Gran'iform, a. refembling a grain or kernel
Gran'it, n. a genus of ftones formed ufually by fragments of quartz, felfpar and mica
Granit'ic, a. pertaining to or like granit
Granitell', n. an aggregate of two fpecies of ftones
Gran'itin, n. an aggregate of three fpecies of ftones
Gran'ilit, n. granits confifting of more than three
Graniv'orous, a. eating or living upon grain (fpecies
Gran'num, Gran'ny, Grand'am, n. grandmother
Grant, v. t. to beftow, give, yield, admit, allow
Grant, n. a thing granted, gift, deed, conceffion
Grant'able, a. that may be granted or yielded

Grantée, n. one to whom a grant is made
Grantor', n. one by whom a grant is made
Gran'ular, a. refembling grains, like feeds (raife
Gran'ulate, v. t. to form into fmall grains, break,
Granulátion, n. the ftate of having fmall round points like grains, the act of reducing to fmall round particles (knobs
Gran'ulate, Granuláted, a. confifting of grains or
Gran'ule, n. a fmall grain, a compact particle
Gran'ularly, ad. in the manner of grains
Grape, n. a fine fruit, the fruit of the vine
Grápeftone, n. the ftone or feed of a grape
Grápefhot, n. a large kind of fhot in clufters
Graph'ic, a. laid down, well delineated, exact
Graph'olite, n. a fpecies of flate
Graphom'eter, n. an Inftrument to find an angle whofe vortex is at the center of it (flukes
Grap'nel, n. a fmall anchor with four or five
Grap'ling, n. an inftrument with barbs to grapple
Grap'ple, v. to lay faft hold of, grafp, fight clofe
Grafp, v. to hold in the hand, gripe, feize, aim
Grafp, n. a gripe of the hand, feizure, hold
Grafs, n. the name of a great variety of plants, many of which are the food of cattle
Grafs, v. to grow over with grafs
Grafs'hopper, n. an infect that hops in the grafs
Grafs'plot, n. a plot of ground with fhort grafs
Grafs'y, a. covered with or having grafs
Grate, n. a partition made with bars, a fireplace
Grate, v. to rub fmall, offend, vex, hurt
Gráteful, a. having a due fenfe of favors, pleafant
Grátefully, ad. with proper gratitude, pleafantly
Gráter, n. a rough inftrument to grate with
Gratificátion, n. pleafure, delight, a reward, a gift
Grat'ify, v. t. to indulge, delight, pleafe, require
Gráting, pa. a. rubbing, vexing, difagrecable
Grátingly, ad. in a difpleafing manner, harfhly
Grátings, n. covering for a hatchway
Grátis, ad. for nothing, without reward, freely
Grat'itude, Grátefulnefs, n. duty to benefactors
Gratúitous, a. voluntary, done freely, not proved
Gratúitoufly, ad. voluntarily, without due proof
Gratúity, n. gift, prefent by way of recompenfe
Grat'ulate, v. t. to congratulate, wifh joy, rejoice
Gratulátion, n. the act of rejoicing with another
Grat'ulatory, a. expreffing joy or pleafure
Grave, n. a flat accent, a place for the dead
Grave, a. ferious, folemn, deep, flow, flat
Grave, v. graved, pret. graved, graven, pa. engrave, carve, clean, bury
Grávecloaths, n. pl. the drefs of the dead
Grav'el, n. a hard fand, very fmall pebbleftones
Grav'el, v. t. to cover with gravel, puzzle, pofe
Grávelefs, a. having no grave, unburied
Grav'elly, ad. abounding with or having gravel
Grávely, ad. ferioufly, folemnly, deeply, plainly
Gráver, n. an engraver, a tool to grave with
Gráveftone, n. a ftone laid over the dead
Gravid'ity, n. pregnancy, heavinefs, largenefs

Gravitate, v. i. to tend to the center, to weigh
Gravitátion, n. the act of tending to the center
Grav'itative, a. weighing down, tending to the center
Gravity, Gráveness, n. weight, ferioufnefs, folem-
Grávy, n. the juce of boiled or roafted meat (nity
Gray or Grey, a. hoary, white mixed with black
Gráybeard, n. an old man, by way of contempt
Gráyifh, a. fomewhat gray
Gráyling, n. a frefh water fifh
Gráynefs or Grey'nefs, n. a grey quality or ftate
Graze, v. i. to eat grafs, touch flightly, glance, fkim
Grázier, n. a feeder of cattle for flaughter
Grázing, n. the act of feeding upon grafs
Greafe n. the foft part of fat, a difeafe in horfes
Greafe, v. t. to fmear with fat, bribe, corrupt
Gréafinefs, n. a greafy ftate, oilinefs, fatnefs
Gréafy, a. fmeared with greafe, oily, fat, heavy
Great, a. large, important, chief, noble, pregnant
Great, n. the grofs, the whole, the whole lump
Greátly, ad. in a great degree, nobly, generoufly
Greátnefs, n. largenefs, dignity, grandeur, pride
Greaves, n. pl. ancient armor ufed for the legs
Grebe, n. a water fowl, a quick diver
Grécian, a. belonging to or produced in Greece
Grécifm, n. a Greek idiom or form of fpeech
Greece, n. a flight of fteps, kind of fur, country
Gréedily, ad. eagerly, ravenoufly, voracioufly
Gréedinefs, n. eagernefs, ravenoufnefs, nearnefs
Grédy, a. eager, ravenous, hungry, covetous
Greek, n. a native of Greece, the greek language
Greek, a. belonging to Greece, Grecian
Green, a. unripe, young, new, frefh, not dry
Green, n. a color, a graffy plain, leaves, branches
Green, v. t. to make or tinge green
Greencloth, n. a board of juftice in England
Gréeneyed, a. having a fort of greenifh eyes
Gréenfinch, n. a kind of fmall finging bird
Gréengage, n. a remarkable lufcious plum
Gréenhoufe, n. a houfe to keep tender plants in
Gréenifh, a. inclining to greennefs, rather green
Gréenifhnefs, n. a greenifh ftate or quality, a wan-
Gréenly, ad. with a greenifh color, wanly   (nefs
Gréennefs, n. a green color, unripenefs, newnefs
Greéaficknefs, n. a difeafe incident to virgins
Gréenfward, n. the turf on which grafs grows
Gréenwood, n. wood as it appears in the fummer
Greet, v. t. to falute, addrefs, congratulate, hail
Gréeting, pa. faluting, addreffing; n. a falutation
Greeze, Grice or Grife, n. a ftep, a flight of fteps
Gregárious, a. going in flocks or herds
Gregórian, a. denoting what pertains to Gregory
Grenáde, n. a fireball, a fmall hand bomb
Grenadiér or Granadiér, n. a tall foot foldier, a bird
Grey'houad, n. a tall fwift dog ufed in courfing
Grid'dle, n. a pan to bake cakes in
Gride, v. i. to cut, make way by cutting, ob.
Grid'elin, a. white and red mixed together
Grid'iron, n. a kind of grate to broil meat upon

Grief, n. a painful fenfe of lofs, forrow, caufe of
    forrow, pain, affliction
Griévance, n. a ftate or caufe of trouble, grief
Grieve, v. to mourn, lament, afflict, hurt, vex
Griévingly, ad. with grief, forrowfully, heavily
Griévous, a: afflictive, heavy, hard to be borne
Griévoufly, ad. painfully, miferably, vexatioufly
Griévoufnefs, n. grief, forrow, heavinefs, mifery
Grif'fin or Grif'fon, n. a fabled animal from a lion
Grig, n. a fmall eel, a merry fellow   (and eagle
Grill, v. t. to broil on a gridiron; n. a fmall fifh,
Grill'ed, Grill'ied, pa. broiled, roafted, teazed
Grill'y, v. t. to broil, roaft, harafs, teaze
Grim, a. ill-looking, horrible, ugly, four, crabbed
Grimáce, n. an air of affectation, a wry mouth
Grimáced, a. diftorted, looking crabbed
Grimalk'in, n. a cat, a little gray old woman
Grime, n. dirt; v. t. to dirty, daub, foil, befmear
Grim'ly, ad. horribly, hideoufly, fourly, fullenly
Grim'nefs, n. dreadfulnefs of countenance, fournefs
Grin, n. an affected laugh, trap, fnare, gin
Grin, v. i. to fet the teeth together, laugh, titter
Grind, v. t. ground, pret. ground, pa. to fharpen,
    rub, reduce to powder, harafs, opprefs
Grinder, n. one who or what grinds, a back-tooth
Grind'ftone, n. a ftone for grinding tools on
Grinet'ta, n. an aquatic fowl of the gallinule kind
Grin'ner, n. one who grins, one who titters
Grin'ningly, ad. in a grinning manner   (opprefs
Gripe, v. t. to hold faft, prefs clofe, fqueeze,
Gripe, n. a grafp, fqueeze, oppreffion; pl. the bel-
Gríper, n. an ufurer, oppreffor, extortioner (lyache
Gríping, n. a holding faft, twitch, colic
Grípingly, ad. with a keen pain in the bowels
Grifs'amber, n. a kind of rich drug, ambergris, ob.
Gris'ly, a. horrible, dreadful, hideous, gray, thin
Grift, n. grain ground or to be ground, profit
Grift'mill, n. a mill for grinding grain
Gris''tle, n. cartilage, a firm fubftance of the
    joints, nofe, &c.
Gris''tlinefs, n. a griftly ftate or quality
Gris''tly, a. like or full of griftles, tough
Grit, n. the coarfe part of meal, fand, duft, a fifh,
    an argillaceous earth or ftone
Grit'tinefs, n. a gritty or rough ftate, fandinefs
Grit'ty, a. full of or having hard particles, fandy
Griz'zle, a. gray, roan; n. a kind of gray color
Griz'zled, Griz'zly, a. gray, mixed with gray, roan
Groan, v. i. to mourn with a hoarfe deep noife
Groan, n. a hoarfe and mournful found, a deep figh
Gróaning, n. the act of fending out groans, a groan
Groat, [grawt] n. a fmall fum, 4d fterling
Grócer, n. a dealer in teas, fugars, liquors, &c.
Grócery, n. wares or goods fold by a grocer
Grog, n. fpirit and water mixed
Grogram, n. a thick ftuff made of filk and hair
Groin, n. the part next the thigh, a grumbling
Grómet, n. a ring formed by the ftrand of a rope
Grou'wel, n. a plant of feveral fpecies

Groom, n. one who cleans and tends horses
Grooms'man, n. an attendant on a bridegroom
Groove, n. a hollow cut with a tool; v.t. to hollow
Grope, v. i. to feel or search for in the dark
Grofs, a. thick, bulky, fat, stupid, dull, shameful
Grofs, n. the whole, total, bulk, twelve dozen
Grofsbeak, n. a bird with funnel shaped bill, the hawfinch
Grofsly, ad. coarfely, shamefully, palpably, badly
Grofincfs, n. coarfenefs, fatnefs, indelicacy
Grot, Grot'to, n. a cavern, a cave for pleasure
Grotefqué or Grotefk' a. ludicrous, odd
Grove, n. a small wood, a walk shaded by trees
Grov'e, v. i. to be mean, to creep on the ground
Grov'eller, n. one who grovels, an abject wretch
Ground, n. the upper part of the earth, foundation, soil, country, floor, cause
Ground, v. t. to lay on the ground, to inftruct
Ground, pret. and pa. paff. of to grind
Ground'edly, Ground'ly, ad. upon firm principles
Ground'floor, n. the lowest story of a house
Groundivy, n. a medical herb, alehoof
Ground'lefs, a. void of foundation or truth, false
Ground'lefsly, ad. without juft cause or reason
Ground'leffnefs, n. a want of due or juft cause
Ground'nut, n. a root like a potatoe
Ground'plot, n. the ground a building ftands on
Ground'rent, n. rent paid for building-ground
Ground'room, n. a room level with the ground
Ground'fel or Grun'fel, n. timber that is next the ground, an herb, a kind of common weed
Ground'work, n. the ground, foundation, cause
Group or Groop, n. a cluster, crowd, huddle
Group or Groop, v. t. to form into a cluster or assemblage
Groufe, n. a fine kind of bird found on heaths
Grout, n. coarse meal, pollard, dregs, an apple
Grow, v. grew, pret. grown, pa. to shoot out, increase, improve, raise, become
Grower, n. one who grows, one who produces
Growl, v. i. to fnarl, grumble, murmur, mutter
Growl'er, n. one who grumbles or complains
Growl'ing, n. the act of fnarling or complaining
Growth, n. vegetation, product, improvement
Grub, n. a small worm, dwarf, dirty person
Grub, v. t. to dig up, to destroy by digging
Grub'ble, v. t. to feel in the dark, grope, ob.
Grudge, v. to envy, give unwillingly, murmur
Grudge, n. an old quarrel, anger, ill-will, envy
Grudg'ing, n. envy, reluctance, a wish, remains
Grudg'ingly, ad. unwillingly, reluctantly, crofsly
Gruel, n. food made of meal boiled in water
Gruff, Grum, a. four, ftern, furly, rough, harsh
Gruff'ly, ad. fourly, furlily, roughly, harfhly
Gruff'nefs, n. a gruff appearance, fternnefs
Grum'ble, v. i. to murmur, mutter, growl, fnarl
Grum'bler, n. one who grumbles or murmurs
Grum'bling, n. a complaint, a noise of difcontent
Grume, n. clotted blood, the thicknefs of a fluid

Grúmous, a. clotted like blood, thick, lumpy
Grunt, Grunt'ing, n. the noise of a hog
Grunt, Grun'tle, v. i. to make a noife like a hog
Grunt'er, n. a person who grunts, a kind of fish
Grútch, v. to grudge, envy, repine; n. ill-will
Gry, n. a meafure, one tenth of a line
Guáiacum, n. a tropical tree and its gum
Guánaco, n. the wild Lama or camel of S. A.
Guána, n. a lizard of the Weft-Indies
Guára, n. a Brazilian bird with a long bill
Guarau'na, n. an aquatic bird of Brazil
Guáva, n. a fpecies of plant, the bay plum
Guaranteé, v. t. to warrant, to undertake for the performance of an agreement
Guar'anty, n. one who warrants of is bound for the fulfilment of a ftipulation
Guar'anty, n. the act of warranting or undertaking to fee ftipulations performed
Guard, n. a watch, defense, caution, border
Guard, v. t. to watch, take care of, defend, adorn
Guard'age, Guard'ianfhip, n. the office of guardian
Guard'ian, n. one who has the care of another
Guard'ian, a. defending, protecting (person
Guardlefs, a. void of defenfe or care, exposed
Guard'fhip, n. a fhip fent to guard a harbour, care
Gubernátion, n. government, management, ob.
Gubernatórial, a. relating to a governor
Gud'geon, n. a small fish, man deceived, bait, pin
Guerd'on, n. a reward, recompenfe, requital, ob.
Guefs, v. t. to conjecture, fuppofe, hit upon
Guefs, n. a conjecture, fuppofition, furmife
Guefs'er, n. one who guesses or conjectures
Guefs'ingly, ad. by or on guefs, uncertainly
Gueft, n. a person who is entertained, a visiter
Gueft'chamber, n. a room kept for entertainment
Gueft'rope, n. a rope to tow with
Gug'gle or Gur'gle, v. i. to gufh out with noise
Guidage, n. the hire or reward given to a guide
Guidarce, n. direction, government, care, advice
Guide, v. t. to direct, conduct, fuperintend, rule
Guide, n. a director, conductor, manager
Guidelefs, a. having no guide, left at large
Guider, n. a guide, director, fuperintendant
Guild, n. a fociety, body, corporation, fraternity
Guild'er, n. a dutch coin value 40 cents
Guile, n. deceit, fraud, craft, cunning, artifice
Guileful, a. deceitful, treacherous, artful, wily
Guilefully, ad. deceitfully, treacheroufly, flily
Guilelefs, a. devoid of guile, harmlefs, innocent
Guil'lemot, n. a water fowl like the auk
Guills, n. a plant, the corn marigold
Guilt, n. an offenfe, crime, fault, wickednefs, vice
Guilt'ily, ad. in a guilty manner, wickedly
Guilt'inefs, n. a ftate of guilt, guilt, wickednefs
Guilt'lefs, a. free from guilt, innocent, upright
Guilt'leffnefs, n. freedom from guilt, innocence
Guilt'y, a. chargeable with guilt, wicked
Guin'ea, n. an Englifh gold coin value four dollars and two thirds; the French guinea or Louis'd'

or, four dollars and sixty cents (guineas

Guin'eadropper, n. one who cheats by dropping

Guin'eahen, n. a fowl of the gallinaceous kind from Africa (the cavy

Guin'eapig, n. a small quadruped from Africa,

Guin'iad, n. a fish of a deep blue and purple color

Guife, n. a manner, habit, custom, practice, dress

Guitar', n. a stringed mufical instrument (ding

Gúla or Góla, n. an ogee or wavy member in building

Gules, a. red, red in heraldry or a coat of arms

Gulf, n. a large deep bay, whirlpool, abyss

Gulf'y, a. full of gulfs or whirlpools, deep

Gull, v. t. to cheat, trick, defraud, impose upon

Gull, n. one eafily cheated, a cheat, fraud, seafowl

Gull'catcher, Gull'er, n. a cheat, impoftor, knave

Gull'et, n. the throat, windpipe, passage for food

Gull'y, v. to run with noise, to wear out or away

Gull'y, n. a channel worn by a current of water

Gull'yhole, n. a place where gutters empty themselves

Gulos'ity, n. gluttony, greediness, ob. (selves

Gulp, v. t. to swallow down eagerly or at once

Gulp, n. what is swallowed at once, one swallow

Gum, n. the juce of trees which becomes hard, is infipid and foluble in water, the fubftance inclofing the teeth

Gum, v. t. to close or smear with gum

Gum'minefs, Gummos'ity, n. a gummy ftate

Gum'mous, Gum'my, a. having gum, clammy

Gumres'in, n. a mixed juce of plants confifting of refin and extractive matter or gum (pot

Gun, n. a cannon, mufket, &c. a great flagon or

Gun'nel, Gun'wale, n. the upper part of a ship's

Gun'ner, n. one ufing a gun, a cannonier (fide

Gun'ning, n. the act of hunting with a gun

Gun'powder, n. powder made for guns

Gun'fhot, n. the reach or range of a fired gun

Gun'fhot, a. made or hit by the fhot of a gun

Gun'fmith, n. a man who makes or fells guns

Gun'ftock, n. a piece of wood to fix a gun in

Gun'ftone, n. the fhot of a cannon made of ftone

Gurge, n. a whirlpool, gulf, deep place, abyfs

Gur'nard, n. a marine fifh of feveral fpecies, having the head covered with bony plates

Gur'rahs, n. India muflins, plain and coarfe, from a yard to 9-8ths in width

Gufh, v. t. to rufh out; n. the act of rufhing out

Gufs'et, n. a fmall bit of cloth to ftrengthen with

Guft, n. the fenfe of tafting, a tafte, love, blaft

Guft'able, a. that may be tafted, agreeable to the

Guftátion, n. the act of tafting, a relifh (tafte

Guft'ful, a. well-tafted, nice, pleafant, agreeable

Guft'o, n. the relifh of a thing, tafte, love, liking

Guft'y, a. ftormy, tempeftuous, rough, foul

Gut, n. the inward paffage of food, gluttony, appe-

Gut, v. to take out the guts, draw, plun'der (tite

Gut'ter, n. a paffage for water, kennel, fpout

Gut'ter, v. t. to form or run in little hollows

Gut'tulous, a. having the form of a fmall drop

Gut'tural, a. belonging to the throat, hoarfe

Guy, n. a rope to keep a heavy body fteady while hoifting or lowering, or to confine a boom forward, &c.

Guz'zle, v. t. to drink much, to eat immoderately

Guz'zler, a great drinker, toper, drunkard

Gymnaftic, Gym'nic, [g foft] a. relating to ftrong

Gy'ral, [g foft] a. whirling, circular (exercifes

Gyrátion, [g foft] n. the act of turning round, a winding (trance

Gyre or Gire, [g foft] n. a circle, ring, turn, fit,

Gybe, [g foft] v. to fhift a boom-fail from one fide of a veffel to the other

Gymnofperm'ous, [g foft] a. having naked feeds

Gymnótus, [g foft] n. a genus of apodal fifh

Gynan'dria, n. a clafs of plants in which the flamens and ftyles are united

Gymnofophift, [g foft] n. an Indian philofopher who went barefooted

Gyp'fum, [g foft] n. plafter-ftone [improperly called plafter of Paris] confifting of calcareous earth and fulphuric acid

Gyp'feous, a. of the nature of gypfum

Gyve, [g foft] v. t. to bind faft, chain; n. a fetter

H

HA, exclam. expreffing wonder, joy or forrow

Hábeas-corp'us, n. a writ of trial or liberty

Haberdafher, n. a dealer in fmall wares

Hab'erdafhery, n. the goods fold by a haberdafher

Haber'geon, n. armor for the neck and breaft

Habil'iment, n. drefs, attire, clothes, garments

Habil'itate, v. t. to qualify, entitle, prepare, ob.

Habilitátion, n. a qualification, fitnefs, ob.

Hab'it, n. an aptitude or difpofition acquired by cuftom, cuftomary ufe, drefs

Hab'it, v. t. to drefs or equip

Hab'itable, a. that may be inhabited, decent, fafe

Hab'itant, Hab'itator, n. an inhabitant, a dweller

Habitátion, n. a place of abode, dwelling, refidence

Habit'ual, a. acquired by habit, cuftomary, ufual

Habit'ually, ad. by habit, by cuftom or ufe, gener-

Habit'uate, v. t. to accuftom, to ufe often (ally

Habit'uated, pa. accuftomed, ufed often, ufed

Hab'itude, n. habit, familiarity, ftate, relation

Hab'nab, ad. at random, by accident or chance

Hack, v. t. to cut irregularly, cut, chop, ufe often

Hack, n. any thing ufed in common, a rack, a crib

Hac'kle, n. an inftrument, raw filk, fkin, fly

Hac'kle, v. t. to drefs flax or hemp

Hack'ney, v. t. to practice or ufe one thing much

Hack'ney, n. a hired horfe, hireling, proftitute

Hack'ney, a. common, let for hire

Had'dock, n. a feafifh of the cod kind

Haft, n. a handle; v. t. to fet or put in a haft

Haft'ing, n. the act of putting or fitting on a haft

Hag, v. t. to fatigue, tire, harafs, torment

Hag, n. a fury, very ugly woman, witch

Hag'gard, n. any thing wild or ugly, a hawk

Hag'gard, Hag'gardly, a. ugly, deformed, lean

Hag'gefs, n. a fheep's head and pluck minced

Hag'gih, *a.* like a hag, frightful, deformed

Hag'gle, *v.* to mangle, cut, chop, bargain tediously

Hag'gler, *n.* one who haggles, one who mangles

Hag'gling, *n.* a mangling, a bargaining hardly

Hagiog'rapher, *n.* a holy or infpired writer

Hail, *n.* frozen rain; *exclam.* all health-be to you

Hail, *v. t.* to pour down hail, falute, call out to

Háilſhot, *n.* fmall ſhot ſcattered about like hail

Háilſtone, *n.* a fingle ball or particle of hail

Háily, *a.* confiſting of or like hail, thick as hail

Háinous, *a.* hateful, odious, enormous

Háinoufly, *ad.* hatefully, vilely

Háinoufnefs, *n.* odioufnefs, enormity

Hair, *n.* one of the coverings of the body, a courſe

Háirbrained, *a.* wild, thoughtlefs, giddy, foolifh

Háirbreadth, *n.* a very fmall breadth or diſtance

Háircloth, *n.* a very prickly cloth made of hair

Háiriff, *n.* clivers or goofegrafs

Háirinefs, *n.* a hairy ſtate or quality, roughnefs

Háirlefs, *a.* deſtitute of hair, fmooth, bare, bald

Háirpowder, *n.* fine powder of flour for the head

Háiry, *a.* covered with or made of hair, rough

Hake, *n.* a marine fiſh with a flender body

Hal'bard or Hal'berd, *n.* a foldier's long battleaxe

Hal'cyon, *a.* happy, quiet, calm, ſtill; *n.* a bird

Hale, *a.* healthy, hearty, robuſt, ſtout, found

Hale, *v. t.* to drag, fee *haul*

Half, *n. pl. halves,* one of two equal parts (both

Half'blood, *n.* relation by one parent and not by

Half'blooded, *a.* mean, bafe, low, degenerate

Half'bred, *a.* mongrel, mixed, imperfeᵭ, mean

Half'faced, *a.* ſhowing only one half of the face

Half'heard, *a.* heard in an imperfeᵭ manner

Half'moon, *n.* the moon at the quarters or half full, an outwork with two faces and a gorge in form of a crefcent

Half-penny, [happenny] *n.* half a penny

Half'pike, *n.* a fmall pike carried by officers

Half'ſtrained, *a.* half-bred, imperfeᵭ, foul, *ob.*

Half'ſword, *n.* a very clofe fight, a warm combat

Half'way, *n.* the middle way; *ad.* in the middle

Half'wit, *n.* a foolifh perfon, fimpleton, blockhead

Halfwit'ted, *a.* filly, foolifh, weak

Halit'uous, *a.* relating to vapor or fmoke, *ob.*

Hall, *n.* a manfion houfe, court, large room (LORD

Hallelújah, *v.* praife the LORD; *n.* praife to the

Halloo, *v. t.* to fet on with ſhouts, to cry out, or call with a loud voice

Hal'low, *v. t.* to confecrate, devote, reverence

Hᵣllucination, *n.* an overfight, blunder, miſtake

Hálo, *n.* a colored circle round the fun or moon

Halt, *v.* to limp, hefitate, ſtop, ſtop in a march

Halt, *n.* a limping, a ſtop in a march; *a.* lame

Halt'er, *n.* a rope, a cord; *v. t.* to put on a halter

Halve, *v. t.* to divide into two equal parts, ſhare

Halves, *n. pl.* of *half;* two parts, an equal ſhare

Ham, *n.* a leg of pork cured, end of the thigh, houfe

Hámated, *a.* hooked, fet with hooks crooked

Hames, *n. pl.* a kind of collar for draft horfes

Ham'let, *n.* a part of a parifh, a fmall village

Ham'mer, *n.* an inſtrument to drive nails, &c. by

Ham'mer, *v.* to beat with a hammer, labor, work

Ham'mering, *n.* a beating with a hammer

Ham'moc, *n.* a fwinging bed ufed in a ſhip

Hamófe, *a.* having hooked briſtles

Hamp'er, *n.* a covered bafket ufed for carriage

Hamp'er, *v. t.* to perplex, entangle, infnare, fet

Hamp'ſter, *n.* the cricetus, a deſtruᵭive rat

Ham'ſtring, *n.* the ſtring or tendon of the ham

Ham'ſtring, *v. t.* to hamſtring, *pret.* hamſtringed, hamſtrung, *pa.* to cut the tendon of the ham

Han'aper, *n.* a treafury, exchequer, office [ENG.]

Hand, *n.* a part of the body, pointer, concern, fet

Hand, *v. i.* to give, deliver, lead, conduᵭ, feize

Hand'barrow, *n.* a barrow borne by hand

Hand'bafket, *n.* a fmall bafket for the hand

Hand'bell, *n.* a bell to be rung in the hand

Hand'breadth, *n.* the exaᵭ breadth of the hand

Hand'cuff, *v. t.* to confine the hands with irons

Hand'ed, *a.* ufing or joining hands, conveyed, conduᵭed

Hand'er, *n.* one who hands to others

Hand'faſt, *n.* hold, cuſtody, confinement, prifon

Hand'full, *n.* as much as the hand can well hold

Hand'gallop, *n.* a gentle eafy gallop

Hand'icraft, *n.* a manual occupation, work, labor

Hand'icraftſman, *n.* a workman, a manufaᵭurer

Hand'ily, *ad.* in a handy manner, ſkilfully

Hand'iwork, *n.* work done by the hand, labor, deed

Hand'kerchief, *n.* a piece of linen or filk ufed to wipe the face, &c. or to wear round the neck

Han'dle, *v. t.* to touch, feel, manage, treat of

Han'dle, *n.* the part of a thing that is held, a hold

Hand'lefs, *a.* having no hand, deſtitute of hands

Hand'maid, *n.* a maid continually waiting or near

Hand'mill, *n.* a fmall mill to grind things by

Hand'faw, *n.* a faw manageable by one hand only

Hand'fel, *v. t.* to ufe a thing the firſt time, *ob.*

Hand'fel, *n.* money for the firſt fale, a firſt fale, *ob.*

Hand'fome, *a.* beautiful, fine, graceful, generous

Hand'fome, *v. t.* to make elegant or neat

Hand'fomely, *ad.* beautifully, elegantly, generoufly

Hand'fomenefs, *n.* beauty, elegance, gracefulnefs

Hand'foming, *pa.* making handfome or neat

Hand'fpike, *n.* a fmall wooden lever for the hand

Hand'writing, *n.* any one's particular writing

Hand'y, *a.* ready, dexterous, ſkilful, convenient

Hang, *v.* hanged, hung, *pret.* hanged, hung, *pa.* to fix upon, put, choke, adorn, float, drag

Hang'er, *n.* a ſhort broadfword, an iron

Hanger-on, *n.* a dependant, flatterer, fycophant

Hang'ings, *n. pl.* ornaments hung againſt walls

Hang'man, *n.* one who hangs, a public executioner

Hank, *n.* a ſkain of thread, &c. tie, wooden ring

Hank'er, *v. t.* to long for or after, to defire much

Hank'ering, *n.* a ſtrong or inceſſant craving

Hanovérian, *n.* a native of Hanover in Germany

Hanovérian, *a.* pertaining to Hanover

Hap, *n.* chance, accident, a misfortune

Hap, v. i. to happen, fall out, come to pass
Haphaz'ard, n. chance, merechance, accident
Hap'lefs, a. unhappy, unlucky, unfortunate, poor
Hap'ly, ad. perhaps, peradventure, by chance
Hap'pen, v. i. to fall out, come to pass, chance
Hap'pily, ad. luckily, well, agreeably, gracefully
Hap'pinefs, n. bleffednefs, content, good fortune
Hap'py, a. bleffed, pleafed, fortunate, ready
Harangue', n. an oration; v. i. to make a fpeech
Haran''guer, n. a perfon who harangues, an orator
Har'afs, v. t. to weary, tire, perplex; n. a watte
Har'binger, n. a forerunner, meffenger, officer
Har'bor, v. to fhelter, lodge, entertain, fecure
Har'bor, Har'borage, n. a port, fhelter, lodging
Har'bormafter, n. an officer who regulates the mooring of fhips, &c.
Hard, a. firm, folid, difficult, unkind, niggardly
Hard, ad. clofe, nearly, diligently, faft, juft
Hard'bound, a. bound tight or faft, coftive
Hard'en, v. to make or grow hard, to confirm
Hard'favored, a. having coarfe features, rough
Hard'handed, a. having hard hands, rough, coarfe
Hard'hearted, a. cruel, mercilefs, inhuman, bafe
Hard'heartednefs, n. cruelty, want of tendernefs
Hard'ihood, Hard'iment, Hard'inefs, n. bravery
Hard'labored, a. much labored or ftudied, (elly
Hard'ly, ad. with difficulty, fcarcely, feverely cru-
Hard'mouthed, a. difobedient to the rein or bit
Hard'nefs, n. a hard quality, feverity, ftinginefs
Hard'fhip, n. injury, oppreffion, cruelty, fatigue
Hard'ware, n. wares made of iron, fteel, brafs, &c.
Hard'wareman, n. a maker or feller of hardware
Hard'y, a. hard, ftrong, ftout, brave, bold, daring
Hare, n. a well known animal; v. t. to terrify
Harebrained, a. giddy, heedlefs, roving, unfettled
Harehearted, a. timorous, fearful, cowardly
Harelip, n. a divided lip like a hare's
Harem, n. a kind of feraglio kept in the eaft
Hareng'iform, a. fhaped like a herring
Har'icot, n. a ragoo of meat and roots
Har'ier or Har'rier, n. a dog for hunting hares
Hark ! exclam. hear ! liften ! attend ; v. i. to liften
Har'lequin, n. a buffoon, a merry-andrew
Har'lequin, v. t. to play odd and amufing tricks
Har'lot, n. a whore, ftrumpet, very loofe woman
Har'lotry, n. the trade of a harlot, a ftrumpet
Harm, n. injury, mifchief; v. t. to hurt, to injure
Harmat'tan, n. a dry north-eaft wind in Africa, deftructive to vegetation
Har'mel, n. the wild Affyrian rue
Harm'ful, a. hurtful, mifchievous, detrimental
Harm'fully, ad. hurtfully, injurioufly, wickedly
Harm'lefs, a. innocent, void of guilt, unhurt, fafe
Harm'lefsly, ad. innocently, without hurt
Harm'leffnefs, n. innocence, freedom from hurt
Harmon'ic, Harmon'ical, a. mufical, accordant
Harmon'ics, n. pl. the doctrin of founds
Harmo'nious, a. mufical, well agreed, adapted
Harmo'nioufly, ad. mufically, agreeably

Har'monift, n. a mufician, a writer of harmonies
Har'monize, v. to make mufical, adjuft, agree
Har'mony, n. agreement, juft proportion of found
Har'nefs, n. traces for horfes, trappings, armor
Har'nefs, v. t. to put on traces, to put on armor
Harp, n. a mufical inftrument, a conftellation
Harp, v. i. to play on the harp, to dwell upon
Harp'er, n. one who harps, a player on the harp
Harp'ings, n. the forepart of the wales of a fhip
Harpoon', n. a barbed fpear to catch whales with
Harpoon', v. t. to ftrike with a harpoon
Harpoon'er, n. one who handles a harpoon
Harp'fichord, n. a fine mufical inftrument
Harp'y, n. a filthy bird, a mean ravenous wretch
Har'quebufs, n. a large hand gun
Har'quebuffier, n. one armed with a harquebufs
Har'ridan, n. a decayed or worn-out ftrumpet
Har'row, n. an inftrument ufed in hufbandry
Har'row, v. t. to break clods with a harrow, tear up, ftrip, lay wafte, ravage, harafs, difturb
Har'rower, n. one who harrows, a kind of hawk
Har'ry, v. t. to teaze, ruffle, daunt, pluuder, rob
Harfh, a. rough, rigorous, four, peevifh, grating
Harfh'ly, ad. in a harfh manner, feverely, crofsly
Harfh'nefs, n. roughnefs, fournefs, peevifhnefs
Hars'let, n. the heart, liver, lights, &c. of a hog
Hart, n. a kind of large ftag, the male of a roe
Hart'beeft, n. a fpecies of gazell, cervine antelope
Harts'horn, n. a chymical fpirit, an herb
Hart'wort, n. the plant wild fpignel
Har'veft, n. the feafon for gathering ripe corn, the crop gathered (or maiz
Har'veft, v. to gather ripe corn, whether wheat
Har'veft-home, n. a fong at the end of harveft
Har'veftlord, n. the head-reaper at the harveft
Hafh, v. t. to mince, cut, mix, drefs in fmall bits
Hafh, n. a kind of dith, minced meat, mixture
Hafp, n. a clafp for a ftaple; v. t. to fhut with a hafp
Hafs'oc, n. a thick mat to kneel on at church
Haft'ate, a. having or like a fpear, pointed
Hafte, Haften, v. to hurry, urge or pufh on, drive
Hafte, Haftinefs, n. hurry, fpeed, paffion, warmth
Haftily, ad. in a hurry, quickly, warmly, rafhly
Haftings, n. pl. peas that come early, an apple
Hafty, a. quick, fpeedy, paffionate, hot, rafh, early
Haftypud'ding, n. milk and flour boiled together,
In An. maiz flour and water boiled together
Hat, n. a part of drefs, a cover for the head
Hat'band, n. a ftring round a hat, a piece of filk
Hat'box, Hat'cafe, n. a flight box for a hat
Hatch, v. to produce young, plot, contrive, fhade
Hatch, n. a brood, half-door, door on a fhip's deck
Hatch'el, v. t. to draw flax through hatchel teeth, vex or hector (flax from tow
Hatch'el, n. an inftrument with long teeth to clean
Hatch'et, n. a fmall kind of ax
Hatch'etface, n. an ugly or very ill-formed face
Hatch'ment, n. an efcutcheon fet up for the dead
Hatch'way, n. the opening in a fhips deck to the hold

Hate, v. t. to dislike greatly, abhor, detest, loathe
Hate, Hátred, n. great dislike, ill-will, malice
Háteful, a. causing hatred, detestable, vile
Hátefully, ad. with great dislike, odiously
Háter, n. one who hates, one who dislikes
Hat'ter, n. a maker of hats; v. t. to harass, ob.
Haught or Haught'y, a. proud, lofty, high, bold
Haught'íly, ad. proudly, loftily, arrogantly, boldly
Haught'inefs, n. great pride, loftinefs, arrogance
Haul, v. t. to pull, to drag by violence; n. a pull
Haulm or Haum, n. the ftraw of peas or beans
Haunch, n. the thigh, hip, hinder part, rear (low
Haunt, n. a place of refort; v. to frequent, to fol-
Haunt'ed, pa. frequented, followed, disturbed
Haunt'er, n. one who frequents a place very much
Hant'boy, [hoboy] n. a wind-inftrument, a ftraw-
berry (procure, contain
Have, v. t. had, pret. had, pa. to poffefs, enjoy, get,
Háven, n. a harbor, fhelter, refuge, retreat
Hávener, n. the overfeer of a haven or port
Hav'er, n. one who poffeffes or holds, oats
Hav'ings, n. a poffeffion, hold, eftate, behavior
Hav'ock, n. waite, ruin, deftruction, flaughter
Haw, n. the berry of a thorn; v. i. to fpeak flowly
Haw'finch, n. the grofs beak, a bird of the pafferine
Hawk, n. a bird of prey, kind of cough (order
Hawk, v. to force up phlegm, carry, fell, catch
Hawk'er, n. one who cries goods in the ftreets
Hawk'weed, n. a plant of feveral kinds
Hawfe, n. the fituation of cables when a fhip is at
Haws'er, n. a fmall cable (anchor
Hawféhole, n. an aperture for a cable
Haw'thorn, n. the kind of thorn that bears haws
Hay, n. grafs dried for fodder, a net, park, dance
Háyloft, n. a fcaffold for hay
Háymaker, n. one who makes or prepares hay
Háymow, Háyrick, Háyftack, n. a mow of hay
Haz'ard, n. chance, accident, danger, a game
Haz'ard, v. to expofe to chance, rifk, adventure
Haz'ardable, a. liable to danger, ob.
Haz'ardous, a. expofed to chance, dangerous
Haz'ardoufly, ad. with chance or danger, boldly
Haze, n. a fog, a mift; v. to be foggy, to frighten
Házel, n. a common plant or tree
Házel, Házelly, a. like hazel, brown, light-brown
Házy, a. foggy, mifty, rimy, thick, dark, gloomy
He, pron. a man that was named before, a male
Head, n. a chief, the top, what contains the brain
Head, v. t. to lead, govern, lop, top, behead, go
in front, have a fource or originate
Head'ach, n. a pain in the head, trouble, forrow
Head'band, n. a fillet or topknot, a band of a book
Head'borough, n. a kind of fubordinate conftable
Head'drefs, n. the drefs of a woman's head
Head'inefs, n. obftinacy, rafhnefs, a ftrong quality
Head'ing, n. timber for the heads of cafks
Head'land, n. a cape, point, ground under hedges
Head'lefs, a. void of a head or chief, obftinate, rafh
Head'long, a. rafh, thoughtlefs; ad. rafhly, haftily

Head'moft, a. moft advanced, moft forward, fi rft
Head'piece, n. armor, a helmet, underftanding
Head'fails, n. the fails on the foremaft or bowfprit
Heads'man, n. one who beheads, an executioner
Head'ftall, n. part of a bridle covering the head
Head'ftone, n. a firft or chief ftone, a graveftone
Head'ftrong, a. ungovernable, obftinate, violent
Head'way, n. the motion of an advancing fhip
Head'workman, n. a firft workman, a foreman
Head'y, a. rafh, hafty, unruly, ftubborn, ftrong
Heal, v. to cure, grow well, foften, reconcile
Héaling, pa. curing, foftening; n. a curing
Health, n. a freedom from ficknefs, purity, wifh
Health'ful, Health'fome, a. free from ficknefs,
ftrong, well-difpofed, wholefome (fomenefs
Health'fulnefs, n. the ftate of being well, whole-
Health'inefs, n. a healthy way, ftate or condition
Health'lefs, a. unhealthy, fickly, weak infirm
Health'y, a. free from ficknefs, hale, found, ftrong
Heap, n. a pile, confufed jumble, clufter, crowd
Heap, v. t. to pile, lay, caft, increafe, add, join
Héapy, a. a lying in or having heaps, large, big
Hear, v. heard, pret. heard, pa. to perceive by the
ear, hearken to, attend to, try
Héarer, n. one who attends to a difcourfe
Héaring, n. the fenfe of receiving founds, a trial
Heark'en, v. i. to liften, attend, pay regard
Héarfay, n. report, rumor, fame, common talk
Hearfe, n. a monument over the dead, ob.
Heart, n. the organ which propels the blood, chief
or inner part, feat of love, affection
Heart'ach, n. deep forrow, grief, affliction, diftrefs
Heart'break, Heart'breaking, n. a very great forrow
Heart'breaker, n. the ringlets of a woman's hair
Heart'burning, n. a pain at the ftomach, difcontent
Heart'dear, a. very dear, fincerely beloved
Heart'eafing, a. giving peace or quiet (good
Heart'en, v. t. to ftir up, encourage, manure, do
Heart'felt, a. felt deep, felt in the confcience
Hearth, n. a place on which a fire is made
Heart'ily, ad. from the heart, fincerely, eagerly
Heart'inefs, n. fincerity, earneftnefs, diligence
Heart'lefs, a. fpiritlefs, void of courage, uneafy
Heart'fick, a. much pained in mind, mortally ill
Heart'ftring, n. the nerve that braces the heart
Heart'ftruck, a. driven to the heart, much afraid
or difmayed, deeply affected
Heart'whole, a. having the affections unfixed, found
Heart'wounded, a. filled with love or grief
Heart'y, a. fincere, warm, healthy, ftrong, hale
Heat, n. warmth, glow, flufh, paffion, rage
Heat, v. t. heat, heated, pret. heat, heated, pa. to
make hot, warm, put into a paffion
Héater, n. a thing that heats, kind of iron, utenfil
Heath, n. a plant, common, common ground
Héathcock, n. a kind of fowl upon heaths, the grous
Héathen, n. a pagan, one deftitute of revelation
Héathen, Héathenifh, a. favage, wild, Gentile
Héathenifm, n. paganifm, ignorance of the true

Héathy, a. full of or abounding with heath (God

Heave, n. a lift, swell, struggle, effort, endeavor

Heave, v. heaved, hove, pret. heaved, hove, pa. to lift, swell, pant, beat, vomit, cast

Heav'en, n. the habitation of the blessed, the sky

Heav'enborn, a. descended from heaven, holy

Heav'enbred, a. produced in heaven, devout

Heav'enbuilt, a. built by the favor of the gods

Heav'endirected, a. directed towards heaven

Heav'enly, a. inhabiting heaven, holy, charming

Heav'enly, ad. in a heavenly manner, divinely

Heav'enward, ad. towards heaven, devoutly

Héaveoffering, n. the first fruits given to a priest

Heav'ily, ad. in a heavy manner, slowly   (ness

Heav'iness, n. weight, affliction, oppression, dull-

Héaving, n. a lifting, swelling, effort to vomit

Heav'y, a. weighty, grievous, full, dull, drowsy

Heav'yhanded, a. having a heavy hand, clumsy

Hebdom'adal, Hebdom'adary, a. weekly

Heb'domad, n. a week, the space of seven days

Heb'etate, v. t. to make dull, dull, blunt, stupify

Heb'etude, n. dullness, bluntness, great heaviness

Hebráic, Hébrew, a. pertaining to the Hebrews

Hébraism, n. a Hebrew idiom or form of speech

Hébraist, Hebri"cian, n. one skilled in Hebrew

Hébrew, n. the language of the Hebrews, a Jew

Hec'atomb, n. a sacrifice of an hundred oxen

Hec'tic, a. habitual, continual, flow; n. a fever

Hec'tor, n. a bully; v. t. to bully, boast, threaten

Hec'toring, n. a bullying, a threatening, a noise

Hed'eral, a. formed of or relating to ivy

Hedge, v. to make a hedge, fence, inclose, shift

Hedge, Hedge'row, n. a fence made with bushes

Hedge'born, a. meanly born, poor, low, obscure

Hedge'hog, n. a rough prickly animal, plant, fish

Hedge'note, n. a word of contempt, low ribaldry

Hedge'pig, n. a small or young hedgehog

Hedg'er, n. one who hedges, one who secures

Hedge'sparrow, n. a sparrow living among bushes

Hedg'ing, n. the act of making hedges

Hedg'ingbill, n. a kind of ax used to hedge with

Heed, v. t. to mind, observe, regard, attend, value

Heed, n. care, attention, caution, notice, respect

Heed'ful, a. attentive, watchful, cautious, wary

Héed'fully, ad. carefully, attentively, cautiously

Heed'less, a. careless, negligent, inattentive, giddy

Héed'lessly, ad. carelessly, inattentively

Héed'lessness, n. carelessness, inattention (to dance

Heel, n. the hind part of the foot, &c. v. to lean,

Héelpiece, v. t. to put a piece on the heel of a shoe

Heft, n. an effort, haft, handle, weight

Hegíra, n. the epoch or date used by the Turks

Heif'er, n. a young cow, a young woman in joke

Heigh'ho! exclam. denoting slight uneasiness

Height or Highth, n. altitude, space upward, utmost degree, tallness

Heighten, v. t. to raise, increase, exalt

Heightening, n. a raising higher, increase

Héinous, a false spelling, see hainous

Heir, [air] n. he who inherits by law

Heir, v. t. to inherit, take by descent

Heir'ess, n. a woman who inherits by law

Heir'less, a. having no heir, wanting an heir

Heir'loom, n. what descends with a freehold, to

Heir'ship, n. the state or right of an heir (the heir

Held, pret. and pa. of to hold

Héliacal, a. relating or belonging to the sun

Hel'ical, a. spiral, twisted, winding   (muses

Heliconian, a. pertaining to Helicon, a hill of the

Heliocent'ric, a. appearing or seen from the sun

Helispher'ical, n. spiral   (a spiral line

Hel'ix, n. a shell fish always floating on the water,

Heliom'eter, n. an instrument to take the diameters of heavenly bodies (hurting the eyes

Héliofcope, n. a telescope to view the sun without

Héliotrope, n. a green filiceous stone, the sunflower

Hell, n. the place of the damned, the grave, prison

Hell'black, a. extremely black, dismal, ob.

Hell'doomed, a. consigned to hell, damned

Hell'ebore, n. a plant, the Christmas-flower

Hel'lenism, n. a peculiarity of the Greek tongue

Hellenis'tic, a. pertaining to the Greeks

Hell'hated, a. hated like hell, quite abhorred, ob.

Hell'hound, n. a dog or agent of hell, a wretch

Hell'ish, a. belonging to hell, very wicked, vile

Hell'ishly, ad. in a hellish manner, very wickedly

Hell'ishness, n. abominable wickedness or behavior, great impiety, base or vile qualities

Hel'lespont, n. the strait between Europe and Asia, by which the Euxine runs into the Mediterranean

Hell'ward, ad. towards hell, in the way to hell

Helm, n. the apparatus by which a ship is steered, consisting of a rudder, and tiller, and a wheel

Helm'ed, a. furnished with a headpiece, guarded

Helm'et, n. armor for the head, a headpiece

Help, v. helped, pret. helped, holpen, pa. to assist, support, supply, heal, cure, avoid

Help, n. assistance, support, relief, remedy, cure

Help'er, n. one who helps or assists, a low servant

Help'ful, a. assisting, useful, wholesome   (help

Help'less, a. wanting power or assistance, weak of

Help'lessness, n. a helpless state, great weakness

Helt'er-skelt'er, ad. confusedly, without any order

Helve, n. a haft, handle, handle of an ax

Helve, v. to fit or furnish with a handle, to haft

Helvet'ic, a. relating to the Swiss or Switzerland, anciently called Helvetia

Hem, n. the edge of a garment, a sudden noise

Hem, v. to close with a hem, shut in, call to

Hem'atite, n. an ore of iron, brown or red

Hematit'ic, a. pertaining to hematite

Hem'ifphere, n. the half of a sphere or globe

Hemifpher'ic, Hemifpher'ical, a. half round

Hemift'ic, n. half a verse, half a line in poetry

Hem'itone, n. in music, a half tone

Hem'lock, n. a poisonous herb, a tree   (flux

Hem'orrhage, n. a great flux of blood, a bloody

Hem'orrhagic, a. pertaining to a flow of blood
Hem'orrhoids, n. pl. the piles, emrods
Hemorrhoid'al, a. pertaining to hemorrhoids
Hemp, n. a plant from which ropes, &c. are made
Hemp'en, a. made of or like hemp, tough
Hen, n. the female of all birds and fowls
Hen'bane, n. a plant, tobacco, a bean
Hence, v. t. to fend far off or away, ob.
Hence, ad. or exclam. from this place or thing
Henceforth, Hencefor'ward, ad. from this time
Hench'man, n. a page, attendant, firname
Hend, v. t. to feize, catch, crowd, furround, ob.
Hendec'agon, n. the endecagon or figure of 11 fides
Hen'harrier, n. a bird of the hawk kind
Hen'harm, Hen'harrier, n. a kind of hawk, a kite
Hen'hearted, a. daftardly, cowardly, fearful, timid
Hen'pecked, a. governed by a wife, dejected, mean
Hen'rooft, n. a houfe or place where poultry reft
Hepat'ic, a. of or relating to the liver, bilious
Hep'atize, v. t. to impregnate with fulphurated
  hydrogenous gas formerly called hepatic gas
Heptan'dria, n. a clafs of plants with hermaphro-
  dite flowers of feven ftamens
Hep'tagon, n. a plain figure of feven equal fides
Heptag'onal, a. having feven angles   (and angles
Heptagyn'ia, n. an order of plants with feven ftyles
Heptan''gular, a. having feven angles
Heptaphyl'lous, a. having feven leaves
Hep'tarchy, n. a government under feven kings
Her, pron. belonging to a female or woman
Her'ald, n. an officer who regulates coats of arms,
  and funerals, harbinger, forerunner
Her'ald, v. to introduce or act like a herald, ob.
Herald'ic, a. relating to heraldry or heralds
Her'aldry, n. the art, duty or office, of a herald
Herb, n. a plant with a fucculent ftalk in diftinc-
  tion from a fhrub and tree, that part of a plant
  which is above the root
Herbáceous, a. belonging to or feeding on herbs,
  foft, perifhing annually
Herb'age, n. herbs, grafs, pafture, tithe of pafture
Herb'aged, a. clothed with plants
Herb'al, n. a treatife on herbs, a book of plants
Herb'alift or Herb'arift, n. one fkilled in herbs
Herb'alize, v. i. to gather herbs, to ftudy botany
Herb'bane, n. a plant of feveral fpecies
Herb'ivorous, a. eating or fubfifting on herbs
Herb'orize, v. i. to fearch for or ftudy plants
Herborizátion, n. the act of feeking and ftudying
  plants, the figure of plants in a mineral
Herb'orized, a. having the form of plants, as a
  mineral herborized
Herb'ous, Herb'y, a. having or like herbs
Hercúlean, a. very great, difficult or dangerous
Hercyn'ian, a. denoting formerly a great foreft
  now in Swabia
Herd, n. a flock, drove, company, keeper of cattle
Herd, v. to affociate, join, unite, run in companies
Herd'man or Herds'man, n. one who keeps herds

Here, ad. in this place or ftate ; n. this place
Héreabouts, ad. about or near this place
Hereaf'ter, ad. in future time ; n. a future ftate
Hereat', ad. at or upon this, upon this account
Hereby', ad. by this, by this thing or means
Hered'itable, Her'itable, a. that may be inherited
Heredit'ament, n. an inheritance, eftate, defcent
Hered'itarily, ad. by way or right of inheritance
Hered'itary, a. defcending or got by inheritance
Herein', Hereintó, ad. in or into this thing
Heremit'ical, a. folitary, retired, devout, pious
Hereof', ad. of or from this thing or perfon
Hereon', Hereupon', ad. on or upon this, forthwith
Heréfiarch, [ch as k] n. a leader in herefy
Her'efy, n. a fundamental error in religion (faith
Her'etic, n. one who holds fundamental errors in
Heret'ical, a. containing herefy, falfe, dangerous
Heretó, Hereuntó, ad. to or unto, this place
Heretofóre, ad. formerly, anciently, long ago, once
Herewith', ad. with this, at the fame time (death
Her'iot, n. a fine paid to the lord of a manor on a
Her'iffon, n. a beam armed with iron fpikes
Her'itage, n. an inheritance, the people of God
Hermaph'rodite, n. two fexes in one perfon, in
  botany a plant having only male and female
  flowers or anther and ftigma
Hermaphrodit'ic, a. pertaining to both fexes
Hermet'ic, Hermet'ical, a. clofed perfectly by
  heating the glafs and twifting it
Hermet'ically, ad. in a hermetical manner (crab
Her'mit, n. a folitary devout perfon, a reclufe, a
Her'mitage, n. an hermit's cell or habitation
Hermit'ical, a. relating to or fuiting an hermit
Hern or Her'on, n. a large bird that deftroys fifh
Héro, n. a brave or worthy man, a great warrior
Her'oefs, Her'oine, n. a brave or very bold woman
Heróic, Heróical, a. brave, fine, noble, fpirited
Heróically, ad. bravely, courageoufly, boldly
Her'oifm, n. the qualities of a hero, bravery
Herpet'ic, a. pertaining to cutaneous fores
Her'ring, n. the name of a fmall feafifh   (here
Hers, pron. the female poffeffive; as, this hat is
Her'fchel, [herfhel] n. a planet difcovered by
  Dr. Herfchel in 1781
Herfchélian, [herfhelian] a. pertaining to Herfchel
Herfe, n. a carriage for corpfes, a lattice befet
  with fpikes to ftop a gate
Herfe, v. t. to put on a herfe, carry to the grave
Hers'ed, pa. put in a herfe, made gloomy or difmal
Herfelf', pron. the female perfonal pronoun
Herfe'like, a. fuitable to funerals, gloomy, dull
Her'fillon, n. a little herfe in fortification
Hes'itate, v. i. to paufe, delay, doubt, flammer
Hefitátion, Hes'itancy, n. a doubt, a ftop in fpeech
Hes'fian, n. a native of Heffe Caffel in Germany
Hes'fian, a. relating to Heffe Caffel
Heft, n. a command, injunction, precept, order
Heteroc'lite, n. an irregular noun, thing or man
Heteroclit'ical, a. irregular, deviating, varying

Het'erodox, a. differing from the true church

Het'erodoxy, n. a difference from found doctrine

Heterogéneal, Heterogéneous, a. unlike in nature

Heterogéneoufnefs, n. a difference in nature or kind

Heterop'tics, n. pl. falfe optics, deception, error

Hetrúrian, a. pertaining to Hetruria, now Tufcany

Hew, v. t. hewed, pret. hewed, hewn, pa. to cut off chips and pieces, peck, hack, chop, fell, labor

Hew'er, n. a perfon who hews wood or ftone

Hex'ade, n. a feries of fix numbers

Hex'agon, n. a figure of fix equal fides or angles

Hexag'onal, a. having fix equal fides or angles

Hexagyn'ia, n. an order of plants having fix ftyles

Hexahédron, n. a folid with fix fides

Hexahédral, a. having fix fides

Hexam'eter, n. a verfe or line confifting of fix feet

Hexan'dria, n. a clafs of plants having hermaph-rodite flowers with fix ftamens

Hexan'gular, a. having fix angles

Hex'aped, n. an animal with fix feet

Hexapet'alous, a. having fix petals

Hexaphyl'lous, a. having fix leaves

Hex'aftyle, n. a building with fix columns in front

Hey ! exclam. a word of joy or exhortation

Hey'day ! exclam. denoting furprife; n. heat

Hiátion, n. the act of gaping or yawning, a gap

Hiátus, n. an aperture, breach, cleft, gap, opening

Hiber'nal, a. belonging or relating to winter

Hiber'nian, n. a native of Ireland

Hiber'nian, a. pertaining to Ireland or the Irifh

Hic'cius-doc'cius, n. a juggler, trickfter, cheat

Hick'ory, n. a tree, a fpecies of walnut

Hick'up, n. a convulfed motion of the ftomach

Hick'up, v. i. to fob with a convulfed ftomach

Hick'wall, n. a fmall fpecies of wood pecker

Hide, v. hid, pret, hid, hidden, pa. to lie or be con-cealed, conceal, cover, withdraw from fight

Hide, n. the fkin of an animal, a meafure of land

Hidebound, a. having the fkin or bark too tight

Hid'eous, a. horrible, dreadful, frightful, fhocking

Hid'eoufly, ad. horribly, dreadfully, fhockingly

Hid'eoufnefs, n. horror, dreadfulnefs

Hidingplace, n. a place of concealment, a hole

Hie, v. i. to haften, make hafte, go faft or quick

Hierarch, [ch as k] n. the chief of a facred order

Hierarch'al, a. pertaining to a divine or ecclefiaftic-al government

Hierarchy, n. a facred government or order

Hieroglyph'ic, n. an emblem, figure, reprefentation

Hieroglyph'ical, a. emblematical, allufive, obfcure

Hig'gle, v. i. to carry about, bargain hard, haggle

Hig'gler, n. one who hawks provifions by retail

High, a. tall, lofty, loud, dear; n. a high place

High'blest, a. greatly bleffed, quite or very happy

High'blown, a. fwelled greatly with wind, full

High'born, a. come of high or noble extraction

High'flier, n. one who is extravagant in opinion

High'flown, a. elevated, proud, affected, nice

High'heaped, a. covered with high piles, large

Highland, n. a high or mountainous country

Highlander, n. a mountain-Scotchman

Highly, ad. with efteem, proudly, ambitioufly

Highmettled, a. high in fpirit, bold, daring, proud

Highminded, Highftomached, a. proud, haughty

Highmoft, a. higheft, topmoft, firft, fartheft

Highnefs, n. height, dignity of nature, a high title

Highplumed, a. wearing high plumes

Highprieft, n. the chief prieft

Highred, a. very or extremely red, very glaring

Highfeafoned, Highftafted, a. hot to the tafte

Highfpirited, a. bold, daring, hot, very warm

Highth, n. highnefs, altitude, elevation

Hight, a. called, named, ftyled, denominated

Highwáter, n. the full flood tide

Highway, n. a great way or road, a public road

Highwáyman, n. one who robs on a public road

Highwrought, a. very neatly finifhed, labored

Hilar'ity, n. gayety, mirth, cheerfulnefs, joy, plea-

Hild'ing, n. a mean cowardly wretch, ob. (fantry

Hill, n. a high land, an eminence, a clufter of plants and the earth raifed about them

Hill, v. t. to draw earth round plants

Hill'ock, n. a little or fmall hill, rifing ground

Hill'y or Hill, a. full of or having hills, irregular

Hilt, n. a handle, a handle of a fword, the very top

Hilum, n. the eye of a bean or other feed

Him'antope, n. an aquatic bird with very long legs

Hin, n. a Jewifh liquid meafure of about ten pints

Hind, n. a fhe to a ftag, boor, fervant; a. backward

Hin'der, v. t. to prevent, ftop, ftay; a. backward

Hin'derance, n. an impediment, ftop, obftruction

Hindermoft, Hindmoft, a. the laft, the lateft

Hin'doo or Hin'du, n. a native of Indoftan

Hin'doo, a. relating to Hindoos or India

Hinge, n. the joint on which a door turns, a point

Hinge, v. to bend as a hinge, hang, reft, turn

Hint, v. to allude, touch upon, intimate, point

Hint, n. a remote fuggeftion, intimation, item

Hip, n. a joint of the thigh, lownefs of fpirits, mel-ancholy, the fruit of a briar

Hip, v. to fprain the hip, difpirit, flope off

Hip'pilaph, n. a quadruped of Norway, like a horfe and a ftag

Hip'pifh, a. low in fpirits, dejected, melancholy

Hip'pifhnefs, n. lownefs of fpirits, dejection

Hippocent'aur, n. a monfter half man half horfe

Hip'podrome, n. a place in Greece for horfe and chariot races

Hip'pogriff, n. a fabulous animal, a winged horfe

Hippopot'amy, n. the river horfe or Behemoth

Hip'roof, n. a roof in which there is an angle

Hip'fhot, a. fprained in the hip, lame, dull

Hire, v. t. to engage for pay; n. wages, juft due

Hireling, n. a mercenary, proftitute, low wretch

Hireling, a. ferving for hire, mercenary, mean

Hir'las, n. the ancient Welch drinking-horn

Hirfúte, a. rough, rugged, hairy

His'pid, a. having ftrong briftles, or prickles

Hifs, v. to cry like a ferpent, explode by hiffes, fhow a diflike

Hifs, n. a noife, noife made by a ferpent, cenfure

Hifs'ing n. a noife or contempt by hiffes

Hift, exclam. an exclamation commanding filence

Hiftórian, Hiftoriog'rapher, n. a writer of hiftory

Hiftor'ically, ad. by way of hiftory, regularly

Hiftor'ify, v. t. to record in hiftory, relate, ob.

Hift'ory, n. a narration of facts, actions, wars, &c.

Hiftrion'ic, a befitting a ftage or players, arch

Hit, v. hit, pret. hit, pa. to ftrike, clafh, fall upon, fucceed, reach the mark

Hit, n. a ftroke, blow, lucky chance, event, game

Hitch, v. to catch, move by jerks, hit, cut, faften

Hitch, n. a kind of knot or noofe, tie, rope

Hithe, n. a place to land goods at, a wharf (Eng.)

Hith'er, ad. to this place or end ; a. nearer, lower

Hith'ermoft, a. neareft this way or place

Hith'erto, ad. to this time, till now, heretofore

Hith'erward, ad. towards this way or place

Hive, n. a cafe to keep bees in, fwarm, company

Hive, v. to put into a hive, take fhelter, join, mix

Hiver, n. one who puts or gets bees into hives

Hiving n. the act of putting bees into hives

Hives, n. the difeafe called rattles or croop

Hoact'li, n. a Mexican bird white and crefted

Hoac'ton, n. a Mexican bird of the aeron kind

Hoact'zin, n. an American bird of the fize of a hen

Hoar, Hóary, a. gray with age, whitifh, mold covered with a white pubefcence

Hoard, v. t. to lay up privately, lay up, keep

Hoard, n. a private flock, hidden ftore, treafure

Hóarder, n. one who lays up in fecret, a churl

Hóarfroft, n. a thin white froft, frozen dew

Hóarinefs, n. a hoary ftate or quality, graynefs

Hoarfe, a. having a rough voice, rough, harfh

Hóarfely, ad. with a rough harfh voice, deeply

Hóarfenefs, n. a roughnefs of voice, harfhnefs

Hob'ble, v. i. to walk lamely, go unevenly, limp

Hob'ble, n. an aukward halting walk, a fcrape

Hob'bler, n. a bad walker, an Irifh horfe-foldier

Hob'bliggly, ad. lamely, aukwardly, poorly, badly

Hob'by, n. a little horfe, a ftupid fellow, a hawk

Hob'byhorfe, n. a fmall horfe, ftick, plaything, favorite thing, ftupid or dull perfon, foil

Hob'goblin, n. a bugl ear, apparition, fpirit, fairy

Hob'nail, n. a broad nail ufed for fhoes

Hob'nailed, a. fet with hobnails, clumfy, rough

Hock, n. a part of bacon, joint, game, fine wine

Hock, Hoc'kle, v. t. to cut the hock, to hamftring

Hócus-pócus, n. a juggler, cheat, deception, trick

Hod, n. a bricklayer's trough ufed for mortar, &c.

Hodge'podge, Hotch'potch, n. a confufed mixture

Hodier'nal, a. of or belonging to this day or time

Hoe, n. a garden tool ufed to cut up weeds

Hoe, v. t. to cut or dig up with a hoe, to weed

Hog, n. a general name of fwine, a mean wretch

Hog, v. i. to bend as a hog's back

Hog'pen, Hog'fty, n. a houfe or place for hogs

Hog'gifh, a. filthy, greedy, brutifh, clownifh

Hog'gifhly, ad. in a hoggifh manner, greedily

Hog'gifhnefs, n. greedinefs, felfifhnefs, brutality

Hog'herd, n. a keeper or feeder of hogs

Hógo or Hógoo, n. a mefs of high relifh, a ftink

Hogs'head, n. a meafure of fixty-three gallons, the puncheon of 110 gallons is fo called

Hog'wafh, n. the wafh or victuals given to fwine

Hoid'en, n. an aukward country-girl ; v. i. to romp

Hoift, v. t. to raife on high, heave up, lift up

Hoift, n. the highth of a fail or flag

Hoit'lallote, n. an American bird of a whitifh color

Hoitzitzil'lin, n. an American bird of moft elegant plumage

Hold, v. held, pret. held, holden, pa. to fupport grafp, keep, retain, detain, flick, continue

Hold, n. a fupport, catch, power, cuftody, place, the interior of a fhip

Hold, exclam. flop! flay! ceafe! leave off! forbear

Hólder, n. one who holds any thing, a tenant

Hóldforth, n. one who fpeaks in public, a talker

Hóldfaft, n. an iron hook, catch, cramp, nail

Hólding, n. a tenure, farm, burden of a fong

Hole, n. a hallow place, cell, mean habitation, fhift

Hol'ibut, n. a large flat fifh of the flounder kind

Hole, v. t. to dig or make holes, to drive into a bag as in billiards

Holeráceous, a. pertaining to pot-herbs

Hólidam, n. a bleffed lady, the Virgin Mary, an oath

Hólily, ad. pioufly, religioufly, facredly, juftly

Hólinefs, n. piety, religion, care, the pope's title

Holló, v. to call to any one, fhout, hoot

Hollo', n. a call to any one at a diftance

Ho'land, n. a kind of fine ftrong linen, a country

Ho'low, a. low within, empty, deceitful, noify

Hol'low, n. a hollow place, hole, opening, cavert

Hol'low, v. to make hollow, fcoop, empty, fhout

Hol'lowly, ad. with hollows, deceitfully, falfely

Hol'lownefs, n. a hollow ftate, deceit

Ho'ly, n. a kind of evergreen tree or fhrub

Ho'lyhock, n. a plant, the rofe mallow

Holm, Holme, n. a kind of oak, the evergreen oak

Hol'ocauft, n. a whole burnt facrifice, a burnt-offer-

Holp'en, pa. paff. of to help, ob.   (ing

Hólfter, n. a leathern cafe for a horfeman's piftols

Hóly, a. pure, pious, religious, devout, facred

Hol'yday, n. an anniverfy feaft, a day of joy, &c.

Hom'age, n. obedience, refpect, fervice to a lord

Hom'age, v. t. to pay homage, honor, refpect

Hom'ager, n. one who pays homage

Home, n. one's own houfe ; ad. to the point, clofe

Hómeborn, Hómebred, a. native, plain, artlefs

Hómefelt, a. felt inwardly, painful, uneafy

Hómelinefs, n. plainnefs, coarfenefs, rudenefs

Hómely, a. inelegant, plain, coarfe ; ad. coarfely

Hómelot, n. the inclofure on which the manfion ftands

Hómemade, a. made at home, coarfe, plain

Homer, n. a Jewifh meafure of about three pints

Homer'ic, a. pertaining to or like Homer the poet, or his verses

Hómefpun, a. made at home, homely, coarfe

Hómefpun, n. a rude, inelegant, ruftic, a clown

Hómeftal, Hómefted, n. the place of a houfe

Hómeward or Hómewards, ad. towards home

Homicídal, a. murderous, bloody, barbarous

Hom'icide, n. murder, deftruction, a murderer

Homilet'ical, a. fociable, converfable, ob (fermon

Hom'ily, n. a difcourfe to be read in churches, a

Hom'moc, n. a fmall detached hill ufually covered with trees   (coarfe and boiled

Hom'mony, n. food made of maiz broken, but

Homogéneous, a. fimilar in nature or kind, like

Homogéneoufnefs, n. joint or like nature

Homol'ogous, a. proportional, fimilar, alike, like

Homon'ymous, a. equivocal, ambiguous, different

Homon'ymy, n. equivocation, ambíguity

Homot'onous, a. equable, correfpondent

Hone, n. a ftone to whet razors on

Hone, v. t. to fharpen on a hone

Hon'eft, a. upright, juft, true, fincere, good, chafte

Hon'eftly, ad. uprightly, juftly, faithfully, truly

Hon'efty, n. juftice, truth, virtue, purity, a flower

Hon'ey, [hunny] n. the fweet juice of vegetables collected by bees, a darling

Hon'ey, v. to cover with honey, to talk kindly

Hon'eybag, n. the bag or ftomach of a bee

Hon'eycomb, n. cells of wax for holding honey

Hon'eycomb, a. full of little cavities, or cells

Hon'eydew, n. a fweet dew or matter found on

Hon'eylefs, a. void of honey, empty   (plants

Hon'eymoon, n. the firft month after marriage

Hon'eyfuckle, n. a genus of plants of many fpecies

Hon'eywort, n. a fpecies of plant

Hon'or, n. reputation, the efteem due to worth, a nice regard to reputation, bravery, chaftity, virtue, rank or dignity, reverence

Hon'or, v. t. to efteem, reverence, dignify, exalt

Hon'orable, a. illuftrious, noble, honeft, generous

Hon'orably, ad. reputably, nobly, generoufly, well

Hon'orary, a. done in conferring honor

Hon'orer, n. one who honors or greatly refpects

Hood, v. t. to drefs in a hood, veil, cover, conceal

Hood, n. a covering for the head, an ornament

Hoodmanblind, n. a play, blindman's buff

Hood'wink, v. t. to blind, hide, cover, deceive

Hoof, n. the horny cover of a horfe's foot, a peck

Hook, n. a bent piece of iron, &c. fnare, trap

Hook, v. t. to fix on a hook, bend, catch, draw

Hook'nofed, a. having the nofe high in the middle

Hoop, n. a circle of wood or iron, an ornament

Hoop, v. t. to bind or fecure with hoops, to fhout

Hoop'ingcough, n. a convulfive cough

Hoo'poe, n. a bird with a beautiful creft (contempt

Hoot, n. a fhout of contempt; v. i. to fhout in

Hop, n. a jump, mean dance, plant   (hops

Hop, v. to leap on one leg, limp, impregnate with

Hope, n. a defire of good accompanied with an

expectation of obtaining it or a belief that it is obtainable, the object of hope

Hope, v. to live in hopes, to expect with defire

Hópeful, a. full of expectation, promifing, good

Hópefully, ad. in a hopeful manner, pleafingly

Hópefulnefs, n. a promife or expectation of good

Hópelefs, a. deftitute of hope, forlorn, abandoned

Hópelefsly, ad. without ground to expect

Hópeleffnefs, n. a hopelefs or loft ftate, defpair

Hóper, n. one who has pleafing expectations

Hop'ground, n. ground fet apart for hops

Hópingly, ad. with hope, with good expectation

Hop'per, n. one who hops, part of a mill, a bafket

Hop'ple, v. t. to tie the feet very near or together

Hóral, Hórary, a. belonging to an hour, hourly

Horde, n. a clan, tribe, fet, crew, migratory crew

Hórehound, n. the name of plants of feveral kinds

Hor'izon, [falfely horizon] n. the line that terminates the fight

Horizon'tal, a. near or parallel to the horizon

Horizon'tally, ad. in a horizontal direction

Horn, n. a part of an ox, ram, &c. an inftrument

Horn'beam, n. a genus of trees of three fpecies

Horr'blend, n. a fpecies of argillaceous earth of a black or green color

Horn'book, n. a book of horn ufed for children

Horn'ed, a. furnifhed with or wearing horns

Horn'er, n. one who works or deals in horns

Horn'et, n. a bee of the wafp kind

Horn'fifh, n. the garfifh or fea needle

Horn'foot, Horn'footed, a. hoofed, firm, very hard

Horn'pipe, n. a kind of quick fingle dance

Horn'flate, n. a gray filiceous ftone

Horn'ftone, n. a filiceous ftone blue or gray

Horn'y, a. made of or like horn, callous, hard

Hórologe, n. an inftrument for telling time by

Horom'etry, n. the art of meafuring time by hours

Hor'ofcope, n. a figure of the heavens at the birth

Hor'rent, a. rough, fharp, ftanding up, horrid

Hor'rible, a. dreadful, terrible, fhocking, hideous

Hor'riblenefs, n. a horrible ftate or quality, horror

Hor'ribly, ad. dreadfully, frightfully, hideoufly

Hor'rid, a. dreadful, hideous, rough, vile, offenfive

Hor'ridly, ad. dreadfully, fhockingly, hideoufly

Hor'ridnefs, n. hideoufnefs, enormity, vilenefs

Horrif'ic, a. caufing horror or dread, horrible

Hor'ror, n. terror, dread, drearinefs

Horfe, n. a quadruped for draft or carriage, a machine of various kinds for fupport, a rope upon a yard for feamen to ftand on, cavalry

Horfe, v. t. to mount, ride, furnifh with horfes

Horfe'back, n. the feat or ftate of riding a horfe

Horfe'bean, n. a fmall bean ufed for horfes

Horfe'boy, n. a boy who dreffes or looks after horfes

Horfe'breaker, n. one who tames horfes for riding

Horfe'cloth, n. a cloth to throw over horfes

Horfe'courfer, n. one who runs or deals in horfes

Horfe'dealer, n. one who deals in horfes, a jockey

Horfe'faced, a. having a large and coarfe face, ugly

Horſe'fly, n. a large fly that ſtings horſes
Horſe'guards, n. cavalry for guards
Horſe'hair, n. the hair of horſes, very ſtrong hair
Horſe'laugh, n. a very loud or violent laugh
Horſe'leech, n. a leech that bites horſes, a farrier
Horſe'litter, n. a carriage hung between two horſes
Horſe'man, n. one who is ſkilled in riding, a rider
Horſe'manſhip, n. the act or art of riding well
Horſe'marten, n. a very large kind of bee
Horſe'meat, n. meat for horſes, very ſtrong food
Horſe'play, n. a coarſe or rough play, rudeneſs
Horſe'pond, n. a pond for watering horſes at
Horſe'race, n. a match of horſes in running
Horſe'radiſh, n. a very hot biting root
Horſe'ſhoe, a ſhoe for horſes, a kind of herb
Horſe'ſtealer, n. a thief that takes away horſes
Horſe'tail, n. a plant of different ſpecies
Horſe'way, Horſe'road, n. a broad and open way
Hortátion, Hor'tative, n. an exhortation, advice
Hor'tative, Hor'tatory, a. tending to exhort or ad-
Hor'ticultor, n. one who cultivates a garden (viſe
Hor'ticulture, n. the culture of a garden
Hor'tulan, a. belonging to or like a garden
Hoſan'na, n. glory to God, a ſhout or ſong of praiſe
Hoſe, n. ſtockings, breeches, a lethern pipe
Hóſen, old pl. of hoſe
Hóſier, n. one who makes or ſells hoſe
Hóſiery, n. ſtockings, ſocks and the like wares
Hos'pitable, a. kind to ſtrangers, friendly, civil
Hos'pitably, ad. in a hoſpitable manner, kindly,
Hos'pital, n. a reception for ſick or poor people
Hoſpital'ity, n. entertainment of ſtrangers, &c.
Hos'pitate, v. i. to reſide under another's roof, ob.
Hóſt, v. i. to take up entertainment, engage, ob.
Hoſt, n. a landlord, matter, army, great number
Hos'tage, n. a pledge for performance of conditions
Hóſtleſs, n. a female hoſt, landlady, miſtreſs
Hos'tile, a. adverſe, oppoſite, warlike, enraged
Hoſtil'ity, n. a ſtate of war, open war, enmity, hate
Hóſting, n. an encounter, engagement, muſter
Hos'tler, n. one who dreſſes horſes at inns
Hos'try, n. a place for horſes of gueſts, a ſtable
Hot, a. having heat, furious, eager, keen, luſtful
Hot'ach, n. pain from preternatural heat
Hot'bed, n. a bed made of earth and dung covered
   with glaſs
Hot'br..ined, a. furious, paſſionate, violent
Hot'cockles, n. pl. a kind of childiſh play
Hotel', n. a palace, an inn for genteel lodgers
Hot'headed, a. hot, paſſionate, violent, vehement
Hot'houſe, n. a place to ſweat and cup in, broth-
   el, a houſe kept warm for plants
Hot'ly, ad. violently, keenly, luſtfully
Hot'mouthed, a. violent, headſtrong, ungovernable
Hot'neſs, n. a hot ſtate or quality, heat, violence
Hot'ſpur, n. a heady paſſionate man, an early pea
Hot'ſpurred, a. heady, paſſionate, raſh, headſtrong
Hove, Hóven, p2. of to heave
Hov'el, n. a ſhed, mean cottage, ſhelter

Hov'el, v. t. to ſhelter or put in a hovel   (der
Hov'er, [huver] v. i. to hang overhead, fly, wan-
Hough, [hok] n. the lower part of the thigh
Hough, v. to hock, hamſtring, cut, break, hawk
Hound, n. a dog uſed for hunting, a fiſh
Hound, v. t. to purſue with hounds, to hunt
Hounds, n. the projecting parts of a maſthead
Hour, n. the twenty-fourth part of a day, time
Hour'glaſs, n. a glaſs of ſand for meaſuring time
Hour'ly, a. done every hour, frequent, common
Hour'ly, ad. every hour, frequently
Houſe, n. a place of abode, the table, a family or
   race, one branch of a legiſlature, a quorum or
   legal number of members to do buſineſs
Houſe, [houze] v. to put under or take ſhelter
Houſe'breaker, n. one who breaks into houſes
Houſe'breaking, n. the act of robbing houſes
Houſe'hold, n. a family living together
Houſe'holder, n. one who rents or holds a houſe
Houſe'holdſtuff, n. furniture, goods, moveables
Houſe'keeper, n. one who has the care of a family
Houſe'keeping, n. the keeping of a houſe, plenty
Houſe'keeping, a. uſeful to or fit for a family
Houſe'leek, n. a plant which grows within doors
Houſe'leſs, a. having no houſe or abode, deſtitute
Houſe'maid, n. a maid to clean the houſe, &c.
Houſe'room, n. a place in a houſe, cover, ſhelter
Houſe'warming, n. a feaſt on entering a houſe
Houſe'wife, Hus'wife, n. a good miſtreſs of a houſe
Houſe'wifery, Hus'wifery, n. female economy
Houſe'wifely, a. pertaining to a houſewife
Hous'ing, n. a putting into a houſe, a horſecloth,
   a line of three ſtrands for ſeizings, &c.
How, ad. in what manner, ſtate, or degree, why
Howbéit, ad. nevertheleſs, notwithſtanding
How'dye, contracted, from how do ye do
Howev'er, ad. nevertheleſs, yet, at leaſt, at all
   events, in what manner or way, in any degree
Hówitzer, n. a mortar mounted on a moveable
   carriage with trunnions on the middle
Howl, v. i. to cry as a dog or wolf, to cry bitterly
Howl, n. the cry of a dog or wolf, a cry of horror
How'let, n. a bird of the owl kind, aſh colored
Howl'ing, n. the noiſe of a dog, &c. a bitter cry
Howſoev'er, ad. in what manner, at leaſt
Hox, v. t. to hough, hamſtring, dirty, daub, ob.
Hoy, n. a coaſting veſſel, a ſmall ſhip, large boat
Hub or Hob, n. the nave of a wheel
Hub'bub, n. a tumult, great noiſe, uproar, riot
Huck, n. the German river trout
Huck'aback, n. a linen with raiſed figures on it
Huc"klebone, n. the hip-bone
Hucs'ter, n. a retailer of ſmall articles of proviſion
Hud'dle, v. to do or put on in a hurry, to crowd
Hud'dle, n. a crowd, collection, confuſion, tumult
Hudibras'tic, a. like Hudibras, doggerel, rough
Hue, n. a color, die, clamor, great noiſe, purſuit
Huff, n. a ſwell of ſudden anger or pride, a pet
Huff, v. to chide, treat with inſolence, bluſter

Huff, Huffer, n. a blusterer, bully, hector, boast
Huffish, a. hectoring, infolent, arrogant, proud
Hug, v. t. to embrace fondly; n. a clofe embrace
Huge, a. vaft, immenfe, very great, large
Hugely, ad. immenfely, enormoufly, greatly, very
Hagenefs, n. vaft bulk or fize, bignefs, greatnefs
Hug'ger-mug'ger, n. fecrecy, privacy; a. confufed
Hulk, v. t. to gut; n. the body of a fhip, a clown
Hull, n. a hufk, pod, outfide, body of a fhip
Hull, v. to hufk, clear, drive to and fro, float,
    pierce the hull with a fhot
Hull'y, a. having hulls or pods, hufky, foul
Hum, v. to fing low, buzz, paufe, mock, deceive
Hum, n. a low noife, a deception
Hûman, a. belonging to or like man
Humâne, a. tender, compaffionate, kind, civil
Humânely, ad. tenderly, kindly, civilly
Hûmaniſt, n. a learned perfon, a grammarian
Human'ity, n. the nature of man, benevolence
Hûmanize, v. t. to foften, make tender, civilize
Humanizâtion, n. the act of humanizing
Hûmankind, n. the whole race of men, mankind
Hûmanly, ad. after the manner of men, kindly
Hum'ble, a. modeft, meek, lowly, low, obfcure
Hum'ble, v. t, to bring down, mortify, fubdue
Hum'blebee, n. a large buzzing bee, an herb
Hum'blemouthed, a. mild, meek, gentle, kind
Hum'bly, ad. without pride, fubmiffively, lowly
Hum'drum, n. a ftupid perfon, a drone; a. dull
Humect', Humect'ate, v. t. to wet, moiften, damp
Humectâtion, n. the act of wetting or moiftening
Hûmeral, a. of or belonging to the fhoulder
Hum'hum, n. a plain coarfe India cotton cloth
Humicubâtion, n. lying on the ground, ob.
Hûmid, a. moift, damp, wet, watery, plafhy
Humid'ity, Hûmidnefs, n. moiftnefs, dampnefs
Humifi'c, a. caufing dampnefs, foftening, moift
Humiliâtion, n. the act of humility, mortification
Humil'iating, a. humbling, mortifying
Humil'ity, Hum'blenefs, n. fubmiffion, modefty
Hum'mer, n. one who hums, one who applauds
Hum'mingbird, n. the fmalleft of all birds
Hûmor, n. moifture, droollery, whim, caprice
Hûmor, v. t. to gratify, footh, comply with, oblige
Hûmoral, a. proeeeding from humors, grofs
Hûmoriſt, n. one who gratifies his humor, or is
    diftinguifhed for humor
Hûmorous, a. jocular, pleafant, droll, whimfical
Hûmoroufly, ad. jocofely, pleafantly, merrily
Hûmorfome, a. peevifh, odd, humorous, droll
Hump, Hump'back, n. a crooked back (ed back
Hump'backed, Hunch'backed, a. having a crook-
Hunch, v. t. to pufh with the elbow, ftrike,
    raife, crook
Hun'dred, a. the number 10 multiplied by 10
Hun'dred, n. the number 100, 10 times 10
Hung, pret. and p t. of to hang
Hungârian, n. a native of Hungary in Europe
Hungârian, a. belonging to Hungary

Hun''ger, n. a defire of food, an eager or keen defire
Hun''ger, v. i. to feel the pain of hunger, to long
Hun''gerbitten, a. pained or weakened by hunger
Hun''gerly, Hun''grily, ad. with a keen appetite
Hun''gerly, Hun''gry, a. defirous of food, ftarved
Hun''gerftarved, Hun''gred, a. pinched by hunger
    or want of food, famifhed, weak
Hunks, n. a fordid mean wretch, m fer, niggard
Hunt, v. to chafe, purfue, fearch, feek, man age
Hunt, n. a chafe, purfuit, fport, pack of hounds
Hunt'er, n. one who chafes animals, a dog, a horfe
Hunt'er, n. a double milled foreft cloth
Hunt'ing, n. the act of chafing with dogs
Hunt'inghorn, n. a horn to cheer hounds with
Hunt'refs, n. a woman who follows the chafe
Hunts'man, n. a perfon who manages a chafe
Hunts'manfhip, n. the qualifications of a hunter
Hur'dle, n. fticks woven together, a gate, a cradle
Hurl, v. t. to throw with violence; n. a riot, noife
Hurl'bat, n. an old kind of weapon, a whirlbat
Hurl'y-burl'y, n. a tumult, noife, buftle, confufion
Hur'ricane, n, a violent ftorm, a great tempeft
Hur'ry, v. to haften, to move on with great hafte
Hur'ry, n. precipitation, hafte, buftle, tumult, ftir
Hurt, n. a bruife, wound, injury, harm, mifchief
Hurt, v. t. hurt, pret. hurt, pa. to bruife, wound,
    injure, harm, pain, affect with lofs, impair
Hurt'ers, n. pieces of wood at the lower en l of a
    platform to prevent the wheels of guncarriages
    from injuring the parapet
Hurt'ful, a. injurious, pernicious, mifchievous
Hurt'fulnefs, n. the quality of doing harm
Hurt'fully, ad. with harm, mifchievoufly
Hur''tle, v. to fkir.nifh, clafh, hit, move violently
Hurt'lefs, a. harmlefs, innocent, inoffenfive, fafe
Hus'band, n. a married man, economift, farmer,
    a fhip's owner having charge of her
Hus'band, v. t. to marry, manage, fave, keep, till
Hus'bandlefs, a. having no hufband, deftitute, lone
Hus'bandly, a. careful, frugal, thrifty, fparing
Hus'bandman, n. one who works in tillage
Hus'bandry, n. tillage, management, frugality
Hufh, v. to appeafe, quiet, forbid; exclam. be ftill
Hufh'money, n. a bribe to hinder information
Hufk, n. the covering of fome fruits, &c. refufe
Hufk, v. t. to ftrip off or cover with hufks
Hufk'ing, n. the act of ftripping maiz, often by a
    number in company
Hufk'y, a. abounding in or having hufks, dry
Huf'far, n. a kind of horfe-foldier, coat, cloak
Hufſy, n. a forry bad woman, wench, kind of bag
Hus'tle, v. t. to fhake, tofs about, mix by fhaking
Huf'wife, v. t. to manage with frugality
Hut, n. a poor cottage, mean abode, hovel, lodge
Hut'ted, a. lodged in huts
Hutch, n. a corn-cheft, rabbit-box, trap, treafure
Huix, v. t. to catch pike by means of a bladder
Huzzâ, [a as in afk] n. a fhout of joy or triumph
Huzzâ, v. to utter or receive with acclamatio s

Hy'acinth, n. a genus of plants, of great variety, cultivated for the flowers, also a genus of pellucid gems

Hyacinth'ine, a. made of or like hyacinths

Hy'ades or Hy'ads, n. a cluster of seven stars in the face of Taurus, a rainy constellation

Hy'aline, a. glassy, crystalline, clear, bright

Hy'alite, n. a white filiceous stone

Hy'bernate, v. i. to pass the winter confined as birds or beasts in a cold climate (ment

Hybernátion n. a remaining in winter in confine-

Hy'bernacle, n. the part of a plant which inclofes the embryo in winter, a bulb or bud, a winter lodge

Hy'brid, n. an animal or plant, the produce of two fpecies, mongrel

Hyb'ridous, a. of a mixed nature, mongrel

Hy'dra, n. a ferpent with many heads, a monfter

Hy'drant, n. a pipe to conduct and deliver water

Hydraul'ic, a. relating to hydraulics, watery

Hydraul'ics, n. the fcience of the motions of fluids and of veffels to convey them

Hydrocar'bonated, n. containing carbonic acid combined with hydrogene

Hy'drocele, n. a kind of watery rupture

Hydroceph'alus, n. a dropfy in the head

Hy'drogene, n. the bafe of inflammable air, an element · which united with oxygene forms

Hydrogénous, a. belonging to hydrogene (water

Hy'drogenated, a. combined with hydrogene

Hydrog'rapher, n. one who draws maps of the fea

Hydrograph'ical, a. relating to a defcription of

Hydrog'raphy, n. a defcription of the feas (water

Hydrol'ogy, n. the fcience of water

Hydrolo"gical, a. pertaining to hydrology

Hy'dromancy, n. a prediction by means of water

Hydroman'tic, a. pertaining to hydromancy

Hy'dromel, n. a liquor from honey and water, mean

Hydrom'eter, n. an inftrument to meafure the gravity, denfity, &c. of fluids

Hydromet'rical, a. pertaining to the hydrometer

Hydrom'etry, n. the menfuration of the gravity, denfity, velocity, &c. of fluids

Hy'drophane, n. a ftone made tranfparent by water

Hydroph'anous, a. rendered tranfparent by immerfion in water

Hy'drophoby, n. a dread of water, canine madnefs

Hydrophóbic, a. pertaining to canine madnefs or dread of water

Hydrop'ic, Hydrop'ical, a. dropical, watery

Hydropneumat'ic, a. denoting a veffel of water, and other apparatus for chemical experiments

Hy'drofcope, n. a water-clock ufed by the ancients

Hydroftat'ic, a. of or relating to hydroftatics

Hydroftat'ics, n. pl. the fcience of weighing fluids

Hydroful'phuret, n. a combination of fulphurated hydrogene with an alkali, earth or metallic oxyd

Hydrot'ic, n. what purges off water or phlegm

Hy'druret, n. a combination of hydrogene with a metallic fubftance

Hyémal, a. pertaining to winter, done in winter

Hyemátion, n. the paffing of a winter

Hy'en, Hyéna, n. a very fierce animal like a wolf

Hygrom'eter, n. an inftrument to meafure the moifture in the air with

Hygrom'etry, n. the meafuring the moifture of air

Hygromet'rical, a. belonging to hygrometry

Hy'grofcope, n. a hygrometer

Hy'men, n. the god of marriage, membrane, fold

Hymenéal, n. a marriage fong

Hymenéal or Hymenéan, a. pertaining to marriage

Hymn, v. t. to praife in fongs of adoration, to fing

Hymn, n. a divine or holy fong, a fong of praife

Hym'nic, a. relating or belonging to hymns

Hyp, v. t. to make melancholy or low, to difpirit

Hypal'lage, n. a change of words or cafes

Hy'perbate, n. a tranfpofition of words

Hyper'bola, n. a fection of a cone made by a plane

Hyperb'ole, Hyperb'oly, n. an exaggeration

Hyperbol'ical, a. exaggerating, bold, extenuating

Hyperbol'ically, ad. in a hyperbolical manner

Hyperbórean, a. northern, very cold

Hypercrit'ic, Hy'per, n. a critic exact beyond reafon

Hypercrit'ical, a. critical beyond ufe, very fevere

Hyper'meter, n. what is above the due ftandard

Hypermet'rical, a. above the ftandard of meafure

Hyperoxy"ginated, a. fuper faturated with oxygene

Hy'phen, n. the mark (-) between words or fyllables

Hyp'ocauft, n. a furnace, ftove, hot houfe (affection

Hypochon'driac, [ch as k] n. one ill of nervous

Hypochon'driac, Hypochon'driacal, a. melancholy, very dejected, low in fpirits, fplenetic

Hypochon'driacifm, n. indigeftion, languor and anxiety from debility

Hypocráterform, a. fhaped like a cup or falver

Hypoc'rify, n. diffimulation, deceit, art, pretence

Hyp'ocrit, n. a diffembler, a deceitful perfon

Hypocrit'ical, a. diffembling, infincere, falfe

Hypocrit'ically, ad. without due fincerity, falfely

Hypogas'tric, a. feated or felt in the lower belly

Hypos'tafis, n. a diftinct fubftance, perfonality

Hypoftat'ic, a. conftitutive, diftinct, perfonal

Hypotenúfe, n. a line in a triangle which fubtends the right angle

Hypoth'efis, n. a fyftem formed upon fuppofition

Hypothet'ical, a. fuppofed, feigned, conditional

Hypothet'ically, ad. upon fuppofition, condition-

Hy'fon, n. a fpecies of green tea (ally

Hy'ffop or Hy'fop, n. a genus of aromatic plants

Hyfter'ic, Hyfter'ical, a. troubled with fits

Hyfter'ics, n. pl. a complaint, fits of women

I

I, pron. ufed in the firft perfon fingular, myfelf

Iam'bic, a. confifting of a long and fhort foot

Iam'bics, n. verfes compofed of a long and fhort fyllable alternately

I'bex, n. a fpecies of goat

Ib'jar, n. an American venomous ferpent

Ib'ijau, *n.* a Brazilian bird of the size of a swallow

I'bis, *n.* a bird of ancient Egypt

Ib'itin, *n.* a large venomous serpent of India

Icárian, *a.* soaring too high for safety, like Icarus

Ice, *v. t.* to turn to ice, to cover with concreted

Ice, *n.* water frozen, sugar that is concreted (sugar

I'cebuilt, *a.* loaded with piles of ice

I'cehouse, *n.* a house made to preserve ice in

Iceland'ic, *n.* the language of Iceland

Iceland'ic, *a.* pertaining to Iceland

Ichneûmon, [ch as k] *n.* a quadruped of the weasel kind, a numerous genus of flies

Ichnograph'ic, [ch as k] describing a plot

Ichnog'raphy, [ch as k] *n.* a ground plot, platform,

I'chor,[ch as k] *n.* a sharp humor, ulcers   (draft

Ich'orous, *a.* sharp, hot, thin, watery, undigested

Ichthyol'ogy, [ch as k] *n.* the science of fish of all kinds

I'cicle, *n.* dripping water frozen and dependent

I'con, *n.* a picture, cut, representation, image

Icon'oclast, *n.* a breaker of Images

Icofan'dria, *n.* a class of plants, hermaphrodite, with twenty or more stamens

Icofahèdron, *n.* a body of twenty equal sides

Icofahèdral, *a.* having twenty equal sides

Ic'terus, *n.* a bird of the size of a thrush

Icter'ic, Icter'ical, *a.* afflicted with the jaundice

Icteri''tious, *a.* yellow, resembling the jaundice

I'cy, *a.* full of or having ice, cold, very backward

Idéa, *n.* a mental imagination, notion, intention

Idéal. *a.* mental, intellectual, imaginary, fond

Idéally, *ad.* in idea, in imagination or thought

Ident'ic, Ident'ical, *a.* the same, not different

Ident'icalness, Ident'ity, *n.* sameness, reality

Ident'ify, *v. t.* to prove to be really the same

Ides, *n. pl.* the 15th day of March, May, July and October, and the 13th of the other months

Id'ioelec'tric, *n.* containing electricity in its natural state

Id'iom, *n.* a particular kind or manner of speech

Idiomat'ic, Idiomat'ical, *a.* peculiar to a tongue

Id'iopathy, *n.* an affection of a part not dependent on another

Idiopath'ic, *a.* having its own disease

Idiopath'ically, *ad.* by means of its own affections

Idiofync'rafy, *n.* a peculiar temper or disposition

Id'iot, *n.* a fool, oaf, changling, a natural

Idiot'ic, *a.* like an idiot, foolish

Id'iocy, *n.* want of reason

Id'iotifm, *n.* peculiarity of expression, idiocy

I'dle, *a.* lazy, unemployed, worthless, trifling

I'dle, *n.* to spend the time in laziness, trifle, waste

I'dleheaded, *a.* foolish, unreasonable, absurd

I'dleness, *n.* laziness, sloth, unreasonableness, folly

I'dler, *n.* a lazy or indolent person, a sluggard

I'dly, *ad.* lazily, carelessly, foolishly, vainly, badly

I'dol, *n.* an image worshipped as a god, a darling

Idol'ater, I'dolift, *n.* a worshipper of idols

Idol'atress, *n.* a female idolater

Idol'atrize, *v. i.* to worship or serve idols

Idol'atrous, *a.* tending or given to idolatry, vain

Idol'atroufly, *ad.* in an idolatrous manner

Idol'atry, *n.* the worship of an idol or creature

I'dolize, *v. t.* to worship as a deity, adore, honor

Idóneous, *a.* fit, meet, proper, suitable, convenient

I'dyl, *n.* a short pastoral poem, an eclogue

Ig'neous, *a.* containing or emitting fire, fiery

Ignes'cent, *a.* yielding fire or sparks

Ignip'otent, *a.* presiding over or directing fire

Ig'nis-fat'uus, *n.* will-with-a-wisp, a delusion

Ig'nite, Ig'nify, *v. t.* to kindle, fire, set on fire, render luminous by fire

Ig'nitible, *a.* that may be set on fire

Igni''tion, *n.* the act of setting on fire, a calcination, a heating to luminousness

Igniv'omous, *a.* vomiting out or ejecting fire

Ignóble, *a.* mean of birth, worthless, base, vile

Ignóbly, *ad.* meanly, disgracefully, basely, vilely

Ignomin'ious, *a.* mean, shameful, disgraceful

Ignomin'ioufly, *ad.* meanly, scandalously, badly

Ig'nominy, *n* disgrace, reproach, shame, infamy

Ignorámus, *n.* a foolish fellow, an indorsement on an indictment, when the jury have not evidence of the facts

Ig'norance, *n.* want of knowledge, unskilfulness

Ig'norant, *a.* wanting knowledge, untaught, rude

Ig'norant, *n.* one who is untaught or unskilled

Ig'norantly, *ad.* without knowledge, art or skill

Ile, *n.* a walk or alley in a church, an ear of corn

Il'iac, Il'iacal, *a.* belonging to the lower bowels

Il'iad, *n.* a fine heroic poem written by Homer

Ill, *a.* bad, fick, disordered, not in health, evil

Ill, *n.* harm, misfortune, misery, wickedness, evil

Ill, *ad.* not rightly, amiss, wickedly, not easily

Illa''cerable, *a.* that cannot be torn or divided

Illapfe', *n.* a gradual entrance, sudden attack, fall

Il'aq'ueate, *v. t.* to entangle, insnare, trap, catch

Illaqueátion, *n.* the act of insnaring, a snare, a trap

Illátion, *n.* an inference, conclusion, deduction

Ill'ative, *a.* that may be drawn or inferred   (tion

Ill'aud'able, *a.* unworthy of praise or commenda-

Illaud'ably, *ad.* unworthily, meanly, basely

Illcondi''tioned, *a.* in a bad order or state

Illégal. *a.* contrary to law, unjust, dishonest, base

Illegal'ity, *n.* contrariety to law, unlawfulness

Illégally, *ad.* in an illegal manner, unjustly

Ille''gible, *a.* that cannot be read or made out

Illegit'imacy, Illegitimátion, *n.* a state of bastardy

Illegit'imate, *a.* unlawful, born out of wedlock

Illev'iable, *a.* that cannot be levied, laid or exacted

Illfávored, *a.* ugly, ordinary, rough, deformed

Illib'eral, *a.* sparing, ungenerous, disingenuous

Illiberal'ity, *n.* parsimony, niggardliness, meanness

Illib'erally, *ad.* meanly, disingenuously

Illi''cit, *a.* unlawful, unfit, improper, contraband

Illight'en, *v. t.* to enlighten, give light, ob.

Illim'itable, *a.* that cannot be bounded, infinit

Illim'itedness, *n.* an exemption from bounds

Illini"tion, n. a tincture, discoloration

Illit'erate, a. unlearned, ignorant, untaught, mean

Illit'eratenefs, Illit'erature, n. a want of learning

Illnature, n. peevishnefs, crossnefs, unkindnefs

Illnátured, a. peevish, crofs, unkind, untractable

Illnáturedly, ad. peevishly, crofsly, unkindly

Ill'nefs, n. sicknefs, diforder, weaknefs, folly, vice

Illo"gical, a. contrary to or ignorant of logic

Illo"gically, ad. in an illogical manner, abfurdly

Ill'ſtarred, a. fated to be unfortunate

Illúde, v. t. to play upon, mock, banter, deceive

Illúme, Illúmin, Illúminate, v. t. to enlighten, to

Illuminátion, n. a giving light, brightnefs (adorn

Illúminative, a. able or tending to give light

Illumináti or Illuminátes, n. formerly a fect in France who relied on fublime prayer for falvation, without other means; recently, affociations of men to deftroy religious inftitutions and fubftitute reafon, men who rely on human perfectibility

Illúminifm, n. the principles of the illuminates

Illúminize, v. t. to initiate in the doctrins of modern Philofophifts

Illúfion, n. a falfe fhow, mockery, cheat, error

Illúfive, a. deceiving by falfe fhow, deceitful, falfe

Illúfory, a. deceiving, impofing on, fraudulent

Illuft'rate, v. t. to brighten, clear up, explain

Illuftrátion, n. an explanation, expofition, glofs

Illuft'rative, a. able to clear, tending to explain

Illuft'ratively, ad. for or by way of explanation

Illuft'rious, a. confpicuous, eminent, famous

Illuft'rioufly, ad. confpicuoufly, nobly, famoufly

Illyr'ian, a. pertaining to a country on the Adriatic, now called Albania, in Turkey

Im is often ufed for in and un, in the fenfe of not, giving to words a contrary fignification

Im'age, n. a ftatue, picture, likenefs, idol, idea

Im'age, v. t. to imagin, conceive, reprefent

Im'agery, n. fenfible reprefentation, fhow, an idea

Ima"ginable, a. poffible to be conceived

Ima"ginant, a. imagining, thinking, forming ideas

Ima"ginary, a. fancied only in the imagination

Imaginátion, n. fancy, notion, idea, a contrivance

Ima"ginative, a. full of imagination, fantaftic

Ima"gin, v. t. to fancy, think, contrive, fcheme

I'man, n. a Turkifh prieft, prefident, head, ruler

Imbánk, v. t. to inclofe or keep up with banks

Imbank'ment, n. an inclofing with banks, a bank

Im'becile, a. weak, languid, impotent

Imbecil'ity, n. weaknefs, feeblenefs, languor, decay

Imbed', v. t. to fink or cover as in a bed

Imbíbe, v. t. to drink or fuck in, admit, drench

Imbíber, n. one who or what drinks or fucks in

Imbibi"tion, n. the act of drinking or fucking in

Imbit'ter, v. t. to make bitter, exafperate, provoke

Imbod'y, v. t. to form into a body, unite, mix

Imbólden, v. t. to give boldnefs, to encourage

Imbor'der, v. t. to furnifh with borders

Imbófom, v. t. to hold in the bofom, carefs, love

Imbound', v. t. to inclofe, clofe, fhut in, ob.

Imbów, v. t. to arch, vault, cover over, ob.

Imbow'er, v. t. to fhelter or cover with trees

Imbówment, n. an imbowing, an arch, a vault, ob.

Im'bricate, a. lapped over each other like tiles

Imbricátion, n. a concave indenture, bend, tiling

Imbrown', v. t. to make brown or dark, to darken

Imbrúe, v. t. to fteep, foak, wet, moiften, dip

Imbrúte, v. t. to fink to brutality, degrade, pollute

Imbúe, v. t. to tincture deep, tinge, feafon, fit

Imitabil'ity, n. an imitable ftate or quality

Im'itable, a. poffible or worthy to be imitated

Im'itary, a. relating or belonging to imitation

Im'itate, v. t. to copy, to endeavor to refemble

Imitátion, n. an attempt to refemble, a copy

Im'itative, a. inclined or tending to copy

Im'itator, n. one who imitates, one who copies

Imac'ulate, a. fpotlefs, pure, undefiled, clear

Imman'acle, v. t. to fetter, fhackle, bind, confine

In'manent, a. inherent, intrinfic, eternal, real

Imman'ifeft, a. not plain, doubtful, obfcure, ob.

Imman'ity, n. barbarity, favagenefs, ob.

Immarcef'fible, a. unfading, undecaying

Immar'tial, a. not warlike, weak, defencelefs

Immafk', v. t. to cover, difguife, conceal, hide

Immatérial, a. void of matter, unimportant, equal

Immaterialifm, n. the doctrin of the exiftence or ftate of immaterial or fpiritual fubftances

Immaterial'ity, n. an immaterial nature

Immaterialized, Immatériate, a. incorporeal

Immatúre, a. unripe, imperfect, too hafty

Immatúrely, ad. too early, too foon, too haftily

Immatúrity, n. unripenefs, incompletenefs, hafte

Immeabil'ity, n. an inability to pafs, ob.   (fured

Immeaſ"ureable, Immenſ'urable, a. not to be mea-

Immeaſ"urably, ad. immenfely, unboundedly

Immechan'ical, [ch as k] a. contrary to mechanics

Immédiacy, n. perfonal greatnefs or power

Immédiate, a. inftant, acting by itfelf, next to

Immédiately, ad. inftantly, without delay, foon

Immed'ical, a. incurable, not to be healed

Immemórial, a. paft the time of memory, ancient

Immenfe', a. unlimited, infinite, huge, vaft

Immenfe'ly, ad. without meafure, infinitely, very

Immens'ity, n. unbounded greatnefs, infinity

Immer'it, n. a want of merit, unworthinefs, ob.

Immerfe' or Immerge', v. t. to plunge, to involve

Immer'fion, n. the act of putting under water

Immefh', v. t. to entangle in mefhes or a net

Immethod'ical, a. having no method, confufed

Immethod'ically, ad. irregularly, confufedly

Im'migrate, v. t. to remove into a country

Immigrátion, n. the act of moving into a country

Im'migrant, n. one who removes into a country

Im'minence, n. a clofe approach, nearnefs

Im'minent, a. impending, near, threatening

Imminútion, n. a diminution, decreafe, failure

Immis'cible, a. incapable of being mixed

Immis"fion, n. the act of fending in, an injection

Immit', v. t. to fend or fquirt into, to injeçt
Immix', Immin'gle, v. t. to mix, mingle, unite
Immix'able, a. that is incapable of being mixed
Immobil'ity, n. unmoveablenefs, ftedfaftnefs, fafety
Immod'erate, a. exceffive, extravagant
Immod'erately, ad. in an exceffive degree, very
Immod'eft, a. unchafte, indecent, impudent
Immod'eftly, ad. without modefty, impudently
Immod'efty, n. a want of modefty, indecency
Im'molate, v. t. to facrifice, flay, kill, offer up
Immo'ation, n. the act of facrificing, a facrifice
Immóment, a. trifling, poffeffing little value, ob.
Immor'al, a. wicked, bad, irreligious, dishoneft
Immoral'ity, n. a want of virtue, vice, lewdnefs
Immor'ally, ad. in an immoral manner
Immor'tal, a. never dying or ending, perpetual
Immortal'ity, n. immortal life or fame
Immor'talize, v. to become or make immortal
Immor'tally, ad. without end, forever, always
Immove'able, a. unfhaken, firm, ftable, unfeeling
Immove'ably, ad. unalterably, firmly, truly, ever
Immúnity, n. a privilege, exemption, freedom
Immúre, v. t. to inclofe, to fhut in; n. an inclofure
Immúfical, a. unmufical, rough, harfh
Immutabil'ity, n. invariablenefs, a conftant ftate
Immútable, a. invariable, unalterable, fixed, firm
Immútably, ad. unchangeably, unalterably
Im'mutate, v. unaltered, unchanged
Imp, n. an offspring, puny devil, fhoot, graft
Imp, v. t. to imitate, enlarge, extend, join
Im'pact, n. a driving together, touching
Impact', v. t. to drive clofe together or very hard
Impáint, v. t. to paint, adorn, decorate, ob.
Impáir, v. t. to leffen, diminifh, injure, hurt
Impáir, Impáirment, n. a diminution, an injury
Impalp'able, a. not perceptible to the touch
Impals'y, v. t. to ftrike with a palfy, to deaden
Impan'nel, v. t. to form a jury
Impar'adife, v. t. to make happy or bleffed
Impar'ity, n. difproportion, inequality, oddnefs
Impark', v. t. to inclofe for or make a park
Imparl'ance, n. a continuation of a fuit in court
from day to day
Impart', v. t. to communicate, give, grant
Impart'ance, n. a communication, grant, fhare
Impar'tial, a. equitable, juft, equal, unbiaffed, fair
Impartial'ity, n. equitablenefs, juftice, fairnefs
Impar'tially, ad. equitably, juftly, properly, fairly
Impart'ible, a. that may be communicated
Impartibil'ity, n. the capacity of being imparted
Impart'ment, n. the act of imparting, a fhare
Impafs'able, a. that cannot be paffed through
Impafs'ible, Impafs'ive, a. incapable of fuffering
Impafs'iblenefs, Impaffibil'ity, n. exemption from
Impas''fioned, a. feized with paffion, warm (pain
Impáfted, a. pafted over, covered with pafte
Impátience, n. uneafinefs, fretfulnefs, heat
Impátient, a. not able to endure, eager, hot, hafty
Impátiently, ad. uneafily, paffionately, eagerly

Impawn', v. t. topawn, to leave as a pledge, ob.
Impéach, v. t. to accufe by a public body, of mal-
conduct in office, to accufe by authority, to cen-
fure [to hinder, ob.]
Impéachable, a. accufable, chargeable
Impéacher, n. one who impeaches or accufes
Impéachment, n. an accufation of malconduct
in office by authority, private cenfure, [hin-
drance, ob.]
Impe arl', v. t. to form like or adorn with pearls
Impeccabil'ity, n. an exemption from all offence
Impec'cable, a. not fubject to fin, perfect, pure
Impéde, v. t. to hinder, obftruct, let, ftop (tion
Impéd'iment, n. an hinderance, obftruction, oppofi-
Impel', v. t. to urge forward, drive on, inftigate
Impel'lent, n. a power that drives forward or on
Impend', v. i. to hang over, be near at hand, await
Impend'ence, n. the ftate of hanging overnearnefs
Impend'ent, a. hanging over, preffing clofely, near
Impenetrabil'ity, n. an impenetrable quality
Impen'etrable, a. not to be pierced or found out
Impen'etrably, ad. with impenetrable hardnefs
Impen'itence, n. a want of remorfe or repentance
Impen'itent, a. void of repentance, obdurate, hard
Impen'itently, ad. without repentance, hardly
Impens'ible, a. free from expence or reward
Imp'erate, a. done with knowledge or willingly, ob.
Imper'ative, a. commanding, ordering, bidding
Imperceptible, a. not to be perceived, minute
Imperceptibly, ad. in an imperceptible manner
Imper'fect, a. incomplete, defective, frail
Imperfec'tion, n. a defect, failure, want, fault
Imper'fectly, ad. not completely or fully, badly
Imper'forate, a. not pierced or bored through
Impérial, a. belonging to an emperor, royal
Impérialift, n. one belonging to an emperor
Impérious, a. haughty, arrogant, lordly, powerful
Impérioufly, ad. infolently, arrogantly, proudly
Impérioufnefs, n. high authority, arrogance, pride
Imper'ifhable, a. not liable to decay or perifh (able
Impermeabil'ity, n. the quality of being imperme-
Imper'meable, a. that cannot be paffed through
Imper'manent, a. not lafting, not durable
Impers'onal, a. having no particular perfon
Impers'onally, ad. in an imperfonal manner
Imperfpic'uous, a. not fufficiently clear or plain
Imperfuáfible, a. not to be perfuaded, obftinate
Impert'inence, n. intrufion, rudenefs, folly, a trifle
Impert'inent, a. meddling, intrufive, faucy, trifling
Impert'inent, n. a meddler, intruder, trifler
Impert'inently, ad. officioufly, without reafon
Impertranf'ible, a. that cannot be paffed through,
Imperturb'able, a. that cannot be difturbed (ob.
Imper'vious, a. unpaffable, thick, inacceffible
Impetuos'ity, Impet'uoufnefs, n. violence, fury
Impet'uous, a. violent, furious, vehement, fierce
Impet'uoufly, ad. violently, vehemently, hotly
Im'petus, n. a violent effort, force, blow, ftroke
Impiety, n. wickednefs, ungodlinefs, irreverence.

Impinge', v. t. to dash or fall against, to clash with

Impin"guate, v. t. to fatten, make fat, ob.

Imp'ious, a. wicked, lewd, profane, irreligious

Imp'iously, ad. wickedly, lewdly, profanely, vilely

Implacabil'ity, n. an inexorable state or quality

Implácable, a. not to be appeafed or pacified

Implácably, ad. with conftant enmity, inexorably

Implant', v. t. toingraft, infert, infix, place, fet

Implaus'ible, a. not fpecious, not appearing true

Implaufibil'ity, n. the not being plaufible

Impléad, v. t. to profecute or fue at law, to indict

Imp'lement, n. a tool, inftrument, utenfil, veffel

Implétion, n. the act of filling up, a full fiate

Implex', a. intricate, entangled, complicated

Implex'ion, n. involution, combination

Imp'licate, v. t. to infold, entangle, embarrafs

Implicátion, n. an involution, fold, tacit inference

Impli"cit, a. refting upon another, involved, real

Impli"citly, ad. abfolutely, by inference

Implóre, v. t. to beg, befeech, entreat, invoke

Implórer, n. one who implores, one who befeeches

Imply', v. t. to comprife, involve, infold, fuggeft

Impois'on, v. t. to corrupt or kill with poifon

Impol'icy, n. inexpedience, unfuitablenefs to the end propofed

Impolíte, a. unpolite, uncivil, rude, rough

Impol'itic, a. imprudent, indifcreet, improper

Impol'iticly, ad. in an impolitic manner, fimply

Impon'derable, a. having no fenfible weight

Impon'derous, a. void of fenfible weight, light

Imporos'ity, n. clofenefs, compactnefs, hardnefs

Imporous, a. free from pores, clofe, compact, hard

Impórt, v. t. to bring from abroad, imply, avail

Im'port, n. a thing imported, meaning, importance

Impórtable, a. that may be imported, [not to be borne, ob.]

Import'ance, n. moment, weight, confequence

Import'ant, a. momentous, weighty, forcible

Import'antly, ad. with importance or confequence

Importátion, n. the act of bringing from abroad

Impórter, n. one who brings things from abroad

Impórtlefs, a. very trifling, having no confequence

Import'unate, a. inceffant in folicitations, urgent

Import'unately, ad. with inceffant folicitation

Import'unatenefs, Importúnity, n. inceffant folicit-

Importúne, v. t. to teafe with folicitations (ation

Imp'rtúne, a. troublefome, urgent, unfeafonable

Importúnely, ad. inceffantly, unfeafonably

Impórtuous, a. void of ports, having no harbor

Impófe, v. t. to enjoin as a duty, lay, put, deceive

Impófe, n. a command, injunction, order, ob.

Impófable, a. that may or is fit to be impofed

Impófer, n. one who impofes, one who enjoins

Impofi"tion, n. an injunction, oppreffion, cheat

Impoffibil'ity, n. an impoffible or abfurd ftate

Impofs'ible, a. impracticable, that cannot be done

Im'poft, n. a duty on goods laid at the time of importation and paid by the importer, any duty or tax, upper part of a pillar

Impos't'humate, v. i. to form an abfcefs, to gather

Impofthumátion, n. the act of forming an abfcefs

Impos'thume, n. an abfcefs, matter gathered

Impos'tor, n. one who affumes a feigned character

Impos'ture, n. a cheat, deception, impofition, trick

Imp'otence, n. want of power, weaknefs, incapacity

Imp'otent, a. weak, feeble, difabled, maimed

Imp'otently, ad. without power, weakly, feebly

Impound', v. t. to fhut up in a pinfold, to confine

Impov'erifh, v. t. to render poor, exhauft, weaken

Impov'erifhment, n. a becoming poor

Imprac'ticable, a. not to be effected by human means, ftubborn

Impracticabil'ity, Imprac'ticablenefs, n. a ftate or quality of being beyond human power or the means propofed

Imp'recate, v. t. to invoke or wifh evil, to curfe

Imprecátion, n. an invocation of evil, a curfe

Imp'recatory, a. relating to imprecation, curfing

Impreci"fion, n. a want of precifion or exactnefs

Impregnabil'ity, n. an impregnable ftate, fafety

Impreg'nable, a. that is not to be taken, unmoved

Impreg'nably, ad. in an impregnable manner

Impreg'nate, v. t. to fill, make fruitful, tincture

Impregnátion, n. the act of making fruitful

Imprejúdicate, a. unprejudiced, impartial, juft, ob.

Imprcparátion, n. a want of preparation, ob.

Imprefcrip'tible, a. not to be impaired or loft by prefcription, not affected by long ufage or neglect (ent of cuftom or ufe

Imprefcriptibil'ity, n. the ftate of being independ-

Imprefs', v. t. to print, ftamp, mark, fix deep, prefs

Im'prefs, n. a forcing into fervice, impreffion, device

Imprefs'ible, a. that may or can be impreffed

Imprefs'ing, n. a forcing into public fervice

Imprefs'ment, n. a forcing into public fervice

Impres"fion, n. a ftamp, motto, edition, influence

Impreff'ive, a. tending or able to imprefs, producing a powerful effect

Impres'fure, n. a mark made by preffure

Im'primis, ad. in the firft place, before the reft

Imprint', v. t. to print, mark, fix deep, imprefs

Imprint'ing, n. a marking, an impreffion

Impris'on, v. t. to fhut up or put in prifon, to confine

Impris'onment, n. confinement in prifon (fiue

Improbabil'ity, n. unlikelihood, abfurdity, folly

Improb'able, a. unlikely, incredible, abfurd, filly

Improb'ably, ad. unlikely, incredibly

Improb'ity, n. dishonefty, bafenefs, wickednefs

Improlif'icate, v. t. to make fruitful, ob.

Impromp'tu, n. an extemporaneous compofition

Improp'er, a. unfit, unqualified, wrong

Improp'erly, ad. unfitly, unfuitably, amifs

Impropriate, v. t. to convert to private ufe, to alienate

Impropriátion, n. church-lands in lay-hands (nate

Impróp'riator, n. a layman having church-lands

Impropriety, n. unfitnefs, inaccuracy, fault

Impros'perous, a. unfuccefsful, unfortunate, ob.

Impros'peroufly, ad. unfuccefsfully, unhappily

Improvable, [o as oo] a. capable of improvement
Improve', v. to make or become better, to advance,
In N. England, to cultivate or occupy
Improve'ment, n. advancement, edification.
Improve'ments, n. pl. the additions to or meliorations of a farm, as buildings, fences, clearings, &c.
Improv'er, n. one who improves or makes better
Improv'idence, Improvi''fion, n. want of forecast
Improv'ident, a. wanting forecast, thoughtlefs
Improv'idently, ad. without due care or thought
Imprúdence, n. a want of prudence, indifcretion
Imprúdent, a. wanting prudence, indifcreet, filly
Imprúdently, ad. indifcreetly, fillily, carelefsly
Im'pudence, Impudi''city, n. fhamelefsnefs, impudent
Im'pudent, a. fhamelefs, faucy, bold (modefty
Im'pudently, ad. fhamelefsly, faucily, very boldly
Impúgn, v. t. to attack, affault, oppofe, difprove
Impuifs'ance, n. impotence, inability, ob.
Im'pulfe, n. a communicated force, motion, idea
Impul'fion, n. an influence on the mind or body
Impuls'ive, a. having the power to impel, moving
Impuls'ively, ad. with impulfe, with force (alty
Impúnity, n. exemption from punifhment or penImpúre, a. unholy, unchafte, lewd, droffy, foul
Impúrely, ad in an impure manner, unchaftly
Impúrity, n. uncleannefs, foulnefs, guilt
Impur'ple, v. t. to color or tinge with purple
Impútable, a. that can be imputed, chargeable
Impútablenefs, n. the quality of being imputable
Imputátion, n. an attribution, cenfure, blame
Impútative, a. that may or can be imputed
Impúte, v. t. to charge upon, attribute, affign
Imputres'cible, a. that cannot be corrupted (ing
In, prefixed to words like un, gives an oppofit meanInabil'ity, n. a want of power, impotence, weaknefs
Inabs'tinence, n. intemperance, extravagance
Inaccefs'ible, a. not to be approached or reached
Inacceffibil'ity, n. the ftate of being inacceffible
Inac'curacy, n. a want of exactnefs, a defect
Inac'curate, a. not accurate, faulty, carelefs
Inac'curately, ad. in an inaccurate manner
Inac'tion, n. a ftate of reft, indolence, idlenefs
Inac'tive, a. unemployed, indolent, fluggifh, idle
Inact'ively, ad. indolently, fluggifhly, idly, dully
Inactiv'ity, n. inaction, fluggifhnefs, idlenefs, eafe
Inad'equate, a. defective, not proportionate, unequal
Inad'equately, ad. defectively, imperfectly (qual
Inadhéfion, n. defect of adhefion
Inadhéfive, a. not adhefive or fticky
Inadmis'fible a. not proper to be admitted
Inadmiffibil'ity, n. a ftate of being inadmiffible
Inadvert'ence, n. inattention, negligence, floth
Inadvert'ent, a. inconfiderate, carelefs, giddy
Inadvert'ently, ad. inconfiderately, negligently
Inal'ienable, a. that cannot be alienated, fixed
Inaliment'al, a. affording no nourifhment
Inal'terable, a. not poffible to be changed
Inalterabil'ity, n. the quality of not admitting alInamifs'ible, a. incapable of being loft (teration

Inamoráto, n. a fond or amorous perfon, a lover
Ináne, a. void, empty, ufelefs, infignificant
Inan'imate, a. void of life or animation
Inani''tion, n. emptinefs, an emptinefs of body
Inan'ity, n. a void fpace, vacuity, emptinefs
Inap'petence, n. a want of appetite or defire
Inap'plicable, a. that cannot be applied, foreign
Inapplicabil'ity, n. the quality of not being applicable
Inappréciable, a. not to be duly eftimated (cable
Inapplication, n. inactivity, indolence, idlenefs
Inap'pofit, a. unfit, unfuitable, improper
Inappropriate, a. unfuitable, unfit
Inappróachable, a. not to be approached
Inapt'itude, n. want of fitnefs
Inarch', v. t. to graft by approach, or by joining
to a ftock a cion without feparating it from the
Inartic'ulate, a. indiftinct, confufed, thick (branch
Inartic'ulately, ad. indiftinctly, confufedly
Inartifi''cial, a. done contrary to art, artlefs, bad
Inartifi''cially, ad. without or contrary to art
Inatten'tion, n. difregard, negligence, careleffnefs
Inattent'ive, a. regardlefs, negligent, carelefs, idle
Inattent'ively, ad. carelefsly, heedlefsly, giddily
Inaud'ible, a. not to be heard, void of found
Inaug'ural, a. relating to inauguration, invefting
Inaug'urate, v. t. to inveft with folemnity, to begin
Inaugurátion, n. an invefture with folemnities
Inaug'uratory, a. pertaining to inauguration
Inaurátion, n. the act of gilding with gold (ble
Inaufpi''cious, a. unlucky, unfortunate, unfavorable
Inaufpi''cioufly, ad. with bad omens of fuccefs
Inaufpi''cioufnefs, n. unluckinefs, a bad omen
In'being, n. inherence, infeparablenefs, reality
In'born, a. implanted by nature, inherited
In'breathed, a. infpired, infufed, poured in
In'bred, a. bred or hatched within, natural
In'ca, n. the name of the princes of Peru, before
the conqueft
Incales'cence, n. an increafing heat, warmth
Incandes'cence, n. a white heat
Incandes'cent, a. white with heat (gle
Incantátion, n. an enchantment, charm, fpell, maIncant'atory, a. dealing by enchantment, magical
Incant'on, v. t. to form or unite to a canton
Incapabil'ity, n. a legal qualification, inability
Incápable, a. unable, not fit, unfit, unqualified
Incapácious, a. having but fmall content, narrow
Incapa''citate, v. t. to difqualify, difable, weaken
Incapa''city, n. inability, a want of proper powers
Incar'cerate, v. t. to imprifon, confine, fhut up
Incarcerátion, n. imprifonment, confinement
Incarn', v. to cover over with or breed flefh, ob.
Incarn'adine, v. t. to die or tinge red, ob. (flefh
Incarn'ate, v. t. to clothe in flefh; pa. clothed in
Incarnátion, n. the act of affuming a human body
Incarn'ative, a. a medicin producing flefh
Incáfe, v. t. to cover, inclofe, infold, furround
In'cavated, a. made hollow, bent round or in
Incavátion, n. the act of hollowing, a hollow made

Incau"tious, a, unwary, heedlefs, carelefs, giddy
Incau"tioufly, ad. unwarily, heedlefsly, giddily
Incau"tioufnefs, n. want of caution or forefight
Incend'iary, n. one who burns houfes or fows ftrife
In'cenfe, n. a ftrong perfume offered to fome deity
Incenfe', v. t. to provoke, enrage, incite, ftir up
Incenfe'ment, n. rage, fury, paffion, heat
Incen'fion, n. the act of kindling or burning
Incens'or, n. one who provokes or inflames
Incens'ory, n. a veffel ufed to burn incenfe in
Incent'ive, n. an incitement, encouragement, fpur
Incent'ive, a. ftirring up, encouraging, enticing
Incep'tion, n. a beginning, an attempt
Incep'tive, a. beginning, noting abeginning
Incert'itude, n. uncertainty, doubtfulnefs, doubt
Incefs'ancy, n. uninterrupted continuance
Incef'fant, a. continual, unceafing, uninterrupted
Incef'fantly, ad. without intermiffion, always
In'ceft, n. a cohabitation of parties prohibited
Inceft'uous, a. guilty of or living in inceft
Inceft'uoufly, ad. with unnatural love or union
Inch, n. the twelfth part of a foot, a fmall piece
Inch, v. to drive, take, give or retreat by inches
Inchant', v. t. to bewitch, facinate, delight
Inchant'ment, n. magical charms, high delight
Inchant'ingly, ad. by way of magic, delightfully
Inchant'refs, n. one who enchants
Inch'ed, pa. having inches in length or breadth
Inch'meal, n. a piece an inch long ; ad. by inches
In'choate [ch as k] v. t. to begin, commence
Inchoátion, n. the act of beginning, an entrance
Inchóative, a. beginning, inceptive
Incíde, v. t. to cut, cut into, hew, divide, feparate
In'cidence, In'cident, n. an accident, a cafualty
In'cident, Incident'al, a. accidental, cafual (way
Incident'ally, In'cidently, ad. occafionally, by the
Incin'erate, v. t. to burn or reduce to afhes
Incinerátion, n. the act of burning to afhes
Incip'ient, a. beginning, commencing, juft rifing
Incircumfpec'tion, n. a want of caution or care
Inciffed, a. cut, made by cutting, carved, jagged
Inci"fion, Incifure, n. a cut, opening, wound
Incifive, a. having the quality of cutting, fharp
Incifor, s. the name of a fharp fore tooth, a cutter
Incitant, n. that which incites or ftimulates
Incitátion, Incitement, n. an incentive, a motive
Incite, v. t. to ftir up, fpur or urge on, animate
Incivil, a. uncivil, unkind, rough, rude
Incivil'ity, n. a want of proper civility, rudenefs
Inciv'ifm, n. unfriendlinefs to a ftate or government
Inclem'ency, n. feverity, roughnefs, hardnefs
Inclem'ent, a. unmerciful, rough, rugged, hard
Inclinable, a. inclined, difpofed, willing, ready
Inclinátion, n. a tendency, flope, affection, defire
Incline, v. to bend, bow, lean, flope, difpofe
Inclip', v. t. to inclofe, furround, hold faft
Inclois'ter, v. t. to fhut up or confine in a cloifter
Inclófe, v. t. to furround, fhut in, fence about
Inclófure, n. a place inclofed, fence, wall

Incloud', v. t. to darken, make dark, obfcure
Inclúde, v. t. to comprehend, take in, inclofe
Inclúfion, n. the act of including, a repetition
Inclúfive, a. comprehending, taking in, inclofing
Inclúfively, ad. together, at one or the fame time
Incoer'cible, a. not to be forced
Incoexift'ence, n. the not exifting together (nefs
Inco"gitancy, n. a want of thought, rafhnefs, giddi-
Inco"gitative, a. wanting in thought, thoughtlefs
Incog'nito, Incog', ad. in a ftate of concealment
Incohérence, n. a want of connection, incongruity
Incohérent, a. unconnected, inconfiftent, loofe
Incohérently, ad. inconfiftently, loofely, badly
Incolúmity, n. fafety, fecurity, foundnefs, ob.
Incombuftibil'ity, n. the power of refifting fire
Incombuft'ible, a. that cannot be confumed by fire
In'come, n. a yearly rent, falary, profit, produce
Incommen'furable, a. that cannot be meafured,
    having no common meafure
Incommen'furate, a. having no common meafure
Incommenfurabil'ity, n. incapacity of being mea-
Incommis'cible, a. that cannot be mixed   (fured
Incommóde, v. t. to hinder, embarrafs, difturb
Incommódious, a. inconvenient, unfit, offenfive
Incommódioufly, ad. inconveniently   (ence
Incommó lioufnefs, Incommod'ity, n. inconveni-
Incommúnicable, a. that cannot be communicated
Incommúnicating, a. having no intercourfe
Incommútable, a. that cannot be exchanged
Incompact', a. not clofe, disjointed, loofe
Incomp'arable, a. above compare, excellent   (ly
Incomp'arably, ad. beyond comparifon, exceeding-
Incompas"fionate, a. void of pity, cruel, bloody
Incompatibil'ity, n. inconfiftency, abfurdity
Incompat'ible, a. inconfiftent, contradictory
Incompat'ibly, ad. inconfiftently, unfuitably
Incom'petency, n. infufficiency, inability
Incom'petent, a. inadequate, unfuitable, unable
Incom'petently, ad. inadequately, unfuitably
Incompléte, a. unfinifhed, imperfect, fhort
Incomplétely, ad. in an imperfect manner
Incomplétenefs, n. an unfinifhed ftate
Incomplex', a. uncompounded, fimple, fingle
Incompliance, n. untractablenefs, difobedience
Incompofed, a. difcompofed, difturbed, rough
Incom'pofit, a. uncompounded, fimple, prime
Incompoffibil'ity, n. inconfiftency, ob.
Incomprehenfibil'ity, Incomprehenfiblenefs, n.
    a incomprehenfible ftate or quality   (tained
Incomprehens'ible, a. not to be conceived or con-
Incomprehens'ibly, ad. inconceivably, obfcurely
Incomprefs'ible, a. not to be preffed into lefs fpace
Incompreffibil'ity, n. the quality of not being ca-
    pable of being reduced to a fmaller compafs
Inconcéalable, a. not to be concealed, open
Inconcéivable, Inconcep'tible, a. incomprehenfible
Inconcéivably, ad. beyond all comprehenfion
Inconclúdent, a. inferring no confequence, weak
Inconclúfive, a. defective, imperfect, weak

Inconclúſively, ad. in an imperfect manner
Inconclúſiveneſs, n. a want of rational conviction
Inconcoc'tion, n. an unripe or undigeſted ſtate
Inconcur'ring, a. not agreeing, not uniting, ob.
Incondens'able, a. not capable of being condenſed
Incon'dite, a. irregular, rude, bare, ob. (reſtrained
Incondi'tional, Incondi'tionate, a. unlimited, un-
Inconfórmity, n. incompliance, untractableneſs
Incongénial, a. not of a like nature, unſuitable
Incon'gruence, Incongrúity, n. inconſiſtency
Incon'gruous, a. inconſiſtent, unfit, abſurd
Inconnex'edly, ad. without connexion, ob.
Incons'equence, n. inconcluſiveneſs, defect, weak-
Inconſequen'tial, a. of no moment (neſs
Incons'equent, a. inconcluſive, not following
Inconſid'erable, a. unworthy of notice, trifling
Inconſid'erableneſs, n. a trifling ſtate, a low value
Inconſid'erate, a. inattentive, careleſs, fooliſh
Inconſid'erately, ad. thoughtleſsly, inattentively
Inconſid'erateneſs, Inconſiderátion, n. a want of
  conſideration, inattention, giddineſs, raſhneſs
Inconſiſt'ency, n. diſagreement, contradiction
Inconſiſt'ent, a. unſuitable, contrary, abſurd, odd
Inconſiſt'ently, ad. contrarily, abſurdly, oddly
Inconſiſt'ing, a. diſagreeing, differing, contrary
Inconſólable, a. not to be comforted, wretched
Inconſólably, ad. in an inconſolable manner
Incons'onancy, n. inconſiſtency, diſagreement
Inconſpic'uous, n. not diſcernible, not viſible
Incons'tancy, n. unſteadineſs, fickleneſs, change
Incons'tant, a. unſteady, fickle, changeable
Incons'tantly, ad. in an inconſtant manner
Inconſúmable, Inconſumpt'ible, a. not to be ſpent
Inconſum'mate, a. not complete or finiſhed
Inconteſt'able or Inconteſt'ible, a. indiſputable
Inconteſt'ibly, ad. beyond all diſpute, certainly
Incontig'uous, a. not joined together, ſeparated
Incont'inence, n. intemperance, unchaſtity, looſe-
Incont'inent, a. unchaſte, looſe, immediate (neſs
Incont'inently, ad. unchaſtly, immediately
Incontrovert'ible, a. indiſputable, certain, real
Incontrovert'ibly, ad. indiſputably, certainly
Inconvénience, n. unfitneſs, diſadvantage (ſome
Inconvénient, a. unfit, diſadvantageous, trouble-
Inconvéniently, ad. unfitly, unſeaſonably
Inconvers'able, a. unſocial, ſhy, ſtiff, formal
Inconvert'ible, a. that cannot be changed, fixed
Inconvin'cibly, ad. that is not to be convinced
Inconvin'cibly, ad. obſtinately (rial, unbodied
Incorp'oral, Incorpóreal, Incorp'orate, a. immate-
Incorp'orate, v. i. to form into one body, join, mix
Incorporátion, n. an union of divers ingredients
Incorpóreally, ad. immaterially, ſpiritually
Incorpſe', v. t. to form into a body, unite, ob.
Incorrect', a. not correct, inaccurate, faulty, bad
Incorrect'ly, ad. in an incorrect manner
Incorrect'neſs, n. inaccuracy, error, careleſſneſs
Incor'rigible, a. bad beyond amendment, vile, baſe
Incor'rigibleneſs, n. a ſad or hopeleſs depravity

Incor'rigibly, ad. beyond all hopes of amendment
Incorrupt', a. free from corruption, pure, honeſt
Incorruptibil'ity, n. an incapacity of decay
Incorrupt'ible, a. that does not admit of decay
Incorrup'tion, n. an exemption from corruption
Incorrupt'ive, a. not liable to corruption
Incorrupt'neſs, n. purity, uprightneſs, honeſty
Incrafs'ate, v. t. to thicken, make thick, increaſe
Incrafs'ate, a. increaſing in thickneſs, thick
Incraſſátion, n. the act or ſtate of thickening
Incraſs'ative, n. a medicin to thicken the blood
Incréaſe, v. to grow, make more or greater, raiſe
Incréaſe, n. an augmentation, addition, produce
Incredibil'ity, n. an incredible ſtate or quality
Incred'ible, a. not to be credited or believed
Incred'ibly, ad. in a manner not to be believed
Incredúlity, n. a hardneſs or refuſal of belief
Incred'ulous, a. hard of or refuſing belief
Incrémable, a. incapable of being burnt, ob.
Inc'rement, n. an increaſe, produce, fluxion, (buke
Increpátion, n. the act of chiding, a reproof, a re-
Incres'cent, Increſs'ant, a. increaſing, ſwelling
Incrim'inate, v. t. to accuſe, to charge in turn
Incruſt', Incruſt'ate, v. t. to cruſt or cover over
Incruſtátion, n. the act of incruſting, a covering
Incrys'talizable, a. that will not form into cryſtals
Inc'ubate, v. i. to ſit upon eggs, brood, hatch
Incubátion, n. the act of ſitting upon eggs
Inc'ubus, n. a diſorder, the night-mare
Inculc'ate, v. t. to enforce, urge, repeat, teach
Inculcátion, n. the act of inculcating
Inculp'able, a. unblamable, juſt, upright, pure
Inculp'atory, a. tending to blame, containing cen-
Incult', a. uncultivated, untilled, rude (ſure
Incum'bency, n. the keeping of a benefice, a lying
Incum'bent, n. one who poſſeſſes a benefice (upon
Incum'bent, a. impoſed as a duty, reſting upon
Incum'ber, v. t. to clog, load, embarraſs
Incum'brance, n. a clog, impediment, load
Incur', v. t. to become liable to, deſerve, occur
Incurabil'ity, Incúrableneſs, n. an impoſſibility of
Incúrable, a. not to be cured, hopeleſs (cure
Incúrably, ad. without cure, without remedy
Incúrious, a. inattentive, careleſs, negligent
Incúriouſneſs, n. want of curioſity
Incur'ſion, n. an invaſion, inroad, attack, ravage
Incurv'ate, v. t. to bow, bend, make crooked
Incurv'ate, a. bent or curved inwards
Incurvátion, n. the act of bowing or bending, a bow
Incurv'ity, n. a bent ſtate, crookedneſs, bend
Indagátion, n. a diligent ſearch, a cloſe inquiry, ob.
In'dagator, n. a ſearcher, ſtrict inquirer, ob.
Indart', v. t. to dart or ſtrike in, inject, ob.
Indebt'ed, a. involved in debt, owing, obliged
Indécency, n. a thing unbecoming, filthineſs
Indécent, a. unbecoming, unfit for the eyes or ears
Indécently, ad. without decency, very unſuitable
Indecid'uous, a. not falling off or ſhed, laſting
Indeci'ſion, n. want of deciſion, doubt, unſettled

ftate (tain, hefitating

Indecif'ive, *a.* not bringing to a final clofe, uncer-
Indeclin'able, *a.* that is not varied by terminations
Indeclin ibil'ity, *n.* incapacity of being declined
Indecompof'able, *a.* not capable of decompofition
Indec'orous, *a.* indecent, unbecoming, unfeemly
Indecorum, *n.* indecency, impropriety
Indéed, *ad.* in truth, in reality, in fact, verily
Indefat'igable, *a.* unwearied, untired, conftant
Indefat'igablenefs, *n.* unweariednefs
Indefat'igably, *ad.* without wearinefs, conftantly
Indefea'fible, *a.* not to be vacated or cut off
Indefect'ible, *a.* not fubject to defect or decay
Indefens'ible, *a.* not to be defended, infamous
Indef'inite, *more correctly* indefinit, *a.* indetermin-
ate, unlimited, boundlefs, uncertain
Indef'initly, *ad.* in an unlimited manner
Indefin'itude, *n.* an unlimited quantity or ftate,*ob.*
Indelib'erate, *a.* unpremeditated, rafh, hafty,fud-
Indel'ible, *a.* not to be effaced or blotted out (den
Indel'ibly, *ad.* in a manner not to be effaced
Indel'icacy, *n.* a want of tafte or proper decency
Indel'icate, *a.* wanting decency, grofs, unrefined
Indel'icately, *ad.* in an indelicate manner
Indemnification, *n.* a fecurity, a reimburfement
Indem'nify, *v. t.* to maintain unhurt, to fecure
Indem'nity, *n.* an exemption from punifhment
Indemons'trable, *a.* that cannot be demonftrated
Indent', *v. t.* to cut irregularly, notch, covenant
Indent', **Indentation**, *n.* an inequality, notch, cut
In'dent, *n.* a certificate for intereft, iffued by the
government of the U. States
Indent'ure,*n.* a kind of covenant or deed (freedom
Independ'ence, *n.* an exemption from control,
Independ'ent, *a.* not fubject to control, free, eafy
Independ'ently, *ad.* without dependence, at eafe
Independ'ents, *n. pl.* a certain religious fociety
Indefert', *n.* a want of merit, unworthinefs, *ob.*
Indes'inently, *ad.* without ceafing, for ever,*ob.*
Indeftruct'ible, *a.* that is not to be deftroyed (tible
Indeftructibil'ity,*n.* the quality of being indeftruc-
Indeterm'inable, *a.* that cannot be fixed or fettled
Indeterm'inate, *a.* indefinit, uncertain, vague
Indeterm'inately, *ad.* in an unfettled manner
Indeter'minatenefs,*n.* the ftate of being indefinite
Indetermination, *n.* a want of determination
Indeterm'ined, *a.* undecided, unfettled, doubtful
Indevotion, *n.* a want of devotion, irreligion
Indevout', *a.* not devout or pious, irreligious
In'dex,*n.* a pointer, hand, mark, table of contents
Indexter'ity, *n.* aukwardnefs, unhandinefs
In'dian, *n.* a native of the Indies, an aboriginal
In'dian, *a.* pertaining to the Indians (of America
In'dicant, *a.* fhowing, pointing out, difcovering
In'dicate, *v. t.* to fhow, point out, difcover, tell
Indication, *n.* a mark, fign, token, note, fymptom
Indic'ative, *a.* fhowing, pointing out, affirming
Indic'atively, *ad.* in an indicative manner
Indict', *v. t.* to accufe of a crime by a grand jury

Indict'ment, *n.* a written formal accufation of a
crime by a grand jury
Indict'able, *a.* that may be indicted by law, or that
for which an indictment will lie (years
Indic'tion, *n.* a declaration, a proclamation, 15
Indif'ference, *n.* unconcernednefs, careleffnefs
Indif'ferent,*a.* unconcerned, regardlefs, impartial,
equal, tolerable, poorly, low
Indif'ferently, *ad.* tolerably, poorly, coolly
In'digence, *n.* need, want, poverty, diftrefs
In'digene,*n.* a native of the country or foil
Indig'enous,*a.* natural to or born in a country
In'digent,*a.* needy, wanting, poor, empty, void
Indigeft'ed, *a.* not digefted, irregular, confufed
Indigeft'ible,*a.* that cannot be digefted, very hard
Indiges'tion,*n.* the ftate of meals unconcocted
Indi''gitate, *v. t.* to point at or out, to fhow, *ob.*
Indigitation, *n.* the act of pointing at or out, *ob.*
Indign, *a.* unworthy, undeferving, *ob.*
Indig'nant, *a.* angry, raging, enraged, fcornful
Indignation,*n.* anger mixed with contempt, rage
Indig'nity,*n.* an infult, contumely, contempt
In'digo,*n.* a plant ufed for dying blue
Indirect', *a.* not ftrait, oblique, unfair, mean
Indirec'tion, **Indirect'nefs**,*n.* unfairnefs, dishonefty
Indirect'ly, *ad.* obliquely, unfairly
Indifcern'ible, *a.* not difcernible, not to be feen
Indifcerp'ible, *a.* that cannot be feparated or torn
Indis'ciplinable, *a.* not capable of receiving difci-
Indifcov'erable, *a.* that cannot be difcovered (plin
Indifcréet, *a.* imprudent, injudicious, incautious
Indifcreet'ly,*ad.* imprudently, foolifhly, fimply
Indifcre''tion,*n.* imprudence,inconfideration,folly
Indifcrim'inate, *a.* undiftinguifhed, confufed
Indifcrim'inately, *ad.* without diftinction
Indifcrim'inating,*a.* not making a diftinction
Indifcrimination, *n.* want of diftinguifhing (lute
Indifpens'able,*a.* not to be fpared, neceffary,abfo-
Indifpens'ably,*ad.* neceffarily, abfolutely, really
Indifpófe, *v. t.* to diforder, difqualify, make unfit
Indifpófed, *pa. a.* difordered, difqualified, averfe
Indifpófednefs, *n.* illnefs, ficknefs, unfitnefs
Indifpofi''tion,*n.* a diforder, ficknefs, diflike
Indifpútabie,*a.* not to be difputed, certain, true
Indifpútably,*ad.* without controverfy, really
Indiffolv'able, *a.* not to be feparated as to its parts
Indiffolubil'ity, **Indifs'olublenefs**,*n.* an indiffoluble
Indifs'oluble, *a.* binding for ever, firm (quality
Indiftinct', *a.* confufed, obfcure (tainty
Indiftinc'tion, **Indiftinct'nefs**, *n.* confufion, uncer-
Indiftinct'ly, *ad.* confufedly, obfcurely, darkly
Indiftinguifh'able, *a.* not to be diftinguifhed
Inditurb'ance,*a.* calmnefs, peace, quiet, repofe
Indite, *v. t.* to compofe, draw up, dictate, accufe
Individ'ual, *a.* not to be divided, numerically one
Individ'ual, *n.* a fingle perfon or thing, a particle
Individual'ity, *n.* a diftinct ftate or exiftence
Individ'ually, *ad.* with feparate exiftence, fingly
Individ'uate, *v. t.* to diftinguifh, feparate, fingle

Individuátion, *. the act of making fingle

Indivin'ity, *n.* a want of divine power or exiftence

Indivifibil'ity, *n.* an impoffibility of divifion

Indivis'ible, *a.* not to be divided   (untractable

Indo''cible, Indo''cil, *a.* incapable of inftruction,

Indocil'ity, *n.* untractablenefs, dulnefs, heavinefs

Indoc'trinate, *v. t.* to teach, inftruct, train, form

Indoctrinátion, *n.* inftruction, information

In'dolence, *n.* lazinefs, idlenefs, inattention, eafe

In'dolent, *a.* lazy, idle, fluggifh, careiefs, liftlefs

In'dolently, *ad.* lazily, idly, carelefsly, heedlefsly

Indorfe', *v. t.* to write on the back of a paper, to affign by indorfement

Indors'able, *a.* that may be indorfed

Indors'er, *n,* one who writes his name on the back of a note or bill of exchange

Indorfe'ment, *n.* the act of writing on the back, writing or name written (ed by indorfement

Indorfeé, *n.* the perfon to whom a note is affign-

In'draught, *n.* a paffage inward, inlet, bay, *ob.*

Indrench', *v. t.* to foak, overwhelm, drown, bury

Indubious, Indúbitable, Indúbitate, *a.* certain

Indúbitably, *ad.* certainly, unqueftionably, really

Indúce, *v. t.* to prevail with or on, lead, introduce

Indúcement, *n.* a motive, incitement, bait, trap

Induct', *v. t.* to bring in, put in poffeffion, admit

Inductile, *a.* that is not capable of being drawn into threads

Inductil'ity, *n.* the quality of being inductile

Induc'tion, *n.* an introduction, a taking poffeffion

Induct'ive, *a.* perfuafive, leading, able to infer

Indúe, *v.* to inveft, fupply, furnifh, equip, digeft

Indulge', *v. t.* to humor, gratify, oblige, favor

Indul'gence, *n.* fondnefs, forbearance, forgivenefs

Indul'gent, *a.* kind, fond, tender, favorable

Indul'gently, *ad.* kindly, fondly, favorably, well

Indurate, *v,* to harden, to grow or make hard

Indurátion, *n.* the act or ftate of hardening, hard-

Indus'trious, *a,* diligent, laborious, defigned (nefs

Indus'trioufly, *ad.* diligently, duly, defignedly

In'duftry, *n.* diligence, attention, an endeavor

Indwell'ing, *n.* a refidence within

Inébriate, *v.* to make or grow drunk, to ftupify

Inébriate, *n.* an habitual drunkard

Inébriant, *n.* that which intoxicates or affects the nerves in the manner of fpirit

Inebriátion, *n.* drunknefs, intoxication, ftupor

Ined'ited, *a.* unpublifhed, not made public

Inef'fable, *a.* inexpreffible, not to be defcribed

Inef'fably, *ad* unfpeakably, inexpreffibly

Ineffect'ive, *a.* producing no effect, ufelefs vain

Ineffect'ual, Inefficácious, *a.* void of power, weak

Ineffect'ually, *ad.* to no end or purpofe, in vain

Ineffect'ualnefs, Inefficacioufnefs, Inefficacy, *n.* a want of effect or power, weaknefs

Ineffervef'cence, *n.* a ftate of not effervefcing

Ineffervef'cent, *a.* not effervefcing

Ineffervef'cible, *a.* not capable of effervefcence

Ineffervefcibil'ity, *n.* the ftate of not being capa-

ble of effervefcence

Ineffi''cient, *a.* not powerful, not effectual

Inelas'tic, *a.* wanting elafticity

Inelafti''city, *n.* the quality of not being elaftic

Inel'igible, *a.* not expedient, that cannot be elected

Ineligibil'ity, *n.* unfitnefs or incapacity to be chofen

Inel'egance, *n.* a want of elegance, clumfinefs

Inel'egant, *a.* mean, contemptible, rough, coarfe

Inel'gantly, *ad.* in an inelegant manner

Inel'oquent, *a.* not eloquent aukward, plain

Inept', *a.* unfit, ufelefs, trifling, fimple, foolifh

Inept'itude, *n.* unfitnefs, unfuitablenefs, weaknefs

Inept'ly, *ad.* unfitly, unfuitably, foolifhly (nefs

Inequal'ity, *n.* unevennefs, difproportion, rough

Ineq'uitable, *a.* contrary to equity or juftice

Inerrabil'ity, Iner'rablenefs, *n.* infallibility

Iner'rable, *a.* exempt from error or miftake

Iner'rably, Iner'ringly, *ad.* without error, fafely

Inert', *a.* fluggifh, dull, heavy, motionlefs, fleepy

Iner'tion, *n.* a want of action, a torpid ftate

Inert'ly, *ad.* fluggifhly, dully, heavily, fleepily

Ines'timable, *a.* that is above all price, is valuable

Inev'ident, *a.* not plain or clear, obfcure, dark

Inevitabil'ity, Inev'itablenefs, *n.* certainty

Inev'itable, *a.* not to be efcaped, certain, fixed

Inev'itably, *ad.* without a poffibility of efcape

Inexact', *a.* not exact or precife

Inexact'nefs, *n.* incorrectnefs, want of precifion

Inexcítable, *a.* not capable of excitement

Inexer'tion, *n.* a want of effort or exertion (ance

Inexecútion, *n.* neglect of execution or perform-

Inexcúfable, *a.* not to be excufed, infamous

Inexcúfably, *ad.* beyond or without excufe

Inexhá'lable, *a.* that cannot be evaporated

Inexhauft'ed, *a.* not drained or emptied, unfpent

Inexhauft'ible, *a.* that cannot be drained or fpent

Inexhauft'ive, *a.* not to be exhaufted or fpent

Inexhauft'lefs, *a.* inexhauftible, not to be fpent

Inexiftence, *n.* a privation of exiftence or being

Inexift'ent, *a.* not exifting, not in actual being

Inex'orable, *a.* not to be moved by entreaty, firm

Inexorabil'ity, *n.* the quality of being inexorable

Inex'orably, *ad.* in an inexorable manner

Inexpédience, *n.* a want of fitnefs, unfuitablenefs

Inexpédient, *a.* improper, unfit, inconvenient

Inexpérience, *n.* a want of experience or fkill

Inexpérienced, *a.* unfkilled, unacquainted

Inexpert', *a.* unfkilful, unfkilled, unhandy, dull

Inex'piable, *a.* that cannot be atoned for, horrid

Inex'piably, *ad.* in an inexpiable manner, vilely

Inex'pleably, *ad.* in an infatiable manner, *b.*

Inex'plicable, *a.* not to be explained, myfterious

Inexpref'sible, *a.* not to be defcribed, unutterable

Inexpref'sibly, *ad.* in an unutterable manner

Inexpref'sive, *a.* not expreffing, not uttering

Inexpug'nable, *a.* that cannot be taken by affault

Inexterm'inable, *a.* not to be exterminated

Inextin''guifhable, *a.* unquenchable, not to be

Inex'tricable, *a,* not to be difentangled (put out

Inéye, v. t. to inoculate, infert a bud, ingraft, ob.

Infallibil'ity, n. an exemption from all error

Infal'lible, a. incapable of miftake, certain, true

Infal'libly, ad. without error or fail, certainly

Infáme, v. t. to defame, flander, ob.

In'famous, a. vile, bafe, fcandalous, notorious

In'famoufly, ad. vilely, fhamefully, fcandaloufly

In'famy, n. difgrace, reproach, wickednefs

In'fancy, n. the firft part of life or being, an origin

In'fant, n. a very young child; a. early, tender

Infant'a, n. a Spanifh or Portuguefe princefs

Infant'icide, n. a murder or murderer of infants

Infant'ile, a. relating to an infant, childifh, filly

In'fantry, n. pl. the foot-foldiers of an army

Infarc'tion, n. the act of ftuffing, fulnefs

Infat'igable, a. indefatigable, unwearied, ob.

Infat'uate, v. t. to ftrike with folly, to bewitch

Infatuátion, n. a deprivation of reafon, weaknefs

Infauft'ing, n. the act of making unlucky, ob.

Infeáfible, a. impracticable, not to be performed

Infect', v. t. to communicate bad qualities, taint,

Infect'er, n. one who or what infects (pollute

Infec'tio, n. volatile matter emitted from difeafed bodies or putrifying fubftances, capable of
caufing difeafe in a healthy body, taint

Infec'tious, Infect'ive, a. contagious, tainting

Infec'tioufly, ad. with or by infection, contagioufly

Infecund'ity, n. barrennefs, fterility

Infeli'city, n. unhappinefs, mifery, calamity

Infer, v. t. to deduce, derive, draw, conclude

In'ference, n. a conclufion drawn from premifes

Infer'able, a. that may be inferred or concluded

Inférior, n. a perfon of lower rank; a. lower, lefs

Inferior'ity, n. a lower ftate of dignity or place

Infer'nal, a. hellifh, very bad, lower, lying below

Infer'tile, Infec'und, a. unfruitful, barren, poor

Infertil'ity, n. unfruitfulnefs, barrennefs, poverty

Infeft', v. t. to difturb, harafs, plague, annoy

Infeudátion, n. the granting of tithes to laymen,
the putting in poffeffion of a fee

In'fidel, n. an unbeliever, heretic, traitor, pagan

In'fidel, a. unbelieving, contradictory, abfurd

Infidel'ity, n. a want of faith, a difbelief in Chrift

Infil'trate, v. to enter by penetrating the interftices

Infiltrátion, n. a penetrating by pores, the fubftance fo entered

In'finite, more correctly infinit, a. unbounded, endlefs, vaft, very great, immenfe

In'finitely, ad. without limits, immenfely

In'finitenefs, Infin'itude, n. boundleffnefs, infinity

Infinites'imal, n. an indefinitly fmall part

Infin'itive, n. a mood in grammar; a. unlimited

Infin'ity, n. an an infinit number, immenfity

Infirm', a. weak, feeble, crazy, fickly, irrefolute

Infirm', v. t. to weaken, enfeeble, fhake, fhatter

Infirm'ary, n. a refidence of the fick, a hofpital

Infirm'ity, n. a weaknefs, failing, fault, difeafé

Infirm'nefs, n. weaknefs, feeblenefs, crazinefs

Infix', v. t. to fix or drive in, faften, implant

Infláme, v. t. to fet on fire, heat, provoke

Inflámer, n. a thing or perfon that inflames

Inflammabil'ity, n. the quality of catching fire

Inflam'mable, a. eafily fet on fire, fiery, hot

Inflammátion, n. an inflamed ftate, heat, fwelling

Inflam'matory, a. able or tending to inflame

Infláte, v. t. to fwell, fwell with wind, puff up

Inflátion, n. a fwelling, fwelled ftate, windinefs

Inflect', v. t. to bend, crook, turn, vary, decline

Inflec'tion, n. the act of bending or varying, a bend

Inflect'ive, a. able to bend or vary, powerful

Inflexibil'ity, Inflex'iblenefs, n. ftiffnefs, obftinacy

Inflex'ible, a. immoveable, not to be altered, firm

Inflex'ibly, ad. invariably, unalterably, firmly

Inflict', v. t. to punifh, lay upon, impofe, dafh

Inflict'er, n. one who inflicts, one who punifhes

Inflic'tion, n. the act of inflicting, a punifhment

Inflict'ive, a. tending or able to inflict

Inflores'cence, n. the manner of flowering or in
which flowers are connected with a plant by
the peduncles

In'fluence, n. an afcendant power, fway, bias, turn

In'fluence, v. t. to have power over, move, bias

In'fluent, a. flowing or running into

Influen'tial, a. exerting influence or power

Influen'za, n. an epidemic cold or catarrh

In'flux, n. the act of flowing in, increafe, power

Infóld, v. t. to involve, inwrap, inclofe, fold up

Infóliate, v. t. to cover or fpread with leaves

Inform', v. t. to tell, acquaint, accufe, animate

Inform', a. unfhapen, fhapelefs, ugly, uncouth

Inform'al, a. informing, accufing, irregular, loofe

Informal'ity, n. want of form or technical manner

Inform'ant, Inform'er, n. one who informs

Informátion, n. intelligence, notice, a charge

Inform'idable, a. not to be feared or dreaded

Inform'ity, n. fhapeleffnefs, irregularity, uglinefs

Inform'ous, a. fhapelefs, irregular, rough, ftrange

Infor'tunate, a. unlucky, unhappy, miferable

Infract', v. t. to break, crufh, violate

Infrac'tion, n. the act of breaking, a violation

Inframund'ane, a. lying or fet beneath the world

Infran'gible, a. not to be broken, durable, firm

Infréquency, n. uncommonnefs, ftrangenefs

Infréquent, a. rare, unufual, uncommon, ftrange

Infri'gidate, v. t. to chill, cool, make cold, ob.

Infrigidátion, n. the act of chilling or cooling, ob.

Infringe', v. t. to violate, break, tranfgrefs

Infringe'ment, n. a violation, breach, tranfgreffion

Infrin'ger, n. a violator, breaker, tranfgreffor

In'fucate, v. t. to paint, paint the face, daub over

Infundibúlliform, a. fhaped like a funnel

Infúriate, v. t. to enrage, to make mad or furious

Infúriate, a. like a fury, mad, raging, enraged

Infufc'ate, v. t. to make black, blacken, darken

Infúfe, v. t. to pour in, put, fteep, tincture, infp ire

Infúfible, a. that may be infufed, that cannot be
fufed or made liquid (ving power of heat

Infufibil'ity, n. the quality of refifting the diffol-

Infūfion, n. the act of pouring or steeping in, the
fubstance infufed or the mixture

Infūfive, a. having the power of infufion, melting

In'gathering, n. a gathering in, harveft-time

Iagem'inate, v. t. to redouble, to repeat, ob.

Ingeminátion, n. the act of repeating, ob.

Ingen'erable,a. not to be brought into exiftence,ob.

Ingen'erated, a. innate, inborn, unbegotten, ob.

Ingénio, n. a houfe or mill where fugar is made

Ingénious, a. poffeffed of genius, witty, curious

Ingénioufly, ad. in an ingenious manner

Ingénioufnefs,n. wittinefs, invention, contrivance

Engen't', a. inborn, native, natural, ob.

Ingenúity,n. wit,acutenefs,[opennefs,candor,ob.]

Ingen'uous, a. open, candid, fair, honeft, noble

Ingen'uoufly, ad. openly, candidly, fairly, freely

Ingen'uoufnefs,n. opennefs, candor, honefty

In'geny, n. wit, genius, acutenefs, ingenuity, ob.

Ingeft', v. t. to throw into the ftomach, to add

Inges'tion, n. a throwing into the ftomach

Inglórious, a. void of glory or honor, mean, bafe

Inglorioufly, ad. difhonorably, with difgrace

In''got, n. a bar or wedge of gold or filver

Ingraft', v. t. to infert a cion of one tree in another, to fix deep, implant

Ingraft'ment, n. the act of ingrafting, a graft

In'grain,v. t. to die in the grain, or before manu-

In'grained, pa. dyed in the raw material (facture

Ingráte, a. ungrateful, unthankful, unpleafant

Ingráte, n. an ungrateful or unthankful perfon

Ingrátiate, v. i. to get into or curry favor

Ingrátiating, n. the act of getting favor (vior

Ingrat'itude, n. unthankfulnefs, ungrateful beha-

Ingrédient, n. a part, a component part of a body

In''grefs, n. an entrance, a power of entering

Ingres''fion,n. the act of entering, entrance

In''guinal, a. belonging to or like the groin

Ingulf', v. t. to fwallow up in or caft into a gulf

Ingur'gitate, v. i. to fwill, to fwallow greedily

Ingurgitátion, n. the act of fwallowing up

Inguft'able, a. that cannot be tafted, infipid

Inhabil'ity, n. unfkilfulnefs, unfitnefs

Inhab'it,v. to dwell or live in, occupy, poffefs

Inhab'itable, a. habitable, [not habitable, ob']

Inhab'itance, n. a dwelling, or refidence

Inhab'itancy, n. legal refidence to acquire the
rights of an inhabitant. [local]

Inhab'itant, Inhab'iter, n. one who dwells in a
place, one who has lived in a town fufficient
time to acquire the rights of citizens, or of
maintenance by the public, if poor, [local]

Inhabitátion, n. the act or place of refidence

Inhále, v. t. to draw in with the breath (mouth

Inháler, n. a veffel for drawing fteam into the

Inharmónious, a. unmufical, not fweet, harfh

Inhére, v. i. to ftick or exift in fomething elfe

Inhérence, Inhéfion, n. an inherent ftate or quality

Inhérent, a. exifting in fomething elfe, innate

Inher'it, v. t. to have by inheritance, to poffefs

Inher'itable, a. obtainable by inheritance

Inher'itance, n. a hereditary poffeffion, a patri-

Inher'itor, n. a man who inherits, an heir (mony

Inher'itrefs, Inher'itrix, n. a female who inherits

Inherfe', v. t. to put into a funeral monument

Iahīb'it, v. t. to prohibit, hinder, reftrain, check

Inhi''bition, n. a prohibition, reftraint, embargo

Inhōld, v. t. inheld, pret. inheld, pa. to hold or
contain within itfelf, ob.

Inhos'pitable, a. unkind to ftrangers, unfeeling

Inhofpital'ity, n. a want of hofpitality or courtefy

Inhúman or Inhumáne, a. barbarous, cruel

Inhuman'ity, n. barbarity, cruelty, unkindnefs

Inhúmanly, ad. barbaroufly, cruelly, unkindly

Inhúmate, Inhúme, v. t. to bury, inter, hide

Inhumátion, n. the act of burying, a digeftion in
a warm fubftance

Inim'ical, a. hoftile, contrary, repugnant, crofs

Inimitabil'ity, n. an inimitable ftate or quality

Inim'itable, a. not to be imitated or copied, very

Inim'itably, ad. very excellent, remarkably (fine

Ini''quitous,a. unjuft, wicked, vile, bafe

Ini''quity, n. injuftice, wickednefs, guilt, fault

Inir'ritable, a. not capable of irritation

Inirritabil'ity, n. the quality of being inirritable

Inir'ritative,a. denoting want of action or irritation

Ini''tial, a. placed at the beginning, firft

Ini''tial, n, the firft letter, of a name

Ini''tiate,v. t. to admit, to inftruct ; a.unpracticed

Initiátion, n. an admiffion, an inftruction

Ini''tiatory, a. tending, ferving or ufed, to initiate

Inject', v. to throw or fquirt in, throw up, caft

Injec'tion, n. the act of injecting, a glyfter

Injudi''cious, a. void of judgement, unwife, filly

Injudi''cioufly, ad. without judgement, fimply

Injunc'tion, n. a command,order,precept,prohibi-

In'jure, v. t. to annoy, hurt ufijuftly, wrong (tion

In'jurer, n. one who hurts another unjuftly

Injúrious, a. unjuft, mifchievous, reproachful

Injúrioufly, ad. hurtfully, wrongfully, bafely, ill

Injúrioufnefs,n. an injurious quality

In'jury, n. hurt, mifchief,detriment, reproach

Injuft'ice,n. injury, wrong, iniquity, dishonefty

Ink, n. a black liquid to write or print with

Ink, v. t. to black, daub or mark with ink

Ink'horn,n. a veffel to hold ink for writing

In''kle, n. a broad tape, a fort of fillet

Ink'ling, n. a hint, intimation, whifper, report

Ink'ftand, n. a veffel to hold ink

Ink'y, a. daubed with or refembling ink, black

In'land, a. fituated remotely or far from the fea

In'land, n. parts that are remote from the fea

In'lander, n. one who lives remote from the fea

Inlap'idate, v. t. to turn to ftone, ob.

Inláw, v. t. to clear from outlawry, to reftore,ob.

Inláy, v. t. inlaid, pret. inlaid, pa. to variegate
wood, &c. checker, infert

In'lay, n. any matter that is inlaid

In'let, n. a paffage, entrance, admiffion

Inlift', v. to engage or enter into military service
Inlift'ment, n. the act of inlisting, the writing containing the terms of entering into service and the names
In'ly, a. internal, secret; ad. internally, secretly
In'mate,n.a lodger,one who lives in the same house
In'moft, In'nermoft, a. deepeft, remoteft
Inn, n. a houfe of entertainment for travellers
Inn, v. to put up at an inn, ftop, houfe, lodge,reft
In'nate, a. inborn, inbred, implanted, natural
Innavigable, a. not to be failed upon, dangerous
In'ner, a. more inward, placed within, nearer
Innerve', v. t. to give nerves, to invigorate
Inn'holder, Inn'keeper, n. one who keeps an inn
In'nings, n. pl. lands recovered from the fea (tity
In'nocence, n. harmleffnefs,purity,integrity,chaf-
In'nocent, a. harmlefs, pure, free from guilt
In'nocent, n. one harmlefs like a child
In'nocently, ad. harmlefsly, without guilt
Innoc'uous, a. innocent, harmlefs, pure, upright
Innoc'uoufly, ad. without mifchievous effects
Innoc'uoufnefs, n. harmleffnefs,innocence, purity
In'novate, v. t. to introduce novelties, to change
Innovation, n. an introduction of novelty, change
In'novator, n. one who introduces novelties
Innox'ious, a. free from harm, harmlefs,innocent
Innox'ioufly, ad. without harm, innocently
Innuend'o, n. an oblique or diftant hint; in law a word to afcertain the precife perfon
Innumerable, Innumerous, a. not to be numbered
Innumerably, ad. without or beyond number
Innutri'tion, n. failure or want of nourifhment
Innutri'tious, a. not nourifhing
Inobferv'able, a. that cannot be perceived or feen
Inobferv'ant, a. not taking notice
Inoc'ulate, v. t. to propagate by infertion
Inoculation, n. the act of inoculating or grafting
Inoc'ulator, n. a perfon who inoculates or grafts
Inodorous, a. wanting fmell, unperfumed
Inoffens'ive, a. giving no fcandal, harmlefs, pure
Inoffens'ively, ad. without offenfe or harm
Inoffens'ivenefs, n. harmleffnefs, innocence
Inoffi''cious, a. contrary to natural duty
Inop'erative, a. not operative, not active
Inop'ulent, a. not wealthy, or very rich
Inord'inancy,Inordination,n.irregularity, oddnefs
Inord'inate a. diforderly, irregular, immoderate
Inord'inately, ad. in an irregular manner
Inorgan'ical, a. devoid of organs or inftruments
Inorgan'ically, ad. in an inorganical manner
Inor'ganized, a. not have organic ftructure
Inofc'ulate, v. t. to unite, join, make to kifs
Inofculation, n. an union, conjunction, kifs
In'queft, n. a judicial or other inquiry, a fearch
Inquietude,n. uneafinefs, reftleffnefs
In'quinate, v. t. to pollute, corrupt, defile, foul
Inquination, n. a pollution, corruption, ftain, blot
Inquire, v.t. to afk, feek out, fearch, examin
Inquirent, a. fearching, examining, inquifitive

Inquirer, n. one who afks, fearches or examins
Inquiry, n. an interrogation, fearch, examination
Inquifi''tion, n. a judicial enquiry, a cruel court
Inquifi''tional, a. relating to the inquifition, cruel
Inquis'itive, a. prying, curious, bufy, diligent
Inquis'itivenefs, n. curiofity, impertinence
Inquis'itor, n. an officer of the inquifition
Inquifitórial, a. making or pertaining to inquiry
Inrail, v. t. to rail in, inclofe with rails
In'road, n. an incurfion, fudden invafion, attack
Infalubrious, a. unhealthy, unwholefome, bad
Infalubrity, n. unhealthinefs, noxioufnefs
Infal'utary, a. not favorable to health, noxious
Infáne, a. mad, diftracted, gone out of one's mind
Infánenefs, Infan'ity, n. madnefs, dotage
Infátiable. Infátiate,a.not to be fatisfied,very gree-
Infátiablenefs, n. a greedinefs not to be fatisfied (dy
Infátiably, ad. with an infatiable greedinefs
Infatisfac'tion, n. a diffatisfied ftate, difcontent,ob.
Infat'urable, a. that cannot be filled or glutted
Infcrbe, v. t. to write in or upon, to dedicate
Infcrip'tion, n. an epitaph, title, thing written
Infcrútable, a. unfearchable, hidden, fecret,dark
Infculp', v. t. to engrave, cut upon, carve, mark
Infculp'ture, n. fculpture, an engraving
In'fect, n. any fmall creeping or flying animal
Infect'ile, a. having the nature of or like infects
Infec'tion, n. the act of cutting into a thing, a cut
Infectiv'orous, a. devouring or feeding on infects
Infectol'oger, n. one who defcribes infects
Infecúre, a. unfafe, dangerous, hazardous
Infecúrely, ad. unfafely, with danger or hazard
Infecúrity, n. a want of fafety, danger, hazard
Infecution, n. the act of purfuing, a purfuit
Infens'ate, a. fenfelefs, ftupid, enraged, mad
Infenfibil'ity, Infens'iblenefs, n. ftupidity, dulnefs
Infens'ible, a. void of fenfe, imperceptible, flow
Infens'ibly, ad. imperceptibly, by flow degrees
Infen'fient, a. not having power of perception
Infeparabil'ity, Infep'arablenefs, n. an infeparable
Infep'arable, a. not to be disjoined, fixed (quality
Infep'arably, ad. in an infeparable manner
Infert', v. t. to put or place among other things
Infer'tion, n. the act of inferting, a thing inferted
Inferv'ient, a. conducive, helping, ufeful, fit
Infhell', v. t. to hide or put in a fhell, ob.
Infhip', v. t. to put into a fhip, fhip, embark, ob.
Infhrine, v. t. to put into a fhrine, inclofe, lay up
Inside, n. the inward part, the part placed within
Infid'ious, a. trecherous, deceitful, fly, unfair
Infid'ioufly, ad. trecheroufly, deceitfully, flily
Infid'ioufnefs, n. trechery, deceit, flinefs, craft
In'fight, n. an infpection, view, knowledge
Infignif'icance, n. a want of meaning, meannefs
Infignif'icant, a. void of meaning, mean, trifling
Infignif'icantly, ad. in an infignificant manner
Infincére, a. deceitful, unfaithful, unfound
Infincer'ity, n. diffimulation, deceit, unfairnefs
Infin'ew, v. t. to ftrengthen, harden, confirm

Infin'uant, _a._ able or tending to gain favor
Infin'uate, _v. t._ to hint artfully, instil, wreath, steal
Infinuâtion, _n._ the act of insinuating, a sly hint
Infin'uative, _a._ stealing upon the affections
Infin'uator, _n._ one who insinuates or hints at
Infip'id, _a._ void of taste or spirit, dull, flat
Infipid'ity, Infip'idness, _n._ a want of taste or spirit
Infip'idly, _ad._ without taste or spirit, dully, flatly
Infip'ience, _n._ folly, foolishness, weakness
Infift', _v._ to stand, dwell, persist in, command
Infist'ent, _a._ placed, standing or resting upon
Infift'ure, _n._ constancy, firmness, regularity, _ob._
Infi"tiency, _n._ an exemption from thirst, _ob._
Infi'tion, _n._ the act of ingrafting, a graft
Ins'itive, _a._ ingrafted, implanted, not natural
Infnâre, _v. t._ to entrap, entangle, catch, inveigle
Infnârer, _n._ one who insnares or draws in
Infobrîety, _n._ drunkenness, intemperance, riot
Infôciable, _a._ averfe to conversation, morofe
Infolâtion, _n._ an exposure to the heat of the sun
Ins'olence, _n._ haughtiness, pride with contempt
Ins'olent, _a._ haughty, proud, overbearing, faucy
Ins'olently, _ad._ haughtily, proudly, fauciiy, rudely
Infolv'able, _a._ that cannot be folved or paid off
Infol'uble, _a._ not able to be diffolved or folved
Infolubil'ity, _n._ the quality of not being diffolvable
Infolv'ency, _n._ an inability to difcharge debts
Infolv'ent, _a._ unable to pay or difcharge debts
Infolv'ent, _n._ one who has not eftate to pay his debts
Infom'nious, _a._ troubled with dreams, reft'efs
Infomuch', _ad._ fo, fo that, to fuch a degree
Infpect', _v. t._ to overlook, view, fearch, examin
Infpec'tion, _n._ overfight, view, furvey, care
Infpect'or, _n._ a fuperintendant, a nice examiner
Infpect'orfhip, Infpect'orate, _n._ the office of infpector
Infper'fion, _n._ a fprinkling upon, a befprinkling
Infphére, _v. t._ to place in a fphere or orb
Infpirable, _a._ that may be drawn in or infufed
Infpirâtion, _n._ a drawing of breath, divine wifdom
Infpîre, _v. t._ to breathe or infufe into, to imprefs
Infpîrer, _n._ one who infpires or encourages
Infpir'it, _v. t._ to animate, encourage, enliven, excite
Infpifs'ate, _v. t._ to thicken, to make thick
Infpiffâtion, _n._ the act of thickening liquids
Inftabil'ity, _n._ ficklenefs, inconftancy, weaknefs
Inftâble, _a._ inconftant, changeable, unfettled
Inftall', _v. t._ to put into poffeffion, inveft, place
Inftallâtion, _n._ the act of putting into poffeffion
Inftall'ment, _n._ the act of inftalling, a payment
Ins'tance, _n._ folicitation, motive, occafion, example
Ins'tance, _v. i._ to produce an example
Ins'tant, _n._ a moment, prefent moment, month
Ins'tant, _a._ prefent, immediate, quick, urgent
Inftantanéity, _n._ an inftantaneous ftate _ob._
Inftantâneous, _a._ done in an inftant, immediate
Inftantâneoufly, Ins'tantly, _ad._ immediately, foon
Inflâte, _v. t._ to place in a certain rank, to inveft
Inftaurâtion, _n._ a reftoration, renewal, repair
Inftead' or Infted', _ad._ in the room or place

Inftéep, _v. t._ to foak, foften, lay in water, &c.
In'ftep, _n._ the upper or higheft part of the foot
Ins'tigate, _v. t._ to tempt to do evil, incite, urge
Infligâtion, _n._ an incitement to a crime, a motive
In'ftigator, _n._ one who incites or ftirs up to ill
Inftil', _v. t._ to infufe by drops, infufe, infinuate
Inftillâtion, _n._ the act of dropping, a thing infufed
Inftimulâtion, _n._ the act of urging on or forward
In'ftinct, _n._ a natural defire, a natural averfion
In'ftinct, Inftinct'ed, _a._ impreffed, animated
Inftinct'ive, _a._ void of the choice of reafon, acting
Inftinct'ively, _ad._ by inftinct (by inftinct
Ins'titute, _v. t._ to eftablifh, appoint, inftruct
Ins'titute, _n._ an eftablifhed law, principle, maxim
Inftitûtion, _n._ an eftablifhment, law, education
Inftitûtionary, _a._ elementary, fundamental
Ins'titutift, _n._ a writer or compofer of inftitutes
Ins'titutor, _n._ one who fettles, one who inftructs
Inftop', _v. t._ to ftop, clofe up, faften, fecure
Inftruct', _v. t._ to teach, tell, train up, model, form
Inftruct'er or Inftruct'or, _n._ one who inftructs
Inftruc'tion, _n._ the act of teaching, direction, order
Inftruct'ive, _a._ conveying knowledge, learned
Inftruct'refs, _n._ a female teacher, a tutorefs
Ins'trument, _n._ a tool, deed of contract, act, means
Inftrument'al, _a._ conducive to fome end (end
Inftrumental'ity, Inftrument'alnefs, _n._ means to an
Inftrument'ally, _ad._ by way of inftrument
Infuccâtion, _n._ a foaking, maceration
Infubordinâtion, _n._ difobedience or want of fub-
   miffion to authority
Infuf'ferable, _a._ not to be borne, deteftable
Infuf'ferably, _ad._ in an infufferable manner
Infuffi"ciency, _n._ inability, incapacity
Infuffi"cient, _a._ incapable, inadequate, unfit
Infuffi"ciently, _ad._ inadequately, unfitly, weakly
Infufflâtion, _n._ the act of breathing upon, breath
Ins'ular, _a._ belonging to or like as ifland, detached
In'fulate, _v. t._ to feparate or fet detached, to
   place upon a non-conducting fubftance
Infulâtion, _n._ the act of infulating or ftate of be-
   ing infulated
In'fult, _n._ infolence, contempt, abufe, an affront
Infult', _v. t._ to treat with infolence, affront, attack
Infult'er, _n._ one who infults another perfon
Infult'ingly, _ad._ with haughty triumph, proudly
Infuperabil'ity, _n._ an infuperable ftate or quality
Infûperable, _a._ that cannot be furmounted, invin-
Infûperably, _ad._ in an infuperable manner (cible
Infuppôrtable, _a._ not to be fupported or borne
Infuppôrtablenefs, _n._ an infufferable quality
Infuppôrtably, _ad._ beyond bearing, fhockingly
Infuppreff'ive, _a._ that is not to be kept under
Infûrable, _a._ proper to be infured
Infûre, _v. t._ to make fure, to fecure againft lofs
Infûrance, _n._ the act of making fure, price of in-
Infû'rer, _n._ one who infures, an under writer (furing
Infûred, _pa._ made fecure againft lofs
Infur'gent, _n._ one who rifes up in rebellion

Insurmount'able, *a.* that cannot be overcome

Insurrec'tion, *n.* domestic rebellion, sedition

Insurrec'tional, *a.* pertaining to insurrection

Insusep'tible, *a.* not having power of perception

Insusceptibil'ity, *n.* the quality of not being susceptible

Insurrátion, *n.* the act of whispering or buzzing

Intact'able, *a.* that is not perceptible by the touch

Intag'lio, *n.* a stone with a figure engraved on it

Intan'gible, *a.* that is not to be touched

Intástable, *a.* that cannot be tasted, insipid

In'teger, intégral, *n.* the whole of any thing

Intégral, *a.* whole, complete, entire, unbroken

Intégrant, *a.* making a part of a whole, necessary

Integ'rity, *n.* honesty, uprightness, entireness

Integ'ument, *n.* a covering, membrane, skin

In'tellect, Intellect'ual, *n.* understanding, perception

Intellec'tion, *n.* the act of understanding (tion

Intellect'ive, *a.* able to understand or perceive

Intellect'ual, *a.* relating to the understanding, ideal

Intellect'ualist, *n.* one who overrates the understanding

Intellect'ually, *ad.* in an intellectual manner

Intel'ligence, *n.* understanding, advice, notice

Intel'ligencer, *n.* one who brings or sends news

Intel'ligent, *a.* knowing, skilful, well informed

Intelligen'tial, *a.* intellectual, unbodied, pure

Intelligibil'ity, Intel'ligibleness, *n.* a possibility or power of being understood

Intel'ligible, *a.* that can be understood, plain

Intel'ligibly, *ad.* clearly, plainly, distinctly

Intemp'erament, *n.* a bad constitution or weather

Intemp'erance, *n.* excess, irregularity, looseness

Intemp erate, *a.* excessive, irregular, drunken

Intemp'erately, *ad.* excessively, immoderately

Intemp'erateness, *n.* an intemperance, irregularity

Intemp'erature, *n.* an excess of some quality

Intend', *v.t.* to design, mean, aim, regard, enforce

Intend'ant, *n.* an officer of high rank, an overseer

Intend'mant, *n.* an intention, design, meaning, aim

Inten'erate, *v.t.* to make tender or soft, *ob.*

Inteneration, *n.* the act of making tender, *ob.*

Inten'ible, *a.* that cannot hold out or be held, *ob.*

Intense', *a.* excessive, vehement, great, close

Intense'ly, Intens'ively, *ad.* to a great degree

Intense'ness, Intent'ness, *n.* closeness, eagerness

Inten'sion, *n.* the act of stretching, a writ

Intens'ity, *n.* strength, extreme degree

Intens'ive, *a.* intent, eager, full of care, stretched

Intent', *n.* using close application, diligent, eager

Intent' *n.* a design, purpose, meaning, drift, aim

Inten'tion, *n.* design, purpose, closeness, eagerness

Inten'tional, *a.* designed, done by or with design

Inten'tionally, *ad.* by or with design, in will

Intent'ive, *a.* diligently applied, close, attentive

Intent'ively, Intent ly, *ad.* closely, eagerly, busily

Intent'ness, *n.* close or constant application

Inter', *v.t.* to bury, to put in or under the ground

In'teract, *n.* intermediate employment or piece

Intercaláry, *a.* inserted, put between, added

Interc'alate, *v.t.* to put in an extraordinary day

Intercalátion, *n.* the insertion of an odd day

Intercéde, *v.i.* to mediate, interpose, entreat

Intercédent, *a.* mediating, going between others

Intercept', *v.t.* to stop, obstruct, seize, cut off

Intercep'tion, *n.* a stoppage, hinderance, seizure

Interces'sion, *n.* a meditation, a prayer for another

Interces'sor, Intercéder, *n.* a mediator, an agent

Intercháin, *v.t.* to chain, join or link together

Interchange', *v.t.* to exchange, barter, succeed to

In'terchange, Interchange'ment, *n.* an exchange

Interchange'able, *a.* given and taken, mutual, alterchange'ably, *ad.* mutually, alternately (nate

Intercip'ient Interci'sion, *n.* what intercepts, *ob.*

Interclúde, *v.t.* to shut out or up, stop, intercept

Intercolumniátion, *n.* the space between pillars

Intercom'mon, *v.i.* to feed at the same table (ly

Intercommúnicate, *v.i.* to communicate mutual-

Intercommunicátion, *n.* mutual communication.

Intercost'al, *a.* placed between the ribs

In'tercourse, *n.* communication, connection

Intercur'rence, *n.* a passage between, a connection.

Intercur'rent, *a.* running or passing between

Intercur'rent, *n.* that which comes between

Intercutáneous, *a.* within the skin

Interdict', *v.t.* to forbid, excommunicate, suspend

In'terdict, Interdic'tion, *n.* a prohibition, a curse

Interdict'ory, *a.* relating to an interdiction

In'terest, *v.t.* to concern, affect, move

In'terest, *n.* a concern, share, part, benefit, advantage, influence, sum for the use of money

In'teresting, *pa.* affecting, moving, concerning

Interfére, *v.i.* to interpose, intermeddle, clash

Interférence, *n.* interposition, mediation

Inter'fluent, Inter'fluous, *a.* flowing between

Interfoliáceous, *a.* between opposit leaves

Interful'gent, Interlúcent, *a.* shining between

Interfúsed, *a.* poured or scattered between

Intérior, *a.* internal, more inward, inner, nearer

Intérior, *n.* the inland part of a country, the inside or parts within

Interjácency, *n.* the act or state of lying between

Interjácent, *a.* lying or extended between

Interjec'tion, *n.* a part of speech, an intervention

In'terim, *n.* the mean time, the mean while, a deed

Interjoin', *v.t.* to join together, to intermarry

Interknowl'edge, *n.* mutual knowledge or skill

Interláce, *v.t.* to intermix, infert, put together

Interlapse', *n.* the time between any two events

Interlard', *v.t.* to insert between, mix, diversify

Interléave, *v.t.* to insert blank leaves between

Interline, *v.t.* to write between lines, to alter

Interlineátion, *n.* a correction wrote between lines

Interlink', *v.t.* to join or mix chains together

Interlocútion, *n.* a dialogue, conference, speech

Interloc'utor, *n.* one who talks with another

Interloc'utory, *a.* consisting of dialogue, previous

Interlópe, *v.* to intercept, prevent right, come in

Interlóper, n. one who interferes wrongfully

In'terlude, n. fomething played between, a farce

Interlúency, n. water running between, a flood

Interlúnar, a. being betwixt old moon and new

Intermar'riage, n. the marriage of one and the giving of another to two different families

Intermar'ry, v. i. to marry one and give another

Intermeátion, n. a flowing or paffing between

Intermed'dle, v. to meddle officioufly, to mix

Intermed'dler, n. an officious intruding perfon

Intermédiacy, n. an interpofition, intervention

Intermédial, Intermédiate, a. intervening, lying between

Intermediátion, n. intervention, common means

Inter'ment, n. a burial, a burying

Intermicátion, n. the act of shining between

Intermigrátion, n. an exchange of place or abode

Interm'inate, a. having no limits, boundlefs

Interm'inable, a. unbounded, admitting of no end

Interminátion, n. a threat, menace, injunction

Intermin'gle, v. t. to mingle, to mix together

Intermis'fion, n. a paufe, a ceffation for a time

Intermifs'ive, Intermit'tent, a. coming by fits

Intermit', v. to ceafe, leave off, difcontinue

Intermit'tent, n. a difeafe with fever that intermits

Intermix', v. to mix, join or be mingled together

Intermixt'ure, n. a mixture of ingredients, a mafs

Intermund'ane, a. fubfifting between two worlds

Intermúral, a. fet, lying or fituate betwixt walls

Intermútual, a. mutual, alternate, interchanged

Intern', Intern'al, a. inward, real, not foreign

Intern'ally, ad. inwardly, within, intellectually

Internécine, a. endeavoring mutual deftruction, ob.

Internécion, n. a maffacre, flaughter, havoc, ob.

In'ternode, n. the fpace betweed the joints of a plant

Internun'cio, n. a meffenger between two parties

Interos'feal, Interos'feous, a. between bones

Interpellátion, n. a fummons, call, hinderance

Interplead, v. i. to difcufs or fettle a previous point

Interpléader, n. a bill in chancery, petitioning that the plaintiffs may interplead

Interp'ólate, v. t. to infert words improperly, to

Interpolátion, n. an addition to an original (add

Interpolátor, n. one who puts in falfe paffages

Interpófal, Interpofi'tion, n. the act of placing between, a ftop, block, hinderance, mediation

Interpófe, v. to place between, fet, offer, mediate

Interpófer, n. one who comes between, a mediator

Inter'pret, v. t. to explain, decipher, tranflate

Inter'pretable, a. capable of interpretation

Interpretátion, n. an explanation, an expofition

Inter'pretative, a. collected by interpretation

Inter'pretatively, ad. as collected by interpretation

Inter'preter, n. an explainer, a tranflator (vacant

Interreg'num, In'terreign, n. the time a throne is

Inter'rogate, v. t. to examin by queftion, to afk

Interrogátion, n. a queftion, a mark, the note (?)

Interrog'ative, n. the pronoun who? what? &c.

Interrog'atively, ad. by way of interrogation

Inter'rogator, n. one who interrogates or inquires

Interrog'atory, n. a queftion, inquiry, fearch

Interrupt', v. t. to ftop, hinder, divide, feparate

Interrupt'edly, ad. with ftoppages or hinderance

Interrup'tion, n. a ftop, hinderance, obftruction

Interfcap'ular, a. placed between the fhoulders

Interfécant, a. cutting or crofing one another

Interfect', v. to divide, cut, crofs, meet and crofs

Interfec'tion, n. a point where lines cut or crofs

Interfem'inate, v. t. to fow between or amongft

Interfert', v. t. to put in between other things

Interfer'tion, n. an infertion, a thing inferted

In'terfpace, n. a fpace between

Interfperfe', v. t. to mix here and there, to fcatter

Interfper'fion, n. a fcattering here and there (tem

Interftel'lar, a. between ftars, beyond the folar fyf-

In'terftice, n. a fpace between things or times

Interfti'tial, a. containing interftices or fpaces

Intertext'ure, n. an interwoven ftate or quality

In'tertie, In'terduce, n. a fmall timber between fummers, &c.

Intertrop'ical, a. lying within the tropics

Intertwine, Intertwift', v. t. to unite by twifting

In'terval, n. a fpace, diftance, refpit, remiffion, low ground between hills, or on the banks of rivers, called alfo bottom

Intervein'ed, a. interfected with veins

Intervéne, v. i. to come between; n. oppofition

Intervénient, a. coming between, interpofed

Interven'tion, n. interpofition, agency, a furprife

Intervert', v. t. to turn or apply another way, ob.

In'terview, n. a fight of each other, a conference

Intervolve', v. t. to wrap one within another

Interwéave, v. t. interwove, pret. interwove, interwoven, pa. to weave one into another

Interwifh', v. t. to wifh mutually to each other, ob.

Inteft'able, a. difqualified to make a will

Inteft'acy, n. a ftate of dying without a will

Inteft'ate, a. dying without leaving a will

Inteft'inal, a. belonging or relating to the guts

Inteft'ine, a. internal, inward, fecret, domeftic

Inteft'ines, n. pl. bowels, entrails, pipes

Inthrall', v. t. to enflave, fhackle, embarrafs (debt

Inthrall'ment, n. flavery, bondage, embarraffmere,

In'timacy, n. a clofe familiarity, friendfhip, union

In'timate, v. t. to hint, point out indirectly, fhow

In'timate, a. inmoft, clofe, near, familiar, dear

In'timate, n. a familiar friend, crony, favorite

In'timately, ad. clofely, nearly, familiarly, well

Intimátion, n. a hint, item, indirect declaration

Intim'idate, v. t. to make fearful, frighten, fcare

Intimidátion, n. the act of intimidating, fear

Intinctiv'ity, n. the quality of not tinging or ftain-

Intíre, Intírely, Intírenefs, fee Entire, &c. (ing

Intol'erable, a. infufferable, extremely bad, vile

Intol'erablenefs, n. an infufferable ftate or quality

Intol'erably, ad. to a degree paft bearing

Intol'erance, n. a want of patience, or of toleration

Intol'eration, n. intolerance, refufal to tolerate

Intol'erant, *a.* impatient, unable to bear, proud

Intóne, *v. i.* to make a flow and protracted noife

Intonâtion, *n.* the act or manner of founding the notes of a mufical fcale

Intort', *v. t.* to twift, wreath, turn, wind, wring

Intor'fion, *n.* a winding, bending or twifting

Intox'icate, *v. t.* to make drunk, bewitch, infatuate

Intoxicâtion, *n.* a drunken ftate, drunkennefs

Intract'able, *a.* untractable, unmanageable, rough

Intract'ablenefs, Intractabil'ity, *n.* a ftate of being unmanageable, indocility

In'trados, *n.* the interior fide of an arch

Intrafoliáceous, *a.* on the infide of leaves

Intranquil'ity, *n.* a want of eafe or quiet, trouble

Intrans'itive, *a.* not paffing from one to another

Intrans'itively, *ad.* without an object following

Intranfmútable, *a.* not to be altered or changed

In'trant, *a.* entering, penetrating

Intreas'ure, *v. t.* to lay up or by, hoard up, *ob.*

Intrench', *v. t.* to fortify with a trench, to encroach

Intrench'ant, *a.* not to be divided or hurt

Intrench'ment, *n.* a fortification with a trench

Intrep'id, *a.* fearlefs, brave, bold, daring, refolute

Iatrepid'ity, Intrep'idnefs, *n.* bravery, boldnefs

Intrep'idly, *ad.* fearlefsly, boldly refolutely

In'tricacy, In'tricatenefs, *n.* difficulty, obfcurity

In'tricate, *v. t.* to perplex, darken, obfcure, *ob.*

In'tricate, Intrins'ecate, *a.* entangled, perplexed

In'tricately, *ad.* in a perplexed or obfcure manner

Intrígue, [intregue] *n.* a plot, fcheme, fecret correfpondence, complication of a fable

Intrígue, *v. i.* to carry on private defigns

Intríguer, *n.* one who intrigues or forms plots

Iatrins'ic, Intrins'ical, *a.* inward, real, folid, genuine

Intrins'ically, *ad.* inwardly, naturally, really, truly

Intróduce, *v. t.* to bring or lead in, to admit

Introdúcer, *n.* one who introduces or makes known

Introduc'tion, *n.* a bringing in or into, a preface

Introduct'ive, Introduct'ory, *a.* previous, paving

Intromit', *v. t.* to fend or let in   (the way

Introfpec'tion, *n.* a view of the infide   (ment

Introfump'tion, *n.* the act of taking in, nourifh-

Introfufcep'tion, *n.* a receiving internally

Introvénient, *a.* entering, coming in or into

Intrúde, *v. i.* to encroach, to come in uninvited

Intrúder, *n.* one who intrudes, an interloper

Intrúfion, *n.* the act of intruding, an encroachment

Intrúfive, *a.* apt to intrude, encroaching

Intruft', *v. t.* to truft, to truft with a fecret, &c.

Intui"tion, *n.* immediate perception or fight

Intúitive, *a.* feeing at once, immediate, clear

Intúitively, *ad.* without any deduction of reafon

Intumes'cence, Inturges'cence, *n.* a fwelling, tu-

Intwíne, *v. t.* to twift or wreath together   (mor

Inunc'tion, *n.* the act of anointing or fmearing

Inunctuos'ity, *n.* a want of unctuofity, or greafinefs

Inun'dant, *a.* overflowing, copious, abundant, full

Inundâtion, *n.* overflow of water, flood, deluge

Inurban'ity, *n.* incivility, clownifhnefs

Inúre, *v. t.* to accuftom, habituate, bring into ufe

Inúrement, *n.* cuftom, habit, practice, ufe

Inurn', *v. t.* to put into an urn, entomb, bury

Inus'tion, *n.* a burning, operation of fire

Inutil'ity, *n.* ufeleffnefs, unprofitablenefs

Inváde, *v. t.* to enter or feize in a hoftile manner

Inváder, *n.* an affailant, encroacher, intruder

In'valid, *n.* one difabled by age, ficknefs or hurt

Inval'id, *a.* weak, void, having no weight or force

In'valided, *a.* rendered invalids, enfeebled

Inval'idate, *v. t.* to weaken or leffen in force

Invalid'ity, Inval'idnefs, *n.* weaknefs

Inval'uable, *a.* very valuable, ineftimable, rare

Inváriable, *a.* unchangeable, unerring, conftant

Invâriablenefs, *n.* unchangeablenefs, conftancy

Inváriably, *ad.* unchangeably, conftantly, really

Invâfion, *n.* hoftile entrance, attack, affault

Invâfive, *a.* entering in a hoftile manner, hoftile

Invect'ive, *n.* a railing fpeech; *a.* abufive, keen

Invect'ively, *ad.* abufively, fatirically, bitterly

Invéigh, [inváy] *v. i.* to exclaim againft, to rail

Inveigh'er, *n.* one who inveighs, a violent railer

Invéigle, *v. t.* to feduce, allure, entice, wheedle

Invéigler, *n.* a feducer, deceiver, allurer, coaxer

Invent', *v. t.* to contrive, find out, feign, forge

Invent'er or Invent'or, *n.* a contriver, a forger

Inven'tion, *n.* a contrivance, difcovery, device

Invent'ive, *a.* quick at contrivance, ready, keen

In'ventory, *n.* a lift or account of feperate articles of goods, ufually of a deceafed perfon

In'ventory, *v. t.* to make a lift or account of arti-

In'verfe, *a.* inverted, reciprocal, contrary   (cles

In'verfely, *ad.* in an inverted order or manner

Inver'fion, *n.* a change, a change of order or place

Invert', *v. t.* to turn upfide down, change, divert

Invert'ent, *n.* a medicin to invert the order of motions

Invert'edly, *ad.* in an inverted order, by inverfion

Inveft', *v. t.* to drefs, adorn, confer, befiege, furround, change the form and condition of money by laying it out in fomething lefs fleeting

Inveft'ient, *a.* clothing, covering, adorning

Inveft'igable, *a.* that may be fearched out

Inveft'igate, *v. t.* to fearch out, explore, difcover

Inveftigâtion, *n.* a fearching out, an examination

Inveft'iture, *n.* the act of giving poffeffion

Inveft'ment, *n.* drefs, clothes, inveftiture, the act of converting money into property lefs fleeting, the fums fo expended

Iaveter'acy, *n.* a long continuance, excefs

Invet'erate, *a.* old, obftinate, fixed, eftablifhed

Invet'erate, *v. t.* to become obftinate by continu-

Invet'eratenefs, *n.* a long continuance   (ance

Invid'ious, *a.* envious, ill-natured, malicious

Invid'ioufly, *ad.* envioufly, odioufly, unkindly

Invid'ioufnefs, *n.* an envious quality, malice, ha-

Invig'orate, *v. t.* to ftrengthen, to animate   (tred

Invigorâtion, *n.* the act of invigorating

Invin'cible, *a.* not to be fubdued, unconquerable

Invin'ciblenefs, n. an invincible ftate or quality
Invin'cibly, ad. unconquerably, firmly, abfolutely
Inviolable, a. not to be hurt, broken or profaned
Inviolably, ad. without breach or failure
Inviolate, a. unhurt, uninjured, unbroken, fafe
In'vious, a. impaffable, untrodden, rough, ob.
Invifc'ate, v. t. to daub with glutinous matter
Invifibil'ity, n. an invifible ftate or quality
Invis'ible, a. that cannot be feen, very diminutive
Invis'ibly, ad. in an invifible manner, darkly
Invitation, n. the act of inviting, a bidding, a call
Invite, v. t. to bid, afk, tempt, allure, perfuade
Inviter, n. one who invites, one who allures
Invitingly, ad. in a pleafing or enticing manner
Invit'rifiable, a not capable of converfion into glafs
Invocation, n. the act of calling upon by prayer
In'voice, n. a bill or lift of goods with the price
    annexed   (with the price of each
In'voice, v. t. to make a lift of particular articles,
Invoke, In'vocate, v. t. to call upon, to pray to
Involve', v. to entangle, engage, mix, raife, imply
In'volucrum, n. a calyx remote from the flower
    as at the origin of an umbel
In'volucret, n. a fmall or partial involucrum
Invol'untarily, ad. unwillingly, not from choice
Invol'untary, a. done unwillingly, not chofen
Involution, n. a complication, a fold, a raifing
In'volute, In'voluted, a. rolled in, as leaves when
    their margins are rolled fpirally inwards
In'volute, n. a curve traced by a ftring unwound
    from a figure
Invul'nerable, a. that cannot be wounded, fecure
In'ward, a. lying within, reflecting, intimate
In'ward, In'wardly, In'wards, ad. within, into
In'wardnefs, n. intimacy, familiarity, nearnefs
In'wards, n. pl. inteftines, the inner parts
Inweave, v. t. inwove, pret. inwove, inwoven,
    pa. to mix in weaving, intwine, infold
Inwood', v. t. to hide or lofe in a wood
Inwrap', v. t. to cover, involve, puzzle, ravifh
Inwreathe, v. t. to furround with a wreath, to in-
Inwrought', a. adorned with work within   (fold
Ion'ic, a. pertaining to Ionia in Afia, denoting an
    order of columns
Ionian, n. a native of Ionia; a. pertaining to it
Ipecacuan'ha, n. a plant, an emetic root
Iras'cible, a. foon angry, apt to be eafily provoked
Iras'ciblenefs, n. an irafcible quality, a warmth
Ire, n. anger, wrath, rage, fury, paffionate hatred
I'reful, a. angry, raging, furious, hot, enraged
Irides'cent, a. having colors like the rainbow
Irides'cently, ad. in the manner of a rainbow
I'ris, n. the rainbow, a flower-de-luce, a circle
I'rifed, a. formed like or containing colors like the
    iris or rainbow
I'rifh, n. the people of Ireland, their language
I'rifh, a. pertaining to Ireland
Irk, v. to vex, grieve, give pain or uneafinefs, ob.
Irk'fome, a. tedious, tirefome, troublefome

Irk'fomenefs, n. tedioufnefs, wearifomenefs, flownefs
I'ron, n. a hard metal, any inftrument made of it
I'ron, v. t. to fmooth with a hot iron, to fhackle
I'ron or I'rony, a. made of or like iron, hard
Iron'ical, a. fpoken by way of irony, fneering
Iron'ically, ad. in an ironical manner, keenly
I'ronmonger, n. one who deals or trade in iron
I'ronmold, n. a yellow mark on linen, an earth
I'ronwort, n. a plant, bafe horehound
I'rony, n. a meaning contrary to words fpoken
Irra'diancy, n. beams of light emitted, a lufter
Irra'diate, v. t. to illuminate, to enlighten
Irradiation, n. an illumination, a giving of light
Irra''tional, a. void of reafon, filly, abfurd, furd
Irrationality, n. folly, foolifhnefs, abfurdnefs
Irra''tionally, ad. without reafon, abfurdly
Irreclaimable, a. not to be reclaimed, fhamelefs
Irreconci'leable, a. that cannot be reconciled
Irreconci'leably, ad. beyond reconciliation
Irreconci'led, a. not reconciled, not atoned for
Irrecov'erable, a. not to be regained or remedied
Irrecov'erably, ad. beyond recovery, abfolutely
Irredeemable, a. that cannot be redeemed
Irredeemability, n. the quality of being not re-
Irreducible, a. that cannot be reduced (deemable
Irrefrag'ble, a. that cannot be denied or confuted
Irrefragably, ad. above confutation or difproof
Irrefutable, a. that cannot be refuted, certain
Irreg'ular, a. immethodical, diforderly, loofe
Irregular'ity, n. a deviation from rule, diforder
Irreg'ularly, ad. in an irregular manner loofely
Irreg'ulate, v. t. to make irregular, ob.
Irrel'ative, a. fingle, fimple, unconnected, lone
Irrel'evant, a. inapplicable, not coming up to
Irrel'evancy, n. inapplicability
Irreli''gion, n. a contempt of religion, impiety
Irreli''gious, a. ungodly, profane, wicked, vile
Irreli''gioufly, ad. without godlinefs, wickedly
Irremeable, a. admitting of no return back
Irremediable, a. not to be remedied or cured, loft
Irremediably, ad. without remedy or cure
Irremifs'ible, a. not to be forgiven, unpardonable
Irremoveable, a. not to be removed or changed
Irremoveabil'ity, n. a ftate of being not removeable
Irreparabil'ity, n. an irreparable or loft ftate
Irrep'arable, a. not to be repaired or recovered
Irrep'arably, ad. beyond all recovery or amends
Irrepealable, a. that cannot be legally repealed
Irrepealabil'ity, n. the quality of being not repeal-
Irreplev'iable, a. not to be replevied   (able
Irreplev'ifable, a. not to be replevied, or bailed
Irreprehens'ible, a. blamelefs, upright, juft, pure
Irreprefent'able, a. that is not to be reprefented
Irreproachable, a. free from reproach, blamelefs
Irreprovable, a. not to be reproved, upright, juft
Irrefiftibil'ity, n. an irrefiftible power or force
Irrefift'ible, Irrefift'lefs, a. fuperior to oppofition
Irrefift'ibly, ad. in an irrefiftible manner
Irrefoluble, a. not to be broken or diffolved, ob.

Irres'olublenefs, n. an irrefoluble quality, ob.

Irrefolv'edly, ad. without fettled determination

Irres'olute, a. unfteady, unfettled, wavering

Irres'olutely, ad. without refolution or firmnefs

Irrefolútion, n. a want of due firmnefs of mind

Irrefpect'ive, a. not regarding circumftances

Irrefpect'ively, ad. without regard to circumftances

Irres'pirable, a. not fit for refpiration

Irrefpons'ible, a. not liable to anfwer

Irretriévable, a. irrecoverable, irreparable (ever

Irretriévably, ad. irrecoverably, irreparably, for

Irrev'erence, n. a want of veneration or refpect

Irrev'erent, a. not paying due reverence, rude

Irrev'erently, ad. without due refpect, rudely

Irrevers'ible, a. not to be changed or called back

Irrevers'ibly, ad. without or beyond change

Irrev'ocable, a. not to be recalled or brought back

Irrevocabil'ity, n. incapacity of being revoked

Irrev'ocably, ad. beyond recall, abfolutely, really

Irrevókable, a. that cannot be revoked

Ir'rigate, v. t. to wet, water, moiften, bedew

Irrigátion, n. the act of watering or moiftening

Irrig'uous, a. watery, watered, wet, dewy, moift

Irri'fion, n. the act of laughing at another, fcorn

Ir'ritable, a. eafily provoked, wafpifh, capable of being eafily excited into action, or contracting upon the application of a power

Irritabil'ity, n. a quality of being capable of irritation, or excitement to action

Ir'ritate, v. t. to provoke, exafperate, vex, excite animal motions

Irritátion, n. provocation, ftimulation, wrath, ire

Ir'ritative, a. accompanied with or produced by increafed action or irritation

Irrórate, v. t. to bedew, moiften, fprinkle, damp

Irrup'tion, n. an invafion, inroad by force, fally

Is'abel, a. of a brownifh yellow with a fhade of

I'fagon, n. a figure of equal angles (brownifh red

Ifchiat'ic, [ch as k] a. pertaining to the hips

Is'aty, n. the arctic or northern fox

Ifch'ury or Ifc'ury, n. a ftoppage of urine

I'fingglafs, n. a tranfparent fubftance made of the founds of fifh, cleanfed and dried

I'fland, more correctly Ieland or Iland, n. land furrounded by water, a large mafs of floating ice

I'flander, n. the inhabitant of an iiland

Ifoch'ronal, Ifoch'ronous, [ch as k] performed in

I'folated, a. detached, ftanding alone (equal times

Ifoperimet'rical, a. having equal circumferences

Ifos'celes, a. having two of the legs or fides equal

Is'raelitifh, a. belonging to Ifrael or the Jews

Is''fue, n. an end, event, trial, difcharge, offspring

Is'fue, v. to come or fend out, arife, proceed

Is'fuable, a. that may iffue, concerning iffues in law

Is'fuelefs, a. having no offspring, childlefs

Ifth'mus, Ift'mus, n. a neck of land joining larger portions of land (mus of Corinth

Ift'mian, a. denoting games celebrated on the Ift-

Ital'ian, n. a native of Italy or the language

Ital'ian, a. pertaining to Italy

Ital'ic, a. relating to Italy, or to a kind of letters

Ital'ics, n. letters or characters which ftand inclining,

Ital'icize, v. t. to write or print in italics (like thefe

Itch, n. a troublefome difeafe, a teazing defire

Itch, v. i. to prick, defire, long much

Itch'y, a. having or infected with the itch

I'tem, n. a hint, caution, new article; ad. alfo

It'erant, a. repeating, done or faying over again

It'erate, v. t. to repeat, to do or fay over again

Iterátion, n. a repetition, a recital over again

Itin'erant, n. one who wanders or travels about

Itin'erate, v. i. to travel about, without a fixed

Itin'erant, Itin'erate, a. wandering, unfettled (home

Itin'erary, n. a book of travels; a. travelling, wan-

Itfelf', pron. of it and felf (dering

I'vory, n. an elephant's tooth; a. made of ivory

Ivoryblack', n. a fine kind of foft blacking

I'vy, n. the name of a common winding plant

J

JAB'BER, v. i. to talk idly, chatter, prate
Jab'ber, Jab'bering, n. idle talk, prate, noife

Jab'berer, n. one who talks unintelligibly or idly

Jab'iric, n. an aquatic fowl of the crane kind

Jácent, a. lying, lying at length, extended

Jácinth, n. a gem, jewel, precious ftone, hyacinth

Jack. n. John, an engine, fifh, lethern can, cup

Jack'al, n. a voracious animal of the canine genus

Jack'anapes, n. a monkey, ape, coxcomb, meddler

Jack'boots, n. pl. very large boots ferving for armor

Jack'daw, n. a kind of black chattering bird

Jack'et, n. a waiftcoat, a kind of fhort clofe coat

Jack'ketch, n. a common hangman

Jackpud'ding, n. a merry-andrew, buffoon, mimic

Jac'obin, n. the member of a private club to overturn or manage government, one who oppofes government in a fecret or unlawful manner or from an unreafonable fpirit of difcontent

Jacobin'ic, Jacobin'ical, a. pertaining to fecret affociations againft government or a factious fpirit

Jac'obinifm, n. unreafonable oppofition to government, an attempt to overthrow or change government by fecret clubs or irregular means

Jac'obite, n. a partifan or favorer of James II.

Jac'obitifm, n. the principles of a jacobite

Jaconet', n. a kind of coarfe muflin

Jactitátion, n. a toffing motion, heave, reftleffnefs

Jaculátion, n. the act of throwing or darting

Jade, n. a bad woman, wench, worthlefs horfe (ifh

Jade, n. a magnefian ftone of a dark green or blu-

Jade, v. to tire, weary, ride down, harafs, fink

Jádifh, a. unruly, vicious, unchafte, loofe

Jagg, v. t. to notch; n. a notch, uevennefs, load

Jag'gednefs, n. a jagged ftate, unevennefs

Jag'ging, n. the act of cutting in notches, a notch

Jaguar', n. the American tiger

Jag'gy, a. notched, indented, uneven, ragged

Jail, n. a prifon, a place of confinement

Jáilbird, n. one who has been confined in jail

Jáiler, *n.* the keeper or mafter of a prifon
Jakes, *n. pl.* a houfe of office, boghoufe, layftall
Jal'ap, *n.* the root of a fpecies of bind-weed ufed in powder as a purgative
Jam, *n.* a conferve of fruit, child's frock, bed
Jam, *v. t.* to confine in or between, to wedge in
Jamb, *n.* the upright poft of a door, a fupporter
Jan"gle, *v. i.* to wrangle, differ, be out of tune
Jan"gler, *n.* a quarrelfome or noify perfon
Jan"gling, *n.* a wrangling, a harfh noife
Jan'izary, *n.* a Turkifh foldier, foot-guard, officer
Jant'y or Jaunt'y, *a.* fhowy, gay, giddy, fluttering
Jan'uary, *n.* the firft month in the year
Japan', *n.* a fine varnifh to work in colors with
Japan', *v.* to varnifh, adorn, fet off, black fhoes
Japan'ner, *n.* one who japans, a fhoeblack
Japanéfe, *n.* a native of Japan, the language
Jap'u, *n.* a Brazilian bird that fufpends its neft
Jar, *v. t.* to clafh, hit, difagree, differ, quarrel
Jar, *n.* a clafh, difcord, harfh found, a veffel
Jar'gon, *n.* gibberifh, nonfenfe, a fpecies of ftone very hard and white
Jargon'ic, *a.* pertaining to jargon
Jas'min, *n.* a fhrub with fragrant flowers
Jas'per, *n.* a beautiful white or green ftone
Jafpidéan, *a.* like jafper, green
Jav'elin, *n.* a kind of dart, fpear, half pike
Jaun'dice, *n.* a diftemper arifing from the liver
Jaun'diced, *a.* affected with the jaundice, yellow
Jaunt, *v. i.* to walk or travel about, to ramble
Jaunt, *n.* a ramble or excurfion, a felly of a wheel
Jaunt'ily, *ad.* airily, gayly, brifkly, nimbly, quickly
Jaunt'inefs, *n.* airinefs, gayety, brifknefs, flutter
Jaw, *n.* the bone inclofing the teeth, noife, talk
Jay, *n.* a bird, a finical and gaudy perfon
Jázel, *n.* a precious ftone of a blue color
Jcal'ous, *a.* fufpicious, fearful, cautious, tender
Jeal'oufy, *n.* fufpicion in love, fufpicious fear,
Jears, *n.* tackles to hoift or lower the lower yards
Jeat, *n.* a foffil of a fine black color (miftruft
Jeer, *v. t.* to fcoff, to rally; *n.* a fcoff, gibe, jeft
Jéeringly, *ad.* in a geering way, with haughtinefs
Jehóvah, *n.* the Hebrew name for GOD, the LORD
Jejúne, *a.* hungry, dry, flat, unaffecting, trifling
Jejúnenefs, *n.* drynefs, poverty, want of matter
Jel'lied, *a.* brought to or like a jelly, glutinous
Jel'ly, *n.* a tranfparent fizy broth, a fweetmeat
Jennérian, *a.* denominating what relates to Dr. Jenner the author of vaccination
Jen'net, *n.* a fmall Spanifh or Barbary horfe
Jen'neting, *n.* a kind of forward or early apple
Jen'ny, *n.* a machine for fpinning many threads at once, ufed in manufactories
Jeat'ling, *n.* a fifh in the Danube, the blue chub
Jeop'ard, *v. t.* to put in danger, hazard, expofe
Jeop'ardous, *a.* dangerous, hazardous, doubtful
Jeop'ardy, *n.* danger, peril, hazard, rifk, doubt
Jer'bo, *n.* a quadruped with very fhort fore legs
Jerk, *v.* to give a quick fmart blow, lafh, throw

Jerk, *n.* a quick and fmart lafh, twitch, quick jolt
Jerk'in, *n.* a jacket, fhort coat, kind of hawk
Jer'fey, *n.* combed wool, woolen yarn, an ifland
Jefs'amin, *n.* a very fragrant fhrub
Jeft', *v. t.* to make merry by words, joke, divert
Jeft, *n.* any thing ludicrous, a joke, a laughing ftock
Jeft'er, *n.* one fond of jefting, a wit, a buffoon
Jeft'ing, *n.* talk to raife laughter, mirth, wit
Jeft'ingly, *ad.* in a jefting or jocofe manner
Jeufit'ical, *a.* fhuffling, equivocal, deceitful, fly
Jes'uitifm, *n.* deceit, artifice, hypocrify, principles of the Jefuits
Jet, *n.* a very black foffil, fpout, court, yard
Jet, *v. i.* to fhoot forward, jolt, ftrut, intrude
Jet'fam, Jet'fon, *n.* goods from a fhipwreck
Jet'ty, *a.* made of jet, like or black as jet
Jew'el, *n.* a precious ftone, a name of fondnefs
Jew'eller, *n.* a man who deals in precious ftones
Jew'ellery, *n.* jewels and trinkets in general
Jéws-harp, *n.* a very fmall mufical inftrument
Jew'ifh, *a.* pertaining to the Jews or Ifraelites
Jib, *n.* the foremaft fail of a veffel
Jib'boom, *n.* a fpar projecting forward of the bowfprit to fupport the jib
Jiboy'a, *n.* an American ferpent of the largeft kind
Jig, *v. i.* to dance nimbly, ; *n.* a quick dance
Jig'ger, *n.* a rope and block to hold a cable as it is drawn in
Jig'maker, *n.* one who dances or plays merrily
Jilt, *v. a.* a deceiving woman ; *v. t.* to deceive
Jin"gle, *v. i.* to found correfpondently, to clink
Jin"gle, *n.* any thing founding, a noife, a rattle
Job, *v.* to do jobs, play the ftockjobber, ftrike, hit
Job, *n.* a piece of chance-work, an affair, a ftab
Job'ber, *n.* a man who jobs or does chance-work
Job'bernowl, *n.* a blockhead, dunce, fimpleton
Joc"key, *n.* one who rides or deals in horfes, a cheat
Joc"key, *v. t.* to cheat, trick, caft, deceive, joftle
Jocófe, Joc'ular, *a.* given to jefting, droll, merry
Jocófely, *ad.* in jeft, drolly, waggifhly, pleafantly
Jocófenefs, Jocos'ity, Jocular'ity, *n.* pleafantry
Joc'und, *a.* merry, gay, lively, fprightly, blithe
Joc'undly, *ad.* merrily, gayly, joyfully, pleafantly
Jog, Jog'gle, *v.* to pufh, fhake, move; *n.* a pufh
Jog'ger, *n.* one who moves flowly or heavily
Johan'nes, *n.* a Portuguefe gold coin value 8 dolls.
Join, *v. t.* to add, unite, clofe, encounter, clafh
Join'der, *n.* a joining, conjunction, union
Join'er, *n.* a perfon who joins wood together
Join'ery, *n.* the art of joining wood together
Joint, *n.* a point where bones, &c. meet, a hinge
Joint, *v. t.* to join, form, cut, divide, feparate
Joint, *a.* fhared among many, combined, united
Joint'ed, *pa.* full of or cut into joints, joined
Jointten'ancy, *n.* a tenure of eftate by unity of interet, title, time and poffeffion
Jointten'aut, *n.* one who holds by joint-tenancy
Joint'er, *n.* an inftrument, a long plane
Joint'ly, *ad.* together, in a body, in conjunction

Joint'refs, *n.* a woman who poffeffes a jointure

Joint'ure, *n.* an eftate or income fettled on a wife

Joift, *n.* a fmall beam to fupport floors

Joke, *v. i.* to jeft, to be merry ; *n.* a jeft, mirth

Jóker, *n.* a jefter, a merry and facetious fellow

Jole, Jowl, *n.* the cheek, face, head of a fifh

Jol'lily, *ad.* in a merry manner, jovially, gayly

Jol'fiment, Jol'linefs, Jol'iity, *n.* merriment, gayety

Jol'ly, *a.* merry, gay, plump, full of flefh

Jolt, *n.* a violent fhock ; *v. t.* to fhake very much

Jólthead, *n.* a blockhead, blunderhead, dunce

Jon'quil, *n.* a fpecies of daffodil

Jor'den, *n.* a pot, veffel, chamberpot

Jófo, *n.* a fmall fifh of the gudgeon kind

Jos''tle, *v. t.* to run againft, pufh, tofs about

Jot, Ióta, *n.* a point, tittle, bit, fmalleft part

Jove, *n.* one of the names of jupiter

Jóvial, *a.* jolly, gay, merry, cheerful, pleafant

Jóvially, *ad.* gayly, merrily, pleafantly, airily

Jóvialnefs, *n.* gayety, merriment, cheerfulnefs, life

Jour'nal, *n.* a diary, book, newfpaper ; *a.* daily

Jour'nalift, *n.* a writer or keeper of a journal

Jour'nalize, *v. i.* to enter or put in a journal

Jour'ney, *n.* a travel by land or fea ; *v. t.* to travel

Jour'neyman, *n.* a hired mechanic or workman

Jour'neywork, *n.* work done by a journeyman, &c.

Jouft, *n.* a mock fight ; *v. i.* to run in the tilt

Joy, *v.* to rejoice, be or make glad, congratulate

Joy, *n.* a lively fenfe of good, caufe of pleafure, gladnefs, happinefs

Joy'ful, *a.* full of joy or mirth, very glad, exulting

Joy'fully, *ad.* with joy, gladly, merrily, gayly

Joy'fulnefs, *n.* great joy, great gladnefs, pleafure

Joy'lefs, *a.* void of joy or pleafure, infipid, fad

Joy'ous, *a.* glad, merry, cheerful, pleafant, joyful

Júbilant, *a.* uttering fongs of triumph, fhouting

Júbilee, *n.* a public periodical feftivity, a feaft

Jocund'ity, *n.* pleafantnefs, agreeablenefs, mirth

Judáical, *a.* of or relating to the Jews, Jewifh

Júdaifm, *n.* the practice of tenets of the Jews

Júdaize, *v. i.* to conform or incline to Judaifm

Jud'dock, *n.* the fmall fnipe

Judge, *n.* one who prefides in a court, an umpire

Judge, *v.* to pafs fentence, doom, decide, difcern

Judg'er, *n.* one who judges or fettles, a juryman

Judge'ment, *n.* a fentence, decifion, opinion, fkill

Júdicatory, *n.* a court or diftribution of juftice

Júdicature, *n.* a power to diftribute juftice

Judi''cial, *a.* belonging to a caufe or trial, legal

Judi''cially, *ad.* in form of or according to law

Judi''ciary, *a.* paffing or forming judgment, legal

Judi''ciary, *n.* that branch of government which is concerned in the determination of fuits

Judi''cious, *a.* prudent, wife, fkilful, rational, fit

Judi''cioufly, *ad.* prudently, wifely, fkilfully

Judi''cioufnefs, *n.* a judicious quality, fkilfulnefs

Jug, *n.* a large drinking veffel, note, meadow

Jug, *v. t.* to drefs a hare in a veffel by fteam (draw

Jug'gle, *v. i.* to play tricks by fleight of hand, to

Jug'gle, *n.* a deception, fallacy, impofture, trick

Jug'gler, *n.* one who juggles, a cheat, a deceiver

Jug'gling, *n.* the act of playing tricks, deceit

Júgular, *a.* belonging or relating to the throat

Júgulate, *v. t.* to cut the throat, kill, murder

Jugulátion, *n.* the act of cutting the throat

Juice or Juce, *n.* fap in vegetables, fluid in animals,

Júicelefs, *a.* void of moifture, dry, infipid (gravy

Júicinefs, *n.* plenty of juice, fulnefs of moifture

Júicy, *a.* full of juice or moifture, moift, rich

Jujúbe, *n.* a tree, ramnus jujuba

Júlap or Júlep, *n.* a kind of liquid medicin

Júlis, *n.* a fmall fifh with a green back

July', *n.* the feventh month of the year

Júmart, *n.* the offspring of a bull and a mare

Jum'ble, *v. t.* to mix or put together confufedly

Jum'ble, *n.* a confufed mixture, a confufed heap

Júment, *n.* a beaft ufed for burden or hufbandry

Jump, *v. i.* to leap, fkip, bound, jolt, agree, tally

Jump, *n.* a leap, fkip, kind of ftays ; *ad.* exactly

Junc'ate, *n.* a cheefecake, any delicacy, ob.

Júnc'ous, *a.* full of or refembling bulrufhes

Junc'tion, *n.* an union, coalition, combination

Junc'ture, *n.* a critical time, ftate, joint, point, un-

June, *n* the fixth month of the year   (ion

Júnior, *a.* younger, later-born, inferior, lower

Júnior, *n.* one younger in years or office

Júniper, *n.* the name of a fhrub or fmall tree

Junk, *n.* a Chinefe fhip, old ropes   (privately

Junk'et, *n.* a private entertainment ; *v. i.* to feaft

Jun'to, *n.* a cabal, faction, party, combination, fet

Júpiter, *n.* a heathen deity, a planet

Júrat, *n.* a magiftrate in fome corporation-towns

Júratory, *a.* giving or relating to an oath

Jurid'ical, *a.* ufed in courts of juftice, legal

Jurid'ically, *ad.* with legal authority or form

Jurifcon'fult, *n.* one who gives his opinion in law

Júrifdic'tion, *n.* legal authority, power, a diftrict

Jurifdic'tional, *a.* pertaining to jurifdiction

Jurifprúdence, *n.* the fcience of or fkill in law

Jurifpru'den'tial, *a.* relating to jurifprudence

Júrift, *n.* a profeffor of civil law, civilian, lawyer

Júror, Júryman, *n.* a perfon who ferves on a jury

Jurucuá, *n.* a Brazilian tortoife very large

Jurúra, *n.* a fmall Brazilian tortoife

Júry, *n. pl.* perfons fworn to deliver truth on fuch evidence as fhall be given before them

Júrymaft, *n.* a temporary maft

Juft, *a.* upright, incorrupt, honeft, exact, orderly

Juft, *n.* a mock fight made on horfeback, a tilt

Juft, *ad.* exactly, really, merely, barely, nearly

Juft'ice, *n.* right, equity, punifhment, an officer

Juft'icefhip, *n.* the rank or office of a juftice

Jufti''ciary, *n.* a perfon who adminifters juftice

Juft'ifiable, *a.* that can be juftified, defenfible

Juft'ifiablenefs, *n.* a poffibility of being defended

Juft'ifiably, *ad.* in a juftifiable manner, right

Juftification, *n.* a defenfe, vindication, fupport

Juft'ifier, *n.* one who juftifies, one who defends

Juft'if'y, v. t. to defend, maintain, free, clear
Jus'tle, v. t. to run against, push about, jostle
Juft'ly, ad. uprightly, honeftly, properly, exactly
Juft'nefs, n. reafonablenefs, propriety, exactnefs
Jut, Jut'ty, v. i. to come or fhoot out of the line
Júvenile, a. young, youthful, gay, brifk, lively
Juvenil'ity, n. youthfulnefs, gayety, brifknefs
Juxtapofi'tion, n. the act of placing near or by

K

KAÄLING, n. a fpecies of ftarling in China
Kah'bos, n. a fifh of a brown color without fcales.
Kal'ender, n. an account or regifter of time
Käli, n. a kind of fea-weed, a marine plant
Kam, a. crooked, turned awry, bent, perverted
Kangaroo' n. an animal of New-Holland, fomewhat refembling the fox and opoffum
Ka'olin, n. a foft earth ufed in China as one of the materials of porcelain
Kaw, v. n. to cry as a raven or crow, to gafp
Kaw, n. the cry of a raven or crow, a gafp
Käta, n. a Syrian bird of the grous kind
Kawn, n. a public inn in Turkey
Kayle, n. a ninepin, the game at ninepins
Keck, v. i. to heave the ftomach, to naufeate
Kec'kle, v. n. to keck, to tie a rope round a cable
Kecks, Kecks'y, n. dry ftalks and fticks, hemlock
Keck'y, a. refembling or having kecks
Kedg'er, n. a fmall anchor ufed in fhallow water
Ked'lock, n. a pernicious field-weed, charlock
Kee, n. kine, cows, all beafts of the cow kind
Keel, n. the loweft timber of a fhip; v. t. to cool
Keelhaul, v. t. to punifh, to drag under the keel
Keen, a. fharp, fine, eager, fevere; v.t. to fharpen
Keenly, ad. fharply, eagerly, bitterly, feverely
Keennefs, n. fharpnefs, eagernefs, vehemence
Keep, v. t. kept, pret. kept, pa. to preferve, fave, maintain, hold, detain, conceal, obey
Keep, n. cuftody, guard, reftraint, a ftrong tower
Keeper, n. one who keeps, one who guards
Keeperfhip, n. the office or duty of a keeper
Keeping, n. cuftody, fupport, protection, feed
Kef'fekil, n. a ftone, white or yellow, which increafes in the fire, of which Turkey pipes are made
Keg or Kag, n. a fmall barrel or cafk, a cag
Kell, n. pottage, what covers the guts, the caul
Kelp, n. falt extracted from calcined fea-weed
Kel'fon or Keelfon, n. the wood next the keel
Kelt'er, n. a prepared or due ftate, order, readinefs
Kemb, v. t. to comb, difentangle, drefs, adorn
Ken, v. to fee or difcover at a diftance, to know
Ken, n. a view, reach of the fight, knowledge
Ken'nel, n. a houfe for dogs, watercourfe, haunt
Ken'nel, v. to lie, dwell, fhut up, enter, get in
Ken'tle, n. in trade a hundred weight
Kent'ledge, n. pigs of iron for ballaft
Kentuck'y, n. a ftate and a river on the fouth of the Ohio

Kept, pret. and pa. paff. of to keep (the head
Ker'chief, n. a headdrefs, a cloth ufed in dreffing
Ker'chiefed, Ker'chieft, a. dreffed, hooded
Kerf, n. the notch cut or fawn away in timber
Kerm'es, n. a fmall animal found on a fpecies of fmall oak in Afia and Europe, ufed in dying red
Kern, n. an Irifh foot-foldier or boor, mill, horn
Kern, v. to form into grains, curdle, falt, corn
Ker'nel, n. the fubftance within a fhell, a knob
Ker'nel, v. to form into kernels, ripen, indent
Ker'fey, n. a coarfe woollen ftuff woven in ribs
Kes'trel, n. a bird of the hawk kind, the ftannel
Ketch, n. a large heavy fhip, an executioner
Ketch'up, n. a fauce for food
Ket'tle, n. a kitchen-veffel to boil things in
Ket'tledrum, n. a very large drum made of brafs
Kev'el, n. a fpecies of antelope, with flat horns
Key, n. a thing to open a lock or explain, part of mufical inftruments, tone in mufic, wharf
Key'age, n. money for lying at a key or wharf
Key'hole, n. a hole in a door, &c. to put a key in
Key'ftone, n. the middle ftone in an arch
Kibe, n. a chap in the heel, fore, chilblain
Kibed, a. with chapped flefh on the heel
Kick, n. a blow or wound made with the foot
Kick, v. t. to ftrike with the foot, to ftrike back
Kick'er, n. one who kicks or ftrikes back
Kick'ing, n. the act of ftriking with the foot
Kick'fhaw, n. a fantaftical difh of meat, a trifle
Kick'fhoe, n. a caperer, buffoon, jackpudding
Kid, n. a young goat, child, apprentice, faggot
Kid, v. t. to bring forth as a goat, to bundle up
Kid'der, n. an engroffer of corn, a huckfter
Kid'dow, n. the guillemot or fea hen
Kid'nap, v. t. to fteal perfons, feduce, decoy
Kid'napper, n. a perfon who fteals perfons
Kid'ney, n. a part of an animal, race, bred, kind
Kid'neybean, n. a garden herb, a French bean
Kid'neyfhaped, a. fhaped like the kidney
Kill'dee, n. a fmall bird fo called
Kil'derkin, n. a liquid meafure of 16 or 18 gallons
Kill, v. t. to deprive of life, to deftroy; n. a kiln
Kill'er, n. one who kills, an animal which fubfifts on the whale
Kil'las, n. a ftone of a pale or greenifh gray
Kil'low, n. a blackifh kind of ftone, a meafure
Kiln, n. a ftove to dry or burn things in
Kiln'dry, v. t. to dry in or at a kiln, to harden
Kim'bow, a. crooked, bent, arched, fet acrofs
Kim'bula, n. a crocodile of beautiful colors
Kin, n. a relation, kindred, clafs, the fame kind
Kind, a. good, tender, obliging, favorable
Kind, n. a race, clafs, nature, fort, way (forth
Kin'dle, v. to fet on or catch fire, provoke, bring
Kin'dler, n. one who lights, one who inflames
Kindly, ad. with good will, tenderly, obligingly
Kindly, a. mild, promifing, favorable, like
Kind'nefs, n. benevolence, favor, love, tendernefs
Kin'dred, n. relation, affinity, relatives, a clafs

Kin'dred, a. related, allied, fimilar, like, congenial
Kine, n. pl. of cow; two or more cows
Kinepock, n. the vaccine difeafe
King, n. a monarch, fupreme governor, herald, card
King, v. t. to fupply with or make a king
King'craft, n. the art or act of governing
King'dom, n. the dominions of a king
King'ed, pa. having or made a king, crowned
King'fifher, n. a fmall very beautiful bird
King'ling, n. a petty king, ufed in contempt
King'ly, a. royal, noble; ad. with an air of royalty
Kingfevil, n. a fcrofulous diforder
King'fhip, n. royalty, monarchy, fovereign power
Kink, n. a twift formed by the twifting of hard
Kink, v. t. to twift into a kink   (twifted threds
Kino, n. an aftringent refin from a tree in Africa, refin, aftringent
Kins'folk, n. pl. relations, perfons related
Kinsman, n. one of the fame race, a male relation
Kins'woman, n. a female related or of the fame fa-
Kirk, n. a church, the church of Scotland (mily
Kir'tle, n. an upper garment, gown, quantity of
Kifs, n. a falute given with the lips   (flax
Kifs, v. t. to falute with the lips, fondle, carefs
Kifs'ing, n. the act of faluting with the lips
Kifs'ingcruft, n. the cruft where two loaves touch
Kit, n. a fmall fiddle, fmall fifhtub, bottle, pail
Kitch'en, n. a room ufed for cooking in
Kitch'engarden, n. a garden to raife plants for food
Kitch'enmaid, n. a maid who cleans the kitchen
Kitch'enftuff, n. fat from pots, vegetables
Kite, n. a bird of prey, a paper bird or flying figure
Kit'ten, n. a young cat; v. i. to bring forth cats
Kitefoot, n. a particular fort of tobacco
Kit'tiwake, n. a bird of the gull kind
Klick, v. i. to make a fmall fharp noife, fnatch,
Klick'ing, n. a regular low fharp noife (call in
Knab, v. t. to gnaw, bite with noife, nibble
Knack, v. to bite, make a quick noife, talk fine
Knack, n. dexterity, art, a nice trick, toy, top
Knack'er, n. a maker of knacks, a collarmaker
Knag, n. a hard knot in wood, ftump, wart
Knag'gy, a. knotty, rough with knots, very hard
Knap, n. a fwelling, prominence, tuft, hill
Knap, Knap'ple, v. to bite, fnap, break fhort
Knap'fack, n. a foldier's bag or pouch
Knap'weed, n. a plant of different kinds
Knar or Knurle, n. a hard knot of wood
Knave, n. a petty rafcal, fcoundrel, card, fervant
Knavery, n. low dishonefty, petty villany, deceit
Knavifh, a. dishoneft, fraudulent, waggifh
Knavifhly, ad. dishoneftly, mifchievoufly
Knavifhnefs, n. dishonefty, deceit, waggifhnefs
Knawel, n. a fpecies of plant
Knead, v. t. to work or mix dough with the hand
Kneadingtrough, n. a trough to work pafte in
Knee, n. the joint between the leg and thigh
Knee, v. t. to put knees, to entrereat by keeling
Kneedeep, a. rifing up or funk down to the knees

Kneehigh, a. to or as high as the knee
Kneel, v. to bend the knee, to reft on the knee
Knee'tribute, n. obeifance fhown by kneeling
Knell, n. the found made by tolling a bell
Knife, n. pl. knives, a fteel, utenfil to cut with
Knight, n. a title of honor; v. t. to create a knight
Knighter'rant, n. a roving adventurous knight
Knighter'rantry, n. the feats of a knighterrant
Knighthood, n. the dignity of a knight
Knightly, a. becoming or fit for a knight, noble,
Knit, v. t. knit, knitted, pret. knit, knitted, pa, to make ftocking-work, join, unite
Knit'ter, n. one who knits or is kept to kn t
Knit'tingneedle, n. a wire ufed to knit with
Knit'tle, n. a ftring to draw or gather a purfe, &c.
Knob, n. the protuberance of a tree, a knot
Knob'bed, Knob'by, a. full of knobs, hard, rough
Knock, v. to hit, ftrike, dafh, beat, clafh, rap
Knock, n. a fudden or loud ftroke, blow, rap
Knock'er, n. one that knocks, a hammer of a door
Knoll, v. to ring or found as a bell; n. a little hill
Knop, n. a tufted top of any thing, tuft, knob
Knot, n. a part tied, hard place in wood, bond, a divifion of the log-line, as five knots an hour is five miles an hour
Knot, v. t. to make knots, tie, faften, form buds
Knot'grafs, n. grafs of various kinds
Knot'ted, Knot'ty, a. full of knots, hard, difficult
Knot'tily, ad. in a knotty, manner, ruggedly
Knot'tinefs, n. a fulnefs of knots, difficulty
Knot'lefs, a. free from knots
Knout, n. a Ruffian punifhment by a lether thong
Know, v. t. knew, pret. known, pa. to underftand, diftinguifh, perceive, find out
Knowable, a. that may be known or difcovered
Knower, n. one who knows or has knowledge
Knowing, pa. fkilful, confcious; n. knowledge
Knowingly, ad. with real knowledge, wilfully
Knowl'edge, n. underftanding, fkill, learning, notice
Knub, Knub'ble, v. t. to beat with the knuckles
Knuc'kle, v. i. to fubmit, yeld, bend, comply
Knuc'kle, n. a joint of the fingers, knee, knot
Knuck'led, a. having knuckles, jointed, hard
Knuff, n. an aukward perfon, clown, boor, ruftic
Knurl'y, a. full of knots, hard
Koba, n. an antelope with horns clofe at the bafe
Kokob, n. a venomous ferpent of America
Kom'manic, n. the crefted lark of Germany
Koran, n. the Mahometan book of faith
Koret, n. a delicious fifh of the E. Indies
Kor'in, n. an antelope with flender fmooth horns
Kraal, n. a village among the Hottentots
Kraken, n. a fuppofed large fea animal
Kragg, n. a fpecies of argillaceous earth

L

LA! exclam. fee! look! n. a note in mufic
Labefac'tion, n. a weakening, downfal, ruin
Label, n. a fhort direction on any thing, a ribbon
Labial, a. uttered by or relating to the lips

Lábial *n.* a letter whofe found is formed by the lips
Lábiate, *a.* having fegments like lips
Lab'ile, *a.* apt to flide or flip, flippery, unftable
Labiodent'al, *a.* pronounced by the lips and teeth
Lábor, *n.* pains, toil, work, childbirth
Lábor, *v.* to toil, work, ftrive, be in travail, beat
Lab'oratory, *n.* a place for chemical operations or manufacturing warlike apparatus, &c.
Láborer, *n.* one who labors or takes pains
Labórious, *a.* diligent in work, difficult, heavy
Labórioufly, *ad.* with labor, with toil, carefully
Labórioufnefs, *n.* great labor, diligence, difficulty
Láborfome, *a.* made with great labor or pains
Lábra, *n.* a lip, brim, brink, fide, edge
Lab'yrinth, *n.* a maze, a place full of windings
Labyrinth'ian, *a.* winding, intricate, perplexed
Lac, *n.* a fubftance like wax formed by an infect in India, ufed in dying fcarlet and fealing wax
Lac'cic, *a.* pertaining to lac or white lac
Lace, *n.* a cord, ornamental trimming of gold, filver or thred curioufly woven, fnare, gin
Lace, *v. t.* to tighten with a lace, trim, beat
La''cedemónian, *n.* a native of Sparta in Greece
La''cedemónian, *a.* relating to Sparta
Láceman, *n.* a man who makes or deals in lace
La''cerable, *a.* that may be rent or torn in pieces
La''cerate, *v. t.* to tear in pieces, rend, deftroy
La''cerate, *a.* formed with irregular fegments as
Laceration, *n.* the act of tearing   (if torn
La''cerative, *a.* tearing, rending, able to tear
Lacer'tus, *n.* the girroc, a fifh of the gar fifh kind
Lach'es or Lach, *n.* in law neglect, negligence
Lach'rymal, [ch as k] *a.* caufing tears, fad
Lach'rymary, *a.* containing or holding tears
Lach'rymatory, *n.* a veffel for containing tears
Lacin'iate, *a.* having irregular incifions
Lack, *v.* to want, to be in want; *n.* want, need
Lack of rupees is one hundred thoufand, the rupee at 55 cents
Lack'brain, *n.* one who wants wit or fenfe, a fool
Lack'er, *n.* a kind of varnifh; *v. t.* to varnifh
Lack'ey, *n.* a footboy, footman, fervant
Lack'ey, *v.* to act as a footboy, to dangle after
Lack'linen, *a.* wanting linen or fhirts, mean
Lack'lufter, *a.* wanting brightnefs, dull, dark
Lacónian, *a.* pertaining to Laconia, a part of Pelopponefus of which Sparta was the capital
Lacon'ic, *a.* fhort, brief, concife, pithy, expreffive
Lacon'ically, *ad.* fhortly, briefly, concifely, tartly
Lacon'icifm, Lacon'ifin, *n.* a concife ftyle
Lac'tant, *a.* fucking, fuckling, giving milk
Lac'tary, *a.* milky, foft, ; *n.* a dairy, a dairy houfe
Lac'tate, *n.* a falt formed by the lactic acid with a bafe
Lac'teal, *n.* a flender veffel that conveys chyle
Lac'teal, Lac'teous, *a.* milky, conveying chyle
Lactef'cence, *n.* a tendency to produce milk or juce, a flowing of juce
Lactef'cent, Lactif'ic, *a.* tending to caufe milk

Lac'tic, *a.* pertaining to four milk or whey
Lacunófe, *a.* furrowed by the finking of the veins
Lac'unar, *n.* an arched roof or ceiling
Lad, *n.* a boy, ftripling, youth, very young man
Lad'der, *n.* a frame made with fteps, a gradual rife
Lade, *v. t.* laded, *pret.* laded, laden, *pa.* to freight, load, empty, throw out with a dipper
Lading, *n.* a freight, load, burden, weight
Ládle, *n.* a large fpoon, veffel, receptacle, flaff
Lá'ly, *n.* a title of honor or refpect, a woman
Láylybird, Ládycow, *n.* a genus of beetles with fpotted wings
Ládyday, *n.* the annunciation of the B. V. Mary
Ládylike, *a.* foft, delicate, elegant, fine, genteel
Ládyfhip, *n.* the ufual title of or addrefs to a lady
Lag, *a.* laft, coming behind, flow, fluggifh, idle
Lag, *n.* the loweft clafs, fagend, one who is laft
Lag, *v. i.* to loiter, ftay behind, move flowly
Lagoon' or Langúne, *n.* a pond or marfh
Láic, Láical, *a.* belonging to the laity or layman
Laid, *pret.* and *pa.* of *to lay*
Lain, *pa. paff.* of *to lie*
Lair, *n.* the bed of a boar or wild beaft, a fhelter
Laird, *n.* a Scotch lord or proprietor of a manor
Láity, *n.* the people as diftinct from the clergy
Lake, *n.* a large inland water, red color, lawn
Lam'a, [a as in afk] *n.* the deity of the Afiatic tartars, a fmall fpecies of camel in S. America
Laman'tin, *n.* a fpecies of the walrus or fea cow
Lamb, *n.* a young fheep, a title of our Savior
Lam'bative or Lam'bitive, *a.* taken by licking
Lam'bent, *a.* playing about, gliding over, licking
Lamb'kin, *n.* a little lamb, a young lamb
Lamb'like, *a.* like a lamb, meek, gentle, humble
Lamdid'al, *a.* like the Greek letter lamda—thus Λ
Lame, *a.* crippled, hobbling, weak, imperfect, bad
Lame, *v. t.* to make lame, cripple, difable, hurt
Lam'el, *n.* a very thin plate or fcale
Lam'ellate, Lam'ellar, *a.* difpofed in thin plates
Lam'ellarly, *ad.* in thin plates
Lam'ellated, *a.* covered with or in form of plates
Lámely, *ad.* in manner of a cripple, imperfectly
Lámenefs, *n.* the ftate of a cripple, imperfection
Lament', *v.* to grieve, weep, mourn, bewail, regret
Lam'entable, *a.* mournful, miferable, pitiful, fad
Lam'entably, *ad.* with forrow, pittifully, fadly
Lamentátion, Lament', *n.* an expreffion of forrow
Lament'er, *n.* one who laments, one who mourns
Lament'ing, *n.* lamentation, mourning, grief
Lam'in, *n.* a thin plate, coat or fcale, cover, table
Lam'inable, *a.* capable of being formed into thin
Lam'inar, *a.* in plates, pertaining to a plate (plates
Lam'inate, Lam'inated, *a.* confifting of plates or thin layers
Lam'mas, *n.* the firft of Auguft, when the parochial clergy collected their tithes in lambs
Lamp, *n.* a veffel, a light made of oil or fpirits
Lamp'black, *n.* the foot of pitch
Lamp'ers, *n.* a fwelling of the throat in horfes

Lampoon', n. abufe, perfonal flander
Lampoon', v. t. to abufe perfonally, libel, ridicule
Lampoon'er, n. a writer of perfonal fatire
Lamp'rel, Lamp'rey, Lamp'ron, n. a kind of eel
Lanârious, a. relating to or bearing wool
Lan'ate, a. covered with a wooly hair
Lance,n. a long fpear; v. t. to pierce,cut,lay open
Lan'ced, pa. opened or cut with a lance, pierced
Lance'ly, a. fuitable to or becoming a lance ob.
Lan'ceolate, a. fhaped like a lance
Lan'cet, n. a furgical inftrument to let blood
Lanch, v. t. to caft as a lance, throw, dart, fet off
Lanch, n. the fliding of a fhip into the water
Land, n. a country, region, earth, ground, urine
Land, v. to fet, put or come on fhore, to arrive
Land'dam, v. t. to ftop urine, ftop, kill, deftroy
Land'ed, a. having an eftate in land, fet on fhore
Land'fall, n. land firft feen as veffels approach
Land'flood, n. a great flood, inundation, overflow
Land'forces, n. pl. foldiers that ferve on land
Lrand'grave, n. a title, German title, count, earl
Landgrâviate, n. the territory of a landgrave
Land'holder, n. a perfon who is poffeffed of land
Land'ing, n. a place to land at, the top of ftairs
Land'jobber, n. one who fpeculates in land
Land'lady,n. the miftrefs of land, an inn, &c.
Land'lefs, a. deftitute of property or fortune,poor
Land'locked, a. fhut in or inclofed by land
Land'lord, n. an owner of land or houfes, a mafter
Land'mark, n. a mark of boundaries or direction
Land'office, n. an office for the difpofal of lands
Land'fcape, n. a profpect of a country, a picture
Land'flip, n. a detached portion of a hill which
  flides down
Land'tax, n. a tax put upon land and houfes
Land'waiter, n. one who watches the landing of
Land'ward, ad. towards or near the land (goods
Lane, n. a narrow ftreet, a clofe paffage or road
Lan'grage or Lan'grel, n. pieces of old iron for
  fhooting from cannon
Lan''guage, n. all human fpeech, a tongue, a ftyle
Lan''guaged, a. knowing various languages
Lan''guagemafter, n. one who teaches languages
Lan''guet, n. a leaden tongue ufed by weavers
Lan''guid, a. faint, weak, feeble, heartlefs, dull
Lan''guidly, ad. faintly, weakly, feebly, heavily
Lan''guidnefs, n. faintnefs, weaknefs, feeblenefs
Lan''guifh, v. t. to melt, pine,droop,lofe ftrength
Lan''guifhingly, ad. meltingly, feebly, tedioufly
Lan''gifhment, Lan''guifh, n. a foftnefs of mien
Lan''guor, n. faintnefs, lownefs, heavinefs (ings
Lan'iard, n. a fhort piece of rope or line for faften-
Lániate, v. t. to tear in pieces, rend, kill, butcher
Laniâtion, n. the act of tearing or butchering
Lanif'erous, Lani''gerous, a. bearing wool, ob.
Lan'ifice, n. a woollen manufacture, fpinning, ob.
Lank, a. not filled, thin, flender, languid, faint
Lank'nefs, n. a want of flefh, thinnefs, flendernefs
Lan'ner, n. a bird of the longwinged hawk kind

Lant'ern,Lant'horn, n. a cafe for a candle; a.thin
Laodicéan, n. a native of Laodicea in Afia
Lap, n. a feat on the thighs, fold, plait, drink
Lap, v. t. to wrap round, fold over, bind, lick up
Lap'dog, n. a little dog for the lap, a favorite
Lap'ful, n. as much as the lap can hold or bear
Lapidârious, a. ftony, confifting of ftones
Lap'idary, a. engraved upon ftone, monumental
Lap'idary, Lap'idift, n. one who deals in gems
Lap'idate, v. t. to ftone, to kill by ftoning
Lapid'eous, a. ftony, like ftone, hard, rough
Lapides'cence, n. a ftony concretion or hardnefs
Lapides'cent, a. turning to ftone, petrifying
Lapidif'ic, Lapidif'ical, a. forming into ftones
Lapidificâtion, n. the act of forming into ftones
Lapid'ify, v. to form or turn to ftone
Lap'lander, n. a native of Lapland in Europe
Lap'per, n. one who laps, one who wraps up
Lap'pet, n. a loofe part of a woman's headdrefs
Lap'ping, n. a licking up with the tongue
Lapfe, v. i. to flip, glide, fall, defcend, go
Lapfe, n. a flip, error, overfight, fall, courfe
Lap'fided, a. having one fide heavier than the
Lap'wing, n. the name of a fwift noify bird (other
Lap'work, n. one thing wrapped over another
Lar'board, n. the left-hand fide of a fhip or boat
Lar'ceny, n. theft, petty theft, petty robbery
Larch, n. a tree, a fpecies of pine
Lard, n. greafe of fwine; v. t. to ftuff with bacon
Lard'er, n. a place where meat is kept, a houfe
Large, a. big, bulky, wide, full, copious, plentiful
Large'ly, ad. abundantly, liberally, extenfively
Large'nefs, n. greatnefs, bulk, widenefs, extent
Lar'gefs, n. a gift, prefent, dole, bounty at harveft
Lark, n. the name of a fmall finging bird
Lark'fpur, n. a genus of plants of feveral fpecies
Larmiér, n. a flat jutting part of a cornifh
Laryngot'omy, n. a cutting open of the windpipe
Lar'ynx, n. a cavity in the throat by which the
  voice is regulated, the windpipe
Lar'um, n. an alarm, a machine that ftrikes loud
Lar'va, n. the caterpillar ftate of infects
Lafcar, n. a feaman in the Eaft Indies
Lafciv'ious, a. wanton, lewd, luftful, fond, foft
Lafciv'ioufly, ad. wantonly, lewdly, loofely, foftly
Lafciv'ioufnefs, n. wantonnefs, luftfulnefs
Lafh, n. a part of a whip, ftroke, fnare, gin
Lafh, v. t. to fcourge, ftrike, fatirize, tie, faften
Lafh'ing, n. a piece of rope for occafional faftening
Lafs, n. a girl, young maid, young woman
Lafs'itude, n. fatigue, wearinefs, languor, weaknefs
Lafs'lorn, a. forfaken or left by a miftrefs
Laft, a. lateft, hindmoft, following the reft, next
Laft, v. t. to continue; n. a mold, load, end
Laft, Laft'ly, ad. in the laft time or place
Laft'age, n. a cuftom paid for freightage, ballaft
Laft'ing, pa. a. continuing, durable, ftrong
Latch, n. a catch for a door; v. t. to faften with a
Latch'et, n. a faftening, a fhoeftring (latch

Late, *a.* out of due time, long, advanced, deceafed
Late, *ad.* far in the day or night, unfeafonably
Lated, *a.* benighted, overtaken by the night, late
Lately, *ad.* not very long ago, juft now
Latenefs, *n.* a late ftate, time far advanced
Lateenfail, a triangular fail
Latent, *a.* fecret, private, hidden, concealed, deep
Lat'eral, *a.* placed upon the fide, paffing fideways
Laterality, *n.* the quality of having diftinct fides
Lat'erally, *ad.* fidewife, on one fide, by the fide
Lat'eran, *n.* one of the Pope's palaces at Rome
Laterifólious, *a.* growing on the fide of a leaf at
Lateri'tious, *a.* of the color of bricks (the bafe
Lath, *v. t.* to cover or line with laths (or tiles
Lath, *n.* a narrow flip of wood to fupport plaiter
Lathe, *n.* a turner's tool, a divifion of a county
Lath'er, *n.* froth of foap and water, a fweat
Lath'er, *v.* to cover with lather, to form a froth
Lath'ing, *n.* a fitting up with laths, an invitation
Lat'iclave, *n.* an ornament on the garments of Roman fenators
Lat'in, *n.* the ancient Roman language
Lat'in, *a.* pertaining to the Roman language
Lat'inifm, *n.* an idiom of the Latin tongue
Lat'inift, *n.* a perfon who is fkilled in Latin
Latin'ity, *n.* the ftyle of the Latin tongue
Lat'inize, *v. i.* to make or turn into Latin
Látion, *n.* a motion or removal in a right line
Látifh, *a.* fomewhat late, growing late
Latiros'trous, *a.* broad-beaked, *ob.*
Lat'itancy, Latitátion, *n.* concealment
Lat'itant, *a.* lurking, lying hid, concealed, clofe
Lat'itude, *n.* breadth, width, room, extent, diftance, the diftance from the equator north and fouth
Latitúdinal, *a.* pertaining to latitude
Latitudinárian, *n.* one who departs from ortho-
Latitudinárian, *a.* unlimited, unconfined (doxy
Látiant, *a.* barking, fnarling, captious, crofs, *ob.*
Latrátion, *n.* the act of barking like a dog, *ob.*
Látria, *n.* the higheft kind of divine worfhip
Lat'ten, *n.* iron plate covered with tin
Lat'ter, *a.* the laft of two, following, late, modern
Lat'terly, *ad.* in latter times or ages, lately
Lat'tice, *n.* a window formed of network
Lat'ticed, *a.* fitted up with a kind of network
Laud, *n.* praife, honor; *v. t.* to praife, extol, blefs
Laud'able, *a.* praifeworthy, commendable, healthy
Laud'ably, *ad.* in a manner that deferves praife
Laud'anum, *n.* tincture of opium, a fleepy portion
Laugh, [laff] *v.* to make that noife which mirth excites
Laugh, *n.* the convulfion caufed by merriment
Laugh'able, *a.* exciting or fit for laughter, droll
Laugh'er, *n.* one who laughs or is merry
Laugh'ingly, *ad.* in a laughing way, cheerfully
Laugh'ingftock, *n.* an object of ridicule, a butt
Laugh'ter, *n.* a convulfive merry noife, fport, jeft
Launch, *fee* lanch
Laun'drefs or Lan'drefs, *n.* a wafherwoman

Laun'dry, *n.* a room to wafh or iron clothes in
Lau'ret, *n.* the royal poet, the king's poet
Lau'reate, Laur'elled, *a.* crowned with laurel
Lau'rel, *n.* the name of an evergreen tree
Lau'riferous, *a.* producing or bringing laurels
Lav'a, [a as in afk] *n.* matter which iffues from a volcano, liquid, but hardening when cool
Lavátion, *n.* the act of wafhing or cleanfing
Lav'atory, *n.* a laundry, a wafh for difeafed parts, a place where gold is obtained by wafhing earth
Lave, *v. t.* to wafh, bathe, lade, draw out
Lavéer, *v. i.* to turn often in a courfe, *ob.*
Lav'ender, *n.* a kind of fweet-fmelling plant
Láver, *n.* a wafhing-veffel, a plant
Lav'ifh, *a.* prodigal, wafteful, indifcreet, wild
Lav'ifh, *v. t.* to wafte, fcatter profufely, fpend
Lav'ifhly, *ad.* in a very extravagant manner
Lav'ifhment, Lav'ifhnefs, *n.* extravagance, wafte
Law, *n.* a rule, order, judicial procefs, juftice
Law'ful, *a.* conformable to law, juft, right, proper
Law'fully, *ad.* in a lawful manner, fitly, fafely
Law'fulnefs, *n.* the allowance of law, law, juftice
Law'giver, Law'maker, *n.* one who makes laws
Law'giving, *a.* making or paffing laws
Law'lefs, *a.* contrary or not fubject to law, difor-
Law'lefsly, *ad.* in a lawlefs manner (derly
Law'leffnefs, *n.* a ftate of being without reftraint
Lawn, *n.* a plain between woods, a fine linen
Lawn'y, *a.* level as a plain or lawn
Law'fuit, *n.* a procefs in law, a conteft
Law'yer, *n.* one who practices law, a pleader
Lax, *a.* loofe, vague, flack; *n.* a loofenefs, a fifh
Lax'ative, *a.* relieving coftivenefs, purging, loofe
Lax'ity, Lax'nefs, *n.* loofenefs, opennefs, flacknefs
Lay, *v.* laid, layed, *pret.* laid, *pa.* to put, place, apply, wager, calm, ftill, bring eggs, contrive
Lay, *n.* a fong, graffy ground, row, wager; *a.* laical
Láyer, *n.* a ftratum, row, bed, fprig, laying hen
Láyman, *n.* one of the laity, a kind of image
Láyftall, *n.* a place kept for dung, a dungill
Lázar, *n.* a perfon afflicted with filthy difeafes
Lázarhoufe, *n.* a houfe kept to receive lazars in
Lazaret', Lazaret'to, *n.* a houfe for the accommo- dation of perfons difeafed, chiefly with infec- tious fevers
Lázily, *ad.* idly, flothfully, fluggifhly, heavily
Lázinefs, *n.* idlenefs, flothfulnefs, fluggifhnefs
Lázing, Lávy, *a.* idle, not willing to work, flow
Laz'ulite, *n.* a fpecies of argillaceous earth or zeo- lite of a blue color
Lea, Lee, Ley, *n.* ground inclofed, a lawn, yarn
Lead, *v.* led, *pret.* led, *pa.* to go firft, guide, con- duct, entice, draw, pafs, fpend
Lead, *n.* a heavy, foft metal, very ductile, a bar of lead for founding
Lead, *v. t.* to cover or fit with lead
Lead'en, *a.* made of lead, heavy, dull, thick, flow
Léader, *n.* a conductor, commander, captain, head
Léading, *pa. a.* going before, principal, chief

Q 2

Léadingftrings, n. pl. ftrings to hold children by
Léadman, n. a man who begins a dance, ob.
Leaf, v. to bear or produce leaves, to put in leaves
Leaf, n. a part of a tree, book, table, thin plate
Léaflefs, a. void of leaves, ftripped of leaves
Léafy or Léavy, a. full of or thick with leaves
League, n. a confederacy, a meafure of three miles
League, v. t. to join, band or confpire together
Léagued, pa. confederated, joined, united
Léagúer, n. the fiege of a town, a confederate
Leak, n. a hole which lets water in or out
Leak, v. i. to let water in or out, drop, run out
Léakage, n. an allowance for lofs by leaks
Léaky, a. letting water in or out, open, talkative
Léamer, n. a dog, a kind of hound
Lean, a. thin, poor, flender; n. meat void of fat
Lean, v. i. to incline, bend, reft againft or upon
Léanlooked, a. looking lean, thin, poor, flender
Léannefs, n. a want of flefh or bulk, thinnefs
Léanto, n. the part of a building which appears to
lean upon another (rufh, comprefs as beafts
Leap, v. leaped, leapt, pret. and pa. to jump, ftart,
Leap, n. a jump, fkip, embrace of animals, trap
Léapfrog, n. the name of a childifh play
Léapyear, n. every fourth even year, the biffextile
Learn, v. to gain knowledge, improve, teach, hear
Learn'ed, pa. a. having learning, fkilled, taught
Learn'edly, ad. with knowledge or fkill, wifely
Learn'er, n. one who is learning any thing
Learn'ing, n. fcholaftic knowledge, reading, fkill
Leafe, n. a temporary contract for land or houfes
Leafe, v. t. to let by leafe, glean, pick up corn
Léafer, n. one who gleans or picks up corn
Leafh, n. a leathern thong, a rope, three things
Leafh, v. t. to bind to hold in a ftring or line
Léafing, n. lies, falfehood deceit (no more
Leaft, a. fmalleft; ad. in the loweft degree to fay
Leath'er, more correctly Leth'er, n. the hide of an
animal dreffed, fkin
Leath'ercoat, n. the name of a very rough apple
Leath'erdreffer, n. a perfon who dreffes leather
Leath'ern, a. made of or refembling leather
Leath'erfeller, n. a perfon who deals in leather
Leath'ery, a. like leather, tough, tenacious
Leave, n. permiffion, liberty, grant, farewel
Leave, v. left pret. left, pa. to quit, forfake, let re-
main, defift, ftop, bequeath
Léaved, a. full of or having leaves, folding
Leav'en, v. t. to ferment, raife, taint
Leav'en or Lev'en, n. dough fermented, a mixture
Léaver, n. one who leaves, one who forfakes
Leaves, n. pl. of leaf
Léavings, n. pl. things left, offals remains
Lech, v. t. to lick, heal, cure, reftore again ob.
Lech'er, n. a man given to lewdnefs.
Lech'erous, a. lewd, luftful, given to luft
Lech'eroufly, ad. lewdly, luftfully, wantonly (nefs
Lech'erousnefs, Lech'ery, n. lewednefs, luft, loof-
Lec'tion, n. a reading, a difference in copies

Lec'tionary, n. the Romifh fervice-book
Lec'ture, v. to read lectures, reprimand, reprove
Lec'ture, n. a difcourfe on a fubject, a reprimand
Lec'turer, n. a teacher by lectures, reader, minifter
Lec'turefhip, n. the office or place of a lecturer
Led, pret. and pa. of to lead
Ledge, n. a fmall molding on the edge, a ridge
Ledg'er, n. a chief book of accounts, a timber
Ledg'er, a. fixed, conftant, lying in one place
Lee, n. the fide or part oppofit to the wind
Lee'board, n. a frame of planks to aid a veffel to
keep her from falling to the leeward
Leech, n. a water-bloodfucker, healer, farrier, the
border or edge of a fail.
Leech'craft, n. the art or act of healing cattle
Leek, n. a common pot-herb, ; a. having leeks
Leer, n. an oblique caft of the eye, learning, hue
Leer, v. i. to look obliquely or archly
Lees, n. dregs, fediment, a fnare, lofs, falfehood
Lee'fhore, n. the fhore towards which the wind
blows
Lee'fide n. the fide of a fhip oppofit to the wind
Lee'tide, n. a tide running with the wind
Leet, n. a lawday, a petty kind of court
Lee'ward, a. being on the fide towards which the
Lee'ward, n. the fide from the wind (wind blows
Lee'way, n. the direction of a courfe to leeward
Left, pret. and pa. of to leave
Left, a. that is oppofit to the right, unlucky
Left'handed, a. ufing the left hand
Left'handednefs, n. an habitual ufe of the left hand
Leg, n. the limb between the knee and foot
Leg'acy, n. a bequeft or thing left by will
Légal, a. done according to law, lawful, juft, due
Legal'ity, Légalnefs, n. lawfulnefs, juftice, right
Légalize, v. t. to make lawful, authorize, adjuft
Légally, ad. according to law, lawfully, duly
Leg'atary, Legatée, n. one who has a legacy left
Leg'ate, n. an ambaffador, efpecially from the pope
Leg'atefhip, n. the office or dignity of a legate
Leg'atine, a. belonging to or made by a legate
Legátion, n. an embaffy, deputation, commiffion
Legátor, n. one who leaves or bequeaths legacies
Légend, n. an infcription, fabulous ftory, tale
Lé'gendary, a. fabulous, incredible, ftrange
Legerdemáin, n. fleight of hand, deception, a trick
Leger'ity, n. lightnefs, nimblenefs, dexterity
Le"gerline, n. an additional line in the mufical fcale
Leg'ged, a. having legs, put on legs, prepared
Le"gible, a. that may be read, apparent, plain
Le"gibly, ad. in a legible manner, plainly, clearly
Légion, n. a body of foldiers, vaft number, hoft
Légionary, a. relating to a legion, very numerous
Le"giflate, v. i. to make or pafs laws, to enact
Le"giflátion, n. the act of giving or paffing laws
Le"giflative, a. lawgiving, paffing laws, proper
Le"giflátor, n. one who makes laws, a lawgiver
Le"giflátrefs, n. a female lawgiver
Le"giflature, n. the power that makes laws

Legit'imacy, *n* a lawful birth, genuineness
Legit'imate, *a.* born in marriage, lawful, proper
Legit'imate, *v. i.* to make lawful, qualify, adopt
Legit'imately, *ad.* lawfully, duly, genuinely
Legitimátion,*n.*legitimacy, the act of legitimating
Leg'mue, *n.* pulfe of any kind, beans, a pericarp with two valves, and feeds fixed to one future only, as a pea-pod
Legúminous, *a.* belonging to or having pulfe
Leis'urable, *a.* done at or having leifure, eafy, *ob.*
Leis'urably, *ad.* at leifure, without hurry, *ob.*
Leis'ure, *n.* freedom from bufinefs, convenience
Leis'urely,*a.*deliberate,flow ; *ad.*flowly,in no hurry
Léman, *n.* a fweetheart, gallant, harlot, *ob.*
Lem'ma, *n.* a previous or affumed propofition
Lem'ming, *n.* a rat in the north of Europe, fome-times migrating (the Grecian fea
Lem'nian, *a.* pertaining to Lemnos, an ifland of
Lem'nifcate, *n.* a curve in form of the figure 8
Lem'on, *n.* the name of a very acid fruit
Lemonáde, *n.* a mixture of water, fugar and lemon
Lend,*v.* lent,*pret.* lent,*pa.* to grant on condition of receiving the fame or an equivalent in kind, to afford or grant
Lend'er, *n.* one who lends any thing to another
Length, *n.* fpace from end to end, the full extent
Length'en, *v.* to grow or make longer, to add
Length'wife, *ad.* in or according to the length
Length'y, *a.* fomewhat long, applied chiefly to writings or difcourfes
Lénient,*a.* affuafive,foftening, mild, gentle
Len'ify, *v. t.* to affuage, mitigate, appeafe, *ob.*
Len'iment, Len'itive, *n.* an affuafive application
Len'itive, *a.* affuafive, eafing, foftening, mild
Len'itude, Len'ity, *n.* mildnefs, mercy, tendernefs
Lens, *n.* a glafs which diverts the rays of light from a direct courfe
Lent, *n.* the time of the long faft ; *pa.* of *to lend*
Lent'en, *a.* ufed in or belonging to lent, fparing
Len'tiform, *n.* in the form of a lens
Lentic'ular, *a.* of the form of lens, or a lentil
Lentic'ularly, *ad.* in the form of a lens, curving
Lent'il, *n.* a fort of pulfe, a kind of coarfe pea
Len'tifk, *n.* a plant, maftic
Lent'itude, *n.* flownefs, fluggifhnefs, heavinefs
Lent'or, *n.* tenacity, fizinefs, flownefs, delay
Lent'ous, *a.* vifcous, tenacious, ropy, clammy
Léonine, *a.* having the nature or color of a lion
Leop'ard or Lep'ard, *n.* a fpotted wild beaft of prey
Lep'er, *n.* one infected with the leprofy
Lep'erous or Lep'rous, *a.* caufing or having a lep-
Lep'id, *a.* pleafant, jocofe, fmart, merry (rofy
Lep'idolite, *n.* a fpecies of argillaceous earth
Léfion, *n.* an injury, bruife, fracture
Lepórean, Lep'orine, *a.* belonging to a hare
Lepros'ity, Lep'rofy,*n.* a diftemper of white fcales
Les'bian, *a.* pertaining to Lefbos, an ifland in the Egean Sea, now Metelin
Lefs, *comparative* of *little ; n,* not quite fo much

Lefs, Lefs'er, *ad.* in a fmaller or lower degree
Leffée, *n.* a perfon who takes the leafe of another
Lefs'en,*v.* to grow or make lefs, fhrink, degrade
Lefs'on, *n.* a tafk to learn or read ; *v. t.* to inftruct
Leffor', *n.* one who grants a leafe to another perfon
Left, *conj.* that not, in cafe that, for fear that
Let, *v.* let, *pret.* let, *pa.* to fuffer, leave, forbear, hinder, hire out
Let, *n.* an hindrance, impediment, obftacle, ftop
Léthal, *a.* mortal, pertaining to death
Lethar'gic, *a.* fleepy, drowfy, heavy, phlegmatic
Lethar'gicnefs,Leth'argy,*n.*a very great drowfinefs
Leth'argied,*a.* thrown into a deep fleep,entranced
Léthe, *n.* forgetfulnefs, a draught of oblivion
Lethif'erous,*a.* deadly,fatal,deftructive,pernicious
Let'ter, *n.* one who lets, a written meffage, plain meaning, foundation of the alphabet,type,mark
Let'ter, *v. t.* to ftamp, mark or adorn with letters
Let'tercafe, *n.* a book to put letters, &c. in
Let'tered, *pa. a.* marked with letters, learned
Let'terfounder, *n.* one who makes letters for print-
Let'ters, *n. pl.* learning, literature (ing
Let'terspat'ent, *n.* a writing open to infpection, conveying fome right
Let'tice or Let'tuce, *n.* a common falad plant
Levant', *a.* eaftern, lying up the Mediterranean
Levant'ine, *a.* pertaining to the eaftern part of the Mediterranean fea
Lev'ee, *n.* a crowd of attendants, vifit, lady's toilet
Lev'el, *a.* even, fmooth, plain, flat, equal, adapted
Lev'el, *v.* to make or lay flat, take aim, direct
Lev'el, *n.* a plain, flat, equality, inftrument
Lev'eller, *n.* one who deftroys due fubordination
Lev'elnefs,*n.* evennefs, an equality of furface
Lev'er, *n.* a mechanical power, beam, rod, balance
Lev'eret, *n.* a young hare, a little hare
Levet', *n.* a blaft or leffon on the trumpet
Lev'iable, *a.* that may be laid or impofed
Levia,han, *n.* the largeft of all fea-monfters (mix
Lev'igate, *v. t.* to reduce to a fine powder, fmooth,
Levigátion, *n.* the act of making fmooth or fine
Lévite, *n.* one come from the tribe of Levi, a prieft
Levit'ical, *a.* prieftly, ritual, judicial, legal
Lev'ity,*n.* lightnefs, inconftancy, vanity, folly
Lev'y,*v.* to raife, collect, impofe, make war
Lev'y, *n.* the act of raifing money, &c. a rate, war
Lewd, *a.* wicked, luftful, obfcene, filthy, laical
Lewd'ly, *ad.* wickedly, badly, luftfully, wantonly
Lewd'nefs,*n.* wickednefs, vilenefs, luftfulnefs
Lewd'fter, Libid'inift, *n.* a lecherous perfon, *ob.*
Lexicog'rapher,*n.* a writer of a dictionary
Lex'icon, *n.* a dictionary, a Greek dictionary
Líable, *a.* fubject, expofed, apt, refponfible
Liablenefs, *n.* a liable ftate, a fubjection
Líablenefs, Liabil'ity, *n.* expofednefs, tendency to, refponfibility, a ftate of being anfwerable
Liar, *n.* one who lies, one who utters falfehoods
Líard, *a.* roan, mingled, fpotted, grey, hoary
Libátion, *n.* an offering made of wine, &c. a tafte

Libel, *v. t.* to defame, lampoon, satirize, institute a process in a court of admiralty, &c.

Libel, *n.* a defamatory satire, a declaration in law

Libellant, *n.* one who brings a libel or suit in an admiralty court

Libeller, *n.* a defamatory writer, a lampooner

Libellous, *a.* defamatory, abusive, scandalous

Liberal, *a.* generous, bountiful, free, genteel

Liberality, *n.* generosity, munificence, kindness

Liberally, *ad.* generously, bountifully, freely

Liberate, *v. t.* to set at liberty, release, deliver

Liberation, *n.* a setting free from restraint

Liberalize, *v. t.* to make liberal, or catholic

Libertin, *a.* licentious, debauched, irreligious

Libertin, *n.* a dissolute liver, wretch, freedman

Libertinism, *n.* licentiousness of life, looseness

Liberty, *n.* freedom, leave, permission, privilege

Libidinous, *a.* lustful, licentious, lewd, wild

Libidinously, *ad.* lustfully, lewdly

Librarian, *n.* one who has the care of a library

Library, *n.* a collection of or place for books

Librate, *v. t.* to poise, balance, level, weigh

Libration, *n.* the state of being balanced, a trembling motion (west of Egypt

Libratory, *a.* moving like a balance or scales

Libyan, *a.* pertaining to ancient Lybia in Africa,

Libyan, *n.* a native of Libya

Lice, *n. pl.* of *louse*

Licence or License, *n.* permission, liberty

License, *v.* to grant leave, set at liberty

Licenser, *n.* one who grants leave or permission

Licentiate, *n.* a graduate in Spain or in physic

Licentiate, *v. t.* to encourage by licence, to permit

Licentious, *a.* unrestrained, loose, presumptuous

Licentiously, *ad.* with too great liberty, lewdly

Licentiousness, *n.* a contempt of just restraint

Lichen, *n.* liver wort, a genus of mosses very numerous on rocks, &c. (beat

Lick, *v. t.* to touch with the tongue, lap, devour,

Lick, *n.* a taste, blow, stroke, a place where cattle lick for salt

Lickerish, *a.* nice, delicate, luxurious, greedy

Lickerishness, *n.* a niceness of taste, daintiness

Licorice, Licorish, *n.* a plant and its juice

Lictor, *n.* a kind of beadle amongst the Romans

Lid, *n.* a cover for a pot, box, &c. a membrane

Lie, *n.* an untruth or falsehood uttered with a criminal intention, a fiction

Lie, *v. i.* to tell a lie, to utter a falsehood

Lie, *v. i.* lay, *pret.* lain, lien, *pa.* to rest, lean, stay, remain, colt, belonging to

Lief, Leave, *ad.* willingly, soon; *a.* beloved, dear

Liege, *n.* a lord, a sovereign; *a.* trusty, faithful

Lieger, *n.* a resident embassador

Lientery, *n.* a great looseness, a very sudden flux

Lier, *n.* one who lies down, one who rests

Lieu, *n.* place, room, stead, exchange, behalf

Lieutenancy, *n.* the office or body of lieutenants

Lieutenant, *n.* a deputy, viceroy, second in rank

Lieutenantship, *n.* the rank or state of a lieutenant

Life, *n.* animation, the state of an organized being while its functions are performed, whether animals or plants, the present state of existence, manner of living, energy, exact likeness, narrative of ones life

Lifeblood, *n.* blood necessary to life, vital blood

Lifeguard, *n.* a prince's or king's body guard

Lifeless, *a.* dead, void of spirit, inactive, dull, heavy

Lifelessly, *ad.* without spirits, dully, heavily

Lifelessness, *n.* deadness, dullness, heaviness, sloth

Lifelike, *a.* resembling life or a living person

Lifestring, *n.* a string imagined to convey life

Lifetime, *n.* the continuance or length of life

Lifeweary, *a.* quite tired of living, very wretched

Lift, *v.* lift, lifted, *pret.* lift, lifted, *pa.* to raise up, exalt, heave, strive, help, rob

Lift, *n.* the act of lifting, a struggle, load, rope, gate

Lifter, *n.* one who lifts or raises up, a crutch

Lig, *v. i.* to lie, to lie in bed or on any place, *ob.*

Ligament, *n.* a band to unite parts together

Ligamental, *a.* composing or like a ligament

Ligation, *n.* the act or state of binding together

Ligature, *n.* a bandage, any thing bound on

Light, *n.* that by which we see or understand, a view

Light, *a.* bright, not heavy, nimble, airy, trifling

Light, *ad.* lightly, cheaply, without difficulty

Light, *v.* lighted, lit, *pret.* lighted, lit, *pa.* to give light, guide by a light, kindle, ease, rest, fall, come down, get off, meet with

Lighten, *v.* to flash with lightning, ease, cheer

Lighter, *n.* a large boat used for unloading ships

Lighterman, *n.* one who manages a lighter

Lightfingered, *a.* thievish, dishonest, knavish

Lightfooted, Lightlegged, *a.* nimble, swift, quick

Lighthead, *a.* delirious, thoughtless, giddy

Lighthearted, *a.* gay, airy, merry, cheerful, easy

Lighthorse, *n.* light armed cavalry (men

Lighthouse, *n.* a building with lights to direct seamen

Lightless, *a.* void of light, dark, dull, gloomy

Lightly, *ad.* nimbly, easily, gaily, with levity

Lightminded, *a.* unsettled in mind, inconstant

Lightness, *n.* want of weight, giddiness, levity

Lightning, *n.* the flash that precedes thunder

Lights, *n. pl.* the lungs, the organs of breathing

Lightsome, *a.* giving light, brisk, airy, cheering

Lightsomeness, *n.* luminousness, cheerfulness

Ligneous, *a.* wooden, made of or like wood

Ligniform, *a.* like, or in the form of wood

Lignify, *v.* to become or convert into wood

Ligulate, *a.* like a bandage or strap (Italy

Ligurian, *a.* pertaining to Liguria, now Genoa, in

Ligure, *n.* a kind of jewel or precious stone

Like, *n.* something that is like, a near approach

Like, *a.* resembling, equal, even, likely, probable

Like, *ad.* in the same manner, fitly, probably

Like, *v.* to be pleased with, approve, choose, gratify

Likelihood, *n.* a probability, an appearance

Likeliness, *n.* probability, a good appearance

Li'kely, *a.* probab'e, well-favored; *ad.* probably
Liken, *v. t.* to make like, compare, resemble
Likenefs, *n.* a refemblance, form, fhow, appearance
Likewife, *ad.* in like manner, alfo, too
Liking, *n.* a plumpnefs, good ftate, tafte, trial
Lilac, *n.* a flowering fhrub
Liliaceous, *a.* like or pertaining to a lily
Lil'lied, *a.* embelifhed with or having lilies
Lil'y, *n.* the name of a beautiful flower
Limation, *n.* the act of filing or polifhing
Limb, *n.* a member, joint, bough, border, edge
Limb, *v. t.* to give limbs, to difmember
Lim'bat, *n.* a cooling periodical wind in Cyprus
Lim'bec, *n.* a veffel ufed to diftil with, a ftill
Limb'ed, *a.* formed with regard to limbs
Lim'ber, *a.* eafily bent, pliant, fupple, yielding
Lim'bernefs, *n.* a bending quality, pliancy
Lim'bers, *n.* fquare holes in a fhips floor timbers, fhafts of a gun-carriage
Lim'bo, *n.* the borders of hell, hell, a prifon
Lime, *n.* a kind of earth obtained from ftones, fhells, &c. a vifcid fubftance, a tree, a fruit
Lime, *v. t.* to cover with lime, fmear, entangle
Limegall, *n.* an infect found on the leaves of the lime tree
Limekiln, *n.* a kiln for burning limeftone, &c. in
Limeftone, *n.* a ftone from which lime is made by expelling the carbonic acid, carbonate of lime
Limetwig, *n.* a twig fmeared over with birdlime
Lim'it, *n.* a bound, border, extent, utmoft reach
Lim'it, *v. t.* to confine within bounds, to reftrain
Lim'itary, *a.* placed at the boundaries, guarding
Limitation, *n.* a reftriction, circumfpection, end
Lim'itlefs, *a.* without limits, boundlefs
Limn, *v. t.* to paint a face, take a likenefs, draw
Lim'ner, *n.* a painter, a facepainter
Limous, *a.* full of or like mud, muddy, flimy
Limp, *a.* pliant, weak; *v. i.* to walk lamely, to halt
Lim'pet, *n.* a genus of teftaceous infects, univalvular
Limp'id, *a.* clear, tranfparent, bright, pure, fine
Limpid'ity, Limp'idnefs, *n.* clearnefs, purenefs
Limp'ingly, *ad.* in a lame or halting manner
Limp'nefs, *n.* limbernefs, weaknefs, foftnefs
Limy, *a.* containing or like lime, glutinous, ropy
Linch'pin, *n.* an iron pin to keep a wheel on the
Lin'den, *n.* a tree, lime-tree, teil-tree (axletree
Line, *n.* a ftring, extenfion in length, trench, verfe, mark, equator, order, progeny, 12th of an inch
Line, *v. t.* to guard within, cover over, impregnate
Lin'eage, *n.* a race, family, defcent, pedigree
Lin'eal, *a.* defcending or going on in a right line
Lineal'ity, *n.* the ftate of being in a line
Lin'eally, *ad.* in a direct line, duly, regularly
Lin'eament, *n.* a feature, a difcriminating mark
Lin'ear, *n.* compofed of or like lines, ftrait
Lin'eate, *a.* marked with lines lengthways
Lineation, *n.* a draft or appearance of lines
Lin'en, *n.* cloth of hemp or flax; *a.* made of linen
Lin'endraper, *n.* a perfon who deals in linen cloth

Ling, *n.* a large feafifh, a kind of heath
Lin''ger, *v.* to droop, loiter, hefitate, protract
Lin''geringly, *ad.* tedioufly, flowly, with delay
Lin''get, *n.* a fmall mafs of metal, a bird
Lin''go, *n.* a language, tongue, fpeech, [*vulgar*]
Linguadent'al, *a.* uttered by the tongue and teeth
Lin''gual, *a.* pertaining to the tongue
Lin'guiform, *a.* in the fhape of a tongue
Lin'guilate, *a.* having the fhape of a tongue
Lin''guift, *n.* a perfon fkilled in different languages
Lin'iment, *n.* a kind of foft ointment, a balfam
Lining, *n.* the inner covering of any thing
Link, *n.* a part of a chain, chain, torch of pitch
Link, *v. t.* to join, unite, connect, combine, fix
Link'boy, *n.* a boy who carries a link or torch
Lin'net, *n.* a genus of fmall finging birds
Lin'feed, *n.* a kind of fmall feed, the feed of flax
Lin'fey-wool'fey, *a.* made of linen and wool
Lin'ftock, *n.* a fhort ftaff with a match at the end
Lint, *n.* a foft flaxen fubftance, linen fcrapings
Lint'el, *n.* the upper crofs part of a door-frame
Lion, *n.* a bold, ftrong carnivorous animal, a fign in the zodiac
Lionefs, *n.* a fhe lion, female lion, fury, fcold
Lip, *n.* the front of the mouth, the edge of a thing
Lip, *v.* to falute with the lips, kifs, bill, fondle
Lip'aris, *n.* an anguiliform fifh
Lip'labor, Lip'wifdom, *n.* talk without wifdom
Lipoth'ymous, *a.* fwooning, fainting, fick, low
Lipoth'ymy, *n.* a fwoon, fainting fit, ficknefs
Lip'pitude, *n.* blearednefs or forenefs of the eyes
Liquefac'tion, *n.* the act of melting, a melted ftate
Li''quefiable, *a.* that may be melted (or clear
Li''quefy, Liquate, *v.* to melt, diffolve, grow foft
Li''quefier, *n.* that which melts or makes liquid
Liques'cency, *n.* an aptnefs to melt or foften
Liques'cent, *a.* melting, diffolving, growing foft
Li''quid, *a.* fluid, foft, melted, diffolved, clear
Li''quid, *n.* any liquid or fluid fubftance, liquor
Li''quidate, *v. t.* to adjuft, fettle, afcertain, reduce to a certain ftandard (known rule
Liquidation, *n.* an adjuftment, reduction to a
Liquid'ity, Li''quidnefs, *n.* a liquid ftate, loofenefs
Li''quids, *n. pl.* the four letters, *l, m, n, r*
Li''quor, *n.* a liquid, ftrong drink; *v. t.* to drench, to moiften
Li''quorice or Li''quorifh, *n.* a plant of feveral kinds
Lifbon, *n.* a kind of wine, capital of Portugal
Lifne, *n.* a cavity, a hollow place, *not ufed*
Lifp, *v. i.* to clip words in their pronunciation
Lifp, *n.* the act of lifping, an imperfect utterance
Lifp'er, *n.* one who lifps or clips his words
Lift, *v.* to cover with lift, inlift, hear, like
Lift, *n.* a roll, catalogue, place for fighting, ftrip of cloth, fillet, coarfe wool, an inclining, a bill of ratable eftate, (Con.)
Lift'ed, *pa.* covered with lift, inlifted, ftripped
Lis'ten, *v.* to hearken, hear, attend to, heed, mind
Lis'tener, *n.* one who hearkens through curiofity

Lift'er, n. one who receives and makes return of ratable eftate. (Con.)

Lift'lefs, a. indifferent, carelefs, heedlefs, flow

Lift'lefsly, ad. without thought, attention or care

Lift'leffnefs, n. indifference, inattention

Lit, pret. and pa. of to light

Lit'any, n. a form of public prayer or fupplication

Lit'eral, a. according to the letter, plain, exact

Lit'eral, Literal'ity, n. the literal plain meaning

Lit'erally, ad. with clofe adherence to the words

Lit'erary, a. relating to letters or learning

Literáti, n. pl. the learned, men of learning (books

Lit'erature, n. learning, reading, fkill in letters or

Lith'arge, n. an oxyd of lead, or lead and oxygene

Lithe, Lithefome, a. pliant, limber, nimble, weak

Lith'er, a. lazy, idle, fluggifh, naughty, ob.

Lith'ic, a. pertaining to the ftone in the bladder

Lith'ate, n. a falt formed by lithic acid and a bafe

Lithog'raphy, n. the act of ingraving upon ftone

Lithol'ogy, n. the fcience of ftones on the earth

Litholo''gic, a. pertaining to the fcience of ftones

Lithol'ogift, n. one fkilled in the fcience of ftones

Lith'omancy, n. a prediction from or by ftones

Lith'omarg'a, n. a fpecies of fine clay

Lithot'omift, n. a perfon who cuts for the ftone

Lithot'omy, n. the cutting for the ftone

Lithontrip'tic, n. a medicin that wears away or breaks the ftone in the bladder

Lithontrip'tic, a. wearing or breaking the ftone

Lithoph'agous, a. eating ftones, as an oftrich

Lit'igant, n. one who is engaged in a lawfuit

Lit'igant, a. engaged or contefting in a lawfuit

Lit'igate, v. to conteft in law, wrangle, debate

Litigation, n. a conteft at law, quarrel, difpute

Liti''gious, a. inclined to 'awfuits, quarrelfome

Liti''gioufly, ad. in a wrangling or crofs manner

Liti''gioufnefs, n. a quarrelfome difpofition

Lit'mus, n. a blue pigment ufed in painting (bird

Lit'orn, n. a fpecies of thrufh, like the hen black

Lit'ter, v. t. to bring forth, fcatter about, cover

Lit'ter, n. a fedan, ftraw, brood of pigs, confufion

Lit'tle, a. fmall, diminutive, trifling, not much

Lit'tle, n. a fmall fpace, fhare or part, mere trifle

Lit'tle, ad. in a fmall degree or quantity

Lit'tlenefs, n. fmallnefs, meannefs, want of dignity

Lit'toral, a. relating to or lying near the feafhore

Lit'urgy, n. a form of common or public prayers

Live, v. i. to be in a ftate of life, exift, laft, fwim

Live, a. living, quick, active, merry, ftrong, firm

Livelihood, n. the means of living, a maintenance

Livelinefs, n. fprightlinefs, brifknefs, life, vigor

Live'long, a. tedious, flow, whole, lafting, durable

Lively, a. brifk, gay, cheerful, vigorous, ftrong

Lively, ad. in a lively or brifk manner

Liv'er, n. one who lives, a part of entrails, a food

Liv'ercolor, n. the color of liver, a very dark red

Liv'ergrown, a. having too great a liver

Liv'erftone, n. a fpecies of barytic ftone, emitting when rubbed, the fmell of alkaline fulphuret

Liv'ery, n. a giving poffeffion, a certain drefs

Liv'eryman, n. one who wears a livery, a freeman

Liv'eryftable, n. a place to let or keep horfes at

Liv'erwort, n. orpine, a plant of feveral kinds

Lives, n. pl. of life (imals

Live'ftock, n. cattle, horfes and fmall domeftic an-

Liv'id, a. difcolored as with a blow, blue, black

Livid'ity, Liv'idnefs, n. a livid color or ftate

Liv'ing, n. a livelihood, a benefice; pa. alive

Liv'ingly, ad. in a living ftate or condition

Liv'er, n. a fmall filver coin, a French coin

Lixiv'ial, Lixiv'ious, a. obtained by lixivium

Lixiv'iate, a. making or refembling a lixivium

Lixiv'iate, v. t. to form or extract a lye

Lixiviátion, n. the act of forming a lye

Lixiv'ium, n. lye made of afhes and water, a falt

Liz'ard, n. a numerous genus of reptiles, with long tapering bodies and fhort legs, amphibious

Loach, n. the cobitis, a fmall fifh

Lo, exclam. look! fee! behold! view!

Load, n. a burden, freight, leading vein in a mine

Load, v. t. loaded, pret. loaded, loaden, pa. to burden, freight, charge, encumber

Load'ftone, n. a ftone having an attracting power

Loaf, n. a quantity or mafs of bread (loam

Loam or Loom, n. a fat earth; v. t. to cover with

Loamy, a. confifting of or like loam, marly

Loan, n. any thing lent, ufe, intereft of money

Loan, v. t. to lend, which fee

Loan'office, n. an office to receive loans of money for the public, keep the accounts and pay the

Loan'officer, n. one who keeps a loan office (intereft

Loath or Loth, a. unwilling, backward, not ready

Loathe or Lothe, v. t. to hate, abhor, diflike, fhun

Loathful, n. hating, hated, odious, difguftful

Loath'ing, n. hatred, abhorrence, diflike, difguft

Loathly, a. hateful, abhorred; ad. unwillingly

Loathnefs, n. unwillingnefs, backwardnefs

Loathfome, a. abhorred, odious, caufing diflike

Loathfomenefs, n. the quality of raifing diflike

* Italic L not filent.

Loaves, n. pl. of loaf

Lob, n. a heavy fellow, large worm, fifh, prifon

Lob, v. t. to let fall in a lazy carelefs manner

Lobate, Lobed, a. divided to the middle in feparate parts, like lobes, with convex margins

Lob'by, n. on opening before a room, antichamber

Lobe, n. a part of the lungs or liver, a divifion

Lobs'ter, n. an admired fhellfifh of the crab kind

Lob'ule, n. a fmall lobe

Local, a. being of or in a place, relating to a place

Local'ity, n. a local ftate, exiftence in a place

Locally, ad. with refpect to place or fituation

Locate, v. t. to place, to felect, furvey or fix the bounds of unfettled land, or to defignate a tract by a writing

Location, n. the act of placing, a fituation, the act of defignating or furveying and bounding land, the tract fo defignated

Loch, [ch as k] n. a lake, a large collection of water

Lock, n. part of a door or gun, a tuft, hug, place, a barrier in a canal

Lock, v. to faften with a lock, grapple, fix, unite, form locks for inland navigation

Lock'er, n. a drawer, cupboard, cheft, box

Lock'et, n. an ornamental lock, a catch or fpring

Lock'ram, n. a fort of very coarfe linen

Locomotion, n. a power or act of changing place

Locomotive, a. changing or able to change place

Loc'ulament, n. a cell for feeds in a capfule

Locuft, n. a very large devouring infect

Lodeftone, n. tin-ftone, ftone containing oxyd of tin

Lodge, n. a fmall houfe in a park, a porter's room, a fociety of free mafons

Lodge, v. to place, lay, fettle, harbor, refide, live

Lodge'ment, n. a placing, a poffeffion of outworks

Lodg'er, n. one who lodges or hires a lodging

Lodg"ing, n. rooms hired, an apartment, a covert

Loft, n. the higheft floor, a convenience

Loft'ily, ad. proudly, highly, on high, fublimely

Loft'inefs, n. pride, haughtinefs, height, fublimity

Loft'y, a. proud, haughty, ftately, high, fublime

Log, n. a piece of wood, dunce, hebrew meafure

Log'arithms, n. pl. the indexes of the ratios of numbers to each other

Logarithmet'ical, a. in the manner of logarithms

Log'book, n. a book ufed to keep a fhip's way in

Log'gats, n. pl. an old and illegal play or game

Log'gerhead, n. a blockhead, dunce, ftupid perfon

Log'gerheaded, a. dull, ftupid, heavy, fimple

Log'houfe, n. a dwelling made of logs

Lo"gic, n. the art of reafoning with propriety

Lo"gical, a. of or belonging to logic, conclufive

Lo"gically, ad. by the rules of logic, truly, fairly

Logi"cian, n. a perfon verfed or fkilled in logic

Logift'ic, a. relating to fexagefimals or algebra

Log'line, n. a line to meafure a fhip's way by

Log'man, n. one who carries a log, a woodman

Logog'raphy, n. a mode of printing by types caft in whole words

Logograph'ic, a. pertaining to logography

Logom'achy, n. a difpute or conteft about words

Log'wood, n. a wood brought from Campeachy

Loin, n. the reins, waift, back of an animal, joint

Loit'er, v. i. to idle away time, linger, lag, delay

Loit'erer, n. one who loiters, an idle lazy perfon

Loll, v. to lean idly, reft, hang out the tongue

Lomentáceous, a. containing flowers which afford beautiful tinctures

Lone, a. fingle, being without company, lonely

Lónelinefs, Lónenefs, n. folitarinefs, dulnefs

Lónely, Lónefome, a. folitary, retired, difmal, dull

Long, ad to a great length, by the fault, becaufe

Long, a. having length, protracted, tedious, flow

Long, v. i. to defire earneftly; n. a kind of note

Longanim'ity, n. long forbearance, great patience

Long'boat, n. the largeft boat belonging to a fhip

Longe or Lunge, n. a full thruft in fencing

Longev'ity, n. great length or extent of life, age

Longévous, a. living a long time, very aged

Long'headed, a. having great extent of thought

Longim'anous, a. having long hands (land

Longprim'er, n. a fort of printing types

Longim'etry, n. the art of meafuring diftances or

Long'ing, n. an earneft defire, an ardent wifh

Long'ingly, Long'ly, ad. with inceffant wifhes

Long'ifh, a. moderately long

Lon'gitude, n. length, diftance from Eaft to Weft

Longitúdinal, a. meafured by or running out in

Long'legged, a. having long legs, tall (length

Longsighted, a. able to fee at a great diftance

Longsightednefs, n. the faculty of feeing very diftant objects

Long'fome, a. long, dilatory, tedious, ob.

Longfuf'fering, a. patient; n. clemency, mercy

Long'ways, Long'wife, ad. in length or extent

Longwind'ed, a. having good breath, tedious, flow

Loo, Lu, n. the name of a game at cards

Loob'ily, a. aukward, clumfy; ad. aukwardly

Loob'y, n. an aukward heavy perfon, clown, lubber

Loof, Luff, v. to bring near or clofe to the wind

Look, v. to behold, fee, watch, feek for, appear

Look, n. a view, appearance, air of the face (jects

Look'ingglafs, n. a glafs that fhows images of objects

Loom, v. i. to appear elevated more than ufual

Loom, n. a weaver's frame for work, tool, bird

Loon, n. a fimple fellow, a fcoundrel, a bird

Loop, n. a noofe for a rope or ftring, an iron ring

Loop'ed, Loop'holed, a. full of holes or noofes

Loop'hole, n. a hole for a ftring, hole, trick, fhift

Loofe, v. to unbind, deliver, free, fet free, fet fail

Loofe, a. unbounded, lax, wild, wanton; n. liberty

Loofe'ly, ad. in a loofe manner, idly, wantonly

Loos'en, v. to let loofe, unite, relax, free, part

Loofe'nefs, n. a laxnefs of body, flux, depravity

Loofe'ftrife, n. a plant of feveral kinds

Lop, v. t. to cut fhort; n. a branch cut off, a flea

Loquácious, a. full of talk, talkative, blabbing

Loquácioufnefs, Loqua"city, n. talkativenefs

Lord, n. GOD, a title of honor, mafter, hufband

Lord, v. t. to domineer, to rule haughtily

Lord'ane, Lord'ant, n. a haughty lazy perfon, ob.

Lord'ing or Lord'ling, n. a little or petty lord

Lord'linefs, n. pride, haughtinefs, dignity, ftate

Lord'ly, a. proud, haughty, ftately, infolent, noble

Lord'ly, ad. proudly, haughtily, defpotically

Lord'fhip, n. a title given to lords, a manor, power

Lore, n. learning, doctrin, inftruction, a leffon

Lor'icate, v. t. to plate or cover over, to fill up

Lorication, n. a covering of a veffel with a cruft for refifting fire, a furface like a mail

Lóris, n. a fmall quadruped of Ceylon

lorn, a. forlorn, lonely, forfaken, left, deferted

lóry, n. a fubordinate genus of the parrot kind

lofe, [looze] v. loft, pret. loft, pa. to fuffer lofs, fail, mifs, let flip, forfeit, bewilder

lofe'able, a. capable of being loft, loofe

los'el, *n.* a fcoundrel, worthlefs fellow, cheat, *ob.*
lófer, *n.* one who lofes or has fuffered lofs
lofs, *n.* damage, hurt, prejudice, forfeiture, a fault
loft, *pa.* no longer perceptible, gone, perifhed
let, *n.* a fortune, ftate, portion, fhare, chance, a
   fhare or divifion of land, a field
lóta, *n.* a fpecies of eel pout
lote, *n.* a tree, herb, feed, pipe
lótion, *n.* the act of wafhing, a medicinal wafh
lot'tery, *n.* a diftribution of prizes made by chance
lótus, *n.* a fpecies of plant, trefoil
loud, *a.* noify, founding, clamorous, turbulent
loud'ly, *ad.* noifily, clamoroufly, violently, hotly
loud'nefs, *n.* a great found or noife, turbulence
lough,[lok] *n.* a lake, a large inland body of water
louis-d'or, *n.* a French gold coin value about 4
   dolls. 50 cents
lounge, *v. i.* to loiter, idle about, idle, live lazily
lounge, *n.* indulgence in indolence
loun'ger, *n.* an idler, an idle lazy perfon   (lice
loufe, *n.* a fmall body animal ; *v. t.* to clear from
lous'ily, *ad.* in a mean or dirty manner, filthily
lous'inefs, *n.* an abounding with lice, meannefs
lous'y, *a.* fwarming with lice, mean, dirty
loufe'wort, *n.* cockfcomb or rattle yellow (wardly
lout, *n.* an aukward fellow; *v. i.* to bow auk-
lout'ifh, *a.* clownifh, aukward, clumfy, heavy
lout'ifhly, *ad.* clownifhly, aukwardly, clumfily
lov'age, *n.* a fpecies of plant
love, [luv] *v. t.* to regard with affection, like, value
love, *n.* a paffion. friendfhip, kindnefs, filk fluff
love'letter, *n.* a letter of courtfhip or fondnefs
love'lily, *ad.* in a lovely manner, amiably, finely
love'linefs, *n.* a lovely quality, amiablenefs
love'lorn, *a.* forfaken of one's love, caft down
love'ly, *a.* exciting love, amiable, fine, delightful
love'monger, *n.* one who deals in affairs of love
lov'er, *n.* one who is in love, one who likes a thing
love'fecret, *n.* a fecret between two lovers
love'fick, *a.* fick or languifhing through love
love'fong, *n.* a fong expreffing or denoting love
love'fuit, *n.* the act of making love, courtfhip
love'tale, *n.* a tale or ftory relating to love
love'thought, *n.* an amorous thought or fancy
love'toy, *n* a fmall prefent made by a lover
love'trick, *n.* an act expreffing love or fondnefs
loving, *pa. a.* fond, affectionate, kind
lovingkindnefs, *n.* tendernefs, mercy, favor, love
lov'ingly, *ad.* fondly, with affection or kindnefs
lov'ingnefs, *n.* affection, tendernefs, kindnefs
low, *a.* little, deep, weak, poor, mean, late, cheap
low, *v.* to bellow, make a noife, fink, lower
low, *ad.* with low voice, meanly, lately, cheaply
low'bred, *a.* vulgar, grofs, unmannerly, mean
low'er, *n.* cloudinefs, gloominefs
low'er, *v. i.* to be cloudy, to frown
low'er, *v.* to bring low, leffen, reduce, fink
low'eringly, *ad.* cloudily, gloomily, heavily, dully
lowermoft, *a.* loweft, deepeft, that is under all

low'ery, *n.* cloudy, threatening rain
lowing, *n.* the noife made by oxen, &c. a bellowing
low'lands, *n. pl.* a low part of a country, a marfh
low'linefs, *n.* humility, a want of dignity, mean-
low'ly, *a.* humble, meek, mild, mean   (nefs
low'ly, *ad.* not highly, humbly, meekly, meanly
lown, *n.* a fcoundrel, rafcal, dull heavy perfon
low'nefs, *n.* a low, weak or mean ftate, dejection
low'fpir'ited, *a.* void of fpirits, caft down, uneafy
low'thoughted, *a.* having low or mean thoughts
lowt, *v.* to overpower, look crofs, pout
low'wines, *n.* the produce of the firft diftillation
   of a fermented liquor, or the firft run of the ftill
loxodrom'ics, *n. pl.* the art of failing by rhumbs
loxodrom'ic, *a.* pertaining to the rhumbline
loy'al, *a.* true or obedient to a fovereign, trufty
loy'alift, *n.* one who is faithful to his king
loy'ally, *ad.* with fidelity, or due fubmiffion
loy'alty, *n.* fidelity, ftrict adherence, fubmiffion
loz'enge, *n.* a medicin made up in fmall pieces,
   a four-cornered figure in heraldry, an ornament
   in brilliants
lub'bard, Lub'ber, *n.* a lazy fturdy fellow, a clown
lub'berly, *a.* lazy and bulky, clumfy, awkward
lub'berly, *ad.* lazily, clumfily, awkwardly
lúbricant, *n.* that which lubricates
lúbric, Lúbricous, *a.* flippery, unfteady, wanton
lúbricate, *v. t.* to make flippery, fmooth, rub
lubri''city, *n.* flipperinefs, inftability, lewdnefs
lubrifac'tion, Lubrification, *n.* the act of lubrica-
luce, *n.* a pike that is full grown   (ting
lúcent, *a.* fhining, bright, glittering, dazzling
lucern', *n.* a kind of ftrong grafs, lamp, candle
lucern'a, *n.* a fifh with a bifid tail and furrowed
lúcid, *a.* fhining, bright, glittering, clear
lucid'ity, Lúcidnefs, *n.* brightnefs, clearnefs
lúcifer, *n.* the name of the devil, the morning-ftar
lucif'erous, Lucif'ic, *a.* giving or caufing light
luck, *n.* chance, accident, fortune, good fortune
luck'ily, *ad.* by good hap, fortunately, favorably
luck'inefs, *n.* good hap, good fortune, fuccefs
luck'lefs, *a.* unfortunate, unhappy, wretched
luck'y, *a.* fortunate, fuccefsful, favorable, happy
lúcrative, *a.* profitable, gainful, bringing gain
lúcre, *n.* profit, gain, advantage, benefit, ufe
lucrif'ic, Lucrif'erous, Lúcrous, *a.* profitable
lúcrine, *a.* pertaining to a lake in Campania
luctation, *n.* a ftruggle, effort, endeavor, conteft
luctif'erous, Luctif'ic, *a.* caufing forrow
lúcubrate, *v. i.* to watch, to ftudy hard and late
lucubrátion, *n.* a nightly ftudy or work from it
lúcubratory, *a.* compofed or done by candlelight
lúculent, *a.* clear, bright, certain, evident, plain
lúdicrous, *a.* merry, fportive, ridiculous, fimple
lúdicroufly, *ad.* in a ludicrous or filly manner
luff, *v.* to put the tiller towards the lee fide, to
   fail nearer to the wind
lug, *v.* to pull or carry with force and difficulty
lug, *n.* a twitch, pull, ear, pole, perch, fmall fifh

Lugg, *n.* an infect like an earth worm but with

Lug'gage, *n.* any thing cumberfome or heavy (legs

Lug'ger, *n.* a veffel with three mafts, a running bowfprit and lug-fails

Lug'fail, *n.* a four-fided fail bent on a yard which hangs obliquely to the maft

Lugúbrious, *a.* mournful, doleful, forrowful, fad

Lúkewarm, *a.* moderately warm, indifferent, cool

Lúkewarmly, *ad.* with indifference or coolnefs

Lúkewarmnefs, *n.* a want of zeal, indifference

Lull, *v. t.* to put to reft, compofe to fleep, allure

Lull'a, Lull'aby, *n.* a nurfe's fong to quiet infants

Lúmachel, *n.* a calcareous ftone compofed of fhells and coral conglutinated

Lumbágo, *n.* a pain in the mufcles of the loins

Lum'bar, *a.* belonging to the lóins

Lum'ber, *v.* to heap carelefsly, fill, move heavily

Lum'ber, *n.* any kind of ufelefs furniture, timber in general, but chiefly fmall timber, as boards flaves, hoops, fcantling, &c.

Lumbri''ciform, *a.* fhaped like an earth worm

Lúminary, *n.* a body that gives or cafts light, a di-

Lúminous, *a.* fhining, bright, enlightened   (vine

Lúminoufnefs, *n.* a ftate of being light or bright

Lump, *n.* a whole piece, the grofs, a heap

Lump, *v. t.* to take or put in the grofs, to join

Lump'fifh, *n.* a thick fifh with a fharp back and tubercles   (lines

Lump'en, *n.* a long fifh greenifh and marked with

Lump'ing, Lump'ifh, *a.* heavy, large, dull, four

Lump'ifhly, *ad.* heavily, ftupidly, fourly

Lump'ifhnefs, *n.* heavinefs, dulnefs, ftupidity

Lump'y, *a.* full of or having lumps, heavy, dull

Lúnacy, *n.* madnefs that is affected by the moon

Lúnar, Lúnary, *a.* relating to or like the moon

Lunárian, *n.* an inhabitant of the moon

Lúnate, Lúnated, *a.* formed like a half moon

Lúnatic, *n.* a madman ; *a.* mad, affected by the

Lunátion, *n.* a revolution of the moon   (moon

Lunch, Lunch'eon, *n.* a large piece of food to eat

Lune, *n.* any thing like a half moon, madnefs

Lunge, *n.* a thruft, a fudden pufh

Lunett', *n.* a half moon in fortification, a blind

Lung'ed, *a.* having lungs, like or refembling lungs

Lungs, *n. pl.* the lights, the parts for breathing

Lúniftice, *n.* the fartheft point of the moon's northing and fouthing in her monthly revolu-

Lung'wort, *n.* a fpecies of plant   (tions

Lunt, *n.* a match-cord to fire great guns with

Lúnular, Lúnulate, *a.* fhaped like a crefcent

Lúpine, *n.* a kind of pulfe, a kind of flower

Lurch, *v.* to lurk, cheat, pilfer, devour, defeat

Lurch, *n.* a forlorn condition, a helplefs ftate, a fudden motion towards one fide

Lurch'er, *n.* a fort of hunting-dog, poacher, thief

Lure, *n.* an enticement ; *v. t.* to entice, to call,

Lúrid, *a.* gloomy, difmal, wan, pale   (hawk

Lurk, *v. i.* to lie in wait as a rogue, to lie clofe

Lurk'er, *n.* one who lies in wait for prey, a thief

Lurk'ingplace, *n.* a fecret place, hiding place, den

Lus'cious, *a.* very fweet, rich, pleafing, immodeft

Lus'cionfnefs, *n.* a very great fweetnefs or richnefs

Lufh, *a.* having a deep color ; *n.* lewdnefs, luxury

Lúfiad. *n.* an epic poem on the difcovery of India

Lufitánian, *n.* a native of Lufitania now Portugal

Lufitánian, *a.* pertaining to Lufitania or Portugal

Lufórious, Lúfory, *a.* ufed in play, fportive, gay

Luft, *n.* a carnal defire; *v. i.* to defire carnally

Luft'ful, *a.* having irregular defires, raifing luft

Luft'fully, *ad.* in a luftful or lecherous manner

Luft'fulnefs, *n.* a luftful or irregular defire, luft

Luft'ed, Luft'ihood, *n.* bodily ftrength, *ob.*

Luft'ily, *ad.* ftoutly, boldly, with courage

Luft'inefs, *n.* ftoutnefs, fturdinefs, ftrength, vigor

Luft'ing, *n.* the act of inordinate defire

Lr.ft'rate, *v. t.* to cleanfe, purify, furvey, view

Luftrátion, *n.* a purification by water, a viewing

Lus'ter, *n.* brightnefs, glofs, renown, a fpace of five years, a fconce

Lus'tring or Lúteftring, *n.* a kind of filk cloth

Luft'rous, *a.* bright, gloffy, fhining, luminous

Luft'y, *a.* ftout, ftrong, powerful, large, healthy

Luft'wort, *n.* a fpecies of plant

Lutárious, *a.* like clay or mud, living in mud

Lute, *v. t.* to clofe or cover with chymift's clay

Lute, *n.* a foft clay, a ftringed mufical inftrument

Lútheran, *n.* a follower or admirer of Luther

Lútheranifm, *n.* the doctrines held by Luther

Lúthern, *n.* a window in the roof of a building

Lútulent, *a.* muddy, foul, turbid, dirty, thick

Lux, Lux'ate, *v. t.* to put out of joint, to disjoint

Luxátion, *n.* a disjointing, a thing disjointed

Luxúriance or Luxúriancy, *n.* excefs, plenty

Luxúriant, *a.* fuperfluoufly plenteous, exuberant

Luxúriate, *v. i.* to grow or fhoot out to excefs

Luxuriátion, *n.* a growing exuberantly or exceeding the natural growth

Luxuríety, Luxúrioufnefs, *n.* great extravagance

Luxúrious, *a.* voluptuous, foftening by pleafure

Luxúrioufly, *ad.* voluptuoufly, delicioufly, highly

Lux'ury, Luxe, *n.* excefs in eating, drefs or pleafure

Lycanth'ropy, *n.* a fpecies of madnefs

Ly''cian, *n.* a native of Lycia in Afia

Ly''cian, *a.* pertaining to Lycia

Lycos'tom, *n.* a Baltic fifh like a herring

Lyd'ian, *n.* a native of Lydia in Afia

Lyd'ian, *a.* pertaining to Lydia   (thro' afhes

Lye, *n.* water impregnated with falt by paffing

Ly'ing, *pa.* of *to lie* ; *n.* the act of telling lies

Lymph, *n.* tranfparent water, a clear fluid

Lymph'ated, *a.* frightened into madnefs, raving

Lymphat'ic, *a.* mad, diftracted ; *n.* a perfon mad

Lymphat'ic, *a.* pertaining to lymph   (lymph

Lymphat'ics, *n.* veffels which convey or fecrete

Lymph'educt, *n.* a veffel to convey lymph

Lynx, *n.* a very fharpfighted fpotted feline beaft

Lyre, *n.* an old mufical inftrument, a harp

Ly'rate, *a.* fhaped like a lyre or harp

R

Lyr'ic, a. pertaining, like or finging, to a harp
Lyr'ic, n. a poet who writes fongs for the harp
Ly'rilt, n. a harper, one who plays on the harp

M

MAC, n. an Irifh or Scotch name for Son
Macáco, n. the great monkey of Angola
Macao, n. the name of a game at cards
Macaróni, n. a fop, fribble, finical fellow, pafte
Macaron'ic, n. a confufed heap or mixture, a jum-
Macaroón, n. a fweet cake, a rude fellow (ble
Macau'co, n. a genus of animals, the lemur
Macaw', n. a bird bred in the Welt-Indies, a parrot
Mac'cabaw, n. a kind of fine fnuff
Mac'cabees, n. two apocryphal books of fcripture
Mace, n. an enfign of authority, ftaff, fine fpice
Máceale, n. ale that is fpiced with mace
Mácebearer, n. an officer, one who carries a mace
Ma''cedonian, n. a native of Macedonia
Ma''cedonian, a. pertaining to Macedonia
Ma''cerate, v. t. to fteep, foak, infufe, make lean
Maceration, n. an infufion, the act of wafting
Mach'inate, [ch as k] v. t. to plan, plot, contrive
Machination, n. a plot, contrivance, artifice
Mach'inift, n. one who plans or contrives
Machine, [mathene] n. any engine to aid human
power in the application of force
Machinery, n. enginery, decorations in a poem
Mack'arel, n. a fine fea fifh
Mackaw', n. a fpecies of tree
Microcofm, n. the world, whole world, univerfe
Maclátion, n. the act of killing beafts for facrifice
Mac'ula, Maculátion, n. a fpot, ftain, pollution
Mac'ulate, Mac''kle, v. t. to fpot, ftain, foil
Maçucáqua, n. the wild hen, a bird of Brazil
Mad, a. difordered in mind, enraged, angry
Mad, Mad'den, v. to make or become mad
Mad'am, n, an addrefs paid to a gentlewoman, a title
Mad'brained, a. hotheaded, giddy, thoughtlefs
Mad'cap, n. a madman, a wild or very giddy perfon
Mad'der, n. a plant much ufed in dying
Made, pret. and pa. of to make
Madefac'tion, n. the act of wetting, wetnefs
Mad'efy, Mad'idate, v. t. to wet, to moiften
Mad'houfe, n. a houfe for keeping mad perfons
Madéira, n. an ifland and the wine it produces
Mad'ly, ad. furioufly, foolifhly, fimply
Mad'man, n. a man deprived of underftanding
Mad'nefs, n. diltraction, fury, paffion, great folly
Mad'repore, n. a fubmarine fubftance of a ftony
hardnefs, branched and full of cells, inhabited
by animals by which it is formed or medufa
Mad'jival, n. a kind of air or fong, a paftoral fong
Mad'woman, n. a woman that is wild or furious
Mad'wort, n. wild buglofs or great goofe grafs
Magazine, [i as e] n. a ftorehoufe, armory, pam-
phlet   (pole which revolve like ftars
Magellan'ic clouds, whitifh clouds near the fouth
Mag'got, n. a fmall worm, grub, whim, odd fancy
Mag'goty, a. full of magots, whimfica', ftrange

Mági, n. pl. wife men, eaftern philofophers
Mágian, n. a wife man, an eaftern philofopher
Mágian, a. pertaining to the Magi
Mágianifm, n. the doctrines of the Magi who
worfhipped the fun
Ma''gic, n. a dealing with fpirits, enchantment
Ma''gic, Ma''gical, a. performed by magic arts
Ma''gically, ad. by the rites, rules, &c. of magic
Magi''cian, n. one fkilled in magic, an enchanter
Magifterial, a. proud, lofty, imperious, very fine
Magifterially, ad. proudly, loftily, arrogantly
Magifterialnefs, n. the airs of a mafter, haughtinefs
Ma''giftery, n. powder wafhed well from its falts
Ma''giftracy, n. the office, ftate, &c. of a magiftrate
Ma''giftrally, ad. defpotically, haughtily, highly
Ma'giftrate, n. one invefted with public authority
Mag'ma, n. drofs, refufe
Magnal'ity, n. the quality of being great or grand
Magnanim'ity, n. greatnefs of mind, bravery
Magnan'imous, a. great in mind, brave, heroic
Magnan'imoufly, ad. bravely, courageoufly, nobly
Magnéfia, n. a fpecies of earth white and fost,
very abforbent and purgative
Magnéfian, a. belonging to magnefia
Mag'net, n. a ftone that attracts iron, iron ore, fteel
Magnet'ic, Magnet'ical, a. attractive, drawing
Magnet'ics, n. the principles or fcience of magne-
tifm   (loadftone
Mag'netifm, n. the power of attraction, or of a
Mag'netize, v. to communicate magnetifm or
become magnetic
Magnif'ic, a. illuftrious, grand, noble
Magnificable, a. that may be magnified
Magnif'ical, n. a great man, a nobleman; a.noble
Magnif'icence, n. grandeur, ftate, fplendor, fhow
Magnif'icent, a. grand in appearance, fplendid
Magnif'icently, ad. pompoufly, fplendidly, finely
Magnif'ico, n. a grandee or nobleman of Venice
Mag'nifier, n. a perfon who extols or praifes, a glafs
that increafes the bulk of a viewed object
Mag'nify, v. to make great, extol, praife, avail
Mag'nitude, n. greatnefs, fize, comparative bulk
Magnólia, n. the tulip tree, beautiful and mageftic
Mag'pie, n. a bird, a very talkative perfon
Magau'ri, n. a Brazilian bird of the ftork kind
Mahog'any, n. a very valuable brown wood
Mahom'etan, n. a follower or favorer of Mahomet
Mahom'etanifm, Mahom'etifm, n. the principles
taught by Mahomet
Maid, n. a virgin, female fervant, fifh
Máiden, n. a maid, virgin, beheading inftrument
Máiden, a. frefh, new, unpolluted, untainted
Máidenhair, n. a plant of feveral kinds
Máidenhead, n. virginity, newnefs, firft ufe
Máidenly, a. modeft, bafhful, timorous, decent
Máidhood, Máidenhood, n. virginity   (a maid
Maidmárian, n. a kind of dance, a boy dreffed like
Máidpale, a. pale as a fick virgin, wan, fickly
Máidfervant, n, a female fervant, drudge, flave

Mail, *n.* armor, a bag of poft-letters ; *v.t.* to arm

Maim, *n.* a privation, defect, lofs, injury, hurt

Maim, *v. t.* to hurt, wound, lame, cripple, cut off

Main, *a.* chief, principal, important, vaft, wide

Main, *n.* the grofs, fum total, chief part, ocean

Mainland, *n.* a continent, largeft part of land

Mainly, *ad.* chiefly, principally, powerfully

Mainmaft, *n.* the chief or middle maft of a fhip

Mainprize, *n.* a deliverance of a prifoner on bail

Mainfail, Mainfheet, *n.* the fail of the mainmaft

Maintain, *v.* to preferve, keep, fupport, uphold

Maintainable, *a.* defenfible, juftifiable, prcper

Maintainer, *n.* a defender, a fupporter

Maintenance, *n.* fuftenance, fupport, help, fupply

Maintop, *n.* the top of the mainmaft of a fhip

Mainyard, *n.* the yard of the mainmaft of a fhip

Majá, *n.* a bird of Cuba of a beautiful yellow

Majeftic, *a.* auguft, ftately, lofty, fublime, royal

Majeftically, *ad.* with dignity, withgrandeur

Ma''jefty, *n.* dignity, grandeur, power, a royal title

Major, *a.* greater, elder, firft, prime, chief

Major *n.* an officer in the army, a term in logic

Majoration, *n.* an increafe, enlargement, extent

Majority, *n.* the rank of major, a great number

Maiz, *n.* Indian corn, native corn of America

Make, *v.* made, *pret.* made, *pa.* to form, create, produce, force, conduce

Make, *n.* a form, ftructure, nature, companion

Makebate, *n.* a maker or promoter of mifchief

Makepeace, *n.* a peacemaker, reconciler, friend

Maker, *n.* one who makes any thing, the Creator

Makeweight, *n.* any thing to make up due weight

Making, *n.* the act of forming, workmanfhip, work

Malabaric, Malabárian, *a.* pertaining to Malabar the weftern coaft of India

Mal'achite, [ch as k] *n.* a green copper ore or copper with aerial acid, capable of a high polifh

Mal'ady, *n.* a difeafe, diftemper, illnefs, ficknefs

Maladminiftration, *n.* bad management of an office

Mal'apert, *a.* faucy, impudent, pert, bold, daring

Mal'apertly, *ad.* faucily, impertinently,, boldly

Mal'apertnefs, *n.* faucinefs, pertnefs, boldnefs

Málar, *a.* pertaining to the cheek (a bafe

Mal'ate, *n.* a falt formed by the malic acid and

Maláyan, *a.* pertaining to the Malays in India

Male, *a.* belonging to the fex that begets young

Male, *n.* the he of any fpecies of creatures

Mal'content, *a.* difcontented, diffatisfied

Mal'content, *n.* one who is difcontented, a rebel

Malcontent'ednefs, *n.* difcontent, difaffection

Maledic'tion, *n.* a curfe, execration, imprecation

Malefact'or, *n.* one who offends againft the law

Malef'ic, *a.* mifchievous, hurtful, deftructive

Maleficence, *n.* a doing mifchief or harm, a difpofition to injure

Maleficent, *a.* doing harm, tending to injure

Malprac'tice, *n.* bad practice, improper behavior

Malev'olence, *n.* ill-will, malignity, fpite, hatred

Malev'olent, *a.* ill-difpofed towards others, vile

Malev'olently, *ad.* with ill-will, malignantly

Málic, *a.* pertaining to apples or the like fru't

Mal'ice, *n.* ill defign or intention, fpite, hatred

Mali''cious, *a.* malevolent, fpiteful, illnatured

Mali''cioully, *ad.* with an intention of mifchief

Mali''cioufnefs, *n.* malice, an ill defign, hatred

Malign, *a.* malicious, unfavorable, infectious

Malign, *v. t.* to hurt, injure, traduce, envy

Malig'nancy, Malig'nity, *n.* malevolence, malice

Malig'nant, *a.* envious, malicious, fatal

Malig'nant, Maligner, *n.* a reviler, an envier

Malig'nantly, Malignly, *ad.* envioufly with ill-will

Malk'in, Maalk'in, *n.* a dirty wench, a mop, ob.

Mall, *v. t.* to ftrike with a mall, beat, hammer

Mall, *n.* a large hammer or beetle

Mull [mal] *n.* a public walk

Mal'lard, *n.* the male or drake of wild ducks

Mal'leable, *a.* that can be extended by hammering

Malleabil'ity, Mal'leablenefs, *n.* the quality of fuffering extenfion by beating

Mal'leate, *v. t.* to hammer

Malleátion, *n.* an extenfion by beating

Mal'let, *n.* a wooden hammer

Mal'low, *n.* the name of many plants

Malm'fey, *n.* a kind of rich fweet wine

Mal'polon, *n.* a fpotted ferpent of Ceylon

Malt, *n.* barley fteeped in water and dried on a kiln

Malt, *v.* to make or be made into malt

Malt'floor, *n.* a floor employed for drying malt on

Mal'tha, *n.* a fpecies of mineral pitch, a fmall fhark

Malt'horfe, *n.* a dull bad horfe, a very flow perfon

Malt'houfe, *n.* a houfe for making malt in

Maltreat, *v. t.* to treat ill or amifs, abufe, injure

Mal'fter, *n.* one who makes or deals in malt

Malváceous, *a.* made of or relating to mallows

Malverfation, *n.* a mean artifice or evafion, a trick

Mam, Mammá, *n.* a word ufed by infants for mother

Mam'mary, *a.* relating to the breaft

Mammee', *n.* the name of feveral plants

Mam'met, *n.* a puppet, a figure dreffed up

Mam'millary, *a.* belonging to or like the paps

Mam'moc, *v. t.* to tear or break quite in pieces

Mam'moc, *n.* a fhapelefs piece, fragment, fcrap

Mam'odis, *n.* coarfe plain India muflins from 7 to 9-8ths in width (wealth

Mam'mon, *n.* riches, money, wealth, the god of

Mam'monift, *n.* one who doats on riches

Mam'moth, *n.* the name given to an animal now extinct, of the elephant kind

Man, *n.* a human being, male, fmall bit of wood

Man, *v.* to furnifh with men ftrengthen, tame

Man'acle, *v. t.* to chain the hands, fhacle, bind

Man'acles, *n. pl.* fetters or chains for the hands

Man'age, *v. t.* to conduct, tranfact, govern, train

Man'age, Man'agement, Man'ager, *n.* conduct, government, dealing, frugality, prudence, care

Man'ageable, *a.* governable, tractable, mild, eafy

Man'ager, *n.* a conductor, leader, frugal perfon

Man'akin, *n.* a tribe of birds of great beauty

Man'atus or Man'ati, *n.* the fea cow or walrus
Manátion, *n.* the act of flowing or iffuing out
Manch'et, *n.* a fmall loaf of fine white bread
Manchineél, *n.* a poifonous tropical tree
Man'cipate, *v. t.* to enflave, bind, tie, fell, yield
Man'ciple, *n.* a purveyor, caterer, kind of fteward
Mandámus, *n.* a writ from the king's bench
Man'darin, *n.* a Chinefe magiftrate or nobleman
Man'date,*n.* a command,order,charge,commiffion
Mandátor, *n.* a commander,orderer,director,ruler
Man'datory, *a.* commanding,ordering, enjoining
Man'dible, *n.* the jaw; *a.* eatable, wholefome
Man'dil, *n.* a kind of Perfian cap or turban
Man'drake, *n.* a plant with very odd roots
Man'drel, *n.* a turner's wooden pulley
Man'ducate, *v. t.* to chew, champ, eat, devour
Manducátion, *n.* the act of chewing or eating
Mane, *n.* the long hair on the neck of a horfe
Man'eater, *n.* one who eats human flefh, a favage
Mánes, *n. pl.* ghofts, fhades, departed fouls, hell
Maneuver, *n.* management, dextrous movement
Maneuver, *v.* to manage with addrefs, to vary pofitions in an army or fleet
Man'ful,*e.* bold, brave, ftout, courageous, daring
Man'fully, *ad.* boldly, ftontly, courageoufly, nobly
Man'fulnefs, *n.* boldnefs, ftoutnefs, great courage
Man'gaby, *n.* a monkey with naked eye lids
Manganéfe, *n.* a whitifh gray metal very hard and difficult to fufe, alfo the oxyd of the metal
Manganéfian, *a.* pertaining to manganefe
Manganíc acid, *a.*a faturated combination of manganefe and oxygene
Mange, *n.* a diftemper, the fcab or itch in cattle
Mánginefs, *n.* a mangy ftate, fcabbinefs, itch
Man'ger, *n.* a wooden trough to feed horfes from
Man'gelwurzel, *n.* a fpecies of large beet
Man'gle, *v. t.* to cut or tear in pieces, alter much, fmooth linen
Man'gle, *n.* an inftrument to fmooth linen
Man'gler, *n.* one who mangles
Man'gling, *n.* the act of mangling, a hacking
Man'go, *n.* a fruit from the E. Indies pickled, a green mufmelon pickled
Mangoftan' or gar'cin, *n.* a beautiful tree
Man'grove or Man'gle, *n.* a genus of trees in the W. Indies growing near water
Mángy, *a.* infected with the mange, fcabby
Man'hater, *n.* one who hates or fhuns mankind
Man'hood, *n.* a man's eftate, courage, refolution
Mániac, *a.* raving with madnefs; *n.* a perfon mad
Mánichéans, [ch as k]*n.* heretics who held to two fupreme principles or deities, light and darknefs
Man'ifeft, *a.* plain, clear, evident, detected
Man'ifeft, *v. t.* to make known, to fhow plainly
Man'ifeft, *n.* an invoice of a cargo
Manifeft'o, *n.* a public proteftation, an edict
Manifeftátion, *n.* a difcovery, a publication
Manifeft'ible, *a.* that may be eafily fhown, plain
Man'ifeftly, *ad.* plainly, clearly, evidently

Man'ifold, *a.* many, divers, repeated, multiplied
Man'ifoldly, *ad.* in a manifold manner, diverfly
Man'ikin, *n.* a little or flender man, a male child
Manillé, *n.* a ring, band, bracelet, name of a card
Man'ioc, *n.* an acrid plant, from the root of which is extracted caffava bread
Man'iple, *n.* a handful, a fmall band of foldiers
Man'is, *n.* a name for the pangolin (in the arts
Manipulátion, *n.* the act of performing operations
Man'killer, Man'queller, Man'flayer, *n.* a murderer
Mankfnd, *n.* the whole human race
Man'lefs, *a.* having no men, unmanned, empty
Man'like, Man'ly, *a.* becoming a man, brave, noble
Man'linefs, *n.* bravery, ftoutnefs, dignity
Man'ly, *ad.* in a manlike manner, with courage
Man'na, *n.* a phyfical drug, gum, delicious food
Man'ner, *n.* a form, cuftom, way, kind, turn, catt
Man'nerift, *n.* one who has a particular manner
Man'nerlinefs, *n.* mannerly behavior, civility
Man'nerly,*a.* civil, complaifant, kind; *ad.* civilly
Man'ners, *n. pl.* ftudied civility, conduct, morals
Man'nifh, *a.* like a man, mafculine, bold, daring
Manom'eter, *n.* an inftrument to fhow the denfity and rarity of the air
Man'or, *n.* a lord's jurifdiction or eftate
Man'orhoufe, *n.* the houfe of the lord of a manor
Manórial or Manérial, *a.* belonging to a manor
Manfe, *n.* a parfonage or vicarage houfe
Man'fin, Man'fionl.o.fe, *n.* a dwelling houfe
Man'flaughter, *n.* the killing of a perfon in a fudden paffion
Manfüetude, *n.* tamenefs, gentlenefs, mildnefs
Man'ta, *n.* a fort of flat fifh which appears like a cloud (penthoufe
Man'telet, *n.* a kind of woman's fhort cloak, a
Man'tiger *n.* a large kind of monkey
Man'tle or Man'tletree, *n.* the part of a chimney in front lying on the jambs
Man'tle, *n.* a cloak; *v.* to froth, cover, revel
Mantol'ogy, *n.* the gift or art of prophefying
Mant'ua, *n.* a woman's gown, a kind of filk
Mant'uamaker, *n.* one who makes women's gowns
Man'tuan, *a.* pertaining to Mantua in Italy
Man'ual, *a.* performed, done or ufed, by the hand
Man'ual, *n.* a fmall or thin book of prayers, &c.
Manúbial, *a.* relating to fpoils taken in war
Manuduction, *n.* a guidance by the hand
Manufac'tural, *a.* relating to manufacture
Manufact'ure, *n.* any thing that is made by art
Manufact'ure, *v. t.* to make or form by art
Manufact'urer, *n.* a maker, artificer, workman
Manumis''fion, *n.* the act of releafing flaves, free-
Man'umit, *v.* to fet free, releafe, difcharge (dom
Manúrable, *a.* that is capable of being cultivated
Manúre, *v. t.* to dung, to enrich; *n.* foil for land
Manúrement, *n.* cultivation, improvement
Man'ufcript, *n.* a written book, written copy, copy
Ma''ny, [menny] *a.* numerous, feveral, fundry
Ma''nycolored, *a.* having many colors, varied

Ma″nycornered, *a.* having feveral corners
Ma″nyheaded, *a.* having feveral heads, ftrange
Ma″nylanguaged, *a.* having many languages
Ma″nypeopled, *a.* very numerous, populous, full
Ma″nytimes, *ad.* often, frequently, repeatedly
Map, *n.* a delineation of lands, feas, countries, &c.
Map, *v. t.* to lay down or make a map, to draw
Máple, *n.* the name of a well known tree
Map′pery *n.* the art of planning and defigning, *ob.*
Mar, *v. t.* to fpoil, injure, hurt, damage, undo
Mar′acan, *n.* a fpecies of parrot in Brazil
Maragon′gis, *n.* a very low priced India muflin 3·4ths in width
Maranátha, *n.* a Jewifh form of anathematizing
Mar′anon, *n.* a river in S. America, the largeft in the world, improperly called Amazon
Maras′mus, *n.* a confumption, decline, flow wafte
Maraud′er, *n.* a plunderer, a plundering foldier
Maraud′ing, *n.* a queft of or fearch after plunder
Maravédi, *n.* a fmall Spanifh copper-coin
Mar′ble, *n.* a fine hard ftone, a little ball of ftone
Mar′ble, *v. t.* to vein, form or ftain, like marble
Mar′ble, *a.* made of or variegated like marble
Mar′blehearted, *a.* very hardhearted, unfeeling
Mar′cafit, *n.* a hard bright foffil, mundic, more ftrictly, an ore of iron or pyrite
Marces′cent, *a.* withering, fading decaying
Marcefs′ible, *a.* that is liable to wither or fade
Mareh, *n.* the third month, a movement of foldiers, proceffion, folemn walk or tune
March, *v.* to move in a military or ftately manner
March′er, *n.* a prefident or head of the marches
March′es, *n. pl.* borders, the limits of a country
Mar′chionefs, [ch as fh] *n.* the lady or wife of a mar-
March′pane, *n.* a kind of fweet bread or cake (quis
Mar′cid, *a.* lean, poor, withered, pining, rotten
Marcid′ity, Mar′cor, *n.* leannefs, a wafte of flefh
Mare, *n.* the female of the horfe kind
Mar′eca, *n.* a fpecies of duck in S. America
Mar′ena, *n.* a fifh fomewhat like a pilchard
Mar′efchal, *n.* the chief commander of an army
Mar′garite, *n.* a pearl, jewel, kind of ftone, daify
Mar′gay, *n.* an American animal of the cat kind
Mar′gent, Mar′gin, *n.* an edge, border, brim, fide
Mar′gin, *v. t.* to form a border, to border
Mar′grave, *n.* put in or relating to the margin
Mar′grave, *n.* a title of fovereignty in Germany
Margráviate, *n.* the territory of a margrave
Marigénous, *a.* produced in or by the fea
Mar′igold, *n.* a plant, the name of a yellow flower
Mar′ikin, *n.* a fpecies of monkey with a mane
Mar′inate, *v. t.* to fry or preferve fifh in oil, &c.
Marine, [marene] *a.* relating to the fea
Marine, *n.* a fea-foldier, body of a fleet, ftate of
Mar′iner, *n.* a failor, a feaman (the navy
Mar′iput, *n.* the zoril, a variety of the fkunk
Mar′ifh, *a.* fenny, boggy, fwampy; *n.* a fen, a bog
Mar′ital, *a.* pertaining to a hufband or marriage
Mar′itime, *a.* marine, naval, joining to the fea

Mar′joram, *n.* a fweet fmelling herb, origanum
Mark, *n.* a coin, a token, object to fhoot at, butt, impreffion, note, proof, evidence
Mark, *v.* to make a mark, note, mind, obferve
Markeé, *n.* a large tent for officers
Mark′er, *n.* one who marks, one who takes notice
Mark′et, *v. i.* to deal at market, purchafe, bargain
Mark′et, *n.* a place and time of fale, rate, price
Mark′etable, *a.* faleable, fit for the market, current in market
Mark′etbell, *n.* a bell to give notice for market
Mark′etcrofs, *n.* a crofs fet up in a market place
Mark′etday, *n.* a day on which a market is held
Mark′etfolks, *n. pl.* the people that go to market
Mark′etman, *n.* one who buys or fells at market
Mark′etplace, *n.* a place where a market is held
Mark′etprice, *n.* the current price of any thing
Mark′ettown, *n.* a town that has a ftated market
Mark′etwoman, *n.* a woman that attends market
Marks′man, *n.* one who can hit a mark, a fhooter
Marl, *n.* a kind of clay, a kind of good manure
Marl, *v.* to lay on marl, to faften with marline
Marláceous, *a.* marly, partaking of marl
Marl′in, *n.* twifted hemp dipped well in pitch
Marl′ing, *v. t.* to wind twine or marlin about a rope
Marl′ite, *n.* a fpecies of marl
Marlit ic, *a.* like or pertaining to marlite
Marl′pit, *n.* a pit out of which marl may be dug
Marl′y, *a.* abounding with or like marl
Mar′malade, *n.* pulp of quinces boiled in fugar
Mar′morated, *a.* covered over with marble
Marmórean, Marmóreous, *a.* relating to marble
Marmófe, *n.* an animal fomewhat like the opoffum
Mar′mofet, *n.* a fmall monkey, an odd figure
Mar′mot, *n.* a quadruped that burrows in the earth
Maroon′, *n.* a free black living on the hills in the W. Indies
Maroon′, *v. t.* to live on a defolate ifland
Marque, *n.* a reprifal, retaliation, revenge, fhip
Mar′quis, *n.* a title of honor next below a duke
Mar′quifate, *n.* the dignity or power of a marquis
Mar′rer, *n.* one who fpoils, defaces or hurts
Mar′riage, *n.* the act of joining man and woman
Mar′riageable, *a.* that is of a fit age to be married
Mar′ried, *pa.* joined in marriage, united, linked
Mar′row, *n.* a fubftance in bones, the quinteffence
Mar′rowbone, *n.* a bone containing marrow, the
Mar′rowfat, *n.* a fine large kind of pea (knee
Mar′rowlefs, *a.* void or deftitute of marrow
Mar′ry, *v.* to join or be joined in marriage, to unite
Marfh, *n.* a fen, bog, fwamp, watery ground
Marfh′al, *v. t.* to range, to rank or put in order
Marfh′al, *n.* an officer of an army, a fheriff
Marfh′aller, *n.* one who ranges in order
Marfh′alfea, *n.* the prifon of a king's marfhal
Marfh′alfhip, *n.* the office or poft of a marfhal
Marfh′mallow, *n.* a kind of plant or herb
Marfh′marigold, *n.* the name of a plant or flower
Marfh′y, *a.* fenny, boggy, fwampy

Mar'fian, a. pertaining to the Marfi, in Germany

Mart, n. a place of public fale, a market; v. t. to buy or fell. (of the weafel kind

Mar'tin, n. a bird of the fwallow kind, an animal

Mar'tial, a. warlike, fuiting war, bold, like iron

Mar'tialift, n. a warrior, fighter, man ufed to arms

Mar'tian, a. pertaining to Campus Martius at Rome

Mart'inet, Mart'let, n. a fmall martin

Mart'ingal, n. a lethern ftrap ufed to curb a horfe

Mart'inmas, n. the feftival or day of St. Martin

Mar'tyr, n. one who dies for the truth, a facrifice

Mar'tyr, v. t. to put to death, murder, kill, flay

Mar'tyrdom, n. the death, honor, &c. of a martyr

Martyrol'ogy, n. a regifter or book of martyrs

Mar'vel, v. i. to wonder; n. a wonder, a flower

Mar'um, n. a plant, penny royal

Mar'vellous, a. wonderful, ftrange, aftonifhing

Mar'velloufly, ad. wonderfully, ftrangely, oddly

Ma'ryland, n. one of the United States

Mafc'uline, a. male, like a man, bold, ftrong

Mafc'ulinely, a. in a mafculine or bold manner

Mafc'ulinenefs, n. mafculine behavior, boldnefs

Mafh, n. falt and water. bran and water, a mefh

Mafh, v. t. to mingle, mix, break, bruife, fqueeze

Mafk, n. a difguife, cover, pretenfe, entertainment

Mafk, v. to difguife, hide, cover, conceal, revel

Mafk'er, n. one who revels in a mafk, a mummer

Mafon, n. one who lays walls of ftone or brick, a member of the fraternity of Freemafons

Mafonry, n. the care of or work done by a mafon, the fcience of Freemafons

Mafon'ic, a. pertaining to mafonry

Maforet'ic, a. pertaining to the Maforites who interpreted the Hebrew fcriptures by traditions, and ufed the vowel points

Mas'querade, n. a mafked affembly, difguife, cover

Mafquerade, v. i. to go or affemble in difguife

Mafquerader, n. a perfon who appears in a mafk

Mafs, v. i. to celebrate or frequent mafs

Mafs, n. a lump, the fervice of the Romifh church

Mafs'acre, v. t. to butcher indifcriminately

Mafs'acre, n. butchery, carnage, murder, havoc

Maffachúfetts, n. one of the United States

Mas'feter, n. a mufcle which raifes the under jaw

Mas'fic, a. pertaining to Mafficus a mountain in Campania in Italy

Mas'ficot, n. an oxyd of lead of a deep yellow

Mafs'inefs, Mafs'ivenefs, n. weight, great bulk

Mafs've, Mafs'y, a. weighty, heavy, bulky, folid

Maffylian, a. pertaining to Maffyla in Africa

Maft, n. the principal fpar in a fhip, erected upon the keel, and fupporting the yards, fails and rigging, the fruit of beech and oak

Maft'ed, a. fitted or furnifhed with a maft

Maft'er, n. the chief in any place or thing

Maft'er, v. t. to conquer, tame, rule, perform

Maft'erdom, n. rule, dominion, power, authority

Maft'erhand, n. a perfon very fkilful in any art

Maft'erjeft, n. the principal or chief jeft

Maft'erkey, n. a key that will open feveral locks

Maft'erleaver, n. a perfon who deferts his mafter

Matt'erlefs, a. having no matter, ungovernable

Maft'erly, a. fkilful, excellent, imperious, proud

Maft'erly, ad. with the fkill of a mafter, cleverly

Matt'erpiece, n. a chief excellence or performance

Maft'erfhip, n. headfhip, fuperiority, fkill, a title

Maft'erftring, n. the principal or chief ftring

Matt'erftroke, n. a capital performance or act

Maft'erteeth, n. pl. the principal or chief teeth

Mas'terwort, n. a plant of feveral kinds

Matt'ery, n. rule, dominion, power, conqueft, fkill

Maft'ful, a. abounding with or having mafts

Matt'icate, v. t. to chew, grind, eat

Maftica'tion, n. the act of chewing or eating

Maft'icatory, a. a medicin to be chewed only

Maft'ic, n. a tree, a refin flowing from the maftic or turpentine tree, ufed in varnifhing, a cement

Maft'iff, n. a very large fierce dog, a tyrant

Matt'lefs, a. not having a maft, bearing no maft

Maft'lin, Mes'lin, Mis'cellane, n. a mixed corn

Mas'toid, a. like a breaft or nipple

Mat, n. fomething made of rufhes, flags or ftraw

Mat, v. t. to cover with mats, to twift together

Mat'achin, n. a very old kind of dance

Mat'adore, n. a term ufed at omber or quadrille

Match, n. a conteft, marriage, what catches fire

Match, v. to pair, couple, marry, fuit, equal

Match'able, a. that may be matched, fuitable

Match'lefs, a. having no equal, incomparable

Match'maker, n. one who makes up matches

Mate, n. a companion, helper, fecond in command

Mate, v. t. to match, equal, marry, fubdue, crofs

Matérial, a. corporeal, effential, important, real

Matérialifm, n. the doctrins of materialifts

Matérialift, n. one who denies fpiritual fubftances

Materiál'ity, n. material or bodily exiftence, body

Matérialize, v. t. to reduce to a ftate of matter

Matérially, ad. in a ftate of matter, effentially

Matérials, n. pl. what any thing is made of, parts

Matériate, a. confifting or compofed of matter

Matériation, n. the act of forming matter

Mater'nal, a. motherly, fond, indulgent, kind

Mater'nity, n. the relation of a mother

Mat'felon, n. a plant, knapweed or hard head

Mathemat'ical, a. relating to the mathematics

Mathemat'ically, ad. according to mathematics

Mathemati''cian, n. one verfed in mathematics

Mathemat'ics, n. pl. the fcience of number and measure

Math'efis, n. the doctrins of mathematics (fure

Mat'in, a. ufed in the morning; n. the morning

Mat'ins, n. pl. morning prayers, early prayers

Mat'rafs, n. a long chymical glafs veffel (ters in

Mátrice, Mátrix n. the womb, a mold to caft letter

Mat'ricide, n. the murder or murderer of a mother

Matric'ulate, v. t. to enter youths in college, to admit

Matric'ulate, n. one who is matriculated (mit

Matriculátion, n. the act of matriculating

Matrimónial, a. nuptial, pertaining to marriage

Matrimónially, ad. by the laws of marriage
Mat'rimony, n. marriage, wedlock, clofe union
Mat'ron, n. a grave and elderly woman, a nurfe
Mat'ronal, a. fuitable to a matron, grave, motherly
Mat'ronly, a. elderly, ancient, careful, kind
Matrofs', n. a common foldier in the artillery
Mat'ter, n. body, materials, a fubject, affair, importance, object, dimenfion, purulent running
Mat'ter, v. to produce matter, fignify, regard
Mat'tery, a. producing matter, corrupt, filthy
Mat'tock, n. a pickax, a tool to grub trees up
Mat'trefs, n. a kind of quilted bed to lie on
Maturátion, n. the act of ripening, fuppuration
Matúrative, a. ripening, digeftion, advancing on
Matúre, a. ripe, full, well digefted , v. t. to ripen
Matúrely, ad. with counfel well digefted, early
Matúrity, n. ripenefs, perfection, underftanding
Mat'weed, n. a fpecies of plant, lygeum
Maud'lin, a. drunk, fuddled, ftupid ; n. a plant
Mau'ger, ad. in open defiance of, notwithftanding
Maul, v. t. to beat in a grofs manner, to bruife
Maul, n. a heavy wooden hammer, a ftick
Maun'der, v. i. to grumble, to murmur, ob.
Maun'dy-Thurs'day, n. Thurfday before Eafter
Maufóleum, n. a pompous monument to the dead
Maw, n. the ventricle of the ftomach, the craw
Maw'kifh, a. unfavory, fickifh, fqueamifh
Maw'kifhnefs, n. a mawkifh quality or ftate, fick-
Maw'mifh, a. foolifh, fimple, idle, naufeous (nefs
Máw-worm, n. a worm that breeds in the ftomach
Max'illary, a. belonging to or like the jawbone
Max'im, n. a general principal or rule, an axiom
Max'imum, n. the greateft ftate or quality
May, an auxiliary verb ; v. t. to go a maying
May, n. the 5th month, the gay part of life, youth
Máyday, n. the firft day of May, a great holiday
Máyflower, n. the name of a very common flower
Máyfly, n. a kind of fly, a kind of infect or bug
Máygame, n. a fport, diverfion, amufement, play
Máying, n. the gathering of flowers on Mayday
Máylily, n. a fweet flower, the lily of the valley
Máyor, n. the chief magiftrate of a corporation
Máyoralty, n. the office, dignity, &c. of a mayor
Máyorefs, n. the wife of a perfon who is mayor
Máypole, n. a long pole to dance round, a tall pole
Maz'agan, n. a fpecies of bean
Máz'ard, n. a part of the face, the jaw, a cherry
Mazarine' or Mazaréne, n. a deep blue, color, paper, difh, tart
Maze, n. a labyrinth, confufion, aftonifhment
Mázy, a. intricate, perplexed, confufed
Me, pron. the objective cafe of I
Méacock, n. an effeminate or uxorious man, ob.
Mead, n. a liquor made from honey, a meadow
Mead'ow or Med'dow, n. a rich grafs-field, low land by rivers or bottom
Méager, a. lean, thin, poor, ftarved
Méagernefs, n. leannefs, thinnefs, poornefs
Meak, n. a kind of hook with a long handle

Meal, n. grain ground to a powder, the food taken at one eating
Meal, v. t. to fprinkle, cover or mix with meal
Méalinefs, n. a mealy ftate or quality, foftnefs
Méalman, n. a perfon who fells or deals in meal
Méaly, a. dufted with meal, foft, pulpy
Méalymouthed, a. unable to fpeak freely, bafhful
Mean, a. low, pitiful, fordid, medial, average
Means, n. medium, method, inftrument, income
Mean, v. t. meant, pret. meant, pa. to intend, defign, have in mind or view
Meand'er, n. a winding place, turn, maze, intricacy
Meand'er, v. i. to wind, turn, run very irregularly
Méaning, n. an intention, defign, purpofe, fenfe
Méanly, ad. without dignity, ungeneroufly, bafely
Méannefs, n. lownefs, pitifulnefs, fordidnefs
Méantime, Méanwhile, ad. in the time paffing between or before
Mcafe, n. the quantity of 500, a manfion-houfe
Méafled, Méafly, a. fpotted with meafles, feabby
Méafles, n. a difeafe in men, fwine and trees
Meas'urable, a. that may be meafured, moderate
Meas'urably, ad. with due meafure, moderately
Meas'ure, n. what gives the quantity of any thing, a cadence in verfe, time in mufic, degree, portion
Meas'ure, Mens'urate, v. t. to compute, allot, take dimenfions, contain in length, &c.
Meas'urelefs, a. immenfe, boundlefs, infinit
Meas'urement, n. a menfuration, the act of meaf-
Meas'urer, n. one who meafures (uring
Meas'ures, n. ways, means, actions, proceedings
Meat, n. flefh to be eaten, food, provifions, fodder
Méated, a. fupplied with meat, fed, foddered
Meathe, n. drink, liquor, any beverage, ob.
Méatoffering, n. an offering that was to be eaten
Mechan'ic, [chas k]n. an artificer, a handicraftfman
Mechan'ical, a. done by mechanics or art
Mechan'ically, ad. in a mechanical manner
Mechani''cian, n. a man who profeffes mechanics
Mechan'ics, n. pl. the fcience or laws of force, or of machinery to apply force
Mech'anifm, n. conftruction of a body or engine
Mecónium, n. juice of poppies, firft excrement
Med'al, n. an extraordinary or ancient coin
Medal'lic, a. pertaining or relating to medals
Medal'lion, n. a large medal or its reprefentation
Med'allift, n. a perfon fkilled in medals
Med'dle, v. i. to interpofe, concern, touch
Med'dler, n. a bufybody in another man's affairs
Med'dlefome, Med'dling, a. officious, bufy
Médial, a. noting a mean or average, alfo one kind of alligation
Médian, a. pertaining to the ancient Media
Médiate, v. to endeavor to reconcile, to limit
Médiate, a. middle, acting as a mean, intervening
Médiately, ad. by a fecondary caufe
Mediátion, n. an interpofition, agency, entreaty
Mediátor, n. an interceffor, kind advifer, manager
Mediatórial, a. of or belonging to a mediator

Mediátorfhip, *n.* the office of a mediator
Mediátrix, *n.* a female mediator or interceffor
Med'ic, *n.* a plant of feveral kinds
Med'icable, *a.* that may be cured or healed
Med'ical, Medi''cinal, *a.* relating to healing
Med'ically, Medi''cinally, *ad.* phyfically (healing
Med'icament, *n.* any thing ufed in medicin or
Medicament'ally, *ad.* after the manner of medicin
Med'icate, *v. t.* to tincture with medicins
Medicéan, *a.* pertaining to the Medici, a noble
family in Italy
Medi''cinable, *a.* having the power of phyfic
Med'icin, *n.* phyfic, a remedy; *v. t.* to phyfic
Medíety, *n.* a mean ftate, half, moiety
Médin, *n.* a fmall old coin, a dry meafure
Medioc'rity, *n.* a middle ftate, moderation
Med'itate, *v. t.* to think, mufe, fcheme, contrive
Meditátion, *n.* contemplation, a feries of thought
Med'itative, *a.* given to meditation, ferious, fad
Mediterránean, *a.* furrounded with land, inland
Médium, *n.* a mean, a middle ftate or place, a kind
of printing paper, average ftate
Med'lar, *n.* the name of a tree or its fruit
Med'ley, *n.* a mixture, mifcellany, hotchpotch
Medul'lary, *a.* pertaining to marrow, pithy, foft
Meed, *n.* a reward, recompenfe, gift, prefent
Meek, *a.* mild, foft, gentle, lowly, humble
Méeken, *v. t.* to make meek, foften, tame, humble
Méekly, *ad.* mildly, foftly, gently, lowly, humbly
Méeknefs, *n.* mildnefs, gentlenefs, eafinefs
Méekfpirited, *a.* meek, mild, gentle, lowly
Méered, *a.* relating to boundaries, limited, fixed
Meet, *v.* met, *pret.* met, *pa.* to come together,
join, unite, face, find, encounter
Meet, *a.* fit, proper, fuitable, becoming
Méeter, *n.* a perfon that meets or accofts another
Méeting, *n.* an affembly, congregation, conflux
Méetinghoufe, *n.* a place of worfhip
Méetly, *ad.* fitly, properly, duly
Méetnefs, *n.* fitnefs, propriety, fuitablenefs
Mégrim, *n.* a painful giddinefs in the head
Méiny, *n.* fervants, a retinue, a family, obf.
Mel'ancholic, Mel'ancholy, [ch as k]*a.* gloomy, dif-
mal, low in fpirits, dejected, calamitous
Mel'ancholy, *n.* a kind of madnefs, gloominefs
Melas'ses, *n.* a fyrup drained from mufcovado fu-
gar, when cooling
Melanúre, *n.* a fmall Mediterranean fifh
Mel'ilot, *n.* a fpecies of plant
Mel'late, *n.* a combination of mellitic acid with an
alkali or earth
Mellit'ic, *a.* pertaining to Melite or honey ftone
Méliorate, *v. t.* to make better, mend, improve, en-
Meliorátion, Melior'ity, *n.* an improvement (rich
Mel'leous, *a.* like honey, fweet
Mellif'erous, *a.* productive of or having honey
Mellificátion, *n.* the act of making honey
Mellif'luent, Mellif'luous, *a.* flowing with honey
Mel'lite, *n.* honey-ftone, mineral of a honey color

Mel'low, *v.* to foften, grow foft, ripen, mature
Mel'low, *a.* foft, full-ripe, nice, merry, drunk
Mel'lownefs, *n.* foftnefs, ripenefs, maturity
Melódious, *a.* harmonious, mufical, very fweet
Melódioufly, *ad.* mufically, harmonioufly, finely
Melódioufnefs, Mel'ody, *n.* fweet mufic, harmony
Mel'odife, *v. t.* to render mufical or harmonious
Mel'on, *n.* the name of a fine delicious fruit
Melt, *v.* melted, *pret.* melted, molten, *pa.* to
make or become liquid, foften, wafte
Melt'er, *n.* one who melts, one who melts metals
Melt'ingly, *ad.* with great feeling or tendernefs
Mem'ber, *n.* a limb, part, head, claufe, one of a body
Mem'berfhip, *n.* the being a member
Membranáceous, *a.* confifting of a membrane
Mem'branate, *a.* flattened like a leaf
Mem'brane, *n.* a web, coat or film of many fibres
Membránous, *a.* confifting of membranes
Mement'o, *n.* a hint to awaken the memory
Memin'na, *n.* a fmall antelope of Ceylon
Mem'oir, *n.* an account of any thing, hint, notice
Mem'orable, *a.* worthy of remembrance, famous
Mem'orably, *ad.* in a memorable manner
Memorand'um, *n.* a note to help the memory
Memórial, *n.* fomething to preferve memory, a to-
ken, a reprefentation of facts, accompanied
with a petition
Memórial, *a.* preferving remembrance, aiding
Memórialift, *n.* one who prefents memorials
Memórialize, *v. t.* to prefent a memorial to
Mem'orize, *v. t.* to commit to memory, to record
Mem'ory, *n.* remembrance, power of recollection
Mem'phian, *a.* pertaining to Memphis, the ancient
capital of Egypt, very dark, a fenfe derived
from the darknefs of Egypt in the days of Mofes
Men, *n. pl.* of man
Men'ace, *v. t.* to threaten, to deter; *n.* a threat
Men'acer, *n.* one who threatens, one who deters
Men'achanite, [ch as k]*n.* a newly difcovered foffil
Menachanit'ic, *a.* pertaining to menachanite
Menáge, *n.* a collection of brute animals
Mend, *v.* to repair, improve, grow better, alter
Menda''city, *n.* falfehood, difpofition to lie
Mend'er, *n.* one who mends, one who improves
Men'dicancy, *n.* beggary, a ftate of begging
Mend'icant, *a.* begging; *n.* a begging friar
Mend'icate, *v. t.* to beg, to afk alms or charity
Mendi''city, *n.* beggary, great want, indigence
Menháden, *n.* a fpecies of fmall fifh
Ménial, *a.* domeftic, low; *n.* a domeftic fervant
Menifc'us, *n.* a lens, concave on one fide and con-
vex on the other
Menol'ogy, *n.* a regifter or account of months
Men'pleafer, *n.* a perfon too fond of pleafing men
Mens'al, *a.* belonging to or done at the table
Mens'trual, *a.* monthly, coming once a month
Mens'truum, *n.* a fubftance which diffolves another
Mens'urable, *a.* meafurable, having limits, finite
Menfurabil'ity, *n.* the capacity of being meafured

Menfurátion, *n.* the act or refult of meafuring
Ment'al, *a.* belonging to the mind, intellectual
Ment'ally, *ad.* in the mind, intellectually, ideally
Men'tion, *n.* an expreffion in words or writing
Men'tion, *v.t.* to exprefs in words or writing
Mentórial, *a.* like Mentor, guiding, counfelling
Mephit'ic, *a.* offenfive, poifonous, noxious
Meph'itifm, Meph'itis, *n.* a noxious quality, or vapor in air, carbonic acid gas
Merc'antant, *n.* a trader, foreign trader, *ob.*
Merc'antile, *a.* trading, commercial, active, bufy
Merc'at, *n.* a market, trade, traffic, *ob.*
Mer'cenarinefs, *n.* a mercenary difpofition
Mer'cenary, *n.* a hireling; *a.* mean, felfifh, greedy
Mer'cer, *n.* one who fells or deals in filks, &c.
Mer'cery, *n.* the trade or goods of a mercer
Mer'chand, Mer'chandize, *v.i.* to trade, to traffick
Mer'chandize, *n.* trade, commerce, wares, goods
Mer'chant, *n.* one who deals in merchandize
Mer'chantable, *a.* fit to be bought or fold
Mer'chantlike, Mer'chantly, *a.* like a merchant
Mer'chantman, *n.* a fhip of trade, trader, merchant
Mer'ciful, *a.* compaffionate, tender, kind, good
Mer'cifully, *ad.* compaffionately, tenderly, kindly
Mer'cifulnefs, *n.* mercy, compaffion, tendernefs
Mer'cilefs, *a.* void of pity, very hardhearted, cruel
Mer'cilefsly, *ad.* in a mercilefs manner, cruelly
Mercúrial, *a.* compofed of quickfilver, fprightly
Mercúrial, *n.* a preparation of quickfilver
Mercúriate, *n.* a combination of the oxyd of mercury, with another fubftance
Mercurificátion, *n.* a mixture with mercury
Merc'ury, *n.* quickfilver, fprightlinefs, a planet
Mer'curic acid, *n.* a faturated combination of mercury and oxygene
Mer'cy, *n.* pity, compaffion, tendernefs, difcretion
Mer'cyfeat, *n.* a table of gold fet over the ark
Mere, *a.* this or that only; *n.* a lake, a boundary
Mérely, *ad.* fimply, fingly, only, folely, barely
Meretri'cious, *a.* lewd, gaudy, falfe
Mergan'fer, *n.* a fpecies of water fowl
Merid'ian, *n.* a line drawn from north to fouth
Merid'ian, Merid'ional, *a.* fouthern, higheft
Merid'ionally, *ad.* in a line with the meridian
Mer'it, *v.t.* to deferve, earn, gain, claim as a right
Mer'it, Meritórioufnefs, *n.* defert, a right, a claim
Meritórious, *a.* deferving of reward or honor, good
Meritórioufly, *ad.* in a deferving manner, juftly
Mer'lin or Mer'ling, *n.* a hawk a fifh [embrafures
Mer'lon, *n.* the part of a parapet between two
Mer'maid, *n.* a fabulous woman, fea-woman, fifh
Mer'man, *n.* a fabulous animal, the fea-man
Mérops, *n.* a bird called bee-eater
Merovin'gian, *a.* noting the family of Merovœus, a race of french kings in the 5th century
Mer'rily, *ad.* cheerfully, jovially, gaily, brifkly
Mer'rimake, *v.i.* to feaft, revel, be jovial, rejoice
Mer'rimac, *n.* a river in N. Hamp. and Maffachufetts
Mer'rymaking, *n.* a meeting for innocent mirth

Mer'riment, Mer'rinefs, *n.* cheerfulnefs, gaity
Mer'ry, *a.* cheerful, laughing, jovial, fuccefsful
Mer'ry-an'drew, *n.* a buffoon, one who plays tricks
Mer'rythought, *n.* a forked bone of a fowl
Mer'fion, *n.* the act of di pping or plunging
Meféems, *v. imp.* fo it appears to me (tery
Mefenter'ic, Meferáic, *a.* relating to the mefen-
Mes'entery, *n.* a membrane which connects the inteftines to the vertebers of the loins
Mefh, *v.t.* to catch or take in a net, to infnare
Mefh, *n.* the fpace between the threads of a net
Mefh'y, *a.* formed of network, reticulated (rye
Mes'lin, *n.* a mixture of grain, chiefly wheat and
Mefs, *n.* a feeding together, portion of food, difh, a number who eat together
Mefs, *v.i.* to join in mefs, to eat or feed together
Mefs'age, *n.* an errand, advice fent, account
Mefs'enger, *n.* one who carries an errand for another
Meffénian, *n.* a native of Meffenia in Greece
Meffi'ah, *n.* the anointed, the CHRIST
Mes'fieurs, *n. pl.* Sirs! Gentlemen! partners
Mefs'mate, *n.* one who eats at the fame table
Mefs'on, *n.* the fecond deity of the American In-
Mefs'uage, *n.* a fmall houfe, any houfe (dians
Meftée, *n.* the offspring of a quadroon by a white man, a perfon of mixed blood
Met, *pret.* and *pa.* of *to meet*
Metacarp'al, *a.* noting the bones and parts of the hand next to the wrift
Métage, *n.* the act of meafuring coals, a meafure
Met'al, *n.* a hard body, gold, filver, &c. courage
Metalep'tic, *a.* acting tranfverfely, tranfverfe
Metal'lic, *a.* pertaining to or confifting of metal
Met'alline, *a.* impregnated with or like metal
Met'allift, *n.* a worker, or one fkilled in metals
Metalizátion, *n.* the forming of metals
Metal'lurgift, *n.* one fkilled in the refining of metals
Metal'liform, *a.* in the form of metal
Met'allize, *v.t.* to form into a metal
Metallog'raphy, *n.* a defcription of metals
Metal'lurgy, *n.* the art of working upon metals
Metallur'gic, *a.* pertaining to the working of metals
Metamorph'ic, *a.* transforming, changing forms
Metamor'phofe, *v.t.* to transform, change, alter
Metamor'phofis, *n.* a transformation, a change
Met'aphor, *n.* a change from natural to figurative
Metaphor'ical, *a.* not literal, figurative, typical
Metaphor'ically, *ad.* in a figurative manner
Met'aphrafe, *n.* a verbal or literal tranflation
Metaphys'ical, *a.* of or relating to metaphyfics
Metaphys'ically, *ad.* according to metaphyfics
Metaphyfi'cian, *n.* one verfed in metaphyfics
Metaphys'ics, *n.* the fcience of immaterial beings
Metas'tafis, *n.* a tranflation or removal of place
Metatars'al, *a.* noting the bones of the foot next to the ankle
Metath'efis, *n.* a tranfpofition, removal, change
Mete, *v.* to meafure, take meafure, allot, dream
Metemfychófis, [ch as k] *n.* a tranfmigration of fouls

Méteor, *n.* a tranfient luminous appearance or fire ball, any phenomenon in the air

Meteor'ic, *a.* pertaining to meteors

Meteorolo'gical, *a.* relating to meteors, fiery

Meteorol'ogy, *n.* the doctrins of meteors (porous

Méteorous, *a.* having the nature of a meteor, va-

Méter, *n.* a perfon appointed to mete, a meafurer

Méter, *n.* the cadence or meafure of verfes, verfe

Métewand, Méteyard, *n.* a rod to meafure with

Metheg'lin, *n.* a drink made of honey and water

Methinks', *v. imp.* I think, it feems or appears

Meth'od, *n.* order, regularity, rule, manner

Method'ical, *a.* ranged in order, regular, exact

Method'ically, *ad.* according to order, exactly

Meth'odife, *v. t.* to difpofe in order, to regulate

Meth'odifm, *n.* the doctrins and worfhip of a de-nomination of chriftians, fo called from their ftrictnefs of life and principles

Meth'odift, *n.* an obferver of method, an adherent to methodifm

Methodift'ic, *a.* like or in the manner of methodifts

Methought', *pret.* of *methinks,* I thought

Meton'ic cycle, the cycle of the moon or 19 years

Metonym'ical, *a.* ufed by way of metonymy

Met'onymy, *n.* the putting of one word for another

Metópe, *n.* a fpace between the tryglyphs of the doric frieze

Met'rical, *a.* pertaining to meter, poetical, fweet

Métrice, *n.* a mufical meafure of fyllables, poetry

Metrop'olis, *n.* the chief city of a country

Metropol'itan, *n.* an archbifhop

Metropol'itan, *a.* belonging to a metropolis

Met'tle, *n.* fpirit, courage, fire, vivacity, livelinefs

Met'tled, *a.* fpirited, courageous, bold, fprightly

Met'tlefome, *a.* fpirited, lively, gay, brifk, airy

Mew, *n.* a cage, coop, inclofure, feafowl

Mew, *v.* to fhut up, molt, caft horns, cry as a cat

Mewl, *v. i.* to fquall or cry as a young child

Mex'ican, *n.* a native of Mexico; *a.* pertaining to it

Mezzotint'o, *n.* a kind of engraving upon copper

Míafm or Mias'ma, *n.* noxious effluvia

Miafmat'ic, *a.* pertaining to noxious effluvia

Míca, *n.* an argillaceous earth, in fhining, thin plates, called alfo glimmer and talck

Micáceous, *a.* like or pertaining to Mica

Micarell', *n.* a fpecies of argillaceous earth

Mice, *n. pl.* of *moufe*

Mich'aelmas, [ch as k]*n.* the feaft day of St. Michael

Miche, *v. i.* to lie hid, hang back, *ob.*

Mich'er, *n.* a very lazy perfon, *ob.*

Mic"kle, *a.* much, great; *n.* a great deal

Míco, *n.* a beautiful fpecies of monkey

Mícrocofm, *n.* the little world, a title of man, man

Microcos'mic falt, the acid of urine or phofphorus

Microg'raphy, *n.* the defcription of objects vifible by a microfcope or telefcope only

Microm'eter, *n.* an inftrument to meafure the mag-nitudes of objects viewed thro' telefcopes and microfcopes.

Mícrophone, Microcous'tic, *n.* an inftrument to increafe fmall founds

Microfcope, *n.* a magnifying optical inftrument

Microfcop'ic, *a.* like a microfcope, magnifying, ve-ry fmall, vifible by the microfcope only

Mid, Mid'dle, Midft, *a.* between two, equally diftant

Mid'courfe, Mid'way, *n.* the middle of the way, half-

Mid'day, *n.* the middle time of the day, noon (way

Mid'dle, Midft, *n.* the middle part, way or time

Mid'dleaged, *a.* being about the middle of life

Mid'dlemoft, Mid'moft, *a.* neareft the middle

Mid'dling, *a.* being of a middle rank, moderate

Mid'heaven, *n.* the middle point of the fky

Mid'land, *a.* fituated in the middle of the land

Mid'leg, *n.* the middle or thick part of the leg

Mid'night, *n.* the middle part or depth of night

Mid'rib, *n.* the main nerve or rib of a leaf

Mid'riff, *n.* what feparates the heart from the body

Mid'fea, *n.* middle of the fea, the Mediterranean

Mid'fhips, *n.* the middle of a fhip, with regard to length or bredth

Mid'fhipman, *n.* an officer on board a man of war

Mid'ftream, *n.* the middle part of a ftream

Mid'fummer, *n.* the fummer-folftice, the longeft

Mid'way, *ad.* in the middle of a paffage (day

Mid'wife, *n.* one who delivers women with child

Mid'wifery, *n.* the art or act of delivering women

Mid'winter, *n.* the winter-folftice, the fhorteft day

Mien, *n.* an air, look, countenance, manner

Miff, *n.* a flight refentment, peevifhnefs

Miff, *v. t.* to affront, to excite flight anger

Might, *pret.* of *may;* power, ftrength, force

Mightily, *ad.* powerfully, ftrongly, vigoroufly

Mightinefs, *n.* power, greatnefs, height of dignity

Mighty, *a.* powerful, ftrong, excellent; *ad.* very

Migonet', *n.* a fpecies of plant

Mígrate, *v. t.* to change place, to remove

Migrátion, *n.* the act of changing place, a removal

Migratory, *a.* roving, wandering, going about

Milanéfe, *n.* the territory of Milan or its inhabitants

Milch, *a.* giving milk, fupplying with milk

Mild, *a.* kind, gentle, calm, foft, mellow, fweet

Mil'dew, *n.* a difeafe in plants, filk, cloth and paper

Mil'dew, *v. t.* to taint with mildew

Mildly, *ad.* kindly, gently, tenderly, foftly, eafily

Mildnefs, *n.* gentlenefs, foftnefs, mellownefs

Mile, *n.* a land meafure or fpace of 1760 yards

Mileage, *n.* fees paid for travel by the mile

Miléfian, *n.* a native of Miletus, formerly the capi-tal of Ionia, in Afia

Mileftone, *n.* a ftone to mark miles on

Mil'foil, *n.* an herb that has many leaves, yarrow

Mil'iary, *a.* like millet, very fmall, numberlefs

Mil'itant, *a.* fighting, engaged in warfare

Mil'itary, *a.* warlike, fuiting a foldier; *n.* the foldiery

Mil'itate, *v. i.* to war, fight, oppofe, contradict

Mili'tia, Mil'ice, *n.* a national force, trainbands

Milk, *n.* a liquid drawn from the teats of females

Milk, *v. t.* to draw milk from a cow, &c. to fuck

Milk'en, a. confifting of milk; n. a houfebreaker
Milk'er, n. one that draws milk from cows, &c.
Milk'inefs, n. foftnefs like that of milk, meeknefs
Milk'livered, a. cowardly, fainthearted
Milk'maid, n. a woman employed in a dairy
Milk'man, n. a man that fells or carries about milk
Milk'pail, n. a veffel ufed to contain or carry milk
Milk'pan, n. a veffel to hold milk in a dairy
Milkpot'tage, n. milk, water, and meal boiled
Milk'fcore, n. a fcored account of milk owed for
Milk'fop, n. an effeminate fribbling man, a fop
Milk'tooth, n. a tooth of a foal 3 months old
Milk'white, a. white as milk, exceeding white
Milk'woman, n. a woman who fells milk about
Milk'wort, n. a plant, fpurge
Milk'y, a. made of, yielding or like milk
Milkywáy, n. a broad white track in the heavens
Mill, n. an engine to grind or cut with, a nominal
    coin of the United States, value the tenth part
    of a cent and the thoufandth of a dollar
Mill, v. t. to grind, beat up, ftamp coin, fteal
Mill'cog, n. the tooth of a wheel ufed for a mill
Mill'dam, n. a dam to keep water for a mill
Millenárian, n. one who holds to the millennium
Mill'enary, a. confifting of or having a thoufand
Millen'ial, a. relating to the millenium or a thoufand
Millen'nium, n. Chrift's reign of a thoufand years
Mill'eped, n. an infect of many feet, a wood loufe
Mill'er, n. one who attends a mill, a fly
Milles'imal, a. a thoufandth, having a thoufand
Mill'et, n. a kind of fifh, a kind of plant
Mill'horfe, n. a horfe that turns or works a mill
Mill'iner, n. one who makes women's caps, &c.
Mill'inery, n. goods that are fold by a millener
Mill'ing, n. a ftamping or polifhing in a mill
Mill'ion, n. the number of 1,000,000, a large fum
Mill'ionth, a. the ten hundred thoufandth
Mill'moth, n. an infect fomewhat like a beetle
Mill'pond, n. a bed of water kept above a mill
Mill'race, n. a canal to convey water to or from a
    mill or the current of water
Mill'ftone, n. a heavy ftone to grind corn with
Mill'teeth, n. pl. very large teeth, the grinders
Milréa or Milrée, n. a Portugal coin, value 124 cents
Milt, n. the fpleen, the fperm of a fifh, a coin
Mime, Mímer, n. a mimic, buffoon, imitator
Mime, Mim'ic, v. t. to ape, imitate, ridicule
Mim'ic, n. one who ludicroufly imitates another
Mim'ic, Mim'ical, a. acting the mimic, imitating
Mim'icry, n. a burlefque imitation, buffoonery
Mi'na, n. a denomination of money in Greece, equal
    to about 18 dollars
Minácious, Min'atory, a. threatening, harfh
Min'aret, n. a fmall fpire or fteeple
Mince, v. to cut very fmall, clip, leffen, palliate
Mince, n. meat cut fmall and heated, a hafh
Min'cingly, ad. in fmall parts, not fully, darkly
Mind, n. intelligent power, opinion, inclination
Mind, v. to mark, heed, regard, attend, incline

Minded, pa. a. regarded, difpofed, inclined, ready
Mindful, a. regardful, obfervant, attentive
Mindlefs, a. regardlefs, inattentive, carelefs
Mindftruck, a. moved or affected in mind
Mine, pron. belonging to me only
Mine, n. a place where minerals are dug, a hole dug
Mine, v. to dig mines, fap, ruin, deftroy flowly
Minedigger, Miner, n. a perfon who digs mines
Min'eral, n. any fubftance dug from mines, a foffil
Min'eral, a. confifting of or like foffil bodies
Min'eralift, n. one who is fkilled in minerals
Min'eralize, v. t. to combine with a mineral in ore
Mineralizátion, n. the procefs of forming an ore by
    a combination of minerals   (metal in ore
Min'eralizer, n. a fubftance which unites with a
Mineral'ogy, n. a treatife on minerals or mines
Mineralo''gic, a. pertaining to mineralogy
Mineral'ogift, n. one who difcribes minerals
Min''gle, v. t. to mix, blend, compound, join, unite
Min''gle, n. a mixture, confufed mafs, medley
Min'iature, n. a reprefentation in a fmall compafs
Min'ikin, a. fmall, diminutive; n. a very fmall pin
Min'im, n. a dwarf, fmall being, note, letter
Min'ion, n. a woman's favorite, a dependent
Min'ious, a. like or refembling redlead
Min'ifh, v. t. to make lefs, impair, ob.
Min'ifter, n. a high officer, clergyman, agent, aider
Min'ifter, v. to give, fupply, yield, attend, ferve
Min'iftrefs, n. a female who difpenfes
Minifté'rial, a. relating to a minifter of church or
Min'iftery, n. an office, charge, fervice   (ftate
Min'iftrant, a. attendant, acting at command
Miniftrá'tion, n. an office, function, agency, act
Min'iftry, n. office, charge, fervice, agency
Min'ium, n. the red oxyd of lead
Mink, n. a fmall quadruped, valued for its fur
Min'now or Men'now, n. a very fmall fifh
Minor, a. lefs, fmall, petty, inconfiderable
Minor, n. one under age, the fecond propofition, a
    beautiful bird of the Eaft Indies
Minor'ity, n. the being under age, a lefs number
Minotaur, n. a fabled monfter, half man, half bull
Mins'ter, n. a cathedral church, monaftery, fociety
Mins'trel, n. an ancient wandering mufician
Mins'trelfey, n. mufic, a company of minftrels
Mint, v. t. to coin, ftamp money, invent, forge
Mint, n. a fweet plant, a place for coining in
Mint'age, n. duty paid for coining, what is coined
Mint'er, Mint'man, n. a coiner, a man who coins
Mint'mafter, n. one who prefides over the coinage
Min'uet, n. a graceful and regular dance
Min'ute, n. 60th part of an hour, a fhort abftract
Min'ute, v. t. to fet down in fhort lines, to note
Minúte, a. fmall, little, trifling, exact, nice
Min'utebook, n. a book to note fhort hints in
Min'utegun, n. a gun that is fired every minute
Min'utely, a. done every minute, fhort
Minútely, ad. to a fmall point, exactly, nicely
Minútenefs, n. fmallnefs, exactnefs, carefulnefs

Minx, *n.* a pert wanton girl, a fhe puppy

Mi'ny, *a.* abounding with mines

Mir'acle, *n.* fome act or event that is beyond the ordinary laws of nature

Mirac'ulous, *a.* fupernatural, wonderful

Mirac'uloufly, *ad,* by miracle, wonderfully

Mirac'uloufnefs, *n.* a miraculous quality or ftate

Mirador, *n.* a balcony, a finall projecting gallery

Mire, *v. t.* to foil with mire, to fix in mud

Mire, *n.* mud, wet dirt, filth, an ant, a pifmire

Mir'ror, *n.* a lookingglafs, a pattern

Mir'rorftone, *n.* a kind of tranfparent ftone

Mirth, *n.* merriment, gaiety, laughter, jollity

Mirth'ful, *a.* merry, gay, cheerful, pleafant, noify

Miry, *a.* full of mire, deep in mud, muddy, dirty

Mis prefixed to words denotes *error* or *wrong*

Mifacceptation, *n.* a taking in a wrong fenfe, a mif-

Mifadvent'ure, *n.* a mifchance, manflaughter [take

Mifadvent'ured, *a.* unfortunate, unlucky, crofs

Mifadvife, *v. t.* to give wrong or bad advice

Mifadvifed, *part.* advifed amifs, ill-directed

Mifaimed, *a.* not duly aimed, not directed right

Mifalliance, *n.* an unnatural alliance or union

Mis'anthrope, *n.* a hater of mankind in general

Mifanth'ropy, *n.* a general averfion to mankind

Mifapplication, *n.* an applying to wrong purpofes

Mifapply', *v. t.* to apply to wrong or bad purpofes

Mifapprehend', *v. t.* not to underfland, to miftake

Mifapprehen'fion, *n.* mifconception, miftake

Mifarrange', *v. t.* to place in a wrong order

Mifarrange ment, *n.* a wrong order

Mifafcribe, *v. t.* to afcribe falfely or wrong

Mifafsign, *v. t.* to affign erroneoufly, or falfely

Mifbecome', *v. i.* mifbecame, *pret.* mifbecome, *pa.* not to come, not to fuit or fit

Mifbegot'ten, *a.* that is unlawfully begotten

Mifbehave, *v. t.* to behave improperly or badly

Mifbehavior, *n.* bad or ill conduct, bad practice

Mifbelief, *n.* a falfe belief, wrong faith, diftruft

Mifbeliever, *n.* one who holds a falfe religion

Mifcall', *v. t.* to call wrong, to name improperly

Mifcalc'ulate, *v. t.* to reckon wrong, to mifcount

Mifcar'riage, *n.* an abortion, failure, defeat, fault

Mifcar'ry, *v. i.* to have an abortion, fail, mifs, err

Mifcaft' *v. t.* mifcaft, *pret.* mifcaft, *pa.* to take a wrong or falfe account, to mifreckon

Mifcellanarian, *n.* a writer of mifcellany

Mifcellanarian, *a.* pertaining to mifcellany

Mifcellaneous, *a.* mixed, formed of various kinds

Mifcellaneoufly, *ad.* in a mixed manner

Mis'cellany, *n.* a collection of various things

Mifchance', *n.* ill fortune, mifhap, misfortune

Mifcharge', *n.* a miftake in charging

Mifcharge', *v. t.* to make a miftake in an entry

Mis'chief, *n.* harm, hurt, difturbance; *v. t.* to hurt

Mis'chiefmaker, *n.* one who makes mifchief

Mis'chievous, *a.* hurtful, deftructive, malicious

Mis'chievoufly, *ad.* hurtfully, wickedly, vilely

Mis'chievoufnefs, *n.* wickednefs, malicioufnefs

Mis'cible, *a.* that can be mixed together

Mifcitation, *n.* a falfe or improper quotation

Mifclaim, *n.* a miftaken or improper claim

Mifconcep'tion, *n.* a falfe opinion, a wrong notion

Mifcon'duct, *n.* bad management, ill behavior

Mifconftruc'tion, *n.* a wrong or bad interpretation

Mifcons'true, *v. t.* to interpret wrong or badly

Mifcount', *v. t.* to count or wreckon wrong

Mis'creance, *n.* unbelief, falfe faith, wickednefs

Mis'creant, *n.* an unbeliever, a bafe vile wretch

Mifcreate, *v. t.* to form badly or unnaturally

Mifdeed, *n.* an evil action, crime, fault, offenfe

Mifdeem, *v. t.* to judge ill or amifs, to miftake

Mifdeemful, *a.* thinking ill of, fufpecting

Mifdemean, *v. i.* to behave ill, act amifs, offend

Mifdemeanor, *n.* a petty offenfe, ill behavior

Mifdevotion, *n.* miftaken devotion, falfe piety

Mifdirect', *v. t.* to direct wrong or improperly

Mifdiftin"guifh, *v. t.* to diftinguifh wrong, to err

Mifdo, *v.* mifdid, *pret.* mifdone, *pa.* to do or act wrong, to commit a fault

Mifdoer, *n.* one who acts amifs, an offender

Mifdoubt', *v. t.* to fufpect; *n.* fufpicion, hefitation

Mifemploy', *v. t.* to ufe to wrong or bad purpofes

Mifemploy'ment, *n.* an improper application or ufe

Mifen'try, *n.* an erroneous entry or charge

Mifer, *n.* one who is covetous to excefs, a wretch

Mis'erable, *a.* unhappy, wretched, ftingy, mean

Mis'erably, *ad.* unhappily, wretchedly, meanly

Mis'ery, *n.* wretchednefs, misfortune, ftinginefs

Misfafh'ion, *v. t.* to make wrong, to fhape amifs

Misform', *v. t.* to form badly or amifs, to deform

Misfor'tune, *n.* calamity, bad luck, a bad event

Misgive', *v. i.* misgave, *pret.* misgiven, *pa.* to fill with doubt, fail, give way

Misgov'ernment, *n.* an ill adminiftration of affairs

Misguidance, *n.* a falfe guidance, a bad direction

Misguide, *v. t.* to direct ill, lead wrong, deceive

Mis'gum or Mis'gurn, *n.* an anguilliform fifh

Mifh'na, *n.* a digeft of Jewifh traditions

Mifh'nic, *a.* relating to the mifhna

Mifhap', *n.* an ill chance, crofs event, calamity

Mifimprove', *v. t.* to ufe to a bad purpofe

Mifimprove'ment, *n.* ill or wrong ufe

Mifinfer', *v. t.* to infer wrong, to err or miftake

Mifinform', *v. t.* to deceive with falfe accounts

Mifinformation, *n.* falfe intelligence, deception

Mifinterp'ret, *v. i.* to interpret in a wrong fenfe

Misjoin, *v. t.* to join unfitly, or improperly

Misjudge', *v. t.* to judge wrong or amifs

Miflay, *v. t.* miflaid, *pret.* miflaid, *pa.* to lay in a wrong or improper place, to lofe

Miflayer, *n.* one who puts in a wrong place

Mif'le, *v. i.* to rain or fall in very fmall drops

Miflead, *v. t.* miflead, *pret.* mifled, *pa.* to lead into error, guide wrong, deceive

Mifleader, *n.* one who mifleads or leads to ill

Miflike, *v. t.* to diflike, difapprove of, condemn

Miflike, *n.* diflike, diftafte, difapprobation

Miſliker, n. one who diſlikes or diſapproves
Mis'ly, a. raining in very ſmall drops, foggy
Miſman'age, v. t. to manage badly, to do wrong
Miſman'agement, n. bad management or conduct
Miſmark', v. t. to mark wrong or improperly
Miſmatch', v. t. to match badly or unſuitably
Miſname, v. t. to call by a wrong name
Miſnomer, n. the miſtake of a name in law proceed-
Miſobſerve', v. t. not to obſerve accurately (ings
Miſor'der, v. t. to conduct ill; n. diſorder
Miſor'derly a. diſorderly, irregular
Miſpend', v. t. miſpent, pret. miſpent, pa. to ſpend
amiſs, waſte, laviſh away
Miſpend'er, n. a prodigal, waſter, laviſh perſon
Miſpenſe, n. the act of ſpending improperly
Miſperſuaſion, n. a wrong notion, a falſe opinion
Miſplace, v. t. to place wrong, miſlay, miſapply
Miſpoint', v. t. to point or divide wrong
Miſprint', v. t. to print wrong or erroneouſly
Miſprint', n. an error in printing
Miſpriſe, v. t. to deſpiſe, ſlight, miſtake, ob.
Miſpri''ſion, n. a contempt, miſtake, overſight
Miſproud, a. uncommonly proud, ob.
Miſquote, v. t. to quote falſely or wrong
Miſrecital, n. an erroneous recital
Miſrecite, v. t. to repeat or relate wrong
Miſreck'on, v. t. to reckon or compute wrong
Miſrelate, v. t. to relate wrong or inaccurately
Miſrelation, n. a falſe or inaccurate account
Miſremem'ber, v. t. not to remember right, to err
Miſreport, v. t. to give a falſe or bad account of
Miſreport, n. a falſe report, falſe account, ſtory
Miſrepreſent', v. t. to repreſent not as a thing is
Miſrepreſentation, n. a wrong repreſentation
Miſrule, n. confuſion, tumult, diſorder, noiſe
Miſs, n. a young or unmarried woman, miſtake, loſs
Miſs, v. not to hit, to eſcape, fail, omit, want
Miſs'al, n. a Romiſh prayer-book, a maſs-book
Miſſay, v. t. miſſaid, pret. miſſaid, pa. to ſay ill or
badly, ſay wrong, blunder
Miſs'engroſs, n. a trifling Saxon or German coin
Miſſerve', v. t. to ſerve unfaithfully or badly
Miſſhape, v. t. misſhaped, pret. misſhaped, mis-
ſhapen, pa. to ſhape or form ill, deform, ſpoil
Miſs'ile, a. that may be thrown by the hand
Miſs'ile, n. a mixture of different colors, a dart
Mis''ſion, n. a ſending, legation, commiſſion
Mis'ſionary, n. a perſon ſent to propagate religion
Miſſiſſip'pi, n. the ſire of rivers, the great river
which bounds the U. States weſtward
Miſs'ive, a. ſuch as may be ſent, thrown or ſhot
Miſs'ive, n. a meſſenger ſent, letter ſent, gift
Miſs'letoe, n. a plant which grows on another
tree and derives ſupport from it
Miſſpeak, v. t. miſſpake, miſſpoke, pret. miſſpo-
ken, miſpoke, pa. to ſpeak wrong or amiſs
Miſt, n. a low thin cloud, fine rain, fog, dimneſs
Miſt, v. t. to cloud, to rain in fine drops
Miſtakable, a. that is or may be miſtaken

Miſtake, n. a miſconception, unintentional error
Miſtake, v. miſtook, pret. miſtaken, pa. to con-
ceive wrong, to err in judgement
Miſtaken, a. when uſed of a perſon denotes wrong,
erroneous; when uſed of a thing, miſconceived
Miſtakenly, ad. by miſtake, erroneouſly
Misſtate, v. t. to ſtate wrong or erroneouſly
Miss âtement, n. an erroneous ſtatement
Miſteach, v. t. miſtaught, pret. miſtaught, pa. to
teach wrong or amiſs, to teach badly
Miſtell', v. t. miſtold, pret. miſtold, pa. to relate
wrong or imperfectly
Miſtemper, v. t. to temper ill, diſtemper, hurt
Mis'ter, n. the common title of addreſs to a man,
corrupted from maſter
Miſterm', v. t. to term wrong, to name erroneouſly
Miſthink', v. t. misthought, pret. misthought, pa-
to think wrong, to think ill of
Misthought', n. a wrong thought, a bad opinion
Miſtime, v. t. not to time right, to time badly
Miſt'ineſs, n. a falling of fine rain, dimneſs, miſt
Miſt'reſs, n. a woman who governs, a concubine
Miſtruſt', n. ſuſpicion, diffidence; v. t. to ſuſpect,
Miſtruſt'ful, a. ſuſpicious, diffident (to doubt
Miſtruſt'fulneſs, n. ſuſpicion, doubt, diffidence
Miſtruſt'leſs, a. confident, unſuſpecting, artleſs
Miſt'y, a. rainy in fine drops, dull, damp, moiſt
Misunderſtand', v. t. misunderſtood, pret. miſun-
derſtood, pa. to misconceive, to miſtake
Misunderſtanding, n. a diſagreement, an error
Miſuſage, Miſuſe, n. ill or bad treatment, abuſe
Miſuſe, v. t. to uſe badly or improperly, to abuſe
Miſuſer, n. an ill uſe, abuſe, wrong application
Mis'y, n. yellow ſulphate of iron (coin
Mite, n. a very ſmall inſect, ſmall thing, particle,
Mith'ridate, n. a medicine good againſt poiſon
Mithridat'ic, a. pertaining to Mithridates king
Mit'igate, v. t. to alleviate, leſſen, eaſe, (of Pontus
Mitigation, n. alleviation, diminution
Miter, n. a biſhop's cap, a term in joinery
Mitered, a. adorned with a miter, cut at 45 degrees
Mit'tens, n. pl. gloves without fingers
Mit'tent, a. ſending forth, emitting, diſcharging
Mit'timus, n. a warrant of commitment to jail
Mitu, n. a Brazilian bird of the turky kind
Mity, a. having or abounding with mites, rotten
Mix, v. t. to mingle, make, form, join, unite
Mix'tion, Mix'ture, n. the act of mixing, things
mixed (ers curved
Mixtilin'ear, a. mixture of lines, ſome ſtrait, oth-
Miz'maze, n. a maze, labyrinth, confuſion
Miz'en, n. the maſt in the ſtern of a ſhip
Miz'zy, n. a bog, quagmire, ſwamp
Moan, v. i. to grieve, to lament, n. a lamentation
Moat, n. a canal or ditch made round a caſtle, &c.
Moat, v. t. to ſurround or ſecure with a moat
Mob, n. a woman's cap, crowd, populace, noiſe
Mob, v. t. to ſcold, haraſs, riot, overbear, preſs
Mob'biſh, v. mean, low, vulgar, noiſy, loud

S

Mobile, n. a mob, rout. fphere, caufe of motion
Mobility, n. the populace, activity, inconfiftency
Moc'cafon or Mog'gafon, n. a fhoe of foft lether without a fole, ornamente lround the ankle
Móchottone, [ch as k] n. a'gray ftone with figures of mofs, fhrubs and branches
Mock, v. t. to deride, mimic, tantalize, deceive
Mock, a. falfe, counterfeit ; n. a ridicule, a jeft
Mock'able, a. expofed to derifion, ridiculous
Mock'er, n. one who mocks, one who derides
Mock'ery, n. derifion, ridicule, fport, vain fhow
Mock'ingly, ad. in the way of mockery or infult
Mock'ingftock, n. a butt chofen for merriment
Módal, a. relating to the mode or form, formal
Modal ity, n. a modal or accidental difference
Mode, n. a form, fafhion, way, ftate, appearance
Mod'el, n. a copy, pattern, reprefentation, mold
Mod'el, v. t. to fafhion, fhape, mold, delineate
Mod'eller, n. a former, defigner, contriver
Mod'erate, a. temperate, fober, mild, reafonable
Mod'erate, v. t. to regulate, govern, allay, calm
Mod'erately, ad. temperately, mildly, reafonably
Modera'ion, n. a forbearance of extremity, care
Moderátor, n. one who reftrains, rules or prefides
Mod'ern, a. late, recent, new, common, mean
Mod'ernize, v. t. to reduce ancient to modern
Mod'ernifm, n. a deviation from ancient cuftom
Mod'erns, n. pl. people of late or prefent times
Mod'eft, a. chafte, diffident, humble, moderate
Mod'eftly, ad. with modefty, chaftely, diffidently
Mod'efty, n. chaftity, diffidence, humility
Mod'eftypiece, n. lace, &c. worn over the bofom
Mod'icum, n. a fmall portion of fhare, a pittance
Med'ifiable, a. that may be modified or formed
Modifica'tion, n. the act of modifying or fhaping
Mod'ify, v. t. to fhape, change the form, foften
Modil'lion or Modil'ion, n. a kind of bracket
Módifh, a. fafhionable, tafty, fine, flafhy, airy, gay
Módifhly, ad. in a modifh manner, fafhionably
Módifhnefs, n. an affectation of the fafhion
Mod'ulate, v. t. to form founds to a key or note
Modulátion, n. agreeable harmony, proportion
Mod'ulator, n. one who forms founds to fome key
Mod'ule, n. a model, reprefentation, meafure taken at pleafure for proportioning columns
Módus, n. a fixed fum paid in lieu of tithes
Mogu', n. the emperor of India, a hord, a clan
Móhair, n. a thread or ftuff made of goat's hair
Moham'medan, n. a follower of Mohammed
Moham'medan, a. belonging to Mahammed
Móhawk, n. a barbarous Indian, favage, ruffian
Moid'ered, a. crazy, bewildered, puzzled, loft
Móidore, n. a Portugal gold coin in value 6 dollars
Mo'ety, n. the half, the one of two equal parts
Moil, v. to toil, drudge, labor, daub, fprinkle
Moift, a. wet in a fmall degree, damp, foft, juicy
Moift'en, v. t. to wet in a fmall degree, to damp
Moift'nefs, n. a trifling wetnefs, a dampnefs
Moift'ure, n. juice, juicinefs, dampnefs

Molaffes, fee melaffes
Mold, n. a white downy fubftance contracted in moift places which the microfcope fhows to be vegetable, alfo fine earth, a form or hallow to give fhape
Mold, v. to model, fhape, knead, contract mold
Móldinefs, n. a moldy condition
Mó'ding, n. a mold, a projection in building and (on guns
Mólder, n. he who gives fhape
Mólder, v. to decay, perifh, turn to duft
Móldy, a. covered with or containing mold
Mole, n. a natural fpot, mound, pier, lump, animal
Mólecaft, Mólehill, n. a hilloc made by a mole
Mólecatcher, n. one who is ufed to catch moles
Mólecule, n. a very minute particle
Móleeyed, a. without eyes, blind
Moleft', v. t. to difturb, trouble, difquiet, plague
Moleftátion, n. difturbance, interruption
Moleft'er, n. one who molefts, one who difturbs
Móletrack, n. the courfe of a mole under ground
Mólewarp, Mó'dwarp, n. an animal, a mole
Mol'lient, a. foftening, affuaging, leffening
Mol'lifiable, a. that may be foftened or eafed
Mollification, n. the act of foftening, mitigation
Mol'lifier, n. what foftens, mitigates or pacifies
Mol'lify, v. t. to foften, affuage, appeafe, quiet
Molt, v. to caft or fhed fethers
Molt'en, melted, obfolete participle of melt
Móly, n. a kind of wild rue or wild garlic (a bafe
Molyb'date, n. a falt formed by molybdic acid with
Molyb'den or Molyb'denite, n. a metal of a whitifh yellow color
Molyb'denous, Molyb'denic acid, a faturated combination of molybden and oxygene (acid
Molyb'denated, a. combined with molybdenous
Mome, n. a dull ftupid perfon, dunce, drone, ob.
Móment, n. a part of time, importance, weight
Mómently, ad. only for or in a moment,
Mómentary, a. lafting a moment
Moment'ous, a. important, weighty, valuable
Mom'mery, n. a farcical entertainment, a mafk
Mon'achal, [ch as k] a. monaftic, monkifh, fevere,
Mon'achifm, n. a monaftic life, ftate or condition
Mon'ad, n. an indivifible thing, unity
Monan'dria, n. a clafs of plants with hermaphrodite flowers with one ftamen (united ftamens
Monadel'phia, n. a clafs of plants with one fet of
Mon'arch, [ch as k] n. a fovereign, king, prince
Mon'archal, Monarch'ial, a. fuiting a monarch,
Monarch'ical, a. vefted in a fingle ruler (regal
Mon'archife, v. i. to play the king, rule, ob.
Mon'archy, n. a government by one, a kingdom
Mon'aftery, n. a religious houfe, a convent
Monaft'ic, a. belonging to a monk or convent
Monaft'ically, ad. reclufely, retiredly, rigidly
Mon'day, [o as u] n. the fecond day of the week
Monécia, n. a clafs of plants which have feparate male and female flowers on the fame plant, as maiz (cafa

Mo"ney, [munny]*n.* metal coined for public ufe,

Mo"neybag, *n.* a bag ufed for money, large purfe

Mo"neychanger, *n.* a broker in money, a banker

Mo"neyed, *a.* rich in money, rich, wealthy

Mo"neyer, *n.* a coiner of or dealer in money

Mo"neylefs, *a.* wanting money, pennylefs, poor

Mo"neymatter, *n.* a matter relating to money

Mo"neyfcrivener, *n.* a raifer of money for others

Mo"neyworth, *n.* a full value a thing valuable

Mon"ger, [o as u] *n.* a dealer, trader, feller, fifh-

Mongoos' *n.* the woolly macauco   (ing-boat

Mon"grel, [o as u] *n.* an animal of a mixed breed

Mon"grel, *a.* that is of a mixed breed, doubtful

Mon'iment, *n.* an infcription, hint, *ob.*

Mon'ifh, *v. t.* to admonifh, advife, caution, *ob.*

Mon'ifher, *n.* one who admonifhes or cautions, *ob.*

Moni"tion, *n.* warning, information, inftruction

Mon'itor, *n.* one who warns others of faults, informs of duty, or gives ufeful hints (warning

Mon'itory, *a.* giving admonition or inftruction,

Mon'itory, *n.* an admonition, caution, warning

Monk, [munk] *n.* one who lives in a monaftery

Monk'ery, *n.* a monaftic life, a reclufe life

Monk'ey, *n.* an ape, baboon, fop, filly fellow

Monk'hood, *n.* the character or ftate of a monk

Monk'ifh, *a.* pertaining to or refembling monks

Mon'ochord, *n.* an inftrument of only one ftring

Mon'ocotyledon, *n.* a plant with one lobe in the feeds

Mon'ocotyled'onous, *a.* having only one lobe in
the feeds

Monoc'ular, Monoc'ulous, *a.* having but one eye

Mon'odon, *n.* an American fifh with a flat body

Mon'ody, *n.* a ditty fung only by one perfon

Monog'amift, *n.* one who difallows fecond marriages

Monog'amous, *a.* having but one hufband or wife

Mon'ogram, *n.* a cypher having one or more letters

Monogyn'ia, *n.* an order of plants with one ftyle

Mon'ologue, *n.* a foliloquy, a feparate fpeech

Monom'achy, *n.* a fingle combat, a duel

Monomial, *n.* in algebra a nomial of one term only

Monopet'alous, *a.* having one petal or flower leaf

Monoph'yllous, *a,* having but one leaf

Monop'olift, Monop'olizer, *n.* one who engroffes a
commodity or trade

Monop'olize, *v. t.* to engrofs, to purchafe the
whole of a commodity in market

Monop'oly, *n.* the fole property of felling, the act
of engroffing all

Monop'tote, *n.* a noun of only one cafe

Monofperm'ous, *a.* having one feed only

Monoftroph'ic, *a,* in unvaried meter   (lable

Monofyllab'ic, Monofyl'labled, *a.* having one fyl-

Monofyl'lable, *n.* a word having only one fyllable

Monoton'ical, Monot'onous, *a.* in a uniform tone

Monot'ony, *n.* a want of variety in cadence

Monfoon', *n.* a periodical wind

Mons'ter, *n.* fomething unnatural, horrible or bad

Mons'ter, *v.* to make or become monftrous

Monftros'ity, *n.* the ftate of being monftrous

Mons'trous, *a.* fhocking, unnatural, irregular

Mons'troufly, *ad.* to a very great or high degree

Mons'troufnefs, *n.* enormity, uncommonnefs

Montéro, *n.* a horfeman's cap, a feaman's cap, *ob.*

Montét, or Montéth, *n.* a veffel to wafh glaffes in, *ob.*

Month, [munth] *n.* the time from one change of
the moon to another, the 12th part of a year,

Month'ly, *a.* happening once a month (4 weeks

Months' mind, *n.* earneft defire or inclination

Mon'ument, *n.* a memorial, tomb, pillar

Monument'al, *a.* preferving memory, memorial

Mood, *n.* a temper of mind, a term in grammar

Mood'y, *a.* being out of humor, angry, mental

Moon, *n.* the great luminary of the night, a month

Moon'beam, *n.* a ray of lunar light

Moon'calf, *n.* a monfter, dolt, fimpleton, fool

Moon'eyed, *a.* having bad, weak or fhort fight

Moon'lefs, *a.* not enlightened by the moon, dark

Moon'light, *a.* illuminated by the moon, light

Moon'light, Moon'fhine, *n.* the light of the moon

Moon'feed, *n.* a fpecies of plant

Moon'fhiny, *a.* enlightened by the moon

Moon'ftruck, *a,* affected by the moon, mad

Mooa'wort, *n.* a plant, fattin-flower, honefty

Moon'y, *a.* having or refembling a moon, horned

Moor, *n.* a black, a marfh, watery ground, heath

Moor, *v.* to faften, place, be fixed with anchors

Moor'hen, *n.* a waterfowl, the gallinule

Moor'ing, *n.* a place where a fhip is anchored

Moor'ifh, Moor'y, *a.* fenny, marfhy, watery, wet

Moor'land, *n.* marfhy or boggy ground, a fen

Moofe, *n.* an American quadruped of the cervine
genus very large

Moot, *v.* to exercife in law-pleadings, to argue

Moot'cafe, *n.* a difputable cafe, an uncertain point

Mop, *v.* to rub with a mop, to make wry mouths

Mop, *n.* an utenfil to clean houfes, a wry mouth

Mope, *v.* to be fpiritlefs or drowfy, ftupify, dull

Mope, Mópus, *n.* a ftupid lifelefs perfon, a drone

Mop'pet, Mop'fy, *n.* a puppet, a name for a girl

Mor'al, *a.* regarding vice or virtue, upright, good

Mor'al, *n.* the inftruction or meaning of a fable

Mor'alift, *n.* one who teaches morality (tue

Moral'ity, *n.* the doctrine of the duties of life, vir-

Mor'alize, Mor'al *v. i.* to make moral reflections

Mor'alizer, *n.* one who moralizes, one who reflects

Mor'ally, *ad.* honeftly, probably, in common, very

Mor'als, *n. pl.* natural principles, duties, manners

Morafs', *n.* a fen, moor, marfh, bog, fwamp

Morafs'y *a.* confifting or partaking of morafs (feet

Morávian, *n.* a native of Moravia, one of a religious

Mor'bid, *a.* difeafed, corrupt, unfound, infectious

Mor'bidnefs, Morbos'ity, *n.* a difeafed ftate

Morbif'ic, *a.* caufing or tending to difeafes

Morbil'lous, *a.* meafly, pertaining to meafles

Mordácious, Mord'icant, *a.* fharp, biting, gnawing

Morda"city, *n.* a biting or pungent quality

Mord'ant, *n.* a falt to fix colors, as alum

Mordication, *s.* the act of biting or corroding

More or Moe, a. greater in degree, number or

More, n. a greater number or quantity [quantity

Moregame, n. a kind of fowls that feed on moors

Morel', n. a black cherry, the name of a plant

Moreland, n. a hilly country, waste ground

Moreover, ad. and conj. likewife, alfo, further

Mor'gray, n. a fish called the rough hound fish

Mor'ibund, a. about to die, dying

Morinel', n. a bird called alfo dotterel

Moring'a, n. a fpecies of plant

Mor'ion, Mur'rion, n. armor for the head, ob.

Morifc'o, n. a dancer of the morris dance, ob.

Morn, Morn'ing, n. the firft part of a day

Morning-gown, n. a loofe gown for the morning

Morning-ftar, n. Venus fhining in the morning

Morofe, a. fullen, four, peevifh, crofs, illnatured

Morofely, ad. fourly, fullenly, peevifhly, crofsly

Morofenefs, n. fournefs, peevifhnefs

Mor'phew, n. a white fcurf, a fmall tawny fpot, ob.

Mor'ris'dance, n. a Moorifh dance, ob.

Mor'row, n. the next day after the prefent one

Morfe, n. the river-horfe, a fpecies of walrus

Mor'fel, n. a fmall quantity or piece, a mouthful

Mort, n. a tune at the death of game, a doxy, much

Mor'tal, a. fubject to death, deadly, violent, human

Mor'tal, n. a man, a human creature

Mortal'icy, n. human nature, death, havoc, wafte

Mor'tally, ad. fatally, extremely, irrecoverably

Mor'tar, n. a cement ufed in buildings, veffel to

    pound in, bomb-cannon, lamp

Mor'tgage, v. t. to pledge real eftate to a creditor

    for fecurity, to pledge

Mor'tgage, n. a pledge of real eftate

Mortgagee, n. one who takes a mortgage

Mor'tgager, n. one who executes a mortgage

Mortiferous, a. deadly, deftructive, fatal

Mortification, n. a gangrene, vexation, humiliation

Mor'tify, v. t. to corrupt, vex, humble, fubdue

Mor'tife, n. a term in joinery, joint, cut, hole

Mor'tife, v. t. to cut or join with a mortife

Mort'main, n. an entailed or unalienable eftate

Mort'pay, n. a payment not made, dead pay, ob.

Mor'trefs, n. a ftrange difh, hodgepodge, olio, ob.

Mor'tuary, n. a gift left at death to a church. &c.

Mofaic, n. a variegated work with pebbles, &c.

Moskatel', n. a plant, hollow root

Mofk, Mofque, n. a Mahometan temple or church

Mofs, n. a fubftance growing on trees; v. t. to

Mofs'inefs, n. a moffy ftate   (cover with mofs

Mofs'grown, a. overgrown with mofs

Mofs'y, a. overgrown with or full of mofs

Moft, a. greateft in number or quantity

Moft, n. the greateft number, part or quantity

Mos'tic, n. a painter's ftaff or ftick to lean on

Moftly, ad. for the greateft part, ufual'y

Mote, n. a fmall particle of matter, atom, court

Moth, n. a fmall winged infect that eats cloth

Moth'eaten, a. eaten or confumed by moths

Moth'er, [o as u] n. a woman who has borne a

child, a vifcous fubftance in vinegar

Moth'er, v. i. to mold; a. native, original

Moth'erhood, n. the ftate or office of a mother

Moth'erlefs, a. having loft or void of a mother

Moth'erly, a. like a mother, kind; ad. tenderly

Moth'ery, a. concreted, moldy, dreggy, foul

Moth'erwort, n. the plant leonurus cardiaca

Moth'y, a. full of moths   [v. t. to propofe

Motion, n. the act of moving, action, a propofal;

Motionlefs, a. deftitute of motion, ftill, dead

Motive, n. the reafon of action; a. moving

Mot'ley or Mot'ly, a. fpeckled, mixed, mingled

Motory, a. giving or caufing motion, moving (vice

Mot'to, n. a fhort fentence prefixed or added, a de-

Mould, [more correctly mold] n. a downy vegetable

    fubftance growing in moift places, a thing to give

    fhape, fine earth

Mould, v. to contract mold, model, fhape, knead

Mould'able, a. that may be molded or formed

Mould'er, n. one who molds, one who forms

Mould'er, v. to turn to duft, perifh in duft, wafte

Mould'inefs, n. a moldy ftate or condition   (non

Mould'ing, n. a projection in building and on can-

Mould'y, a. overgrown with concretions, white

Moult, Mue, v. t. to fhed, drop or lofe fethers

Mound, n. a fence raifed to fortify or defend, a ball

Mount, n. a hill, heap, raifed walk, bank, weight

Mount, v. to get on horfeback, afcend, rife, fet,

    to place on a carriage, as a gun

Mount'ain, n. a high hill; a. found on mountains

Mountaineer, n. a highlander, ruftic, plunderer

Mount'ainet, n. a little mountain, hill, hillock

Mount'ainous, a. hilly, irregular, huge, bulky

Mount'ainoufnefs, n. a mountainous or high ftate

Mount'ant, a. rifing on high or aloft, rifing up, ob.

Mount'ebank, v. t. to cheat, gull, impofe upon

Mount'ebank, n. a ftage-doctor, quack, cheat

Mount'er, n. one who mounts, one who afcends

Mount'y, n. the rife or afcent made by a hawk

Mourn, v. to grieve, lament, bewail, wear black

Mourner, n. one who mourns or follows a corpfe

Mournful, a. lamentable, forrowful, fad, dull

Mournfully, Mourn'ingly, ad. with forrow, fadly

Mourning, n. a drefs of forrow, forrow, grief

Moufe, n. a fmall quadruped; v. i. to catch mice

Moufe'ear, n. the name of feveral plants

Moufe'hunt, Mous'er, n. one that catches mice

Moufe'tail, n. a fpecies of plant

Moufe'trap, n. a trap to catch mice with

Mouth, n. the aperture in the head where food is

    received, an entrance, opening, wry face, cry

Mouth, v. to mutter, grumble, fpeak big, chew

Mouth'ed, a. furnifhed with a mouth, borne down

Mouth'friend, n. a pretended friend   (by noife

Mouth'ful, a. what the mouth can hold at once

Mouth'honor, n. pretended honor or regard

Mouth'ing, n. a grumbling, a fpeaking full

Mouth'lefs, a. deftitute of or having no mouth

Mouth'made, a. expreffed without fincerity

Move, [moov] v. to change place, pafs, walk, ftir, ftir up, excite, affect, vex, propofe

Móveable, a capable of being moved, changeable

Móveables, n. pl. goods, furniture of any kind

Móvelefs, a. that cannot be moved, unmoved, fixed

Móvement, n. a motion, a manner or act of moving

Móvent, n. a mover, that which moves; a. moving

Móver, Mótor, n. one who moves, propofes, &c.

Móving, pa. paffing, exciting, affecting

Móvingly, ad. pathetically, feelingly, deeply

Mow, n. a heap of hay or corn, ftack, wry mouth

Mow, v. t. to make or pile on a mow

Mow, v. mowed, pret. mowed, mown, pa. to cut down with a fythe, to level or deftroy in great numbers at once

Mówer, n. one who mows, or cuts grafs

Mox'a or Mox'o, n. a valuable Indian mofs

Moyle, n. a mule, graft, cion, ob.

Muca"ginous, a. pertaining to mucus, flimy (many

Much, ad. greatly, often, nearly; a. large, long,

Much, n. a great deal, fum, quantity, burden

Much'what, ad. near, nearly, almoft, wellnigh

Múcilage, n. a flimy fubftance, gum diffolved

Mucila"ginous, a. flimy, vifcous, ropy, tough, foft

Muck, n. dung for manure, dirt, any filthy thing

Muck, v. t. to manure with muck, dung, daub

Muck'ender, n. a dirty pocket-handkerchief, ob.

Muck'er, v. i. to hoard or get with meannefs, ob.

Muck'hill, n. a dunghill, a large piece of dirt

Muck'inefs, n. naftinefs, filthinefs, dirtinefs, dirt

Muc"kle, a. much, having much, great, large

Muckfweat, n. a very great or profufe fweat

Muck'worm, n. a worm living in dung, a mifer

Muck'y, a. full of muck, nafty, filthy, dirty, foul

Múcous, Múculent, a. flimy, vifcous, ropy, thick

Múcron-te, a. narrowed to a fharp point

Múcu, n. a brazilian fifh of the lamprey kind

Múcus, n. a flimy fubftance, flimy moifture, fnot

Mud, n. wet dirt, ftreet-dirt, flime, mire, filth

Mud, v. t. to cover with mud, make dirty, daub

Mud'dily, ad. dirti'y, foully, with foul mixture

Mud'dinefs, n. dirtinefs, foulnefs, thicknefs

Mud'dle, v. t. to make half drunk, ftup'fy, grope

Mud'dled, pa. a. made drunk, ftupified, heavy

Mud'dy, v. t. to make muddy, foul, cloud, difturb

Mud'dy, a. dirty, thick, dull, cloudy; n. a bird

Mud'fifh, n. a fifh of the cyprin kind and one of the

Mud'fucker, n. the name of a feafowl (trout kind

Mud'wall, n. a wall built of mud only, a bird

Mud'walled, a. having or fenced by a mudwall

Mud'wort, n. a fpecies of plantain

Muff, n. a warm cover of fkin, &c. for the hands

Muff'in, n. a nice light cake eaten with tea

Muffle, n. a fmall earthen oven or veffel

Muffle, v. to wrap up, blindfold, hide, flutter

Muffler, n. a kind of cover for the face or chin

Mufflon, n. the wild fheep or mufmon

Muf'ti, n. a Mahometan high or chief prieft

Mug, n. a cup ufed to drink out of, fog, mift

Mug'gent, n. a fpecies of frefh water duck

Múgil, n. a fifh called alfo mullet

Mug'gifh, Mug'gy, a. moift, damp, mo'dy, clofe

Mug'houfe, n. a place to drink ale at, an alehoufe

Múgient, a. lowing, bellowing, roaring

Mug'weed, n. a fpecies of plant

Mug'wort, n. a fpecies of artemifia

Malat'to, n. one who is born of a black and a white

Mul'berry, n. the name of a tree or its fruit

Mulct, v. t. to fine; n. a fine, penalty, forfeit

Mule, n. an animal between an afs and a mare

Múlebird, n. a hybrid produced by the canary and linnet, &c.

Muletéer, n. a mule-driver, a keeper of mules

Mulieb"rity, n. womanhood, tendernefs, foftnefs

Múlifh, a. like a mule, fullen, ftubborn

Mull, v. t. to warm, fpice and fweeten, wine or ale

Mull'ar, n. a ftone or ftick for grinding colors

Mul'len, n. a plant, a fpecies of ftone

Mul'lers, n. a genus of fifh of the thoracic order

Mull'et, n. a very fine lufcious feafifh

Mull'igrubs, n. a twifting of the guts, fullennefs

Mult.in"gular, a. having many corners or angles

Multicap'fular, a. having many capfules

Multifárious, a. having great muliplicity

Mu'tifárioufly, ad. in various refpects, diverfly

Mult.fárioufnefs, n. a great diverfity or variety

Mult'ifid, a. divided into many parts

Mult'iform, a. having many fhapes or appearance 's

Mult'iformly, ad. with many fhapes or forms

Multiflórous, a. bearing many flowers

Multigen'erous, a. having feveral kinds

Multijúgous, a. confifting of many pairs

Multilat'eral, a. having many fides

Multiloc'ular, a. having many cells for feeds

Maltinómial, a. confifting of many names or terms

Mu'tip'arous, a. bringing forth many at a birth

Multipart'ite, a. divided into feveral parts

Mult'iped, n. an infect with many feet, a wood-

Mult'iple, a. containing feveral times (loufe

Mult'ipliable, a. capable of being multiplied

Multiplicand', n. a number given to be multiplied

Multip'licate, n. what contains more than one, having a multiplied corol

Multiplication, n. the act or art of multiplying

Multiplicator, n. that by which one multiplies

Multipli"cious, a. manifold, various, different

Multipli"city, n. more than one, a great variety

Mult'iplier, n. one who multiplies, a multiplicator

Mult'iply, v. t. to increafe or grow in number

Multip'otent, a. poffeffed of very great power

Multifil'iquous, a. having many pods

Mult'itude, n. a great number, a crowd, the vulgar

Multitúdinous, a. manifold, various (valves

Mul'tivalve, n. an animal with a fhell of many

Multivalv'úlar, Mul'tivalv, a. having many valves

Mu'toc'ular, a. having feveral eyes, full of eyes

Mult'ure, n. a toll or fee taken for grindii g corn

Mum, exclam. hufh; n. ale brewed from wheat

S 2

Mura'ble, v. to speak inwardly, mutter, chew fast
Mum'ber, n a flow or bad speaker, a mutterer
Mumm, v. t. to put on a mask, mask, go masked
Mummer, n. one who goes masked, a masker
Mum'm'ery, v. a masking. farce, buffoonery, frolic
Mumm'y, n. an Egyptian embalmed corpse, a wax
Mump, v. t. to nibble, speak low and quick, ob.
Mump'er, n. one that mumps, a genteel beggar, ob.
Mump'ish, a. glum, sullen, sour, cross, obstinate
Mumps, n. pl. fallennefs, a difeafe of the neck
Munch, v. i. to eat fast and much
Mund, n. peace, quiet, reft, eafe, ob.
Mund'ane, a. belonging to this world, worldly
Mund'atory, Mundificative, a. able to cleanfe
Mund'ic, n. a hard or stony substance, a marcasite
Mundification, Mundation, n. the act of cleansing
Mund'ify, v. t. to make clean, cleanfe, purify
Munerary, a. relating to a gift, bribe, or reward
Mun'grel, fee mongrel
Muni'cipal, a. belonging to a corporation or city
Municipal'ity, n. a corporate body, a diftrict in
    France and its inhabitants
Munificence, n. liberality, generofity, bounty
Munif'icent, a. liberal, generous, bountiful
Munif'icently, ad. in a liberal or kind manner
Muniment, n. a defenfe, fupport, hold, title, deed
Munite, v. t. to strengthen, fortify, fecure, ob.
Muni'tion, n. a fortification, ammunition
Mural, a. pertaining or relating to a wall
Mur'der, n. a killing unlawfully with malice
Mur'der, v. t. to kill unlawfully with premedita-
    ted malice   (meditated purpofe
Mur'derer, n. one who kills with malice and pre-
Mur'derous a. guilty of murder, bloody, cruel
Mure, v. t. to wall in or up; n. a wall, a defenfe
Muriacite, n. a ftone compofed of falt, fand and
    gypfum
Muriate, n. a falt formed by the muriatic acid and
Muriated, a. combined with muriatic acid (abafe
Muriatic, a. having the nature of or like brine
Muricate, a. full of fharp points, prickly
Murine, a. pertaining to mice
Murin, n. the leffer opoffum of S. America
Murk, n. darknefs, gloominefs, dry hufks of fruit
Murk'y, a. dark, cloudy, gloomy, wanting light
Mur'mur, v. i. to grumble, mutter, complain, pant
Mur'mur, n. a grumbling, private complaint, noife
Mur'murer, n. a grumbler, complainer, repiner
Mur'muring, n. a grumbling, a low deep noife
Mur'rain, n. a plague amongst cattle, a quick rot
Mur'rey, a. darkly red, purplish; n. a dark red
Mufcadel' or Mufcatel', n. a grape and its wine
Mufc'adin, n. a fweet grape, fweet wine, a pear
Mus'cardin, r. the leffer fpecies of dormoufe
Mufcat', n. a fpecies of grape, and wine, a pear
Mus'cle, n. a flefhy fiber, a well known fhellfish
Mufcovádo, n. unrefined fugar of the W. Indies
Mufc'ular, Mufc'ulous, a. full of mufcles, brawny
Mufe, n. the power of poetry, deep thought, ftudy

Mufe, v. i. to ponder, think clofe, paufe, wonder
Mufea or Musia, n. curious mofaic work
Mufeful, a. wrapt up in deep thought, very abfent
Muféum, n. a repofitory of curiofities, a library
Mush, n. food of maiz, flower and water boiled (local)
Mufh'room, n. a fpungy plant, an upftart
Mufic, n. harmony, the fcience of founds, muficians
Mufical, a. harmonious, melodious, fweet
Mufically, ad. harmonioufly, fweetly, finely
Mufi'cian, n. one who is fkilled in mufic
Muficmafter, n. one who profeffes to teach mufic
Mufk, n. an animal fomewhat like a goat and deer,
    a perfume found in a fack on the animal
Mufk'et, n. a foldier's hand-gun, a kind of hawk
Mufketéer, n. a foldier armed with a mufket
Mufkétoe, n. a vexatious infect
Mufketoon', n. a fhort gun with a very large bore
Mufk'melon, n. a very fragrant melon
Mufk'rat, n. a quadruped, the mufquafh
Mufk'ox, n. a fpecies of the bovine genus about
    Hudfon's bay, having the fmell of mufk
Mufk'rofe, n. a very fragrant rofe
Mufk'feed, n. a plant, hibifcus
Mufk'wood, n. a fpecies of plant
Mufk'y, a. like mufk, fweetfcented, fragrant
Mus'lin, n. a fine kind of cloth made of cotton
Mus'lin, a. made of muflin
Muflinet', n. a coarfe cotton cloth
Mus'mon, n. the mufflon or wild fheep
Mufs'ac, n. a liquor much ufed by the Chinefe
Mufs'ulman, n. a Mahometan believer or title
Muft, verb. imperf. to be obliged   (or wort
Muft, v. to make or grow moldy; n. new wine
Mus'tac, n. a fmall tufted monkey
Muftáches or Muftáchoes, n. pl. whifkers, hair
Muft'ard, n. the name of a plant, feed and flower
Muft'ardpot, n. a pot to put made muftard in
Muft'er, v. t. to review, affemble, raife, gather
Muft'er, n. a review and regifter of forces   (tered
Muft'erbook, n. a book in which foldiers are regif-
Muft'ermafter, n. one who fuperintends a mufter
Muft'erroll, n. a correct lift or regifter of forces
Muft'ily, ad. in a mufty or moldy manner
Muft'inefs, n. moldinefs, dampnefs, foulnefs
Muft'y, a. fpoiled with damp, moldy, ftale, dull
Mutability, Mutablenefs, n. changeablenefs
Mútable, a. changeable, unfettled, inconftant
Mutátion, n. a change of ftate, an alteration
Mute, a. dumb, fpeechlefs, filent, not fpeaking
Mute, n. one filent, a letter without a found, dung
Mute, v. i. to dung as birds, void, difcharge
Mútely, ad. dumbly, filently, without fpeaking
Mútilate, v. t. to maim, cut off, leffen, diminifh
Mútilate, a. not producing a corol
Mútilated, Mútilous, a. maimed, defective, lame
Mutilátion, n. the deprivation of a limb or part
Mútine, Mutinéer, n. a mover of fedition, a rebel
Mútinous, a. feditious, turbulent, diforderly
Mútinoufly, ad. feditioufly, turbulently, noifily

Mútiny, v. i. to rise up against lawful authority
Mútiny, n. a revolt or refiftance of authority among foldiers and feamen
Mut'ter, v. to grumble, fpeak confufedly, repine
Mut'terer, n. a grumbler, murmurer, repiner
Mut'tering, n. a grumbling, murmuring, noife
Mut'ton, n. the flefh or meat of a fheep, a fheep
Mut'tonfift, n. a very large, coarfe and red hand
Mútual, a. reciprocal ,acting in return, equal, like
Mutual'ity, n. a mutual kindnefs, a return made
Mútually, ad. reciprocally, in return, by turns
Mútule, n. a fquare modillion in the doric frieze
Muz'zle, v. to bind up the mouth, fecure, fondle
Muz'zle, n. a mouth, fpout, kind of halter
Myol'ogy, n. the doctrin of the mufcles
Myr'iad, n. the number of ten thoufand, infinity
Myr'midon, n. a rude ruffian, conftable, helper
Myrrh, n. a kind of ftrong aromatic gum
Myrrh'ine, a. made of or like myrrhine ftone
Myr"tle, n. a fragrant kind of fhrub or tree
Myr'tiform, u. refembling myrtle berries
My'rus, n. a fpecies of fea ferpent
Myfélf, pron. I myfelf, I only, not another perfon
Myft'agogue, n. an interpreter of myfteries
Myftérious, a. that is not eafily underftood
Myftérioufly, ad. obfcurely, very darkly
Myftérioufnefs, n. obfcurity, an artful difficulty
Myft'erize, v. t. to explain or form myfteries
Myft'ery, n. a fecret, obfcurity, wonder, trade
Myft'ic, Myft'ical, a. fecret, obfcure, dark
Myft'ically, ad. by fome fecret meaning, darkly
Myft'icalnefs, n. a myftical ftate, a dark quality
Mys'ticifm, n. obfcurity of doctrins
Mityle'nean, n. a native of Mitylene, the capital of Lefbos, a of Mitylene
Mytholo"gical, a. relating or belonging to fables
Mythol'ogift, n. a framer or interpreter of fables
Mythol'ogize, v. i. to relate or explain fables
Mythol'ogy, n. a fyftem or explanation of fables

N

NAB, v. t. to catch by furprife, catch, bite
Nábob, n. a prince in India, fubordinate to the fubahs, a man of great wealth
Nádir, n. the point oppofit to the zenith
Nag, n. a faddle horfe, a little or young horfe
Náid, n. a water nymph
Nail, n. a kind of horn on the fingers and toes, iron pin, ftud, bofs, the 16th part of a yard
Nail, v. t. to faften, fecure or ftud with nails
Náiler, n. a maker of or dealer in nails
Náked, a. uncovered, bare, unarmed, open, plain
Nákedly, ad. barely, fimply, plainly, evidently
Nákednefs, n. a want of covering, plain evidence
Námaz, n. the common prayer ufed by the Turks
Name, v. t. to mention by name, call, utter, tell
Name, n. an appellation, title, reputation, renown
Námelefs, a. having no name, unnamed
Námely, ad. particularly, to wit, that is to fay
Námer, n. one who names, one who appoints

Námefake, n. a perfon who is of the fame name
Nankeén, n. a fpecies of cotton cloth from China
Nap, n. a fhort fleep, a down on cloth (cheat
Nap, v. to take a nap, be off one's guard, raife,
Nape, n. the joint of the neck behind (ble
Naph'tha, n. a bituminous mineral, very inflamma-
Nap'kin, n. linen to wipe the face or hands on
Nap'lefs, a. threadbare, much worn, fhabby
Nap'py, a. having a nap, foft, frothy, fpumy
Narcifs'us, n. a fine flower, the daffodil-flower
Narcot'ic, a. ftupifying, opiate, caufing fleep, eafing
Narcot'ic, n. a ftupifying medicin, an opiate
Nard, n. an odoriferous fhrub, a fweet ointment
Nare, n. a natural cavity in the nofe, a noftril
Nar'rable, a. that may be related or told (tory
Narration, Nar'rative, n. an account, relation, hif-
Nar'rative, a. relating, defcriptive, expreffive
Nar'ratively, ad. by way of narrative or relation
Narrátor, n. a relater, teller, reciter, repeater
Nar'row, a. not broad, not wide, covetous, near
Nar'row, v. t. to contract, limit, diminifh, cut
Nar'rowly, ad. clofely, nearly, fparingly, meanly
Nar'rowminded, a. meanfpirited, ungenerous
Nar'rownefs, n. a want of breadth, meannefs,
Nar'rows, n. a ftrait or narrow paffage (greedinefs
Nar'wal, n. the fea unicorn, a fifh with a horn pro-
jecting from its nofe
Náfal, a. belonging or relating to the nofe
Nas'cent, a. beginning to exift or grow
Náfeberry, n. a fpecies of tree
Naft'ily, ad. dirtily, filthily, obfcenely, lewdly
Naft'inefs, n. dirtinefs, filthinefs, filth, obfcenity
Naftur'tion, n. a fpecies of crefs
Naft'y, a. dirty, filthy, naufeous, obfcene, lewd
Nas'us, n. a fifh like the chub
Nátal, a. relating to nativity or birth, native
Natali'tious, a. relating to a perfon's birthday
Nátant, a. fwimming, floating on water
Natátion, n. a fwimming, the act of fwimming
Nath'lefs, ad. neverthelefs, notwithftanding, ob-
Nátion, n. a body of people united under one prince
or government, or their ftate or kingdom
Na"tional, a. public, favoring one's own people
Na"tionally, ad. with regard to a whole nation
Nátron, n. foda or mineral alkali
Nátive, n. one born in any place; a. natural, real
Nativ'ity, n. birth, bondage, a figure, a pofition
Nat'ural, a. produced by nature, bafeborn, eafy
Nat'ural, n. an idiot, fool, native quality or gift
Nat'uralift, n. one who ftudies natural philofophy
Naturalizátion, n. admiffion to native privileges
Nat'uralize, v. t. to admit to native privileges
Nat'urally, ad. without affectation, fpontaneoufly
Nat'uralnefs, n. natural ftate, conformity to truth
Náture, n. the native ftate of any thing, conftitu-
tion, difpofition, regular courfe, ftate or fyftem
of the world, natural affection, fort, kind
Naught, a. worthlefs, corrupt, lewd ; n. nothing
Naught'ily, ad. badly, corruptly, wickedly, vilely

Naught'inefs, a. badnefs, wickednefs, lewdnefs
Naught'y, a. bad, corrupt, wicked, lewd, vile
Naum'achy, n. a feafight, a mock feafight
Naus'ea, n. a ficknefs at the ftomach, a difguft
Naus'eate, v. to grow fqueamifh, loathe, abhor
Naufeáting, n. a naufea, difguft
Naus'eous, a. loathfome, difguftful, offenfive
Naus'eoufly, ad. with difguft, offenfively, badly
Naus'eoufnefs, n. loathfomenefs, difguft, hatred
Naut'ical, a. pertaining to feamen or fhips
Naut'ilus, n, a fhellfifh that has oars and a fail
Nával, a. confifting of or belonging to fhips
Nave, n. the middle part of a wheel or church
Nável, n. a part of the body, middle, center
Návelltring, n. the ligament which attaches a fetus
　　to the parent
Návelwort, n. a plant of feveral kinds
Navic'ular, a. fhaped like a boat, cymbiform
Nav'ew, n. a plant, a fpecies of cabbage
Nav'igable, a. paffable for fhips or boats
Nav'igate, v. to fail, manage, direct, pilot fhips
Navigátion, n. the act or art of paffing by water
Nav'igator, n. a feaman, one who pilots a fhip
Návy, n. a fleet of fhips of war only, a force by fea
Nay, ad. no, by no means, not only fo but more
Náyword, n. a denial, by-word, reproach, jeft
Nazaréne, n. a native of Nazareth, one of a fect of
　　Jews who mingled judaifm and chriftianity
Naz'arite, n. one of the Jews who profeffed an ex-
　　traordinary purity of life and devotion
Naz'aritifm, n. the doctrins and practice of the
　　Nazarites
Neaf, n. a feaft, hand when clencked, ob.
Neal, v. t. to temper by fire or a gradual heat
Neap, a. low, decreafing, fcanty, deficient
Néaptide, n. a low tide, a fhort or flack tide
Neapol'itan, n. a native of Naples in Italy
Neapol'itan, a. pertaining to Naples
Near, a. not diftant, clofe, intimate, niggardly
Near, Near'ly, ad. at hand, clofely, fparingly
Néarnefs, n. clofenefs, niggardlinefs, avarice
Neat, a. clean, fpruce, nice; n. an ox, cow, &c.
Néatherd, n. one who keeps herds, a cowkeeper
Néatly, ad. cleanly, fprucely, nicely, artfully
Néatnefs, n. cleanlinefs, fprucenefs, elegance
Neb, n. a nofe, mouth, bill or beak of a bird
Neb'ule, n. a cloudinefs, a thin cloud
Nebulos'ity, n. cloudinefs, miftinefs
Neb'ulous, a. cloudy, mifty, hazy, dim, dark, dull
Ne''ceffaries, n. pl. things needful to fupport life
Ne''ceffarily, ad. from neceffity, unavoidably
Nc''ceffary, a. needful, proper, conclufive, fatal
Neceffitárian, n. a perfon who denies free agency
Necefs'itate, v. t. to make neceffary, compel, force
Necefs'itated, pa. forced by neceffity, obliged
Neceffitátion, n. a making neceffary, compulfion
Necefs'itous, a. preffed with poverty, needy, low
Necefs'itoufnefs, Necefs'itude, n. povérty, want
Necefs'ity, n. poverty, want, diftrefs, compulfion

Neck, n. a part of the body, of land, &c. a point
Neck'beef, n. the coarfe or hard flefh of the neck
Neck'cloth, n. a thing worn about men's necks
Neck'lace, n. a woman's ornament for the neck
Necrol'ogy, n. an account of the dead
Necrolo''gical, a. pertaining to necrology
Nec'romancer, n. a magician, a conjurer
Nec'romancy, n. magic, conjuration, enchantment
Nec'romant'ic, a. of or relating to necromancy
Nec'tar, n. the feigned drink of the gods, a fweet
Nec'tared, a. tinged or mixed with nectar (drink
Nectáreous, Nec'tarin, a. fweet as nectar, fine
Nectarif'erous, a. producing nectaries
Nec'tary, n. that part of a plant which produces a
　　fweet juce or honey
Nectif'erous, a. producing nectar
Nec'tarin, n. a very fine fruit of the plum-kind.
Need, v. to want, lack, require, be neceffitated
Need, Néedinefs, n. neceffity, want, exigence
Néeder, n. one who needs or wants any thing
Néedful, a. indifpenfibly requifit, neceffary, fit
Néedfully, ad. with need or want, neceffarily
Néedily, ad. in need, in want, in poverty, in diftrefs
Nee''dle, n. a thing ufed for fewing with, a fmall
　　fteel bar or wire ufed in a mariner's compafs
Néedle, v. to form into needles, as in cryftals
Nee''dleful, n. a fhort piece of filk, thread, &c.
Néedlefifh, n. a fifh with the middle of the body
　　hexangular
Nee''dlemaker, Néedler, n. one who makes needles
Need'lefs, a. unneceffary, not requifit, ufelefs
Néedlefsly, ad. without need, unneceffarily
Néedleffnefs, n. an unneceffary ftate or quality
Nee''dlework, n. work done with a needle
Needs, ad. from need, neceffarily, indifpenfably
Néedy, a. neceffitous, poor, diftreffed, low
Néefe, v. i. to fneeze; n. a nofe, cape, headland
Nef, n. the body of a church, a nave of a wheel
Nefand'ous, Nefárious, a. abominable, wicked
Negátion, n. a denial, a defcription by negative
Neg'ative, n. a propofition that denies; a. denying
Neg'ative, v. t. to deny, refufe, reject, caft out
Neg'atively, ad. with denial, by means of denial
Neglect', v. t. to omit, let flip, difregard, flight
Neglect', n. omiffion, careleffnefs, coldnefs
Neglect'er, n. one who neglects, one who flights
Neglect'ful, a. heedlefs, inattentive, difregarding
Neglect'ive, a. inattentive to, regardlefs of
Neg'ligence, n. a habit of acting careleſsly, folly
Neg'ligent, a. carelefs, heedlefs, inattentive, idle
Neg'ligently, ad. careleſsly, heedlefsly, remifsly
Negótiable, a. that may be negotiated or paffed
　　from one to another by affignment
Negótiate or Negóciate, v. t. to traffic, trade, treat
　　with, tranfact, make, manage
Negotiátion, n. a trading, treaty of bufinefs, care
Negótiator, n. one employed to treat or manage
Négrefs, n. a female black or African
Négro or Néger, n. an African, or his defcendant of

full blood, a black man

Negus, *n.* wine, water, fugar, nutmeg and lemon

Neif, *n.* the fift, a bond-woman, a female flave

Neigh, [na] *v. i.* to cry as a horfe

Neigh, *n.* the voice of a horfe

Neigh'bor, [nabor] *n.* one who lives near another

Neigh'bor, *v. i.* to live near, border upon, adjoin

Neigh'borhood, *n.* a people or place adjoining

Neighboring, *a.* near, living near

Neigh'borly, *a.* civil, kind, obliging; *ad.* civilly

Neither, *n.* not either, no one; *conj.* nor

Neméan, *a.* pertaining to Nemea, in Greece

Nem'ine-contradicent'e, none oppofing

Nem'oral, *a.* relating or belonging to a grove

Nelo'gical, *a.* pertaining to neology

Neol'ogy, *n.* the introduction of new words

Neol'ogift, *n.* he who ufes new terms in language

Néophite, *n.* that which is newly planted

Neoter'ic, *a.* novel, late, modern, frefh, recent, *ob.*

Nep, *n.* a plant, catmint

Nepenth'e, *n.* a drug that can expel all pain or care

Neph'ew, *n.* the fon of a brother or fifter

Nephrit'ic, *a.* pertaining to the kidneys

Nephrit'ic, *n.* a medicin good againft the ftone

Nep'otifm, *n.* a fondnefs or affection for nephews

Neptúnian, *a.* of or relating to the ocean or water

Neptu'nian, Nep'tunift, *n.* one who believes that the ocean once covered the earth

Nerf'ling, *n.* a frefh water fifh of Germany

Nérite, *n.* a genus of univalve fhell-fifh

Nerve, *n.* an organ of fenfation, a whitifh veffel

Néreid, *n.* a fea nymph

Nerve *v. t.* to give nerves, ftrength or vigor

Nervófe, *a.* having fimple unbranched nerves

Nerve'lefs, *a.* void of ftrength, weak, infipid

Nerv'ous, Nerv'y, *a.* ftrong, vigorous, robuft, having the nerves affected or difeafed

Nerv'oufnefs, *n.* great ftrength, weaknefs

Nes"cience, *n.* ignorance, a want of knowledge

Nefs, *n.* a headland, point, nofe   (build nefts

Neft, *n.* a bed, box of drawers, abode; *v. i.* to

Neft'egg, *n.* an egg left in the neft of a bird

Neft"le, *v.* to lie clofe, fettle, cherifh, move

Neft'ling, *n.* a bird juft hatched, a clofe perfon

Neftórian, *n.* one of a fect who denied Mary to be the mother of Chrift

Net, *n.* a device for fifhing, &c. *a.* neat, real

Net, *v.* to make nets, to catch in a net

Neth'er, *a.* lower, placed lower, infernal

Neth'ermoft, *a.* loweft, moft infernal

Net'ting, *n.* a complication of ropes interfecting each other   (fting

Net'tle, *n.* a ftinging plant; *v. t.* to provoke, to

Net'work, *n.* work made in the manner of nets

Nev'er, *ad.* at no time, in no degree, not even

Nev'ermeaning, *a.* having no meaning or defign

Neverthelefs', *ad.* notwithftanding that, however

Neúter, Neútral, *a.* indifferent, being of neither

Neúter, Neútral, *n.* one who ftands neuter (party

Neutral'ity, *n.* a ftate of abfolute indifference

Neútralize, *v. t.* to render neuter, to deftroy the properties of a body or bodies by mixture

Neutralizátion, *n.* the deftroying of the qualities of bodies by combination

New, *a.* frefh, late, modern, repaired, uncommon

New'el, *n.* the upright poft in a ftaircafe

New'fangled, *a.* newly formed, novel, affected

New'fanglednefs, *n.* a foolifh love of novelty

New'fafhioned, *a.* lately come into fafhion, fine

New'grown, *a.* lately grown, juft fprung up

New-Hamp'fhire, *n.* one of the United States

New-Jer'fey, *n.* one of the United States

New'ly, *ad.* frefhly, lately, juft or even now

Newmood'el, *v. t.* to form or make anew

New'nefs, *n.* frefhnefs, novelty, a reformation

News, *n.* frefh accounts of tranfactions

News'monger, *n.* a dealer in news, a bufy body

News'paper, *n.* a public print to circulate news

Newt, *n.* a fmall water lizard

Newto'nian, *n.* a follower of the Great Newton

Newto'nian, *a.* produced by or pertaining to Newton

New-year's-gift, *n.* a prefent on new-year's day

New-York', *n.* one of the United States and its metropolis

Next, *a.* neareft in place; *ad.* in the next place

Nib, *n.* a point of a pen, point, end, beak of a bird

Nib, *v.* to make or cut a nib, point, bill

Nib'bed, *pa. a.* having a nib, pointed, fharp

Nib'ble, *v.* to eat flowly, bite at, carp at

Nib'bler, *n.* one that bites a little at a time, a critic

Nice, *a.* exact, refined, fqueamifh, finical, fine

Nícely, *ad.* accurately, minutely, delicately

Nicenefs, *n.* accuracy, exactnefs, care, delicacy

Nicety, *n.* accuracy, minutenefs, delicacy, dainty

Nich, *n.* a hollow for a ftatue to ftand in

Nick, *n.* a notch, cut, fcore, exact point, Nicholas

Nick, *v. t.* to cut in nicks, notch, fit, hit, trick

Nick'el, *n.* a metal of a grayifh white color

Nick'elic acid, a faturated combination of nickel and oxygene

Nick'name, *n.* a byname; *v. t.* to give a byname

N ctate, *v. i.* to wink, to twinkle with the eyes

Nide, *n.* a brood, efpecially that of pheafants

Nidificátion, *n.* the act or art of building nefts

Nid'orous, *a.* tafting or fmelling like roaft meat

Nid'ulant, *a.* neftling, as feeds in the pulp of a berry

Nidulátion, *n.* the time of remaining in a neft

Niece, *n.* the daughter of a brother or fifter

Nig'gard, *n.* a mifer; *v. a.* to ftint, bound confine

Nig'gard, Nig'gardly, *a.* fordid, mean   (oufnefs

Nig'gardlinefs, Nig'gardnefs, *n.* meannefs, covet-

Nig'gardly, *ad.* ford'd y, meanly, fparingly

Nigh, *a.* near, not diftant, allied by blood

Nigh, Nighly, *ad.* nearly, clofely, within a little

Nighnefs, *n.* a nearnefs or clofenefs of, fituation

Night, *n.* the time of darknefs, gloominefs, death

Nightbrawler, *n.* a perfon who quarrels by night

Nightcap, *n.* a cap worn in bed or in an undrefs

Nightcrow, n. a bird that cries in the night
Nightdew, n. a dew that falls in the night
Nightdog, n. a dog that hunts in the night
Nightdrefs, n. a drefs worn only at night
Nighted, a. clouded, darkened, dark, black
Nightfaring, a. travelling by or in the night
Nightfire, n. a kind of meteor, will-with-a-wifp
Nightfoundered, a. loft by or in the night
Nightgown, n. a very loofe wide gown, an undrefs
Nighthag, n. a witch that wanders in the night
Nightingale, n. a fmall bird that fings fweetly
Nightly, ad. every night, by or in the night
Nightly, a. done by night, acting by night
Nightman, n. one who empties privies by night
Nightmare, n. a morbid oppreffion of the breaft
Nightpiece, n. a picture of a view in the night
Nightrail, n. a linen covering for the fhoulders
Nightraven, n. a night bird, a fort of owl
Nightrule, n. a difturbance made in the night
Nightfhade, n. the name of many plants, fome of them poifonous
Nightwalker, n. a ftrumpet who walks at night
Nightwarbling, a. finging by or in the night
Nightward, a. drawing towards night, dufkifh
Nightwatch, n. three hours of the night
Nigres'cent, a. growing or making black
Nihil'ity, n. nothingnefs, a trifle, nonexiftence
Nilom'eter, n. an inftrument to meafure the rife of the Nile during the floods
Nill, v. t. not to will, to refufe, ob.
Nim, v. t. to fteal, pilfer, filch, ob.
Nim'ble, a. active, brifk, ready, quick, fpeedy, fwift
Nim'blefooted, a. nimble, active, quick, fpeedy
Nim'blenefs, n. activity, quicknefs, fpeed, hafte
Nim'blewitted, a. quick, ready, eager to fpeak
Nim'bly, ad. actively, readily, quickly, fpeedily
Nin'compoop, n. a blockhead, fimpleton, fool
Nine, a. the number of eight and one
Ninefold, a. repeated or doubled nine times
Ninepins, n. pl. a play with nine pins and a bowl
Ninefcore, a. twenty repeated nine times, 180
Nineteen, a. nine and ten, nine added to ten
Nineteenth, a. noting the number nineteen
Ninetieth, a. the ninth ten times told
Ninety, a. ten taken or repeated nine times
Nin'ny, Nin'nyhammer, n. a fimpleton, a fool
Ninth, a. what in numbers precedes the tenth
Nip, n. a plant, ill fmelling ragwort
Nip, v. t. to pinch, blaft, deftroy, vex, ridicule
Nip, n. a pinch, bite, fmall cut, blaft, taunt, nib
Nip'per, n. one who nips or pinches, a keen fatirift
Nip'pers, n. pl. an inftrument, fmall pinchers
Nip'pingly, ad. bitterly, feverely, tartly, keenly
Nip'ple, n. an orifice or end of a teat, teat, dug
Nip'plewort, n. a plant, wartwort
Nis'an, n. a Jewifh month-anfwering to March and April
Nis'berry, n. a fpecies of tree
Nit, n. the egg of a loufe or any little animal
Nitency, n. brightnefs, an endeavor, a fpring

Nit'id, a. bright, fhining, gay, fine, neat, clean
Niter, n. a mineral and very cooling falt, faltpeter
Nitrous, Nitry, a. impregnated with or like niter
Nitrate, n. a falt formed by nitric acid and a bafe
Ni'trated, a. combined with niter
Nitric acid is niter faturated with oxygene
Ni'trous acid, is niter not faturated with oxygene
Ni'trite, n. a falt formed by the nitrous acid, with
Ni'trogene, n. azote, or the element of niter (a bafe
Nitrogenous, a. pertaining to nitrogene
Ni'tromuriat'ic acid, a mixture of nitric and muriatic acids
Nit'tily, ad. in a nitty manner, loufily, meanly
Nit'ty, a. abounding with or refembling nits
Nival, a. abounding with or like fnow, white
Niv'eous, a. fnowy, like or white as fnow, fair
No, ad. a word of denial, not ; a. none, not any
Nob l'itate, v. t. to ennoble, to make famous
Nobil'ity, n. perfons of high rank, dignity, fame
Noble, a. great, illuftrious, grand, brave, generous
Noble, n. a perfon of high rank, a coin
Nobleman, n. a man of high rank or great birth
Noblenefs, n. greatnefs, dignity, boldnefs, worth
Nobleffe, n. the body of nobles, nobility, dignity
Nobly, ad. illuftrioufly, grandly, bravely
Nobody, n. not any one whatever, not any perfon
Nocent, Nocive, Noc'uous, a. guilty, hurtful, ob.
Nock, n. a notch, flit, cut, hole, ob.
Noctambulation, n. a walking in fleep
Noctam'bulift, n. a perfon who walks in his fleep
Noctid'ial, a. containing a night and a day
Noc'tiluca, n. phofphorus which fhines at night without the previous aid of folar rays
Noc'tuary, n. an account of night affairs
Noc'tule, n. a large fpecies of bat
Noc'turn, n. devotion performed by night
Nocturn'al, a. nightly, in the night
Nocturn'al, n. an inftrument of obfervation by night
Nod, v. i. to bend the head, be drowfy, fleep
Nod, n. a quick declination of the head, a fign
Nod'der, n. one who nods, one who makes figns
Nod'dle, Noll, n. the head; by way of contempt
Nod'dy, n. a fimpleton, a fpecies of gull
Node, n. a knot, knob, fwelling, interfection
Nodofe, Nodous, a. knotty, full of knots, hard
Nodos'ity, n. a knottinefs, a great complication
Nod'ule, n. a fmall knot, or irregular lump
Nod'ular, a. pertaining to or in form of a nodule
Nog'gen, a. hard, rough, harfh, troublefome
Nog'gin, n. a fmall wooden cup or mug, a fmall
Noi'er, n. one who annoys or hurts, ob. (meafure
Noife, n. a found, outcry, clamor, fquabble
Noife, v. to found loud, bawl out, fpread a report
Noife'ful, a. loud, high, clamorous, troublefome
Noife'lefs, a. making no noife, filent, quiet, eafy
Noife'maker, n. a noify and troublefome perfon
Nois'ily, ad. in a noify manner, troublefomely
Nois'inefs, n. loudnefs of found, difturbance

Nois'ome, a. noxious, offenfive, naſty, ſtinking

Nois'omely, ad. offenfively, with a naſty ſtench

Nois'omenefs, n. offenſivenefs, naſtinefs, ſtench

Nois'y, a. clamorous, turbulent, troublefome

Nolens-vólens, whether a perfon will or no

Noli"tion, n. unwillingnefs, reluctance, not ufed

Nomad'ic, a. paſtoral, fubſiſting by feeding flocks and herds, wandering as the Tatars

Nom'bles, n. pl. the entrails of a deer

Nomenclátor, n. one who names perfons, &c. right

Nom'enclature, n. the act of naming, a vocabulary

Nomenclátural, a. pertaining to a nomenclature

Nómial, n. à ſingle name or term in mathematics

Nom'inal, a. exiſting only ln name, not real, titular

Nom'inaliſt, n. one of a fect who denied all exiſtences but names

Nom'inally, ad. in or by name only, titularly

Nom'inate, v. to name, propofe, appoint, entitle

Nominátion, n. a naming, the power of appointing, in Connecticut, a liſt of men felected by choice as candidates for council or congrefs

Nom'inative, a. naming, the firſt cafe in grammar

Nominée, n. one named, appointed or deſignated, as the nominee of a life annuity

Non'age, n. minority in point of age   (ecliptic

Nonages'imal, a. noting the 90th degree of the

Non'agon, n. a figure having 9 fides and angles

Nonappéarance, v. the omiſſion of due appearance

Nonattend'ance, n. an omiſſion of attendance

Nonce, n. a purpofe, intent, defign, drift, ob.

Noncompliance, n. neglect of compliance

Nonconduct'or, n. a fubſtance which does not tranfmit another fubſtance, efpecially electricity

Nonconduct'ing, n. not tranfmitting another fub-

Noncontágious, a. not infecting   (ſtance

Noncontágioufnefs, n. the ſtate of not being communicable by infection

Nonconform'iſt, n. a perfon who does not conform to the worſhip of an eſtabliſhed church

Nonconform'ity, n. a refufal to join in opinion

Nondefcript', a. that has not yet been defcribed

None, a. not any, not one, not even one befides

Nonelec'tric, n. a conductor of electricity

Nonent'ity, n. nonexiſtence, a want of being

Nones, n. pl. in the Roman calender, were the feventh of March, May, July and October, and the fifth of the other months

None'fuch, n. a very extraordinary perfon, &c.

Nonexiſt'ence, n. a want or abfence of exiſtence

Nonjúring, a. refufing to fwear allegiance

Nonjúror, n. one who refufes to fwear allegiance.

Nonnat'urals, n. pl. things that enter not into the nature of difeafes, though they may caufe them; as air, meat, drink, fleep, exercife, &c.

Nonparéil, n. an apple, a fort of printing-letter

Non'plus, n. a puzzle; v. t. to puzzle, to confound

Nonponderos'ity, n. levity, the having no weight

Nonregard'ance, n. a want of due or juſt regard

Non.res'idence, n. an abfence from fome charge, or an eſtate   (ſtate or with his charge

Nonres'ident, n. one who does not refide on his ef-

Nonreſiſt'ance, n. paſſive obedience, fubmiſſion

Non'fenfe, n. words without connected meaning,

Nonfens'ical, a. unmeaning, foolifh, filly, trifling

Nonfolútion, n. a failure in or want of folution

Non'fparing, a. cruel, mercilefs, unfeeling

Non'fuit, n. a non-appearance of the plaintiff in a fuit, when called in court

Non'fuit, v. t. to adjudge that the plaintiff does not profecute his fuit, upon default of appearance

Nonúfer, n. a neglect of the duties of an office

Nook, n. a corner, covert, retreat, part of land

Noon, n. the middle point or hour of the day

Noon'day, Noon'tide, n. midday, twelve o'clock

Noon'day, Noon'tide, a. meridional, the higheſt

Noofe, v. t. to knot; n. a running knot, a trap

Nópal, n. the cochineel fig

Nor, conj. a negative particle, neither, not even

Norm'al, a. perpendicular, forming a right angle, relating to rudiments or principles

North, n. the part of the earth oppofit the fouth

North, North'erly, North'ern, North'ward, a. lying towards the north, tending to the north

North'ing, n. the diſtance of a planet from the equator northward, diſtance north

North'ſtar, m. the ſtar neareſt the northern pole

Northum'brian, a. pertaining to Northumberland

North'wind, n. the wind that blows from the north

Norwégian, n. a native of Norway; a. pertaining to Norway   (fcent

Nofe, n. a part of the face; v. to bluſter, oppofe,

Nófebleed, n. a difcharge of blood from the nofe

Nófefiſh, n. a fiſh with a flat blunt fnout

Nófegay, n. a bunch of flowers, a pofy

Nófelefs, a. having no nofe, deſtitute of a nofe

Nofol'ogy, n. a fyſtematic claſſification of difeafes

Nofolo'gical, a. pertaining to Nofology

Nofol'ogiſt, n. one who claſſifies difeafes

Nofopoet'ic, n. caufing or productive of difeafes

Nos'tril, n. the inward cavity of the nofe

Nos'trum, n. a medicin, the ingredients of which are kept fecret

Not, ad. a particle of denying or refuſing

Not'able, a. memorable, buſtling, active, careful

Not'ablenefs, Notabil'ity, n. diligence, contrivance

Not'ably, ad. remarkably, with diligence or care

Nótary, n. one who proteſts bills or draws contracts

Notátion, n. the act of noting down, a meaning

Notch, v. t. to cut in fmall hollows; n. a nick

Note, n. a mark, token, written paper, found in mufic, abbreviation, explanatory annotation, an obligation without feal

Note, v. t. to fet down, obferve, attend, charge

Nóted, pa. a. fet down, celebrated, remarkable

Noth'ing, n. not any thing, a mere trifle, nonentity

Noth'ingnefs, n. a thing of no value, nonexiſtence

Nótice, n. regard, advice, information, warning

Nótice, v. t. to fee, regard, obferve, attend

Noticeable, a. that may be observed
Notification, n. the act of making known, a sign
Notify, v. t. to make known, declare, publish
Notion, n. a sentiment, opinion, idea, sense
Notional, a. imaginary, ideal, conceived, fond
Notionality, n. an empty or ungrounded opinion
Notionally, ad. in notion, in idea or conception
Notoriety, Notorioufness, n. public knowledge
Notorious, a. publicly known, plain, infamous
Notoriously, ad. in a notorious or base manner
Nott, n. a quantity of thred, confiding of 40 rounds
  of a reel, the 20th. of a run, or 80 yards
Notwithstanding, conj. in spite of, nevertheless
Nought, [nawt] n. not any thing, nothing
Noun, n. the name of things in grammar
Nourish, v. t. to support with food, to cherish
Nourishable, a. that may be nourished or fed
Nourishing, a. affording nutriment, cherishing
Nourishment, n. food, sustenance, support, help
Nousel, v.t. to entrap, confine, bring up, ob.
Novaculite, n. Turkey hone, a species of shittus
Novel, a. new, strange, appendant to the code
Novel, n. a feigned story or tale, a law to the code
Novelist, n. a writer of novels, an innovator
Novelty, n. a new thing or state, newness
November, n the eeventh month of the year
Novenary, n. the number nine; a. relating to nine
  * Italic N not silent
Novercal, a. relating to or like a stepmother
Novice, n. one unlearned or unskilled, a beginner
Noviciate, n. the state or condition of a novice
Novity, n. novelty, newness, freshness, ob.
Now, ad. at this very time; n. the present time
Nowadays, ad. now, in the present age or time
Now'ed, a. knotted, tied with knots, ob.
Nowhere, ad. not in any place, not in existence
Nowise, ad. not in any manner, by no means
Noxious, a. hurtful, destructive, criminal, guilty
Noxioufnefs, n. hurtfulnefs, a destructive quality
Noyeau, [noeyo] n. a rich cordial
Noz'zle, n. a nose, snout, front, point, end
Nub, n. a knob, a protuberance
Nub'ble, v.t. to bruise with fighting, bang, beat
Nub'by, a. full of knobs, or points
Nubiferous, a. bringing clouds, heavy, stormy
Nubile, a. marriageable, fit for marriage, grown
Nubilous, a. cloudy, overcast, dark, gloomy, dull
Nuciferous, a. bearing or producing nuts
Nucleus, n. the body of a comet, a central part
Nugacity or Nugality, n. trifling talk, futility
Nugatory, a. trifling, futile, insignificant, vain
Nuisance, n. that which annoys, see nusance
Null, n. a thing of no force or meaning, a cipher
Null, v. t. to annul, to annihilate; a. void, having
Nullity, n. a want of force or efficacy   (no force
Numb, a. benumbed, torpid, cold, chill, dead
Numb, v. t. to make numb, chill, stupify, deaden
Num'ber, v.t. to count, tell over, reckon, add
Num'ber, n. many units added, poetry, harmony

Num'berer, n. one who numbers or reckons
Num'berlefs, a. not to be numbered, innumerable
Num'bers, n. the fourth book of the Old Testament
Numb'nefs, Numb'ednefs, n. stupefaction, deadnefs
Numerable, a. that may be numbered or reckoned
Numeral, a. confiding of or relating to number
Nu'meral, n. a letter denoting a number, as L for 50
Numerally, ad. according to number, by numbers
Numerary, a. belonging to a certain number
Numeration, n. the art or act of numbering
Numerator, n. a number that measures others
Numerical, a. numeral, denoting famenefs
Numerically, ad. by a famenefs in number
Numerist, n. one who is well skilled in numbers
Numerosity, n. a numerous state, plenty, harmony
Numerous, a. containing many, musical, sweet
Numidian, n. a native of Numidia in Africa
Numidian, a. pertaining to Numidia
Numismatic, a. pertaining to coins or money
Num'mary, a. belonging to or containing money
Num'skull, n. a dunce, blockhead, dolt, head
Nun, n. a religious recluse woman, a small bird
Nunch'ion, n. victuals eaten between meals
Nun'ciature, n. the office or state of a nuncio
Nun'cio or Nun'ciate, n. a popes embassador
Nuncupative, Nuncupatory, a. verbally declared
Nun'nery, n. a place for the residence of nuns
Nuptial, a. pertaining or relating to marriage
Nuptials, n. a marriage, marriage-rites   (person
Nurse, n. one who takes care of a child or a sick
Nurse, Nour'sle, v. t. to bring up a child, to feed
Nurse'pond, n. a pond to keep young fish in
Nurser, n. one who nurses or feeds, a prompter
Nursery, n. the act of nursing, a room in which
  children are kept, a plantation of young trees
Nursling, n. one nurfed tenderly up, a fondling
Nurture, v. t. to train or bring up, educate, nurfe
Nurture, n. food, diet, nourishment, education
Nusance, n. that which annoys, the fource of continual or durable injury or inconvenience
Nuzzle, v. t. to fondle, cherish, carefs, hug, love
Nut, n. a fruit in a shell, a part of a screw
Nut, v. i. to go a nutting, to gather nuts
Nutant, a. nodding, declining
Nutation, n. a nodding, tremulous motion, shake
Nut'brown, a. brown like a ripe nut, very brown
Nut'crackers, n. pl. an instrument to break nuts
Nut'gall, n. the excrefcence of an oak   (with
Nut'hatch, n. a bird of the pye kind
Nut'meg, n. a very warm fine spice
Nutrication, n. the manner or state of feeding
Nutrient, n. that which feeds or nourishes
Nutriment, n. food, nourishment, aliment, fuel
Nutrimental, a. affording nourishment, good, rich
Nutrition, n. the quality or act of nourishing
Nutritious, Nutritive, a. nourishing, good, rich
Nutriture, n. the power or state of nourishing
Nut'tree, n. a tree that bears nuts
Nut'wood, n. the popular name of hickory

Nuz'zle, *v.* to nurfe, to go with the nofe down
Nyl'gaw, *n.* a quadruped like a cow and deer
Nymph, *n.* a goddefs of the woods, lady, virgin

O

OAF, *n.* a changling, filly fellow, idiot, fool
    O'afifh, *a.* dull, ftupid, weak, filly, foolifh
O'afifhnefs, *n.* dullnefs, ftupidity, weaknefs, folly
Oak, *n.* the name of a tree or its wood
O'akapple, *n.* a fpungy excrefcence ufual on oaks
O'aken, *a.* made of or gathered from the oak
O'akum, *n.* old ropes or cords quite untwifted
Oar, *n.* an inftrument ufed to row with
Oar, *v. t.* to row, to move or impel by rowing
Oaft, Oft, Ouft, *n.* a kiln to dry hops or malt on
Oat'cake, *n.* a cake that is made of oatmeal
O'aten, *a.* like or bearing oats, made of oatmeal
Oath, *n.* a folemn or a profane appeal to heaven
O'athable, *a.* that may take an oath, *ob.*
O'athbreaking, *n.* the breach of an oath, perjury
O'atmalt, *n.* malt that is made of oats
O'atmeal, *n.* flower of oats, a kind of herb
Oats, *n. pl.* a fpecies of grain well known
Obcord'ate, *a.* fhaped like a heart, with the apex
    downward
Obduce, *v. t.* to draw over, cover, conceal, hide
Obduc'tion, *n.* the act of drawing or laying over
Ob'duracy, Obduration, *n.* hardnefs of heart
Ob'durate, *a.* hardhearted, impenitent, ftubborn
Ob'durately, *ad.* ftubbornly, inflexibly
Ob'duratenefs, *n.* ftubbornnefs, hardnefs of heart
Obdured, *a.* hardened, inflexible, rough
Obedience, *n.* dutifulnefs, fubmiffion, compliance
Obedient, *a.* fubmiffive, obfequious, compliant
Obedien'tial, *a.* relating to obedience or refpect
Obediently, *ad.* with obedience, fubmiffively
Obeifance, *n.* an act of reverence, bow, courtefy
Ob'elifk, *n.* a pyramid, a mark ufed in printing
Oberrátion, *n.* the act of wandering up and down
Obefe, *a.* fat, loaden with flefh, grofs, heavy
Obefenefs, Obefity, *n.* fatnefs, grofsnefs
O'bey', [obáy] *v. t.* to fubmit to, obferve, regard
Obfufcate, *v. t.* to make dark, darken, obfcure
Obfufcátion, *n.* the act of darkening or obfcuring
Ob'ject, *n.* that on which we are employed, a matter
Object', *v. t.* to oppofe, charge with, urge   (object
Ob'jectglafs, *n.* the glafs in a telefcope next to the
Objec'tion, *n.* an oppofition, charge, fault, defect
Objective, *a.* propofed as or having an object
Objectively, *ad.* by way of object or objection
Object'or, *n.* one who objects, one who oppofes
Ob'it, *n.* death, funeral rites, an anniverfary
Obit'ual, *a.* relating to death or the time of it
Obit'uary, *n.* a regifter of deaths
Objurátion, *n.* a binding or fecuriug by oath
Objurg'ate, *v. t.* to chide, rebuke, reprove, fcold
Objurgátion, *n.* the act of chiding, a reproof
Obláda, *n.* a fifh variegated with lines
Obláte, *a.* flatted about the poles, like a fpheroid
Oblátion, *n.* an offering, facrifice, toil, fubfidy

Obleðátion, *n.* delight, pleafure, recreation
Ob'ligate, *v. t.* to bind, force, compel, oblige
O ligátion, Obligement, *n.* an engagement, bord,
Ob'ligatory, *a.* binding, compelling   (f.vor
Ob'ige, *v.* to bind, force, compel, do a favor
Obligée, *n.* one to whom a bond is executed
Obliging, *pa. a.* forcing, civil, kind, good
Obligingly, *ad.* civilly, complaifantly, kindly
Obligingnefs, *n.* civility, complaifance, force
Obligor', *n.* one who executes a bond or is bound
    by contract
Ob'iquátion, Obliquenefs, Obli''quity, *n.* an oblique
    ftate, a deviation from moral rectitude
Oblique, [obiíke] *a.* not direct, not perpendicu'ar
Obliquely, *ad.* not directly, not perpendicularly
Obliquenefs, Obliq'uity, *n.* deviation from a direct
    or perpendicular line or from rectitude
Oblit'erate, *v. t.* to blot out, efface, rafe, deftroy
Obliterátion, *n.* the act of blotting any thing out
Obliv'ial, Ob vious, *a.* caufing forgetfulnefs
Obliv'ion, *n.* forgetfulnefs, a general pardon
Ob'long, *a.* longer than broad; *n.* a long fquare
Ob'longly, *ad.* in an oblong form, ftate or direction
Ob'longifh, *a.* fomewhat oblong
Ob'longnefs, *n.* a ftate of being oblong
Ob'loquy, *n.* flander, a cenforious fpeech
Obmutef'cence, *n.* a lofs of fpeech, filence
Obnox'ious, *a.* liable, expofed, fubject, offenfive
Obnox'ioufly, *ad.* in an obnoxious manner
Obnox'ioufnefs, *n.* liablenefs to punifhment
Obnubilate, *v. t.* to cloud over, darken, obfcure
Obnubilátion, *n.* an obfcuring by clouds
Obóvate, *a.* inverfely ovate, or having the fmaller
    end downwards next the ftem
Obfcéne, *a.* immodeft, filthy, nafty, difgufting
Obfcénely, *ad.* in an immodeft manner, filthily
Obfcénenefs, Obfcen'ity, *n.* ribaldry, filthinefs
Obfcurátion, *n.* the act of darkening, darknefs
Obfcúre, *a.* dark, gloomy, difficult, unknown
Obfcúre, *v. t.* to darken, to make lefs intelligible
Obfcúrely, *ad.* darkly, imperfectly, privately
Obfcúrenefs, Obfcúrity, *n.* darknefs, privacy
Obfecrátion, *n.* an entreaty, fupplication, prayer
Obfequies, *n. pl.* funeral rites or folemnities
Obféquious, *a.* obedient, comp'afant, ready
Obféquioufly, *ad.* obediently, with funeral rites
Obféquioufnefs, *n.* ready obedience, complafance
Obferv'able, *a.* remarkable, plain, vifible, noted
Obferv'ably, *ad.* in a manner deferving of notice
Obferv'ance, *n.* attention, refpect, performance
Obferv'ant, *a.* attentive, diligent, heedful, fond
Obferv'ant, *n.* a flavifh or very carefal attendant
Obfervátion, *n.* a noting, notice, heed, remark, note
Obfervátor, Obferv'er, *n.* one that obferves   (tions
Obferv'atory, *n.* a place for aftronomical obferva-
Obferve', *v.* to watch, mind, mark, fee, obey
Obferv'ingly, *ad.* attentively, carefully, clofely
Obfef''fion, *n.* the act of befieging, a clofe attack
Obfolef'cent, *a.* growing obfolete

Obfidian, a. pertaining to a fiege
Obfidian, n. a filicious ftone, black or grayifh black
Obfolete, a. worn or grown out of ufe, difufed
Obfo'etenefs, n. a ftate of being difufed
Obstacle, n. an obftruction, bar, let, hindrance
Obftetric, a. pertaining to midwifery
Obstinacy, n. ftubbornnefs, perverfenefs
Obstinate, a. ftubborn, refolute, fixed, firm
Obstinately, ad. ftubbornly inflexibly, fternly
Obftipation, n. the act of filling or ftopping up
Obftrep'erous, a. noify, loud, bawling, clamorous
Obftrep'eroufly, ad. noifily, clamoroufly
Obftrep'eroufnefs, n. loud noife, clamor
Obftriction, n. an obligation, engagement, bond
Obftruct, v. t. to hinder, ftop, block up
Obftruc'tion, Obftructive, n. hindrance, obftacle
Obftructive, a. hindering, ftopping up, oppofing
Obs'truent, a. ftopping, blocking up, obftructing
Obftupefac'tion, n. a ftate of being ftupefied
Obftupefactive, a. ftupifying, overpowering
Obtain, v. to gain, get, acquire, procure, prevail
Obtainable, a. that may be obtained or procured
Obtainment, n. the act of obtaining or procuring
Obtend, v. t. to oppofe, hold out, pretend, ob
Obtenebration, n. the act of darkening, darknefs
Obten'fion, n. oppofition, denial, pretenfe, ob.
Obteft, v. t. to befeech, entreat, beg hard
Obteftation, n. a fupplication, prayer, entreaty
Obtrectation, n. defamation, detraction, fcandal
Obtrude, v. t. to thruft into, force, impofe
Obtruder, n. one who has no right to enter
Obtrufion, n. a breaking in upon by force
Obtrufive, a. difpofed or tending to intrude upon
Obtund, v. t. to blunt, dull, deaden, break, quell
Obtufe, a. not pointed, blunt, dull, flat, heavy
Obtufely, ad. without a point, bluntly, dully
Obtufenefs, n. bluntnefs, dulnefs, heavinefs
Obtufion, n. the act of blunting, bluntnefs
Obun.brate, v. t. to fhade over, cloud, darken, hide
Oovert, v. t. to turn upwards or againft, to turn
Ob'verfe, a. having the bafe narrower than the top
Ob'verfe, n. the face of a coin, oppofed to reverfe
Ob'viate, v. to meet, prevent, hinder, anfwer
Ob'vious, a. evident, clear, plain, eafy, open
Ob'vioufly, ad. evidently, plainly, apparently
Ob'vioufnefs, n. evidence, clearnefs, plainnefs
Ob'volute, a. rolled together, fo that the margins
    embrace each other, as leaves of plants
O cafion, n. a caufe, need, opportunity, incident
Occafion, v. t. to caufe, produce, effect, influence
Occafional, a. cafual, accidental, incidental
Occafionally, ad. upon accafion, now and then
Occafioner, n. one who caufes or promotes
Occafive, a. weftern, towards the fetting of a planet
Occecation, n. the act of blinding, ob.
Oc'cident, n. the weft, a. weftern, fetting
Occidental, Occid'uous, a. weftern, weft, fetting
O cip'ital, a. pertaining to the back part of the fkull
Occlude, v. t. to fhut up or againft, to clofe

Occlufe, pa. a. fhut up or againft, clofed
Occlufion, n. a clofing or fhutting up
Occult'nefs, n. the ftate of being hid, fecretnefs
Occult', a. fecret, hidden, unknown, myfterious
Occultation, n. the act or time of concealment
Oc'cupancy, n. poffeffion, the act of feizing on
Oc'cupant, n. one who holds or takes poffeffion
Oc'cupate, v. t. to hold, poffefs, enjoy, feize on
Occupation, n. a bufinefs, employment, trade, art
Oc'cupier, n. one who occupies, one who poffeffes
Oc'cupy, v. t. to hold, ufe, poffefs, employ, follow
Occur', v. i. to come, arife, happen, meet
Occur'rence, Occur'rent, n. any thing that happens
Occur'fion, n. a clafh, dafh, mutual blow or ftroke
O'cean, [o'fhun] n. the largeft body of water on
    the globe   (fea
O'cean, Ocean'ic, O'ceanous, a. pertaining to the
O'celated, a. having or refembling eyes, ob.
O'celot, n. the Mexican panther, or catamount
O'cher, [o'ker] n. a kind of earth, fine, fmooth
    and foft, of various colors
O'cherous, O'chery, a. like or containing ocher
Oc'tagon, n. a figure having eight fides and angles
Octag'onal, a. having eight fides or angles
Octahedron, n. a body with eight equal fides
Octahedral, a. having eight equal fides
Octan"gular, a. having eight angles or corners
Octan'dria, n. a clafs of plants having hermaphro-
    dite flowers with eight ftamens
Oc'tant, n. an afpect including 45 degrees
Oc'tave, n. the eighth day after, an eighth in mufic
Octavo, n. a fheet when folded into eight leaves
Octen'nial, a. happening every eighth year
Oc'tile, n. an afpect of planets diftant an eighth of a
    circle or 45 degrees
October, n. the tenth month of the year
Oc'tofid, a. divided into eight parts or fegments
Octoloc'ular, a. having eight cells for feeds
Octonoc'ular, a. having eight eyes
Octopet'alous, a. having eight petals
Octoradiated, a. having eight rays
Octofperm'ous, a. containing eight feeds
Oc'toftyle, n. a range of eight columns
Oc'tuple, a. eight-fold, eight times as many
Oc'ular, a. known by or depending on the eye
Oc'ularly, ad. by obfervation of the eye, by fight
Oc'uliform, a. refembling an eye
Oc'culift, n. one who cures diftempered eyes
Odd, a. uneven, particular, unaccountable, ftrange
Odd'ly, ad. unevenly, particularly, ftrangely
Odd'ity, n. a particularity, a ftrange perfon
Odd'nefs, n. an odd ftate, particularity, ftrangenefs
Odds, n. more than even number or wager
Ode, n. a fhort poem, a poem to be fung to mufic
O'dious, a. hateful, abominable, deteftable, vile
O'dioufly, ad. hatefully, abominably, hainoufly
O'dioufnefs, O'dium, n. hatred, difgrace, blame
Od'or, n. a fcent, fmell, fragrance
O'dorating, a. diffufing odor, fragrant

Odorif'erous, a. fragrant, fweet, perfumed
Odorif'eroufnefs, n. fragrance, fweetnefs of fmell
Odoros'ity, O'doroufnefs, n. that which occafions the fenfation of fmell
O'dorous, O'dorate, a. fragrant, perfumed, fcented
Oecon'omy, fee economy
Oecumen'ical, fee ecumenical
Oeil'iad, n. a glance, wink, token by the eye, ob.
O'er, ad. a contraction of over (from
Of, pr. concerning, among, according to, by, in,
Off, ad. fignifying diftance, not on or near, from
Off'al, n. wafte meat, refufe, entrails, carrion
Offend', v. to difpleafe, affront, tranfgrefs, fin
Offend'er, n. one who offends or tranfgreffes
Offenfe', n. a crime, fault, injury, difguft, affront
Offenfe'ful, a. injurious, hurtful, mifchievous
Offenfe'lefs, a. inoffenfive, innocent, harmlefs
Offens'ive, a. difpleafing, invading, injurious
Offens'ively, ad. in an offenfive manner
Offens'ivenefs, n. a caufe of difguft, mifchief
Of'fer, v. to prefent, propofe, try, bid, facrifice
Of'fer, n. a propofal, tender, attempt, price bidden
Of'ferer, n. one who makes an offer or facrifices
Of'fering, n. a facrifice, oblation, prefent, gift
Of'fertory, n. the act of offering, a thing offered
Of'fice, n. a public employment, bufinefs, duty
Of'fice, v. t. to perform, act, do, difcharge
Of'ficer, n. a man in office, a commander in the ar-
Of'ficer, n. to furnifh with officers (my
Of'ficerlike, a. like or becoming an officer
Of'ficered, a. fupplied with commanders
Offi''cial, a. relating to an office, conducive
Offi''cial, n. an officer in an ecclefiaftical court
Official'ity, n. the charge or duty of an official
Offi''cially, ad. by way of office, from authority
Offi''ciate, v. to perform another's duty, to give
Offi''cinal, a. ufed in or relating to fhops
Offi''cious, a. importunately forward, bufy, kind
Offi''cioufly, ad. with unafked kindnefs, readily
Offi''cioufnefs, n. great forwardnefs of civility
Off'ing, n. a fea-term for the open or full fea
Off'fcouring, n. the refufe of any thing, filth, dirt
Off'fet, n. a fprout from the root of a plant, a dif-
tance from a line in furveying
Off'fpring, n. a propagation, generation, race, fruit
Oft, Oft'en, Oft'entimes, Oft'times, ad. frequently,
ufually, moftly, many or feveral times
Ogee', n. a molding of two members, one round,
the other hollow
O'gle, v. t. to look at with pleafure, to look flily
O'gler, n. one who ogles, a fly or fond gazer
O'gling, n. the act of viewing flily or obliquely
Ogy''gian, a. relating to Ogyges, king of Beotia,
or the great inundation in his time
Oh! exclam. expreffive of forrow, furprife or pain
Oil, n. the juce of olive, &c. any thing unctuous
Oil, v. t. to fmear, anoint or foften with oil
Oil'bag, n. a gland in birds containing an oil
Oil'color, n. a colored fubftance ground up with oil

Oil'inefs, n. greafinefs, lubricity, fmoothnefs
Oil'man, n. a man who deals in oils
Oil'fhop, n. a fhop where oils are fold
Oil'y, a. containing oil, greafy, rich, glib, fmooth
Oint, v. t. to anoint, to fmear or daub over
Oint'ment, n. a kind of falve to anoint with
Old, O'lden, a. ancient, long practifed, long ago
O'ldfafhioned, a. gone out of fafhion, obfolete
O'ldnefs, n an old ftate, old age, antiquity
O'liander, n. the rofe-bay, a genus of plants
Olea''ginous, O'leofe, a. oily, unctuous, greafy
Oleas'ter, n. a plant, the wild olive
O'lénean, a. pertaining to Olenum in Peloponnefus
Olerá'ceous, a. of pot-herbs or confifting of them
Olfact'ory, a. having the fenfe of fmelling
Ol'iban; n. a gum refin from a fpecies of juniper
O'lid, O'lidous, a. fmelling ftrong, ob.
Oligarch'ical, [ch as k]a. pertaining to an oligarchy
Ol'igarchy, n. a government in the hands of few
Ol'io, n. a medley of meat, herbs and roots
Ol'itory, a. belonging to a kitchen garden
Olivaft'er, a. dark-brown; n. a wild olive
Ol'ive n. a tree or its fruit, an emblem of peace
Ol'iveyard, n. a place to cultivate or keep olives in
Ol'ivin, n. a filiceous ftone of a light brownifh
Olymp'iad, n. the fpace or term of four years (green
Olymp'ian, a. pertaining to Olympia a town in
Greece, and to olympus a mountain
Olymp'ic, a. pertaining to Olympia, and the
gamesthere celebrated
O'mber, n. a game at cards, the name of a fifh
Ombrom'eter, n. an inftrument to meafure the
quantity of rain that falls
Oméga, a. the laft letter of the Greek alphabet
Om'elet, n. a pancake made of eggs
O'men, n. a good or bad fign, token, prognoftic
O'mened, a. containing omens or prognoftics
O'mer, n. a Hebrew meafure of three wine quarts
Om'inate, v. i. to forebode, prognofticate, ob.
Ominátion, n. a foreboding, omen, prognoftic, ob.
Om'inous, a. foreboding ill, forethowing ill, bad
Om'inoufly, ad. with good or bad omens, frigh
Omis'fible, a. that may be omitted or left (f uay
Omis''fion, Omit'tance, n. neglect, forbearance
Omit', v. t. to leave out or off, pafs by, neglect
Omnifárious, a. containing all kinds or forts
Omnif'ic, a. all-creating, doing all things
Omnigénous, a. confifting of all kinds or forts
Omnip'otence, Omnip'otency, n. almighty power
Omnip'otent, a. almighty, all-powerful
Omnipres'ence, n. unbounded prefence, ubiquity
Omnipres'ent, a. prefent in every place at once
O mnis''cience, n. infinite wifdom or knowledge
Omnis''cient, a. knowing all things or actions
Om'nium, n. the aggregate of certain proportions
of ftocks in the funds
O nniv'orous, a. fwallowing things indifcrimi ately
O nol'ogy, n. fimilarity, agreement, proportion
On, pr. upon; ad. forward, in due progreffion

On'ager, n. a name of the wild afs (formerly
Once, [wunc:] ad. at one time, at the fame time,
Once or Ounce, n. a carnivorous quadruped of
the feline genus
One. [wun] a. fingle, different, any; n. a perfon,
Oneeyed, a. having only one eye (&c. an unit
Oneirocrit'ic, n. an interpreter of dreams, ob.
Oneirocrit'ical, a. interpreting dreams, ob.
One'nefs, n. the quality of being one, unity
On'erate, v. t. to load, burden, lay upon, opprefs
On'erofe, On'erous, a. heavy, burdenfome, hard
Onion, n. a plant having a bulbous root (fingle
Only, ad. fimply, fingly; a. this and no more
On'omancy, n. a divination of names, ob.
Onomant'ic, Onomant'ical, a. predicting by names
On'fet, n. an attack, affault, attempt, appendage
Onfet', v.t. to fet upon, attack, begin, attempt, ob.
On'flaught, n. a fierce attack, onfet, ftorm, ob.
Ontol'ogy, n. the fcience of being, metaphyfics
On'ward, ad, forward, progreffively, in advance
O'nyx, n. a femi pellucid gem, nail, hoof, fore
Ooze, n. a foft mud, flime, fpring, foft flow
Ooze, v. i. to drop out flowly, to run gently
Oozy, a. muddy, flimy, dirty, plafhy, moift
Opacate, v. t. to darken, obfcure, fhade, ob.
Opake, [opaque] a. not tranfparent, obfcure
Opakenefs, Opa"city, n. the quality of not tranf-
mitting rays of light
O'pal, n. a filiceous ftone in the form of a pebble
of various colors
Opalef'cent, a. refembling opal in color
O'palline, a. like or pertaining to opal
Ope, ufed in poetry for open
O'pen.v. to fet open, unlock, divide, explain, begin
O'pen, a. unfhut, unclofed, uncovered, plain, clear
O'pener, n. one who or what opens, an interpreter
O'pen-eyed, a watchful, attentive, vigilant, wary
O'pen-handed, a. generous, liberal, free, kind
O'penhearted, a. honeft, candid, generous, free
O'pening, n. a place opened, breach, way, dawn
O penly, ad. publicly, evidently, plainly, clearly
O'penmouthed, a. talkative, ravenous, furious
O'pennefs, n. freedom from difguife, clearnefs
Op'era, n. a kind of mufical entertainment
Op'erable, a. that may be done, practicable, ob.
Op'erant, a. laboring, active, bufy, able to prod
Op'erate, v. to work, act, perform, effect, ftir
Operátion, n. a work, action, agency, effect
Op'erative, a. having the power of acting, ftrong
Op'erator, n. one who operates, one who effects
Operófe, a. laborious, troublefome, tedious
Oper'culate, a. having an operculum or cover
Ophid'ion, n. a fifh like an eel but fhorter
Ophioph'agous, a. eating or feeding on ferpents
O'phite, n. marble with fpots like a ferpent
Ophthal'mic, a. relating to or fit for the eyes
Ophthal'my, n. an inflamation of the eyes
O'piate, n. a medicine caufing fleep; a. caufing
Opi'ficer, n. an artift, workman, maker (fleep

Op'inator, n. one who holds an opinion, ob.
Opíne, v. i. to think, believe, judge, ob.
Opinias'ter, n. one fond of his opinion, ob.
Opin'iative, Opin'ionative, a. ftiff in opinion
Opin'iator, Opin'ionift, n. one ftiff in opinion
Opiniáter, a. obftinate, ftubborn, ftiff, ob.
Opin'iatry, n. obftinacy, ftubbornnefs, ob.
Opin'ion, n. a notion, fentiment, judgment
Opin'ionated, a. obftinate, ftubborn, bigoted
O'pium, n. the diftilled juce of Turkifh poppies
Opobal'fam, n. a refin from a tree in Arabia
Opos'fum, n. a quadruped which carries her young
in a bag under her belly
Oppig'norate, v. t. to pawn, pledge, bind, ob.
Oppilátion, n. an obftruction, matter heaped up
Op'pilative, a. obftructing, ftopping
Op'ponent, a. adverfe, oppofit, oppofing, croffing
Op'ponent, n. an antagonift, competitor, rival
Opportúne, a. feafonable, convenient, fit, proper
Opportúnely, ad. feafonably, conveniently, fitly
Opportúnity, n. a fit place or time, convenience
Oppófe, v. to act againft, withftand, object
Oppófer, n. one who oppofes, an antagonift, a rival
Op'pofite, more correctly oppofit; a. facing, con-
trary, adverfe, crofs, repugnant
Op'pofit, n. an opponent, a thing contrary
Op'pofitly, ad. in an oppofit manner, crofsly
Oppofi"tion, n. refiftance, contradiction, a party
oppofing, fituation in front, contrariety
Oppos'itifólious, a. growing oppofit to the leaves
Oppofi"tionift, n. one who belongs to a party op-
pofed to the ruling power or party
Opprefs', v. t. to injure, crufh by hardfhip, fubdue
Oppres"fion, n. cruelty, hardfhip, heavinefs
Opprefs'ive, a. cruel, fevere, heavy, unjuft
Opprefs'or, n. one who oppreffes, a tyrant
Oppróbrious, a. reproachful, difgraceful, vile
Oppróbrioufly, ad. reproachfully, difgracefully
Opróbrioufnefs, n. reproachfulnefs, fcurrility
Oppróbrium, n. reproach, difgrace, infamy
Oppúgn, v. t. to oppofe, attack, refift, confute
Oppug'nancy, n. oppofition, refiftance, cavil
Oppúgner, n. one who oppofes, one who attacks
Op'tative, a. expreffive of defire, wifhing
Op'tic, n. an organ or inftrument of or for fight
Op'tic, Op'tical, a. relating to optics or vifion
Opti"cian, n. a perfon who is fkilled in optics
Op'tics, n. the fcience or doctrin of vifion
Op'timacy, n. nobility, the whole body of nobles
Op'timifm, n. the opinion that all is for the beft
Op'tion, n. a choice, liberty of choofing, will
Op'tional, a. left to free choice or election
O'pulence or Op'ulency, n. wealth, riches
Op'ulent, a. wealthy, rich, affluent, abundant
Op'ulently, ad. richly, with fplendor
Or, n. gold in heraldry; conj. either
O'rach, n. a plant of feveral fpecies (ter oracles
Or'acle, n. a wife fentence or perfon; v. i. to ut-
Orac'ular, Orac'ulous, a. uttering oracles, wife

Orac'uloufly, ad. in manner of an oracle, wifely
Or'aifon or Or'ifon, n. a prayer, fupplication, wifh
O'ral, a. delivered by the mouth only, not written
O'rally, ad. by word of mouth, without writing
O'ran out'ang, n. the largeft of the ape kind, and the brute moft like the human fpecies
Or'ange, n. a fine well known fruit
Or'angery, n. a plantation of orange treees
Or'angepeel, n. the fkin or rind of an orange
Orátion, n. a rhetorical fpeech, harangue, addrefs
Or'ator, n. a fpeaker, eloquent perfon, petitioner
Oratórial, Orator'ical, a. becoming an orator, rhetorical, florid, eloquent
Oratório, n. a kind of facred drama fet to mufic
Or'atory, n. the fcience of rhetoric, a place for
Orb, n. a fphere, circle, wheel, the eye (prayer
Or'bate, a. deprived, childlefs, fatherlefs
Orbátion, n. a deprivation, a lofs of parents, &c.
Or'bed, a. rounded, formed into a circle, circular
Orbic'ular, a. fpherical, circular, round,
Orbic'ularly, ad. circularly, fpherically
Or'ic'ulate, a. round, like an orb
Orbic'ulate, v. t. to form round or into an orb
Or'bis or Orb'fifh, n. a fifh of a circular form
Or'bit, n. the line in which a planet moves, a track
Or'bital, Orbit'ual, a. like or pertaining to an orbit
Or'bitar, a. noting a part near the orbit of the eye
Or'chard, n. a garden or place of fruit trees
Or'chefter or Or'cheftra, [ch as k] n. a gallery for muficians or the muficians collectiv'ly
Or'charding, n. orchards in general, the cultivation of an orchard (nium in Greece
Orchoménean, [ch as k] a. pertaining to Orchome-
    * Italic O not filent.
O'dáin, v. t. to appoint, eftablifh, fettle, inveft
Or'deal, n. a trial of innocence by fire or water
O:'der, n. a command, method, rule, rank, clafs
O:'der, v. t. ro bid, teil, direct, regulate, fet apart
O:'derer, n. one who orders, one who reguiates
O:'derlefs, a. irregular, diforderly, void of rule
O:'derly, a. regular, methodical; ad. regularly
Or'ders, n. pl priefthood, ftate of the clergy
Or'dinable, a. that may be appointed or fettled
O:'dinal, n a book of rites; a. noting due order
Or'dinance, n. a law, rule, appointment, holy rite
O:'dinarily, ad. ufually, according to fixed ru'e
Or'dinary, a. common, ufual, mean, ugly, plain
Or'dinary, n. a judge, eating houfe, price of a meal
Or'dinate, a. regular, methodical; v. t. to appoint
Or'dinates, n. right lines parallel and cutting curves in a number of points
Ordinátion, n. the act of ordaining, order, fet ru'e
Ord'nance, n. cannon, artillery, mortars
Or'donnance, n. difpofition of figures in pictures
Or'dure, n. animal dung, filth, naftinefs
Ore, n. metal in its mineral ftate, a fmall coin
Orei'lar, n. a fmall bat with long ears
Or'gal, n. argol, lees of wine dried, tartar
Or'gan, n. a natural or a mufical inftrument

Or'ganbuilder, n. a perfon who makes organs
Organ'ic, Organ'ical, a. inftrumental, conducive
Organ'ically, ad. by means of inftruments
Or'ganifm, n. an organical ftructure or form
Or'ganift, n. a perfon who plays on an organ
Organizátion, n. a ftructure, a formation
Or'ganize, v. t. to conftruct, form, frame
Or'panpipe, n. the pipe or tube of an organ
Or'gafm, n. a fudden exertion, violence, force
Or'gies, n. mad rites of Bacchus, frantic revels
Orgil'lous, a. proud, haughty, arrogant, ob.
Or'gues, n. long timbers fhod with pointed iron hung over a gate-way to be let down on the approach of an enemy
O'rient, a. eaftern, rifing, bright, fhining
Orient'al, a. placed in or coming from the eaft
Orient'al, n. an inhabitant or native of the eaft
O:ient'alifm, n. a peculiar idiom of the eaft
Orient'alift, n. one fkilled in the eaftern languages
Oriental'ity, n. an oriental ftate or fituation
Or'ifice, n. an opening, perforation, mouth (leaves
Or'igan, n. the plant wild marjoram or oil of its
Or'igin, n. a beginning, rife, fource, defcent, ftock
Ori"ginal, n. a fource, a firft copy; a. primitive,
Original'ity, n. the quality of being original (firft
Ori"ginally, ad. at firft, primarily, chiefly
Ori"ginary, a. primitive, productive, caufing
Ori"ginat, v. to begin, arife, fpring, give rife to
Originátion, n. a bringing into exiftence, a firft caufe (baftions that have cafemates
Oril'lon, n a rounding of earth on the fhoulder of
O'riole, n a beautiful bird of America
O'rion or Orion, n a fouthern conftellation (ital
Or'let or Or'lo, n. a fillet under the ovolo of a cap-
Or'lop, n. the middle deck of a fhip (faly
Ormérian, a. pertaining to the Ormenium in The:-
Or'nament, v. t. to adorn, embellifh, drefs, fet off
Or'nament, Or'nature, n. decoration, grace, honor
Ornament'al, a. tending to adorn, graceful
Ornament'ally, ad. in a manner to adorn
O:'namented, O'rnate, pa. adorned, decked
Ornithol'ogy, n. the fcience or account of birds
Orol'ogy, n. the fcience or a defcription of moun-
    tains (tains
O.olo"gical, a. pertaining to a defcription of moun-
Orol'ogift, n. a defcriber of mountains
Or'phan, n. a fatherlefs child; a. bereft of parents
Orpphéan, Or'phic, a. pertaining to Orpheus the great mufician of Greece
Or'pheus, n. a fifh of a thick flat figure
Or'piment, n. fulphuret of arfenic, 80 parts of ful-
    phur and 20 of arfenic
Or'pine, n. a plant of feveral kinds, livelong
or'rer, n. an inftrument to fhow the revolutions of the planets
or'ris, n. gold and filver lace, a plant, a flower
or'thodox, a. found in doctrin or belief, true
or'thodoxly, ad. with foundnefs of opinion
or'thodoxy, n. true belief, foundnefs of doctrin

T 2

orthodrom'ics, n. the art of failing in the arch of a great circle or by the shortest course

or'thoepy, n. the art of just pronunciation

er'thoepist, n. one skilled in pronunciation

orthogon, n. a right-angled or squared figure

orthog'onal, a. rightangled, rectangular

orthog'rapher, n. one who spells grammatically

orthographical, a. rightly spelled, rightly drawn

orthographically, ad. according to rule, truly, orthog'raphy, n. right spelling or writing (exactly

o'rtive, a. rising as a planet or star, easterly

o'rtolan, n. a small but very delicate bird

oscillation, n. the vibration of a pendulum

os'cillatory, a. moving like a pendulum, waving

os'citancy, oscitation, n. a yawning, carelessness

os'citant, a. yawning, sleepy, sluggish, heavy, dull

osculation, n. the act of kissing, a close contract

os'culatory, a. pertaining to kissing or contact

o'sier or o'zier, n. a tree of the willow kind

os'mund, n. a plant, the flowering fern

os'pray, n. a species of eagle

os'seous, a. bony, like or made of bone, stony

os'sicle, n. a small or little bone, a stone of fruit

ossific, a. making or converting to bone

ossification, n. the act of changing into bone

os'sifrage, n. a strong fierce kind of eagle

os'sify, v. to change, turn or harden into bone

ossiv'orous, a. devouring or swallowing bones

os'suary, n. a place kept for the bones of the dead

ostens'ible, a. that may be shown, apparent, seem-

osten'sibly, ad. apparently, seemingly (ing

ostens'ive, a. tending to show, betokening

os'tent, n. a show, appearance, token, prodigy, ob.

ostent'ate, v. t. to show with parade, to display, ob.

ostentation, n. outward or vain show, parade

ostentatious, a. fond of show, pompous, proud

ostentatiously, ad. with pomp or parade, vainly

os'teocolla, n. a petrefaction in the form of roots of trees

osteol'ogy, n. a description of the human bones

osteolo'gic, a. pertaining to osteology

os'tiary n. the mouth of a river, a doorkeeper

os'tler, n. one who takes care of horses at inns

os'tracism, n. a banishment by votes written on

os'tracite, n. a fossil oyster shell (shells

os'trich, n. a large bird with elegant fethers, and wings too short for flight

otacous'tic, n. an instrument to help hearing

oth'er, [o as u] a. not the same, different, diverse

oth'ergates, ad. in another manner

oth'erguise, ad. of another kind

oth'erwhere, ad. in another place, elsewhere

oth'erwise, ad. in a different manner or degree

ot'a or a'tyr, n. the essential oil of roses

oto'mo, n. a bird of Germany, as large as a pigeon

ot'ter, n. a strong amphibious animal

ot'toman, a. belonging to the Turks

Ought, [aut] n. any thing, mistake for aught

Ought, v. i. to be obliged, become, be fit

Ounce, n. the sixteenth of a pound, avordupois, and the fourteenth of a pound, troy, see once

Ouphe, n. a fairy, elf, goblin, ob.

Ouph'en, a. elfish, like an elf, like a fairy, ob.

Our, pron. pertaining or relating to us

Ourself', pron. used in royal style for myself

Ourselves', pron. recip. we, not any other persons

Ousel, n. a black bird

Oust, v. t. to cast or put out, vacate, take away

Ous'ter, n. a dispossessing

Out, ad. and pr. abroad, not at home, from, in an

Out, v. to drive away, to deprive, be gone (error

Outact', v. t. to do or go beyond, excel, exceed

Outbal'ance, v. t. to outweigh, to preponderate

Outbid, v. t. outbade, outbid, pret. outbid, out-
bidden, pa. to bid more than any other

Out'bound, a. going far or on a distant voyage

Outbráve, v. t. to bear down, dash, bully, dare

Outbrázen, v. t. to bear down with impudence

Out'break, n. a breaking out, breach, eruption

Outbréathe, v, i. to breathe the longer, to die

Out'cast, a. cast out, banished, expelled •

Out'cast, n. a person who is banished or rejected

Outcraft', v. t. to excel or outdo in cunning

Out'cry, n. a cry of distress, public clamor, sale

Outdáre, v. t. to venture beyond, beat, bully

Outdáte, v. t. to make old or void, to antiquate

Outdó, [outdoo] v. t. outdid, pret. outdone, pa.
to excel, surpass, go beyond, beat

Outdwell', v. i. outdwelled, outdwelt, pret. outdwelt, pa. to stay beyond the due time

Out'er, a. that is without, outward, more remote

Out'erly, ad. towards or near the outside, far off

Outfáce, v. t. to bear or stare down, to brave out

Out'fall, n. a fall of water, canal, ditch, quarrel

Outfawn', v. t. to exceed in fawning or flattery

Out'fits, n. pl. the expenses of equipping and fur-
nishing a ship, &c.

Outfly', v. t. outflew, pret. outflown, pa. to fly beyond, leave behind, exceed

Out'form, n. an outward appearance, a pretense

Outfrown', v. t. to frown down, overbear, deject

Out'gate, n. an outlet, passage out, place of escape

Outgen'eral, v. t. to beat in or by generalship

Outgive', v. t. outgave, pret. outgiven, pa. to surpass in giving, to give most

Outgó, v. t. outwent, pret. outgone, pa. to surpass, excel, overreach, cheat

Outgrów, v. t. outgrew, pret. outgrown, pa. to
surpass or exceed in growth

Out'guard, n. the advanced guard of an army

Outher'od, v. t. to exceed in absurdity or cruelty

Outjest', v. t. to exceed or surpass in jesting

Outknáve, v. t. to surpass or outdo in knavery

Outland'ish, a. foreign, rustic, coarse

Outlast', v. t. to surpass in duration, to outlive

Out'law, n. one excluded the benefit of the law

Out'law, v. t. to deprive of the benefit of the law

Out'lawry, n. a depriving of the protection of the law

Outléap, *v. t.* to furpafs or outdo in leaping

Out'leap, *n.* a fally out, iffue from, flight, efcape

Out'let, *n.* a paffage or difcharge outwards, a gate

Out'line, *n.* the firft line of a device or figure

Outlive', *v. t.* to live longeft or after, to furvive

Outlook', *v. t.* to face down, outftare, browbeat

Outlus'ter, *v. t.* to exceed in lufter or brightnefs

Out'lying, *a.* placed out of order, not yet paid

Outmarch', *v. t.* to march quicker, to leave behind

Outmea"sure, *v. t.* to exceed in meafure

Out'moft, Out'ermoft, *a.* fartheft from the middle

Outnum'ber, *v. t.* to exceed or outdo in number

Outpáce, *v. t.* to outgo, outwalk, leave behind

Out'part, *n.* a part lying near or on the outfide

Out'parters, *n. pl.* a kind of freebooters or thieves

Outpafs', *v. t.* to go beyond, exceed

Outpóur, *v. t.* to emit, to fead out in a ftream

Outpóuring, *n.* a pouring out, diffufion

Outprize, *v. t.* to prize or value too highly

Out'rage, *v. t.* to injure greatly, to infult grofsly

Out'rage, *n.* violence, fury, tumultuous mifchief

Outrágeous, *a.* violent, furious, mad, enormous

Outrágeoufly, *ad.* violently, furioufly, tumultu-

Outrágeoufnefs, *n.* violence, fury, rage (oufly

Outréach, *v. t.* to go beyond, exceed, cheat, gull

Outreck'on, *v. t.* to exceed in reckoning

Outríde, *v. t.* outrid, outrode, *pret.* outridden, *pa.* to ride the fafteft, to leave behind

Out'rider, *n.* a rider for others, fervant, bailiff

Out'rigger,*n.* a beam or boom thruft out from a fhip

Outright, *ad.* immediately, directly, completely

Out'road, *n.* a deviation, excurfion, ramble, trip

Outróar, *v. t.* to exceed or outdo in roaring

Outroot', *v. t.* to root or pull up, to deftroy

Outrun', *v. t.* outran, *pret.* outrun, *pa.* to beat or leave behind in a race

Outfail, *v. t.* to beat or leave behind in failing

Outfcorn', *v. t.* to bear down by contempt

Outfell', *v. t.* outfold, *pret.* outfold, *pa.* to fell for more or a better price

Out'fet, *n.* the firft fetting out or beginning

Outfhine, *v. t.* outfhined, outfhone, *pret.* and *pa.* to excel in lufter or brightnefs

Outfhoot', *v. t.* outfhot, *pret.* outfhot, *pa.* to exceed or pafs in fhooting

Out'fide, *n.* the outward part, fhow, appearance

Outfit', *v. t.* outfat, *pret.* outfat, outfitten, *pa.* to fit longer or beyond the time

Outfléep, *v. i.* outflept, *pret.* outflept, *pa.* to fleep beyond the proper time

Outfpéak, *v. t.* outfpake, outfpoke, *pret.* outfpoken, *pa.* to fpeak the longer, to outtalk

Outfpórt, *v. i.* to exceed or outdo in fporting

Outfpread', *v. t.* outfpread, *pret.* outfpread, *pa.* to fpread open, extend, diffufe

Outftand', *v.* outftood, *pret.* outftood, *pa.* to ftand beyond proper time, to refift

Outftand'ing, *pa.* ftanding out, left unpaid

Outftáre, *v. t.* to put out of countenance by ftaring

Out'ftreet, *n.* a ftreet lying at the end of a town

Outftretch', *v. t.* to extend, enlarge, fpread out

Outftrip', *v. t.* to outgo, leave behind, excel

Outfweár, *v. t.* outfware, outfwore, *pret.* outfworn, *pa.* to overpower by fwearing

Outfwéeten, *v. t.* to exceed in fweetnefs

Outtalk', *v. t.* to overpower or outdo by talk

Outtongue', *v. t.* to bear down by noife or talk

Outval'uc, *v. t.* to value or efteem too highly

Outven'om, *v. t.* to exceed in venom or poifon

Outvie, *v. t.* to excel, exceed, furpafs, go beyond

Outvill'ain, *v. t.* to exceed in villany or roguery

Outvoice', *v. t.* to outroar, to bawl or cry louder

Outvóte, *v. t.* to furpafs or exceed in votes

Outwalk', *v. t.* to leave in walking, to go fafteft

Out'wall, *n.* the outward part of a building

Out'ward, *a.* lying on the outfide, apparent, foreign

Out'ward, *ad.* to the outer parts; *n.* the outfide

Out'wardbound, *a.* going from a port or country

Out'wardly, *ad.* in outward manner, apparently

Out'wards, *ad.* towards the outparts or outfide

Outwatch', *v. t.* to exceed in watching

Outweár, *v. t.* outware, outwore, *pret.* outworn, *pa.* to wear longer

Outwéigh, [outway] *v. t.* to exceed in weight

Outwit', *v. t.* to cheat, to overcome by cunning

Out'work, *n.* a fortification neareft to the enemy

Outwórn, *a.* deftroyed by ufe or age, gone

Outworth', *v. t.* to excel in virtue or value

Out'wrought, *a.* outdone, exceeded in power

o'val, *n.* a figure like an egg ; *a.* like an egg

ovárious, *a.* confifting of or refembling eggs

o'vary, *n.* the feat of eggs or of impregnation

o'vate, *a.* nearly oval, with one end elliptical, the other narrower

ovátion, *n.* a leffer kind of triumph for victory (in

ov'en,[o as u]*n.* an arched place for baking things

o'ver, *pr.* and *ad.* more, above, upon, before, paft

overabound', *v. i.* to abound more than enough

overact', *v. t.* to act or do more than enough

o'veralls, *n.* a kind of long clofe trowfers

o'veranxious, *a.* too anxious, too eager

overarch', *v. t.* to cover over with an arch

overawe', *v. t.* to keep in awe, keep under, ftop

overbal'ance, *v. t.* to outweigh, to preponderate

o'verbalance, *n.* fomething more than equivalent

o'verbattle, *a.* too fruitful, too rich, ob.

overbeár, *v. t.* to overbore, *pret.* overborne, *pa.* to bear down, fubdue, keep in awe

overbid', *v. i.* overbade, overbid, *pret.* overbid, overbidden, *pa.* to bid too much

o'verboard, *ad.* out of the fhip, off the fhip

overboil', *v. a.* to boil too much or too long

overbó'd, *a.* too bold, daring, impudent, faucy

o'verbulk', *v. t.* to bear down by bulk, ob.

overbur'den, *v. t.* to burden or load too much

overbuy', *v. t.* to overbought, *pret.* overbought, *pa.* to buy at too dear or high a rate, ob.

overcar'ry, *v. t.* to carry too far, to hurry too far

overcaſt', *v. a.* overcaſt, *pret.* overcaſt, *pa.* to few over, cloud, darken

overcharge', *v.i.* to rate too high, to fill too full

overcloud', *v. t.* to cover with clouds, to darken

overcome', *v. t.* overcame, *pret.* overcome, *pa.* to ſubdue, conquer, vanquiſh, beat

overcount', *v. t.* to rate or value too high

overdo, [overdoo]*v.t.*overdid,*pret.* overdone,*pa.* to do more than enough, to do too much

overdreſs', *v. t.* to dreſs or adorn laviſhly

    * Italic O not ſilent

Overdrive, *v. t.* overdrave, overdrove ; *pret.* overdriven ; *pa.* to drive too hard or faſt

Overemp'ty, *v. t.* to make or render too empty

Overeye, *v. t.* to ſuperintend, obſerve, look to

O'verfall, *n.* a ſteep fall of water, a cataract

Overfeed, *v. t.* overfed ; *pret.* overfed ; *pa.* to feed too much, cram, glut, ſtuff

Overfloat, *v. i.* to float, ſwim, overflow, paſs over

Overflow, *v. t.* to run over, deluge, be too full

O'verflow, *n.* an inundation, deluge, exuberance

Overflowing, *n.* copiouſneſs, a very great plenty

Overflowingly, *ad.* redundantly, exuberantly

Overfly, *v. t.* overflew ; *pret.* overflown ; *pa.* to paſs over or croſs by flight

Overfor'wardneſs, *n.* too great forwardneſs, haſte

Overget', *v. t.* overgat, overgot, *pret.* overgotten *pa.* to come up with, overtake, reach, *ob.*

Overglance', *v. t.* to look haſtily or very ſoon over

Overgo, *v.t.* overwent ; *pret.* overgone ; *pa.* to ſurpaſs, exceed, excel, outdo, beat

O'vergraſt, *a.* grown over with graſs, *ob.*

Overgrow, *v. t.* overgrew ; *pret.* overgrown ; *pa.* to grow beyond the natural ſize

O'vergrown, *pa.* too large or bulky, very proud

O'vergrowth, *n.* an improper or uncommon ſize

Overhale, *ſee* overhaul

Overhang', *v.* overhanged, overhung; *pret.* and *pa.* to jut over or out, project, hang out

Overhard'en, *v. t.* to make or render too hard

Overhaul' *v. t.* to turn over and examin, to looſen, to gain upon or overtake

Overhaul'ing *n.* a turning over for examination

Overhead', *ad.* aloft, above, in a place above

Overhear, *v. t.* overheard ; *pret.* overheard ; *pa.* to hear ſecretly or only by chance

overheat, *v. t.* to heat too or very much (extaſy

overjoy', *v. t.* to tranſport, to raviſh ; *n.* tranſport,

overlabor, *v. t.* to take too much pains, to drudge

overlade, *v. t.* overladed, *pret.* overladed, overladen, *pa.* to overburden, to overload

overlarge', *a.* too large or great, vaſt, huge, groſs

overlaſh'ingly, *ad.* with exaggeration, *ob.*

overlay, *v. t.* overlaid, *pret.* overlaid, *pa.* to ſmother, oppreſs by weight, cover

overleap, *v. t.* to leap over, to beat in jumping

o'verlether, *n.* the upperlether of a ſhoe

overlive, *v.* to live too long, live longer, ſurvive

o'verliver, *n.* one who lives longeſt or ſurvives

overload, *v. t.* overloaded, *pret.* overloaded, overloaden, *pa.* to load too much

overlong', *a.* too or very long, too long continued

overlook', *v. t.* to peruſe, examin, review, ſuperintend, neglect, paſs by indulgently, excuſe

overlook'er, *n.* one who overlooks, watches, &c.

overmaſt'ed, *a.* carrying too much maſt

overmaſt'er, *v. t.* to ſubdue, conquer, beat, govern

overmatch', *v. t.* to be too powerful, to conquer

o'vermatch, *n.* a perſon of ſuperior ſtrength, &c.

o'vermoſt, *a.* placed over the reſt, higheſt, firſt

overmuch', *ad.* in too great a degree ; *a.* too much

overname, *v. t.* to name in a ſeries, to reckon over

overnight, *n.* the night before, the night now paſt

overof fice, *v. t.* to behave haughtily, *ob.*

overoffi'cious, *a.* too officious, too forward

overpaſs', *v. t.* to overlook, omit, flight, neglect

overpay, *v. t.* overpaid, *pret.* overpaid, *pa.* to pay more than the juſt price

overpeer, *v. a.* to overlook, view, hover over

overperch', *v. t.* to fly over or beyond, to paſs over

o'verplus, *n.* what is left or more than ſufficient

overply', *v. t.* to ply or work too cloſely

overpoiſe', *v. t.* to outweigh, weigh more, outdo

o'verpoiſe, *n.* a preponderant weight or power

overpow'er, *v. t.* to oppreſs by power, to conquer

overpreſs', *v.t.* to overwhelm, cruſh, deſtroy, ruin

overprize, *v.t.* to prize, value or love, too much

overrank', *a.* too rank, very ſtrong or offenſive

overrate, *v. t.* to rate too much or too high

overreach, *v.* to go beyond, deceive, cheat

overreacher, *n* one who overreaches, a cheat

overread, *v. t.* overread, *pret.* overread, *pa.* to read quite through, to peruſe

overred', *v.* to make red all over, to redden over

Overripen, *v.* to make or grow too ripe, to ſpoil

Overroaſt, *v. t.* to roaſt too much or too long

Overrule, *v. t.* to ſuperintend, ſuperſede, perſuade

Overrun', *v. t.* overran, *pret.* overrun, *pa.* to outrun, overſpread, ravage, lay waſte

Overſat'urated, *a.* more than ſaturated

Overſee, *v. t.* overſaw, *pret.* overſeen, *pa.* to overlook, manage, omit

Overſeen, *pa.* overlooked, declared, miſtaken

Overſeer, *n.* a ſuperintendant, clerk, pariſh-officer

Overſet', *v.* overſet, *pret.* overſet, *pa.* to fall off from the baſis, to overturn

Overſhade, *v. t.* to cover with darkneſs, to hide

Overſhad'ow, *v. t.* to cover, ſhelter, hide, protect

Overſhoot', *v.* overſhot, *pret.* overſhot, *pa.* to go beyond or too far, paſs, aſſert too much

O'verſhot, *a.* an overſhot mill or wheel is one which receives the water a little beyond the top on the deſcent, ſo that the water is *ſhot over* the wheel

O'verſight, *n.* a miſtake, error, fault, inſpection

Overſize, *v. t.* to ſize over, to ſurpaſs in bulk

Overſkip', *v. t.* to ſkip over, paſs by, ſlip, eſcape

Overſleep, *v. i.* overſlept, *pret.* overſlept, *pa.* to

sleep too long or too much

Overslip', v. t. to pass over unnoticed, to neglect

Oversnow, v. t. oversnowed, pret. oversnowed, oversnown, pa. to cover with snow, ob.

Oversold, a, fold for or at too high a price, ob.

Oversoon, ad. too soon, too early, too hastily

Overspent', a. greatly wearied, quite harrassed

Overspread', v. t. overspread, pret. overspread, pa. to cover over, scatter over, fill

Overstand', v. i. overstood, pret. overstood, pa. to stand too much upon terms, ob.

Overstare, v. t. to outstare, to stare wildly, ob.

Overstock', v. t. to fill or put too full, to crowd

Overstrain, v. t. to stretch or extend too far

Oversway, v. t. to overrule, govern, dissuade

Overswell', v. t. to rise above, to overflow

O'vert, a. open, public, apparent, manifest, plain

Overtake, v. t. overtook, pret. overtaken, pa. to come up with, to catch

Overtask', v. t. to give too great or too long a task

Overtax', v. t. to tax too much or too high

Overthrow, v. t. overthrew, pret. overthrown, pa. to throw down, defeat, destroy

O'verthrow, n. a defeat, ruin, destruction, havoc

O'verthwart, a. opposit, adverse, perverse, cross

O'verthwartly, ad. perversely, crossly, across

O'verthwartness, n. perverseness, crossness

O'vertly, ad. openly, publicly, honestly, plainly

Overtop', v. t. to exceed in height, to surpass

Overtrip', v. t. to walk lightly or nimbly over

O'verture, n. an opening, proposal, piece of music

Overturn', v. t. to throw down, destroy, conquer

O'verturner, n. one who throws down or destroys

Overvalue, v. t. to value, rate or esteem too high

Overveil', [overvail] v. t. to veil over (out

Overwatch', v. t. to want sleep too long, to weary

Overweak, a. too weak or feeble, unable

Overweath'er, v. t. to batter by bad weather

Overween, v. i. to think too highly or fondly

Overweigh', [overway] v. t. to outweigh

O'verweight', n. more than weight, preponderance

Overwhelm', v. t. to crush, subdue, overpower

Overwhelm'ingly, ad. in a destructive manner

Overworn, a. worn quite out, spoiled by time

Overwrought', a. labored too much, too fine

O'viform, a. like an egg, shaped like an egg, oval

Ovip'arous, a. that bringeth forth eggs or by eggs

O'volo, n. a round molding, the quarter of a circle, called also a quarter round

Owe, v. t. owed, pret. owed, owen, pa. to be in debt, be obliged, pay to, own

O'wing, pa. now due, to be ascribed to as a cause

Owl, Owl'et, n. a kind of bird that flies by night

Owl'er, n. a name in England for one that exports wool contrary to law

Own, pron. as my own, their own, our own, &c.

Own, v. t. to acknowledge, confess, claim, possess

O'wner, n. one to whom a thing justly belongs

O'wnership, n. property, right, lawful possession

Owse, n. bark of oak beaten into small pieces

Ows'er, n. bark and water mixed in a tanpit

Ox, n. Ox'en, n. pl. a castrated bull or bulls

Ox'alate, n. a salt formed by the oxalic acid and

Oxal'ic, a. pertaining to sorrel (a base

Ox'eye, n. a plant, a small cloud, presaging rain

Ox'fly, n. a fly hatched under the skin of cattle

Ox'gang, n. a quantity, twenty acres of land

Ox'lip, n. a yellow flower, the cowslip

Ox'ycrate, n. vinegar and water mixed together

Ox'yd, n. a substance combined with oxygene, calx, rust of metals [form an oxyd

Ox'ydate, v. to combine with oxygene and

Ox'ydable, a. capable of combining with oxygene

Oxyda'tion, n. the act or process of uniting with oxygene [ing principle of other substances

Ox'ygene, n. the base of vital air and the acidifying

Oxyge'nous, a. pertaining to oxygene

Oxy''genate, v. t. to combine oxygene with [with

Oxygena'tion, n. the act of combining oxygene

Oxy''genant, n. that which causes oxygenation

Oxymu'riate, n. a salt formed by oxygene and muriatic acid [atic acid

Oxymuriat'ic, a. composed of oxygene and muriatic

Ox'ymel, n. vinegar and honey boiled together

Oy'er, v. i. to hear; n. a court, commission, trust

Oyes', ad. hear ye, attend, observe, regard, heed

Oys'ter, n. a bivalvular shell-fish

Oys'terwench, n. a woman who sells oysters

P

PAB'ULAR. Pab'ulous, a. affording food

Paca', [a as in ask] n. a small quadruped of America, somewhat like a hare and a pig

Pac'can', n. an American tree and its nut

Pacated, a. appeased, pacified, calmed, mild

Pace, n. a step, gait, degree, measure of five feet

Pace, v. i. to move gently, to measure by steps

Paced, n. having or taught a certain kind of gait

Pacer, n. one who or that which paces, a horse

Pacif'ic, n. a peaceable, peaceful, gentle, mild [Asia

Pacif'ic, n. the great ocean between America and

Pacifica'tion, n. the act of making peace, quiet

Pa''cificator, n. a peacemaker, mediator, adviser

Pa''cifier, n. one who pacifies, one who appeases

Pa''cify, v. t. to appease, still anger, make easy

Pack, n. a large bundle, load, burden, 52 cards, a number of hounds, set, crew

Pack, v. t. to bind up for carriage, to sort cards, to put down meat in salt, to pick a jury

Pack'age, n. a large pack or bale, a thing or charge made for packing

Pack'cloth, n. a cloth for packing goods in

Pack'er, n. one who packs meat, goods, &c.

Pack'et, n. a small pack, a parcel of letters, a vessel for dispatches; in America, a coasting vessel for passengers (dle

Pack'et, v. t. to ply with a packet, put up in a bun-

Pack'etboat, n. a boat for advice or passengers

Pack'horse, n. a horse of burden, drudge, slave

Pack'faddle, *n.* a faddle for carrying burdens on

Pack'thred, *n.* a ftrong thred for packing with

Páco or Pácos, *n.* the fheep of S. America, fhaped like a camel

Pact, Pac'tion, *n.* a barg in, covenant, agreement

Pad, *n.* an eafy-paced horfe, faddle, path, robber

Pad, *v.* to travel gently, beat a way fmooth, rob

Pad'ar, *n.* grouts, very coarfe flour, pollard, *ob.*

Pad'der, *n.* a foot-highwayman, footpad, robber

Pad'dle, *v. i.* to play in water, row, beat, move

Pad'dle, *n.* an oar ufed by a fingle rower, a ftaff

Pad'dler, *n.* one who paddles, one who moves

Pad'dock, *n.* a large frog, toad, inclofure, a plant

Pad'lock, *n.* a lock; *v. t.* to faften with a padlock

Págan, *n.* a heathen; *a.* heathenifh, favage, wild

Páganifm, *n.* heathenifm (fide of a leaf

Page, *n.* a boy attendant on a great perfon, one

Page, *v. t.* to mark the pages of a book, to ferve

Págeant, *n.* a fpectacle of entertainments, a fhow

Págeant, *a.* fhowy, pompous; *v. t.* to exhibit

Págeantry, *n.* fhow, pomp, finery, vanity, folly

Píglls, *n.* a plant, cowflips

Pa"ginal, *a.* confifting of or refembling pages

Págod, Pagóda, *n.* a monument, tower, temple or idol in the E. Indies, a filver coin value 175 or

Paid, *pret.* and *pa. paff.* of *to pay* (200 cents

Pail, *n.* a wooden veffel for water, milk, &c.

Páilful, *n.* the quantity which a pail will hold

Pailmail, *fee* pell-mell

Pain, *n.* a fenfation of uneafinefs, toil, penalty

Pain, *v. t.* to make uneafy, afflict, torment, hurt

Páinful, *a.* full of pain, afflictive, difficult, hard

Painfully, *ad.* with pain, uneafily, laborioufly

Páinfulnefs, *n.* pain, affliction, forrow, induftry

Páinim, *n.* a pagan, an infidel; *a.* pagan, grofs

Páinlefs, *a.* void of pain or labor, eafy, fimple

Páinftaker, *n.* a laborious or induftrious perfon

Páinftaking, *a.* laborious, induftrious, active

Paint, *v. t.* to color, adorn, reprefent, defcribe

Paint, *n.* colors mixed together for painting

Páinter, *n.* one who paints or profeffes painting, a rope to faften a boat

Páinting, *n.* the art of laying on colors, a picture

Páinture, *n.* the art or bufinefs of painting

Pair, *n.* two things fuiting one another, a couple

Pair, *v. t.* to join in couples, couple, unite, fuit

Pal'ace, *n.* a royal or very grand houfe

Paláceous, *a.* royal, noble, grand, fplendid, *ob.*

Palanquin' or Palankin', *n.* a covered carriage in India, borne on the fhoulders of men

Pal'atable, *a.* pleafing to the tafte, agreeable, nice

Pal'ate, *n.* the inftrument of tafte, tafte, relifh

Pala'tial, Pal'atine, *a.* pertaining to the palate

Palat'ic, *a.* belonging or relating to the palate

Palat'inate, *n.* the country of a prince Palatine

Pal'atine, *n.* a letter formed by the palate

Pal'atines, *n. pl.* inhabitants of a palatinate

Pale, *a.* wanting frefh color, whitifh, faint

Pale, *n.* a flip of wood, inclofure, jurifdiction

Pale, *v. t.* to inclofe with pales, to make pale

Paleáceous, Páleous, *a.* chaffy, like chaff

Páleeyed, *a.* having bad or dim eyes, dimfighted

Pálefaced, *a.* fickly-looking, pale, whitifh, wan

Pálely, *ad.* in a pale manner, wanly, faintly

Pal'endar, *n.* a kind of fmall coafting veffel, *ob.*

Pálenefs, *n.* whitenefs, wannefs, ficklinefs

Pales'trian, *a.* belonging to wreftling

Pal'et, *n.* the board for a painter's colors

Pal'frey or Pal'fry, *n.* a fmall horfe trained for la-

Pal'freyed, *a.* riding on or having a palfrey [dies

Palification, *n.* the act of paling in or round

Pal'inode or Pal'inody, *n.* a fong, a recantation

Palifáde, *n.* pales fet up for inclofure or defenfe

Palifáde, *v. t.* to inclofe or fence with palifades

Pálifh, Pály, *a.* fomewhat pale, whitifh fickly

Pall, *n.* a cloak of ftate, a covering for the dead

Pall, *v.* to cloak, hide, cloy, weaken, grow vapid

Palla'dium, *n.* a ftatue of Pallas in ancient Troy, which was effential to its fafety, a bulwark, effectual defenfe (the goddefs Pallas

Palládian, *a.* pertaining to the palladium, or to

Pal'lat, *n.* a nut, the nut of a watch

Pal'let, *n.* a fmall low bed, fmall meafure

Pal'liament, *n.* a robe, garment, drefs, *ob.*

Pal'liate, *v. t.* to cloak, cover, extenuate, excufe

Palliátion, *n.* an extenuation, an imperfect cure

Pal'liative, *n.* fomething mitigating; *a.* extenu-

Pal'lid, *a.* faint in color, pale, wan, weak (ating

Pallmall', *n.* a game with an iron ball

Palm, *n.* a tree, victory, part of the hand, 3 inches

Palm, *v. t.* to cheat, impofe on, conceal, handle

Palm'ar, *a.* relating to a palm or handbreadth

Palm'ate or Palm'ated. *a.* fpreading like the open hand, with branches like fingers

Palm'er, *n.* a cheat, pilgrim, deer's crown, ferula

Palm'erworm, *n.* a worm covered with hair

Palmet'to, *n.* a fpecies of the palm-tree

Palmif'erous, *a.* bearing or producing palms

Palm'iped, *a.* webfooted, filmed as ducks, &c.

Palm'ift, *n.* the palm fquirrel of Barbary

Palm'ifter, *n.* one who pretends to palmiftry

Palm'iftry, *n.* a telling of fortunes by the hands

Palm'funday, *n.* the laft funday in lent

Palm'y, *a.* abounding with or bearing palms

Palpabil'ity, Palp'ablenefs, *n.* a palpable quality

Palp'able, *a.* that may be felt, plain, grofs, coarfe

Palp'ably, *ad.* feelingly, clearly, plainly, grofsly

Palp'itate, *v. i.* to beat as the heart, pant, flutter

Palpitátion, *n.* a beating or pafting of the heart

Pals'grave, *n.* a German title of honor, a count

Pals'ical, Pals'ied, *a.* afflicted with the palfy

Pal'fy, *n.* a privation of the power of action

Pal'fy, *v. t.* to deftroy the power of action, paralize

Palt'er, *v.* to fhift, dodge, trifle, fpend, fquander

Palt'rinefs, *n.* meannefs, pitifulnefs, bafenefs

Palt'ry, *a.* mean, pitiful, defpicable, low

Pam, *n.* the name of a card, the knave of clubs

Pam'pelmoe, *n.* a fhaddock, a fpecies of citrus

Pamp'er, *v. t.* to feed delicately, glut, indulge
Pamp'erer, *n.* one who pampers, one who indulges
Pamph'let, *n.* a small book ; *v.i.* to write pamphlets
Pamphletéer, *n.* a writer of pamphlets, a scribbler
Pamphyl'ian, *n.* a native of Pamphylia, in Afia
Pamphyl'ian, *a.* pertaining to Pamphylia
Pamp'us, *n.* a small fish with a round spotted tongue
Pan, *v. t.* to join or clofe together, to unite
Pan, *n.* a kitchen-veffel, hole, part of a lock
Panacéa, *n.* an univerfal medicin, an herb
Panáda or Panádo, *n.* bread boiled in water
Pan'cake, *n.* a kind of thin cake fried in a pan (ing
Panch, *n.* a mat to fave fpars or rigging from wear-
Pancrat'ical, *a.* excelling in exercifes, almighty
Panc'reas, *n.* the fweetbread of an animal
Pancreat'ic, *a.* contained in or like the pancreas
Pandemónium, *n.* the council-chamber of the de-
Pan'dect, *n.* a complete treatife, a digeft (vils
Pandem'ic, *a.* incident to a whole people, general
Pan'der, *n.* a pimp; *v. t.* to pimp
Pan'derly, *a.* pimping, pimplike, lewd, luftful
Pandiculátion, *n.* a yawning or ftretching, reftleff-
Pan'durform, *a.* fhaped like a guitar (nefs
Pane, *n.* a fquare of glafs, a mixture of fquares
Panegyr'ic, [g as j] *n.* an eulogy, encomium, praife
Panegyr'ical, *a.* containing or beftowing praife
Panegyr'ift, *n.* one who beftows panegyrics
Pane"gyrize, *v.t.* to praife, beftow commendation
Pan'el, *n.* a fquare of wainfcot, &c. a jury-roll
Pang, *n.* extreme or fudden pain, torture
Pang, *v. t.* to put to great pain, to torture
Pan'golin, *n.* an animal of E. Indies, with a long body, fhort legs, and covered with fcales
Fan'ic, *n.* a violent fright without a juft caufe
Pán'ic, *a.* violent without due caufe, groundlefs
Pan'icle, *n.* a loofe fpike of grafs, or beard on which feeds hang
Pan'icled, Panic'ulate, *a.* having flowers in panicles
Fannáde, *n.* the curvet of a prancing horfe
Pan'ael, *n.* a fort of mean faddle, ftomach, pipe
Pan'nier, *n.* a kind of bafket carried on horfes
Panomphéan, *a.* hearing all voices, a title of Jove
Pan'nier, *n.* a kind of bafket carried on horfes
Pan'oply, *n.* complete armor or harnefs
Pan'fy, *n.* a violet of three colors
Pant, *v. i.* to beat at the heart, long, wifh
Pant, *n.* the act of beating by the heart (fpinet
Pantaloon', *n.* a man's garment, buffoon, Danifh
Pantheis'tic, *a.* pertaining to pantheifm
Pan'theifm, *n.* a fyftem of principles in which the Univerfe was confidered as God, and its parts as his members
Pan'theift, *n.* a believer in pantheifm
Pan'theon, *n.* a temple of all the heathen gods
Panth'er, *n.* a fpotted and very fierce wild beaft
Pant'ile, *n.* a guttertile for houfes
Pant'ler, *n.* one who has the care of bread
Pant'ofle, *n.* a kind of loofe eafy fhoe, a flipper
Pan'tomime, *n.* mimicry, dumb fhow, a mimic

Pant'ry, *n.* a fmall room to put provifions in
Pan'urgy, *n.* complete fkill, fubtilty, craftinefs
Pap, *n.* a nipple, the pulp of fruit, infant's meat
Papá, *n.* a name for father, a Ruffian prieft
Pápacy, *n.* the popedom or dignity of pope
Pápal, *a.* belonging to the pope, popifh, Romifh
Papan', *n.* a beautiful duck of the Eaft Indies
Papavérean, Papav'erous, *a.* refembling poppies
Papaw', *n.* a tree and its fruit
Páper, *n.* a fubftance made of rags ; *a.* flight, thin
Páper, *v. t.* to hang or cover with paper, to note
Pápermaker, *n.* a man who makes paper for fale
Pápermill, *n.* a mill ufed to make paper in
Páperftainer, *n.* one who ftains or colors paper
Papes'cent, *a.* containing or producing pap, foft
Páphian, *a.* pertaining to Paphos, a city of Cyprus
Páphlago'nian, *n.* a native of Paphlagonia
Pap'il, *n.* a fmall pap, or nipple
Papilionáceous, *a.* refembling a butterfly
Pap'illary, *a.* having emulgent veffels, like a nipple
Papil'lous, Papillófe, *a.* covered with dots like nipples
Pápift, *n.* one who adheres to popery
Papift'ical, *a.* popifh, adhering to the pope
Pápiftry, *n.* the religion of Roman Catholics
Pappoos', *n.* the indian name of a child
Pap'pofe, Pap'pous, *a.* having foft and light down
Pap'py, *a.* foft, fpongy, jucy, eafily divided
Papyrus, *n.* a plant of different kinds
Par, *n.* a ftate of equality, an equal quantity
Par'able, *a.* that is eafily procured, *ob.*
Par'able, *n.* a fimilitude, a figurative fpeech
Parab'ola, *n.* one of the three conic fectons (abola
Parabol'ic, *a.* having the form or qualities of a par-
Parabol'ical, *a.* expreffed in parables, allufive
Parabol'ically, *ad.* by way of parable, allufively
Parab'olifm, *n.* divifion of the terms of an equation by a known quantity involved in the firft term
Parab'oloid, *n.* a figure generated from a parabola
Paracent'rical, *a.* deviating from circularity
Parach'ronifm, [ch as k] *n.* an error in chronology
Parachúte, *n.* a thing to defcend through the air by
Par'aclet, *n.* a comforter, an advocate
Paráde, *n.* a fhow, pomp, military order, guard, a place for affembling or exercifing troops
Paráde, *v. t.* to affemble and arrange, exhibit
Par'adife, *n.* the garden of Eden, a place of blifs
Paradis'ical, *a.* fuiting paradife, quite heavenly
Par'adox, *n.* an affertion contrary to appearance
Paradox'ical, *a.* inclined to contrarieties, ftrange
Paradox'ically, *ad.* in a paradoxical manner
Paradoxol'ogy, *n.* the ufe of paradoxes, oddnefs
Par'adrome, *n.* an open gallery or paffage
Parago"gic, *a.* additional, noting an addition
Par'agon, *v. t.* to compare, to equal ; *n.* a model
Par'agraph, *n.* a diftinct part of a difcourfe, a fection
Par'agraph, *v. t.* to form or write paragraphs
Par'alize, *v. t.* to affect as with palfy, to check action and the power of acting
Parallact'ic, *a.* pertaining to parallaxes

Par'allax, *n.* the difference between the true and apparent place of any of the heavenly bodies

Par'allel, *n.* a line at the fame diftance from fome other line, line for latitude, &c. refemblance

Par'allel, *v.* to preferve the fame direction, equal, compare; *a.* lying in the fame direction, equal

Par'allelifin,*n.* the ftate of being parallel or like

Parallel'ogram, *n.* a right-lined figure of four fides, the oppofit ones parallel

Par'allel'opip'ed, *n.* a folid figure under fix parallelograms the oppofits of which are equal and parallel

Paral'ogifm, Paral'ogy,*n.* falfe or bad reafoning

Paral'o_ize, *v. i.* to argue fophiftically or falfely

Paralyt'ic, *n.* one who is afflicted with a palfy

Paralyt'ic, Paralyt'ical, *a.* palfied,having the palfy

Param'eter, *n.* a conftant right line in each of the conic fections

Par'amount, *n.* a chief; *a.* chief, fuperior

Paramour, [ou as oo] *n.* a lover, wooer, miftrefs

Par'anymph, *n.* a brideman, fupporter,helper, *ob.*

Par'apet, *n.* a wall of defenfe, a wall breaft-high

Paraphernália, *n. pl.* goods in a wife's difpofal

Par'aphrafe, *n.* an interpretation in many words

Par'aphrafe, *v. t.* to interpret fully or at large

Par'aphraft, *n.* a diffufe or large interpreter

Paraphraft'ic, Paraphraft'ical, *a.* explanatory

Paraphras'tically, *ad.* in the manner of paraphrafe

P.raphren'itis, *n.* an inflammation of the diaphram

Par'afang, *n.* a Perfian meafure from 3 to 6 miles

Par'afite, *n.* a flatterer of great men, a fawner, a plant growing on another

Parafit'ic, Parafit'ical, *a.* flattering,fawning

P.r'afol, *n.* an umbrella to guard againft the fun

Par'at, *n.* a fith of the mullet kind in Brazil

Par'boil, *v. t.* to half boil, to boil only in part

Par'cel, *n.* a fmall bundle, lot, fet, company (rope

Par'celling,*v.* flips of canvas tarred to bind round a

Par'cel, *v. t.* to divide into portions, parts or fets

Par'cenary, *n.* a joint tenure or inheritance

Par'cener, *n.* one who holds eftate in coparcenary

Parch, *v.* to fcorch, become fcorched, grow dry

Parch'ment, *n.* fkins of fheep dreffed for writing

Pard, P.rd'ale, *n.* a fierce fpotted beaft, a leopard

Pard'on,*n.* forgivenefs, a remiffion of penalty

Pard'on, *v. t.* to forgive. excufe, pafs by, remit

Pard'onable, *a.* that may be forgiven, excufable

Pard'onablenefs, *n.* a pardonable ftate or quality

Pard'onably, *ad.* with or by pardon, excufably

P.rd'oner, *n.* one who forgives another perfon

Pare, *v. t.* to cut off the furface, cut, diminifh

Paregor'ic, *a.* having power to affuage pain

Paragor'ic,*n.* a ftimulating and foporific medicin

Paren'chyma, [ch as k] *n.* fpungy fubftance, the pith of plants

Parenchym'atous, *a.* porous, fpungy, pithy, foft

Párent, *n.* a father or mother, fource, head, caufe

Par'entage, *n.* birth, extraction, defcent, kindred

Parent'al, *a.* becoming parents, affectionate, fond

Parenth'efis, *n.* a fentence included thus ()

Parenthet'ical,*a.* put or included in a parenthefis

Párer, *n.* a tool to cut away the furface by

Par'get, [g hard] *n.* a plafter,plafter ftone

Par'gip, *n.* a fith fomewhat like the fea bream

Parhélion, Parhélium, *n.* a mock or falfe fun

Párian, *a.* pertaining to Paros in the Egean fea

Pariétal, *a.* making walls, relating to a bone

Páring, *n.* a thing that is pared off, a rind

Par'ifh, *n.* a particular diftrict or divifion of land under a minifter having the cure of fouls, a religious fociety or corporation

Par'ifh, *a.* belonging to or maintained by a parifh

Parifh'ioner, *more correctly* Parifh'oner, *n.* one belonging to a parifh

Paris'ian, *n.* a native or inhabitant of Paris

Paris'ian, *a.* pertaining to Paris in France

Parifyllab'ical, *a.* having equal or like fyllables

Par'itor, *n.* a fummoner of the courts of civil law

Par'ity, *n.* equality, refemblance, likenefs

Park,*n.* an enclofed ground for deer, &c. a net

Park, *v. t.* to inclofe in, or make into a park

Park'er, *n.* the keeper or overfeer of a park

Parle or Par'ley, *n.* a conference, talk, oral treaty

Par'ley, *v. i.* to talk, to treat by word of mouth

Par'liament, *n.* the chief affembly of England

Parliament'ary *a,* pertaining to a parliament

Par'lor, *n.* a lower room kept for entertainments

Par'lous, *a.* fprightly, keen, tart, witty, waggifh

Parmefan', *a.* pertaining to Parma in Italy

Parnas'ian,*a.* belonging to parnaffus a mountain in Greece facred to the poets

Par'nops,*n.* a fpecies of wafp found among fruits

Paróchial [ch as k] *a.* belonging to a parifh

Par'ody,*n.* a byrlefque change of another's words

Par'ody, *v. t.* to copy or do by way of parody

Parokeét, *n.* a clafs of fmall parrots

Paróle, *n.* words given as an affurance

Paróle, *a.* by word of mouth, verbal, oral (letters

Paronon'afy, *n.* a play upon words, a change of

Paron'ymous, *a.* refembling another word, like

Parot'id, *a.* falivary, fituated near the ears

Par'oxyfin,*n.* a fit, the periodical return of a fit

Par'rel, *n.* a machine to faften a fail-yard to the

Parrici'dal, *a.* of or relating to parricide (maft

Par'ricide, *n.* the murder or murderer of a father

Par'rot, *n.* a genus of birds of numerous varieties, remarkable for the faculty of imitating the hu, man voice

Par'rot fifh, *n.* a greenifh fith with a hooked fnout

Par'ry, *v. t.* to put by a thruft, ward off, fence off

Parfe, *v. t.* to refolve by the rules of grammar

Parfimónious, *a.* frugal, fparing, near, covetous

Parfimónioufly, *ad.* frugally, fparingly, meanly

Parfimónioufnefs, Pars'imony,*n.* frugality, nig-

Pars'ley, *n.* a numerous clafs of plants (gardlinefs

Pars'nip, *n.* a well known garden root

Pars'on, *n.* a clergyman, prieft, minifter

Pars'onage, *n.* the houfe or benefice of a parfon

Part, *n*. a portion, member, party, fpace, conduct
Part, *v. t.* to fhare, divide, feparate, go away, quit
Part'age, *n.* the act of parting, a divifion
Partáke, *w.* partook, *pret.* partaken, *pa.* to have
 or take a part, fhare, admit to
Partáker, *n.* a fharer, affociate, accomplice, ally
Part'er, *n.* one who parts, one who feparates
Parterre', *n.* a flower garden, plot, level ground
Parth'ian, *n.* a native of Parthia in Afia
Parth'ian, *a.* belonging to Parthia, now Perfia
Par'tial, *a.* inclined to favor, unjuft, imperfect
Partial'ity, *n.* an unequal judgment, injuftice
Par'tialize, *v. t.* to make partial, bias, incline, *ob.*
Par'tially, *ad.* in a partial manner, in part only
Part'ible or Part'able, *a.* divifible, feparable
Parti''cipable, *a.* that may be fhared or divided, *ob.*
Parti''cipant, *a.* fharing, having fome fhare
Parti''cipate, *v.* to partake, to have a fhare
Participátion, *n.* a partaking of, a divifion
Particip'ial, *a.* having the nature of a participle
Particip'ially, *ad.* in the manner of a participle
Part'iciple, *n.* a word partaking of a noun and verb
Part'icle, *n.* a fmall part or word, an atom
Partic'ular, *a.* fingular, intimate, individual
Partic'ular, *n.* a point, circumftance, individual
Particula'rity, *n.* fomething peculiar (fpecify
Partic'ularize, *v. t.* to mention particulars, to
Partic'ularly, *ad.* diftinctly, fingly, eminently
Part'ifan, *n.* a partyman, head of a party, ftaff
Part'ite, *a.* divided, feparated into parts
Parti''tion, *v. t.* to divide into diftinct parts
Parti''tion, *n.* a divifion, thing that divides, part
Part'let, *n.* a hen, ruff for the neck, loofe collar
Part'ly, Part, *ad.* in part, in fome meafure
Part'ner, *n.* a fharer, a dancing mate ; *v. t.* to join
Part'nerfhip, *n.* union in trade, joint intereft
Part'ners, *n. pl.* pieces of plank nailed round mafts
 and capterns on a fhip's deck
Partook, *pret.* of *to partake*
Part'ridge, *n.* a genus of birds of feveral fpecies
Parts, *n. pl.* qualities, faculties, diftricts, regions
Parturient, *a.* that is about to bring forth
Parturi''tion, *n.* the act or ftate of bringing forth
Part'y, *n.* a felect affembly, fet, detachment, fide
Part'ycolored or Part'icolored, *a.* having different
Part'yman, *n.* a factious or bufy perfon (colors
Part'ywall, *n.* a wall that feparates two buildings
Par'u, *n.* a broad flat fifh of America
Par'vitude, Par'vity, *n.* littlenefs, minutenefs, *ob.*
Pas, *n.* a ftep, a right of precedence, *ob.*
Pas'chal, [ch as k] *a.* relating to the paffover
Pafh, *v. t.* to ftrike, *ob.*
Pafhaw', *n.* a bafhaw, a Turkifh governor [fr. pacha]
Pafhaw'lic, *n.* the jurifdiction of a Pafhaw
Pas'quil, Pas'quin, Pasquinàde, *n.* a keen lampoon
Pafs, *v.* to go, make way, proceed, fpend, omit,
 vanifh, excel, go beyond, tranfact, enact
Pafs, *n.* a paffage, road, licenfe, pufh, condition
Pafs'able, *a.* that may be paffed, tolerable

Paffáde or Paffádo, *n.* a pufh, thruft, gift, alms
Pafs'age, *n.* a journey by water, road, act of paffing,
 courfe, incident, a claufe or fentence
Pafs'enger, *n.* one who paffes in a carriage
Pafs'er, *n.* one who paffes by or over, a traveller
Pas'ferine, *a.* like or belonging to fwallows
Paffibil'ity, Pafs'iblenefs, *n.* the power of fuffering
 or being acted on by external agents
Pafs'ible, *a.* that may fuffer or be impreffed
Pafs'ing, *pa.* exceeding, furpaffing, very
Pafs'ing, *n.* the act of going or travelling
Pafs'ingbell, *n.* a bell rung at the death of a perfon
Pas''fion, *n.* fury, anger, zeal, love, luft, fuffering
Pas''fionate, *a.* moved by paffion, foon angry, fond
Pas''fionately, *ad.* angrily, vehemently, fondly
Pas''fionatenefs, *n.* an aptnefs to be in a paffion
Pas''fioning, *a.* earneftly wifhing, fondly defiring
Pas''fion-week, *n.* the week before Eafther
Pafs'ive, *a.* fubmiffive, meek, not oppofing
Pafs'ively, *ad.* fubmiffively, humbly (fuffering
Pafs'ivenefs, Paffiv'ity, *n.* fubmiffion, a power of
Pafs'over, *n.* a great Jewifh feftival to commemo-
 rate God's paffing by the Ifraelites when he
 fmote the firft-born of the Egyptians
Pafs'port, *n.* a permiffion in writing to pafs or go
Paft, *pa.* not prefent, gone through, fpent
Pafte, *n.* a thick mixture of folids and fluids, a ce-
Pafte, *v. t.* to faften or ftick with pafte (ment
Páfteboard, *n.* a thick and ftrong kind of paper
Paft'ern, *n.* a part of the leg, the heel of a horfe
Paft'il, *n.* a roll of pafte, kind of pencil, crayon
Paft'ime, *n.* a fport, diverfion, amufement, game
Paft'inate, *v. i.* to dig in a garden, prepare, *not ufed*
Paftinátion, *n.* the act of digging the earth
Paft'or, *n.* a fhepherd, a minifter of a congregation
Paft'oral, *a.* rural, relating to the cure of fouls
Paft'oral, *n.* a kind of poem, rural fong, bucolic
Páftry, *n.* baked pafte, pies, a making of pies
Páftrycook, *n.* one who makes or fells pies, &c.
Paft'urable, *a.* that is fit or may ferve for pafture
Paft'urage, *n.* land kept to be grazed, feed
Paft'ure, *n.* land ufed for grazing, feed, education
Paft'ure, *v.* to put in a pafture, graze, feed, fatten
Paft'y, *n.* a raifed pie, a pie raifed without a difh
Pat, *a.* fit, exact, ready; *ad.* fitly, patly
Pat, *v. t.* to tap, to clap; *n.* a light blow
Patacoon', *n.* a Spanifh coin of 104 cents
Patagónian, *n.* a native of Patagonia the extreme
 fouthern part of America
Patavin'ity, *n.* a Paduan idiom ufed by Livy
Patch, *n.* a piece to cover a hole or fore with, a bit
Patch, *v.* to put on patches, piece, mend, botch
Patch'er, *n.* one who patches or mends, a botcher
Patch'ery, *n.* botched or bungling work, forgery
Patch'work, *n.* bits of different cloth fewed together
Pate, *n.* the head or its fkin, a kind of half moon
Patefac'tion, *n.* the act or ftate of laying open
Patel'liform, *a.* in fhape of a faucer or difh
Pat'en, *n.* a place to put bread on at the altar

V

Pat'ent, a. open, public, appropriated, exclufive
Pat'ent, n. a grant of an exclufive right, a charter
Pat'ent, v. t. to make grants of, under authority
Patentée, n. one who has a patent granted him
Pater'nal, a. fatherly, affectionate, hereditary
Pater'nity, n. fatherfhip, the relation of a father
Paternos'ter, n. the Lord's prayer, a great bead
Path, Path'way, n. a footroad, road, track, way
Pathet'ic, Pathet'ical, a. affecting, tender
Pathet'ically, ad. in a moving manner, tenderly
Pathet'icalnefs, n. earneftnefs, energy, feeling
Path'lefs, a. having no path, untrod, unknown
Pathognomon'ic,a. proper and peculiar to a difeafe
Pathol'ogy, n. a minute defcription of difeafes
Patholo"gic,a. pertaining to the nature of difeafes
Pathol'ogift, n. one who treats of pathology
Pathos, n. warmth, paffion, feeling, tendernefs
Pat'ible, a. that may be borne, fufferable
Pátience, n. the power or act of enduring or wait-
  ing without difcontent, calmnefs, conftancy
Pátient, a. not eafily moved, refigned (ed perfon
Pátient, n. one who receives impreffions, a difeaf-
Pátient, v. t. to compofe or be patient, ob.
Pátiently, ad. without murmuring, quietly
Pat'ine, n. the cover of a chalice, a plant
Pat'ly, ad. feafonably, fitly, readily (rior bifhop
Pátriarch, [ch as k] n. a head of a family, a fupe-
Patriarch'al, a. belonging to patriarchs (triarchs
Patriarch'ate, Pátriarchy, n. a jurifdiction of pa-
Patri"cian,a. fenatorial, noble ; n. a nobleman
Patrimónial, a. derived by inheritance
Pat'rimony, n. an eftate coming by inheritance
Pat'riot, n. a lover of his country, a benefactor
Pat'riot, Patriot'ic, a. having patriotifm, noble
Pat'riotifm, n. a love and zeal for one's country
Patrôl,n. a guard kept to walk the rounds
Patrôl, v. i. to guard, to go the rounds
Pat'ron,n. a fupporter, defender, benefactor, faint
Pat'ronage, n. fupport, protection, donation
Pat'ronal, a. fupporting, guarding, defending
Pat'ronefs, n. a female patron or defender
Pat'ronife, v. t. to fupport, protect, favor, aid
Patronym'ic,n. a name derived from anceftors
Pat'ten,a. the bafe of a pillar, a clog fhod with iron
Pat'tepan, n. a pan to bake fmall pies in
Pat'ter, v. i. to beat or make a noife like hail
Pat'tern, n. a fpecimen, example, figure ; v. i. to
Pat'ulous,a. open, wide, fpreading (copy
Pau'city,n. fewnefs, fmallnefs of number
Paunch,n. the belly ; v. t. to take out the paunch
Paup'er, n. a poor perfon, one who receives alms
Paufe,n. a ftop,a break ; v. to wait,ftop,deliberate
Paus'er, v. one who paufes, one who deliberates
Pav'an or Pav'in, n. a grave kind of dance
Pave, v. t. to lay with ftones, prepare, make eafy
Pávement, n. a paved way, a ftone or brick floor
Páver, n. one who paves or lays ftones
Pavil'ion, n. a tent, moveable houfe, main part
Pavil'ion, v. t. to furnifh with or put in tents

Paw, n. the foot of a beaft, the hand
Paw, v. to handle roughly, ftrike, fawn, flatter
Paw'ed, pa. a. handled, flattered, having paws
Pawl,n.a bar of wood or iron to fupport a windlafs
Pawn, n. a pledge left for fecurity, a chefsman
Pawn, v. t. to pledge, to leave or give fecurity
Pawn'broker,n. one who lends money upon goods
Pay, v. t. paid, payed, pret. and pa. to difcharge a
  debt, atone, reward, fuffer, beat, drub
Pay, n. wages, hire, money for fervices, payment
Páyable,a. proper to be paid,due, that is to be paid
Páyday, n. a day for paying debts or wages upon
Payeé, n. the perfon to whom a bill is made paya-
  ble (pay
Páyer, Páymafter, n. one who pays, or is bound to
Páyment, n. the act of paying, reward
Páyfer,n. one that weighs,one that poifes, ob.
Pea, n. Peas or Peafe, pl. a kind of pulfe of nume-
  rous kinds for the table
Peace, n. a refpit from war, quiet, reft, content
Peace, exclam. denoting or commanding peace
Péaceable,a. free from war, quiet, goodnatured
Péaceablenefs, Péacefulnefs, n. quietnefs,eafe
Péaceably, ad. without difturbance, quietly, eafily
Péaceful, a. quiet,eafy, mild, undifturbed, ftill
Péacefully, ad. quietly, calmly, mildly, gently
Péacemaker, n. one who makes or reftores peace
Péaceoffering, n. a facrifice to make atonement
Péaceofficer, n. an officer who keeps the peace
Péaceparted, a. fent out of the world in peace
Peach, n. a delicious ftone fruit of great variety
Peach for impeach, not ufed
Péachcolored, a. like a peach in color, blooming
Péachick, n. a chicken of the breed of peacocks
Péacock, n. a fowl very beautiful in its fethers
Péahen, n. the hen or female of the peacock
Peak, n. the top of a hill, forepart of a headdrefs,
  upper part of a fail, yard or gaff
Peak, v. i. to look fickly or meanly, to fneak, to
  raife a yard or gaff
Péaking, pa. a. fneaking, mean, fickly, poorly
Peal, n. a fucceffion of loud founds, noife, ring
Peal, v. i. to play loud, to affail with noife
Péan, n. a fong of praife or triumph
Pear, n. a well known fruit
Pearl, n. a gem in fhellfifh, color, film, letter
Pearl'ed, a. fet or adorned with pearls
Pearl'eyed, a. having a fpeck or film on the eye
Pearl'y, a. abounding with or like pearls
Peármain, n. the name of an admired appl
Péartree, n. a tree that bears or produces pears
Péas'ant, n. one who lives by rural labor, a ruftic
Péas'antry, n. country people, ruftics, clowns
Péafecod, Péafhell, n. a hull that contains peafe
Péafehaum,Péafeftraw, n. the ftraw of peafe
Péafepudding, n. a pudding made of peafe
Peat,n. a fpecies of turf ufed for fuel, a net
Peb'ble, Peb'bleftone, n. a fort of hard fmall ftone
Peb'bled, a. covered or abounding with pebbles

Peb'bly, a. full of, rough with or like pebbles
Peccabil'ity, n. a ftate or poffibility of finning
Pec'cable, a. liable to fin, fubject to error, frail
Peccadill'o, n. a petty fault or crime, a miftake
Pec'cancy, n. a bad quality, a difordered habit
Pec'cant, a. criminal, guilty, faulty, corrupt
Pec'cary, n. a quadruped of Mexico like a hog
Peccávi, n. a form of afking pardon for a fault
Pech'blend or Pitch'blend, n. an ore of uranite
Peck, n. a fourth part of a bufhel, a deal
Peck, v. t. to ftrike with the beak, eat, pufh, cavil
Peck'er, n. one that pecks, a woodpecker
Pec'tinal, Pec'tinate, a. formed like a comb
Pec'toral, a. belonging to the breaft, ftomachic
Pec'toral, n. a ftomachic medicin, a breaftplate
Pec'ulate, v. t. to defraud the public of property
   entrufted to one's care
Peculátion, n. embezzlement of the public money
Pec'ulator, n. one who embezzles public property
   entrufted to his care
Peculiar, n. property, fomething exempted
Pecú'iar, a. appropriate, particular, fingular, odd
Peculiar'ity, Pecúliarnefs, n. particularity, oddnefs
Pecúliarize, v. t. to make peculiar or diftinct
Pecúliarly, ad. particularly, fingly, oddly
Pecúliars, n. an ecclefiaftical court
Pecúniary, a. relating to or confifting of money
Ped, n. a fmall packfaddle, hamper, bafket
Ped'agogue, n. a fchoolmafter, teacher, pedant
Ped'agogue, v. i. to teach or tell fupercilioufly
Ped'agogy, n. the office of a pedagogue, difciplin
Pédal, n. one of the large pipes of an organ
Pédal, a. a foot high, belonging to a foot
Ped'ant, n. one vainly oftentatious of learning
Pedant'ic, a. like a pedant, conceited, vain, proud
Pedantically, ad. in a pedantic manner
Ped'antifm, Ped'antry, n. pedantic behavior
Pédate, a. divided like toes on a foot
Ped'atifid, a. having the parts united by a mem-
Ped'dle, v. i. to travel and retail goods   (brane
Pederéro, Pateréo, n. a fwivel-gun ufed in fhips
Ped'eftal, n. the bafe of a ftatue or pillar
Pedes'trial, Pedes'trious, a. going on foot
Pedes'trian, n. one who walks much
Ped'icle, or Ped'icel, n. the ftalk which fupports a
   fingle flower, when there are feveral on a ped-
Pedic'u'ar, Pedic'ulous, a. loufy, having lice [uncle
Ped'igree, n. a genealogy, lineage, defcent, race
Ped'iment, n. an ornamental crowning of fronts
Ped'lar or Ped'ler, n. one who travels to fell goods
Ped'lery, n. wares fold by pedlers
Ped'ling, n. travelling and felling goods
Pedobap'tifm, n. infant baptifm
Pedobap'tift, n. one who holds to infant baptifm
Pedom'eter, n. an inftrument to meafure diftances
   by the fteps in walking   [plants
Pedun'cle, n. the footftalk of the fructification of
Pedun'cular, a. pertaining to a peduncle
Pedun'culate, a. growing on footftalks

Peel, v. t. to take or fcale off, flay, plunder, rob
Peel, n. a rind, firefhovel, board ufed by bakers
Péeler, n. one that ftrips off or flays, a robber
Peep, n. a fly look, the firft appearance
Peep, v. i. to make the firft appearance, look, cry
Péepers, n. chickens breaking the fhell, the eyes
Péephole, Péepinghole, n. a hole to peep through
Peer, v. i. to come juft in fight, peep, appear
Peer, n. an equal, nobleman, lord   (of peers
Péerage, Péerdom, n. the dignity of a peer, born
Péerefs, n. a woman ennobled, a peer's lady
Péerlefs, a. having no equal, excellent, noble
Péevifh, a. wafpifh, crofs, very hard to pleafe
Péevifhly, ad. wafpifhly, crofsly, fretfully
Péevifhnefs, n. wafpifhnefs, fretfulnefs, anger
Peg, n. a wooden pin, a nickname for Margaret
Peg, v. t. to faften with a peg, pin down, clofe
Pégafus, n. in poetry a horfe with wings
Pehlav'ic, a. pertaining to the pehlava a polifhed
   dialect of the Perfian language
Pekan' n. a quadruped of the weefel kind
Pelas'gian, Pelas'gic, a. pertaining to the Pelafgi,
   early fettlers of Greece
Pélian, a. pertaining to Peleus or his fon Achilles
Pelf, n. money, riches, flock, food, paltry ftuff
Pel'ican, n. a bird with a bag attached to its under
   mandible, of feveral fpecies
Pell, n. a fkin, hide, roll, record [houfe, ob.]
Pell'et, n. a little ball or bullet, a mark
Pell'eted, a. confifting of or having pellets
Pell'icle, n. a thin fkin, film, fragment, bit
Pel'litory, n. a plant of many varieties
Pellmell', ad. faft, confufedly, without any order
Pells, n. pl. an office in the exchequer
Pellúcid, a. tranfparent, clear, bright, pure
Pellúcidnefs, n. tranfparency, clearnefs, brightnefs
Pelágian, a. pertaining to the ocean
Pelágian, n. one of a fect who held that the confe-
   quences of Adam's fin were limited to himfelf
Pelágianifm, n. the doctrins of Pelagius
Peloponnéfian, a. pertaining to Peloponnefus
Pelt, n. a fkin, a hide; v. t. to throw, to caft
Pelt'ate, a. like a fhield, when the footftalk is in-
   ferted into the difk of the leaf
Pelt'ing, pa. a. throwing, [pitiful, paltry, ob.]
Pelt'monger, n. a dealer in raw hides or fkins
Pen, v. t. p. penned, to write or compofe
Pen, v. t. pa. pent, to confine, inclofe, fhut in
Pénal, a. inflicting or denouncing punifhment, re-
   lating to the punifhment of crimes
Pen'alty, n. punifhment, cenfure, forfeiture
Pen'ance, n. a mortification, grief, atonement
Pen'cafe, n. a cafe to carry or put pens in
Pence, n. pl. of penny   (to paint
Pen'cil, n. a tool for drawing and painting; v. t.
Pen'cilled, a. radiated, having pencils of rays
Pen'cilform, a. in the fhape of a pencil
Pen'dant or Pendent, n. an earing, a pendulum

Pen'dant or Pen'dent, a. hanging, jutting out
Pen'dence or Pen'dency, n. inclination, fu'pence
Pen'ding, a. depending, undecided, unfettled
Pendulo'vity, Pen'duloufnefs, n. a hanging ftate
Pen'dulous, a. hanging, fufpended, moving
Pen'dulum, n. the vibrating regulator of time in a clock
Penetrabil'ity, n. a fufceptibility of impreffion
Pen'etrable, a. that may be pierced or underftood
Pen'etrails, n. pl. the inward parts, entrails, ob.
Pen'etrancy, n. the power of piercing or entering
Pen'etrant, a. having the power to pierce, fharp
Pen'etrate, v. t. to pierce, enter, dive, underftand
Penetrátion, n. a piercing, acutenefs, fagacity
Pen'etrative, a. piercing, fubtle, acute, fagacious
Pen'fifh, n. a kind of eelpout, with a fmooth fkin
Pen'guin, n. a clafs of birds with fhort wings, a plant
Pen'ine, a. denominating the higheft of the alps, Mount Blanc, the great St. Bernard, &c.
Penins'ula, n. a land almoft furrounded by water
Penin'fular, a. in the ftate of a peninfula
Penin'fulate, v. t. to form a peninfuia
Penins'ulated, pa. nearly furrounded by water
Pen'itence, n. repentance, a forrow for fin
Pen'itent, a. repentant, forrowful for an offenfe
Pen'itent, n. one forrowful for fin committed
Peniten'tial, a. expreffing repentance, forrowful
Peniten'tial, n. a book directing the due penance
Peniten'tiary, n. one who does penance, a confeffor
Peniten'tiary, a. penitential, forrowful
Pen'itently, ad. with repentance, devoutly, lowly
Pen'knife, n. a knife ufed to cut pens with
Pen'man, n. one who teaches writing, a writer
Pen'manfhip, n. the act, art or ufe of writing
Pen'nant, n. a flag, a rope to hoift up things by
Pen'nate, a. winged, furnifhed with wings, even
Pen'ner, n. a writer, compofer, author, pencafe
Pen'niform, a. like a quill or fether
Pen'ni'efs, a. having no money, poor, wretched
Pen'non, n. a painted flag, fmall flag, enfign
Pennfylvánia, n. one of the U. States
Pennfylvánian, n. a citizen of Pennfylvania
Pennfylvánian, a. belonging to Pennfylvania
Pen'ny, n. the 12th part of a fhilling
Pen'nypon, n. one who carries letters from the poft-office for a trifling fum
Pennyroy'al, n. an aromatic plant
Pen'nywort, n. marfh or water nave'wort
Pen'nyweight, n. 24 grains in Troy weight
Pen'nywife, a. hazarding much to fave but little
Pen'nyworth, n. enough for a penny, a good bargain
Pens'il or Pens'ile, a. hanging, fufpended
Pens'ilenefs, Penfil'ity, n. a hanging ftate
Pen'fion, v. t. to fupport by a yearly allowance
Pen'fion, n. a fettled yearly allowance, a falary
Pen'fionary, n. a chief magiftrate in Dutch cities
Pen'fionary, a. maintained or kept by a penfion
Pen'fioner, n. one who has or lives on a penfion
Pens'itate, v. t. to weigh, deliberate, revolve, ob.

Pens'ive, a. forrowful, thoughtful, ferions
Pens'ively, ad. with melancholy, fadly, ferioufly
Pens'ivenefs, n. melancholy, thoughtfulnefs
Pent, pret. and pa. paff. of to pen (five ftrings
Pent'achord, [ch as k] n. an inftrument having
Pen'tacoccous, a. containing five grains
Pent'agon, n. a figure having five equal angles
Pentag'onal, Pentan''gular, a. having five angles
Pen'tagraph, n. an inftrument to copy or reduce the fize of a plan, print, &c.
Pentagyn'ia, n. an order of plants having five ftyles
Pentahédron, n. a figure with five equal fides
Pentahédral, a. having five equal fides
Pentahédrous, a. having five fides or five bafes
Pentan'dria, n. a clafs of plants with hermaphrodite flowers and five ftamens
Pentam'eter, n. a verfe confifting of five feet
Pent'angle, n. a figure with five angles
Pentapet'alous, a. having five petals
Pentaph'yllous, a. having five leaves
Pent'aftyle, n. a work with five columns (the bible
Pent'ateuch, [ch as k] n. the five firft books of
Pent'ecoft, n. Whitfuntide, a high Jewifh feftival
Pent'ecoftal, a. belonging to Whitfuntide
Pent'houfe, Pent'ice, n. a floping fhed or roof
Penult', n. the laft fyllable but one
Penult'imate, a. of the laft fyllable but one
Penum'bra, n. an imperfect or faint fhadow
Penúrious, a. fparing, niggardly, mean, fcanty
Penúrioufly, ad. in a niggardly manner, meanly
Penúrioufnefs, n. parfimony, niggardlinefs, care
Pen'ury, n. poverty, indigence, great want
Péony, n. a plant, pæonia
Péople, n. perfons in general, the vulgar, a nation
Péople, v. t. to ftock or fill with inhabitants
Pepaftic, n. a medicin given to help digeftion
Pep'per, n. a fpice, a plant of many kinds
Pep'per, v. t. to fprinkle with pepper, warm, beat
Pep'perbox, n. a box ufed for holding pepper
Pep'percorn, n. a grain of pepper, a thing of little
Pep'permint, n. a very hot kind of mint (value
Pep'tic, a. digeftive, promoting digeftion, eafing
Peracute, a. very fharp or keen, very violent
Peradvent'ure, ad. perhaps, percafe, by chance
Per'agrate, v. i. to travel or rove about, ob.
Peragrátion, the act of paffing over or about
Peram'bulate, v. t. to walk through, view, furvey
Perambulátion, n. a paffing through, a furvey
Perambulátor, n. a pedometer or inftrument for meafuring diftances in walking
Percáfe, ad. perchance, by chance, perhaps, ob.
Percéivable, a. that may be perceived or feen
Percéive, v. t. to obferve, fee, difcover, know
Perceptibil'ity, n. the power or act of perceiving
Percep'tible, a. that may be perceived or feen
Percep'tibly, ad. in a manner to be perceived
Percep'tion, n. knowledge, a notion, idea, view
Percep'tive, a. that is able or tends to perceive
Perceptiv'ity, n. the power of perceiving (red

Perch, *n.* a fish, bird's roost, pole, 5 1-2 yards, a
Perch, *v.* to light down or sit as a bird, to roost
Perchance', *ad.* perhaps, percase, peradventure
Percip'ient, *a.* perceiving, able to perceive, quick
Perc'olate, *v.* to strain or pass as through a sieve
Percolátion, *n.* a purification made by a straining
Percuss', *v. t.* to strike, to dash against, *ob.*
Percus'sion, *n.* a striking, stroke, knock, found
Percútient, *a.* able to strike, striking, smiting
Per'difoil, *n.* a plant which casts its leaves
Perdi'tion, *n.* destruction, ruin, loss, death
Perdúe, *ad.* closely, secretly, in wait, in ambush
Per'dulous, *a.* lost, thrown away, cast off, *ob.*
Perdúrable, *a.* very lasting, continuing long
Perdúrably, *ad.* in a very lasting manner, firmly
Perdurátion, *n.* a long or lasting continuance
Per'egrinate, *v. i.* to travel into far countries
Peregrinátion, *n.* a travel made to foreign lands
Per'egrinator, *n.* a traveller into foreign parts
Per'egrine, *a.* foreign, outlandish, strange, new
Perempt', *v. t.* to kill, slay, crush, destroy, *ob.*
Peremp'tion, *n.* a killing, extinction, crush, *ob.*
Per'emptorily, *ad.* absolutely, positively
Per'emptoriness, *n.* positiveness, determination
Per'emptory, *a.* absolute, positive, final
Peren'nial, *a.* durable, perpetual, in botany lasting more than two years
Peren'nity, *n.* perpetuity, a perpetual duration
Per'fect, *a.* complete, blameless, pure, holy, safe
Per'fect, *v. t.* to complete, finish, instruct fully
Per'fecter, *n.* one who makes perfect or complete
Perfectible, *a.* that may be made perfect
Perfectib'lity, *n.* the capacity of becoming perfect
Perfec'tion, *n.* a perfect state, excellence
Perfec'tionate, *v. t.* to perfect, to complete, *not used*
Perfec tionist, *n.* one who believes in perfectibility
Perfec'tive, *a.* conducive to perfection, perfecting
Perfec'tively, *ad.* in a perfective manner
Per'fectly, *ad.* completely, exactly, fully, totally
Per'fectness, *n.* completeness, skill, goodness
Perfi'cient, *a.* in effect, effectual
Perfid'ious, *a.* treacherous, false to trust, base
Perfid'iously, *ad.* by breach of faith (treachery
Perfid'iousness, Per'fidy, *n.* a breach of faith,
Perfláte, *v. t.* to blow through, to blow very hard
Perflátion, *n.* the act of blowing through
Perfóliate, *a.* having the base of the leaf surrounding the stem
Per'forate, *v. t.* to pierce or run through, to bore
Per'forate, *a.* having many small holes
Perforátion, *n.* the act of boring, a place bored
Per'forator, *n.* a surgical instrument for piercing
Perfórce, *ad.* by force, by constraint, violently
Perform', *v.* to do, execute, discharge, succeed
Perform'able, *a.* practicable, that may be done
Perform'ance, *n.* the act of performing, a work
Perform'er, *n.* one who performs, one who plays
Per'fricate, *v. t.* to rub thoroughly or all over
Perfúme, *n.* a sweet odor or smell; *v. t.* to scent

Perfúmer, *n.* one who sells or deals in perfumes
Perfúmery, *n.* perfumes in general
Perfunc'torily, *ad.* carelessly, negligently, *ob.*
Perfunc'toriness, *n.* carelessness, negligence, *ob.*
Perfunc'tory, *a.* slight, careless, negligent, *ob.*
Perfúse, *v. t.* to sprinkle, tincture, overspread
Perhaps', *ad.* perchance, peradventure, it may be
Per'iapt, *n.* a charm, a charm against diseases, *ob.*
Per'ianth, Perianthy, *n.* a calyx surrounding the fructification of plants
Per'iauger, *n.* a sort of canoo made of two trunks of trees hollowed and united, also a long narrow ferry boat
Pericard'ium, *n.* the membrane inclosing the heart
Per'icarp, *n.* the case which contains the seeds
Pericránium, *n.* a membrane covering the skull
Peric'ulous, *a.* dangerous, hazardous, perilous, *ob.*
Periécians, *n.* inhabitants of the opposit side of the globe in the same parallel of latitude
Per'idot, *n.* another name of the Chrysolite
Per'igee, *n.* the place of a planet nearest the earth
Perihé:ion, *n.* the place of a planet nearest the sun
Per'il, *n.* danger, hazard, jeopardy, risk
Per'ilous, *a.* full of danger, hazardous, very small
Per'ilously, *ad.* with danger or hazard, wittily
Per'ilousness, *n.* a state of danger or hazard
Perim'eter, *n.* the circumference of a figure
Périod, *n.* a circuit, epocha, date, end, full point
Period'ical, *a.* regular, fixed, stated, set, circular
Period'ically, *ad.* at stated periods, at fixed times
Perios'teum, *n.* a membrane covering the bones
Peripatet'ic, *a.* relating to Aristotle, &c. walking
Peripatet'ic, *n.* an adherent to Aristotle
Periph'ery, *n.* a circumference, a compass
Peripher'ical, *a.* pertaining to the circumference
Periph'rasis, *n.* a circumlocution, a tediousness
Periphrast'ic, *a.* expressed in many words
Peripneúmony, *n.* an inflammation of the lungs
Perís'cians, *n.* inhabitants of the earth, whose shadows move round every day without disappearing
Per'ish, *v.* to decay, die, go to ruin, be destroyed
Per'ishable, *a.* liable to perish, subject to decay
Per'ishableness, *n.* a liableness to perish or decay
Peristalt'ic, *a.* spiral, wormlike, rolling round
Per'istyle, *n.* a circular order or range of pillars
Perisys'toly, *n.* the pause between two pulsations
Peritonéum, *n.* the membrane inclosing the intestines
Peritóneal, *a.* pertaining to the peritoneum (tunes
Per'jure, *v. t.* to forswear, to take a false oath
Per'jure or Per'jurer, *n.* one who swears falsely
Per'jury, Perjurátion, *n.* a forswearing one's self
Per'iwig, *n.* false hair worn on the head, a wig
Per'iwig, *v. t.* to dress the head with false hair
Per'iwinkle, *n.* a small shellfish, sea-snail, plant
Perk, *v.* to hold up the head affectedly, to dress
Perk, *a.* lively, brisk, holding up the head
Per'manence, Perman"sion, *n.* duration, continuance
Per'manent, *a.* durable, lasting, constant (ance

Per'manently, *ad.* durably, laftingly, conftantly
Per'meable, *a.* that may be paffed through by a fluid
Per'meant, *a.* paffing or piercing through (fluid
Per'meate, *v. t.* to pafs through as a fluid
Permis'fion, Permit'tance, *n.* a grant of liberty
Permifs'ive, *a.* granting leave or liberty
Permifs'ively, *ad.* by permiffion, with allowance
Permis'tion or Permix'tion, *n.* the act of mixing
Permit', *v. t.* to allow, grant, fuffer, give up
Permit', *n.* a warrant, licence, leave
Permutátion, *n.* an exchange of one for another
Perni''cious, *a.* deftructive, mifchievous, fwift
Perni''cioufly, *ad.* dettructively, ruinoufly, badly
Perni''cioufnefs, *n.* a pernicious or bad quality
Perni''city, *n.* fwiftnefs of motion, fpeed, hafte
Pernoctátion, *n.* the act of paffing the night
Perorátion, *n.* the clofe or end of an oration
Perpend', *v. t.* to weigh well in the mind, *ob.*
Perpendic'ular, *a.* paffing at right angles, upright
Perpendic'ular, *n.* any thing directly upright
Perpendicul.rity, *n.* a perpendicular ftate
Perpendic'ularly, *ad.* in a perpendicular manner
Perpenfation, Perpen''fion, *n.* a ferious confidera-
Perpetrate, *v. t.* to do or commit a crime (tion
Perpetrátion, *n.* the commiffion of a crime, guilt
Perp'etrator, *n.* one who perpetrates or commits
Perpet'ual, *a.* continual, never ceafing, endlefs
Perpet'ually, *ad.* conftantly, inceffantly, for ever
Perpet'uate, *v. t.* to make perpetual, to eternize
Perpetuátion, *n.* the act of rendering perpetual
Perpetúity, *n.* a duration through all futurity
Perplex', *v. t.* to diftract, difturb, puzzle, vex
Perplex'ed, Perplex', *pa. a.* diftracted, intricate
Perplex'edly, *ad.* in an intricate manner, crofsly
Perplex'ednefs, *n.* embarraffment, intricacy, care
Perplex'ity, *n.* diftraction, anxiety, difficulty
Per'quifit, *n* a prefent, a fee beyond the falary
Per'ry, *n.* a very pleafant liquor made of pears
Perfecute, *v. t.* to purfue with enmity, to harafs
Perfecútion, *n.* the act of perfecuting, oppreffion
Pers'ecutor, *n.* one who perfecutes or difturbs
Perfepo'litan, *a.* pertaining to ancient Perfepolis
Perfevérance, *n.* fteadinefs, conftancy, firmnefs
Perfevérant, *a.* perfitting, conftant, refolute, firm
Perfevére, *v. i.* to perfift, go on, continue
Perfevéringly, *a.* with conftancy, without remiffion
Per''fian, *a.* of or belonging to Perfia
Per''fian, *n.* a native or the language of Perfia
Perfim'mon, *n.* a tree and its fruit
Perfift', *v. i.* to perfevere, go on, continue firm
Perfift'ance or Perfift'ence, *n.* perfeverance, obftinacy
Perfift'ent, Perfift'ing, *a.* enduring, not decaying
Perfift'ive, *a.* perfevering, fteady, firm
Pers'on, *n.* a man or woman, the fhape of a body
Pers'onable, *a.* handfome, graceful, defending
Pers'onage, *n.* a perfon, appearance, character
Pers'onal, *a.* belonging to him or her, peculiar
Perfonal'ity, *n.* the individuality of a perfon
Per'fonally, *ad.* in perfon, in prefence, fingly

Pers'onate, *a.* mafked, labiate with the lips clofed
Pers'onate, *v. t.* to reprefent, counterfeit, feign
Perfonátion, *n.* a counterfeiting another perfon
Perfonificátion, *n.* a change of things to perfons
Perfon'ify, *v. t.* to change from things to perfons
Perfpec'tive, *a.* of or relating to vifion, optical
Per fpec'tive, *n.* a fpying-glafs, view, appearance
Perfpicácious, *a.* quickfighted, fharpfighted, keen
Perfpicácioufnefs, Perfpica''city, *n.* quickfighted-
Pers'picil, *n.* an optical glafs, *ob.* (nefs
Perfpicúity, *n.* clearnefs, plainnefs, tranfparency
Perfpic'uous, *a.* clear, plain, evident, eafily feen
Perfpic'uoufly, *ad.* clearly, plainly, evidently
Perfpic'uoufnefs, *n.* clearnefs, plainnefs
Perfpírable, *a.* that may be emitted by the pores
Perfpirabil'ity, *n.* the quality of being perfpirable
Perfpirátion, *n.* the act of fweating, a great heat
Perfpírative, *a.* caufing or tending to perfpire
Perfpíre, *v. i.* to fweat, become hot, get vent, pafs
Perftringe', *v. t.* to graze upon, to glance upon
Perfuáde, *v. t.* to bring to an opinion, to influence
Perfuáder, *n.* an important or ftrong advifer
Perfuáfible, *a.* that may be perfuaded or induced
Perfuáfion, *n.* the act of perfuading, an opinion
Perfuáfive, *n.* an argument to perfuade
Perfuáfive, Perfuáfory, *a.* tending to perfuade
Perfuáfively, *ad.* fo as to perfuade, pleafingly
Perfuáfivenefs, *n.* force or power of perfuafion
Perfultátion, *n.* an eruption of the blood through
Pert, *a.* fmart, brifk, lively, faucy (the veffels
Pertáin, *v. i.* to belong, relate, concern, extend
Pertinácious, *a.* obftinate, ftiff, refolute, fteady
Pertinácioufly, *ad.* obftinately, ftubbornly, ftiffly
Pertinácioufnefs, Pertina''city, Pert'inacy, *n.* obfti-
nacy, ftubbornnefs, conftancy, firmnefs
Pert'inence or Pert'inency, *n.* propriety, fitnefs
Pert'inent, *a.* juft to the purpofe, fit, befonging
Pert'inently, *ad.* to the purpofe, fitly, aptly, duly
Pert'ly, *ad.* fmartly, brifkly, readily, faucily
Pert'nefs, *n.* fmartnefs, brifknefs, faucinefs
Perturb', *v. t.* to difquiet, difturb, vex, confufe
Perturbátion, *n.* difquiet, diforder, confufion
Perturb'ed, *a.* difquieted, difturbed, vexed, uneafy
Pertúfe, *a.* punched, having hollow dots
Pertúfion, *n.* the act of punching, a hole fo made
Perúke, *n.* a hairy covering for the head, a wig
Perúkemaker, *n.* a maker of periwigs, a barber
Perúfal, *n.* the act of reading over or examining
Perúfe, *v. t.* to read over, examin, obferve
Perúfer, *n.* a reader over, examiner, clofe obferver
Perúvian, *n.* a native of Peru in South America
Perúvian, *a.* belonging to Peru
Perváde, *v. t.* to pafs through or over, to poffefs
Perváfion, *n.* the act of paffing through or over
Perváfive, *a.* able or tending to pervade, paffing
Perverfe', *a.* crofs, obftinate, ftubborn, petulent
Perverfe'ly, *ad.* vexatioufly, crofsly, obftinately
Perverfe'nefs, Pervers'ity, *n.* crofsnefs, obftinacy
Perver''fion, *n.* a change for the worfe, abufe

Pervert', v. t. to turn from the right, to corrupt
Pervert'er, n. one who perverts, one who corrupts
Pervert'ible, a. that may be perverted or turned
Perveftigátion, n. a thorough examination
Pervicácious, a. fpitefully obftinate, ftubborn
Pervicácioufly, ad. with fpiteful obftinacy
Pervicácioufnefs, Pervica''city, n. perverfe obftina-
Per'vious, a. admitting paffage, pervading (cy
Per'vioufnefs, n. a pervious quality or ftate
Pefáde, n. a particular motion made by a horfe
Péfo, n. a coin, value about 132 cents
Peft, n. a plague, mifchief, bane, deftruction, ruin
Peft'er, v. t. to plague, teaze, harafs, difturb
Peft'erer, n. one who pefters, one who plagues
Peft'erous, a. troublefome, cumberfome, odious
Peft'houfe, n. a hofpital for infectious perfons
Peftiferous, a. deftructive, deadly, malignant
Peft'ilence, n. a contagious diftemper, the plague
Peft'ilent, Peft'ilential, a. infectious, pernicious
Peftillátion, n. the act of pounding in a mortar
Pes''tle, n. a tool to beat in a morter, a gammon
Pet, n. a flight paffion or anger, whim, cade lamb
Pétal, n. a leaf of a flower, or flower leaf
Pétalform, a. in fhape of a petal
Pétalled, a. furnifhed with petals
Pet'alifm, n. a banifhment by writing votes on
leaves, an ancient practice in Syracufe
Pet'alline, a. pertaining to or being on a petal
Petar' or Petard', n. an engine to blow up places by
Petéchial. [ch as k] a. fpotted with a peftilence
Pet'it, a. fmall, inconfiderable, trifling, mean
Pet'iole, n. a little footftalk, or footftalk of a leaf
Pet'iolar, a. proceeding from a footftalk, as a tendril
Pet'iolate, a. growing on a footftalk as a leaf
Peti''tion, n. a prayer, requeft, entreaty, article
Peti''tion, v. t. to fupplicate, folicit, entreat, beg
Peti''tionarily, ad. by way of begging the queftion
Peti''tionary, Pet'itory, a. fupplicating, petitioning
Petitioneé, n. the perfon cited to defend in a peti-
Peti''tioner, n. one who offers a petition (tion
Pet'rel, n. a tribe of aquatic fowls
Petrifac'tion, Petrificátion, n. a becoming ftone
Petrifact'ive, Petrific'ic, a. able to turn to ftone
Pet'rify, v. to change to ftone, to become ftone
Pet'rilite, n. a fpecies of felfpar of a brownifh red
Petres'cence, n. a hardening into ftone
Petres'cent, a. turning into ftone, hardening
Pétrol, n. rock oil, a liquid inflammable oily fub-
ftance iffuing from the earth
Pet'ronel, n. a piftol, a very fmall or light gun
Pétrofilex, n. rock-ftone, a mixed earth
Petrofili''ceous, a. pertaining to rock-ftone
Pet'ticoat, n. an under garment worn by women
Pet'tifogger, n. a petty attorney, a petty lawyer
Pet'tifogging, a. low, mean, little, unbecoming
Pet'tinefs, n. fmallnefs, littlenefs, meannefs
Pet'tifh, Pet'tle, a. froward, fretful, peevifh, crofs
Pet'tifhnefs, n. fretfulnefs, peevifhnefs, croffnefs
Pet'titoes, n. pl. the feet of a fucking pig, the feet

Pet'to, n. the breaft, privacy, fecrecy, referve
Pet'ty, a. fmall, little, trifling, inconfiderable, low
Pet'tychaps, n. a bird in the north of England
Pet'ulance or Pet'ulency, n. faucinefs, peevifhnefs
Pet'ulent, a. faucy, perverfe, peevifh, wanton
Pet'ulantly, ad. perverfely, peevifhly, wantonly
Petun'fi, n. a ftone or earth ufed in making china
Pew, n. an inclofed or referved feat in a church
Pew, v. t. to cover or furnifh with pews
Pew'et, n. a fpecies of the lapwing, the black-cap
Pew'ter, n. a compofition of lead, brafs and tin, or
tin and antimony
Pew'terer, n. one who works in or fells pewter
Pháeton, n. a high and open carriage of pleafure
PhagedEn'ic, a. eating flefh, corroding
Phalan'ger, n. a fpecies of opoffum in the E. Indies
Phálanx, n. a fquare troop of men clofely embodied
Phal'arope, n. a bird with fcolloped membranes
on its toes
Phant'afm, n. a vain imagination, whim, vifion
Phant'om, n. an aparition, ghoft, fancied vifion
Pharifáical, a. externally religious, deceitful
Pharifáically, ad. with great oftentation, vainly
Phar'ifaifm, n. the principles or practice of the
Pharifees, oftentation of religion
Pharmacol'ogift, n. one who writes upon drugs
Pharmacopéia, n. a treatife upon drugs
Pharmacop'olift, n. one who fells medicins
Pharmaceu'tical, a. pertaining to pharmacy
Phar'macy, n. the act of preparing medicins
Pháros, n. a lighthoufe, watchtower, beacon
Pharyngot'omy, n. a cutting open the windpipe
Pháfels, n. pl. a plant, french beans
Pháfes, n. appearances or pofitions of the moon, &c.
Phafm, n. an appearance, a fancied apparition
Phat'agin, n. the leffer or long tailed pangolin
Pheas'ant, n. a genus of gallinaceous birds
Phebéan, a. pertaining to Phœbus or Apollo
Pheefe, v. t. to comb, fleece, curry, trim, ob.
Phénean, a. pertaining to Pheneum in Arcadia
Pheni''cian, n. a native of Phenice, on the eaftern
fhore of the Mediterranean
Pheni''cian, a. pertaining to Phenice
Phénix, n. a fabulous bird of antiquity (or fight
Phenom'enon, n. any appearance, a fingular event
Phíal, n. a fmall glafs bottle
Philadel'phia, n. the chief city of Pennfylvania
Philadel'phian, n. a citizen of Philadelphia
Philanthrop'ie, a. humane, loving mankind
Philan'thropift, n. a perfon of univerfal benevo-
lence (courtefy
Philan'thropy, n. the love of mankind, humanity,
Phil'ibeg, n. a kind of fmall or fhort petticoat
Phil'ippine, a. denoting a vaft clufter of iflands in
the Pacific, near the Afiatic coaft
Philip'pian, n. a native of Philippi in Macedonia
Philiftines, n. inhabitants of Paleftine, afterwards
Philip'pic, n. an invective, a tart declamation [Judea
Philol'oger, Philol'ogift, n. a grammarian, a critic

Philolo"gical, a. grammatical, critical, nice
Philol'ogy, n. grammatical learning, criticifm
Philomath, n. a lover of learning or fcience
Philom'athy, n. a love of learning
Philomath'ic, a. relating to a love of fcience
Phil'omel, n. a name of the nightingale
Phil'omot, a. brownifh, like a dead leaf   (rem
Philos'opheme, n. a principle of reafoning, a theo-
Philos'opher, n. one who is fkilled in philofophy
Philofopher's-ftone, n. a pretended ftone that will turn all other metals into gold, a myftery
Philofoph'ical, a. of philofophy, rational, nice
Philofoph'ically, ad. rationally, wifely, properly
Philos'ophize, v. i. to reafon like a philofopher
Philos'ophy, n. knowledge moral or natural
Philos'ophifm, n. the love or practice of fophiftry
Philos'ophift, n. one who practices fophiftry
Philofophis'tical, a. pertaining to the practice of fophiftry   (love
Philt'er, n. a love charm or potion; v. t. to caufe
Phiz, n. the face, vifage, countenance
Phlebot'omift, n. one who lets blood
Phlebot'omize, v. t. to let blood, to open a vein
Phlebot'omy, n. blood-letting, an opening of a vein
Phlegm, n. a watery humor of the body
Phlegm'agogues, n. pl. medicins to clear phlegm
Phlegmat'ic, a. abounding in phlegm, dull, heavy
Phleg'matifm, n. dullnefs, heavinefs
Phleg'mon, n. an inflammation, a hot fwelling
Phleg'monous, a. inflammatory, very hot, burning
Phleme, n. a farrier's inftrument to bleed with
Phlogis'ton, [g as j] n. an element fuppofed by fome to be the principle of inflammability or matter of fire and heat
Phlogis'tie, a. inflaming, pertaining to phlogifton
Phlogis'tian, n. a believer in phlogifton
Phlogis'ticate, v. t. to combine phlogifton with
Phlogiftication, n. the act of combining with phlo-gifton   (taining to Phocis
Phocian, n. a native of Phocis in Greece; a. per-
Phon'ics, n. the fcience of founds, acouftics
Phonocamp'tic, a. able to change or alterfound
Phos'phor, n. the morning ftar
Phos'phorus or Phos'phor, n. a fimple combuftible fubftance of a c'ear tranfparent yellowifh col-or exhibiting a faint light in the dark
Phos'phate, n. a falt formed by phofphoric acid, and a bafe of earth, alkali or metal
Phos'phite, n. a falt formed by phofphorous acid and a falifiable bafe   (phofphorus
Phos'phorate, Phos'phorize, v. t. to combine with
Phos'phorated, a. combined with phofphorus
Phofphorefce', v. i. to emit light without heat, as phofphorus   (phofphorus
Phofphores'cence, n. a luminoufnefs like that of
Phofphores'cent, a. fhining, luminous like phof-phorus   (acid
Phos'pholite, n. an earth united with phofphoric
Phofphor'ic, a. denoting an acid formed by a fat-

urated combination of phofphorus and oxygene
Phos'phorite, n. a fpecies of phofpholite
Phos'phorous, a. denoting an acid, formed by a combination of phofphorus and oxygene
Phos'phoret, n. a combination of phofphorus with another fubftance without oxygene
Phrafe, n. a mode of fpeech, a ftyle; v. t. to ftyle,
Phrafelefs, a. not to be defcribed   (to term
Phrafeol'ogy, n. a mode of fpeech, diction, ftyle
Phrenet'ic, a. mad, frantic, diftracted, furious
Phren'etis, Phren'fy or Phren'zy, n. madnefs
Phren'ic, a. pertaining to the diaphram
Phthis'ic, n. a confumption, a fhortnefs of breath
Phthis'ical, a. confumptive, fhortbreathed
Phthi'sis, n. a confumption or wafting difeafe
Phylact'ery, n. a fcroll infcribed with a fentence
Phylloph'orous, a. bearing leaves   (man
Phyfian'throphy, n. the fcience of the nature of
Phys'eter, n. a genus of cetaceous fifh or whales
Phys'ic, n. the art of healing, a medicin, a purge
Phys'ic, v. t. to purge with phyfic, cleanfe, cure
Phys'ical, a. medicinal, relating to nature
Phys'ically, ad. naturally, by natural operation
Phyfi'cian, n. one who profeffes the art of healing
Phys'ics, n. pl. natural philofophy, divinity
Phyfiog'nomift, n. a judge of men by their faces
Phyfiognomon'ical, a. relating to phyfiognomy
Phyfiog'nomy, n. the art of judging by the face,
Phyfiolo"gical, a. relating to phyfiology (the face
Phyfiol'ogift, n. a writer on natural philofophy
Phyfiol'ogy, n. the doctrin of phyfics or nature
Phytiv'orous, a. that feeds on vegetables
Phyto'ogy, n. a defcription of plants, botany
Phytol'ogift, a. a botanift
Piacle, n. a great crime, hain th fault, facrifice, ob.
Piac'ular, a. very wicked, atrocious, expiatory
Piaft'er, n. a foreign coin, value about 80 cents
Piation, n. an atoning or purging by facrifice
Piaz'za, n. a fhort walk under arches, a portico
Pica, n. the green ficknefs, a printing letter, a bird
Picaroon', n. a robber, plund..rer, freebooter, thief
Pick, v. to choofe, gather, feparate, clean, ftrike, pull, rob, open, eat flowly or a very little
Pick'ax, n. a kind of ax that has a fharp point
Pick'ed or Piked, a. fharp at the end, pointed
Pick'eer, v. t. to rob, to make a flying kirmifh
Pick'er, n. one who picks, a robber, a pickax
Pick'erel, n. a common name of the pike
Pick'et, n. a fharpened poft or ftake, an out guard
Pick'et, v. t. to inclofe with pickets
Pic"kle, n. a thing pickled, falt liquor, brine, ftate
Pic"kle, v. t. to preferve in pickle, feafon, imbue
Pick'lock, n. a tool or perfon that picks locks
Pick'pocket, n. one that fteals out of a pocket
Pick'thank, n. a very officious perfon, a flatterer, ob.
Pick'tooth, n. an inftrument to clean the teeth by
Pict, n. a perfon that has the body painted over
Pictorial, a. produced, done or drawn by a painter
Pict'ure, n. a refemblance in colors; v. t. to paint

Picturefque', a. full of diverfified figures
Pid'dle, v. i. to feed fqueamifhly, pick, trifle
Pid'dler, n. one that eats little, a trifler
Pie, n. a cruft baked with fomething in it, a bird
Piebald, a. diverfified in color, particolored
Piece, n. a patch, part, performance, coin, gun
Piece, v. f. to enlarge, add, join, clofe, fupply
Piécelefs, a. that is not made of pieces, whole, ob.
Piécemeal, a. fingle, divided ; ad. in or by pieces
Pied, a. particolored, fpeckled, fpotted, marked
Piednefs, n. an odd diverfity or mixture of colors
Piéled, a. having very fhort hair, fhortened, ob.
Pier, n. the column or fupport of an arch, a wharf
    or mound in a river or the fea
Pierce, v. to enter, bore, broach, force, affect
Pier'cer, n. a perfon who or that which pierceth
Pier'cingly, ad. keenly, fharply, acutely, ftrongly
Pier'cingnefs, n. the power of piercing or forcing
Pietifm, n. an affectation of piety, fuperftition
Piety, Pioufnefs, n. duty to GOD or to parents
Pig, n. a young boar or fow, a mafs of lead or iron
Pig, v. t. to bring forth pigs, farrow, fleep, lay
Pi'geon, n. a genus of birds, wild and domeftic
Pi'geonhoufe, n. a houfe or building for pigeons
Pi'geonlivered, a. mild, meek, foft, gentle, tame, ob.
Pig'gen or Pig'gin, n. a wooden veffel, a dipper
Pight, a. pitched, fixed, determined, fettled, ob.
Pig'ment, n. paint, colors for painting the face
Pig'my, n. a very little perfon ; a. very fmall, puny
Pig'nut, n. the name of a plant, an earth nut
Pigus, n. a fifh refembling the carp
Pigwid'geon, n. any thing fmall ; a. very little, ob.
Pike, n. a lance ufed by foldiers, fork, a fifh of fev-
    eral fpecies, with long bodies and very voracious
Pikeman, n. a foldier armed with a pike
Pikeftaff, n. the wooden handle of a pike, any thing
Pilaft'er, n. a fmall fquare column   (eafy
Pilaw', n. a famous Turkifh difh, an ointment
Pilch or Pilcher, n. a cloak lined with fur, ob.
Pilch'ard, n. a fmall fifh like a herring
Pile, n. a heap, edifice, piece of wood, nap, figure
Pile, v. t. to heap or lay upon, heap, raife up
Pil'eate, Pil'eated, a. covered with or like a cap
Pileworm, n. a worm found in the piles of Holland
Pilf'er, v. i. to fteal, to fteal trifling things
Pilf'erer, n. one who fteals petty things, a mean
Pilf'ering, Pilf'ery, n. petty theft   (thief
Pil'grim, v. i. to ramble, wander, rove, travel
Pil'grim, n. one who vifits the fhrines of faints
Pil'grimage, n. a journey to vifit fhrines, travel
Pill, n. a fmall ball of phyfic ; v. t. to rob, to peal
Pill'age, n. plunder; v. t. to plunder, rifle, rob
Pill'ager, n. one who pillages, one who plunders
Pill'ar, n. a column, prop, fupport, defender
Pill'ared, a. fupported by or like pillars
Pillgar'lic, n. a name of ridicule or contempt
Pill'ion, n. a cufhion for women to ride on behind
    a perfon
Pill'ory, n. an inftrument or place of punifhment

Pill'ory, v. t. to punifh with or put in the pillory
Pill'ow, n. a thing to lay the head on ; v. t. to reft
Pill'owbeer, Pill'owcafe, n. the cover of a pillow
Pilôfe, a. hairy, covered with hairs
Pilos'ity, n. a hairy ftate, hairinefs, roughnefs
Pilot, n. one who fteers a fhip ; v. t. to conduct
Pilotage, n. the pay, fkill or office of a pilot
Pilotfifh, n. a fifh of the fize of a mackarel
Piment'o, n. all-fpice, Jamaica-pepper
Pimp, n. a pander, he-bawd, procurer, low wretch
Pimp, v. i. to provide gratifications for others
Pim'pillo, n. a plant, the cactus
Pim'pinel, n. a plant of many fpecies
Pimp'ing, a. little, mean, petty, fnivelling, forry
Pim'ple, n. a fmall red puftule upon the fkin
Pim'pled, a. full of pimples
Pimp'like, a. like a pimp, infamous, vile
Pin, n. a pointed fhort piece of wire, peg, ftrain
Pin, v. t. to faften or clofe with pins, fix, pen
Pinârian, a. pertaining to Pinarius, a prieft of Arca-
    dia who prefided over facrifices (fee pinchers]
Pin'cers, n. an inftrument to draw nails [ill formed,
Pinch, v. to fqueeze, prefs, gall, hurt, be frugal
Pinch, n. a painful fqueeze, gripe, difficulty, trial
Pinch'beck, n. a compofition of copper and zink
Pinch'ers, n. an inftrument to draw nails
Pinch'fift, Pinch'penny, n. a mifer, a covetous man
Pin'cufhion, n. a thing ufed to ftick pins in
Pindar'ic, a. like Pindar, lofty, fublime, bold
Pin'duft, n. duft rifing from cutting pins
Pine, n. a tree ; v. i. to languifh, to wafte
Pineafter, n. a fpecies of pine, pinus fylveftris
Pin'fethered, a. having very young fethers
Pin'fold, n. a confinement for cattle that ftray
Pin'guid, a. fat, unctuous, greafy, large, plump
Pin'hole, n. a fmall hole made by a pin
Pin'ion, n. a wing, quill, tooth of a wheel, fetter
Pin'ion, v. t. to bind the wing, bind, tie, fhackle
Pin'ionift, n. a bird, a winged animal
Pinirôlo, n. an Italian fifh like a fand piper
Pink, n. a flower, color, a veffel with a narrow ftern
Pink, v. to ftamp with fmall holes, to wink
Pink'er, v. i. to fquint, look afkew, ogle, eye
Pin'maker, n. one who makes pins
Pin'money, n. an allowance for a wife's pocket
Pin'nace, n. a man of war's boat, a fmall floop
Pin'nacle, n. a turret, fpire, high-fpiring point
Pin'nate, a. having leaflets along the fide like fethers
Pin'natifid, a. divided like the plumes of a fether
    into lateral, oblong fegments
Pin'nacled, a. adorned with pinacles
Pin'ner, n. a pinmaker, lappet, cap
Pint, n. half a quart, twelve ounces, a pound
Pioneer, n. a military perfon to clear ways, &c.
Pious, a. doing the duties of religion, religious
Pioufly, ad. in a pious manner, religioufly
Pip, n. a fpot on cards, leaf, difeafe of fowls
Pip, v. to fpot, mark, chirp or cry like a bird
Pipe, n. a tube, mufical inftrument, 2 hogfheads

Pipe, v. to play on a pipe, play, cry, whine, moan
Pipefish, n. a genus of fish with a long tubular nose
Piper, n. one who plays on a pipe, a fish
Pip'erin, n. a concretion of volcanic ashes
Piping, a. weak, feeble, hot; ad. quite, very
Piping, n. a playing on a pipe, a whining noise
Pipis'trel, n. the smallest of the bat kind
Pip'kin, n. a small earthern boiler or pot
Pip'peridge, n. a shrub, a tree
Pip'pin, n. the name of an admired apple
Piq'uancy, n. a piquant quality, poignancy, wit
Piq'uant, [pik'ant] a. poignant, pricking, severe
Piq'uantly, ad. sharply, tartly, with resentment
Pique, [peek] v. t. to offend, vex, provoke, sting
Pique, n. a grudge, enmity, ill-will, point, nicety
Piquéerer, Pickéerer, n. a robber, not used
Piquet', [pikett']n. a game at cards
Piracy, n. a robbery on the sea, a robbery (der
Pírate, n. a sea-robber, any robber; v. i. to plun-
Pirat'ical, a. predatory, plundering, thievish
Pirat'ically, ad. in the manner of piracy
Pisc'ary, n. a privilege or liberty to catch fish
Piscátion, n. the act, art or practice of fishing
Pisc'atory, a. belonging to fish or fishing
Pis'cine, a. belonging to fish, fishy
Pisciv'erous, a. eating fish, living upon fish
Pish, v. i. to show contempt by a kind of hiss
Pish, n. an expression of contempt; exclam. imply-
Pis'iform, a. in the shape of a pea (ing contempt
Pis'olith, n. a calcareous stalactite of a gray color
Pis'mire, n. an insect, ant, emmet
Piss, n. urine, v. to make water
Pis'olite, n. a sort of freestone, like the roe of fish
Pistáchio, n. a fragrant nut brought from Syria
Pis'til, n. the style or pointal of a plant, containing
    the stigma, which receives the fecundating dust
    of the stamen
Pistillátion, n. the act of pounding in a mortar
Pistilláceous, a. growing on the germ or seed bud
Pistilliferous, a. bearing pistils without stamens
Pist'ol, n. a weapon, the smallest of all firearms
Pist'ol, v. t. to shoot or engage with a pistol
Pistóle, n. a Spanish coin of 3 dolls. 73 cts.
Pistolet', n. a small pistol
Pist'on, n. a part of a pump or syringe which ex-
    hausts the air of a tube and causes suction
Pit, n. a hole, deep place, hollow part, dint, grave
Pit, v. to sink in hollows, dint, challenge, set
Pit'apat, n. a flutter, a quick step; ad. in a flutter
Pitch, n. a kind of resin, size, height, rate, bar
Pitch, v. to smear over with pitch, fix, agree, cast,
    throw, drop, light, fall
Pitch'er, n. a large earthern pot, a pointed iron bar
Pitch'fork, n. a long fork to pitch hay, &c.
Pitch'stone, n. a siliceous stone of a grayish black
Pitch'y, a. smeared with or like pitch, dismal
Pit'coal, n. any kind of coal dug out of a pit
Pit'eous, a. sorrowful, tender, pitiful, woful
Pit'eously, ad. in a piteous manner, sadly

Pit'fal, n. a pit dug and covered over, trap, snare
Pit'fish, n. a fish of the size of a smelt
Pith, n. the marrow of a plant, strength, weight
Pith'ily, ad. with strength, with force or cogency
Pith'iness, n. energy, strength, force, fulness
Pith'less, a. wanting pith or force, weak, flat
Pith'y, a. consisting of pith, energetic, forcible
Pit'iable, a. deserving pity, mournful, wretched
Pit'iful, a. tender, paltry, despicable, wretched
Pit'ifully, ad. in a pitiful manner, meanly, badly
Pit'ifulness, n. tenderness, mercy, despicableness
Pit'iless, a. devoid of pity, mercy or compassion
Pit'ilessly, ad. without pity or mercy, cruelly
Pit'man, n. a man who works in pits, a sawyer
Pit'saw, n. a large saw to be used by two men
Pit'tance, n. a small allowance, a little portion
Pitshitous, Pituitary, a. consisting of phlegm
Pit'y, n. compassion, sympathy, concern, mercy
Pit'y, v. t. to compassionate misery, to bewail
Piv'ot, n. a pin upon which a thing turns round.
Pix, n. a box that contains the host, chest, pitch
Placabil'ity, n. a willingness to be appeased
Plácable, a. that may be appeased or pacified
Placart', n. an edict, proclamation, manifesto
Plácate, v. t. to appease, pacify, quiet, reconcile
Place, n. locality, residence, rank, office, state of
    being, space in general, room, part, ground
Place, v. to rank, order, fix, establish, put out
Placen'tal, a. belonging to the placenta, the part
    by which circulation is carried on between the
    parent and fœtus
Placentátion, n. the disposition of the cotyledons
    in seeds when they begin to grow
Pla"cid, a. calm, mild, gentle, quiet, easy, soft
Placid'ity, Pla"cidness, n. a placid quality or state
Pla"cidly, ad. calmly, mildly, quietly, patiently
Pla"cit, n. a decree, determination, ordinance, ob.
Plack'et, Pla"quet, n. the opening in a garment
Plágiarism, n. a theft, especially in books
Plágiary, n. one guilty of plagiarism
Plague, n. a pestilence, vexation, trouble, misery
Plague, v. t. to teaze, trouble, vex, hurt, afflict
Plaguily, ad. vexatiously, horribly, dreadfully
Plaguy, a. vexatious, troublesome, horrible, vile
Plaice, n. a seafish, a kind of flat fish
Plaid, n. a variegated stuff, a Scotch dress
Plain, a. smooth, flat, clear, evident, homely
Plain, n. a level ground, field of battle, square
Plain, Plain'ly, ad. sincerely, clearly, bluntly
Plain, v. t. to make smooth, level, lament
Plaindealing, n. downright honesty; a. sincere
Pláining, pa. making smooth; n. a complaint
Plainness, n. flatness, clearness, simplicity
Plaint, n. a complaint, lamentation, cry
Pláintful, a. complaining, uneasy, sorrowful, sad
Plaintiff, n. one who commences a suit at law
Plaintiff, Pláintive, a. sorrowful, mournful
Plainwork, n. needlework, work not figured
Plait or Pleet, n. a fold; v. t. to fold, to weave

Plan, *n.* a fcheme, projeƈt, draft, model, plot

Plan, *v. t.* to fcheme, form in defign, contrive

Planch'ed, *a.* made of boards, laid with boards, *ob.*

Planch'er, *n.* a flat board, plank, piece of wood, *ob.*

Plane, *v. t.* to fmooth, to level; *n.* a tool, a tree

Plan'et, *n.* a ftar which revolves about a center in an orbit nearly circular   (of the planets

Planetárium, *n.* a machine to reprefent the orbits

Planim'etry, *n.* the meafuring of furfaces

Plan'etary, Planet'ical, *a.* belonging to planets

Plan'etftruck, *a.* blafted, aftonifhed, amazed

Planipet'alous, *a.* having plain flat petals

Plan'ifphere, *n.* a fphere projeƈted upon a plain

Plank, *n.* a thick board; *v. t.* to lay with planks

Plan'ner, *n.* one who plans, one who fchemes

Plan'ning *n.* a defign, formation, contrivance

Planocon'ical, *a.* flat and conical on different fides

Planocon'vex, *a.* flat and convex on different fides

Planohorizon'tal, *a.* fmooth or even and horizontal

Planofub'ulate, *a.* fmooth and awlfhaped

Plant, *n.* a vegetable produƈtion, herb, tree, foot

Plant, *v. t.* to fet, place, fix, fettle, people, point

Plant'able, *a.* capable of or fit for planting

Plant'ain, *n.* an herb, a Weft-Indian tree

Plant'al, *a.* belonging to or refembling plants

Plantátion, *n.* a place that is planted, a colony, a cultivated eftate or farm

Plant'cane, *n.* a cane of the firft growth from original plants fet in the earth, *W. Indies*

Plant'er, *n.* one who fets or cultivates, a farmer

Plant'erſhip, *n.* the bufinefs of a planter

Plant'icle, *n.* a young plant or plant in embryo

Plant'ing, *n.* the aƈt of fetting in the ground

Plaſh, *n.* a fmall puddle of water, a cut branch

Plaſh, *v. t.* to fplaſh, to cut and lay branches

Plaſh'y, *a.* wet, watery, filled with puddles

Plafin, *n.* a mold for metals   (on linen, &c.

Plas'ter, *n.* lime prepared to cover walls, a falve

Plas'ter, *v. t.* to cover or daub with plafter, &c.

Plas'terer, *n.* one who covers walls with plafter

Plas'ter of Paris, a mixture of feveral forts of gypfum, ufed alfo for gypfum

Plas'tic, *a.* forming, able to form, creative (form

Plasti''city, *n.* the quality of being fufceptible of

Plas'tran or Plas'tron, *n.* a piece of ftuffed lether

Plat, *v. t.* to interweave; *n.* a piece of ground

Plat'band, *n.* a border of flowers or other plants, the lintel of a door or window

Plate, *n.* wrought filver, a difh to eat on, a prize

Plate, *v. t.* to cover with or beat into plates

Plat'en, *n.* a part of a printing prefs by which the impreffion is made

Plat'form, *n.* an horizontal plain, level, flat roof, a fyftem of church difciplin, [Con.]

Plátin, [platína] *n.* a very hard metal heavier than gold, and nearly refembling filver in color

Platon'ic, *d.* relating to Plato, chafte, pure, refined

Plátoniſm, *n.* the doƈtrins of Plato

Plátoniſt, *n.* an adherent to the opinions of Plato

Plátonize, *v.* to reafon like or adopt the fyftem of Plato

Platoon', *n.* a fmall fquare body of mufketeers

Plat'ter, *n.* a large broad flat difh

Plat'terfaced, *a.* having a very large broad face

Plat'ypus, *n.* a quadruped of New-Holland with jaws elongated into the fhape of a duck's bill

Plaud'it, *n.* applaufe, praife, approbation, a clap

Plaud'itory, *a.* praifing, commending, extolling

Plaufibil'ity, Plaus'iblenefs, *n.* appearance of right

Plaus'ible, *a.* fpecious, fair, fuperficially pleafing

Plaus'ibly, *ad.* fpecioufly, with a fair fhow

Plaus'ive, *a.* applauding, praifing, plaufible, fair

Play, *v.* to fport, toy, trifle, mock, aƈt, perform

Play, *n.* fport, recreation, a game, a drama, room

Play'book, *n.* a book which contains plays only

Play'day, *n.* a day exempted from tafks or labor

Play'debt, *n.* a debt contraƈted by gaming

Play'er, *n.* one who plays, one who performs

Play'fellow, *n.* a eompanion or crony in youth

Play'ful, Play'fome, *a.* full of play, fportive, gay

Play'game, *n.* a play or game of mere children

Play'houfe, *n.* a houfe ufed for aƈting plays in

Play'pleafure, *n.* an idle or trifling amufement

Play'thing, *n.* a thing to play with, toy, trifle

Play'wright, *n.* one who makes or writes plays

Plea, *n.* an excufe, allegation, form of pleading

Pleach, *v. t.* to bend, to interweave branches, *ob.*

Plead, *v.* to defend, difcufs, argue, allege, fay

Pleadable, *a.* that may be pleaded, alleged, or faid

Plead'er, *n.* one who pleads, one who alleges

Plead'ing *n.* the aƈt or form of pleading caufes

Pleas'ant, *a.* delightful, gay, cheerful, trifling

Pleas'antly, *ad* in a pleafant manner or place

Pleas'antnefs, *n.* delightfulnefs, cheerfulnefs

Pleas'antry, *n.* cheerfulnefs, humor, merriment

Pleafe, *v.* to give pleafure, delight, content, like

Pléafeman, *n.* an officious perfon, a flatterer

Pléafer, *n.* one who pleafes or courts favor

Pléafingly, *ad.* in a manner fo as to pleafe

Pleas'urable, *a.* delightful, fine, cheerful   (pleafe

Pleas'ure, *n.* delight, gratification, choice; *v. t.* to

Pleas'ureboat, *n.* a boat for amufement in failing

Pleas'urecarriage, *n.* a carriage for pleafure

Plebéian, Plébean, *a.* vulgar, common, low, mean

Plebéian, *n.* one of the common people

Pledge, *n.* a pawn; *v. t.* to pawn, to invite to drink

Pledg'ee, *n.* the perfon to whom any thing is pledged

Pledg'er, *n.* he who pledges or pawns

Pledg'et, *n.* a fmall piece of lint for a wound

Pleet, *n.* a fold; *v. t.* to fold, lay in folds

Plei'ades, *n.* a northern conftellation, the feven ftars

Plénarily, *ad.* fully, completely, entirely, totally

Plénary, *ad.* full, complete; *n.* a decifive procedure

Pleni'lunary, *a.* relating to the full moon

Plenip'otence, *n.* fulnefs of power

Plenip'otent, *a.* invefted with full power

Plenipoten'tiary, *n.* one invefted with full power

Plénift, *n.* one who holds fpace to be full of matter

Plen'itude, n. fulness, completeness, repletion
Plent'eous, a. abundant, copious, fertile (oufly
Plent'eoufly, Plent'ifully, ad. abundantly, copi-
Plent'iful, a. abundant ,copious, fruitful, rich
Plent'y, Plent'eoufnefs, n. abundance, fruitfulnefs
Plen'ty, a. abundant, in great quantity
Pléonafm, n. a figure, a redundancy of expreffion
Pleonas'tic, a. redundant in expreffion
Pleth'ora, Pleth'ory, n. a too full habit of body
Plethoret'ic, Pleth'oric, a. having a full habit
Plefirify, n. an inflamation of the pleura or fide
Pleurit'ic, a. difeafed with or having a pleurify
Plex'iform,a. in the form of network, complicated
Pli'cate, a. formed like folds, plaited
Pliable, a. flexible, eafy to be bent or led (bent
Pliablenefs, Pliancy, Pliantnefs, n. eafinefs to be
Pliant, a. flexible, bending, limber, eafy to be per-
Pliers, n. pl. nippers, fmall pinchers (fuaded
Plight v. t. to pledge, engage, weave, braid
Plight, n. a condition, cafe, pledge, fold, plait
Plinth, n. the foot or loweft part of a pillar
Plod, v. i. to toil, drudge, labor, ftudy clofely
Plod'der, n. a dull or heavy, but laborious perfon
Plod'ding, n. clofe drudgery or ftudy, hard labor
Plot, n. a ftratagem, intrigue, confpiracy, plat
Plot, v. t. to fcheme, plan, project, contrive
Plot'ter, n. a fchemer, contriver, confpirator
Plover, n. a bird of feveral fpecies
Plow, v. t. to turn up with a plow
Plow, n. an inftrument of hufbandry or joinery
Plow'boy, n. a boy who drives a team in plowing
Plow'land, n. land for grain, a quantity of land
Plow'man, n. a perfon who holds the plow
Plow'fhare, n. one of the irons of a plow
Pluck, v. to fnatch, pull, ftrip off fethers, take
Pluck, n. a quick pull, the heart, liver and lights
Plug, v. t. to ftop with a plug ; n. a ftopple
Plum, n. a fruit, raifin, 100,000l. Engl. money
Plumage. n. fethers, a bunch of fethers
Plumb, n. a leaden weight on a line, a plummet
Plumb, v. t. to found, to adjuft ; ad. perpendicular
Plumba'ginous, a. like or containing plumbago
Plumbago, n. carburet of iron, or iron and carbon,
    called alfo black lead
Plumb'er, n. a perfon who works upon lead
Plumb'ery, n. work for or done by a plumber
Plumbif'erous, a. producing lead
Plumb'line, n. a line with a weight at the end
Plum'cake, n. a cake made up with raifins, &c.
Plume, n. a fether, down, token of honor, pride
Plume, v. to adjuft fethers, adorn, ftrip, pride
Plumealum, n. a mineral ftone, a kind of afbeftos
Plumiped, n. a bird with fethers on the feet
Plum'met, n. a leaden weight, leaden pencil, ball
Plumofe, a. covered with pappus or foft down
Plumos'ity, Plumoufnefs, n. a fethered ftate
Plump, a. fat, fleek, comely ; n. a clutter, a tuft
Plump, v. to fatten, fwell, increafe, fall at once
Plump, ad. with a fudden fall, quickly, at once

Plump'er, n. what plumps out, a fudden ftroke
Plump'ly, ad. with plumpnefs, without referve
Plump'nefs, n. fatnefs, fulnefs, fleeknefs
Plum'porridge, n. porridge made with plums
Plum'pudding, n. a pudding made with plums
Plump'y, a. rather plump, fat, jolly, full
Plúmule, n. the leaf bud, or afcending part of the
    corcle of a plant
Plúmy, Plúmous, a. fethery, like fethers
Plun'der, v. t. to pillage, to rob like an enemy
Plun'der, n. fpoil gotten in war or by violence
Plun'derer, n. a hoftile pillager, robber, fpoiler
Plunge, v. to fink or rife fuddenly, dive, dip, put
Plunge, n. the act of finking under water, diftrefs
Plun'ger, n. a brafs cylinder ufed as a forcer in
Plunk'et,n.a fort of fine blue color; a.blue (pumps
Plúral, a. having more than one, many, feveral
Plúralift, n. he that holds more livings than one
Plura'lity, n. a number more than one, more cures
    of fouls than one, a number greater than any
    other, but lefs than half
Plúrally, ad. in a plural manner
Plurilit'eral, n. a word of more letters than three
Plufh, n. fhag, a fort of very ftrong rough cloth
Pluton'ic, a. denoting the fyftem of the plutonifts
Plutonift, n. one who afcribes the formation of
    mountains to eruptions of fire
Plúvial, Plúvious,a. rainy,wet,fhowery
Plúvial, n. a cap, a prieft's cope
Pluviam'eter, n. a rain gage to afcertain the quan-
    tity of water falling in rain (bent, a plait
Ply, v. to work clofely, bend, offer fervice; n. a
Pneumat'ic, a. moved by or confifting of wind,
    pertaining to elaftic fluids (fluids in general
Pneumat'ics, n. the doctrin of the air or of elaftic
Pneumatol'ogy, n. the fcience of fpiritual being
Poach, v. to boil flightly, fteal,game, ftab,be damp
Poacher, n. one who kills game unlawfully
Poachinefs, n. foftnefs of earth, ftickinefs
Poaching. n. the act of killing game unlawfully
Poachy, a. foft as earth, yielding to the feet, moift
Pock, n. a puftule, fcab, mark, dint (to fteal
Pock'et, n. a fmall bag; v. t. to put in a pocket,
Pock'etbook, n. a writing-book for the pocket
Pock'etglafs, n. a lookingglafs for the pocket
Pock'hole, n. a mark left by the fmall pox
Pock'inefs, n. a pocky ftate or quality
Pock'wood, n. a hard wood, lignumvita
Pock'y, a. infected with or having the pox, foul
Poc'ulent, a. fit for drinking, drinkable, ob.
Pod, v. t. to fill, fwell, pick; n. a cafe of feeds
Podag'rical, a. gouty, relating to or like the gout
Pod'der, n. one who gathers peafe, &c. in pods
Podge, n. a puddle, plafh, watery or dirty place
Póem, n. a work or compofition written in verfe
Póefy, n. the art of writing poems, poetry, verfe
Póet, n. a writer of poems, a compofer of verfes
Póetafter, n. a petty poet, a poor pitiful rhymer
Póetefs or Póetrefs, n. a female writer of poetry

Poet'ical, a. expressed in or relating to poetry
Poet'ically, ad. in a poetical manner, musically
Póetize, v. i. to write or attempt poetry
Póetry, n. metrical composition, rhyme, poems
Poign'ancy, n. a poignant quality, sharpness
Poign'ant, a. sharp, biting, severe, satirical, keen
Point, n. a sharp end, indivisible part of time or space, nicety, critical moment, stop in writing
Point, v. to sharpen, level, direct, note, divide
Point'ed, pa. a. divided by points, sharp, keen
Point'edly, ad. in a pointed manner, directly
Point'edness, n. sharpness, smartness, keenness
Point'el, n. a thing on a point, pencil, pen
Point'er, n. a thing that points, index, dog
Point'ingstock, n. an object of ridicule or mirth
Point'less, a. having no point, blunt, dull
Pois'on, n. venom, what destroys or injures life
Pois'on, v. t. to infect with poison, to corrupt
Pois'oner, n. one who poisons, one who corrupts
Pois'onous, a. venomous, destructive, deadly
Pois'onously, ad. with a poisonous quality, badly
Poit'rel, n. a breastplate, a kind of graving tool
Poize or Poise, v. t. to weigh, balance, level
Poize, n. a weight, balance, regulating power
Poke, n. a small bag, pocket, gown, a plant
Poke, v. t. to feel in the dark, search out, stir up
Póker, n. a kind of iron bar to stir a fire with
Póking, pa. feeling; n. the act of feeling out
Pólacre, n. a ship with three masts without tops or cross trees
Pólar, Pólary, a. near to or issuing from the pole
Polar'ity, n. a tendency to point to the pole
Pole, n. a staff, perch, five yards and a half, extremity of the earth, point, native of Poland
Pole, v. t. to furnish, fasten or stick with poles
Póleax, n. an ax that is fixed upon a long pole
Pólecat, n. a quadruped of the wesel kind
Póleclipt, a. clipt upon the head, cut short
Póledavy, n. a sort of canvas or very coarse cloth
Pólemarch, [ch as k] n. a magistrate in Athens who had the care of strangers
Polem'ic, n. a disputant, wrangler, great talker
Polem'ic, Polem'ical, a. controversial, disputative
Pólestar, n. a star near the pole, guide, director
Police, [i as ee] n. the government of a city or place
Pol'iced, a. regulated, governed, ruled (ning
Pol'icy, n. the art of government, prudence, cun-
Pólish, a. pertaining to Poland in Europe
Pol'ish, v. t. to make smooth and glossy, to refine
Pol'ish, n. an artificial gloss, elegance, turn
Pol'isher, n. one who gives a gloss or refines
Pol'ishing, n. the act of giving a polish
Políte, a. desirous to please, of genteel manners, well bred, [in the sense of glossy, smooth, ob.]
Politely, ad. genteelly, elegantly, civilly, neatly
Politeness, n. gentility, good breeding, elegance, civilities proceeding from a desire to please
Pol'itic, a. shrewd, cunning, wise, political
Polit'ical, a. relating to a state as a corporate body,

and to public affairs
Polit'ically, Pol'iticly, ad. with policy, cunningly
Politi'cian, n. one who is versed in politics
Pol'itics, n. the science or art of government
Pol'iture, n. the act or art of polishing, a polish
Pol'ity, n. civil constitution, civil government
Poll, n. the head, a register of heads or of voices
Poll, v. to lop the tops of trees, cut off or shorten, hair, shear, take a list of voters, vote, strip
Pol'lack, n. a fish of two species
Pol'lard, n. a tree lopped, fine bran, fish
Pollá ver, n. fawning behavior, gross flattery
Pol'len, n. the farin or fecundating dust of the sta-
Pollenif'erous, a. producing pollen (mens of plants
Pol'lenger, n. brushwood, a pollard, a cut tree
Póller, n. one who votes, a robber, a plunderer
Pollúte, v. t. to defile, taint, corrupt, pervert
Pollúter, n. a defiler, corrupter, perverter
Pollútion, n. the act of defiling, defilement, guilt
Polonáise or Polonése, n. a sort of dress, a gown
Poltroon', n. a coward, scoundrel, bird
Poltroon'ery, n. cowardliness, meanness, baseness
Pol'verin, n. the ashes of a plant from the Levant used in making white glass
Polyacous'tic, n. an instrument to multiply sounds
Polyan'dria, n. a class of plants with many stamens
Polyanth'us, n. the name of a beautiful flower
Polycotylédon, n. a seed with many lobes
Polycotyléd'onous, a. having many lobes
Polydel'phia, n. a class of plants with stamens united in three or more filaments
Polygam'ia, n. a class of plants with hermaphrodite flowers, and also with male or female or both
Polygam'ian, a. belonging to the class polygamia
Polyg'amist, n. he who has more than one wife
Polyg'amy, n. a plurality of wives at one time
Polygénous, a. of differerent kinds or forts
Pol'yglot, a. written in several languages; n. a bird
Pol'yglot, n. a book containing many languages
Pol'ygon, n. a figure having many angles or sides
Polyg'onal, a. containing many angles or sides
Pol'ygram, n. a figure made up of several lines
Polyg'raphy, n. the art of writing in cyphers or multiplying copies
Polygraph'ic, a. pertaining to polypraphy
Polygyn'ia, n. an order of plants with many pistils
Polyhédron, n. a solid with many sides
Polyhédral, Polyhédrous, a. having many sides
Polynómial, a. containing many names or terms
Polyop'trum, n. a glass through which objects appear multiplied
Polypet'alous, a. having many petals
Polyph onism, n. a multiplicity of sounds
Polyph'yllous, a. having many leaves
Pol'ypus, n. a sea animal, a disease in the nose
Pol'yscope, n. a glass which makes a single object appear as many
Polysperm'ous, a. having many seeds

Pol'yfyllable, n. a word that has may fyllables
Polyfyllab'ic, a. pertaining to a word of many
fyllables (many arts
Polytech'nic, [ch as k] a. noting or embracing
Pol'ytheifm, n. a belief in a plurality of gods
Pol'ytheift, n. one who holds a plurality of gods
Pomáceous, a. confifting of or having apples
Pomáde, n. a fragrant ointment made of apples
Pomand'er, n. a little ball of feveral perfumes
Pomátum, n. an ointment made from hog's lard
Pome'granate, n. the name of a tree or its fruit
Pomif'erous, a. bearing or producing apples
Pom'mel, n. a round knob on a fword or faddle
Pom'mel, v. t. to bruife, beat, bang, thump
Pomp, n. fplendor, oftentation, parade, pride
Pom'pholyx, n. white ca'x or flowers of zink
Pompos'ity, Pomp'oufnefs, n. affected greatnefs
Pomp'ous, a. fplendid, grand, affected, proud
Pomp'oufly, ad. fplendidly, magnificently, finely
Pom'water, n. the name of a large apple
Pond, n. a ftanding water, pool, fmall lake
Pond'er, v. t. to confider, think, mufe, weigh
Pond'erable, a. capable of being weighed
Pond'eral, a. eftimated by weight, weighed out
Pon'derance, n. weight, ponderoufnefs
Ponderátion, n. the act of weighing or valuing
Ponderos'ity, Pond'eroufnefs, n. weight, heavinefs
Pond'erous, a. weighty, heavy, forcible, ftrong
Pónent, a. weftern, tending to the weft, fetting, ob.
Pong'o, n. a name of the ouran-outang
Pon'iard, n. a dagger; v. t. to ftab with a dagger
Pont'age, n. a toll of tax for repairing bridges
Pon'tic, a. noting the Euxine or Black fea
Pont'iff, n. a chief-prieft, a high prieft, the pope
Pontif'ical, a. belonging to a pontiff or bridge
Pont'fical, n. a book of epifcopal rites or forms
Pontíficate, n. the papal dignity, popedom
Pont'ifice, n. the ftructure of a bridge, a bridge
Pon'tine or Pomp'tine, a. noting a large marfh be-
tween Rome and Naples
Pontoon', n. a boat lined with tin to form a tempo-
rary bridge, a low flat veffel ufed in careening
fhips
Pôny, n. a fmall or little horfe, an eafy nag
Pood, n. a Ruffian weight of 40 pounds, equal to
36 pounds Englifh
Pool, n. a ftanding water, pond, term ufed at cards
Poop, n. the ftern or hindmoft part of a fhip
Poor, a. lean, indigent, mean, paltry, unhappy
Poor, n. a fmall fifh confidered as a nufance
Poor'ly, a. rather indifpofed, indifcrent, ill
Poor'ly, ad. without fpirit, meanly, indifferently
Poor'nefs, n. poverty, want, meannefs, barrennefs
Poor'fpirited, a. meanfpirited, mean, cowardly
Poor'fpiritednefs, n. meannefs, cowardlinefs
Pop, n. a fmall fmart found from a gun, &c.
Pop, v. to come or go quickly or flily, to fhift
Pope, n. the bifhop of Rome, the name of a fifh
Pópedom, n. the jurifdiction or dignity of a pope

Pópery, Pápifm, Pápiftry, n. the popifh religion
Pop'gun, n. a child's wooden gun
Popinátion, n. the act of frequenting taverns, ob.
Pop'injay, n. a parrot, woodpecker, fimple fop
Pópifh, a. Romifh, taught by the pope, fuited to
Pópifhly, ad. in a popifh manner (popery
Pop'lar, n. the name of a tree; a. made of poplar
Pop'ple, n. a plant, cockle
Pop'py, n. the name of a plant or its flower
Pop'ulace, n. the common people, the multitude
Pop'ular, a. pleafing to the people, general
Popular'ity, n. the favor or love of the people
Pop'ularly, ad. in a popular or vulgar manner
Pop'ulate, v. i. to breed or increafe in people
Populátion, n. the number of inhabitants
Pop'ulous, a. full of people, very well inhabited
Pop'uloufly, ad. in a populous manner or ftate
Pop'uloufnefs, n. an abounding with inhabitants
Por'celain or Por'celan, china ware, an herb
Por'cellanite, n. a fpecies of jafper, a filiceous ftone
Porch, n. an entrance with a roof, a portico
Por'cine, a. pertaining to fwine (quills
Por'cupine, n. a genus of quadrupeds covered with
Por'cupinefifh, n. a fifh covered with fpines
Pore, n. a paffage; v. i. to look very near or in-
Por'gy, n. a fifh of the gilthead kind (tenfely
Pórinefs, a. a pory ftate, a fulnefs of pores
Pórifm, n. a general theorem, a general rule
Pork, n. a kind of animal food, fwine's flefh
Pórkeater, n. one who is fond of eating pork
Pórker, Pórket, Pórkling, n. a young hog, a pig
Poros'ity, Póroufnefs, n. a pory ftate
Pórous, Póry, a. abounding with or like pores
Por'pefs, n. a fea hog, a fifh of the delphine genus
Porphyrit'ic, Porphyráceous, a. pertaining to or
like porphyry
Por'phyry, n. a ftone of various kinds containing
grains or dots of felfpar
Porráceous, a. like or having leeks, greenifh
Por'ret, n. a fcallion, leek, fmall green onion
Por'ridge, Pot'tage, n. a kind of broth or milk
Por'ringer, Pot'tager, n. a veffel for fpoonmeat
Port, n. a harbor, gate, wine, carriage, the larboard
fide of a fhip, opening for guns
Port, v. t. to carry in form, to turn to the left
Pórtable, a. that may be carried, fupportable
Pórtablenefs, n. the ftate of being portable
Pórtage, n. the price of carriage, a porthole, a
carrying place round a fall (of the great door
Port'ail, n. the face of a church viewed on the fide
Pórtal, n. a gate, leffer gate, arch of a gate
Pórtance, n. port, carriage, behavior
Pórtafs, n. a kind of prayerbook, a breviary, ob.
Pórtative, a. that may be carried
Portcull'is, v. t. to bar, to fhut up; n. a drawbridge
Porte, n. a port, the court of the Turkifh emperor
Portend', v. t. to betoken, denote, forefhow
Porten'fion, n. the act of forefhowing, an omen
Por'tent, n. an omen or token of ill, fign, prodigy

Portent'ous, _a._ foreboding, ominous, monftrous

Pórter, _n._ one who has the charge of a gate, a carrier of burdens, a kind of ftrong beer

Pórterage, _n._ money paid for or to a porter

Portfólio, _n._ a portable cafe for papers

Pórthole, _n._ a hole in the fide of a fhip for cannon

Por'tico, _n._ a piazza, a kind of covered walk (dow

Pórtion, _n._ a part, a fortune; _v. t._ to divide, to en-

Pórtlid, _n._ the door which fhuts a port

Pórtlinefs, _n._ noble mien, grandeur of demeanor

Pórtly, _a._ grand of mien, ftately, bulky, fwelling

Portmant'eau, _n._ a bag to carry cloaths in

Pórtrait, uórtraiture, _n._ a picture from real life

Portráy, _v. t._ to paint, draw, adorn with pictures

Pórtrefs, _n._ the female guardian of a gate

Pórtreve, _n._ the fteward of a feaport, a governor

Por'tuguefe, _n. fing._ and _pl._ a native or the language of Portugal

Por'tuguefe, _a._ belonging to Portugal

Póry, _a._ containing or full of pores

Pofe, _v. t._ to puzzle, perplex, oppofe, fuppofe

Pófer, _n._ a puzzler, one who afks hard queftions

Pos'ited, _a._ placed, put, fet, laid, ranged, fituated

Pofi"tion, _n._ a fituation, principle laid down, rule

Pofi"tional, _a._ refpecting pofition or fituation

Pos'itive, _a._ abfolute, real, certain, obftinate

Pos'itively, _ad._ abfolutely, really, certainly; truly

Pos'itivenefs, Pofitiv'ity, _n._ obftinacy, confidence, certainty

Pos'net, _n._ a little bafon, porringer, fkillet, _ob._

Pos'polite, _n._ militia in Poland confifting of the gentry

Pof'e,e, _n._ an armed power, large body, fet, rabble

Poffefs', _v. t._ to get or give poffeffion, have, enjoy

Poffes"fion, _n._ the having in one's own power

Poffes"fioner, _n._ one who has property in a thing

Poffefs'ive, Poffefs'ory, _a._ having poffeffion

Poffefs'or, _n._ an owner, mafter, proprietor, keeper

Pofs'et, _n._ milk curdled with beer, or wine

Pofs'et, _v. t._ to curdle, break, turn, change, alter

Poffibil'ity, _n._ a poffible ftate or thing

Pofs'ible, _a._ having the power to be or do, likely

Pofs'ibly, _ad._ by any power, perhaps, probably

Poft, _n._ a meffenger, office, place, piece of timber, a fpecies of paper, letter paper

Poft, _v._ to haften, ftation, put, expofe, delay, carry accounts to a ledger

Póftage, _n._ money paid for letters fent by the poft

Póftboy, _n._ a boy who carries letters, a driver of a Poftcháife, [ch as fh] _n._ a light body-carriage (chaife

Poftdáte, _v. t._ to date later than the juft time

Poftdilúvian, _a._ living or being after the flood

Poftdilúvian, _n._ a perfon that lived after the flood

Pófter, _n._ a perfon who travels haftily, a courier

Poftérior, _a._ following, placed after, later

Pofterior'ity, _n._ the ftate of being pofterior

Poftériors, _n. pl._ the hinder parts, the breech

Pofter'ity, _n._ fucceeding generations, offspring

Pos'tern, _n._ a fmall back gate, a little door (life

Poftexift'ence, _n._ future or later exiftence, future

Póftfix, _n._ a fuffix, fomething added at the end

Poftfix', _v. t._ to add or annex at the end

Pófthackney, _n._ a hired pofthorfe, a jade

Pófthafte, _n._ full fpeed; _ad._ very faft or quick

Pófthorfe, _n._ a horfe kept to ride poft with

Pófthoufe, _n._ a houfe kept to take in letters

Pos'thumous, _a._ publifhed after a perfon's death

Pos'tic, _a._ backward, added or done afterwards, _ob._

Pos'til, _n._ a glofs, comment, marginal note, _ob._

Pos'til, _v. t._ to illuftrate with notes, _ob._

Pos'tiller, _n._ one who gloffes, one who illuftrates, _ob._

Poftil'lion, _n._ one who rides the firft coach horfe

Poft'lim'inous, _a._ done or contrived fubfequently

Póftman, _n._ a man who delivers out poft-letters

Póftmafter, _n._ one who fuperintends a poft-office

Póftmafter-gen'eral, _n._ the head poftmafter of all

Poftmerid'ian, _a._ being or done in the afternoon

Póft-office, _n._ a place where letters are delivered for conveyance, or received from a diftance

Poftpóne, _v. t._ to put off, defer, delay, lay afide

Poftpónement, _n._ a putting off, delay to another

Póftfcript, _n._ a writing added to a letter (time

Pófttown, _n._ a town where a poft-office is kept

Pos'tulate, _n._ fomething affumed; _v. t._ to affume

Pos'tulant, _n._ a candidate, one who c aims

Poftulátion, _n._ an affumption, a demand

Pos'tulatory, _a._ affumed or taken without proof

Poftulátum, _n._ a principle taken without proof

Pos'ture, _n._ an attitude, fituation, ftate, place

Pos'ture, _v. t._ to put in a particular fituation

Pos'turemafter, _n._ one who diftorts his limbs

Pófy, or Pófey, _n._ a motto on a ring, a nofegay

Pot, _n._ a veffel for boiling or holding liquids, a fmall kind of paper

Pot, _v. t._ to preferve in pots, feafon meats, drink

Pótable, Pot'ulent, _a._ fit to drink, drinkable

Pótablenefs, _n._ the quality of being drinkable

Potag'ro, _n._ a kind of Weft-India pickle (of plants

Pot'afh, _n._ a fixed alkali obtained from the afhes

Potátion, _n._ a drinking-bout, draft, good dofe

Potátoe, _n._ a well known efculent root

Pot'bellied, _a._ having a big or prominent belly

Pot'belly, _n._ a large or prominent belly

Potch, _v. t._ to poach, boil, drefs, thruft, pufh

Pot'companion, _n._ a fellow-drinker, a crony

Pótelot, _n._ an ore, fulphuret of molybden

Pótency, _n._ power, might, ftrength, efficacy, ability

Pótent, _a._ powerful, ftrong, forcible, efficacious

Pot'entate, _n._ a fovereign, prince, monarch, king

Poten'tial, _a._ denoting poffibility, powerful, able

Potential'ity, Poten'tialnefs, _n._ poffibility, power

Poten'tially, _ad._ in power, in effect, in reality

Pótently, _ad._ powerfully, ftrongly, efficacioufly

Pótentnefs, _n._ power, might, great ftrength

Poth'er, _v. i._ to make a ftir; _n._ a buftle, a ftir

Pot'herb, _n._ an herb fit to be boiled for food

Pot'hook, _n._ a hook to hang a pot on, bad writing

Pótion, _n._ a draft, efpecially in phyfic, a dofe

Pot'lid, n. the lid of a pot, the cover of a pot
Bot'sherd, n. a piece of some broken earthen pot
Pot'stone, n. a species of magnesian stone
Pot'tage, n. usually called porridge, which see
Pot'ter, n. a man who makes earthen vessels
Pot'tery, n. the works or business of a potter
Pot'ting, n. the act of drinking, toping, drunken-
Pot'tle, n. a measure of four pints   (ness
Pot'valiant, a. made courageous only by liquor
Pouch, n. a small bag, purse, pocket, the paunch
Pouch, v. to pocket, swallow, pout, frown
Pouch'mouthed, a. having thick pouting lips
Poult, n. the name of a young chicken, a chick
Poult'rer, n. one who sells fowls ready picked
Poult'ice, n. a soft application; v. t. to apply a
Poult'ry, n. all sorts of fowls, a place   (poultice
Pounce, n. the claw of a bird, a powdered gum
Pounce, v. t. to sprinkle with pounce, arm with
   claws, pierce, seize
Pounce'box, n. a box with holes used for pounce
Pound, n. a weight of 16 ounces avordupois, and
   14 of troy, sum of money, pinfold, place
Pound, v. t. to beat with a pestle, beat, shut up
Pound'age, n. a sum deducted from a pound, a fee
Pound'er, n. a pestle, cannon, large pear
Pour, v. to empty, fall heavily, run, rush out
Pout, n. a four look, fort of fish, young bird
Pout, v. i. to look sullen, make a lip, frown, hang
Pov'erty, n. want, necessity, meanness, a defect
Pow'der, n. fine dust, dust of starch, gunpowder
Pow'der, v. to sprinkle with powder, reduce to
   dust, salt, or sprinkle with salt
Pow'derbox, n. a box to keep hair-powder in
Pow'dercheit, n. a chest for gunpowder in a ship
Pow'derhorn, n. a horn for holding gunpowder
Pow'deringtub, n. a tub or vessel for salted meat
Pow'dermill, n. a mill to make gunpowder in
Pow'derroom, n. a room where powder is kept
Pow'dery, a. dusty, white, easily crumbled, soft
Pow'er, n. command, government, influence,
   reach, strength, ability, a host, a potentate
Pow'erful, a. mighty, strong, potent, efficacious
Pow'erfully, ad. mightily, strongly, efficaciously
Pow'erfulness, n. great power, strength, efficacy
Pow'erless, a. weak, helpless, defenseless
Pow'ow, n. a dance or a priest among the Indians
Pox, n. the veneral disease, pustules
Prac'ticable, a. performable, possible, assailable
Practicabil'ity, Prac'ticableness, n. the possibility
   of being performed by human means
Prac'ticably, ad. in a manner to be performed
Prac'tical, Prac'tic, a. relating to performance
Prac'tically, ad. by or in practice, in fact
Prac'tice, n. habitual use, custom, exercise, a rule
Prac'tice, v. t. to do, perform, use, exercise, try
Prac'ticer, n. one who practices
Prac'tisant, n. an agent, ob.
Practi'tioner, n. one engaged in any art or business
Pragmat'ical, a. meddling, very busy, impertinent

Pragmat'ically, ad. busily, impertinently,
Pragmat'icalness, n. a disposition to meddle
Prairy, n. natural meadow, or a plain naturally
   destitute of trees
Praise, n. commendation, renown, honor, glory
Praise, v. t. to commend, applaud, extol, glorify
Praiseful, a. commendable, laudable, worthy, good
Praiser, n. one who praises, one who commends
Praiseworthy, a. deserving praise, commendable
Prame, n. a kind of boat, a flat-bottomed boat
Prance, v. i. to spring and move in high mettle
Pran'cer, n. a horse that prances or capers about
Prank, n. a frolic, a wicked deed; v. t. to adorn
Prank'ed, Prankt, pa. dressed, clad, decorated
Prase, n. a species of blueish chrysolite
Prate, v. i. to talk idly; n. talk, talkativeness
Prater, n. an idle or great talker, a chatterer
Prat'ic, n. a release from quarantine, permission
   to trade
Prating, n. the act of talking much, idle talk
Pratingly, ad. in a prating or talkative manner
Prat'tle, v. i. to chatter like an infant; n. childish
Prat'tler, n. one who prattles, a chatterer   (talk
Prav'ity, n. depravity, corruption, wickedness
Prawn, n. a kind of fine shellfish, a large shrimp
Pray, v. to offer up prayers, entreat, beseech
Prayer, n. a petition, request, entreaty
Prayerbook, n. a book with forms of prayer in it
Prayerless, a. not praying, not using prayers
Pre, in composition denotes before
Preach, v. to deliver a public discourse, to prate
Preach, n. a sermon, religious discourse, discourse
Preacher, n. a person who preaches, a minister
Preachment, n. a sermon in contempt, talk, prate
Preamble, n. an introduction   (amination
Preapprehen'sion, n. an opinion formed before ex-
Preb'end, n. a stipend in cathedral churches
Preb'endary, n. a stipendiary of a cathedral
Precarious, a. uncertain, doubtful, dependent
Precariously, ad. by dependence, uncertainly
Precariousness, n. a precarious state, uncertainty
Precative, a. praying, expressing intreaty
Precau'tion, n. a preventive measure, a warning
Precau'tion, v. t. to warn beforehand
Preeau'tionary, a. consisting in previous caution
Precedaneous, a. previous, antecedent, going before
Precede, v. t. to go before in rank or time
Precedence, n. the foremost place, priority, lead
Precedent, a. going before, foregoing, former
Pre''cedent, n. an example, rule, foregoing act
Precedently, ad. beforehand, in time anterior
Precentor, n. one who leads a choir, a chanter
Precept, n. a command, instruction, rule, law
Precep'tial, a. consisting of or having precepts, ob.
Precept'ive, a. giving or containing precepts
Precept'or, n. a teacher, instructor, tutor, master
Preces'sion, n. a going before, an advancement
Precinct, n. a boundary, outward limit, division
Pre''cious, a. valuable, costly, dear, nice, fine

Pre"cioufly, ad. in a precious manner, dearly
Pre"cioufnefs, n. valuableaefs, worth, great value
Pre"cipe, n. a kind of writ, command, direction
Pre"cipice, n. a headlong or perpendicular fall
Precip'ient, a. directing, commanding
Precip'itance, n. rath hafte, hurry, violent fury
Precip'itant, a. rath, hafty, hurried, unadvifed
Precip'itant, n. any fubftance which caufes another fubftance in folution to fall to-the bottom in a concrete ftate
Precip'itable, a. that may be thrown to the bottom
Precipitabil'ity, n. the quality of being capable of being thrown to the bottom
Precip'itate, n. red oxyd of mercury
Precip'itate, v. t. to throw down headlong, hurry, haften, to feparate one fubftance from others in folution, and throw it to the bottom
Precip'itate, a. hafty, violent, headftrong
Precip'itately, ad. in a blind hurry, rafhly
Precipitatioa, n. blind or rafh hafte, hurry, a fall
Precip'itous, a. hafty, tending to danger, fteep
Precife, a. exact, ftrict, nice, ftiff, formal, finical
Precifely, ad. exactly, accurately, nicely, formally
Precifenefs, n. exactnefs, rigid nicety, formality
Preci'tion, n. exact limitation, exactnefs, care
Precifive, a. exactly or nicely limiting, exact
Preclude, v. t. to prevent from entering, ftop, prevent (tion, hinderance
Preclufion, n. a prevention from entering, preven-
Preclufive, a. preventing beforehand, hindering
Precocious, a. ripe early or before the time, ob.
Preco"city, n. a very or too early ripenefs, ob.
Precogitation, n. previous thought or confideration
Precog'nita, n. pl. things previoufly known
Precogni"tion, n. a foreknowledge, an inquiry
Preconceit, n. an opinion formed beforehand
Preconceive, v. t. to form an opinion beforehand
Preconcep'tion, n. a previous thought or opinion
Preconcert', v. t. to concert or fettle beforehand
Preconfign, v. t. to confign beforehand
Precon'tract, n. a prior contract or bargain
Precontract', v. t. to contract or bind beforehand
Precurfe', n. a forerunning, a going before, ob.
Precurs'or, n. a forerunner, harbinger, courier
Predaceous, a. living by prey or plunder, favage
Predal, a. robbing, plundering, preying
Predation, n. the act of robbing or plundering
Pred'atory, a. plundering, preying, rapacious
Predeceafed, a. deceafed before a certain time
Predecefs'or, n. one going before, an anceftor
Predeftinarian, Predeftinator, n. one who holds the doctrin of predeftination (ibly
Predes'tinate, Predes'tine, v. t. to decree irresift-
Predeftination, n. preordination, a fatal decree
Predetermination, n. a previous determination
Predeterm'in, v. t. to doom by previous decrees
P. edial, a. belonging to or growing from farms
Pred'icable, n. a logical term ufed in affirmation
Pred'icable, a. that may be affirmed or declared

Predicabil'ity, n. the capacity of being attributed
Predic'ament, n. a clafs, arrangement, kind, ftate
Predicament'al, a. relating to predicaments
Pred'icant, n. one who affirms, one who declares
Pred'icant, a. affirming, declaring, preaching
Pred'icate, n. what is affirmed of any fubject
Pred'icate, v. t. to affirm, declare, teach
Predication, n. an affirmation, a declaration
Predict', v. t. to foretel, prophefy, forefhow
Predic'tion, n. a foretelling, prophefy, token
Predict'ive, a. foretelling, having power to predict
Predict' or, n. one who foretels or prophefies
Prediges'tion, n. a digeftion performed too foon
Predilec'tion, n. prepoffeffion in favor of any thing
Predifpofe, v. t. to incline or adopt beforehand
redifpofi"tion, n. a previous or prior adaption
Predom'inance, n. prevalence, afcendency
Pecdom'inant, a. prevalent, afcendant, overruling
Predom'inate, v. i. to prevail, govern, rule
Preelect', v. t. to elect or choofe beforehand
Preem'inence, n. fuperiority, precedence, power
Preem'inent, a. excellent above others, principal
Preem'inently, ad. in a preeminent degree
Preemp'tion, n. a right of buying before another
Preen, v. t. to drefs or trim as birds their fethers
Preengage, v. t. to engage firft or beforehand
Preengagement, n. a previous or prior obligation
Preeftablifh, v. t. to fettle or fix beforehand
Preeftablifhment, n. a previous fettlement
Preexift', v. i. to exift beforehand or in another
Preexiftence, n. previous exiftence (ftate
Preexift'ent, a. exifting or being before
Preface, n. a kind of introduction to a book
Preface, v. t. to introduce a treatife, to cover
Prefacer, n. the writer or fpeaker of a preface
Prefatory, a. done by way of preface, introductory
Prefect, n. a governor, mayor, commander
Prefecture, n. the office or jurifdiction of a prefect
Prefer', v. t. to regard more, exalt, promote, offer
Pref'erable, a. eligible before another, better
Pref'erably, ad. in or with preference (another
Pref'erence, Pref'erablenefs, n. eftimation above
Prefer'ment, n. advancement, a place of honor
Prefiguration, n. a foregoing reprefentation
Prefig'ure, v. t. to reprefent or fhow beforehand
Prefine, v. t. to limit or folve beforehand, ob.
Prefix', v. t. to place before, fix, fettle, appoint
Prefix, n. a particle placed before a word
Preform', v. t. to form or fafhion beforehand
Preg'nancy, n. a being with young, fruitfulnefs
Preg'nant, a. breeding young, fertile, full, clear
Preg'nantly, ad. fruitfully, fully, clearly, plainly
Preguftation, n. the act of tafting firft or before
Prehenfile, a. grafping, adapted to clafp
Prehnite, n. a filiceous ftone of an apple green
Prejudge', v. t. to judge or condemn beforehand
Prejudgement, n. a prior determination, precedent
Prejudicate, a. formed by prejudice, prepoffeffed
Prejudicate, v. t. to determin without evidence

Prejudication, *n.* the act of judging beforehand
Pre"judice, *n.* prepoffeffion, damage, injury, hurt
Pre"judice, *v. t.* to fill with prejudice, to injure
Prejudi"cial, *a.* injurious, hurtful, contrary
Prélacy, *n.* the dignity of a prelate, epifcopacy
Prélate, *n.* a bifhop, high ecclefiattic, dignitary
Prelat'ical, *a.* relating to a prelate or bifhop
Prelátion, *n.* the act of fetting before, preference
Prelect', *v. i.* to difcourfe, explain, comment
Prelec'tion, *n.* a reading, lecture, leffon, fermon
Prelibátion, *n.* a pouring out before, a foretafte
Prelim'inary, *a.* previous, introductory
Prelim inary, *n.* a firft ftep, article, condition
Prelúde, *v. i.* to ferve by way of introduction
Prélude, Prelfidium, *n.* an introduction
Prelúdious, Prelúfive, *a.* previous, introductory
Prematúre, *a.* ripe too foon, too early, too hafty
Prematúrely, *ad.* too early, too foon, too haftily
Prematúrenefs, Prematúrity, *n.* a premature ftate
Premed'itate, *v. t.* to think beforehand, contrive
Premeditátion, *n.* a meditating beforehand
Premer'it, *v. t.* to merit or deferve beforehand
Prem'ices, *n. pl.* firft fruits of the earth
Prémier, *a.* firft, chief, leading, principal, capital
Prémier, *n.* a chief perfon, head, prime minifter
Premífe, *v. t.* to lay down premifes, to preface
Prem'ifes, *n. pl.* antecedent matter, houfes, &c.
Prem'ifs, *n.* an antecedent propofition or term
Prémium, *n.* an advance to a bargain, a bounty
Premon'ifh, *v. t.* to warn or advife beforehand
Premon'ifhment, Premoni"tion, *n.* previous notice
Premons'trate, *v. a.* previoufly advifing or giving notice
Premons'trate, *v. t.* to fhow or tell beforehand
Premorfe', *a.* ending abruptly, as certain roots
Premunire, *n.* a kind of writ, penalty, difficulty
Prenom'inate, *v. t.* to forename, to name firft
Prenominátion, *n.* the name firft or beforehand
Prenótion, *n.* a previous idea or knowledge
Prent'ice, *n.* one bound to a mafter for inftruction
Prent'icefhip, *n.* the fervitude of a prentice
Prenunciátion, *n.* a declaration beforehand
Preoc'cupancy, *n.* a firft or previous poffeffion
Preoc'cupate, *v. t.* to anticipate, prepoffefs
Preoccupátion, *n.* a prepoffeffion, prejudice, bias
Preoc'cupy, *v. t.* to get or have firft poffeffion
Preom'inate, *v. t.* to prognofticate, *ob.*
Preopin'ion, *n.* a prepoffeffion, prejudice, notion
Preordáin, *v. t.* to ordain or appoint beforehand
Preor'dinance, *n.* an antecedent determination
Preordinátion, *n.* a decreeing beforehand
Preparátion, *n.* a making ready for fome purpofe
Prepar'ative, *n.* fomething ufed to pave the way
Prepar'ative, *a.* able or tending to prepare (oufly
Prepar'atively, *ad.* by way of preparation, previ-
Prepáre, *v. t.* to make fit, qualify, form, provide
Prepáre, *n.* a preparation, a previous meafure, *ob.*
Prepáredly, *ad.* with due preparation, previoufly
Prepárednefs, *n.* a ftate of being prepared
Prepárer, *n.* one who or that which prepares

Prepenfe', *a.* preconceived, contrived beforehand
Prepond'er, Prepond'erate, *v. t.* to outweigh,
  overbalance, overpower, exceed, pafs, prevail
Prepond'erance, Preponderátion, *n.* greater weight
Prepond'erant, *a.* overbalancing, exceeding
Prepofi"tion, *n.* a particle governing fome cafe
Prepoffefs', *v. t.* to prejudice, bias, influence
Prepoffes'fion, *n.* a firft poffeffion, prejudice, bias
Prepos'terous, *a.* abfurd, perverted, wrong
Prepos'teroufly, *ad.* abfurdly, foolifhly, ftrangely
Prepos'teroufnefs, *n.* a prepofterous quality
Prépotency, *n.* greater power or force, fuperiority
Prépuce, *n.* what covers the glans, the forefkin
Prerequire, *v. t.* to demand or afk previoufly
Prere"quifit, *n.* fomething previoufly neceffary
Prere"quifit, *a.* that is previoufly neceffary
Prerog'ative, *n.* a peculiar privilege, a juft right
Prerog'atived, *a.* having fome peculiar privilege
Préfage, Preságement, *n.* a prognoftic, an omen
Preságe, *v. t.* to forebode, foretoken, foretel
Preságeful, *a.* foreboding, cautious, provident
Pres'byter, *n.* an elder, prieft, bifhop, prefbyteriarn
Prefbyterial, *a.* relating to a prefbyter or prieft
Prefbytérian, *n.* a follower or admirer of Calvin
Prefbytérian, *a.* fuitable to Calvin's doctrins
Pres'bytery, *n.* a body of paftors and lay elders
Prefci'ence, *n.* a knowledge of future events
Prefci'ent, *a.* foreknowing, prophetical
Préfcious, *a.* foreknowing
Prefcind', *v. t.* to cut off or before, abftract, divide
Prefcind'ent, *a.* cutting off or from, abftracting
Prefcribe, *v.* to order, direct medically, fet, fix,
  claim by prefcription or immemorial ufe
Préfcript, *a.* ordered, directed, fet; *n.* a direction
Prefcrip'tion, *n.* a medical receipt, cuftom, right
  by long continued poffeffion, limitation, rule
Prefcrip'tive, *a.* confifting in long ufage or enjoy-
  ment, immemorial
Pres'eance, *n.* precedence in place, priority, *ob.*
Pres'ence, *n.* a being prefent, fight, look, readinefs
Pres'ence-chámber, *n.* a room to receive company
Pres'ent, *a.* near at hand, now being, ready
Pres'ent, *n.* a free gift, a royal mandate or letter
Prefent', *v.* to give, prefer, exhibit, offer (ed
Prefent'able, Prefent'ative, *a.* that may be prefent-
Prefentáneous, *a.* ready, quick, immediate
Prefentátion, *n.* the gift of a benefice, an exhibition
Prefentée, *n.* one prefented to a benefice
Prefent'er, *n.* one that prefents, one that offers
Prefen'tial, *a.* fuppofing actual or real prefence
Prefential'ity, *n.* the ftate of being prefent
Prefen'tiate, *v. t.* to make or render prefent
Prefen'timent, *n.* a previous idea, apprehenfion,
  or impreffion on the mind
Pres'ently, *ad.* fhortly, foon after (ation
Prefent'ment, *n.* the act of prefenting, a reprefent-
Pres'entnefs, *n.* prefence of mind, readinefs
Prefervátion, *n.* the act or care of preferving
Preferv'ative, *n.* what has the power to preferve

Preferv'ative, a. able or tending to preserve

Preferve, v. t. to keep, fave, defend, keep fruits

Preferve, n. a fruit preferved with fugar

Preferv'er, n. one who preferves, one who guards

Prefi'de, v. i. to fuperintend, direct, manage

Pres'idency, n. fuperintendance, direction, care, the office or term of office of a prefident

Pres'ident, n. one who is at the head of a fociety, the firft magiftrate of the United States

Prefiden'tial, a. pertaining to a prefident

Pres'identfhip, n. the place or office of a prefident

Prefid'ial, n. a court of judicature, a tribunal

Prefid'ial, a. of, or belonging to a garrifon

Prefig'nify, v. t. to fignify beforehand

Prefs, v. t. to fqueeze, crufh, crowd, urge, force

Prefs, n. an inftrument for prefling, a cafe for clothes, crowd, act of forcing men into fervice, inftrument ufed for printing

Prefs'bed, n. a bed that fhuts clofe up in a cafe

Prefs'er, n. one who preffes or works at prefs

Prefs'gang, n. a crew that prefs men into public fer-

Prefs'ing, pa. a. fqueezing, crufhing, urgent (vice

Prefs'ingly, ad. with force, clofely, urgently

Prefs'fion, n. the act of prefling, a great weight

Prefs'itant, a. weighing down, gravitating, ob.

Prefs'man, n. a printer that works at the prefs

Prefs'money, n. money paid to prefs foldiers

Prefs'fure, n. weight, force, impreffion, affliction

Preft, n a loan, a prieft ; pa. preffed, ready, neat

Preft'o, ad. quick, foon, at once, without delay

Prefûmable, a. that may be prefumed or fuppofed

Prefûmably, ad. without examination or proof

Prefûme, v. t. to fuppofe, venture, depend

Prefûmer, n. an arrogant or confident perfon

Prefûming, pa. a. fuppofing, confident, bold

Prefump'tion, Prefump'tuoufnefs, n. arrogance, confidence, boldnefs, probablenefs, fufpicion

Prefump'tive, a. fuppofed, bold, probable, likely

Prefump'tuous, a. arrogant, infolent, irreverent

Prefump'tuoufly, ad. arrogantly, irreverently

Prefump'tuoufnefs, n. rafhnefs, excefs of confidence

Prefuppofal, n. a fuppofal previoufly formed

Prefuppofe, v. t. to fuppofe as previous or true

Prefurmife, n. a furmife previoufly formed

Pretenfe, n. a fhowing what is not real, a claim

Pretend, v. to play the hypocrit, feign, counterfeit, allege falfely, fay, claim, hold before

Pretend'edly, ad. in a pretended manner, falfely

Pretend'er, n. one who pretends or lays claim

Pretend'ingly, ad. arrogantly, prefumptuoufly

Preten'fion, n. a claim, right, pretenfe

Preterimper'fect, a. that is not yet perfectly paft

Preteri''tion, n. a going by, an omiffion, ob.

Preterlaps'ed, a. paft and gone, paft by or over

Preterlegal, a. illegal, contrary to law

Pretermis'fion, n. an omitting or paffing over

Pretermit', v. t. to pafs by or over, omit, neglect

Preternat'ural, a. extraordinary, irregular

Preternat'ually, ad. out of the order of nature

Preterper'fect, Préterit, a. that is abfolutely paft

Preterpluper'fect, a. more than perfectly paft

Prétext, n. a pretenfe, excufe, cloke, fhow

Prétor, n. a Roman judge or chief ruler, a mayor

Prétorfhip, n. the office of a pretor

Iiretorian, a. belonging to a pretor, judicial

Pret'tily, ad. neatly, elegantly, pleafingly, well

Pret'tinefs, n. beauty that is without dignity

Pret'ty, a. neat, beautiful, handfome, comely

Pret'ty, ad. in fome fmall degree, nearly, almoft

Pretyp'efy, v. t. to fhow or point out beforehand

Prevail, v. i. to take place, induce, overcome

Prevailing, p a. having influence, predominant

Prevailment, Prev'alence, n. influence, fuperiority

Prev'alent, a. predominant, powerful, victorious

Prev'alently, ad. powerfully, forcibly, ftrongly

Prevar'icate, v. i. to cavil, fhuffle, quibble, waver

Prevarication, n. the act of fhuffling, cavil, deceit

Prevar'icator, n. a fhuffler, quibbler, caviller

Prevénient, a. going before, preventive, hindering

Prevent', v. t. to hinder, ftop, anticipate

Prevent'able, a. that may or can be prevented

Prevent'er, n. one who prevents or hinders

Preven'tion, n. the act of going before, hinderance, ftop, anticipation, prejudice (dote

Prevent'ive, a. hindering, prefervative ; n. an anti-

Prevent'ively, ad. in a preventive manner

Prévious, a. going before, prior, antecedent, firft

Prévioufly, ad. before, beforehand, antecedently

Prey, [pray] n. fomething to be devoured, plunder

Prey, v. i. to wafte, corrode, hurt, rob, plunder

Priapifm, n. a preternatural tention of the penis

Price, n. a rate, worth, value, eftimation, reward

Prick, v. to pierce, fpur, incite, affect with remorfe, pain, hurt, make acid, mark

Prick, n. a puncture, point, print, mark, fting

Prick'er, n. a fharp inftrument, a light herfeman

Prick'et, n. a buck in his 2d year, a bottle-bafket

Prick'le, n. a very fmall fharp point, thorn, brier

Prick'linefs, n. a prickly ftate or quality

Prick'ly, a. full of or having fharp points, rough

Prick'fong, n. a fong pricked or fet to mufic

Pride, n. felf-efteem, loftinefs of manner, elevation, that in which one glories

Pride, v. i. to be proud of, rate too high, boaft

Prier, n. one who examins very narrowly

Prieft, n. a perfon who officiates at the altar

Prieftcraft, n. a priefly act or trick, pious fraud

Prieftefs, n. a woman that officiated in heathen

Priefthood, n. the office or order of priefts (rites

Prieftlinefs, n. the appearance of a prieft

Prieftly, a. becoming or like a prieft, facerdotal

Prieftridden, a. managed by priefts

Prig, v. to fteal, to haggle ; n. a conceited fellow

Prig'gifh, a. pert, conceited, pragmatical, faucy

Prill, v. i. to gore, n. a turbot, pron. brill

Prim, a. formal, precife, demure, affectedly nice

Prim, v. i. to form or deck to an affected nicety

Primacy, Primatefhip, n. a chief ecclefiaftical fta-

Prímage, n. the freight of a ship, a duty (tion
Prímarily, ad. originally, in the first intention
Prímary, a. original, first, chief, first in station
Primary, n. a quill fether of a bird
Prímate, n. a first or chief bishop, an archbishop
Prime, n. the dawn of day, first or best part, spring,
  height of perfection, first canonical hour
Prime, v. t. to put powder into the pan of a gun
  or cannon, to lay the first colors on in painting
Prime, Primal, a. first, principal, best, excellent
Prímely, ad. originally, first, chiefly, excellently
Prímeness, n. precedence, excellence, dignity
Prim'er, n. a first book for children, an office
Priméro, n. the name of an old game at cards
Primest, a. best, most excellent, choicest, chiefest
Priméval, a. such as was at first, original, prior
Primigénous, a. original, of first formation
Príming, n. first coat of paint, &c. powder laid to
  communicate fire to the charge
Primi''tial, a. relating to the first fruits
Prim'itive, a. ancient, original, native, formal
Prim'itively, ad. originally, primarily, at first
Prim'itiveness, n. antiquity, affected formality
Prim'ness, n. precifeness, demurenefs, affectation
Primogénial, a. first-born, original, conttituent
Primogen'iture, n. first birth, ob.
Primogen'iture, n. the first birth, eldership (ginning
Primor'dial, Primor'diate, a. existing from the be-
Prim'rose, n. the name of a flower and plant
Prince, n. a king's son, fovereign, chief ruler
Prince, v. i. to play the prince, to take state, ob.
Prince'dom, n. the dignity or power of a prince
Prince'like, a. like or becoming a prince, noble
Prince'ling, n. a poor or petty prince, a lordling
Prince'ly, a. royal, grand, august, noble, generous
Prin'cefs, n. a prince's wife, a king's daughter
Prin'cipal, a. chief, capital, eflential, princely
Prin'cipal, n. a head or chief man, a capital fum
Principal'ity, n. a prince's domain, fovereignty
Prin'cipally, ad. chiefly, above all, above the rest
Principiátion, n. a reducing into elemental parts
Prin'ciple, n. a fundamental truth, original caufe,
  motive, ground of action, opinion, tenet, rule
Prin'ciple, v. t. to inftruct, teach, fix in a tenet
Prin'cipling, pa. imprinting upon the mind
Prin'cock, Prin'cox, n. a pert young coxcomb, ob.
Prink, v. t. to drefs for show, to affect stately airs
Print, v. t. to mark by impreffion, to publish
Print, n. a mark made by impreffion, a picture
Print'er, n. one who prints books or stains linen
Print'ing, n. the impreffing of books or cloth, &c.
Print'lefs, a. leaving no mark or impreffion
Prior, a. former, going before, antecedent, first
Prior, n. a religious title amongft monks
Priorefs, n. a kind of governefs amongft nuns
Prior'ity, n. a being first in rank, precedence
Prior'ship, n. the office, quality or state of a prior
Priory, n. a convent that is governed by a prior
Prífage, n. a cuftom upon lawful prizes or wine, ob.

Prifm, n. an oblong folid, under more than four
  planes, whofe bafes are equal and parallel
Prifmat'ic, a. like or formed by a prifm
Prifmat'ically, ad. in the form or shape of a prifm
Prifm'oid, n. a folid body like a prifm
Pris'my, a. like or pertaining to a prifin
Pris'on, n. a jail, place of confinement, fast hold
Pris'on, v. t. to shut up in hold, confine, enchain
Prifonbáfe, n. a boyish play, called alfo prifonbars
Pris'oner, n. one who is under arreft, a captive
Pris'onhoufe, n. a jail to confine prifoners in
Pris'onment, n. imprifonment, confinement, ob.
Prift'ine, a. ancient, original, first, accuftomed
Prith'ee, abbrev. for I pray thee
Prit'tleprattle, n. a common or idle talk, chat
Privacy, Privatenefs, n. fecrecy, privity, retreat
Privádo, n. a private or fecret friend, ob.
Private, a. fecret, clandeftine, retired
Private, n. a fecret place, a fecret meffage
Privatéer, n. a ship of war belonging to private
  citizens, commiffioned to take prizes, &c.
Privately, ad. in private, fecretly, clandeftinely
Privátion, n. a lofs, deftruction, want
Priv'ative, a. caufing privation or lofs, negative
Priv'atively, ad. by abfence or want, negatively
Priv'et, n. the primp, a plant, an evergreen
Priv'ilege, n. a peculiar advantage, a public right
Priv'ilege, v. to grant a privilege, free, exempt
Priv'ily, ad. fecretly, privately, clandeftinely
Priv'ity, n. knowledge, private communication
Priv'y, a. admitted to fecrets, confcious, private
Priv'y, n. a neceffary houfe (an enemy
Prize, n. a reward to merit, fomething taken from
Prize, v. t. to value, efteem, regard, honor, rate
Prizer, n. one who values or efteems a thing
Prizefighter, n. one who fights for a fet reward
Prízepry, v. t. to raife by a lever, to pry
Probabil'ity, n. likelihood, an appearance of truth
Prob'able, a. likely, like to be or to be true
Prob'ably, ad. in all likelihood, perhaps
Próbat or Próbate, n. the proof or copy of a will,
  a court for the trial of wills and diftribution of
  eftates of deceafed perfons
Probátion, n. a proof, trial, evidence, teftimony
Probátionary, a. ferving for trial
Probátioner, n. one who is upon trial, a novice
Probátionership, n. the state of a probationer
Próbative, a. proving, confifting in proof
Próbatory, a. relating to proof or trial
Probátum eft, latin, it is tried and fully proved
Probe, n. a furgeon's inftrument, a flender wire
Probe, v. t. to try with a probe, try, feel, fearch
Prob'ity, n. honefty, fincerity, veracity, goodnefs
Prob'lem, n. a queftion propofed for folution
Problemat'ical, a. uncertain, difputable, difputed
Problemat'ically, ad. in a problematical manner
Probos'cis, n. a fnout, the trunk of an elephant
Procácious, a. faucy, pert, impudent, loofe
Proca''city, n. faucinefs, petulance, impudence

Precatarc'tic, *a.* forerunning, antecedent, prior

Procédure, *n.* a manner of proceeding, progrefs

Procéed, *v. i.* to go on, profecute, take effect

Procéeder, *n.* a perfon who proceeds

Procéeding, *n.* a tranfaction, act, legal procefs

Procéeds, *n. pl.* money or value arifing from a fale

Procep'tion, *n.* the act of taking firft, *ob.*

Procer'ity, *n.* tallnefs, height of ftature, length

Pro"cefs, *n.* a method, progrefs, courfe, order, knob

Proces"fion, *n.* a folemn train, march, ftep, order

Proces"fional, Proces"fionary, *a.* belonging to or confifting in proceffion

Pro"ceffverb'al, *n.* regular form in public acts

Pr6cinct, *n.* a complete preparation for action *ob.*

Procláim, *v. t.* to publifh folemnly, declare, tell

Procláimer, *n.* one who makes proclamation

Proclamátion, *n.* a publication by authority, public declaration, notice

Proclíve, Proclívous, *a.* inclinable, inclined

Proclívity, *n.* a tendency, readinefs, fteepnefs

Procon'ful, *n.* a Roman officer who governed a province with the powers of a conful

Procon'fular, *a.* pertaining to a proconful

Procon'fulfhip, *n.* the office of a proconful

Procraft'inate, *v. t.* to put off, defer, delay, ftop

Procraftinátion, *n.* a delay, ftop, dilatorinefs

Procraftinátor, *n.* a dilatory perfon

Prócreant, *a.* productive, fruitful, pregnant

Prócreate, *v. t.* to generate, beget, get, produce

Procreátion, *n.* a generation, production, caufe

Procreátive, *a.* generative, productive, caufing

Procreátivenefs, *n.* the power of generation

Procreátor, *n.* one who begets, one who produces

Proc'tor, *n.* an attorney in the fpiritual court, an

Proc'tor, *v. t.* to manage (officer in a univerfity

Proc'torfhip, *n.* the office or honor of a proctor

Procum'bent, *a.* lying down or along, prone, flat

Procúrable, *a.* obtainable, acquirable, acceffible

Procurátion, Procúrement, *n.* the act of procuring

Procurátor, *n.* a manager, agent, factor, officer

Procuratórial, *a.* made or done by a procurator

Procurátorfhip, *n.* the office of a procurator

Procúre, *v.* to obtain, get, manage, perfuade

Procúrer, *n.* one who procures, a pimp, a pander

Procúrefs, *n.* a bawd, a lewd feducing woman

Prod'igal, *a.* profufe, wafteful, lavifh, expenfive

Prod'igal, *n.* a fpendthrift, wafter, lavifh perfon

Prodigal'ity, *n.* profufenefs, wafte, extravagance

Prod'igally, *ad.* profufely, lavifhly, idly

Prodi"gious, *a.* amazing, aftonifhing, monftrous

Prodi"gioufly, *ad.* amazingly, enormoufly, very

Prodi"gioufnefs, *n.* a prodigious ftate, largenefs

Prod'igy, *n.* a furprifing thing, wonder, monfter

Prodi"tion, *n.* treafon, trechery, deceitfulnefs

Prod'itor, *n.* a traitor, a trecherous perfon

Proditórious, *a.* trecherous, betraying fecrets

Prodúce, *v. t.* to bring forth, bear, generate, fhow

Prod'uce, *n.* a product, amount, profit, gain, fruit

Brodúcent, *n.* one who exhibits or offers

Prodúcer, *n.* one who produces or generates

Prodúcible, *a.* capable of being produced

Produciblenefs, *n.* the ftate of being preducible

Prod'uct, *n.* a thing produced, work, effect, fruit

Produc'tion, *n.* the act of producing, a product

Productive, *a.* generative, fertile, beneficial

Próem, *n.* a preface, introduction, entrance (ence

Profanátion, *n.* a violation of facred things, irrevere

Profáne, *a.* ungodly, wicked, polluted, common

Profáne, *v. t.* to pollute, violate, mifapply, abufe

Profánely, *ad.* unholy, wickedly, irreverently

Profánenefs, *n.* impiety, wickednefs, ill language

Profáner, *n.* a polluter, violator, defiler, abufer

Profec'tion, *n.* an advancement, courfe, departure

Profefs', *v. t.* to declare, proteft, exercife

Profefs'edly, *ad.* with full intention, openly

Profes"fion, *n.* a declaration, opinion, vocation

Profes"fional, *a.* relating to a profeffion or art

Profefs'or, *n.* a public teacher or lecturer, one who makes open declaration of faith

Profefsórial, *a.* pertaining to a profeffor

Profefs'orfhip, *n.* the office of a public teacher

Prof'fer, *v. t.* to offer, tender, propofe, attempt

Prof'fer, *n.* an offer, effay, attempt, feafon

Prof'ferer, *n.* one who offers or propofes

Profi"ciency, *n.* improvement, progrefs, profit

Profi"cient, *n.* one who makes improvement

Profic'uous, *a.* advantageous, beneficial, ufeful

Prófile, *v. t.* to draw or reprefent in profile

Prófile, *n.* the fideface, a half face

Prof'it, Prof'itablenefs, *n.* gain, advantage, benefit

Prof'it, *v.* to benefit, improve, gain advantage

Prof'itable, *a.* gainful, lucrative, advantageous

Prof'itably, *ad.* beneficially, advantageoufly

Prof'itlefs, *a.* void of gain or advantage, ufelefs

Prof'ligacy, Prof'ligatenefs, *n.* debauchery

Prof'ligate, *a.* abandoned, loft to virtue (away

Prof'ligate, *n.* an abandoned wretch, *v. t.* to drive

Prof'ligately, *ad.* fhamefully, lewdly, loofely

Prof'luence, *n.* a progrefs, courfe, ftore, plenty

Prof'luent, *a.* flowing on or forward, proceeding

Profound', *a.* deep, low, learned, humble, lowly

Profound', *n.* the fea, the abyfs; *v. i.* to dive into

Profound'ly, *ad.* with deep infight or concern

Profound'nefs, Profund'ity, *n.* deepnefs, depth

Profúfe, *a.* lavifh, prodigal, abundant

Profúfe, *v. t.* to beftow in abundance, to lavifh

Profúfely, *ad.* prodigally, with exuberance, very

Profúfenefs, *n.* lavifhnefs, prodigality, wafte

Profúfion, *n.* profufenefs, exuberant plenty

Prog, *v. i.* to rob, fteal, fhift for provifion, *ob.*

Prog, *n.* victuals, provifions of any kind, *ob.*

Progen'itor, *n.* an anceftor, a forefather

Progen'iture, *n.* a begetting or birth

Pro"geny, *n.* an offspring race, iffue, generation

Prognófis, *n.* in difeafes, prognoftic figns

Prognoft'ic, *a.* foretelling, foreboding, fhowing

Prognoft'ic, *n.* a prediction in difeafes, a fign

Prognoft'icable, *a.* that may or can be foretold

Prognoſt'icate, *v. t.* to foretel, foreſhow, gueſs
Prognoſticátion, *n.* the act or art of foreſhowing
Prognoſt'icator, *n.* one who foretels or infers
Prog'reſs, *n.* a courſe, advancement, journey, way
Progreſs', *v. i.* to move forward, advance, paſs
Progres'ſion, Progreſs'iveneſs, *n.* a progreſs
Progres'ſional, *a.* advancing, increaſing, adding
Progreſs'ive, *a.* going on or forward, advancing
Progreſs'ively, *ad.* in or by a regular courſe
Progreſs'iveneſs, *n.* a ſtate of advancing
Prohib'it, *v. t.* to forbid, debar, hinder
Prohibi'tion, *n.* the act of forbidding or hindering
Prohib'itory, *a.* implying prohibition, forbidding
Project', *v.* to jut out, threw out, plan, contrive
Proj'ect, *n.* a ſcheme, plan, contrivance, deſign
Project'ile, *n.* a body put in motion; *a.* impelled
Projec'tiles, *n.* the ſcience which treats of the motions of bodies projected
Projec'tion, *n.* the act of ſhooting forward, a plan
Project'ure, *n.* a ſtanding out f.om a plain ſurface
Project'or, *n.* one who forms ſchemes or deſigns
Proin, *v. t.* to lop, cut, prune, trim, *ob.*
Prolapſe', *v. t.* to extend or jut out too much
Proláte, *v. t.* to pronounce, ſay, utter, *ob.*
Pró'late, *a.* lengthened at two oppoſit points
Prolátion, *n.* a pronunciation, utterance, delay
Prolegom'ena, *n.* previous obſervations, prefaces
Prolep'ſis, *n.* an anticipation of objections
Prolep'tical, *a.* previous, antecedent, obviating
Prolep'tically, *ad.* by way of anticipation
Proletárious, *a.* mean, wretched, vulgar, low, *ob.*
Prolif'ic, Prolif'ical, *a.* fruitful, generative, rich
Prolif'ically, *ad.* in a prolific or fruitful manner
Prolif'erous, *a.* producing young, as one flower produces another
Prolificátion, *n.* a producing of young
Prolíx, (Prolix'ious, *ob.*) *a.* long, tedious, dilatory
Prolix'ity, Prolix'neſs, *n.* tedieuſneſs, a tireſome
Prolix'ly, *ad.* at great length, tedieuſly (length
Proloc'utor, *n.* the ſpeaker of a convocation
Proloc'utorſhip, *n.* the office of a prolocutor
Prólogue, *n.* a preface, the introduction to a play
Prólogue, *v. t.* to introduce with formal preface
Prolong', *v. t.* to lengthen out in time, continue
Prolon'gate, *v. t.* to lengthen or extend in ſpace
Prolongátion, *n.* a delay to a longer time, extent
Prolúſion, *n.* a prelude, a diverting performance
Promethéan, *a.* pertaining to Prometheus, who ſtole fire from the ſun
Prom'inence, *n.* a protuberance, a part jutting out
Prom'inent, *a.* ſtanding out, conſpicuous
Promiſc'uous, *a.* mingled together, confuſed
Promiſc'uouſly, *ad.* indiſcriminately, confuſedly
Promiſc'uouſneſs, *n.* a promiſcuous ſtate
Prom'iſe, *n.* a declaration which binds the promiſ-er in law or honor (give reaſon to expect
Prom'iſe, *v.* to give one's word, aſſure, engage,
Prom'iſebreach, *n.* a violation of promiſe, deceit
Prom'iſer, *n.* one who makes a promiſe or paſſes

Prom'iſſorily, *ad.* by way of promiſe (his word
Prom'iſſory, *a.* containing or making a promiſe
Prom'ontory, *n.* a headland, cape, high land, hill
Promóte, *v. t.* to forward, advance, raiſe, prefer
Promóter, *n.* an encourager, advancer, informer
Promótion, *n.* advancement, preferment, honor
Promótive, *a.* tending to advance or encourage
Promóve, *v. t.* to promote, advance, exalt, *ob.*
Prompt, *v. t.* to aſſiſt, remind, tell, incite
Prompt, *a.* ready, quick, ſharp, told down, preſent
Prompt'er, *n.* one who reminds a public ſpeaker
Prompt'itude, *n.* promptneſs, readineſs, quickneſs
Prompt'ly, *ad.* readily, quickly, immediately
Prompt'neſs, *n.* readineſs, quickneſs, alacrity
Prompt'uary, *n.* a magazine, ſtorehouſe, buttery
Prompt'ure, *n.* a ſuggeſtion, motion, *ob.*
Promul'gate, Promulge', *v. t.* to publiſh, to make
Promulgátion, *n.* a publication, notice (known
Promulgátor, Promul'ger, *n.* one who publiſhes
Pronátor, *n.* a muſcle which turns the palm of the hand downwards
Prone, *a.* bending downwards, ſloping, inclined
Próneneſs, Prónity, *n.* an inclination, a deſcent
Prong, *n.* a branch of a fork, fork, pitchfork
Pronom'inal, *a.* belonging to or like a pronoun
Prónoun, *n.* a word uſed in the place of a noun
Pronounce', *v. t.* to ſpeak, utter, declare
Pronoun'ceable, *a.* that may be pronounced
Pronoun'cer, *n.* one who pronounces or utters
Pronunciátion, *n.* the act or mode of utterance
Proof, *n.* evidence, teſt, a rough ſheet of print
Proof, *a.* able to reſiſt, impenetrable, rough, hard
Proofleſs, *a.* not proved, wanting evidence
Prop, *n.* a ſupport, that on which a thing reſts
Prop, *v. t.* to ſupport, ſuſtain, bear or keep up
Prop'agable, *a.* that may be ſpread or extended
Prop'agate, *v. t.* to generate, ſpread, extend
Propagátion, *n.* generation, production, increaſe
Prop'agator, *n.* a ſpreader, extender, producer
Propel', *v. t.* to drive or puſh forward, to urge
Propend', *v. i.* to incline to ſome part, tend, *ob.*
Propend'ency, *n.* a tendency of deſire, proneneſs
Propenſe', *a.* inclined, diſpoſed, prone (dency
Propen'ſion, Propenſ'ity, *n.* an inclination, a ten-
Prop'er, *a.* one's own, peculiar, fit, juſt, plain
Prop'erly, *ad.* fitly, ſuitably, duly, in a ſtrict ſenſe
Prop'erneſs, *n.* a proper or fit ſtate, propriety
Prop'erty, *n.* a right of poſſeſſion, quality, in the W. Indies and U. States, a plantation, eſtate
Prop'erty, *v. t.* to inveſt with qualities, to retain,
Propháne, *ſee* profane (*ob.*
Proph'eſy, *n.* a prediction of a thing (preach
Proph'eſy, (Proph'etize, *ob.*) *v. t.* to predict, foretel,
Proph'eſying, *n.* the act of foretelling events
Proph'et, *n.* a man who foretels future events, a
Proph'eteſs, *n.* a female prophet (divine teacher
Prophet'ic, Prophet'ical, *a.* foretelling events
Prophet'ically, *ad.* in the manner of a propheſy
Prophylac'tic, *a.* preventive, preſervative

PRO   [—239—]   PRO

Propin"quity, *n.* nearnefs, clofenefs, kindred
Propi"tiable, *a.* that may be atoned or appeafed
Propi"tiate, *v. t.* to atone, induce to favor, gain
Propitiation, *n.* an atonement for fome crime
Propi"tiator, *n.* one who atones or appeafes
Propi"tiatory, *a.* able to atone or make kind
Propi"tiatory, *n.* the mercy-feat in the temple
Propi"tious, *a.* favorable, kind, merciful, good
Propi"tioufly, *ad.* favorably, kindly, gently
Propi"tioufnefs, *n.* favorablenefs, favor, kindnefs
Próplafm, *n.* a mold, matrix, model, pattern, *ob.*
Propónent, *n.* one who makes a propofal, *not ufed*
Propórtion, *n.* an equal part, ratio, fymmetry, fize
Propórtion, *v. t.* to adjuft parts, fit, fuit, fet
Propórtionable, *a.* adjufted, fitted, fuitable
Propórtionably, *ad.* according to due proportion
Propórtional, *a.* having due proportion, adjufted
Propórtional, *n.* a quantity in exact proportion
Proportionality, *n.* a proportional quality
Propórtionally, *ad.* in a ftated or due degree
Propórtionate, *v. t.* to adjuft by a ratio, *ob.*
Propórtionate, *a.* proportional, correfpondent,
Propórtionatenefs, *n.* a correfpondent ftate, *ob.*
Propófal, *n.* a fcheme propounded, an offer
Propófe, *v.* to offer for confideration, form, mean
Propófer, *n.* one who offers for confideration
Propofi"tion, *n.* a thing propofed, an offer
Propofi"tional, *a.* confidered as a propofition
Propound, *v. t.* to propofe, exhibit, offer
Propound'er, *n.* he who propofes or offers
Propréfect, *n.* a prefect's deputy   (right
Proprietary, Proprietor, *n.* a poffeffor in his own
Proprietary, *a.* belonging to fome certain owner
Proprietrefs, *n.* a female proprietor, *not ufed*
Propriety, *n.* fitnefs, juftnefs, exclufive right
Propt, Prop'ped, *ad.* fuftained or held by a prop
Propúgn, *v. t.* to defend, fupport, vindicate, *ob.*
Propugnation, *n.* a defenfe, fupport, affiftance, *ob.*
Propug'ner, *n.* a defender, fupporter, vindicator, *ob.*
Propul'fion, *n.* the act of driving off or forward
Prore, *n.* the prow, head, forepart of a fhip, a bone
Prorogation, *n.* a putting off, prolongation, delay
Prorógue, *v. t.* to put off, protract, prolong, delay
Prorup'tion, *n.* the act of burfting out or from
Profáic, *a.* belonging to or written in profe
Profcríbe, *v. t.* to doom to death, to outlaw
Profcríber, *n.* one who dooms to deftruction
Profcrip'tion, *n.* a doom to death, a confifcation
Profe, *n.* language not confined to fixed numbers
Profe, *a.* formed of profe, unreftrained, free
Pros'ecute, *v. t.* to purfue, follow, fue, indict
Profecútion, *n.* a purfuit, procefs, criminal fuit
Pros'ecutor, *n.* one who purfues, one who fues
Pros'elyte, *v. t.* to convert, bring over, turn
Pros'elyte, *n.* one converted to a new opinion
Pros'elytize, *v. t.* to convert to one's own opinion
Pros'elytifm, *n.* the practice of making converts
Profemination, *n.* a propagation by feed, *ob.*
Profódian, *n.* one fkilled in the art of profody

Pros'ody, *n.* the art of metrical compofition
Pros'opopy, *n.* profonification, a fpeaking of inanimate things as if animated
Pros'pect, *n.* a view, an object of view, ground of expectation, reafon to hope
Profpect'ive, *a.* viewing at a diftance, provident
Profpect'us, *n.* a fummary account of a new publication
Pros'per, *v.* to thrive, fucceed, favor, blefs
Profper'ity, *n.* fuccefs, good fortune, happinefs
Pros'perous, *a.* fuccefsful, fortunate, lucky
Pros'peroufly, *ad.* fuccefsfully, fortunately, well
Pros'tate, *a.* ftanding before, as the proftate gland fituated before the bladder
Profternation, *n.* a throwing down, a dejection
Pros'titute, *v. t.* to fell or expofe to lewdnefs, debafe, make common
Pros'titute, *a.* vicious for hire, fold to vice, vile
Pros'titute, *n.* a public ftrumpet, a mere hireling
Proftitution, *n.* act of proftituting, debafement
Pros'trate, *v.* to lay flat, fall down, kneel
Pros'trate, *a.* lying with the face to the ground
Proftration, *n.* the act of adoration, a dejection
Próftyle, *n.* a range of columns in front
Protat'ic, *a.* previous, beginning, introductory, *ob.*
Protect', *v. t.* to defend, fhield, cover from harm
Protec'tion, *n.* a defenfe, fhelter, paffport
Protect'ive, *a.* defenfive, fheltering, covering
Protect'or, *n.* a defender, helper, fupport, regent
Protect'orate, *n.* a government by a protector
Protect'orfhip, *n.* the office of a protector
Protect'refs, *n.* a female protector or patron
Protend', *v. t.* to hold out, ftretch forth, defer
Proteft', *v.* to declare, affirm, vow, fhow, prove
Proteft', *n.* a folemn or formal declaration, as of diffenting members of the houfe of lords, of a matter of a veffel, againft a feizure, of the holder of a note not duly paid
Prot'eftant, *a.* belonging to or like proteftants
Prot'eftant, *n.* one who protefts againft popery
Prot'eftantifm, *n.* the religion of proteftants
Proteftation, *n.* a folem declaration, a vow
Proteft'er, *n.* one who protefts, one who declares
Prothon'otary, *n.* a chief notary, a regifter
Prótocol, *n.* the original copy of a writing, a title
Prótomartyr, *n.* the firft martyr, St. Stephen
Prótoplaft, *n.* a thing firft formed, an original, *ob.*
Prótotype, *n.* the original of fome copy, a model
Protract', *v.* to lengthen in time, prolong, draw out
Protract'er, *n.* one who protracts, an inftrument for laying down angles on paper, &c.
Protrac'tion, *n.* a lengthening out, delay, ftop
Protract'ive, *a.* fpinning out, delaying, dilatory
Protrep'tical, *a.* advifing, perfuading, *ob.*
Protrúde, *v.* to thruft, pufh or extend forward
Protrúfion, *n.* the act of thrufting on, a pufh
Protrúfive, *a.* impelling forward or outward
Protúberance, *n.* a fwelling above the reft, a knot
Protúberant, *a.* fwelling out, prominent, raifed
Protúberate, *v. i.* to fwell out, to ftand full out

Proud, *a.* elated, haughty, conceited, grand, lofty, high, daring, eager for the male, hot, exuberant

Proud'ly, *ad.* in a proud manner, haughtily

Prove, [prooV] *v.* to try, experience, to make certain by evidence, put to the test

Prove'able, *a.* that may be proved or tried

Proved'itor, *n.* one who provides, a purveyor

Provedóre, *n.* a provider or purveyor, *ob.*

Prov'ender, *n.* food for brute animals, meal, &c.

Próver, *n.* one who tries, an inspector, (Mass.)

Prov'erb, *n.* a maxim, an old or common saying

Prov'erb, *v. t.* to mention in or use as a proverb

Proverb'ial, *a.* mentioned in a proverb, common

Proverb'ialist, *n.* one who deals in proverbs

Proverb'ially, *ad.* in or by a proverb, by maxims

Provide, *v.* to procure, furnish, prepare, stipulate

Provided, *pa.* furnished, on condition

Prov'idence, *n.* God's care, foresight, prudence

Provident, *a.* forecasting, cautious, frugal, wise

Providen'tial, *a.* effected by providence, happy

Providen'tially, *ad.* by the care of providence

Prov'idently, *ad.* with wise or careful precaution

Provider, *n.* one who provides, one who procures

Prov'ince, *n.* a region, a conquered country, office

Provin'cial, *a.* belonging to a province or district

Provin'cial, *n.* a spiritual or chief governor, an inhabitant of a province

Provin'cialism, *n.* a peculiarity of speech in a province or district of country

Provin'ciate, *v. t.* to turn to or make a province, *ob.*

Provi'sion, *n.* a providing beforehand, measure taken, stores laid up, meat, also, food, stipulation

Provi'sion, *v. t.* to furnish with food

Provi'sional, *a.* serving for present use, wary

Provi'sionally, *ad.* with a proviso, temporarily

Provi'so, *n.* a stipulation, provision, caution, grant

Provi'sor, *n.* one who has the care of providing

Provocátion, *n.* a cause of or for anger, an appeal

Provócative, *n.* a thing to revive a bad appetite

Provócative, *a.* tending to revive a bad appetite

Provóke, *v. t.* to rouse, enrage, vex, challenge

Provóker, *n.* one who provokes, one who stirs up

Provóking, *pa.* exciting or tending to excite wrath

Provókingly, *ad.* so as to raise anger, crossly

Provóst, *n.* a chief of any body, an executioner

Provôst'ship, *n.* the place or office of a provost

Prow, *n.* the fore part of a ship, a vessel in the E.

Prow'ess, *n.* bravery, courage, valor, vigor (ladies

Prow'est, *a.* bravest, boldest, most courageous, *ob.*

Prowl, *v.* to rove about, seek for prey, plunder

Prowl'er, *n.* one who prowls or seeks for prey

Prox'imate, (Prox'ime, *ob.*) *a.* next, immediate,

Prox'imately, *ad.* without intervention, nearly.

Proxim'ity, *n.* nearness, close approach, kindred

Prox'y, *n.* a substitute or deputy for another

Pruce, *n.* a kind of lether, Prussian lether, *ob.*

Prude, *n.* a woman who is over affected and nice

Prúdence, *n.* wisdom, discretion, wariness

Prúdent, *a.* practically wise, discreet, cautious

Pruden'tial, *a.* done upon principles of prudence

Pruden'tially, *ad.* according to prudence, wisely

Pruden'tials, *n. pl.* maxims of prudence, affairs to be managed by discretion

Prúdently, *ad.* wisely, discreetly, judiciously

Prúdery, *n.* too much affectation, shiness, coyness

Prúdish, *a.* like a prude, affectedly grave, formal

Prune, *n.* a dried plum; *v. t.* to lop, dress, trim

Prunel'lo, *n.* a silken stuff, a sort of plum

Prúner, *n.* one who lops trees, one who cuts off

Prunif'erous, *a.* bearing or producing plums

Prúninghook, *n.* a hook or knife used to lop trees

Prúrience, Prúriency, *n.* an itching or great desire

Prúrient, *a.* itching, hot, eager, warm, curious

Prus'sian, *n.* a native of Prussia; *a.* pertaining to it

Prus'sic, *a.* denominating a certain acid obtained from Prussian blue (and a salifiable base

Prus'siate, *n.* a neutral salt formed of Prussic acid

Prússiáted, *a.* combined with the prussic acid

Pry, *v.* to look into with close inspection, to raise with a lever

Prytáne, *n.* a president of the senate in Athens

Psalm, *n.* a kind of sacred song, a sacred hymn

Psalm'ist, *n.* a writer of psalms, a singer of psalms

Psalm'ody, *n.* the act or art of singing psalms

Psalt'er, *n.* a book, a book of psalms

Psalt'ery, *n.* a kind of harp used for psalms

Pseúdo, *a.* false, counterfeit, pretended, forged

Pseudog'raphy, *n.* a writing of falsehood

Pseudol'ogy, *n.* falsehood of speech, deceit, a lie

Pseudon'ymous, *a.* relating to fictitious names

Pshaw, *n.* an expression of contempt or dislike

Pshaw, *exclam.* expressing contempt or dislike

Psychol'ogy, [ch as k] *n.* the doctrins of spirit or

Psycho'o'gical, *a.* pertaining to psychology (mind

Ptar'migan, *n.* a bird of northern climates

Ptis'an, *n.* a cooling drink made from raisins, &c.

Ptolemáic, *a.* relating Ptolomy the geographer (iva

Pty'alism, *n.* salivation, increased secretion of saliva

Púberty, *n.* ripe age in the sexes

Pubes'cence, *n.* a state of puberty, the hairy, woolly, downy substance on plants

Pubes'cent, *a.* arriving at puberty, downy

Pub'lic, *a.* open, notorious, common, general

Pub'lic, *n.* the body of a nation, an open view

Pub'lican, *n.* a victualler, officer, tollgatherer

Publicátion, *n.* a publishing, edition, work

Publi'city, *n.* a public state, notoriety

Pub'licly, *ad.* openly, in full view, notoriously

Pub'licness, *n.* a public or open state, notoriety

Pub'licspirited, *a.* regarding public good, noble

Pub'lish, *v. t.* to make known, declare, set forth

Pub'lisher, *n.* one who publishes or puts out a book

Pub'lishment, *n.* notice of intended marriage, [local]

Puccoon', *n.* a plant, bloodwort

Puck, *n.* a supposed spirit, fairy, sprite

Púcelage, *n.* the state of virginity, maidenhood

Púceron, *n.* the vine-fretter, plant-louse or aphis

Puck'er, *v. t.* to plait, to fold; *n.* a fold, a nest

Pud'der, *n.* a tumult, a buftle; *v. i.* to pother
Pud'ding, *n.* a kind of food, gut fluffed, coil
Pud'dingpie, *n.* a pudding with meat in it
Pud'dingftone, *n.* a collection of pebbles of the filiceous kind cemented by a like fubftance
Pud'dingtime, *n.* dinnertime, the nick of time
Pud'dle, *n.* a dirty plafh or fettle of water, a pool
Pud'dle, *v. t.* to make muddy, dirty, daub
Pud'dly, *a.* wet, muddy, dirty, miry, foul
Púdency, Pudi"city, *n.* modefly, chaftity, purity
Púefellow, *n.* a partner, companion, crony, *ob.*
Púerile *a.* childifh, boyifh, giddy, trifling, fimple
Púeril'ity, *n.* childifhnefs, boyifhnefs, folly
Puer'peral, *a.* pertaining to childbirth
Puerp'erous, *a.* bearing children, lying in, fick
Púet, *n.* a kind of waterfowl, a fort of plover
Puff, *n.* a blaft of wind, any thing porous, a tool to powder hair with, undeferved praife
Puff, *v. t.* to blow, fwell with wind, praife much
Puff'er, *n.* one who puffs, a boafter, a deceiver
Puffin, *n.* a waterfowl, fifh, fuzzball
Puff'y, *a.* windy, flatulent, tumid, fwelled, big
Pug, *n.* a Dutch hog, monkey, thing beloved
Pugh, *exclam.* denoting contempt or diflike
Púgil, *n.* a champion, fighter, fmall handful
Púgilifm, *n.* boxing, fighting with the fift
Púgilift, *n.* a boxer, a fighter with the fift
Pugilis'tic, *a.* pertaining to boxing or fift fighting
Pugnácious, *a.* fighting, prone to refift
Puifne, [puny] *a.* younger, fmall, petty, lower
Puifs'ance, *n.* power, ftrength, force, valor
Puifs'ant, *a.* powerful, ftrong, forcible, brave
Puifs'antly, *ad.* powerfully, forcibly, valiantly
Puke, *v. i.* to fpew, vomit, caft up, throw up
Puke, Púker, *n.* a medicin caufing to vomit
Pul'chritude, *n.* beauty, grace, comelinefs, fhow
Pule, *v. i.* to whine, cry, cry like a chicken
Pulkhá, *n.* a Laplander's travelling fled
Pull, *v. t.* to pluck, draw violently, drag, degrade
Pull, *n.* the act of pulling, a pluck, effort
Pull'er, *n.* one who pulls or plucks, a flanderer
Pull'et, *n.* a young hen, young fowl, clofe room
Pull'ey, *n.* a fmall wheel for a running cord
Pul'licat, *n.* a fort of filk handkerchief
Pull'ulate, *v. i.* to bud, fpring, fhoot out, appear
Pullulátion, *n.* a budding, the germination of buds
Pul'monary, *a.* belonging to the lungs
Pulmon'ic, *a.* pertaining to or affecting the lungs
Pulp, *n.* the foft part of fruit, any foft mafs
Pulp, *v. t.* to feparate the pulp from the berry as in coffee works (from
Pulp'it, [u as in full] *n.* an exalted place to fpeak
Pulp'ous, Pulp'y, *a.* full of pulp, foft, pappy, rich
Pulp'oufnefs, *n.* a pulpy ftate or quality, foftnefs
Puls'ate, *v. i.* to beat as the artery, to pulfe
Pulfátion, Pul'fion, *n.* the act of driving forward, a motion or beat of the pulfe
Puls'ative, *a.* beating, throbbing
Pulfe, *v.* to beat as the pulfe, to drive forward

Pulfe, *n.* a beating of the blood, peafe, &c.
Pultáceous, *a.* macerated, diffolved, nearly fluid
Pul've rable, *a.* that may be reduced to powder
Pul'verate, *a.* covered with duft or the like fubftance
Pulverizátion, *n.* a reduction to powder or duft
Pul'verize, *v. t.* to reduce to powder or duft
Pul'verous, *a.* confifting of duft, powdery
Pulver'ulent, *a.* confifting of duft or powder
Pul'vil, *v. t.* to perfume; *n.* a fweet fcent
Púma, *n.* a rapacious quadruped, the panther
Pum'ice, *n.* a fpungy ftone full of holes, apples or other fruit bruifed or mafhed
Pumi"ceous, *a.* confifting of or like pumice
Pum'kin, *n.* a large kind of melon
Pum'mel, *n.* a knob, a protuberant part
Pum'mel, *v. t.* to beat, thump, bruife
Pump, *n.* a water-engine, a very thin fhoe
Pump, *v.* to work a pump, to difcover artfully
Pump'er, *n.* a perfon or inftrument that pumps
Pun, *n.* a quibble, a low or ludicrous repartee
Pun, *v. i.* to quibble, quirk, play upon words
Punch *n.* an inftrument, liquor, buffoon, puppet,
Punch, *v. t.* to bore a hole with a punch (horfe
Punch'bowl, *n.* a bowl ufed to make punch in
Punch'eon, *n.* a tool to make a hole, a large cafk
Pun'chin, *n.* a fhort timber for fupporting weights
Punchinel'lo, *n.* a fquab fellow, a ftage puppet
Punc'tate, *a.* fprinkled with hollow dots or points
Punctil'io, *n.* ceremony, exactnefs, nicety
Punctil'ious, *a.* ceremonious, exact, nice
Punctil'ioufnefs, *n.* exactnefs, precifenefs in form
Punctil'ioufly, *ad.* in an exact, formal manner
Punc'to, *n.* the point in fencing, ceremony, form
Punc'tual, *a.* exact, fcrupulous, ftrict, nice
Punctual'ity, Punc'tualnefs, *n.* exactnefs, nicety
Punc'tually, *ad.* exactly, fcrupuloufly, nicely
Punc'tuate, *a.* having fpots or points
Punctuátion, *n.* the act or method of pointing
Punc'tulate, *v. t.* to mark with fmall fpots, *ob.*
Punc'ture, *n.* a fmall prick, little hole, fracture
Punc'ture, *v. t.* to prick or perforate with a pointed inftrument
Pun'gency, *n.* the power of pricking, fharpnefs
Pun'gent, *a.* pricking, fharp, tart, keen, fevere
Púnic, *a.* falfe, trecherous, faithlefs, deceitful, pertaining to ancient carthage
Púninefs, *n.* fmallnefs, pettinefs, weaknefs
Pun'ifh, *v. t.* to chaftife, beat, inflict penalties
Pun'ifhable, *a.* worthy or capable of punifhment
Pun'ifher, *n.* one who inflicts punifhment
Pun'ifhment, *n.* any thing inflicted for a crime
Puni"tion, *n.* the act of punifhing, punifhment
Púnitive, Púnitory, *a.* inflicting punifhment
Punk, *n.* a ftrumpet, common proftitute
Puns'ter, *n.* one who puns, one who loves puns
Punt, *n.* a fmall flat-bottomed boat
Punt, *v. i.* to play at baffet or omber
Púny, *a.* fmall, little, petty, fickly, weak tender
Púny, *n.* a mere novice, an unexperienced perfon

X

Pup, n. a very young or little dog, a puppy
Pup, v. i. to bring forth puppies, whelp, cub
Púpil, n. the apple of the eye, a fcholar, a ward
Púpilage, n. the ftate of a fcholar, wardfhip
Púpilary, a. pertaining to or having a fcholar
Pup'pet, n. a fmall doll, wooden image, child
Pup'petman, n. the mafter of a puppetfhow
Pup'petfhow, n. a kind of mock play by images
Pup'py, n. a whelp, faucy ignorant fellow, fop
Pup'pyheaded, a. dull, heavy   (ous cement
Pur'beckitone, n. a hard fandftone with a calcare-
Pur'blind, Póreblind, a. nearfighted, fhortfighted
Pur'blindnefs, n. a ftate of being nearfighted
Pur'chafe, v. to obtain for a confideration, to buy
Pur'chafe, n. a thing bought, an obtaining by giv-
    ing an equivalent, the power of a lever in me-
    chanics, an obtaining of real eftate by one's own
    act, and not by defcent
Pur'chafeable, a. that may bought for money
Pur'chafer, n. one who buys or makes a purchafe,
    one who obtains lands by his own act or agree-
    ment
Pure, a. unfullied, clear, clean, uncorrupt, chafte
Púrely, ad. in a pure manner, merely, fimply
Púrenefs, n. a pure ftate, clearnefs, innocence
Pur'fle, Pur'flew, n. a border in embroidered work
Pur''fle, v. t. to work or adorn with a needle
Purgátion, n. the act of cleanfing or purifying
Purg'ative, a. tending to purge, cleanfing
Purg'ative, n. a medicin tending to purge
Purg'atory, n. a place of purgation after death
Purge, n. a medicin, a medicin caufing ftools
Purge, v. to cleanfe, purify, clear from guilt, clear,
    clarify, difcharge by ftool, have ftools
Pur'ger, n. a perfon who clears away, a purge
Pur'ging, n. the act of cleanfing, a loofenefs
Purificátion, n. the act of making pure or clean
Purificative, Purificatory, a. tending to cleanfe
Púrifier, n. what purifies, a cleanfer, a refiner
Púriform, a. like pus, in the form of pus
Púrify, v. to make or grow pure, clear, refine
Púrim, n. the feaft of lots among the Jews to cele-
    brate their efcape from Haman's plot
Púritan, n. a rigid diffenter, one very ftrict
Púritan'ical, a. relating to puritans, demure
Púritanifm, n. the opinions or practice of puritans
Púrity, n. clearnefs, innocence, chaftity, virtue
Purl, n. a fort of lace, border, bitter malt liquor
Purl, v. i. to flow with a gentle noife, to adorn
Pur'lieu, n. an inclofure, diftrict, border, edge
Pur'ling, n. the noife of a gentle rippling current
Pur'lins, n. pl. infide braces to fupport rafters
Purloin', v. t. to fteal, pi'fer, thieve privately
Purloin'er, n. one who takes privately, a thief
Purp'arty, n. a fhare, part in a divifion, partition
Pur'ple, a. red tinged with blue, red, livid
Pur'ple, n. a purple color, a royal garb, dignity
Pur'ple, v. t. to color with purple, to make red
Pur'ples, n. pl. purple or livid fpots in a fever

Purp'lifh, a. fomewhat purple, like purple
Pur'port, n. a defign, meaning, tendency
Pur'port, v. t. to intend, defign, mean, tend, fhow
Pur'pofe, n. an intention, defign, effect, example
Pur'pofe, v. t. to intend, defign, mean, refolve
Pur'pofely, ad. on purpofe, by or with defign
Pu'prefs'ture, n. in law a certain fpecies of nufance
Pur'prife, n. an inclofure, the compafs of a manor
Purr, v. i. to murmur like a cat; n. a bird, cider
Purfe, v. t. to put into a purfe, draw, contract
Purfe, n. a fmall bag ufed for money, a gift, a
    prize or fum to be run for at a horfe race
Purfe'net, n. a net that draws up like a purfe
Purfe'proud, a. puffed up or elated with riches
Purs'er, n. an officer on board a fhip
Purs'inefs, n. a diforder, a fhortnefs of breath
Purs'lain, n. a well known plant of many kinds
Purfúable, a. capable of being purfued
Purfúance, n. a profecution, procefs, confequence
Purfúant, a. done in confequence, agreeable
Purfúe, v. to follow, chafe, profecute, proceed
Purfúer, n. one who follows in a hoftile manner
Purfúit, n. a chafe, profecution, act of following
Par'fuivant, n. a herald, an attendant on heralds
Pars'y, a. fhortbreathed and fat, grofs, heavy
Purt'enance, n. an appurtenance, a pluck (provide
Purvey', [ey as a] v. to buy provifions, procure,
Purvey'ance, n. a procurement of provifions
Purvey'or, n. one who provides victuals, a pimp
Pur'view, n. extent of meaning or intended pro-
    vifion, body of a law
Púrulence or Púrulency, n. a generation of pus
Púrulent, a. confifting of pus or corrupt matter
Pus, n. matter from a well digefted fore
Pufh, v. to thruft, prefs forward, go, urge, teaze
Pufh, n. a thruft, affault, trial, need, pimple, fpot
Pufh'ing, pa. a. thrufting, enterprifing, eager
Pufh'pin, n. a childifh play by pufhing pins
Pufillanim'ity, n. cowardice, meannefs of fpirit
Pufillan'imous, a. cowardly, mean fpirited, low
Pufs, n. a cat, hare, naughty or dirty woman (tules
Pus'tulated, a. having puftules, fpotted with puf-
Puft'ule, n. a pimple or red fpot, a fmall fwelling
Puft'ulous, a. full of or having pimples, fore
Put, v. put, pret. put, pa. to lay, place, fet, repofe,
    commit, add, propofe, apply, incite
Put, n. an action of diftrefs, fhift, game, clown
Pútage, n. the act of whoredom, proftitution, ob.
Pútanifm, n. the trade or life of a proftitute, ob
Pútative, a. fuppofed, reputed, reckoned, deemed
Pútid, a. mean, low, worthlefs, bafe, ob.
Put'log, n. a log ufed in a bricklayer's fcaffold
Pútred'inous, a. rotten, ftinking, offenfive
Putrefac'tion, n. a rotting ftate, rottennefs
Putrefact'ive, a. making rotten, rotting, fpoiling
Pútrefy or Pútrify, v. t. to rot, to corrupt
Putres'cence, n. the ftate of rotting, corruption
Putres'cent, a. growing rotten, corrupting
Pútrid, a. rotten, corrupt, offenfive, difguftful

Putrid'ity, Pútridnefs, *n.* rottennefs, corruption
Put'ter. *n.* one who puts or places, an inftigator
Put'tingftone, *n.* a large ftone thrown by hand
Put'toc, *n.* a buzzard (to faften with putty
Put'ty, *n.* a kind of cement ufed by glaziers; *v. t.*
Puz'zle, *n.* a perplexity, embarraffment, riddle
Puz'zle, *v. t.* to perplex, embarrafs, confound
Puz'zler, *n.* one who puzzles, one who perplexes
Puz'zolan, *n.* a loofe porous volcanic ftone
Pye, *n.* an order of birds with convex flatted bills
Pygarg'us or Pygarg', *n.* a bird of the vultur kind
Pygméan, *a.* of or like a pygmy, dwarfifh, puny
Pyg'my, *n.* a kind of fabulous perfon, a dwarf
Pylórus, *n.* the lower orifice of the ftomach
Pylor'ic, *a.* pertaining to the pylorus
Pyl'ian, *a.* pertaining to Pylos in Peloponnefus
Pyr'amid, *n.* a fquare pillar ending in a point
Pyram'idal, *a.* [*an ill formed word*]
Pyramid'ical, *a.* like a pyramid
Pyramid'ically, *ad.* in the form of a pyramid
Pyram'idoid, *n.* a folid figure formed by the rotation of a femiparabola about its bafe or greateft ordinate
Pyre, *n.* a pile to be burnt, a funeral pile
Pyrenéan, *a.* pertaining to the Pyrenees, high mountains between France and Spain
Pyr'ite, *n.* a fireftone, a fulphuret of iron or other metal, the name given it in modern chemiftry
Pyr'itous, Pyrit'ical, Pyritáceous, *a.* pertaining to, confifting of or refembling pyrite
Pyritif'erous, *a.* producing or containing pyrite
Pyritol'ogy, *n.* a treatife on pyrite (tilling wood
Pyrolig'nous, *n.* denoting an acid obtained by dif-
Pyrolig'nite, *n.* a compound of the pyrolignous acid with another fubftance (heat
Pyrol'ogift, *n.* a believer in the doctrin of latent
Pyr'omancy, *n.* a divination by means of fire
Pyrom'eter, *n.* an inftrument to meafure the expanfion of bodies by heat
Pyromu'cous, *a.* denoting an acid obtained by diftilling fugar or any fweet juce
Pyromúcite, *n.* a compound of pyromucous acid and other fubftance
Pyr'ophane, *n.* a ftone rendered tranfparent in fire
Pyroph'anous, *a.* rendered tranfparent by fire
Pyroph'orus, *n.* a fubftance which takes fire on expofure to air
Pyrophor'ic, *a.* like or pertaining to pyrophorus
Pyrotar'tarous, *a.* denoting an acid obtained by diftilling pure tartarite of potafh
Pyrotar'trite, *n.* a compound of pyrotartarous acid and other fubftance
Pyrotech'nical, [ch as k] *a.* relating to fireworks
Pyrotech'nics, *n. pl.* the art of making fireworks
Pyr'otechny, *n.* the art of making fireworks
Pyrrhon'ic, *a.* pertaining to pyrrhonifin
Pyr'rhonift, *n.* one who doubts of things, a fceptic
Pyr'rhonifm, *n.* fcepticifm, univerfal doubt
Pythegórean, *n.* a follower of Pythagoras

Pythagórean, *a.* pertaining to Pythagoras
Pyth'ian, *a.* pertaining to Pythia the prieftefs of Apollo at Delphi, and to Pythius, a name of Apollo
Pyx, *n.* a box or veffel wherein the hoft is kept

Q

Q *abbrev.* for queftion
Quab, *n.* a fifh in Ruffian rivers
Quac'hil'to, *n.* a beautiful bird in S. America
Quack, *v. i.* to cry like a duck, brag, phyfic
Quack, *n.* a bold but ignorant pretender to phyfic
Quack'ery, *n.* mean or bad acts in phyfic, deceit
Quack'falver, *n.* a man who boafts of falves, *ob.*
Quadrages'ima, *n.* Lent confifting of 40 days
Quadrages'imal, *a.* belonging to or ufed in Lent
Quad'rangle, *n.* a figure that has four right angles
Quadran'gular, *a.* having four right angles
Quad'rant, *n.* a fourth part, a marine inftrument, an arch of 90 degrees, a piece of metal to fill fpaces in printing
Quadrant'al, *a.* having a fourth part of a circle
Quad'rat, *n.* an inftrument called geometrical
Quad'rate, *a.* fquare, fuited, fitted, adapted (fquare
Quad'rate, *v. i.* to fquare, fuit, fit, agree
Quadrat'ic, *a.* relating to or including a fquare
Quad'rature, *n.* the act of fquaring, fquarenefs, the quartering of the moon
Quadren'nial, *a.* happening once every four years
Quad'rible, *a.* that may be fquared or completed
Quadricap'fular, *a.* having four capfules
Quadrident'ate, *a.* having four indentations
Quad'rifid, *a.* divided into four fegments
Quadrijúgous, *a.* having four pair or pair of petioles
Quadrilat'eral, *a.* having four fides or angles
Quadrill', *n.* a game at cards
Quadrilit'eral, *a.* confifting of five letters
Quad'rilobe, *a.* having four lobes
Quadriloc'ular, *a.* having four cells for feeds
Quadripart'ite, *a.* divided into four parts
Quadriparti'tion, *n.* a dividing into four equal parts
Quad'rireme, *n.* a veffel with four benches of oars
Quadrivalv'ular, Quad'rivalve, *a.* having four valves
Quadroon', *n.* the offspring of a mulatto woman by a white man
Quad'rum, *n.* a gritftone with a calcareous cement
Quad'ruped, *n.* any beaft going on four feet
Quad'ruple, *a.* fourfold, told or taken four times
Quad'ruple, *v. t.* to take or repeat four times
Quadrúplicate, *a.* fourfold, four times repeated
Quadrúplicate, *v. t.* to make fourfold
Quad'ruply, *ad.* in a fourfold ftate or proportion
Quaff, *v. t.* to drink, drink hard, tipple, tope
Quaff'er, *v. i.* to feel out; *n.* a perfon who quaffs
Quag'gy, *a.* boggy, fwampy, fenny, marfhy, foft
Quag'mire, *n.* a bog, boggy place, fhaking marfa
Quáhog, *n.* the popular name of a large clam
Quail, *n.* a bird; [*v.* to languifh, crufh, quell, *ob.*]
Quáilpipe, *n.* a pipe ufed to allure quails by
Quaint, *a.* nice, pretty, fubtle, artful, exact, odd

Quáintly, ad. nicely, prettily, artfully, exactly
Quáintnefs, n. a petty elegance, nicety, fubtility
Quake, v.i. to fhake with cold or fear; n.a fhudder
Quáker, n. cne of the fect of friends
Quákerifm, n. the fyftem or manners of quakers
Qualificátion, n. an accomplifhment, a capacity
Quál'ify, v.t. to make fit, leffen, abate, foften
Quál'ity, n. nature relatively confidered, property, efficacy, rank, birth, temper, difpofition
Qualm, n. a fudden fit of ficknefs, a faintnefs
Quálmifh, a. feized with a fickly languor, fick
Quand'ary, n. a doubt, uncertainty, difficulty
Quant'itive, a. valued according to the quantity
Quant'ity, n. bulk, weight, a part, portion, meafure of time obferved in pronouncing fyllables
Quant'um, n. a quantity, amount, fufficiency
Quar'antin, n. reftraint of intercourfe impofed on a veffel arriving in port, originally 40 days
Quar'antin, v.t. to reftrain a veffel from intercourfe
Quar'rel, n. a brawl, difpute, conteft, ftrife, fcuffle
Quar'rel, v.i. to brawl, debate, find fault, fight
Quar'relous, Quar'relfome, a. inclined to quarrel
Quar'relfomenefs, n. a quarrelfome difpofition
Quar'ry, n. a ftone mine, kind of arrow, fquare
Quar'ry, v.t. to dig from a quarry, [to prey upon,
Quar'ryman, n. one who digs ftones in a quarry (ob.]
Quart, n. a forth part of a gallon, a fequence
Quart'an, n. a fourth day ague; a. every fourth day
Quartátion, n. the procefs of refining a metal by mixing one fourth with three fourths of another metal (timber, mercy, part, region
Quart'er, n. a fourthpart, meafure of eight bufhels,
Quar'ters, n. lodgings, a ftation
Quar'ter, v.t. to divide or break into four parts, lodge, diet, ftation, fix, bear as an appendage
Quart'erage, n. a quarterly allowance or payment
Quar'terday, n. the day that completes three months or quarter of a year
Quar'terdeck, n. the fhort upper deck of a fhip
Quart'erly, a. happening every three months
Quart'erly, ad. once in the quarter of a year
Quart'ermafter, n. one who regulates quarters for
Quart'ern, n. the fourth part of a pint (men
Quart'erftaff n. an ancient ftaff of defenfe
Quar'tile, n. an afpect of planets diftant one fourth of a circle or 90 degrees
Quart'o, n. the fize of a fheet when twice doubled
Quartz, n. a filiceous ftone fo hard as to emit fparks with fteel (or like quartz
Quartz'ous, Quartz'y, Quartzófe, a. pertaining to
Quafh, v. to crufh, fubdue, annul, be fhaken
Quate, n. an inftrument of play, a quoit
Quáterconfin, n. a diftant relation, a friend
Quatern', a. confifting of four (four
Quater'nary, Quater'nion, Quater'nity, n. number
Quátrain, n. four lines that rhyme alternately
Quáver, v.i. to fhake the voice, to vibrate
Quáver, n. a note in mufic, a fhake
Quay, n. a key for landing goods at

Quean, n. a low worthlefs woman, ftrumpet, drab
Quéafinefs, n. a ficknefs of ftomach, greafinefs
Quéafy, a. fqueamifh, faftidious, greafy
Queck, v.i. to fhrink, fhow pain, ob.
Queen, n. the wife of a king, a fovereign princefs
Queénbee, n. the chief bee in a fwarm
Queer, a. odd, ftrange, particular, droll, original
Quéerly, ad. oddly, ftrangely, particularly, fhily
Quéernefs, n. oddnefs, ftrangenefs, particularity
Quell, v. to crufh, fubdue, appeafe; n. murder
Quell'er, n. one who crufhes or fubdues
Quel'quechofe, n. a trifle, mere trifle, kickfhaw
Quench, v.t. quenched, quencht, pret. and pa. to extinguifh, cool, allay, deftroy
Quench'able, a. that may be quenched or cooled
Quench'er, n. one who or that which quenches
Quench'lefs, a. that cannot be extinguifhed
Quer'citron, n. the yellow oak of America
Quer'ele, n. a complaint made to a court, a writ
Querimónious, a. complaining, making moan
Querimónioufly, ad. with complaint or moan
Quérift, n. an inquirer, an afker of queftions
Quern or Querns, n. a handmill, a churn
Querp'o, n. a drefs clofe to the body, a waiftcoat
Quer'ulous, a. habitually complaining, mournful
Quer'uloufly, ad. by way of complaint
Quer'uloufnefs, n. a complaining mournfully
Quéry, n. a queftion, a doubt put to be cleared up
Quéry, v.t. to put or afk queftions, to doubt of
Queft, n. a fearch, [empannelled jury, requeft, ob.]
Queft'ant, Queft'rift, n. a feeker, inquirer, ob.
Queft'ion, n. an interrogatory, inquiry, doubt
Queft'ion, v.t. to afk, inquire, examin, doubt
Queft'ionable, a. doubtful, difputable, fufpicious
Queft'ionary, a. afking queftions, inquiring
Queft'ionlefs, ad. without doubt or controverfy
Queft'man, n. a ftater of lawfuits, inquirer, officer
Queft'or, n. an officer, a Roman public treafurer
Queft'orfhip, n. the office of a Roman treafurer
Queft'uary, a. ftudious of profit, greedy, ob.
Quib, n. a farcafm, gibe, taunt (a pun
Quib'ble, v.i. to equivocate, to pun; n. an evafion,
Quib'bler, n. an equivocator, fhuffler, punfter
Quick, a. fwift, active, ready, living; ad. readily
Quick, n. any fenfible part, living flefh, a plant
Quick'en, v. to make or become alive, to haften
Quick'ener, n. who or what quickens or haftens
Quick'lime, n. lime unquenched or unflaked
Quick'ly, ad. nimbly, fpeedily, foon, immediately
Quick'nefs, n. fpeed, brifknefs, readinefs, pungency
Quick'fand, n. a finking or fhaking fand
Quick'fet, n. a thorn-plant fet to grow
Quick'fighted, a. having a fharp fight, keen
Quick'fightednefs, n. fharpnefs of fight
Quick'filver, n. a white fluid mineral, mercury
Quick'filvered, a. overlaid with quickfilver
Quid'dity, n. the effence, a trifling nicety, a cavil
Quid pro quo, in law, a confideration or equivalent
Quief'cence or Quief'cency, n. quiet, reft, repofe

Quies'cent, *a.* quiet, ftill, refting, lying in repofe
Quiet, *a.* ftill, calm, eafy, unmolefted, fafe
Quiet, *n.* reft, repofe, tranquility, eafe, fecurity
Quiet, *v. t.* to ftill, calm, pacify, lull, put to reft
Quietifm, *n.* the opinion of the Quietifts, quiet
Quietift, *n.* one who places religion in quiet
Quietly, *ad.* calmly, peaceably, gently, fecurely
Quietnefs, Quietude, *n.* calm, reft, repofe
Quiétus, *n.* a full difcharge, anfwer, reft, death
Quill, *n.* the hard and ftrong fether of the wing
Quill'et, *n.* a fubtility, nicety, quibble (together
Quilt, *n.* the cover of a bed ; *v. t.* to few two cloths
Quinary, *a.* confifting of or relating to five
Quince, *n.* the name of a tree or its fruit
Quin'cunx, *n.* a fort of plantation, order, five
    twelfths of any thing (gles
Quindec'agon, *n.* a figure with 15 fides and 15 an-
Quinde"cemvirs, *n.* fifteen officers in Rome who
    prefided over facrifices
Quindecem'virate, *n.* the office of fifteen
Quinquages'ima, *n.* a name of Shrove-funday
Quinquan"gular, *a.* having five corners or fides
Quinquartic'ular, *a.* confifting of five articles
Quinquecap'fular, *a.* having five capfules
Quinquedent'ate, *a.* divided into five fegments
Quinquefárious, *a.* opening into five parts
Quin'quefid, *a.* divided into five parts (ments
Quin'quelobe, *a.* having five lobes, or convex feg-
Quinqueloc'ular, *a.* having five cells for feeds
Quinquepar'tite, *a.* divided into five parts (valves
Quinquevalv'ular, Quin'quevalve, *a.* having five
Quin'quevirs, *n.* five priefts in Rome who facrifi-
    ced to the dead
Quinquen'nial, *a.* lafting or happening in 5 years
Quin'fy, *n.* a very dangerous difeafe in the throat
Quint, *n.* a fequence of five ufed at piquet
Quint'ain or Quint'in, *n.* a poft with a turning top
Quint'al, *n.* a hundred pounds, a kentle
Quintes'sence, *n.* the virtue of any thing extracted
Quinteffen'tial, *a.* confifting of the quinteffence
Quin'tile, *n.* the afpect of planets diftant 72 de-
    grees or a fifth part of a circle
Quint'uple, *a.* fivefold, told or holding five times
Quip, *v. t.* to rally ; *n.* a carcafm, gibe, fharp jeft, *ob.*
Quire, *n.* a body of fingers, twenty-four fheets
Quire, *v. i.* to fing in concert or in a body
Quir'ifter, *n.* one who fings in concert, a chorifter
Quirk, *n.* a fubtilty, nicety, quibble, light tune
Quir'pel, *n.* the Indian ferret, an animal of the
    weefel kind
Quit, *v. t.* quit, quitted, *pret.* quit, quitted, *pa.* to
    leave, remove, difcharge, give up
Quit'claim, *n.* a releafe of claim by deed (deed
Quit'claim, *v. t.* to releafe a claim to an eftate by
Quite, *ad.* complete!y, entirely ; *v. t.* to repay
Quit'rent, *n.* a fmall rent referved to manors
Quits, *ad.* quite even in bets, upon equal terms
Quit'tance, *n.* a difcharge from a debt, a receipt, *ob.*
Quit'tance, *v. t.* to repay, return, requite, *ob.*

Quiv'er, *n.* a cafe for arrows ; [*a.* nimble, active, *ob.*
Quiv'er, *v. t.* to fhake, tremble, fhiver, fhudder
Quiv'ered, *a.* fheathed in or having a quiver
Quob, *v. i.* to move as an embryo, *not ufed*
Quod'libet, *n.* a fubtility, nice point, quirk, pun
Queif, *v. t.* to drefs with a headdrefs, to cap
Queif, Qeoif'fure, *n.* a kind of headdrefs, a cap
Quoin, *n.* a corner, wedge, warlike inftrument
Quoit, *n.* a kind of horfefhoe to pitch at a mark
Quoit, *v.* to play at quoits, throw, caft, pitch
Quoll, *n.* an animal like the polecat in N. Holland
Quon'dam, *a.* having been formerly, former, old
Quórum, *n.* a fpecial commiffion of juftices, the
    number of members of a council or corporation
    required to tranfact bufinefs
Quóta, *n.* a fhare, rate, proportion, part, fum
Quotátion, *n.* a citation, paffage quoted, paffage
Quote, *v. t.* to cite or recite the words of another
Quóter, *n.* one who quotes or cites from another
Quoth, *verb. imperf.* for *fay* or *faid*
Quotid'ian, *n.* daily, happening every day
Quotid'ian, *n.* a fever which returns every day
Quótient, *n.* the number arifing from a divifion
Quur'batos, *n.* a bird in Africa like the king-fifher

R

R Abáte, *v. i.* to recover a hawk to the fift
    Rabáto, *n.* a kind of ruff for the neck, *ob.*
Rab'bet, *n.* a joint in carpentry, groove, cut
Rab'bet, *v. i.* to make a rabbet-joint, join, pare
Rab'bi or Rab'bin, *n.* a Jewifh doctor
Rabbin'ical, *a.* relating to Rabbins, fabulous, ob-
Rab'binite, *n.* a follower of the Rabbins (fcure
Rab'bit, *n.* a fmall quadruped well known
Rab'ble, *n.* an affembly of low people, a crowd
Rabdol'ogy, *n.* a method of performing mathe-
    matical operations by little fquare rods
Raccoon', *n.* a quadruped valued for its fur
Race, *n.* a running match, family, generation, fet,
    progrefs, train, root, tafte, a ftrong current
Race, *v. i.* to run or contend in a race, to run
Rácehorfe, *n.* a horfe bred to run for prizes
Racemátion, *n.* a formation of clufters, a clufter
Ra"ceme, *n.* a clufter or bunch of berries, a pedun-
    cle with fhort branches
Ra"cemous, *a.* in bunches, full of bunches
Rácer, *n.* a runner, a man who runs a racehorfe
Ráceginger, *n.* ginger in the root
Rácinefs, *n.* a racy ftate or quality, roughnefs
Rack, *n.* an engine for torture, extreme pain, a
    frame for hay or bottles, kind of diftaff, pace, a
    fpirituous liquor
Rack, *v. t.* to torture, torment, fcrew, draw off
Rack'et, *n.* a noife, a thing to ftrike a tennis-ball
Rack'rent, *n.* a rent raifed to the utmoft value
Rack'renter, *n.* one who pays to the utmoft rent
Rácy, *a.* ftrong, retaining flavor, rough, rich
Rádial, *a.* pertaining to the radius, or fore arm
Rádiance or Rádiancy, *n.* a fparkling lufter
Rádiant, *a.* emitting rays, fhining, fparkling

Rádiate, v. i. to emit rays, fhine, fparkle, fhoot
Rádiated, a. adorned with or having rays
Rádiated, Rádiate, flower, is one whofe florets of
the difk are tubular, and thofe of the radius li-
gulate
Radiátion, n. an emiffion of rays, a beamy lufter
Rad'ical, a. original, implanted by nature, inborn
Rad'ical, n. a radical word, root, primary element
Radical'ity, n. a radical ftate or quality (or bafe
Rad'ically, ad. originally, primitively, by nature
Rad'icant, a. rooting, taking root
Rad'icate, Rad'ical, a. proceeding from the root
Rad'icate, v. to root, take root, plant deeply
Radicátion, n. the act of fixing deeply or firmly
Radicátion, n. the difpofition of the roots of a plant
Rad'icle, n. the germ of the root in plants
Radiom'eter, n. the foreftaff, an inftrument for
taking the altitude of celeftial bodies
Rad'difh, n. the name of a well known root
Rádius, a line, the femidiameter of a circle, the
ligulate margin of a compound flower, a bone
of the fore arm
Raff, v. to fweep, fnatch, take haftily, huddle up
Raf'fle, v. i. to caft dice for a prize, rifk, put in
Raf'fle, n. a lottery by cafting dice for prizes
Raft, n. a float of wood; a. bereft, deprived, rent
Raft'er, n. a fecondary roof-timber of a houfe
Raft'ered, a. built or furnifhed with rafters
Rag, n. a worn-out piece of cloth, ftone, herd
Ragamuff'in, n. a paltry mean fellow, a wretch
Rage, n. violent anger, fury, paffion, great heat
Rage, v. i. to be in a fury, fume, ravage, cheat
Rágeful, a. furious, violent, very hot, enraged
Rágg, n. a fpecies of trap or ferrilite
Rag'ged, a. dreffed in rags, mean, rent, rugged
Rag'gednefs, n. a ragged ftate, great poverty
Rágingly, ad. in a raging manner, furioufly, hotly
Rag'man, n. a dealer in rags, madnefs,
Ragoó, Ragoút, n. a high feafoned ftewed meat
Rag'ftone, n. a ftone to fmooth the edge of a tool
Rag'wort, n. nip, an ill fmelling plant
Rail, n. a narrow piece of wood or iron, fupported
by pofts, a genus of birds
Rail, v. t. to inclofe with rails, infult, abufe
Ráiler, n. one who rails or ufes bad language
Ráillery, Ral'lery, n. fatirical mirth, flight fatire
Ráiment, n. drefs, vefture, clothes, garments, at-
Rain, n. water falling from the clouds (tire
Rain, v. i. to fall as rain, to drop from the clouds
Ráinbow, n. a various colored arch in the clouds
Ráindeer, n. a large ferviceable deer, fee rane
Ráininefs, n. a rainy ftate, wetnefs, wet weather
Ráinwater, n. a water arifing or had from rain
Ráiny, a. tending or apt to rain, fhowery, wet
Raife, v. t. to lift, fet, ftir up, erect, levy, collect
Ráifer, n. one who raifes, what ferves to raife up
Ráifin, n. a kind of dried fruit, a dried grape
Rájah, n. a native Hindoo prince in India
Rake, n. a kind of tool with teeth, a loofe man

Rake, v. to gather or clear with a rake, fearch
eagerly, fcour, pafs with violence, cover, get
Rákehell, n. a very debauched fellow, a wretch
Ráker, n. one who rakes, a kind of fcavenger
Rákifh, a. loofe, debauched, lewd, thoughtlefs
Rákifhnefs, n. a rakifh difpofition or behavior
Ral'ly, v. to chide in a facetious manner, ridicule,
banter, reunite difordered troops, put in order
Ral'lery, n. banter, a laughing at one in good humor
Ram, n. a male fheep, a tool to batter walls with
Ram, v. t. to drive with violence, to fill clofe
Ram'ble, n. a wandering excurfion, journey, walk
Ram'ble, v. i. to rove, ftroll, wander, walk
Ram'bler, n. one who rambles about, a rover
Ram'bling, n. the act of rambling, a wandering
Ramificátion, n. a branching or fpreading out, the
manner of branching in plants
Ram'ify, v. t. to feparate or part into branches
Ram'mer, n. a ftick to force the charge into a gun
Ram'mifh, a. fmelling ftrong, rank, offenfive
Ram'mifhnefs, n. a rammifh ftate or quality
Ramoon', n. an American tree
Rámous, Ramófe, Rámeous, a. full of branches
Ramp, v. i. to climb, gambol, frifk, fee romp
Ramp, n. a leap, fpring, arch, romp
Ram'pancy, n. exuberance of growth or action
Ramp'ant, a. wanton, frifky, exuberant, ready to
Ramp'art, n. a wall round fortified places (attack
Ramp'art, Ramp'ire, v. t. to fortify with ramparts,
Ramp'ion, n. a plant of various kinds (ob.
Ram'fons, n. a plant, a fpecies of allium
Ran, pret. of to run
Ranch, v. t. to fprain, force open, injure, ob.
Ran'cid, a. ftrong fcented, ftinking, mufty
Ran'cidnefs, Rancid'ity, n. a rancid quality
Ranc'or, n. malignity, hatred, fpite, virulence
Ranc'orous, a. malignant, moft or very fpitefu
Rand, n. the border or feam of a fhoe
Rand'om, a. done by chance; ad. without aim
Rand'om, n. the want of direction, hazard, chance,
range (vated above a horizontal direction
Rand'omfhot, a. fhot with the axis of a gun ele-
Ráne, n. a fpecies of deer in the north of Europe,
Afia and America, improperly called reindeer
Rang, pret. of to ring (extent, diftance, compafs
Range, n. a rank, excurfion, path, kitchen-grate,
Range, v. to place in order, wander, rove
Ran'ger, n. one who ranges, a foldier, a dog
Ran'ging, n. the act of placing in order
Rank, a. ftrong fcented, ftrong, luxuriant, full
Rank, n. a line of men, row, range of fubordina-
tion, degree of dignity, clafs, order, place
Rank, v. to place in a row, fet, range, be ranged
Ran'kle, v. i. to fefter, corrupt, be inflamed
Rank'ly, ad. offenfively, coarfely, grofsly
Rank'nefs, n. a rank fmell, exuberant growth
Rans'ack, v. t. to fearch narrowly, to plunder
Rans'om, n. a price paid for liberty; v. t. to redeem
Rans'omlefs, a. free or exempt from ranfom

Rant, _n._ an extravagant flight of words, a noise
Rant, _v. i._ to rave or talk violently, roar, rage
Rant'er, _n._ one who rants, a very noisy person
Rant'ipole, _n._ a giddy, roving, talkative person, _ob._
Rant'ipole, _v. i._ to run about wildly; _a._ giddy, _ob._
Ranunc'ulus, _n._ a fine flower, the crowfoot
Rap, _n._ a quick and smart blow, a sudden knock
Rap, _v. i._ to strike smartly, batter, enrapture
Rapacious, _a._ seizing by violence, very greedy
Rapáciously, _ad._ ravenously, greedily
Rapácioufnefs, Rapa''city, _n._ ravenoufnefs
Rape, _n._ a violent defloration, a carrying away, a
Rap'id, _a._ swift, quick, violent, strong   (plant
Rapid'ity, Rap'idnefs, _n._ swiftnefs, quicknefs
Rap'idly, _ad._ swiftly, with a quick motion
Rap'ids, _n. pl._ a part of a river where the water is
   rapid over a moderate descent·
Rápier, _n._ a small sword used only in thrusting
Rap'il, Rapil'lo, _n._ pulverized volcanic subfances
Rap'ine, _n._ plunder, pillage, violence, open force
Rappeé, _n._ a coarse kind of snuff
Rap'ping, _n._ a striking with a quick smart blow
Rappórt, _n._ a relation, reference, proportion, _not_
Rap'fody, _fee_ Rhapfody   (_uſed_
Rapt, _a._ carried away in ecftacy
Rapt, Rapt'ure, _v. i._ to put in ecftacy, to ravish
Rapt'ure, _n._ ecftacy, transport, rapidity, hafte
Rapt'ured, _pa._ ravished, mad spoiler, delighted
Rapt'urous, _a._ ecftatic, transporting, delightful
Rare, _a._ uncommon, scarce, fine, thin, raw
Ráreefhow, _n._ a show that is carried in a box
Rarefac'tion, _n._ expanfion of the parts of a body
Rarefac'tive, _a._ tending or able to rarefy
Rárefiable, _a._ that is capable of rarefaction
Rúrefy, _v._ to make or become thin, expand, dilate
Rárely, _ad._ feldom, finely, nicely, accurately
Rárenefs, Rárity, _n._ uncommonnefs, fcarcity
Ráreripe, _a._ early ripe; _n._ an early fruit
Rafc'al, _n._ a villain, fcoundrel, mean or bad fellow
Rafcal'ion, _n._ a very low wretch
Rafcal'ity, _n._ villany, the loweft of the people
Rafc'ally, _a._ mean, worthlefs, vile, dishoneft
Rafe, _v. t._ to erase, blot out, ruin, deftroy, fkim
Rafh, _a._ precipitate, hafty; _n._ an eruption, fatin
Rafh'er, _n._ a thin flice of bacon, a very thin cut
Rafh'ly, _ad._ haftily, violently, without thought
Rafh'nefs, _n._ haftinefs, inconfiderate warmth
Rafp, _n._ a berry, a rough file for bread, wood, &c.
Rafp, _v. t._ to rub or file with a rafp, to clean off
Rafp'atory, _n._ a little rafp, a furgeon's rafp·
Rafp'berry, _n._ a fpecies of bramble and its fruit
Ráfure, _n._ the act of fcraping out, a dafh, a blot
Rat, _n._ a very fierce animal of the moufe kind
Rátable, _a._ that may be put at a certain value, lia-
   ble to be taxed.
Rátably, _ad._ at a certain rate, proportionably
Ratafi'a, _n._ a kind of liquor, a delicious cordial
Ratan', _n._ a kind of ftick, a fmall Indian cane
Rat'catcher, _n._ one who goes about to catch rats·

Ratch, _n._ a wheel in clocks with 12 fangs to lift
   the detents, and make the clock ftrike
Ratch'et, _n._ a tooth at the bottom of the fufec or
   barrel of a watch to ftop it in winding up
Ratch'il, _n._ among miners, fragments of ftone
Rate, _n._ a price, value, proportion, tax, way, or-
   der or clafs in a navy, as a firft rate fhip
Rate, _v. t._ to value, tax, fcold, chide, reprove
Ratel', _n._ an animal of the weefel kind, the fitzler
Rath, _a._ early, coming before the time, _ob._
Rath'er, _ad._ more willingly, efpecially, chiefly
Ratification, _n._ the act of ratifying, confirmation
Rat'ifier, _n._ one who ratifies, one who confirms
Rat'ify, _v. t._ to confirm, fettle, eftablifh, fix·
Rátio, _n._ a proportion, rate, relation, regard
Ratiocination, _n._ the act of reafoning, a debate, a
   deducing of confequences   (gularly
Ratio''cinative, _a._ argumentative, advancing re-
Ration, _n._ an allowance of provifions to men in
   naval or land fervice, confifting of meat, drink,
   &c. for one day
Ra'tional, _a._ agreeable to reafon, having reafon
Ra'tionalift, _n._ one who acts wholly upon reafon
Rationality, _n._ the power of reafoning, reafonable-
Ra'tionally, _ad._ reafonably, with reafon   (nefs
Rat'lings, _n._ the fmall cords of fhrouds forming a
Rats'bane, _n._ a poifon for rats, arfenic   (ladder
Rattéen, _n._ a thick woollen ftuff twilled·
Rattinet', _n._ a twifted ftuff thinner than ratteen
Rat'tle, _v._ to make a noife, clatter, rail, fcold
Rat'tle, _n._ a quick noife, loud empty talk, talka-
   tive perfon, child's plaything, herb
Rat'tleheaded, _a._ noify, talkative, giddy, unfteady
Rat'tlefnake, _n._ a very dangerous kind of ferpent
Ratoon', _n._ a fhoot from the root or ftole of the
   fugar cane
Ratoon' _v. i._ to put forth ratoons, [W. Indies]
Rau''city, _n._ hoarfenefs, a loud and harfh noife
Raught, _a._ reached, fnatched, fnapped, rent, _ob·_
Rav'age, _v. t._ to fpoil, pillage, plunder, lay wafte
Rav'age, _n._ fpoil, plunder, wafte, ruin, havoc
Rav'ager, _n._ a mad fpoiler, plunderer, deftroyer
Rave, _v. i._ to be mad, rage, dote, be very fond of
Rave, _n._ the upper fide timber of the body of a cart
Rav'el, _v. t._ to difentangle, untwift, unweave
Rav'elin, _n._ a kind of half-moon in fortification
Ráven, _n._ a carrion-fowl; _v. t._ to devour greedily
Rávenfifh, _n._ a fifh with a mouth like a bird
Rav'enous, _a._ voracious, raging, very hungry
Rav'enoufly, _ad._ with raging voracity, greedily
Rav'enoufnefs, _n._ a furious or very great voracity
Ráven'sduck, _n._ a fpecies of thin duck for light fails
Rav'in, _n._ prey, plunder, pillage, rapacioufnefs, a
   hollow, deep and long
Rávingly, _ad._ with frenzy, with or in diftraction
Rav'ifh, _v. t._ to violate chaftity, take by force,
Rav'ifher, _n._ a perfon who ravifhes   [tranfport
Rav'ifhment, _n._ the act of ravifhing, tranfport
Raw, _a._ unfubdued by fire, chill, fore, ignorant

Raw'boned, *a.* having large bones with little flesh
Raw'head, *n.* a word of terror used to children
Raw'ly, *ad.* in a raw manner, sorely, newly
Raw'nefs, *n.* a raw ftate, unfkilfulnefs, novelty
Ray, *n.* a beam of light, line, fifh, herb, leaf
Ray, *v. t.* to ftreak, mark with long lines, adorn
Raze, *n.* a head or whole root of ginger
Raze, *v. t.* to overthrow, deftroy, ruin, efface
Razor, *n.* a tool to fhave the beard with
Razorbill, *n.* a water-fowl, a fpecies of duck
Razorfifh, *n.* a fifh with a compreffed body
Razure, *n.* the act of erafing, a fcratch, a mark
Re, *in compofition, indicates repetition*
Reabforb', *v. t.* to abforb what has been fecreted
Reabforp'tion, *n.* the act of abforbing a fecond time
Reaccefs', *n.* a vifit renewed, a readmiffion
Reach, *v.* to hold out, extend, arrive at, vomit
Reach, *n.* power, ability, extent, fetch, fcheme
Reach', *v. t.* to return an impulfe, repel, refift
Reac'tion, *n.* the reciprocation of an impulfe
Read, *v.* read, *pret,* read, *pa.* to perufe, difcover, perceive, learn fully
Read, *pa.* perufed, learned from reading, feen
Readep'tion, *n.* the act of regaining, a recovery, *ob.*
Reader, *n.* a perfon who reads, a ftudious perfon
Readerfhip, *n.* the office of reading prayers
Read'ily, *ad.* with fpeed, without delay, eafily
Read'inefs, *n.* a being ready, ftate of preparation, freedom from obftruction, willingnefs, will
Reading, *n.* ftudy, a lecture, a variation of copies
Readmis''fion, *n.* the act of admitting again
Readmit', *v. t.* to admit again, to let in again
Readorn', *v. t.* to adorn anew, to deck anew
Read'y, *a.* prepared, willing, near; *ad.* readily
Reaffirm'ance, *n.* a fecond or frefh affirmation
Reagent, *n.* a fubftance employed to precipitate another in a folution, or detect the ingredients of a mixture
Real, *a.* true, certain, fure, genuine, immoveable
Real'gar, *n.* red fulphuret of arfenic, *ob.*
Real'ity, *n.* truth, certainty, abfolute exiftence
Realize, *v. t.* to bring into being or act, to fave
Realization, *n.* the act of realizing
Really, *ad.* truly, certainly, actually, verily
Realm, *n.* a ftate, kingdom, kingly government
Realty, *n.* the condition of freehold or *real* eftate, oppofed to *perfonal,* [in the fenfe of loyalty, *ob.*]
Ream, *n.* the quantity of twenty quires of paper
Rean'imate, *v. t.* to reftore back to life, to revive
Reanimation, *n.* a reftoring to life, renewal of fpirits
Reannex', *v. t.* to annex again, to join again
Reap, *v. t.* to cut down grain, gather, obtain, get
Reaper, *n.* one who reaps, one who gathers
Reapinghook, *n.* a hook ufed to reap with
Reapply, *v. t.* to apply again
Reapplication, *n.* a fecond application
Rear, *n.* a hinder troop, laft clafs; *a.* raw, early
Rear, *v. t.* to raife or move up, elevate, roufe, ftir up, bring to maturity, educate, inftruct

Rearad'miral, *n.* an admiral of the third divifion
Rearmoufe, Raremoufe, *n.* a bat [a defenfe
Rearward, *ad.* towards the end or tail; *n.* the rear,
Reafcend', *v. t.* to claim, mount or go up again
Reafon, *n.* the faculty of thinking, a caufe, motive, propriety, juftice, moderation
Reafon, *v.* to argue or examin rationally
Reafonable, *a.* endued with reafon, rational, juft
Reafonablenefs, *n.* reafon, propriety, moderation
Reafonably, *ad.* agreeable to reafon, moderately
Reafoner, *n.* one who reafons, one who argues
Reafoning, *n.* an act of reafon, an argument
Reafonlefs, *a.* void of reafon, foolifh, abfurd
Reaffem'ble, *v. t.* to affemble or collect again
Reaffert', *v. t.* to affert again, to affirm again
Reaffim'ilate, *v. t.* to make to refemble again
Reaffimilation, *n.* a fecond affimilation
Reaffume, *v. t.* to refume, retake, take again
Reaffump'tion, *n.* the act of reaffuming
Reaffure, *v. t.* to affure or promife again
Reaffurance, *n.* a fecond infurance of property before infured
Reave, *v. t.* to take by ftealth or violence, *ob.*
Rebaptize, *v. i.* to baptize again [baptifm
Rebaptization, *n.* a repetition of baptifm, a fecond
Rebate, *v. t.* to blunt, deprive of keennefs, leffen
Rebate, Rebatement, *n.* difcount for pay in hand
Rebec, *n.* a fiddle of three ftrings
Reb'el, *n.* one who oppofes lawful authority
Rebel', *v.* to oppofe lawful authority, to revolt
Rebel'ler, *n.* one who rebels, one who oppofes
Rebel'lion, *n.* oppofition to lawful authority
Rebel'lious, *a.* oppofing lawful authority, vile
Rebel'liously, *ad.* by way of rebellion
Rebel'low, *v. i.* to bellow in return, to echo back
Reblofs'om, *v. i.* to bloffom again, to bud afrefh
Rebound', *v. i.* to fpring or fly back, reverberate,
Rebound, *n.* the act of flying back (recoil
Rebuff', *n.* a denial, quick and fudden refiftance
Rebuff', *v.* to beat back, repel, oppofe, difcourage
Rebuild, *v. t.* rebuilded, rebuilt, *pret.* rebuilt, *pa.* to build over again, renew, repair
Rebukable, *a.* deferving of rebuke or reproof
Rebuke, *v. t.* to reprove for a fault, *n.* a reproof
Rebuker, *n.* one who rebukes, one who reproves
Rebus, *n.* a kind of riddle, a ridiculous picture
Rebut', *v. t.* to drive back, oppofe or repel, reply to a furrejoinder [that which repels
Rebut'ter, *n.* defendants anfwer to a furrejoinder,
Recall', *n.* the act of calling over or back again
Recall', *v. t.* to call back, call home, revoke
Recant', *v. t.* to retract an opinion, to recall
Recantation, *n.* the act of retracting an opinion
Recant'er, *n.* one who recants or retracts
Recapit'ulate, *v. t.* to repeat again diftinctly
Recapitulation, *n.* a diftinct repetition, a detail
Recap'tion, *n.* a fecond feizure or diftrefs [taken
Recap'tor, *n.* one who retakes, what was before
Recap'ture, *n.* a taking of what has been taken before

Recap'ture, v. t. to take what has been before taken

Recar'ry, v. t. to carry back, to carry again

Recéde, v. i. give back, depart, retreat, defift

Recéipt, n. a reception, admiffion, acquittance

Reoéipt, v. t. to give a receipt for

Recéivable, a. capable of being received

Recéive, v. t. to take, get, admit, hold, entertain

Recéived, pa. taken, admitted, allowed, held

Recéiver, n. one who receives, a partaker with a thief, a veffel which receives the product of diftillation, &c.

Recel'ebrate, v. t. to celebrate again

Récency, n. a new ftate, newnefs, latenefs

Recen'fion, n. an enumeration, review, clofe view

Récent, a. new, frefh, late, not long paffed

Récently, ad. newly, frefhly, lately, juft now

Récentefs, n. newnefs, frefhnefs, latenefs

Recep'tacle, n. a place to receive things in, the bafe which fupports the fructification of a plant

Receptac'ular, a. pertaining to the receptacle, growing on it, as the nectary of a plant

Receptibil'ity, n. a poffibility of receiving

Recep'tion, n. the act of receiving, treatment

Recep'tive, a. capable of receiving, fit to receive

Recep'tory, a. generally received or admitted

Recefs', n. a retirement, retreat, fecret place

Reces"fion, n. the act of retreating or departing, the act of ceding back

Rechange, v. t. to change again, to pay twice

Recharge', v. t. to attack anew, to accufe in return

Rechéat, n. a calling hounds off a wrong fcent

Recidivate, a. a backfliding, a relapfe, ob.

Re"cipe, n. a medical bill, prefcription, receipt

Recip'ient, n. a receiver, a veffel ufed to receive

Recip'rocal, a. alternate, mutual, inverfe, equal

Recip'rocally, ad. mutually, interchangeably

Recip'rocalnefs, Recipro"city, n. a mutual return

Recip'rocate, v. i. to act mutually or by turns

Reciprocátion, n. an alteration, a return

Reci"fion, n. a cutting off, a making void   [tion

Recítal, Recitátion, Recíte, n. rehearfal, repetition

Recit'ative or Recitativo, n. a mufical fpeaking

Recíte, v. t. to rehearfe, repeat, fay, enumerate

Recíter, n. one who recites, one who repeats

Reck, v. to regard, mind, heed, care, value, ob.

Reck'lefs, a. heedlefs, carelefs, unmoved, hard, ob.

Reck'leffnefs, n. careleffnefs, negligence, ob.

Reck'on, v. t. to count, number, compute, calculate, caft, efteem, depend

Reck'oner, n. one who reckons, one who fettles

Reck'oning, n. a computation, fhot, eftimation, account of a fhips courfe

Recláim, v. to reform, correct, recall, cry out

Reclamátion, n. a reclaiming, reformation, cry

Reclinátion, n. a bearing backward from an upright pofition

Reclíne, v. i. to lean fideways or back, to reft

Reclíne or Reclíned, a. fet in a leaning pofture

Rec'linate, a. reclined, bending down

Reclinátion, n. an inclining

Reclófe, v. t. to clofe again, to clofe up anew

Reclúde, v. t. to open, unlock, unbar, ob.

Reclúfe, a. fhut up, retired, religious, devout

Reclúfe, n. one fhut up or retired, a devout perfon

Recoagulátion, n. a fecond coagulation

Recogni"tion, n. an acknowledgment, a review

Recog'nizance, n. a bond of record, token, badge

Recog'nize, v. t. to acknowledge, to recollect

Recog'nized, pa. acknowledged, bound by record

Recoil', v. i. to rufh or fall back, fail, fhrink

Recoil', n. a rebound, return, motion backward

Recoin', v. t. to coin over again or afrefh

Recoin'age, n. the act of coining over again

Recollect', v. t. to recover in the memory, to bethink, call to mind, gather again

Recollec'tion, n. a recovery of notion, memory

Recombine, v. t. to combine or form again

Recombina'tion, n. a fecond combination

Recom'fort, v. to comfort again, to give ftrength

Recommence', v. t. to begin again or afrefh

Recommence'ment, n. the act of beginning again

Recommend', v. t. to commend to another

Recommend'able, a. worthy of recommendation

Recommendátion, n. the act of recommending

Recommend'atory, a. tending to recommend

Recommend'er, n. a perfon who recommends

Recommis'fion, v. t. to commiffion a fecond time.

Recommit', v. t. to commit anew, to fend back

Recommit'ment, n. a fecond commitment

Recommu'nicate, v. t. to communicate again

Rec'ompenfe, n. a compenfation, an equivalent

Rec'ompenfe, v. t. to repay, pay, requite, redeem

Recompílement, n. a new or frefh compilation

Recompófe, v. t. to quiet again, to fettle anew

Reconcíle, v. t. to make men or things agree

Reconcíleable, a. confiftent, capable of kindnefs

Reconcíleablenefs, n. a difpofition to love or friendfhip

Reconcílement, n. a reconciliation   (fhip

Reconcíler, n. a perfon who reconciles

Reconciliátion, n. a renewal of love, atonement

Reconcíliatory, a. able or tending to reconcile

Recondenfe', v. t. to condenfe anew or over again

Recon'dite, a. fecret, obftrufe, dark, profound

Recon'ditory, n. a ftorehoufe, repofitory, magazine

Reconduct', v. t. to conduct back or again

Reconjoin', v. t. to join over again or anew

Reconnoi'ter, v. t. to furvey, view, examin

Recon"quer, v. t. to conquer again, to beat afrefh

Recons'ecrate, v. t. to confecrate again or afrefh

Reconfíder, v. t. to review, confider again

Reconfiderátion, n. a fecond view or confideration

Reconvert, v. t. to convert again

Reconver'fion, n. a fecond converfion

Reconvéne, v. t. to convene or affemble anew

Reconvey', v. t, to convey or fend back again

Record', v. t. to regifter folemnly, enrol, celebrate

Rec'ord, n. a regifter, authentic enrolment, proof

Recordátion, n. a remembrance, memory, ob.

Record'er, n. one who records, a law officer, a lute

Recouch', v. i. to lie down again, to sleep afresh

Recov'er, [o as u] v. to grow well, get again, regain

Recov'erable, a. that may be restored or regained

Recov'ery, n. a restoration from sickness, a deed

Récount', v. t. to relate, describe, tell distinctly

Recount'ment, n. relation, recital, account

Recöurse, n. access, application for help, return

Rec'reant, a. cowardly, meanspirited, false, base

Rec'reant, n, a false wretch, apostate, miser

Rec'reate, v. t. to amuse, delight, refresh, revive

Recreätion, n. amusement, diversion, relief, ease

Rec'reative, a. amusing, diverting, refreshing

Rec'rement, n. dross, filth, refuse, useless parts

Recrement'al, Recrementi''tious, a. drossy

Recrim'inate, v. i. to return an accusation

Recriminätion, n. an accusation retorted back

Recrim'inator, n. one who retorts a charge

Recrudes'cent, a. growing painful or bad again

Recruit', v. t. to repair, replace, supply, fill up

Recruit', n. a new inlisted soldier, a new supply

Red'angle, n. a figure with angles of 90 degrees

Rectan''gular, a. having one or more right angles

Rectan''gularly, ad. in a rectangular manner

Rect'ifiable, a. that is capable to be set right

Rectificätion, n. the act or art of setting right, purification by distilling or subliming

Rect'ifier, n. one who rectifies or sets right

Rect'ify, v. t. to make right, correct, measure, purify by distillation or sublimation

Rectilin'ear, a. consisting of right lines

Rect'itude, n. straitness, uprightness, integrity

Rect'or, n. a minister of a parish, ruler, president

Rectörial, a. belonging to a rector

Rect'orship, n. the office or rank of a rector

Rect'ory, n. a kind of church living

Recubation, Recum'bency, n. a lying down, repose

Recum'bent, a. lying down or along, leaning

Recur', v. i. to have recourse, return, arise

Recüre, v. t. to recover, n. a cure, a recovery

Recur'rence, Recur'rency, Recur'sion, n. a return

Recur'rent, a. returning, running back

Recur'rent, n. a branch of nerves faom the thorax

Recurv'ate, a. bent downwards or outwards

Recurvätion, Recurv'ity, n. a bending back

Recurv'ous, a. bent or turned back, crooked

Recurv'iroster, n. a bird whose beak bends upwards

Recüsant, n. one who refuses to communicate

Recüse, v. to refuse, deny, reject, oppose, ob.

Red, n. a high or glaring color; a. like blood

Red'ans or Red'ant, n. saw-like or indented work in fortifications

Redar'gue, v. t. to refute, confute, disprove

Red'breast, a. a common small bird, a robin

Red'coat, n. a british soldier by way of contempt

Red'den, v. to make or grow red, blush, fume

Re'dient, a. returning, coming again

Red'dish, a. somewhat red, inclining to redness

Red'dishness, n. a tendency to redness

Reddi''tion, Rendi''tion, n. a surrender, a restitu-
tion

Red'ditive, a. answering to an interrogative (tion

Red'dle, n. a red calciform ore of iron, called also red chalk

Rede, n. counsel, advice, v. t. to advise, help, ob.

Redéem, v. t. to ransom, recover, rescue, save

Redéemable, a. that may or can be redeemed

Redéemer, n. one who ransoms, our Saviour

Redeliv'er, v. t. to deliver back, give back, restore

Redemand', v. t. to demand or ask back again

Redemp'tion, n. a ransom, release, purchase of God's favor by means of the death of Christ

Redemp'tioner, n. one who redeems himself by services, or whose services are sold to pay certain expenses

Redemp'tory, a. of or belonging to redemption

Redent'ed, a. formed with redents or saw work

Red'eye, n. a fish of a red color, especially the iris

Red'haired, a. having the hair of a red color, fiery

Redhot', a. very hot, heated to redness, violent

Redintégrate, a. renewed, restored, fresh, ob.

Redintégrate, v. t. to renew, restore, repair, ob.

Redintegrätion, n. a renovation, a restored state

Redisséisin, n. a second disseisin, a writ against a redisseisor

Redisséis'or, n. one who disseises a second time

Redis'solve, v. t. to dissolve a second time

Redlead', n. minium or red oxyd of lead, composed of 88 parts of lead and 12 of oxygene

Red'ness, n. the quality of being red, heat, fever

Red'olence or Red'olency, n. a very sweet scent

Red'olent, a. sweetscented, smelling fragrantly

Redoub'le, v. t. to make double, to repeat often

Redout', n. the outwork of a fortification

Redout'able, a. formidable, terrible to enemies

Redout'ed, a. dreaded, reverenced, awful

Reëound', v. i. to conduce, contribute, arise

Red'pole, n. a bird with a red head

Redress', v. t. to set right, correct, relieve, heal

Redress', n. reformation, relief, remedy, amends

Redress'ive, a. tending to redress, relieving

Red'shank, n. an aquatic fowl with reddish legs

Red'short, a. brittle when red hot

Red'start, n. a song bird of several species

Red'streak, n. a sort of apple and cider

Redüce, v. t. to lessen, lower, subdue, bring back

Redücement, n. the act of lessening or subduing

Redücer, n. one who reduces, one who lessens

Redücible, a. that is possible to be reduced

Reduc'tion, n. the act of reducing, a bringing back, of restoring or reviving of metals from a state the calx, a rule or art of bringing various denominations to one

Reduc'tive, a. tending or able to reduce

Reduc'tively, ad. by reduction, by consequence

Redun'dance or Redun'dancy, n. superfluity

Redun'dant, a. superabundant, superfluous, too full

Redun'dantly, ad. superabundantly, superfluously

Redüplicate, v. t. to double or fold over and over

Redupiiçâtion, *n.* the act of doubling often over
Redúplicative, *a.* doubling over, double, twofold
Red'wing, *n.* the wind thruſh, or ſwine pipe
Reech'o, [ch as k] *v. i.* to echo back, to ſend back
Reed, *n.* a plant, ſmall pipe, arrow, meaſure
Reed'ify, *v. t.* to rebuild, to build over again
Reedleſs, *a.* void of reeds, bare, naked, expoſed
Reedy, *a.* abounding with or having reeds
Reef, *v. t.* to draw in ſails, reduce, contract, fold
Reef, *n.* a part of a ſail rolled up, a chain of rocks
Reek, *n.* ſmoke, ſteam, a rick, *v. i.* to ſmoke
Reeky, Reechy, *a.* ſmoky, black, dark, tanned
Reel, *n.* a frame to wind yarn, &c. upon, a dance
Reel, *v.* to wind on a reel, ſtagger, ſlip, incline
Reelect', *v. t.* to elect again, to chooſe over again
Reelec'tion, *n.* a freſh election, a repeated choice
Reel'igible, *a.* capable of being elected again to the
 ſame office   (the ſame office
Reeligibil'ity, *n.* capacity of being again elected to
Reembark', *v. t.* to take ſhipping again, to ſhip
Reemit', *v. t.* to emit again   (again
Reenact', *v. t.* to enact again or anew
Reenac'tion, *n.* a ſecond paſſing of a law
Reenfórce, *v. t.* to ſend freſh forces, to recruit
Reenfórcement, *n.* a freſh ſupply, a recruit
Reenjoy', *v. t.* to enjoy over again or afreſh
Reen'ter, *v.* to enter again or anew, to return to
Reenthróne, *v. t.* to place again on a throne
Reen'trance, *n.* the act of entering again or anew
Reeſtab'liſh, *v. t.* to eſtabliſh or fix again
Reeſtab'liſhment, *n.* a reeſtabliſhing, a reſtoration
Reeve, *v. t.* to paſs the end of a rope thro a hole
Reeve or Reve, *n.* a ſteward, bailiff, aſſiſtant
Reexam'in, *v. t.* to examin over again or afreſh
Reexcíte, *v. t.* to renew excitement, excite again
Reexpórt, *v. t.* to export what has been imported
Reexportátion, *n.* the exportation of an import
Refect', *v. t.* to refreſh, repair, recruit, reſtore
Refec'tion, *n.* refreſhment, a repaſt, meal, food
Refect'ive, *a.* refreſhing ; *n.* a reſtorative (ment
Refect'ory, *a.* an eating-room, a place of refreſh-
Refel', *v. t.* to refute, diſprove, repreſs, *ob.*
Refer', *v.* to leave, ſend, direct, reſpect
Ref'erable, *a.* that may be referred
Referée, *n.* one to whom any thing is referred
Ref'erence, *n.* the act of referring, a relation, a
 hearing before referees
Referend'ary, *n.* a referee, an ancient officer
Referment', *v. t.* to ferment again or afreſh
Refer'rible, *a.* that may be conſidered by reference
Refi'ne, *v. t.* to clear from droſs, purify, improve
Refi'nedly, *ad.* with affected elegance, neatly
Refi'nement, *n.* a purifying, an improvement
Refi'ner, *n.* one who refines or clears, a purifier
Refi'nery, *n.* the place and apparatus of refining
Refit', *v. t.* to repair, mend, reſtore after damage
Reflect', *v.* to think, conſider, reproach, caſt back
Reflect'ent, *a.* bending back, flying back
Reflect'ible, *a.* capable of being turned back

Reflect'ing, *pa.* caſting back, conſidering
Reflec'tion, *n.* thought, conſideration, cenſure
Reflect'ive, *a.* conſidering things paſt, reflecting
Reflect'or, *n.* one who or that which reflects
Reflex, *n.* a reflection, *ob.*
Re'flex, *a.* directed backwards
Reflexibil'ity, *n.* a reflexible ſtate or quality
Reflex'ible, *a.* capable of being thrown back
Reflex'ity, *n.* capacity of being reflected
Reflex'ive, *a.* reſpecting ſomething paſt
Reflex'ively, *ad.* in a backward direction
Réfloat, *n.* a flowing back, reflux, ebb, turn
Reflores'cence, *n.* a flouriſhing or bloſſoming again
Reflour'iſh, *v. t.* to flouriſh anew
Reflów, *v. i.* to flow back, flow again, return
Refluctuation, *n.* a flowing back
Ref'luent, *a.* flowing or running back again
Réflux, *n.* a backward courſe of water, ebb of tide
Reform, *v. t.* to mend, amend, correct, reduce
Reform', *n.* a reformation, change, diſcharge
Reformátion, *n.* amendment of life or religion
Reform'er, *n.* one who makes a reformation
Refract', *v. t.* to break the courſe of rays (gle
Refract'ed, *a.* in botany, bent back to an acute an-
Refrac'tion, *n.* a variation of the rays of light from
 a direct courſe
Refract'ive, *a.* tending or able to refract
Refract'orineſs, *n.* a ſullen or wilful obſtinacy
Refract'ory, *a.* obſtinate, contumacious, perverſe,
 applied to metals, difficult to fuſe
Refráin, *v.* to hold back, forbear, abſtain
Refrangibil'ity, *n.* the capacity of being refracted
Refran'gible, *a.* capable of being refracted
Refreſh', *v. t.* to revive, cheer, repair, feed, cool
Refreſh'er, *n.* one who or that which refreſhes
Refreſh'ing, *pa.* giving ſpirits, renewing life
Refreſh'ment, *n.* food, nouriſhment, reſt, relief
Refri''gerant, *n.* a cooling medicin
Refri''gerant, *a.* cooling, refreſhing, cheering
Refri''gerate, *v. t.* to cool, allay, refreſh
Refrigerátion, *n.* the act of cooling, a cool ſtate
Refri''gerative, Refri''geratory, *a.* able to cool
Refri''gerátor, *n.* a veſſel for cooling, a cooler
Refri''geratory, *n.* any thing that cools, a veſſel for
 cooling diſtilled ſpirits
Reft, *pa.* taken away, deprived, *ob.*
Ref'uge, *v. t.* to protect, *n.* a ſhelter from danger
Refugée, *n.* one who flies or is driven from home
Reful'gence, *n.* great brightneſs, ſplendor, luſter
Reful'gent, *a.* very bright, ſplendid, glittering
Refund', *v. t.* to pour or pay back, repay, reſtore
Refúſal, *n.* the firſt right of choice, option, denial
Refuſe, *a.* worthleſs remains, *a.* worthleſs
Refúſe, *v. t.* not to accept of, to reject, to deny
Refúſer, *n.* one who refuſes, one who rejects
Refútable, *a.* capable of refutation, or diſproof
Refutátion, *n.* the act of refuting an aſſertion
Refúte, *v. t.* to prove falſe, diſprove, confute
Regáin, *v. t.* to get or find again, to recover

Régal, a. royal, kingly, n. an inſtrument, a feaſt
Regále, v. t. to refreſh, entertain, treat, gratify
Regálement, n. a refreſhment, an entertainment
Regália, n. pl. the enſigns or rights of royalty
Regal'ity, n. royalty, ſovereignty, grandeur, ſtate
Regard', v. t, to eſteem, reſpect, value, obſerve
Regard', n. eſteem, reſpect, attention, look, view
Regard'able, a. deſerving of notice obſervable, ob.
Regard'er, n. one who regards, one who reſpects
Regard'ful, a. attentive, taking notice   (fully
Regard'fully, ad. reſpectfully, attentively, care-
Regard'leſs, a. inattentive, heedleſs, negligent
Regat'ta, n. a grand rowing or ſailing match
Régency, n. government, vicarious authority
Regen'erate, v. t. to make anew, to renew
Regen'erate, pa. a. renewed, born by grace
Regenerátion, n. the new birth, birth by grace
Régent, n. a governor, rular, royal vicar, prince
Régent, a. ruling for or by another, governing
Régentſhip, n. deputed government or power
Regerm'inate, v. to germinate again
Regermination, n. a budding or ſprouting again
Re''gible, a. capable of being governed
Re''gicide, n. the murderer or murder of a king
Re''gimen, n. a diet uſed in time of ſicknefs, rule
Re''giment, n. a body of ſoldiers, polity, rule
Re''giment, v. t. to form into a regiment
Regiment'al, a. belonging to a regiment, military
Re''giment'als, n. pl. the uniform of a regiment
Région, n. a tract of land or ſpace, country, rank
Re''giſter, n. a liſt, record, keeper of a regiſter, co-
    reſpondence of columns on oppoſit ſides of a ſheet
    in printing
Re''giſter, v. t. to put in a regiſter, to record
Re''giſter, n. a hole and valve in a ſtove &c. to
    regulate the admiſſion of air
Re''giſterſhip, n. the office of a regiſter
Re''giſtrar, n. the regiſter of a univerſity
Re''giſtry, n. the act of regiſtering, facts recorded
Reg'let, n. a thin ledge of wood uſed by printers
Reg'nant, a. reigning, prevalent, predominant
Regorge', v. t. to vomit up, to ſwallow eagerly
Regraft', v. t. to graft over again or afreſh
Regraſt', v. t. to grant back, to grant over again
Regráte, v. t. to foreſtall, engrofs, offend, hurt
Regráter, n. a foreſtaller, engroſſer, huckſter
Regréet, n. a return of ſalutation : v. t. to reſalute
Regrefs', v. i. to return, to go or come back, ob.
Régrefs, Regref''ſion, n. a return, a going back
Regrefs'ive, a. returning, going or coming back
Regret', n. grief, ſorrow, vexation, diſlike
Regret', v. t. to feel ſorry at, hurt in mind
Reguerd'on, n. a reward; v. t. to reward, ob.
Reguerd'oned, pa. rewarded, compenſated, ob.
Reg'ular, a. agreeable to rule, orderly, exact
Reg'ular, n. one who obſerves ſome rule of life
Regular'ity, n. order, method, exactneſs
Reg'ularly, ad. methodically, juſtly, conſtantly
Reg'ulars, n. ſtanding troops, oppoſed to militia

Reg'ulate, v. t. to adjuſt by rule, order, direct
Regulátion, Reg'lement, n. a method, form, rule
Reg'ulator, n. a perſon or thing that regulates
Reg'ulus, n. pure metal ſeparated from other
    matters, a bird, a ſtar
Reg'uline, a- pertaining to regulus
Reg'ulize, v. i. to reduce to regulus, to ſeparate
    the pure metal from other matter
Regur'gitate, v. to throw or be poured back
Regurgitátion, n. a pouring back
Rehéar, v. t. reheard, pret. reheard, pa. to hear
    over again, to hear twice
Rehéaring, n. a ſecond hearing or trial
Rehears'al, n. a previous recital, repetition, relation
Rehearſe', v. t. to recite previouſly, to repeat
Reject', v. t. to caſt off, diſcard, diſmifs, refuſe
Rejec'tion, n. the act of caſting off, a refuſal
Reject'ive, a. caſting off or away
Reign, [rane] n. the time of kingly government
Reign, v. i. to rule as a king, obtain, prevail
Reimbod'y, v. t. to imbody again   [penfe
Reimburſe', v. t. to repay, to repair loſs or ex-
Reimburs'able, a. that may be repaid
Reimburſe'ment, n. a repayment, a reparation
Reimpreg'nate, v. t. to impregnate or fill anew
Reimpreſ''ſion, n. a repeated impreſſion
Reinfec'tious, a. capable of infecting again
Rein, [rane] n. part of a bridle, the act of governing
Rein, v. t. to govern, rule, reſtrain, control, run
Rein'deer, n. falſe ſpelling, ſee rane
Reinliſt', v. t. to inliſt thoſe who were before inliſted
Reinliſtment, n. a ſecond inliſtment
Reins, n. pl. the kidneys, loins, hips, lower back
Reinſert', v. t. to inſert again or afreſh
Reinſpire, v. t. to inſpire anew, animate, excite
Reinſtall', v. t. to ſet or put again in poſſeſſion
Reinſtáte, v. t. to replace in a former ſtate
Reinſtátement, n. a replacing in a former ſtate
Reintégrate, v. t. to renew, repair, reſtore,
Reinveſt', v. t. to inveſt again or anew
Reit'erate, v. t. to repeat, to do again and again
Reiterátion, n. a frequent repetition of a thing
Rejoice', v. to be glad, exult, make glad, cheer
Rejoic'er, n. one who rejoices or makes glad
Rejoin', v. to join or meet again, reply, anſwer
Rejoin'der, n. a reply to an anſwer, a ſecond anſwer
Rejólt, n. a ſhock, concuſſion, ſtroke
Rejudge', v. t. to reexamin, review, hear again
Rejuvenes'cence, n. a renewal of youth
Rekin'dle, v. t. to kindle or inflame again
Relapſe', v. i. to fall back into vice or ſickneſs
Relapſe', n. a return to vice, a return of illneſs
Reláte, v. to tell, recite, refer, belong
Reláter, n. a teller, informer, reciter, repeater
Relátion, n. a narration, tale, kindred, reference
Relátionſhip, n. the ſtate of being related
Rel'ative, n. a relation, what contains relation
Rel'ative, a. having a relation, reſpecting
Rel'atively, ad. with relation, with reſpect

Relax', v. to flacken, remit, abate, weaken
Relax', Relax'ed, pa. flackened, weakened
Relaxátion, n. a remiffion from ftudy, a ceffation
Relãy, n. horfes placed to relieve others, a gap
Reléafe, v. t. to fet free from reftraint, eafe, quit
Reléafe, n. a difmiffion, difcharge, acquittal, a deed of difcharge or quit claim
Rel'egate, v. t. to banifh, exile, fend away, remove
Relegátion, n. banifhment, exile, removal
Relent', v. i. to feel compaffion, foften, melt, turn
Relent'lefs, a. unmerciful, unpitying, cruel
Rel'evant, a. relieving, helping, pertinent
Rel'evancy, n. pertinence, aid, fupport
Reliance, n. truft, dependance, confidence
Rel'ics, n. pl. remains, the remains of bodies
Rel'ict, n. a widow, a woman left in widowhood
Relief, n. fuccor, help, mitigation, fine, relievo
Reliévable, a. capable or deferving of relief
Reliéve, v. t. to fuccor, help, eafe, free, change
Reliéver, n. one that relieves, one that eafes
Reliévo, n. the prominence of a picture or figure
Relight, v. t. relighted, relit, pret. and pa. to light afrefh or over again
Reli"gion, n. a fyftem of faith and worfhip, obedience to divine commands, from love to a Supreme Being and moral excellence
Reli"gionift, n. a perfon bigoted to any religion
Reli"gious, a. believing in, reverencing and obeying a Supreme Being, pious, devout, holy, bound by vows
Reli"gioufly, ad. pioufly, devoutly, ftrictly
Relin"quifh, v. t. to quit, give up, forfake, releafe
Relin"quifhment, n. the act of forfaking
Rel'iquary, n. a fhrine or cafket kept for relics
Rel'ifh, n. a tafte, liking, delight, manner, caft
Rel'ifh, v. to give or have a flavor, feafon, like
Rel'ifhable, a. that may be relifhed, pleafant, nice
Relóan, v. t. to lend a fecond time
Relóan, n. a fecond loan of a thing
Relúcent, a. fhining, tranfparent, clear
Reluct', Reluct'ate, v. i. to ftruggle againft, to refift
Reluct'ance or Reluct'ancy, n. unwillingnefs
Reluct'ant, a. unwilling, averfe to, refifting
Reluct'antly, ad. in a reluctant or crofs manner
Reluctátion, n. a ftruggle, refiftance, averfion
Relúme, Relúmin, v. t. to light anew, to rekindle
Rely', v. i. to put truft in, to depend
Remáin, v. i. to continue, endure, be left, await
Remáinder, n. what is left, a balance, an eftate to veft on the determination of another
Remáins, n. pl. what is left, relics, a dead body
Remáke, v. t. remade, pret. remade, pa. to make anew or over again
Remand', v. t. to fend, command or call, back
Rem'anent, n. a part remaining, a remnant, ob.
Remark', v. t. to obferve, mind, note, point out
Remark', n. an obfervation, note, notice, token
Remark'able, a. obfervable, worthy of notice, odd
Remark'ablenefs, n. a remarkable quality

Remark'ably, ad. obfervably, uncommonly, very
Remark'er, n. one who remarks or obferves
Remaft'icate, v. t. to chew a fecond time
Remédiable, a. that may be remedied or cured
Remédiate, a. affording a remedy, medicinal
Rem'edilefs, a. void of all remedy, irreparable
Rem'edy, n. a medicin, cure, help, reparation
Rem'edy, v. t. to cure, to remove a complaint
Remelt', v. t. to melt a fecond time
Remem'ber, v. t. to call to or keep in mind
Remem'berer, n. one who remembers or retains
Remem'brance, n. recollection, account preferved
Remem'brancer, n. one who puts in mind, a clerk
Remi'grate, v. i. to remove or rove back again
Remigrátion, n. a removal or return back again
Remínd, v. t. to put in mind, tell, hint
Reminis'cence, n. recollection, a recovery of ideas
Reminifcen'tial, a. relating to recollection
Remifs', a. flothful, carelefs, backward, relaxed
Remifs'ible, a. that can admit of forgivenefs
Remis"fion, n. forgivenefs, pardon, abatement
Remifs'ly, ad. carelefsly, negligently, flackly
Remifs'nefs, n. carelefnefs, negligence, coldnefs
Remit', v. to forgive, give up, reftore, fend money to a diftant place, relax, flacken, abate
Remit'tal, n. a giving back, remiffion
Remit'tance, n. money, &c. fent to a diftant place
Remit'ter, n. one who remits, a recovery of a right by operation of law
Rem'nant, n. what is left, a refidue; a. remaining
Remolt'en, a. melted afrefh or over again
Remons'trance, n. a reprefentation, a difcovery
Remon'ftrant, n. one who remonftrates
Remons'trate, v. i. to object, to fhow reafons
Rem'ora, n. an obftacle, ob. the fucking fifh
Remorfe', n. uneafinefs, fting, check, tendernefs
Remorfe'ful, a. tender, compaffionate, pitiful, kind
Remors'elefs, a. unmerciful, hard, cruel, favage
Remóte, a. diftant, far off, far, foreign, abftracted
Remótely, ad. not nearly, at a diftance, far
Remótenefs, Remóvednefs, n. a diftance, a fpace
Remótion, n. the act of removing or changing
Remov'able, [o as oo] a. that may be removed
Removabíl'ity, n. the capacity of being removed or difplaced
Remov'al, n. the act of moving, a difmiffion
Remov'e, v. to change place, go from place to place, place at a diftance, take or carry away
Remóve, n. a change of place, the act of moving
Romov'er, n. one who removes, one who moves
Remount', v. t. to mount again, to fupply horfes
Remúnerable, a. fit or proper to be rewarded
Remunerabil'ity, n. capacity of receiving reward
Remúnerate, v. t. to reward, requite, repay
Remunerátion, n. a reward, a requital (ward
Remúnerative, a. tending to reward, giving re-
Remur'mur, v. t. to utter back in murmurs
Rénal, a. pertaining to the kidneys
Ren'ard, n. a fox, a fly or cunning perfon

Renas'cent, *a.* riling or springing up anew

Renas'cency, *n.* a renewal of growth

Rencount'er, *n.* a perfonal oppofition, fudden combat, cafual engagement; *v. i.* to meet with

Rend, *v. t.* rent, *pret.* rent, *pa.* to tear, to tear or pull afunder with violence

Rend'er, *v. t.* to return, repay, make, tranflate

Rend'er, *n.* one who rends or tears, a furrender

Rend'ezvous, *n.* a place appointed for meeting at

Ren'dezvous, *v. t.* to colleft or affemble as troops

Renegáde or Renegádo, *n.* an apoftate, a revolter

Renége, *v. t.* to difown, deny, refufe, *ob.*

Renew', *v. t.* to make new, begin again, repeat

Renew'able, *a.* that may be renewed or repeated

Renew'al, *n.* the aft of renewing, a change

Ren'iform, *a.* fhaped like the kidneys

Ren'itency, *n.* refiftance, oppofition, a ftruggle

Ren'itent, *a.* refifting, oppofing, repelling

Ren'net, *n.* an apple, the juice of a calf's maw

Ren'ovate, *v. t.* to renew, to reftore to firft ftate

Renovátion, *n.* the aft of renewing, a renewal

Renounce', *v. t.* to difown, difclaim, give up, quit

Renounce', *n.* the aft of not following fuit

Renounce'ment, *n.* the aft of renouncing, hate

Renown', *v. t.* to make famous, to make noted

Renown', *n.* fame, praife, note, charafter, merit

Renown'ed, *pa. a.* celebrated, famed, eminent

Rent, *v.* to hold by paying a rent, tear, blufter

Rent, *n.* money paid for houfe or land, a revenue, income, yearly payment, place torn, flit, hole

Rent'al, *n.* an account or fchedule of an eftate let

Rent'charge, *n.* a charge fettled upon an eftate

Rent er, *n.* one who holds by paying rent, a tenant

Ren'ter, *v. t.* to few the edges of cloth without doubling them, to work new warp into damaged tapeftry (of cloth in a delicate manner

Ren'tering, *n.* fine drawing, or joining pieces

Renúmerate, *v. t.* to pay back, to count again

Renunciátion, *n.* the aft of renouncing, a difavow-

Reordáin, *v. t.* to ordain again or afrefh (al

Reordinátion, *n.* a repeated or fecond ordination

Reor'ganize, *v. t.* to organize a fecond time

Reorganizátion, *n.* the organizing of what has been diforganized

Repa"cify, *v. t.* to pacify again, to appeafe again

Repack', *v. t.* to pack a fecond time

Repack'er, *n.* one who packs over again

Repáid, *pret.* and *pa.* of *to repay*

Repáir, *v.* to mend, refit, fill up anew, go to

Repáir, *n.* a reparation, fupply of lofs, abode

Repáirable, *a.* that may be repaired or mended

Repáirer, *n.* one who mends, one who reftores

Repand', *a.* bending back, without angles

Repand'ity, *n.* a being bent back, a crookednefs

Repand'ous, *a.* bent upwards or back, crooked

Rep'arable, *a.* that may be amended or retrieved

Reparátion, *n.* the aft of reftoring, reftitution, a-

Repar'ative, *n.* what makes amends (mends

Repartée, *n.* a witty reply; *v. i.* to reply fmartly

Repafs', *v.* to pafs again, pafs back, return

Repaft', *n.* a meal, the aft of eating; *v. t.* to feed

Repaft'ure, *n.* an entertainment, feaft, treat ob.

Repáy, *v. t.* repaid, *pret.* repaid, *pa.* to pay back,

Repáyable, *a.* to be repaid (requite, recompenfe

Repáyment, *n.* the aft of repaying, a fum repaid

Repéal, *n.* an abolition, abrogation, recall

Repéal, *v. t.* to make void, annul, revoke, recall

Repéalable, *a.* that may be repealed or annulled

Repealabil'ity, *n.* capacity of being repealed

Repéat, *v.* to rehearfe, tell, fay, do or try again

Repéatedly, *ad.* over and over, frequently, often

Repéater, *n.* one who repeats, a kind of watch

Repel', *v.* to drive back, refift, prevent

Repel'lency, *n.* the quality of a fubftance which expands, feparates or repels, the principle of repulfion

Repel'lent, *n.* a medicin with a repelling power

Repel'lent, *a.* able or tending to repel

Répent, *a.* creeping, growing horizontally

Repent', *v.* to think on or exprefs with forrow

Repent'ance, *n.* forrow for paft fins, penitence

Repent'ant, *a.* forrowful for fin, penitent

Repent'ing, *n.* the aft of forrowing for fin

Repéople, *v. t.* to ftock or fill anew with people

Repercufs', *v.* to drive or beat back, to rebound

Repercus"fion, *n.* a driving back, a rebound

Repercufs'ive, *a.* able to drive back, rebounding

Rep'ertory, *n.* a book of records, treafury, ftore

Repetend', *n.* the parts of decimals continually re-

Repeti"tion, *n.* the aft of repeating, a recital (peated

Repíne, *v. i.* to fret, grieve, murmur, grumble

Repíner, *n.* one who repines, one who murmurs

Repláce, *v. t.* to put again in due place, to fupply

Repláit, *v. t.* to plait or fold over other parts

Replant', *v. t.* to plant anew or over again

Repléad, *v. t.* to plead a fecond time

Repléader, *n.* a fecond plea or courfe of pleading

Replen'ifh, *v.* to fill, fatisfy, ftock, become ftocked

Repléte, *a.* full, completely filled, replenifhed

Replétenefs, Replétion, *n.* a full or too full ftate

Replev'in, *n.* a writ to recover poffeffion of a dif-

Replev'iable, Replev'ifable, *a.* that can be replevied (trefs, the fuit or aftion

Replev'y, *v. t.* to obtain a releafe of a diftrefs, upon fecurity

Replication, *n.* a reply, repercuffion, rebound

Reply', *v. t.* to anfwer, return for anfwer, rejoin

Reply', *n.* an anfwer, a return made to an anfwer

Reply'er, *n.* one who replies, one who anfwers

Repol'ifh, *v. t.* to polifh again or anew

Repórt, *v.* to noife abroad, tell, relate, return

Repórt, *n.* a rumor, talk, fame, account, noife

Repórter, *n.* one who reports, one who relates, a book of reports of law-cafes

Repórtingly, *ad.* by report, by common fame only

Repófal, *n.* the aft of repofing or refting, reft

Repófe, *v.* to lay to reft, lay up, put, place

Repófe, *n.* fleep, quiet, reft, the caufe of reft

Repos'it, v. t. to lodge as in a place of safety
Repofi"tion, n. the act of replacing or setting
Repos'itory, n. a place where any thing is safely
Repoffefs', v. t. to poffefs or get again (laid up
Reprehend', v.t. to reprove, chide, blame, cenfure
Reprehend'er, n. a reprover, blamer, cenfurer
Reprehens'ible, a. culpable, blamable, wrong
Reprehens'iblenefs, n. blamablenefs, liablenefs to
Reprehens'ibly, ad. blamably (cenfure
Reprehen'fion, n. reproof, open blame, cenfure
Reprehens'ive, a. containing reproof or blame
Reprefent', v. to fhow, exhibit, appear for another
Reprefentátion, n. likenefs, account, appearance
for another, a whole body of delegates
Reprefent'ative, a. put in the place of another
Reprefent'ative, n. a fubstitute in power, a deputy
Reprefent'atively, ad. by means of a deputy or dep-
Reprefent'er, n. one who exhibits, a deputy (uties
Reprefent'ment, n. an image, figure, likenefs
Reprefs, v.t. to crufh, fubdue, curb, reftrain
Reprefs', Repres"fion, n. the act of crufhing
Reprefs'ive, a. able or tending to reprefs
Repriéve, v. t. to refpit from punifhment
Repriéve, n. a refpit, a delay of fentence, eafe
Rep'rimand, n. a reproof, reprehenfion, blame
Reprimand', v. t. to chide, rebuke, reprove, check
Reprint', v. t. to print a new or frefh edition
Reprífal, Reprífe, n. feizure by way of recompenfe
Repróach, v. t. to upbraid, cenfure, condemn
Repróach, n. cenfure, blame, difgrace, fcandal
Repróachable, a. deferving reproach, difgraceful
Repróacher, n. one who reproaches or upbraids
Repróachful, a. fcurrilous, abufive, infamous
Repróachfully, ad. fcurriloufly, ignominioufly
Rep'robate, n. a man abandoned to wickednefs
Rep'robate, a. loft to virtue, abandoned, vile
Rep'robate, v. t. to difallow, condemn, abandon
Rep'robatenefs, n. a reprobate ftate, a loft ftate
Reprobátion, n. a being abandoned to deftruction
Reprodúce, v. t. to produce anew or over again
Reproduc'tion, n. the act of producing again
Reproof', n. blame, rebuke, reprehenfion, check
Reprov'able, [o as oo] a. deferving of reproof
Reprove, v. t. to blame, cenfure, chide, condemn
Repróver, n. one who reproves, one who blames
Reprúne, v. t. to prune again or a fecond time
Rep'tile, n. a creeping thing, a very mean perfon
Rep'tile, a. creeping, grovelling, vulgar, low
Repub'lic, n. a commonwealth or ftate governed
by reprefentatives elected by the people
Repub'lican, n. a favorer of a commonwealth
Repub'lican, a. placing government in the people
Repub'licanifm, n. a fyftem of republican govern-
ment, attachment to that fyftem
Republicátion, n. a fecond publication
Repub'lifh, v. t. to publifh what has been publifhed
Repúdiable, a. fit to be put away or rejected
Repúdiate, v.t. to divorce, put away, reject, refufe
Repudiátion, n. a divorce, rejection, refufal

Repug'nance, n. contrariety, unwillingnefs
Repug'nant, a. contrary, oppofit, difobedient
Repug'nantly, ad. contradictorily, unwillingly
Repul'ulate, v. i. to bud again, ob.
Repullulátion, n. the act of budding anew, ob.
Repulfe', n. a being driven off, rejection, denial
Repulfe', v. t. to beat back, drive off, reject
Repuí'fion, n. the act of driving off from itfelf
Repuls'ive, Repuls'ory, a. able to repel, forbidding
Repul'fivenefs, n. the quality of repelling
Repur'chafe, v. t. to buy back, to buy over again
Repur'chafe, n. a buying back what one has fold
Rep'utable, a. honorable, being of good report
Rep'utably, ad. with reputation, with credit
Reputátion, n. honor, credit, good character, merit
Repúte, v. t. to account, efteem, reckon, think
Repúte, n. reputation, good character, opinion
Repútelefs, a. difgraceful, difhonorable, ob.
Requeft', n. an entreaty, petition, demand, credit
Requeft', v. t. to folicit, petition, defire, afk
Requick'en, v. t. to quicken again, revive, raife
Re"quiem, n. a prayer for the dead, reft, peace
Requírable, a. fit to be required or afked
Require, v. t. to demand, afk, make neceffary
Re"quifit, a. neceffary; n. any thing neceffary
Re"quifitly, ad. in a requifit or fit manner
Re"quifitnefs, n. neceffity, propriety, expedience
Requifi"tion, n. a requiring, requeft, claim
Requis'itive, a. implying requifition
Requítal, n. a retaliation, recompenfe, reward
Re quíte, v. t. to recompenfe, reward, fatisfy
Re'reward, n. the rear or laft troop of an army
Refáil, v. t. to fail back, fail over again, return
Refale, n. a fale over again, a fale at fecond hand
Refalúte, v. t. to falute again or afrefh
Refcind', v. t. to cut off, abrogate, repeal
Refcis"fion, n. a cutting off, abrogation, repeal
Refcifs'ory, a. able or tending to cut off
Refcríbe, v. t. to write back, to copy again, ob
Réfcript, n. an edict of an emperor, &c.
Res'cue, v. t. to deliver by force, free, fave
Res'cue, n. a deliverance from reftraint
Refearch', n. diligent inquiry, or examination
Refearch', v. t. to examin or inquire again
Refeat, v. t. to feat or place again, to replace
Refeizure, n. a repeated or fecond feizure
Refem'blance, n. a likenefs, fimilitude, picture
Refem'ble, v. to be like, have a likenefs, liken
Refend', v.t. refent, pret. refent, pa. to fend back,
to fend over again
Refent', v. t. to take as an affront, take ill, hate
Refent'er, n. one who refents or takes ill [voked
Refent'ful, Refent'ive, a. malicious, eafily pro-
Refent'ingly, ad. with refentment, with anger
Refent'ment, n. a deep fenfe of injury, anger
Refervátion, n. a referve, fomething kept back
Referv'atory, n. a place where any thing is kept
Referve', v. t. to keep in ftore, lay up, fave, retain
Referve', n. a ftore untouched, exception, model y

Referv'ed, *pa. a.* excepted, modeft, fullen, clofe
Referv'edly, *ad.* with referve, cautioufly, coldly
Referv'edneſs, *n.* referve, clofeneſs, coldneſs
Reſervoir, *n.* a large baſon or confervatory of water
Refet'tle, *v. t.* to fettle over again or afreſh
Refet'tlement, *n.* the act of fettling over again
Refhip', *v. t.* to ſhip what has been ſhipped or imported
Refhip'ment, *n.* re-exportation, a fecond ſhipment
Refi'de, *v. i.* to live in a place, dwell, fubfide
Res'idence, Res'iance, *n.* a place of abode, abode
Res'ident, *a.* refiding, dwelling
Res'ident, *n.* a dweller, agent, public minifter
Refiden'tiary, *a.* holding or obliged to refidence
Refid'ual, *n.* what remains; *a.* remaining, left
Refid'uary, *a.* entitled to the refidue of an eftate
Res'idue, *n.* a remaining part, a remainder
Refid'uum, *n.* the remains, or refidue
Refi'gn, *v. t.* to give or yield up, yield, fubmit
Refignation, *n.* the act of refigning, fubmiffion
Refi'gner, *n.* one who refigns, one who gives up
Refi'gnment, *n.* the act of refigning, fubmiffion
Res'ilah, *n.* an ancient patriarchal coin
Refil'ience, *n.* a leaping back, rebound, recoil
Refil'ient, *a.* leaping back, rebounding, recoiling
Res'in, *n.* the dried juice of trees, of an oily nature and foluble in fpirits
Refinif'erous, *a.* producing refin
Res'ino extrac'tive, *a.* noting extractive matter when refin predominates
Res'inous, Res'iny, *a.* containing or like refin
Res'inoufly, *ad.* in a refinous manner
Refipis'cence, *n.* repentance, penitence, grief
Refift', *v.* to oppofe, withftand, act againft, deny
Refift'ance, *n.* oppofition, the power which refifts
Refiftibil'ity, *n.* the ftate or quality of refifting
Refift'ible, *a.* that may be refifted or withſtood
Refift'lefs, *a.* that cannot be refifted or oppofed
Res'oluble, *a.* that may be melted or diffolved
Res'olute, *a.* fteady, firm, courageous, bold
Res'olutely, *ad.* fteadily, firmly, courageoufly
Res'oluteneſs, *n.* a fixed determination, bravery
Refolu'tion, *n.* determination, courage, diffolution, performance of a problem
Refolv'able, *a.* that may be folved or feparated
Refolve', *v.* to determin, folve, anfwer, diffolve
Refolve', *n.* a refolution, determination, defign
Refolv'edly, *ad.* with firmnefs, with conftancy
Refolv'edneſs, *n.* firmnefs, refolution, conftancy
Refolv'ent, Res'olutive, *a.* able to diffolve
Refolv'er, *n.* one who refolves, one who anfwers
Res'onance, *n.* a found fent back again, an echo
Res'onant, *a.* refounding, echoing back
Reforb', *v. t.* to fuck back, to fwallow up again
Refort', *v. i.* to repair, have recourfe, revert
Refort', *n.* a concourfe, affembly, meeting, fpring
Refound', *v.* to found again, echo, ring, celebrate
Refource, *n.* a refort, retreat, expedient, means
Refow, *v. t.* refowed, *pret.* refowed, refown, *pa.*

to fow afreſh or over again
Refpeak, *v. t.* refpake, refpoke, *pret.* refpoken, *pa.* to fpeak again, anfwer, reply
Refpect, *v.* to regard, confider, relate, belong
Refpect, *n.* regard, efteem, reverence, relation
Refpect'able, *a.* deferving of refpect or regard
Refpectabil'ity, *n.* the quality of deferving refpect
Refpect'er, *n.* one who has a partial regard
Refpect'ful, *a.* full of duty or outward civility
Refpect'fully, *ad.* with refpect, with efteem
Refpect'ive, *a.* particular, relative, accurate
Refpect'ively, *ad.* particularly, relatively, nicely
Refpira'tion, *n.* a breathing, a relief from toil
Refpire, *v. i.* to breathe, to take reft from toil
Refpi'rable, *a.* that may be breathed, fit to be breathed or for fupporting animal life
Refpi'ratory, *a.* ferving for refpiration
Res'pit, *n.* a reprieve, delay, paufe, interval, eafe
Res'pit, *v. t.* to fufpend, delay, put off, paufe
Refplen'dence or Refplen'dency, *n.* lufter, brightnefs
Refplen'dent, *a.* bright, fhining, glaring
Refplen'dently, *ad.* with lufter, very brightly
Refplit', *v. t.* to fplit a fecond time
Refpond', *v. i.* to anfwer, reply, correfpond, fuit
Refpond'ent, *n.* an anfwerer in a fuit or debate
Refponfe', *n.* an alternate anfwer, reply, return
Refponfibil'ity, Refpons'iblenefs; *n.* liability to anſwer or to pay, ability to pay [pay
Refpons'ible, *a.* anfwerable, accountable, able to
Refpon'fion, *n.* the act of anfwering, a reply
Refpons'ive, Refpons'ory, *a.* anfwering, fuited to
Reft, *n.* fleep, repofe, quiet, fupport, remainder
Reft, *n.* others, thofe not included, remainder
Reft, *v.* to fleep, die, be at eafe, be ftill, compofe, lay at reft, eafe, lean, depend, remain
Reftag'nant, *a.* remaining without motion, *ob.*
Reftag'nate, *v. i.* to ftand without flowing, *ob.*
Res'tant, *a.* remaining, as footftalks after the flower has fallen
Reftaura'tion, *n.* a recovery of a former ftate, *ob.*
Reftem', *v. t.* to force back againft the current
Reft'ful, *a.* full at reft, quiet, eafy [born, at reft
Reft'iff, Reft'ive, Reft'y, *a.* unwilling to ftir, ftubborn
Reft'inefs, Reft'ivenefs, *n.* an obftinate reluctance
Reftitu'tion, *n.* the act of reftoring or recovering
Reft'lefs, *a.* void of reft, uneafy, unfettled
Reft'lefsly, *ad.* in a reftlefs manner, uneafily
Reft'lefsnefs, *n.* a want of reft, unfteadinefs
Reftor'able, *a.* that may or fhould be reftored
Reftora'tion, *n.* a placing in a former ftate, a recovery
Reftor'ative, *a.* able to recruit life [ery
Reftor'ative, *a.* a medicin to reftore vigor
Reftore', *v. t.* to bring or give back, to retrieve
Reftor'er, *n.* one who reftores or gives back
Reftrain', *v. t.* to withhold, keep in, curb, fupprefs
Reftrain'able, *a.* that may be reftrained, gentle
Reftrain'edly, *ad.* with reftraint, with bounds
Reftrain'er, *n.* one who reftrains or keeps in
Reftraint, *n.* an abridgement of liberty, force

Reſtrict', v. t. to limit, confine, ſtint, bound, tie
Reſtric'tion, n. a limitation, confinement, tie
Reſtrict'ive, a. expreſſing limitation, aſtringent
Reſtrict'ively, ad. with reſtriction or limitation
Reſtrin'gent, a. tending to bind, bracing
Reſublime, v. t. to ſublime a ſecond time
Reſult', v. i. to fly back, follow, ariſe, accrue
Reſult', n. a flying back, conſequence, concluſion
Reſúmable, a. that may be taken up again
Reſúme, v. t. to take back, to begin again
Reſump'tion, n. the act of reſuming or taking a-
Reſupíne, a. having the face upwards   (gain
Reſúpinate, a. having the upper ſide turned down-
     wards   (ſide turned to the ground
Reſupinátion, n. the ſtate of having the upper
Reſurrec'tion, n. a return from the grave, a revival
Reſurvey', v. t. to ſurvey again, to review
Reſus'citate, v. to ſtir up anew, revive, raiſe again
Reſuſcitátion, n. a ſtirring up anew, a reviving
Retáil, v. t. to divide or ſell out in ſmall parcels
Retáil, n. a ſale by ſmall quantities or pieces
Retáiler, n. a perſon who retails, a publiſher
Retáin, v. t. to keep, hold in cuſtody or memory,
    deſerve, hire, fee, keep in pay, continue
Retáiner, n. a dependent, ſervant, previous fee
Retáke, v. t. retook, pret. retaken, pa. to take
    again, to take back again
Retal'iate, v. t. to repay, requite, make a return
Retaliátion, n. a keen return of like for like
Retard', v. to delay, hinder ſtop, ſtay back, puff to
Retardátion, n. the act of delaying, a hindrance
Retard'er, n. one who obſtructs, one who hinders
Retch, v. t. to vomit, force up, ſtrain, ſtretch
Retch'leſs, a. careleſs, flothful, lazy, wicked, ob.
Retec'tion, n. the act of diſcovering to the view, ob.
Retent', n. that which is retained
Reten'tion, n. a retaining, the memory, cuſtody
Retent'ive, a. able to retain, faithful
Retent'iveneſs, n. the power of retaining
Retic'ula, Ret'icule, n. a contrivance to meaſure
    the quantity of an ecliptſe
Retic'ular, Rétiform, a. made in form of a net
Retic'ulate, a. made of or like network, open
Reticulátion, n. network or work reſembling it
Ret'ina, n. the expanſion of nerves at the bottom
    of the eye by which viſion is produced
Ret'inue, n. a train of attendants   (tirement
Retire, v. to retreat, to withdraw; n. a retreat, re-
Retired, pa. a. withdrawn, private, lonely
Retiredneſs, n. ſolitude, retreat, privacy, ſecrecy
Retirement, n. a private abode or manner of life
Retóld, pa. told or related over again
Retort', n. a cenſure returned, a glaſs veſſel
Retort', v. t. to throw back, to return an argument
Retort'er, n. one who retorts or throws back
Retoſs', v. t. to toſs back, to throw back again
Retouch', v. t. to improve by new touches
Retráce, v. t. to trace back, to trace over again
Retract', v. t. to recant, recall, reſume, deny

Retractátion, n. a recantation, a contraction
Retrac'tile, a. capable of being drawn back
Retrac'tion, n. a withdrawing of a queſtion
Retréat, n. a retiring, a place of retirement, cafe
Retréat, v. i. to retire, withdraw, go off
Retrench', v. t. to reduce, leſſen, cut off, confine
Retrench'ment, n. a reduction, an intrenchment
Ret'ribute, v. t. to pay back, to recompenſe
Retribútion, n. a repayment, requital, reward
Retrib'utive, Retrib'utory, a. repaying, rewarding
Retriévable, a. that may be retrieved
Retriéve, v. t. to recover, regain, repair, recall
Retroac'tive, a. affecting what is paſt, retroſpective
Retrocéde, v. t. to cede or grant back
Retroceſ'ſion, n. the act of going or ceding back
Retroduc'tion, n. the act of leading or bringing
Ret'roflex, a. bent back or variouſly bent (back
Ret'rofract, a. bent back as if broke
Retrogradátion, n. the act of going backwards
Ret'rograde, a. going backwards, contrary, croſs
Ret'rograde, v. i. to go backward, to turn back
Retrogreſ'ſion, n. the act of going backwards
Retropuls'ive, a. repelling, driving back
Ret'roſpect, n. a view of things paſt, a review
Retroſpec'tion, n. the act of looking backwards
Retroſpec'tive, a. looking backwards, reviewing
Ret'roverted, a. turned back
Retund', v. t. to blunt, turn the edge, weaken
Return', v. to come or go back, ſend back, tranſ-
    mit, convey, repay, make anſwer, retort
Return', n. the act of coming back, profit, repay-
    ment, reſtitution, requital, anſwer, relapſe
Return'able, a. allowed to be returned back
Return'er, n. one who returns, one who remits
Retúſe, a. blunt, not pointed
Reunite, v. t. to unite again or a ſecond time
Reúnion, n. a ſecond union (matter a ſecond time
Revac'cinate, v. t. to inoculate with cow-pock
Revaccinátion, n. a ſecond vaccination
Reveál, v. t. to make known, diſcloſe, ſhow, tell
Reveáler, n. one who reveals, one who diſcove s
Rev'el, v. i. to carouſe; n. a looſe and noiſy feaſt
Rev'el, v. t. to draw back or off, retract, ob.
Revelátion, n. a communication of ſacred truth
Rev'eller, n. one who feaſts with noiſy jollity
Rev'elrout, n. a mob, unlawful aſſembly, noiſe
Rev'elry, n. looſe or noiſy jollity, feſtive mirth
Reven'dicate, v. t. to reclaim or regain what was
    taken away
Revendicátion, n. a claiming what has been loſt
Revenge', n. a malicious return of an injury
Revenge', v. to return an injury, avenge, puniſh
Revenge'ful, a. full of revenge, vindictive, cruel
Revenge'fully, Reven'gingly, ad. with revenge
Revenge'fulneſs, n. a revengeful diſpoſition
Revenge'ment, n. a return of injury, vengeance, ob.
Reven'ger, n. one who avenges crimes or injuries
Rev'enue, n. the income of a prince or ſtate, [pri
    vate income, ob.]

Reverb'erate, v. t. to rebound, to resound [reverb,
R. verb'erant, Reverb'erate, a. beating back
Reverberátion, n. the act of beating or driving back
Reverb'eratory, a. beating back, returning
Revére, v. t. to reverence, venerate, honor, love
Rev'erence, n. a veneration, respect, honor, title of the clergy, bow, courtesy, act of obeisance
Rev'erence, v. t. to regard with awful respect
Rev'erencer, n. one who regards with reverence
Rev'erend, a. deserving or entitled to reverence
Rev'erend, n. a clergy man, minister, divine
Rev'erent, a. expressing veneration, humble, low
Reveren'tial, a. expressing reverence or regard
Reveren'tially, ad. with a show of reverence
Rev'erently, ad. with awe, respectfully, humbly
Revérer, n. one who reveres, one who venerates
Reverié or Rev'ery, n. irregular or loose thought
Revers'al, n. a change, a change of sentence
Reverse', v. to invert, change, over turn, repeal
Reverse', n. the opposit side, change, vicissitude
Reverse', a. contrary, opposit
Revers'ed, pa. turned upside down, repealed
Revers'ible, a. that may be reversed or repealed
Rever'sion, n. a right of succession, a succession
Rever'sionary, a. having a right in succession
Revert', v. t. to return, to turn over; n. a return
Revert'ent, n. a medicin which restores inverted motion
Re ert'ible, a. returnable, that may return back
Revert'ive, a. returning back, causing to return
Re est', v. t. to clothe, to put again in possession
Revest'iary, n. a place for vestments, a wardrobe
Revet'ment, n. a strong wall or the outside of a rampart to support the earth
Revibráte, v. to vibrate back again or in return
Revibrátion, n. a vibration back again
Revic'tion, n. a return to life, revival, ob.
Revict'ual, v. t. to stock again with provisions
Review', v. t. to reexamin, survey, look again
Review', n. a reexamination, survey, smallbook
Review'er, n. one who reviews, a kind of critic
Revíle, v. t. to villify, to reproach; n. reproach
Reviler, n. one who reviles, one who reproaches
Revíling, n. the act of villifying, reproach
Revíingly, ad. in an opprobrious manner
Revisal, Revi'sion, n. a reexamination, a review
Revíse, v. t. to reexamin, review, read again
Revíse, n. a proof that is reexamined, a review
Revíser, n. one who examins, a superintendent
Revi'sional, a. pertaining to a revisal
Revis'it, v. t. to visit again or once more
Revíval, n. a return to life, a restoration
Revíve, v. to return to life, restore, renew, cheer
Revíver, n. one who revives, one who invigorates
Revivificátion, n. the act of calling back to life
Revíving, pa. recovering, restoring, comforting
Revivis'cency, n. a renewal or recovery of life
Revíves'cent, a. reviving, regaining life or action
Revíver, n. the act or process of reviving a suit in court

Rev'ocable, a. that may be recalled or repealed
Rev'ocate, v. t. to recall, call back, repeal, alter
Revocátion, Revókement, n. a recalling, a repeal
Revóke, v. t. to recall, withdraw, reverse, repeal
Revóke, n. an omission to follow suit
Revókeable, a. that may be recalled
Revolt', n. a change of sides, a desertion
Revolt', v. i. to desert, go or fall of, rebel
Revolt'er, n. one who changes sides, a deserter
Revolve', v. to perform a revolution, to consider
Rev'olute, a. rolled back or downwards
Revolútion, n. a returning motion, rotation, turn, change of government in a state (ernment
Revolutionary, a. pertaining to a change of gov-
Revolútionize, v. t. to effect a change of govern-
Revolútionist, n. one engaged in a revolution (ment
Revom'it, v. t. to vomit again, to vomit up again
Revul'sion, n. a turning back of humors, a change
Reward', v. t. to recompense, satisfy, pay, repay
Reward', n. a recompense, return, punishment
Reward'able, a. worthy of reward, meritorious
Reward'er, n. one who rewards, one who repays
Reword', v. t. to repeat in the same words. ob.
Reys, n. the master of an Egyptian bark or ship
Rhabarb'arate, a. tinctured with rhubarb, ob.
Rhab'domancy, n. a divination by a wand, ob.
Rhapfod'ical, a. like a rhapsody, extravagant
Rhap'sodist, n. one who writes rhapsodies
Rhap'sody, n. an irregular unconnected writing
Rhénish, a. denoting wine produced near the Rhine
Rhétian, a. pertaining to Rhetia now the country of the Grisons and Tyrolese on the Alps
Rhet'oric, n. the art of speaking properly, oratory
Rhetor'ical, a. pertaining to rhetoric, oratorical
Rhetor'ically, ad. duly as an orator, figuratively
Rhetor'icate, v. i. to play the orator, affect, ob.
Rhetori'cian, n. one who teaches rhetoric
Rhetori'cian, a. sniting a master of rhetoric
Rheum, n. thin watery matter from the mouth
Rheumat'ic, a. troubled with the rheumatism
Rheum'atism, n. a very acute painful disorder
Rheum'y, a. full of rheum, having sharp moisture
Rhino'ceros, n. a large animal, the unicorn
Rhóde-Island, n. one of the U. States, an island
Rhódian, n. a native of Rhodes, an island in the
Rhódian, a. pertaining to Rhodes (Mediterranean
Rhomb, n. a quadrangular figure with equal sides, and two angles accute and two obtuse
Rhom'bic, a. resembling or shaped like a rhomb
Rhom'boid, n. a figure with four sides, the opposit ones only equal
Rhomboid'al, a. like or belonging to a rhomb
Rhom'bo, n. an Italian fish of the turbot kind
Rhúbarb, n. a medicinal purgative root
Rhumb, n. a vertical circle of a place or the point in which such a circle intersects the horizon, a point of compass (compass
Rhumbline, n. a line prolonged from a point of

R*h*yme, *n.* harmony of verfes, meter, poetry
R*h*yme, *v. i.* to make verfes, jingle, agree
R*h*y'mer, *n.* one who makes rhymes, a poet
R*h*yth'mical, *a.* harmonious, mufical, fine
R*h*yth'mus, *n.* proportion between the parts of mu-
Rib, *n.* a bone in the body, a timber in fhips (fic
Rib'ald, *n.* a loofe and mean wretch, *ob.*
Rib'aldry, *n.* rude brutal language, obfcenity
Rib'bed, *a.* made with ribs, tightened, fecured
Rib'bon, Rib'and, *n.* a fillet of filk, fafh, piece
Rib'roaft, *v. t.* to beat foundly, ufed in droll ftyle
Rib'wort, *n.* the ribbed plantain
Rice, *n.* a well known efculent grain, a twig
Rícebird, *n.* a bird of the fize of a greenfinch
Rich, *a.* wealthy, fruitful, valuable, fweet, nice
Rich'es, *n.* plenty of money or poffeffions
Rich'ly, *ad.* plenteoufly, abundantly, fplendidly
Rich'nefs, *n.* opulence, fruitfulnefs, finery, fweet-
Rick, *n.* a heap of grain or hay, ftack, pile (nefs
Rick'ets, *n.* a diftemper of the joints in children
Rick'ety, *a.* troubled with the rickets, weak
Rid, *v. t.* rid, *pret.* rid, *pa.* to fet free, free, difen-
gage, clear, drive away, deftroy
Rid'dance, *n.* a clearing away, deliverance, end
Rid'dle, *v. t.* to folve, fift, run through a fieve
Rid'dle, *n.* a puzzling odd queftion, a wide fieve
Rid'dlingly, *ad.* in an obfcure manner, darkly
Ride, *v. i.* rid, rode, *pret.* ridden, *pa.* to be carried
on horfeback, or in a vehicle, to float
Ride, *v. t.* to carry, to make fubfervient
Rideau, Ridóe, *n.* a fmall mound or trench
Rider, *n.* one who rides a horfe, a horfe, timber
Ridge, *n.* the upper part of a flope, top, wrinkle
Ridge, *v. t.* to form a ridge, to throw up a ridge
Ridg'el or Ridg'il, *n.* a ram only half caftrated
Ridg'y, *a.* rifing or having a ridge, floping
Rid'icule, *n.* laughter with contempt
Rid'icule, *v. t.* to expofe to laughter, to banter
Ridic'ulous, *a.* exciting laughter, odd, filly, mean
Ridic'uloufly, *ad.* in a low contemptible manner
Ridic'nloufnefs, *n.* a ridiculous quality, folly
Ríding, *pa.* of *to ride*
Rídingcoat, *n.* a large over coat
Rifinghood, *n.* a woman's long over cloke
Rídot'to, *v. n.* a mufical entertainment, an opera
Rife, *a.* prevalent, predominant, common
Rifely, *ad.* prevalently, commonly, abundantly
Rifenefs, *n.* prevalence, frequency, abundance
Rifle, *n.* a gun, the infide of whofe barrel has fpiral
channels
Rifle, *v. t.* to pillage, plunder, fpoil, rob, pick
Rifleman, *n.* one who ufes a rifle
Rifler, *n.* a pillager, plunderer, fpoiler, robber
Rift, *n.* a cleft, a breach; *v.* to cleave, burft, belch
Rift'y, *a.* having rifts or fiffures
Rig, *n.* a back, top of a hill, ridicule, romp, horfe
Rig, *v. t.* to fit with rigging, trim, drefs, adorn
Rigadoon', *n.* a kind of quick French dance
Rigátion, *n.* the act of watering or moiftening

Rig'ger, *n.* one who rigs, dreffes or adorns
Rig'ging, *n.* the ropes and tackling of a fhip
Rig'gifh, *a.* wanton, whorifh, loofe, lewd, wild
Rig'gle, *v. i.* to move backwards and forwards
Right, *a.* fit, proper, true, juft, happy, ftrait
Right, *ad.* properly, truly, juftly, directly, very
Right, *n.* juftice, a juft claim, privilege, preroga-
tive, intereft, property, power, the fide not left,
a tract of land, freedom from error
Right, *v. t.* to relieve from wrong, adjuft, repelac
Right, *v. i.* to take a proper pofition
Righteous, [richus] *a.* juft, honeft, virtuous, pious
Righteoufly, *ad.* juftly, honeftly, fitly, virtuoufly
Righteoufnefs, *n.* juftice, honefty, virtue, piety
Rightful, *a.* having a right or juft claim, juft
Rightfully, *ad.* according to right and juftice
Rightfulnefs, *n.* rectitude, juftice, honefty
Rightly, *ad.* properly, juftly, uprightly, exactly
Rightnefs, *n.* a conformity to truth, ftraitnefs
Ri''gid, *a.* ftrict, exact, ftiff, ftern, fevere
Rigid'ity, Ri''gidnefs, *n.* ftrictnefs, feverity
Ri''gidly, *ad.* ftrictly, exactly, fternly, feverely
Rig'let, *n.* a flat and thin fquare piece of wood
Rig'marole, *a.* confufed, unconnected, irregular
Rig'or, *n.* ftrictnefs, feverity, a fhivering with cold
Rig'orous, *a.* ftrict, harfh, fevere, cruel
Rig'oroufly, *ad.* ftrictly, harfhly, feverely
Rill, *v. i.* to run in rills or fmall ftreams
Rill, Rill'et, *n.* a fmall brook, a fmall ftream
Riim, *n.* a border, edge, fide, margin, boundary
Rime, *n.* a hoarfroft, fog, chink, hole, rhyme
Rimófe, Rímous, *a.* full of clefts or chinks
Rim''ple, *v.* to pucker, plait, wither, wrinkle
Rímy, *a.* foggy, hazy, mifty, ftreamy, hoary
Rind, *n.* bark, a hufk; *v. t.* to bark, fkin, hufk
Rin'dle, *n.* a fmall gutter, a fmall watercourfe
Ring, *n.* a circle, ornament, found, fet of bells
Ring, *v.* rang, rung, *pret.* ringed, rung, *pa.* to fit
with rings, ftrike a bell, tinkle, clink, found,
make a ruftic, echo, refound
Ring'bolt, *n.* a bolt to which a ring is faftened
Ring'dove, *n.* a kind of pigeon, a woodpigeon
Rin'gent, *a.* gaping, opening as a cleft
Ring'er, *n.* one who rings, one fkilled in ringing
Ring'leader, *n.* the head of a mob or in mifchief
Ring'let, *n.* a fmall ring, a fmall circle or curl
Ring'ftreaked, *a.* circularly ftreaked or marked
Ring'tail, *n.* a bird of the hawk kind
Ring'worm, *n.* a circular tetter, diforder, mark
Rinfe, *v. t.* to wafh, wafh out foap, &c. cleanfe
Rins'er, *n.* one who rinfes, one who wafhes out
Ríot, *n.* fedition, tumult, uproar, very noify mirth
Ríot, *v. i.* to raife fedition or uproar, to revel
Ríoter, *n.* one who makes a riot or difturbance
Ríotous, *a.* feditious, noify, licentious, luxurious
Ríotoufly, *ad.* feditioufly, noifily, luxurioufly
Ríotoufnefs, *n.* a ftate of or difpofition to riot
Rip, *v. t* to tear up, cut up or afunder, difclofe
Ripe, *a.* mature, fit for ufe, complete, finifhed

Ripe, Rípen, *v.* to grow or make ripe, to fwell

Rípely, *ad.* at full growth, at the fit or due time

Rípenefs, *n.* maturity, perfection, fulnefs, fitnefs

Riphéan, *a.* an epithet anciently applied to mountains of Scythia, or as fome fuppofe, to forefts, their fituation is indeterminate

Rip'per, *n.* one who rips up, one who difclofes

Rip'ple, *v.* to run gently over, fret, rub off, clean

Ript, *pa.* torn up, cut open, unfewed, difclofed

Rife, *v.* rofe, *pret.* rifen, *pa.* to get up, grow, fwell, increafe, be improved, afcend, be exalted

Rife, *n.* the act of rifing, afcent, firft appearance, beginning, birth, fource, increafe, advance

Rifer, *n.* one who rifes, the upright of a ftair

Rifibility, *n.* the quality of laughing, laughter

Rifible, *a.* exciting laughter, laughable, ridiculous

Rifk, *n.* hazard, chance, danger

Rifk, *v. t.* to hazard, expofe to chance, endanger

Rifk'er, *n.* one who hazards, one who endangers

Rite, *n.* a folemn act of religion, ceremony, form

Rit'ual, *n.* a book of rites or religious ceremonies

Rit'ual, *a.* folemnly ceremonious, formal, ufual

Rit'ualift, *n.* one fkilled in religious ceremonies

Riv'age, *n.* a bank, fhore, coaft, voyage, toil, *ob.*

Rival, *n.* a competitor; *a.* making the fame claim

Rival, *v.* to be a competitor, oppofe, emulate

Rívalry or Rívalty, *n.* competion, emulation

Rívalfhip, *n.* the ftate or character of a rival

Rive, *v.* rived, *pret.* rived, riven, *pa.* to cleave, fplit, be fplit, thruft, ftab

Riv'el, *v. t.* to contract into wrinkles, to fhrink

Riv'er, *n.* a large ftream or current of water

Riv'erdragon, *n.* the king of Egypt, a crocodile

Riv'ergod, *n.* the tutelar deity of a river

Riv'et, *n.* a kind of pin clenched at both ends

Riv'et, *v. t.* to faften with rivets, clench, fecure

Riv'ulet, *n.* a fmall river or ftream, a brook

Rixátion, *n.* the act of quarrelling or brawling

Rix'dollar, *n.* a German coin, in value 1 dollar

Roach, *n.* the name of a fmall river-fifh

Road, *n.* a way for travelling on, anchorage fome diftance from fhore

Róader, *n.* a veffel at anchor in a road

Roam, *v. i.* to ramble, rove, wander, range, go

Roan, *a.* bay, forrel, or black fpotted, mixed

Roar, *v. i.* to make a loud noife, bellow, cry out

Roar, *n.* a loud noife or found, outcry, clamor

Róaring, *n.* the cry of a wild beaft, a great noife

Róary, Rórid, *a.* dewy, moift with dew, *ob.*

Roaft, *v. t.* to drefs meat before the fire, heat much, banter feverely, teafe

Roaft, *n.* a thing roafted, a bufinefs; *a.* roafted

Rob, *v. t.* to take from the perfon of another, forcibly, felonioufly, and by putting him in fear, to take unlawfully, to ftrip or deprive

Rob, *n.* infpiffated juces of fruit, a thicknefs

Rob'ber, *n.* a thief, a perfon who takes by force

Rob'bery, *n.* forcible taking from the perfon of another, an unlawful taking

Robe, *v. t.* to drefs pompoufly, drefs, inveft

Robe, *n.* a long veft or gown, a drefs of dignity

Rob'in, Robinred'breaft, *n.* a common bird

Rob'orant, *n.* a medicin for giving ftrength

Robuft', *a.* ftrong, ftout, lufty, vigorous, violent

Robuft'nefs, *n.* ftrength, luftinefs, vigor, power

Roc'ambole, *n.* a wild garlic, a Spanifh garlic

Róche alum, *n.* a purer fort of alum

Ro"chet, *n.* a bifhop's furplice, fifh, roach

Rock, *n.* a vaft ftone, protection, defenfe, diftaff

Rock, *v.* to fhake, reel, move a cradle, quiet

Rock'er, *n.* a fhaker, one who rocks a cradle, &c.

Rock'et, *n.* a kind of artificial firework, a plant

Rock'fifh, *n.* a fifh living about rocks

Rock'lefs, *a.* void of rocks, fmooth, plain, even

Rock'ruby, *n.* a precious ftone, a kind of garnet

Rock'falt, *n.* a hard falt, a mineral falt

Rock'work, *n.* a fort of building imitating rocks

Rock'y, *a.* full of or having rocks, ftony, hard

Rod, *n.* a twig, inftrument of correction, perch, pole

Rode, *pret* of *to ride*

Rodomontáde, *n.* boafting, noife, blufter, rant

Rodomontáde, *v. i.* to brag, boaft, blufter, rant

Roe, *n.* the female of the hart, the eggs of fifh

Rogátion, *n.* a fupplication, a requeft, the litany

Rogátion week, *n.* the week before Whitfunday

Rogue, *n.* a knave, rafcal, wag; *v. i.* to wander

Róguery, *n.* knavery, knavifh tricks, waggery

Róguefhip, *n.* the qualities or acts of a rogue

Róguifh, Róguy, *a.* knavifh, vagrant, wanton

Róguifhnefs, *n.* the qualities of a rogue

Roil, *v. t.* to render turbid by ftirring up lees, to difturb the mind and excite anger

Roift, *v. i.* to blufter, fwagger, *ob.*

Roift'erer, *n.* a noify bluftering man, bully, *ob.*

Roll, *n.* a thing rolling, turn, mafs made round, public regifter, catalogue, chronicle, office

Roll, *v.* to fold, turn, move in a circle, run, level

Róller, *n.* a thing that turns round on its own axis, thing to roll with, bandage, a fillet, a bird

Róllingpin, *n.* a round piece of wood for paftry

Róilingprefs, *n.* a prefs for printing pictures

Róllypolly, *n.* a fort of game

Rom'age, *n.* a tumult, buftle, ftir, *fee* rummage

Romal', *n.* a fpecies of filk handkerchief

Róman, *n.* a native or inhabitant of Rome

Róman, *a.* relating to Rome or the Romans

Rómance, *n.* a fiction, fable, fabulous ftory

Rómance, *v. i.* to tell or write fables

Roman'cer, *n.* a forger of tales

Rómanift, *n.* one who profeffes popery, a papift

Rómanize, *v.* to latinize, to write or ufe latin, to become Roman (the Grifons in Swifferland

Romanfh', *n.* a dialect of the Latin, fpoken among

Romant'ic, *a.* wild, irregular, improbable, falfe

Romant'icnefs, *n.* a romantic ftate, wildnefs

Rómifh, *a.* of or belonging to Rome, popifh

Romp, *n.* a rude and aukward girl, boifterous play

Romp, *v. i.* to play rudely or boifteroufly

Romp'ing, *n.* rough noify play, rudenefs, noife
Rondeau, [rondo] *n.* a kind of ancient poetry
Ron''dle, *n.* a round ball, round tower, fong
Ron'ion or Ron'yon, *n.* a fat bulky woman, *ob.*
Rood, *n.* the fourth of an acre in fquare meafure, *improperly ufed alfo for* rod or perch
Roof, *n.* the cover of a houfe, palate of the mouth
Roof, *v. t.* to cover or inclofe with a roof
Roofing, *n.* timber of or for a roof
Roof'y, *a.* having roofs, fupplied with roofs
Rook. *n.* a bird, cheat, low cheffman ; *v.t.* to cheat
Rook'ery, *n.* a nurfery of rooks, cheating, deceit
Room, *n.* fpace, place, ftead, chamber, apartment
Room'age, Room'inefs, *n.* a roomy ftate, fpace
Room'y, *a.* fpacious, capacious, wide, large, full
Rooft, *n.* a place whereon birds reft, bed, fleep
Rooft, *v. i.* to reft as a bird, fleep, lodge
Root, *n.* the part from which vegetables fpring, original or firft caufe, firft anceftor, bottom
Root, *v.* to take root, imprefs, dig up, deftroy
Root'ed, *pa. a.* fixed deep, radical, deftroyed
Root'edly, *ad.* deeply, fixedly, firmly, ftrongly
Rope, *n.* a cord, halter, row of things dependent
Rope, *v.i.* to form into filaments, to become ropy
Rópedancer, *n.* an artift who dances on a rope
Rópemaker, *n.* one who makes ropes to fell
Rópery, Rópetrick, *n.* a trick deferving a halter
Rópewalk, *n.* a place in which ropes are made
Rópeyarn, *n.* the threds for the ftrands of a rope
Rópinefs, *n.* a ropy ftate, a glutinous quality
Rópy, *a.* vifcous, glutinous, clammy, flimy, tough
Roquelafire, Ro''quelo, *n.* a fort of man's cloke
Róral, *a.* pertaining to dew, dewy
Rorátion, *n.* a falling of dew, a bedewing, dew
Rorif'erous, *a.* producing or caufing dew, wet
Rofáceous, *a.* refembling or pertaining to a rofe
Rófary, *n.* a fet of beads containing 15 paternofters and 150 ave-maries, mafs, devotion
Ros'cid, *a.* abounding with or having dew, dewy
Rofe, *n.* a very fweet flower ; *pret* of *to rife*
Rófeate, *a.* full of or like rofes, rofy, blooming
Rófebay, *n.* the name of feveral plants
Rófed, *a.* made or painted red, reddened, flufhed
Rófemary, *n.* a fragrant medicinal plant
Rófet, *n.* a kind of red color ufed by painters
Rófetree, *n.* a tree that produces rofes
Rófewater, *n.* water diftilled from rofes
Roficru'cian, *n.* a vifionary philofopher [rofin
Ros'in, *n.* infpiffated turpentine ; *v. t.* to rub with
Ros'tel, *n.* the defcending part of the heart of a feed
Rofs, *n.* the external rough part of bark
Roffet', *n.* the large ternate bat
Roft'rated, *a.* adorned with the beaks of fhips
Roft'rum, *n.* the beak of a bird, a fhip's head
Rófy, *a.* like a rofe, red as a rofe, red, charming
Rot, *v.* rotted, *pret.* rotted, rotten, *pa.* to putrefy, perifh, corrupt, bring to corruption
Rot, *n.* a diftemper in fheep, putrefaction
Rótary, *a.* turning round like a wheel

Rotate, *a.* whirled, wheel-fhaped
Rotátion, *n.* a whirling round, courfe, turn
Rótative, *a.* in manner of a wheel, rotary
Rotátor, *n.* who or what gives a circular motion
Rotátoplane, *a.* wheel fhaped and flat without a tube
Rote, *n.* repetition of words without rule or meaning, [a harp, *ob.*]
Rot'oco, *n.* an eaftern weight of 5lb.
Rot'ten, *pa. a.* perifhed, putrid, unfound
Rot'tennefs, *n.* a rotten ftate, putrefaction
Rot'tenftone, *n.* a foft ftone ufed in polifhing, &c. called alfo Tripoly, from that country
Rotund', *a.* round, circular; *n.* a rotundo
Rotund'ity, *n.* roundnefs, circularity, fphericity
Rotund'o a round building, round, pantheon
Rove, *v. i.* to ramble, wander, range, walk about
Róver, *n.* a wanderer, fickle perfon, pirate
Rouge, [rooge] *n.* a red paint ufed for the face
Rough, [ruff] *a.* rugged, uneven, harfh, fevere, ftormy
Rough'caft, *n.* a rough model, a rough plafter
Rough'caft, *v. t.* roughcaft, *pret.* and *pa.* to form by way of effay, to plafter roughly
Rough'draft, *n.* a draught only in its rudiments
Rough'draw, *v. t.* rough drew, *pret.* roughdrawn, *pa.* to draw or trace coarfely
Rough'en, *v.* to make or become rough
Rough-hewn, *a.* unfinifhed, unpolifhed, rude
Rough'ly, *ad.* ruggedly, harfhly, rudely, ill
Rough'nefs, *a.* unevennefs, harfhnefs, feverity
Rough'wrought, *a.* wrought or done coarfely
Roun'ceval, *n.* a kind of large rich pea
Round, *a.* like a circle, fmooth, large, full, plain
Round, *n.* a circle, orb, diftrict, courfe, rundle
Round, *ad.* in a circle, every way ; *pr.* about
Round, *v.* to make or go round, furround, raife
Round'about, *a.* ample, extenfive, indirect, loofe
Round'elay, *n.* a kind of ancient poetry, a dance
Round'er, *n.* an inclofure, circumference, circuit
Round'head, *n.* a puritan in Oliver's time
Round'houfe, *n.* a room, poop of a fhip
Round'ifh, Round'ing, *a.* fomewhat or rather round
Round'ly, *ad.* in a plain manner, in good earneft
Round'nefs, *n.* circularity, fmoothnefs, opennefs
Round'ridge, *v.t.* to form round ridges by plowing
Roup, *n.* a difeafe in poultry, public fale, auction
Roufe or Rouze, *v. t.* to ftir up, excite, wake
Roufe, *n.* too much liquor, a wile, a trick, deceit
Rous'er, *n.* one who roufes, one who ftirs up
Rout, *n.* a defeat, clamorous multitude, fquabble, riot, noife, affembly for gaming
Rout, *v.* to defeat, root up, affemble in crowds
Route, *n.* a road, way, courfe, march, journey
Row, *n.* a number of things ranged in a line
Row, *v.* to impel with or ufe oars ; *a.* rough
Row'el, *n.* the point of a fpur, a feton, an iffue
Row'el, *v. t.* to keep open by a feton
Row'en, *n.* the fecond growth of grafs in a feafon
Rówer, *n.* one who rows or manages an oar
Row'lyrag, *n.* a ftone of a dark gray color

Roy'al, a. regal, kingly, becoming a king, noble
Roy'al, n. a large kind of paper, a fail above the top gallant-fail
Roy'alift, n. an adherent to a king, a loyal perfon
Roy'alize, v. t. to make or render royal
Roy'ally, ad. in a royal manner, nobly [a king
Roy'alty, n. kingfhip, the office, ftate or right of
Roy'alties, n. pl. the rights of a king
Royn'ifh, a. mean, paltry, forry, rude, ob.
Rub'bleftone, n. a fpecies of fandftone
Rub, v. to clean, fcour, polifh, fret, get through
Rub, n. an impediment, difficulty, act of rubbing
Rub'ber, n. one who rubs, a cloth to rub with
Rub'bifh, n. ruins of buildings, a worthlefs thing
Ru'bellite, n. a filiceous ftone of a red color
Rubes'cent, a. growing, or becoming red
Rubicel', n. a fpecies of the ruby of a reddifh color
Rúbicund, Rúbiform, a. inclined to rednefs, red
Rúbied, Rúbious, a. red as a ruby, a ruddy
Rubifácient, n. that which makes red
Rubific, a. making or coloring red, reddening
Rubify, Rúbricate, v. t. to make or color red
Rúble, n. a Ruffian coin, value one dollar
Rúbric, a. red ; n. directions in the common prayer
Rub'ftone, n. a ftone to clean or fharpen with
Rúby, n. a preciousred ftone, a blotch ; a. red
Ructátion, n. the act of belching, a belch
Rudd, n. a fifh of the cyprin kind
Rud'der, n. the thing that fteers a fhip, a fieve
Rud'dinefs, n. a ruddy ftate or quality
Rud'dle, n. a kind of red earth or chalk
Rud'dy, a. approaching to rednefs, frefh, yellow
Rude, a rough, brutal, harfh, uncivil, ignorant
Rúdely, ad. in a rude manner, roughly, violently
Rúdenefs, n. incivility, violence, ignorance
Rúdefby, n. a rúde child or girl, romp, ob.
Rúdiments, n. the firft principles of a fcience
Rudiment'al, a. relating to firft principles, chief
Rue, v. to grieve for, regret, lament ; n. an herb
Rúeful, a. mournful, forrowful, woful, difmal
Rúefully, ad. mournfully, forrowfully, difmaily
Rúefulnefs, n. mournfulnefs, forrowfulnefs, woe
Ruelle', n. a private affembly, circle, ftreet, ob.
Ruff, n. a linen ornament, plain ftate, bird, fifh
Ruff, v. to trump at cards, ftrike, hit, wound
Ruffian, a. brutal, favage ; v. i. to act brutally
Ruffian, n. a brutal fellow, robber, murderer
Ruf'fle, v. t. to diforder, flutter, fret, vex, plait
Ruf'fle, n. an ornament for the hands, a tumult
Ruffling, or Ruffing, n. a particular beat of a drum
Rúfous, a. red, of a reddifh color
Rug, n. a rough woollen coverlet for beds
Rug'ged, a. rough, uneven, four, harfh, ftormy
Rug'gedly, ad. roughly, unevenly, fourly, harfhly
Rug'gednefs, n. roughnefs, afperity, fournefs
Rúgine, n. a kind of rafp, a furgeon's rafp
Rugófe, a. full of wrinkles, rough, uneven
Rúin, n. deftruction, overthrow, fall, bane, lofs
Rúin, v. to deftroy, demolifh, fpoil, run to ruin

Rúinate, v. t. to ruin, fubvert, bring to poverty
Ruinátion, n. ruin, deftruction, fubverfion
Rúinous, a. fallen to ruin, deftructive, pernicious
Rúinoufly, ad. with ruin, deftructively
Rule, n. government, command, direction, law
Rule, v. to govern, manage, direct, draw lines
Rúler, n. a governor, an inftrument to rule lines
Rum, n. ardent fpirit diftilled from cane juce
Rum'ble, v. i. to make a hoarfe low noife
Rum'bling, n. a hoarfe low noife, a noife
Rúminant, a. chewing the cud, meditating
Rúminate, v. i. to chew the cud, reflect, mufe
Rumination, n. meditation, reflection, deep ftudy
Rum'mage, n. a clofe or active fearch for things
Rum'mage, v. t. to fearch diligently, to empty
Rum'mer, n. a kind of drinking cup, a large glafs
Rúmor, n. a report, talk, noife
Rúmor, v. t. to report, to fpread a report
Rúmorer, n. a fpreader of reports, a teller
Rump, n. the buttocks, tail, tail of a fowl
Rum'ple, v. t. to crufh out of fhape, to creafe
Rum'ple, n. a rough plait, fold, pucker, wrinkle
Run, v. to move or flow fwiftly, rufh, contend, pafs, have a general reception, pierce or ftab, drive faft, form in a mold, incur, afcertain an imaginary line, fnuggle
Run, n. a courfe, cadence, reception, fuccefs, a fkain of 20 knots, unufual demands upon a bank, the aft part of a fhips bottom, a fmall ftream
Run'agate, n. a runaway, fugitive, apoftate, rebel
Run'away, n. a fugitive, deferter, mean coward
Run'cinate, a. having lobes convex before and ftrait behind
Run'dle, n. the ftep of a ladder, a round, a ball
Rund'let or Run'let, n a fmall barrel or cafk
Rung, pret. and pa. of to ring
Rung, n. a fhip's floor timber
Rúnic, a. denoting the language, &c. of the ancient people of the north of Europe
Run'nel, n. a rivulet, fmall brook, pollard
Run'ner, n. one who runs, a fhoot, rope, ftone, bird
Run'net, n. a liquor ufed to coagulate milk with
Run'ning, n. that which comes off at one diftilling
Run'ning-rigging, is that part of rigging which runs through blocks, &c.
Run'nion, n. a paltry or fcurvy wretch, a rafcal
Runt, n. a fmall pig, a fhort perfon, a bird
Rupée, n. an Indian coin in value 55 cents
Rup'tion, n. a breach, a diffolution [to burft
Rup'ture, n. a breach of peace, burftennefs ; v. t.
Rúral, a. country, like the country, retired
Rufh, n. a violent courfe, plant, worthlefs thing
Rufh, v. i. to pafs or move with violence
Rufh'light, n. a candle made with a rufh-wick
Rufh'y, a. abounding with or made of rufhes
Rufk, n. a kind of bifcuit, a kind of hard bread
Ruf'fet, a. reddifh, ruftic, coarfe ; n. a country
Ruf'feting, n. a very rough apple [drefs
Ruffian, n. a native of Ruffia, in the north of Europe

Rus'fian, *a*. pertaining to Ruffia

Ruft, *n*. an oxyd of a metal, or oxygene and a metal combined, calx

Ruft, *v*. to gather ruft, make rufty, canker, fpoil

Ruft'ic, *a*. rural, clowaifh, plain ; *n*. a clown

Ruft'ical, *a*. rude, unmannerly, boifterous, favage

Ruft'ically, *ad*. rudely, inelegantly [try

Ruft'icate, *v*. to refide in or banifh into the coun-

Rufti''city, *n*. a rural appearance, clownifhnefs

Rus'tic-work, in building, is where the face of the ftones is picked with an inftrument

Ruft'ily, *ad*. in a rufty manner

Ruft'inefs, *n*. a rufty quality or ftate

Rus'tle, *v. i*. to make a low rattling noife

Ruft'y, *a*. covered with ruft, brown, weakened

Rut, *v. i*. to defire to copulate, to cry like deer

Rut, *n*. a track of a wheel, the copulation of deer

Ruth, *n*. pity, tendernefs, mercy, fadnefs, forrow

Rúthful, *a*. pitiful, rueful, woful, fad, forrowful

Rúthfully, *ad*. miferably, fadly, forrowfully

Rúthlefs, *a*. pitilefs, mercilefs, cruel, barbarous

Rúthlefsly, *ad*. without pity or mercy, cruelly

Rúthleffnefs, *n*. a want of pity or mercy, cruelty

Rut'tifh, *a*. wanton, luftful, lecherous, unchafte

Rutúlian, *a*. pertaining to the Rutuli, a people of Latium in Italy, whofe capital was Ardea

Ry'al, *n*. a Spanifh coin worth 10 cents

Ry'der, *n*. a claufe added to a bill in Parliament

Rye, *n*. a coarfe and black kind of grain

Ry'egrafs, *n*. a kind of very ftrong grafs

Ry'ot, *n*. a renter of land in India, who has a permanent leafe, at a fixed rent

S

SAB'aoth, *n. pl*. armies, hofts

Sab'bath, *n*. Sunday, a day of reft and worfhip

Sab'bathbreaker, *n*. one who violates the fabbath

Sabbat'ical, *a*. belonging to the fabbath or to reft

Sabbatárian, *n*. a feventh-day baptift

Sab'batifm, *n*. a keeping of the fabbath, reft, eafe

Sabéan or Sábian, *a*. pertaining to Saba in Arabia, famous for aromatic plants

Sábianifm, Sábiifm, *n*. the fyftem of oriental religion confifting in the worfhip of the heavenly bodies and the elements

Sáber, *n*. a cimetar, falchion, fhort broad fword

Sábine, *a*. pertaining to the Sabines, N. E of Rome

Sáble, *n*. an animal of the weefel genus, or his fur

Sáble, *a*. black, dark, dufky

Sac'charine, [ck as k] *a*. like or pertaining to fugar

Saccholac'tic, *a*. denoting an acid obtained from the fugar of milk [acid with a bafe

Sac'cholate, *n*. a falt formed by the faccholactic

Sacerdótal, *a*. prieftly, belonging to a prieft

Sach'el, *n*. a fmall fack or bag

Sáchem, *n*. a prince, the chief of an Indian tribe

Sack, *n*. a bag of 3 bufhels, quantity, woman's robe, ftorm of a town, plunder, canary-wine

Sack, *v. t*. to put into facks, take by ftorm, rob

Sack'but, *n*. an old mufical inftrument a pipe

Sack'cloth *n*. a cloth ufed for facks or mourning

Sack'er, *n*. one who plunders or takes by ftorm

Sack'ful, *n*. a fack filled, a fulnefs to the very top

Sack'ing, *n*. cloth for facks, a taking by ftorm

Sack'poffet, *n*. a poffet made of fack, milk, &c.

Sac'rament, *n*. an oath, the Lord's fupper, baptifm

Sacrament'al, *a*. relating to a facrament

Sacrament'ally, *ad*. in the manner of a facrament

Sácred, *a*. holy, folemn, confecrated, inviolable

Sácredly, *ad*. holily, religioufly, purely, inviolably

Sácrednefs, *n*. a facred ftate, holinefs, fanctity

Sacrif'icable, *a*. that may be properly facrificed

Sácrif'icator, *n*. one who offers up a facrifice

Sacrif'icature, *n*. whatever relates to facrificing

Sac'rifice, *v. t*. to offer or give up, kill, deftroy

Sac'rifice, *n*. any thing offered up or deftroyed

Sac'rificer, *n*. one who facrifices or offers up

Sacrifi''cial, *a*. pertaining to or doing facrifice

Sac'rilege, *n*. the robbery of a church or chapel

Sacrile''gious, *a*. violating a thing made facred

Sacrile''gioufly, *ad*. with facrilege

Sácring, *a*. confecrating, *vb*.

Sácringbell, *n*. a bell that is rung before the hoft

Sácrift, Sac'riftan, *n*. one who is intrufted with the utenfils and care of a church, a fexton

Sac'rifty, *n*. the veftry room of a church

Sad, *a*. forrowful, dull, heavy, wretched, vile

Sad'den, *v. t*. to make fad, make gloomy, deepen

Sad'dle, *n*. a feat put on a horfe's back, a joint

Sad'dle, *v. t*. to put on a faddle, load, burden

Sad'dlebacked, *a*. having a low or deep back

Sad'dler, *n*. one who makes or fells faddles, &c.

Sadducéan, *a*. pertaining to the Sadducees

Sad'ly, *ad*. forrowfully, miferably, badly, ill

Sad'nefs, *n*. forrow, heavinefs, dejection

Safe, *a*. free from danger ; *n*. a kind of buttery

Safecon'duct, *n*. a convoy, guard, paffport, pafs

Sáfeguard, *n*. a defenfe, convoy, paffport ; *v. t*. to

Sáfely, *ad*. in a fafe manner, fecurely [guard

Sáfenefs, *n*. an exemption from danger, fecurity

Sáfety, *n*. a freedom from danger or hurt, cuftody

Saf'flower, *n*. a deep red fecula feparated from the yellow matter of plants, called alfo Spanifh red and China lake

Saf'fron, *n*. a phyfical plant ; *a*. like faffron, yellow

Sag, *v*. to load, burden, hang heavy, doubt

Sagácious, *a*. quick of fcent or thought, acute

Sagácioufly, *ad*. with quick fcent, acutely, keenly

Sagácioufnefs, Saga''city, *n*. acutenefs, keennefs

Sagap'enum, *n*. a concrete juce in tears or maffes

Sage, *n*. a plant, a man of wifdom ; *a*. wife, grave

Sàgely, *ad*. wifely, prudently, difcreetly, gravely

Sàgenefs, *n*. wifdom, prudence, fkill, gravity

Sag''gittary, *n*. an archer, centaur, conftellation

Sa''gitate, *a*. fhaped like an arrow

Sa''gital, *a*. like or pertaining to an arrow

Ságo, *n*. a fecula or dry powder obtained from a fpecies of Palmtree in the Moluccas, &c.

Sagoin', *n*. a genus of fmall monkey

Sáic or Sáick, *n.* a kind of Turkifh veffel, a ketch

Said, *pret.* and *pa. pff.* of *to fay*

Sail, *n.* a canvas-fheet, fhip, veffel, wing

Sail, *v. i.* to move with fails, fwim, fly, pafs

Sáiler or Sáilor, *n.* a feaman, one ufed to the fea

Sáiling, *n.* the aĉt or art of failing

Sáilmaker, *n.* one whofe bufinefs is to make fails

Sáilyard, *n.* a fpar to extend a fail with

Sáim, *n.* a hog's lard, the fat of fwine, [*local*]

Sáinfoin, *n.* a fort of grafs, a ftrong fodder

Saint, *n.* one eminent for piety, a fort of puritan

Saint, *v.* to canonize, to appear very pious or holy

Sáinted, *pa. a.* canònized, adored, facred

Sáintlike, Sáintly, *a.* refembling a faint, devout

Sáintfhip, *n.* the charaĉter or ftate of a faint

Sáke, *n.* caufe, purpofe, account, regard, end

Sáker, *n.* a kind of cannon, a kind of hawk, *ob.*

Salácious, *a.* lecherous, luftful, wanton, lewd

Salácioufly, *ad.* luftfully, wantonly, lewdly

Sala"city, *n.* lechery, luft, wantonnefs, eagernefs

Sal'ad, Sall'et, *n.* a food compofed of raw herbs

Sal'amander, *n.* a kind of lizard, a kitchen utenfil

Salaman'drine, *a.* like a falamander, fiery

Salamin'ian, *a.* pertaining to Salamin in Greece

Sal'ary, *n.* a ftated hire, a periodical payment

Sale, *n.* the aĉt of felling, a vent, market, price

Sale, *a.* fold or bought, oppofed to homemade

Sáleable, *a.* fit for fale, having quick fale

Sáleablenefs, *n.* a faleable ftate or quality

Sal'ep or Saloop, *n.* the roots of a fpecies of orchis

Sálefman, *n.* one who fells ready-made clothes

Salentin'ian, *a.* pertaining to the Salentini, a people of Calabria, in the fouth of Italy

Sálework, *n:* work made for fale, carelefs work

Sal'ic, *a.* denoting an old law in France which pre cluded females from the crown

Sálient, *a.* leaping, beating, projeĉting

Sal'ify, *v. t.* to form a neutral falt by combining an acid with an alkali, earth or metal

Sal'ifiable, *a.* capable of combining with an acid to form a neutral falt

Salificátion, *n.* the aĉt of falifying

Salíne, *a.* confifting of, like or conftituting falt

Salíne, *n.* a falt fpring   (and falt

Salinoterréne, *a.* denoting a compound of earth

Salinif'erous, *a.* producing falt

Salin'iform, *a.* like or in the form of falt

Salíte, *v. t.* to feafon or impregnate with falt

Salíted, *a.* combined with falt   (glands

Sal'iva or Sal'ive, *n.* fpittle, juce feparated by the

Salíval, Salívous, *a.* relating to or like fpittle

Sal'ivary, *a.* pertaining to the fpittle

Sal'ivate, *v. t.* to purge by the falival glands

Salivátion, *n.* a purging or curing by fpitting

Sállow, *n.* a kind of willow; *a.* yellow, fickly

Sal'lownefs, *n.* yellow nefs, a fickly palenefs

Sal'ly, *n.* an iffue from a place, efcape, flafh, ring

Sal'ly, *v. i.* to make an eruption, rufh out, iffue out

Sal'lyport, *n.* a gate to make fallies from

Salmagun'di, *n.* a mixture of herrings, apples, &c.

Salm'on, [fammon] *n.* a large and very delicious fifh

Salmontrout', *n.* a trout of the falmon kind

Saloon', *n.* a large or fpacious hall

Salp'a, *n.* a fifh of a bluifh green color

Sals'afy, *n.* garden goats beard

Salfoa"cid, *a.* confifting of faltnefs and fournefs

Salt, *n.* a fubftance which affeĉts the tafte, diffolves in water and cryftalizes, the fpecies are nume- rous and various, alfo wit, tafte, a veffel to hold

Salt, *a.* having the tafte of falt, luftful, wanton (falt

Salt, *v. t.* to feafon, mix or fprinkle with falt

Salt'ant, *a.* leaping, jumping, dancing, *ob.*

Saltátion, *n.* the aĉt of jumping or dancing, *ob.*

Salt'atory, *a.* relating to leaping or dancing, *ob.*

Salt'cat, *n.* a heap of falt, a large lump of falt

Salt'cellar, *n.* a kind of cup to hold falt at table

Salt'er, *n.* one who falts, one who fells falt

Salt'ern, *n.* a falt-work, a place where falt is made

Saltinbanc'o, *n.* a quack, mountebank, *ob.*

Salt'ifh, Salfúginous, *a.* fomewhat falt, not frefh

Szlt'ifhly, Salt'ly, *ad.* in a falt ftate or manner

Salt'ifhnefs, *n.* a faltifh ftate or quality

Salt'lefs, *a.* void of falt, frefh, infipid, fimple

Salt'nefs, *n.* a falt ftate, the tafte of falt

Salt'pan, Salt'pit, *n.* a place where falt is made

Saltpéter, *n.* a mineral falt, niter

Salts, *n.* falt water flowing up rivers, [S. C.]

Salt'wort, *n.* a plant, milkwort, fea-chick-weed

Salúbrious, *a.* wholefome, healthful, falutary

Salúbrioufnefs, *n.* healthfulnefs

Salúbrity, *n.* wholefomenefs, healthfulnefs

Sal'utary, *a.* wholefome, healthful, proper, fafe

Salutátion, *n.* a faluting courteoufly, a greeting

Salúte, *v. t.* to greet, hail, addrefs, pleafe, kifs

Salúte, *n.* a falutation, greeting, addrefs, kifs

Salutif'erous, *a.* bringing health, healthy, good

Salvabil'ity, *n.* a poffibility or ftate to be faved

Sal'vable, *a.* that may be faved or preferved

Sal'vage, *n.* a reward for faving wrecked goods

Sal'vage, *a.* favage, wild, uncivilized, rude, *ob.*

Salvátion, *n.* a prefervation from eternal death

Sal'vatory, *n.* a place where a thing is preferved

Salve, *n.* a plafter, help, remedy, cure

Salve, *v. t.* to help or fave by a falve, to cure

Sal'ver, *n.* a piece of plate with a foot, a faver

Sal'vo, *n.* a plea, excufe, refervation, exception

Samar'itan, *n.* an inhabitant of Samaria, chiefly one of the foreigners, fettled there by the Affy- rian king

Samar'itan, *a.* pertaining to Samaria, humane

Sam'bo, *n.* the offspring of a black and a mulat- to [W. Indies]

Same, *a.* of the like kind, mentioned before

Sáme nefs, *n.* the fame ftate or quality, identity

Sámiel, *n.* a hot and fatal wind in Arabia

Sam'fet, *n.* a fifh of the falmon kind, the branlin

Samp, *n.* maiz broken coarfe, boiled and mixed with milk, &c.

Sam'phire, n. a plant, sea fennel   (similar
Sam"ple, n. a specimen ; v. t. to show something
Samp'ler, n. a piece of girl's needlework, a pattern
San'able, a. that may be healed or cured
Sanation, n. the act of healing or curing, a cure
San'ative, a. healing, curing, powerful to cure
Sanctification, n. the act of making holy, purity
Sanc'tifier, n. one who sanctifies or makes holy, a
    title given or applied to the Holy Ghost
Sanc'tify, v. t. to make holy, purify, devote
Sanctimonious, a. appearing holy, faintly, devout
Sanctimoniously, ad. with grave austerity
Sanc'timony, n. holiness, a scrupulous austerity
Sanc'tion, n. a ratification, confirmation, decree
Sanc'tion, v. t. to ratify, confirm, support
Sanc'titude, Sanc'tity, n. holiness, piety, purity
Sanc'tuarise, v. t. to shelter, protect, defend, ob.
Sanc'tuary, n. a holy place, a refuge for criminals
Sanc'tuary, a. of or belonging to a sanctuary
Sand, n. a soft gravelly earth, barren land
Sand, v. t. to cover or sprinkle with sand
Sand'al, n. a loose open shoe, a kind of slipper
San'darac, n. a resin obtained from the juniper tree,
    also a beautiful fossil
Sand'bath, n. a bath made by sand
Sand'blind, a. having very short sight, purblind
Sand'box, n. a box for sand, a tree
Sand'ed, pa. covered or sprinkled with sand
Sand'erling, n. a bird of the plover kind
Sandemanian, n. a follower of Sandeman, [local]
Sand'ers, n. a valuable sort of Indian wood
Sand'iver, n. the superfluous salts cast up in glass-
Sand'ish, a. like sand, gritty, loose   [making
Sand'piper, n. a bird with a long slender bill
Sand'stone, n. a stone that consists of small grains
Sand'wort, n. a plant, arenaria
Sand'y, a. abounding, with or like sand
Sane, a. sound in mind, healthy, whole, sober
Sang, pret. of to sing
San'giac, n. a Turkish governor of a province
Sanguif'erous, a. conveying or carrying blood
Sanguification, n. the production of blood
San"guifier, n. a thing that produces blood
Sanguif'luous, a. floating or running with blood
San"guify, v. i. to produce or cause blood
San"guinary, a. bloody, murderous, cruel, horrid
San'guine, a. full of or like blood, confident
San'guineness, Sanguin'ity, n. heat, confidence
Sanguin'eous, a. like blood, bloody, sanguine
San'hedrim, n. the supreme council of the Jews
San'icle, n. a plant of various species
Sanies, n. a thin matter issuing from a wound
Sanious, a. running with thin matter, corrupt
San'ity, n. soundness of mind or body, health
Sank, pret. of to sink
San'nahs, n. India muslins of various qualities
Sans'crit or Shans'crit, n. the ancient language of
    India, now used only by the bramins
Sap, n. the vital juice of plants, a military mine

Sap, v. t. to undermine, subvert, destroy, ruin
Sapajo', n. a kind of monkey with prehensile tails
Sap'id, a. well tasted, savory, palatable, pleasing
Sapid'ity, Sap'idness, n. tastefulness, savor
Sapience, n. wisdom, knowledge, prudence
Sapient, a. wise, sage, skilled, knowing, prudent
Sap'less, a. void of sap, dry, old, husky, simple
Sap'ling, n. a young tree, a poor simple person
Saponaceous, Sap'onary, a. soapy, like soap
Sap'onule, n. a combination of volatile or essential
    oil with some base
Sapor, n. a taste, savor, relish, stimulating quality
Saporif'ic, a. occasioning or producing taste
Saporos'ity, n. the quality of a body which occa-
    sions the sensation of taste
Sap'pare, n. a species of argillaceous earth
Sap'phic, a. pertaining to Sappho a Grecian poetess
Sapph'ire, n. a blue precious stone
Sap'phirine, a. made of or resembling sapphire
Sap'piness, n. a sappy or juicy state, simpleness
Sap'py, a. full of sap, juicy, young, simple
Saraband', n. a Spanish dance, tune, slow measure
Saracen'ic, a. pertaining to the Saracens or Arabi-
Saragoy', n. the opossum of the Molucca isles   (ans
Sar'casm, n. a gibe, taunt, scoff, keen reproach
Sarcast'ic, Sarcast'ical, a. taunting, severe, keen
Sarcast'ically, ad. tauntingly, severely. keenly
Sarce'net, n. a fine thin tough woven silk
Sar'cocol, n. a yellow, semitransparent, solid sub-
    stance between sugar and gum
Sarcoph'agous, a. eating or feeding on flesh
Sarcoph'agy, n. the practice or act of eating flesh
Sarcot'ic, a. producing or causing new flesh
Sar'dan, n. a fish like the herring
Sar'dine, Sar'donyx, n. a precious stone, a color
Sardin'ian, n. a native of Sardinia
Sardin'ian, a. pertaining to Sardinia
Sarg'us, n. a fish with brown transverse rings
Sark, n. a shirt, a large seafish, the shark
Sar'lac, n. the grunting ox of Tartary
Sarmatian, Sarmat'ic, a. noting the Sarmatians,
    tribes of Asia who settled Russia and Poland
Sarmentose, a. full of twigs at the joints   (Sparta
Saron'ic, a. denoting a gulf between Attica and
Sar'rasin, n. a portcullis or herse, see herse
Sarsaparill'a, n. the name of a plant and tree
Sarse, n. a fine hair sieve ; v. t. to sift, ob.
Sash, n. a silk belt, silk band, part of a window
Sassafras, n. a species of the laurel
Sas'soral, n. a species of pigeon called rock pigeon
Sat, pret. of to sit
Satan, n. a name of the devil, the prince of hell
Satan'ic, Satan'ical, a. devilish, infernal, hellish
Satch'el or Sa"chel, n. a little sack, a little bag
Sate, Satiate, v. t. to glut, saturate, fill, satisfy
Sat'ellite, n. a small planet revolving about a larg
    a follower or dependant
Satelli'tious, a. consisting of or having satellites
Satiety, n. a glut, fulness, disgust, hatred

Sat'in, n. a kind of very foft, clofe and fhining filk

Satinet', n. a thin fatin

Sat'ire, n. a poem that cenfures vice or folly

Satir'ic; Satir'ical, a. fevere, keen, cenforious

Satir'ically, ad. with intention to cenfure or vilify

Sat'irift, n. one who writes or utters fatires

Sat'irize, v. t. to cenfure as in a fatire, to abufe

Satisfac'tion, n. content, pleafure, delight, comfort, atonement, recompenfe, amends

Satisfac'tive, a. yielding fatisfaction, fatisfying

Satisfac'torily, ad. to fatisfaction, pleafingly

Satisfac'torinefs, n. the power of fatisfying

Satisfac'tory, a. giving content, making amends

Sat'isfy, v. t. to content, pleafe, feed to the full, atone, pay, reward, recompenfe, convince

Sâtive, a. relating to fowing, fown, fet, planted

Sat'rap, n. a peer, nobleman, governor, viceroy

Sat'rapy, n. a province in Perfia or jurifdiction of a fatrap

Sat'urable, a. that can receive more or be filled

Sat'urate, v. t. to fill till no more can be received

Saturátion, n. a ftate of being filled or fupplied

Sat'urday, n. the laft or feventh day of the week

Satúrity, n. a full ftate, fulnefs, glut, ob.

Sat'urn, n. a planet, lead in chymiftry, dark color

Saturn'ian, a. relating to Saturn, fimple, rude

Sat'urnine, a. grave, dull, heavy, melancholy

Sat'urnite, n. a fubftance feparated from lead ore by torrefaction

Sat'yr, n. a fylvan god, beaft, monkey, fatire

Sauce, n. fomething to improve the relifh of food

Sauce, v. t. to accompany with fauce, to pleafe

Sauce'box, n. a faucy or impertinent perfon, flirt,

Sauce'pan, n. a pan to make fauce, &c. in (minx

Sau"cer, n. a fmall plate ufed for a teacup

Sau"cily, ad. pertly, impertinently, impudently

Sau"cinefs, n. impertinence, impudence, boldnefs

Sau"cy, a. pert, impudent, infolent, rude, bold

Saun'ders, n. a tree or a red dye extracted from it

Saunt'er, v. i. to loiter, idle, wander about idly

Saus'age, n. minced meat ftuffed in a gut

Sav'age, a. wild, uncultivated, cruel, barbarous

Sav'age, v. t. to make cruel or barbarous [not ufed]

Sav'age, n. a perfon uncivilized, a genus of flies

Sav'agely, ad. cruelly, barbaroufly, inhumanly

Sav'agenefs, Sav'agery, n. great cruelty, barbarity

Savan'na, n. an open meadow, a pafture ground

Save, v. to preferve from danger or ruin, refcue, lay up, keep frugally, fpare, except

Sáveall, n. a fmall pan to fave candle ends on

Sav'elin, n. a fifh with a black back

Sáver, n. one who faves, a preferver, a gatherer

Savin, n. a plant or tree of feveral varieties

Sáving, a. frugal, careful, near, excepting

Sávingly, ad. in a faving manner, frugally, clofely

Sávingnefs, n. frugality, great care, parfimony

Sávior, n. He who faves mankind, a redeemer

Sávor, n. a tafte, fcent, odor, fmell

Sávor, v. to have a tafte or fmell, tafte, relifh, like,

feafon, betoken, refemble, exhibit, fhow

Sávorily, ad. with a guft, with a pleafing relifh

Sávory, a. pleafing to the fmell or tafte, nice

Sávery, n. a garden plant, the fatureja

Savoy', n. a fort of colewort, a fort of cabbage

Savoy'ard, n. an inhabitant of Savoy

Saw, n. a toothed inftrument, faying, maxim

Saw, v. t. fawed, pret. fawed, fawn, pa. to cut with a faw; pret. of to fee

Saw'duft, n. duft arifing from fawing wood (teeth

Saw'fifh, n. a fifh with a long beak of bone fet with

Saw'fly, n. a genus of flies with a ferrated mouth

Saw'pit, n. a place where large wood is fawed

Saw'wort, n. a fpecies of plant, the feratula

Saw'yer, n. one who faws, one who faws timber

Sax'ifrage, n. an herb good againft the ftone, a tree

Sax'ifragous, a. diffolvent of or good for the ftone

Sax'on, n. one of the people who conquered England in the fixth century, their language

Sax'on, a. pertaining to the Saxons

Sax'onifm, n. a faxon idiom or phrafe

Say, v. t. faid, pret. faid, pa. to fpeak, utter, pronounce, tell, allege

Say, n. a fpeech, fample, proof, trial, thin ftuff

Sáying, n. a proverb, maxim, expreffion, opinion

Scab, n. an incruftation over a fore, itch, mange

Scab, v. i. to grow a hard fkin over a fore

Scab'bard, n. the fheath of a fword, a cafe, a cover

Scab'bed, a. covered with fcabs, paltry, forry

Scab'binefs, n. a fcabby ftate or quality

Scab'by, a. difeafed with fcabs, itch or mange

Scábious, a. itchy, leprous; n. a plant

Scábrous, a. rough, rugged, harfh, unmufical

Scad, n. the horfe mackarel

Scaf'fold, n. a temporary ftage or frame of wood

Scaf'foldage, n. a gallery, a kind of hollow floor

Scaf'folding, n. a fupport made for workmen

Scaláde, n. a ftorm of a place made with ladders

Scálary, a. proceeding by or like fteps

Scald, [as aw] v. t. to burn with hot liquids

Scald, n. a burn with liquids, a fcurf on the head an ancient bard or poet of the north of Europe

Scald, a. fcurvy, paltry, ob.

Scale, n. a part of the covering of a fifh, cruft, balance, regular gradation, gamut, line of diftances, degree of a circle, ladder, fcalade

Scale, v. t. to fcrape off fcales, pare, peel, mount

Scáled, pa. having fcales like fifh, mounted

Scaléne, n. a triangle with all its fides unequal

Scalénous, a. pertaining to a fcalene

Scálinefs, n. a fcaly ftate, roughnefs

Scal'lion, n. a kind of fmall green onion

Scal'lop, n. fee fcollop

Scalp, n. the fkull, the fkin and flefh on the fkull

Scalp, v. t. to cut the fkin off the fkull

Scalp'el, n. a knife ufed in furgery

Scalp'er, n. a furgeons fcraping knife

Scály, a. covered with or having fcales, rough

Scam'ble, v. to fcramble, fhift aukwardly, maul, ob.

Scam'mel, n. a kind of bird

Scam'mony, n. a plant, a gum refin from the plant

Scamp'er, v. i. to run away with fear and fpeed

Scan, v. t. to examin nicely, canvafs, meafure

Scan'dal, n. a difgrace, a reproachful afperfion

Scan'dal, Scan'dalize, v. t. to difgrace, to defame

Scan'dalous, a. difgraceful, fhameful, bafe, vile

Scan'daloufly, ad. fhamefully, cenforioufly

Scan'dent, a. climbing, creeping up

Scant, v. t. to limit, ftraiten, reftrain, confine

Scant, a. narrow, fcanty ; ad. fcarcely, hardly

Scant'ily, ad. narrowly, fparingly, niggardly

Scant'inefs, Scant'nefs, n. narrownefs, fmallnefs

Scant'let, n. a fmall quantity, piece or pattern

Scant'ling, n. timber cut into a fmall fize

Scant'ly, ad. fcarcely, hardly, nearly, penurioufly

Scant'y, a. narrow, fmall, poor, fparing, near

Scape, v. i. to efcape; n. an efcape, a flight

Scape, n. a ftalk which bears t'ke fructification with-

Scapelefs, a. deftitute of a fcape   (out leaves

Scapement, n. the method of communicating the impulfe of wheels to the pendulum of a clock

Scap'ular, n. a fether near the junction of the wing with the body, lying on the back

Scap'ular, Scap'ulary, a. belonging to the fhoulder

Scap'ulary, n. a badge worn on the fhoulder

Scar, n. the mark of a burn or cut, a rock

Scar, v. t. to mark with wounds or fores

Scar'amouch, n. a buffoon in motley drefs

Scarce, a. uncommon, rare, not plentiful, dear

Scarce, Scárcely, ad. hardly, rarely, fcantily

Scárcenefs, Scárcity, n. rarenefs, want

Scare, v. t. to frighten, terrify, alarm, difturb

Scárecrow, n. an image to frighten birds, a gull

Scarf, v. t. to drefs or throw on loofely, to join

Scarf, n. a loofe covering for the fhoulders

Scarf'fkin, n. the thin outward fkin, the cuticle

Scarification, n. a flight incifion with a lancet

Scar'ificator, n. an inftrument ufed in cupping

Scar'ifier, n. one who fcarifies, one who cups

Scar'ify, v. t. to lance or cut the fkin, cup, open

Scárious, a. dry and rough to the touch

Scar'let, n. a color deeply red, but not fhining

Scar'let, a. being of a deep red color

Scar'let bean, n. a kind of red bean, a garden plant

Scarlet féver, n. a fever attended with a red fkin and fore throat, vulgarly called canker rafh

Scarleti'nous, a. of a fcarlet color as in fcarlet fever

Scar'let oak, n. a tree, a fpecies of the oak

Scarp, n. the flope before a ditch

Scárus, n. a fish living among rocks   (with fcates

Scate, n. an iron to flide with, a fish ; v. i. to flide

Scath, n. wafte, damage, ob.

Scath, v. t. to wafte, damage, deftroy, ob.

Scath'ful, a. deftructive, mifchievous

Scat'ter, v. t. to fpread, fprinkle, difperfe, caft

Scat'terer, n. one who fcatters, one who difperfes

Scat'teringly, ad. difperfedly, loofely, irregularly

Scaup, n. a fowl of the duck kind

Scav'age, n. a duty for permiffion to fell gocds

Scav'enger, n. a perfon employed to clean ftreets

Scel'erat, n. a villain, knave, wicked wretch, ob.

Scene, n. an appearance, part of a play, the ftage

Scénery, n. reprefentation, imagery, appearance

Scen'ic, Scen'ical, a. theatrical, dramatic, acted

Scénift, n. one who defcribes or views fcenes

Scenograph'ical, a. drawn in perfpective

Scenog'raphy, n. the art of perfpective

Scent, n. fmell, a chafe by fmell; v. i. to perfume

Scep'ter, n. a royal enfign carried in the hand, a conftellation

Scep'tered, a. marked with or having a fcepter

Scep'tic, n. one who doubts of every thing, efpe-cially of the truth of revelation

Scep'tical, a. doubting, hefitating to admit the truth of an opinion or fyftem

Scep'tically, ad. in a fceptical manner

Scep'ticifm, n. doubt, hefitation to admit the truth of revealed religion

Scep'ticize, v. t. to doubt, to be fceptical

Sched'ule, [ch as k] n. a fmall fcroll, an inventory

Scheme, [ch as k] n. a plan, project, contrivance,

Scheme, v. t. to plan, project, contrive, plot (figure

Schémer, n. a projector, contriver, defigner, head

Schéfis, n. habitude, the ftate of a thing, ob.

Schirros'ity, n. an induration of the glands   (hard

Schir'rous, [ch as k] a. having an indurated gland,

Schifm, n. a feparation, a divifion in the church

Schis'matic, n. one who feparates from the church

Schifmat'ic, Schifmat'ical, a. feparated, divided

Schifmat'ically, ad. in a fchifmatical manner

Schol'ar, [ch as k] n. a difciple, man of learning, a pupil, one who has a liberal education

Schol'arfhip, n. learning, exhibition for a fcholar

Scholaft'ic, Scholaft'ical, a. belonging to a fchool

Scholaft'ically, ad. in the method of fchools

Schóliaft, [ch as k] n. a writer of fcholiums or fhort notes

Schólion, Schólium, Schóly, n. an explanatory

Schóly, v. i. to write explanatory notes, ob. (note

School, [ch as k] n. a place for education

School, v. t. to inftruct, teach, reprove

School'boy, n. a boy at fchool, learner, novice

School'day, n. a day or age to fend youth to fchool

School'fellow, n. one bred up at the fame fchool

School'man, n. a man verfed in fchool divinity

School'mafter, n. a man who teaches a fchool

School'miftrefs, n. a woman who teaches a fchool

Schoon'er, [ch as k] n. a veffel with two mafts and a fail to each extended by a gaff and boom

Sciag'raphy, n. the fection of a building, the art of finding out the hour by means of a fhadow

Sciath'eric, a. belonging or relating to a fundial

Sciat'ic, Sciat'ical, a. troubled with the hip gout

Science, n. knowledge, deep learning, fkill, art

Sciences, n. pl. grammar, logic, rhetoric, arith-metic, geometry, aftronomy and mufic

Scien'tial, a. producing or relating to fcience, ob.

Scientific, *a.* producing knowledge, masterly
Scientifically, *ad.* conformable to science
Scimeter, *n. fee* cimetar
Scintillate, *v. i.* to sparkle, to throw out sparks
Scintillation, *n.* the act of sparkling or shining
Sciolist, *n.* a mere smatterer in any science
Sciolous, *a.* knowing things only superficially, *ob.*
Sciomachy, (ch as k.)*n.* a battle with a shadow
Scion, *n.* a small twig, shoot, sprout, graft, cion
Scioptrics, *n.* the science of exhibiting images through a hole in a darkened room
Scioptic, *a.* pertaining to the camera obscura
Sciffars or Sciffors, *n. pl.* a small pair of shears
Scissible, Scissile, *a.* that may be cut or divided
Scission, *n.* the act of cutting or dividing
Scissure, *n.* a crack, rent, fissure, cleft, cut, slit
Sclerotic, *a.* hard. firm, tough, hardening
Scobiform, *a.* in the form of saw dust
Scoff, *v. t.* to laugh with scorn, ridicule, deride
Scoff, *n.* an expression of scorn, ridicule, derision
Scoffer, *n.* a saucy scorner, derider, mocker
Scoffingly, *ad.* in scorn, contempt or ridicule
Scold, *v.* to chide, find fault, brawl, quarrel
Scold, *n.* a cross quarrelsome woman, clamor
Scollop, *n.* a fish, an indenting; *v. t.* to indent
Scolopenders, *n.* a genus of insects without wings
Sconce, *n.* a fort, hanging candlestick, looking-
Sconce, *v. t.* to fine, to mulct   (glass, the head
Scoop, *n.* a kind of large ladle, sweep, stroke, dash
Scoop, *v. t.* to cut hollow or deep, lade, empty
Scooper, *n.* one who scoops, a waterfowl
Scope, *n.* a drift, intention, liberty, room, sally
Scopulous, *a.* rocky, full of rocks, craggy, rough
Scorbutic, *a.* diseased with or having the scurvy
Scorbutically, *ad.* with a tendency to the scurvy
Scorch, *v.* to burn slightly, to be dried too much
Score, *n.* a line drawn, notch, draft, account, debt, fake, motive, reason, the number twenty
Score, *v. t.* to set down, mark, impute, charge
Scoriaceous, *a.* like dross, drossy
Scorification, *n.* the act or process of forming dross
Scoriform, *a.* like or in the form of dross
Scorify, *v.* to form into dross
Scorious, *a.* drossy, foul, refuse, worthless (metals
Scory, *n.* dross, mixed mass floating on melted
Scorn, *n.* contempt; *v. t.* to despise, slight, scoff
Scorner, *n.* a despiser, ridiculer, scoffer, infidel
Scornful, *a.* contemptuous, haughty, insolent
Scornfully, *ad.* contemptuously, insolently
Scornfulness, *n.* scornful or insolent behavior
Scorpion, *n.* a reptile animal, venomous insect, feafish, sign of the zodiac, scourge, punishment
Scortatory, *a.* pertaining to lewdness
Scot, *v. t.* to stop a wheel by some obstacle
Scot, *n.* a Scotchman, shot, part, share, payment
Scotch, *v. t.* to cut slightly, to cut off; *n.* a slight
Scotch, *n.* of or belonging to Scotland   (cut
Scoter, *n.* a fowl of the duck genus
Scotfree, *a.* excused from paying, free, clear, safe

Scotia, *n.* a semicircular cavity or channel between the tores in the bases of columns
Scotomy, *n.* a swimming or giddiness in the head
Scotticism, *n.* a Scotch idiom or mode of speech
Scottish, *a.* pertaining to Scotland or the Scots
Scoundrel, *n.* a mean low fellow, villain, rogue
Scour, *v.* to clean by rubbing, cleanse, purge, pass over swiftly, scamper, run fast, rove, rake
Scourer, *n.* one who scours or cleans, a purge
Scourge, *n.* a whip, lash, punishment, punisher
Scourge, *v. t.* to whip, lash, beat, chastise, punish
Scourger, *n.* one who scourges, one who lashes
Scout, *n.* one who observes an enemy's actions
Scout, *v. i.* to reconnoiter privately, to sneer at
Scovel, *n.* a kind of mop to sweep an oven with, *ob.*
Scow, *n.* a large flat-bottomed boat
Scow, *v. t.* to transport in a scow
Scowl, *v. i.* to frown, to look angry; *n.* a frown
Scowlingly, *ad.* in a sullen manner, angrily
Scrabble, *v. i.* to scratch, to paw with the hands
Scrag, *n.* any thing thin, the neck, sharp point
Scragged, Scraggy, *a.* thin, lean, rough, uneven
Scragginess, *n.* leanness, roughness, hardness
Scramble, *v. i.* to catch eagerly, contend, climb
Scramble, *n.* an eager contest to get any thing
Scrambler, *n.* one who scrambles for any thing
Scranch, *v. t.* to grind harshly between the teeth
Scrannel, *a.* vile, grating, *ob.*
Scrap, *n.* a little piece, bit, crum, fragment
Scrape, *v.* to pare lightly, erase, shave, make an aukward bow or disagreeable noise, court, get
Scrape, *n.* a difficulty, perplexity, hobble, distress
Scraper, *n.* a thing with which we pare, clear or erase, an iron to clean on, miser, vile fidler
Scratch, *v. t.* to rub with the nails, &c. write badly, mark out lines; *n.* a very slight wound
Scratches, *n. pl.* cracked scabs in a horse's foot
Scratchingly, *ad.* with the action of scratching
Scraw, *n.* the surface, a cut turf, *ob.*   (writing
Scrawl, *v.* to write or draw badly, to creep; *n.* bad
Scrawler, *n.* a hasty or inelegant writer
Scray, *n.* a bird, the sea swallow
Screak, *v. i.* to make a shrill or hoarse noise
Scream, *v. i.* to cry out violently or shrilly
Scream, *n.* a quick shrill cry from fear, &c.   (cry
Screamers, *n.* a genus of fowls so called from their
Screech, *v. i.* to shriek, cry, cry as an owl, hoot
Screech, *n.* a harsh and horrid cry, shout, hoot
Screechowl, *n.* an owl that hoots by night
Screen, *v. t.* to shelter, hide, conceal, sift, riddle
Screen, *n.* a thing that conceals or saves, a riddle
Screw, *v. t.* to turn or fasten with a screw, deform by contortions, extort, squeeze, oppress
Screw, *a.* a mechanical power with spiral threds
Scribble, *n.* bad or careless writing, a scrawl
Scribble, *v. t.* to write without care or beauty
Scribbler, *n.* a bad writer, a mean or petty author
Scribe, *n.* a writer, public notary, divine teacher
Scribe, *v. t.* to mark by a model or rule, to fit one

piece to another

Scrimer, *n.* a gladiator, a fencing-master, *ob.*

Scrine, *n.* a bookcase, a repository for writings, *ob.*

Scrip, *n.* a small bag, small writing, schedule

Scrip'tory, *a.* relating to writing, written, penned

Scrip'tural, *a.* contained in the bible, holy, divine

Scrip'turalist, *n.* one who adheres litterally to scripture and makes it the foundation of all philosophy

Scrip'ture, *n.* sacred writings, holy writ, the bible

Scriv'ener, *n.* one who draws contracts for money

Scrof'ulous, *a.* troubled with sores, ulcers, &c.

Scroll, *n.* a writing wrapped up, roll, wreath

Scrótum, *n.* the purse or membrane that incloses the testicles, a skin, bag, cist, case

Scroyle, *n.* a mean fellow, rascal, rebel, *ob.*

Scrub, *n.* a mean fellow, a broom worn out

Scrub, *v.* to rub hard, to ease or clean by rubbing

Scrub'by, *a.* mean, sorry, dirty, worthless, vile

Scrúple, *n.* a doubt, a weight of twenty grains

Scrúple, *v.* to doubt, hesitate, boggle, question

Scrúpler, *n.* one who scruples, one who doubts

Scrupulos'ity, *n.* doubt, fear of acting, niceness

Scrúpulous, *a.* doubtful, cautious, careful, nice

Scrúpulously, *ad.* cautiously, carefully, nicely

Scrútable, *a.* discoverable by inquiry   (inquirer

Scrutátor, Scrutinéer, *n.* an examiner, searcher,

Scrútinize, *v. t.* to examin diligently, to search

Scrútinous, *a.* inquisitive, captious, careful, nice

Scrútiny, *n.* an examination, search, inquiry

Scrutóire, *n.* a case of drawers for papers

Scud, *n.* a small flying cloud, a sudden shower

Scud, *v. i.* to fly as a cloud before the wind

Scuf'fle, *n.* a confused quarrel, broil, fray

Scuf'fle, *v. i.* to fight confusedly, to contend

Sculk, *v. i.* to lurk secretly, lie close, hide

Sculk'er, *n.* one who sculks, a lurker   (a shoal

Scull, *n.* the arched bone of the head, a small oar,

Scull, *v.t.* to impel a boat by a single oar at the stern

Scull'cap, *n.* a small cap for the head, a nightcap

Scull'er, *n.* a small boat managed by one rower

Scull'ery, *n.* a place to wash and keep things in

Scull'ion, *n.* a cook's servant, a low mean drudge

Sculp, *v. t.* to carve, to engrave; *n.* a cut, a print

Sculp'tile, *a.* made by carving or engraving

Sculp'tor, *n.* a carver, engraver, cutter, former

Sculp'ture, *v. t.* to cut, to engrave; *n.* carved work

Scum, *n.* froth, dross, refuse, dregs of this people

Scum, *v. t.* to take off the scum or foulness

Scum'mer, *n.* one who scums or clears, a skimmer

Scum'mings, *n.* matter skimmed from the surface

Scup'pers, *n.* the channels and holes in a ships side to carry water off of the deck

Scurf, *n.* a kind of dry scab, scale, adherent stain

Scurf'iness, *n.* a scurfy state or quality

Scurf'y, *a.* covered with or like scurf

Scur'ril, Scur'rilous, *a.* abusive, scandalous

Scurril'ity, *n.* gross language, vile abuse

Scur'rilously, *ad.* with gross reproach, abusively

Scur'vily, *ad.* meanly, pitifully, basely, vilely

Scur'viness, *n.* meanness, baseness, vileness

Scur'vy, *n.* a distemper; *a.* scabbed, vile, worthless

Scur'vygrass, *n.* a plant good against the scurvy

Scut, *n.* the tail of a hare, &c. a loose woman

Scútage, *n.* shield, service or expedition money

Scutch'eon, *n.* a shield represented in heraldry

Scutel'lated, *a.* divided into small surfaces

Scútiform, *a.* shaped like a shield

Scut'tle, *v. i.* to run about in a hurry, to cut holes in a ships bottom, to sink by letting in water

Scut'tle, *n.* a thing for coals, grate, quick place, a small hatch way   ('Tartary

Scyth'ian, *n.* a native of Scythia, now Russia and

Scyth'ian, Scyth'ic, *a.* pertaining to Scythia

Sea, *n.* the ocean, an inland water, deluge

Séabear, *n.* an animal of the bear kind

Séabeaten, *a.* beaten or dashed by the waves

Séaboat, *n.* a boat or vessel able to bear the sea

Séabord, *n.* the shore or edge of the sea

Séabord, *a.* bordering on the sea

Séaborn, *a.* born of or produced by the sea

Séaboy, *n.* a boy employed on shipboard

Séabreach, *n.* a breach made by the sea

Séabreeze, *n.* a breeze or wind from the sea

Séabuilt, *a.* built for the sea or for sailing

Séacalf, *n.* a kind of sea-animal, the seal-fish

Séacap, *n.* a cap made to be worn on shipboard

Séachart, *n.* a map or delineation of the seacoast, and of the ocean and islands placed in the sea

Séacoal, *n.* coal that is brought or carried by the sea

Séacoast, *n.* the edge or side of the sea, the shore

Séacompass, *n.* the mariner's compass

Séacow, *n.* a large animal, the manatus

Séadog, *n.* a kind of fierce sea-animal, a shark

Seaencir'cled, *a.* surrounded by the sea

Séafarer, *n.* a sailor, mariner, traveller by the sea

Séafaring, *a.* using or travelling over the seas

Séafight, *n.* a fight or battle on the sea

Séafish, *n.* a fish that lives or breeds in the sea

Séafowl, *n.* a bird that lives principally at sea

Séagirt, *a.* surrounded or shut in by the sea

Séagrass, *n.* an aquatic plant

Séagreen, *a.* being of the sea-color, rather green

Séagull, *n.* the name of a common sea-fowl

Séahedgehog, *n.* a very rough sea-shellfish

Séahen, *n.* another name of the guillemot

Séahorse, *n.* the morse, a large sea-animal

Seal, *n.* a stamp, mark, confirmation, sea-calf

Seal, *v.* to fix a seal, close, settle, confirm, ratify

Séaling, *n.* the killing of seals

Séalingvoyage, *n.* a voyage for killing seals

Séalion, *n.* a marine animal with a mane

Séalingwax, *n.* a wax used to seal letters, &c. with

Seam, *n.* what joins two pieces together, a scar, measure of 8 bushels, load, tallow, lard, net

Seam, *v. t.* to join or fix together, mark, scar

Séamaid, *n.* a kind of sea-animal, a mermaid

Séaman, *n.* a mariner, sailor, animal, mermaid

Séamanship, *n.* the qualifications of a good seaman

Scamarge, *n.* the brink or fide of the fea, a cliff
Scamark, *n.* a mark fet to direct failors at fea
Scamew, *n.* a kind of feafowl, a feagull
Seamlefs, *a.* having no feam, entire, whole, even
Seamonfter, *n.* a ftrange odd animal of the fea
Seamoufe, *n.* the aphrodite, an infect of an oval form
Seamfter, Seamftrefs, *n.* one who lives by fewing
Seamy, *a.* having a feam, full of feams, rough
Sean, *n.* a fifhing net, fometimes written *feine*
Seanymph, *n.* a nymph or goddefs of the fea
Seaooze, *n.* mud of the fea, filth upon the fhore
Seapiece, *n.* a picture or draft of a fea affair
Seaport, *n.* a port for fhips on the fea fhore
Seapye, *n.* a difh of pafte and bits of meat boiled
Sear, *v. t.* to burn, to fcorch; *a.* dry, withered
Searce, *v. t.* to fift, to fift finely; *n.* a fine fieve
Search, *v.* to feek, look, inquire, examin, find
Search, *n.* the act of feeking, a queft, an inquiry
Searcher, *n.* one who fearches, an examiner
Searcloth, *n.* a large ftrengthening plafter
Searifk, *n.* a rifk or hazard at fea, a venture
Searoom, *n.* plenty of room at fea, an open fea
Seafervice, *n.* naval employment, naval war
Seafhell, *n.* a fhell found on the feafhore
Seafhore, *n.* the coaft or fide of the fea, the fhore
Seafick, *a.* fick from the motion of the fea
Seaficknefs, *n.* ficknefs caufed by the fea
Seafide, *n.* the fide or edge of the fea
Seafon, *n.* a fourth part of the year, fit time, relifh
Seafon, *v. t.* to give a relifh to, qualify, make fit
Seafonable, *a.* fuited to the time, proper, fit
Seafonablenefs, *n.* fitnefs of time, opportunity
Seafonably, *ad.* in due or juft time, properly, fitly
Seafoner, *n.* one who feafons or gives a relifh
Seafoning, *n.* that which gives a relifh, a trial
Seafurgeon, *n.* a furgeon employed on fhipboard
Seafurrounded, *a.* furrounded with the fea
Seat, *n.* a chair, bench, poft, manfion, refidence
Seat, *v. t.* to place on or in a feat, fix, fettle, plan
Seaterm, *n.* a term or word of art ufed by feamen
Seaward, *ad.* towards the fea, near or by the fea
Seawater, *n.* the water of the fea, falt water
Seaworthy, *a.* fit for a voyage, or for fea
Sebaceous, *a.* fat, pertaining to fat
Sebacic, *a.* denoting an an acid obtained from fat
Sebate, *n.* a falt formed by febacic acid and a bafe
Sebeften, *n.* the affyrian plum
Secant, *a.* dividing into two parts, cutting
Secant, *n.* a line drawn from the center of a circle
  till it cuts a tangent to the circle; a line which
Secede, *v. i.* to depart, to withdraw (cuts another
Seceder, *n.* one who departs, one who feparates
Secern, *v. t.* to feparate fine from grofs matter
Secernent, *n.* that which promotes fecretions
Secession, *n.* the act of withdrawing from
Secle, *n.* a century, a hundred years, *ob.*
Seclude, *v. t.* to exclude, feparate, fhut up
Seclufion, *n.* the act of fecluding or feparating
Second, *v. t.* to fupport, affift, forward, follow

Second, *a.* next to the firft, inferior; *n.* a perfon
  that backs another, the 60th part of a minute
Secondarily, *ad.* in the fecond order or place
Secondary, *a.* fecond, inferior, lefs; *n.* a deputy
Secondary, *n.* a fether growing on the fecond part
  of the wing
Secondhand, *a.* not original, borrowed, derived
Secondhand, *n.* the fecond place of order or time,
  the fecond place in poffeffion
Secondly, *ad.* in the fecond or next place
Secondrate, *n.* a fecond order in dignity; *a.* fecond
Secondfight, *n.* a power to forefee things future
Secondfighted, *a.* endued with fecondfight
Secrecy, *n.* clofe filence, privacy, retirement
Secret, *a.* concealed, unfeen, private, faithful
Secret, *n.* a thing unknown; *v. t.* to keep private
Secretary, *n.* one who writes for another in bufi-
  nefs, an indian bird of the fize of a turky
Secretaryfhip, *n.* the office or poft of a fecretary
Secrete, *v. t.* to hide, conceal, feparate
Secretion, *n.* a feparation of animal juces, juce
Secretift, *n.* a dealer in fecrets, a fecret perfon, *ob.*
Secretitious, *a.* feparated by animal fecretion
Secretly, *ad.* in a fecret manner, privately, clofely
Secretnefs, *n.* privacy, a faculty of keeping fecrets
Secretory, *a.* performing the office of fecretion
Sect, *n.* a body of men united in certain tenets
Sectarifm, *n.* a difpofition or tendency to fchifm
Sectarian, *n.* one of a fect, a feparate
Sectarian, *a.* pertaining to a fect
Sectary, *n.* one who joins with fchifmatics
Sectator, *n.* a follower, difciple, pupil, imitator
Section, *n.* a cutting, part cut, divifion
Sector, *n.* a portion of a circle between two radiu-
  fes and their included arc, an inftrument to find
  proportional quantities of a like kind
Secular, *a.* worldly, laical, not bound by vows
Secularity, *n.* worldlinefs, a worldly ftate
Secularize, *v. t.* to convert from ecclefiaftical to
  fecular ufe   (ecclefiaftical to a fecular ufe
Secularization, *n.* the act of converting from an
Secundine, *n.* the afterbirth or burden, a cake
Secure, *a.* free from fear or danger, fafe, carelefs
Secure, *v. t.* to make faft, fave, protect, enfure
Securely, *ad.* without danger, fear or care, fafely
Securement, *n.* a caufe of fafety, fafety, *ob.*
Securiform, *a.* in the fhape of an ax
Security, *n.* a fafety, protection, defenfe, pledge
Sedan, *n.* a kind of clofe chair for carriage
Sedate, *a.* calm, quiet, ferene, undifturbed, eafy
Sedately, *ad.* calmly, quietly, compofedly
Sedatenefs, *n.* calmnefs, ferenity, compofure
Sedative, *a.* compofing, fettling, eafing, relieving
Sedative, *n.* that which compofes or weakens
Sedentary, *a.* fitting much, inactive, fluggifh
Sedge, *n.* a kind of narrow flag, a long grafs
Sedgy, *a.* overgrown with or like fedge
Sediment, *n.* what fettles at the bottom of liquids
Sedition, *n.* a tumult, infurrection, commotion

Sedi"tious, *a.* factious with tumult, turbulent
Sedi"tiously, *ad.* with factious turbulence, noisily
Sedi"tiousness, *n.* a seditious disposition, faction
Sedúce, *v. t.* to lead astray by arts, entice from duty, debauch
Sedúcement, *n.* the act, art or means of seducing
Sedúcer, *n.* one who draws aside from the right
Sedúcible, *a.* capable of being seduced
Seduc'tion, *n.* the act or art of seducing, deceit
Sedúlity, *n.* diligence, industry, application
Sed'ulous, *a.* diligent, industrious, laborious
Sed'ulously, *ad.* diligently, industriously, busily
See, *n.* the diocese of a bishop or archbishop
See, *v.* saw, *pret.* seen, *pa.* to perceive by the eye, observe, discern, penetrate, attend
Seed *n.* what produces plants and animals, an original, generation, offspring, race, extraction
Seed, *v.* to produce seed, to shed or sow seed
Seedcake, *n.* a kind of sweet seedy cake
Seediness, *a.* a seedy state or quality
Seedling, *n.* a plant springing from seed
Seedlip or Seed'lop, *n.* a vessel used to put seed in
Seedpearl, *n.* small or trifling grains of pearl
Seedplot, *n.* a ground on which seeds are sown
Seedsman, *n.* a person who deals in seeds, a sower
Seedtime, Seed'ness, *n.* the fit season for sowing
Seedy, *a.* abounding with or resembling seed
Seeing, *n.* the act of perceiving, sight, vision
Seeing, *pa.* of *to see*, since, because that
Seek, *v. t.* sought, *pret.* sought, *pa.* to look for, search, endeavor after, go to
Seeker, *n.* one who seeks, an inquirer
Seeksorrow, *n.* a man who causes himself sorrow
Seel, *v.* to close the eyes, lean on one side, roll, *ob.*
Seem, *v. i.* to appear, have resemblance, pretend
Seemer, *n.* one who appears, one who pretends
Seeming, *n.* an appearance, show, opinion, sense
Seemingly, *ad.* in appearance, show or pretense
Seemingness, *n.* a fair appearance, a fair outside
Seemliness, *n.* comeliness, grace, beauty, decency
Seemly, *a.* comely, becoming, decent, proper, fit
Seemly, *ad.* in a decent or proper manner, fitly
Seen, *pa. a.* perceived, beheld, skilled, versed
Seer, *n.* a person who sees, prophet, teat of a cow
See'saw, *n.* a reciprocating motion, alternate play
See'saw *v. i.* to move up and down, to trump
Seeth, *v.* seethed, sod, *pret.* seethed, sodden, *pa.* to boil, to make or be hot
Seether, *n.* a boiler, a pot to boil things in
Segar', *n. see* cigar
Seg'ment, *n.* a piece cut off or contained
Seg'regate, *v. t.* to separate, set apart, remove
Segrátion, *n.* the act of separating or reserving
Seigneúrial, *a.* invested with large powers, great
Seignior, [seneyur] *n.* a lord with the Italians, a Turkish emperor
Seigniorage, *n.* authority, power, rule
Seigniory, or Signiory, *n.* a lordship, dominion
Seignorise, *v. t.* to lord or domineer over

Seine, *n.* a large fishing net
Seizable, *a.* that may be seized on or taken away
Seize, *v. t.* to take by force, catch, fasten, join
Seizin or Seisin, *n.* the act of taking possession
Seizing, *n.* cords for fastening ropes together
Seizure, *n.* the act of seizing, a thing seized, force
Sejúgous, *a.* pinnate with six pair of leaflets
Sejunc'tion, *n.* a disunion, separation
Sel'dom, *ad.* rarely, not often, now and then
Sel'domness, *n.* rareness, infrequency, uncommonness
Seld'thown, *a.* shown but seldom, *ob.* (ness
Select', *v. t.* to choose in preference, pick, cull
Select', *a.* well chosen, picked, culled, choice
Selec'tion, *n.* the act of choosing, a choice made
Select'man, *n.* a town officer in New England; the selectmen are the executive officers of towns
Select'ness, *n.* choiceness, a particular value
Select'or, *n.* one who selects, one who chooses out
Sel'enite, *n.* sulphate of lime, fossil of various species
Selenit'ical, *a.* pertaining to selenite
Selenog'raphy, *n.* a description of the moon
Self, *pron. a.* one's own person, the very same
Selfev'ident, *a.* evident of or in itself, quite clear
Selfin'terest, *n.* private interest, selfishness
Self in'terested, *a.* particularly concerned, selfish
Self'ish, *a.* regarding self interest supremely
Self'ishly, *ad.* with self love, niggardly, meanly
Self'ishness, *n.* self love only, mean covetousness
Se f love', *n.* the love of one's self alone
Selfmur'der, *n.* the murder of one's self (sion
Selfrepel'ling, *a.* having an innate power of repul-
Self'same, *a.* numerically the same, the very same
Sell, *v. t.* sold, *pret.* sold, *pa.* to part with for a price, trade or deal in, deliver up
Sell'ander, *n.* a dry scab in the pastern of a horse
Sell'er, *n.* one who sells, deals in, or delivers up
Sel'vage, *n.* the edge of cloth, a hank of rope
Selves, *pl.* of *self*
Sem'blable, *a.* resembling, like, likely, fair, *ob.*
Sem'blably, *ad.* with resemblance or likeness, *ob.*
Sem'blance, *n.* resemblance, likeness, show
Sem'blant, Sem'blative, *a.* resembling, like, *ob.*
Sem'ble, *v.* to resemble, to make like, *ob.*
Sem'i, *a.* half, containing, &c. only half
Semiacid'ified, *a.* half acidified
Semiamplex'icaul, *a.* half surrounding the stem
Sem'iannular, *a.* half-round, half-circular
Semiap'erture, *n.* the half of an aperture
Sem'ibreve, Sem'ibrief, *n.* a note, two minims
Semical'cined, *a.* half calcined
Sem'icircle, *n.* the half of a circle, an instrument
Sem'icircular, *a.* like half a circle, half-round
Sem'icolon, *n.* a point made or marked thus (;)
Semicolum'nar, *a.* flat on one side and round on the other
Semicompact', *a.* half compact or indurated
Semicrustáceous, *a.* half crustaceous
Semicylin'drical, *a.* half cylindrical
Sem'idiameter, *n.* the half of a diameter, a radius

Sem'idiapen'te, *n.* in mufic, an imperfect fifth

Semidiapáfon, *n.* an imperfect octave, or an octave diminifhed by a lefter femitone

Sem'idiaphonous, *a.* half-clear, half-tranfparent

Semidiatefs'aron, *n.* a defective fourth (6 to 5

Sem'iditone, *n.* a lefter third, having its terms as

Sem'idouble, *a.* half-folemn among Romaniíts

Semiflos'cular, *a.* having petals half hollow and half flat

Sem'iffuid, *a.* imperfectly fluid or flowing, thick

Sem'iformed, *a.* half-formed

Semiin'durated, *a.* half-hardened

Semilentic'ular, *a.* half-convex, or like a lens

Sem'ilunar or Semilúnary, *a.* like a half-moon

Sem'imetal, *n.* an imperfect metal

Semimetal'lic, *a.* partially metallic

Sem'inal, *a.* containing or like feed, radical, firft

Seminal'ity, *n.* nature of feed, power of producing

Sem'inary, *n.* a feedplot, flock, college, fchool

Seminátion, *n.* the difperfion of the feeds of plants

Seminif'erous, *a.* producing feed

Seminific, Seminif'ical, *a.* productive of feed

Seminificátion, *n.* a propagation by feed

Semiorbic'ular, *a.* in fhape of a half-fphere

Semioxy"genated, *a.* half-faturated with oxygene

Sem'iopáeous, Semiopáke, *a.* half-tranfparent

Semies'seous, *a.* bony, half as hard as a bone

Semióvate, *a.* half egg-fhaped

Semipalm'ate, *a.* half-palmate or webbed

Sem'iped, *n.* a half-foot in poetry

Sem'ipellucid, *a.* not quite clear, not very bright

Sem'ipellucid'ity, *n.* a ftate of being imperfectly

Sem'iperfpicuous, *a.* not quite plain or clear (clear

Sem'iquaver, *n.* half the quantity of a quaver

Semifpher'ical, *n.* in form of half a fphere

Semifex'tile, *n.* one twelfth of a circle

Sem'itone, *n.* half a tone, half a note in mufic

Semiton'ic, *a.* pertaining to a femitone

Semitranspárent, *a.* half tranfparent

Sem'itranspárency, *n.* half tranfparency

Semivitrifac'tion, *n.* a fubftance half vitrified

Semivit'rified, *a.* half vitrified or turned to glafs

Semivócal, *a.* half vocal or founding

Sem'ivowel, *n.* a confonant with imperfect found

Semperviírent, *a.* ever green

Sempiter'nal, *a.* everlafting, perpetual, endlefs

Sempiter'nity, *n.* an eternal or endlefs duration

Séna or Sen'na, *n.* the leaves of the caffia

Sénary, *a.* containing or belonging to fix

Sen'ate, *n.* an affembly of counfellors, fenators, a branch of the congrefs of the United States, and of the legiflatures of feveral States

Sen'atehoufe, *n.* a houfe where the fenate meet

Sen'ator, *n.* a public counfellor, &c. an alderman, a member of a fenate

Senatórial or Senatórian, *a.* belonging to fenators or parliament-men, grave, venerable

Send, *v. t.* fent, *pret.* fent, *pa.* to difpatch, let fly, commiffion, propagate

Send'er, *n.* one who fends, one who difpatches

Sen'eclude, *n.* old age, ancientnefs, antiquity

Senegal', *n.* gum fenegal, a gum from Africa

Sen'eka, *n.* a plant, fnakeroot or milkwort

Senes'cence, *n.* a growing old, decay by time or age

Sen'efchal, *n.* a fteward, head-bailif, magiftrate

Sen'green, *n.* the houfeleek

Sénile, *a.* belonging to or confequent on old age

Sénior, *a.* older than another; *n.* one who is older

Senior'ity, *n.* elderfhip, priority of birth or order

Senoc'ular, *a.* having or relating to fix eyes

Senfátion, *n.* perception by means of the fenfes

Senfe, *n.* a faculty of perceiving, meaning, opinion

Sens'ed, *a.* perceived or conveyed by the fenfes

Senfe'ful, *a.* full of fenfe, reafonable, judicious

Senfe'lefs, *a.* void of fenfe, filly, doltifh, ftupid

Senfe'lefsly, *ad.* in a fenfelefs manner, ftupidly

Senfe'leffnefs, *n.* folly, ftupidity, abfurdity

Senfibil'ity, Sens'iblenefs, *n.* quicknefs of fenfation

Sens'ible, *a.* wife, judicious, convinced, bodily, perceptible by the fenfes, eafily moved

Sens'ibly, *ad.* with fenfe, perceptibly, judicioufly

Sens'itive, *a.* having fenfe, produced by fenfation

Sens'itively, *ad.* in a fenfitive manner (the touch

Sens'itiveplant, *n.* mimofa, a plant which fhrinks at

Senfórial, *a.* pertaining to the fenforium, or the fource of animal motions (fenfation

Senfórium, Sens'ory, *n.* the feat of fenfe, organ of

Sens'ual, *a.* pleafing to the fenfes, carnal, lewd

Sens'ualift, *n.* one devoted to carnal pleafures

Sensual'ity, *n.* an addiction to carnal pleafures

Sens'ualize, *v. t.* to fink into fenfual pleafures

Sens'ually, *ad.* in a fenfual manner, carnally

Sens'uous, *a.* pathetic, full of paffion, tender

Sent, *pret.* and *pa. paff.* of *to fend* (period

Sent'ence, *n.* a decifion, condemnation, maxim,

Sent'ence, *v. t.* to condemn, doom, confign

Senten'tial, *a.* pertaining to or making a period

Senten'tiousity, Senten'tioufnefs, *n.* pithinefs, con-

Senten'tious, *a.* fhort and energetic (cifenefs

Senten'tioufly, *ad.* with ftriking brevity, pithily

Sen'tient, *a.* perceiving; *n.* one who perceives

Sent'iment, *n.* a thought, opinion, idea, judgment

Sentiment'al, *a.* thoughtful, reflecting, fenfible

Sentimen'talift, *n.* one fond of fentiment

Sent'inel, Sent'ry, *n.* a foldier on guard, a watch

Sent'rybox, *n.* a box or ftand for a fentinel

Separabil'ity, *n.* the quality of admitting difunion

Sep'arable, *a.* capable or poffible to be difunited

Sep'arablenefs, *n.* a capacity of being feparated

Sep'arate, *v. t.* to divide, disjoin, part, fet apart

Sep'arate, *a.* divided, difunited, difengaged

Sep'arate, *n.* a feceder from a church

Sep'arately, *ad.* diftinctly, fingly, apart, afunder

Sep'aratenefs, *n.* a feparate ftate

Separátion, *n.* a disjunction, parting, divorce

Sep'aratift, *n.* a fchifmatic, diffenter, feceder

Sep'arator, *n.* one who feparates or divides

Sep'aratory, *a.* ufed in or relating to feparation

Sepoy', n. a native foldier or militia of India

Seps, n. a fpecies of venomous lizard

Sept, n. a clan, race, breed, generation, number

September, n. the ninth month of the year (feven

Sep'tenary, a. confiting of feven; n. the number

Septen'nial, a. lafting or happening in feven years

Septent'rion, n. the northern part, the great bear

Septent'rional, a. northern, relating to the north

Septent'rionally, ad. towards or near the north

Septent'rionate, v. i. to tend or go to the north

Sept'foil, n. the plant tormentil

Sep'tic, a. caufing or promoting putrefaction

Sep'tics, n. fuch things as promote putrefaction

Septilat'eral, a. having feven fides (feventy

Septua''genary, Septuages'imal, a. confiting of

Septuages'ima, n. the 9th funday after eafter

Sep'tuagint, n. a Gr. verfion of the Old Teftament

Sep'tuary, n. a week, any thing compofed of feven

Sep'tuple, a. fevenfold, feven times as much

Sepul'chral, a. monumental, relating to burial

Sep'ulcher, n. a grave, a tomb; v. t. to bury

Sepul'ture, n. the act of burying, interment

Sequacious, a. following, attendant, pliant, tough

Sequa''city, n. pliablenefs, obedience, toughnefs

Séquel, n. a fucceeding part, clofe, confequence

Séquence, n. a feries, an order of fucceffion

Séquent, n. a follower; a. following, fucceeding

Seqweft'er, v. t. to fet apart, feparate, withdraw

Sequeft'rable, a. that may be fequeftered or fepa-

Sequeft'rate, v. t. to fequefter] (rated

Sequeftrátion, n. a deprivation of profits

Sequeftrátor, n. one who deprives of profits

Séquin, n. a Venetian and Turkifh gold coin

Seragl'io, n. a houfe kept for women of pleafure

Ser'aph, n. one of the higheft orders of angels

Seraph'ic, Seraph'ical, a. angelical, fublime

Ser'aphim, n. pl. angels of a certain exalted order

Serafs', n. an indian bird of the crane kind

Sere, Seer, a. dry, withered, brittle, yellow, ob.

Serenáde, v. t. to entertain with mufic (night

Serenáde or Serenáte, n. mufic by lovers in the

Seréne, v. t. to calm, quiet, ftill, clear, brighten

Seréne, a. calm, undifturbed, quiet, clear, fair

Seréne, n. a calm clear fky, a calm evening

Serénely, ad. calmly, quietly, coolly (peace

Serénenefs, Serenitude, Serenity, n. calmnefs,

Serf, n. a fervant or flave employed in hufbandry

Serge, n. a thin woollen cloth or ftuff

Ser'geant, n. a petty officer in the army, degree

in law of the higheft rank under a judge, title

Ser'geantry, n. a tenure of lands by perfonal fervice

Serge'maker, n. a man who manufactures ferges

Seri''ceous, a. filky, covered with foft hairs

Séries, n. a fequence, courfe, order, continuance

Ser'in, n. a fong bird of Italy and Germany

Sérious, a. grave, fober, folemn, earneft, weighty

Sérioufly, ad. gravely, folemnly, in earneft

Sérioufnefs, n. gravity, folemnity, earneftnefs

Ser'mon, v. to lecture, to talk, ob.

Ser'mon, n. a pious difcourfe, a lecture

Ser'monize, v. i. to make or preach a fermon

Ser'monizer, n. a writer of fermons

Seroon', n. a fquare bale or package

Serof'ity, n. the thin or watery part of the blood

Sérous, a. relating to or like ferum, thin, watery

Serp'ent, n. a genus of reptiles, amphibious and

breathing through the mouth (or dotted

Ser'pentine, n. a fpecies of magnefian ftone, veined

Serp'entine, a. winding like a ferpent, fpiral

Ser'pentize, v. i. to wind in a ferpentine form

Serpi''genous, a. difeafed with or having a tetter

Serr'ate, a. jagged like a faw, having teeth

Serr'ature, n. an indenting like faw teeth

Ser'rulate, a. finely ferrate, with fmall teeth

Serr'ing, n. the act of driving clofe together, ob.

Ser'tin, n. a fpecies of bat

Serv'al, n. an animal like the lynx and panther

Serv'ant, n. a perfon who ferves, a term of civility

Serve, v. t. to attend on at command, obey, affift

Serv'er, n. a utenfil to ferve with tea or glaffes

Serv'ice, n. a menial office, command, duty, office

of devotion, benefit, ufe, order of difhes

Ser'viceable, a. ufeful, good, fit, active, officious

Serv'iceablenefs, n. ufefulnefs, officioufnefs

Serv'ile, a. flavifh, dependant, cringing, fawning

Serv'ile, n. a letter added for the inflection of words

Serv'ilely, ad. flavifhly, meanly, abjectly, bafely

Serv'ilenefs, Servil'ity, n. flavifhnefs, dependance

Serv'ingman, n. a man fervant, a menial fervant

Serv'itor, n. the loweft order or rank in a college

Serv'itude, n. flavery, bondage, an apprenticefhip

Sérum, n. the thin watery part of the blood, whey

Sefáme, n. oily grain, a plant

Sefqual'ter, Sefquialt'eral, a. one and a half

Sefquidúplicate, a. noting a ratio in which the

greater term contains the leffer twice and a

half, as 50 to 20 (bombaft

Sefquipedálian, a. containing a foot and a half,

Sefquip'licate, a. in the ratio of one and a half to one

Sefquiter'tional, a. noting the ratio of one and a

Sefs, n. a rate, a tax; v. t. to affefs, ob. (third

Sef'file, a. growing on the ftem, without a footftalk

Ses''fion, n. act or time of fitting

Ses'terce, n. a Roman denomination of money

Set, v. t. fet, pret. fet, pa. to place, put, plant, fix,

value, difappear, fall below the horizon

Set, pa. a. placed, planted, fixed, regular, formal

Set, n. a number of things or perfons fuited to each

other, living plant, game, wager at dice

Setáceous, a. fet with ftrong hairs, briftly, refem-

bling brittles (another

Set'off, n. an account or demand to fet againft

Séton, n. a kind of iffue, a rowel in the neck

Setófe, a. fet with ftrong hairs, briftly

Settée, n. a long feat with a back, a kind of fhip

Set'ter, n. one that fets, a kind of dog for game

Set'terwort, n. bears foot, a fetid hellebore

Set'ting n. the paffing of a planet below the horizon

Set'tle, *n.* a long feat; a bench with a back

Set'tle, *v.* to fix, eftablifh, confirm, agree upon, compofe, calm, adjuft, pay, reft, fink, lower

Set'tlednefs, *n.* a fettled ftate, a fettlement

Set'tlement, *n.* a fixed place of abode, reft. colony, factory, agreement, income, jointure, a place inhabited

Sev'en, *a* noting one more than fix

Sev'enfold, *a.* taken feven times; *ad.* feven times

Sev'ennight, Sen'night, *n.* feven nights and days

Sev'enfcore, *a.* twenty repeated feven times

Sev'enteen, *a.* ten and feven added together

Sev'enthly, *ad.* in the feventh place or order

Sev'enty, *a.* ten added or repeated feven times

Sev'er, *v. t.* to part by force, part, difjoin, divide

Sev'eral, *a.* many, different, diftinct (ulars

Sev'eral, *n.* a ftate of feparation, inclofure, partic-

Sev'erally, *ad.* feparately, diftinctly, minutely

Sev'eralty, Sev'erance, *n.* a partition, a feparation

Sevére, *a.* cruel, rigid, ftrict, fharp, painful

Sevérely, *ad.* with feverity, painfully (fharpnefs

Sevérenefs, Sever'ity, *n.* cruel treatment, rigor,

Sew or Soe, *v. t.* to join with a needle and thred

Sew'er, *n.* one who fews, an officer at feafts, paffage for water, drain, hole

Sex, *n.* the diftinction betwixt male and female

Sex'agenary, *a.* pertaining to fixty

Sexages'ima, *n.* the fecond Sunday before Lent

Sexages'imal, *a.* numbered by fixties, the fixtieth

Sex'angled, Sexan''gular, *a.* having fix angles

Sexen'nial, *a.* lafting or happening in fix years

Sex'fid, *a.* divided into fix fegments

Sexloc'ular, *a.* having fix cells for feeds

Sex'tant, *n.* the fixth part or portion of a circle

Sex'tile, *n.* the diftance of 60 degrees or two figns

Sex'ton, *n.* an under officer of a church

Sex'tonfhip, *n.* the office or place of a fexton

Sex'tuple, *a.* fixfold, told or repeated fix times

Sex'ual, *a.* pertaining to the fexes and to the doctrin of fexes in plants (in plants

Sex'ualift, *n.* an adherent to the doctrin of fexes

Sexual'ity, *n.* the ftate or diftinction of fex

Shab'bily, *ad.* meanly, defpicably, raggedly

Shab'binefs, *n.* meannefs, paltrinefs, raggednefs

Shab'by, *a.* mean, paltry, defpicable, ragged

Shack, *n.* winter pafturage, Eng. maft, a fhiftlefs fellow

Shac''kle, *v. t.* to chain, fetter, bind, entangle

Shac''kles, *n. pl.* chains, fetters, rings, dificulties

Shad, *n. fing.* and *pl.* a fpecies of fifh well known

Shad'dock, *n.* a fpecies of orange, pampelmoe

Shade, *n.* a fhadow, fhelter, fcreen, cool, darknefs, likenefs, foul in a ftate of feparation, ghoft

Shade, *v. t.* to cover from light or heat, protect, fhelter, fcreen, hide, paint in obfcure colors

Shádinefs, *n.* a fhady ftate, coolnefs

Shad'ow, *n.* a fhade, darknefs, faint reprefentation, type, infeparable companion, ghoft, protection

Shad'ow, *v. t.* to fhade, darken, fcreen, reprefent

Shad'owy, *a.* full of fhade, gloomy, heavy, faint

Shády. *a.* fecure from too much light or heat, cool

Shaft, *n.* an arrow, weapon, paffáge into a mine, ftrait part of a column, a bird

Shag, *n.* a rough hair, rough cloth, a water fowl

Shag'ged, Shag'gy, *a.* hairy, rough, rugged

Shag'ginefs, *n.* a fhaggy ftate or quality, roughnefs

Shagréen, *v.* to provoke, vex, be vexed, chagrin

Shagréen, *n.* a kind of very rough fifh-fkin

Shaik, *n.* in the eaft, an old man or a chief

Shake, *v.* fhook, *pret.* fhaken, *pa.* to caufe to move or totter, move to and fro, tofs, agitate, tremble, trill, caft off, weaken

Shake, *n.* a motion given and received, fhock, trill,

Sháker, *n.* a perfon or thing that fhakes (flaw

Sháky, Sháken, *a.* fplit; having fiffures

Shale, [error for *fhell*] *n.* a hufk, a fpecies of fhiftus or ftate of a deep black color

Shalloon', *n.* a flight woolen fluff ufed for linings

Shalloóp or Shal'lop, *n.* a kind of boat, a floop

Shal'low, *a.* not deep, filly, weak, trifling, empty

Shal'low, *n.* a fhoal, fhelf, fand bank, flat, ford

Shal'lowbrained, *a.* foolifh, filly, weak, trifling

Shal'lowly, *ad.* with no great depth, fimply (nefs

Shal'lownefs, *n.* want of depth or thought, weak-

Shalm or Shawm, *n.* a mufical pipe, a cornet, *ob.*

Shalóte, *n.* a kind of garlic or fine fmall onion

Shalt, *the fecond perfon fingular* of *fhall*

Sham, *v. t.* to counterfeit, pretend, cheat

Sham, *n.* a pretenfe, lie, impofture, delufion, trick

Sham, *a.* falfe, counterfeit, pretended, contrived

Sham'anifm, *n.* the religion of the Eaftern Tartars, which recognizes an author of nature, who governs it by inferior deities

Sham'bles, *n. pl.* a butchery, a place to buy meat at

Sham'bling, *a.* moving aukwardly, fhuffling

Sham'bling, *n.* a fhuffling and aukward gait

Shame, *n.* an apprehenfion or fenfe of difgrace, caufe of fhame, ignominy, reproach

Shame, *v.* to make afhamed, confound, difgrace

Shámefaced, *a.* bafhful, modeft, fheepifh, fimple

Shámefacednefs, *n.* bafhfulnefs, great modefty

Shámeful, *a.* difgraceful, reproachful, infamous

Shámefully, *ad.* difgracefully, infamoufly, ill

Shámelefs, *a.* frontlefs, impudent, immodeft, vile

Shámeleffnefs, *n.* impudence, immodefty, folly

Sham'mylether, *n.* the fkin of a fhamois tanned

Sham'ois, *n.* a wild goat, lether made of its fkin

Sham'rock, *n.* a three-leaved Irifh grafs

Shan'achy, *n.* a very old Caledonian bard

Shank, *n.* the handle of a tool, the joint of the leg, or of an iron bar or cylinder

Shape, *v. t.* fhaped, *pret.* fhaped, fhapen, *pa.* to form, mold, caft, create, conceive

Shape, *n.* a form, make, ftate, external appearance

Shápelefs, *a.* wanting regularity of form, ugly

Shápelinefs, *n.* beauty, proportion of form

Shápely, *a.* well formed or proportioned

Shápefmith, *n.* one who improves the form

Shard, *n.* a piece of a pot, plant, fish, gap, *ob.*

Shard'born, *a.* born or produced among shards, *ob.*

Shard'ed, *a.* inhabiting or like shards, sealed, *ob.*

Share, *n.* a part, portion, dividend, plow iron

Share, *v. t.* to portion, divide, cut, partake

Shareholder, *n.* one who holds or owns a share (ner

Sharer, *n.* one who shares, a divider, partaker, part-

Shark, *n.* a voracious fish, tricking fellow, trick

Shark, *v.* to cheat, trick, gull, pick up eagerly

Sharp, *n.* a sharp or acute sound, sword, needle

Sharp, *a.* keen, piercing, acute, fevere, four, lean

Sharp, *v.* to sharpen, make keen, cheat, trick

Sharp'edged, *a.* having a sharp edge, keen, fine

Sharp'en, *v. t.* to edge, point, make quick, raise

Sharp'er, *n.* a petty thief, tricking fellow, cheat

Sharp'ly, *ad.* keenly, crofsly, feverely, painfully

Sharp'nefs, *n.* keennefs, harfhnefs, feverity, pain

Sharpfet', *a.* hungry, eager, keen in defire

Sharpfi'ghted, *a.* having quick fight, keen, acute

Shas'ter, *n.* a facred book among the Hindoos, containing comments on the vedam or bible ; principles of their religion, &c.

Shat'ter, *v.* to break into pieces, fhake, be broken

Shat'terbrained, Shat'terpated, *a.* giddy, crazy

Shat'tery, *a.* eafily broken, not compact, loofe

Shave, *v. t.* fhaved, *pret.* fhaved, fhaven, *pa.* to cut clofe off with a razor, pare, ftrip

Sháveling, *n.* a perfon fhaved, young fellow, friar

Sháver, *n.* one who fhaves, a fharp dealer, a cheat

Sháving, *n.* a thin flice pared off, a cutting off

Shaw, *n.* a thicket, fmall wood, grove, *ob.*

Shawl, *n.* a cloth of cotton or filk to cover the neck

She, *pron.* the pronoun perfonal ufed for a female

Sheaf, *n.* a fmall bundle of new-cut grain, a heap

Sheaf, *v. t.* to gather or bind into fheaves, to heap

Shear, *v. t.* fheared, fhore, *pret.* fheared, fhorn, *pa.* to clip, cut, fnip, take off, reap, mow

Sheard, *n.* a broken piece of an earthen veffel

Shearer, *n.* a perfon that fhears fheep or cloth

Shearman, *n.* a man who fhears or finishes cloth

Shears, *n. pl.* a fharp inftrument with two blades, an engine to hoift heavy weights

Shearwater, *n.* a fowl of the weft of England

Sheatfish, *n.* a fish with a long flimy body

Sheath, *n.* a cafe for any thing, fcabbard, fifh

Sheath or Sheathe, *v. t.* to put into a fheath

Sheathing, *n.* the covering of a fhips bottom

Sheathwinged, *a.* having hard cafes fet over the

Sheathy, *a.* forming or like a fheath   (wings

Sheave, *n.* a wheel in the block of a pulley

Shed, *n.* a fmall flight building, a fhelter

Shed, *v. t.* fhed, *pret.* fhed, *pa.* to fpill, pour out, fcatter, caft, let fall

Shed'der, *n.* one who fheds, one who fpills

Sheen, *n.* brightnefs, fplendor, lufter, fhow, *ob.*

Sheen or Sheeny, *a.* bright, glittering, fhining, *ob.*

Sheep, *n.* a genus of ufeful animals, a dolt

Sheepbite, *v. i.* to practice petty thefts, *ob.*

Sheepbiter, *n.* a petty thief, a mean wretch, *ob.*

Sheepcot or fold, *n.* a place ufed to pen fheep in

Sheephook, *n.* a hook to lay hold on a fheep's legs

Sheepifh, *a.* fhamefaced, bafhful, fimple

Sheepifhnefs, *n.* fhamefacednefs, bafhfulnefs

Sheepmafter, *n.* a mafter or owner of fheep

Sheepfeye, *n.* a loving fly look, an oblique view

Sheepshead, *n.* a table fifh much valued

Sheepfhank, *n.* a knot in a rope

Sheepfhearing, *n.* the time of fhearing fheep

Sheepwalk, *n.* a place of pafture ufed for fheep

Sheer, *a.* clear, pure, real ; *ad.* clean, quick

Sheer, *v.* to deviate from a courfe, move fideways

Sheer, *n.* the curve of a fhips fide or deck length-ways   (fails

Sheet, *n.* a rope faftened to the lower corners of

Sheet, *n.* linen for a bed, a fail, a piece of paper

Sheet, *v. t.* to cover or furnifh with fheets

Sheetanch'or, *n.* the largeft anchor, chief fupport

Sheetiron, *n.* iron in a thin plate

Sheetlead', *n.* lead in a thin plate

Shek'el, *n.* a Jewifh coin, in value 55 cents

Shelf, *pl.* fhelves, *n.* a board ufed to lay things on, fandbank in the fea, rock under fhallow water till

Shelf'y or Shelv'y, *a.* full of rocks and fhoals

Shell, *v.* to take out of or caft the fhell

Shell, *n.* a hard covering, a fuperficial part

Shell'drake or Shil'drake, *n.* a fpecies of duck

Shell'fifh, *n.* any fifh covered with a fhell

Shell'y, *a.* abounding with or confifting of fhells

Shelt'er, *n.* a place of fafety, cover, defenfe

Shelt'er, *v. t.* to cover, defend, protect, harbor

Shelt'erlefs, *a.* expofed without hope or refuge

Shelv'ing, *a.* floping, flanting, having a declivity

Shend, *v. t.* to ruin, fpoil, overpower, difgrace, *ob.*

Shent, *pa.* ruined, crufhed, difgraced, *ob.* (minifter

Shep'herd, *n.* one that tends fheep, a fwain, lover,

Shep'herdefs, *n.* a female fhepherd, a rural lafs,

Shep'herdifh, *a.* like a fhepherd, paftoral, rural, *ob.*

Shep'herdy, *n.* the office or duty of a fhepherd, *ob.*

Sher'bet, *n.* a mixture of acid, fugar and water

Sher'iff, *n.* a chief county-officer charged with the keeping of the peace and execution of writs

Sher'iffalty, Sher'iffdom, *n.* the office of a fheriff

Sher'ry, *n.* a Spanifh wine from Xera

Shew, *fee* fhow

Shield, *n.* a buckler, protection, defenfe, defender

Shield, *v. t.* to protect, defend, keep, fecure, cover

Shift, *v.* to change, alter, move, put off, provide

Shift, *n.* an evafion, artifice, woman's body linen

Shift'er, *n.* an artful fcheming perfon, a trickfter

Shift'ing, *n.* a change of place or linen, artifice, art

Shift'lefs, *a.* wanting means to act or live, poor

Shil'ling, *n.* a filver coin, a nominal fum of twelve pence, of various value .

Shil'lifhalli, *a.* wavering, indeterminate, trifling

Shily, *ad.* with fhinefs, cautioufly, cunningly

Shin, *n.* the forepart of the bone of the leg

Shine, *v. i.* fhined, fhone, *pret.* and *pa.* to glitter, glare, be bright and without clouds, be confpic-

nous or propitious, appear
Shine, n. luſter, brightneſs, beauty, fair weather
Shineſs, n. reſervedneſs, coyneſs, backwardneſs
Shin"gle, n. a thin board to cover houſes with
Shin"gle, v. t. to cover with ſhingles
Ship"gles, n. pl. a kind of diſtemper, a tetter
Shiny, a. bright, ſplendid, luminous, ſhining
Ship, n. a veſſel with three maſts, ſquare rigged
Ship, v. t. to put on board a ſhip, ſend, tranſport
Ship'board, ad. on board a ſhip, in or into a ſhip
Suip'boy, n. a boy that ſerves or lives in a ſhip
Ship'leſs, a. without ſhips
Ship'man, n. a ſeaman, ſailor, mariner, tar
Ship'maſter, n. the maſter or captain of a ſhip
Ship'ment, n. the act of ſhipping, articles ſhipped
Ship'money, n. a tax levied for fitting out ſhips
Ship'ping, n. veſſels for navigation, a paſſage
Ship'wreck, n. the loſs of a ſhip, deſtruction, ruin
Ship'wreck, v. to ſuffer ſhipwreck, deſtroy, ruin
Ship'wright, n. a ſhip-carpenter, a ſhip builder
Shire, n. a county, what is under only one ſheriff
Shirl, ſee ſhorl
Shir'ly, n. a bird, the greater bullfinch
Shirt, n. a part of dreſs, a man's body linen
Shirt, v. t. to put on or furniſh with a ſhirt
Shirt'leſs, a. not worth or not having a ſhirt
Shiſt, Shiſt'us, n. a ſpecies of ſtone, flate
Shiſt'ic, Shiſtoſe, Shiſt'ous, a. of the nature of flate
Shit'tim, n. a very precious Arabian wood
Shive, n. a ſlice, ſplinter, plate; v. t. to ſhiver
Shiv'er, n. a ſhivering, very ſmall piece, wheel, a
　ſpecies of hard blackiſh clay
Shiv'er, v. to break into ſhivers, ſhake, tremble
Shiv'ering, n. the act of breaking, a ſhaking fit
Shiv'ery, a. eaſily broken, crazy, not compact
Shoal, v. i. to crowd, preſs, grow or be ſhallow
Shoal, n. a crowd, ſandbank, ſhallow; a. ſhallow
Shoalineſs, n. a ſhoaly ſtate, ſhallowneſs, lowneſs
Shoaly, a. full of or having ſhallows, ſhallow
Shock, n. a concuſſion, conflict, pile of ſheaves
Shock, v. t. to ſhake, affect, diſguſt, pile up
Shock'ing, pa. a. ſhaking, diſguſtful, dreadful
Shock'ingly, ad. in a ſhocking manner, dreadfully
Shoe, [ſhoo] v. t. ſhod, ſhoed, pret. ſhod, ſhoed,
　pa. to fit or cover with ſhoes
Shoe, n. an outward covering for the foot or for
　the runner of a ſled or other utenſil, or engine
Shoe'black, Shoe'boy, n. a perſon who cleans ſhoes
Shoe'inghorn, n. a horn to draw on ſhoes, ob.
Shoe'leſs, a. deſtitute of ſhoes
Shoe'maker, n. one who makes ſhoes
Shoe'ſtring, Shoe'tie, n. a ſtring to tie the ſhoe
Shog, v. t. to ſhake ſuddenly; n. a concuſſion, ob.
Shone, pret. and pa. of to ſhine
Shook, pret. of to ſhake　　　　　　　　(caſk
Shook, n. a bundle of ſtaves packed in form of a
Shoot, v. ſhot pret. ſhot, pa. to let off, diſcharge
　from a gun, dart, paſs, puſh forward, jut out,
　ſprout, twitch, kill

Shoot, n. a branch iſſued from the main ſtock
Shoot'er, n. one who ſhoots, a gunner, an archer
Shoot'ing, n. the killing of game with a gun
Shop, n. a place for ſale of wares or for work
Shop'board, n. a kind of table uſed to work upon
Shop'book, n. a book for a tradeſman's accounts
Shop'keeper, n. one who ſells in a ſhop by retail
Shop'lifter, n. one who ſteals goods out of a ſhop
Shop'man, n. a journeyman to a ſhopkeeper, a pet-
　ty trader
Shore, n. a coaſt, drain, buttreſs, prop; v. t. to prop
Shoreleſs, a. having no coaſt, widely extended
Shorl, n. a ſpecies of ſiliceous ſtone of a black color
Shorláceous, a. like or pertaining to ſhorl
Shorl'ite, n. a ſiliceous ſtone of a whitiſh color
Shorn, pa. of to ſhear
Short, a. not long, ſcanty, defective, low, brittle
Short, n. an account in ſhort or in few words
Short'breathed, a. having the breath ſhort, purfy
Short'en, v. t. to make ſhort, lop, cut off, contract
Short'faced, a. having a ſhort or flat face
Short'hand, n. a ſhort method of writing
Short'lived, a. not living or continuing long
Short'ly, ad. quickly, ſoon, briefly, in few words
Short'neſs, n. the quality of being ſhort, conciſe-
　neſs, a want of memory, imperfection, defect
Shorts, n. the bran and coarſe parts of wheat meal
Short'fighted, a. unable to ſee far, imprudent, weak
Short'fightedneſs, n. a defect of ſight or prudence
Short'waiſted, a. having a ſhort waiſt or body
Short'winded, a. breathing very faſt, aſthmatic
Shory, a. lying near or upon the ſhore, ob.
Shot, pret. and pa. of to ſhoot　　　(oning, charge
Shot, n. the act of ſhooting, a bullet, ball, reck-
Shot'free, a. excuſed a ſhare of the reckoning
Shot'ten, pa. having caſt the ſpawn, curled, thin
Shough, [ſhock] n. a very ſhaggy dog, ſhock
Should, [ſhood] an auxiliary, denoting intention
　or duty
Shoulder, n. a joint to connect the body and arm
Shoulder, v. t. to lay on the ſhoulder, puſh, crowd
Shoulderbelt, n. a belt that croſſes the ſhoulder
Shoulderblade, n. the ſcapula, a bone
Shoulderclapper, n. one who affects a familiarity
Shoulderknot, n. a knot of lace on the ſhoulder
Shoulderſhotten, a. ſtrained in the ſhoulder
Shoulderſlip, n. a diſlocation of the ſhoulder
Shout, v. i. to cry in triumph, cry out, huzza
Shout, n. a cry of rejoicing, &c. a loud noiſe
Shout'er, n. one who ſhouts in triumph or joy
Shove, [ſhuv] v. t. to puſh forcibly, drive forward
Shove, n. the act of ſhoving, a puſh, a thruſt
Shov'el, [ſhuvl] n. a utenſil broader than a ſpade
Shov'el, v. t. to throw with a ſhovel, to heap up
Shov'elboard, n. a long table to play upon, a game
Shov'eler, n. a fowl of the duck kind
Show, v. ſhowed, pret. ſhowed, ſhown, pa. to ex-
　hibit to view, appear, prove, tell, teach
Show, n. a ſight, exhibition, appearance, promp

Showbread, n. twelve loaves of bread representing the twelve tribes of Israel

Show'er, n. a fall of rain, a liberal diftribution

Show'er, v. t. to rain, wet, pour down, diftribute

Show'ery, a. rainy, wet, uncertain, unfettled

Shówily, ad. in a fhowy manner, gaudily, finely

Shówinefs, n. a fhowy ftate or quality, finery

Shówifh, Shówy, a. fplendid, gaudy, oftentatious

Shown, pa. paff. of to fhow

Shrank, pret. of to fhrink

Shred, v. t. fhred, pret. fhred, pa. to cut into fmall pieces, cut fmall, mince

Shred, n. a fmall piece or bit cut off, a fragment

Shrew, n. a peevifh, vexatious woman, an animal like a moufe

Shrewd, a. having the qualities of a fhrew, cunning, artful, fly, fubtle, pinching, painful

Shrewd'ly, ad. cunningly, artfully, vexatioufly

Shrewd'nefs, n. arcknefs, fly c·nning, petulance

Shrew'ifh, a. like a fhrew, peevifh, crofs

Shrewifhly, ad. peevifhly, crofsly, frowardly

Shrew'ifhnefs, n. peevifhnefs, clamoroufnefs

Shriek, v. i. to fcream; n. a cry of anguifh or horror

Shrift, n. a confeffion of fins made to a prieft, ob.

Shrike, n. a genus of birds, the tyrant or butcher (bird

Shrill, a. giving a piercing found, fharp

Shrill, v, i. to pierce the ear with a fharp found

Shrill'nefs, n. a fhrill quality, a fharp noife

Shrill'y, ad. with a fhrill noife, loudly, fharply

Shrimp, n. a fmall fhellfifh, dwarf, very little man

Shrine, n. a depofitory of relics, a temple

Shriik, v. i. fhrank, fhrunk, pret. fhrunk, fhrunken, pa. to grow lefs, withdraw, be in fear

Shrink, n. a quick contraction of the body

Shrink'age, n. a fhrinking, contraction

Shrive, v. i. fhrove, pret. fhrived, fhriven, pa. to hear a confeffion, confefs, reveal

Shriv'el, v. to contract or run up into wrinkles

Shriver, n, one who hears confeffion ob.

Shroud, n. a burial cloth, cover, fhelter

Shroud, n. a large rope from the fide of a fhip to the head of a maft for fupport

Shroud or Shrowd, v. to drefs the dead, defend, protect, fave, conceal, fhelter, take fhelter

Shróvetide, n. the Tuefday before Lent, from fhrove the pret. of fhrive, the time of confeffion

Shrub, n. a bufh, a fpirit with acid and fugar mixed

Shrub, v. t. to cudgel, bang, beat foundly

Shrub'bery, n. a place planted with fhrubs, fhrubs

Shrub'by, a. full of fhrubs or fmall trees in general

Shrug, v. t. to contract, raife, draw up

Shrug, n. a contracted motion of the fhoulders

Shrunk, Shrunk'en, pa. of to fhrink

Shud'der, v. i. to quake, fhake, quiver, tremble

Shud'der, Shud'dering, n. fhaking, a fhivering

Shuf'fle, v. to change the pofition of cards, mix, fhake, prevaricate, evade, fhift off, cheat

Shuf'fle, n. a difordering of things, fhake, trick

Shuf'flecap, n. a kind of game, a very low game

Shuf'fler, n. one who evades, one who plays tricks

Shuf'flingly, ad. with an irregular gait, meanly

Shun, v. t. to avoid, endeavor to efcape, pufh

Shun'lefs, a. not to be avoided, unavoidable

Shut, v. fhut, pret. fhut, pa. to clofe, bar, ftop, faften, confine, contract

Shut, pa. a. clofed, confined, free, clear, rid

Shut, n. the act of fhutting, a door, cover, pig

Shut'ter, n. one who fhuts, a cover for a window

Shut'tle, n. a weaver's inftrument to fhoot by

Shut'tlecock, n. a cork with fethers to be ftruck with a battledore, a play

Shy, a. not familiar, referved, coy, wary, jealous

Shy'ly, Shy'nefs, fee fhily, fhinefs

Siaméfe, n. a native of Siam in Afia

Siamefe, a. pertaining to Siam

Sibérian, n. a native of Siberia in Afia

Sibérian, a. pertaining to Siberia

Sib'ilant, a. hiffing, making a hiffing noife

Sibilátion, n. the act of hiffing, a hiffing found

Sib'ylline, a. pertaining to the Sybils ancient propheteffes (in Sicily and Italy

Sicánian, a. pertaining to the Sicani who fettled

Sic'cative, a. drying, n. that which makes dry

Sic'city, n. drynefs, drouth, a want of moifture

Sicil'ian, n. a native of Sicily, a lively air or dance

Sicil'ian, a. pertaining to Sicily

Sice n. a term ufed at dice, the number fix

Sick, a. afflicted with a difeafe, ill, low, difgufted

Sick, v. i. to grow, fall or make fick, to ficken

Sick'en, v. to grow or make fick, decline, decay

Sick'ifh, a. rather fick, qualmifh, languid

Sic'kle, n. a reaping hook, a kook to cut grain with

Sic'kleman, Sick'ler, n. one who reaps, a reaper

Sick'linefs, n. a tendency to ficknefs, weaknefs

Sick'ly, a. fomewhat difordered, unhealthy, faint

Sick'ly, ad. in a fickly condition; v. t. to diforder

Sick'nefs, n. a difeafe, fome diforder of the body

Side, n. the rib part of animals, an edge, a party

Side, a. not direct, awry; v. i. to take part with

Sideboard, n. a fide table for convenience

Sidebox, n. a box or feat on one fide of a theater

Sidelong, a. lateral, oblique, not placed in front

Sid'eral, Sidéreal, Sidérean, a. ftarry, bright

Sid'erated, a. blafted, planetftruck, benumed, ob.

Siderátion, n. a blaft, a fudden mortification, ob.

Sid'erite, n. phofphate of iron or iron combined with phofphoric acid

Siderit'ic, a. pertaining to or confifting of fiderite

Siderocal'cite, n. a calcareous earth combined with

Sidefaddle, n. a woman's faddle for a horfe (iron

Sidefman, n. an affiftant to a churchwarden

Sideways, ad. on or with one fide

Sidle, v. i. to go with the fide firft or on one fide

Sidling, pa. with the fide firft, on a flope

Siege, n. the befieging of any place, a feat, a ftool

Sienite, n. a ftone compofed of quartz, hornblend and felfpar

Sieve, n. a bolter, fearce, thing ufed to fift with

Sift, v. t. to put through a fieve, part,examin,try
Sift'er,n. one who fifts or examins, a fieve
Sigh, v. i. to exprefs grief with the breath, to la-
Sigh, n. a mournful breathing, a deep fob (ment
Sight, n. perception by the eye, the act of feeing, an open view, the eye, a fhow, a fpectacle, hole
Sightfulnefs, n. clearnefs of fight, fightlinefs
Sightlefs, a. blind, unfightly, offenfive, horrid
Sightlinefs, n. a comely or graceful appearance
Sightly, a. pleafing to the eye, ftriking, comely
Si'gil, n. a feal, mark, kind of charm
Sign, n. a token, fymbol, device, miracle, conftellation containing 30 degrees or the 12th part of the zodiac
Sign, v. t. to fubfcribe, ratify by writing, mark
Sig'nal, n. a fign that gives notice, token, mark
Sig'nal, a. eminent, remarkable, memorable
Signal'ity, n. a remarkable quality or property,ob.
Sig'nalize, v. t. to make eminent, to diftinguifh
Sig'nally, ad. eminently, remarkably, notably
Signation,n. the act of betokening, a fign,a mark
Sig'natory, a. relating to a feal, ufed in fealing
Sig'nature, n. a mark, a name figned, a letter to diftinguifh fheets in printing
Sig'naturift, n. one who is fond of fignatures, ob.
Signer, n. one who figns or fubfcribes his name
Sig'net,n.a feal,efpecially a king's, fign,mark
Significance, n. importance,force, meaning
Significant, a. important, betokening, expreffive
Significantly, ad. with great force of expreffion
Significátion, n. a meaning by figns or words
Significative, a. fhowing by a fign, forcible,full
Sig'nify, v. to mean, exprefs, avail,make known
Signpoft, n. the poft on which a fign hangs
Silence, n. taciturnity, fecrecy, ftillnefs, quiet
Silence, v. t. to make filent, to ftill
Silent, a. mute, dumb, ftill, quiet, weak, ufelefs
Silently, ad. without noife or words, quietly
Siléne, n. catchfly, a genus of plants
Siléfia, n. a fpecies of thin coarfe linen
Siléfian, n. a native of Silefia in Pruffia
Siléfian, a. pertaining to Silefia
Silex, n. a genus of ftones of the flint kind
Sili'cious, a. pertaining to filex, of the genus of filex, flinty (feeds grow to both futures
Si'licle, n. a bivalvular pericarp or pod, whofe
Sili'cify, v. t. to form into filex or flint (of filex
Silicíferous, a. producing or united with a portion
Silicicalcáreous, a. confifting of filicious and calcareous matter (magnefia
Silic'murite,n. an earth compounded of filex and
Silic'ulous, a. having or pertaining to filicles
Sil'iqua, n. a pod or pericarp, whofe feeds are attached alternately to both futures
Sil'iquofe. Sil'iquous, a.having or formed in a pod
Suk, n. the produce of worms,the ftuff made of it
Silk. Silk'en, a. made of or dreffed in filk, foft
Silk'mercer,n. a retailer or feller of filk
Silk'weaver,n. one who makes filken ftuffs

Silk'worm, n. a worm that yields or produces filk
Silk'y, a. made of or like filk, foft, fmooth
Sill,n. the bottom of a doorcafe, a threfhold, the foundation timber of a building
Sill'abub or Sill'ibub, n. a poffet made of new milk
Sill'ily, ad. fimply,foolifhly, ridiculoufly, idly
Sill'inefs, n, fimplenefs, weaknefs, harmlefs folly
Sill'y, a. fimple, weak, witlefs, foolifh, harmlefs
Silûre, n. a kind of fifh with beards
Sil'van, a. woody, inhabiting woods, ruftic, wild
Sil'ver, n. a white hard metal, money made of it
Sil'ver, a. made of filver, white, beguiling, foft
Sil'ver, v. t. to cover with leaf-filver, to gild
Sil'verbeater, n. one who beats filver into leaves
Sil'vering, n. a covering or gilding with filver
Sil'verly, a. of or like filver, white, bright, fhining
Sil'verfmith, n. one who works or deals in filver
Sil'very, a. refembling or wafhed with filver
Simár or Simáre, n. a woman's loofe robe, ob.
Sim'ilar, a. like, refembling, homogeneous, equal
Similar'ity, n. a likenefs, like ftate, refemblance
Sim'ilarly, ad. in a fimilar or like manner
Sim'ile, n. a comparifon made for illuftration
Simil'itude, n. likenefs, refemblance, comparifon
Similitúdinary, a. relating to fimilitude, like
Sim'mer, v. i. to boil very gently or flowly
Sim'nel, n. a kind of fweet cake, a fine kind of bun
Simon'ical, a. partaking of the crime of fimony
Sim'ony, n. a buying or felling church preferment
Simoom',n.a hot,fuffocating wind in fandy defarts
Símous, a. having a flat or fnub nofe, bent up, ob.
Simp'er,v.i.to fmile like a fool, to look pleafantly
Simp'er, n. a kind of fmile, a foolifh fmile
Sim''ple, a. artlefs, plain, filly, fingle, unmingled
Sim''ple, n. a fingle ingredient, herb, plant, drug
Sim''ple, v. i. to gather phyfical herbs, ob.
Sim''plenefs, n. a fimple ftate, weaknefs, folly
Simp'ler, Simp'lift, n. one who gathers herbs
Sim''pleton,n. a filly or foolifh perfon, oaf, trifler
Simpli''city, n. plainnefs, want of cunning, folly
Sim'plify, v. t. to make fimple, free from com-
Simplification,n.the act of making fimple(plexnefs
Simp'ly, ad. without art, fillily, only, merely
Sim'ular, n. one who counterfeits or pretends, ob.
Sim'ulate, v. t. to counterfeit, diffemble, pretend
Simulátion, n. hypocrify, deceit, mere pretence
Simultáneous, a. acting or exifting together
Simultáneoufly, ad. at the fame time, in union
Sin, n. a tranfgreffion of the law of God, guilt
Sin, v. i. to tranfgrefs the laws of God, to offend
Sin'apifm, n. a cataplafm of muftard feed, &c.
Since, ad. becaufe, before this, ago; pr. after
Sincére, a. honeft, true, uncorrupt, pure, unhurt
Sincérely, ad. honeftly, plainly, without deceit
Sincer'ity, a. honefty, plainnefs, purity of mind
Sindéan, Sindet'ic, a. pertaining to the Sindy the ancient Indus, a large river of Hindooftan
Sin'don,n. fine linen, a wrapper of fine linen, ob.
Sine, n. a geometrical line from the end of an arc

perpendicular to the radius,being half the chord of double the arc

Sinecure, *n*. an office without employment

Sin'ew, *n*. a tendon, mufcle, nerve,ligament,bond

Sin'ew, *v. t.* to join, link or faften with finews

Sin'ewed, *pa.* furnifhed with or having finews

Sin'ewy, *a.* like finews, nervous, ftrong, powerful

Sin'ful, *a.* unholy, wicked, profane, guilty, vile

Sin'fully, *ad.* in a finful manner, wickedly

Sin'fulnefs, *n.* wickednefs, an alienation from God

Singaléfe,*n.* a native of Ceylon; *a.* pertaining to it

Sing, *v.* fang, fung, *pret.* fung, *pa.* to form the voice to melody, celebrate, defcribe in verfe

Singe, *v. t.* to fcorch, burn flightly, burn off

Sing'er,*n.* one who fings, one fkilled in finging

Sing'ingmafter, *n.* a man who teaches to fing

Sin''gle, *a.* alone, unmarried, fimple, uncorrupt

Sin''gle, *v. t.* to feparate, felect, take from others

Sin''glenefs, *n.* fimplicity, fincerity, purity of heart

Sin''gly, *ad.* individually, barely, honeftly, fairly

Sin''gular, *a.* only one, particular, odd, queer,rare

Singular'ity, *n.* particularity, uacommonnefs

Sin''gularly, *ad.* particularly, oddly, ftrangely

Sin'ifter, *a.* left, unjuft, unfair, perverfe, unlucky

Sinis'trous, *a.* abfurd, perverfe, headftrong

Sinis'troufly, *ad.* towards the left hand, abfurdly

Sink, *v.* fank, funk, *pret.* funk, *pa.* to fall gradually, fettle, decline, diminifh, deprefs, degrade, fupprefs, conceal, plunge, pierce, dig

Sink, *n.* the head of a drain, a place of filth

Sink'ingfund, *n.* a fund or revenue to reduce a public debt

Sin'lefs, *a.* exempt from fin, innocent, pure, holy

Sin'leffnefs, *n.* an exemption from fin, purity

Sin'ner,*n.*one who fins, an offender, a tranfgreffor

Sin'offering, *n.* an offering made to atone for fin

Sin'ople,*n.* a fpecies of dark red jafper   (animals

Sinóvia, *n.* the liquid which lubricates the joints of

Sin'uate, *v. t.* to bend in and out, wind, turn

Sin'uate, *a.* having the edge fcolloped

Sinuátion, Sinuos'ity, *n.* a bending in and out

Sin'uous, *a.* bending in and out, winding, turning

Sinus, *n.* a bay, gulf, fold, opening, winding hole

Sip, *n.* a very fmall draft, fmall mouthful, tafte

Sip, *v. t.* to drink a little at a time, to tafte

Siphon or Sy'phon, *n.* a pipe with two legs of unequal lengths to draw liquors out of the top of a veffel

Sir, *n.* a word of refpect ufed to men, title, man

Sire, *n.* a father, title of kings, male of beafts

Sir'en,*n.* a goddefs famed for finging, an enticer, a fpecies of lizard in Carolina

Sir'en, *a.* belonging to a firen, enticing

Sir'ius, *n.* a very bright ftar, the great dogftar

Siroc, Siroc'co, *n.* the fouth-eaft or Syrian wind

Sir'up, *n.* any juce boiled with fugar

Sir'rah, *n.* a name of reproach or infult

Sir'upy, *a.* refembling or fmeared with firup

Sifk'in, *n.* another name of the aberdavin

Sis'ter, *n.* a woman born of the fame parents, a woman of the fame nature, faith or fociety

Sis'terhood, *n.* women of the fame order or fociety

Sis'terly, *a.* like or becoming a fifter, kind, fond

Sit, *v.* fat, *pret.* fat, fitten, *pa.* to be in a local pofition, perch, reft, ftay, brood

Site,*n.* fituation, pofition, ftate, pofture, fpot

Sith, Sith'ence, *ad.* fince, feeing, becaufe, that, *ob.*

Sit'ter, *n.* a perfon that fits, a bird that is brooding

Sit'ting,*n.* the act of refting on a feat, ftay, feffions

Sit'uate or Sit'uated,*a.* placed, feated, fet, lying

Situátion, *n.* a pofition, local ftate, condition

Six, *a.* one more than five, half a dozen

Six'fold, *a.* taken fix times, fix times as much

Six'pence, *n.* a fmall filver coin, half a fhilling

Six'fcore, *a.* twenty added or repeated fix times

Sixtéen, *a.* fix and ten added or joined together

Sixteenth, *a.* the fixth in order after the tenth

Sixth,*n.* a fixth part; *a.* the next after the fifth

Sixth'ly, *ad.* in the fixth place or order

Six'tieth, *a.* the tenth repeated fix times

Six'ty, *a.* ten added or repeated fix times   (fcore

Size, *n.* bulk, bignefs, a glutinous fubftance, a

Size, *v. t.* to fmear with fize, adjuft, fix, take up

Sizeable, *a.* reafonably or decently bulky, juft

Sizer, *n.* the loweft rank of ftudents in a college

Sizinefs,*n.* glutinoufnefs, ropinefs, thicknefs

Sizy, *a.* glutinous, vifcous, ropy, tough, thick

Skain or Skein, *n.* a fmall knot of thred, &c.

Skáinfmate, *n.* a meffmate, companion, *ob.*

Skate, *n.* a fort of flat fifh, a kind of fliding fhoe

Skate, *v. i.* to flide on the ice by fkates

Skean,*n.* an Irifh fhort fword, a knife

Skel'eton,*n.* the human bones entire,one very thin

Sketch, *n.* the outlines, rough draft, firft plan

Sketch, *v. t.* to draw out roughly, mark out, plan

Skew, *v. i.* to fquint, leer, look difdainfully, *ob.*

Skew'er,*n.* a kind of pin to trufs meat, &c. with

Skew'er, *v. t.* to faften or fecure with fkewers

Skid,*n.* a timber to flide heavy weights on

Skiff, *n.* a kind of fmall light boat, a fhallop

Skil'ful, *a.* knowing, experienced, dexterous

Skil'fully, *ad.* with fkill or art, dexteroufly

Skil'fulnefs,*n.* fkill, dexterity, ability, art

Skill, *v. t.* to be knowing, differ, fignify (or ftudy

Skill'ed, *pa.* knowing, acquainted with, verfed

Skill'efs,*a.* wanting fkill or art, ignorant, filly

Skill'et, *n.* a kind of kettle or boiler

Skim, *n.* the froth or drofs of boiling liquor

Skim, *v.* to take off the fkim, pafs, fly quickly

Skim'mer, *n.* a ladle to take off the fkim with

Skim'milk, *n.* milk deprived of its cream

Skim'mings,*n.* matter fkimmed off of liq'rs

Skin, *n.* a covering of flefh, hide, rind, body

Skin, *v. t.* to flay, uncover, heal or cover o'er

Skin'flint, *n.* a very niggardly perfon

Skink, *n* a fmall fpecies of lizard

Skink,*n.*any thing potable; *v. i.* to ferve drink,*ob.*

Skink'er,n. a perfon that ferves drink to others,ob.
Skin'ned,pa. a. covered with fkin, flayed
Skin'ner, n. a dealer in fkins, a fellmonger
Skin'ninefs, n. a fkinny ftate, leannefs, thinnefs
Skin'ny, a. full of fkin, wanting flefh, thin
Skip, v. i. to leap, bound, pafs; n. a light leap
Skip'jack, n. an upftart, a fervant, a fkipping fifh
Skip'kennel, n. a footboy, footman, fervant
Skip'per,n. a mafter of a fhip, failor, feaman
Skir'mifh, n. a flight engagement,encounter,fight
Skir'mifh, v. i. to fight loofely or in fmall parties
Skirr or Skirre,v.t.to fcour, feud, run in hafte, ob.
Skir'ret, n. a fpecies of parfnip
Skirt,n.a border, edge, extremity; v.t. to border
Skit, n. a whim, fancy, jeft, lampoon, ob.
Skit'tifh, a. eafily frightened, fhy, frifky, wanton
Skit'tifhly, ad. fhily, un'teadily, fickly, wanfonly
Skit'tifhnefs, n. fhinefs, reftivenefs, wantonnefs
Skit'tles, n. a game like ninepins
Skreen, n. a coarfe fieve, fhelter, protection
Skreen, v. t. to fift, fhade, fhelter, hide, protect
Skue,a. oblique, fidelong; v. i. to leer, to fquint
Skulk, v. i. to hide, lurk in fear, lie clofe
Skull n. the bone that inclofes the brain, a fhoal
Skunk, n. a quadruped remarkable for its fmell
Sky, n. the heavens, clouds, firmame.it, weather
Sky'color, n. the color of the fky, an azure color
Sky'colored, a. colored like the fky, blue, azure
Sky'dyed, Sky'ifh, a. colored like the fky, bluifh
Sky'ed, a. enveloped or furrounded by the fkies
Sky'lark, n. a lark that mounts in air and fings
Sky'light, n. a window in the roof or deck
Sky'rocket, n. a firework that rifes very high
Slab, n. a table of ftone, the outfide cut of a log made by fawing
Slab'ber, v. to flaver, drivel, fpill, fhed, fmear
Slab'bering, n. a daubing with fpittle or filth
Slab'by, a. wet, plafhy, dirty, filthy, ropy, thick
Slack, a. loofe, relaxed, remifs, flow   (unbend
Slack, Slack'en, v. to loofen,be remifs,flag,abate,
Slack'en, n. drofs, fcoria of metals
Slack, n. coal broken into fmall parts or pieces
Slack'ly, ad. loofely, negligently, backwardly
Slack'nefs, n. loofenefs, remiffnefs, want of care
Slack'water, n. the ftate of tide when the current has nearly ceafed
Slag, n. the drofs or refufe of metals
Slain,pa. of to flay
Slake, v. to quench, extinguifh, become relaxed, [when ufed of lime, pron. flak]
Slam, n. the winning of all the tricks in a hand
Slam, v. to win all the tricks, fhut hard, crufh
Slan'der, v. t. to injure reputation by falfehood
Slan'der, n. a falfe invective, reproach, difgrace
Slan'derer, n. one who flanders or belies another
Slan'derous, a. uttering reproachful falfehoods injurious to one's good name
Slan'deroufly, ad. with falfe reproach, abufively
Slang,pret. of to fling

Slang, n. vulgar language, cant phrafes, [low]
Slant, v.t. to flope, to form or caft obliquely
Slant, Slant'ing, a. oblique, floping, inclining
Slant'ly, Slant'wife, ad. in a floping direction
Slap, v. t. to ftrike or beat with the open hand
Slap, n. a blow; ad. with a violent fudden blow
Slapdafh, ad. all at once, plump, very fuddenly
Slafh, v. to cut long cuts, lafh, ftrike at random
Slafh, n. a wound, cut, cut in cloth, lafh   (ones
Slat n. a thin piece of timber connecting larger
Slate, n. a grey ftone; v. t. to cover with flates
Slater, n. one who covers houfes with flates
Slat'tern, n. a negligent nafty woman, a flut
Slat'tern, v. t. to wafte by negligence
Slat'ternly, a. negligent in drefs, fluttifh
Slaty, æ. having the nature of or like flate
Slaughter,n. deftruction by the fword, havoc
Slaughter, v. t. to flay, kill, kill with the fword
Slaughter'houfe, n. a place for killing beafts in
Slaughter'erman,n. one employed in killing beafts
Slaughter'erous, a. deftructive, murderous, bloody
Slave, n. one deprived of freedom, a drudge
Slave, v. i. to drudge, toil, toil much, work hard
Slav'er, v. i. to drivel, to emit fpittle; n. fpittle
Slav'erer, n. a driveller, fimpleton, idiot
Slavery, n. the condition of a flave, fervitude
Slavifh, a. fervile, mean, bafe, dependant, clofe
Slavifhly, ad. fervilely, meanly, pitifully, bafely
Slavifhnefs, n. fervility, meannefs, bafenefs
Slavonian, Slavon'ic, a. pertaining to the Slavons or Slavi, the anceftors of the prefent Ruffians and Poles   (fians and Poles
Slavonian, Slavon'ic, n. the language of the Ruf-
Slay, v. t. flew, pret. flain, pa. to kill, put to death, murder, butcher
Slay, Slaie, n. a weaver's reed to clofe work with
Slayer, n. a killer, murderer, deftroyer, butcher
Sleave,n. filk or thread untwifted, a fifh
Sleazy, a. thin, flight, flimfy, badly wrought
Sled, n. a carriage moving on runners
Sled, v.t. to convey on a fled
Sled'ded, a. mounted upon or riding on a fled
Sled'ding, n. the act of conveying on a fled, fnow convenient for fleds to pafs
Sledge, n. a fled, low carriage, very large hammer
Sleek, a. fmooth, gloffy, fat; v. t. to make fmooth
Sleekly, ad. in a fleek manner, fmoothly, foftly
Sleeknefs,n. a fmooth ftate or quality, fatnefs
Sleep, n. repofe, flumber, reft, eafe, quiet, death
Sleep, v. i. flept, pret. flept, pa. to fufpend the mental powers by reft   (a floor-timber
Sleeper, n. one who fleeps, a lazy inactive drone,
Sleepily, ad. drowfily, heavily, ftupidly, lazily
Sleepinefs, n. drowfinefs, heavinefs, dulnefs
Sleeping, n. the act of taking reft in fleep, fleep
Sleeplefs, a. wanting or void of fleep, watchful
Sleepy, a. caufing fleep, drowfy, heavy, fluggifh
Sleet,n. fmall fnow or hail, rain and fnow mixed
Sleety, a. bringing or caufing fleet

Sleeve, *n.* the covering of the arm; *v. t.* to put in fleeves

Sleevebutton, *n.* a button to fasten the fleeve

Sleeveless, *a.* wanting fleeves, fimple, foolish

Sleight, *n.* dexterous practice, artifice, art, cunning

Slen'der, *a.* thin, flight, fmall, weak, fparing, poor

Slen'derly, *ad.* without much bulk, flightly, poorly

Slen'derness, *n.* thinnefs, want of bulk, flightnefs

Slept, *pret.* and *pa.* of *to fleep*

Slew, *pret.* of *to flay* (veyance on fnow

Sley [flay] *n.* a vehicle moving on runners for con-

Sley, *v.* to ride or convey in a fley (for fleying

Sley'ing, *n.* a riding in a fley, a ftate of fnow fit

Sley, Sleave, *v. t.* to part or twist into threds

Slice, *v. t.* to cut into thin pieces, cut off, divide

Slice, *n.* a broad piece cut off, a kitchen-utenfil

Slich, *n.* the ore of a metal pounded for working

Slid'der, *v. i.* to flide, to flide with interruption

Slide, *v. i.* flid, *pret.* flid, flidden, *pa.* to move on a fmooth or flippery furface, to pafs on fmoothly or inadvertently

Slide, *n.* a fmooth eafy paffage, even courfe, flow

Slider, *n.* a perfon who or that which flides

Slight, *a.* thin, weak, trifling, fmall, worthlefs

Slight, *n.* neglect, contempt, an artifice, a trick

Slight, *v.* to neglect, difregard, fcorn, do carelefsly

Slightingly, *ad.* with or in contempt, with fcorn

Slightly, *ad.* weakly, badly, carelefsly, coolly

Slightnefs, *n.* weaknefs, a want of due attention

Slim, *a.* flender, thin of fhape, weak, crafty

Slime, *a.* a glutinous fubftance, foft mud, mire

Sliminefs, *n.* vifcofity, a glutinous ftate or matter

Slimy, *a.* vifcous, glutinous, ropy, clammy, foft

Slinefs, *n.* defigning artifice, low cunning, craft

Sling, *n.* a miffive weapon for ftones, throw, caft

Sling, *v. t.* flang, flung, *pret.* flung, *pa.* to throw by a fling, to hang by cords

Sling'er, *n.* one who flings or ufes a fling

Sling'ing, *n.* the act or art of flinging

Slink, *v.* flank, flunk, *pret.* flunk, *pa.* to caft the young, fteal out of the way, fneak away

Slink'ing, *pa.* cafting, ftealing or fneaking away

Slip, *v.* to flide, difplace, commit a miftake, fteal away, let loofe, lofe, pafs over, efcape, ftrip

Slip, *n.* a falfe ftep, miftake, efcape, twig, narrow piece, a narrow entrance, a defcent

Slip'board, *n.* a board fliding in grooves

Slip'knot, *n.* a knot that flips, a knot with a bow

Slip'per, *n.* a kind of loofe fhoe, a morning-fhoe

Slip'perinefs, *n.* want of firm footing, uncertainty

Slip'pery, *a.* apt to make one flip, unftable

Slip'fhod, *a.* not having the fhoes pulled up, loofe

Slip'flop, *n.* bad or infipid liquor, poor ftuff

Slit, *n.* a long cut or rent, a long narrow opening

Slit, *v. t.* flit, *pret.* flit, flitted, *pa.* to cut or rend lengthwife, divide, fplit

Sliv'er, *v.* to divide longways, fplit, creep

Sliv'er, *n.* a flice cut off, a piece rent off

Sloat, *n.* an under-timber of a cart

Slob'ber, *v.* to flaver, to wet with fpittle; *n.* flave

Sloe, *n.* the fruit of the black-thorn, a four plum

Sloke, *n.* a fpecies of plant, ulva

Sloop, *n.* a veffel having but one maft

Slop, *v. t.* to make a puddle, fpill, dafh, fwallow

Slop, *n.* a puddle, wetnefs, mean liquor, clothing

Slope, *a.* oblique, flanting, fhelving, declining

Slope, *n.* a flanting form, declivity, defcent

Slope, *v. t.* to cut or run obliquely, to incline

Slope, Slopewife, Sloping, *ad.* obliquely

Slopenefs, *n.* a flanting ftate, declivity, defcent

Slop'py, *a.* miry and wet, plafhy, dirty, filthy, nafty

Slot, *n.* the track of a deer

Sloth, *n.* idlenefs, naftinefs, a very flow animal

Sloth'ful, *a.* idle, lazy, indolent, fluggifh, nafty

Sloth'fully, *ad.* with or in floth, idly, lazily, filthily

Sloth'fulnefs, *n.* idlenefs, lazinefs, filthinefs

Slouch, *n.* a man who looks heavy and clownifh

Slouch'ing, *a.* walking aukwardly and heavily

Slov'en, [o as u] *n.* one dirtily or carelefsly dreffed

Slov'enlinefs, Slov'enry, *n.* a neglect of drefs

Slov'enly, *a.* negligent of neatnefs, nafty, filthy

Slov'enly, *ad.* in a dirty or inelegant manner

Slough, *n.* a deep miry place, the fkin which a fer-

Slough'y, *a.* miry, boggy, muddy (pent cafts off

Slow, *a.* not fwift, tardy, tedious, long, dull, heavy

Slow, *v. i.* to delay, defer, put off, omit, neglect

Slow or Slowly, *ad.* tardily, fluggifhly, heavily

Slowneſs, *n.* a want of due fpeed, dulnefs, delay

Slowworm, *n.* a blindworm, a flow and fmall viper

Slub'ber, *v. t.* to do carelefsly, daub, ftain, foil

Sludge, *n.* mire, dirt, dirt mixed with water

Sluce, *n.* a vent or channel for water

Slue, *v. t.* to turn on an axis, to turn round

Slug, *n.* a fort of fnail, flow lazy wretch, drone, ball

Slug'gard, *n.* an idle fleepy perfon, drone, flug

Slug'gardize, *v. t.* to make idle or dronifh

Slug'gifh, *a.* lazy, flothful, fleepy, dull, heavy

Slug'gifhly, *ad.* lazily, flothfully, heavily

Slug'gifhnefs, *n.* lazinefs, dulnefs, heavinefs

Sluice or Sluce, *n.* a vent for water, lock, floodgate

Sluice, *v. t.* to throw out water, caft, let out

Sluicy, *a.* falling in ftreams, running faft out

Slumber, *v.* to fleep lightly, dofe, reft, ftupify

Slumber, *n.* a light or unfound fleep, repofe, eafe

Slumberous, Slumbery, *a.* caufing fleep, fleepy

Slump, *v. i.* to fink or fall into water or mud, through ice or other hard furface, [N. E.]

Slung, *pret.* and *pa.* of *fling*

Slunk, *pret.* and *pa.* of *to flink* (notes

Slur, *n.* flight, difgrace, a curve line connecting

Slur, *v. t.* to fully, cheat, pafs lightly

Slut, *n.* a low dirty woman, a word of contempt

Slut'tifh, *a.* nafty, dirty, filthy, indecent, mean

Slut'tifhly, *ad.* in a fluttifh manner, naftily

Slut'tifhnefs, Slut'tery, *n.* naftinefs, dirtinefs, filth

Sly, *a.* cunning, artful, crafty, infidious, waggifh

Sly'boots, *n.* a cunning or waggifh perfon

Sly'ly or Slily, *ad.* with fecret artifice, cunningly

Smack, *v.* to kifs, crack, make a fmart noife, beat, tafte, relifh, have a peculiar tafte or quality

Smack, *n.* a kifs, crack, ftroke, tafte, favor, fhip

Small, *a.* little, fhort, flender, weak, mean, petty

Small, *n.* the fmall or narrow part of a thing

Small'age or Smell'age, *n.* a plant of the parfley

Small'beer, *n.* a weak beer (genus

Small'coal, *n.* fmall charcoal to light fires with

Small'craft, *n.* a veffel lefs than a fhip, any fmall

Small'craft, *a.* relating to fmall veffels (veffel

Small'nefs, *n.* littlenefs, weaknefs, infignificance

Smallpox', *n.* an eruptive contagious difeafe

Small'y, *ad.* in a little or low degree, *ob.*

S.nalt, *n.* a very beautiful blue glafs, of cobalt, flint and potafh fufed together

Smarag'dine, *a.* made of or like an emerald, green

Smaris, *n.* a fifh of a dark green color

Smart, *a.* quick, active, brifk, witty, keen, fharp

Smart, *n.* an active perfon; *v. i.* to feel quick pain

Smart'ly, *ad.* brifkly, wittily, fharply, tartly

Smart'nefs, *n.* livelinefs, vigor, wittinefs, keennefs

Smatch, *n.* a tafte, tincture, twang, fmattering

Smat'ter, *v. i.* to have a fuperficial knowledge

Smat'ter, *n.* a fuperficial or trifling knowledge

Smat'terer, *n.* one who has but a flight knowledge

Smat'tering, *n.* a very flight knowledge, a tafte

Smear, *v. t.* to daub, foil, defile, pollute, cover

Sméardab, *n.* a dab or fpecies of broad fifh

Sméary, *a.* dauby, fticky, clammy, tough, nafty

Smeeth, *v. t.* to fmoke, to blacken with fmoke

Smell, *v. t.* fmelled, fmelt, *pret.* and *pa.* to perceive by means of the nofe

Smell, *n.* the power or act of fmelling, fcent, odor

Smell'feaft, *n.* one who haunts good tables, an epicure

Smelt, *pret.* and *pa. paff.* of *to fmell*

Smelt, *v. t.* to extract metal from ore; *n.* a feafifh

Smelt'er, *n.* one who fmelts or melts ore

Smerk or Smirk, *v. i.* to fmile, to fmile wantonly

Smew, *n.* the englifh name of the bird mergus

Smile, *v. i.* to look gay or joyous, fmirk, fneer

Smile, *n.* a look of pleafure or kindnefs

Smilingly, *ad.* with a look of pleafure, pleafingly

Smirch, *v. t.* to foil, daub, pollute, cloud, fully

Smirk, *v. i.* to look affectedly foft

Smirk'er, *n.* one who fmirks or looks pleafantly

Smite, *v. t.* fmote, *pret.* fmit, fmitten, *pa.* to ftrike, hit, dafh, afflict, blaft, kill

Smiter, *n.* one who fmites or afflicts, the arm

Smith, *n.* one who works in metals or forges

Smith'ery, *n.* a fmith's workfhop, and work

Smit'ten, *pa. paff.* of *to fmite* (a woman

Smock, *n.* a woman's body-linen, a fhift; *a.* like

Smock'faced, *a.* palefaced, beardlefs, maidenly

Smoke, *n.* an exhalation from burning bodies

Smoke, *v.* to emit fmoke, trouble with or hang in fmoke, burn, ufe tobacco, difcover, ridicule

Smókedry, *v. t.* to dry or harden in the fmoke

Smókelefs, *a.* having no fmoke (the fmoke

Smóker, *n.* one who fmokes tobacco, or dries in

Smókejack, *n.* an engine for turning a fpit by the force of the afcending current of air in a chimney

Smóky, *a.* emitting or full of fmoke, offenfive

Smooth, *a.* even on the furface, foft, flattering

Smooth, *v. t.* to make even or eafy, calm, flatter

Smooth'en, *v. t.* to make fmooth or even, *ob.*

Smooth'faced, *a.* having a fine fmooth face, fat, placid

Smooth'ly, *ad.* evenly, calmly, gently, eafily

Smooth'nefs, *n.* evennefs, mildnefs, gentlenefs,

Smote, *pret.* of *to fmite* (foftnefs

Smoth'er, [o as u] *v. t.* to fuffocate, fupprefs

Smoth'er, *n.* a fmoke, thick duft, fuppreffion

Smóuldering, *a.* burning without much vent

Smug, *a.* nice, fpruce, neat, clean, tricked up, *ob.*

Smug'gle, *v. t.* to import or export goods without paying the duties, run, convey privately

Smug'gler, *n.* one who fmuggles goods, a veffel employed in fmuggling

Smug'gling, *n.* the act of running goods

Smug'ly, *ad.* nicely, fprucely, neatly, cleanly, *ob.*

Smug'nefs, *n.* fprucenefs, neatnefs, cleannefs, *ob.*

Smut, *n.* foot, a fpot, mildew, obfcenity, ribaldry

Smut, *v. t.* to mark with fmut, to caufe mildew

Smutch, *v. t.* to black with fmoke, daub, fmut

Smut'tily, *ad.* dirtily, filthily, obfcenely

Smut'tinefs, *n.* foil from fmoke, obfcenenefs

Smut'ty, *a.* black, mildewed, filthy, immodeft, vile

Snack, *n.* a fhare, a part; *v. t.* to fnatch (bridle

Snaf'fle, *n.* a bridle that croffes the nofe; *v. t.* to

Snag, *n.* a tooth ftanding out, knot, knob, fnail

Snag'ged, Snag'gy, *a.* full of fnags or fharp points

Snail, *n.* a teftaceous infect, flow perfon, drone

Snaillike, *a.* in the manner of a fnail, flow

Snake, *n.* a ferpent, a fly perfon

Snákeroot, *n.* the name of a medical root

Snáky, *a.* refembling a fnake, having fnakes, fly

Snap, *v.* to break at once, bite, catch at, found,

Snap, *n.* the act of breaking, bite, catch (chide

Snap'dragon, *n.* a kind of play, a kind of plant

Snap'per, *n.* one who fnaps, a peevifh perfon, a fifh

Snap'pifh, *a.* eager to bite, tart, peevifh, crofs

Snap'pifhly, *ad.* eagerly, tartly, peevifhly, crofsly

Snap'pifhnefs, *n.* a fnappifh temper, peevifhnefs

Snare, *n.* a gin, trap, net; *v. t.* to entangle, trap,

Snarl, *v.* to growl like a cur, fnap, entangle (prune

Snarl'er, *n.* one who fnarls, a crofs furly fellow

Snáry, *a.* entangling, infidious, trecherous, fly

Snaft or Snat, *n.* the fnuff of a candle, *ob.*

Snatch, *v.* fnatched, fnatcht, *pret.* and *pa.* to feize haftily upon, catch eagerly, to

Snatch, *n.* a hafty catch, broken part, bit, fit, quip

Snatch'block, *n.* a kind of pulley in a fhip

Snatch'er, *n.* one who fnatches or takes haftily

Sneak, *v. i.* to creep flily, lurk about (fneaks

Snéaker, *n.* a large veffel of drink, a perfon who

Snéaking, *a.* mean, fervile, covetous

Snéakingly, *ad.* flily, meanly, fervilely, bafely

Snéakup, *n.* an infidious mean fcoundrel, *ob.*

Sneap, *v. t.* to reprove, check; *n.* a reprimand, *ob.*

Sneer, v. i. to fhow contempt by laughing, to rid

Sneer, n. contempt, a fcornful look (icule

Sneerer, n. one who fneers, one who ridicules

Sneerful, a. contemptuous, fcornful, infolent

Sneeze, v. i. to emit wind audibly by the nofe

Sneeze, n. an emiffion of wind audibly by the nofe

Snick and Snee, n. a combat with knives, ob.

Snick'er, v. i. to laugh filly or contemptuoufly

Sniff, v. i. to draw the breath audibly by the nofe

Snig'gle, v. i. to fifh for eels with a bait

Snip, v. t. to cut, to cut at once with fciffors

Snip, n. a fingle cut, fmall fhred, fhare, fnack, part

Snipe, n. a fmall delicate bird, blockhead, fool

Snip'pet, n. a fmall fhare or part, fragment, bit

Snip'fnap, n. a tart dialogue or debate, a quarrel

Snite, n. a bird, a fnipe ; v. i. to blow the nofe, ob.

Sniv'el, n. the running of the nofe, fnot, naftinefs

Sniv'el, v. i. to run at the nofe, to cry like a child

Sniv'eller, n. one who fnivels, a foolifh weeper

Snore, n. a noife made through the nofe in fleep

Snore, v. i. to breathe hard through the nofe

Snort, v. i. to blow through the nofe like a horfe

Snot, n. the mucous difcharge of the nofe, filth

Snot'ty, a. full of fnot, nafty, dirty, filthy, mean

Snout, n. the nofe of a beaft, a nofe, nozle, end

Snout'ed, a. having or fitted with a fnout

Snout'fair, a. painted, fet off with paint or wafhes

Snow, n. water frozen in flakes, a fmall fhip

Snow, v. i. to defcend in congealed flakes, to fall

Snow'ball, n. a lump of fnow, a plant

Snow'bird, n. a bird which appears in time of fnow

Snow'broth, n. fnow melted into water, fleet, cold

Snowdrop, n. a white flower (liquor

Snow'fhoe, n. a light frame to walk with on fnow

Snow'flip, n. a body of fnow fliding from a hill

Snow'white, a. white as fnow, very white or fair

Snow'y, a. white as or abounding with fnow

Snub, v. to check, reprimand, chide, nip, fob

Snub, n. a check, reprimand, knot in wood, jagg

Snudge, v. i. to lie idle, clofe or fnug, ftoop, ob.

Snuff, n. the burnt or burning wick of a candle, a

candle's end, tobacco powdered, perverfe re-

fentment (offenfe

Snuff, v. to crop, fmell, draw breath, fnort, take

Snuff'box, n. a box to hold or carry fnuff in

Snuff'ers, n. pl. an inftrument to crop candles with

Snuf'fle, v. i. to fpeak or breath through the nofe

Snuf'fles, n. obftruction of the nofe by mucus

Snug, a. clofe, private, concealed, hidden, fly

Snug, Snug'gle, v. i. to lie very clofe or warm

So, ad. and conj. in like manner, thus, provided

Soak, v. to fteep, lie fteeped, wet, drench, drain

Soap, n. a compound of oil and alkali, or oil and

earth, and metallic oxyds, ufed in cleanfing,

medicins, &c.

Soap, v. t. to rub over or wafh with foap

Soapboiler, n. a maker of foap, a feller of foap

Soapftone, n. a ftone of the magnefian genus, ufu-

ally white or yellow, lapis ollaris

Soapfuds, n. pl. water well impregnated with foap

Soapy, a. covered with or refembling foap

Soapwort, n. a plant, faponaria

Soar, v. i. to fly aloft, to rife high ; n. a high flight

Sob, v. to cry with convulfive forrow, figh, wet

Sob, n. a convulfive figh or cry, a very deep figh

Sob'by, a. moift, wet, foft with water

Sober, a. temperate, found in mind, calm, grave

Sober, v. t. to make fober or ferious, calm, quiet

Soberly, ad. temperately, moderately, coolly

Sobernefs, Sobriety, n. temperance, coolnefs

Soc'age or Soc'cage, n. an ancient tenure of lands

Sociable, a. converfable, familiar, friendly, kind

Sociabil'ity, n. difpofition for fociety or converfation

Sociablenefs, n. good fellowfhip, kindnefs

Sociably, ad. converfably, as a companion

Social, a. familiar in converfation, fit for fociety

Society, n. company, fraternity, partnerfhip, union

Socin'ian, n. a follower or admirer of Socinus who

denied the divinity of Chrift

Socin'ianifm, n. the doctrins held by Socinus

Sock, n. a high theatrical fhoe, falfe ftocking, iron

Sock'et, n. a hollow to receive a thing in, a cafe

Sock'etchifel, n. a ftronger fort of chifel

Soc'man, n. one who holds lands by foccage

Soc'otrine, a. denoting the pureft kind of aloes

Socrat'ic, a. in the manner of Socrates who gave

inftruction by afking queftions

Sod, n. a piece of turf, turf, clod, furface of land

Sod, Sod'den, pret. and pa. of to feeth (falt

Soda, n. mineral fixed alkali, the bafis of common

Sodal'ity, n. fociety, fellowfhip, intercourfe

Sod'der or Sol'der, n. a cement to unite bodies

Sod'der, v. t. to unite by fodder

Sod'omite, n. one who is guilty of fodomy

Sod'omy, n. a hainous unnatural crime, buggery

Soe, v. t. to unite with a needle and thred

Sofa, n. a fplendid feat covered with carpets, feat,

Soft, a. fmooth, tender, eafy, gentle, fimple (bed

Soft, ufed for, be gentle, forbear

Soft'en, v. to moke foft or eafy, leffen, relent

Soft'ly, ad. tenderly, kindly, gently, flowly, mildly

Soft'ner, n. one who palliates, a moderator

Soft'nefs, n. a foft quality, mildnefs, effeminacy

Soho, exclam. ufed as a form of calling to any one

Soil, v. t. to daub, ftain, pollute, fully, manure

Soil, n. dung, compoft, dirt, land, earth, country

Soil'inefs, Soil'ure, n. a ftain, pollution, foulnefs

Sojourn', n. a temporary refidence, a fhort abode, ob.

Sojourn', v. i. to live at home, refide

Sojourn'er, n. a temporary dweller, refident

Sojourn'ing, n. the act of living or refiding

Sol, n. the name of a note in mufic, a french coin

Sol'ace, v. t. to comfort, cheer, amufe, recreate

Sol'ace, n. comfort, alleviation, pleafure, delight

Sol'andgoofe, n. a fpecies of the goofe kind

Sol'ano, n. a hot S. E. wind in Spain, which pro-

duces inflammatory effects on men

Solar, a. of or belonging to the fun, bright

Sold, *pret.* and *pa. pass.* of *to sell*

Sold'an, *n.* the emperor of the Turks, a sultan

Sol'danel, *n.* a species of plant

Sóldier, [foljer] *n.* a man engaged in military service, a private as opposed to an officer, a brave warrior

Sóldierlike, *a.* like a foldier, warlike, fierce, bold

Sóldierly, *a.* becoming a foldier, warlike, bold

Sóldierfhip, *n.* the military character or ftate

Sóldiery, *n.* a body of foldiers, army, foldierfhip

Sole, *n.* the bottom of the foot or of a fhoe, a fifh

Sole, *v. t.* to furnifh fhoes with new foles

Sole, *a.* fingle, alone, only, fimple, not married

Sol'ecifm, *n.* an impropriety or badnefs of fpeech

Sólely, *ad.* fingly, only, feparately, without others

Sol'emn, *a.* awful, religioufly grave, very ferious

Sol'emnefs, *n.* a folemn manner, awfulnefs

Solem'nity, *n.* awfulnefs, pomp, dignity, gravity

Solemnizátion, *n.* a celebration, performance

Sol'emnize, *v. t.* to celebrate, to perform religiouf-

Sol'emnly, *ad.* awfully, with formal ftate (ly

Sóleneſs, *n.* the ftate of being alone

Soli'cit, *v. t.* to entreat, beg, afk, excite, difturb

Solicitátion, *n.* importunity, prayer, excitement

Soli'citor, *n.* one who petitions or acts for another

Soli'citous, *a.* anxious, careful, uneafy, concerned

Soli'citoufly, *ad.* anxioufly, carefully, uneafily

Soli'citrefs, *n.* a lady who petitions for another

Soli'citude, *n.* anxiety, earneftnefs, uneafinefs

Sol'id, *a.* firm, compact, found, true, grave (body

Sol'id, *n.* that which comprehends the whole, a

Solid'ify, *v.* to become or make folid (folid

Solidificátion, *n.* the act of making or becoming

Solid'ity, *n.* fulnefs of matter, firmnefs, truth

Sol'idly, *ad.* firmly, compactly, foundly, truly

Sol'idnefs, *n.* folidity, gravity, ferioufnefs, truth

Solidun''gulous, *a.* wholehoofed, entire, firm

Solifid'ian, *n.* one who holds faith only without

Solil'oquy, *n.* a talking to one's felf (works, *ob.*

Sol'iped, *n.* an animal whofe feet are not cloven

Solitáire, *n.* an ornament for the neck, an hermit

Sol'itarily, *ad.* in folitude, without company

Sol'itarinefs, *n.* folitude, lonelinefs, retirement

Sol'itary, *a.* retired, difmal, fingle; *n.* an hermit

Sol'itude, *n.* a folitary life, lonely place, defert

Sol'lar or Sol'ar, *n.* an upper room, garret, roof

Sólo, *n.* a tune played or fung by only one perfon

Sol'ftice, *n.* the ftate of the fun at its fartheft diftance from the equator in June and December

Solfti'tial, *a.* of or belonging to the folftice

Solv'able, *a.* poffible to be refolved, payable

Solubil'ity, *n.* a fufceptibility of being diffolved in a fluid

Sol'uble, *a.* capable of being diffolved in a fluid

Solve, *v. t.* to refolve, clear up, explain, loofen

Solv'ency, *n.* an ability to pay all debts or claims

Solvend, *n.* a fubftance to be diffolved

Solv'ent, *a.* able to pay debts, diffolving, eafing

Solv'ent, *n.* a fluid which diffolves a fubftance

Solúte, *a.* loofened, loofe, relaxed, free, eafy, gay

Solútion, *n.* explanation, anfwer, the procefs of diffolving, the ftate of a body diffolved in a fluid, or the mixture

Sol'utive, *a.* laxative, caufing relaxation or eafe

Solymǽan, *a.* pertaining to Solyma in Lycia

Sómber, *a.* dull, dark, gloomy, clouded, overcaft

Some, [fum] *a.* more or lefs, one, not many, certain

Some'body, *n.* an indifcriminate perfon, a perfon

Some'how, *ad.* in one way or other (of note

Som'erfault, Som'erfet, *n.* a kind of active leap

Some'thing, *n.* more or lefs, part; *ad.* rather

Some'time, *ad.* once, formerly, heretofore, long

Some'times, *ad.* now and then (fome degree

Some'what, *n.* fomething, more or lefs; *ad.* in

Some'where, *ad.* in fome place or other, in being

Somnabulátion, *n.* a walking in fleep

Somnab'ulifm, *n.* the act or practice of walking in

Somnab'ulift, *n.* a walker in fleep (fleep

Somnif'erous, Somnif'ic, *a.* caufing fleep, opiate

Som'nolence or Som'nolency, *n.* fleepinefs, heavi-

Son, [fun] *n.* a male-child, native, defcendant (nefs

Sonáta, *n.* a tune or mufic for inftruments only

Son-in-law, *n.* one married to a perfon's daughter

Son'fhip, *n.* the ftate, duty or character of a fon

Song, *n.* a poem modulated by the voice, lay, note

Song'ifh, *a.* containing or confifting of fongs, *ob.*

Songs'ter, *n.* a finger of fongs, finger, poor finger

Songs'trefs, *n.* a female finger of fongs

Son'net, *n.* a fhort poem, a poem of 14 lines

Sonneteer, *n.* a trifling poet, a poet in contempt

Sonorif'ic, Sonif'erous, *a.* giving or caufing found

Sonórous, *a.* giving a loud and full found, grand

Sonóroufly, *ad.* with a high found, loudly, fhrilly

Sonóroufnefs, *n.* a high and full found, loudnefs

Soon, *a.* fpeedy, quick, ready, immediate

Soon, *ad.* fhortly, readily, early

Soop, *n.* a food made of flefh and vegetables boiled

Soot, Sut, *n.* a fubftance formed by combuftion, confifting of oil, carbon, &c. *v. t.* to cover with

Soot'ed, *pa.* covered or fmeared with foot (foot

Soot'erkin, *n.* a kind of falfe or pretended birth

Sooth, *n.* truth, reality; *a.* pleafant, *ob.*

Soothe, *v. t.* to flatter, pleafe, calm, foften, gratify

Sooth'er, *n.* a flatterer, appeafer, calmer, pacifier

Sooth'fay, *v. i.* to foretel, predict, divine

Sooth'fayer, *n.* a predictor, diviner, fortuneteller

Sooth'faying, *n.* the foretelling of future events

Soot'inefs, *n.* a footy ftate or quality, blacknefs

Soot'y, *a.* covered with or like foot, black, dark

Sop, *n.* bread fteeped in liquor, a thing to pacify by

Sop, *v. t.* to fteep or foak in liquor, dip, wet

Soph'imore, *n.* a ftudent in college of the 2d. year

Sóphi, *n.* the title of the emperor of Perfia

Soph'ifm, *n.* a keen fallacious argument, a fubtilty

Soph'ift, *n.* a profeffor of philofophy, caviller, foph

Soph'ifter, *n.* a fophift, a keen infidious logician

Sophift'ical, *a.* fallacious, logically deceitful

Sophift'ically, *ad.* with keen or fallacious fubtilty

Sophift'icate, v. t. to adulterate ; a. adulterated
Sophiftication, n. the act of adu tering, fallacy
Soph'iftry, n. a fallacy, a fallacious argument
Soporif'erous, Soporif'ic, a. caufing fleep, opiate
Sor'bent, n. that which promotes abforption
Sor'cerer, x. a magician, enchanter, conjurer
Sor'cerefs, n. an enchantrefs, witch, hag
Sor'cery, n. magic, enchantment, witchcraft (ob.
Sord, n. a piece of turf, graffy ground ; a. reddifh,
Sord'es, n. foulnefs, dregs, naftinefs, filthinefs
Sord'id, a. niggardly, mean, nafty, filthy, vile
Sor'didly, a. niggardly, nearly, meanly, filthily
Sor'didnefs, n. niggardlinefs, meannefs, naftinefs
Sore, n. a place tender and painful, wound, buck
Sore, a. tender to the touch, painful, grievous
Sorcé, n. a bird, the little water hen
Sor'el, n. a fallow buck, a buck of the third year
Sorely, Sore, ad. with pain or vehemence, much
Sorenefs, n. the tendernefs of a hurt or cut, pain
Sorg'o, n. a fpecies of plant
Sorites, n. argument heaped on argument, a heap
Sor'rel, n. a four plant, a reddifh color
Sor'rily, ad. meanly, poorly, wretchedly, badly
Sor'rinefs, n. meannefs, wretchednefs, badnefs
Sor'row, n. grief, trouble, mourning, fadnefs, pain
Sor'row, v. i. to grieve, wail, be fad or dejected
Sor'rowed, a. accompanied with forrow, mourned
Sor'rowful, a. expreffing grief, mournful, fad, dull
Sor'rowfully, ad. in a forrowful manner
Sor'rowfulnefs, n. forrow, grief, fadnefs
Sor'ry, a. grieved, uneafy, poor, vile, worthlefs
Sort, n. a kind, fpecies, rank, lot, company, fet
Sort, v. t. to difpofe in claffes, adjuft, fuit, fit
Sort'al, a. relating to fome fort of fpecies, ob.
Sort'ance, n. agreeablenefs, fuitablenefs, fitnefs, ob.
Sort'ilege, n. the act of drawing lots, forcery, ob.
Sort'ment, n. a parcel duly forted, diftribution, ob.
Sofhong' or Souchong', n. a kind of tea of a mid-
  dle quality
Sofs, v. i. to fall plump into a feat, to fit lazily
Sot, n. a drunkard, toper, blockhead, dull fellow
Sot, v. to befot, ftupify, drink, tipple, ob.
Sot'tifh, a. given to liquor, dull, ftupid, fenfelefs
Sot'tifhly, ad. dully, ftupidly, heavily, fenfelefsly
Sot'tifhnefs, n. dulnefs, ftupidity, drunkennefs
Sough, n. a fubterraneous drain, fewer, ob.
Sought, [fawt] pret. and pa. paff. of to feek
Soul, n. the immortal part of man, fpirit, life, a
Soul'ed, a. furnifhed with a foul or mind (being
Soul'lefs, a. fpiritlefs, heavy, mean, narrow
Soul'fcot, Soul'fhot, n. money paid for a requiem, ob.
Sound, a. healthy, whole, ftout, right, juft, faft
Sound, n. a noife, probe, a narrow arm of the fea,
  air bladder cf fifh
Sound, v. t. to make or yield a noife, celebrate
  by found, play on, fearch for bottom with a lead
Sound'ing, pa. making a found, examining
Sound'ingboard, n. a board to propagate found by
Sound'ings, n. pl. a part of the ocean in which a

line will reach the bottom, alfo the kind of
  ground found by founding
Sound'ly, ad. heartily, ftoutly, truly, well,
Sound'nefs, n. health, ftrength, truth, rectitude
Soup or Soop, n. a broth, a decoction of flefh for
  the table
Sour, a. acid, tart, crabbed, peevifh, painful
Sour, v. to make or grow four or difcontented
Source, n. a fpring, head, origin, firft caufe, root
Sour'ifh, a. rather four, rather harfh or crofs
Sour'ly, ad. with fournefs, harfhly, crofsly
Sour'nefs, n. acidity, crabbednefs, aufterity (trifle
Sous [foo] n. a fmall coin, French penny, mere
Soufe, ad. with fudden violence, all at once
Soufe, n. a pickle made of falt, water and vinegar
Soufe, v. t. to fteep in foufe, duck in water, fall
Sout'errain, n. a grotto, cave, not ufed (region
South, n. the place where the fun is at noon, fouth
South, ad. from or towards the fouth ; a. fouthern
Southéaft, n. the point between the fouth and eaft
South'erly, Southern, a. lying from or to the fouth
South'ernwood, n. a plant of ftrong fcent
South'ing, a. approaching or going to the fouth
South'ing, n. a courfe or diftance fouth
South'moft, a. lying or going neareft to the fouth
South'fay, fee foothfay
South'ward, South'wardly, ad. towards the fouth
Southweft, n. the point between fouth and weft
Sov'ereiga, [fuverun] n. a fupreme lord, a king
Sov'ereign, a. fupreme in power
Sov'reignty, n. the higheft place, fupremacy
Sow, n. a female of the hog, large piece of lead,
  tub, infect (befprinkle, fpread, propagate
Sew, v. t. fowed, pret. fowed, fown, pa. to fcatter,
Sower, n. one who fows feed, one who promotes
Sow'ins, n. pl. a four flummery, foured oatmeal, ob.
Sowl, v. t. to pull or twich by the ears, ob.
Space, n. local extenfion, diftance, room, time
Spacious, a. large, great, extenfive, roomy, wide
Spacioufnefs, n. extent, roominefs, loftinefs
Spad'dle, n. a fmall inftrument, a little fpade
Spade, n. a fhovel for digging, fuit at cards, deer
Spadeful, n. as much as a fpade will hold
Spadi''ceous, a. having a light red color, reddifh,
  having a receptacle within a fpathe
Spadill'e or Spadill'o, n. the ace of fpades
Spadix, n. a receptacle proceeding from a fpath
Spake, pret. of to fpeak
Spall, n. a joint of the body, the fhoulder, ob.
Spalt, n. a whitifh ftone ufed in melting metals
Spalt, a. of loofe texture, fcaly, eafily fplit
Span, n. a hand's breadth, 9 inches, a fhort time
Span, v. t. to meafure by the fingers extended
Span, pret. of to fpin
Span'drel, n. the fpace between the curve of an
  arch and the right lines inclofing it
Span'farthing, n. a kind of low childifh game
Span''gle, n. a fmall bofs of fhining metal, tinfel
Span''gle, v. t. to cover or fet with fpangles

Span'iard, n. a native of Spain
Span'iel, n. a dog for sport, a very sneaking person
Span'iel, v. i. to fawn upon, cringe, cajole
Span'ish, a. coming from or belonging to Spain
Span'ish, n. an earth used in making bricks, the language of Spain
Spank, v. t. to beat, to slap with the open hand
Spank'er, n. a small or trifling coin, a large sail
Spank'ing, a. large, big, jolly, strong, fine, spruce
Span'ner, n. one who spans, the lock of a fusee
Spar, n. stones which break into regular shape
Spar, n. a small beam, bar, spoke, tree, glass
Spar, v. to shut, bar, fight, quarrel, cry
Spar'adrap, n. a cerecloth, a large plaster   (ity
Spare, a. scanty, lean, thin, superfluous; n. frugal-
Spare, v. t. to be frugal, save, omit, allow, forgive
Spárenefs, n. a spare or thin state, leanness, care
Spárer, n. one who strives to avoid, expence
Spárerib, n. ribs of pork with little flesh left on
Spargefac'tion, n. the act of sprinkling, moisture
Spáring, a. frugal, niggardly, near, scarce, scanty
Spáring, Spáringnefs, n. frugality, nearness
Spáringly, ad. frugally, scantily, cautiously
Spark, n. a particle of fire or light, gay lad, lover
Spark'ful, Spark'ish, a. lively, brisk, airy, gay, fine
Spar'kle, n. a spark, a small particle of fire
Spar'kle, v. i. to emit sparks, glitter, shine
Spark'ler, n. one who sparkles, one who shines
Spark'lingly, ad. with bright or twinkling luster
Spark'lingnefs, n. a bright twinkling luster
Spar'row, n. a genus of birds of the paserine order
Spar'rowhawk, n. a species of short winged hawk
Spar'ry, a. confifting of or resembling spar
Sparfe, a. thin, scattered here and there
Spart'an, n. a native of Sparta
Spart'an, a. pertaining to Sparta, hardy, undaunted
Spasm, n. a convulsion, involuntary contraction,
Spasmod'ic, Spasmod'ical, a. convulsive   (cramp
Spat, n. the young of shellfish, a stone; pret. of spit
Spáthe, [a as in ask] n. a calyx like a sheath, bursting lengthwise
Spatháceous, a. having calyx like a sheath
Spath'iform, a. resembling a sheath
Spátiate, v. i. to rove, range, ramble at large
Spat'ter, v. to bespatter, sprinkle, dash, spit slander
Spat'terdafhes, n. pl. coverings for the legs
Spat'ula, n. a spreading slice used by apothecaries
Spav'in, n. a disease in horses, a kind of swelling
Spaw, n. a well or spring of fine mineral water
Spawl, v. i. to spit much or frequently; n. spittle
Spawn, n. the eggs of fish, offspring, children
Spawn, v. i. to shed spawn, breed, produce, issue
Spawn'er, n. a female fish, a fish that spawns
Spay, v. t. to castrate a female animal, geld, cut
Speak, v. spake, spoke, pret. spoken, pa. to talk, utter, pronounce, address, celebrate
Spéakable, a. able to speak, fit to be spoken
Spéaker, n. one who speaks, one who teaches, the president of a branch of legislature

Spéaking, pa. talking, conveying words, declaring
Spear, n. a long pointed weapon, a lance
Spear, v. t. to kill with a spear, sprout, shoot
Spéargrafs, n. a long and stiff grass
Spéarman, n. a person who fights with a spear
Spéarmint, n. a species of hot mint
Spe"cial, a. peculiar, particular, singular, brave
Spe"cially, ad. peculiarly, particularly, chiefly
Special'ity, n. a particular state
Spe"cialty, n. a special contract or evidence of a debt under seal, the debt
Spécie, n. coined money of any kind
Spécies, n. a sort, kind, class, order, letter, money
Specif'ic, a. distinguishing one sort from another
Specif'ic, n. a remedy adapted to some one disease
Specif'ically, ad. according to the species, specially
Specif'icate, v. t. to distinguish particularly
Specificátion, n. a particular notation or mention,
Spe"cify, v. t. to particularize, to mention (a sample
Spe"cimen, n. a sample, proof, part of the whole
Spécious, a. showy, plausible, striking, pleasing
Spéciously, ad. with a good appearance, plausibly
Speck, n. a small spot, a stain; v. t. to spot, to mark
Spec"kle, n. a very small speck or spot, a little mark
Spec"kle, v. t. to mark with speckles, to spot
Spec"kled, pa. full of small spots, spotted
Spec'tacle, n. a gazing stock, a glass for the fight
Spec'tacled, a. furnished with spectacles   (fight
Spectátion, n. regard, respect, notice, a view, a
Spectátor, Spectátrefs, n. a looker on, a beholder
Spectátorship, n. the act or office of beholding
Spec'ter, n. an apparition, spirit, ghost
Spec'trum, n. an image, visible form
Spec'ular, a. like a speculum, affifting the fight
Spec'ulate, v. to meditate, consider, hazard, to purchase in expectation of a rife of price
Speculátion, n. a mental view, examination, spy, the act or practice of buying things, and relying for profit on an increase of price, opposed to regular trade in which the profit is the difference between the wholesail and retail prices
Spec'ulatist, n. one who forms theories
Spec'ulator, n. one who speculates or buys at hazard
Spec'ulative, a. contemplative, serious, notional
Spec'ulatively, ad. in a speculative manner (ment
Spec'ulum, n. a mirror, lookingglafs, table, instru-
Speech, n. articulate utterance, talk, an oration
Spéechlefs, a. not having power to speak, dumb
Spéechleffnefs, n. the state of being speechless
Spéechmaker, n. a maker of speeches, an orator
Speed, v. sped, pret. sped, pa. to hasten, give or have success, affist, aid
Speed, n. quicknefs, hafte, difpatch, fuccefs, issue
Spéedily, ad. quickly, hastily, readily, soon
Spéedinefs, n. a speedy quality, quicknefs, hafte
Spéedy, a. quick, ready, nimble, active, dexterous
Spéerage, n. another name of asparagus
Speek, n. a spike, a long nail; v. t. to spike
Spell, n. a charm, turn at work, change, tale, story

Spell, v. fpelled, fpelt, pret. and pa. to charm, form words of letters, take a turn at

Spell'er, n. one who fpells, one who forms words

Spell'ing, n. the act of writing words properly

Spelt, v. t. to fplit, break in pieces, fever, ob.

Spelt'er, n. a kind of femi-metal, zink

Spend, v. t. fpent, pret. fpent, pa. to expend, confume, wafte, pafs, fatigue

Spend'er, n. one who fpends or waftes, a prodigal

Spend'thrift, n. a prodigal, prodigal lavifher, rake

Spérable, a. that may be hoped for, ob.

Sperm, n. feed by which a fpecies is propagated, the head matter of a whale (from oily matter

Spermacéti, n. the brain of certain whales purified

Spermat'ic, Spermat'ical, a. full of fperm, feminal

Sperm'atize, v. i. to yield or throw out feed, ob.

Spet, v. t. to pour out largely; n. a great flow, ob.

Spew, v. t. to caft or throw up, vomit, eject

Spha''celate, v. to gangrene, mortify, corrupt

Spha''celus, Spha''celátion, n. a mortification

Sphenoid', a. refembling a wedge

Sphere, v. t. to place in a fphere, to make round

Sphere, n. a globe, orb, circuit, compafs, province

Spher'ic, Spher'ical, a. globular, circular, round

Spher'ically, ad. in the form of a fphere, roundly

Spher'icalnefs, Spheri''city, n. a round ftate

Spher'ics, n. the doctrin of the fphere

Spheroid', n. a body almoft of a fpherical form

Spheroid'al, Spheroid'ical, a. having the form of a

Spher'ule, n. a fmall fphere, a little globe (fpheroid

Spic'ate, a. having flowers in fpikes

Spice, n. an aromatic fubftance ufed in fauces, a

Spice, v. t. to feafon or mix with fpice (fmatch

Spicer, n. one who fpices, one who deals in fpices

Spicery, n. the commodity or repofitory of fpices

Spicif'erous, a. bearing ears of grain or flowers

Spick and Span, ad. quite, entirely, totally, very

Spicy, a. like, producing or abounding with fpice

Spider, n. the name of a well known infect

Spig'nel, n. a plant, hartwort

Spig'ol, n. a fifh, a fpecies of perch

Spig'ot, n. a peg to put into a faffet, pin, ftopple

Spike, n. an ear of corn, great nail, pointed iron

Spike, v. t. to faften, fet or fpoil with fpikes

Spikelets, n. fmall fpikes of a large one

Spik'enard, n. a plant of feveral fpecies

Spile, n. a peg or pin to ftop a hole in a cafk

Spill, n. a fmall quantity, fhiver, thin bar, gift, ob.

Spill, v. fpilled, fpilt, pret, and pa. to fhed, be loft by fhedding, wafte, lavifh

Spill'er, n. one who fpills, a kind of fifhing line

Spilth, n. any thing fpilled or wafted, wafte

Spin, v. fpan, fpun, pret. fpun, pa. to draw out in threds, ftream out, protract, whirl

Spin'age, n. the name of a garden herb

Spinal, a. belonging to the fpine or backbone

Spin'dle, n. a pin to form thred on, axis, ftalk

Spin'dle, v. i. to grow thin an tall, to fhoot out

Spin'dlefhanked, a. having very fmall or thin legs

Spine, n. the backbone, a thorn, a fharp point

Spines'cent, a. hard and fharp like a thorn

Spin'net, n. a mufical inftrument, a fmall harpficord

Spinif'erous, a. bearing or producing thorn

Spin'ner n. a perfon that fpins, a longlegged fpider

Spin'ning, n. the act of drawing out in threds

Spin'olet, n. a fmall bird of the lark kind

Spinos'ity, n. a thorny perplexity, crabbednefs

Spi'nozifm, n. the principles of Spinoza a deift

Spins'ter, n. a woman who fpins, a maiden woman

Spiny, Spinous, a. thorny, perplexed, difficult

Spíracle, n. a breathing hole, fmall vent, pore

Spiral, a. winding upwards, turning, curved

Spiral, n. a curve line winding and receding from

Spirally, ad. in a fpiral or winding form (its center

Spire, v. i. to fhoot out pyramidically

Spire, n. a round pyramid, wreath, twift, curve

Spir'it, n. a ghoft, foul, breath, life, courage, vigor

Spir'it, v. t. to animate, encourage, excite, roufe

Spir'itally, ad. with or by means of the breath, ob.

Spir'ited, a. lively, full of fire, bold, ftirred (linefs

Spir'itednefs, Spir'itfulnefs, n. livelinefs, fpright-

Spir'itlefs, a. dejected, depreft, very dull, inactive

Spir'itous, a. refined, fine, active, lively, ardent

Spir'itoufnefs, finenefs, activity, ardor, heat

Spir'its, n. pl. inflammable liquors, livelinefs, life

Spir'itual, a. incorporeal, heavenly, pure, mental

Spiritual'ity, n. immateriality, a pure act of the foul, that which belongs to an ecclefiaftic

Spiritualizátion, n. the act or art of fpiritualizing

Spir'itualize, v. t. to apply to a religious fenfe

Spir'itually, ad. without bodily groffnefs, purely,

Spir'itualty, n. a fpiritual ftate ob. (divinely

Spir'ituous, a. full of fpirits, fiery, hot, diftilled

Spirt, v. t. to ftream or throw out in a jet

Spiry, a. pyramidical, wreathed, curled, winding

Spifs, a. thick, clofe, firm, compact, grofs, ob.

Spifs'ated, a. infpiffated, thickened

Spifs'itude, n. thicknefs, clofenefs, groffnefs

Spit, n. an iron prong for roafting, a depth of earth

Spit, v. fpat, fpit, pret. fpit, fpitted, fpitten, pa. to put upon a fpit, to throw out fpittle

Spitch'cock, n. an eel cut into pieces and roafted

Spite, n. malice, malicioufnefs, rancor, defiance

Spite, v. t. to treat malicioufly, thwart, offend

Spiteful, a. malicious, malignant, illnatured, crofs

Spitefully, ad. malicioufly, malignantly, crofsly

Spitefulnefs, n. malice, malignancy, fpite

Spit'tal, n. a charitable foundation, a hofpital

Spit'ted, pa. put on a fpit, pierced, fhot out

Spit'ter, n. one who fpits, a young or male deer

Spit'tle, n. the moifture of the mouth

Spit'venom, n. poifon ejected from the mouth

Splafh, v. t. to daub with water or dirt, wet, dirty

Splafh'y, a. full of little pools or dirty water

Spláyfooted, a. having the feet broad or turned in

Spláymouthed, a. the mouth made wide by defign

Spleen, n. the milt, fpite, anger, hip, melancholy

Spléened, a. deprived of the fpleen, gentle, kind

Spleenful, Spleen'y, a. angry, hot, peevish, fretful
Spleenlefs, a. kind, civil, obliging, gentle; mild
Spleenwort, n. a plant of feveral fpecies
Splen'dent, a. fhining, bright, gloffy, famous
Splen'did, a. fhowy, magnificent, fumptuous
Splen'didly, ad. magnificently, fumptuoufly
Splen'dor, n. luſter, magnificence, pomp (fretful
Splenetic, Spleenifh, a. full of fpleen, peevifh,
Splen'ic, a. belonging to or like the fpleen, dull
Splen'itive, a. paffionate, hot, violent, furious, ob.
Splice, n. two ropes or lines joined without a knot
Splice, v. t. to join, to join ropes without a knot,
   join trees in a fence by interlocking their
   branches
Splint, n. a thin bit of wood ufed by furgeons
Splint, Splint'er, v. t. to fecure by fplints, to fhiver
Splint'er, n. a thin piece of wood broken off
Splin'tery, a. confifting of or like fplinters
Split, v. t. fplit, pret. fplit, fplitted, pa. to divide,
   break in pieces, dafh, crack
Split'ter, n. one who fplits, a buſtle, ſtir, tumult
Splut'ter, n. a confufed angry fpeech, buſtle, ſtir
Spoil, v. to rob, ſtrip, mar, decay, perifh, corrupt
Spoil, n. plunder, wafte, corruption, a flough
Spoil'er, n. one who fpoils, a robber, a plunderer
Spoke, n. a bar or ray in a wheel; pret. of to fpeak
Spokefman, n. a perfon who fpeaks for another
Spoliate, v. i. to rob, plunder, fpoil, lay wafte
Spoliation, n. a robbing or plundering, plunder
Spon'dee, n. a foot in poetry of two long fyllables
Spon'dyl, n. a tribe of bivalvular fhell fifh
Spon'dyle, n. a verteber, joint of the backbone
Sponge, n. fee fpunge
Sponfal, a. relating to a fpoufe or matrimony
Spon'fion, n. the act of becoming furety for ano-
Spons'or, n. a furety, proxy, godfather (ther
Spontaneous, a. voluntary, free, unforced
Spontaneoufly, ad. voluntarily, freely, willngly
Spontaneoufnefs, Spontaneity, n. voluntarinefs
Spool, n. a weaver's quill; v. t. to wind yarn
Spool'er, n. one who winds thred upon fpools
Spoom, v. i. to pafs on fwiftly, to raife froth, ob.
Spoon, n. a kind of ladle to eat liquids with
Spoon'bill, n. a bird with a beak like a fpoon
Spoon'drift. n. a fprinkling of water fwept from
   the furface of waves in a tempeft
Spoon'ful, n. as much as a fpoon can hold at once
Spoon'meat, n. any liquid food eaten with fpoons
Spoon'wort, n. fcurvy grafs
Sporadic, a. occurring in fingle inftances, fcattered
Sport, n. diverfion, paſtime, jeft, game, gingle
Sport, v. to play, make merry, divert, trifle, game
Sportful, a. merry, gay, frifky frolicfome, wanton
Sportfully, ad. merrily, cheerfully, wantonly
Sportfulnefs, Sportivenefs, n. frolic, wantonnefs
Sportive, a. merry, gay, airy, wanton, ludicrous
Sportfman, n. a man who is fond of hunting, &c.
Sportule, n. alms, a dole by great men, gift, ob.
Spot, n. a fpeck, blot, ftain, difgrace, certain place

Spot, v. to mark, ftain, daub, corrupt, difgrace
Spot'tednefs, n. a ftate of being full of fpots
Spot'lefs, a. pure, immaculate, holy, upright, juft
Spot'ty, a. full of fpots, marked with fpots
Spous'al, a. nuptial, matrimonial; n. marriage
Spoufe, n. a hufband, wife, married perfon
Spous'ed, a. efpoufed, married, wedded
Spoufe'lefs, a. having no hufband or wife, fingle
Spont, n. a wooden gutter, pipe, mouth, waterfal
Spont, v. to run out with violence, to iffue out
Spout'ing, n. the act of pouring out, harangue
Sprain, n. a violent extenfion of the tendons
Sprain, v. t. to ftretch the ligaments violently, to
Sprang, pret. of to fpring (ftrain
Sprat, n. a fmall and well known fifh
Sprawl, v. i. to tumble with agitation, to ftruggle
Spray, n. the drops of water driven from a wave
Spread, n. an extent, expanfion of parts, compafs
Spread, v. fpread, pret. fpread, pa. to extend,
   ftretch, cover, propagate, publifh
Spread'er, n. one who fpreads, one who publifhes
Sprent, pa. fprinkled, befprinkled, fcattered
Sprig, n. a fmall branch, twig, flip, fhoot, fpray
Sprig, v. t. to work in or form fprigs, to adorn
Sprig'gy, a. full of or having fprigs (with fprigs
Spright or Sprite, n. an apparition; v. t. to haunt
Sprighted, pa. haunted with fpirits, frightened
Sprightful, a. brifk, lively, gay, airy, merry
Sprightfully, ad. brifkly, gaily, airily, vigoroufly
Sprightlinefs, n. brifknefs, livelinefs, gaity, vigor
Sprightly, a. brifk, lively, gay, airy, fharp, active
Spring, v. fprang, fprung, pret. fprung, pa. to
   grow, arife, ftart, bound, leap, fire a mine, crack
   a maft or yard
Spring, n. a feafon of the year, elaſtic force, leap,
   fkip, leak, fountain, fource, rife, caufe, original,
   a tranfverfe crack in a maft or yard, a rope from
   a fhip's ftern to a cable
Springe, n. a gin, fnare, noofe to catch by a jerk
Spring'er, n. one who roufes game, the white an-
Spring'halt, n. a lamenefs in a horfe's legs (telope
Spring'inefs, n. a fpringing power, elafticity
Sprin'gle, n. a fpringe, fnare, elaftic noofe
Spring'tide, n. a tide at the new moon, a high tide
Sprin'gy, a. full of or containing fprings, elaftic
Sprin'kle, v. to wet with drops of liquor, fcatter
   in fmall drops, befprinkle, bedew
Sprink'ling, n. a wetting gently, a fmall quantity
Sprit, v. i. to fhoot; n. a fhoot, fprout, fpirit
Sprite, n. a fpirit, an apparition, cheerfulnefs
Spriteful, a. brifk, lively, gay, merry
Spritefully, ad. brifkly, gaily, fprightfully
Spritefulnefs, n. brifknefs, livelinefs, gayety
Sprightly, a. lively, gay, brifk, merry
Sprit'fail, n. the fail on the bowfprit of a fhip
Sprout, v. i. to fhoot out by vegetation, bud, grow
Sprout, n. a fhoot of a vegetable after it is crept
Spruce, a. neat, nice, trim, clean; n. a kind of fir
Sprucebeer, n. beer tinctured with boughs of fir

Sprúcely, *ad.* in a fpruce manner, neatly
Sprúcenefs, *n.* neatnefs in drefs
Sprung, *pret.* and *pa. paff.* of *to fpring*
Sprunt, *n.* any thing fhort and ftiff; *a.* lively, gay
Spry, *a.* nimble, brifk, quick in action
Spud, *n.* a kind of fhort knife, a poor forry wretch
Spume, *n.* froth, foam, fcum ; *v. i.* to froth, to foam
Spumef'cence, *n.* foam, froth, act of foaming
Spúmous, Spúmy, *a.* frothy, foamy, empty, vain
Spun, *pret.* and *pa. paff.* of *to fpin*
Spunge, *n.* an animal fubftance growing in water compofed of firm elaftic fibers, remarkable for imbibing water, fifty fpecies are known
Spunge, *v.* to wipe with a fpunge, live upon others
Spun'ger, *n.* a hanger on for maintenance
Spun'ginefs, *n.* moifture with foftnefs
Spun'gy, *a.* moift and foft, imbibing moifture
Spun'ginghoufe, *n.* a bailiff's houfe to put debtors
Spunk or Sponk, *n.* rotten wood, touchwood (in
Spur, *n.* a prick, fharp point, incitement, motive
Spur, *v.* to prick with a fpur, urge, incite, go faft
Spur'galled, *a.* hurt or torn by a fpur, fore
Spurge, *n.* a plant, milk wort, dwarf bay
Spúrious, *a.* falfe, counterfeit, illegitimate
Spúrioufly, *ad.* in a fpurious manner, falfely
Spúrioufnefs, *n.* a fpurious ftate or quality
Spur'ling, *n.* the name of a fmall feafifh
Spurn, *v. t.* to kick, fcorn, treat contemptuoufly
Spurn'ing, *n.* infolent or haughty treatment, pride
Spur'rier, *n.* one who makes or deals in fpurs
Spur'ry, *n.* a fpecies of plant
Spurt, *v.* to fly or throw out in a quick ftream
Spurt, *n.* a quick ftream, ftart, fudden fit, hurry
Sputátion, *n.* the act of fpitting or fpurting out, *ob.*
Sput'ter, *v.* to throw out fpittle in fpeaking, &c.
Sput'terer, *n.* one who fputters or talks very faft
Spy, *n.* one who watches another's actions
Spy, *v. t.* to difcover, fee at a diftance, examin
Spy'boat, *n.* a boat fent out to obtain intelligence
Spy'glafs, Spy'ingglafs, *n.* a kind of telefcope
Squab, *a.* thick and ftout, fat, fhort, unfeathered
Squab, *n.* a couch, a young pigeon
Squab, *v. i.* to fall down plump or heavily
Squab'bifh, Squab'by, *a.* thick, heavy, flefhy, fat
Squab'ble, *v. i.* to wrangle, debate peevifhly, brawl
Squab'ble, *n.* a wrangle, a petty quarrel or brawl
Squab'bler, *n.* a quarrelfome or brawling fellow
Squabpíe, *n.* a pie made of fquabs
Squad'ron, *n.* a part of a fleet, a part of an army
Squad'roned, *a.* formed into or having fquadrons
Squac'co, *n.* a large fierce bird
Squal'id, *a.* foul, nafty, filthy, dirty, illfavored
Squall, *n.* a fudden guft of wind, ftorm, loud fcream
Squall, Squeal, *v. i.* to fcream fuddenly or loudly
Squall'y, *a.* windy, gufty, ftormy, tempeftuous
Squálor, *n.* naftinefs, filthinefs, coarfenefs, horror
Squami"gerous, *a.* bearing or having fcales
Squam'iform, *a.* in the fhape of fcales
Squamófe, Squámous, *a.* fcaly, rough, hard, dry

Squan'der, *v. t.* to fpend lavifhly, fpend, diffipate
Squan'derer, *n.* a prodigal waiter, a fpendthrift
Square, *a.* having right angles, equal, very ftout
Square, *n.* a regular figure, a kind of inftrument
Square, *v. t.* to form with right angles, fit, adjuft
Squárenefs, *n.* a fquare ftate, evennefs, ftoutnefs
Squárer, *n.* a fwaggering perfon, boafter, bully
Squárifh, *a.* fomewhat fquare, nearly fquare
Squarrófe, *a.* ragged, fcaly, fcurfy
Squafh, *n.* a fudden fall, pulp, fruit, animal
Squafh, *v. t.* to make into pulp, crufh, put an end to
Squat, *v. i.* to cower, to fit clofe to the ground
Squat, *n.* the pofture of cowering, tin ore, bruife
Squat, *a.* cowering, clofe, near, fhort and thick
Squat'ter, *n.* one who fettles upon land without a title, [local]
Squeak, *v. i.* to cry out fhrilly, to betray a fecret
Squeak, *n.* a fhrill and quick cry, a cry of pain
Squéamifh, *a.* faftidious, nice, eafily difgufted
Squéamifhly, *ad.* faftidioufly, nicely, fickly
Squéamifhnefs, *n.* delicacy, nicenefs, ficknefs
Squeeze, *v. t.* to prefs clofe, crufh, opprefs
Squeeze, *n.* a preffure, compreffion, clofe hug
Squelch, *n.* a fudden and heavy fall, crafh, *ob.*
Squib, *n.* a paper of wildfire, a puffing fellow, ri-
Squill, *n.* a fea onion, fifh, infect (dicule
Squin'ancy, *n.* the name of a difeafe, a quinfy, *ob.*
Squint, *v. i.* to look obliquely ; *a.* looking afquint
Squint'eyed, *a.* having an oblique fight, indirect
Squintfégo, *a.* fquinting, looking obliquely, *ob.*
Squin'y, *v. i.* to look afquint, to fquint, *ob.*
Squire, *v. t.* to wait upon, attend, conduct, lead
Squire, *n.* a title, title of gentility, attendant
Squir'rel, [i as u] *n.* a fmall nimble animal (to prate
Squirt, [i as u] *v.* to throw out in a quick ftream,
Squirt, *n.* an inftrument to fquirt with, a fmall
Squirt'er, *n.* one who plies a fquirt (quick ftream
Stab, *v. t.* to wound mortally or mifchievoufly
Stab, *n.* a wound with a fharp weapon, a fly hurt
Stab'ber, *n.* one who ftabs, a fly fecret murderer
Stabil'iment, *n.* ftability, firmnefs, fupport, prop
Stabil'ity, Stáblenefs, *n.* firmnefs, conftancy
Stáble, *a.* fixed, firm, fure, fteady, ftrong, durable
Stáble, *n.* an apartment or building for beafts
Stáble, *v.* to put in, keep or live in a ftable
Stábleboy, Stábleman, *n.* one employed in a ftable
Stab'lifh, *v. t.* to eftablifh, confirm, fix, fettle, *ob.*
Stack, *n.* a large pile, rick, quantity, number
Stack, *v. t.* to pile up, pile up in ricks, ftumble
Stac'te, *n.* a fweetfmelling gum from myrtles
Stad'dle, *n.* a fmall ftrait tree, a young tree
Stad'dled, *a.* abounding with young trees
Stádium, *n.* a furlong or forty rods
Stadt'holder, *n.* the chief magiftrate in Holland
Stadt'holderate, *n.* the office of the ftadtholder
Staff, *pl.* ftaves, *n.* a ftick, prop, ftay, enfign of office, ftanza
Staff'ifh, *a.* ftiff, harfh, formal, firm, *ob.*
Stag, *n.* a red male deer, the male of the hind

Stage, n. a theater, place for public tranfactions or a reit on a journey, floor, ftep, courfe, life, a carriage running regularly for paffengers

Stage, v. t. to exhibit publicly, difplay, fhow, act

Stagecoach, n. a coach that travels by fet ftages

Stageplay, n. a play, a theatrical entertainment

Stageplayer, n. an actor upon a theater

Stager, n. a practitioner, player, actor, comedian

Staggard, n. the name of a ftag four years old

Stagger, v. to reel, doubt, hefitate, fhock, alarm

Staggers, n. pl. a difeafe in horfes, giddinefs

Stagnant, a. not flowing, motionlefs, ftill, calm

Stagnate, v. i. to have no courfe, lie ftill, ftop

Stagnation, n. a ftop of motion, ftop, ceflation

Stagyrite, n. an appellation given to Ariftotle from the place of his birth

Staid, pret. and pa. of to ftay

Staid, a. fober, grave, compofed, fteady, ob.

Staidnefs, n. fobriety, gravity, regularity, ob.

Stain, v. to blot, fpot, daub, die, pollute, difgrace

Stain, n. a blot, fpot, blur, mark, taint, infamy

Stainer, n. a perfon who ftains or blots, a polluter

Stainlefs, a. free from blots, fin or reproach, pure

Stair, n. a ftep made to afcend by

Staircafe, n. a fet of ftairs, a place for ftairs

Stake, n. a poft, wager, bet, pledge, hazard, anvil

Stake, v. to wound with ftakes, to fet or bet

Stalactic, a. refembling ftalactite, like icicles

Stalactite, n. fpar in the form of icicles

Stalactitic, a. in the form of ftalactite

Stalagmite, n. fpar in the form of drops

Stalder, n. a wooden frame to fet cafks on

Stale, a. old, long kept, vapid, corrupt, ftinking

Stale, n. urine, old beer, a handle, ftep, proftitute

Stale, v. to make water as a horfe, to wear out

Stalely, ad. in a ftale manner or ftate, of old

Stalenefs, n. an old or bad ftate, oldnefs, fournefs

Stalk, [ftauk] v. i. to walk proudly, to ftrut

Stalk, n. a proud ftep, ftrut, ftem of a plant, &c.

Stalkinghorfe, n. a horfe to fcreen, mafk, fcreen

Stalky, a. hard like a ftalk, refembling a ftalk

Stall, v. to keep in a ftall, live, inveft, glut, cloy

Stall, n. a crib for a horfe or ox, feat, booth, fhed

Stallfeed, v. t. to feed or fatten in a ftable

Stallfed, a. fed in a ftall, fed with dry food only

Stallion, n. a male horfe, gallant, bully

Stamen, pl. Stamens, n. the filament of a flower fupporting the anthers which contain the fecundating duft or pollen

Stamened, a. furnifhed with flamens

Staminal, a. confifting in or pertaining to ftamens

Stamina, n. folids of the body, threds of plants

Stamineous, a. confifting of or like threds

Stamineous flower, is one which has no corol

Staminiferous flower, is one which has ftamens without a piftil

Stammer, v. i. to hefitate in fpeaking, to ftutter

Stammerer, n. one who fpeaks with hefitation

Stammering, n. a ftop or impediment in fpeech

Stamp, v. t. to ftrike with the foot, pound, mark

Stamp, n. an inftrument to make an impreffion, thing ftamped, legal mark, cut, form, value

Stamper, n. an inftrument ufed for pounding

Stamping, n. the act of ftriking, an impreffion

Stanch, v. to ftop blood, ftop, ceafe, fatisfy, cloy

Stanch, a. found, firm, ftrong, determined, true

Stanchion, n. a fmall poft or upright fupporter

Stanchlefs, a. that cannot be ftopped, dreadful

Stanchnefs, n. foundnefs, firmnefs, refolution

Stand, v. ftood, pret. ftood, pa. to be on the feet, ftop, remain, offer as a candidate, perfift, be confiftent, abide, fuffer, direct a courfe

Stand, n. a ftop, halt, ftation, poft, difficulty, prop, a mufket and its apparatus

Standard, n. an enfign in war, teft, tree left

Standardbearer, n. a man who carries a ftandard

Standel or Standil, n. a tree of a long ftanding, ob.

Stander, n. one who ftands, a tree left ftanding

Standing, n. continuance, ftay, ftation, condition

Standing, pa. a. fet on the feet, fettled, lafting,

Standifh, n. a cafe to hold pens and ink (ftagnant

Stang, n. a perch, 5 1-2 yards in length, a cowlftaff

Stank, pret. of to ftink

Stannary, a. relating to a tinwork; n. a tinmine

Stannel, n. the reftrel, a fpecies of hawk

Stannic, a. pertaining to tin or the acid of tin

Stanza, n. a ftaff or fet of verfes, an entire ftrain

Stapazin, n. a bird, a fpecies of warbler

Staple, n. a fettled mart of goods, the texture or thred of cotton, wool, &c. an iron loop

Staple, a. eftablifhed in commerce, fettled

Star, n. a body fet in the heavens, the mark (*)

Star, v. t. to fet or adorn with ftars

Starboard, n. the right fide of a fhip or boat (with

Starch, n. a thing made of flour to ftiffen linen

Starch, v. t. to ftiffen with ftarch; a. ftiff, formal

Starchamber, n. a kind of court in England

Starched pa. ftiffened with ftarch, ftiff, formal

Starcher, n. one who ftiffens linen with ftarch

Starching, n. the act of ftiffening with ftarch

Starchly, ad. ftiffly, in a formal manner

Starchnefs, n. ftiffnefs, precifenefs, formality

Stare, v. i. to look with wonder or impudence

Stare, n. a fixed or wild look, a bird

Starer, n. one who ftares, an eager or wild gazer

Stargazer, n. an aftronomer, aftrologer, wizard

Stargazing, n. the act of obferving the ftars

Stargrafs, n. ftarry duck meat

Starjelly, n. a plant

Starwort, n. a plant, after

Stark, a. ftiff, fixed, quite, entire

Starkly, ad. ftiffly, ftrongly, firmly, ob.

Starlefs, a. having no light from the ftars, dark

Starlight, n. light afforded by means of the ftars

Starlight, a. lighted by the ftars, bright, clear, fine

Starlike, a. like a ftar, pointed, fhining, bright

Starling, n. a genus of birds, a defenfe to piers in a bridge.

Star'oft, n. a feudatory, one who holds a fief
Star'ofty, n. a fief, an eftate held by feudal fervice
Star'paved, a. paved or ftudded with ftars
Star'proof, a. not admitting the light of the ftars
Star'red, a. decorated with or influenced by ftars
Star'ring, a. fhining with or like ftars, bright
Star'ry, a. adorned with or refembling ftars
Star'fhoot, n. an emiffion from a ftar, a jelly, ob.
Start, v. to wince, fhrink, leap, move fuddenly, fet off or out, fly, alarm, bring within purfuit, let out a liquid
Start, n. a motion of terror, the act of fetting out
Start'er, n. one who fhrinks from his purpofe
Start'ful, a. apt to ftart, fkittifh
Start'fulnefs, n. pronenefs to ftart
Start'ing, n. the act of ftarting
Start'ingly, ad. with fudden ftarts or fits, quickly
Start'ifh or Start'lifh, a. apt to ftart, unfteady, fhy
Star"tle, v. to ftart, fhrink, fright, be frightened
Star"tle, n. a ftart, fhock, impreffion, fudden alarm
Start'up, n. one who comes fuddenly into notice
Starve, v. to perifh or kill with hunger, [with cold, Eng.]
Starve'ling, n. one in want of nourifhment
Starv'ing, pa. killing with or dying of hunger
Star'wort, n. a plant
State, n. a condition, grandeur, pomp, a kingdom or republic, civil power, body of a nation
State, v. t. to reprefent, propofe, fettle, regulate
Statelinefs, n. grandeur, affected dignity, pride
Stately, ad. with or in ftate, majeftically, proudly
Stately, a. auguft, pompous, lofty, elevated, proud
Statement, n. the act of ftating, an arrangement, an account of particulars
Statefman, n. a man employed in public affairs
Statefwoman, n. a woman who meddles in public matters, a bufy female politician, ob.
Stateroom, n. an apartment in fhips
Stat'ic, Stat'ical, a. of or relating to weighing
Stat'ics, n. pl. the fcience of weighing bodies (ter
Station, n. the act of ftanding, poft, rank, charac-
Station, v. t. to fix in a certain place, place, poft
Stationary, a. fixed, fettled, ftanding ftill
Stationer, n. one who fells paper, &c. a bookfeller
Statift, n. a ftatefman, a man publicly employed
Statis'tical, a. exhibiting or relating to a ftate of fociety or a people (condition of a people
Statis'tics, n. pl. a ftatement or view of the civil
Stat'uary, n. the art of carving images, a carver
Stat'ue, n. an image of metal, ftone or wood
Stat'ue, v. t. to place or form as a ftatue, ob.
Stat'ure, n. the natural height of any thing, fize
Stat'utable, a. done according to ftatute, legal, juft
Stat'ute, n. an act of the legiflature, law, decree
Stau'rolite, n. a filiceous ftone white or gray
Stave, v. to break into pieces, fpoil, part, pufh off
Staves, n. pl. of ftaff
Stay, v. ftaid, ftayed, pret. and pa. to continue in a place, ftop, prevent, reft, depend, prop

Stay, n. a continuance, ftep, prop, fhip-tackling
Stayed, pa. ftopped, propped, ferious, fteady
Stayedly, ad. gravely, compofedly, foberly, folidly
Stayednefs, n. gravity, folidity, fteadinefs
Stayer, n. one who ftops or fupports
Staymaker, n. a maker of ftays (a fhip
Stays, n. pl. of ftay, a woman's bodice, ropes in a
Stead or Sted, n. a place, room, turn, ufe, help,
Stead, v. t. to help, aid, fupport, ob. (frame
Stead'faft or Sted'faft, a. conftant, fixed firm
Stead'fatily, ad. conftantly, firmly, refolutely, ful-
Stead'faftnefs, n. conftancy, firmnefs, courage (ly
Stead'ily, ad. without variation, without fhaking
Stead'inefs, n. conftancy, firmnefs, uniformity
Stead'y, a. not wavering, conftant, fixed, firm, fure
Stead'y, v. t. to make fteady, hold faft, fupport
Steak, Stake, n. a flice of flefh to fry or broil
Steal, v. ftole, pret. ftolen, pa. to take from anoth-
er unlawfully and privately with felonious in-
tent, gain by art, come or pafs fi'ently
Stealer, n. a perfon who fteals, thief, rogue, rafcal
Steal'ing, ad. flily, in an imperceptible manner
Stealth or Stelth, n. a fecret act, theft, a ftealing
Stealth'y, a. performed by ftealth, clandeftine, fly
Steam, n. the fmoke or heat of hot liquor, vapor
Steam, v. i. to fend up or pafs in vapor, to fume
Steatite, n. foap ftone, a fpecies of magnefian earth
Steatit'ic, a. pertaining to fteatite
Sted, n. room or place
Sted'dy, a. firm, conftant, not wavering
Sted'dy, v. t. to make or keep firm
Sted'dily, ad. firmly, conftantly
Sted'dinefs, n. firmnefs, conftancy, uniformity
Sted'faft, a. firm in a place or condition
Sted'faftly, ad. firmly, immoveably
Sted'faftnefs, n. firmnefs of refolution
Steed, n. a horfe, a horfe kept for ftate or war
Steel, n. iron combined with a fmall portion of carbon, armor, weapons, hardnefs
Steel, v. t. to edge with fteel, make hard, harden
Steely, a. made of fteel, firm, hard, unmerciful
Steelyard, n. an iron rod to weigh goods with
Steep, a. approaching to a perpendicular, flanting
Steep, n. a precipice; v. t. to foak, dip, infufe
Steep, n. a mixture for fteeping feeds, &c.
Steeper, n. a vat or ciftern to fteep in, [W. Indies]
Stee"ple, n. the turret or fpire of a church
Steepnefs, n. a fteep defcent, a great declivity
Steepy, a. fteep, perpendicular, inclining, floping
Steer, n. a young bullock; v. t. to direct a courfe
Steerage, n. the act of fteering, care, part of a fhip
Steerfman, Steerfmate, n. one who fteers a fhip
Stellar or Stel'lary, a. ftarry, relating to the ftars
Stel'late, a. radiated like a ftar, verticillate
Stellif'erous, a. having or abounding with ftars
Stel'liform, Stel'lular, a. like a ftar, radiated
Stem, n. a ftalk, family, race, generation, prow
Stem, v. t. to oppofe a current, ftop, keep back
Stench, n. a ftink, bad fmell; v. t. to make to ftink

Stenog'raphy, n. the art of writing fhort-hand
Stenog'rapher, n. a fhort hand writer
Stentorophon'ic,a. fpeaking or founding loudly,ob.
Step, v. to move the feet, walk, advance, fix the foot of a maft in the keel
Step, n. a footftep, pace, gait, round of a ladder
Step'child, n. a fon-in-law, a daughter-in-law
Step'dame, Step'mother,n. a mother by marriage
Step'father,n. a father-in-law,a father by marriage
Stepp, n. an extenfive level plain in Afia
Step'pingftone, n. a ftone to fave from dirt or wet
Step'ftone,n. a ftone to ftep on in entering a houfe
Stercoráceous, Stercorárious, a. relating to dung
Stercorátion, n. the act of dunging or manuring
Stereog'raphy, n. art of drawing folids on a plane
Stercograph'ic,a. delineated on a plain
Stereom'etry, n. the art of meafuring folid bodies
Ster'il, a. barren, unfruitful, poor, dry, fhallow
Steril'ity, n. barrennefs, unfruitfulnefs, drynefs
Ster'ilize, v. t. to make barren or unfruitful
Ster'let, n. a fifh of the Cafpian fea
Ster'ling, n. Englifh coin, a ftandard rate,a defenfe
Ster'ling, a. genuine, lawful, pure
Stern, a. fevere in look, harfh, cruel, afflictive
Stern, n. the hinder part of a fhip. tail, direction
Stern'age, n. the fteerage, the hind part in a fhip
Stern'chafe, n.a gun to fire from the ftern of a fhip
Stern'ly, ad. in a ftern manner, harfhly, feverely
Stern'moft, a. moft aftern, laft
Stern'nefs, n. harfhnefs, morofenefs, feverenefs
Stern'poft, n. the timber which fupports the rud-
Stern'on, Stern'um, n. the breaft bone   (der
Sternutátion, n. the act or effort of fneezing
Sternútative, Sternútatory, a. caufing to fneeze
Stew, v. to drefs, to feeth or be feethed flowly
Stew, n. a food, brothel, hothoufe, finall pond
Stew'ard,n. a man who manages another's eftate, one who provides victuals
Stew'ardfhip, n. the office or poft of a fteward
Stew'ing, n. the act of feething over a flow fire
Stib'ial, a. antimonial, like or having antimony
Stib'iated, a. impregnated with antimony
Stick, n. a fmall piece of wood, fmall tree, ftaff
Stick, v. ftuck, pret. ftuck, pa. to faften, fix, ad-here, ftop, fcruple, ftab, kill
Stick'inefs, n. an adhefive or glutinous quality
Stic'kleback, n. a fmall fifh of feveral fpecies
Stic'kle, v. i. to ftrive, conteft, take pains, trim
Stick'ler, n. one who takes part in a conteft
Stick'ling, n. a contending for with eagernefs
Stick'y, a. vifcous,adhefive,glutinous,ropy,tough
Stiff, a. ftubborn, harfh, ftrong, hard,thick,formal
Stiff'en, v. to make ftiff, to grow or become ftiff
Stiff'ening, n. a making ftiff, a thing to ftiffen
Stiff'hearted, a. obftinate, ftubborn, inexorable
Stiff'ly, ad. ftubbornly, inflexibly, rigidly
Stiff'necked, a. ftubborn, obftinate, rebellious
Stiff'nefs,n. obftinacy, harfhnefs, hardnefs, form-
Stifle, v. t. to fupprefs, conceal, extinguifh (ality

Stifle, n. the joint of a horfe next to the buttock
Stig'ma, n. a mark of infamy, brand,difgrace,the top of the piftil in a flower
Stigmat'ic, Stigmat'ical, a. branded with infamy
Stig'matize, v. t. to mark with infamy, to brand
Stilar,a. relating to or like the ftile of a fundial
Stile, n. ftepsinto a field, the pin of a fundial, an
Stilet'to, n. a fmall kind of dagger   (upright
Still, v. t. to calm, quiet, appeafe, filence, diftil.
Still, a. calm, quiet, filent, motionlefs, eafy, dead
Still, ad. till this time, till now, ever, continually
Still, n. a veffel for diftillation, calm, filence
Still'atory, n. a ftill, a kind of laboratory, ob.
Still'born, a. born dead, dead in the very birth
Still'icide,n. dropping, a fucceffion of drops, ob.
Stillicid'ious, a. dropping, falling in drops, ob.
Still'nefs,n. a calm, calmnefs,quietnefs, filence
Still'ftand, n. an abfence of motion, a calmnefs,ob.
Still'y, ad. with ftillnefs, calmly, quietly, filently
Stilts,n. pl. walking fupports ufed by boys, props
Stim'ulant, a. exciting or increafing action (tion
Stim'ulant, n. that which excites or increafes ac-
Stim'ulate, v. t. to prick, excite, ftir up, fpur on
Stimulátion, n. an excitement, motive, pungency
Sting, v. t. ftang, ftung, pret. ftung, pa. to pierce with a fting, pierce, wound, pain, hurt
Sting, n. an animal's weapon, wound, point
Stin'gily, [g as j] ad. covetoufly, meanly, fordidly
Stin'ginefs, n. covetoufnefs, nearnefs, meannefs
Sting'lefs, a. having no fting, harmlefs, innocent
Stin''go, n. ftrong beer, a name for fine old beer
Sting'ray, n. a fifh of the cartilaginous kind
Stin'gy,a. covetous, greedy, niggardly, mean
Stink, n. a nafty or offenfive fmell
Stink, v. i. ftank, ftunk, pret. ftunk, pa. to emit an offenfive fmell
Stink'ing'ly, ad. with a ftink, naftily, offenfively
Stint, n. a bound, limit, reftraint, proportion,part
Stint, v. t. to bound, limit, fix, reftrain, confine
Stipe, n. the filament which connects the down with a feed, the ftem of a leaf, or frond
Stipend, n. a fettled pay, falary, wages, income
Stipend'iary, a. receiving a ftipend, hireling
Stipend'iary, n. one who ferves for a ftipend
Stip'itate, a. fupported by a ftipe
Stip'tic, n. an aftringent medicine or lotion
Stip'tic, Stip'tical, a. ftopping or ftanching blood
Stipuláceous, Stip'ular,a. formed of ftipules
Stip'ulate, v. t. to covenant, contract, bargain
Stip'ulate, a. containing ftipules
Stipulátion,n. a contract, agreement, bargain, the fituation and ftructure of the ftipules of plants
Stip'ule, n. a leaf or fcale at the bafe of a petiole or peduncle
Stir, v. to move, go on, incite, animate, rife
Stir, n. a tumult, buftle, agitation, uproar, noife
Stir'ious, a. refembling or hanging like icicles
Stirp, n. a race, family,generation,iffue,root,ftalk
Stir'rer, n. one in motion, an early rifer, an inciter

Stir'rup, *n.* a kind of iron for a horfeman's foot

Stitch, *v. t.* to few loofely or flightly

Stitch, *n.* a fingle pafs of a needle in fewing, or one turn of thred round a needle in knitting, in plowing, a fpace between furrows

Stitch'ery, *n.* needlework, in contempt

Stitch'ing, *n.* the act of fewing, needlework

Stith''y, *n.* an anvil, *v. t.* to forge on an anvil, *ob.*

Stive, *v. t.* to fhut up quite clofe, make hot, *ob.*

Stiver, *n.* a Dutch coin about a cent value, a trifle

Stoat, *n.* an animal of the weefel kind, the ermin

Stoccádo, *n.* a ftab, a thruft with a rapier

Stock, *n.* a log, trunk, linen for the neck, ftem, lineage, family, pack, quantity, fund, tally, property or intereft in a joint capital or fund, cattle, animals fhipped, in W. Indies flaves on a plantation

Stock, *v. t.* to ftore, lay in ftore, furnifh, root up

Stock'ade, *n.* a fharpened poft or ftake fet in the earth, a line of ftockades

Stockáde, *v. t.* to fortify with pofts (in the funds

Stock'broker, *n.* a broker who buys and fells ftocks

Stock'dove, *n.* a bird, ringdove, wood pigeon

Stock'fifh, *n.* a cod dried very hard without falt

Stock'ing, *n.* a well known covering for the leg

Stock'ing, *v. t.* to drefs in or cover with ftockings

Stock'jobber, *n.* one who buys ftock or money

Stock'ifh, *a.* hard, blockifh, ftupid, heavy, perverfe

Stock'lock, *n.* a lock fixed in wood (funds

Stocks, *n. pl.* a wooden frame for punifhment, the

Stockftill, *a.* ftill as a ftock, quite motionlefs

Stóic, *n.* a philofopher of the fect of Zeno

Stóical, *a.* relating to the Stoics, unfeeling

Stóicifm, *n.* the opinions or maxims of the Stoics

Stole, *n.* a royal robe, a long veft, a root or ftump,

Stólen, *pa.* taken away privately and felonioufly

Stolid'ity, *n.* foolifhnefs, folly, ftupidity, *ob.*

Stoloniferous, *a.* producing fhoots from the root

Stom'ach, [o as u] *n.* the organ of digeftion, appetite, fullennefs, obftinacy, anger, haughtinefs

Stom'ach, [ch as k] *v.* to refent, be angry, bear, like

Stom'ached, *pa.* filled with refentment, angry

Stom'acher, *n.* an ornament worn upon the breaft

Stom'achful, *a.* loth to fubmit, fullen, peevifh

Stomach'ic, *a.* relating to or ftrengthening the

Stomach'ic, *n.* a medicin for the ftomach (ftomach

Stomp, *v.* to beat with the foot

Stomp, *n.* a beat or hard ftep of the foot

Stond, *n.* a ftand, ftation, poft, *ob.*

Stone, *n.* a concretion of earth, as clay, lime, filex, &c. ufually combined with fome kind of air, and often with fulphur or a metal; ftones are hard, infoluble in water, indu&ile and unmalleable ; alfo a concretion in the kidneys or bladder, a cafe containing the kernel of a feed, a tefticle, a weight of 14 lb. [in Eng. the ftone is 8, 12, 14 or 16 lb.]

Stone, *a.* made of or like ftone

Stone, *v. t.* to pelt or kill with ftones, to harden

Stóneblind, *a.* quite blind, not able to fee at all

Stónechatter, *n.* a bird fo named from its chattering

Stóneutter, *n.* one who hews or works in ftone

Stónedead, *a.* lifelefs as a ftone

Stónefruit, *n.* any fruit that has a ftone in it

Stónehorfe, *n.* a horfe that has not been caftrated

Stónepit, *n.* a quarry from which ftones are dug

Stónepitch, *n.* a very hard kind of pitch

Stóneftill, *a.* ftill or motionlefs as a ftone

Stónework, *n.* what is built or made with ftone

Stóninefs, *n.* a ftony ftate, roughnefs

Stóny, *a.* made or full of ftones, very hard, cruel

Stsod, *pret.* and *pa.* of *to ftand*

Stool, *n.* a feat without a back, an evacuation

Stool'ball, *n.* a kind of play with ftools and balls

Stoop, *v. i.* to bend down, lean, fink, light, yield

Stoop, *n.* the act of ftooping, fall, veffel of liquor

Stoop'ingly, *ad.* with a little inclination, meanly

Stop, *v* to hinder from going on, ftand ftill, fupprefs, ftay, regulate, clofe

Stop, *n.* a ceffation of motion, paufe, prohibition, obftacle, point in writing, regulation in mufic

Stop'cock, *n.* a pipe ftopped by a cock that turns

Stop'page, *n.* the ftate of being ftopped, delay, ftop

Stop'per, *n.* a ftopple, a fhort rope

Stop'ple, *n.* what ftops the mouth of a veffel

Stórax or Sty'rax, *n.* a tree and very fragrant gum

Store, *n.* plenty, accumulated ftock, a warehoufe, fhop, the contents of a fhop

Store, *v. t.* to furnifh, ftock, lay up ; *a.* laid up

Stórehoufe, *n.* a repofitory, magazine, warehoufe

Stórekeeper, *n.* a man who has the care of ftores

Stóried, *pa.* adorned with hiftorical pictures, told

Stork, *n.* a bird of the heron kind of feveral fpecies

Storm, *n.* a tempeft, tumult, affault, fury, diftrefs

Storm, *v.* to attack or take by open force, to rage

Storm'y, *a.* tempeftuous, boifterous, paffionate, hot

Story, *n.* a hiftory, tale, fiction, lie, part of a houfe

Story, *v. t.* to relate, tell, defcribe, range in order

Storyteller, *n.* one who tells a ftory or lie, a liar

Stound, *n.* forrow, aftonifhment, feafon, *ob.* (beer

Stout, *a.* ftrong, valiant, brave, refolute ; *n.* ftrong

Stout'ly, *ad.* ftrongly, luftily, boldly, obftinately

Stout'nefs, *n.* ftrength, bravery, courage, obftinacy

Stove, *n.* a place to make a fire in, hothoufe, ftew

Stove, *v. t.* to keep an artificial heat, to keep warm

Stov'er, [ftuver] *n.* fodder for cattle

Stow, *v. t.* to lay up, lay in order and clofe, place

Stówage, *n.* a place to lay up in, a being laid up

Strábifm, *n.* a fquinting, a looking obliquely

Strad'dle, *v. i.* to walk wide and very aukwardly

Strag'gle, *v. i.* to wander, ramble, rove, go aftray

Strag'gler, *n.* one who quits his company, a rover

Straight, *f. e* ftrait (tighten, force, conftrain, exert

Strain, *v. t.* to fprain, weaken, fqueeze, filter,

Strain, *n.* a fprain, force, ftyle, fong, race, rank

Stráiner, *n.* an inftrument for filtration

Strait, *a.* direct, not crooked, narrow, rigorous,

Strait, *n.* a narrow pafs, frith, difficulty (difficult

B b 2

Stráiten, *v. t.* to make direct or narrow, to distress
Stráitlaced, *a.* stiff, formal, narrow, constrained
Stráitly, *ad.* narrowly, closely, strictly, directly
Stráitnefs, *n.* directness, narrowness, rigor, want
S.ráitwaistcoat, *v. t.* to confine in a strait waistcoat
S ráitway, *ad.* immediately, soon, forthwith
Strake, *n.* a plate of iron, seam, bredth, track
Strand, *v.* to drive or be driven on shore, to wreck
Strand, *n.* the verge or shore of the sea, a thred or twist of a rope.
Strange, *a.* wonderful, odd, new, foreign, referved
Strángely, *ad.* wonderfully, oddly, uncommonly
Strángenefs, *n.* wonder, shinefs, ignorance
Stránger, *n.* a foreigner, guest, one unacquainted
Stránger, *v. t.* to estrange, alienate, remove, *ob.*
Stran"gle, *v. t.* to choke, suffocate, kill, supprefs
Stran"gler, *n.* one who strangles or supprefses
Stran"gles, *n. pl.* a difeafe in horfes, hard fwelling
Strangulátion, *n.* the act of killing by strangling
Stran"gury, *n.* a difficulty in making water
Strap, *n.* a long slip of lether or cloth
Strap, *v. t.* to beat with a strap, beat, chastife
Strappáda, *n.* a chastifement with a strap, a rack
Strap'ping, *a.* well grown, large, big, bulky, stout
Strat'agem, *n.* an artifice, trick, means to deceive
Strátum, *pl.* Stratums or Strata, *n.* a bed or layer of earth, covering, row
Strátify, *v. t.* to form stratums arrange in layers
Stratificátion, *n.* the act of forming layers, a state of being in layers
Straw, *n.* a stalk of grain, trifle, worthlefs thing
Straw, *fee* strow
Straw'berry, *n.* the name of a fine cooling fruit
Straw'built, *a.* built or made of straw
Straw'color, *n.* a light yellow color, a yellownefs
Straw'colored, *a.* having the color of straw
Straw'y, *a.* like straw, made of or having straw
Stray, *v. i.* to go astray, wander, err, deviate
Stray, *n.* a beast that is lost by wandering away
Streak, *n.* a line of color, stripe, ray, mark, track
Streak, *v. t.* to stripe, dapple, variegate, stretch
Streaky, *a.* striped, dappled, variegated, motley
Stream, *n.* a running water, current, courfe, force
Stream, *v.* to run, flow, iffue continually, streak
Streamer, *n.* a thin flag, pennant, ensign, ornament
Streamy, *a.* running fast, flowing with a current
Street, *n.* a road, way, paved way between houfes
Streetwalker, *n.* a common prostitute, a whore
Strength, *n.* force, power, armament (confirm
Strength'en, *v.* to make or grow strong, animate,
Strength'ener, *n.* one who or what gives strength
Strength'lefs, *a.* deprived of strength, very weak
Stren'uous, *a.* bold, brave, active, zealous, eager
Stren'uously, *ad.* actively, vigorously, vehemently
Strépent, *a.* resounding, making a loud noife
Strep'erous, *a.* noify, loud, hoarfe, harfh, jarring
Strefs, *n.* force, violence, dependance, storm
Stretch, *v. t.* to extend, strain, expand, difplay, advance as a ship clofe hauled under a prefs of

fail (a tack in failing
Stretch, *n.* an extension, effort, more than truth,
Stretch'er, *n.* one who stretches, a support, a brick
Strew, *v. t.* strewed, *pret.* strewed, strewn, *pa.* to fcatter, fpread by fcattering, cast (*ob.*
Strew'ment, *n.* what is strewed or fcattered about,
Stríæ, *n. pl.* fmall channels in cocklefhells, &c.
Stríate, Striated, *a.* formed into striæ, channelled
Stríature, *n.* a difposition of striæ or channels
Strick'en, *pa.* struck, fmitten, hurt, advanced, *ob.*
Stric"kle, *n.* a thing to strike grain level with
Strict, *a.* fevere, clofe, tight, exact, accurate, nice
Strict'ly, *ad.* feverely, rigorously, clofely, exactly
Strict'nefs, *n.* feverity, rigor, clofenefs, exactnefs
Strict'ure, *n.* a contraction, portion, flight touch
Stride, *n.* a long step, a wide stretch of the legs
Stride, *v.* strid, strode, *pret.* stridden, *pa.* to make long steps, open the legs wide, crofs
Strid'ulous, *a.* making a fmall creaking noife
Strife, *n.* contention, conteft, difcord, endeavor
Strifeful, *a.* contentious, quarrelfome, crofs
Strig'ment, *n.* fcrapings, drofs, refufe
Strigófe, *a.* having stiff hairs or prickles
Strike, *n.* four pecks, a bufhel, a strickle
Strike, *v.* struck, *pret.* struck, *pa.* to hit with a blow, dafh, stamp, found, affect, run afhore, lower, let fail or furrender, W. Indies to lade liquor into a cooler
Stríker, *n.* one who strikes, a quarrelfome man
Stríking, *pa.* beating, affecting, furprifing, fine
String, *n.* a flender rope, cord, line, nerve, feries, fet
String, *v. t.* strung, *pret.* stringed, strung, *pa.* to furnifh with or put on strings, file, tighten
Strin'gent, *a.* binding, contracting, forcing
String'halt, *n.* a diforder in horfes, twitch, catch
String'lefs, *a.* having no strings, unbent, let loofe
String'y, *a.* consisting of fmall threds, fibrous
Strip, *v. t.* to make naked, bare, peel, diveft, rob
Strip, *n.* a narrow fhred, flip, little piece, bit
Stripe, *v. t.* to variegate with different lines
Stripe, *n.* a variation of color, line, lafh, blow
Strip'ling, *n.* a youth, a young or very weak man
Strive, *v. i.* strived, strove, *pret.* striven, *pa.* to struggle, endeavor, vie, emulate
Strob'il, *n.* a fcaly pericarp as the cone of a pine
Strob'ilform, *a.* fhaped like a strobil
Stroke, *n.* a blow, found of a clock, touch, dafh, line
Stroke, *v. t.* to rub gently or tenderly, footh, calm
Stroll, *v. i.* to rove, ramble, wander, go
Stroll, *n.* a ramble, walk, excursion·
Stróller, *n.* a rover, wanderer, vagrant, vagabond
Strong, *a.* vigorous, robust, potent, able, firm. full
Strong'fisted, *a.* having a strong hand, powerful
Strong'hand, *n.* power, strength, force, violence
Strong'ly, *ad.* powerfully, forcibly, fully, eagerly
Strong'fcented, *a.* having a powerful fmell
Strong'water, *n.* fpirits, distilled fpirits, a cordial
Stron'tite or Stron'thian, *n.* a distinct fpecies of earth of a whitifh or light green color

Strontit'ic, Stron'thian, *a.* pertaining to fttrontite

Stron'thianite, *n.* ftronthian combined with fixed air   (to hang a block by

Strop,*n.*a ftrap, a rope fpliced into a circular wreath

Stróphe, *n.* a ftanza, the firft member of a poem

Strove, *pret.* of *to ftrive*

Strout, *v.* to ftrut, which fee

Strow, *v. t.* ftrowed, *pret.* ftrowed, ftrown, *pa.* to ftrew, fcatter, fpread, throw about

Struck,*pret.* and *pa. paff.* of *to ftrike*

Struc'ture, *n.* a building, edifice, pile, form, make

Scrug'gle, *v. i.* to ftrive, endeavor, be in diftrefs

Strug'gle, *n.* a conteft, labor, effort, agony, trial

Strámous, *a.* having a fwelling in the glands

Strump'et,*n.*a proftitute, a whore, *v.t.* to debauch

Strung, *pret.* and *pa. paff.* of *to ftring*

Strut, *n.* a proud affected walk, ftatelinefs, pomp

Strut, *v. i.* to walk affectedly, parade, fwell

Strúthious, *a.* pertaining to the oftrich

Stub, *v. t.* to root or dig up ; *n.* a ftump, log, block

Stub'bed, *pa. a.* rooted up, fhort and thick

Stub'bednefs, *n.* a ftubbed ftate or quality

Stub'ble, *n.* the ftalks of grain left after reaping

Stub'born, *a.* obftinate, firm, hard, rugged, crofs

Stub'bornly, *ad.* obftinately, firmly, perverfely

Stub'bornnefs, *n.* obftinacy, firmnefs, perverfenefs

Stub'by, *a.* covered with fhort and thick bits

Stub'nail, *n.* a fhort nail, a nail that is broken off

Stuc'co,*n.*a fine plafter for walls,a fine plafterwork

Stuc'co, *v. t.* to plafter or overlay with ftucco

Stuck, *pret.* and *pa. paff.* of *to ftick*

Stud, *n.* a place for or fet of horfes, button for fhirt-fleeves, ornamental nail, poft

Stud, *v. t.* to adorn or fet with ftuds

Stud'dingfail, *n.* a fail extended beyond the fkirts of the principal fails

Stúdent,*n.* a fcholar, learner, bookifh man

Stud'ied, *pa.* learned, labored, confidered

Stud'ier, *n.* one who ftudies, a ftudent

Stúdious, *a.* bookifh, diligent, attentive, defirous

Stúdioufly, *ad.* diligently, attentively, carefully

Stúdioufnefs, *n.* a careful addiction to ftudy, ftudy

Stud'y, *n.* an apartment for books, application to books, thought, attention, contrivance

Stud'y, *v.* to mufe, meditate, confider attentively

Stuff, *n.* any thing, furniture, medicin, texture

Stuff, *v. t.* to fill, cram, fwell, feed gluttonoufly

Stuffing, *n.* relifhing ingredients put into meat

Stult'ify, *v. t.* to become or render foolifh

Stum, *n.* wine unfermented, new or vapid wine

Stum, *v. t.* to renew wine by new fermentation

Stum'ble, *v.* to trip in walking, make to trip, err

Stum'ble, *n.* a trip, flip, falfe ftep, blunder, failure

Stum'bler, *n.* one who ftumbles or miftakes

Stum'blingblock, *n.* a caufe of offenfe, an offenfe

Stump,*n.* a block, the remaining part of a joint

Stump'y, *a.* full of ftumps, hard, ftiff, ftrong, firm

Stun, *v.t.* to make fenfelefs with a blow, to ftupify

Stung, *pret.* and *pa. paff.* of *to fling*

Stunk, *pret.* and *pa. paff.* of *to ftink*

Stunt, *v. t.* to hinder from or ftop in the growth

Stupe, *n.* warm medicaments for a hurt or fore

Stupe, *v. t.* to drefs with or ufe ftupes, to foment

Stupefac'tion,*n.* infenfibility, ftupidity, dulnefs

Stupefac'tive, *a.* caufing infenfibility, very ftrong

Stupen'dous, *a.* wonderful, amazing, aftonifhing

Stúpid,*a.* dull, heavy, flow, blockifh, fenfelefs

Stúpid'ity,*n.* dulnefs, heavinefs of mind, weaknefs

Stúpidly,*ad.* dully, heavily, fimply, fenfelefsly

Stúpifier, *n.* one who or what occafions ftupidity

Stúpify or Stúpefy, *v. t.* to make ftupid, dull, benumb, aftonifh, difmay

Stúpor, *n.* a deprivation of fenfe, maze, ftupidity

Stúprate, *v.* to ravifh, force, deflour, violate, ruin

Stuprátion,*n.* a rape, ravifhment, violation, ruin

Stur'dily, *ad.* hardily, ftoutly, boldly, refolutely

Stur'dinefs,*n.* ftoutnefs, luftinefs, brutal ftrength

Stur'dy, *a.* hardy, ftout, ftrong, ftiff, bold, brutal

Stur'geon, *n.* the name of a large fifh

Sturk, *n.* a young ox or heifer, [Scotch]

Stut, Stut'ter, *v. i.* to ftammer, to fpeak badly

Stut'terer, *n.* one who ftutters, a ftammerer (foar

Sty, *n.* a place for hogs ; *v.* to fhut up in a fty, to

Sty"gian, *a.* hellifh, infernal, dark, black, difmal

Style, *n.* a manner of writing, title, pin of a dial, the filament of a piftil, manner, mode of reckoning time

Style, *v. t.* to call, term, name, denominate

Styloid' or Sty'liform, *a.* like a ftyle or pin

Styp'tic,*n.* an aftringent medicin or lotion

Styp'tic, *a.* able to flop blood, aftringent, ftrong

Stypti"city,*n.* the power of ftanching blood

Súable, *a.* that may be fued, fubject to anfwer in court   (il procefs

Suabil'ity, *n.* liability to be fued, fubjection to civ-

Suáfible, *a.* that may be eafily perfuaded

Suáfive, *a.* tending or able to perfuade, pleafing

Suáfory, *a.* having a tendency to perfuade

Suav'ity, *n.* fweetnefs, pleafantnefs, good temper

Sub, prefixed to words denotes *under* or *lefs*

Suba"cid, *a.* rather acid,fomewhat four or tart

Subac'rid, *a.* fomewhat fharp or pungent   (crufh

Subact', *v. t.* to reduce, fubdue, bring under,

Subac'tion,*n.* the act of reducing or fubduing

Súbah or Subah'dar, *n.* a viceroy in India, next in rank to the Mogul

Súbahfhip or Súbah, *n.* the jurifdiction of a Subah

Subaltern'ate, *a.* fucceffive, fucceeding by turns

Subal'tern,*n.* inferior officer, inferior judge

Subal'tern, *a.* fubordinate, inferior, fucceeding

Subaquat'ic, Subáqueous, *a.* being under water

Subax'illary,*a.* placed under the axil

Sub'beadle,*n.* an inferior or lower beadle

Subceles'tial, *a.* placed under the heavens or fkies

Sub'chanter, *n.* the deputy of a precentor   (bone

Subclávian, *a.* lying under the fhoulder or collar

Subconftellátion,*n.* an inferior conftellation

Subcontract'ed, *a.* contracted or engaged again

Subcont'rary, *a.* contrary in a lower degree, fimilar

Subcord'ate, *a.* fomewhat like a heart in fhape

Subcutáneous, *a.* lying or being under the fkin

Subcutic'ular, *a.* under the cuticle or fcarf-fkin

Sub'deacon, *n.* an order in the church of Rome

Sub'dean, *n.* a dean's deputy or fubftitute

Subdivers'ify, *v. t.* to diverfify or alter over again

Subdivide, *v. t.* to divide a part, to divide again

Subdivi'"fion, *n.* the act of fubdividing   (ful

Sub'dolous, *a.* crafty, cunning, artful, fly, deceit-

Subdúce or Subduct', *v. t.* to take or draw away

Subduc'tion, *n.* the act of taking away, fubtraction

Subdúe, *v. t.* to conquer, reduce, tame, opprefs

Subdúement, *n.* the act of fubduing, *ob.*

Subdúer, *n.* one who fubdues, one who conquers

Subdúple, *a.* half, one out of two

Subdúplicate, *a.* in the ratio of the fquare roots

Subéqual, *a.* nearly equal, approaching equality

Súberate, *n.* a falt formed by fuberic acid and a bafe

Súberic, *a.* denoting the acid of cork

Suberófe, *a.* as if fomewhat gnawed

Súberous, *a.* corky, foft and elaftic

Subfúfc, *a.* fomewhat brown or tawny, dufkifh

Subinfeudátion, *n.* a fale or feffment made by a tenant or feffee, referving rent to himfelf

Subitáneous, *a.* fudden, hafty, unexpected

Subjácent, *a.* lying or placed under, fubject to

Subject', *v.* to put under, enflave, fubmit, expofe

Sub'ject, *a.* placed under, liable, apt, expofed, open

Sub'ject, *n.* one who is under the dominion of another, a matter in debate, a thing treated of

Subjec'tion, *n.* a being under government, the act

Subject'ive, *a.* relating to a fubject   (of fubduing

Subingres'"fion, *n.* a fecret or private entrance

Subjoin', *v. t.* to add at the end, to add afterwards

Sub'jugate, *v.* to conquer, enflave, fubdue, humble

Subjugátion, *n.* the act of fubduing or humbling

Subjunc'tion, *n.* the act of fubjoining or adding

Subjunc'tive, *a.* fubjoined, put after, added

Sub'lanate, *a.* fomewhat woolly

Sublaps'ary, *a.* done or made after the fall of man

Sublátion, *n.* the act of taking away or raifing up

Sublevátion, *n.* the act of raifing up or on high

Subligátion, *n.* the act of binding underneath

Sublímable, *a.* that may be fublimed or refined

Sublímablenefs, *n.* what admits of fublimation

Sub'limate, *n.* muriate of mercury, or mercury and muriatic acid combined

Sub'limate, *v. t.* to refine folid fubftances by heat

Sublimátion, *n.* the act of expelling the finer parts of folid bodies by heat, fublimation of folids refembles the diftillation of fluids

Sublime, *a.* high in ftyle or excellence, proud

Sublíme, *n.* a lofty or grand ftyle, fublimity

Sublíme, *v. t.* to fublimate, raife, exalt, improve

Sublímely, *ad.* loftily, grandly, nobly, proudly

Sublímenefs, Sublim'ity, *n.* loftinefs, excellence

Sublin'"gual, *a.* placed or lying under the tongue

Sub'lunary, *a.* fituate under the moon, terreftrial

Submarine', *a.* lying, put or acting under the fea

Submerge', Submerfe', *v. t.* to put under, to drown

Submerfe', *a.* under water

Submer'fion, *n.* the act of plunging or drowning

Submin'ifter, *v.* to ferve under, fupply, afford, yield

Submifs', Submifs'ive, *a.* humble, lowly, refigned

Submis'"fion, *n.* refignation, obedience   (humbly

Submifs'ly, Submifs'ively, *ad.* with fubmiffion,

Submifs'ivenefs, *n.* humility, obfequioufnefs

Submit', *v.* to yield, refign, humble, refer, fink

Submult'iple, *n.* a number or quantity contained in another a certain number of times, or an aliquot part of it

Subnas'cent, *a.* growing underneath

Subnorm'al, *n.* a fubperpendicular, or a line under the perpendicular to a curve

Subnúde, *a.* almoft bare of leaves

Suboc'tave, Suboctúple, *a.* one out of eight

Suboc'ular, *a.* placed under the eye

Suborbic'ulate, *a.* almoft orbiculate

Subor'dinacy or Subor'dinancy, *n.* inferiority

Subor'dinate, *a.* inferior, lower, lefs, fubject

Subor'dinate, *v. t.* to range or put under another

Subor'dinately, *ad.* in a fubordinate manner

Subordinátion, *n.* a fubordinate ftate, inferiority

Suborn', *v. t.* to procure by falfe means, to fet up

Subornátion, *n.* the act of feducing to a bafe action,

Suborn'er, *n.* one who fuborns others   (collufion

Subóvate, *a.* almoft or nearly ovate

Subpéna, *n.* a writ that commands attendance

Subpet'iolate, *a.* having a very fhort petiole

Subquad'ruple, *a.* a fourth, that has one out of four

Subquin'tuple, *a.* a fifth, that has one out of five

Subramófe, *a.* having few branches

Subrect'or, *n.* the deputy or fubftitute of a rector

Subrep'tion, *n.* the act of obtaining by furprife or

Subrepti'"tious, *a.* fraudulently obtained   (deceit

Sub'rogate, *v. t.* to depute in the place of another

Subrogátion, *n.* a putting in the place of another

Subrotund', *a.* almoft round

Subfcríbe, *v. t.* to fign, atteft, confent, limit

Subfcríber, *n.* one who fubfcribes or contributes

Subfcríp'tion, *n.* an underwriting, atteftation, confent, joint contribution, help

Subfect'ion, *n.* an inferior fection, a lefs divifion

Subfec'utive, *a.* following in train or due order

Subfep'tuple, *a.* a feventh, one out of feven

Sub'fequence, *n.* the ftate of following in due order

Sub'fequent, *a.* following in due order, pofterior

Sub'fequently, *ad.* in confequence

Subfes'file, *a.* with very fhort footftalks (mentally

Subferve', *v. i.* to ferve fubordinately or inftru-

Subferv'ience, *n.* an inftrumental ufe, a fitnefs

Subferv'ient, *a.* fubordinate, inftrumental, ufeful

Subferv'iently, *ad.* in a fubordinate manner

Subfex'tuple, *a.* a fixth, containing one out of fix

Subfíde, *v. i.* to fink, tend downwards, ceafe, end

Sub'fidence, *n.* a finking, a tendency downwards

Subfíd'iary, *a.* affiftant, helping, brought in aid

Sub'fidy, *n.* an aid in money, a grant of money
Sub'fidize, *v. t.* to pay a fubfidy to, or live by a fubfidy
Subfign, *v. t.* to fign under or below, to fign after
Subfift', *v.* to continue, to have the means to live
Subfift'ence, *n.* real being, the means of fupport
Subfift'ent, *a.* having a real being, being, exiftent
Subs'tance, *n.* being, an effential part, fomething folid, body, matter, wealth, the means of life
Subftan'tial, *a.* real, folid, corporeal, ftrong, rich
Subftantial'ity, *n.* reality, materiality, corporeity
Subftan'tialize, *v. t.* to reduce to reality, to realize
Subftan'tially, *ad.* really, truly, ftrongly
Subftan'tialnefs, *n.* firmnefs, ftrength, real power
Subftan'tials, *n. pl.* effential or material parts
Subftan'tiate, *v. t.* to make to exift, confirm, real-
Subs'tantive, *n.* a noun betokening a thing   (ize
Subs'tantive, *a.* betokening exiftence, real, folid
Subs'titute, *n.* one who acts for another, a deputy, one thing ufed in place of another
Subs'titute, *v. t.* to put in the place of another
Subftitution, *n.* a putting one thing for another
Subftract', *v, t.* to take away part, deduct
Subftrac'tion, *n.* a taking away part, deduction, a rule in arithmetic
Subftract'ive, *a.* taking away, deducting
Subftruc'tion, *n.* an underbuilding, prop, fupport
Sub'ftyle, *n.* the line on which a gnomon ftands
Subfty'lar, *n.* under the ftyle or gnomon
Subfult'ive, *a.* abounding, leaping up, bubbling up
Subfult'orily, *ad.* in a bounding manner, loofely
Subfult'ory, *a.* bounding, moving by fits or ftarts
Subtan'gent, *n.* a line limited between the tangent and ordinate to the point and contact
Subtend', *v. i.* to lie or be extended under
Subtenfe', *n.* the chord of an arch, a bowftring
Subtep'id, *a.* moderately warm
Sub'terfuge, *n.* a fhift, excufe, evafion, trick
Subterráneous, Sub'terrany, *a.* lying beneath the furface of the earth
Subterran'ity, *n.* a place lying under ground
Subt'ile, *a.* thin, fine, refined, piercing, cunning
Subt'ilely or Subt'illy, *ad.* finely, cunningly, artfully
Subtil'iate, *v. t.* to make fubtile or fine, *ob.*
Subtiliátion, *n.* the act or making thin or fine, *ob.*
Subt'ilize, *v. t.* to make thin, refine, ufe fubtilty
Subt'ilty, Subt'ilenefs, *n.* thinnefs, finefs, cunning
Su'btle, *a.* fly, cunning, artful, thin, pure, refined
Subt'ly, *ad.* flily, cunningly, artfully, nicely
Subtract', *v. t.* to deduct, better written, *fubftract*, like *abftract*   (a withholding
Subtrac'tion, *n.* the taking of a fum or part away,
Subtract'ive, *a.* withdrawing, deducting
Subtrahend', *n.* a number that is to be fubtracted
Subtri'ple, *a.* a third, containing one part in three
Subtriplicate, *a.* in the ratio of the cubes
Sub'ulate, *a.* fhaped like an awl
Suburb'an, *a.* inhabiting the fuburbs of a place
Sub'urbs, *n. pl.* the confines or outparts of a city

Subvar'iety, *n.* the divifion of a variety
Subventáneous, *a.* addle, windy, *ob.*
Subven'tion, *n.* a fupply, fubfidy, aid, help, relief
Subver'fion, *n.* an overthrow, ruin, deftruction
Subvers'ive, *a.* tending to overturn or ruin   (rupt
Subvert', Subverfe', *v. t.* to overturn, deftroy, cor-
Subvert'er, *n.* an overthrower, deftroyer, enemy
Sub'worker, *n.* an underworker, laborer, helper
Succedáneous, *a.* fupplying the place, relieving
Succedáneum, *n.* what ferves for fomething elfe
Succeed', *v.* to follow in order, profper, turn out
Succeeder, *n.* one who fucceeds, one who profpers
Succefs', *n.* profperity, fortune, luck, event
Succefs'ful, *a.* profperous, fortunate, happy, kind
Succefs'fully, *ad.* profperoufly, luckily, happily
Succefs'fulnefs, *n.* a happy conclufion, fuccefs
Succes'fion, *n.* a feries, order, rightful inheritance
Succefs'ive, *a.* following in order, inheriting
Succefs'ively, *ad.* in regular order, in due courfe
Succefs'ivenefs, *n.* a regular continuation or order
Succefs'lefs, *a.* unfortunate, unlucky, unhappy
Succefs'or, *n.* one who fucceeds to another
Succid'uous, *a.* ready to fall, ready to fail off
Succif'erous, *a.* bearing or conveying fap   (cife
Succinct', *a.* girded up, prepared, fhort, brief, con-
Succinct'ly, *ad.* fhortly, briefly, concifely, clofely
Succinct'nefs, *n.* brevity, concifenefs   (and a bafe
Suc'cinate, *n.* a falt formed by the fuccinic acid
Succin'ic, *a.* denoting the acid of amber
Suc'cinous, *a.* pertaining to amber
Suc'cinated, *a.* impregnated with fuccinic acid
Suc'cory, *n.* a cooling herb or plant, wild endive
Suc'cor, *v. t.* to help, aid, affift, relieve
Suc'cor, *n.* aid, affiftance, help, one who helps
Suc'corer, *n.* one who fuccors, one who helps
Suc'corlefs, *a.* void of help or friends, deftitute
Suc'cotafh, *n.* a mixture of new foft maiz and
Suc'culency, *n.* jucinefs   (beans boiled
Suc'culent, *a.* jucy, full of juce, moift, plump
Succumb', *v. i.* to yield, give up, fink or fall under
Succuffátion, *n.* a trotting, a fhaking, trot, *ob.*
Succus'fion, *n.* a fhaking, fhake, fhock, jolt
Such, *pron.* being of that kind, like this, fimilar
Suck, *v.* to draw in, to drain ; *n.* the act of fucking
Suck'er, *n.* any thing that draws in, a fhoot, a fifh
Suck'et, *n.* a fweetmeat, conferve, preferve
Suck'ingbottle, *n.* a bottle ufed inftead of the breaft
Suc'kle, *v. t.* to nurfe at the breaft, to bring up
Suck'ling, *n.* one who is fed by the pap, a nurfling
Suc'tion, *n.* the act of fucking or drawing in
Sudátion, *n.* the act of fweating, a great heat
Súdatory, *a.* fweating, moift ; *n.* a fweating bath
Sud'den, *a.* coming without notice, hafty, violent
Sud'den, *n.* fomething quite unexpected, a furprife
Sud'denly, *ad.* in an unexpected manner, quickly
Sud'dennefs, *n.* a fudden manner, hafte, hurry
Sudet'ic, *a.* denoting mountains of Bohemia
Sudorif'ic, *a.* caufing or provoking fweat
Sudórous, *a.* confifting of or like fweat, *ob.*

Suds, *n.* a mixture of foap and water, a difficulty
Sue, *v.* to profecute by law, entreat, beg, requeft
Súet, *n.* hard fat, the fat about the loins
Súety, *a.* confifting of or like fuet, fat, greafy
Suf'fer, *v. t.* to bear, undergo, let, allow, permit
Suf'ferable, *a.* tolerable, that may be endured
Suf'ferably, *ad.* tolerably, with or by endurance
Suf'ferance, *n.* permiffion, patience, mifery, pain
Suf'ferer, *n.* one who fuffers or endures, a lofer
Suf'fering, *n.* pain fuffered, diftrefs, an execution
Suffi'ce, *v. i.* to be enough, fatisfy, pleafe, fupply
Suffi''ciency, *n.* enough, an adequate fupply, pride
Suffi''cient, *a.* enough, equal to, qualified, fit
Suffi''ciently, *ad.* well enough, tolerably, duly
Suf'fix, *n.* a letter or fyllable annexed
Suffix', *v. t.* to add, annex or fubjoin
Suf'focate, *v. t.* to choke, ftifle, fmother, kill
Suffocátion, *n.* the act of choking or fmothering
Suf'focative, *a.* able or tending to choke
Suf'fragan, *n.* a bifhop under fome metropolitan
Suf'fragate, *v. t.* to vote or agree with, *ob.*
Suf'frage, *n.* a vote, voice, approbation
Suffra''ginous, *a.* relating to the knee-joint of beafts
Suffrúticous, *a.* half or part fhrubby, the root per-
   manent and branches fomewhat withering
Suffumigátion, *n.* a fume raifed by means of fire, *ob.*
Suffúmige, *n.* a medical fume raifed from herbs, *ob.*
Suffúfe, *v. t.* to fpread or cover over, tinge, die
Suffúfion, *n.* the act of overfpreading, a dimnefs
Súgar, [fhooger] *n.* the juce of cane reduced to a
   concrete ftate, confifting of falt and mucilage,
   any thing very fweet
Súgar, *v. t.* to fweeten or mix with fugar
Súgarcane, *n.* the cane or reed which affords fugar
Súgarmite, *n.* a winglefs infect, lepifma
Sug'arplum, *n.* a kind of trifling fweetmeat
Sug'ary, *a.* tafting of fugar, fweet, pleafant
Suggeft', *v. t.* to hint, intimate, inform fecretly,
Sugges'tion, *n.* a hint, intimation, notice (feduce
Suggeft'ive, *a.* containing intimations
Su''gillate, *v. t.* to beat black and blue, *ob.*
Súicide, *n.* felf-murder, a felf-murderer
Súillage or Sul'liage, *n.* filth, *ob.*
Súing, *n.* the act of profecuting, [a foaking thro', *ob.*]
Suit, *n.* a fet, retinue, courtfhip, requeft, procefs
Suit, *v.* to fit, be fitted, adapt, agree, accord, drefs
Súitable, *a.* fit, proper, agreeable, according with
Súitablenefs, *n.* fitnefs, propriety, agreeablenefs
Súitably, *ad.* fitly, properly, agreeably, according
Súiter or Súitor, *n.* a wooer, petitioner, fuppliant
Súiting, *n.* the act of fuiting or fitting, courtfhip
Súitrefs, *n.* a female petitioner or fuppliant
Sulc'ate or Sulc'ated, *a.* furrowed, channelled
Sulk'y, *a.* fullen, four, morofe, gloomy, obftinate
Sull'en, *a.* four, gloomy, heavy, obftinate, angry
Sull'enly, *ad.* fourly, morofely, gloomily, angrily
Sull'ennefs, Sull'ens, *n.* morofenefs, gloominefs
Sull'y, *v. t.* to foil, fpot, tarnifh; *n.* a foil, a fpot
Sulph'ate, *n.* a neutral falt formed by fulphuric

acid and a bafe, as fulphate of lime or of iron
Sulphat'ic, *a.* pertaining to a fulphate (with a bafe
Sulph'ite, *n.* a combination of fulphurous acid
Sulph'ur, *n.* called alfo brimftone, is a fimple com-
   buftible fubftance, yellow, brittle, infoluble in
   water, but fufible in heat
Sulph'urated, *a.* combined with fulphur
Sulph'uret, *n.* a combination of fulphur with an
   alkaline, earthy or metallic bafe
Sulph'uric, *a.* denoting an acid formed by fulphur
   faturated with oxygene
Sulph'urous, *a.* like or containing fulphur, alfo de-
   noting an acid formed by fulphur underfatura-
   ted with oxygene
Sulphúreous, *a. formerly ufed for* fulphurous
Sulph'uroufnefs, *n.* a fulphurous ftate or quality
Sulph'ury, *a.* partaking of or having fulphur
Sult'an, *n.* the name of the Turkifh emperor
Sultána, Sult'anefs, *n.* the emprefs of the Turks
Sult'anry, *n.* an eaftern empire or dominion
Sult'rinefs, *n.* a fultry ftate or quality, great heat
Sult'ry, *a.* hot and clofe, hot and cloudy, very hot
Sum, *n.* the whole, amount, abftract, height
Sum, *v.* to add together, reckon, comprife
Súmac, *n.* plants of feveral fpecies
Sum'lefs, *a.* that cannot be computed, infinite
Sum'marily, *ad.* fhortly, briefly, concifely
Sum'mary, *a.* fhort, brief; *n.* an abridgment
Sum'mer, *n.* the fecond feafon, a principal beam
Sum'mer, *v.* to pafs the fummer, to keep warm
Sum'merhoufe, *n.* a fmall houfe in a garden, &c.
Sum'merfet, *n.* a high leap with heels over head
Sum'mit, *n.* the top of any thing, the utmoft height
Sum'mon, *v. t.* to call by authority, cite, roufe
Sum'moner, *n.* one who fummons, one who cites
Sum'mons, *n. fing.* a call of authority, call, citation
Sump'ter, *n.* a horfe of burden or ftate, a packhorfe
Sump'tion, *n.* the act of taking or affuming
Sump'tuary, *a.* regulating the way of living
Sump'tuoufnefs, *n.* coftlinefs, elegance
Sump'tuous, *a.* coftly, expenfive, fplendid
Sump'tuoufly, *ad.* expenfively, finely, fplendidly
Sun, *n.* the luminary of the day, a hot funny place
Sun, *v. t.* to expofe to or warm in the fun
Sun'beam, *n.* a ray of light coming from the fun
Sun'beat, *a.* fhone upon or tanned by the fun
Sun'bright, *a.* bright as the fun, very bright
Sun'burning, *n.* the effect of the fun on the face
Sun'burnt, *a.* tanned by the fun, made brown
Sun'day, *n.* the fun's day, the chriftian fabbath
Sun'der, *v. t.* to part, feparate, divide; *n.* two parts
Sun'dial, *n.* a plate to fhow time by the fun   (ent
Sun'dry, *a.* feveral, many, various, divers, differ-
Sun'fifh, *n.* a name of the diodon
Sun'flower, *n.* a flower that turns with the fun
Sung, *pret.* and *pa. paff.* of *to fing*
Sunk, *pret.* and *pa. paff.* of *to fink*
Sun'lefs, *a.* wanting the fun, gloomy, dull, dark
Sun'like, *a.* made like the fun, refembling the fun

Sun'ny, a. expofed to the fun, bright, clear, fine
Sun'rife, Sun'rifing, n. the beginning of morning
Sun'fet, n. the beginning of evening, the clofe of
Sun'fhine, n. the action of the fun, profperity (day
Sun'fhiny, a. bright with or as the fun, clear, fine
Sup, v. to drink by fups, to eat or give a fupper
Sup, n. a mouthful of liquor, fmall draft, tafte
Súper, in compofition denotes *above* or *over*
Súperable, a. that may be conquered or excelled
Superabound', v. i. to have more than enough
Superabun'dance, n. more than enough, fulnefs
Superabun'dant, a. more than enough, exceffive
Superabun'dantly, ad. in a fuperabundant manner
Superadd', v. t. to add over and above, join, annex
Superaddi'tion, n. a fuperadding, a thing added
Superadvénient, a. coming in aid of (than a year, *ob*.
Superan'nuate, v. to impair by age, to laft more
Superan'nuated, pa. difqualified by age, very old
Superannuátion, n. a difqualification from years
Superb', a. magnificent, grand, pompous, ftately
Superb'ly, ad. in a fuperb manner, finely, proudly
Supercar'go, n. an officer deputed to manage trade
Superceles'tial, a. placed above the firmament
Supercil'iary, a. placed above the eyelid
Supercil'ious, a. haughty, arbitrary, dictatorial
Supercil'ioufly, ad. haughtily, contemptuoufly
Supercil'ioufnefs, n. haughtinefs, great pride
Superconcep'tion, n. conception upon conception
Supercons'equence, n. a remote confequence, *ob*.
Supercres'cence, n. what grows on a growing thing,
Superem'inence, n. uncommon eminence (*ob*.
Superem'inent, a. eminent in a very high degree
Superer'ogate, v. i. to do more than duty requires
Supererogátion, n. the act of doing more than duty
Supererog'atory, a. more than ftrict duty or need
Superex'cellent, a. excellent in a very high degree
Superexcres'cence, n. what grows on fuperfluoufly
Superfétate, v. i. to conceive after a conception
Superfétation, n. one conception made on another
Súperfice, Superfi''cies, n. the furface, the outfide
Superfi''cial, a. lying on the furface, fhallow, flight
Superficial'ity, Superfi''cialnefs, n. fhallownefs
Superfi''cially, ad. without going deep, flightly
Súperfine, a. eminently or very fine, very excellent
Superflúitance, n. a floating above or upon, *ob*.
Superflúitant, a. floating above or on the top, *ob*.
Superflúity, Super'fluoufnefs, n. excefs, overplus
Super'fluous, a. unneceffary, more than enough
Super'fluoufly, ad. in a fuperfluous manner
Súperflux, n. what is more than is really wanted
Superhúman, a. more than human, divine
Superimpófe, v. t. to lay or impofe upon fomething
Superimpofi''tion, n. a laying or being placed upon
Superincum'bent, a. lying or refting on fomething
Superindúce, v. t. to bring in as an addition
Superinduc'tion, n. the act or art of fuperinducing
Superinftitútion, n. one inftitution upon another
Superintend', v. i. to overfee, to take the care
Superintend'ency, n. the act of overfeeing

Superintend'ant, n. an overfeer, a manager
Supérior, n. one who is older or higher in rank, one who excels
Supérior, a. higher, greater, preferable (grade
Superior'ity, n. advantage, preference, higher
Superlátion, n. exaggeration, excefs, *ob*.
Super'lative, a. expreffing the higheft degree
Super'latively, ad. in or with the higheft degree
Superlúnar, a. placed above the moon or world
Super'nal, a. placed above, celeftial, heavenly
Supernátant, a. fwimming above or on the top ;
Supernatátion, n. the act of fwimming on the top
Supernat'ural, a. being above nature, miraculous
Supernat'urally, ad. in a fupernatural manner
Supernúmerary, a. being above the ftated number
Superpartic'ular, a. noting a ratio when the excefs of the greater term is unit
Superpar'tient, a. noting a ratio when the excefs of the greater term is more than unit
Súperplant, n. a plant growing on another plant
Superpofi''tion, n. a placing above, fituation above, that which is placed upon fomething elfe
Superproportion, n. overplus of proportion
Superpurgátion, n. more purgation than enough
Superreflec'tion, n. the reflection of an image that had been reflected before (ing paper
Superroy'al, a. denoting the largeft kind of print-
Superfáliency, n. the act of leaping on any thing
Superfat'urate, v. t. to faturate to excefs
Superfaturátion, n. the act of faturating to excefs, or ftate of being fo faturated
Superfcríbe, v. t. to write at top or on the outfide
Superfcrip'tion, n. a writing on the outfide, a di-
Superféde, v. t. to fet afide, to make void (rection
Superferv'iceable, a. too officious, too meddling
Superfti''tion, n. falfe devotion or religion, bigotry
Superfti''tious, a. addicted to fuperftition, bigoted, fcrupulous, fanciful
Superfti''tioufly, ad. in a fuperftitious manner
Superftráin, v. t. to ftrain or ftretch too much
Superftráining, n. the act of ftraining too much
Superftruct, v. t. to build on any thing, to erect
Superftruc'tion, n. a building raifed on any thing
Superftruct'ive, a. built or raifed on any thing
Superftruct'ure, n. what is built on any thing
Supervacáneous, a. needlefs, unneceffary, vain
Supervéne, v. i. to come extraneoufly, to furprife
Supervénient, a. coming fuddenly, additional
Superven'tion, n. a coming upon one fuddenly
Supervífe, v. t. to overfee, overlook, fuperintend
Supervifal, Supervi''fion, n. infpection, fuperintend-ence (cife
Supervífor, n. an overfeer, infpector, officer of ex-
Supervíve, v. i. to overlive, outlive, furvive
Supinátion, n. the act of turning upfide down
Supinátor, n. a mufcle which turns the palm of the hand upwards
Súpine, n. a kind of verbal word in grammar
Supíne, a. having the face up, indolent, carelefs

Supinely, *ad.* with the face upward, carelefsly, idly

Supineness, *n.* carcleffnefs, indolence, floth

Suppedaneous, *a.* placed under the feet, *ob.*

Sup'per, *n.* the evening meal, one who fups

Sup'perlefs, *a.* going without fupper, hungry

Supplant', *v. t.* to difplace by craft, to undermine

Supplant'er, *n.* one who fupplants or undermines

Supplantation, *n.* the act of fupplanting

Sup'ple, *a.* pliant, flexible, limber, foft, fawning

Sup'ple, *v.* to grow or make pliant or foft, to bend

Sup'plement, *n.* an addition to fupply fome defect

Supplement'al, Supplement'ary, *a.* additional

Sup'plenefs, *n.* a fupple ftate or quality, activity

Sup'pletory, *n.* what ferves to fill up deficiencies

Sup'pliant, *a.* entreating, befeeching, begging

Sup'pliant or Sup'plicant, *n.* an humble petitioner

Sup'plicate, *v. t.* to implore, entreat, befeech, beg

Supplication, *n.* an humble petition, fuit or requeft

Sup'plicatory, *a.* tending to fupplicate, humble

Supply', *v. t.* to fill up, afford, furnifh, relieve

Supply', *n.* a relief of want, aid, fupport, recruit

Support', *n.* a prop, help, maintenance, fupply

Support', *v. t.* to prop up, fuftain, bear maintain

Support'able, *a.* tolerable, moderate (port, *ob.*)

Support'ance, Support'ation, *n.* maintenance, fup-

Support'er, *n.* one who fupports, a defender, a prop

Suppof'able, *a.* that may be fuppofed or granted

Suppofe, Suppof'al, *n.* a fuppofition, an imagination

Suppofe, *v.* to lay down without proof, to imagin

Suppofer, *n.* one who fuppofes, one who imagins

Suppofi"tion, *n.* fomething fuppofed or laid down

Supofiti"tious, *a.* not genuine, illegitimate, falfe

Suppos'itive, *a.* implying a fuppofition

Suppos'itively, *ad.* with, by or upon fuppofition

Suppos'itory, *n.* a folid or dry glyfter (fecret

Supprefs', *v. t.* to crufh, fubdue, conceal, keep

Suppres"fion, *n.* the act of fuppreffing or crufhing

Supprefs'or, *n.* one who fuppreffes, one who crufhes

Sup'purate, *v. i.* to generate or grow into matter

Suppuration, *n.* a ripening into matter or pus

Sup'purative, *a.* generating matter, digeftive

Supputation, *n.* a reckoning, computatio, *ob.*

Suppute, *v. t.* to reckon, compute, calculate, *ob.*

Supraax'illary, *a.* growing above the axil

Supradecompound', *a.* more than compound

Suprafoliaceous, *a.* growing above a leaf

Supramun'dane, *a.* fet above the world, heavenly

Supraren'al, *a.* placed over the kidneys

Supravul'gar, *a.* placed above the vulgar, rich

Suprem'acy, *n.* the higheft authority or place

Supreme, *a.* higheft, chief, principal, main

Supreme, *n.* the fupreme or divine Being, GOD

Supremely, *ad.* in the higheft degree

Suraddi"tion, *n.* fomething added to a name, *ob.*

Sural, *a.* belonging to or like the calf of the leg

Surance, *n.* a warrant, fecurity, affurance, *ob.*

Surbate, *v.* to harafs, fatigue, hurt, bruife, batter, *ob.*

Surcease, *n.* a ceffation, ftop, end, conclufion, *ob.*

Surcease, *v. i.* to be at an end, ceafe, ftop, leave off

Surcharge', *v. t.* to overcharge, to load too much

Surcharge', *n.* too great a charge or burden

Sur'cingle, *n.* an upper girt, a girdle of a caffoc

Sur"cle, *n.* a fhoot, twig, fucker, fmall branch, *ob.*

Sur'coat, *n.* a fhort coat worn over other drefs, *ob.*

Surd, *a.* deaf, unheard, foolifh, incommenfurable

Surd, *n.* an incommenfurable number

Surd'ity, *n.* deafnefs, dulnefs, heavinefs, ftupidity

Sure, *a.* certain, true, confident, affured, fafe, fecure

Sure or Surely, *ad.* certainly, undoubtedly, fafely

Surefooted, *a.* treading firmly, not ftumbling, fafe

Surenefs, *n.* certainty, truth, faithfulnefs, fafety

Suretifhip, *n.* the act of being bound for another

Surety, *n.* a bondfman, bail, fecurity againft lofs

Surf, *n.* waves or fwell of the fea breaking on fhore

Sur'face, *n.* the outfide of a thing, fhallownefs

Sur'feit, *n.* ficknefs occafioned by great fulnefs

Sur'feit, *v. t.* to make fick with eating, to difguft

Sur'feiter, *n.* one who riots, a great glutton

Sur'feitwater, *n.* a fimple water to cure furfeits

Surge, *n.* a fwelling fea, a wave; *v. i.* to rife high

Sur'geon, *n.* one who cures by manual operations

Sur'gery, *n.* the art or practice of curing fuch dif-eafes or affections of the body as require the ufe of inftruments or manual operations

Sur'gy, *a.* rifing in billows, fwelling high, rough

Suricate, *n.* an animal refembling the ichneumon, the fourtoed weefel

Sur'lily, *ad.* in a morofe or perverfe manner

Sur'linefs, *n.* morofenefs, croffnefs, illnature

Sur'ling, *n.* a furly perfon, a morofe fellow, *ob.*

Sur'ly, *a.* morofe, four, crabbed, rough, uncivil

Sur'malot, *n.* a large brown rat

Surmife, *v. t.* to fufpect, imagin, fuppofe, think

Surmife, *n.* a fufpicion, an imperfect notion

Surmount', *v. t.* to conquer, overcome, furpafs,

Surmount'able, *a.* conquerable, paffable (exceed

Surmul'let, *n.* a fifh much admired by the Romans

Sur'name, *n.* a family name, one added to the ori-ginal baptifmal name

Surname, *v. t.* to name by an appellation added

Surpafs', *v.* to pafs or go beyond, beat, excel, exceed

Sur'plice, *n.* a white garment ufed by a minifter

Sur'plus, Surplus'age, *n.* an overplus, a remainder

Surprifal, Surprife, *n.* aftonifhment, wonder

Surprife or Surprize, *v. t.* to take unawares, per-plex, aftonifh, amaze

Surprifing, *pa.* aftonifhing, amazing, wonderful

Surprifingly, *ad.* aftonifhingly, wonderfully

Sur'quedry, *n.* pride, infolence, conceit, *ob.*

Surrebut'ter, *n.* a plaintiff's reply to the defendant's rebutter

Surrejoin'der, *n.* a plaintiff's anfwer to a defend-ant's rejoinder

Surren'der, *v. t.* to yield or deliver up, to refign

Surren'der, Surren'dry, *n.* the act of furrendering

Surrep'tion, *n.* ftelth, a fudden invafion, *ob.*

Surrepti"tious, *a.* done by ftelth, clandeftine

Surrepti"tioufly, *ad.* by ftelth, fraudulently

Sur'rogate, *n.* a deputy, a delegate, a county officer who has the probate of wills, [N. Y.]

Surround', *v.* to environ, encompass, inclose, befet

Surfolid, *n.* the fifth power of any affigned root

Surtout or Surtoot, *n.* a clofe over coat

Survéne, *v. i.* to fupervene, to be added, *ob.*

Survey', [furvay] *v. t.* to overlook, view, meafure

Sur'vey, *n.* a view, profpect, meafure, plan or draft of what is meafured, diftrict for collection of the cuftoms

Survey'or, *n.* an overfeer, a meafurer of land, an infpector of the weight and quantity of goods or of highways, &c.

Survey'orfhip, *n.* the office or duty of a furveyor

Survíve, *v.* to live after or longer, to outlive

Survivency, *n.* furvivorfhip, a furviving

Survíver or Survívor, *n.* one who outlives another

Survívorfhip, *n.* the ftate of furviving another

Sufceptibil'ity, *n.* the quality or ftate of admitting

Sufcep'tible, Sufcep'tive, *a.* capable of admitting

Sufceptiv'ity, *n.* capacity of receiving

Sufcep'tion, *n.* the act or art of taking in hand

Surfcip'ient, *a.* receiving, admitting, undertaking

Sus'citate, *v. t.* to roufe, excite, ftir up, awake

Sus'lik, *n.* a fpotted animal of the rat kind

Sufpect', *a.* doubtful, uncertain ; *n.* fufpicion, *ob.*

Surfpect, *v.* to imagin, miftruft, fear, think guilty

Sufpend', *v. t.* to hang, ftop, delay, put off, deprive

Sufpenfe', *n.* uncertainty, doubt, ftop, delay, fear

Sufpenfe', *a.* held in doubt, kept from proceeding

Sufpens'ible, *a.* capable of being fufpended

Sufpenfibil'ity, *n.* capacity of being fufpended

Sufpen'fion, *n.* the act of hanging up, a ceffation for a time, a temporary privation of an office

Sufpens'ory, *a.* fufpended, hung up, hanging by

Sufpi'cion, *n.* the act of fufpecting, miftruft (ous

Sufpi'cious, *a.* inclined or liable to fufpicion, jeal-

Sufpi'cioufly, *ad.* with fufpicion, doubtfully

Sufpi'cioufnes, *n.* a tendency to fufpicion, doubt

Sufpiration, *n.* the act of breathing deep, a figh, *ob.*

Sufpíre, *v. i.* to breath hard or deep, figh, fob, *ob.*

Suftáin, *v. t.* to bear, endure, uphold, fupport

Suftáinable, *a.* that may be fuftained or fupported

Suftáiner, *n.* one who fuftains, one who fuffers

Suft'enance, *n.* maintenance, food, the ufe of food

Suftentátion, *n.* fupport, affiftance, maintenance

Sut, *n.* the matter which is collected from fmoke

Sut'ty, *a.* like or confifting of fut, black

Sut'ler, *n.* one who fells provifions to foldiers

Sut'tle, *n.* the neat or juft weight of commodities

Súture, *n.* a fewing, feam, juncture

Swab or Swob, *n.* an ordinary mop, a bean fhell

Swab, *v. t.* to clean with a mop, to mop

Swábian, *n.* a native of Swabia in Germany

Swábian, *a.* pertaining to Swabia

Swab'ber, *n.* a mopper or cleaner of decks

Swad'dle, *v. t.* to fwathe, bind about, beat, cudgel

Swad'dle, *n.* clothes bound round the body

Swad'dlingband, *n.* a cloth for a new-born child

Swag, *v.* to fink down by its weight, to lie heavy

Swag'ger, *v. i.* to boaft, brag, bully, blufter, be noify

Swag'gerer, *n.* a boafter, bully, hector, noify fellow

Swag'gy, *a.* hanging down heavily, heavy, lumpy

Swain, *n.* a paftoral youth, youth, lover, fervant

Swal'low, *n.* a genus of birds, fifh, throat, voracity, gulf

Swal'low, *v. t.* to take down the throat, to take in

Swam or Swum, *pret.* of *to fwim*

Swamp, *n.* a marfh, bog, fen, foft watery ground

Swamp'y, *a.* marfhy, boggy, fenny, watery, foft

Swan, *n.* a very large white water fowl

Swans'down, *n.* a fine foft thick woollen cloth

Swan'fkin, *n.* a fine and very foft kind of flannel

Swap, *v. t.* to exchange, barter, fwop

Sward, *n.* the furface of the ground, the fkin of

Sware, *pret.* of *to fwear* (bacon

Swarm, *n.* a crowd, multitude, great number, prefs

Swarm, *v. i.* to crowd, throng, abound, breed

Swart, Swarth, *a.* tawny, gloomy; *v. t.* to blacken

Swarth'inefs, *n.* tawninefs, darknefs of the fkin

Swarth'y, *a.* tawny, dufkifh, dark of complexion

Swafh'ing, *a.* huge, fhowy, [*vulgar*]

Swafh'er, *n.* a blufterer, noify fellow, hector, bully

Swath, *n.* a line of grafs cut down, a fillet

Swathe, *v. t.* to bind faft with rollers or bands

Sway, *v.* to govern, rule, wield, hang heavy, lean

Sway, *n.* power, command, rule, influence, direction

Sweal, *v. t.* to melt, blaze away, finge

Swear, *v.* fware, fwore, *pret.* fworn, *pa.* to utter oaths, to declare or put upon oath

Sweárer, *n.* one who fwears or utters oaths

Sweat, *n.* a matter from the pores, drudgery, toil

Sweat, *v.* fweat, fweated, *pret.* and *pa.* to emit or put into a fweat, warm, drudge, toil, labor

Sweat'inefs, *n.* a fweaty ftate, moifture, great heat

Sweat'y, *a.* moift with fweat, hot, laborious, hard

Swéde, *n.* a native of Sweden (of Sweden

Swédifh, *a.* pertaining to Sweden ; *n.* the language

Sweep, *v.* fweeped, fwept, *pret.* and *pa.* to clean with a befom, pafs quickly over, rufh over, pafs with pomp, fetch a long ftroke

Sweep, *n.* the direction of a motion, deftruction, a large oar, a range

Sweepings, *n. pl.* what is fwept away, filth, refufe

Sweepnet, *n.* a very large kind of net

Sweepftake, *n.* one who gets or wins all

Sweepy, *a.* paffing with great violence or fpeed

Sweet, *a.* grateful to the tafte, fmell, ear or eye, pleafant, nice, fine, mild, foft, not ftale, frefh

Sweet, *n.* fweetnefs, perfume, a word of fondnefs

Sweetbread, *n.* the pancreas of a calf

Sweetbriar, *n.* the name of a fragrant fhrub

Sweeten, *v.* to make or become fweet, to palliate

Sweetener, *n.* one who or that which fweetens

Sweetheart, *n.* a lover, miftrefs, wooer, fondling

Sweeting, *n.* a word of endearment, a fine apple

Sweetifh, *a.* fomewhat fweet or palatable

Sweetly, *ad.* in a fweet manner, delightfully, well

C c

Sweetmar'joram, *n.* a fragrant plant
Sweetmeat, *n.* a fruit that is preserved with sugar
Sweetnefs, *n.* a fweet quality, mildnefs, melody
Sweet, *n.* canejuce, melaffes or other fweet vegetable fubftance
Sweetfcented, *a.* having a fweet fmell, fragrant
Sweetfmelling, *a.* fmelling fweetly, fragrant
Sweetwil'liam, *n.* the name of a garden flower
Sweetwil'low, *n.* a plant, gale, Dutch myrt'e
Swell, *v.* fwelled, *pret.* fwelled, fwollen, fwoln, *pa.* to make or grow bigger, rife, increafe
Swell, *n.* an extenfion of bulk, an increafe, anger, a wave or rolling of the fea
Swelling, *n.* a place or thing fwelled, rife, pain
Swelt'er, *v.* to nearly melt or perifh with heat
Swelt'ry, *a.* almoft melting with heat
Swept, *pret.* and *pa.* of *to fweep*
Swerd, *v. i.* to grow or produce a green turf, *ob.*
Swerve, *v. i.* to wander, rove, deviate, fly, climb
Swift, *a.* quick, fpeedy, nimble; *n.* a bird, a cur-
Swift, *v. t.* to faften bars to a capftern (rent
Swift'er, *n.* a rope to faften bars to a capftern or to encircle a boat, an outward fhroud
Swift'ly, *ad.* quickly, fpeedily, nimbly
Swift'nefs, *n.* rapidity, quicknefs, fpeed, activity
Swig, *v. i.* to drink by large drafts, to fwill
Swill, *v.* to drink luxurioufly, drench, inebriate
Swill, *n.* a luxurious draft, a wafh for hogs
Swill'er, *n.* a luxurious or hoggifh drinker
Swim, *v. i.* fwam, fwum, *pret.* fwum, *pa.* to float or move on water, glide, flow, be dizzy
Swim or Swimin, *n.* the bladder of fifhes
Swim'mer, *n.* one who fwims or can fwim
Swim'ming, *n.* a motion on or in water, a dizzinefs
Swim'mingly, *ad.* without obftruction, fmoothly
Swin'dle, *v. t.* to cheat or defraud grofsly or with deliberate artifice
Swin'dler, *n.* one who lives by defrauding, a cheat
Swine, *n.* a hog, pig, hoggifh fellow, mean wretch
Swineherd, *n.* a keeper of fwine, a feeder of hogs
Swing, *n.* a waving motion, unreftrained liberty
Swing, *v.* fwang, fwung, *pret.* fwung, *pa.* to wave or move loofely, to whirl round
Swinge, *v. t.* to whip, to punifh; *n.* a fway, a fweep
Swinge'buckler, *n.* a bully, a bluftering fellow
Swing'er, *n.* one who fwings, one who whirls
Swin'ging, *pa.* waving, very great, huge, large
Swin'gingly, *ad.* vaftly, hugely, largely, greatly
Swin"gle, *v.* to fwing in pleafure, dangle, beat flax
Swin"glingknife, *n.* a tool ufed in dreffing flax
Swin"glingtow, *n.* the coarfe part of flax
Swinifh, *a.* refembling fwine, hoggifh, brutal, grofs
Swink, *v.* to toil, labor, tire; *n.* toil, drudgery, *ob.*
Swifs, *n.* a native of Switzerland, the language of
Swifs, *a.* pertaining to Switzerland (the country
Switch, *n.* a flexible fmall twig; *v. t.* to lafh
Swiv'el, *n.* a thing to turn round upon, ring, gun
Swiv'el, *v.* to turn upon a movable pin
Swob, *n.* a mop to clean floors or guns

Swob, *v. t.* to clean a floor or gun, &c.
Swob'ber, *n.* a term at cards, a fweeper of decks
Swollen, Swoln, *pa. paff.* of *to fwell, ob.*
Swoon, *v. i.* to faint, to ficken; *n.* a fainting fit
Swoop, *v. t.* to fall at once upon, catch up, ftrike
Swoop, *n.* the fudden fall or dafh of a bird of prey
Swop, *v. t.* to exchange, change, barter
Sword, *n.* a fharp weapon, the vengeance of juftice
Swordbearer, *n.* one who bears a fword of ftate
Swordcutler, *n.* one who makes or deals in fwords
Sworded, *a.* girt with or having a fword
Sworder, *n.* a cutthroat, ruffian, foldier, *ob.*
Swordfifh, *n.* a fifh with a long bone iffuing from his head
Swordknot, *n.* a knot of ribbon on a fword's hilt
Swordlaw, *n.* violence, force, ftrength, power
Swordman, *n.* a fighter with fwords, foldier, fencer
Swordplayer, *n.* a prizefighter, gladiator, fencer
Swore, *pret.* of *to fwear*
Sworn, *pa.* of *to fwear*
Swofh, *n.* a narrow or fhallow channel, [Carolina]
Swung, *pret.* and *pa. paff.* of *to fwing*
Syc'amore, *n.* a tree, the maple, and by fome the name is given to the button wood
Syc'ophant, *n.* a flatterer, a parafite; *v. i.* to flatter
Sycophant'ic, *a.* flattering, wheedling, paraftical
Sydnean, *a.* denoting a fpecies of white earth from Sydney Cove in South Wales
Syllab'ic, Syllab'ical, *a.* confifting of fyllables
Syllabication, *n.* the act of forming fyllables
Syl'lable, *n.* one articulation in a word, tittle, jot
Syl'lable, *v. t.* to utter diftinctly, articulate, *ob.*
Syl'labub, *n.* a drink made of wine and milk
Syl'labus, *n.* an abftract, the heads of a lecture
Syl'logifm, *n.* an argument of three propofitions
Syllogis'tical, *a.* confifting of a fyllogifm, logical
Syllogis'tically, *ad.* in form of a fyllogifm, clofely
Syl'logize, *v. i.* to argue fyllogiftically or clofely
Sylph, *n.* a kind of fairy nymph, a woodnymph
Syl'van, *a.* woody, belonging to the woods, fhady,
Syl'van, *n.* a god of the woods, rural god, fatyr (wild
Syl'vanite, *n.* a femi-metal newly difcovered
Sym'bol, *n.* a type, emblem, fign, abftract, creed
Symbol'ical, *a.* typical, expreffing by or in figns
Symbol'ically, *ad.* by fymbols, typically, allufively
Symbolization, *n.* a reprefentation, a refemblance
Sym'bolize, *v.* to reprefent, refemble, fuit (tion
Symmetrian, Sym'metrift, *n.* one fond of propor-
Symmet'rical, Sym'metral, *a.* proportionate, true
Sym'metrize, *v. t.* to reduce to due proportion
Sym'metry, *n.* proportion, harmony, good temper
Sympathet'ic, *a.* having mutual fenfation, tender
Sympathet'ically, *ad.* with fympathy, tenderly
Sym'pathize, *v. i.* to feel with or for another
Sym'pathy, *n.* a fellow-feeling, compaffion
Symph'onious, *a.* harmonious, mufical, pleafing
Symph'ony, *n.* harmony of founds, agreement
Sympófiac, *a.* relating to merry meetings, jovial, *ob.*
Symp'tom, *n.* a fign, mark, token, indication, proof

Symptomat'ic, *a.* denoting a symptom and not the primary caufe

Spmptomat'ically, *ad.* in the nature of a fymptom

Syn'agogue, *n.* a place fet apart for Jewifh worfhip

Syn'agris, *n.* a fifh with a fharp back

Synale'pha, *n.* a contraction or excifion of a fylla-

Synax'is, *n.* a congregation, the Lord's fupper(ble

Synchron'ical, [ch as k] *a.* happening at the fame time

Synch'ronifm, *n.* a concurrence or union of events

Synch'ronize, *v. i.* to agree in point of time

Synchronous, *a.* exifting at the fame time

Synchronoufly, *ad.* at the fame time

Syncopation, *n.* in mufic an interruption of the regular meafure or inverting the order of notes in a bar, connection of notes in different bars

Syn'copated, *a.* inverted, having inverted order

Sync'ope, *n.* a fainting fit, the cutting off a part

Sync'opift, *n.* one who contracts words

Syn'dic, *n.* a deputy, agent, magiftrate, alderman

Syn'dicate, *v. t.* to judge, doom, cenfure, execute

Syn'drome, *n.* a concurrence in action, union

Synec'doche, [ch as k] *n.* a part taken or put for the whole

Synecdoch'ical, *a.* of or relating to fynecdoche

Syngenéfia, *n.* a clafs of plants whofe anthers are united in a cylinder

Syn'od, *n.* an ecclefiaftical affembly, a union

Synod'ical, *a.* relating to or done by a fynod

Synod'icalmonth, the interval from one change of the moon to another

Synod'ically, *ad.* by the authority of a fynod

Syn'onym, *n.* a name which has the fame meaning with another

Synon'ymife, *v. t.* to exprefs by different words

Synon'ymous, *a.* the fame in fignification, like

Synon'imoufly, *ad.* in the fame fenfe

Synon'ymy, *n.* the quality of having the fame meaning

Synop'fis, *n.* a general or fhort view of all parts

Synop'tical, *a.* fhowing many parts at one view

Synóvia, *n.* the nutritious juce proper to any part

Syntac'tic, Syntac'tical, *a.* pertaining to fyntax

Synt'ax, *n.* a fyftem, order, conftruction of words

Synth'efis, *n.* the act of compounding or joining

Synthet'ical, *a.* compounding, conjoining

Syn'thetize, *v. t.* to unite in regular ftructure

Syph'ilis, *n.* the venereal difeafe

Syphilit'ic, *a.* pertaining to fyphilis

Syracúfan, *n.* a native of Syracufe in Sicily

Syracúfan, *a.* pertaining to Syracufe

Syr'iac, *n.* the ancient language of Syria

Syr'iac, *a.* denoting the Syrian tongue or a verfion of the fcriptures in that tongue

Syr'ian, *n.* a native of Syria in Afia

Syr'ian, *a.* pertaining to Syria

Syr'inge, *n.* a pipe to fquirt or inject liquids with

Syr'inge, *v. t.* to wafh or fquirt with a fyringe

Syrt'is, *n.* a quickfand, fhelf in the fea, gulf

Syft'em, *n.* a method, fcheme, plan, theory, treatife

Syftemat'ic, *n.* one who likes or obferves fyftem

Syftemat'ical, *a.* methodical, connected, regular

Syftemat'ically, *ad.* in form of a fyftem, regularly

Sys'tematift, Sys'temmáker, *n.* a framer of a fyftem

Sys'temmonger, *n.* one over fond of forming fyftems

Syft'emizer, *n.* he who reduces to fyftem or order

Syft'emize, *v. t.* to reduce into a regular fyftem

Sys'tile, *n.* a placing of colums with fpaces between them of 2 diameters and 4 modules

Syft'ole, Sys'toly, *n.* the contraction of the heart, the act of fhortening a long fyllable

Sythe, *n.* an inftrument to cut grafs, &c.

Syz'ygy, *n.* the conjunction or oppofition of a planet

T

Tab'by, *n.* a kind of waved filk; *c.* brindled

Tab'by, *v. t.* to give a waving appearance to filk by paffing it under rollers engraved

Tabefac'tion, *n.* a wafting or pining away

Tab'efy, *v. t.* to wafte or pine away, to confume

Tab'erd or Tab'ard, *n.* a herald's coat or gown

Tab'ernacle, *v.* to enfhrine, live, dwell, abide

Tab'ernacle, *n.* a tent, temporary place of worfhip,

Tab'id, *a.* wafted by difeafe, confumptive (veffel

Tab'lature, *n.* a painting on walls or cielings

Table, *n.* a flat furface, board or frame to eat on, fare, index, fynopfis, fet of numbers

Table, *v.* to board, to note or fet down regularly

Táblebeer, *n.* fmall beer for common drinking

Táblebook, *n.* a book to grave or note down on

Tablecloth, *n.* a linen cloth to fpread on a table

Tab'leman, *n.* a bit of wood, a man at drafts

Tábler, *n.* one who boards at another perfon's houfe

Tables, *n. pl.* a board ufed for back gammon

Tab'let, *n.* a little table, the form of a medicin

Tábletalk, *n.* converfation at table, chitchat

Tábling, *n.* a broad hem on the fkirts of fails

Taboo', *n.* a prohibition, interdict

Taboo', *v. t.* to forbid, hold facred and inviolable

Tábor, *v. i.* to play on a tabor, to beat quick

Tábor, Tab'oret, Tab'orin, Tábret, *n.* a kind of fmall drum beaten with only one ftick

Táborer, *n.* one who beats or plays on a tabor

Tab'ular, *a.* formed in tables, fquares or plates

Tab'ulated, *a.* noted down, having a flat furface

Tacamahac', *n.* a refin, a tree

Tach or Tache, *n.* a catch, hook, loop, button, trick

Ta'cit, *a.* filent, implied though not expreffed

Ta'citly, *ad.* filently, by implication, in effect

T. citurn'ity, *n.* habitual filence, referve, fecrecy

Tack, *n.* a fmall nail, rope, turn of a fhip, leafe

Tack, *v. t.* to faften, join, unite, few, turn about

Tac'kle, *v. t.* to faddle, accooter, fit out, prepare

Tac'kle, *n.* ropes of a fhip, inftruments, a pulley

Tack'ied, *pa.* made of ropes, joined, accootered

Tack'ling, *n.* furniture, implements, a harnefs

Tac'tic, *a.* relating to the art of war, military

Tac'tics, *n. pl.* the art of ranging in order of battle

Tac'tile, *a.* that may be touched or felt

Tac'tion, *n.* the act of touching or feeling
Tad'pole, *n.* a young and shapeless frog
Taf'ferel, *n.* the upper part of a ship's stern
Taf'feta or Taf'fety, *n.* a sort of thin silk
Tag, *n.* metal at the end of a lace, a paltry thing
Tag, *v. t.* to fix or put a tag on, to join together
Tag'tail, *n.* a kind of variegated worm
Tail, *v. t.* to pull by the tail; *n.* the hinder part
Tail'age or Tal'lage, *n.* a tax, tribute, toll, share
Tailor, *n.* one who makes men's cloaths
Taint, *v. t.* to infect, corrupt, fully, stain, spoil
Taint, *n.* a tincture, infection, stain, spot, blemish
Taintless, *a.* free from taint or infection, found
Tainture, *n.* a taint, defilement, stain, spot, tinge
Tajacu, *n.* the peccary or Mexican hog
Take, *v.* took, *pret.* taken, *pa.* to receive, seize, trap, suppose, hire, please
Taker, *n.* one who takes, one who uses or assumes
Taking, *pa.* receiving, arresting, engaging
Taking, *n.* a seizure, distress, difficulty, fright
Talapoin', *n.* a priest of Siam, a monkey
Tal'bot, *n.* a spotted dog with a turned-up tail, *ob.*
Talc or Talck, *n.* a magnesian earth consisting of broad flat smooth lamens or plates
Talck'ite, *n.* a species of talck of a loose form
Talck'ic, *a.* like or consisting of talck (reckoning
Tale, *n.* a story, fable, received number or value,
Talebearer, *n.* an officious informer, a liar
Talebearing *n.* the act of informing officiously
Tal'ent, *n.* a certain weight or sum, gift, faculty
Tal'isman, *n.* a magical character, image, charm
Talisman'ic, *a.* magical, secret, hidden, occult
Talk, [tauk] *v.* to speak, prate, converse, discourse
Talk, *n.* speech, conversation, discourse, tale, a public conference with or among Indians, and an official verbal communication
Talk'ative, *a.* full of talk, prating, noisy, cheerful
Talk'ativeness, *n.* a talkative quality or temper
Talk'er, *n.* a prater, a noisy or boasting person
Talk'ing, *n.* the act of speaking, oral conversation
Tall, *a.* high in stature, lofty, lusty, sturdy, stout
Tal'lage, *n.* a tax, toll or tribute
Tal'low, *n.* the hard fat of an animal, chiefly that of the bovine species and sheep
Tal'low, *v. t.* to smear or grease with tallow
Tal'lowcandle, *n.* a candle made of tallow
Tal'lowchandler, *n.* a maker of tallow candles
Tal'lowish, *a.* having the nature of tallow, greasy
Tal'ly, *n.* two sticks equally notched, what suits
Tal'ly, *v.* to fit or be fitted, suit, agree, score
Tal'lyman, *n.* one who sells for weekly payment
Tal'mud, *n.* the book of Jewish traditions
Tal'mudic, *a.* relating to the talmud
Tal'mudist, *n.* one versed in the talmud
Tall'ness, *n.* a tall state, height of stature
Tal'on, *n.* the claw of a bird of prey, a member
Tal'us, *n.* the slope of a work as of a wall
Tam'arin, *n.* a small monkey with large ears
Tam'arind, *n.* a kind of four Indian fruit

Tam'arisk, *n.* a plant of two species
Tam'borin, *n.* a small drum, fine sieve, a dance
Tam'bour, *n.* a capital of a column, a box in a porch, a kind of embroidery on a cushion
Tam'bour, *v. t.* to embroider with a tambour
Tame, *a.* not wild, gentle, dull, spiritless, subdued
Tame, *v. t.* to make gentle, humble, subdue, crush
Tameable, *a.* that may be tamed or brought under
Tamely, *ad.* meanly, mildly, without resistance
Tameness, *n.* a tame quality, meanness
Tamer, *n.* one who tames or humbles, a conqueror
Tam'kin, *n.* a stopper for a great gun's mouth
Tam'my, *n.* a thin kind of woollen stuff
Tamp'er, *v. i.* to meddle with, practice upon, try
Tam'tam, *n.* a large flat drum among the Hindoos
Tan, *v.* to cure skins, become brown, turn, beat
Tan, *n.* bark which has been used in tanning, a substance in gall nuts, &c.
Tang, *n.* a strong taste, relish, sound; *v. t.* to ring
Tang, *n.* a fish of a rhomboidal form
Tan'gent, *n.* a line perpendicular to radius or which touches a curve
Tangibil'ity, *n.* a being perceptible by the touch
Tan'gible, *a.* perceptible by the touch, harmless
Tan'gle, *v.* to embroil, ensnare, mix, entangle
Tan'gle, *n.* a knot of things mingled, a sea-weed
Tank, *n.* a reservoir of water, large bason, cistern
Tank'ard, *n.* a large drinking vessel with a cover
Tan'ner, *n.* one who tans hides for lether
Tan'pit, *n.* a pit used for a tanner's work
Tan'rec, *n.* an Indian quadruped larger than a rat
Tan'sy, *n.* the name of a common garden herb
Tant, *n.* a small spider of a scarlet color (tion
Tant'alism, *n.* the punishment of Tantalus, decep-
Tan'talite, *n.* a mineral of a bluish or dark gray color
Tantalium, *n.* a metal lately discovered
Tan'talize, *v. t.* to teaze with false hopes
Tan'tamount, *a.* equivalent, worth full as much
Tan'tiv'y, *ad.* with haste, with great or full speed, *ob.*
Tant'ling, *n.* one hoping for unattainable things, *ob.*
Tan'yard, *n.* a yard used for the business of a tanner
Tap, *v. t.* to touch softly, pierce, broach, open
Tap, *n.* a rap, gentle blow, noise, small pipe, run
Tape, *n.* a narrow linen, fillet, a kind of fine inkle
Tap'er, *n.* a light, a waxcandle; *a.* sloping regularly
Tap'er, *v. i.* to grow smaller by regular degrees
Tap'erness, *n.* a tapering state or quality
Tap'estry, *n.* a cloth woven in figures, hangings
Tap'eti, *n.* an American animal of the hare kind
Tap'house, *n.* a house for selling liquors
Tap'ir, *n.* an American amphibious quadruped of the size of a mule and resembling the hippopotomy
Tap'root, *n.* the principal or chief stem of a root
Tap'ster, *n.* one who taps, one who draws beer
Tar, *n.* the juce of the pine obtained by a suffocating heat, a sailor
Tar, *v.* to smear or daub with tar, tease, provoke
Tarabe, *n.* a large parrot with a red head

Taraquíra, *n.* a species of lizard in America (sic

Tarant'ula, *n.* a spider whose bite is cured by music

Tarant'ulate, *v. t.* to excite or govern emotions by music

Tar'digrade, Tar'digradous, *a.* moving slowly, *ob.*

Tar'dily, *ad.* slowly, sluggishly, dully, heavily

Tar'diness, Tar'dity, *n.* slowness, sluggishness

Tar'dy, *a.* slow, dilatory, criminal; *v. t.* to delay

Tare, *n.* a weed an allowance in weight for the cask, &c. in which goods are packed

Tare, *v. t.* to mark the weight of tare

Tare, *pret.* of *to tear*

Taren'tine, *n.* a native of Tarentim in Italy

Targe or Targ'et, *n.* a kind of buckler or shield

Tar'gum, *n.* the Chaldee paraphrase on the pentateuch (thority

Tar'if or Tar'iff, *n.* a table of duties fixed by authority

Tar'nish, *v.* to sully, soil, lose brightness or luster

Tarpawl'ing, *n.* a cloth covered with tar, a sailor

Tarpéian, *a.* denoting a steep rock in Rome (ment

Tar'ras or Ter'ras, *n.* a volcanic earth used as a cement

Tar'riance, *n.* a stay, delay, stop, hindrance, *ob.*

Tar'rier, *n.* one who tarries, a kind of small dog

Tar'rock, *n.* a fowl of the gull kind

Tar'ry, *v.* to stay, continue, delay, stop; wait, live

Tars'el, *n.* a fierce bird, a kind of hawk

Tart, *a.* sour, acid, keen, severe; *n.* a small fruit pie

Tart'an, *n.* a kind of soft woollen stuff

Tart'an, *n.* a kind of small coasting ship

Tar'tar, *n.* a concretion on the sides of vessels in which wine is fermented, a native of Tartary, spelt also Tatar (Tartary

Tartar'ic, Tartárian, Tatar'ic, *a.* pertaining to

Tartárean, Tartáreous, *a.* hellish, infernal

Tar'tarin, *n.* vegetable fixed alkali or potash

Tar'tarinated, *a.* combined with tartarin

Tart'arous, *a.* consisting of or containing tartar, denoting the acid of tartar

Tar'tarize, *v. t.* to impregnate with tartar

Tart'ly, *ad.* sharply, sourly, keenly, severely (ture

Tart'ness, *n.* sharpness, sourness, keenness, illnature

Tar'trite, *n.* a salt formed by tartarous acid with a base

Task, *n.* a business imposed, employment, labor

Task, *v. t.* to impose something to be done, to set

Task'master, *n.* one who imposes tasks on others

Tass'el, *n.* an ornamental bunch of silk, &c hawk,

Tass'eled, *a.* adorned with or having tassels (board

Tástable, *a.* that may be tasted, savory, nice

Taste, *v.* to try the relish, essay, prove, feel, enjoy

Taste, *n.* the sense of tasting or relishing, discernment, judgement, a trial, experiment, piece, bit

Tásted, *pa.* having a particular taste or relish

Tásteful, *a.* having a high relish, savory, nice

Tástefulness, *n.* a palatable or high taste

Tásteless, *a.* having little or no relish, insipid

Tástelessness, *n.* a want of taste or relish, insipidity

Táster, *n.* one who tastes, a little cup, a dram cup

Tat'ter, *v. t.* to tear, to rend; *n.* a loose rag

Tatterdemal'lion, *n.* a ragged shabby fellow

Tat'tle, *v. i.* to prate, to talk idly; *n.* trifling talk

Tat'tler, *n.* a prater, gossip, telltale, busy body

Tattoo', *n.* a sound of drum ordering to quarters

Pattoo', *v. t.* to puncture and stain the skin in various figures, a practice among savages

Tau, *n.* the toad fish of the jugular genus

Taught, *pret.* and *pa. pass.* of *to teach*

Taunt, *v. t.* to insult, revile, rail at, ridicule, scoff

Taunt, *n.* an insult, reproach, saucy answer, scoff

Taunt'er, *n.* one who taunts, a saucy answer

Taunt'ingly, *ad.* with insult, revilingly, saucily

Taúrian, *a.* pertaining to Mount Taurus in Asia

Tau'rus, *n.* the bull, a sign in the zodiac

Tautolo"gical, *a.* repeating often the same thing

Tautol'ogy, *n.* a repetition of the same sense

Tav'ern, *n.* a house of entertainment for travellers, an inn, a house for the sale of liquors

Tav'ernkéeper, *n.* an inn holder

Tav'ernman, *n.* a man who keeps a tavern, a toper

Taw, *v. t.* to dress white lether; *n.* a boy's marble

Taw'driness, *n.* a tawdry dress, tinsel finery

Taw'dry, *a.* meanly showy or fine, gaudy

Taw'er, *n.* a tanner or dresser of white lether

Taw'ney, Taw'ny, *a.* yellowish, brownish, reddish

Tax, *n.* an impost, duty, tribute, censure, charge

Tax, *v. t.* to lay a tax, impose, accuse, charge

Tax'able, *a.* that may be taxed, chargeable

Taxátion, *n.* the act of laying a tax, a valuation

Tax'er, *n.* one who taxes, one who inspects bills

Tax'gatherer, *n.* one employed to gather in taxes

Táylor, *n.* one who makes clothes for men

Tea, *n.* a Chinese plant, a decoction of the tea or other plant

Téaboard, *n.* a board to put teacups, &c. on

Teach, *v. t.* taught, *pret.* taught, *pa.* to instruct, show, tell, inform, declare

Téachable, *a.* willing to be taught, tractable

Téachableness, *n.* a willingness or aptness to learn

Teache, *n.* the last boiler in sugar works

Téacher, *n.* a master, instructor, tutor, preacher

Téacup, *n.* a small cup used to drink tea out of

Tead, Tede, *n.* a torch, flambeau, *ob.*

Téague, *n.* an Irishman by way of contempt

Teak, *n.* a timber tree of Birman in Asia equal or superior to the oak of Europe and America

Teal, *n.* the name of a fowl of the duck kind

Team, *n.* cattle or horses attached to a cart, sled, waggon, &c. flock, number

Téapot, *n.* a pot in which tea is made

Tear, *n.* water from the eye, moisture, a rent

Tear, *v.* tare, tore, *pret.* torn, *pa.* to rend or pull in pieces, spoil, rave, rage

Téarfalling, *a.* shedding tears, tender, feeling

Téarful, *a.* full of tears, weeping, heavy, sad

Téarless, *a.* void of tears, dry, unfeeling, cruel

Tease, Teaze, *v. t.* to comb wool, search, torment

Téasel, *n.* a useful plant to dress cloth with

Téaser, *n.* one who teases, vexes or provokes

Téafpoon, *n.* a fmall fpoon ufed in drinking tea
Teat, *n.* the dug of a beaft, a nipple, the breaft
Téatable, *n.* a table for holding tea furniture
Tech'nical, [ch as k] *a.* belonging to arts and fci-
Tech'y, *a.* peevifh, eafily provoked, fretful (ences
Teólon'ic, *a.* pertaining to building or framing
Ted, *v. t.* to lay mown grafs in rows, to fpread
Ted'der, *n.* a rope to give a beaft a certain range
 in feeding
Ted'der, *v. t.* to tie or limit to a fpot in feeding
Te Deum, n. a kind of hymn ufed in the Liturgy
Tédious, *a.* flow, dilatory, tirefome, wearifome
Tédioufly, *ad.* flowly, in a flow irkfome manner
Tédioufnefs, *n.* flownefs, tirefomenefs, irkfomenefs
Teem, *v.* to be big, bring forth, pour out, abound
Téemful, *a.* pregnant, heavy, fruitful, brimful
Téemlefs, *a.* barren, unfruitful, worthlefs, ufelefs
Teen, *n.* forrow, grief; *v.* to excite, kindle, fence
Teens, *n. pl.* the years between twelve and twenty
Teeth, *n. pl.* of *tooth; v. i.* to breed or put in teeth
Teg'ular, *a.* like or pertaining to tiles or a roof
Teg'ularly, *ad.* like tiles or a roof
Teg'ument, *n.* a covering, outward part, cafe
Teh-hé, *v. i.* to laugh, titter, grin; *n.* a laugh
Teint, *n.* a color, touch of a pencil. *fee* tint
Telamónian, *a.* pertaining to Telamon king of
 Salamin and father of Teucer and Ajax
Télary, *a.* like a web, fpinning webs, *ob.*
Tel'egraph, *n.* a machine for communicating in-
 telligence with fignals for letters
Telegraph'ic, *a.* pertaining to a telegraph
Tel'efcope, *n.* an optical inftrument for viewing
 diftant objeóls, increafing the powers of vifion
Telefcop'ical, *a.* pertaining to or feen only by a
 telefcope (form, report, count, reckon
Tell, *v. t.* told, *pret.* told, *pa.* to relate, utter, in-
Tell'er, *n.* one who tells or counts, an officer who
 receives and pays money in a bank
Tell'tale, *n.* an officious informer, a bufy body
Tel'lur or Tellurium, *n.* a metal lately difcovered
 of a grayifh white color
Temerárious, *a.* rafh, hafty, heedlefs, headftrong
Temerity, *n.* rafhnefs, haftinefs, heedleffnefs
Temp'er, *n.* a due mixture, frame of mind, difpo-
 fition, calmnefs, moderation
Temp'er, *v. t.* to mix, qualify, make fit, mollify
Temp'erament, *n.* a conftitution, ftate, medium
Témperament'al, *a.* conftitutional, real
Temp'e.ance, *a.* moderate indulgence of appe-
 tites or paffions
Temp'erate, *a.* moderate, fober, cool, calm, quiet
Temp'erately, *ad.* moderately, coolly, calmly
Tem'peratenefs, *n.* moderate ftate or quality,
 temperance
Temp'erature, *n.* temperament, moderation, ftate
Tem'pered, *pa.* well hardened by fire, difpofed
Temp'eft, *n.* a violent wind, ftorm, tumult, buftle
Temp'eft, *v. t.* to difturb as by a tempeft, to raife
Temp'eftbeaten, *a.* fhattered or toft by ftorms

Tempeftiv'ity, *n.* feafonablenefs, due time, fitnefs
Temp'efttoft, *a.* toft or driven about by ftorms
Tempeft'uous, *a.* ftormy, turbulent (nefs
Tempeft'uoufnefs, *n.* tempeftuous weather, rough-
Temp'lar, *n.* a ftudent at law living in a temple
Tem"ple, *n.* a church, building, fide of the head
Temp'let, *n.* a fmall piece of timber in a building
Temp'oral, *a.* not eternal, not ecclefiaftical, not
 fpiritua', worldly, pertaining to the temples or
 to time
Temporal'ity, Temp'orals, *n.* fecular poffeffions
Temp'orally, *ad.* with refpeót to time or this life
Temp'orary, *a.* continuing only for a time, fleeting
Temp'orize, *v.* to comply with the time, to delay
Temp'orizer, *n.* a timeferver, trimmer, turncoat
Tempt, *v. t.* to entice to ill, provoke, try, prove
Temptátion, *n.* the aót of tempting, a bait, a trial
Tempt'er, *n.* one who tempts, an enticer, Satan
Tem'ulent, *a.* intoxicated, fuddled, drunk
Ten, *a.* twice five
Ten'able, *a.* that may be held or maintained (gardly
Tenácious, *a.* holding faft, obftinate, adhefive, nig-
Tenácioufly, *ad.* in a tenacious manner, firmly
Tenácioufnefs, *n.* ftiffnefs, obftinacy, firmnefs
Tena"city, *n.* ftiffnefs in opinion, adherence
Tenáil, *n.* an outwork in fortification, confifting
 of two parallel fides, with a reentering angle
Tenaillon', *n.* a work like a lunett on each fide of
 the ravelin
Ten'ancy, *n.* a temporary poffeffion or tenure
Ten'ant, *n.* one who holds from or rents of another
Ten'ant, *v. t.* to hold on conditions, to rent
Ten'antable, *a.* fit to be rented
Ten'antlefs, *a.* unoccupied, uninhabited, empty
Ten'antry, *n.* tenants in general
Tench, *n.* the name of a delicious pond-fifh
Tend, *v.* to attend, wait, move, load, conduce
Tend'ance, *n.* attendance, the aót of waiting upon
Tend'ence or Tend'ency, *n.* a drift, fcope, courfe
Tend'er, *a.* foft, fore, kind, fond, nice, young
Tend'er, *v. t.* to offer, exhibit, hold, efteem, value
Tend'er, *n.* a propofal for acceptance, offer, regard,
 a veffel that fupplies a fhip with ftores
Tend'erhearted, *a.* compaffionate, kind, foft, good
Tend'erling, *n.* a fondling, the firft horns of a deer
Tend'erly, *ad.* gently, foftly, kindly, fondly
Tend'ernefs, *n.* foftnefs, forenefs, kindnefs
Tend'inous, *a.* containing tendons, finewy, ftrong
Tend'on, *n.* a finew, a general ligature of joints
Ten'drac, *n.* an animal of the hedgehog kind
Tend'ril, *n.* the clafp of a vine, &c.
Ten'ement, *n.* a houfe, apartment, whatever ef-
 tate may be held
Tenement'al, *a.* that is or may be held by tenants
Tenement'ary, *a.* ufually let to or held by tenants
Tenef'mus, *n.* a frequent wanting to go to ftool
Ten'et, *n.* a pofition, opinion, principle, doótrin
Ten'nis, *n.* a fort of play with a racket and ball
Ten'on, *n.* that which fills up a mortife

Ten'or, *n.* a continuity of flate, courfe, purport, drift, part in mufic

Tenfe, *n.* a diftinction of time ; *a.* ftretched, ftiff

Tenfe'nefs, *n.* a tenfe flate, tightnefs, ftiffnefs

Tens'ible, Tens'ile, *a.* that is capable of extenfion

Ten'fion, Tens'ure, *n.* the act of ftretching, extent

Tens'ive, *a.* giving a fenfation of ftiffnefs, tight

Tens'or, *n.* a mufcle which turns the thigh

Tent, *n.* a pavilion, moveable habitation, roll of lint to put into a fore, very fweet red wine

Tent, *v.* to lodge in a tent, fill with tent, tend

Tentátion, *n.* a temptation, attempt, trial, proof

Tent'ative, *a.* trying, effaying ; *n.* a trial, an effay

Tent'ed, *pa.* covered with or containing tents

Tent'er, *n.* a frame, iron hook, difficulty, trouble

Tent'er, *v. t.* to ftretch on hooks, to extend

Tenth, *a.* the ordinal of ten, firft after the ninth

Tenth, *n.* a tenth part, a tax or tribute of that part

Tenth'ly, *ad.* in the tenth place

Tenúity, *n.* thinnefs, fmallnefs, minutenefs

Ten'uous, *a.* thin, flender, fmall, minute (eftate

Ten'ure. *n.* a condition by which a man enjoys an

Tep'id, *a.* hottifh, warm, lukewarm, not zealous

Tep'idnefs, Tepid'ity, *n.* a gentle heat, lukewarm-

Terce, *a.* a veffel containing 42 gallons (nefs

Tercemájor, *n.* a fequence of the three beft cards

Terebinth'ine, *a.* mixed with or like turpentine

Ter'ebrate, *v. t.* to bore, pierce, perforate, *ob.*

Terebrátion, *n.* the act of boring a hole, *ob.*

Teréde, *n.* a fea worm which penetrates the bot-

Teréte, *a.* cylindrical, tapering (toms of fhips

Térek, *n.* a water fowl, webfooted, with long legs

Tergem'inal, Tergem'inate, *a.* threefold, three-double

Ter'gem'inous, *a.* treble, threefold, having three

Tergiverfátion, *n.* a fhift, fetch, evafion, excufe

Term, *n.* a limit, boundary, word, member, condition, article, number, time, time for feats of juftice and exercifes at an univerfity, an eftate for years

Term, *v. t.* to call, name, denominate, ftyle

Term'or, *n.* one entitled to an eftate for years

Term'agancy, *n.* turbulence, croffnefs, great noife

Term'agant, *n.* a fcold ; *a.* turbulent, furious

Term'er, *n.* one who attends the term of a court

Term'inal, *a.* ending, growing at the end

Term'inate, *v.* to limit, bound, conclude, end

Termination, *n.* a limiting, term, conclufion, end

Term'inator, *n.* in aftronomy, the circle of illumination. (tors

Term'iner, *n.* a determining or trial of malefac-

Term'lefs, *a.* unlimited, boundlefs, endlefs

Term'ly, *ad.* term by term, in every county

Tern, *n.* a water fowl of feveral varieties

Tern, *a.* three, confifting of three

Tern'ary, Tern'ion, *n.* the number three

Tern'ate, *a.* divided into three, having three leaf-

Tern'ate, *n.* a fpecies of bat (lets on a petiole

Ter'race, *n.* a fmall graffy hill or mount, a flat roof

Ter'raced, *a.* made with or having terraces

Terráqueous, *a.* compofed of land and water

Ter'rel, *n.* a little earth, or globular magnet

Terréne, Ter'reous, *a.* belonging to or confifting

Terréne, *n.* the furface of the earth (of earth

Terres'trial, *a.* belonging to the earth, worldly

Terres'trify, *v. t.* to reduce to the flate of earth, *ob.*

Ter'rible, *a.* formidable, dreadful, exceffive

Ter'riblenefs, *n.* formidablenefs, dreadfulnefs

Ter'ribly, *ad.* formidably, dreadfully, violently

Ter'rier, *n.* a dog which purfues game into their burrows, a furvey of land, an auger, *ob.*

Terrif'ic, *a.* caufing terror or fear, dreadful

Ter'rify, *v. t.* to fright, make afraid, fcare, fhock

Terri'genous, *a.* born of or produced by the earth

Territórial, *a.* relating to or having a territory

Ter'ritory, *n.* land, a diftrict, country, dominion

Ter'ror, *n.* dread, fear, the caufe of fear

Terfe, *a.* fmooth, neat, cleanly written, exact

Terten'ant, *n.* a tenant who occupies land

Ter'tials, *n.* fethers near the junction of the wing with the body

Ter'tian, *a.* returning or coming every third day

Ter'tiate, *v. t.* to examin the thicknefs of metal at the muzzle of a gun

Tefs'ellate, *a.* chequered, variegated by fquares

Teft, *n.* a cupel to try metals, trial, means of trial

Teft, *v. t.* to compare with a ftandard, try, prove

Teft'able, *a.* that may be divifed or given by will

Teftáceous, *a.* confifting of fhells, having hard entire fhells as an oyfter

Teft'ament, *n.* a will, covenant, name of holy writ

Teftament'ary, *a.* given by or relating to a will

Teft'ate, *a.* having made a will, leaving a will

Teftátor, *n.* a man who leaves or gives by will

Teftátrix, *n.* a woman who leaves or gives by will

Teft'ed, *a.* tried by a teft, tried, proved, witneffed

Teft'er, *n.* a top-cover of a bed, headpiece

Teft'icle, *n.* a ftone, organ of feed in animals

Teftic'ulate, *a.* fhaped like a tefticle

Teftificátion, *n.* the act of witneffing or proving

Teftifier, *n.* one who teftifies, declares or proves

Teft'ify, *v.* to witnefs, give evidence, prove, fhow

Teft'ily, *ad.* peevifhly, crofsly, feurly, morofely

Teftimónial, *n.* a certificate of one's character

Teftimony, *n.* evidence, proof, profeffion ; *v. t.* to

Teft'inefs, *n.* peevifhnefs, morofenefs (witnefs

Teft'y, *a.* peevifh, crofs, fretful, four, morofe

Tetch'inefs, *n.* peevifhnefs, fretfulnefs

Tetch'y, *a.* peevifh, eafily provoked, fretful

Tetaug', *n.* the rock or black fifh

Tete, *n.* falfe hair for the head of a woman

Tête-a-tête, *n.* check by jole, clofenefs, nearnefs

Teth'er, *fee* Tedder (in mufic

Tet'rachord, [ch as k] *n.* an interval of four tones

Tetradiapáfon, *n.* a a quadruple eighth or 29th

Tetradynam'ia, *n.* a clafs of plants in which four ftamens are longer than the others

Tet'ragon, *n.* a figure of four fides, a fquare afpect

Tetrag'onal, *a.* having 4 angles or fides, fquare
Tet'ragonifm, *n.* the quadrative of the circle
Tetragyn'ia, *n.* an order of plants with four piftils
Tetrahédron, *n.* a figure with four equal fides
Tetrahédral, *a.* having four equal fides
Tetram'eter, *a.* confifting of four meafures
Tetran'dria, *n.* a clafs of plants with hermaphrodite flowers of four males or ftamens
Tetrapet'alous, *a.* containing 4 petals or leaves
Tetraph'yllous, *a.* having four leaves
Tet'rarch, [ch as k] *n.* a governor of a tetrarchate
Tetrarch'ate, *n.* a fourth part or fhare of a province
Tetrafperm'ous, *a.* having four feeds
Tetras'tich, *n.* a ftanza of four verfes or lines
Tet'rical, Tet'ricous, *a.* crabbed, perverfe, *ob.*
Tetri''city, *n.* crabbeddefs, fournefs, illnature, *ob.*
Tet'rodon, *n.* a fifh of the cartilaginous kind
Tet'ter, *n.* a kind of ringworm, fcab, fcurf, fore
Tet'ter, *v. t.* to affect with tetters
Teúthys, *n.* fifh with a truncate head
Teuton'ic, *a.* denoting what belonged to the Teutons, ancient Germans
Tew, *v. t.* to work, toil, pull, beat, foften, *ob.*
Tew, *n.* an iron chain, any kind of materials, *ob.*
Tew'el, *n.* an iron pipe put at the back of a forge, *ob.*
Tew'taw, *v. t.* to beat, break flax, drefs, *ob.*
Text, *n.* a fentence, portion, part, original writing
Text'copy, *n.* a copy written in text hand
Text'hand, *n.* a large hand, a large kind of writing
Text'ile, *a.* woven, that may be woven or plaited
Text'man, *n.* one ready at the quotation of texts
Text'rine, *a.* relating to the act or art of weaving
Text'uarift, Text'uary, *n.* one verfed in fcripture
Text'uary, *a.* contained in a text, authoritative
Text'ure, *n.* a manner of weaving, web, form
Tham'muz, *n.* a Jewifh month, anfwering to part of June and July
Than, *ad.* placed or employed only in comparifon
Thane, *n.* a Saxon title of honor, baron, freeholder
Thank, *v. t.* to give or return thanks
Thank'ful, *a.* full of gratitude, grateful, pleafed
Thank'fully, *ad.* with a lively fenfe of favor
Thank'fulnefs, *n.* gratitude, acknowledgment
Thank'lefs, *a.* unthankful, ungrateful, defpifed
Thank'leffnefs, *n.* ingratitude (of fome mercy
Thank'offering, *n.* an offering in acknowledgment
Thanks, *n. pl.* an acknowledgment of fome favor
Thankfgiv'ing, *n.* a celebration of mercy, praife, a day fet apart for rendering thanks
Thank'worthy, *a.* worthy or deferving of thanks
Tháfian, *a.* pertaining to Thafos, a fertile ifland in the Egean fea, near Thrace
That, *pron.* which, who, the thing ; *conj.* becaufe
Thatch, *n.* ftraw ufed for the covering of a houfe
Thatch, *v. t.* to cover a houfe, &c. with ftraw
Thatch'er, *n.* one who covers places with ftraw
Thatch'ing, *n.* the act of covering with ftraw
Thaw, *v. i.* to melt, diffolve, give way, relent, calm
Thaw, *n.* the diffolution of a froft, a melting

The, *article,* denoting fome particular thing, &c.
Théater, *n.* a playhoufe, ftage, place for fhows
Theat'ric, Theat'rical, *a.* fuiting or like a theater
Theat'rically, *ad.* in a theatrical manner
Théban, *n.* a native of Thebes in Greece
Théban, *a.* pertaining to Thebes
Thee, *pron.* the oblique cafe *fing.* of *thou*
Theft, *n.* the act of ftealing, a thing ftolen, diff'Their, *pron. pl.* of *them* (honefty
Théifm, *n.* the belief of the exiftence of a God
Théift, *n.* one who believes in a God
Theift'ical, *a.* pertaining to a theift
Them, *pron. pl.* the oblique cafe of *they*
Theme, *n.* a fubject, tafk, differtation, power, root
Themfelves', *pron. pl.* their very felves, them alone
Then, *ad.* at that time, in that cafe
Thence, *ad.* from that place, for that reafon
Thence'forth, Thencefor'ward, *ad.* from that time
Theoc'racy, *n.* a government under God himfelf
Theocrat'ical, *a.* relating to a theocracy, divine
Theod'olite, *n.* an inftrument to take heights by
Theog'ony. *n.* the feigned generation of the gods
Theolo''gical, *a.* relating to theology, divine
Theolo''gically, *ad.* by or according to theology
Theol'ogift, Théalogue, *n.* a divine, a minifter
Theol'ogize, *v. i.* to frame a fyftem of theology
Theol'ogy, *n.* divinity, the fcience of divine things
Theom'achy, *n.* the battle of the gods and giants
Théorbo, *n.* a kind of inftrument, a large lute
Théorem, *n.* a pofition of acknowledged truth
Theoremat'ical, *a.* of or relating to theorems
Theoret'ic, Theoret'ical, Theor'ical, *a.* fpeculative
Theoret'ically, *ad.* in or by theory, fpeculatively
Théorift, Théoric, *n.* a fpeculatift, a fchemer
Théorize, *v. i.* to form a theory, to fpeculate
Théory, *n.* fpeculation, ftudy, a fcheme, a plan
Theofoph'ifm, *n.* pretenfion to divine illumination, enthufiafm
Theofoph'ift, *n.* one who pretends to divine illumination and interprets fcripture allegorically
Theofoph'ic, *a.* pertaining to theofophifts
Therapeut'ic, *a.* relating to the art or act of curing
There, [thare] *ad.* in that place, at that time, once
Thereabout', *ad.* near that place or that number
Thereaf'ter, *ad.* according or agreeably to that
Thereat', *ad.* at that place, on that account, then
Thereby', *ad.* by that, for that caufe or reafon, fo
There'fore, *ad.* for this reafon, in confequence
Therefrom', *ad.* from that, from this, from thence
Therein', *ad.* in that, in this, in that very thing
Thereinto', *ad.* into that, into this, in addition to
Thereof', *ad.* of that, of this, of that very thing
Thereon', Thereupon', *ad.* on that, on this, then
Thereout', *ad.* out of that, out of this, from thence
Thereto, Thereunto, *ad.* to or unto that or this
Thereun'der, *ad.* under that, under this, beneath
Therewith', *ad.* with that, with this, immediately
Therewithal', *ad.* over and above, alfo, with that
Theriacal, *a.* of or like treacle, medicinal, phyfical

Therm'al, a. pertaining to heat, warm

Therm'olamp, n. an inftrument to furnifh light by means of inflammable gas

Thermom'eter, n. an inftrument to meafure heat

Thermomet'rical, a. belonging to or like a thermometer, relating to the meafure of heat

Ther'mofcope, n. an inftrument to difcover heat

Thefalian, a. pertaining to Theffaly in Greece

Thefe, pron. pl. of this

Thefis, n. a theme, fubject, propofition, pofitidn

Thes'pian, a. relating to Thefpis, the inventor of

Theffalónian, n. a native of Theffalonica (tragedy

Theffalónian, a. pertaining to Theffalonica

Theur'gical, a. relating to the working of miracles

Théurgy, n. the power of performing fupernatural things by an intercourfe with the Deity

Thew, n. manners, quality, brawn, a ftoel, ob.

They, [thay] pron. perfons or things at large

Thick, a. grofs, muddy, clofe, n. the thickeft part

Thick, ad. faft, clofely, frequently, often, deeply

Thick'en, v. to make or grow thick, muddy, or

Thick'et, n. a very clofe wood, a clofe tuft (clofe

Thick'headed, a. having a thick head, ftupid, dull

Thick'ifh, a. rather thick, rather dull or heavy

Thick'ly, ad. to a great quantity, clofely, deeply

Thick'nefs, n. groffnefs, denfity, clofenefs, weight

Thick'fcull, n. a ftupid perfon, blockhead, dunce

Thick'fculled, a. ftupid, dull, heavy, flow, fimple

Thick'fet, a. clofely planted, near; n. a fuftian

Thick'fkin, n. a courfe grofs man, a blockhead

Thick'fprung, a. fprung up clofe together

Thief, n. a perfon who fteals, a blemifh in a candle

Thiéfcatcher, n. one who catches or takes thieves

Thieve, v. i. to practife theft, fteal, pilfer, take

Thiévery, n. the practice or art of ftealing, theft

Thiévifh, a. given to ftealing, dishoneft, fecret

Thiévifhly, ad. dishoneftly, bafely, privately, flily

Thiévifhnefs, n. a fondnefs for ftealing, bafenefs

Thigh, n. the part between the leg and body

Thill, n. a beam, the fhafts of a waggon or cart

Thill'horfe, Thill'er, n. a horfe between the fhafts

Thim'ble, n. a cap ufed on the needle-finger, a ring

Thin, a. not thick, lean, flim, flender, fmall, rare

Thin, v. t. to make thin, attenuate, rarefy

Thin, Thin'ly, ad. not thickly or clofely, rarely

Thine, pron. relating or belonging to thee

Thing, n. whatever is, any kind of matter

Think, v. thought, pret. thought, pa. to have ideas, judge, imagin, believe, mufe, reflect

Think'er, n. one who thinks in a certain manner

Think'ing, n. an imagination, judgment, opinion

Thin'nefs, n. a thin ftate, rarenefs, fcarcity, want

Third, [thurd] a. the next in order to the fecond

Third, n. a third part, the 60th part of a fecond

Third'ly, ad. in the third place, in the third order

Thirds, n. pl. a third part of an eftate belonging to the widow of a deceafed perfon

Thirl, [thurl] v. t. to pierce, bore, perforate

Thirft, [thurft] n. pain from want of drink, defire

Thirft, v. i. to feel the want of drink, to defire

Thirft'inefs, n. a thirfty ftate, thirft

Thirft'y, a. fuffering the want of drink, very eager

Thirtéen, a. ten and three added together

Thirtéenth, a. the third in order after the tenth

Thir'ty, [thurty] a. twenty and ten, ten repeated

This, pron. that which is prefent or near (thrice

This"tle, n. a very prickly weed, plant, order

This"tly, a. overgrown with or like thiftles

Thith'er, ad. to that place, to that point or end

Thith'erto, ad. fo far, thus far, to that end

Thith'erward, ad. towards that place or fpot

Tho or Though, n. grant, admit, be it fo

Thole, v. i. to wait, to bear; n. a pin of a boat

Thómift, n. a difciple of Thomas Aquinas

Thong, n. a ftring or thin ftrap of lether

Thora'ic, a. belonging or relating to the breaft

Thóral, a. relating to the bed, relating to Venus

Thorn, n. a fmall and prickly tree, a difficult point

Thorn'back, n. a fifh with fpines on the back

Thorn'hedge, n. a hedge or fence of thorns

Thorn'y, a. full of thorns, prickly, difficult, hard

Thor'ough, [thurro] a. perfect, complete

Thor'oughfare, n. a paffage quite through a place

Thor'oughly, ad. completely, fully, truly (plete

Thor'oughpaced, Through'paced, a. perfect, com-

Thor'oughfped, a. finifhed in principles, perfect

Thor'oughftitch, ad. completely, fully, entirely

Thorp, n. a village, fmall country-town, name

Thos, n. an animal of the wolf kind

Thofe, pron. pl. of that (we fpeak

Thou, pron. the fecond perfon, the perfon to whom

Thou, v. t. to addrefs or treat with familiarity

Though, an old verb in the imperative mode, more correctly written tho; grant, admit, fuppofe

Thought, [thaut] pret. and pa. paff. of to think

Thought, n. the act of thinking, an idea, fentiment, opinion, purpofe, view, expectation, care

Thought'ful, a. contemplative, anxious, careful

Thought'fully, ad. with thoughtfulnefs, with care

Thought'fulnefs, n. meditation, carefulnefs

Thought'lefs, a. carelefs, giddy, airy, dull, ftupid

Thought'lefsly, ad. without thought, carelefsly

Thought'lefsnefs, n. a want of thought or care

Thou'ghtfick, a. uneafy with or from reflection

Thous'and, n. and a. ten hundred, a great many

Thrácian, n. a native of Thrace, now in Turkey

Thrácian, a. pertaining to Thrace

Thral'dom, n. flavery, fervitude, bondage, trouble

Thrall, n. bondage, a flave; v. t. to enflave

Thrafh, v. to beat grain, heat, drub, toil

Thrafh'er, n. one who thrafhes, a kind of fifh

Thrafh'ingfloor, n. a place ufed to beat grain on

Thrafon'ical, a. boafting, bragging, bluftering, big

Thread or Thred, n. a fmall twift, uniform tenor

Thread, v. t. to put in or upon a thread, fix, pierce

Thread'bare, a. worn out, fhabby, mean, hackneyd

Thread'en, a. made of or refembling thread

Threat or Thret, n. a menace, a denunciation of ill

Threat'en, v. t. to menace, to denounce some evil

Threat'ener, n. one who threatens or denounces

Threat'eningly, ad. in a threatening manner

Threat'ful, a. full of threats, minacious, angry

Three, a. two and one

Three'cornered, a. having three corners

Three'fold, a. thrice repeated, consisting of three

Three'pence, n. a penny thrice told, a silver coin

Three'penny, a. worth only threepence, mean, low

Three'pile, n. a very strong kind of velvet, ob.

Three'piled, a. heaped up, set thick, very strong

Three'score, a. twenty repeated thrice, sixty

Thresh'old, n. a step, gate, door, entrance, begin-

Threw, pret. of to throw (ning

Thrice, ad. three times over, at three times, very

Thril, v. t. to slide through a narrow passage

Thrift, n. frugality, prudence, care, profit, a plant

Thrift'ily, ad. frugally, sparingly, carefully

Thrift'iness, n. frugality, good husbandry, thrift

Thrift'less, a. profuse, lavish, extravagant, wild

Thrift'y, a. frugal, sparing, careful, thriving

Thrill, v. to pierce, bore, penetrate, tingle, sun

Thrill, n. a thrilling, a warbling, a kind of tool

Thrivsa, n. a fish of the herring kind

Thrive, v. i. thrived, throve, pret. thriven, pa. to profper, succeed, grow rich or fat

Thriver, n. one who thrives, one who grows rich

Thrivingly, ad. in a thriving or profperous way

Throat, n. the forepart of the neck, the windpipe, the part of a gaff next the maft

Throb, v. i. to heave, to beat ; n. a heave, a beat

Throe, n. the pain of childbearing, pain, agony

Throe, v. i. to put in agonies, pain, shoot, beat

Throne, n. the feat of kings, princes or bishops

Throne, v. to enthrone, fet on a throne, exalt

Throng, n. a crowd, multitude, prefs of people

Throng, v. to crowd, to incommode with crowds

Throng'ing, n. the act of crowding together

Thros'tle, n. a small singing bird, the thrush

Throt'tle, n. the windpipe, the throat

Throt'tle, v. t. to take by the throat, choke, kill

Throve, pret. of to thrive

Through, pr. from end to end, by means of, by

Throughlighted, a. lighted on both sides, ob.

Throughly, ad. completely, fully, sincerely, ob.

Throughout', pr. quite or completely through

Throughout', ad. every where, in every part, fully

Throw, v. t. threw, pret. thrown, pa. to fling, caft, tofs, drive, turn, twift, reject, repofe

Throw, n. a caft, stroke, hit, fall, effort, fally, fpace

Thrower, n. one who throws or cafts, a throwfter

Throwfter, n. one who twifts filk, thread, &c.

Thrum, n. the ends of a weaver's threads, bad yarn

Thrum, v. i. to play badly on an inftrument, to infert thrums or fmall cords

Thrush, n. a fine finging bird, a diforder

Thruft, v. thruft, pret. thruft, pa. to push, shove, ftab, compel, intrude

Thruft, n. a shove, hoftile attack, affault, thirft

Thruft'er, n. one who thrufts, one who attacks

Thry'fallow, v. t. to plow a third time in fummer

Thumb, more correctly thum, n. the fhort and ftrong finger of the hand

Thum, v. t. to handle aukwardly or very much

Thum'band, n. a band as thick as a man's thum

Thum'ftal, n. a cap for the forefinger, a thimble

Thum'erftone, n. a filiceous ftone of a brown color

Thump, v. to beat or fall with a dull heavy blow

Thump, n. a heavy blow or knock, a hard ftroke

Thump'er, n. one who thumps, a large thing

Thump'ing, pa. a. beating, knocking, large, big

Thun'der, n. a loud noife made in the clouds

Thun'der, v. to make thunder, emit with noife,

Thun'derbolt, n. lightning, fulmination (denounce

Thun'derclap, n. a clap or explofion of thunder

Thun'derer, n. the power that produces thunder

Thun'dering, a. loud, noify, terrible, threatning

Thun'derous, a. producing or caufing thunder

Thun'derfhower, n. rain attended with thunder

Thun'derftone, n. a ftone difcharged by thunder

Thun'derftrike, v. t. thunderftruck, pret. thunderftruck, pa. to ftrike or blaft with lightning, to confound

Thurif'erous, a. producing frankincenfe

Thurification, n. the act of fuming with incenfe

Thurs'day, n. the fifth day of the week

Thus, ad. fo, in this manner, to this degree

Thwack, v. t. to bang, beat, ftrike hard, thrafh

Thwack, n. a bang, hard blow, heavy ftroke

Thwart, a. tranfverfe, crofs, perverfe, mifchievous

Thwart, v. to crofs, traverfe, oppofe, interfere

Thwart'ingly, ad. with oppofition, crofsly, acrofs

Thy, pron. relating to thee, or belonging to thee

Thyme, n. the name of a fragrant herb

Thy'my, a. abounding with thyme, fragrant

Thyfelf', pron. recip. belonging to thee only

Tiar or Tiara, n. a diadem, cap, headdrefs, crown

Tib'etan, a. pertaining to Tibet in Afia

Tib'ial, a. relating to a pipe or the fhin-bone

Tib'uro, n. a fish of the fhark kind

Tice, v. t. to allure, draw over, entice, ob.

Tick, n. a fcore, account, dogloufe, noife, ticken

Tick, v. i. to run a fcore, truft, ftrike, beat

Tick'en, Tick'ing, n. a ftrong cloth for bedcafes

Tick'et, n. a token of right on the delivery of which admiffion is granted, fign, mark, note

Tick'et, v. t. to mark by, put on or affix a ticket

Tic'kle, v. t. to affect with pleafure, pleafe, move

Tic'kle, a. wavering, tottering, unfteady, unftable

Tick'lifh, a. eafily tickled, uncertain, critical

Tick'lifhnefs, n. a ticklifh ftate or quality

Tick'tack, n. a game at tables, a fmall low noife

Tid, a. tender, foft, delicate, nice, delicious, ob.

Tid'dle, v. t. to ufe or do tenderly, fondle, trifle

Tide, n. a flux and reflux of the fea, ftream, flood

Tide, v. to drive with the ftream, tofs, flow out

Tidewaiter, n. a cuftomhoufe-officer

Tidily, ad. neatly, cleanly, decently, readily, well

Tidinefs, *n.* neatnefs, cleanlinefs, readinefs, fkill

Tidings, *n. pl.* news, intelligence, account, notice

Tidy, *a.* neat, cleanly, ready, feafonable, timely

Tie, *v. t.* to bind, faften, hold, hinder, reftrain

Tie, *v.* an obligation, bond, reftraint, knot, rope

Tier, *n.* a row or rank of guns in a fhip, a fet, row of the fame altitude

Tierce, *n.* a third part of a pipe, fequence of three cards, hour, thruft in fencing

Tiff, *n.* liquor, drink, a pet, quarrel, difpute

Tiff, *v. i.* to be in a pet, quarrel, differ, difpute

Tiffany, *n.* a very thin kind of filk   (pacious

Tiger, *n.* an animal of the feline kind, very ra-

Tigerfooted, *a.* haftening to devour, furious, mad

Tight, *a.* tenfe, clofe, difficult, cleanly dreffed, tidy

Tighten, *v. t.* to make tight or clofe, to ftraiten

Tighter, *n.* a ftring to tie women's hair with

Tightifh, *a.* rather tight, neat, pretty well

Tightly, *ad.* clofely, narrowly, neatly, tidily

Tightnefs, *n.* clofenefs, compactnefs, difficulty

Tigrefs, *n.* a wild beaft, female tiger, fury

Tike, *n.* a clown, bullock, heifer, infect, dog's name

Tile, *n.* a plate of burnt clay to cover houfes with

Tile, *v. t.* to cover or fecure with tiles, to guard

Tiler, *n.* one who tiles, a freemafon's porter

Tiling, *n.* the act of laying tiles, a roof covered with

Till, *n.* a money-box in a fhop, a fhelf   (tiles

Till, *conj.* until, to the time or degree; *pr.* unto

Till, *v. t.* to cultivate, plow, dig, turn up, fow

Tillable, *a.* that may be tilled or cultivated

Tillage, *n.* the act or art of tilling land, culture

Tiller, *n.* a plowman, handle of a rudder, till

Tiller, *v. i.* to put forth fhoots or cions

Tilling, *n.* the act of cultivating land, culture

Tillyvalley, *a.* trifling, impertinent, filly, foolifh

Tilman, *n.* a man who tills land, a hufbandman

Tilt, *n.* a cover of a boat, military game, thruft

Tilt, *v.* to cover, turn up, incline, fall, thruft

Tilted, *pa.* ftooping forward, inclined, raifed

Tilter, *n.* one who tilts, one who thrufts or fights

Tilth, *n.* culture, hufbandry; *a.* tilled, cultivated

Timber, *n.* wood fit to build with, a main beam

Timber, *v.* to furnifh with timber, light, perch

Timbered, *pa.* having timber, built, formed

Timberhead, *n.* the top of a fhips timber above the gunnel

Timberfaw, *n.* a kind of worm that breeds in wood

Timberyard, *n.* a place where timber is kept

Timbrel, *n.* a kind of mufical inftrument, a drum

Time, *n.* the meafure of duration, an age, a feafon

Time, *v. t.* to meafure, regulate, fuit, adapt, fit

Timeful, *a.* timely, early, feafonable, proper

Timekeeper, *n.* a clock or watch

Timelefs, *a.* untimely, unfeafonable, improper

Timelefsly, *ad.* unfeafonably, improperly, badly

Timely, *ad.* betimes, early, foon, feafonably

Timely, Timous, *a.* early enough, feafonable

Timepiece, *n.* a clock or watch

Timepleafer, *n.* one who complies fervilely

Timeferver, *n.* a timepleafer, changeling, turncoat

Timeferving, *a.* meanly complying with power

Timid, *a.* timorous, fearful, deftitute of courage

Timidity, *n.* fearfulnefs, habitual cowardice

Timorous, *a.* fearful, bafhful, fcrupulous, nice

Timoroufly, *ad.* with fear or caution, fcrupuloufly

Timoroufnefs, *n.* fearfulnefs, timidity, caution

Tin, *n.* a whitifh gray metal, very malleable and

Tin, *v. t.* to cover with tin   (flexible

Tincal or Tincar, *n.* crude or impure borax

Tinfoil, *n.* tin beat into thin plates

Tinct, *v. t.* to color, die, ftain, imbue, tincture

Tinct, *n.* a color, die, ftain, fpot, tincture

Tincture, *n.* a color, infufion, extract from drugs

Tincture, *v. t.* to tinge, color, die, imbue, infect

Tinder, *n.* burnt linen, what eafily catches fire

Tine, *n.* the tooth of a harrow, a prong, diftrefs

Tine, *v. t.* to kindle, fet on fire. *ob.*

Tineman, *n.* a night-officer of a foreft

Tinge, *v. t.* to impregnate or imbue with color

Tinge, *n.* a color, die, ftain, fmatch, tafte

Tingent, *a.* able to tinge or color

Tingle, *v. i.* to feel a fharp pain, fhoot, tinkle

Tink, *v. i.* to make a fharp or fhrill found, to tin-

Tinker, *n.* a mender of kettles or pans   (kle

Tinkle, *v. i.* to found, make a noife, clink, tink

Tinkling, *n.* a found, fharp and quick noife, clink

Tinman, *n.* one who manufactures or deals in tin

Tinmine, Tinwork, *n.* a place that produces tin

Tinner, *n.* one who works in the tinmines

Tinfel, *n.* lace refembling a falfe lufter

Tinfel, *v. t.* to adorn with cheap ornaments

Tint, *n.* a color, die, ftain, dafh, tincture   (der

Tiny, [teeny] *a.* diminutive, puny, little, fmall, tien-

Tip, *n.* a top, end, extremity, point, tap, ftroke

Tip, *v.* to top, end, cover on the end, point, tap

Tip, *v. t.* to lower on one end as a cart

Tippet, *n.* a kind of covering for a woman's neck

Tipple, *n.* drink, liquor; *v. i.* to drink to excefs

Tippled, *pa. a.* fuddled, muddled, drunk, tipfy

Tippler, *n.* a drinker, drunkard, toper, fot

Tipftaff, *n.* an officer, kind of conftable, ftaff

Tipfy, *a.* almoft drunk or fuddled, merry, drunk

Tiptoe, *n.* the end of the toes, a very filent gait

Tire, *n.* a rank, row, headdrefs, furniture, band

Tire, *v.* to fatigue or be fatigued, harafs, drefs

Tirednefs, *n.* a tired ftate, wearinefs, fatigue

Tirefome, *a.* wearifome, troublefome, tedious

Tirefomenefs, *n.* wearifomenefs, tedioufnefs, flow-

Tirewoman, *n.* one who makes headdreffes (nefs

Tiringroom, *n.* a room ufed by players to drefs in

'Tis, a contraction of *it is*   (and of Oct.

Tifri, *n.* a Jewifh month anfwering to part of Sept.

Tiffue, *v. t.* to interweave, variegate, adorn

Tiffue, *n.* cloth or filk wrought with gold or filver

Tit, *n.* a fmall horfe, woman, little bird

Titanic, Titanian, *a.* relating to the Titans, gi-

    ants or children of Anac   (red color

Titanite, *n.* a new difcovered foffil of a brownifh

Titanit'ic, a. pertaining to titanite
Tit'bit, n. a delicate bit, delicacy, very nice food
Tithable or Titheable, a. subject to pay tithes
Tithe, n. the tenth part of any thing, a portion
Tithe, v. to pay or take the tenth part, to tax
Tithegatherer, n. one used to collect tithes
Tither, n. one who gathers or sets out tithes
Tithing. n. a part of a parish, district, tithe
Tithingman, n. a parish officer, an officer to keep order in church
Tit'illate, v. i. to tickle, move, please very much
Titillation, n. the act of tickling, great pleasure
Tit'lark, n. a musical bird, the meddow lark
Title, n. an appellation, name of honor, claim of right, general head of particulars, first page
Title, v. t. to name, call, entitle, honor, adorn
Titleless, a. wanting a title or name, common
Titlepage, n. the page containing the title of a
Tit'mouse, n. a genus of small birds   (book
Tit'ter, v. i. to laugh secretly, to giggle
Tit'ter, Tit'tering, n. restrained laughter, a weed
Tit'terer, n. one who titters, one who giggles
Tit'tle, n. a point, dot, small particle
Tit'tletattle, n. idle talk, prattle, a gossip
Tit'tletattle, v. i. to prate or talk idly, to report
Tit'ular or Tit'ulary, a. honorary, nominal
Tit'ularly, ad. in title only, nominally
Tit'ulary, n. one who has a title or right
Tiv'y, ad. tantivy, with great haste or speed, ob.
To, ad. and pr. unto, towards, forward, at, with
Toad, n. a quadruped with a broad body and short legs of several species, living in grass, water, or on trees   (than its body
Toadfish, n. the fishing frog, whose head is bigger
Toadflax, n. a plant, a species of snap-dragon
Toadstone, n. a genus of earth of a brownish gray color
Toadstool, n. a soft fungous plant like a mushroom
Toast, v. t. to heat at a fire, to name a health
Toast, n. bread toasted, a health proposed, a lady
Toaster, n. one who toasts, a utensil to toast with
Tobac'co, n. a plant much used for smoaking, &c.
Tobac'conist, n. a dealer in or seller of tobacco
Toc'sin, n. a bell to give alarm
Tod, n. a bush, thick shrub, fox, weight of 28lb.
Tod'dy, n. a mixture of spirit and water sweetened, the juice of the coco
Tody, n. a genus of American birds
Toe, n. one of the divided extremities of the foot
Tockáy, n. a beautiful species of lizard
Tofore, ad. before, heretofore, formerly, ob.
Toft, n. a place where a message has once stood
Togated, Toged, a. dressed in or wearing a gown
Together, ad. in company, in concert, at once
Toil, v. to drudge, work, labor, be weary with labor
Toil, n. hard labor, labor, fatigue, a net, a snare
Toil'et, n. a dressing-table, a cloth upon a table
Toil'some, a. laborious, wearisome, fatiguing, dull
Toil'somely, ad. in a hard laborious manner

Toil'someness, n. laboriousness, trouble, fatigue
Toise, n. a French measure of 6 French feet
Tokay, n. wine made at Tokay in Hungary
Token, n. a sign, note, mark, evidence, memorial
Token, v. to betoken, denote, show, make known
Told, pa. related, mentioned, said, made known
Tole, v. t. to train up, to draw on by slow degrees
Tol'erable, a. supportable, passable, not very bad
Tol'erableness, n. a tolerable state or quality
Tol'erably, ad. moderately well, not very badly
Tol'erance, n. the act or power of enduring
Tol'erate, v. to allow, permit, endure, suffer, bear
Toleration, n. allowance, permission, sufferance
Toll, n. an excise upon goods, fee, found of a bell
Toll, v. to pay toll, exact, ring a bell, take away
Tollbooth, n. a market or town house, prison, jail
Toll'gatherer, n. one who gathers or takes toll
Tolutation, n. the act of pacing or ambling
Tolú, n. a tree which yields a balsam
Tom'ahawk, n. an instrument, an Indian hatchet
Tom'ahawk, v. t. to cut or kill with a tomahawk
Tomáto, n. the love apple, a species of solanum
Tomb, [toom] n. a repository or monument for the dead
Tomb'less, a. wanting a tomb, unburied, exposed
Tomb'boy, n. a wild romping girl, a mean fellow
Tomb'stone, n. a stone laid over or near the dead
Tome, n. a book, volume, distinct volume
Tomentóse, a. downy, covered with down
Tam'pion, n. the stopper of a cannon
Tomtit', n. the name of a small bird, a titmouse
Ton, see Tun
Tone, n. a note, sound, accent, whine, cry, state
Toneless, a. having no tone or sound, unmusical
Tong, n. the catch or fastening of a buckle
Tongs, n. pl. an instrument to hold fire, &c. with
Tongue, or more correctly tung, n. an organ of speech, language, point, what projects out
Tongue, v. to chide, scold, rate, talk, prate
Ton'gued, pa. a. having a tongue, scolded, rated
Tongue'less, a. wanting a tongue, speechless, un-
Tongue'pad, n. a great talker, a prater   (named
Tongue'tied, a. having a lisping or bad speech
Ton'ic, a. of or relating to sounds, extended, elastic
Ton'ic, n. a medicin to increase strength
Ton'nage, see Tunnage
Tonquinése, n. a native of Tonquin
Tonquinése, a. pertaining to Tonquin
Ton'sil, n. a gland in the throat, called almond
Tons'ure, n. the act of clipping or shaving hair
Tontine', n. a raising of money on or by annuities
Too, ad. over and above, likewise, also, besides
Took, pret. of to take   (wretch
Tool, n. an instrument, hireling, mean person,
Tool, v. t. to shape with a tool
Tooth, n. a small bone set in the mouth, a palate
Tooth, v. t. to indent, lock in each other, chew
Tooth'ach, n. a very gnawing pain in the teeth
Tooth'drawer, n. one who pulls out carious teeth

Tooth'ed, *pa.* having teeth, indented, fharp
Tooth'edge, *n.* the fenfation in the teeth made by grating
Tooth'lefs, *a.* deprived of or wanting teeth
Tooth'pick, *n.* an inftrument to clean teeth with
Tooth'fome, *a.* palata'ble, grateful, pleafant, nice
Top, *n.* the higheft part, a pinnacle, furface, toy
Top, *v.* to excel, cover, crop, fnuff, rife up, tip
Tóparch, [ch as k] *n.* the head man of a place
Tópaz, *n.* a precious ftone of a gold color
Tope, *b. i.* to drink to excefs, to drink very hard
Tope, *n.* a large vora^cious fifh
Tóper, *n.* a drunkard, hard drinker, mere fot
Tópet, *n.* a fmall bird, the crefted titmoufe
Top'ful, *a.* full to the very top or brim, quite full
Topgal'lant, *n.* the higheft fail, any thing elevated
Topháceous, *a.* gritty, fandy, ftony, rough, hard
Top'heavy, *a.* too heavy at the top, drunk, tipfy
Tóphet, *n.* hell, a place ufed for facrifices
Tóphi, *n.* duckften, a ftone formed by earth depofited from water; called alfo tufa or trafs
Top'ic, *n.* a general head of difcourfe, a plafter
Top'ical, *a.* local, limited, fixed, applied, general
Top'ically, *ad.* with application to fome one part
Tó; ing, *n.* the act or cuftom of drinking hard
Top'knot, *n.* a folded ribbon on a woman's head
Top'lefs, *a.* having no top, broken off or down
Top'man, *n.* a man placed in the top of a fhip
Top'moft, *a.* uppermoft, higheft, chiefeft, firft
Topog'rapher, *n.* a defcriber of particular places
Topographic, *a.* pertaining to local defcription
Topograph'ically, *ad.* by way of local defcription
Topog'raphy, *n.* a defcription of particular places
Top'ping, *a.* noble, fine, gallant, haughty
Top'pingly, *ad.* finely, bravely, very well, gaily
Top'ple, *v. i.* to tumble down, fall, fall forward
Top'proud, *a.* exceedingly proud, very haughty
Top'fail, *a.* a fail extended acrofs the topmaft by a yard above and below
Topfytur'vy, *ad.* with bottom upwards, invertedly
Torch, *n.* a large waxlight, flambeau, link, ftaff
Torch'bearer, *n.* one who bears or carries a torch
Torch'er, *n.* one who gives light by torches, the fun
Torch'light, *n.* a light made with torches
Tore, *n.* an after growth of grafs, which perifhes in winter, a molding
Tor'ment, *n.* torture, anguifh, great pain, mifery
Torment', *v. t.* to put to pain, torture, teafe, vex
Torment'er, *n.* one who torments, one who teafes
Tor'mentil, *n.* a genus of plants, feptfoil
Tornádo, *n.* a hurricane, whirlwind, fquall, ftorm
Torófe, *a.* bunching out, protuberant
Torpédo, *n.* the cramp-fifh or electric ray, whofe touch gives an electrical fhock
Tor'pent, *a.* benumbed, dull, inactive (tion
Tor'pent, *n.* that which diminifhes irritative exer-
Torpes'cent, Tor'pid, *a.* benumbed, inactive
Tor'pidnefs, Tor'pitude, *n.* a fluggifh or dull ftate
Tor'por, *n.* numbnefs, dulnefs, inactivity, lazinefs

Torporif'ic, *a.* tending to produce torpor
Torrefac'tion, *n.* the act of fcorching or roafting
Tor'refy, *v. t.* to fcorch, parch, dry, roaft
Tor'rent, *n.* a fudden or very rapid ftream, a crowd
Tor'rent, *a.* rolling in a very rapid ftream
Torricel'lian, *a.* denoting what relates to Torricelli, a philofopher who demonftrated the preffure of the atmofphere
Tor'rid, *a.* burning, hot, fcorched, parched, dried
Torrid'ity, Tor'ridnefs, *n.* a parched or hot ftate
Tor'fel, *n.* any thing in a twifted form, a fupport
Tor'fion, Tor'tion, *n.* a wreathed ftate, torment
Ters'ten, *n.* an iron ore of bright bluifh black, &c.
Tórt, *n.* hurt, mifchief, injury, wrong, calamity
Tor'tile, Tor'tive, *a.* twifted, twined, wreathed
Tor'toife, *n.* a genus of amphibious reptiles, covered with a cruft, an old military defence
Tor'toifefhell, *n.* the fhell of a tortoife
Tortuos'ity, Tor'tuoufnefs, *n.* a wreathed ftate
Tor'tuous, *a.* twifted, wreathed, mifchievous
Tor'ture, *n.* torment, anguifh, pain, a punifhment
Tor'ture, *v. t.* to punifh by torture, diftrefs, vex
Tor'turer, *n.* one who tortures, one who torments
Tórus or Tore, *n.* a large round molding in building
Torv'ity, *n.* fournefs of afpect, fternnefs of look, *ob.*
Torv'ous, *a.* four of afpect, ftern, auftere, fevere, *ob.*
Tóry, *n.* an advocate for the ancient conftitution of the ftate and church of England, In Am. a royalift during the revolution
Tóryifm, *n.* the principles of a tory
Tofs, *v.* to fling, caft, agitate, keep in play, wince
Tofs, *n.* an affected caft of the head, throw, pet
Tofs'er, *n.* one who flings or throws up
Tofs'pot, *n.* a toper, drunkard, great drinker
Tott, *pret.* and *pa.* of *to tofs* (the amount
Tótal, *a.* whole, complete, full; *n.* the whole,
Total'ity, *n.* a total ftate, the whole, the amount
Tótally, *ad.* wholly, fully, completely, utterly,
T'other, contraction of *the other* (entirely
Tote, *v. t.* to carry, convey, remove [*Virg. &c.*]
Tot'ter, *v. i.* to fhake, to be in danger of falling
Tot'tery, Tot'ty, *a.* fhaking, unfteady, dizzy
Touch, *v.* to join to, reach, feel, affect, move, mark out, cenfure, infect, try, ftrike, mend
Touch, *n.* the act of touching, the fenfe of feeling
Touch'hole, *n.* a hole to difcharge firearms by
Touch'inefs, *n.* peevifhnefs, irafcibility, croffnefs
Touch'ing, *pa. a.* affecting; *pz.* with refpect to
Touch'ingly, *ad.* feelingly, affectingly, movingly
Touch'needle, *n.* a fmall bar of gold, filver and copper combined, to try the purity of metals by marking
Touch'ftone, *n.* a ftone to try metals by, teft, trial
Touch'wood, *n.* rotten wood that foon takes fire
Touch'y, *a.* foon provoked, peevifh, crofs, ftrange
Tough, [tuff] *a.* not brittle, ftiff, ftrong, clammy
Tough'en, *v* to grow or make tough, to harden
Tough'ly, *ad.* in a tough manner, with toughnefs
Tough'nefs, *n.* firmnefs, tenacity, clamminefs

Toupée, Toupet', *n.* an artificial lock of hair
Tour or Toor, *n.* a roving journey, ramble, turn
Tour'ist, *n.* a maker of tours, a writer of tours
Tour'malin or Tur'malin, *n.* a species of siliceous stone remarkable for its electrical properties
Tourn'ament, *n.* a tilt, military sport, encounter
Tourn'iquet, *n.* a kind of bandage, a turnstile
Touse, *v. t.* to pull, haul, drag, tear, rend, tose
Tow, *n.* the coarse and broken parts of flax and hemp separated by a hatchel
Tow, *v. t.* to draw forward by means of a rope
Tow'ard, Tow'ardly, *a.* ready to do, forward, apt
Tow'ardliness, Tow'ardness, *n.* tractableness
Tow'ards, *ad.* and *pr.* in a direction to, nearly
Tow'el, *n.* a cloth to wipe the hands, &c. on
Tow'er, *n.* a high building, citadel, high headdress
Tow'er, *v. i.* to soar, mount, ascend, rise high
Tow'ered, *a.* adorned with or guarded by towers
Tow'ery, *a.* guarded with or having towers (pinion
Towheé, *n.* a species of the bunting, the black
Tow'line, Tow'rope, *n.* a rope to tow with
Town, *n.* a collection of houses, a district of certain limits, the inhabitants or the legal voters of a town (has charge of the records, &c.
Town'clerk', *n.* a register or officer of a town who
Town'house, *n.* a house for town business, a hall
Town'ship, *n.* the territory or land of a town
Towns'man, *n.* a man who is of the same town
Town'talk, *n.* the common discourse of a place
Toy, *n.* a trifle, plaything, play, folly, odd fancy
Toy, *v. i.* to dally amorously, play, sport, trifle
Toy'ish, *a.* wanton, loose, trifling, simple, foolish
Toy'ishness, *n.* wantonness, a trifling behavior
Toy'shop, *n.* a shop or place where toys are sold
Trace, *v. t.* to follow, mark out, draw, walk over
Trace, *n.* a mark, sign, token, footstep, remains
Tracer, *n.* one who traces, one who marks out
Traces, *n. pl.* the straps of a harness for drawing
Trachot'omy, [ch as k] *n.* a cutting of the wind-
Track, *n.* a beaten path, road, rut, mark left (pipe
Track *v. t.* to follow by marks left, to draw
Track'ingscout, *n.* a vessel drawn by a rope
Track'less, *a.* not marked out, untrodden, desert
Tract, *n.* a region, course, extent, treatise, book
Tract'able, *a.* manageable, governable, palpable
Tractability, *n.* the quality of being docile
Tract'ableness, *n.* a tractable quality, compliance
Tract'ably, *ad.* with ready compliance, gently
Tract'ate, *n.* a tract, treatise, essay, small book
Tract'ile, *a.* that may be drawn out, pliant, soft
Tractility, *n.* the quality of being drawn out
Trac'tion, *n.* the act of drawing, a being drawn
Trade, *n.* commerce, business, employment, art, men of the same occupation
Trade, *v.* to buy, sell, deal, traffic, act for money
Traded, *pa.* versed, practiced, accustomed
Trader, *n.* one who trades, a trading vessel
Tradesfolk, *n. pl.* people employed in trade
Tradesman, *n.* a shop keeper in Eng. but in Am.

more generally a mechanic
Tradewind, *n.* a wind which blows the whole year from the same point or a periodical wind, a monsoon
Trading, *n.* the act of carrying on trade
Tradi''tion, *n.* an oral or verbal account of things
Tradi''tional, *a.* delivered down by tradition, oral
Tradi''tionally, *ad.* by transmission from age to age
Tradi''tionary, *a.* delivered by tradition
Tradi''tionary, *n.* one who adheres to traditions
Trad'itive, *a.* that may be handed from age to age
Traduce, *v. t.* to censure, defame, misrepresent
Traducement, *n.* false censure, slander, scandal
Tradúcent, *a.* traducing, slandering, censuring
Tradúcer, *n.* one who traduces, one who slanders
Tradúcible, *a.* that may be traduced or derived
Tradúcingly, *ad.* slanderously, slightingly
Traduc'tion, *n.* derivation, propagation, tradition
Traf'fick, *n.* trade, commerce, commodities, wares
Traf'fick, *v. i.* to trade, deal, practice commerce
Traf'ficker, *n.* one who trades, a trader, a dealer
Trag'acanth, *n.* goats thorn, a plant and its gum
Tragédian, *n.* a composer or actor of tragedies
Trag'edy, *n.* a serious drama, a mournful event
Tra''gic, *a.* pertaining to tragedy
Tra''gical, *a.* mournful, calamitous, sad
Tra''gically, *ad.* in a tragical manner, heavily
Tra''gicalness, *n.* mournfulness, sadness, misery
Tragicom'edy, *n.* a merry and serious drama
Tragicom'ical, *a.* consisting of mirth and sorrow
Tragicom'ically, *ad.* in a tragicomical manner
Traject, *v. t.* to cast through, throw, convey over, *ob.*
Tra''ject, *n.* a ferry, a passage or conveyance over, *ob.*
Trajec'tion, *n.* emission, the act of darting through
Traject'ory, *n.* a curve line described by a comet
Trail, *v.* to drag, to draw or be drawn along
Trail, *n.* any thing drawn behind or to a length, a track of a hunter, scent left, board, arbor
Train, *v. t.* to form, breed, draw, entice, bring up
Train, *n.* the tail of a bird or a gown, a retinue, great number, procession, line, way
Trainband', *n.* a trained band, the militia
Train'bearer, *n.* one who bears or holds up a train
Train'oil, *n.* oil drawn from the fat of whales
Train'y, *a.* belonging to trainoil, greasy, fat, nasty
Traipse, *v. i.* to walk in a sluttish manner, to go
Trait, *n.* a stroke, touch, line, outline, sketch
Tráitor, *n.* a person who betrays his trust
Tráitorly, Tráitorous, *a.* trecherous, deceitful
Tráitorously, *ad.* trecherously, falsely, basely
Tráitress, *n.* a trecherous or very false woman
Tralati''tious, *a.* not literal, metaphorical, *ob.*
Tralati''tiously, *ad.* metaphorically, figuratively, *ob.*
Tralin'eate, *v.* to turn aside or from, to deviate, *ob.*
Tram'mel, *v.* to shackle, catch, take, intercept
Tram'mel, *n.* shackles for a horse, a long net
Tramontáne, *a.* beyond or over the mountain
Tram'ple, *v. t.* to tread upon, underfoot or quickly
Tramp'ler, *n.* one who treads down or underfoot

Trance, *n.* a vifion, ecftacy, rapture, joy
Tran"ced, *a.* lying in a trance, enraptured
Tran"gram, *n.* an odd intricate thing, trifle, *ob.*
Tian"quil, *a.* peaceful, undifturbed, quiet, calm
Tranquil'lity, *n.* peace of mind, quiet, calmnefs
Tran"quillize, *v. t.* to quiet, calm, harmonize
Tranfact', *v. t.* to manage, negotiate, perform, do
Tranfac'tion, *n.* a management, negotiation, act
Tranfact'or, *n.* one who tranfacts or manages
Tranfalleganean, *a.* beyond the Allegany mountain
Tranfalp'ine, *a.* fituated beyond the Alps with regard to Rofne, that is, on the north or weft of the Alps
Tranfanimation, *n.* a changing of the foul
Tranfatlan'tic, *a.* beyond the Atlantic Ocean
Tranfcend', *v.* to furpafs, excel, go beyond, climb
Tranfcend'ence or Tranfcend'ency, *n.* excellence
Tranfcend'ent, *a.* furpafing, very excellent
Tranfcendent'al, *a.* furpafing, noting quantities which cannot be expreffed or fixed to any equation, and are indeterminate
Tranfcend'ently, *ad.* eminently, excellently
Trans'colate, *v. t.* to ftrain through a fieve
Tranfcrfbe, *v. t.* to copy, to write from or over
Tranfcrfber, *n.* one who writes from a copy, a copy
Tran'fcript, *n.* a copy from an original (pier
Tranfcript'ively, *ad.* in the manner of or by a copy
Tranfcur', *v. i.* to run to and fro, rove, *ob.*
Tranfcur'fion, *n.* a pafing beyond limits, a ramble
Tranfduc'tion, *n.* the act of conveying over
Tranfelementation, *n.* a change of elements, *ob.*
Tranfex'ion, *n.* a change of fex or nature, *ob.*
Transfer', *v. t.* to make over, remove, tranfport
Trans'fer, *n.* the act of making over to another
Transfer'rable, *a.* that may or can be transferred
Transferreé, *n.* he to whom a transfer is made
Transfiguration, *n.* a change of form, a change
Transfig'ure, *v. t.* to transform, to change the
Transfix', *v. t.* to pierce through, to kill (fhape
Transform', *v.* to change the fhape, to be changed
Transformation, *n.* a change of form or ftate
Transfretation, *n.* a paffage made over a fea, *ob.*
Transfufe, *v. t.* to pour into another, to change
Transfufion, *n.* the act of pouring into another
Tranfgrefs', *v.* to violate, break, offend, go beyond
Tranfgref'fion, *n.* a violation, offenfe, fin, crime
Tranfgref'five, *a.* apt to break laws, guilty
Tranfgref'for, *n.* a lawbreaker, offender, finner
Tranfhip', *v. t.* to carry from one fhip to another
Tranfhip'ment, *n.* the act of transferring from one fhip to another
Tran"fient, *a.* foon paft, very fhort, momentary
Tran"fiently, *ad.* with fhort paffage, flightly
Tranfil'ience, *n.* a leap from one thing to another
Trans'it, *n.* the paffage by or over of a planet
Tranfi'tion, *n.* a paffage, removal, change, leap
Trans'itive, *a.* having the power of pafing over
Trans'itorily, *ad.* with a fhort continuance
Trans'itory, *a.* continuing a fhort time, fleeting

Tranflate, *v. t.* to remove, turn, render, interpret
Tranflation, *n.* a removal, change, verfion
Tranflator, *n.* one who turns into another language
Trans'latory, *a.* transferring, changing, moving
Tranflocation, *n.* a mutual exchange of place
Tranflucency, *n.* tranfparency, great clearnefs
Tranflucent, Tranflucid, *a.* tranfparent, very clear
Tranfmarine', *a.* lying or found beyond fea, foreign
Tranfmew, *v. t.* to transform, change, alter, *ob.*
Tranfmi'grant, *a.* removing from place to place
Trans'migrate, *v. i.* to pafs from place to place, or from one body or form to another
Tranfmigration, *n.* a paffage from place to place, or from one form or body to another
Tranfmis'fible, *a.* that may be tranfmitted
Tranfmis'fion, *n.* the act of tranfmitting
Tranfmis'five, *a.* tranfmitted, fent, derived
Tranfmit', *v. t.* to fend from one place to another
Tranfmit'tal, *n.* a tranfmiffion, a conveyance
Tranfmutable, *a.* capable of being changed
Tranfmutation, *n.* change into another fubftance
Tranfmute, *v. t.* to change to another fubftance
Tranfmuter, *n.* one who tranfmutes or changes
Trans'om, *n.* a lintel over a doorcafe, a beam acrofs the ftern poft of a fhip, or acrofs a window, vane of a crofs-ftaff (clearnefs
Tranfparency, *n.* the power of tranfmitting light,
Tranfparent, Tranfpic'uous, *a.* that may be feen through, clear, pellucid
Tranfpierce', *v. t.* to penetrate, go through, pafs
Tranfpiration, *n.* an emiffion in or by vapor
Tranfpire, *v.* to emit in vapor, to become known
Tranfplace, *v. t.* to remove to fome other place
Tranfplant', *v. t.* to plant in another place (ance
Tranfplantation, *n.* the act of removing, convey-
Tranfplant'er, *n.* one who tranfplants or removes
Trans'port, *n.* a criminal banifhed, ecftafy, rapture, delight, fhip to carry foldiers in, carriage
Tranfport', *v. t.* to banifh, to ravifh with pleafure, carry or convey
Tranfport'able, *a.* that may be tranfported
Tranfport'ance, *n.* a conveyance, removal, *ob.*
Tranfportation, *n.* banifhment, carriage, fury, rage
Tranfport'er, *n.* one who tranfports or removes
Tranfpofal, *n.* the act of difplacing, a changing of place or order
Tranfpofe, *v. t.* to difplace, to change places
Tranfpofi'tion, *n.* the act of difp'acing, a change
Transfhape, *v. t.* to change or vary the fhape, *ob.*
Tranfubftan'tiate, *v. t.* to change the fubftance
Tranfubftantiation, *n.* a change of fubftance
Tranfudation, *n.* the act of pafing out in fweat
Tranfude, *v. i.* to fweat or pafs through in fweat
Tranfump'tion, *n.* a taking from place to place
Tranfvec'tion, *n.* the act of conveying over
Tranfvers'al, *a.* running acrofs or over (tion-
Tranfvers'ally, Tranfverfe'ly, *ad.* in a crofs direc-
Trans'verfe, *a.* crofs, lying in a crofs direction
Trap, *n.* a fnare, ambufh, device, plaything, play,

a fpecies of argillaceous ftone or jafper

Trap, v. t. to infnare, catch, take, adorn, drefs

'Trap'door, n. a door made in a floor or roof

'Trapes, n. a flattern, idle nafty woman, traipfe

'Trapézium, n. a figure bounded by four unequal right lines   (trapezium

Trapéziform, Trapezoid'al, a. in the form of a

Trapezoid', n. a figure having two parallel fides, or an irregular figure having 4 fides not parallel

'Trap'pings, n. pl. ornaments, finery, drefs, attire

'Trappófe, a. like or pertaining to trap

'Trap'ftick, n. a boy's plaything, a very fmall leg

'Trafh, n. bad fruit, a worthlefs thing, drofs

'Trafh, v. t. to lop, crop, crufh, humble, ob.

'Trafh'y, a. vile, bad, worthlefs, ufelefs, trifling

'Trafs, n. a gray or yellowifh porous ftone

Traumat'ic, a. of, relating to, or good for wounds

'Trav'ail, v. to toil, labor, harafs, tire, bear a chit'd'

'Trav'ail, n. toil, work, labor, labor in childbirth

'Trav'el, v. i. to make a journey, pafs, toil

'Trav'el, n. a journey, labor; pl. account of journeys

Trav'eller, n. one who travels or goes journeys

Trav'eltainted, a. fatigued, wearied, haraffed, ob.

Trav'erfe, ad. and pr. athwart, croffwife, acrofs

Trav'erfe, a. lying acrofs; n. any thing fet acrofs

Trav'erfe, v. to crofs, fail acrofs, wander over, ufe a pofture of oppofition, turn, furvey, examin

Trav'erfable, a. that may be traverfed or denied

Trav'erfefailing, is failing in different directions

Trav'efty, a. burlefqued, ridiculed, ridiculous

Trav'efty, n. a burlefque tranflation

'Tray, n. a hollow trou gh of wood ; v. t. to betray

Tráytrip, n. a kind of play, game, fport, ob.

Treach'erous, more correctly Trech'erous, a. faithlefs, pérfidious. falfe, bafe

Treach'eroufly, ad. faith'efsly, perfidicufly, bafely

Treach'ery, n. perfidy, deceit, fraud, breach of faith

Tréacle, n. the fpume of fugar in refineries, a medicin   (path

Tread, more correctly Tred, n. a ftep with the foot,

Tread, v. trod, pret. trod, trodden, pa. to fet the foot, walk, beat, crufh, cover

Tread'er, n. one who treads, one who ftruts about

Trea'dle or Tred'dle, n. a part of a loom, the fperm of a cock

Tréafon, n. the higheft crime againft a ftate, including a violation of allegiance and an attempt to overthrow the government; it has different fenfes in different countries

Tréafonable, a. having the nature of treafon

Treas'ure, n. wealth laid up, a ftore, abundance

Treas'ure, v t. to lay up, hoard, provide a fupply

Treas'ury, n. a place where public money, or a company fund is kept   (or a company fund

Treas'urer, n. an officer who keeps public money,

Treas'urerfhip, n. the office of treafurer

Treat, v. to negotiate, fettle, entertain, difcourfe

Treat, n. an entertainment given, feaft, pleafure

Tréatable, a. not violent, calm, moderate, eafy

Tréatife, n. a difcourfe, written difcourfe, book

Tréatment, n. ufage, behavior, management

Tréaty, n. a negociation, contract, entreaty

Tre'ble, a. threefold ; n. a fharp found, note, bell

Tre'ble, v. to multiply by three, to make threefold

Tre'blenefs, n. a treble or threefold ftate   (fold

Treb'ly, ad. in a treble manner, thrice over

Tree, n. the largeft of plants, with a ligneous ftem and branches

Treen, n. pl. trees ; a. made of wood, wooden, ob.

Teénail, n. a wooden pin, fee Trunnel

Tréfoil, n. a plant with three leaves

Treil'lage, n. pales to fupport efpaliers by

Trel'lis, n. a lattice-work of iron or wood   (totter

Trem'ble, v. i. to fhake, quake, fhudder, quiver,

Trem'bling, n. a fhaking or quivering

Trem'blingly, ad. fo as to fhake with fear

Treme'rdous, a. awful, dreadful, horrible, vile

Tremea'doufly, ad. in a tremendous manner

Trem'olite, n. a fpecies of ftone from Mount Tremola in the Alps

Trémor, n. a fhaking or quivering motion, fear

Trem'ulous, a. trembling, fhaking, quivering

Trench, v. t. to make a trench, cut, divide, part

Trench, n. a ditch, cut, defenfe to cover foldiers

Trench'ant, a. cutting, fharp, keen, quick, ob.

Trench'er, n. a wooden plate to cut meat on

Trench'erfly, n. one who haunts tables, a parafite

Trench'erman, n. a great eater, glutton, devourer

Trench'ermate, n. a table-companion, a meffmate

Trend, v. i. to tend, to lie in a particular direction

Trent'al, n. thirty maffes in thirty days for the dead

Trepan', n. a furgeon's inftrument, trap, fnare

Trepan', v. t. to cut with a trepan, catch, entrap

Trepan'ner, n. one who trepans, one who entraps

Treph'ine, n. an inftrument, a fmall trepan

Trep'id, a. trembling, quaking, afraid, fearful

Trepidátion, n. a ftate of trembling and terror

Tres'pafs, v. to fin, offend, enter or go unlawfully

Tres'pafs, n. a fin, offenfe, fault, unlawful entry

Tres'paffer, n. one who trefpaffes or offends

Trefs'es, n. pl. long locks, knots or curls of hair

Tres'tle, n. a frame to fupport any thing on

Tret, n. an allowance in weight for wafte or refufe

Trev'et or Triv'et, n. a ftool with three legs

Trey, [tray] n. the three at cards or dice

Tri'able, a. capable of trial or legal examination

Tri'ad, n. the number three. three united, Trinity

Tri'al, n. a temptation, teft of virtue, experiment

Trian'dria, n. a clafs of plants having hermaphrodite flowers and three ftamens

Triangle, Trigon, n. a figure bounded by three lines and containing three angles

Trian'gular, Trig'onal, a. that has three angles

Tribe, n. a certain body of people, number, fet

Trib'let, n. a tool for making rings with

Tribom'eter, n. an inftrument to meafure friction

Trib'rach [ch as k] n. a poetic foot of three fhort fyllables

Tribulâtion, *n.* diſtreſs, uneaſineſs, care, vexation
Tribúnal, *n.* the ſeat of a judge, a court of juſtice
Trib'unary, *a.* pertaining to tribunes
Trib'unate, *n.* a branch of the legiſlature in France
Trib'une, *n.* a Roman officer civil and military
Trib'uneſhip, *n.* the office or ſtate of a tribune
Tribuni'tial, Tribuni'tious, *a.* ſuiting a tribune
Trib'utary, *a.* paying tribute, paid, ſubject, contributing, furniſhing a part
Trib'utary, *n.* one who pays tribute, tax, toll, &c.
Trib'ute, *n.* a tax impoſed on a conquered country by the victor or on a ſubject ſtate by treaty or compulſion
Trice, *n.* a very ſhort time, moment, inſtant, ſtroke
Tricap'ſular, *a.* having three capſules
Trichot'omous, [ch as k] *a.* divided into three parts
Trichot'omy, *n.* a diviſion into three equal parts
Trick, *n.* a cheat, fraud, artifice, juggle, habit
Trick, *v. t.* to cheat, deceive, dreſs, adorn, ſet off
Trick'er, Trick'ſter, *n.* one who tricks or cheats
Trick'ing, *n.* a cheating, dreſs, ornament, finery
Trick'iſh, *a.* knaviſhly artful or cunning, ſly
Tric''kle, *v. i.* to run, to fall or run down in drops
Trick'ſy, *a.* briſk, active, nimble, pretty, ſweet
Tricoc'cous, *a.* having three cells and grains
Tricus'pidate, Tricus'pid, *a.* ending in three points
Tride, *a.* ſhort, ſwift, fleet, quick, active, ready
Tride''cile, *n.* three tenths of a circle
Trident, *n.* a three forked ſcepter, a ſort of curve
Trident'ate, *a.* having three limbs or teeth
Triden'tine, *a.* pertaining to the Trent on the eaſtern Alps
Trien'nial, *a.* laſting or being every three years
Trier, *n.* one who tries or examins, a teſt
Trifallow, *v. t.* to plow land three times over
Trifárious, *a.* in three parts
T'rifid, *a.* ſplit or divided into three parts
Trifle, *v. i.* to act or ſpend fooliſhly, idle, mock
Trifle, *n.* a thing of little moment or value
Trifler, *n.* one who acts or talks fooliſhly, an idler
Trifling, *pa. a.* ſhuffling, wanting worth, mean
Trifling, *n.* employment about trifles, deceit
Triflingly, *ad.* without importance, meanly
Triflingneſs, *n.* giddineſs, ſimplicity, meanneſs
Triflorous, *a.* bearing three flowers
Triform, *a.* having a triple form or ſhape, triple
Trig, *v.* to ſtop or faſten a wheel, to ſet a mark
Trig'ger, Trick'er, *n.* the catch of a wheel or gun
Trig'la, *n.* a genus of fiſhes of the thoracic order
Triglyph, *n.* an ornament on the Doric freeze, with two channels and three legs
Trigonom'eter, *n.* an inſtrument to reſolve problems in dialling and trigonometry
Trigonomet'rical, *a.* relating to trigonometry
Trigonomet'rically *ad.* by trigonometry
Trigonom'etry, *n.* the art of meaſuring triangles
Trig'onous, Trig'onal, *a.* having three angles or
Trijúgous, *a.* having three pairs (corners
Trihêdron, *n.* a figure with three equal ſides

Trihêdral, *a.* having three equal ſides
Trilat'eral, *a.* having three ſides or three angles
Trill, *n.* a quaver; *v.* to quaver, ſhake, trickle
Trill'ion, *n.* a million of millions of millions
Tri'lobe, *a.* having three lobes
Triloc'ular, *a.* having three cells for ſeeds
Trim, *a.* nice, ſpruce, ſmug, neat, neatly dreſſed
Trim, *v.* to dreſs, deck, fit out, ſhave, balance a veſſel, temporize or fluctuate between two
Trim, *n.* dreſs, ornament, ſtate, condition
Trim'ly, *ad.* nicely, ſprucely, ſmugly, neatly, finely
Trim'mer, *n.* one who trims, a turncoat, a timber
Trim'ming, *n.* lace, &c. put on clothes, heſitation
Trinac'rian, *a.* pertaining to Sicily
Trine, *a.* belonging to the number three (grees
Trine, *n.* an aſpect of two planets diſtant 120 degrees
Trine, *v. t.* to put in a trine aſpect or a trigon
Tri'nerve, Tri'nerved, Trinerv'ate, *a.* having three nerves or unbranched veſſels
Trinitárian, *n.* one who believes in the Trinity
Trin'ity, *n.* three perſons united in one GODHEAD
Trink'et, *n.* a toy, thing of ſmall value, trifle
Trinômial, *a.* containing three terms or names
Tri'o, *n.* a concert of three parts, three
Triob'olar, *a.* mean, vile, worthleſs, common, *ob.*
Trioc'tile, *n.* three eighths of a circle
Trip, *v.* to ſtumble, miſtake, err, ſtrike up the feet, ſupplant, detect, go nimbly
Trip, *n.* a ſtumble, miſtake, error, ſhort voyage
Trip'artite, *a.* divided into three parts or ſhares
Tripe, *n.* a food, the paunch of an ox, &c. the belly
Tripet'alous, *a.* having three petals
Triph'yl'ous, *a.* having three leaves
Tr.pin'nate, *a.* having a triple ſeries of wings, having bipinnate leaves on each ſide
Tri''ple, *a.* treble, threefold, taken three times
Tri''ple, *v. t.* to treble, to make threefold
Trip'lenerve, *a.* having three nerves, each branching into three
Trip'let, *n.* three of a kind, three lines in poetry
Trip'licate, *a.* thrice as much, trebled, cubed
Triplicâtion, *n.* the act of trebling or cubing
Tripli'city, *n.* trebleneſs, a threefold ſtate
Tri'pod, Tripos, *n.* a ſeat or ſtool with three feet
Trip'oli, *n.* a city, a ſpecies of argillaceous earth
Trip'oline, *a.* pertaining to Tripoli in Africa
Trip'per, *n.* one who trips, one who walks nimbly
Trip'ping, *n.* a quick walking, a light dance
Trip'ping, *a.* ſupplanting, paſſing quickly, nimble
Trip'pingly, *ad.* faſt, quick'y, nimbly, with agility
Trip'thong, *n.* a union of three vowels
Trip'tote, *n.* a noun which has only three caſes
Triquêtrous, *a.* having three plain ſides
Trireme, *n.* a veſſel with three benches of oars
Triſec'tion, *n.* a diviſion into three equal parts
Triſperm'ous, *a.* bearing three ſeeds
Triſt'ful, *a.* ſad, heavy, gloomy, melancholy, *ob.*
Triſpaſt, Triſpaſt'ion, *n.* a machine with three pulTriſule, *n.* any thing having three points,

Trifyllable, *n.* a word containing three fyllables
Trifyllab'ic, *a.* pertaining to a trifyllable
Trite, *a.* common, old, ftale, threadbare, worn out
'Tritely, *ad.* in a trite manner, commonly, ftalely
Tritenefs, *n.* a trite ftate, great commonnefs
Tritern'ate, *a.* having three ternate leaflets, or the three divifions of a triple petiole divided into threes
Trithéifm, *n.* the worfhip or belief of three gods
Triton, *n.* a fea god, a trumpeter to Neptune, a beautiful fong bird of the W. Indies
Tritone, *n.* in mufic, falfe concord confifting of a greater third and a greater tone
'Trit'urable, *a.* that is poffible to be pounded
Trit'urate, *v.t.* to pound, bruife, reduce to powder
Trituration, *n.* a rubbing to powder, a thrafhing
Triturium, *n.* a veffel for feparating liquors of different denfities
Trfumph, *n.* joy or pomp for fuccefs, a conqueft
Triumph, *v. i.* to exult, glory, rejoice for victory
Triumph'al, *n.* a triumph, a token of victory
Triumph'al, *a.* ufed in celebrating victory, grand
Triumph'ant, *a.* celebrating a victory, victorious
Triumph'antly, *ad.* in a triumphant manner
Tri'umpher, *n.* one who triumphs, one who exults
Trfumvir, *n.* one of three men in the fame office
Trium'viral, *a.* pertaining to a triumvirate
Trium'virate, *n.* a government by three men
Trfune, *a.* three in one, three joined in one
Triv'ial, *a.* trifling, inconfiderable, worthlefs
Trivially, *ad.* triflingly, lightly, meanly, vulgarly
Triv'ialnefs, *n.* lightnefs, lownefs, commonnefs
Trivalv'ular, Trivalve, *a.* having three valves
Troat, *v. i.* to cry out, to cry like rutting bucks
Trócar, *n.* a furgical inftrument for dropfies
Trocháic, Trocháical, [ch as k] *a.* confifting of trochees (bone
Trochan'ter, [ch as k] *n.* a projection of the thigh
Trochée, *n.* a foot of a long and fhort fyllable
Tróchil, *n.* a hollow ring round a column next to the tore
Trochil'ics, *n. pl.* the fcience of rotary motion, *ob.*
Tróchifh, Tróchifk, *n.* a kind of medical lozenge, *ob.*
Trochoid, *n.* another name for the cycloid
Troch'leary, [ch as k] *a.* refembling a pulley
Trod, Trod'den, *pret.* and *pa. paff.* of *to tread*
Trog'lodyte, *n.* one who inhabits only caves
Troj'an, *n.* a native of ancient Troy
'Troj'an, *a.* pertaining to Troy
Troll, *v.* to move circularly, roll, rove, fifh for pike
Trol'lop, *n.* a flattern, a flovenly woman or drefs
Tromp, *n.* a blowing machine formed by a hollow tree, ufed in furnaces
Trom'pil, *n.* an aperture in a tromp
Troop, *n.* a body of foldiers, a number of people
Troop, *v. i.* to march in a body, go in hafte, flock
Troop'er, *n.* a horfe-foldier, horfeman, good rider
Trope, *n.* a figure ufed in fpeech, turn, change
Trophied, *a.* adorned with trophies, fine

Trophy, *n.* fomething taken in battle, an ornament
Tropic, *n.* the line which bounds the fun's courfe north and fouth of the equator
Trop'ical, *a.* placed near the tropics, figurative
Tropolo"gical, *a.* varied by tropes, moral
Tropol'ogy, *n.* a variation by tropes or figures
Troffers, *fee* Trowfers
Trot, *v. t.* to ride in a trot, to walk faft (woman
Trot, *n.* a jolting high pace of a horfe, walk, old
Troth, *n.* truth, faith, faithfulnefs, a petty oath, *ob.*
Troth'lefs, *a.* faithlefs, falfe, trecherous, bafe, *ob.*
Froth'plight, *a.* betrothed, efpoufed, contracted, *ob.*
Trot'ter, *n.* a trotting horfe, a fheep's foot
Trou"ble, *v. t.* to perplex, difturb, vex, afflict, fue
Trou"ble, *n.* calamity, difturbance, inconvenience
Troub'ler, Trou"bleftate, *n.* one who gives trouble, one who makes difturbance, a makebate
Trou"blefome, *a.* vexatious, tirefome, teafing, fad
Trou"blefomely, *ad.* in a troublefome manner
Trou"blefomenefs, *n.* vexatioufnefs, uneafinefs
Troub'lous, *a.* tumultuous, mad, confufed, mixed
Trough, [trauf] *n.* a veffel, long hollowed thing
Troul, *v. t.* to move faft, roll, *fee* troll
Trounce, *v. i.* to punifh, beat, harafs, fue, cheat
Trout, *n.* a fine fifh, an honeft filly fellow
Trout'ftream, *n.* a river in which trouts breed
Tróver, *n.* an action for goods that are found and not delivered to the owner upon demand made
Trow, *v. i.* to imagin, think, conceive, fuppofe
Trow'el, *n.* a tool to lay bricks in mortar with
Trow'fers *n. pl.* a loofe garment for men in lieu of breeches
Troy, Troy'weight, *n.* a weight of 12 oz. to the lb.
Trúant, *n.* one who keeps from fchool, an idler
Trúant, *a.* idle, lazy, flothful, loitering, carelefs
Trúant, *v. i.* to idle, be lazy, loiter, keep from duty
Trúantfhip, *n.* idlenefs, negligence, careleffnefs
Trub'tail, *n.* a fhort fquat woman, a fat woman
Truce, *n.* a temporary peace, intermiffion, ftop, reft
Trucidátion, *n.* the act of killing, cruel murder
Truck, *v. t.* to exchange ; *n.* an exchange of goods
Truck'ing, *n.* the act of exchanging commodities
Truc"kle, *v. t.* to fubmit, yield, creep, roll
Truc"klebed, *n.* a low bed that runs under another
Truck, *n.* a circular piece of wood for various purpofes, a low carriage fo called from its wheels, or trucks
Truck'man, *n.* one who manages a truck
Truc'ulent, *a.* cruel, barbarous, terrible of afpect
Trudge, *v. i.* to jog on heavily, go, walk, moil
True, *a.* certain, faithful, fteady, exact, genuine
Trúeborn, *a.* having a right by birth, lawful
Trúebred, *a.* coming of a good or right breed
Trúehearted, *a.* honeft, faithful, fincere, upright
Trúeheartednefs, *n.* honefty, faithfulnefs
Trúenefs, *n.* honefty, faithfulnefs, fincerity
Trúepenny, *n.* a worthy honeft fellow, a friend
Truffle, *n.* a kind of fubterraneous mufhroom
Trug or Trugg, *n.* a tray, hod, ancient meafure

Truifn, *n.* a moft undoubted truth, certainty, fact
Trull, *n.* a low vagrant ftrumpet; *v.t.* to trundle
Trúly, *ad.* really, certainly, indeed, exactly, even
Trump, *n.* a trumpet, turn-up card, expedient
Trump, *v. t.* to play a trump, devife, forge
Trump'ery, *n.* trifles, trath, idle talk, falfehood
Trump'et, *n.* a fhrill mufical inftrument
Trump'et, *v. t.* to found, proclaim, tell abroad
Trump'eter, *n.* one who founds a trumpet or praife
Trump'ettongued, *a.* fpeaking very loud or high
Trunc'ate, *v. t.* to cut fhort, lop, maim, mangle
Trunc'ate, *a.* cut off fhort, ending abruptly
Truncâtion, *n.* the act of lopping or maiming
Trunch'eon, *n.* a fhort ftaff, ftaff of command, club
Trunch'eon, *v. t.* to beat with a truncheon
Truncheonéer, *n.* one armed with a truncheon
Trun'dle, *v. i.* to twirl, roll, bowl, turn round
Trun'dle, *n.* any round rolling thing, a carriage
Trun'dlebed, *n.* a bed on trundles
Trun'dletail, *n.* a name of a dog, round tail
Trun'dling, *n.* the act of twirling or rolling on
Trunk, *n.* the body of any thing, a fort of cheft,
the probofcis of an elephant, a long tube
Trunk'ed, *a.* having a trunk, cut off, maimed
Trunk'hofe, *n.* very large breeches worn formerly
Trun'uel, *n.* a long wooden pin to fatten a fhip's
plunks
Trun'nions, *n. pl.* the knobs upon great guns
Trúfion, *n.* the act of thrufting or pufhing forward
Trufs, *n.* a bandage for ruptures, a bundle of hay,
a machine to pull a yard clofe to the maft
Trufs, *v.* to pack clofe, gird, fkewer, fratch up
Truft, *n.* confidence, credit, charge, care
Truft, *v. t.* to confide, rely, believe, credit, fell
upon credit, commit to any one's care
Truftée, *n.* one who is intrufted with any thing
Truft'er, *n.* one who trufts, one who credits
Truft'ily, *ad.* faithfully, honeftly, fincerely
Truft'inefs, *n.* fidelity, honefty, integrity, purity
Truft'y, *a.* fit to be trufted, faithful, honeft, true
Truth, *n.* reality, certainty, faithfulnefs, honefty
Truthlefs, *a.* deftitute of veracity, lying
Trutinâtior, *n.* the act of weighing or balancing, *ob.*
Trútine, *n.* a method to rectify nativities, *ob.*
Try, *v. t.* to examin, prove, endeavor, attempt
Tub, *n.* a wooden veffel of various fizes and ufes
Tube, *n.* a pipe, fiphon, long hollow body, hole
Túbercle, *n.* a fmall fwelling or tumor, a pimple
Túberculate, Túberculous, *a.* having pimples or
fmall fwellings
Túberofe, *n.* a fweet fmelling flower, a plant
Túberous, *a.* full of knobs or fwellings, knotty
Túbuliform, *a.* in the fhape of a tube
Túbular, Túbulate, Túbulous, *a.* long and hollow
Túbule, *n.* a fmall tube, a fmall pipe (like a pipe
Tucan', *n.* a genus of birds with a large bill
Tuck, *n.* a kind of long narrow fword, net, fold
Tuck, *v. t.* to lie clofe, inclofe, fold, draw, full
Tuck'er, *n.* a flip of linen, &c. about the breaft

Tuck'et, *n.* a voluntary in mufic, prelude, firft
Túefday, *n.* the third day of the week (piece
Túfa, *n.* a ftone confifting of volcanic matter con-
Tufáceous, *a.* pertaining to or like tufa (creted
Tuffoon' or Ty'phon, *n.* a violent tempeft or tor-
nado
Tuft, *n.* a clufter of trees, grafs, hair, &c. a clump
Tuft, *v. t.* to adorn, make or plant with a tuft
Tuftaf fety, *n.* a tufted or fhaggy kind of filk
Tuft'ed, *pa.* adorned or covered with tufts
Tuft'y, *a.* growing in tufts or clufters, bufhy
Tug, *v.* to pull, pluck, draw, contend, labor
Tug, *n.* a pull, pull with force, effort, waggon
Tui'tion, *n.* inftruction, guardianfhip, protection
Túlip, *n.* a large and beautiful flower (a tulip
Túliptree, *n.* a tree in America having flowers like
Tum'ble, *n.* a fall, caft, downfal, accident
Tum'ble, *v.* to fall, throw down, roll, turn over
Tum'bler, *n.* one who fhows feats of tumbling, a
glafs, a dog
Tum'brel or Tum'bril, *n.* a dungcart, a dunghill
Tumefac'tion, *n.* the act of fwelling, a fwelling
Túmefy, *v.* to make to fwell, fwell, rife, puff up
Túmid, *a.* fwelled, puffed up, big, pompous, proud
Túmor, *n.* a morbid fwelling, puffy grandeur, pride
Túmorous, *a.* fwelling, falfely magnificent, vain
Túmular, *a.* pertaining to artificial hillocks
Túmulate, *v.* to bury, inter, fwell, rife, *ob.*
Tumulófe, *a.* full of hills, hilly, irregular, rough
Túmult, *n.* a wild commotion, riet, buftle, ftir
Tumult'uarily, *ad.* in a tumultuary manner
Tumult'uarinefs, *n.* turbulence, confufion, noife
Tumult'uary, *a.* confufed, diforderly, riotous, noify
Tumultuátion, *n.* a very confufed agitation, a riot
Tumult'uous, *a.* turbulent, hot, violent, noify
Tumult'uoufly, *ad.* with confufion and violence
Tun, *n.* a cafk of four hogfheads, 10 hundred
weight, a fpace in a fhip to contain a tun
Tun, *v. t.* to put into a cafk, to barrel up drink
Túnable, *a.* harmonious, mufical, fweet, pleafing
Túnablenefs, *n.* harmony, melodioufnefs, mufic
Túnably, *ad.* harmonioufly, melodioufly, fweetly
Tun'bellied, *a.* having a very large belly, heavy
Tune, *n.* harmony, an air, order, ftate, fit temper
Tune, *v. t.* to put into a mufical ftate, prepare, fing
Túneful, *a.* harmonious, melodious, mufical
Túnelefs, *a.* deftitute of harmony, harfh, rough
Túner, *n.* one who tunes or prepares, one who fings
Tung, *n.* the inftrument of fpeech, language, an
infect (or fteel gray color
Tung'ften or Tungften'ite, *n.* a metal of a brown
Tung'ftic or Tung'ftenic, *a.* pertaining to tungften
Tung'ftate, *n.* a falt compofed of tungftenic acid
and a bafe
Tungúfian, *a.* pertaining to the Tungufes, a race
of Afiatics near the fources of the Amur
Túnic, *n.* a child's upper garment, waiftcoat, fkin
Túnicate, *a.* having tunics or covers lying over
each other

Túnicle, *n.* a cover, integument, cafe, thin fkin
Tunis'ian, *n.* a native of Tunis
Funis'ian, *a.* pertaining to Tunis
Tun'nage, *n.* amount of tuns, money paid by the (ton
Tun'nel, *n.* a funnel, part of a chimney, wide net
Tun'nel, *v.* to form like a tunnel, catch, net, fill
Tun'ny, *n.* the name of a feafifh
Tup, *v.* to butt or cover like a ram ; *n.* a ram
Túpelo, *n.* a tree, a fpecies of nyffa
Táraco, *n.* a bird with elegant plumage
Tur'ban, *n.* the head covering ufed by the Turks
Tur'baned, *a.* wearing or having a turban
Tur'bary, *n.* the right or privilege of digging turf
Tur'bid, *a.* thick, muddy, foul, difturbed
Tur'bidnefs, *n.* thicknefs, muddinefs, foulnefs (top
Tur'binate, *a.* twifted, fpiral, made like a cone or
Tur'bith, *n.* yellow precipitate, a purgative herb
Tur'hot, *n.* a much admired feafifh
Tur'bulence or Tur'bulency, *n.* tumult, confufion
Tur'bulent, *a.* tumultuous, agitated, violent
Tur'bulently, *ad.* tumultuoufly, with confufion
Tur'cifm, *n.* the religion of the Turks, Mahomet-
   anifm
Turcoma'nic, *a.* pertaining to Turcomania, now
   Armenia in Afia and its inhabitants the Turco-
   mans
Turf, *n.* a clod covered with grafs, peat, cloth
Turf, *v. t.* to cover or adorn with turfs
Turf'y, *a.* full of or having turfs, like turf, green
Tur'gent, *a.* fwelling, protuberant, jutting out
Turgef'cence, *n.* the act of fwelling, a fwelled ftate
Tur'gid, *a.* tumid, fwelled, bloated, bombaftic, big
Tur'gidnefs, *n.* a turgid or fwelled ftate, bombaft
Turioniferous, *a.* producing fhoots
Turk, *n.* a native or inhabitant of Turkey
Turk'ifh, *a.* pertaining to Turkey or the Turks
Turk'ois or Turc'ois, *n.* a fine blue ftone
Turk'y, *n.* a genus of large fowls natives of Am.
Turm, *n.* a troop, body, great number, *ob.*
Tur'malin, *n.* a filiceous ftone of remarkable elec-
   trical properties
Turm'eric, *n.* an Indian root ufed in dying
Turmoil', *n.* trouble, difturbance, ftir, uneaffnefs
Turmoil', *v.* to labor hard, toil, weary, difturb
Turn, *v. t.* to move round, form, change, transform
Turn, *n.* the act of moving about, change, chance
Turn'coat *n.* an apoftate, one who changes fides
Turn'er, *n.* one who turns in a lathe
Turn'ing, *n.* a winding, a bending, a curdling
Turn'ingnefs, *n.* the ftate or quality of turning, *ob.*
Turn'ip, *n.* the name of a good well known root
Turn'pike, *n.* a toll-gate fet on a road, a road on
   which a turnpike is erected
Turn'pike, *v. t.* to form or erect a turnpike
Turn'fick, *a.* quite giddy, lightheaded, whirling
Turn'fpit, *n.* one who turns a fpit, a kind of dog
Turn'fole, *n.* a plant, the wart wort, a dye
Turn'ftile, *n.* a kind of turning or whirling ftile
Turp'entine, *n.* a clear gum from the pine

Turp'itude, *n.* inherent vilenefs, great bafenefs
Turquoife', *n.* ivory penetrated with the blue calx
   of copper
Tur'ret, *n.* a fmall tower, a little eminence
Tur'reted, *a.* having a turret, built like a tower
Tur'tle, *n.* a kind of dove, turtledove, fea-tortoife
Tur'tledove, *n.* a fpecies of dove, a fort of pigeon
Tufc'an, *a.* denoting an order in architecture, or
   the moft fimple columns ; pertaining to Tufca-
   ny it Italy
Tus'can, *n.* a native of Tufcany
Tufh or Tufk, *n.* a fang, a very large foretooth
Tufh, Tut, *exclam.* expreffing diflike
Tufk'ed, Tufk'y, *a.* furnifhed with tufks, hoftile
Tútelage, *n.* guardianfhip, care, protection, fupport
Tútelar, Tútelary, *a.* guarding, protecting, kind
Tutenag', *n.* a mineral compofed of zink and iron
Tútor, *n.* one who inftructs youths, a preceptor
Tútor, *v. t.* to teach, inftruct, bring up, chide
Tútorage, *n.* the office of a tutor, education
Tútorefs, *n.* an inftructrefs, miftrefs, governefs
Tútoring, *n.* the act of inftructing, education
Tut'fan, *n.* a plant, park-leaves
Tut'ty, *n.* flowers of zink, nofegay, pofey
Tuz or Tuzz, *n.* a lock, bunch or tuft of hair
Twain, *a.* two, both ; *ad.* in two parts, afunder
Twang, *v. i.* to found fharply or with an accent
Twang, *n.* a fharp quick found, a ftrange accent
Twang, *ad.* with a fharp and quick found
Twang'ing, *n.* the act of founding fharply
Twang'ling, *a.* contemptibly noify, troublefome
Twank, *v. i.* to make to found, clank, twang
'Twas, contraction of *it was*
Twat'tle, *v. i.* to prate, gabble, chatter, talk idly
Tweag or Tweak, *v. t.* to pinch, fqueeze, perplex
Tweag or Tweak, *n.* a pinch, perplexity, diftrefs
Twee'dle, *v. t.* to handle lightly or foftly
Tweedledum', Tweedledee, *n.* a mufician in con-
Tweezers, *n. pl.* nippers, fmall pinchers (tempt
Twelfth, *a.* the fecond in order after the tenth
Twelfth'tide, *n.* the twelfth day, the Epiphany
Twelve, *a.* two and ten, fix repeated twice
Twelve'month, *n.* a year of folar months (times
Twelve'pence, *n.* a fhilling, a penny taken twelve
Twelve'penny, *a.* fold for or valued at a fhilling
Twelve'fcore, *a.* twenty repeated twelve times
Twen'ty, *a.* twice ten, ten taken or added twice
Twibil, *n.* a halberd, an iron tool ufed by paviers
Twice, *ad.* two times, double, over again, once
Twid'dle, *v. t.* to tweedle, to touch lightly (more
Twig, *n.* a fmall fhoot of a branch, fwitch, fprout
Twig'gen, *a.* made of or refembling twigs
Twig'gy, *a.* full of or having twigs, like twigs
Twilight, *n.* a light before and after the fun is feen
Twilight, *a.* deeply fhaded, obfcure, dufky, dull
Twill, *v. t.* to weave in ribs or ridges
Twin, *n.* one of two born or produced together
Tw'n, *v.* to bring two, pair, be paired, depart
Twin'born, *a.* born at one or the fame birth

Twine, v. to twift, wrap, wind, bend, unite
Twine, n. a twift, twifted thread, clofe embrace
Twinge, v. t. to tweak, pinch, torment, diftrefs
Twinge, n. a tweak, fharp fudden pain, pinch, gripe
Twink, n. a quick motion of the eye, a moment
Twin'kle, v. i. to open and fhut the eye, to fparkle
Twink'ling, n. a motion of the eye, a fpark of light
Twin'ling, n. the name of a twin-lamb
Twin'ner, n. one who breeds or produces twins
Twirl, v. t. to turn or move round, to whirl
Twirl, n. a quick circular motion, turn, twift
Twift, v. t. to form by complication, wind, turn
Twift, n. thread made by winding together, a
Twift'er, n. one who twifts   (twitch, cord, twig
Twit, v. t. to reproach, upbraid, fneer at, flout
Twitch, v. t. to fnatch, pluck forcibly, fhoot pain
Twitch, n. a quick or fudden pull, twinge, pain
Twit'ter, v. i. to make a noife like fwallows
Twit'ter, n. a diforder of paffion, fit of laughter,
   fear, fright, confufion, agitation, fret
Twit'tletwattle, n. idle talk, gabble, tattle; v. i.
Twixt, contraction of betwixt   (to prate
Two'edged, a. having an edge on both the fides
Two'fold, a. double; ad. doubly, twice, two times
Two'handed, a. big, bulky, enormous, very ftrong
Two'pence, n. a penny twice told, a filver coin
Tychon'ic, [ch as k] a. pertaining to Tycho
   Brahe or his fyftem of aftronomy
Tym'bal, n. a large drum, a kind of kettle-drum
Tymp'an, n. a printer's frame, pannel, ornament,
   area of a pediment, a wheel with pins to turn a
   windlafs
Tymp'anum, n. a drum, drum of the ear, wheel
Tymp'any, n. a difeafe, a hard fwelling of the belly
Type, n. an emblem, token, ftamp, printing-letter
Typ'ical, a. emblematical, figurative, refembling
Typ'ically, ad. in a figurative manner, allufively
Typ'ify, v. t. to figure out, point out, reprefent
Typog'rapher, n. one who prints, a printer
Typograph'ical, a. belonging to types or printing
Typograph'ically, ad. after the way of printers
Typog'raphy, n. the art of printing with letters
Tyr'annefs, n. a female tyrant
Tyran'nic, Tyran'nical, a. like a tyrant, defpotic
Tyran'nically, ad. cruelly, defpotically
Tyran'nicide, n. one who murders a tyrant
Tyr'annize, v. i. to act the tyrant, rule arbitrarily
Tyr'annous, a. cruel, arbitrary, defpotic
Tyr'anny, n. cruel government, unjuft feverity, rig-
Ty'rant, n. a cruel defpotic ruler, an oppreffor (or
Tyr'ian, n. a native of Tyre
Tyr'ian, a. pertaining to Tyre
Tyr'rhene, a. pertaining to Tufcany in Italy
Ty'ro, n. a beginner, novice, ftudent, apprentice
Tyrolefe, n. an inhabitant of Tyrol, in Auftria
Tyrolefe, a. pertaining to Tyrol and its people
Tzar, n. the emperor of Ruffia [true pron. of
   czar]

U

U'BERTY, [u as yu] n. abundance, plenteouf-
   nefs, great ftore
Ubication, Ubiety, [u as yu] n. a relation to a place
Ubi'qui'tary, [u as yu] a. exifting every where
Ubi'quitary, [u as yu] n. one who exifts every
   where   (niprefence
Ubi'quity, [u as yu] n. a being in every place, om-
Ud'der, n. the dugs of a cow or other large animal
Ug'lily, ad. with deformity, offenfively, filthily
Ug'linefs, n. deformity, horridnefs, depravity
Ug'ly, a. deformed, horrid, offenfive to the fight
Ukáfe, n. a proclamation or royal order in Ruffia
Ul'cer, n. a bad running fore, a dangerous fore
Ul'cerate, v. t. to difeafe with or turn to fores
Ulceration, n. a breaking out into fores, a bad fore
Ul'cered, a. grown ulcerous, having ulcers
Ul'cerous, a. afflicted with very bad fores, corrupt
Ul'cufcle, n. a little ulcer or fore
Uli'ginous, a. flimy, foft, muddy, fenny, moorifh
Ul'lage, n. in gaging, is what a cafk wants of being
Ulterior, a. farther, lying beyond, further   (full
Ult'imate, a. the laft, final, concluding, extreme
Ult'imately, ad. in the laft ftate or confequence
Ultimátum, n. a final anfwer, final refolution, end
Ultim'ity, n. a laft ftage or ftate, a laft confequence
Ultramarine, n. a very fine blue; a. foreign, blue
Ultramon'tane, a. beyond the mountains
Ultramun'dane, a. fituate beyond the world
Ultróneous, a. fpontaneous, voluntary, willing, free
Ululátion, n. the act of howling like a wolf
Um'bel, n. an umbrella, or mode of flowering,
   when a number of florets rife on footftalks fo as
   to form an umbrella
Um'bellar, a. pertaining to or like an umbel
Umbelliferous, a. producing umbels
Um'bellate, a. containing an umbel   (cle
Um'bellule, n. a little umbel, or umbel of a pedun-
Um'ber, n. an African crow of the fize of a crow
Um'ber, n. a yellow color, fifh, mongrel, animal
Um'bered, a. painted with umber, fhaded, clouded
Umbil'ic, Umbil'ical, a. belonging to the naval
Umbil'icate, a. connected by a cord
Um'bles, n. pl. entrails, entrails of deer, humbles
Um'bo, n. the point or top of a buckler, a buckler
Um'brage, n. a fhadow, color, offenfe, refentment
Uubrágeous, Umbráical, Um'brofe, a. fhady, dark
Umbrágeoufnefs, Umbros'ity, n. fhadinefs, fhade
Um'brel, Umbrel'la, n. a cover from the fun, &c.
Ump'irage, n. final decifion by a fingle perfon
Ump'ire, n. an arbitrator, one who decides difputes
Un, prefixed to words has the force of not or a
   negative
Unabáfed, a. not abafed, not humbled, proud
Unabafh'ed, a. not afhamed, undaunted, very bold
Unáble, a. not able, incapable, impotent, weak
Unabol'ifhed, a. remaining in full force, left
Unaccent'ed, a. not having an accent
Unaccept'able, a. not acceptable, unwelcome

Unaccept'ablenefs, a. an unacceptable ftate
Unaccept'ably, ad. in an unwelcome manner
Unaccept'ed, a. not accepted or received,rejected
Unaccefs'iblenefs, n. an inacceffible ftate [ences
Unaccom'modated, a. not furnifhed with conveni-
Unaccom'modating, a. not compliant or obliging
Unaccomp'anied, a.unattended, fingle,alone,dull
Unaccomp'lifhed, a. unfinifhed, undone, aukward
Unaccount'able, a. not explicable, ftrange, odd
Unaccount'ablenefs, n. ftrangenefs,oddnefs
Unaccount'ably, ad. ftrangely,oddly, unufually
Unaccred'ited, a. not received, not authorized
Unac'curate, a. not exact, incorrect, confufed
Unaccus'tomed, a. not ufed, unufual,new,ftrange
Unacknowl'edged, a.not owned, not confeffed,de-
Unacquaintance, n. a want of knowledge (nied
Unacquainted, a. not known, unufual, ignorant
Unact'ive, a. not brifk, heavy, having no efficacy
Unadjuft'ed, a. not adjufted or fettled
Unadmired, a. not regarded with love or honor
Unadmon'ifhed, a. not admonifhed
Unadored, a. not worfhipped, neglected, flighted
Unadvifable, a. not expedient
Unadvifed, a. indifcreet, imprudent, foolifh, rafh
Unadvifedly, ad. indifcreetly, inconfiderately
Unaerated, a. not combined with carbonic acid
Unaf'fable, a. unfociable, ftern, haughty, proud
Unaffect'ed, a.not touched,unmoved, candid,real
Unaided, a. not affifted, not helped, fingle, alone
Unalienable, a. that cannot be alienated, fixed
Unallied, a. having no ally or affiftant, left alone
Unalloy'ed, a. not alloyed or mixed
Unalt'erable, a.that cannot or may not be altered
Unalt'erably, ad. in an unalterable manner, really
Unalt'ered, a. not altered, unchanged, fixed
Unambig'uous, a. not ambiguous, plain, clear
Unambi'tious, a. not ambitious, not defirous
Unambi'tioufnefs, n. want of ambition
Unamufing, a. unpleafing, uninftructive, dull
Unamufive, a. not tending to amufe, tedious, dull
Unanal'ogous, n. not analogous
Unan'imalized, a. not formed into an animal
Unanim'ity, [u as yu] n. agreement in mind
Unan'imous, a. being of one mind or fentiment
Unan'imoufly, ad. with one mind, all agreeing
Unannealed, a. not prepared, not hardened, foft
Unanoint'ed, a. wanting extreme unction
Unans'werable, a. not to be refuted, certain, true
Unans'wered, a. not anfwered, not confuted
Unappall'ed, a. not daunted, not difmayed, bold
Unappar'elled, a. not dreffed, naked, bare
Unappar'ent, a. not vifible, concealed, obfcure
Unappeafable, a. that is not to be pacified, ftiff
Unappeafed, a. not appeafed, not pacified, ftern
Unapplied, a. not applied
Unapprehens'ive, a. not apprehending, dull
Unapproachable, a. not to be approached
Unapproached, a. inacceffible, not to be come at
Unappropriated, a. not appropriated, vacant

Unapproved, a. not approved, difliked, hated
Unapt', a. unfit, unfuitable, improper, heavy, dull
Unargued, a.not argued or difputed,not cenfured
Unarm'ed, a. having no armor, defencelefs, weak
Unart'ful, a. void of art, fkill or cunning, plain
Unafk'ed, a. not afked, not defired, not requefted
Unafcertained, a. not made certain
Unafcertainable, a. not reducible to certainty
Unafpiring, a. not ambitious, humble, contented
Unaffailable,a. that cannot be affailed or attacked
Unaffailed, a. not attacked or affaulted, fecure
Unaffift'ed, a. not affifted, not helped, alone, fingle
Unaffift'ing, a. giving no affiftance or help
Unaffociated, a. not united or affociated
Unaffured, a. not confident, not to be trufted in
Unattainable, a. not to be obtained or acquired
Unattempt'ed, a. not attempted, not tried,untried
Unattend'ed, a. having no retinue, fingle, alone
Unavailable, Unavailing, a. ufelefs, vain, trifling
Unaven'ged, a. not avenged or fatisfied
Unavert'ed, a. not turned away
Unavoid'able, a. not to be fhunned, inevitable
Unavow'ed, a. not owned or acknowledged
Unauth'orized, a. not fupported by due authority
Unaware or Unawares, ad. fuddenly,unexpectedly
Unaw'ed, a. dauntlefs, having no fear or regard
Unback'ed, a. untamed, not fupported, left alone
Unbal'laft, v. t. to difcharge ballaft
Unbaptized, a. not baptized, not having baptifm
Unbar', v. to remove or take off a bar, to unbolt
Unbarb'ed, a. not fhaven, bare, relieved, fet free
Unbated, a. not repreffed, not blunted
Unbat'tered, a. not injured by blows, found,entire
Unbeaten, a. not beaten, unhurt, untredden
Unbecom'ing, a. unfuitable, improper, indecent
Unbecom'ingly, ad. in an unfit manner
Unbed', v. t. to raife, get or take from a bed
Unbefit'ting, a. not fit, unbecoming, unfuitable
Unbeget', v. t. to deprive of exiftence, kill, end
Unbegot'ten, a. not generated, not born, eternal
Unbelief, n. want of belief, infidelity, incredulity
Unbelieve, v. t. not to believe, not to think real
Unbeliever, n. an infidel, a vile or wicked perfon
Unbend', v. t. unbended, unbent, pret. unbended,
   unbent, pa. to relax, flacken, eafe
Unbend'ing, pa. a. relaxing, eafing, ftiff
Unbeneficed, a. not enjoying or having a benefice
Unbenev'olent, a.-not kind or good, unmerciful
Unbenighted,a.not vifited by darknefs,light,clear
Unbenign, a. unkind, malevolent, malignant
Unbent', pa. relaxed, unftrung, unfubdued
Unbequeathed, a. not given by will
Unbefeeming, a. unbecoming, indecent,improper
Unbefought', a. not fought or entreated, unafked
Unbewailed, a. not bewailed, not lamented
Unbias, v. t. to remove prejudice, to undeceive
Unbid', Unbid'den, a. not bidden, uninvited
Unbig'oted, a. not bigotted, free from bigotry
Unbind, v. t. unbound, pret. unbound, pa. to

untie, unloofe, fet free, feparate (ders
Unbifh'op, v. t. to deprive of a bifhopric or of orders
Unbit', v. t. to remove a bit, to loofe a cablefrom the bits
Unbit'ted, a. unbridled, unreftrained, loofe
Unblámable, a. not blamable or guilty, innocent
Unblem'ifhed, a. free from blemifh or reproach,
Unblench'ed, a. not difgraced, unfoiled (pure
Unbleft', a. wretched, unhappy, miferable, poor
Unblood'fied, n. not ftained or fouled with blood
Unblos'foming, a. not bearing bloffoms
Unblówn, a. not blown, not yet opened, unripe
Unblunt'ed, a. not blunted, not dulled, fharp, keen
Unbod'ied, a. freed from the body, fpiritual
Unbóit, v. t. to take out or remove bolts, to unbar
Unbolt'ed, pa. a. opened, not fifted or refined
Unbon'neted, a. having no bonnet or hat on, bare
Unbook'ifh, a. not fond of books, unlearned, dull
Unborn', a. not yet brought into life or exiftence
Unbor'rowed, a. not borrowed, genuine, original
Unbos'om, v. t. to reveal in confidence, to vent
Unbot'tomed, a. having no bottom, unfollid, loofe
Unbought', a. not bought, obtained without money
Unbound', a. not bound, wanting a cover, loofe
Unbound'ed, a. unlimited, unreftrained, general
Unbound'edly, ad. without bounds or limits
Unbound'ednefs, n. an unlimited extent or liberty
Unbow'ed, a. not bent, not arched, ftrait, even
Unbow'el, v. t. to take out the bowels, to gut
Unbráce, v. t. to loofe, relax, fet free, unfold
Unbráided, a. not braided, difentangled, unfaded
Unbranch'ed, a. not fhooting into branches
Unbréathed, a. not breathed, not duly exercifed
Unbred', a. not duly taught, badly educated, rude
Unbréeched, a. wanting or not put into breeches
Unbríbed, a. not influenced by money, upright
Unbrídled, a. not reftrained, free, loofe, licentious
Unbróke or Unbróken, a. whole, not fubdued
Unbro"therly, a. not like a brother, unkind, cruel
Unbuc'kle, v. t. to loofe a buckle, fet free, eafe
Unbuild', v. t. unbuilded, unbuilt, pret. and pa.
　　to pull or take down, raze, deftroy
Unbuilt', a. not built, not yet erected, unfinifhed
Unburied, a. not buried, not put into a grave
Unburn'ing, a. not confuming away by fire
Unburnt', a. not burnt, not confumed by fire, fafe
Unbur'then, v. t. to rid of a burden, eafe, difclofe
Unbut'ton, v. t. to loofe buttons, open, let loofe
Uncalcined, a. not calcined, not hardened by fire
Uncall'ed, a. not called, not fent for, uninvited
Uncalm', v. t. to difturb, enrage, provoke, roufe
Uncan'celled, a. not erafed, not blotted out, left
Uncan'did, a. not candid, not fair, partial
Uncanon'ical, a. not canonical, not approved of
Uncan'opied, a. not covered with a canopy
Uncap', v. t. to remove a cap or cover
Uncápable, a. incapable, unable, improper, unfit
Uncar'nate, a. not carnal or luftful, not flefhly
Uncáfe, v. t. to uncover, take off or out, flay

Uncaught', a. not caught, not yet taken, loofe
Uncau"tious, a. incautious, unwary, heedlefs, foolifh
Uncaus'ed, a. not having a caufe or author (ifh
Uncen'trical, a. not centrical, diftant from the center
Uncert'ain, a. not certain, doubtful, unfettled
Uncert'ained, a. made uncertain, not cleared up
Uncert'ainly, ad. in an uncertain ftate or manner
Uncert'ainty, n. dubioufnefs, doubt, contingency
Unchâin, v. t. to fet free from chains, to releafe
Unchange'able, a. that cannot be changed, fixed
Unchange'ablenefs, n. an unalterable quality
Unchange'ably, ad. without change, fixedly, ever
Unchang'ed, a. not changed, unaltered, fixed, true
Unchang'ing, a. fuffering no alteration, fixed, fafe
Uncharacderis'tic, a. not exhibiting a character
Uncharge', v. t. to retract an accufation, recant,
Unchar'itable, a. having no mercy, unkind (draw
Unchar'itablenefs, n. a want of charity or love
Unchar'itably, ad. without charity, unkindly
Unchåry, a. incautious, unwary, unguarded, ob.
Unchâfte, a. lewd, luftful, impure, immodeft, vile
Unchas'tity, n. lewdnefs, luft, immodefty
Unchâftly, ad. lewdly, luftfully, immodeftly
Uncheck'ed, a. not checked, unreftrained, loofe
Uncheerfulnefs, n. melancholy, dejection, want of
Unchew'ed, a. not chewed, not eaten (fpirit
Unchfld, v. t. to deprive or bereave of children
Unchris'tian, a. contrary to Chriftianity, vile
Unchris'tiannefs, n. a contrariety to Chriftianity
Un'cinate, a. hooked at the end
Uncir'cumcifed, a. not circumcifed, hardened
Uncircumci"fion, n. a want of circumcifion
Uncircumfcríbed, a. not limited, unbounded
Uneir'cumfpect, a. not cautious, carelefs, fimple
Uncircumftan'tial, a. not important, trifling, lax
Unciv'il, a. unkind, unpolite, uncourteous, rude
Uncivilizâtion, n. a want of civilization
Unciv'ilized, a. rude, rough, indecent, barbarous
Unciv'illy, ad. unkindly, unpolitely, rudely, badly
Unclâimed, a. not claimed or demanded
Unclar'ified, a. not refined, not purified, thick
Unclafs'ic, Unclafs'ical, a. not claffical, not pure
Un"cle, n. a father's brother, a mother's brother
Unclêan, a. not clean, filthy, wicked, lewd (fin
Unclean'linefs, Uncléannefs, n. want of cleannefs,
Unclean'ly, a. foul, filthy, nafty, dirty, unchafte
Uncleans'ed, a. not cleanfed or purified, impure
Unclench', v. t. to open the hand, raife up, undo
Unclew', v. t. to undo, unfold, unravel a fecret
Unclip'ped, a. not clipped, not cut, whole, full
Unclog', v. t. to difencumber, free, fet at liberty
Unclois'ter, v. t. to fet at liberty, fet free, deliver
Unclôfe, v. t. to open, fet open, difclofe, expofe
Unclôfed, pa. a. fet open, void of inclofures
Unclôthe, v. t. unclad, unclothed, pret. and pa.
　　to make naked, ftrip, bare, take off
Unclôthed, pa. a. ftripped, made bare, naked (fine
Uncloud'ed, Uncloud'y, a. free from clouds, clear,

Uncloud'ednefs, *n.* a freedom from clouds
Unclutch', *v. t.* to open, to open the clofed hand
Uncôated, *a.* not coated or covered
Uncock'ed, *a.* not cocked, not formed to a point
Uncoif', *v. t.* to pull off the cap, bare, lay bare
Uncoil', *v. t.* to unfold, difengage, unravel, open
Uncoin'ed, *a.* not coined, not ftamped or marked
Uncolle&ed, *a.* not collected, not gathered, loofe
Uncol'ored, *a.* not colored, unftained, plain, pure
Uncômbed, *a.* not parted with a comb, rough
Uncombîned, *a.* not combined, fimple
Uncome'linefs, *n.* a want of comelinefs or grace
Uncome'ly, *a.* not comely, ungraceful, ugly, bad
Uncom'fortable, *a.* difmal, gloomy, miferable, fad
Uncom'fortablenefs, *n.* an uncomfortable ftate
Uncom'fortably, *ad.* in an uncomfortable manner
Uncommand'ed, *a.* not commanded, not ordered
Uncommend'ed, *a.* not praifed or commended
Uncommer'cial, *a.* not carrying on trade
Uncom'mon, *a.* not frequent, unufual, rare, odd
Uncom'monly, *ad.* in an uncommon manner
Uncom'monnefs, *n.* an uncommon or rare ftate
Uncommúnicated, *a.* not communicated or told
Uncompa&', *a.* not compact, not clofe, loofe
Uncomp'anied, *a.* having no companion, alone, fad
Uncompel'led, *a.* not forced or obliged, left free
Uncom'penfated, *a.* not rewarded or paid
Uncom'plafantly, *ad.* uncivily, unpolitely
Uncompléte, *a.* not finifhed, not perfe& or exa&
Uncompound'ed, *a.* not intricate, unmixed, fimple
Uncomprehens'ive, *a.* unable to comprehend
Uncomprefs'ed, *a.* not comprefled, loofe, large, full
Unconcéivable, *a.* not to be underftood, myfterious
Unconcéivablenefs, *n.* an unconceivable ftate
Unconcéived, *a.* not conceived or imagined, dark
Unconcern', *n.* indifference, negligence, negle&
Unconcern'ed, *a.* unmoved, indifferent, eafy
Unconcern'edly, *ad.* without concern, eafily
Unconcern'ednefs, *n.* a freedom from concern
Unconcern'ing, *a.* not affecting, not interefting
Unconcern'ment, *n.* a ftate of having no concern
Unconcludent, Unconcluding, *a.* not decifive
Unconcludingnefs, *n.* an inconclufive ftate
Unconco&'ed, *a.* not conco&ed, undigefted
Uncondi"tional, *a.* without conditions, abfolute
Unconfined, *a.* not confined, unreftrained, free
Unconform', *a.* not conformable, unlike, abfurd
Unconform'able, *a.* inconfiftent, not conforming
Unconform'ity, *n.* want of conformity
Unconfufed, *a.* not confufed or embarrafled
Unconfútable, *a.* not capable of refutation
Uncongéaled, *a.* not congealed or côncreted
Unconne&'ed, *a.* not joined or united, not coherent
Unçonníving, *a.* not conniving, not winking at
Uncon'querable, *a.* that cannot be conquered
Uncon'fcionable, *a.* unreafonable, unjuft, vaft
Uncon'fcionablenefs, *n.* an unconfcionable quality, unreafonablenefs, injuftice, largenefs
Uncon'fcionably, *ad.* unreafonably, unjuftly, very

Uncon'fcious, *a.* not perceiving or knowing
Uncon'fcioufnefs, *n.* a not perceiving
Uncon'fecrated, *a.* not dedicated or devoted
Unconfent'ed, *a.* not yielded or agreed to
Unconfent'ing, *a.* not confenting or agreeing
Unconfid'ered, *a.* not confidered or refle&ed on
Uncon'fonant, *a.* inconfiftent, not agreeing
Uncon'ftant, *a.* fickle, changeable, faithlefs
Unconftitútional, *a.* not agreeable to the conftitution   (the conftitution
Unconftitutional'ity, *n.* the quality of being againft
Unconftráined, *a.* free from compulfion
Unconftráinedly, *ad.* without reftraint or force
Unconftráint, *n.* freedom from reftraint, eafe
Unconfult'ing, *a.* taking no advice, rafh, foolifh
Unconfúmed, *a.* not confumed or deftroyed
Unconfum'inate, *a.* not confummated
Uncontem'ned, *a.* not defpifed
Uncontent'ed, *a.* not contented or fatisfied
Uncontent'ingnefs, *n.* want of power to fatisfy
Unconteft'able, *a.* not controvertible, indifputable
Unconteft'ed, *a.* not difputed, evident
Uncon'trite, *a.* not penitent for fin
Uncontróllable, *a.* not to be refifted or governed
Uncontróllably, *ad.* without power of controlling
Uncontrólled, *a.* not ruled or reftrained
Uncontrólledly, *ad.* without controll
Uncon'troverted, *a.* undifputed, admitted
Unconvert'ed, *a.* not converted, not regenerated
Unconvert'ible, *a.* not to be converted or changed
Unconvers'able, *a.* not focial or difpofed to converfe
Unconvin'ced, *a.* not convinced or perfuaded
Uncord', *v. t.* to loofe from cords
Uncorre&'ed, *a.* not freed from errors
Uncorrupt', *a.* honeft, pure, fincere, upright
Uncorrupt'ed, *a.* not corrupted, pure, genuine
Uncorrupt'nefs, *n.* purity, uprightnefs
Uncoun'fellable, *a.* not to be advifed, headftrong
Uncount'able, *a.* numberlefs, infinite, endlefs
Uncount'erfeit, *a.* not counterfeit, genuine, true
Uncou'ple, *v. t.* to loofe or free from couples
Uncourt'eous, *a.* unpolite, rough, rude, uncivil
Uncourt'eoufly, *ad.* uncivilly, unpolitely
Uncourt'linefs, *n.* roughnefs, rudenefs, incivility
Uncourt'ly, *a.* unpolifhed, rough, aukward, rude
Uncouth', [uncooth] *a.* aukward, ftrange, unufual
Uncouth'ly, *ad.* in an aukward or ftrange manner
Uncouth'nefs, *n.* aukwardnefs, oddnefs, harfhnefs
Uncov'er, *v. t.* to remove covering, make naked
Uncreâte, *a.* never created, eternal, everlafting
Uncreâte, *v. t.* to deprive of exiftence, kill, deftroy
Uncreâted, *pa.* a. not yet created, not yet born,
Uncred'itablenefs, *n.* a want of reputation   (killed
Uncrop'ped, *a.* not cropped, fallow, not gathered
Uncrofs'ed, *a.* not crofied, not cancelled
Uncrowd'ed, *a.* not crowded, having room, eafy
Uncrown', *v. t.* to deprive of a crown, to dethrone
Uncrys'talized, *a.* not cryftalized
Unc'tion, *n.* the a& of anointing, an cintment

Unctuos'ity, Unc'tuousnefs, *n.* oilinefs, greafinefs

Unc'tuous, *a.* fat, oily, greafy, clammy, foft

Uncull'ed, *a.* not gathered, not felected, left, frefh

Unculp'able, *a.* not deferving of blame, blamelefs

Uncult'ivated, *a.* not cultivated, uncivilized, rude

Uncum'bered, *a.* not embarraffed or loaded

Uncurb'able, *a.* not to be curbed or checked

Uncurb'ed, *a.* not reftrained, licentious, fierce, hot

Uncurl, *v. t.* to deftroy curls, ftrip off, untwift

Uncur'rent, *a.* not current, not paffable, bad, bafe

Uncurfe', *v. t.* to free or releafe from a curfe

Uncurtailed, *a.* not curtailed, not fhortened, full

Uncut', *a.* not cut, whole, entire, full, rough, fhaggy

Undam', *v. t.* to open banks, to fet loofe or free

Undam'aged, *a.* unhurt, fafe, whole, entire, found

Un'date, Un'dated, *a.* waved, rifing and falling

Undaunt'ed, *a.* not daunted, very bold, daring, firm

Undaunt'edly, *ad.* without fear, very boldly, nobly

Undaz'zled, *a.* not dazzled, unaffected, unmoved

Undéaf, *v. t.* to free from or cure of deafnefs

Undebauch'ed, *a.* not corrupted by debauchery

Undec'agon, *n.* a figure of eleven fides

Undecáyed, *a.* not decayed, not mortified, found

Undecáying, *a.* not fuffering decay, lafting, firm

Undecéive, *v. t.* to fet right, fet free, inform juftly

Undecéivable, *a.* not liable to be deceived or im-

Undecéived, *pa.* fet right, not cheated (pofed on

Undecíded, *a.* undetermined, unfettled, vague

Undecífive, *a.* not conclufive, imperfect, defective

Undeck', *v. t.* to undrefs, to ftrip or diveft of finery

Undeck'ed, *a.* not ornamented or adorned, plain

Undeclíned, *a.* not declined, never varied, fixed

Undecompófed, *a.* not decompofed or feparated

Undecompófable, *a.* not admitting of decompofition

Undec'orated, *a.* unadorned, plain, fimple, artlefs

Undecy'pherable, *a.* not to be decyphered

Unded'icated, *a.* not dedicated, not confecrated

Undéeded, *a.* not fignalized by actions, obfcure

Undefáced, *a.* not disfigured, not blotted out, left

Undeféafible, *a.* not defeafible, true, certain

Undefi'ed, *a.* not defied, not dared, not challenged

Undefi'led, *a.* not polluted, not corrupted, pure

Undefi'nable, *a.* that cannot be defined or limited

Undefi'ned, *a.* not defined, unlimited, loofe, vague

Undel'egated, *a.* not delegated or granted

Undeform'ed, *a.* not deformed or disfigured, fair

Undefráyed, *a.* not defrayed, not fettled or paid

Undelib'erated, *a.* not carefully or duly confidered

Undeliberatin , *a.* without deliberating

Undelighted, *a.* not pleafed, unaffected, unfeeling

Undelightful, *a.* not giving pleafure, unpleafant

Undeliv'ered, *a.* not delivered or communicated

Undemol'ifhed, *a.* not deftroyed or broken down

Undemons'trable, *a.* not to be demonftrated, falfe

Undeníable, *a.* that cannot be gainfaid, certain

Undeníably, *ad.* certainly, truly, beyond doubt

Undeplóred, *a.* not lamented, not bewailed

Undeprávéd, *a.* not corrupted, innocent, pure

Undeprived, *a.* not deprived, not ftripped

Un'der, *ad.* and *pr.* beneath, below, lefs; *a.* inferi-

Un'deraction, *n.* a fubordinate action (or, lower

Underbeár, *v. t.* underbore, *pret.* underborne, *pa.*
to fupport, endure, guard, line

Underbid', *v. t.* underbade, underbid, *pret.* underbid, underbidden, *part.* to bid or offer lefs

Un'derbrufh, *n.* fhrubs and fma'l trees in a foreft

Un'derclerk, *n.* a fubordinate or inferior clerk

Undercur'rent, *n.* a current below the furface

Underdó, *v. t.* underdid, *pret.* underdone, *pa.* to
do lefs than is requifite or fit

Un'derfaction, *n.* a fubordinate or lefs faction

Underfarm'er, *n.* a fubordinate farmer

Un'derfellow, *n.* a poor, ignorant or forry wretch

Un'derfilling, *n.* the lower part of a building

Un'derfoot, *ad.* under the feet, to a difadvantage

Underfur'nifh, *v.* to furnifh with or give too little

Undergird', *v. t.* undergirded, undergirt, *pret.*
and *part.* to bind or faften the bottom

Undergó, *v.* underwent, *pret.* undergone, *pa.*
to fuffer, endure, bear, fuftain, feel

Un'derground, *n.* a fubterraneous fpace or place

Un'derground, *ad.* under the ground, in the grave

Un'dergrowth, *n.* a growth under trees, &c.

Un'derhand, *a.* fly, cunning, private, fecret (ly

Un'derhand, *ad.* flily, fecretly, fraudulently, mean-

Un'derhanded, *a.* fly, infidious, mean

Underíved, *a.* not borrowed, original, pure, new

Un'derlaborer, *n.* a lower, poor or petty, workman

Underláy, *v. t.* underlaid, *pret.* underlaid, *pa.* to
lay under, ftrengthen, fupport

Underlet', *v. t.* to let or leave under another

Underline, *v. t.* to draw a line under, fcore, mark

Un'derling, *n.* an inferior drudge, a mean perfon

Undermine, *v. t.* to fap, injure fecretly, deftroy, ruin

Un'derminer, *n.* one that faps, a fecret enemy

Un'dermoft, *a.* loweft, meaneft, bafeft, weakeft

Undernéath, *ad.* below, beneath, lefs; *pr.* under

Underof'ficer, *n.* an inferior or petty officer

Underog'atory, *a.* not derogatory, not leffening

Un'derpart, *n.* a low or the loweft part, the bottom

Underpet'ticoat, *n.* a fmall coat next to the body

Underpin', *v. t.* to prop, fupport, lay the founda-

Underpin'ning, *n.* foundation wall, prop (tion wall

Un'derplot, *n.* a feries of events fubfervient to the
main plot of a play, a clandeftine fcheme

Underpráife, *v. t.* to praife below defert, to under-

Underprize, *v. t.* to undervalue, to degrade (rate

Underprop', *v.* to prop or pin up, fupport, fuftain

Underproportioned, *a.* having too little proportion

Un'derpuller, *n.* an inferior puller, drudge, flave

Underráte, *v. t.* to rate too low, to value too low

Un'derrate, *n.* a price lefs than the proper value

Underfat'urated, *a.* not fully faturated

Underfec'retary, *n.* a fubordinate fecretary

Underfell', *v. i.* underfold, *pret.* underfold, *pa.* to
fell cheaper or below the value

Underferv'ant, *n.* a lower or inferior fervant

E e

Underset', v. t. underset, pret. underset, pa. to set or put under, prop, support

Un'derfetter, Un'derfetting, n. a prop, a pedeftal

Underfher'iff, n. the deputy of a fheriff

Underfhoot', a. moved by water paffing under

Un'derfhrub, n. a low fhrub

Un'derfong, n. the burden of a fong, a chorus

Underftand', v. underftood, pret. underftood, pa. to comprehend fully, to be informed

Underftand'ing, n. intellectual powers, fkill

Underftand'ing, pa. a. knowing, wife, fkilful

Underftand'ingly, ad. with knowledge or fkill

Un'derftrapper, n. an inferior or petty agent

Undertáke, v. undertook, pret. undertaken, pa. to engage in, take charge, promife

Undertáker, n. one who undertakes, a manager

Undertáking. n. an enterprife, bufinefs, affair

Underten'ant, n. a fecondary or lower tenant

Undertreas'urer, n. a fubordinate treafurer

Underval'ue, v. t. to rate too low, flight, defpife

Un'dervalue, n. a too low rate, a too fmall price

Un'dervaluer, n. one who undervalues or flights

Underwent', pret. of to undergo

Un'derwood, n. low wood, bufhes amongft timber-trees

Un'derwork, n. petty affairs, a bafe defign [trees

underwork', v. t. underworked, underwrought, pret. and pa. to work for lefs, to undermine

Un'derworker, n. an underworkman, a drudge

Un'derwork'man, n. an inferior laborer, a drudge

Underwrite, v. t. underwrote, pret. underwritten, pa. to write under another, to infure

Un'derwriter, n. one who underwrites, an infurer

Un'derwriting, n. the act of infuring fhips, &c.

Undefcríbed, a. not defcribed, unknown, confufed

Undefcríed, a. undifcovered, unfeen, unknown

Undeferv'ed, a. not juftly merited, not incurred

undeferv'edly, ad. without defert, unjuftly

Undeferv'er, n. a perfon of little or no merit

Undeferv'ing, a. not deferving, worthlefs, vile

Undefi'gned, a. not defigned, not intended

Undefi'gning, a. fincere, honeft, upright, plain

Undefi'rable, a. not to be defired, not to be wifhed

Undefi'red, a. not wifhed, not afked or folicited

Undefi'ring, a. not wifhing, negligent, carelefs

undeftroy'able, a. not to be deftroyed, fixed, firm

undeftroy'ed, a. not deftroyed, not wafted, fafe

Undeterm'inable, a. impoffible to be decided

Undeterm'inate, a. unfettled, indefinit, loofe

Undeterm'inatenefs, Undeterminátion, n. uncertainty

undeterm'ined, a. unfettled, undecided [tainty

Undevóted, a. not devoted or fated, not given up

Undex'trous, n. not dextrous, clumfy

Undiaph'anous, a. not tranfparent, dark, dull

undid', pr. t. of to undo

Undigeft'ed, a. not digefted, not concocted, frefh

Undimin'ifhed, a. not diminifhed, entire, whole

Undimin'ifhable, a. not capable of diminution

Undint'ed, a. not marked by a blow, fmooth

Undip'ped, a. not dipped, not plunged, dry

Undirect'ed, a. not directed, not fet right

Undifcern'ed, a. not difcerned, unobferved, unfeen

Undifcern'ible, a. not to be difcerned, invifible

Undifcern'ibly, ad. invifibly, imperceptibly

Undifcern'ing, a. inattentive, injudicious, dull

Undis'ciplined, a. uninftructed, not duly trained

undifcov'erable, a. not to be found out, dark

Undifcov'ered, a. not difcovered, not found out

Undifcréet, a. imprudent, foolifh, indifcreet, ob.

Undifguifed, a. open, artlefs, fincere, honeft

Undifhon'ored, a. not dishonored, not difgraced

Undifob'liging, a. inoffenfive, harmlefs, worthy, ob.

undifpútable, a. not to be controverted

Undiffem'bling, a. not difguifing, frank

Undiffolv'able, a. not capable of diffolution

Undiffolv'ed, a. not diffolved or melted

Undis'fipated, a. not diffipated or fcattered

Undifturb'ed, a. not difturbed, unmolefted, quiet

Undo, [undoo] v. t. undid, pret. undone, pa. to take to pieces, ruin, fpoil, hurt, explain

Undóer, n. one who undoes, one who ruins, a foe

Undóne, [undun] pa. a. ruined, not yet begun

Undoubt'edly, ad. without doubt, certainly

Undoubt'ful, a. not doubtful, certain

Undréamed, a. not thought of, not cared for

Undrefs', v. t. to take off the clothes, to ftrip

Un'drefs, n. a loofe or negligent drefs

Undrofs'y, a. not droffy, pure, clear

Undrown'ed, a. not drowned

Un'dulate, v. t. to roll or move as a wave, to wave

Un'dulate, Un'dulated, a. waving, rifing & falling

Un'dulating, a. moving like waves, rifing & falling

Un'dulatingly, ad. in the manner of waves

Undulátion, n. a motion like that of waves

Un'dulatory, a. waving, moving like a wave

Unéafinefs, n. a ftate of difquiet, trouble, care

Unéafily, ad. in an uneafy manner or ftate

Unéafy, a. unhappy, difturbed, painful, reftlefs

Unéaten, a. not eaten or devoured, left, untouched

Unéath, ad. not eafily, hardly, fcarce, beneath, ob.

Uned'ifying, a. not improving, not inftructing

Uned'ucated, a. having had no education

Unelaf'tic, a. not elaftic, not having a fpring

Unelect'ed, a. not elected, not chofen or preferred

unel'igible, a not worthy to be chofen

Unembar'raffed, a. free from embarraffment

Unemploy'ed, a. not employed, difengaged

Unemp'tiable, a. not to be exhaufted, very deep

unencum'ber, v. t. to difengage, to fet at liberty

Unendow'ed, a. not endowed, not invefted, poor

Unengáged, a. not engaged, not appropriated, free

unengáging, a. not engaging or inviting

Unenjoy'ed, a. not enjoyed, not poffeffed or held

Unenjoy'ing, a. having no enjoyment, not ufing

Unenlarg'ed, a. not enlarged, contracted, mean

Unenlightened, a. not enlightened, dark, dull

Unenflaved, a. not inthralled, free, roving, loofe

Unen'terprizing, a. not enterprizing

Unentertáining, a. giving no delight, very dull

Unentertáiningnefs, n. the quality of being dull
Unen'vied, a. not envied, exempt from envy
Unen'vious, a. free from envy
Unéquable, a. different from itfelf, diverfe
Unéqual, a. not equal, uneven, partial, unjuft
Unéqualable, a. not to be equalled or paralleled
Unéqualled, a. unparalle'ed, fupreme, fuperior
Unéqually, ad. irregularly, in different degrees
Unéqualnefs, n. inequality, irregularity, oddnefs
Une'quitable, a. not juft or right, unfair, partial
Unequiv'ocal, a. not equivocal, plain, honeft
Unerr'ablenefs, n. an incapacity of erring, truth
Unerr'ing, a. not miftaking, certain, invariable
Unerr'ingly, ad. without miftake, certainly
Unefchew'able, a. not to be avoided, certain, ob.
Unefpied, a. not efpied, not difcovered, unfeen
Uneffen'tial, a. not effential, void of life
Uneftab'lifhed, a. not eftablifhed, uncertain
Unéven, a. not even, unequal, irregular, rough
Unévenly, ad. in an uneven manner
Unévennefs, n. inequality, roughnefs, change
Unev'itable, a. not to be avoided, fixed, certain
Unexact'ed, a. not exacted, not forced, quite free
Unexam'ined, a. not examined, not looked over
Unexamp'led, a. having no example or precedent
Unexcep'tionable, a. not liable to objection
Unexco'gitable, a. that cannot be found out, ob.
Unex'ecuted, a. not executed, not performed
Unexemp'lified, a. not known by example, unpro-
Unex'ercifed, a. not exercifed or practiced (ved
Unexert'ed, a. not exerted or exercifed
Unexempt', a. not free, not privileged, liable to
Unexhauft'ed, a. not drained, not fpent or gone
Unex'orcifed, a. not exorcifed, not caft out
Unexpand'ed, a. not fpread or laid out, confufed
Unexpect'ed, a. not expected, not hoped, fudden
Unexpect'edly, ad. without hope, fuddenly
Unexpect'ednefs, n. fuddennefs, a fudden ftate
Unexpec'torating, a. not difcharging from the
    throat or lungs
Unexpédient, a. unfit, improper, inconvenient
Unexpend'ed, a. not laid out or expended
Unexpérienced, a. not experienced, not verfed
Unexpert', a. aukward, unhandy, wanting fkill
Unexplóred, a. not fearched out, unknown, new
Unexpófed, a. not laid open, not fubjected
Unexprefs'ible, Unexprefs'ive, a. unutterable, big
Unextend'ed, a. having no dimenfions, confined
Unextinct', a. not extinct, or extinguifhed
Unextin'guifhable, a. that cannot be put out
Unextin'guifhed, a. not quenched, not put out
Unex'tirpated, a. not extirpated, not rooted out
Unfáded, a. not withered or decayed, frefh, new
Unfáding, a. not liable to fade or change color
Unfáiling, a. not miffing, abiding, certain, true
Unfáir, a. not fair, dishoneft, difingenuous
Unfáirly, ad. not in a fair manner
Unfáirnefs, n. unfair or dishoneft behavior
Unfáithful, a. trecherous, dishoneft, impious

Unfáithfully, ad. trecheroufly, deceitfully, bafely
Unfáithfulnefs, n. trechery, deccit, impiety
Unfal'lowed, a. not fallowed, not duly prepared
Unfamil'iar, a. uncommon, unaccuftomed
Unfafh'ionable, a. not modifh, droll, obfolete
Unfafh'ionablenefs, n. a deviation from the mode-
Unfafh'ionably, ad. not according to the fafhion
Unfafh'ioned, a. not fafhioned or formed by art:
Unfaft'en, v. t. to unloofe, fet free, unfix, open
Unfath'ered, a. fatherlefs, having no owner
Unfath'omable, a. not to be founded, very deep
Unfath'omably, ad. fo as not to be founded
Unfath'omed, a. not fathomed, not founded
Unfatígued, a. not fatigued, unwearied, untired
Unfávorable, ad. not favorable, unpromifing, bad
Unfávorably, a. not favorably, unkindly, badly
Unféared, a. not feared, flighted, defpifed
Unféafible, a. impracticable, not to be done
Unfeth'ered, a. naked or void of fethers, bare
Unféatured, a. wanting regular features, deformed
Unfed', n. not fed, not fupplied with food, hungry
Unfée'd, a. not fee'd, not bribed, left unpaid
Unféeling, a. void of feeling, infenfible, cruel
Unféelingly, ad. in an unfeeling manner
Unféelingnefs, n. infenfibility, cruelty
Unfeign'ed, a. not pretended, real, fincere, honeft
Unfeign'edly, ad. really, truly, fincerely, honeftly
Unfelt', a. not felt, not perceived, fimple, eafy
Unfen'ced, a. not inclofed, left open, defencelefs
Unferment'ed, a. not fermented, not leavened
Unfert'ile, a. unfruitful. barren, bare, wafte
Unfet'ter, v. t. to free from fhackles, to unchain
Unfig'ured, a. plain, reprefenting no animal form
Unfil'ial, a. unfuitable to a fon, difobedient
Unfill'ed, a. not filled, not fupplied, empty, void
Unfin'ifhed, a. wanting the laft hand, imperfect
Unfíred, a. not heated, or inflamed
Unfírm', a. not ftable, weak, feeble, old, infirm
Unfírm'nefs, n. a weak ftate, inftability, change
Unfit', a. improper, unfuitable, unqualified
Unfit', v. t. to make unfit, difqualify, difable
Unfit'ly, ad. not properly, improperly, unfuitably
Unfit'nefs, n. a want of qualification or propriety
Unfit'ting, pa. difqualifying, unbecoming
Unfix', v. t. to loofen, feparate, unbar, make fluid
Unfix'ed, pa. loofened, unfettled, wandering
Unfledg'ed, a. not covered with fethers, bare
Unflefh'ed, a. not covered with flefh, lean, not ufed
Unfoil'ed, a. not fubdued, not conquered (to kill
Unfóld, v. t. to expand, difplay, difcover, tell
Unfólding, pa. directing to unfold, opening
Unfólding, n. a difclofure
Unfool', v. t. to reftore from folly, to undeceive
Unforbid'den, a. not forbidden, allowed, legal
Unforbid'dennefs, n. an unforbidden ftate, lawful-
Unfórced, a. not compelled, not feigned (nefs.
Unfórcible, a. wanting ftrength, weak, feeble
Unfórdable, a. not to be forded
Unforebóding, a. giving no omens or figns

Unforewarn'ed, *a.* not previously warned
Unforeknown, *a.* not foreseen by prescience
Unforeséen, *a.* not foreseen, not known before
Unfóreskinned, *a.* not circumcised, not marked
Unfor'feited, *a.* not forfeited, preserved, saved
Unforgiv'ing, *a.* implacable, inexorable, cruel
Unforgot', Unforgot'ten, *a.* not lost to memory
Unform'ed, *a.* not shaped or modified, shapeless
Unforfáken, *a.* not deserted, supported, affifted
Unfor'tified, *a.* not fortified, weak, defenceless
Unfor'tunate, *a.* unprosperous, wanting luck
Unfor'tunately, *ad.* without good luck, unhappily
Unfor'tunateness, *n.* bad or ill fortune, ill luck
Unfos'tered, *a.* not foftered, nourished or patronized
Unfought', *a.* not fought, not yet determined
Unfoul'ed, *a.* not foiled, clean, uncorrupt, pure
Unfound', *a.* not found, not met with, quite loft
Unfound'ed, *a.* not founded, having no foundation
Unfrámable, *a.* not to be framed or molded
Unfrámed, *a.* not framed, not formed or fafhioned
Unfrank'ed, *a.* not franked, not free or exempt
Unfréquent, *a.* not common, unufual, rare
Unfrequent', *v. t.* to ceafe to frequent, to leave
Unfrequent'ed, *a.* rarely visited, forfaken
Unfréquently, *ad.* uncommonly, rarely, seldom
Unfriend'ed, *a.* wanting friends, deftitute, poor
Unfriend'linefs, *n.* a want of kindnefs or regard
Unfriend'ly, *a.* unkind, uncivil, unfavorable
Unfrózen, *a.* not frozen, not congealed, fluid, open
Unfrúitful, *a.* not fruitful, barren, wafte, wild
Unfrúitfulnefs, *n.* unprofitablenefs, barrennefs
Unfulfill'ed, *a.* not fulfilled, not completed, left
Unfúmed, *a.* not fumigated or fmoked
Unfund'ed, *a.* not funded, having no permanent provifion made for the interefl
Unfurl', *v. t.* to expand, unfold, fpread, open
Unfur'nifh, *v. t.* to ftrip, bare, diveft, deprive
Unfur'nifhed, *pa. a.* ftripped, void of furniture
Unfúfed, *a.* not fufed or diffolved by heat
Ungáin, Ungáinly, *a.* aukward, uncouth, clumfy
Ungall'ed, *a.* not galled, unwounded, unhurt
Ungar'nifhed, *a.* not garnifhed, unadorned, plain
Ungar'tered, *a.* not gartered, loofe, flovenly
Ungath'ered, *a.* not picked or pulled, growing
Ungen'erate or Ungen'erated, *a.* unbegotten, eter-
Ungen'erative, *a.* begetting nothing, barren (nal
Ungen'erous, *a.* illiberal, mean, ignominious
Ungénial, *a.* unfavorable, unfriendly, unkind
Ungentéel, *a.* not genteel, unbecoming, rude
Ungentéelly, *ad.* unpolitely, uncivilly, rudely
Ungen''tle, *a.* fkittifh, wild, harfh, rude, rugged
Ungen''tlemanlike, Ungen''tlemanly, *a.* not becoming a gentleman, illiberal, mean, low
Ungen''tlenefs, *n.* harfhnefs, rudenefs, incivility
Ungent'ly, *ad.* harfhly, roughly, rudely, feverely
Ungeomet'rical, *a.* not geometrical, bungling
Ungild'ed, *a.* not overlaid with gold, &c. plain
Ungird', *v. t.* ungirded, ungirt, *pret.* and *pa.* to loofe a girdle or girth, to untie

Ungirt', *pa. a.* untied, loofely dreffed, loofe, free
Ungiv'ing, *a.* not bringing gifts, niggardly, mean
Unglázed, *a.* not glazed, without a glaze or glofs
Unglórified, *a.* not glorified, not praifed
Unglov'ed, *a.* having the hand naked, uncovered
Unglúe, *v. t.* to feparate a place glued, to loofen
Ungod', *v. t.* to diveft or ftrip of divinity
Ungod'lily, *ad.* impioufly, wickedly, badly
Ungod'linefs, *n.* impiety, profanenefs, wickednefs
Ungod'ly, *a.* irreligious, unholy, profane, wicked
Ungóred, *a.* unwounded with a horn, unhurt
Ungorg'ed, *a.* not glutted, not fated, not filled
Ungot', Ungotten, *a.* not acquired, unbegotten
Ungov'ernable, *a.* not to be ruled, unruly, wild
Ungov'erned, *a.* unbridled, rude, licentious, loofe
Ungráceful, *a.* wanting beauty or air, aukward
Ungrácefully, *ad.* aukwardly, clumfily, badly
Ungrácefulnefs, *n.* inelegance, aukwardnefs
Ungrácious, *a.* unacceptable, offenfive, wicked
Ungrammat'ical, *a.* not agreeable to grammar
Ungrant'ed, *a.* not allowed, not given, ftill left
Ungráteful, *a.* unthankful, vile, unpleafant
Ungratefully, *ad.* with ingratitude, unpleafingly
Ungratefulnefs, *n.* ingratitude, unacceptablenefs
Ungrávely, *ad.* without ferioufaefs, giddily
Unground'ed, *a.* having no ground or foundation
Ungrudg'ingly, *ad.* heartily, cheerfully, readily
Unguard'ed, *a.* not defended, carelefs, unwary
Unguard'edly, *ad.* incautioufly, carelefsly
Un''guent, *n.* an ointment, liquid falve, perfume
Unguent'ous, *a.* like or confifting of unguent
Unguic'ulate, *a.* clawed, having claws
Unguic'ular, *a.* of the length of a nail
Unguid'ed, *a.* not directed or led by a guide
Un'gulate, *a.* fhaped like a hoof
 Unguil'ty, *a.* not guilty, innocent
Unhab'itable, *a.* uninhabitable
Unhack'ed, *a.* not cut or notched
Unhal'low, *v. t.* to profane, make common
Unhal'lowed, *a.* unholy, profane
Unhand', *v. t.* to let go, or loofe from the hand
Unhand'inefs, *n.* clumfinefs, a want of dexterity
Unhand'fome, *a.* illiberal, ungraceful, aukward
Unhand'y, *a.* not handy, not dexterous, aukward
Unhang, *v. t.* to take from hinges, or faftening
Unhang'ed, Un'hung, *a.* not hanged, not hung
Unhap'pied, *a.* made unhappy, made miferable
Unhap'pily, *ad.* in an unhappy manner
Unhap'pinefs, *n.* calamity, wretchednefs
Unhap'py, *a.* unfortunate, diftreffed, miferable
Unharbored, *a.* not fheltered, affording no harbor
Unhard'ened, *a.* not hardened
Unhard'y, *a.* not hardy, feeble, tender
Unharm'ed, *a.* not hurt, unhurt, uninjured, fafe
Unharm'ful, *a.* unable to do hurt, innocent, kind
Unharmónious, *a.* unmufical, harfh, grating
Unhar'nefs, *v. t.* to take off harnefs, to difarm
Unhaz'arded, *a.* not ventured, not put in danger
Unhatch'ed, *a.* not yet brought forth

Unhead', v. t. to take out the head, as of a cask
Unhealth'ful, unhealth'y, a. wanting health, fickly
Unhealth'fulnefs, n. infalubrity, ficklinefs
Unhealth'inefs, n. an unhealthy ftate, ficklinefs
Unhéard, a. not heard, unknown, uncommon
Unheárt, v. t. to difcourage, deprefs, alarm, hurt
Unhéated, a. not heated, not made hot, quite cold
Unhéeded, a. not minded, difregarded, flighted
Unhéedful, a. inattentive, carelefs, giddy, wild
Unhéeding, a. carelefs, negligent, thoughtlefs
Unhéedy, a. rafh, fudden, precipitate, thoughtlefs
Unhelp'ed, a. unaffifted, unfupported, alone
Unhelp'ful, a. not helping, giving no affiftance
Unhewn', a. not hewn, not fhaped or formed
Unhídebound, a. loofe, lax of maw, capacious
Unhinge', v. t. to throw from hinges, to difplace
Unhóard, v. t. to fteal, take away, difclofe, produce
Unhólily, ad. in an unholy manner, profanely
Unhólinefs, n. profanenefs, wickednefs
Unhóly, a. profane, impious, lewd, vile, wicked
Unhon'ored, a. not treated with honor or refpeĉt
Unhoop', v. t. to divcft of or ftrip off hoops
Unhóped, a. not hoped for, more than expeĉted
Unhópeful, a. giving no room to hope, unprom-
Unhorfe', v. t. to throw out of faddle   ifing
Unhos'pitable, a. not hofpitable, unfriendly
Unhos'tile, a. not belonging to an enemy, kind
Unhoufe', v. t. to drive out of a habitation
Unhous'ed, pa. a. driven out, homelefs, free
Unhous'eled, a. going without the facrament, ob.
Unhum'bled, a. not humbled, haughty, proud
Unhurt', a. not hurt, free from harm, quite fafe
Unhurt'ful, a. doing no harm, harmlefs, innocent
Unhurt'fully, ad. without harm, innocently
Unicap'fular, [u as yu] a. having one capfule
U'nicorn, [u as yu] n. a beaft with only one horn, fifh, bird
U'niform, [u as yu] a. fimilar, equable, confiftent
U'niform, n. the drefs of a band of foldiers, which is alike in all   (nefs
Uniform'ity, n. a conformity to one pattern, fame-
U'niformly, ad. in an uniform manner, evenly
Uniflórous, [u as yu] a. having one flower only
Unilat'eral, [u as yu] a. having one fide only
Uniloc'ular, [u as yu] a. having one cell only
Unigénous, a. of one kind, of the fame genus
Unima"ginable, a. not to be imagined or thought
Unima"ginably, ad. in an unimagined degree
Unim'itable, a. not to be imitated, inimitable
Unimmor'tal, a. not immortal, frail, fading
Unimpáirable, a. not liable to be impaired, firm
Unimpáired, a. not impaired, entire
Unimpas'fioned, a. not having paffions, temperate
Unimpéached, a. not impeached, not accufed
Unimpéachable, a. not to be impeached or charged
Unimplóred, a. not folicited or implored
Unimpört'ant, a. not important, trifling, mean
Unimportúned, a. not folicited, not much afked
Unimpreg'nated, a. not impregnated

Unimprefs'ive, a. not impreffive, not forcible
Unimpróvable, a. not to be improved, very bad
Unimprov'ablenefs, n. a ftate of not being capable of improvement
Unimpróved, a. not improved, taught or occupied
Uninchant'ed, a. not inchanted
Unincréafable, a. not to be increafed, boundlefs
Unincum'bered, a. not fubjeĉt to incumbrance or
Unindéared, a. not endeared   (debts
Unindif'ferent, a. partial, addiĉted, fond of
Unindors'ed, a. not indorfed
Unindus'trious, a. not induftrious, idle, lazy
Uninfec'tious, a. not infeĉtious or catching
Uninfec'ted, a. not infeĉted, pure, wholefome
Uninflámed, a. not fet on fire, not at all burnt
Uninflam'mable, a. not capable of being fired
Uninform'ed, a. not informed, not enlightened
Uningen'uous, a. illiberal, unfair, not honeft
Uninhab'itable, a. that is not fit to be inhabited
Uninhab'itablenefs, n. an uninhabitable ftate
Uninhab'ited, a. having no dwellers, empty, void
Unini"tiated, a. not initiated
Unin'jured, a. not injured, unhurt, fafe, fecure
Uninfcribed, a. not infcribed, not written upon
Uninfpired, a. not infpired, not canonical, falfe
Uninftruĉt'ed, a. not inftruĉted, uhtaught, rude
Uninftruĉt'ive, a. not edifying, not teaching
Unin'fulated, a. not infulated, or detached
Unintell'igent, a. not knowing, not fkilful
Unintell'igible, a. that cannot be underftood
Unintelligibil'ity, n. an unintelligible quality
Unintell'igibly, ad. fo as not to be underftood
Uninten'tional, a. not intentional, not defigned
Uninten'tionally, ad. without intention
Unin'terefted, a. not having intereft or concern
Unin'terefting, a. not affeĉting the heart, dull
Unintermit'ted, a. uninterrupted, continued, reg-
Uninter'mix'ed, a. not mingled, feparate   (ular
Uninterrupt'ed, a. not interrupted, continued
Uninterrupt'edly, ad. without obftruĉtion, duly
Unintrench'ed, a. not intrenched, expofed, open
Uninúred, a. not inured, or accuftomed
Uninvent'ed, a. not invented
Uninvers'ible, a. not to be overfet
Uninveft'igable, a. not to be fearched out
Uninvid'ious, a. not invidious
Uninvíted, a. not invited, not afked, not defired
U'nion, [u as yu] n. the aĉt of uniting, concord
Unip'arous, a. bringing forth only one at a birth
Unir'ritated, a. not irritated or fretted
Unir'ritating, a. not irritating or exciting
U'nifon, [u as yu] a. founding alone or the fame
U'nifon, n. an unvaried note, agreement, concert
U'nit, [u as yu] n. the number one
Unitárian, [u as yu] n. one who denies the trinity, and afcribes divinity to one fupreme God only
Unitárian, a. pertaining to the doĉtrin of one per- fon only in the godhead
Uníte, v. to form or grow into one, join, agree

Unitedly, *ad.* with union or consent, together
Uniter, *n.* one who or that which unites
Uni"tion, *n.* the act or power of uniting, union
U'nitive, *a.* able or tending to unite, binding
u'nity, *n.* the state of being one, concord, tenor
U'nivalve, [u as yu] *n.* an animal with one shell
u'nivalve, Univalv'ular, *a.* having one shell (whole
Univers'al, [u as yu] *a.* all, total, general; *n.* the
Univers'alism, *n.* the belief that all men will be saved
Univers'alist, *n.* an adherent to universalism
Univerfal'ity, *n.* a universal state, generality
Univers'ally, *ad.* invariably, without exception
U'niverfe, *n.* a general system of things, the world
Univers'ity, *n.* a general school of liberal arts, &c.
Univ'ocal, [u as yu] *a.* having one meaning, certain
Univ'ocally, *ad.* in one sense or tenor, in one term
Unjoint'ed, *a.* disjointed, broken, having no joint
Unjoy'ous, *a.* void of joy, gloomy, dismal, heavy
Unjudg'ed, *a.* not judically determined
Unjust', *a.* contrary to justice, dishonest, partial
Unjust'ifiable, *a.* not to be justified, very bad, base
Unjust'ifiablenefs, *n.* an unjustifiable state, bad-
Unjust'ly, *ad.* contrary to justice or right (nefs
Unken'nel, *v. t.* to drive from a hole, to roufe
Unkept', *a.* not kept, not obferved, not regarded
Unkind, *a.* not kind, not obliging or civil, cruel
Unkindly, *a.* without kindnefs or due affection
Unkindly, *a.* unnatural, unfavorable, crofs
Unkindnefs, *n.* a want of good-will, malignity
Unking', *v. t.* to depofe a king, to dethrone
Unkifs'ed, *a.* not kiffed, not faluted, not loved
Unknightly, *a.* not becoming a knight, mean
Unknit', *v. t.* unknit, unknitted, *pret.* and *pa.* to
ravel, unweave, open, feparate
Unknot', *v. t.* to free from knots, untie, loofen
Unknow, *v. t.* unknew, *pret.* unknown, *pa.* to
ceafe to know longer, to forget
Unknowable, *a.* that cannot be known, fecret
Unknowing, *a.* ignorant, unlearned, unqualified
Unknowingly, *ad.* ignorantly, undesignedly
Unknown, *a.* not known or noted, undifcovered
Unlabored, *a.* not duly confidered, voluntary
Unlace, *v. t.* to loofe a thing laced up, to cut up
Unlade, *v. t.* unladed, *pret.* unladed, unladen, *pa.*
to unload, take off, empty, put out
Unlaid, *a.* not laid, not placed or put, not pacified
Unlament'ed, *a.* not lamented, not deplored, for-
Unlard'ed, *a.* not intermixed (gotten
Unlatch', *v. t.* to open a latch, to lift up
Unlav'ifh, *a.* not wafteful, faving
Unlaw'ful, *a.* contrary to law, unjust, unfair
Unlaw'fully, *ad.* in an unlawful or bad manner
Unlaw'fulnefs, *n.* a contrariety to law, injuftice
Unlearn', *v. t.* to forget, lofe, let flip, let go, undo
Unlearn'ed, *a.* not learned, ignorant, grofs, heavy
Unlearn'edly, *ad.* ignorantly, grofsly, rudely
Unleav'ened, *a.* not leavened, not fermented
Unleis'urednefs, *n.* a want of leifure, *ob.*
Unlefs, *an old verb in the infinitive mode,* except,

remove, difmifs, releafe, equivalent to, *if not*
Unlefs'oned, *a.* uninftructed, not duly taught
Unlet'tered, *a.* unlearned, ignorant, not marked
Unlev'elled, *a.* not cut or made even, rough
Unlibid'inous, *a.* not luftful, chafte, pure, good
Unlicenfed, *a.* having no licenfe, having no leave
Unlick'ed, *a.* not licked, not formed, fhapelefs
Unlighted, *a.* not lighted, not kindled, very dark
Unlightfome, *a.* dark, gloomy, difmal
Unlike, *a.* not like, unlikely, improbable
Unlikelihood, Unlikelinefs, *n.* improbability, (bly
Unlikely, *a.* not likely, improbable; *ad.* improba-
Unlikenefs, *n.* a want of likenefs or refemblance
Unlim'itable, *a.* admitting of no bounds, infinite
Unlim'ited, *a.* not limited, unbounded, undefined
Unlim'itedly, *ad.* without limits or bounds
Unlin'eal, *a.* not going in due order of fucceffion
Unlink', *v. t.* to disjoin, open, untwift, break
Unliq'nefied, *a.* not melted or diffolved, hard
Un'located, *a.* not fixed or defined in regard to
place, not located or appropriated by choice
Unload, *v. t.* unloaded, *pret.* unloaded, unleaden,
pa. to difburden, to put or take off
Unlock', *v. t.* to open a lock, folve, clear, explain
Unlook'ed, *a.* not expected, not forefeen, ftrange
Unloofable, *a.* not to be loofed, very faft or firm
Unloofe', *v.* to loofe, fet loofe, eafe, fall in pieces
Unlov'ed, *a.* not loved, difliked, difregarded
Unlove'linefs, *n.* an inability to excite love, ugli-
Unlove'ly, *a.* unable to excite love (nefs
Unluck'ily, *ad.* with bad luck, unfortunately
Unluck'inefs, *n.* bad luck, unfortunatenefs
Unluck'y, *a.* unfortunate, mifchievous, waggifh
Unluft'rous, *a.* wanting lufter, not bright, dull
Unluft'y, *a.* not lufty, flight, flim, flender, weak
Unmade, *a.* not made or created, deprived of form
Unmagnet'ic, *a.* not having magnetic properties
Unmaimed, *a.* not maimed, unhurt, whole
Unmakable, *a.* impoffible to be made, *ob.*
Unmake, *v. t.* unmade, *pret.* unmade, *pa.* to
deprive of form or quality, to deftroy
Unmal'leable, *a.* not capable of being hammered
into a plate (by beating
Unmalleabil'ity, *n.* incapacity of being extended
Unman', *v.* to deprive of rational powers or of
ftrength and courage
Unman'ageable, *a.* not manageable, ftubborn
Unman'aged, *a.* not broken in, not at all tutored
Unman'like, Unman'ly, *a.* unbecoming a man
Unman'nered, *a.* rude, grofs, rough, uncivil, brutal
Unman'nerlinefs, *n.* rudenefs, a breach of civility
Unman'nerly, *a.* ill-bred, uncivil; *ad.* uncivilly
Unmanured, *a.* not manured or cultivated, poor
Unmark'ed, *a.* not marked, not regarded, not feen
Unmark'etable, *a.* not faleable or fit for the market
Unmar'red, *a.* not marred or impaired
Unmar'ried, *a.* not married, fingle, lonely
Unmafk', *v. t.* to remove a difguife, to fhow plainly
Unmafk'ed, *pa. a.* not mafked, naked, open

Unmaſt'erable, a. not to be ſubdued or tamed
Unmaſt'ered, a. not ſubdued or conquered, free
Unmatch'able, a. not to be matched or equalled
Unmatch'ed, a. matchleſs, having no equal, fine
Unmeaning, a. having no meaning, inſipid, poor
Unmeant', a. not meant, not intended or deſigned
Unmeaſ'urable, a. unbounded, infinite, endleſs
Unmeaſ'urably, ad. beyond meaſure
Unmeaſ'ured, a. not meaſured, plentiful, large
Unmechan'ical, [ch as k] a. not mechanical
Unmed'dled, a. not touched, not altered
Unmed'dling, a. not meddling, not officious
Unmed'itated, a. not formed by previous thought
Unméet, a. unworthy, unfit, unbecoming
Unméetly ad. not ſuitably, not fitly
Unmell'owed, a. not fully or duly ripened, hard
Unmelt'ed, a. not melted, not diſſolved, hard
Unmen'tioned, a. not told, not at all named (ble
Unmer'chantable, a. not fit for the market, unſalea-
Unmer'ciful, a. cruel, ſevere, unconſcionable
Unmer'cifully, ad. without mercy, with cruelty
Unmer'cifulneſs, n. cruelty, a want of clemency
Unmer'itable, a. having no merit, worthleſs, bad
Unmer'ited, a. not deſerved, unjuſt, cruel (ice
Unmer'itedneſs, n. an unmerited event, &c. injuſt-
Unmetal'lic, a. not metallic or belonging to metals
Unmet'alized, a. not formed into a metal
Unmilk'ed, a. not milked, full, loaded
Unmil'led, a. not milled, not indented or grained
Unminded, a. unheeded, diſregarded, ſlighted
Unmindful, a. heedleſs, inattentive, negligent
Unmin"gle, v. t. to ſeparate or part things mixed
Unmin"gl able, a. that cannot be mixed
Unmin"gled, pa. a. not mixed, ſeparated, pure
Unmiſry, a. not fouled with dirt, clean, dry
Unmiſtruſt'ing, a. not ſuſpecting
Unmit'igated, a. not ſoftened, not leſſened
Unmix'ed, a. not mixed or mingled, pure, entire
Unmóaned, a. not lamented
Unmod'iſiable, a. not to be modified
Unmóiſt, a. not moiſt, not wet, quite dry
Unmoiſt'ened, a. not moiſtened, not wetted
Unmóld, v. t. to change or alter as to the form
Unmoleſt'ed, a. free from all diſturbance, eaſy
Unmóor, v. t. to heave up an anchor, to weigh
Unmor'alized, a. not tutored by morality, groſs
Unmor'tgaged, a. not mortgaged, quite clear, free
Unmor'tified, a. not ſubdued by ſorrow, eaſy
Unmóurned, a. not mourned for, unlamented
Unmove'able, a. that cannot be removed, fixed
Unmove'ableneſs, n. an unmoveable or ſafe ſtate
Unmóved, a. not moved, unaffected, firm
Unmóving, a. not moving, unaffecting, dull
Unmuf'fle, v. t. to take a covering off the face
Unmuſical, a. not harmonious, harſh, rough
Unmuz'zle, v. t. to take off a muzzle, to ſet looſe
Unnámed, a. not mentioned, not ſpoken of
Unnátive, a. not native, not natural, forced
Unnat'ural, a. contrary to nature, forced, cruel

Unnat'uralize, v. t. to diveſt of natural feelings
Unnat'uralized, a. not naturalized or made a citizen
Unnat'urally, ad. in oppoſition to nature, cruelly
Unnat'uralneſs, n. a contrariety to nature, cruelty
Unnav'igable, a. not to be navigated or ſailed
Unnav'igated, a. not failed upon
Unne"ceſſarily, ad. without neceſſity or need
Unne"ceſſarineſs, n. needleſſneſs, uſeleſſneſs
Un"neceſſary, a. needleſs, uſeleſs, trifling
Unneigh'borly, a. not neighborly, not kind
Unneigh'borly, ad. in an unneighborly manner
Unnerv'ate, Unnerv'ed, a. weak, feeble, faint
Unnerve', v. t. to weaken, enfeeble, diſcourage
Unneútral, a. not neutral, not unintereſted
Unnóble, a. not noble, ignoble, low, mean, baſe
Unnóted, a. not noted, not obſerved or regarded
Unnóticed, a. not obſerved or regarded
Unnum'bered, a. not numbered, numberleſs, vaſt
Unobey'ed, a. not obeyed, reſiſted, ſlighted
Unobject'ed, a. not charged as a fault, allowed
Unobnox'ious, a. not liable, not expoſed, free
Unobſcúred, a. not obſcured, bright
Unobſéquiouſneſs, n. diſobedience, contradiction
Unobſerv'able, a. not to be obſerved or perceived
Unobſerv'ant, a. not obſequious, inattentive
Unobſerv'ed, a. not ſeen, not attended to
Unobſerv'ing, a. unheedful, inattentive, ſimple
Unobſtruct'ed, a. not at all hindered, not ſtopped
Unobſtruct'ive, a. not raiſing any obſtacle, kind
Unobtáined, a. not acquired, not gained, left
Unob'vious, a. not readily occurring, not plain
Unoc'cupied, a. unpoſſeſſed, uninhabited
Unoffend'ing, a. harmleſs, innocent, civil, kind
Unof'fered, a. not offered, not preſented
Unoffi"cial, a. not official, not authorized by the
Unóil, v. t. to clear or free from oil (proper officer
Unópened, a. not opened, cloſed, ſhut, ſecured
Unópening, a. not opening, not purgative
Unop'erative, a. producing no effect, very weak
Unoppóſed, a. not oppoſed, not withſtood, yielded
Unoppreſs'ed, a. not oppreſſed
Unor'derly, a. diſorderly, irregular, wild, rude
Unor'dinary, a. uncommon, unuſual, rare
Unor'ganized, a. not organized, not duly formed
Unori"ginal, a. having no birth, not generated
Unor'thodox, a. not holding pure doctrin
Unówed, a. not owed, not due, cleared or paid off
Unówned, a. not owned, having no owner, left
Unoxy"genated, a. not combined with oxygene
Unpack', v. t. to open things packed, to unload
Unpack'ed, pa. not packed, opened, unloaded
Unpáid, a. not paid, not diſcharged, ſtill due
Unpáined, a. ſuffering no pain, being quite at eaſe
Unpáinful, a. not painful, giving no pain
Unpal'atable, a. nauſeous, diſguſting, ſickly, bad
Unpall'ed, a. not deadened
Unpar'adiſe, v. t. to render unhappy or wretched
Unpar'agoned, a. unequalled, unmatched, noble
Unpar'alleled, a. having no equal, unmatched

Unpard'enable, a. not to be forgiven, very bad
Unpard'onable, ad. beyond forgivenefs, bafely
Unpard'oned, a. not forgiven, not difcharged
Unpard'oning, a. not forgiving (parliament
Unparliament'arinefs, n. a contrariety to rules of
Unparliament'ary, a. contrary to rules of parlia-
Unpart'ed, a. not divided or feparated (ment
Unpar'tial, a. juft, fair, honeft, good, impartial, ob.
Unpar'tially, ad. juftly, fairly, duly, impartially, ob.
Unpafs'able, a. admitting no paffage, impaffable
Unpas"fionate, a. free from paffion, quite calm
Unpas"fionately, ad. without paffion, calmly
Unpath'ied, a. untrod, untracked, fmooth, even
Unpat'ronifed, a. not patronifed, unfupported
Unpáved, a. not paved, not covered with ftone
Unpawn'ed, a. not laid in pawn, not pledged, fafe
Unpáy, v. t. to undo, pay back
Unpéaceable, a. quarrelfome, crofs, troublefome
Unpeg', v. t. to pull or let out a peg, to open
Unpelt'ed, a. not pelted, unhurt, unmolefted
Unpen'fioned, a. not penfioned, quite neglected
Unpéople, v. t. to drive off or deftroy inhabitants
Unperceivable, a. that cannot be perceived
Unperceived, a. unfeen, unobferved, hidden
Unperceivedly, ad. fo as not to be perceived
Unper'fect, a. incomplete, not full, imperfect
Unper'fectnefs, n. an imperfect ftate, a defect
Unper'forated, a. not perforated, not having holes
Unperform'ed, a. not performed, not done, left
Unper'ifhable, a. not perifhable, lafting, durable
Unper'jured, a. not perjured, not forfworn
Unperplex'ed, a. not embarraffed, compofed
Unperfpirable, a. that cannot be fweated through
Unperfuádable, a. not to be perfuaded, obftinate
Unpet'rified, a. not turned into ftone (phy
Unphilofoph'ical, a. not conformable to philofo-
Unphilofoph'ically, a. contrary to philofophy
Unphilofoph'icalnefs, n. a being contrary to philo-
    fophy, imperfectnefs, abfurdnefs (pher
Unphilos'ophize, v. t. to degrade from a philofo-
Unpier'ced, a. not pierced, found, whole, entire
Unpill'ared, a. divefted of pillars, not fupported
Unpill'owed, a. wanting a pillow, hard, uneafy
Unpin', v. t. to open what is pinned, to loofen
Unpink'ed, a. not pinked, not fet off or adorned
Unpit'ied, a. not pitied, unlamented, undeplored
Unpit'ifully, ad. without pity or mercy, cruelly
Unpit'ying, a having no compaffion, cruel, hard
Unpláced, a. having no place or employment
Unplágued, a. not tormented, not vexed, happy
Unplant'ed, a. not planted, not fet, fpontaneous
Unplatt'ered, a. not plaftered, bare, naked
Unplaus'ible, a. not plaufible, unlikely. falfe
Unplaus'ive, a. not approving, not commending
Unpleas'ant, a. not pleafant, uneafy, troublefome
Unpleas'antly, ad. crofsly, uneafily, uncivilly
Unpleas'antnefs, n. a want of pleafing qualities
Unpléafed, a. not pleafed, not delighted
Unpléafing, a. not pleafing, offenfive, difgufting

Unpléafingly, ad. in an unpleafing manner
Unpliant, a. not bending to another, very ftiff
Unplow'ed, a. not plowed, not duly prepared
Unplúme, v. t. to ftrip off plumes, ftrip, degrade
Unpoet'ical, a. not becoming a poet or poetry
Unpol'icied, a. not having policy, or civil govern-
    ment
Unpol'ifhed, a. not polifhed, uncivilized, rough
Unpolíte, a. not polite, uncivil, rude, ftrange
Unpolítely, ad. in an unpolite manner
Unpollúted, a. not defiled, not corrupted, pure
Unpop'ular, a. not popular, difliked, hated, odious
Unpórtable, a. not to be carried or borne
Unpoffefs'ed, a. not held or enjoyed, not obtained
Unpoffefs'ing, a. having no poffeffion, deftitute
Unpow'dered, a. not powdered
Unprac'ticable, a. not feafible, not to be done
Unprac'ticed, a. not fkilled by ufe, unfkilled
Unpráifed, a. not praifed, not celebrated
Unprecárious, a. not depending on another, fure
Unpre"cedented, a. not having a precedent, new
Unpredict', v. t. to retract a prediction made
Unprefer'red, a. not advanced or promoted, low
Unpreg'nant, a. unprolific, unfruitful, poor
Unprejúdicate, a. not prepoffeffed, candid, fair
Unpre"judiced, a. free from prejudice, unbiaffed
Unprelat'ical, a. not becoming or like a prelate
Unpremed'itated, a. not ftudied beforehand
Unprepáred, a. not prepared, not fitted, rough
Unprepáredness, n. the ftate of being unprepared
Unprepoffefs'ed, a. not prepoffeffed, impartial
Unpreffed, a. not preffed, not forced, free, loofe
Unpretend'ing, a. not claiming diftinction, plain
Unprevailing, a. being of no force, vain, difliked
Unprevent'ed, a. not prevented, not hindered
Unprincely, ad. unfuitable to or unlike a prince
Unprin'cipled, a. not duly inftructed, profligate
Unprint'ed, a. not yet printed, not publifhed
Unprifable, a. having little eftimation or value
Unpris'oned, a. fet free from confinement, free
Unprized, a. not prized or valued, not regarded
Unprocláimed, a. not publicly declared, fecret
Unprofáned, a. not profaned or violated, facred
Unprofes'fional, a. not belonging to ones profeffion
Unprof'itable, a. ufelefs, vain, ferving no purpofe
Unprof'itablenefs, n. ufelefsnefs, infignificance
Unprof'itably, ad. ufelefsly, to no good purpofe
Unprof'ited, a. not profited, having no gain
Unprohib'ited, a. not forbidden, lawful, right
Unprolif'ic, a. not fruitful, unfruitful, barren
Unprom'ifing, a. not promifing, unfavorable
Unpronoun'ced, a. not uttered, not fpoken
Unprop', v. t. to remove a prop or pillars
Unprop'er, a. not proper or peculiar, ob.
Unprop'erly, ad. unfitly, amifs, improperly, ob.
Unpropi'tious, a. unfavorable, inaufpicious
Unpropi'tioufly, ad. unfavorably, unkindly
Unproportionable, a. wanting due proportion
Unproportionate, a. difproportioned

Unproportioned, a. not proportioned, not fuited
Unpropófed, a. not propofed, not yet declared
Unprop'ped, a. not fupported by props, loofe
Unpros'perous, a. unfortunate, unfuccefsful, bad
Unpros'peroufly, ad. unfuccefsfully, badly
Unpros'tituted, a. not debafed or degraded
Unprotect'ed, a. not protected, unfupported
Unprov'ed, a. not proved by argument, falfe
Unprovíde, v. t. to diveſt of qualifications
Unprovided, a. not provided, not furnifhed
Unprov'ident, a. thoughtlefs, giddy, improvident
Unprovóked, a. not provoked, not difpleafed
Unprúned, a. not pruned, not cut or lopped, long
Unpub'lic, a. not generally known, private
Unpub'lifhed, a. not yet given out to the public
Unpunctual'ity, n. a want of punctuality
Unpun'ifhed, a. not punifhed, excufed, free, fafe
Unpun'ifhing, a. not punifhing
Unpur'chafed, a. not purchafed, unbought, left
Unpur'ged, a. not purged, not cleanfed, foul
Unpúrified, a. not purified, not cleanfed, foul
Unpurfúed, a. not purfued, not followed, quitted
Unpútrified, a. not rotten, not corrupted, found
Unqual'ified, a. not qualified, unfit, improper
Unqual'ify, v. t. to diveſt of qualification
Unquar'rellable, a. not to be attacked, firm, ob.
Unquéen, v. t. to depofe or degrade a queen
Unquell'ed, a. not quelled, unfubdued, furious
Unquench'able, a. net to be quenched or put out
Unquench'ablenefs, n. an unquenchable quality
Unquench'ed, a. not extinguifhed, not put out
Unqueſt'ionable, a. not to be doubted, certain
Unqueſt'ionably, ad. without doubt, certainly
Unqueſt'ioned, a. not afked, not doubted
Unquick', a. not quick, flow, dull, motionlefs
Unquick'ened, a. not animated, not moving
Unquíet, a. reftlefs, difturbed, diffatisfied, uneafy
Unquíetly, ad. without reft, troublefomely
Unquíetnefs, n. reftleffnefs, uneafinefs, trouble
Unrack'ed, a. not racked, not poured off the lees
Unráked, a. not drawn together, not covered
Unran'facked, a. not plundered or pillaged
Unrav'el, v. t. to difentangle, explain, clear up
Unrav'elment, n. development of a plot
Unrázored, a. not fhaven, rough, filthy, nafty
Unréached, a. not reached, not attained to
Unread', a. not read, not learned, untaught
Unread'inefs, n. a want of readinefs or preparation
Unread'y, a. not ready, unfit, ungain, aukward
Unréal, a. not real, unfubftantial, fancied, vain
Unréafonable, a. unjuft, exorbitant, immoderate
Unréafonablenefs, n. inconfiftency with reafon
Unréafonably, ad. unjuftly, immoderately
Unréave, v. t. to difentangle, let loofe, unwind
Unrebáted, a. not blunted, continued, firm
Unrebúkable, a. not blamable, innocent, upright
Unreceíved, a. not received, not admitted, loft
Unreclaimed, a. not reformed, not turned, wild
Unrec'ompenfed, a. not recompenfed or rewarded

Unreconcíleable, a. implacable, inconfiftent
Unreconcíled, a. not reconciled, left at variance
Unrecord'ed, a. not recorded, unregiftered
Unrecount'ed, a. not related, not told or recited
Unrecrúitable, a. not to be recruited, quite loft
Unrecúring, a. not to be cured or remedied ob.
Unredéemed, a. not redeemed, not ranfomed
Unredrefs'ed, a. not redreffed, or relieved
Unredúced, a. not reduced, not leffened, entire
Unréeve, v. t. to take a rope from a hole
Unreform'able, a. not to be reformed, worthlefs
Unreform'ed, a. not reformed, not amended
Unrefract'ed, a. not refracted, not broken
Unrefrefh'ed, a. not comforted or relieved, weak
Unrefrefh'ing, a. not refrefhing, not invigorating
Unregard'ed, a. unheeded, neglected, flighted
Unregard'ful, a. heedlefs, difregardful
Unregen'erate, a. not regenerate, wicked, bad
Unre"giftered, a. not entered in a regiter
Unrein'ed, a. not reftrained by a bridle, loofe
Unreláted, a. not related, or connected
Unrel'ative, a. not relating, or concerning
Unrelent'ing, a. feeling no pity, hard, cruel, ſtern
Unreliévable, a. admitting of no eafe or excufe
Unreliéved, a. not fuccored or helped, not eafed
Unremark'able, a. not worthy of notice, fimple
Unremédiable, a. admitting of no remedy or cure
Unremem'bering, a. having no memory, forgetful
Unremem'brance, n. a want of memory, forgetful-
Unremit'ted, a. not remitted, not abated [nefs
Unremit'ting, a. not ceafing or remitting
Unremóvable, a. not to be taken away, fixed, fure
Unremóvably, ad. fo as not to be removed, fixedly
Unremóved, a. not removed, not taken away
Unrepáid, a. not paid back, not compenfated
Unrepéaled, a. not repealed, not revoked, left
Unrepent'ed, a. not repented of [forry for
Unrepent'ing, Unrepent'ant, a. not penitent, not
Unrepíning, a. not complaining or lamenting
Unreplen'ifhed, a. not filled again, empty, void
Unrepriévable, a. not to be reprieved, loft, gone
Unrepriéved, a. not reprieved or refpited
Unreproached, a. not upbraided; not cenfured
Unreprov'able, a. not liable to blame, pure
Unreprov'ed, a. not cenfured, not blamed
Unrepug'nant, a. not oppofit, not contrary
Unrep'utable, a. not creditable, difgraceful, ob.
Unrequeſt'ed, a. not afked or defired, unfought
Unrequitable, a. not to be requited or fully paid
Unrequi'ted, a. not repaid, or recompenfed
Unrefent'ed, a. not refented or heeded, forgiven
Unreferv'ed, a. not referved, open, frank, free
Unreferv'edly, ad. openly, without limitation
Unreferv'ednefs, n. opennefs, franknefs, candor
Unrefiſt'ed, a. not oppofed, obeyed, refiſtlefs
Unrefiſt'ing, a. not making refiſtance, paſſive
Unrefolv'able, a. not to be folved or cleared up
Unrefolv'ed, a. undetermined, not cleared up
Unrefolv'ing, a. not refolving, not determining

Unrespec'tive, a. taking little notice, careless
Unres'pited, a. not respited or relieved
Unrespons'ible, a. not answerable, not able to answer
Unrest', n. a want of rest, disquiet, uneasiness, ob.
Unrestored, a. not restored, not cleared, left
Unrestrainable, a. not to be restrained
Unrestrained, a. not confined, licentious, loose
Unrestraint, n. a freedom from restraint, ease
Unretrach'ed, a. not revoked, not recalled, held
Unrevealed, a. not revealed, not told about
Unreven'ged, a. not revenged, forgiven, pardoned
Unrev'erend, a. irreverent, disrespectful, rude
Unrev'erendly, ad. disrespectfully, slightingly
Unrevers'ed, a. not revoked, not repealed, full
Unrevi'ved, a. not revived or called to life
Unrevoked, a. not revoked, not recalled
Unreward'ed, a. not rewarded, not recompensed
Unrid'dle, v. t. to solve a difficulty, to explain
Unrig', v. t. to strip off tackling, to undress
Unright'eous, a. unjust, sinful, wicked, base
Unright'eously, ad. unjustly, sinfully, wickedly
Unright'eousness, n. injustice, wickedness, vice
Unright'ful, a. not right or just, unjust wrong
Unring', v. t. unrang, unrung, pret. unrung, pa.
  to take or strip off a ring, to free
Unrip', v. t. to rip open, cut open, disclose, tell
Unripe, a. not yet ripe, sour, hard, too early
Unripened, a. not ripened, not matured, young
Unripeness, n. a want of due ripeness, sourness
Unrivalled, a. having no rival, having no equal
Unriv'et, v. t. to free from rivets, loosen, clear
Unrol, v. t. to open any thing rolled up
Unromant'ic, a. not romantic, simple, plain
Unroof', v. t. to take off a roof, to uncover a house
Unroost'ed, a. driven from or fallen off a roost
Unroot', v. t. to tear from the root, to root out
Unrough, a. not rough, smooth, even, uniform
Unround'ed, a. not made round, uneven, irregular
Unroy'al, a. not royal, unprincely, unfit, mean
Unruf'fle, v. i. to cease from commotion, to calm
Unruf'fled, a. not tumultuous, calm, unmoved
Unruled, a. not set under government, wanton
Unruliness, n. an unruly state or temper
Unruly, a. ungovernable, licentious, loose, wild
Unru'minated, a. not chewed well, or digested
Unsafe, a. not safe, hazardous, dangerous, wrong
Unsafe'ly, ad. not safely or securely, dangerously
Unsafe'ty, n. danger, exposure to injury
Unsaid, a. not said or uttered, unmentioned
Unsale'able, a. not meeting with quick sale
Unsalt'ed, a. not salted, fresh, insipid, tasteless
Unsanc'tified, a. unholy, impure, not consecrated
Unsanc'tioned, a. not confirmed or sanctioned
Unsan'daled, a. without sandals, uncovered
Unsated, a. not sated or satisfied, insatiate
Unsatiable, a. not to be satisfied or pleased, vast
Unsatisfac'torily, ad. so as not to satisfy
Unsatisfac'toriness, n. a failure of satisfaction
Unsatisfac'tory, a. not affording satisfaction

Unsat'isfied, a. not satisfied, discontented
Unsat'isfiedness, n. an unsatisfied state, trouble
Unsat'isfying, a. not able to satisfy or please
Unsat'urated, a. not filled or saturated
Unsa'voriness, n. a bad taste or smell, insipidness
Unsa'vory, a. tasteless, insipid, disgustful
Unsay, v. t. unsaid, pret. unsaid, pa. to retract, recall,
  recant, alter, deny
Unsca'ly, a. having no scales, smooth, soft, fine
Unscan'ned, a. not measured, not computed
Unscar'red, a. not marked with scars or wounds
Unscholast'ic, a. not bred to literature, absurd
Unschool'ed, a. untaught, unlearned, unskilled
Unscientif'ic, a. not according to rules of science
Unscientif'ically, ad. in an unscientific manner
Unscorch'ed, a. not touched by fire, not burnt
Unscor'ified, a. not formed into dross
Unscreened, a. unsheltered, unprotected, bare
Unscrew', v. t. to take out a screw, or loosen
Unscrip'tural, a. not agreeable to the scriptures
Unseal, v. t. to open a seal or any thing sealed
Unsealed, pa. not sealed, having the seal broken
Unseam, v. t. to rip up a seam, to cut open a seam
Unsearch'able, a. not to be explored, hidden, dark
Unsearch'ableness, n. an unsearchable state or place
Unsearch'ed, a. not searched, or examined
Unseasonable, a. untimely, unfit, late
Unseasonableness, n. a disagreement with time
Unseasonably, ad. not seasonably, improperly
Unseasoned, a. not salted, &c. fresh, ill-timed
Unseated, a. having no bottom, not settled
Unsec'onded, a. not seconded, unsupported
Unsec'ret, v. t. to disclose, to divulge; a. not trusty
Unsecure, a. not secure, unsafe, hazardous
Unseduced, a. not drawn away to evil, innocent
Unsee'ing, a. wanting the power of sight, blind
Unseem, v. i. not to seem, not to appear
Unseeming, pa. not seeming, not appearing
Unseem'liness, n. indecency, uncomeliness, fault
Unseem'ly, a. indecent, unbecoming, uncomely
Unseemly, ad. in an unbecoming or bad manner
Unseen, a. not seen, invisible, unexperienced
Unself'ing, a. pulling down self, humbling, low
Unself'ish, a. not governed by private interest
Unsensible, a. insensible, unfeeling, ob.
Unsent', a. not sent, not dispatched, left behind
Unsep'arable, a. not to be parted, not to be divided
Unsep'arated, a. not parted, not divided, entire
Unserv'iceable, a. useless, being of no advantage
Unserv'iceably, ad. without any use or advantage
Unserv'iceableness, n. uselessness, unfitness
Unset', a. not set, not placed, not appointed
Unset'tle, v. t. to make uncertain, to overthrow
Unset'tled, a. not established or fixed, having no
  inhabitants, or occupiers
Unset'tledness, n. irresolution, fluctuation, change
Unsev'ered, a. not parted or divided, entire
Unsex', v. to change or alter the sex, to transform
Unshac'kle, v. t. to loose from chains or bands

unfhad'owed, a. not fhadowed, not darkened
unfhakeable, a. not to be fhaken, fixed, firm
unfhaked, unfhaken, a. not fhaken, unmoved
unfhamed, a. not fhamed, not abafhed, very bold
unfhape, v. t. to diforder, derange
unfhapen, a. misfhapen, deformed, ugly
unfhared, a. not divided in common, not parted
unfheath, v. t. to draw out of a fcabbard
unfhed', a. not fhed, not fpilt, not caft, not loft
unfhelt'ered, a. wanting protection, expofed, open
unfhip', v. t. to take out of a fhip, remove
unfhock'ed, a. not frighted, not difgufted or hurt
unfhod', a. having no fhoes on the feet, barefoot
unfhook', a. not fhaken, not cracked, clear, fine
unfhorn', a. not clipped, not fhaven, rough
unfhot', a. not hit by fhot, not killed, alive, fafe
unfhout', v. i. to retract a fhout, ftop, give over
unfhow'ered, a. not watered by means of fhowers
unfhrink'ing, a. not recoiling back, firm, ftrong
unfhun'able, a. not to be avoided or efcaped, fure
unfhun'ned, a. not fhunned, unavoidable
unfhut', a. not fhut, unfaftened, unclofed, open
unfift'ed, a. not fifted, unexamined, untried
unfi'ght, a. not feeing, blind, unfeen, invifible
unfi'ghted, a. not feen, invifible, obfcure   (mity
unfi'ghtlinefs, n. difagreeablenefs, uglinefs, defor-
unfi'ghtly, a. difagreeable to the fight, ugly
unfincére, a. not fincere, deceitful, falfe
unfincérely, ad. without fincerity, falfely
unfincer'ity, n. falfenefs, a cheat, adulteration
unfin'ew, v. t. to deprive of ftrength, to weaken
unfin'ewed, a. unnerved, nervelefs, weak, feeble
unfin'ged, a. not finged, not fcorched, not burnt
unfink'ing a. not finking, floating, quite light
unfin'ning, a. having no fin, pure, perfect, upright
unfized, a. not fized
unfkil'ful, a. wanting knowledge or art, clumfy
unfkil'fully, ad. without knowledge or art, badly
unfkil'fulnefs, n. a want of fkill or art, ignorance
unfkill'ed, a. wanting fkill or knowledge, fimple
unflain, a. not flain, not killed, preferved, fafe
unflak'ed, a. not quenched, not put out, burning
unfléeping, a. ever wakeful, awake, watchful
unfling', v. t. to take off flings
unflip'ping, a. not liable to flip, faft, firm, fafe
unfmirch'ed, a. unftained, unpolluted, clean
unfmóked, a. not fmoked, not dried in fmoke
unfóber, a. not fober
unfóciable, a. not fociable, reserved, furly
unfóciably, ad. with referve, fhily, furlily
unfócial, a. not ufeful or agreeable in fociety
unfoil'ed, a. unftained, unpolluted, clean, neat
unfóld, a. not fold, not difpofed of, left behind
unfóldierlike, a. unbecoming a foldier, mean
unfoli'cited, a. not afked or requefted
unfoli'citous, a. not folicitous, not anxious, eafy
unfol'id, a. not coherent or firm, fluid, loofe
unfolv'ed, a. not folved, not explained
unfóunable, a. that cannot be founded, broken

unfophift'icated, a. not adulterated, not mixed
unfort'ed, a. not forted, not feparated, mixed
unfought', a. not fought, not fearched for
unfound', a. rotten, wanting health, not honeft,
    infincere, not true, not orthodox, erroneous
unfound'ed, a. not tried by a plummet or lead
unfound'nefs, n. corruption, weaknefs, error, mif-
unfour'ed, a. not made four, not morofe   (take
unfów'ed, unfówn, a. not fown, having no feed
unfpáred, a. not fpared, made free with, ufed
unfpáring, a. not parfimonious, lavifh, profufe
unfpéak, v. t. unfpake, unfpoke, pret. unfpoken,
    pa. to retract, recant, revoke, forbid
unfpéakable, a. not to be expreffed, very great
unfpéakably, ad. inexpreffibly, very greatly, very
unfpe'cified, a. not particularly mentioned
unfpec'ulative, a. not theoretical, plain, fimple
unfped', a. not fped or difpatched, unfuccefsful
unfpent', a. not wafted or diminifhed, left, fafe
unfphére, v. t. to remove from its orb or place
unfpíed, a. not feen, not difcovered, hidden
unfpilt', a. not fpilt, not fhed, not fpoiled, left
unfpir'it, v. t. to deprefs, deject, caft down, hurt
unfpoil'ed, a. not plundered, not marred or hurt
unfpot'ted, a. not fpotted, not ftained with fin
unfquáred, a. not formed, irregular, rough
unftáble, a. not fixed, inconftant, irrefolute
unftáid, a. not ftaid or fteady, changeable, fickle
unftáidnefs, n. thoughtleffnefs, indifcretion, folly
unftained, a. not ftained, not dyed, clean, pure
unftáte, v. t. to put out of ftate, difplace, alter
unftat'utable, a. contrary to ftatute, illegal
unftaunch'ed, or unftanch'ed, a. not ftopped
unftead'faft or unfted'faft, a. not faft, irrefolute
unftead'ily or unfted'dily, ad. inconftantly   (ftancy
unftead'inefs or unfted'dinefs, n. a want of con-
unftead'y or unfted'dy, a. not fixed, irrefolute,
unftéeped, a. not fteeped, not foaked, frefh, dry
unftim'ulating, a. not exciting action
unfting', v. t. unftung, pret. unftung, pa. to take
    out a fting, eafe from, cure
unftint'ed, a. not limited, not confined, free
unftir'red, a. not ftirred, unfhaken, unmoved
unftitch', v. t. to open by picking out ftitches
unftoop'ing, a. not bending, not yielding, proud
unftop', v. t. to free from obftructions, to open
unftop'ped, pa. meeting no refiftance, opened
unftóred, a. not laid up in ftore, not fupplied
unftrained, a. not forced, eafy, natural, proper
unftráitened, a. not ftraitened, unconfined, eafy
unftrength'ened, a. unfupported, unaffifted
unftring', v. t. unftrung, pret. unftringed, unftrung
    pa. to relax ftrings, untie, loofe
unftruck', a. not ftruck, unaffected, unmoved
unftud'ied, a. not ftudied, not labored, quite eafy
unftuff'ed, a. unfilled, unfurnifhed, empty
unfubdúed, a. not fubdued, not conquered, fafe
unfubject'ed, a. not fubdued, not reduced to power
unfub'fidized, a. not receiving fubfidies

Unfubftan'tial, *a.* not folid, not real, empty, poor
Unfubmers'ible, *a.* that cannot be funk
Unfubmit'ting, *a.* not yielding
Unfucceeded, *a.* not fucceeded, not followed
Unfuccefs'ful, *a.* not fuccefsful, unfortunate
Unfuccefs'fully, *ad.* unfortunately, unluckily
Unfuccefs'fulnefs, *n.* a want of fuccefs, a failure
Unfuccefs'ive, *a.* not according to flux of parts
Unfuck'ed, *a.* not having the breaft drawn, full
Unfuf'ferable, *a.* not fufferable, intolerable, vile
Unfuf'ferably, *ad.* fo as not to be endured
Unfuffi''cience, *n.* an inability to anfwer fome end
Unfuffi''cient, *a.* unable, inadequate, unfit, weak
Unfug'ared, *a.* not fweetened with fugar, four
Unfuitable, *a.* unfit, improper, inadequate
Unfuitablenefs, *n.* unfitnefs, incongruity, error
Unfuitably, *ad.* in an unfuitable manner, badly
Unfuiting, *a.* not fitting, not becoming
Unfull'ied, *a.* not fouled, not difgraced, pure
Unfung', *a.* not yet recited in fong or verfe
Unfun'ned, *a.* not expofed to the fun, damp, cold
Unfuper'fluous, *a.* not more than enough, proper
Unfuppórtable, *a.* not to be endured, intolerable
Unfuppórted, *a.* unfuftained, unaffifted, alone
Unfúre, *a.* not fure or certain, not fixed, unfafe
Unfurmount'able, *a.* that cannot be overcome
Unfufcep'tible, *a.* not liable to admit, incapable
Unfufpeĉ', Unfufpeĉ'ed, *a.* not fufpeĉed
Unfufpeĉ'edly, *ad.* in an unfufpeĉed manner
Unfufpeĉ'ing, *a.* not fufpeĉting, not thinking
Unfufpi''cious, *a.* having no fufpicion, open, eafy
Unfuftáined, *a.* not fupported, not feconded
Unfwáyable, *a.* not to be fwayed or influenced
Unfwáyed, *a.* not fwayed, not led, not wielded
Unfweár, *v. t.* unfware, unfwore, *pret.* unfworn,
    pa. to recant a thing already fworn
Unfweat', *v. t.* unfweat, unfweated, *pret.* and *pa.*
    to cool on eafe after fatigue
Unfwórn, *a.* not fworn, not bound by an oath
Unfyftemat'ical, *a.* not reduced to fyftem, abfurd
Untáinted, *a.* unfullied, unftained, pure, good
Untáken, *a.* not taken, not apprehended, left
Untalk'ed-of, *a.* not mentioned in the world
Untámeable, *a.* not to be tamed or fubdued, vile
Untámed, *a.* not tamed, unfubdued, haughty
Untan''gle, *v. t.* to loofe from intricacy, to free
Untar'nifhed, *a.* not foiled or tarnifhed, clean
Untáfted, *a.* not tafted, not touched, left
Untáfting, *a.* not trying by means of the palate
Untaught', *a.* not taught, uninftruĉed, ignorant
Untéach, *v. t.* untaught, *pret.* untaught, *pa.* to
    make to forget, to unlearn
Untem'perate, *a.* without moderation, intemperate
Untem'pered, *a.* not tempered, not hardened
Untem'pering, *a.* not molding or fhaping
Untempt'ed, *a.* not tempted, not embarraffed
Unten'able, *a.* not capable of defence, weak
Unten'antable, *a.* not fit to be inhabited
Unten'anted, *a.* having no tenant, quite empty

Untend'ed, *a.* being without attendance, alone
Untend'er, *a.* wanting compaffion, cruel, unkind
Untend'ered, *a.* not tendered, not offered, tough
Untent', *v. t.* to bring or drive out of a tent
Untent'ed, *a.* having no medicaments applied
Unter'rified, *a.* not affrighted, dauntlefs, brave
Unthank'ed, *a.* not repaid with acknowledgment
Unthank'ful, *a.* ungrateful, difpleafing, carelefs
Unthank'fully, *ad.* ungratefully, negligently
Unthank'fulnefs, *n.* ingratitude, negleĉ of thanks
Unthaw'ed, *a.* not thawed, not diffolved, hard
Unthink'ing, *a.* thoughtlefs, carelefs, giddy, idle
Unthink'ingnefs, *n.* want of thought or refleĉion
Unthorn'y, *a.* not obftruĉed by prickles (peĉed
Unthought'of, *a.* not regarded, not minded, unex-
Unthread', *v. t.* to free from a thread, loofe, cafe
Unthreat'ened, *a.* not threatened, not alarmed
Un'thrift, *n.* a fpendthrift, prodigal, wafter, rake
Unthrift' or Unthrift'y, *a.* extravagant, lavifh
Unthrift'ily, *ad.* without frugality
Unthríving, *a.* not thriving, not profpering, poor
Unthróne, *v. t.* to pull or take from a throne
Untídy, *a.* not tidy or neat
Untie or Unty', *v. t.* to unbind, loofen, refolve
Untied, *pa.* not bound or faftened, loofened, open
Until', *ad.* to the time that, to the place that
Untill'ed, *a.* not tilled, uncultivated, fallow
Untímely, *a.* happening before the proper time
Untímely, *ad.* before natural time, improperly
Untin'ged, *a.* not tinged or ftained, not affeĉed
Untírable, *a.* not to be wearied, indefatigable
Untíred, *a.* not tired, not made weary, frefh
Untítled, *a.* having no title or honor, unknown
Un'to, *prep.* and *ad.* to, until, to the time that
Untóld, *a.* not told, not revealed, not reckoned
Untooth'fome, *a.* not toothfome, unpleafant
Untouch'ed, *a.* not touched, not affeĉed
Untóward, *a.* froward, vexation, crofs, aukward
Untow'ardly, *ad.* perverfely; *a.* perverfe, aukward
Unto'w'ardnefs, *n.* perverfenefs, aukwardnefs
Untráceable, *a.* that cannot be traced, intricate
Untráced, *a.* not traced, not marked out
Untrack'ed, *a.* not tracked or marked out, untrod
Untraĉ'able, *a.* ungovernable, unruly, rough
Untraĉ'ablenefs, *n.* an untraĉable difpofition
Untraĉ'ably, *ad.* in an untraĉable manner
Untráded, *a.* not ufual or cuftomary, ob.
Untráding, *a.* not engaged in trade or commerce
Untráined, *a.* not trained or inftruĉed, rough
Untransfer'rable, *a.* not transferrable, fixed, fure
Untransfer'red, *a.* not transferred, or conveyed
Untranflátable, *a.* not capable of being tranflated
Untranfp'árent, *a.* not tranfparent, cloudy
Untrav'elled, *a.* unfrequented, not having been
    abroad (*pa.* to go back in the very fame fteps
Untread', *v. t.* untrod, *pret.* untrod, untrodden,
Untreas'ured, *a.* not treafured, not laid up, fpent
Untríed, *a.* not tried, not attempted, unknown
Untrim'med, *a.* not trimmed, plain, not fhaven

Untrfumphable, a. allowing no triumph, firm
Untrod', Untrod'den, a. not trodden, fmooth
Untroll'ed, a. not rolled or run along, not bowled
Untroub'led, a. not difturbed, unmoved, clear
Untrúe, a. not true, falfe, unfaithful, deceitful
Untrúly, ad. falfely, unfaithfully, deceitfully
Untrufs'ed, a. not truffed or tied up
Untruth'inefs, n. unfaithfulnefs, deceitfulnefs
Untruft'y, a. not trufty, unfaithful, falfe, giddy
Untrúth, n. a falfhood, falfity, falfe affertion, lie
Untuck'ered, a. not having a tucker, open, bare
Untúnable, a. unmufical, unharmonious, harfh
Untúne, v. t. to put out of tune, diforder, hurt
Unturn'ed, a. not turned, unchanged, obftinate
Untútored, a. uninftructed, untaught
Untwine, Untwift', v. t. to feparate things involved
Unúniform, a. wanting uniformity, irregular
Unur'ged, a. not urged, not preffed, not incited
Unúfed, [unyuzed] a. unemployed, difufed
Unúfeful, a. ferving no ufe or purpofe, ufelefs
Unúfual, [unyuzual] a. uncommon, rare,
Unúfually, ad. uncommonly, rarely (nefs
Unúfualnefs, n. uncommonnefs, rarenefs, ftrange-
Unut'terable, a. inexpreffible, not to be declared
Unvái, v. t. to throw off a vail, uncover, fhow
Unval'uable, a. that is above price, ineftimable
Unval'ued, a. not valued, not prized, flighted
Unvan"qu'fhed, a. not conquered, not fubdued
Unváriable, a. unchangeable, certain, invariable
Unváried, a. not diverfified, unchanged, fixed
Unváriegated, a. not variegated, not altered
Unvar'nifhed, a. not covered with varnifh
Unvárying, a. not varying, not liable to change
Unvéil, [unvail] v. t. to difclofe, fhow, difcover
Unveil'edly, ad. plainly, without difguife
Unven'erable, a. not worthy of refpect
Unvent'ilated, a. not fanned by the wind or air
Unver'itable, a. untrue, fa fe, deceitful, bafe, ob.
Unvers'ed, a. not acquainted with, unfkilled
Unvex'ed, a. not vexed, unprovoked, unmoved
Unvíolated, a. uninjure l, unhurt, unbroken
Unvir'tuous, a. wanting virtue, bad, wicked, vile
Unvis'ited, a. not reforted to, unfrequented
Unvi'tiated, a. not vitiated, not corrupted
Unvit'rified, a. not converted to glafs
Unvoy'ageable, a. not to be paffed over, dangerous
Unvul'nerable, a. that cannot be wounded
Unwákened, a. not waked, not roufed from fleep
Unwall'ed, a. not having walls, open, bare
Unwárily, ad. without proper caution, carelefsly
Unwárinefs, n. a want of due caution, careleffnefs
Unwar'like, a. not like or fit for war, impotent
Unwarn'ed, a. not warned, not cautioned
Unwar'rantable, a. unjuftifiable, indefenfible
Unwar'rantably, ad. not juftifiably, wrong
Unwar'ranted, a. not warranted, uncertain
Unwáry, a. wanting caution, precipitate, hafty
Unwafh'ed or Unwafh'en, a. not wafhed, dirty
Unwáfted, a. not diminifhed, not leffened

Unwáiting, a. not wafting, not growing lefs
Unwáyed, a. not ufed to travelling or the road, ob.
Unweákened, a. not weakened, not leffened
Unweap'oned, a. not furnifhed with arms, weak
Unwéariable, a. that cannot be tired or fatigued
Unwéaried, a. untired, indefatigable, refrefhed
Unwéariedly, ad. without fatigue or remiffion
Unwéary, v. t. to refrefh after wearinefs ; a. not
Unwed', Unwed'ded, a. unmarried, fingle (weary
Unwedge'able, a. not to be cloven by wedges
Unwéeded, a. not cleared from weeds, foul
Unwéeting, a. unknowing, infenfible, ignorant
Unweigh'ed, a. not weighed, not confidered
Unweigh'ing, a. inconfiderate, thoughtlefs, idle
Unwelc'ome, a. not pleafing, not at all grateful
Unwell', a. not well, difordered, fick, afflicted
Unwept', Unweeped, a. not wept, not lamented
Unwet', a. not wet, not moift, dry, hard
Unwhipt', a. not whipped, not corrected
Unwhólefome, a. not wholefome, unhealthy
Unwhólefomenefs, n. an unwholefome ftate
Unwiéldly, ad. heavily, with great difficulty
Unwiéldinefs, n. a difficulty to move or be moved
Unwiéldy, a. unmanageable, bulky, ponderous
Unwill'ed, a. not produced by the will
Unwill'ing, a. not willing, not inclined, loth
Unwill'ingly, ad. not with good will, backwardly
Unwill'ingnefs, n. a difinclination, backwardnefs
Unwind, v. t. unwound, pret. unwound, pa. to
untwift, untwine, difentangle
Unwiped, a. not wiped, not cleaned, dirty, foul
Unwife, a. defective in wifdom, weak, foolifh
Unwifely, ad. not wifely, imprudently, fimply
Unwifh', v. t. to wifh what is not to be, to revoke
Unwifh'ed, pa. not defired, not fought
Unwift', a. unthought of, unapprized
Unwit', v. t. to deprive of wit or underftanding
Unwithdraw'ing, a. continuing liberal or kind
Unwithftood', a. not oppofed, not refifted
Unwit'nefled, a. wanting evidence or due notice
Unwit'tingly, ad. not willingly, ignorantly
Unwit'ty, a. deftitute of wit, coarfe, homely
Unwont'ed, a. uncommon, unufual, rare
Unwork'ing, a. living without work or labor
Unworfh'ipped, a. not adored, not duly honored
Unwor'thily, ad. without due regard, vilely
Unwor'thinefs, n. a want of due merit, vilenefs
Unwor'thy, a. undeferving, unfuitable, mean, vile
Unwound', pa. untwifted, untwined
Unwound'ed, a. not wounded, unhurt, very fafe
Unwréath, v. t. to untwift, untwine, difengage
Unwrin'kle, v. t. to reduce wrinkles, make fmooth
Unwriting, a. not pretending to be an author
Unwrit'ten, a. not written, traditional, verbal
Unwrought', [unrawt] a. not manufactured
Unwrung', a. not wrung or pinched, unhurt
Unyiélded, a. not yielded, not given up, held out
Unyiélding, a. not pliant, not bending
Unyóke, v. t. to loofe from a yoke, free, disjoin

Unyóked, pa. a. freed, unreſtrained, licentious
Unzóned, a. not bound with a girdle, loofe, eafy
Up, ad. out of bed, aloft, above, on
Upbeár, v.t. upbore, pret. upborne, pa. to raiſe up or aloft, ſupport, uphold
Upbráid, v.t. to reproach, twit, charge, chide
Upbráidingly, ad. by way of reproach, croſsly
Upcaſt', v.t. upcaſt, pret. upcaſt, pa. to caſt up, to throw upwards
Up'caſt, n. a throw, caſt, caſt at bowls, event, end
Updraw', v.t. to draw up, raiſe
Upgrów, v.t. to grow up
Up'hand, a. lifted up or ſupported by the hand
Uphéave, v.t. to heave or lift up
Upheld', pa. ſuſtained, ſupported, maintained
Uphill', a. difficult, hard, laborious, troubleſome
Uphóld, v.t. upheld, pret. upheld, upholden, pa. to lift on high, ſupport, ſave, keep
Uphólder, n. a ſupporter, defender, undertaker
Uphólſterer, n. one who furniſhes houſes, beds, &c.
Up'land, n. higher ground; a. higher, high, raiſed
Upland'iſh, a. mountainous, hilly, high, aſcending
Upláy, v.t. uplaid, pret. uplaid, pa. to lay up, hoard up, preſerve, fecure
Uplead, v.t. to conduct upwards
Uplift', v.t. uplift, uplifted, pret. and pa. to lift up or high, raiſe aloft, raiſe
Up'moſt, a. uppermoſt, topmoſt, higheſt, chiefeſt
Upon', pr. on, not under, with reſpect to, near to
Up'per, a. higher in place, ſuperior to, leading
Up'perlether, n. the upper ſoft lether of a ſhoe
Up'permoſt, a. higheſt in place, power, &c. firſt
Up'piſh, a. proud, lofty, high, haughty, arrogant
Up'piſhneſs, n. pride, loftineſs, haughtineſs
Upráiſe, v.t. to raiſe up, exalt, advance, promote
Upreár, v.t. to rear or raiſe on high, to build up
Up'right, n. an upright poſt, model, draft
Upright, a. ſet ſtrait up, erected, honeſt, juſt
Uprighteouſly, ad. in an upright manner
Uprightly, ad. perpendicularly, honeſtly, juſtly
Uprightneſs, n. perpendicularity, honeſty, truth
Upríſe, v.i. uproſe, pret. upriſen, pa. to riſe from a feat, come up, aſcend
Up'riſe, Up'riſing, n. the act or time of riſing
Up'roar, n. tumult, confuſion; v.t. to confuſe
Uprólled, a. rolled up
Uproot', v.t. to root up, grub up, tear up, deſtroy
Uprouſe', v.i. to awaken from ſleep, to excite
Up'ſhot, n. a concluſion, end, event, amount, total
Up'ſide, n. the upper ſide, the upper or near part
Upſpring, v.t. to ſpring up
Up'ſpring, n. a man ſuddenly raiſed or exalted
Up'ſtand, v.i. upſtood, pret. upſtood, pa. to ſtand up, to ſtand or be erected
Upſtart', v.i. to ſtart or ſpring up ſuddenly
Up'ſtart, n. one who is ſuddenly raiſed to wealth
Upſtáy, v.t. upſtaid, upſtayed, pret. and pa. to ſuſtain, ſupport, uphold, defend
Upſwarm', v.t. to raiſe in a ſwarm, to rouſe up

Upturn', v.t. to turn or throw up, to furrow
Up'ward, a. directed higher, more; ad. more; n.
Upwhirl'ed, a. whirled upwards (the top
U'ral, Urálian, a. noting a chain of mountains which divide Europe from Aſia, on the North
U'ranite, [u as yu] n. a metal of a dark gray color
Uranit'ic, a. pertaining to uranite
Urban'ity, n. politeneſs, elegance, civility
Ur'ceolate, a. ſhaped like a pitcher
Urch'in, n. a hedgehog, brat, child in anger, &c.
U'reter, [u as yu] n. a veſſel which conveys urine from the kidney to the bladder
Ure, [u as yu] n. practice, uſe, cuſtom, habit, fate
U'rethra, [u as yu] n. a tube for the paſſage of the urine
Urge, v.t. to preſs, ſolicit, aſk, incite, provoke
Ur'gency, n. a preſſure of difficulty or haſte
Ur'gent, a. preſſing, earneſt, importunate, eager
Ur'gently, ad. cloſely, eagerly, vehemently, vio-
Ur'ger, n. one who urges, one who incites (lently
U'rinal, [u as yu] n. a bottle to keep urine for in- ſpection
U'rinary, a. relating or belonging to urine
U'rinative, a. working by or provoking urine
U'rinator, n. one who ſwims under water, a diver
U'rine, n. animal water; v.i. to make water
U'rinous, a. partaking of or like urine
Urn, n. a veſſel for the aſhes of the dead, &c.
U'roſcopy, n. an examination made of urine
Ur'ry, n. a kind of black clay found near coals
Urs'a, n. the bear, a conſtellation, greater and leſ- ſer, near the North Pole
Ur'ſiform, a. in ſhape like a bear
Ur'ſine, a. pertaining to a bear
Ur'ſuline, a. denoting an order of nuns
U'rus or Ure, n. the wild bull
Us, oblique caſe of we (ment
U'ſage, [u as yu] n. cuſtom, faſhion, practice, treat-
U'ſager, n. one who has any thing in truſt only
U'ſance, [u as yu] n. uſe, uſury, intereſt for mon- ey, a ſpace
Uſe, [yuſe] n. ſervice, employment, practice, intereſt
Uſe, [yuze] v.t. to employ, frequent, treat, behave
U'ſeful, a. ſerviceable, conducive, convenient
U'ſefully, ad. in a way ſo as to help, ſerviceably
U'ſefulneſs, n. a conduciveneſs to ſome end, uſe
U'ſeleſs, a. anſwering no end or purpoſe, vain
U'ſeleſsly, ad. without anſwering any good end
U'ſeleſsneſs, n. unſerviceableneſs, unprofitableneſs
U'ſer, n. one who uſes, one who employs
Uſh'er, n. an under-teacher, introducer, ſervant
Uſh'er, v.t. to introduce, bring in, forerun
Uſquebáugh, n. a compound hot ſpirit
Uſt'ion, n. the act of burning, a burnt ſtate, heat
Uſtórious, a. having the quality of burning, hot
U'ſual, [u as yu] a. common, cuſtomary, frequent
U'ſually, a. commonly, cuſtomarily, generally
U'ſualneſs, n. a uſual ſtate, commonneſs
Uſucap'tion, [u as yu] n. acquiſition by long uſe

U'sufruct, [u as yu] n. a temporary use or profit of a thing

Usufruct'uary, n. one who has a temporary use

U'sure, [u as yu] v. i. to practice or encourage usury

U'surer, n. one who practices usury, a mean wretch

Usúrious, a. exorbitantly greedy, griping, mean

Usúriousness, n. a desire of exorbitant profit

Usurp', [u as yu] v. t. to hold without right, to seize upon by violence

Usurpátion, n. an illegal possession, seizure, force

Usurp'er, n. one who possesses another's right

Usurp'ingly, ad. without just claim or right

U'sury, [u as yu] n. money paid for the use of money beyond lawful interest (thing

Uten'sil, [u as yu] n. an instrument for any use, tool,

U'terine, [u as yu] a. belonging to the womb, related

Utíl'ity, [u as yu] n. usefulness, convenience, profit, worth

U'tis, n. a bustle, stir, noise, disturbance, ob.

Ut'most, a. highest, most; n. most that can be

Utópian, [u as yu] a. chimerical, imaginary, fancied

U'tricle, [u as yu] n. a small bag, cell or bottle

Utric'ular, a. furnished with glandular vessels like small bags or bottles

Ut'ter, a. outward, extreme, complete, full, entire

Ut'ter, v. t. to speak, say, discover, sell, publish

Ut'terable, a. that may be uttered or expressed

Ut'terance, n. a pronunciation, fale, extremity

Ut'terer, n. a speaker, divulger, discoverer, seller

Ut'terly, ad. perfectly, completely, fully, entirely

Ut'termost, a. utmost, most remote, extreme

Ut'termost, n. the greatest degree, the worst part

Uxórious, a. submissive to or very fond of a wife

Uxóriously, ad. fondly submissive to a wife

Uxóriousness, n. fond submission to a wife

V

VA'cancy, n. a vacant place, a time of leisure

Vácant, a. empty, free, disengaged, idle

Vácate, v. t. to make vacant, quit, annul, defeat

Vacátion, n. leisure, ease, intermission, a recess

Vac'cine, n. the cow-pox, kine-pox

Vac'cine, a. denoting the cow-pox (the cow-pox

Vac'cinate, v. t. to inocculate with the virus of

Vaccinátion, n. the act of inocculating with cow-pox-matter

Va"cillancy, Vacillátion, n. a reeling or staggering

Vacuátion, n. the act of emptying, an evacuation

Vac'uist, n. one who holds or maintains a vacuum

Vacúity, n. emptiness, space unfilled, want, defect

Vac'uous, a. empty, void, unfilled, hollow

Vac'uum, n. a void, space that is without matter

Vade, v. i. to go or pass away, vanish, fade, ob.

Váde-mécum, n. the title of a little book

Vag'abond, n. a vagrant, a wanderer; a. strolling

Vagáry, n. a wild sudden frolic, freak, odd whim

Va"ginal, a. sheathed, pertaining to a sheath

Va"ginant, Va"ginate, a. forming a sheath, as a leaf whose base incloses the stem

Vágous, a. wandering, roving, unsettled, vagrant

Vágrancy, n. a vagrant state or condition

Vágrant, n. one unsettled in habitation, a beggar

Vágrant, a. wandering, roving, void of occupation

Vague, a. wandering, unsettled, indefinit

Vail, n. a covering to conceal, mask, perquisit

Vail, v. to cover, hide, let fall, yield, give place

Vain, a. conceited, proud, fruitless, ineffectual

Vainglórious, a. vain or proud without due merit

Vainglóry, n. empty pride, great vanity, folly

Vainly, ad. without effect, proudly, foolishly

Vainness, n. the state of being vain, vanity

Váivode, n. a prince of the Dacian provinces

Val'ance, n. what hangs round the tester of a bed

Val'ance, v. t. to adorn or hang with valances

Vale, n. a valley, low ground, kind of trough

Valedic'tion, n. a bidding farewel, farewel, leave

Val'entine, n. a choice made on Valentine's day

Valérian, n. the name of a medicinal plant

Val'et, n. a waiting-man, footman, servant, stick

Valetudinárian, a. sickly, weakly, infirm, crazy

Valetudinárian, Valetúdinary, n. one of a sickly constitution

Val'iant, a. courageous, brave, bold, noble, stout

Val'iantly, ad. with personal strength, bravely

Val'iantness, n. valor, courage, bravery, boldness

Val'id, a. weighty, conclusive, prevalent, good

Valíd'ity, Val'idness, n. strength, force, certainty

Val'lancy, n. a very large wig; a. large, covering

Val'ley, n. a hollow between two hills, a gutter

Val'or, n. courage, bravery, prowess

Val'orous, a. valiant, courageous, brave, bold, stout

Val'uable, a. having or worthy of value, precious

Val'uableness, n. a valuable quality, value

Valuátion, n. a value of a thing, an apprisement

Val'uator, Val'uer, n. one who values, an appriser

Val'ue, n. a price, worth, rate, esteem

Val'ue, v. t. to fix a price, rate, apprise, esteem

Val'ueless, a. having no value, worthless, trifling

Val'uing, n. the act of setting a price, valuation

Valve, n. a folding-door, the cover of a siphon

Valv'ular, Valv'ed, a. containing valves, like a valve

Valv'ule or Valve'let, n. a little valve, a division of a pericarp

Vamp, n. the upper-lether of a shoe

Vamp, v. t. to mend up old things, piece, patch

Vamp'er, n. one who vamps up, one who mends

Vam'pire, n. a species of large bat, said to suck the blood of animals when asleep

Vam'pirism, n. the practice of vampires

Van, n. the front of an army, a large fan, a wing

Van, v. t. to winnow corn, fan, sift, clean, dress

Van'dal, n. a cruel ferocious savage person

Van'dalism, n. cruelty, indiscriminate destruction

Vandal'ic, a. denoting the cities on the south shore of the Baltic, where the Vandals once lived

Vane, n. a plate that turns with the wind, a van

Van'guard, n. the front or first line of an army in

Vanil'la, n. the name of a plant, a nut (array

Van'ish, v. i. to disappear, pass or go away be lost,

Van'ity, *n.* emptinefs, pride, arrogance, falfehood
Van''quifh, *v. t.* to conquer, fubdue, overcome
Van''quifher, *n.* one who conquers or fubdues
Van'fire, *n.* a fpecies of weefel in Madagafcar
Vant'age, *n.* profit, gain, fuperiority, convenience
Vant'brafs, Vam'brace, *n.* armor for the arms, *ob.*
Vap'id, *a.* flat, palled, dead, worthlefs, fpiritlefs
Vapid'ity, Vap'idnefs, *n.* flatnefs, dulnefs, want of
    fpirit   (heat, fume
Vapor, *n.* a fluid rendered volatile and elaftic by
Vapor, *v.* to fly off in fume, bully, brag
Vaperation, *n.* the act of paffing in vapor
Vaporer, *n.* a boafter, bragger, vain noify perfon
Vaporific, *a.* forming vaper, raifing vapor
Vaporifh, *a.* fplenetic, humorfome, fickle, ftrange
Vap'orize, *v.* to convert into vapor by heat, or to
    pafs off in vapor   (vapor
Vaporization, *n.* the procefs of converting into
Vaporous, *a.* full of or like vapor, fumy, windy
Vapors, *n. pl.* hyfteric fits, fits, whims
Vapulation, *n.* the act of beating or whipping *ob.*
Vari, *n.* the ruffed Macauco, a fpecies of monkey
Variable, *a.* changeable, inconftant, fickle
Variablenefs, *n.* changeablenefs, inconftancy, levity
Variably, *ad.* changeably, inconftantly, fickly
Variance, *n.* difagreement, diffenfion, difcord
Variation, *n.* a change, difference, deviation, turn
Varicous, Varicofe, *a.* fwelled, tumefied
Variegate, *v. t.* to diverfify with colors or objects
Variegation, *n.* a diverfity, mixture of colors
Variety, *n.* change, difference, variation, mixture
Variolite, *n.* a ftone with rounded protuberances
Various, *a.* changeable, different, diverfified
Varioufly, *ad.* in a different or another manner
Varix, *n.* a dilatation or fwelling of a vein
Varlet, *n.* a fcoundrel, villain, footman, valet
Varletry, *n.* the rabble, a crowd
Varnifh, *n.* a fhining liquid fubftance, cover. glofs
Varnifh, *v. t.* to fet a glofs, adorn, cover, palliate
Varnifher, *q.* a perfon who varnifhes   (agree
Vary, *v.* to change, altar, diverfify, deviate, dif-
Vary, *v.* change, alteration, difference, *ob.*
Vafc'ular, *a.* confifting of or full of veffels
Vafcularity, *n.* the ftate of being vafcular
Vafculiferous, *a.* having a peculiar veffel for feed
Vafe, *n.* a veffel with a foot to it, pot, ornament
Vas'fal, *n.* a fubject, dependent, flave; *a.* fervile
Vas'falage, *n.* the ftate of a vaffal, flavery, fealty
Vaft, *n.* an empty wafte, an empty part or fpace
Vaft or Vaft'y, *a.* very great, huge, enormous, large
Vaftation, *n.* the act of laying wafte or fpoiling
Vaft'nefs, *n.* immenfity, width, extent
Vaftly, *ad.* greatly, to a great degree, very much
Vat, *n.* a large veffel, brewer's working tub, fat
Vat'ican, *n.* a magnificent palace of the pope in
Vat'icide, *n.* a murderer of poets or prophets (Rome
Vati''cinal, *a.* containing prophefy
Vati''cinate, *v. t.* to prophefy, foretel, divine
Vault, *n.* a cellar, cave, grave, arch, leap, jump

Vault, *v.* to arch, arch over, leap, jump, tumble
Vault'age, *n.* vaulted work, an arched cellar
Vault'ed, Vault'y, *a.* arched, like an arch, hollow
Vault'er, *n.* a leaper, jumper, fkipper, tumbler
Vaun'mure, *n.* a falfe wall, breaftwork, bulwark, *ob.*
Vaunt or Vant, *v.* to boaft, brag, talk largely, difplay
Vaunt, *n.* a boaft, vain oftentation, firft part
Vaunt'er, *n.* a boafter, braggart, braggadocio
Vaunt'ing, *n.* boafting, oftentation, parade
Vaunt'ingly, *ad.* boaftingly, with vain oftentation
Vav'afor, *n.* a lord next in rank to a baron
Vaward, *n.* the forepart, forefront, face, *ob.*
Veal, *n.* the flefh of a calf killed for the table
Vec'tion, Vectitation, *n.* the act of carrying, carriage
Vec'ture, *n.* carriage, conveyance, removal, a fare
Veda, *n.* a facred book among the Hindoos, of which
    there are four
Vedet', *n.* a fentinel on horfeback, a fcout
Veer, *v.* to turn about, turn, change, let out
Vegetabil'ity, *n.* vegetable ftate or nature, growth
Ve''getable, *n.* a plant; *a.* of or belonging to plants
Ve''getate, *v. i.* to grow as plants   (of plants
Vegetation, Ve''getativenefs, *n.* a growth like that
Vegete, *a.* active, vigorous, fprightly, lively, quick
Ve''getive, *a.* vegetable; *n.* a vegetable, a plant
Vehemence, *n.* violence, force, eagernefs, heat
Vehement, *a.* violent, furious, eager, earneft
Vehemently, *ad.* violently, furioufly, eagerly
Vehicle, *n.* a carriage, conveyance
Vehicled, *a.* conveyed in a vehicle
Veil, [vail] *v. t.* to cover, hide, conceal, inveft
Veil, *n.* a cover to conceal the face; *fee* Vail
Vein, [vane] *n.* a hollow veffel which returns the
    blood to the heart, courfe of metal in a mine,
    row, ftreak, current, turn of mind, ftrain
Vein'ed, Vein'y, *a.* full of veins, variegated
Vein'lefs, *a.* deftitute of veins
Vel'eity, *n.* the loweft degree of defire, a defire
Vel'licate, *v. t.* to twitch, pluck, pull, ftimulate
Vellication, *n.* the act of twitching or ftimulating
Vel'lum, *n.* parchment, a fine kind of parchment
Veloc'ity, *n.* fpeed, fwiftnefs, quicknefs of motion
Vel'vet, Velure, *n.* a filk with a thick pile upon it
Vel'vet, *a.* made of velvet, foft; *v. i.* to paint vel-
Velveteen, *n.* cloth made of cotten and linen   (vet
Vel'vety, *a.* like velvet, foft, fmooth
Venal, *a.* pertaining to veins, mercenary, bafe
Venal'ity, *n.* mercenarinefs, fordidnefs, meannefs
Venat'ic, *a.* relating to hunting or chafing, wild
Venation, *n.* the act or practice of hunting
Vend, *v. t.* to fell, fet or offer to fale, put off
Vendean, *n.* pertaining to La Vendee in France
Vendée, *n.* one to whom any thing is fold
Vend'er, *n.* one who fells or puts off, a feller
Vend'ible, *a.* faleable, that may be fold, proper to
Vend'iblenefs, *n.* a faleable ftate or quality (be fold
Venditation, *n.* a boafted or artful difplay, parade
Vendi''tion, *n.* the act of felling any thing, a fale

Venéer, *v. t.* to cover neatly with thin wood
Venéer, *n.* thin wood to cover or inlay with
Venefi"cial, *a.* acting by poifon, bewitching
Venefi"cioufly,*ad.* with or by poifon, by witchcraft
Vénenate, *v. t.* to poifon, to kill by poifon, *ob.*
Venenátion, *n.* the act of poifoning, poifon, venom
Venéne, Venenófe, *a.* poifonous, venomous
Ven'erable, *a.* deferving of reverence, refpectable
Ven'erablenefs, *n.* a venerable quality
Ven'crably, *ad.* in a venerable manner, honorably
Ven'crate, *v.t.* to reverence,refpect greatly,honor
Venerátion, *n.* a reverend or awful regard, honor
Ven'erator, *n.* one who venerates or refpects
Venéreal,*a.*relating to love,[relating to copper,*ob.*]
Venéreous, *a.* relating to venery or luft, luftful
Ven'cry, *n.* the pleafure of the bed, luft, hunting
Venefec'tion, *n.* the act of letting blood, a bleeding
Venétian, *n.* a native of Venice, a city and ftate
Venétian, *a.* pertaining to Venice
Véney,*n.* a bout, turn, pufh, thruft, near place
Venge, *v. t.* to avenge, punifh, chaftife, *ob.*
Venge'able, *a.* revengeful, malicious, fpiteful, *ob.*
Venge'ance, *n.* punifhment, vehemence
Venge'ful, *a.* revengeful, vindictive, malicious
Véniable, Vénial, *a.* pardonable, excufable
Ven'ifon, *n.* the flefh of deer and other beafts of
Ven'om, *n.* poifon; *v. t.* to poifon, to kill (chafe
Ven'omous, *a.* poifonous, deftructive, malignant
Ven'omoufly, *ad.* poifonoufly, mifchievoufly
Vénous, *a.* contained in or pertaining to a vein
Venófe, *a.* furnifhed with veins
Vent, *n.* a hole, opening, paffage, difcharge, fale
Vent, *v. t.* to let out, open, publifh, fell, fnuff
Ventan'na, *n.* a place that gives light, a window
Vent'iduct, *n.* a paffage for the wind by pipes
Vent'ilate, *v. t.* to fan, winnow, cool, examin
Ventilátion, *n.* the act of fanning or cooling, a vent
Vent'ilator, *n.* an inftrument to fupply frefh air
Ventófenefs, Ventos'ity, *n.* windinefs, airinefs
Vent'ricle,*n.* the ftomach, a cavity in the heart
Ventricófe, *a.* inflated, fwelled as with air
Ventril'oquifm, *n.* the art or practice of fpeaking
   fo that the voice appears to come from a diftant
   part of the room
Ventril'oquift, *n.* one who practices ventriloquifm
Ventril'oquous, *a.* pertaining to ventriloquifm
Vent'ure,*v.* to fend a venture, rifk, expofe, dare
Vent'ure, *n.* a thing at ftake, hazard, hap, chance
Vent'urer, *n.* one who ventures, one who hazards
Vent'urefome, Vent'urous, *a.* daring, bold, fearlefs
Vent'uroufly, *ad.* daringly, boldly, hardily, nobly
Vent'uroufnefs, *n.* a willingnefs or readinefs to run
   hazard, daringnefs, boldnefs, hardinefs
Ven'ue, *n.* the place in which a caufe is to be tried
Vénus, *n.* the goddefs of love, a planet (ing truth
Vera"city,*n.* difpofition to truth, or habit of fpeak-
Verb, *n.* one of the 8 parts of fpeech, which fig-
   nifies doing, fuffering or being, in things, &c.
Verb'al, *a.* derived of or from a verb, fpoken, oral

Verbal'ity,*n.* mere or bare words, a verbal promife
Verb'ally, *ad.* by word of mouth, word by word
Verbátim, *ad.* word for word, literally, truly
Verb'erate, *v. t.* to beat, chaftife, correct, *ob.*
Verberátion, *n.* the act of beating, blows, ftripes
Verbófe, *a.* full of words, prolix, tedious, long
Verbos'ity, *n.* much empty talk, prate, prolixity
Ver'dant, *a.* green, flourifhing, beautiful
Verd'iter, *n.* a preparation of copper ufed as a
   pale green or blue
Ver'derer or Ver'de-or, *n.* a kind of foreft-officer
Ver'dict, *n.* a determination by a jury, a judgment
Ver'digris, *n.* the acetite of copper, the acetous
   acid combined with copper
Ver'dure, *n.* a green color, greennefs of trees, &c.
Ver'durous, *a.* green, covered with or like green
Verge, *n.* a rod,feargeant's mace,brink,edge,com-
Verge, *v. i.* to bend downwards, to tend (pafs
Ver'ger, *n.* a macebearer in cathedrals, &c.
Verificátion,*n.* a confirmation by due evidence
Ver'ify, *v. t.* to confirm, prove true, juftify, enter
Ver'goloo, *n.* a very rich pear
Ver'ily, *ad.* truly, certainly, really, confidently
Verifim'ilar,*a.* probable, likely, credible, apparent
Verifimil'itude, *n.* probability, likelihood
Ver'itable, *a.* agreeable to fact, true, certain
Ver'ity,*n.* truth, certainty,reality,a true affertion
Ver'juce, *n.* a liquor made of crab apples
Vermicel'li, *n.* a pafte made like threds, a foop
Vermic'ular, *a.* like or acting like a worm, fpiral
Vermic'ulate, *v.t.* to inlay wood, &c. to checker
Vermiculátion,*n.* a fpiral motion, twift, gripe
Ver'micule,*n.* a fmall infect,a little worm or grub
Vermic'ulous,*a.* full of little worms or grubs
Verm'iform, *a.* refembling a worm in form
Vermil'ion, *n.* fulphuret of mercury,or cinnabar,
   a beautiful red color
Vermil'ion, *v. t.* to die red, to tinge red
Ver'min,*n.*fmall noxious animals.—it is *fing.* or *pl.*
Verminátion, *n.* a breeding of vermin or worms
Ver'minous, *a.* breeding vermin, filthy, nafty
Vermip'arous, *a.* producing worms or grubs
Vernac'ular, *a.* belonging to one's own country
Ver'nal, *a.* belonging to the fpring (blooming
Ver'nant,*a.* flourifhing as in the fpring, green,
Vernátion, *n.* the difpofition of leaves in the buds
   of plants
Vernicófe, *a.* warty, having knobs or warts
Verniér, *n.* a fcale or divifion fo called
Vernil'ity, *n.* very fervile behavior, meannefs
Vers'al,*a.* univerfal, all, total, whole [*vulgar*]
Vers'atile, *a.* turning round, variable, fickle
Verfatil'ity, *n.* a verfatile ftate, aptnefs to change
Verfe,*n.*poetry, a paragraph; *v. t.* to tell in verfe
Vers'ed, *a.* fkilled, well learned, well practiced
Verfe'man,*n.* a writer or author of verfes, a poet
Verfificátion, *n.* the act or art of making verfes
Vers'ifier, *n.* a maker of verfes a petty poet
Vers'ify, *v.* to make verfe, to defcribe in verfe

Ver'fion, n. the act of tranflating, a tranflation
Vert, n. a green color, a green twig; a. green
Ver'teber, n. a fingle joint of the back bone or neck
Ver'.ebral, a. relating to the fpine or backbone
Vert'ex, n. zenith, point overhead, top of any thing, any point
Vert'ible, a. capable of being turned round
Vert'ical, a. placed in the zenith, perpendicular
Vertical'ity, n. a vertical ftate, perpendicularity
Vert'ically, ad. in the zenith, perpendicularly
Ver'ticil, n. a whirl, a fpecies of inflorefcence in which the flower growsin a whirl or ring
Verti''cillate, a. whirled, having a flower in fhape of a ring
Verti''city, n. the act of turning about, a rotation
Verti''ginous, a. giddy, turning round, whirling
Ver'tigo, n. a giddinefs, a quick whirling motion
Ver'vain, n. the name of a plant, a magic herb
Ver'vel or Var'vel, n. a label tied to a hawk
Ver'y, a. true, real, the fame, in a great degree
Ves'icate, v. t. to blifter, puff up, fwell, rife
Vefication, n. the act of bliftering or fwelling up
Ves'icatory, n. a bliftering medicin, a cupping-
Ves'icle, n. a fmall cuticle filled or inflated (glafs
Vefic'ular, a. hollow like a bladder, inflated
Vefic'ulate, a. containing veficles, bladdery
Ves'per, n. the evening, the evening-ftar, Venus
Ves'pers, n. pl. evening prayers, evening fervice
Ves'pertin, a. of or relating to the evening
Vefs'el, n. any thing ufed to hold liquors, the containing parts of an animal body, a fhip, a flip
Vefs'el, v. t. to put into a veffel, ob.
Veft, n. a garment, kind of fmall coat, crop
Veft, v. to drefs, deck, adorn, beftow, inveft, take effect as a title or become fixed
Veft'al, n. a pure virgin, a facred or holy virgin
Veft'al, a. denoting pure virginity or holinefs
Veft'iary, n. a dreffing-room, wardrobe, veftry
Veft'ible or Veft'ibule, n. a porch, an entrance
Veft'ige, n. a footftep, trace, mark, little cavity
Veft'ment, n. a garment, a prieft'supper robe
Veft'ry, n. a room adjoining to a church, people legally affembled in it, a meeting, an affembly
Veft'ure, n. a garment, habit, drefs, allowance, veft
Vefuvien, a. pertaining to Vefuvius, a volcano near Naples   (fuvius
Vefuvian, n. a filiceous ftone, white garnet of Ve-
Vetch, n. a leguminous plant, a kind of bad pea
Vetch'ling, n. a plant of different fpecies
Vetch'y, a. abounding with or like vetches
Vet'eran, n. an old foldier, one long practiced
Vet'eran, a. long practiced, long experienced, old
Vet'erinary, Veterinarian, a. pertaining to difeafes of horfes and cattle
Veterinarian, n. one fkilled in difeafes of cattle
Veto, n. a prohibition, a forbidding
Vex, v. t. to provoke, difquiet, plague, torment
Vexation, n. the act or caufe of plaguing or teafing
Vexatious, a. provoking, troublefome, afflictive

Vexatioufly, ad. in a vexatious manner
Vexatioufnefs, n. perverfenefs, uneafinefs, trouble
Vex'er, n. one who vexes or provokes, a difturber
Vex'il, n. a flag or ftandard, the upright petal of a papilionaceous flower
Vex'illary, n. an enfign, a ftandard bearer
Vex'illary, a. pertaining to an enfign or ftandard
Vexillation, n. a company under an enfign
Vial, n. a fmall bottle; v. t. to inclofe in a vial
Viands, n. pl. meat dreffed, meat, food, victuals
Viat'ic, a. relating to a journey or travelling
Viat'icum, n. provifion for a journey, a rite
Vibrate, v. to move to and fro, quiver, brandifh
Vibratil'ity, n. a difpofition to preternatural motion or vibration
Vibration, n. a moving with quick return, a fhake
Vibratory, a. confifting in vibration, moving back and forth
Vic'ar, n. a fubftitute, a deputy, the minifter of a parifh where the great tithes are impropriated
Vic'arage, n. the benefice of a vicar, a church-living
Vicarial, a. belonging to a vicar, fmall
Vicarious, a. deputed, delegated, inferior, lower
Vic'arfhip, n. the office or miniftry of a vicar
Vice, n. wickednefs, an iron prefs, gripe, newel
Vice, v. i. to draw with or put into a vice
Vice, in compofition fignifies fecond in rank
Viceadmiral, n. the fecond commander of a fleet
Viceadmiralty, n. the office of a viceadmiral
Vicead'miralty, a. denoting a fubordinate admiralty court
Viceagent, n. one who acts for another, a deputy
Viced, a. wicked, corrupt, debauched, abandoned
Vicegerency, n. the office or duty of a vicegerent
Vicegerent, a. acting in the room of another
Vicegerent, n. one acting by fubftitution   (fities
Vicechan'cellor, n. a fecond magiftrate in univer-
Vicenary, a. belonging to or containing twenty
Viceroy, n. the agent or fubftitute of a king
Viceroy'alty, n. the dignity or poft of a viceroy
Viceroyfhfp, n. the office or jurifdiction of a vice-
Vicety, n. nicety, exactnefs, ob.   (roy
Vi''cinage, n. neighborhood, people in a neighbor-
Vi''cinal, Vicine, a. near, adjoining, bordering (hood
Vicin'ity, n. neighborhood, nearnefs, clofenefs
Vi''cious, a. faulty, immoral, wicked, unruly
Vi''cioufly, ad. immorally, wickedly
Vi''cioufnefs, n. corrupt habit, wickednefs
Vicifs'itude, n. a change, revolution, fucceffion
Vic'tim, n. a facrifice, fomething deftroyed
Vic'tor, n. one who gets the better, a conqueror
Victorious, a. conquering, fuperior, triumphant
Victorioufly, ad. fuccefsfully, triumphantly
Vic'tory, n. conqueft, fuccefs, triumph, honor
Vic'trefs, n. a female that conquers or overcomes
Vict'ual or Vit'tle, v. t. to provide with victuals
Vict'ual, Vict'uals, n. provifions, food, meat
Vict'ualler, n. a provider of victuals, publican, a fhip which furnifhes another with ftores

Videl'icet, *ad.* to wit, that is, namely, *viz.*

Vie, *v. i.* to conteft, contend, ftrive, rival, invite

View, *v. t.* to fee, perceive, look, furvey, examin

View, *n.* a fight, profpect, furvey, difplay, defign

View'ing, *n.* the act of beholding or furveying

Vi''gil, *n.* the eve before a holyday, watch, wake

Vi''gilance, Vi''gilancy, *n.* watchfulnefs, heed, care

Vi''gilant, *a.* watchful, circumfpect, diligent

Vi''gilantly, *ad.* watchfully, attentively, warily

Vignet', *n.* a wreath of leaves or flowers

Vig'or, *n.* force, ftrength, efficacy

Vig'orous, *a.* forcible full of ftrength or life

Vig'oroufly, *ad.* with force, forcibly, ftoutly

Vig'oroufnefs, *n.* vigor, force, ftrength, ftoutnefs

Vile, *a.* bafe, wicked, worthlefs, fordid, mean

Viled, *a.* abufive, fcurrilous, fcandalous, horrid

Vilely, *ad.* bafely, fhamefully, badly, meanly

Vilenefs, *n.* bafenefs, wickednefs, defpicablenefs

Vil'ify, *v. t.* to debafe, defame, abufe, undervalue,

Vill, Vill'a, *n.* a country-feat, a village   (flight

Vill'age, *n.* a fmall collection of country houfes

Vill'ager, *n.* an inhabitant of a village, a ruftic

Vill'agery, *n.* the diftrict or extent of a village

Vill'ain, *n.* a vile wicked wretch, fervant, flave

Vill'anage, *n.* bafe fervitude, bafenefs, infamy

Vill'anize, *v. t.* to debafe, degrade, defame, revile

Vill'anous, *a.* bafe, vile, wicked

Vill'anoufly, *ad.* bafely, infamoufly, wickedly

Vill'any, *n.* bafenefs, wickednefs

Villat'ic, *a.* belonging to villages, homely, mean

Vil'lenage, *n.* a tenure of land by bafe fervices

Villófe, Vill'ous, *a.* hairy, fhaggy, rough, horrid

Vimin'eous, *a.* made of or refembling twigs

Vin'cible, *a.* conquerable, that may be overcome

Vindémial, *a.* relating or belonging to a vintage

Vindémiate, *v. i.* to gather or order the vintage

Vindemiation, *n.* the gathering of grapes

Vin'dicate, *v. t.* to juftify, clear, affert, defend,
    [revenge, punifh, *ob.*]

Vindication, *n.* a juftification, defenfe, affertion

Vin'dicative, *a.* revengeful, malicious, fpiteful

Vin'dicator, *n.* one who vindicates, an affertor

Vin'dicatory, *a.* afferting, avenging, fevere

Vindic'tive, *a.* revengeful, given to revenge

Vindic'tively, *ad.* revengefully, malicioufly, cru-

Vindic'tivenefs, *n.* a vindictive difpofition   (elly

Vine, *n.* a plant that produces grapes

Vinedreffer, *n.* one who trims or cultivates vines

Vinefretter, *n.* the aphis or plant loufe

Vin'egar, *n.* the acid of vegetables   (vines

Vine'yard or Vin'yard, *n.* a ground planted with

Vínous, *a.* of or having the quality of wine

Vint'age, *n.* the produce of vines, time of gather-
    ing grapes

Vint'ager, *n.* one who gathers the vintage

Vint'ner, *n.* one who fells wine, &c. by retail

Vint'ry, *n.* a place for the fale of wine, a cellar

Viol, *n.* a ftringed mufical inftrument, a device

Violable, *a.* that may be violated or injured

Violáceous, *a.* refembling or like violets   (ßour

Violate, *v. t.* to injure, hurt, infringe, ravifh, de-

Violátion, *n.* an infringement, tranfgreffion, rape

Vfolator, *n.* one who violates, one who ravifhes

Violence, *n.* force, fury, outrage, injury, an attack

Violent, *a.* forcible, furious, outrageous, fharp

Violently, *ad.* with force or fury, vehemently, faft

Violet, *n.* a fweet-fmelling flower

Violln', *n.* a fweet mufical inftrument, a fiddle

Violift, *n.* one who plays upon the viol or violin

Violoncel'lo, *n.* a mufical inftrument   (thing

Viper, *n.* a ferpent, adder, mifchievous perfon or

Víperine, Víperous, *a.* of or in quality like a viper

Virágo, *n.* a very bold refolute woman, a termagant

Vírelay, *n.* a French poem of two rhymes only

Vírent, *a.* green, verdant, unfaded, blooming

Virge, *n.* a dean's mace, a white rod or ftaff

Virg'ate, *a.* having many twigs

Vir'gin, *v. i.* to play the virgin, to be very coy

Vir'gin, *n.* a maid unacquainted with man, a fign

Vir'gin, *a.* maidenly, untouched, pure, unmingled

Vir'ginal, *a.* an old ftringed mufical inftrument, *ob.*

Vir'ginal, *a.* maiden, maidenly; *v. i.* to hit or

Virgin'ity, *n.* maidenhood   (ftrike gently

Virgin'ia, *n.* one of the United States of America

Virgin'ian, *n.* a native of Virginia

Virgin'ian, *a.* belonging to Virginia

Vir'go, *n.* the virgin, a fign in the zodiac

Virid'ity, *n.* greennefs, verdure

Vírile, *a.* manly, fuiting a man, bold, courageous

Viril'ity, *n.* manhood, the power of procreation

Virt'ual, *a.* effectual, powerful, equivalent, real

Virtual'ity, *n.* a virtual ftate, efficacy, power

Virt'ually, *ad.* effectually, in reality, not formally

Virt'uate, *v. t.* to make efficacious or ftrong, *ob.*

Virt'ue, *n.* moral goodnefs, force, efficacy, valor

Virt'uelefs, *a.* wanting virtue or efficacy, weak

Virtuófo, *n.* one fkilled in curiofities, &c.

Virt'uous, *a.* morally good, upright, devout, chafte

Virt'uoufly, *ad.* in a virtuous manner   (temper

Vir'ulence or Vir'ulency, *n.* malignit, a wicked

Vir'ulent, *a.* malignant, inexorable, venomous

Vir'ulently, *ad.* malignantly, with bitternefs

Virus, *n.* foul matter from ulcers, poifon

Vis'age, *n.* the face, countenance, look, afpect

Vis'cerate, *v. t.* to embowel, take out the bowels,

Vis'cid, *a.* glutinous, adhefive, fticky   (gut

Vifcid'ity, Vifcos'ity, *n.* glutinoufnefs, tenacity

Vifcount', *n.* a degree of nobility next to an earl

Vifcount'efs, *n.* a vifcount's wife or lady

Vis'cous, *a.* glutinous, adhefive, clammy

Vifh'nou, *n.* in the Hindoo fyftem of faith, one of
    the three beings forming a fort of trinity, the
    preferver

Vifibil'ity, Vis'iblenefs, *n.* a vifible ftate or quality

Vis'ible, *a.* apparent, plain, confpicuous, clear

Vis'ibly, *ad.* plainly, confpicuoufly, clearly, openly

Vi''fion, *n.* fight, a phantom, ghoft, dream, reve-

Vi''fionary, *a.* imaginary, feen in a dream   (lation

Vi'fionary, Vi''fionift, n. one difturbed in thought
Vis'it, v. to go to fee, furvey, view, afflict, punifh
Vis'it, n. the act of going to fee any perfon
Vis'itable, a. liable to be vifited or punifhed
Vis'itant, n. one who vifits or goes to fee another
Vifitátion, n. the act of vifiting, a vifit, a judgement
Vifitatórial, a. belonging to a judicial vifiter
Vis'iter or Vis'itor, n. one who vifits, a judge
Vis'iting, n. the act of paying vifits or judging
Vifive, a. formed by or relating to vifion, feen
Vis'ne, n. a brandy, a wine mixed with brandy
Vis'on, n. an American animal of the weafel kind
Vis'or, n. a mafk, difguife, concealment
Vis'ored, a. mafked, difguifed, concealed, hidden
Vift'a or Vift'o, n. a walk or profpect through trees
Vis'ual, a. belonging to the fight, exercifing fight
Vit al, a. neceffary or belonging to life, effential
Vital'ity, n. the power or act of fubfifting in life
Vitally, ad. in a manner to give life, effentially
Vitals, n. pl. parts effential to life, effence
Vi''tiate, v. t. to deprave, corrupt, defile, deflour
Vitiátion, n. a fpoiling, depravation, corruption
Vitilitigátion, n. a contention in law, difpute, ob.
Vitios'ity, n. depravity, corruption, wickednefs
Vi''tious, a. corrupt, wicked, mifchievous
Vi''tioufly, ad. corruptly, wickedly, vilely, badly
Vi''tioufnefs, n. corruptnefs, wickednefs, vice
Vit'reous, a. glaffy, refembling or as clear as glafs
Vit'reoufnefs, n. a glaffy ftate or quality
Vitres'cence, n. glaffinefs, a tendency to become
Vitres'cent, a. glaffy, tending to glafs   (glafs
Vitrifac'tion, n. the act of vitrifying, a fubftance
    vitrified
Vit'rificate, v. to turn into or become glafs, ob.
Vit'rify, v. to convert into glafs-or become glafs
    by heat
Vit'rifiable, a. capable of changing into glafs (glafs
Vitrificátion, n. the act of becoming or forming
Vit'riform, a. having the form of glafs
Vit'riol, n. a compound of fulphuric acid and a
    metal with a portion of water and oxygene
Vit'riolated, a. impregnated with vitriol (vitriol
Vitriol'ic, Vitríolous, a. containing vitriol, like
Vitriol'ic acid, now called fulphuric acid
Vit'riolize, v. to form into or become vitriol
Vitriolizátion, n. the act of forming or becoming
Vit'riolizable, a. capable of becoming vitriol (vitriol
Vit'uline, a. belonging to or like a calf
Vitúperable, a. blameworthy, cenfurable, faulty
Vitúperate, v. t. to blame, cenfure, find fault with
Vivácious, a. lively, fprightly, gay, brifk, active
Viva''city, n. livelinefs, fprightlinefs, brifknefs
Vive, a. lively, forcible, ftrong, preffing urgent
Vivency, n. a manner of fupporting life, life
vives, n. pl. a diftemper among horfes
viv'id, a. lively, fprightly, quick, active, merry
viv'idly, ad. with life or fpirit, quickly, gaily
viv'idnefs, n. life, livelinefs, fprightlinefs, vigor

vivif'ic, a. giving or caufing life, making alive
vivificátion, n. the act of giving life, animation
viv'ify, v. to make alive, animate, quicken, ftir up
vivip'arous, a. that brings forth the young alive
vix'en, n. a fcold, froward child, young fox
viz, ad. to wit, that is, namely, videlicet
viz'ard, n. a mafk to difguife the face; v. t. to mafk
viz'arded, pa. mafked, difguifed in a mafk, hid
viz'ier, n. the Ottoman prime or chief minifter
vócable, n. a word, name, term, noun   (words
vocab'ulary, n. a little dictionary or collection of
vócal, a. having a voice, modulated by the voice
vocal'ity, Vócalnefs, n. the power of utterance
vócalize, v. t. to form into voice, to modulate
vócally, ad. by the voice, in words, articulately
vocátion, n. a calling, fummons, employment
voc'ative, n. the cafe of nouns ufed in calling
vocif'erate, v. i. to bawl, fhout, make a noife
vociferátion, n. a bawling, noife, outcry, clamor
vocif'erous, a. noify, loud, clamorous, turbulent
vogue, n. fafhion, mode, efteem, credit, repute
voice, n. the found from the mouth, a cry, a vote
voice, v. to fhout, clamor, murmur, report, vote
voi'ced, pa. furnifhed with a voice, voted
void, a. empty, unoccupied, deftitute, vain, null
void, n. an empty fpace, emptinefs, vacuum
void, v. t. to quit, leave, emit, evacuate, annul
void'able, a. that may be voided or annulled
void'er, n. a veffel to carry table furniture in
void'nefs, n. a void ftate, emptinefs, nullity
voi'ture, n. a carriage, conveyance, ob.
volal'kali, n. volatile alkali, by contraction
vólant, a. flying, quick, active, nimble
vol'atile, a. flying, evaporating, lively, fickle
vol'atile, n. a flying or winged creature
volatil'ity, n. an evaporation, changeablenefs, a
    difpofition to fly off in vapor
volatilizátion, n. the act of making volatile
vol'atilize, v. t. to make volatile or very fubtle
vol'canift, n. one verfed in the ftudy of volcanoes,
    one who believes in the effect of fire in forming
    mountains, &c.   (canic origin
volcan'ity, n. the ftate of being volcanic, or of vol-
vol'canize, v. to undergo or fubject to the action
    of volcanic fire   (nic heat
volcanizátion, n. the procefs of undergoing volca-
vol'cáno, n. a mountain which emits fire and lava
vole, n. a deal at cards that wins all the tricks
vólery or vólary, n. a flight of birds, a large cage
volitátion, n. the act or power of flying, flight
voli''tion, n. the act of willing, power to choofe
vol'itive, a. having power to will or choofe
vol'ley, n. a burft of fhot; v. i. to throw out, to
vol'lied, pa. difcharged with a volley (difcharge
vols'cian, a. pertaining to the ancient Volfci, a peo-
    ple of Italy, fouth eaft of Rome
volt, n. a certain tread of a horfe, round, fpring
voltáic, a. pertaining to Volta, the inventor of the
    pile for exhibiting Galvanifm

volubil'ity, *n.* fluency, quicknefs, mutability

vol'uble, *a.* fluent in words, nimble, rolling

vol'ume, *n.* a book, any compact matter, dimenfion

volúminous, *a.* confifting of many volumes, big

voltuminoufly, *ad.* in many volumes, very largely

vol'untarily, *ad.* of one's own accord, kindly

vol'untarinefs, *n.* willingnefs, readinefs

voluntar'ity, *n.* a faculty exifting in the fentorium of producing motion by an act of the will

vol'untary, *a.* acting by choice, willing, ready

vol'untary, *n.* mufic played at will, a volunteer

volunteér, *n.* a foldier ferving of his own accord

volunteér, *v. i.* to go willingly for a foldier

volup'tuary, *n.* one given to luxury or pleafure

volup'tuous, *a.* luxurious, fenfual, extravagant

volup'tuoufly, *ad.* luxurioufly, fenfually, grofsly

volup'tuoufnefs, *n.* luxurioufnefs, extravagance

volúte, *n.* a fpiral fcroll ufed as an ornament in building

volv'ic, *a.* denoting a fpecies of ftone or lava

vom'it, *v. t.* to caft out of the ftomach (thrown up

vom'it, *n.* a medicin to caufe to vomit, matter

vom'iting, *n.* the act of cafting from the ftomach

vomi''tion, *n.* the act or power of vomiting

vom'itive, vom'itory, *a.* caufing to vomit

vorácious, *a.* greedy to eat, ravenous, very keen

voràcioufly, *ad.* ravenoufly, greedily, eagerly

voràcioufnefs, vora''city, *n.* ravenoufnefs

vor'tex, *n.* a whirlpool, whirlwind, whirling motion

vor'tical, *a.* having a whirling motion, whirling

vôtarefs, vôtrefs, *n.* a female votary, friend, &c.

vôtaríft, vôtary, *n.* one devoted to any fervice

vôtary, *a.* confequent or relating to a vow

vote, *v.* to give or choofe by votes, *n.* a voice

vôter, *n.* one who has a right to give a vote

vôting, *n.* a giving of or choofing by votes

vôtive, *a.* given or done by vow, vowed   (atteft

vouch, *n.* a warrant, atteftation ; *v.* to witnefs, to

vouch'er, *n.* one who or what witneffeth, a warrant

vouchfafe, *v.* to condefcend, deign, grant, give

vouchfáfement, *n.* a condefcenfion, grant, gift

vow, *n.* a folemn promife, a religious promife

vow, *v. t.* to make a vow, proteft, confecrate

vow'el, *n.* a letter which is utterable by itfelf

voy'age, *n.* a travel by fea, an undertaking, gain

voy'age, *v. i.* to travel by fea, pafs over, go over

voy'ager, *n.* a traveller by fea, failor, mariner

vul'can, *n.* the god of fubterraneous fire and metals, the fabled author of fmiths work

vulcánian, vulcan'ic, *a.* pertaining to Vulcan, or to the theory which afcribes the origin of ftones, &c to fire

vul'caniſt, *n.* one who believes in the formation of mountains, &c. by volcanoes or internal fire

vul'gar, *a.* common, ordinary, mean, low, trivial

vul'gar, *n.* the common or lower people, rabble

vul'garifm, *n.* a vulgar or mean expreffion

vul'gar'ity, vul'garnefs, *n.* meannefs, rudenefs

vul'garly, *ad.* commonly, meanly, badly, rudely

vul'gate, *n.* a noted latin verfion of the bible

vul'nerable, *a.* that may be wounded or injured

vul'nerary, *a.* ufeful in the cure of wounds

vul'nerary, *n.* a medicin for wounds

vul'nerate, *v. t.* to wound, hurt, injure, maim

vulnerátion, *n.* the act of wounding or hurting

vulp'inary, *a.* cunning, crafty, artful, fly, fubtle

vulpíne, *a.* belonging to a fox, crafty, artful

vult'ur, *n.* a genus of fowls of the hawk kind

vult'urine, *a.* relating to vultures, very rapacious

W

WACK'EN, *n.* a fpecies of argillaceous earth

Wad, *n.* paper or tow to ftop the charge of a gun, black lead, a bundle, a plant

Wad, *v. t.* to ram with wad, to mark with wad

Wad'ding, *n.* a coarfe ftuff, infide of a coat, wad

Wad'dle or Wab'ble, *v. i.* to walk like a duck

Wad'dlingly, *ad.* with irregular gait or motion

Wade, *v. i.* to walk in a fubftance that yields to the feet, to walk or go with difficulty

Wáfer, *n.* a thin dried pafte, cake, bread

Wáfer, *v. t.* to faften or feal with wafers   (body

Waft, *v.* to carry over, float, beckon ; *n.* a floating

Waft'age, *n.* carriage by water or in air

Waft'ure, *n.* the act of waving or floating, play

Wag, *n.* a merry droll, an arch or queer fellow

Wag, *v. i.* to move or fhake flightly, move, ftir

Wage, *v. t.* to lay a wager, engage in, make, hire

Wáger, *n.* a bet, an offer upon oath ; *v. t.* to bet

Wáges, *n.* hire or reward of fervice   (pranks

Wag'gery, Wag'gifhnefs, *n.* wantonnefs, merry

Wag'gifh, *a.* frolicfome, fportive, wanton, merry

Wag'gifhly, *ad.* in a waggifh manner, wantonly

Wag'gle, *v. i.* to move up and down, to waddle

Wag'gon, *n.* a four-wheel carriage for burdens

Wag'gon, *v.* to convey in a waggon, ufe a waggon

Wag'goner, *n.* the driver or matter of a waggon

Wag'goning, *n.* the bufinefs of ufing waggons

Wag'tail, *n.* a genus of fmall birds

Waid, *a.* crufhed, hurt with weight, maimed, *ob.*

Waif, *n.* goods that are found loft and not claimed

Wail, *v. t.* to lament, grieve, forrow, bewail

Wail, Wailing, *n.* lamentation, audible forrow

Wáilful, *a.* mournful, forrowful, lamentable, fad

Wain, *n.* a fort of cart or waggon, a fet of ftars

Wáinrope, *n.* a rope belonging to a waggon

Wáinfcot, *n.* a lining for rooms, a kind of oak

Wáinfcot, *v. t.* to line or fit walls with boards

Waift, *n.* the fmalleft part of the body below the ribs, middle floor of a fhip, middle deck

Wáiftcoat, *n.* a garment worn under a coat

Wáifter, *n.* a feaman ftationed in the waift of a fhip

Wait, *v.* to ftay, attend, expect, watch ; *n.* ambufh

Wáiter, *n.* an attendant, fervant, plate

Wáiting, *pa.* ftaying, ferving, attending

Wáitingmaid, *n.* an upper fervant attending a lady

Waits, *n. pl.* nightly muficians, nightly mufic

Wake, *v.* to ceafe to fleep, watch, roufe, awake

Wake, *n.* a watch, feaft, merriment, mark, track

Wákeful, a. not sleeping well, watchful, awake
Wákefully, ad. in a wakeful manner
Wákefulnefs, n. a want of sleep, watchfulnefs
Wáken, v. to wake, roufe from fleep, excite
Wale, n. a rifing part in cloth, &c. timber, knot,
planks on a fhip's fide (pear
Walk, [wauk] v.i. to go by leifurely fteps, to ap-
Walk, n. the act of walking, gait, path to walk in,
in W. Indies, a plantation
Walk'er, n. one that walks, an officer, a forefter
Walk'ing, n. the act of moving by regular fteps
Walk'ingftick, n. a ftick or ftaff to walk with, a
Walk'mill, n. a kind of mill, a fulling-mill (cane
Wall, [a as aw] n. a partition of brick, &c. fence,
defenfe
Wall, v t. to inclofe or defend with a wall
Wallcréeper, n. a bird that climbs up walls
Wal'let, n. a kind of bag, knapfack, double pouch
Wall'eyed, a. having large white eyes
Wall'flower, n. a fine large garden-flower
Wall'fruit, n. fruit that is ripened on a wall
Wall'ing, n. walls in general, materials for walls
Wáll-loufe, n. the name of an infect of many feet
Wal'lop, v.i. to boil, bubble up, roll, dance
Wal'low, v.i. to roll in mire, to live in filth
Wal'low, n. a kind of rolling walk, a waddling
Wal'lowing, n. the act of rolling or tumbling
Wal'lowifh, a. muddy, filthy
Wal'nut, n. a large and admired kind of nut
Wal'rus or Wal'tron, n. the morfe or fea horfe
Wam'ble, v.i. to roll with ficknefs, move, rife
Wampee, n. a plant, a fpecies of arum
Wamp'um, n. current money amongft Indians
Wan, a. languid of look, pale, fickly, blank
Wand, n. a long flender ftaff or rod, a fmall ftick
Wand'er, v. to rove, ramble, go aftray, travel
Wand'erer, n. a rover, rambler, traveller (viation
Wand'ering, n. uncertainty, a miftaken way, a de-
Wand'eroo, n. a baboon of Ceylon and Malabar
Wand'fu, n. a black monkey of Ceylon
Wane, v.i. to grow lefs ; n. a decreafe or decline
Wan'ly, ad. in a wan manner, palely, fickly
Wan'ned, a. made wan, turned pale or fick
Wan'nefs, n. palenefs, languor, ficklinefs
Wan'nifh, a. of a wan color, fomewhat wan (fhort
Want, v. to be without, need, fail, wifh for, be
Want, n. need, poverty, lack, deficiency, a mole
Want'ing, pa. a. ftanding in need, deftitute, defi-
cient, abfent
Want'lefs, a. free from want, fupplied
Want'on, v.i. to revel, frifk, play lafcivioufly, toy
Want'on, n. a ftrumpet, whoremonger, trifler
Want'on, a. licentious, luftful, loofe, fportive
Wan'tonize, v.i. to behave wantonly, ob.
Want'only, ad. in a wanton or licentious manner
Want'onnefs, n. licentioufnefs, luft, waggery
Want'y, n. a broad lethern girth, a furcingle
Wap'acut, n. the fpotted owl of Hudfon's Bay
Wáped, Wápid, a. dejected, crufhed, fee Whop

Wap'entake, n. divifion of a country, a hundred
War, n. open hoftility, fighting, combat, forces
War, v.i. to make or carry on war, to fight
War'ble, v. to quaver a found, fhake, fing, purl
Warb'ler, n. a fine finger, fongfter, finging bird
Warb'ling, n. the act of fhaking notes or finging
Ward, n. a watch, diftrict of a town, garrifon, cuf-
tody, part of a lock, perfon under a guardian
Ward, v. to watch, guard, act on the defenfive
Ward'en, n. a head-officer, keeper, guardian
Ward'er, n. a keeper, beadle, guard, truncheon
Ward'mote, n. a ward-meeting, a court held
Ward'robe, n. a place in which apparel is kept
Ward'fhip, n. guardianfhip, pupilage, reftraint
Ware, a. wary, cautious, wife ; v.i. to beware
Ware, v.t. to change a fhips courfe by turning her
ftern to the wind
Wárehoufe, n. a ftorehoufe for merchandife
Wárehoufe, v. t. to depofit or fecure in a ftore
Wares, n. pl. goods to be fold, any merchandife
War'fare, n. military fervice and life, a conflict
War'fare, v. i. to lead a military life, to fight (war
War'hoop, n. a favage yell ufed on entering upon
War'ily, ad. cautioufly, carefully, cunningly
Warinefs, n. cautioufnefs, forefight, cunning, art |
War'fin, n. a monkey of S. America
War'like, a. difpofed to or fit for war, military
Warm, a. rather hot, furious, zealous, fanciful
Warm, v.t. to heat moderately, to make hot
Warm'ingpan, n. a pan to warm a bed with
Warm'ly, ad. with warmth, zealoufly, eagerly
Warmth, n. a gentle heat, paffion, zeal, fondnefs
Warn, v.t. to caution, give notice, tell, order
Warn'ing, n. a caution, previous notice, advice
Warp, n. the thred that croffes the woof, a rope
Warp, v. t. to turn, pervert, contract, prepare,
change or move with a warp
War'proof, n. valor tried by war
War'rant, n. a writ of caption, authority, right
War'rant, v. to juftify, authorize, fecure, affure
War'rantable, a. juftifiable, defenfible, right, fit
War'rantablenefs, n. a juftifiable ftate, propriety
War'rantably, a. juftifiably, properly, fuitably
War'rantife, n. fecurity, authority, warranty, ob.
War'ranty, n. a deed of fecurity for a contract, act
of fecuring
Warráy, v.t. to make war upon, moleft, ob.
War'ren, n. a park or inclofure for rabbits
War'rener, n. one who has the care of a warren
War'rior, n. a military man, foldier, champion
Wart, n. a carneous excrefcence on the flefh
Wart'ed, a. covered with little excrefcences
War'ty, a. grown over with or like warts, hard
War'worn, a. worn with war, much battered
War'y, a. cautious, fcrupulous, nice, prudent, wife
Was, pret. of to be
Wafh, [wofh] v.t. wafhed, pret. wafhed, wafhen,
pa. to cleanfe with water, purify, whiten, color
Wafh, n. a thing to wafh with, ftain, bog, food, in.

W. Indies, a mixture of dunder, melasses, water and scummings for distillation

Wash'ball, n. a ball of soap, &c. to wash with

Wash'board, n. a board on a wall next the floor or on the top of a boat

Wash'er, n. one that washes or cleanses

Wash'erwoman, n. a woman who washes for hire

Wash'y, a. watery, damp, soft, bad, weak, infirm

Wasp, [wosp] n. a genus of insects with stings, a petulant person

Wasp'ish, a. peevish, cross, touchy, fretful

Wasp'ishly, ad. in a waspish manner, peevishly

Wasp'ishness, n. a peevishness, morofeness, a sting

Wass'ail, n. a drink made of apples, sugar and ale

Wass'ailer, n. a toper, drunkard, great drinker

Wast, second person singular pret. of to be

Waste, v. to spend, diminish, destroy, dwindle

Waste, a. desolate, wild, uncultivated, ruinated

Waste, n. desolate ground, a wanton destruction

Wasteful, a. lavish, destructive, unoccupied

Wastefully, ad. lavishly, prodigally, diffolutely

Wastefulness, n. prodigality, a needless expense

Waster, n. a lavish consumer, prodigal, destroyer

Was'trel, n. ground not inclosed, a common, ob.

Watch, [wotch] n. a guard, sentinel, pocket-time-piece, the space of time in which one person watches

Watch, v. not to sleep, to guard, tend, observe

Watch'er, n. one who watches or observes

Watch'et, a. pale or light blue, somewhat blue

Watch'ful, a. attentive, careful, close, wakeful

Watch'fully, ad. with watchfulness or care

Watch'fulness, n. great care, a want of due sleep

Watch'house, n. a place to set the night-watch

Watch'ing, n. a guarding, an inability to sleep

Watch'maker, n. one who makes watches

Watch'man, n. a night-guard, guard, sentinel

Watch'tower, n. a tower for a sentinel to stand up-

Watch'word, n. a sentinel's night-word (on

Water, [a as aw] n. a compound substance, when pure, composed of 85 parts of oxygene, and 15 of hydrogene, urine, lutter of a diamond, glofs on dyed filk

Water, v. to give or take in water, wet, foak, long

Waterage, n. money paid for carriage by water

Watercolors, n. pl. colors ufed with water only

Watercourse, n. a channel or paffage for water

Waterer, n. one who waters, one who moistens

Waterfall, n. a fall of water, cataract, cascade

Waterfly, n. an insect that is seen on water

Waterfowl, n. a fowl that breeds near waters

Watergruel, n. food made of meal and water

Waterineſs, Waterishneſs, n. moisture, wetneſs

Waterish, a. resembling water, moist, insipid

Waterlogged, a. full of water, inactive, yielding to the waves (ner

Waterman, n. a boatman, ferryman, sailor, mari-

Watermark, n. the mark or limit of a flood

Watermill, n. a mill turned by means of water

Waterpot, n. a pot or vessel to hold water

Waterrat, n. a rat that makes holes in banks

Waterfapphire, n. a kind of blue precious stone

Waterspout, n. a collection of water at sea, in a vertical column, driven furiously by a whirl-wind

Waterwork, n. a hydraulic performance

Watery, a. abounding with water, thin, insipid

Wat'tle, v. t. to bind, fix or form with twigs

Wat'tlebird, n. a bird of New Zealand

Wat'tles, n. pl. hurdles of willows, a cock's gills

Wave, v. to play loosely, float, beckon, put off

Wave, n. a billow at sea, &c. inequality, hollow

Waved, pa. moved loosely, variegated, put off

Waver, v. i. to be unsettled, float, move loosely

Waverer, n. one who is unsettled in his opinion

Waveloaf, n. a loaf for a waveoffering

Waveoffering, n. an offering to be waved

Waveworn, a. worn by waves

Wavy, a. rising in waves or inequalities, loose

Wawl, v. i. to cry, scream, howl, whine, mew

Wax, n. a tenacious matter gathered from bees, or formed artificially

Wax, v. waxed, pret. waxed, waxen, pa. to smear over with wax, grow, become

Wax'candle, Wax'light, n. a candle of wax

Wax'ed or Wax'en, pa. a. made of wax, grown

Way, n. a road, passage, means, method, custom

Wayfarer, n. a traveller, passenger, stranger

Wayfaring, a. travelling, journeying, passing by

Waylay, v. t. waylaid, pret. waylaid, pa. to lie in wait, to beset by ambush

Wayless, a. having no road, pathless, untrod

Waymark, n. a mark set to direct travellers by

Ways and means, the title of a committee to devise the mode of raising money for public uses

Wayward, a. froward, unruly, peevish, morose

Waywardly, a. frowardly, peevishly, crossly

Waywardneſs, n. frowardneſs, unrulineſs, peev-ishneſs, croſſneſs

Waywiser, n. an instrument to measure distances on a road, a pedometer or perambulator

We, pl. of I

Weak, a. feeble, unfortified, inconclusive, pliant

Weaken, v. t. to make weak, enfeeble, injure

Weakheart'ed, a. dispirited, scrupulous

Weakling, n. a weak or feeble creature

Weakly, ad. feebly; a. feeble, infirm, sickly

Weakneſs, n. a feebleneſs, defect, failing, fault

Weakside, n. a foible, defect, infirmity (stripe

Weal, n. happineſs, profperity, ſtate, mark of a

Weald, Wald, Walt, n. a woody part, wood, grove

Wealth or Welth, n. riches, money, goods, any poſſeſſions

Wealthily, ad. richly, abundantly, plentifully

Wealth'ineſs, n. richneſs, abundance, plenty, ſtore

Wealth'y, a. rich, opulent, abundant, plentiful

Wean, v. t. to deprive of the breaſt, to take

Weanling, n. a child or animal newly weaned

Weap'on, *n.* an inftrument of offenfe or defenfe
Weap'oned, *a.* furnifhed with weapons or arms
Weap'onlefs, *a.* having no weapon, unarmed, bare
Weap'onfalve, *n.* a falve faid to cure wounds after touching the weapon that made them
Wear, *v.* ware, wore, *pret.* worn, *pa.* to wafte, have or put on, carry, hold out, bring to
Wear, *n.* the act of wearing, a great dam of water
Weãrer, *n.* one who wears or ufes any thing
Wéarinefs, *n.* a tired ftate, fatigue, heavinefs
Wearing, *n.* the act of wafting or ufing, clothes
Wéarifh, *a.* boggy, marfhy, fenny, watery, foft
Wéarifome, *a.* tedious, tirefome, troublefome
Wéarifomely, *ad.* tedioufly, flowly, with fatigue
Wéarifomenefs, *n.* tedioufnefs, a tired ftate
Weary, *v. t.* to tire, to harafs; *a.* tired, tirefome
Wea''fand, Wea''zon, *n.* the windpipe, the gullet
Wéafel, *fee* Weefel (ftorm
Weath'er or Weth'er, *n.* a ftate of the air, tempeft,
Weath'er, *a.* being or lying to windward
Weath'er, *v. t.* to pafs with difficulty, to gain, fail round to windward
Weath'erbeaten, *a.* feafoned with bad weather
Weath'ercock, *n.* a vane on a fpire, a very fickle
Weath'erdriven, *a.* forced by a ftorm (perfon
Weath'ergage, *n.* a thing that fhows the weather
Weath'erglafs, *n.* a glafs to fhow the weather by
Weath'ermoft, *a.* fartheft to windward
Weath'erfpy, *n.* a ftargazer, aftrologer, wizard
Weath'erwife, *a.* able to foretel the weather (ther
Weath'erwifer, *n.* any thing forefhewing the wea-
Weave, *v. t.* weft, wove, *pret.* weaved, weft, wove, woven, *pa.* to form by texture, plait, infert
Wéaver, *n.* one who makes threds into cloth
Wéaving, *n.* the act of making into cloth, &c.
Web, *n.* any thing woven, a film, a fkin
Web'bed, *a.* joined by a web, joined by a film
Web'footed, *a.* having films between the toes
Webs'ter, *n.* one who weaves cloth, a weaver
Wed, *v. t.* to marry, join in marriage, unite
Wed'ding, *n.* a marriage, nuptial feftivities
Wedge, *n.* a body with a fharp edge, mafs, ingot
Wedge, *v. t.* to faften or cleave with wedges
Wedge'fhaped, Wedge'form, *a.* in form of a wedge
Wed'lock, *n.* the married ftate, matrimony
Wednes'day, *n.* the fourth day of the week
Wee, *a.* little, fmall, diminutive, puny, *ob.*
Weed, *n.* a ufelefs herb, mourning drefs, veil
Weed, *v. t.* to pull up weeds, root out, clear
Wéeder, *n.* one who weeds, one who takes away
Wéedhook, *n.* a hook to root up weeds with
Wéedlefs, *a.* free from weeds, clean, very neat
Wéedy, *a.* abounding with weeds, foul, rough
Week, *n.* the fpace or compafs of feven days
Wéekday, *n.* any day except Sunday (a week
Wéekly, *a.* done, &c. every week; *ad.* once in
Weel, *n.* a whirlpool, a kind of trap or net for fifh
Ween, *v. i.* to think, fuppofe, imagin, deem
Weep, *v. i.* wept, *pret.* wept, *pa.* to fhed tears,

fhed moifture, bewail, lament, mourn
Wéeper, *n.* a mourner, a white border of linen
Wéerifh, *a.* infipid, weak, four, furly, *ob.*
Wéefel, *n.* a genus of quadrupeds with flender bodies, a particular fpecies of this genus
Weet, Wéeten, *v. i.* to know, to be fenfible of, *ob.*
Wéevil, *n.* an infect injurious to grain
Weft, *n.* a thing woven, the woof of cloth, goods or cattle which have no owner, a gentle blaft
Weft'age, *n.* a texture (min, judge, heave up
Weigh, [way] *v.* to try the weight, confider, ex-
Weigh, Wey, *n.* a weight, meafure, way, paffage
Weigh'able, *a.* that may be weiged
Weigh'ed, *pa.* examined by weight, confidered
Weight, *n.* a mafs by which bodies are weighed, heavinefs of a thing, preffure, importance
Weight'ed, [wated] *a.* preffed with or fubjected to weight
Weight'ily, *ad.* heavily, ftrongly, importantly
Weight'inefs, *n.* heavinefs, force, importance
Weight'lefs, *a.* light, unimportant, very trifling
Weight'y, *a.* heavy, ftrong, important, rigorous
Wel'come, *a.* received with gladnefs, grateful
Wel'come, *n.* a kind reception; *v. t.* to receive
Wel'come, *exclam.* ufed to a vifitor (kindly
Wel'comenefs, *n.* the act of making welcome, a kind reception, gratefulnefs, pleafure
Wel'comer, *n.* one who bids or makes welcome
We'd, *v.* to beat one mafs into another, to join firmly with the aid of extreme heat
Weld, Would, *n.* a dyer's weed for yellow
Wel'fare, *n.* happinefs, profperity, fuccefs, health
Welk'ed, *a.* wrinkled, wreathed, clouded, *ob.*
Welk'in, *n.* the fky, the vifible regions of the air
Welk'ing, *a.* clouding, weak, languifhing, faint, *ob.*
Well, *n.* a fpring, fource, cavity; *v. i.* to fpring
Well, *a.* not fick, recovered, happy, convenient
Well, *ad.* not amifs, rightly, properly, fufficient'y
Well'aday, *exclam.* denoting grief, pity, &c. alas!
Well'béing, *n.* happinefs, fatisfaction, profperity
Well'born, *a.* not meanly born or defcended
Well'bred, *a.* properly educated, polite, civil
Well'done, *exclam.* denoting praife, fupport, &c.
Well'favored, *a.* beautiful, handfome, pleafing
Well'met', *exclam.* denoting falutation, joy, &c.
Well'nigh, *ad.* almoft, nearly, in a manner
Well'pent', *a.* fpent virtuoufly or properly
Well'fpring, *n.* a fpring, fountain, fource, caufe
Well'will'er, *n.* one who means well or kindly
Well'wifh', *n.* a good wifh, a wifh of happinefs
Well'wifh'er, *n.* one who wifhes good (border
Welt, *n.* a border, a felvage; *v. t.* to few with a
Welt'er, *v. i.* to roll in blood, mire or water
Wem, *n.* a fpot, fcar, hurt, damage, fault, *ob.*
Wen, *n.* a flefhy excrefcence on animals
Wench, *n.* a young woman, a ftrumpet
Wench'er, *a.* a fornicator, loofe fellow
Wench'ing, *n.* a following of bad women
Wend, *v. i.* to go, pafs from, turn round, *ob.*

Wen'nel, *n.* an animal newly taken from its dam
Wen'ny, *a.* having the nature of or like a wen
Went, *pret.* of *to go*
Wept, *pret.* and *pa.* of *to weep*
Were, *pret.* of *to be* (for homicide
Wer'egild, *n.* a compensation in money or goods
Wert, *second perf. sing.* of the *pret.* of *to be*
West, *n.* the region or part where the sun sets
West, *a.* situate towards the sunset; *ad.* to the west
West'ering, *a.* tending towards the west
West'erling, West'erly, *a.* passing, &c. to the west
West'ern, *a.* westerly, coming from the west
West'ward, West'wardly, *ad.* towards the west
Wet, *a.* rainy, moist; *n.* rain, water, moisture
Wet, *v.* wet, wetted, *pret.* wet, wetted, *pa.* to
rain, moisten, make to drink, drench
Weth'er, *n.* a castrated ram, a gelded sheep
Wet'nefs, *n.* a wet state, rain, moisture
Wet'tish, *a.* rather wet, rather moist, dull, heavy
Wex, *v. t.* to grow, increase, wax [*not to be ufed*]
Note. In words beginning with *wh*, the *h* is
pronounced before *w*, hwale [hooale] and fo
were thefe letters written in the Saxon
Whale, *n.* the largeft of all fifh, monfter, mark
Whaly, *a.* marked with or in ftreaks, variegated
Whame, *n.* a fpecies of fly, tabanus
Wharf, *n.* a bank or place to land goods at
Wharf, *v.* to make a wharf
Wharf'age, *n.* rates paid for landing at a wharf
Wharf'ing, *n.* wharves in general
Wharf'inger, *n.* a keeper or owner of a wharf
What, *pron.* that which, which part, partly
Whatev'er, Whatfoev'er, *pron.* this or that, any
Wheal, *n.* a puftule, infect, inftrument
Wheat, *n.* bread-corn, the fineft of grains
Wheatear, *n.* a very delicate fmall bird, a warbler
Wheaten, *a.* made of or like wheat
Wheedle, *v. t.* to coax, to entice by foft words
Wheedler, *n.* one who wheedles, one who coaxes
Wheedling, *n.* the act of coaxing, flattery
Wheel, *n.* an inftrument for torture and fpinning,
round body, compafs about, revolution
Wheel, *v.* to move on wheels, to take a round
Wheelbarrow, *n.* a carriage of only one wheel
Wheelcarriage, *n.* a carriage moving on wheels
Wheeler, Wheelwright, *n.* a maker of wheels
Wheeling, *n.* the act of turning a body of men
Wheelfhaped, *a.* in form of a wheel
Wheely, *a.* like a wheel, round, circular
Wheeze, *v. i.* to breathe hard or with a noife
Whelk, *n.* a protuberance, mark, puftule, fhellfifh
Whelm, *v. t.* to cover, bury, deftroy, turn down
Whelm'y, *a.* overwhelming, apt to overwhelm
Whelp, *n.* a puppy, cub, young man, fon, piece
Whelp, *v. t.* to bring young as a bitch, to pup
When, *ad.* at what time, at the fame time
Whence, *ad.* from what place, fource, book, &c.
Whencefoev'er, *ad.* from what place foever
Whenev'er, Whenfoev'er, *ad.* at whatfoever time

Where, *ad.* at or in which place, at what place
Where, *n.* a place, ftate, fpace, abode, fituation
Whereabouts', *ad.* near what or which place
Whereas', *ad.* but on the contrary, at which place
Whereat', *ad.* at or on which, whereupon
Whereby', *ad.* by which, by the means of which
Where'fore, *ad.* for which or what reafon, fo that
Wherein', *ad.* in which, in which thing or place
Wherein'to, *ad.* into which (fome place
Where'nefs, *n.* what or fome place, exiftence in
Whereof', *ad.* of or for which, concerning which
Whereon', Whereupon, *ad.* on or upon which
Where'fo, Wherefoev'er, *ad.* in what place foever
Whereto, Whereunto, *ad.* to which, unto which
Wherev'er, *ad.* at whatfoever place, wherefoever
Wherewith', Wherewithal', *ad.* with or by which
Wher'ret, *v. t.* to teaze, hurry, vex, box the ear
Wher'reting, *n.* the act of teazing or boxing
Wher'ry, *n.* a light river-boat for paffengers
Wher'ry, *v. t.* to convey over in a very fmall boat
Whet, *v. t.* to fharpen, edge, provoke, incite
Whet, *n.* the act of fharpening, dram before a meal
Wheth'er, *pron.* which of the two; *ad.* fome way
Whet'ftone, *n.* a ftone to fharpen edge tools
Whet'ter, *n.* one who fharpens knives, &c. (white
Whey, [whay] *n.* the ferous part of milk, thin and
Whey'ey, Whey'ifh, *a.* like whey, watery, thin
Which, *pron.* who, that, whether of two things
Whichev'er, Whichfoev'er, *pron.* one or the other,
Whiff, *n.* a puff, blaft, a fifh; *v. t.* to blow out
Whif'fle, *v. t.* to prevaricate, fhuffle, trick, play
Whif'fler, *n.* a fhuffler, trickfter, fifer, marcher
Whif'fling, *n.* a fhuffling, inconftancy (ed for draft
Whif'fletree, *n.* the bar to which traces are faften-
Whig, *n.* a party man oppofed to a tory, whey, a
friend to the revolution in America
Whig'gifh, *a.* inclined to whiggifm, fpirited
Whig'gifm, *n.* the principles of the whigs
While, *n.* time, a fpace of time; *v. i.* to loiter
While, Whiles, Whilft, *ad.* as long, as long as
Whilere, *ad.* a little while ago, not very long ago
Whilom, *ad.* of or in old time, formerly, once, *ob.*
Whim, Whim'fey, *n.* an odd fancy, caprice, freak
Whimp'er, *v. i.* to cry low, to cry as a child
Whimp'ering, *n.* the act of crying like a child
Whimp'led, *a.* diftorted, diftorted with crying, *ob.*
Whim'fical, *a.* capricious, oddly fanciful, odd
Whim'fically, *ad.* in a whimfical manner, oddly
Whim'ficalnefs, *n.* a whimfical temper, oddnefs
Whin, *n.* a fhrub, a prickly fhrub, furze
Whin'brel, *n.* an aquatic bird like a curlew
Whin'eat, *a.* a bird, a fpecies of warbler
Whine, *v. i.* to moan meanly; *n.* a mean complaint
Whin'nie, *v. t.* to make crooked, bend, turn, *ob.*
Whin'ny, *v. i.* to make a noife like a horfe
Whin'ftone, *n.* a fpecies of trap
Whin'yard, *n.* a large crooked fword, a cimeter
Whip, *n.* a fcourge or lafh with one thong
Whip, *v.* to cut with a whip, correct with a rod,

G g

laih, take or move nimbly, few flightly
Whip'cord, n. a cord to make whiplashes with
Whip'grafting, n. a particular kind of grafting
Whip'hand, n. an advantage over another perfon
Whip'lash, n. a lash on the fmall end of a whip
Whip'per, n. one who whips, one who beats
Whip'pingpoft, n. a poft ufed to whip vagrants at
Whip'powill, n. a bird, fo called from its fong
Whip'faw, n. a large faw for two perfons
Whips'ter, n. a fharper, fhuffler, nimble fellow
Whip'ftock, n. a rod to which a whip is tied
Whipt, pret. and pa. of to whip
Whirl, v. to turn or run round rapidly
Whirl, n. a rapid turning or circumvolution, a
  wood, hook for twifting, form of a flower
Whirl'bat, n. a thing whirled round for a blow
Whirl'blaft, n. a whirling guft of wind
Whirl'ed, a. having leaves or flowers around a
  ftalk like a whirl, verticillate
Whirl'igig, n. a whirling plaything for children
Whirl'pool, n. water that moves circularly
Whirl'wind, n. a ftormy wind moving circularly
Whir'ring, n. a noife made by a pheafant's wings
Whifk, n. a fmall befom, a kind of tippet
Whifk, v. t. to bruih with a whifk, fweep, run
Whifk'er, n. one who whifks, hair on the lips
Whifk'ing, pa. a brufhing, paffing quick, large
Whifk'y, n. a fpirit diftilled from grain
Whis'per, v. i. to fpeak in a low voice
Whis'per, n. a low foft voice, a fpeaking foftly
Whis'perer, n. one who fpeaks low or talks fecretly
Whis'pering, n. the act of talking in whifpers
Whift, n. a game; a. filent, ftill; exclam. be ftill
Whis''tle, v. to blow a whiftle, to found fhrill
Whis''tle, n. a fmall pipe to whiftle with, a call
Whis''tler, n. one who whiftles or calls by a whiftle
Whit, n. a point, jot, tittle, fmall part, little bit
White, a. fnowy, pale, pure   (or an egg
White, n. a white color, the white part of the eye,
Whitebait, n. a very fmall delicate fifh
Whitelead, n. an oxyd of lead, ufed in painting
Whitelivered, a. malicious, feeb'e, cowardly
Whitelimed, a. covered with plafter or whitewafh
Whitely, a. coming near to white, pale, fickly
Whitemeat, n. a milky diet, fowl, veal, fifh, &c.
Whiten, White, v. to make or grow white
Whitener, n. one who whitens, one who bleaches
Whitenefs, n. a white ftate, palenefs
Whitepot, n. a kind of food from milk, eggs, &c.
Whitethorn, n. a kind of thorn, the hawthorn
Whitethroat, n. a bird, a fpecies of motacilla
Whitewafh, v. t. to make white, adorn, clear, fet
Whitewafh, n. a wafh to make white   (free
Whitewafhing, n. the act of whitening walls
Whitewine, n. wine made from white grapes
Whitewood, n. a timber tree
Whith'er, ad. to what place or degree, how far
Whitherfoev'er, ad. to whatfoever place or end
Whiting, n. a fmall feafifh, a kind of foft chalk

Whitifh, a. fomewhat or tending to white, pale
Whitifhnefs, n. a tendency to white, palenefs
Whit'lether, n. a lether dreft with alum
Whit'low, n. a hot fwelling at the end of a finger
Whit'fter, n. a whitener, a bleacher of linen
Whit'funtide, n. a feftival, the feaft of pentecoft
Whit'tle, n. a knife, a blanket; v. t. to cut, to drefs
Whit'tling, n. the act of cutting or fharpening
Whiz, v. i. to make a loud humming noife; n. a
Who, [hoo] pron. which perfon (humming noife
Whoev'er, pron. any perfon, any perfon whatever
Whole, [hole] n. the total, all of a thing, a fum,
Whole, a. total, all, reftored to health, well, kindly
Wholefooted, a. having the hoof not cloven
Wholefale, n. a fale in the grofs or by the lump
Wholefome, a. contributing to health, falutary
Who!efomely, ad. in a wholefome manner
Wholefomenefs, n. a wholefome quality, healthi-
Wholly, ad. totally, completely, perfectly   (nefs
Whom, [hoom] objective cafe of who
Whomfoev'er, pron. any perfon whatever, whom
Whoop, [hoop] n. a fhout of purfuit; v. i. to fhout
  with infult
Whoop'ing, n. a fhouting with joy or infult
Whop, Whap, or A'whap, ad. an old word for a hea-
  vy fall, or the manner of falling, ftill ufed by
  the vulgar   (man
Whore, [hore] n. a ftrumpet, proftitute, loofe wo-
Whore, v. i. to converfe carnally and unlawfully
Whoredom, n. a playing the whore, adultery, &c.
Whoremonger, Whoremafter, n. one who whores
Whorefon, n. a baftard; a. crofs, fpurious, falfe
Whoring, n. the act of following bad women
Whorifh, a. unchafte, incontinent, loofe, wicked
Whor'tleberry, Whort, n. a bilberry, fhrub, bufh
Whofe, [hooze] pron. gen. of who and which
Whofo, Whofoev'er, pron. any perfon
Whur or Whurr, v. i. to pronounce the letter r
  with too much force, make a noife, fnarl, growl
Whur'ring, n. a noife made by partridges rifing
Why, ad. wherefore, for what reafon
Wick, n. the cotton or fnuff of a candle or lamp
Wick'ed, a. given to vice, bad, curfed, pernicious
Wick'edly, ad. in a wicked manner, corruptly
Wick'ednefs, n. vice, guilt, moral ill, corruption
Wick'er, a. made of fmall willows or twigs
Wick'et, n. a fmall door, a fmall part of a gate
Wide, a. broad, extended, remote, far, deviating
W.de, Widely, ad. remotely, far, at a diftance, very
Widen v. to make or grow wide, extend
Widenefs, Width, n. breadth, a large extent
Wid''geon, n. a waterfowl, dupe, fimpleton
Wid'ow, v. t. to deprive of any thing, ftrip, endow
Wid'ow, n. a woman whofe hufband is dead
Wid'ower, n. a man whofe wife is dead
Wid'owhood, n. the ftate of a widow or widower
Wid'owhunter, n. one who hunts after widows for
  the fake of their jointures or fortunes only
Wid'owmaker, n. one who makes women widows

Widow'scham'ber, *n*. certain effects of a deceased perfon falling to his widow in London

Wield, *v. t.* to ufe with full power, to fway

Wieldlefs, *a.* heavy, not manageable

Wieldy, *a.* that may be wielded, manageable

Wiery, *a.* made of or drawn into wire, marfhy

Wife, *n.* a married woman, a low mean woman

Wig, *n.* a hair-covering for the head, a cake

Wight, *n.* a perfon, a being; *a.* nimble, fwift

Wi''geon, *n.* a bird of the duck kind

Wig'wam, *n.* a fort of mean cabin, an Indian cabin

Wild, *a.* not tame, defert, favage, turbulent, fierce, licentious, loofe; fickle, flrange, fanciful

Wild, *n.* a defert, wafte, bad uninhabited country

Wil'der, *v.* to lofe, to puzzle in an unknown track

Wil'dernefs, *n.* a tract of folitude and favagenefs

Wildfire, *n.* gunpowder rolled up wet, a difeafe

Wildfowl, *n.* wild ducks and fowls of the like kind

Wildgoofechafe, *n.* a vain or very foolifh purfuit

Wilding, *n.* a wild and very four apple

Wildly, *ad.* irregularly, badly, without judgment

Wildnefs, *n.* favagenefs, fiercenefs, fury, rudenefs

Wile, *n.* a trick, deceit, fraud, fhift, cunning, art

Wil'ful, *a.* defigned, ftubborn, unruly, tenacious

Wil'fully, *ad.* on purpofe, obftinately, ftubbornly

Wil'fulnefs, *n.* obftinacy, perverfenefs, croffnefs

Wilily, *ad.* flily, cunningly, archly, fraudulently

Wilinefs, *n.* cunning, craft, guile, deceit, fraud

Wilk, *n.* a fpecies of fhell fifh

Will, *n.* a choice, command, bequeft, teftament

Will, *v. t.* to defire, command, direct, purpofe

Will'ing, *a.* inclined, ready, confenting

Will'ing, *n.* the act of defiring or choofing

Will'ingly, *ad.* readily, with one's own confent

Will'ingnefs, *n.* defire, readinefs, confent

Will'ow, *n.* the name of a common tree

Will-with-a-wifp, *n.* a kind of fiery meteor

Wily, *a.* fly, cunning, arch, artful, crafty

Wim'ble, *n.* an inftrument to bore holes with (*ing*

Wim'men, *n. pl.* of wimman, *the old and true fpell-*

Wim''ple, *n.* a hood; *v. t.* to draw over, to veil

Win, *v. t.* won, *pret.* won, *pa.* to gain, get, get by conqueft or play

Wince or Winch, *v. i.* to fhrink from pain, kick,

Winch, *n.* a handle to turn a mill or fcrew (fpurn

Wind, *n.* a current of air, breath or refpiration, flatulence, publicity.

Wind, *v. t.* wound, *pret.* wound, *pa.* to turn round, twift, infinuate, unfold, blow

Wind'age, *n.* the difference between the diameter of a piece and a ball or fhell

Wind'bound, *a.* confined by contrary winds

Wind'egg, *n.* an egg addle or not duly impregnated

Winder, *n.* one who or what winds, a plant

Wind'fal, *n.* fruit blown off or down, a good event

Wind'flower, *n.* a kind of flower, the anemony

Wind'gun, *n.* a gun difcharged by compreffed air

Wind'inefs, *n.* a fulnefs of wind, wind, coldnefs

Winding, *n.* a turning about, turn, purfuit

Windingfheet, *n.* a fheet to wrap the dead in

Wind'inefs, *n.* a flate of being windy, flatulence

Wind'las, *n.* a machine to raife large weights by

Win''dle, *n.* a fpindle, kind of machine, reel

Wind'gall, *n.* a foft tumor on a horfes fetlo ? joint

Wind'mill, *n.* a mill turned by the wind alone

Wind'ow, *n.* an opening to give light to a building

Win'dow, *v. i.* to make or place at windows, to open (a window

Win'dowblind, *n.* that which obfcures the light of

Win'dowframe, *n.* the frame which fupports the

Win'dowglafs, *n.* glafs in panes for windows (fafhes

Win'dowfafh, *n.* a thin piece of wood to hold the panes of glafs (window

Win'dowfhutter, *n.* a frame or board to clofe a

Wind'row, *n.* a row of grafs raked together

Wind'pipe, *n.* the paffage for the breath

Wind'ward, *a.* lying towards the wind

Wind'ward, *ad.* towards or near the wind

Windy, *a.* breeding wind, flormy, airy, fwelled

Wine, *n.* the fermented juce of the grape

Winebibber, *n.* a great drinker of wine

Winemerchant, *n.* one who deals in wines

Wing, *n.* a limb of a bird, fide of an army, flight

Wing, *v.* to furnifh with wings, fly, wound, hurt

Wing'ed, Wing'y, *a.* having wings, wounded, hurt

Wing'er, *n.* a fmall cafk ftowed in the fides of a fhips hold

Wing'fhell, *n.* the fhell for the wings of infects

Wink, *v. i.* to fhut the eyes, clofe, connive, hint

Wink, *n.* a hint by the motion of one eye, a token

Wink'ingly, *ad.* with the eyes nearly clofed

Win'ner, *n.* one who wins, one who gains or gets

Win'ning, *a.* attractive, charming; *n.* a fum won

Win'now, *v. t.* to fan, fift, part, feparate, examin

Win'ter, *n.* the laft and cold feafon of the year, a part of a printing prefs, on which the carriage

Wint'er, *v.* to pafs, flay or feed in, the winter (refts

Win'terkill, *v. t.* to kill by means of winter, as grain

Wint'erly, Wint'ry, *a.* fuitable to winter, cold

Win'tering, *n.* the hybernacle of plants, or bud

Win'terlodge, *n.* the bud or hybernacle of a plant which protects the gem of the young plant during winter

Winy, *a.* having the tafte of wine, like wine.

Wipe, *v. t.* to clean by rubbing, clear away, cheat

Wipe, *n.* a rub, ftroke, blow, reproof, bird

Wiper, *n.* a perfon that wipes, a thing wiped with

Wire, *n.* a metal drawn into fmall bars or threds

Wiredraw, *v. t.* wiredrew, *pret.* wiredrawn, *pa.* to form wire, draw by art, gull

Wiredrawer, *n.* one who draws out or makes wire

Wis, *v. i.* wift, *pret.* to know; *ad.* verily, truly

Wis'dom, *n.* the power of judging rightly, fenfe

Wife, *a.* judging rightly, fkilful, prudent, grave

Wife, *n.* a manner, a way of being or acting

Wifeacre, *n.* a foolifh fellow, fimpleton, dunce

Wifely, *ad.* judicioufly, prudently, fitly, gravely

Wifh, *n.* a longing or eager defire, a thing defired

Wifh, _v._ to have a ftrong defire, long for, afk

Wifh'er, _n._ one who wifhes or longs for, a defirer

Wifh'ful, _a._ fhowing ftrong defire, longing, eager

Wifh'fully, _ad._ with longing defire, earneftly

Wifk'et or Whifk'et, _n._ a bafket, a kind of fcuttle

Wifp, _n._ a fmall bundle of ftraw or hay, a wreath

Wift, _pret._ of _to wis_ (defire

Wift'ful, _a._ earneft, attentive, full of thought or

Wift'fully, Wift'ly, _ad._ earneftly, attentively

Wis'tit, _n._ a fmall ftriated monkey

Wit, _n._ a man of genius, quicknefs of fancy, &c.
underftanding, fenfe, judgment

Wit, _v. i._ to know, underftand, blame

Witch, _v. t._ to bewitch, enchant, charm, take, hurt

Witch, _n._ a woman accufed of magical arts, a hag

Witch'craft, _n._ the practice of witches, a charm

Witch'ery, _n._ witchcraft, enchantment, a charm

Wit'cracker, _n._ one who cracks a jeft, a jefter

Wit'craft, _n._ invention, contrivance, cunning, art

With, _prep._ by, denoting the caufe or means

Withal', _ad._ along with the reft, befides, alfo, above

Withdraw, _v. t._ withdrew, _pret._ withdrawn, _pa._
to draw back or off, retire, retreat

Withdraw'ingroom, _n._ a room for retirement

Withe, _n._ a flexible band, a twig

With'er, _v._ to fade, pine away, die, make to fade

With'erednefs, _n._ a withered ftate (horfe

With'ers, _n._ the joining of the fhoulder bones of a

Withhold, _v. t._ withheld, _pret._ withheld, with-
holden, _p._ to keep back, ftop, ftay, reftrain

Within', _prep._ in, inwardly, in the inner part

Within'fide, _ad._ in the inward parts (unlefs

Without', _prep._ and _ad._ out, not within compafs of,

Withftand', _v. t._ withftood, _pret._ withftood, _pa._
to oppofe, refift, reftrain, hinder

Withftand'er, _n._ an opponent, foe, refifting power

With'y, _a._ like a withe, flexible, tough

With'y, _n._ a tree, the white willow

Wit'lefs, _a._ wanting underftanding, foolifh, filly

Wit'ling, _n._ a pretender to wit, fimpleton, idler

Wit'nefs, _n._ teftimony, atteftation, an evidence

Wit'nefs, _v._ to bear teftimony, atteft, affirm, fay

Wit'fnapper, _n._ one who affects wit or repartee

Wit'ted, _a._ having wit, endued with wit, keen

Wit'ticifm, _n._ a mean device or low attempt at wit

Wit'tily, _ad._ keealy, artfully, ingenioufly

Wit'tinefs, _n._ fmartnefs, keennefs, wit

Wit'tingly, _ad._ knowingly, by defign, on purpofe

Wit'tol or Wit'tal, _n._ a mean contented cuckold, _ob._

Wit'tolly, _a._ cuckoldly, mean, poor, defpicable, _ob._

Wit'ty, _a._ fmart, keen, tart, farcaftic, ingenious

Wit'worm, _n._ one who feeds on or likes wit

Wive, _v._ to take for or match to a wife, to marry

Wively, _a._ belonging to, like or becoming, a wife

Wives, _n. pl._ of _wife_

Wiz'ard, _n._ a conjurer, enchanter, cunningman

Wo or Woe, _n._ grief, forrow, mifery, pain, a curfe

Wead, _n._ a plant ufed in dying a blue color

Wo'ful, _a._ forrowful, fad, calamitous, wretched

Wo'fully, _ad._ fadly, mournfully, wretchedly, very

Wo'fulnefs, _n._ a fad or difmal ftate, wretchednefs

Wold, _n._ a plain and open country, a down, _ob._

Wolf, [woolf] _n._ a rapacious animal of the canine
kind, an ulcer

Wolf'dog, _n._ a large dog kept to guard fheep

Wolf'fifh, _n._ a large voracious fifh

Wolf'ifh or Wolv'ifh, _a._ like a wolf, ravenous

Wolfs'bane, _n._ a very poifonous herb

Wol'fram, _n._ an ore of tungften, a mineral

Wolve ene, _n._ a carniverous animal, the glutton

Wom'an, [wooman] _n._ a female of the human race

Wom'an, _v. t._ to make pliant like a woman

Wom'aned, _a._ united with or made like a woman

Wom'anhater, _n._ one who hates all womankind

Wom'anhood, _n._ the qualites or ftate of women

Wom'anife, _v. t._ to play the woman, foften, melt

Wom'anifh, _a._ fuitable to a woman, delicate, fofe

Wom'ankind, _n._ the female fex, the female fpecies

Wom'anly, _a._ becoming a woman, not girlifh

Wom'at or Wom'back, _n._ a quadruped of New-
Holland like a fmall bear (conception

Womb, [woomb] _n._ the place of generation or

Womb, _v. t._ to inclofe, contain, breed in fecret

Womb'y, _a._ like a womb, capacious, large big

Wom'en, _n. pl._ of _woman._ _The primitive and
correct orthography is wimmen_

Won, [wun] _pret._ and _pa. paff._ of _to win_

Won'der, _v. i._ to be aftonifhed, to admire (tion

Won'der, Won'derment, _n._ amazement, admira-

Won'derful, _a._ amazing, aftonifhing, ftrange

Wonder'fully, _ad._ in a wonderful manner, oddly

Won'derfulnefs, _n._ ftrangenefs, wonder

Won'derous, Won'drous, _a._ marvellous, ftrange

Won'derftruck, _a._ amazed, aftonifhed, furprifed

Won'droufly, _ad._ to a ftrange degree, ftrangely

Wont, a contraction of _will not_

Wont, [wunt] _v. i._ to be accuftomed; _n._ cuftom,
ufe, habit

Wont'ed, _pa._ accuftomed, ufed, ufual, common

Wont'ednefs, _n._ the ftate of being accuftomed to

Woo, _v._ to court, make love to, fue, entreat, afk

Wood, _n._ a place filled with timber, a collection of
growing trees, the harder parts of trees

Wood'afhes, _n. pl._ afhes from burnt wood

Wood'bind or Wood'bine, _n._ a fhrub, honeyfuckle

Wood'chat, _n._ a fpecies of the butcher bird

Wood'chuck, _n._ an animal of the marmot tribe

Wood'cock, _n._ a fine bird of paffage

Wood'drink, _n._ a decoction of medicinal woods

Wood'ed, _a._ fupplied or thick with wood, rough

Wood'en, _a._ made of wood, hard, clumfy, thick

Wood'fretter, _n._ a noify infect or worm

Wood'hole, _n._ a hole or place where wood is laid

Wood'inefs, _n._ a woody ftate, roughnefs

Wood'ing, _n._ a taking in or procuring of wood

Wood'land, _n._ land that is covered with wood

Wood'lark, _n._ a lark that frequents woods

Wood'loufe, _n._ vermin in and about old wood

Wood'man, *n.* a sportsman, hunter, officer, bailiff
Wood'monger, *n.* a seller of wood for firing, &c.
Wood'note, *n.* a wild note, wild sweet music
Wood'nymph, *n.* a nymph of the woods, a dryad
Wood'offering, *n.* wood that is burnt upon altars
Wood'pecker, *n.* a bird that picks insects from trees, and pecks a hole for its nest
Wood'pigeon, *n.* a kind of wild pigeon
Wood'reve, *n.* a steward or overseer of a wood
Wood'fare, *n.* the froth or spittle seen upon herbs
Wood'sere, *n.* the time when trees have little sap
Wood'stone, *n.* a blackish gray filiceous stone
Wood'shock, *n.* the fisher or wejack, a quadruped of the weefel genus, in N. America
Wood'y, *a.* abounding with or like wood, rough
Woo'er, *n.* one who courts a woman, a lover
Woof, *n.* the threds that crofs the warp, a texture
Woo'ing, *n.* the act of making love, fondnefs
Woo'ingly, *ad.* with earnest entreaty, pleasingly
Wool, *n.* the fleece of a sheep, very short thick hair
Wool'comber, *n.* one who lives by combing wool
Woold, *v.t.* to wind a piece of rope about a mast or yard, when fished or confifting of several pieces
Woold'ing, *n.* a rope round a mast or yard
Wool'fel, *n.* a skin with the wool still on
Wool'len, *a.* made of wool ; *n.* cloth made of wool
Wool'lendraper, *n.* one who deals in woollen goods
Wool'linefs, *n.* a woolly state or quality
Wool'ly, *a.* resembling or confifting of wool
Wool'pack, *n.* a pack or bag of wool, a soft feat
Wool'stapler, *n.* one who trades or deals in wool
Wool'trade, *n.* the trade of dealing in wool
Wool'ward, *ad.* in wool, with wool next the skin. *ob.*
Word, [wurd] *n.* a fingle part of speech, talk, mef-fage, fign, promise, declaration, account, the scripture
Word, *v.* to exprefs properly, describe, difpute, talk
Word'catcher, *n.* a caviller at words, a petty critic
Wore, *pret.* of *to wear*
Work, [wurk] *v.* worked, wrought, *pret.* and *pa.* to labor, toil, do, raife, ferment, be agitated, take effect, produce, make way, embroider
Work, *n.* labor, toil, employment, a deed, a book, materials of labor, effect, treatment
Work'er, *n.* one who works, one who labors
Work'fellow, *n.* one engaged in the fame work
Work'houfe, *n.* a receptacle for parifh-poor
Work'ingday, *n.* a day for working on, a week-day
Work'man, *n.* a maker of any thing, laborer, artift
Work'manlike, *a.* like a workman, good, proper
Work'manly, *ad.* skilfully, well ; *a.* skilful, proper
Work'manfhip, *n.* work, manufacture, skill, art
Work'fhop, *n.* a fhop for performing work in
Work'woman, *n.* a woman skilled in needlework
World, [wurld] *n.* the universe, the earth, mankind, a great multitude, the public, courfe of life, a continent, time
World'linefs, *n.* covetoufnefs, greedinefs, concern
World'ling, *n.* a wretch who idolizes his money

World'ly, *a.* bent upon this world, fordid, huma
World'ly, *ad.* with relation to the prefent life
World'ly minded, *a.* much addicted to this world
Worm, [wurm] *n.* an infect, grub, pipe, fpiral thing, inward torment ; *v. i.* to act flowly
Worm'eaten, *a.* gnawed by worms, worthlefs
Worm'like, *a.* like a worm, fpiral, twisted
Worm'wood, *n.* a very bitter herb
Worm'y, *a.* full of worms, having or like worms
Worn, *pa. paff.* of *to wear*
Wor'nil, *n.* a maggot, a worm bred in cows
Wor'ral, *n.* an animal of the lizard kind in Egypt
Wor'ry, [wurry] *v.t.* to tear, mangle, harafs, teafe
Worfe, [wurfe] *a.* more bad, more ill; *v.t.* to worst, overcome, *ob.*
Worfe, *ad.* in a more bad manner, state or degree
Wor'fhip, *more correctly* wurfhip, *n.* religious reverence, ador tion, dignity, refpect, a term of honor, a term of irony
Wor'fhip, *v.* to adore, perform adoration, refpect
Wor'fhipful, *a.* refpected for dignity or office
Wor'fhipfully, *ad.* refpectfully, honorably
Wor'fhipper, *n.* one who worfhips or adores
Worst, [wurft] *a.* moft vile, moft ill, moft wicked
Worft, *n.* the moft diftreffed or wicked state
Worft, *v.t.* to defeat, beat, overthrow, overcome
Worft'ed, [woofted] *n.* woollen yarn, yarn fpun from combed wool
Wort, [wurt] *n.* ale or beer not fermented, an herb
orth, [wurth] *a.* deferving of, equal in value or price
Worth, *n.* value, price importance, merit, defert
Wor'thied, *a.* made worthy, honored, exalted
Wor'thily, *ad.* defervedly, fuitably, juftly, well
Wor'thinef, *n.* worth, defert, excellence, virtue
Worth'lefs, *a.* unworthy, undeferving, mean, vile
Worth'leffnefs, *n.* a want of worth or value
Wor'thy, *a.* deferving, good, valuable; *v.t.* to exalt
Wor'thy, *n.* a man honorable or deferving praife
Wot, *v.i.* to know, to be fenfible or aware of
Wove, *pret.* and *pa. paff.* of *to weave*
Would, [wood] *pret.* of *will*, auxilia y
Would'ing, *n.* a difpofition, inclination, wifh, *ob.*
Wound, *n.* a hurt ; *v.t.* to hurt by violence
Wound, *pret.* and *pa.* of *to wind*
Wound'lefs, *a.* free from wounds, unhurt
Wound'wort, *n.* a plant of several fpecies
Note.—*W* before *r* is not founded
Wrack, *n.* fea-weed, a grafs (torture
Wrack, *n.* a lofs of a fhip, ruin; *v. t.* to wreck, to
Wran"gle, *n.* a perverfe difpute, fquabble, quarrel
Wran"gle, *v.i.* to difpute peevifhly, to fquabble
Wrang'ler, *n.* a peevifh and difputative perfon
Wrang'ling, *n.* the act of difputing perverfely
Wrap, *v. t.* to roll together, contain, inclofe
Wrap'per, *n.* one who wraps up, a thin cover
Wrafs, *n.* a fifh, the old wife, or fea tench
Wrath, *n.* anger, rage, fury, vengeance
Wrath'ful, *a.* angry, raging, enraged, furious

Wrath'fully, ad. angrily, furiously, paffionately
Wrath'fulnefs, n. great anger, fury, paffion
Wrath'lefs, a. free from anger, meek, kind
Wreak, v.t. to revenge, to execute; n. revenge, fury
Wréakful, a. revengeful, malicious, very angry
Wréaklefs, a. unrevenging, impotent, weak
Wreath, n. any thing twifted, a roll, garland, tail
Wreath or Wreathe, v.t. wreathed, pret. wreath-
ed, wreathen, pa. to twift, interweave, curl
Wréathy, a. fpiral, twifted, curled, involved
Wreck, v. to fuffer wreck or lofs, deftroy, ruin
Wreck, n. a fhipwreck, ruin, lofs, goods wrecked
Wreck'full, a. making wreck, deftructive
Wren, n. the name of a very fmall bird
Wrench, v.t. to pull by force, force, wreft, fprain
Wrench, n. a violent twift, turn or pull, fprain, trap
Wreft, v.t. to twift by violence, turn, force, writhe
Wreft, n. a diftortion, violence, active power
Wreft'er, n. one who wrefts, one who diftorts
Wres''tle, v.i. to ftruggle, to throw with the arms
extended, to ftrive with effort
Wres''tler, n. one who wreftles, one who ftruggles
Wres''tling, n. the act or exercife of wreftling
Wretch, n. a miferable or worthlefs perfon
Wretched, a. miferable, worthlefs, defpicable, vile
Wretch'edly, ad. miferably, meanly, defpicably, ill
Wretch'ednefs, n. mifery, diftrefs, defpicablenefs
Wretch'lefs, a. carelefs, heedlefs, void of care
Wrig'gle, v.i. to move to and fro in the joints
Wrig'gling, n. the act of twifting to and fro
Wright, n. a workman, an artificer in wood
Wring, v.t. wrung, pret. wringed, wrung, pa. to
twift, turn round, fqueeze, prefs, writhe, dif-
tort, torture, harafs, diftrefs, extort
Wring'er, n. one who fqueezes water out of cloth
Wrin''kle, n. a creafe in cloth, the face, &c. a fur-
Wrin''kle, v.t. to caufe wrinkles or creafes (row
Wrift, n. the joint of the hand next the arm
Wrift'band, n. a faftening at or about the wrift
Writ, n. fcripture, a legal procefs or inftrument
Write, v. writ, wrote, pret. writ; written, pa. to
form letters and words with a pen or ftyle, en-
grave, compofe, imprefs
Writer, n. one who writes, an author
Writhe, v. writhed, pret. writhed, writhen, pa. to
twift, diftort, wreft, be in agony or torture
Writing, n. any thing written with pen and ink
Writingmafter, n. a perfon who teaches to write
Writings, n. pl. conveyances of lands, any written
Writ'ten, pa. paff. of to write paper
Wriskled, a. wrinkled, withered, fhrunk, rough
Wrohg, n. injury, injuftice, an error, a miftake
Wrong, a. not right, not true, unfit; v.t. to injure
Wrong, Wrong'ly, ad. amifs, improperly
Wrongdóer, n. an injurious or wicked perfon
Wrong'er, n. one who does wrong or injures
Wrong'ful, a. wrong, unjuft, dishoneft, injurious
Wrong'fully, ad. unjuftly, injurious, hurtfully
Wrong'headed, a. having a perverfe underftanding

Wronghead'ednefs, n. perverfenefs, obftinacy in
Wrong'lefsly, ad. without injury to any one (error
Wrong'nefs, n. a wrong difpofition, error
Wrote, pret. of to write
Wroth, a. very angry, enraged, provoked, vexed
Wroth'ful, a. full of wrath, angry, ob.
Wroth'fully, ad. in great anger, ob.
Wrought, [rawt] pa. worked, performed, manu-
Wrung, pret. and pa. of to wring factured
Wry, a. crooked, diftorted, wrefted; v.t. to turn
Wry'neck, n. a genus of birds of the pye kind
Wry'necked, a. having the neck diftorted

X.

XEBEC', n. a fmall three-mafted veffel in the
Mediterranean

Y

YACH T, [yot] n. a fmall fhip for pleafure, &c.
Yáger, n. a hunter, a foldier [Ger.]
Yam, n. a Weft-Indian root
Yam'boo, n. a genus of plants, with fruit like a plum
Yapoon', n. caffia, or fouth fea tea
Yard, n. ground enclofed to a houfe, a meafure of
three feet, a pole to hang fails upon
Yard'wand, n. a ftick to meafure a yard by, a yard
Yare, a. dexterous, ready, nimble, eager, covetous
Yárely, ad. dexteroufly, fkilfully, covetoufly
Yarn, n. fpun wool or flax, coarfe woollen thred
Yar'rifh, a. having a rough and dry tafte
Yar'row, n. a plant of many leaves
Yaw, v.i. to rife in blifters, breaking in white
froth as cane juce in fugar works [W. Indies]
Yawl, n. a fhip's boat; v.i. to bawl, yell, roar, cry
Yawn, v.i. to gape, to open wide; n. a gaping (out
Yawn'ing, pa. gaping, fleepy, flumbering, dull
Yawn'ing, n. the act of gaping with noife
Yaws, n. the African name for a rafpberry, a dif-
eafe among the Africans
Yclad', a. clad, clothed, dreffed, covered, ob.
Yclep'ed, a. called, named, denominated, ob.
Ye, nom. pl. of thou
Yea, ad. yes, furely, certainly, truly, verily, indeed
Yean, v.i. to bring forth young as fheep
Yeanling, n. the young of fheep, a young lamb
Year, n. the fpace of twelve calendar months
Yéarbook, n. the name of certain books contain-
ing reports of Englifh law cafes
Yéarling, a. being a year old; n. a beaft a year old
Yéarly, ad. once every year; a. lafting a year
Yearn, v.i. to feel great uneafinefs, grieve, bark
Yearn'ing, n. an emotion of tendernefs, pity
Yeaft or Yeft, s. the flower of malt-liquor when
working, barm, the foam of the troubled fea
Yéafty or Yeft'y, a. fmeared with yeaft, frothy
Yelk or Yolk, n. the yellow part of an egg
Yell, v.i. to cry aloud with agony or horror, to howl
Yell, n. a cry of horror or diftrefs, a fhriek
Yelling, n. the act of fhrieking or howling
Yell'ow, n. a bright color; a. bright, like gold
Yell'owboy, n. a piece of gold-coin, a guinea

Yel'lowham'mer, *n.* a fmall bird
Yell'owifh, *a.* tending or approaching to yellow
Yell'owifhnefs, Yell'ownefs, *n.* a yellow ftate, &c.
Yell'ows, *n. pl.* a difeafe in horfes   (jealoufy
Yelp, *v. i.* to bark as a hound, cry, chatter
Yelp'ing, *n.* the act of barking as a beagle or fox
Ye6man,*n.* a gentleman-farmer,freeholder,officer
Ye6manry, *n.* the collective body of yeomen
Yerk, *v.* to throw out a horfe's hind leg, to jerk
Yes, *ad.* a term of affirmation, yea, truly, verily
Yes'ter, Yes'terday,*ad.* on the day laft paft
Yes'terday, *n.* the day laft paft, the day before this
Yes'ternight, *ad.* on or in the night laft paft
Yet,*conj.* however, notwithftanding, neverthelefs
Yet,*ad.* befide, once more, ftill, at leaft, after all
Yew, Eugh,*n.* the name of a very hardy tree
Yew'en, *a.* made of or refembling yew, tough
Yex, *v. i.* to hickup, fob, heave, figh, groan, yux
Yield, *v.* to afford, produce, give up, furrender
Yielder,*n.* one who yields, one who gives up
Yoke,*n.* a bandage on the neck, chain, bond,bondage, mark of fervitude, couple, pair
Yoke, *v. t.* to couple or join together, to enflave
Yokefellow,*n.* a companion in labor, a mate
Yoking,*n.* the act of joining by a yoke
Yon, Yond, Yond'er, *a.* being within view, far
Yore, *ad.* of long time paft, of old time, formerly
You, *pron. fecond perfon, fing. and plu.*
Young, *a.* not old, youthful, tender, ignorant
Young, *n.* the offspring of any creature
Young'er, *a.* more young, not fo old, more weak
Young'eft,*a.* the moft young of all, the very laft
Young'ifh, *a.* femewhat or rather young, tender
Young'ly, *ad.* early in life, betimes, ignorantly
Youngs'ter, Younk'er, *n.* a young perfon, a novice
Your, [yure] *pron.* onging to or relating to you
Yourfelf',*pron.* you, even you, you only, you alone
Youth, *n.* tender age, one who is paft childhood
Youthful, *a.* young, brifk, frolicfome, vigorous
Youthfully, *ad.* in a youthful manner, brifkly
Youthfulnefs,*n.* a youthful ftate, brifknefs
Youthier,*a.* younger, more youthful, *ob.*
Youthiy or Youth'y, *a.* young, youthful, early
Ytrotan'talite, *n.* a mineral found in kidney-form
   maffes
Yule, *n.* the time of Chriftmas, the firft of Auguft
Yux, *n.* the hickup; *v. i.* to hickup, fob, figh

Z

ZAC'CHO, [ch as k] *n.* the loweft part of the
   pedeftal of a column
Zacynth'ian, *a.* pertaining to Zacynthia now Zante an ifland near the W. fhore of Greece
Zaf'fer,*n.* a dark gray oxyd of cobalt
Zany, *a.* a buffoon, a filly or noify fellow
Zapote, *n.* in Mexico a generic name of fruits which are roundifh and contain a hard ftone, the fpecies are various
Zar'nich,*n.* a fubftance in which orpiment is found
Zeal, Zeal'oufnefs, *n.* heat for a perfon or caufe
Zeal'ot, *n.* one who is full of zeal, a fanatic

Zeal'ous, *a.* ardently paffionate, hot, warm, eager
Zeal'oufly, *ad.* with all one's might, very eagerly
Zebra or Zeber,*n.* a quadruped of the equine genus beautifully ftriped
Zebu, *n.* an animal of the bovine kind
Zechin, *n.* a Venetian gold-coin
Zedoary, *n.* the name of a fpicy plant
Zem'indar,*n.* a feudatory or landholder in India, who governs a diftrict and collects taxes
Zem'indary, *n.* the jurifdiction of a Zemindar
Zen'ith,*n.* a point in the heavens directly overhead
Zeph'yr, Zeph'yrus,*n.* a foft wind, the weft wind
Zeolite, *n.* a filiceous ftone of a white or red color
Zeolit'ic, *a.* confifting of or like zeolite
Zeolit'iform, *a.* like zeolite in form
Zerd'a, *n.* an animal of Africa of the canine genus
Zero,*n.* the name of a cypher
Zert'a, *n.* an Italian fifh like a chub
Zerum'bet,*n.* wild ginger
Zeft, *n.* orange peel cut thin, a relifh, a divifion
Zeft *v. t.* to relifh, to give a relifh
Zeta,*n.* a greek letter, parlor, dining room
Zetet'ic, *a.* proceeding by enquiry, feeking
Zeug'ma, *n.* a figure in grammar, ellipfis, defect
Zeus, *n.* a genus of fifhes
Zib'et, *n.* a feline animal of the civet tribe
Zig'zag, *a.* turning fhort, winding, fpiral, fharp
Zig'zag, *n.* a thing or place having fhort turns
Zim'ent, *a.* impregnated with copper
Zink or Zinc, *n.* a metal of a bluifh white colorufed with copper to form brafs, pinch beck,&c.
Zink'y, *a.* like or pertaining to zink
Zirc'on, *n.* a fine white earth obtained from the jargon and hyacinth
Ziv'el,*n.* a marmot without ears
Ziv'olo, *n.* a bird like the yellow hammer
Zoc'co, Zocle or Socle,*n.* a fquare body under the bafe of a pedeftal. &c.
Zodiac, *n.* the fun's track in the twelve figns, a
Zodiacal, *a.* pertaining to the zodiac   (fpace
Zone, *n.* a girdle, belt, divifion of the earth, difeafe
Zoog'rapher,*n.* one who defcribes animals
Zoog'raphy, *n.* a minute defcription of animals
Zoolo'gical, *a.* relating to zoology   (mals
Zool'ogift,*n.* one verfed in the knowledge of animals
Zool'ogy,*n.* a fcientific treatife about animals
Zoon'ic,*a.* pertaining to animals, as zoonic acid obtained from animal fubftances   (life
Zoon'omy,*n.* the fcience of animals or of animal
Zoophite, *n.* a kind of fubftance partaking of
: the nature both of plants and animals
Zoophor'ic, *n.* a column fupporting the figure of an animal
Zooph'orus,*n.* a part between the architrave and cornifh on which are carved figures of animals
Zoot'omift, *n.* one who diffects brute beafts
Zoot'omy, *n.* a diffection of the bodies of beafts
Zoril', *n.* an animal of the weefel or fkunk tribe
Zygomat'ic, Zigomat'ic, *a.* pertaining to a cavity in a bone of the temples like a yoke

A TABLE

Of the Moneys of the principal commercial countries in the world, with the value of each in sterling and in cents, with the fractional parts of cents in decimals.

Note. An Afterisk is prefixed or annexed to *imaginary* money, or *money of account,* not reprefented by a real coin.

UNITED STATES.

An Eagle, a gold coin, *equal to* 10 dols. 247 1-2 gr. fine gold.
A half eagle,   do. - - - - 5 dols. 123 6-8 do.
A quarter eagle, do. - - - - 2 1-2 dols. 61 7-8 do.
A dollar, a filver coin, - - - 100 cents, 347 4-16 gr. pure filver
A half dollar,   do. - - - 50 cents, 185 10-16 do.
A quarter dollar, do. - - - 25 cents, 92 13-16 do.
A dime,   do. - - - 10 cents, 37 2-16 do.
A cent, a copper coin, - - - 10 mills, * 208 grains.
A mill * the tenth of a cent, and the thoufandth of a dollar.

ENGLAND AND SCOTLAND.
Sterling value reduced to Cents and Decimals.

Sterling.		Cents. Dec.	Sterling.	Cents, Dec.
1 Farthing	*equal to*	00, 4627	10 Pence - - - -	18, 51
2 Farthings		00, 9355	11 Pence - - - -	20, 361
3 Farthings		01, 3882	12 Pence or 1 Shilling - -	22, 222
4 Farthings or a penny		01, 851	A crown or 5 fhillings - -	111, 16
2 Pence		03, 702	* A pound or 20 fhillings -	444, 444
3 Pence		05, 553	A guinea or 21 fhillings -	466, 666
4 Pence, a groat,		07, 404		
5 Pence		09, 255	Irifh money is lefs in value by one thirteenth—
6 Pence		11, 106	a fhilling fterling being 13 pence Irifh—a pound
7 Pence		12, 957	Irifh is 18 f. 5 d. 1-2 Sterling—and an Englifh guin-
8 Pence		14, 808	ea, 22 f. 9 d. Irifh.
9 Pence		16, 659	

FLANDERS, or BELGIUM.
Oftend, Antwerp, Ghent, Bruffels, &c.

			£. Sterling.	Cents. Dec.
A pening*		*equal to*	0 0 0 9-160 -	00 104
An urch	is 4 peningens		0 0 0 9-40 -	00 416
A grot*	8 peningens		0 0 0 9-20 -	00 833
A petard	2 grots		0 0 0 9-10 -	01 666
A fcalin*	6 petards		0 0 5 2-5 -	10
A fcalin	7 petards		0 0 6 3-10 -	11 666
A florin*	40 grotes		0 1 6 - -	33 333
A ducat	17 1-2 fcalins		0 9 3 - -	205 553
A pound flemifh*	240 grotes		0 9 0 - -	200

HOLLAND AND ZEALAND.
Amfterdam, Rotterdam, Middleburg, &c.

	equal to	£. Sterling	St. Dec.
A pening* is	-	0 0 0 21-320	00 12
A grote* -	8 peningens	0 0 0 21-40	00 97
A ftiver -	2 grotes	0 0 1 1-20	01 94
A fcalin -	6 ftivers	0 0 6 3-10	11 64
A guilder or florin -	20 ftivers	0 1 9	38 8
A rix dollar -	50 ftivers	0 4 4 1-2	97
A dry guilder -	60 ftivers	0 5 3	116 65
A ducat. -	10 ftivers	0 9 2 1-4	207 86
A pound flemifh* -	6 guilders	0 10 6	233 33
A gold ducat or ducattoo: -	-	1 16 0	800
A fovereign -	-	1 7 0	600

GERMANY.
Hamburgh, Bremen, Lubec, Altona, &c.

	equal to	£. Sterling	St. Dec.
* A tryling is	-	0 0 0 3-128	00 045
A fixling -	2 trylings	0 0 0 3-64	00 091
A fening -	2 fexlings	0 0 0 3-32	01 83
A fhilling Lub. -	12 fenings	0 0 1 1-8	02 083
A marc -	16 fhillings	0 1 6	33 333
A fletch dollar -	2 marcs	0 3 0	66 666
A rix dollar -	3 marcs	0 4 6	100
A ducat -	6 1-2 marcs	0 9 4 1-2	208 325
A pound flem -	120 fhilungs	0 11 3	250

HANOVER.
Lunenburg, Zell, &c.

	equal to	£. Sterling	St. Dec.
A fening is	-	0 0 0 4-48	00 27
A dreyer -	3 fenings	0 0 0 7-16	00 81
A marien -	8 fenings	0 0 1 1-6	02 16
A grofh -	12 fenings	0 0 1 3-4	03 24
A geld -	16 grothen	0 2 4	51 85
A rix dollar -	24 grothen	0 3 6	77 76
A ducat -	4 guldens	0 9 4	207 4

SAXONY.
Holftein, Drefden, Leipfic, Wifmar, &c.

	equal to	£. Sterling	Cts. Dec.
A heller is	-	0 0 0 7-96	00 135
A fening -	2 hellers	0 0 0 7-48	00 27
A dreyer -	6 hellers	0 0 0 7-16	00 81
A marien -	16 hellers	0 0 1 1-6	02 16
A grofh -	12 fenings	0 0 1 3-4	03 24
A gould -	16 grofhen	0 2 4	51 85
* A rix dollar -	24 grofhen	0 3 6	77 76
A fpecie dollar -	32 grofhen	0 4 8	103 7
A ducat -	4 goulds	0 9 4	207 4

Brandenburg, Pomerania, Berlin, Stettin, &c.

	equal to	£. Sterling	Cts. Dec.
A denier is	-	0 0 0 7-270	00 048
A polchen -	9 deniers	0 0 0 7-30	00 43
A grofh -	18 deniers	0 0 0 7-15	00 86
An abrafs -	3 polchens	0 0 0 7-10	01 29
A marc -	20 grofhen	0 0 9 1-3	17 28
A florin -	30 grofhen	0 1 2	25 92
* A rix dollar -	90 grofhen	0 3 6	77 76
An albefus -	108 grofhen	0 4 2 2-5	92 90
A ducat -	8 florins	0 9 4	207 4

Cologne, Mentz, Triers, Liege, Munich, Munfter, &c.

	equal to	£. Sterling	Cts. Dec.
A dute is	-	0 0 0 7-80	00 16
A cruitzer -	3 dutes	0 0 0 21-80	00 48
An alb -	2 cruitzers	0 0 0 21-40	00 96
A fiver -	8 dutes	0 0 0 7-10	01 29
A piapert -	3 fivers	0 0 2 1-10	03 88
A copfluck -	4 piaperts	0 0 8 2-5	15 55
A guilder -	40 ftivers	0 2 4	51 85
A hard dollar -	2 guilders	0 4 8	103 7
A ducat -	4 guilders	0 9 4	207 4

BOHEMIA, SILESIA and HUNGARY.

Coin	Equal to	£. Sterling equal to	Cents. Dec.
A fening	is —	0 0 0 7-60	00 215
A dreyer	2 fenings	0 0 0 7-30	00 43
A groh	3 fenings	0 0 0 7-20	00 645
A cruitzer	4 fenings	0 0 0 7-15	00 86
A white groh	2 cruitzers	0 0 0 14-15	01 72
A gould	60 cruitzers	0 2 4	51 85
A rix dollar*	90 cruitzers	0 3 6	77 76
A hard dollar	2 goulds	0 4 8	103 7
A ducat	4 goulds	0 9 4	207 4

AUSTRIA AND SWABIA.

Vienna, Trieft, Augfburg, &c.

Coin	Equal to	£. Sterling equal to	Cents. Dec.
A fening	is —	0 0 0 7-60	00 215
A dreyer	2 fenings	0 0 0 7-30	00 43
A cruitzer	4 fenings	0 0 0 7-15	00 86
A grofh	14 fenings	0 0 1 19-30	03 14
A batzen	4 cruitzers	0 0 1 13-15	03 44
A gould	15 batzen	0 2 4	51 85
A rix dollar	90 cruitzers	0 3 6	77 77
A fpecie dollar	30 batzen	0 4 8	103 7
A ducat	60 batzen	0 9 4	207 4

FRANCONIA.

Frankfort, Nuremburg, Bettingen, &c.

Coin	Equal to	£. Sterling equal to	Cents. Dec.
A fening equal to	—	0 0 0 7-60	00 215
A cruitzer	is 4 fenings	0 0 0 7-15	00 86
A keyser grofh	3 cruitzers	0 0 1 2-5	02 58
A batzen	4 cruitzers	0 0 1 13-15	03 44
An ort gould	15 cruitzers	0 0 7	12 96
A gould	60 cruitzers	0 2 4	51 85
A rix dollar*	90 cruitzers	0 3 6	77 76
A hard dollar	2 goulds	0 4 8	103 7
A ducat	240 cruitzers	0 9 4	207 4

POLAND AND PRUSSIA.

Warfaw, Cracow, Dantzic, Koningfberg, &c.

Coin	Equal to	£. Sterling equal to	Cents. Dec.
A fhelon	is —	0 0 0 7-45	00 287
A groh	3 fhelons	0 0 0 7-15	00 861
A couftic	5 grohen	0 0 0 2 1-3	04 32
A tinfe	3 couftics	0 0 0 7	12 96
An ort	18 grohen	0 0 0 8 4-5	15 55
A florin	30 grohen	0 1 2	25 92
A rix dollar*	90 grohen	0 3 6	77 76
A ducat	8 florins	0 9 4	207 4
A Frederic D'or	5 rix dollars	0 17 6	388 8

LIVONIA.

Riga, Revel, Narva, &c.

Coin	Equal to	£. Sterling equal to	Cents. Dec.
A blacken	is —	0 0 0 7-90	00 143
A groh	6 blackens	0 0 0 7-15	00 858
A vorden	9 blackens	0 0 0 7-10	01 287
A whiten	2 grofhen	0 0 0 14-15	01 72
A marc	6 grofhen	0 0 0 2 4-5	05 16
A florin	30 grofhen	0 1 2	25 92
A rix dollar*	90 grofhen	0 3 6	77 76
An albertus	108 grofhen	0 4 2 2-5	93 14
A copper plate dollar	64 whitens	0 4 11 3-4	110 64

DENMARK, NORWAY.

Copenhagen, Bergen, &c.

Coin	Equal to	£. Sterling equal to	Cents. Dec.
A fkilling	is —	0 0 0 9-16	01 04
A duggen	6 fkillings	0 0 0 3 3-8	06 24
A marc*	16 fkillings	0 0 0 9	16 66
A rix mark	20 fkillings	0 0 0 11 1-4	20 83
A rix ort	24 fkillings	0 1 1 1-2	25
A crown	4 marcs	0 3 0	66 65
A rix dollar	6 marcs	0 4 6	100
A ducat	11 marcs	0 8 3	183 34
A hat ducat	14 marcs	0 10 6	233 33

FRANCE.
Paris, Lyons, Marseilles, Bourdeaux, &c.

Ancient Coins and denominations.

			£. Sterling.	Cts. Dec.
A denier		equal to	0 0 0 1-24	00 077
A liard	is 3 deniers		0 0 0 1-8	00 232
A dardene	2 liards		0 0 0 1-4	00 463
A fol	12 deniers		0 0 0 1-2	00 925
A livre tournois*	20 fols		0 0 10	18 517
An ecu of exchange 60 fols			0 2 6	55
An ecu or crown	6 livres		0 5 0	110
A piftole*	10 livres		0 8 4	185 17
A louis d'or	24 livres		1 0 0	444 44

New Coins and Denominations. £. Ster.

		£. Ster.	Cts. Dec.
A centim or 1,100th of a franc		0 0 0 81-800	00 187
A decim	10 centims	0 0 1 1-80	01 874
A fol	5 centims	0 0 0	00 987
A franc	10 decims	0 0 10 1-8	18 741

Silver Coins.

		Cts. Dec.
Five francs	0 4 2	92 53
Two francs	0 1 8 1-2	37 48
One franc	0 0 10 1-8	18 74
3-4 of a franc	0 0 7 19-32	14 01
1-2 of a franc	0 0 5 1-16	9 37
1-4 of a franc	0 0 2 17-32	4 68

Gold Coins.

		Cts. Dec.
40 francs	1 13 9	733 19
20 francs	0 16 10 1-2	366 59

PORTUGAL.
Lisbon, Oporto, &c.

			£. Sterling.	Cts. Dec.
A re		equal to	0 0 0 27-400	00 125
A half vintin 10 rez		is	0 0 0 27-40	01 25
A vintin	20 rez		0 0 1 7-20	02 5
A teftoon	5 vintins		0 0 6 3-4	12 5
A crufade of ex 4 teftoons			0 2 3	50
A new crufade 24 vintins			0 2 8 2-5	60
A milree*	10 teftoons		0 5 7 1-2	125
A moidore	48 teftoons		1 7 0	600
A joanefe	64 teftoons		1 16 0	800

SWEDEN AND LAPLAND.
Stockholm, Upfal, Thorn, &c.

			£. Sterling.	Cents. Dec.
A runftic		equal to	0 0 0 7-36	00 35
A fliver	2 runflics		0 0 0 7-18	00 72
A copper marc	8 runflics		0 0 1 5-9	02 88
A filver marc	3 copper do.		0 0 4 2-3	08 64
A copper dollar	4 copper marcs		0 0 6 2-9	11 52
A caroline	9 copper marcs		0 1 2	25 92
A filver dollar	3 copper dollars		0 1 6 2-3	34 56
A rix dollar	3 filver dollars		0 4 8	103 7
A ducat	3 rix dollars		0 9 4	207 4

RUSSIA.
Peterfburg, Mofcow, Archangel, &c.

			£. Sterling.	Cnts. Dec.
A polufca	is	equal to	0 0 0 27-200	00 25
A denufca	2 polufcas		0 0 0 27-100	00 5
A copec*	2 denufcas		0 0 0 27-50	01
An altin	3 copecs		0 0 0 31-50	03
A grievener	10 copecs		0 0 5 2-5	10
A polpotin	25 copecs		0 1 11-2	25
A poltin	50 copecs		0 2 3	50
A ruble	100 copecs		0 4 6	100
A zervonitz	2 rubles		0 9 0	200

SWITZERLAND.
Bafil or Bafle, Zurich, &c.

			£. Sterling.	Cnts. Dec.
A rap		equal to	0 0 0 1-24	00 08
A fenning	is 3 rapen		0 0 0 1-8	00 24
A cruitzer	4 fenings		0 0 0 1-2	00 926
A fol*	12 fenings		0 0 1 1-2	02 77
A coarfe batzen	15 fenings		0 0 1 7-8	03 46
A good batzen	18 fenings		0 0 2 1-4	04 16
A livre*	20 fols		0 2 6	55 55
A gulden	60 cruitzers		0 2 6	55 55
A rix dollar	108 cruitzers		0 4 6	100

SPAIN.

Madrid, Cadiz, Seville, &c.

New plate.

			£. Ster.	Cts. Dec.
A maravedie*	- equal to	0 0 0	43-272	00 06
A quartil	is 2 maravedie	0 0 0	43-136	00 8
A rial	- 34 maravedie	0 0 5	3-8	03 18
A pistarine	2 rials -	0 0 10	3-4	15 92
A piaster of ex*	8 rials -	0 3 7		23 88
A dollar	10 rials -	0 4 6		79 6
A ducat of ex*	375 maradevies	0 4 11	1-2	92 6
A pistole of ex*	32 rials -	0 14 4		136 12
A pistole	36 rials -	0 16 1	1-2	320

Velon.

			£. Ster.	Cts. Dec.
A maravedic*	equal to	0 0 0	23-272	00 156
An ocha°o	is 2 maravedies	0 0 0	23-136	00 3
A quartil	4 maravedies	0 0 0	23-68	00 6
A rial velon*	34 maravedies	0 0 2	7-8	05 27
A piaster of ex*	15 rials	0 3 7	1-8	80 33
A piaster	512 maravedies	0 3 7	5-17	320
A pistole of ex*	60 rials	0 14 4		372
A pistole	70 rials	0 16 9		

Old plate.

Barcelona, Saragossa, Valencia, &c.

			£. Ster.	Cts. Dec.
A maravedie	is - equal to	0 0 0	27-128	00 39
A soldo	- 16 maravedie	0 0 3	3-8	06 24
A rial	- 2 soldos	0 0 6	3-4	12 50
A dollar	16 soldos	0 4 6		100
A libra*	20 soldos	0 5 7	1-2	125
A ducat*	21 soldos	0 5 10	7-8	131 25
A pistole	60 soldos	0 16 10		375

ITALY.

Genoa, Novi, St. Remo, Corsica, &c.

			£. Ster.	Cts. Dec.
A denari	- equal to	0 0 0	43-1200	00 115
A foldi	12 denari	0 0 0	43-100	00 345
A chevelet	4 foldi	0 0 1	18-25	01 388
A lire*	20 foldi	0 0 8	3-5	16 66
A teftoon	30 foldi	0 1 0	9-10	27 77
A croifade	5 lires	0 3 7		100
A pezzo of ex*	115 foldi	0 4 2		116 66
A genouine	6 teftoons	0 6 2	2-5	361 1
A pistole	20 lires	0 14 4		444 44

Piedmont, Savoy, Sardinia, Turin, &c.

			£. Ster.	Cts. Dec.
A denari	- equal to	0 0 0	1-16	00 064
A quatrini	3 denari	0 0 0	3-16	00 256
A foldi	12 denari	0 0 0	3-4	00 72
A florin*	12 foldi	0 0 0	9	01 28
A lire*	20 foldi	0 1 3		10 24
A fcudi	6 florins	0 4 6		15 43
A ducattoon	7 florins	0 5 3		92 6
A pistole	13 lires	0 16 3		115 7
A louis d'or	16 lires	1 0 0		339 5

Leghorn, Florence, &c.

			£. Ster.	Cts. Dec.
A denari	equal to	0 0 0	5-144	00 064
A quatrini	4 denari	0 0 0	5-36	00 256
A foldi	12 denari	0 0 0	5-12	00 72
A craca	5 quatrini	0 0 0	25-36	01 28
A quilo	8 cracas	0 0 5	5-9	10 24
A lire*	20 foldi	0 0 8	1-3	15 43
A piafter of ex	6 lires	0 4 2		92 6
A ducat	7 1-2 lires	0 5 2	1-2	115 7
A pistole	22 lires	0 15 6		339 5

TURKEY.

	equal to	£. Ster.	Cu. Dec.
A mangar is	—	0 0 0 3-20	00 28
An asper*	4 mangars	0 0 0 3-5	01 12
A parac	3 aspers	0 0 1 4-5	03 33
A bettic	5 aspers	0 0 3	05 55
An oftic	10 aspers	0 0 6	11 11
A folota	20 aspers	0 1 0	22 22
A piafter*	80 aspers	0 4 0	88 88
A caragrouch	100 aspers	0 5 0	111 1
A xeriff	10 folotas	0 10 0	222 22

ARABIA.

Mecca, Mocha, &c.

	equal to	£. Ster.	Cu. Dec.
A carret is	—	0 0 0 1-8	00 23
A caveer	5 1-2 carrets	0 0 0 27-400	01 26
A comathee	7 carrets	0 0 0 9-10	01 61
A larin	80 carrets	0 0 10 1-8	18 74
An abyfi	18 comathees	0 1 4 1-5	29 7
A piafter*	60 comathees	0 4 6	100
A dollar	80 caveers	0 4 6	100
A fequin	100 comathees	0 7 6	166 66
A tomond*	80 larins	3 7 6	1500

PERSIA.

	equal to	£. Ster.	Cu. Dec.
A coz is	—	0 0 0 2-5	00 74
A bitti	4 coz	0 0 1 2-5	02 95
A thahee	10 coz	0 0 4	07 4
A mamooda	20 coz	0 0 8	14 81
A larin	25 coz	0 0 10	18 51
Anabafhee	4 fhahees	0 1 4	29 62
An or	5 abafhees	0 6 8	148 13*
A bovello	12 abafhees	0 16 0	355 55
A tomond*	50 abafhees	3 6 8	1481 5

Rome, Ancona, Civita Vecchia, &c.

	equal to	£. Ster.	Cu. Dec.
A quatrini is	—	0 0 0 3-20	00 28
A bayoc	5 quatrini	0 0 0 3-4	01 4
A julio	8 bayocs	0 0 6	11 11
A ftamped julio	10 bayocs	0 0 7 1-2	13 88
A teftoon	24 bayocs	0 1 6	33 33
A crown current	10 julios	0 5 0	111 11
A crown ftamped*	12 julios	0 6 0	133 33
A chequin	18 julios	0 9 0	200
A piftole	31 julios	0 15 6	336 8

NAPLES.

	equal to	£. Ster.	Cu. Dec.
A quatrini is	—	0 0 0 2-1	00 23
A grain	3 quatrini	0 0 0 2-5	00 7
A carlin	10 grains	0 0 4	07 4
A paulo	40 quatrini	0 0 5 1-3	09 87
A tarin	20 grains	0 0 8	14 81
A teftoon	40 grains	0 1 4	29 62
A ducat of ex.	100 grains	0 3 4	74 07
A piftole	23 tarins	0 15 4	340 58
A fpanifh piftole	25 tarins	0 16 9	368 35

H h

VENICE.

	equal to	£. Ster.	Cu. Dec.
A picoli is	—	0 0 0 1-36	00 051
A foldi	12 picoli	0 0 0 1-3	00 617
A gros*	6 1-2 foldi	0 0 2 1-6	04 01
A jule	18 foldi	0 0 6	11 11
A lire*	20 foldi	0 0 6 2-3	12 35
A teftoon	3 jules	0 1 6	33 33
A ducat current	124 foldi	0 3 5 1-3	76 85
A ducat of ex.	24 gros	0 4 4	96 28
A chequin	17 lires	0 9 5 1-3	2:0

INDIA.

Guzarat, Surat, Cambay, &c.

	equal to	£	s	d	frac	Cts. Dec.
A pecka	*is*					
A piee	2 peckas	0	0	0	15-64	00 414
A fanam	4 pices	0	0	0	15-32	00 828
A viz	5 pices	0	0	1	7-8	03 33
An ana	16 pices	0	0	2	11-32	04 55
A rupee	4 anas	0	0	7	1-2	13 88
A crown	2 rupees	0	2	6		55
A pagoda	14 anas	0	5	0		111 1
A gold rupee	4 pagodas	0	8	9		194 45
		1	15	0		777 78

Bombay, &c.

	equal to	£	s	d	frac	Cts. Dec.
A budgrook	*is*					
A rez*	2 budgrooks	0	0	0	27-800	00 06
A pice	5 rez	0	0	0	27-400	00 125
A laree	16 pices	0	0	0	27-80	00 62
A quarter	20 pices	0	0	0	2-5	10
A xeraphim	240 rez	0	0	6	3-4	12 5
A rupee	4 quarters	0	0	4	1-5	30
A pagoda	14 quarters	0	2	3		50
A gold rupee	60 quarters	0	7	10 1-2		175
		0	13	9		750

Coromandel. Madras, Pondicherry, &c.

	equal to	£	s	d	frac	Cts. Dec.
A cash	*is*					
A viz	5 cash	0	0	0	3-80	00 07
A pice	2 viz	0	0	0	3-16	00 34
A pical	6 pices	0	0	0	3-8	00 68
A faaam	8 pices	0	0	2	1-4	04 12
A rupee	10 fanams	0	0	3		05 55
A crown	2 rupees	0	2	6		55
A pagoda	36 fanams	0	5	0		111 1
A gold rupee	4 pagoda	0	9	0		200
		1	16	0		800

BENGAL.

Calcutta, Callicut, &c.

	equal to	£	s	d	frac	Cts. Der.
A pice	*is*					
A fanam	4 pices	0	0	0	5-32	00 29
A viz	6 pices	0	0	0	5-8	01 13
An ana	12 pices	0	0	0	15-16	01 73
A fiano	10 anas	0	0	1	7-8	03 47
A rupee	16 anas	0	1	6	3-4	34 72
An ecu	2 rupees	0	2	6		55
A crown	2 rupees	0	5	0		111 1
A pagoda	56 anas	0	5	0		111 1
		0	8	9		194 3

SIAM.

Pegu, Malacca, Sumatra, Java, &c.

	equal to	£	s	d	frac	Cts. Der.
A cori	*is*					
A fettee	10 cori	0	0	0	3-500	00 01
A falteleer	125 fettees	0	0	0	3-50	00 11
A fooco	250 fettees	0	0	7	1-2	13 75
A tical	500 fettees	0	1	3		27 76
A dollar	900 fettees	0	2	6		55
A rial	2 ticals	0	4	6		100
An ecu	4 fotcos	0	5	0		111 1
A crown	8 faltcleers	0	5	0		111 1

CHINA.

	equal to	£	s	d	frac	Cts. Der.
A caxa	*is*					
A candareen	10 caxa	0	0	0	2-25	00 148
A mace	10 candareens	0	0	0	4-5	01 48
A rupee	37 1-2 candareens	0	0	8		14 8
A rix dollar	70 candareens	0	2	6		55
An ecu	7 maces	0	4	8		103 7
A crown	2 rupees	0	4	8		103 7
A talc*	10 maces	0	5	0		111 1
		0	6	8		148 12

JAPAN.

	equal to	£. s. d. (Str.)	Cts. Dec.
A piti is	—	0 0 0 1-5	00 37
A mace	20 pitis	0 0 4	07 4
An oz. of silver	15 maces	0 5 00	111 1
A tale	20 maces	0 6 8	148 12
An ingot	30 maces	0 9 8 2-3	214 92
An oz. of gold	13 oz. of silver	3 3	1400
A japanese	2 oz. of gold	6 6	2800
A double	2 japanese	12 12	5600
A lattee*	21 oz. of gold	66 3	29400

AFRICA.
Egypt, Cairo, Alexandria, &c.

	equal to	£. s. d. (Str.)	Cts. Dec.
An asper is	—	0 0 0 5-9	01 028
A medin	3 aspers	0 0 1 2-3	03 084
An Italian ducat	24 medins	0 3 4	74 07
A piastre*	80 aspers	0 4 0	88 88
A dollar	30 medins	0 4 6	100 1
An ecu	96 aspers	0 5 0	111 1
A crown	36 medins	0 10 0	222 22
A sultanin	200 aspers	0 10 6	233 33
A pargo dollar	70 medins		

BARBARY.
Algiers, Tunis, Tripoly, &c.

	equal to	£. s. d. (Str.)	Cts. Dec.
An asper is	—	0 0 0 5-9	01 028
A medin	3 aspers	0 0 1 2-3	03 088
A rial, old plate	10 aspers	0 0 6 3-4	12 5
A double	2 rials	0 1 1 1-2	25
A dollar	4 doubles	0 4 6	100
A silver chequin	24 medins	0 3 4	74 07
A zequin	180 aspers	0 8 10	196 3
A pistole	15 doubles	0 16 9	373

MOROCCO.
Fez, Tangiers, Sallee, Mequines, &c.

	equal to	£. s. d. (Str.)	Ctr. Dec.
A fluce is	—	0 0 0 1-12	00 15
A blanquil	24 fluces	0 0 2	03 7
An ounce	4 blanquils	0 0 8	14 8
An octave	7 blanquils	0 1 2	25 9
A quarto	14 blanquils	0 2 4	51 8
A medio	2 quartos	0 4 8	103 7
A dollar	28 blanquils	0 4 6	100
A zequin	56 blanquils	0 9 0	200
A pistolé	100 blanquils	0 16 9	373

ENGLISH ISLANDS.
Jamaica, Barbadoes, &c.

	equal to	£. s. d. (Str.)	Ctr. Dec.
A half penny* is	—	0 0 0 1-2	00 65
A penny	—	0 0 1	01 3
A bitt	7 1-2 pence	0 0 5 3-8	09 82
A shilling	12 pence	0 0 8 12-20	15 76
A dollar	75 pence	0 4 6	100
A crown	7 shillings	0 5 0	111 1
A pound	20 shillings	0 14 3	316 66
A pistole	24 shillings	0 16 9	373
A guinea	30 shillings	1 1 0	466 66

FRENCH ISLANDS.
Hayti, Martinico, &c.

	equal to	£. s. d. (Str.)	Ctr. Dec.
One half sol is	—	0 0 0 1-5	00 35
A half scalin	7 1-2 sols	0 0 2 11-16	05 2
A scalin	15 sols	0 0 5 3-8	10 41
A livre*	20 sols	0 0 7 5-16	13 89
A dollar	7 livres	0 4 6	100
An ecu	8 livres	0 4 10 1-2	108 3
A pistole	26 livres	0 16 9	373
A louis d'or	32 livres	1 0 0	441 44

ENGLISH MEASURE OF LENGTH.

Note. The meafures marked with an afterifk are not ufed in the United States.

3 barley corns	1 inch
12 inches	1 foot
3 feet	1 yard
5 1-2 yards	1 pole, perch or rod
40 rods or perches	1 furlong
8 furlongs	1 mile
4 inches	1 hand
6 feet	1 fathom
3 miles	1 league

60 nautical or geographical miles 1 degree. 69 1-3 ftatute miles 1 degree nearly.

Note. The weights and meafures of the United States, are the fame as the ftandard weights and meafures in England.

CLOTH MEASURE.

2 1-4 inches	1 nail
4 nails	1 quarter
4 quarters	1 yard
3 quarters	1 ell flemifh
5 quarters	1 ell englifh
6 quarters	1 ell french

SQUARE MEASURE.

144 inches	1 foot
9 feet	1 yard
30 1-4 yards	1 pole
40 poles or rods	1 rood
4 roods	1 aker

Gunter's chain for meafuring land contains 100 links, each 7 inches. 92 decimals, which make 4 rods or perches, 22 yards, or 66 feet. Hence an aker contains 10 fquare chains, 160 fquare rods, 4840 fquare yards, 100,000 fquare links.

WINE MEASURE.

4 gills	1 pint
2 pints	1 quart
4 quarts	1 gallon
42 gallons	1 tierce
1 1-2 tierce, or 63 gal.	1 hogshead
1 1-3 hogshead or 84 gal	1 puncheon
1 1-3 puncheon, or 126 gal.	1 pipe
2 pipes	1 tun
231 cubic inches	1 gallon
10 gallons	1 anker*
18 gallons	1 runlet*
31 1⁄2 gallons	1 barrel

ALE AND BEER MEASURE.

2 pints	1 quart	
4 quarts	1 gallon	
9 gallons	1 firkia	
2 firkins	18 gal.	1 kilderkin*
2 kilderkins	36 gal.	1 barrel
1 1-2 barrels	54 gal.	1 hogshead
1 1-3 hogsheads	72 gal.	1 puncheon
1 1-2 puncheon	108 gal.	1 butt

The ale gallon contains 282 cubic inches.

Note. The hogshead of 63 gallons and the puncheon of 84 gallons are not ufed with us. The cafk of 108 or 110 gallons is called a hogshead or a puncheon.

DRY MEASURE.

8 pints	1 gallon
2 gallons	1 peck
4 pecks	1 bufhel
4 bufhels	1 coom
2 cooms	1 quarter*
5 quarters	1 wey*
2 weys	1 laft*

The gallon contains 272 1⁄4 cubic inches, Winchefter meafure.

TABLE OF TROY WEIGHT.

As ufed by Goldfmiths.

24 grains gr.	1 pennyweight dwt.
20 dwt.	1 ounce oz.
12 oz.	1 pound lb.

As ufed by Apothecaries.

20 grains	1 fcruple Ә
3 Ә	1 dram ʒ
8 ʒ	1 ounce ʒ
12 ʒ	1 pound lb.

TABLE OF AVORDUPOIS WEIGHT.

16 drams	1 oz.
16 oz.	1 lb.
28 pounds	1 quarter qr.
4 qrs.	1 hundred cwt.
20 cwt.	1 tun

175 troy pounds is 144 pounds avordupois
175 troy ounces 192 avordupois
1 pound troy 5760 grains
1 pound avordup. 7000 grains
1 ounce avordup. contains 437 1-2 grains
1 dram avordup. contains 27 34-375 grs.
1 troy pound contains 13 oz. 2.651428576 drams avordupois.
1 avordupois lb. contains 1 lb. 2 oz. 1

dwts 16 grains troy

For some purposes the troy grain is thus divided.

The grain into 20 mites
The mite into 24 droits
The droit into 20 periots
The periot into 20 blanks

The dealers in wool in England, use the following weights:

The sack containing 2 weighs*
The weigh   6 1-2 tods*
The tod   2 stones*
The stone   2 cloves*
The clove   7 pounds

12 sacks make a last or 4368 pounds
56 lb. of old hay or 60 lb. of new hay make a truss*
40 lb. of straw make a truss
36 trusses make a load of hay or straw
14 lb. make a stone
5 lb. of glass make a stone. *Note.—these weights are not used in America.*

The old Paris pound was to the English troy pound as 21 to 16, and to the avordupois pound as 27 to 25. It therefore contained 7560 grains troy. The pound was divided into 2 marcs, the marc into 8 ounces, the ounce into 8 gros or drams the dram into 3 deniers or penny weights.

ANCIENT WEIGHTS.

Jewish weights reduced to Troy weight.

	lb.	oz.	dwt.	gr.
Shekel	0	0	9	2 4-7
Manch	2	3	6	10 2-7
Talent	113	10	1	10 2-7

GRECIAN & ROMAN WEIGHTS

Reduced to Troy weight.

	lb.	oz.	dwt.	gr.
Lentes	0	0	0	0 35-112
Siliquæ	0	0	0	3 1-28
Obolus	0	0	0	9 3-28
Scriptulum	0	0	0	18 3-14
Drachma	0	0	2	6 9-14
Sextula	0	0	3	0 6-7
Sicilicus	0	0	4	13 2-7
Duella	0	0	6	1 5-7
Uncia	0	0	18	5 1-7
Libra	0	10	18	13 5-7

Ancient Roman measure of length.

	Eng. yds.	ft.	inch.	& 10ths.
Digitus transverfus	0	0	0	7266
Uncia 1 1-3 digitus	0	0	0	9688
Palmus minor 3 uncia	0	0	2	9063
Pes or foot 4 palms	0	0	11	6255
Palmipes 1 1-4 Pes	0	1	2	5319
Cubitus 1 1-5 palmipes	0	1	5	4383
Gradus 1 2-3 cubitus	0	2	5	0639
Passus 2 gradus	1	1	10	1278
Stadium 125 passus	201	2	5	975
Milliare or mile 8 stadiums 1614	1	11	8	

Roman square measure.

	feet.	Eng. roods.	poles.	feet.
As	28800	2	18 250	05
Deunx	26400	2	10 183	85
Dextrans	24000	2	2 117	54
Dodrans	21600	1	34 51	42
Bes	19200	1	25 257	46
Septunx	16800	1	17 191	25
Semis	14400	1	9 125	03
Quincunx	12000	1	1 58	82
Triens	9600	0	32 264	85
Quadrans	7200	0	24 198	64
Sextans	4800	0	16 132	43
Uncia	2400	0	8 66	21

The actus major was squal to a semis, 14400 feet.
The clima 3600 feet equal to a sescuncia
The actus minimus was 4800 feet, equal to a sextans.
A scruple contained 100 square feet

Grecian measures of length.

	Eng. yds.	ft.	inches.
A digit	0	0	0 7558
A doron or dachme 4 digits	0	0	3 0232
A lichas 2 1-2 dorons	0	0	7 5581
An orthodoron 1 1-10 lichas	0	0	8 3130
A spitham 1 1-10 ortho doron	0	0	9 0697
A foot 1 1-3 spitham	0	1	0 0929
A cubit	0	1	6035
A pygon 1 1-9 cubit	0	1	3 1162
A cubit larger 1 1-5 pygon	0	1	6 1391
A pace 4 cubits	2	0	0 5573
A stadium 100 paces	201	1	7 73
A mile 8 stadiums	1612	1	2 24

The stadium contained 125 geometrical paces or 625 Roman feet, and answered to our furlong. But the stadium was of different lengths in different times and places.

The Grecian square measure was the plethron or aker, whose contents are not certain—some suppose it to contain 1444, others 10,000 square feet. The aroura was half the plethron. The Egyptian aroura was the square of 100 cubits.

Scripture measures of length.

	Eng. yds.	ft.	inch.	dec.
Digit	0	0	0	912
A palm 4 digits	0	0	3	648
A span 3 palms	0	0	10	944
A cubit 2 spans	0	1	9	888
A fathom 4 cubits	2	1	3	552
Ezekiel's rod	3	1	11	328
An Arabian pole	4	2	7	104
A schenus or measuring-line	48	1	11	04

A Jewish Sabbath day's journey 1216 yards.
A day's journey 33 miles, 288 yards.

Jewish reduced to English wine measure.

	gal.	pts.	solid	inch.
A caph	0	0 5-8	0	177
A log 1 1-3 caph	0	0 5-6	0	211
A cab 4 logs	0	3 1-3	0	844
A hin 3 cabs	1	2	2	533
A seah 2 hins	2	4	5	067
A bath or epha 3 seahs	7	4	15	2
A coron or chomer 10 baths	75	5	7	265

Attic reduced to English wine measure.

		gal.	pts.
A cochliarion		0	1-120
A cheme	2 cochliarions	0	1-60
A myſtron	1 1-4 cheme	0	1-48
A conche	2 myſtrons	0	1-24
A cyathos	2 conches	0	1-12
An oxybaphon	1 1-2 cyathos	0	1-8
A cotyle	4 oxy baphons	0	1-2
A xeſtes	2 cotyles	0	1
A chous	6 xeſtes	0	6
A metretes	12 chous	9	0

Roman reduced to English wine measure.

		gal.	pts.
A ligula		0	1 48
A cyathus	4 liqulas	0	1-12
An acetabulum	1 1-2 cyathus	0	1-8
A quartarius	2 acetabulums	0	1-4
A hemina	2 quartariuſes	0	1-2
A fextarius	2 heminas	0	1
A congius	6 fextariuſes	0	6
An urna	4 congiuſes	3	0
An amphora	2 urnas	6	0
A culeus	20 amphoras	120	0

Proportion of the weights of the chief cities of Europe to that of Amſterdam.

100 pounds of Amſterdam or 109 pound avordupois Engliſh, are equal to

108 lb. of Alicant	100 of Dort	120 of Montpelier
105 of Antwerp	97 of Dublin	125 of Muſcovy
120 of Archangel	97 of Edinburgh	100 of Nantz
120 of Avignon	143 of Florence	169 of Naples
98 of Baſil	98 of Frankfort.	100 of Paris
100 of Bayonne	89 of Geneva	112 1-2 fo Revel
166 of Bergamo	163 of Genoa	109 of Riga
97 of Berg. op Zoom	102 of Hamburgh	100 of Rochelle
95 1-4 of Bergen, Norway	125 of Koningsberg	146 of Rome
100 of Bilboa	105 of Leipſic	100 of Rotterdam
105 of Bois le duc	106 of Leyden	96 of Rouen
151 of Bologna	143 of Leghorn	100 of St. Malo
100 of Bourdeaux	106 of Liſbon	100 of St. Sebaſtian
103 of Bremen	109 of London.	158 1-7 of Saragoſſa
125 of Breſlaw	105 of Lubeck	100 of Seville.
105 of Bruges	141 1-2 of Lucca	114 of Smyrna
105 of Bruſſels	116 of Lyons	110 of Stetin
105 of Cadiz	114 of Madrid	81 of Stockholm
105 of Cologne	105 of Malines	118 of Thouloufe
107 1-2 of Copenhagen	123 1-2 of Marſeilles	151 of Turin
87 of Conſtantinople	154 of Meſſina	158 1-2 of Valencia
113 1-2 of Dantzic	168 of Milan	182 of Venice

DRY MEASURE.
Scripture reduced to English.

			pecks.	gl.	pts.
A gachal	equal to	0 0 0	37-110		
A cab	is	20 gachals	0 0 2	5-6	
A gomer		1 4-5 cabs	0 0 5	1-10	
A feah		3 1-3 gomers	1 0 1		
An epha		3 feahs	3 0 3		
A letech		5 ephas	16 0 0		
A chomer or coron		2 letech	32 0 1		
The attic medimnos			4 0 6		
The Roman modius			1 0 0		

MEASURES OF LENGTH.
Ancient and foreign meafures reduced to Eng. yards.
The Englifh mile being 1760 yds. or 5280 feet.

	Eng. yds.	dec.
Ancient Roman mile or 1000 paces	1610	348
Olympic ftadium or 1-8 Rom. mile	201	2935
Stadium 1-10th. of the Roman mile	161	0348
Stadium the 1100th. part of a degree	111	2
Jewifh rifin 7 1-2 to a Roman mile	212	731
Gallic leuca or league 1 1-2 R. mile	2415	522
Ger. raft or common French league	4831	044
Perfian parafang 2 gallic leagues	4831	044
Egyptian fchene 4 Roman miles	6441	392
German league 2 rafts	9662	088
Ger. mile or league 200 rhenifh yds.	8239	846
Arab. m. ufed in time of the crufades	2415	713
Modern Roman mile	1628	466
Mod. Gr. m. of 7 olympic ftadiums	1409	0545
Modern French league 2500 toifes	5328	75
Turkifh mile or verft of Ruffia	1409	0515
Span. league 4 ancient Rom. miles	6441	392
Large league of Spain 5 do.	8051	74

The ancient Roman mile confifted of 1000 paces of 5 feet each, or 4 feet 9 inches and 994 decimals Englifh meafure.

The French toife is 6 French feet, or 6 feet 4 inches and 734 decimals Englifh.

Long meafure of various countries reduced to Engl.

		ft.	Eng. inch, & dec.	
Ancient Roman foot		0	11	626
Greek	do.	1	0	090
Arabic	do.	0	10	544
Alexandria	do.	1	2	112
Paris	do.	1	0	789
Leyden or Rynland		1	0	361
Amfterdam	do.	0	11	304
Antwerp	do.	0	11	352
Dort	do.	1	2	208
Boulogne	do.	1	2	974
Turin	do.	1	8	222
Venice	do.	1	1	677
Padua	do.	1	4	866
Verona	do.	1	0	444

Sweden	do.	1	2	701
Lorrain	do.	0	11	496
Middleburgh	do.	0	11	892
Strafburgh	do.	0	11	040
Bremen	do.	0	11	568
Cologn	do.	0	11	448
Frankfort on main	0	11	376
Spanifh	do.	1	0	012
Toledo	do.	0	10	788
Bononia	do.	1	2	448
Mantua	do.	1	6	838
Dantzic	do	0	11	328
Copenhagen	do.	0	11	580
Riga	do.	1	9	972
Prague	do.	1	0	312
Lyons	ell	3	11	604
Bologna	do	2	0	912
Amfterdam	do.	2	3	228
Antwerp	do.	2	3	276
Rynland or Leyden	ell	2	3	120
Frankfort	do.	1	9	912
Hamburgh	do.	1	10	860
Leipfic	do.	2	3	120
Lubeck	do.	1	10	896
Nuremberg	do.	2	2	724
Bavaria	do.	0	11	448
Vienna	do.	1	0	636
Bononia	do.	2	1	764
Dantzic	do.	1	10	836
Florence	brace or ell	1	10	956
Spanifh	palm	0	9	021
Genoa	do.	0	9	960
Naples	do.	0	10	316
Modern Roman	do.	0	8	798
Spanifh	vare	3	0	040
Lifbon	do.	2	9	000
Gibraltar	do.	2	9	120
Toledo	do.	2	8	220
Caftile	do.	2	8	949
Naples	brace	2	1	200
Naples	canna	6	10	560
Milan	calamus	6	6	528
Flor. Braccio da panna	1	10	954
Ruffia	archine	2	4	242
Rome Palmodi Arcteti	0	8	784
Parma	cubit	1	10	392
China	do.	1	0	192
Cairo	do.	1	9	888
Old Babylonian	do.	1	6	240
Turkifh Pike, larger	2	2	400
Turkifh Pike, fmaller	2	1	572
Perfian	arifh	3	2	364

NEW FRENCH WEIGHTS AND MEASURES.

A variety of weights and measures having been used in the different provinces of France, under the ancient form of government, the new govt. has ordained new standards of weights and measures, founded on nature, and therefore permanent. The standard of measure is a meridional circle of the earth, which has been, for this purpose, accurately ascertained by men of science, and particularly in 1797, by the mensuration of degrees of latitude between Dunkirk and Barcelonia. The whole circle, divided into 40 million parts, or the quadrant of 90 degrees, into ten million parts, gives the unity of length, called a *meter*, which is equal to 36 inches French, and 11,296 lines, equal to 39 inches and 371 decimal parts English.

			Eng. Inch. Dec.
A millim'eter* is the 100th part of a meter			03937
A centim'eter	the 100th part of a meter		39371
A decim'eter	the 10th part of a meter	3	93710
A METER			39 37100
A decam'eter	10	meters	393 71000
A Hecatom'eter	100	meters	3937 10000
A Chiliom'eter †	1000	meters	39371 00000
A myriom'eter	10,000	meters	393710 00000
A grade or degree of the meridian			
equal to 100,000 meters, or 1,			
100th of the quadrant			3937100 00000

* *The new French denominations are reduced to English orthography, and accentuation.* † Ch have the sound of k.

The meter thus being in English inches, 39 371 or 3 feet, 3 inches, and 371 decimals.

		Mls. Fur. Yds. Ft In. Dc.
The decam'eter	is	0 0 10 2 9 7
The hecatom'eter		0 0 109 1 1
The chiliom'eter		0 4 213 1 10 2
The myriom'eter		6 1 156 0 6
The grade or decimal degree of the meridian		62 1 23 2 8

MEASURES OF CAPACITY.

A cube whose side is one tenth of a meter, that is, a cubic decimeter, constitutes the unity of measures of capacity. It is called a *liter*, and contains 61 cubic inches and 028 decimals.*

		Eng. Cubic Inches Dec.
A millil'iter or 1.1000th. part of a liter		06103
A centil'iter	1.100th. of a liter	61028
A decil'eter	1.10th. of a liter	6.10280
A lit'er, a cubic decimeter		61.02800
A decal'iter	10 liters	610.28000

A hecatol'iter	100 liters	6102.80000
A chiliol'iter	1000 liters	61028.00000
A myriol'iter	10,000 liters	610280.00000

The English pint, wine measure, contains 28 cubic inches, and 875 decimals. The liter therefore is 2 pints and nearly one eighth of a pint.—Hence

A decal'iter *is equal to* Gal. 2. & 64.44-231 cubic inches, more than 9 quarts.

A Hecatol'iter Gal. 26. 4.44-231 cubic inches.

A chiliol'iter Gal. 264. & 44-231 cubic inch.

* Authorites do not perfectly agree in the fractions. Pinkerton gives 0242 as the decimals of this measure.

WEIGHTS.

The unity of weight is a *gram*. It is precisely the weight of a quantity of pure water equal to a cubic centimeter, which is the 1.100th of a meter, and is equal to 15 grains and 444 decimals troy.

		Gr. Dec.
A mill'igram is 1.1000th. of a gram		0.0154
A cent'igram	1.100th. of a gram	0.1544
A de''cigram	1.10th. of a gram	1.5444
A gram, a cubic centimeter		15.4440
A dec'agram	10 grams	154.4402
A hec'togram	100 grams	1544.4023
A chil'ogram	1000 grams	15444.0234
A myri'gram	10,000 grams	154440.2344

A gram being equal to 15 grains, 444 decim. troy.

A decagram 6 dwt. 10 gr. 44 dec. *equal to* 5 drams 65 dec. avordupois.

		lb. oz. dr.
A hec'togram	*equal to*	0 3 8 -5 avor.
A chilogram		2 3 5 avor.
A myriogram		22 1 15 avor.

100 myriograms make a tun, wanting 32 lb. 8.

LAND MEASURE.

The unity is an *are*, which is a square decameter, equal to 3 perches, 95 decimals. The de''ciare is a tenth of the are—the cent'iare is a hundredth of the are, and equal to a square meter. The mill'iare is 1.1000th. of the are. The dec'are is equal to 10 ares; the hec'tare to 100 ares and equal to 2 akers, 1 rood 35 perches, 4 decimals English. The chil'are is equal to 1000 ares, the myriare, to 10,000 ares.

For fire-wood the stere is the unity of measure. It is equal to a cubic meter, containing 35 cubic feet English, and 3171 decimals. The de''cestere is the tenth of a stere.

JEWISH MONTHS.

The Jews, Greeks and Romans made use of the synodical month which is, the time between two conjunctions of the sun and moon, that is, the space of time from one change of the moon to another. This month is equal to 29 days, 12 hours, 44 minutes, 3 seconds and 11 thirds. To avoid fractions, the ancients made their months to confist alternately of 29 and 30 days.

The Hebrews had their facred and civil year, in which the months were differently arranged. The facred year began at the fpring equinox, fo that the months do not corefpond exactly with ours. The following is the order of the months

IN THE SACRED YEAR.

1 *Nifan* or *Abib anfwering to the latter part of March and beginning of April*,

2	Jiar	April and May
3	Sivan	May and June
4	Thammuz	June and July
5	Ab	July and Auguft
6	Elul	Auguft and September
7	Tifri	September and October
8	Marfhevan	October and November
9	Cafleu	November and Dec.
10	Thebet	December and January
11	Sebat	January and February
12	Adar	February and March

IN THE CIVIL YEAR.

1	Tifri *anfw.*	September and October
2	Marfhevan	October and November
3	Cafleu	November and Dec.
4	Thebet	December and January

5	Sebat	January and February
6	Adar	February and March
7	Nifan	March and April
8	Jiar	April and May
9	Sivan	May and June
10	Thammuz	June and July
11	Ab	July and Auguft
12	Elul	Auguft and September

The Athenian year began with the firft new moon after the fummer folftice, fo that the firft month anfwered to the latter part of June and the beginning of July. The following was the order of the months with the days in each.

1	Hecatombeon	30	June and July
2	Melagilnion	29	July and Auguft
3	Boedromion	30	Auguft and Sept.
4	Memacterion	29	Sept. and Oct.
5	Panepfion	30	October and Nov.
6	Anthefterion	29	Nov. and Dec.
7	Pofideon	30	Dec and Jan.
8	Gamelion	29	January and Feb.
9	Elaphebolion	30	Feb. and March
10	Munichion	29	May and April
11	Thargelion	30	April and May
12	Skirrophorion	29	May and June

NUMBER OF INHABITANTS IN THE SEVERAL STATES.

| | 1790. | | 1800. | |
	Blacks &c.	Total.	Blacks. &c.	Total.
Vermont		85,539	557	154,465
New Hampfhire	788	141,885	860	183,858
Maine	538	96,540	818	151,719
Maffachufetts	5,463	378,787	6452	422,845
Rhode Ifland	4,355	68,825	3684	69,122
Connecticut	5,572	237,946	6281	251,002
New York	25,978	340,120	30,987	586,050
New Jerfey	14,215	184,139	16,824	211,149
Pennfylvania	10,274	434,373	16,270	602,545
Delaware	12,786	590,096	14,421	64,273
Maryland	111,079	319,728	127,694	349,692
Virginia	305,493	747,610	367,475	886,149
North Carolina	105,547	393,751	140,329	478,103
South Carolina	108,895	249,073	149,336	345,591
Georgia	29,662	82,548	61,618	162,686
Kentucky	12,544	73,677	41,084	220,959
Tenneffee			13,893	105,602

Territory N. W. of Ohio, total 45,365.—Indiana, total 6,407.—Miffifippi Territory, total 8,850.—Total in 1790—3,929,326—in 1800—5,305,482.

The Roman Calendar, as established by Romulus and as corrected by Numa Pompilius, was a very imperfect division of the year and introduced such confusion, as to require a thorough reform. In the reigns of Julius Cesar, and his successor, Augustus, this reformation was effected, and.the division of the year and the names of the months, were established nearly as they now stand in most of the countries of Europe.

By the Romans, each month was divided into *calends*, *nones* and *ides*. The *calends* were the first day of the month. The nones fell on the 7th. and the ides on the 15th. of March, May, July and October; but in the other months, the nones were on the 5th. and the ides on the 13th.

The following Table exhibits the Roman manner of dating.

Days.	March, May, July, October,	January, August, December.	April, June, Sept. November.	February,
1	Calendæ.	Calendæ	Calendæ.	Calendæ.
2	6 Non	4 Non	4 Non	4 Non
3	5 Non	3 Non	3 Non	3 Non
4	4 Non	prid. Non	prid. Non	prid. Non
5	3 Non	Nonæ	Nonæ	Nonæ
6	pridie Non	8 Id	8 Id	8 Id
7	Nonæ	7 Id	7 Id	7 Id
8	8 Id	6 Id	6 Id	6 Id
9	7 Id	5 Id	5 Id	5 Id
10	6 Id	4 Id	4 Id	4 Id
11	5 Id	3 Id	3 Id	3 Id
12	4 Id	prid Idus	prid. Id	prid. Id
13	3 Id	Idus	Idus	Idus
14	pridie Idus	19 Cal	18 Cal	16 Cal
15	Idus	18 Cal	17 Cal	15 Cal
16	17 Cal	17 Cal	16 Cal	14 Cal
17	16 Cal	16 Cal	15 Cal	13 Cal
18	15 Cal	15 Cal	14 Cal	12 Cal
19	14 Cal	14 Cal	13 Cal	11 Cal
20	13 Cal	13 Cal	12 Cal	10 Cal
21	12 Cal	12 Cal	11 Cal	9 Cal
22	11 Cal	11 Cal	10 Cal	8 Cal
23	10 Cal	10 Cal	9 Cal	7 Cal
24	9 Cal	9 Cal	8 Cal	6 Cal
25	8 Cal	8 Cal	7 Cal	5 Cal
26	7 Cal	7 Cal	6 Cal	4 Cal
27	6 Cal	6 Cal	5 Cal	3 Cal
28	5 Cal	5 Cal	4 Cal	prid. Cal
29	4 Cal	4 Cal	3 Cal	
30	3 Cal	3 Cal	prid. Cal	
31	prid. Cal	prid. Cal		

In applying this table to use, the reader will observe that the word *ante*, or *before*, is understood before the words Calendas, Idus, and Nonas—Thus, " 6 Non," stands for 6th. *before the nones*; " 8 Id " for 8th. before the ides. The calends are to be reckoned to the following months; thus, 17 Cal. Aprilis stands for the 17th. before the Calends or first day of April. Pridie denotes the day before; as pridie Id the day before the ides; pridie Cal. the day before the Calends.

LIST OF THE

POST-OFFICES

𝕴𝖓 𝖙𝖍𝖊 𝖀𝖓𝖎𝖙𝖊𝖉 𝕾𝖙𝖆𝖙𝖊𝖘;

With the COUNTIES in which they are fituated, and their DIS-
TANCES from WASHINGTON CITY.

AARONSBURG, *Center*, P.	238	Athol, *Worcefter*, Ms.	455
Abbeville, c. h. *Abbeville*, S. C.	645	Atfion, *Burlington*, N. J.	175
Abingdon, *Wafhington*, Vir.	408	Attleboro' *Briftol*, Ms.	447
Abbottftown, *York*, P.	93	Augufta, *Kennebeck* Ma.	667
Accomac c. h. *Accomac*, Vir.	197	Augufta, *Richmond*, G.	596
Acquafco, *Prince George*, Md.	39	Aurelius, *Cayuga*, N. Y.	448
Addifon, *Addifon*, Vt.	509	Auftinville, *Wythe*, Vir.	366
Air Mount. *Bottourt*, Vir.	267	Averyfboro' *Cumberland*, N. C.	329
Albany, *Albany*, N. Y.	400	Bairditown, *Nelfon*, K.	619
Alexandria, *Huntingdon*, P.	218	Ballfton, *Saratoga*, N. Y.	428
Alexandria, *Alexandria*, Col.	10	Balltown Springs, *Saratoga*, N. Y.	432
Alfred, *York*, Ma.	576	Baltimore, *Baltimore*, Md.	43
Allemance, *Guilford*, N. C.	326	Bangor, *Hancock*, Ma.	760
Allensfrefh, *Charles*, Md.	43	Baretfields, *Liberty*, S. C.	414
Allentown, *Monmouth*, N. J.	188	Barnet, *Caledonia*, Vt.	596
Allentown, *Northampton*, P.	190	Barnftable, *Barnftable*, Ms.	509
Amboy, *Middlefex*, N. J.	219	Barre, *Orange*, Vt.	591
Amherft, *Hillfboro'* N. H.	512	Barre, *Worcefter*, Ms.	469
Amherft c. h. *Amherft*, Vir.	200	Bafkenridge, *Somerfet*, N. J.	230
Amherft Springs, *Amherft*, Vir.	230	Bafon Harbour, *Addifon*, Vt.	524
Andover, *Effex*, Ms.	579	Batavia, *Green*, N. Y.	398
Annapolis, *Ann Arundel*, Md.	40	Bath, *Lincoln*, Ma.	646
Aquia, *Stafford*, Vir.	47	Bath, *Grafton*, N. H.	589
Afh, c. h. *Afh*, N. C.	473	Bath, *Steuben*, N. Y.	497
Afhford, *Windham*, C.	399	Bath c. h. *Bath*, Vir.	227
Afhville, *Buncombe*, N. C.	549	Bath, *Beaufort*, N. C.	338
Afylum, *Luzerne*, P.	327	Battletown, *Frederick*, Vir.	79
Athens, *Luzerne*, P.	350	Beaufort, *Beaufort*, S. C.	629
Athens, *Clark*, G.	684	Beavertown, *Beaver*, P.	282

Bedford, *Weſt Cheſter*, N. Y.	285
Bedford, *Bedford*, P.	150
Bel-air, *Harford*, Md.	77
Belcherton, *Hampſhire*, Ms.	419
Belfaſt, *Hancock*, Ma.	728
Belfont, *Center*, P.	259
Belville, *Mifflin*, P.	190
Bellows Falls, *Windham*, Vt.	578
Belvidere, *Suſſex*, N. J.	220
Bennedict, *Charles*, Md.	47
Bennington, *Bennington*, Vt.	421
Benſon, *Rutland*, Vt.	482
Bent Creek, *Buckingham*, Vir.	243
Berkley Springs, *Berkley*, Vir.	104
Berlin, *Hartford*, C.	354
Berlin, *Adams*, P.	98
Berwick, *York*, Ma.	556
Berwick, *Luzerne*, P.	234
Bethania, *Stokes*, N. C.	380
Bethlehem, *Northampton*, P.	196
Bethlehem ⋈ roads, *Southampton*, Vir.	219
Beverly, *Eſſex*, Ms.	301
Biddeford, *York*, Ma.	585
Big Eddy Grove, *Livingſton*, K.	811
Big Praires, *Randolph*, I. T.	933
Billerica, *Middleſex*, Ms.	500
Blackburn Springs, *Jackſon*, T.	655
Black Swamp, *St. Peter's par.* S. C.	631
Bladenſburg, *Prince George*, Md.	6
Blandford, *Hampſhire*, Ms.	400
Bloomfield, *Ontario*, N. Y.	459
Bluehill, *Hancock*, Ma.	774
Boonesburg, *Wyſhington*, Md.	62
Booneton, *Morris*, N. J.	246
Bordentown, *Burlington*, N. J.	181
Boſcawen, *Hillſboro'* N. H.	560
Boſton, *Suffolk*, Ms.	481
Boſtwicks, *Stokes*, N. C.	290
Bourbonton, *Bourbon*, K.	528
Bowling Green, *Caroline*, Vir.	84
Bowling Green, *Warren*, K.	808
Boyer's ſulpher ſprings, *Bath*, Vir.	291
Brackenridge c. h. *Brackenridge*, K.	699
Braintrem, *Luzerne*, P.	303
Brandon, *Rutland*, Vt.	595
Brattleboro' *Windham*, Vt.	455
Brick Meeting Houſe, *Cecil*, Md.	108
Bridgehampton, *Suffolk*, N. Y.	348
Bridgeport, *Fairfield*, C.	304
Bridgetown, *Cumberland*, Ma.	641
Bridgetown, (W.) *Cumberland*, N. J.	185
Bridgetown, *Kent*, Md.	120
Bridgewater, *Plymouth*, Ms.	474
Bridge branch, *Suſſex*, D.	144
Briſtol, *Lincoln*, Ma.	665
Briſtol, *Addiſon*, Vt.	521
Briſtol, *Briſtol*, R. I.	450
Briſtol, *Bucks*, P.	166
Broadfield, *Weſtmoreland*, Vir.	96

Broadus's mills, *Caroline*, Vir.	97
Broadkill, *Suſſex*, D.	166
Brook c. h. *Brook*, Vir.	305
Brookfield, *Worceſter*, Ms.	428
Brookfield, *Fairfield*, C.	332
Brookhaven, *Suffolk*, N. Y.	317
Brookington, *Amelia*, Vir.	182
Brooklyn, *Windham*, C.	412
Brooklyn, *Kings*, N. Y.	243
Brookville, *Montgomery*, Md.	20
Brownſburg, *Rockbridge*, V.	200
Brown's ⋈ roads, *Roſs*, O.	442
Brownſville, *Fayette*, P.	244
Brownſville, *Oneida*, N. Y.	590
Brunſwick, *Cumberland*, Ma.	634
Brunſwick, *Glynn*, G.	752
Buckfield, *Cumberland*, Ma.	660
Buckingham c. h. *Buckingham*, Vir.	223
Buckland, *Prince William*, Vir.	42
Buckſtown, *Hancock*, Ma.	743
Burlington, *Chittenden*, Vt.	541
Burlington, *Otſego*, N. Y.	473
Burlington, *Burlington*, N. J.	170
Burſontown, *Bucks*, P.	195
Buſtletown, *Philadelphia*, P.	160
Butternutts, *Otſego*, N. Y.	440
Burville, *Anderſon*, T.	570
Buxton, *York*, Ma.	620
Cabarras c. h. *Csbarras*, N. C.	439
Cabbin Point, *Surry*, Vir.	183
Cabellſburg, *Amherſt*, Vir.	215
Cahokia, *St. Clair*, I. T.	963
Ca Ira, *Cumberland*, V.	190
Cambridge, *Franklin*, Vt.	559
Cambridge, *Middleſex*, Ms.	477
Cambridge, *Waſhington*, N. Y.	433
Cambridge, *Dorcheſter*, Md.	100
Cambridge, *Abbevile*, S. C.	602
Camden, *Lincoln*, Ma.	709
Camden, *Kerſhaw diſt.* S. C.	476
Campbell c. h. *Campbell*, K.	525
Campbell's Station, *Rowan*, T.	567
Campbell Town, *Edgefield*, S. C.	576
Canaan, *Kennebeck*, Ma.	700
Canaan, *Grafton*, N. H.	563
Canaan, *Litchfield*, C.	368
Canandaigua, *Ontario*, N. Y.	446
Canfield, *Trumbull*, O.	311
Canonſburg, *Waſhington*, P.	265
Canterbury, *Windham*, C.	412
Canton, *Norfolk*, Ms.	482
Cantwell's Bridge, *New Caſtle*, D.	141
Cape May c. h. *Cape May*. N. J.	231
Cape Iſland, *Cape May*, N. J.	245
Carliſle, *Cumberland*, P.	124
Carthage or Moore c. h. *Moore*, N. C.	391
Cartertville, *Cumberland*, Vir.	182
Caſtine, *Hancock*, Ma.	761
Caſwell c. h. *Caſwell*, N. C.	309

Catawiffee, *Northumberland*, P.	218	City Point, *Prince George*, Vir.	169
Catharineftown, *Tioga*, N. Y.	390	Clairemont, *Chefhire*, N. H.	495
Catfkill, *Green*, N. Y.	383	Clarkfburg, *Montgomery*, Md.	29
Cavendifh, *Windfor*, Vt.	498	Clarkfburg, *Harrifon*, Vir.	258
Catawba Springs, *Lincoln*, N. C.	495	Clarkfburg, *Jackfon*, G.	704
Cayuga, *Cayuga*, N. Y.	439	Clarks Ferry, *Cumberland*, P.	154
Cazenovia, *Chenango*, N. Y.	494	Clarkfville, *Montgomery*, T.	790
Centerville, *Queen Anns*, Md.	72	Claverack, *Columbia*, N. Y.	380
Centreville, *Fairfax*, Vir.	26	Clermont, *Columbia*, N. Y.	361
Centrefurnace, *Centre*, P.	267	Clinton, *Dutchefs*, N. Y.	340
Centre Harhour, *Strafford*, N. H.	586	Cochranfville, *Chefter*, P.	137
Chamberfburg, *Franklin*, P.	92	Cohaffet, *Norfolk*, Ms.	505
Champlaintown, *Clinton*, N. Y.	591	Colchefter, *New-London*, C.	374
Chandlerfville, *Wafhington*, Ma.	815	Colchefter, *Fairfax*, Vir.	26
Chapel Hill, *Orange*, N. C.	319	Colerain, *Bertie*, N. C.	270
Chaptico, *St. Mary's*, Md.	56	Colefville, *Chefterfield*, Vir.	152
Charlefburg, *Montgomery*, Md.	26	Columbia, *Wafhington*, Ma.	833
Charles City, *Charles City*, Vir.	167	Columbia, *Lancafter*, P.	106
Charlefton, *Charlefton*, S. C.	538	Columbia, *Fluvannah*, Vir.	136
Charleftown, *Chefhire*, N. H.	485	Columbia, *Richland*, S. C.	511
Charleftown, *Wafhington*, R. I.	408	Columbia c. h. *Columbia*, G.	621
Charleftown, *Cecil*, Md.	86	Conajohary, *Montgomery*, N. Y.	457
Charleftown, *Jefferfon*, Vir.	73	Concord, *Rockingham*, N. H.	552
Charlton, *Saratoga*, N. Y.	426	Concord, *Middlefex*, Ms.	490
Charlotte, *Chittenden*, Vt.	529	Concord, *Suffex*, D.	159
Charlotte c. h. *Charlotte*, Vir.	233	Connelfville, *Fayette*, P.	220
Charlotte, *Meclenburg*, N. C.	460	Coopers Ferry, *Gloucefter*, N. J.	149
Charlotte Hall, *St. Mary's*, Md.	55	Cooperftown, *Otfego*, N. Y.	467
Charlottefville, *Albemarle*, Vir.	157	Coofawhatchy, *Beaufort*, S. C.	608
Chatham, *Barnftable*, Ms.	529	Cootftown, *Berks*, P.	166
Chatham, *Chefter*, P.	131	Cornwall, *Litchfield*, C.	355
Chatham c. h. *Chatham*, N. C.	315	Coryell's Ferry, *Hunterdon*, N. J.	180
Chatham, *Chefterfield*, S. C.	427	Coventry, *Tolland*, C.	385
Cheaks ✕ roads, *Hawkins*, T.	501	Crab Orchard, *Wafhington*, Vir.	391
Chelmsford, *Middlefex*, Ms.	596	Crag Font, *Sumner*, T.	704
Chelfea landing, *New-London*, C.	397	Crefapfburb, *Allegany*, Md.	155
Chemongo, *Tioga*, N. Y.	360	Crewfville, *Goochland*, Vir.	122
Chenango point, *Tioga*, N. Y.	385	Crofs Keys, *Southampton*, Vir.	220
Cheraw c. h. *Darlington*, S. C.	424	Crown Point, *Effex*, N. Y.	502
Cherry valley, *Otfego*, N. Y.	455	Culpeper, *Culpeper*, Vir.	76
Chefter, *Kennebeck*, Ma.	693	Cumberland, *Allegany*, Md.	143
Chefter, *Rockingham*, N. H.	528	Cumberland c. h. *Cumberland*, Vir.	184
Chefter, *Windfor*, Vt.	490	Cumberland Gap, *Claiborne*, T.	528
Chefter, *Orange*, N. Y.	291	Dagfboro' *Suffex*, D.	168
Chefter, *Delaware*, P.	430	Danbury, *Fairfield*, C.	315
Chefter c. h. *Chefter*, S. C.	534	Danby, *Rutland*, Vt.	460
Chefterfield, *Chefhire*, N. H.	460	Dandridge, *Jefferfon*, T.	565
Chefterfield, *Effex*, N. J.	547	Danville, *Caledonia*, Vt.	607
Chefterfield, *Caroline*, Vir	102	Danville, *Northumberland*, P.	210
Cheftertown, *Kent*, Md.	89	Danville, *Pittfylvania*, Vir.	302
Chickefaw Nation, M. T.	987	Danville, *Mercer*, K.	609
Chiles'burg, *Caroline*, Vir.	90	Darien, *M Intofh*, G.	709
Chilicotha, *Rofs*, O.	420	Darlington c. h. *Darlington*, S. C.	438
Chriftiana, *New-Caftle*, D.	108	Darnes, *Montgomery*, Md.	24
Chriftian c. h. *Chriftian*, K.	816	Davifburg, *Chriftian*, K.	816
Chriftianfville, *Mecklenburg*, Vir.	243	Davis's, *Mecklenburg*, Vir.	234
Church Hill, *Queen Anns*, Md.	82	Dayton, *Hamilton*, O.	575
Cincinnati, *Hamilton*, O.	515	Dedham, *Norfolk*, Ms.	469
Cinthiania, *Harrifon*, K.	590	Deerfield, *Hampfhire*, Ms.	430

Deerfield Street, Cumberland, N. J. 178
Delhi, Delaware, N. Y. 450
Denney'sville, Washington, Ma. 880
Dennis, Barnstable, Ms. 517
Dennis's Creek, Cape May, N. J. 219
Denton, Caroline, Md. 101
Derby, New-Haven, C. 341
Deruyter, Chenango, N. Y. 466
Detroit, I. T. 818
Dighton, Bristol, Ms. 463
Dixhills, Suffolk, N. Y. 289
Dixons Springs, Smith, T. 691
Doniphan's, King George, Vir. 76
Double Bridge, Lunenburg, Vir. 225
Douty's Falls, York, Ma. 563
Dover, Stratford, N. H. 550
Dover, Kent, D. 141
Downington, Chester, P. 150
Doylestown, Bucks, P. 172
Dracut, Middlesex, Ms. 511
Dresden, Lincoln, Ma. 664
Dripping Spring, Warren, K. 855
Duanesburg, Albany, N. Y. 424
Duck Creek, Kent, D. 153
Dumfries, Prince William, Vir. 36
Dunkirk, King & Queen, Vir. 116
Dunstable, Hillsboro' N. H. 520
Durham, Strafford, N. H. 544
Durham, New-Haven, C. 348
Durlock, Schoharie, N. Y. 449
Duxbury, Plymouth, Ms. 520
East Greenwich, Kent, R. I. 442
East Haddam, Middlesex, C. 362
Eastham, Barnstable, Ms. 537
Easton, Bristol, Ms. 469
Easton, Northampton, P. 206
Easton, Talbot, Md. 81
Eastport, Washington, Ma. 897
Eddington, Hancock, Ma. 764
Edenton, Chowan, N. C. 294
Eddyville, Livingston, K. 821
Edgarton, Dukes, Ms. 532
Edgefield c. h. Edgefield, S. C 571
Edisto, Orange, S C. 577
Elberton, Elbert, G. 671
Elizabeth City, Pasquotank, N. C. 299
Elizabethtown, Essex, N. J. 226
Elizabethtown, Essex, N. Y. 529
Elizabethtown, Lancaster, P. 135
Elizabethtown, Washington, Md. 70
Elizabethtown, Bladen, N. C. 391
Elizabethtown, or } Carter, T. 473
   Carter c. h.
Ellisville, Cumberland, P. 156
Elkton, Cecil, Md. 96
Elkrun Church, Fauquier, Vir. 68
Elicotts, Baltimore, Md. 41
Emittsburg, Frederick, Md. 81
Frostburg, Franklin, Vt. 576

Epping, Rockingham, N. H. 540
Epsom, Rockingham, N. H. 556
Essex c. h. Essex, Vir. 531
Everitts Bridge, Nansemond, Vir. 266
Exeter, Rockingham, N. H. 532
Fabius, Onondaga, N. Y. 477
Fairfax, Franklin, Vt. 563
Fairfax c. h. Fairfax, Vir. 14
Fairfield, Franklin, Vt. 573
Fairfield, Fairfield, C. 508
Fairfield or Millers, Adams, P. 83
Fairfield, Rockbridge, Vir. 210
Fairhaven, Rutland, Vt. 474
Falmouth, Barnstable, Ms. 515
Falmouth, Cumberland, Ma. 608
Falmouth, Stafford, Vir. 61
Farmington, Kennebeck, Ma. 603
Farmington, Hartford, C. 366
Farmville, Prince Edward, Vir. 210
Farnham, Richmond, Vir. 159
Fauquier c. h. Fauquier, Vir. 51
Fayette, Kennebeck, Ma. 677
Fayetteville, Cumberland, N. C. 351
Fincastle, Botetourt, Vir. 255
Fireplace, Suffolk, N. Y. 311
Fishkill, Dutchess, N. Y. 312
Fishkill landing, Dutchess, N. Y. 306
Fleming, Fleming, K. 503
Flemington, Hunterdon, N. J. 192
Florida, Orange, N. Y. 280
Fort Ann, Washington, N. Y. 459
Fort Blount, Smith, T. 671
Fort George, Washington, N. Y. 447
Fort George, Washington, N. Y. 465
Fort Massac, Randolph, I. T. 870
Fort Miller, Washington, N. Y. 439
Fort Wilkinson, Hancock, G. 702
Francistown, Hillsboro' N. H. 524
Frankford, Philadelphia, P. 152
Frankfort, Hancock, Ma. 748
Frankfort, Hampshire, Vir. 147
Frankfort, Franklin, K. 560
Franklin, Delaware, N. Y. 447
Franklin, Venango, P. 322
Franklin, O. 560
Franklin, Pendleton, Vir. 191
Franklin c. h. Franklin, G. 701
Franklin, Williamson, T. 755
Frederica, Kent, D. 129
Frederica, St. Simonds I. G. 727
Fredericksburg, Spottsylvania, Vir. 62
Fredericktown, Frederick, Md. 44
Freehold, Green, N. Y. 399
Freehold, Monmouth, N. J. 210
Freeport, Cumberland, Ma. 625
Front Royal, Frederick, Vir. 104
Fryberg, York, Ma. 648
Gaines's X Roads, Culpeper, Vir. 94
Gallatin, Sumner, T. 714

Galway, *Saratoga*, N. Y.	436
Gap, *Lancaſter*, P.	133
Gardiner, *Kennebeck*, Ma.	673
Gates c. h. *Gates*, N. C.	280
Gee's Bridge, *Brunſwic*, Vir.	211
Genefee c. h. *Genefee*, N. Y.	496
Geneva, *Ontario*, N. Y.	432
Genito Bridge, *Powhatan*, Vir.	166
Georgetown, *Lincoln*, Ma.	656
Georgetown, *Beaver*, P.	294
Georgetown, *Suſſex*, D.	158
Georgetown, *Scott*, K.	586
Georgetown, *Georgetown*, S. C.	480
Georgetown, *Warren*, G.	705
Georgetown, *Waſhington*, Col.	2
Georgetown ⅹ Roads, *Kent*, Md.	105
German Flats, *Herkimer*, N. Y.	479
Germania, *Culpeper*, Vir.	82
Germanton, *Stokes*, N. C.	371
Gettiſburg, *Adams*, P.	90
Gilmantown, *Strafford*, N. H.	584
Glafgow, *Barren*, K.	841
Gloucefter, *Eſſex*, Ms.	515
Gloucefter, *Gloucefter*, Vir.	175
Goldfon's, *Brunſwick*, Vir.	207
Goochland c. h. *Goochland*, Vir.	142
Gorham, *Cumberland*, Ma.	613
Goſhen, *Orange*, N. Y.	285
Goſhen, *Loudon*, Vir.	37
Gouldſboro', *Hancock*, Ma.	808
Gowen's Store, *Greenville*, S. C.	536
Grafton, *Grafton*, N. H.	570
Granville, *Waſhington*, N. Y.	458
Gray, *Cumberland*, Ma.	618
Grayfon c. h. *Grayfon*, Vir.	386
Great Barrington, *Berkſhire*, Ms.	368
Great Bridge, *Norfolk*, Vir.	251
Great Mill, *St. Mary's*, Md.	80
Green, *Kennebeck*, Ma.	642
Greenbriar c. h. *Greenbriar*, Vir.	300
Green Caftle, *Franklin*, P.	81
Greenfield, *Hampſhire*, Ms.	435
Greenfield, *Saratoga*, N. Y.	448
Greenſboro' *Caroline*, Md.	109
Greenſboro' Green, G.	674
Greenſburg, *Weſt Cheſter*, N. Y.	264
Greenſburg, *Weſtmoreland*, P.	221
Greenſburg, *Green*, K.	875
Greenville, *Mecklenburg*, K.	766
Greenville, *Pitt*, N. C.	298
Greenville, *Green*, T.	474
Greenville, *Jefferſon*, M. T	1217
Greenville c. h. *Greenville*, S. C.	577
Greenwich, *Fairfield*, C.	280
Grindſtone Ford, *Pickering*, M. T.	1177
Groton, *Middleſex*, Ms.	508
Guilford, *New-Haven*, C.	349
Hackettſtown, *Suſſex*, N. J.	260
Hackinſac, *Bergen*, N. J.	253

Haddam, *Middleſex*, C.	366
Haddonfield, *Gloucefter*, N. J.	152
Hadley, *Saratoga*, N. Y.	460
Hadley, *Hampſhire*, Ms.	418
Haleyſburg, *Lunenburg*, Vir.	235
Halfway-fwamp, *Sumpter*, S. C.	595
Halifax, *Dauphin*, P.	160
Halifax, *Halifax*, N. C.	237
Halifax c. h. *Halifax*, Vir.	262
Hallowell, *Kennebeck*, Ma.	670
Hamburg, *Suſſex*, N. J.	257
Hamburg, *Berks*, P.	167
Hamilton, *Eſſex*, Ms.	506
Hamilton, *Shenango*, N. Y.	467
Hamilton, *Hamilton*, O.	540
Hampden, *Hancock*, Ma.	754
Hampton, *Elizabeth City*, Vir.	213
Hancock, *Waſhington*, Md.	100
Hanover, *Grafton*, N. H.	541
Hanover, *Plymouth*, Ms.	507
Hanover, *York*, P.	86
Hanover c. h. *Hanover*, Vir.	109
Hanovertown, *Hanover*, Vir.	157
Harden c. h. *Harden*, K.	659
Harford, *Harford*, Md.	68
Harper's Ferry, *Berkley*, Vir.	65
Harpersfield, *Delaware*, N. Y.	440
Harriſburg, *Dauphin*, P.	142
Harris's, *Brunſwich*, Vir.	189
Harrodſburg, *Mercer*, K.	599
Hartford, *Hartford*, C.	370
Hartford, *Ontario*, N. Y.	474
Hartford, *Ohio*, K.	736
Hartland, *Windſor*, Vt.	533
Harwich, *Barnſtable*, Ms.	522
Harwinton, *Litchfield*, C.	352
Haverhill, *Grafton*, N. H.	576
Haverhill, *Eſſex*, Ms.	514
Havre de Grace, *Harford*, Md.	80
Hawsbill Mills, *Shenandoah*, Vir.	150
Hawkins c. h. *Hawkins*, T.	477
Haw River, *Orange*, N. C.	330
Haymarket, *Prince William*, Vir.	38
Haywoodſboro' *Chatham*, N. C.	305
Head of Saffafrass *Kent*, Md.	109
Hebron, *Tolland*, C.	390
Hebron, *Waſhington*, N. Y.	452
Hector, *Cayuga*, N. Y.	398
Hempſtead, *Queen*, N. Y.	264
Henderfon, *Henderfon*, K.	786
Henderfontown, *Montgomery*, N. C.	455
Henderfonville, *Nottaway*, Vir.	204
Henderfonville, *Sumner*, T.	720
Henry c. h. or Martinfville, *Henry*, Vir.	330
Hertford, *Perquimans*, N. C.	312
Herkimer, *Herkimer*, N. Y.	475
Hicksford, *Greenville*, Vir.	209
Hillſboro' *Loudon*, Vir.	33
Hillſboro' *Orange*, N. C.	306

Hillsboro' Hillsboro' N. H.	521	Kingston, Ulster, N. Y.	331
Hillsdale, Columbia, N. Y.	380	King and Queen, King & Queen, Vir.	127
Hills Ironworks, York, S. C.	480	Kingstree, Williamsboro', S. C.	480
Hilltop, Charles, Md.	39	King William c. h. King William, Vir.	128
Hinesburg, Chittenden, Vt.	526	Kinsale, Westmoreland, Vir.	145
Hingham, Suffolk, Ms.	500	Kingston, Lenoir, N. C.	390
Hiram, York, Ma.	634	Knoxville, Knox, T.	547
Hogton, Martin, N. C.	272	Kortwright, Delaware, N. Y.	447
Holmes hole, Dukes, Ms.	524	Lancaster, Grafton, N. H.	626
Holmesburg, Philadelphia, P.	150	Lancaster, Worcester, Ms.	462
Hope, Suffex, N. J.	225	Lancaster, Onandago, N. Y.	416
Horntown, Accomac, Vir.	174	Lancaster, Lancaster, P.	117
Hudson, Columbia, N. Y.	376	Lancaster, Garrard, K.	621
Hungarytown, Lunenburg, Vir.	215	Lancaster c. h. Lancaster, Vir.	193
Huntingdon, Huntingdon, P.	210	Lancaster c. h. Lancaster, S. C.	505
Huntington, Chittenden, Vt.	526	Lanesboro', Berkshire, Ms.	393
Huntington, Fairfield, C.	317	Lansingburg, Rensselear, N. Y.	409
Huntington, Suffolk, N. Y.	282	Laureltown, Sussex, D.	153
Huntington, Calvert, Md.	46	Laurens c. h. Laurens, S. C.	588
Huntington south, Suffolk, N. Y.	282	Laytons, Essex, Vir.	99
Huntsville, Surry, N. C.	390	Lebanon, York, Ma.	570
Huntsburg, Franklin, Vt.	587	Lebanon, Grafton, N. H.	551
Hyde c. h. Hyde, N. C.	364	Lebanon, Windam, C.	395
Indiantown, Currituck, N. C.	286	Lebanon, Dauphin, P.	167
Ingles Ferry, Montgomery, Vir.	315	Leedstown, Westmoreland, Vir.	105
Ipswich, Essex, Ms.	511	Leesburg, Loudon, Vir.	43
Islip, Suffolk, N. Y.	290	Lee's Mills, Washington, N. C.	323
Jacksonboro' Colleton, S C.	573	Lee, c. h. Lee, Vir.	460
Jacksonboro' Scriven, G.	653	Leicester, Worcester, Ms.	440
Jaffray, Cheshire, N. H.	486	Lemington, York, Ma.	610
Jamaica, Queens, N. Y.	254	Lenox, Berkshire, Ms.	380
Jamestown, Prince Edward, Vir.	212	Lenox Castle, Rockingham, N. C.	325
Jay, Essex, N. Y.	541	Leominster, Worcester, Ms.	471
Jeffersonton, Cu'peper, Vir.	61	Leonardtown, St. Marys, Md.	68
Jeffersontown, Jackson, G.	714	Lewisburg, Northumberland, P.	207
Jeffersonville, Jefferson, I. T.	628	Lewistown, Lincoln, Ma.	636
Jenkinton, Montgomery, P.	156	Lewistown, Sussex, D.	178
Jericho, Chittenden, Vt.	544	Lewistown, Mifflin, P.	177
Jericho, Queens, N. Y.	272	Lexington, Rockbridge, Vir.	213
Jerusalem, Ontario, N. Y.	434	Lexington, Rowan, N. C.	399
Jerusalem, Southampton, Vir.	210	Lexington, Fayette, K.	548
Jonesboro, Washington, T.	448	Lexington, Oglethorp, G.	665
Jonesburg, Camden, N. C.	296	Leyden, Oneida, N. Y.	530
Jones's Store, Warren, N. C.	254	Liberty, Bedford, Vir.	265
Jonestown, Dauphin, P.	174	Libertytown, Frederick, Md.	44
Johnsonburg, Morris, N J.	256	Ligonton, Amelia, Vir.	202
Johnston, Montgomery, N. Y.	442	Lilly Point, King William, Vir.	134
Kanhawa, c. h. Kanhawa, Vir.	406	Limerick, York, Ma.	604
Kaskaskia, Randolph, I. T.	903	Lincolnton, Lincoln, N. C.	458
Keen, Cheshire, N. H.	472	Lincolnton, Lincoln, G.	636
Kent Island, Queen Anns, Md.	52	Lincolnville, Hancock, Ma.	716
Kempsville, Princess Ann, Vir.	243	Lindsey's Store, Albemarle, Vir.	144
Kennebunk, York, Ma.	580	Lisle, Tioga, N. Y.	404
Kennets Square, Chester, P.	128	Litchfield, Litchfield, C.	343
Killingworth, Middlesex, C.	358	Little Britain, Orange, N. Y.	294
Kinderhook, Columbia, N. Y.	384	Little Falls Mohawk, Herkimer, N. Y.	487
King George, c. h. King George, Vir.	84	Littleton, Grafton, N. H.	609
Kingston, Rockingham, N. H.	526	Littleton, Middlesex, Ms.	508
Kingston, Plymouth, Ms.	520	Lloyds, Essex, Vir.	94

94

Newbury c. h. *Newbury*, S. C.	556	Northumberland c. h. *Northumberland*, Vir.	175
Newburyport, *Essex*, Ms.	523	North W. Fork Bridge, *Sussex*, D.	124
New Canton, *Buckingham*, Vir.	198	North W. River Bridge, *Norfolk*, Vir.	264
New Casco, *Cumberland*, Ma.	613	North Yarmouth, *Cumberland*, Ma.	617
New Castle, *Lincoln*, Ma.	671	Norway, *Cumberland*, Ma.	659
New Castle, *New Castle*, D.	122	Norwalk, *Fairfield*, C.	298
New Found Mills, *Hanover*, Vir.	112	Norway Plains, *Strafford*, N. H.	560
New Garden, *Chester*, P.	125	Norwich, *New London*, C.	399
New Geneva, *Fayette*, P.	230	Nottingham, *Rockingham*, N. H.	554
New Germantown, *Hunterdon*, N. J.	214	Nottingham, *Prince George*, Md.	27
New Gloucester, *Cumberland*, Ma.	617	Nottingham West, *Hillsboro'* N. H.	521
New Hartford, *Litchfield*, C.	388	Oldtown, *Allegany*, Md.	134
New Hampton, *Hunterdon*, N. J.	217	Onondaga, *Onondaga*, N. Y.	470
New Haven, *Addison*, Vt.	520	Oquago, *Tioga*, N. Y.	407
New Haven, *New Haven*, C.	331	Orangeburg, *Orange*, S. C.	547
New Holland, *Lancaster*, P.	129	Orange c. h. *Orange*, Vir.	127
New Ipswich, *Hillsboro'* N. H.	499	Orford, *Grafton*, N. H.	559
New Kent c. h. *New Kent*, Vir.	145	Orleans, *Barnstable*, Ms.	533
New Lancaster, *Ross*, O.	449	Orrington, *Hancock*, Ma.	755
New Lebanon, *Columbia*, N. Y.	394	Orofville, *Granger*, T.	501
New Lebanon, *Camden*, N. C.	279	Orwell, *Rutland*, Vt.	490
New London, *New London*, C.	385	Offipee, *Strafford*, N. H.	580
New London, *Campbell*, Vir.	250	Owego, *Tioga*, N. Y.	362
New Market & Roads, *Chester*, P.	116	Oxford c. h. *Orange*, N. C.	270
New Market, *Rockingham*, N. H.	536	Ovid, *Cayuga*, N. Y.	408
New Market, *Frederick*, Md.	55	Painted Post, *Steuben*, N. Y.	385
New Market, *Dorchester*, Md.	112	Painville, *Amelia*, Vir.	197
New Market, *Shenandoah*, Vir.	132	Palatine, *Montgomery*, N. Y.	466
New Market, *Ross*, O.	465	Palmyra, *Montgomery*, T.	802
New Mills, *Burlington*, N. J.	172	Paris, *Cumberland*, Ma.	667
New Milford, *Lincoln*, Ma.	670	Paris, *Oneida*, N. Y.	485
New Milford, *Litchfield*, C.	325	Paris, *Loudon*, Vir.	59
Newport, *Newport*, R. I.	436	Parfon, *York*, Ma.	595
Newport, *New Castle*, D.	114	Pasquotank, *Pasquotank*, N. C.	308
Newport, *Cocke*, T.	529	Passamaquoddy, *Washington*, Ma.	908
New Rochelle, *West Chester*, N. Y.	264	Patrick c. h. *Patrick*, Vir.	353
New Salem, *Hampshire*, Ms.	468	Patucket Bridge, *Middlesex*, Ms.	508
New Sharon, *Kennebec*, Ma.	590	Peacham, *Caledonia*, Vt.	600
Newtown, *Fairfield*, C.	325	Peekskill, *West Chester*, N. Y.	292
Newtown, *Tioga*, N. Y.	370	Pelham, *Rockingham*, N. H.	515
Newtown, *Sussex*, N. J.	244	Pendleton c. h. *Pendleton*, K.	565
Newtown, *Bucks*, P.	176	Pendleton, *Pendleton*, S. C.	603
Newtown, (Trap,) *Frederick*, Md.	55	Pennington, *Hunterdon*, N. J.	183
Newtown, *King & Queen*, Vir.	107	Perkinsonville, *Amelia*, Vir.	192
New York, *Albemarle*, Vir.	167	Peru, *Clinton*, N. Y.	550
New York City, *New York*, N. Y.	242	Peterfboro' *Hillsboro'* N. H.	424
Niagara, *Genesee*, N. Y.	544	Peterfburg, *York*, P.	79
Nixonton, *Pasquotank*, N. C.	310	Peterfburg, *Dinwiddie*, Vir.	157
Norfolk, *Norfolk*, Vir.	231	Peterfburg, *Elbert*, G.	648
Normans's Store, *Granville*, Vir.	276	Petersham, *Worcester*, Ms.	463
Norridgewock, *Kennebeck*, Ma.	710	Pettepauge, *Middlesex*, C.	368
Norristown, *Montgomery*, P.	163	Peytonfbug, *Pittsylvania*, Vir.	320
Northampton, *Hampshire*, Ms.	414	Philadelphia, *Philadelphia*, P.	146
Northampton c. h. *Northampton*, Vir.	239	Pickensville, *Pendleton*, S. C.	591
North End, *Matthews*, Vir.	185	Pinckneyville, S. C.	512
Northfield, *Hampshire*, Ms.	465	Pifcataway, *Prince George*, Md.	18
Northford, *New Haven*, C.	340	Pitch landing, *Hertford*, N. C.	260
Northport, *Hancock*, Ma.	722	Pittsburg, *Allegany*, P.	252
Northumberland, *Northumberland*, P.	199	Pittsfield, *Berkshire*, Ms.	388

Town	Page
Pittfgrove, *Salem*, N. J.	171
Pittfylvania c. h. *Pittfylvania*, Vir.	300
Pittfylvaniaold c. h. *Pittfylvania*, Vir.	305
Pittiton, *Kennebeck*, Ma.	673
Pittiton, *Hunterdon*, N. J.	199
Pittiton, *Luzerne*, P.	269
Plainfield, *Windham*, C.	414
Plattfburg, *Clinton*, N. Y.	566
Plumftead, *Bucks*, P.	178
Plymouth, *Grafton*, N. H.	597
Plymouth, *Plymouth*, Ms.	515
Plymouth, *Washington*, N. C.	314
Pocotaligo, *Beaufort*, S. C.	602
Poland or Minot, *Cumberland*, Ma.	636
Pomfret, *Windham*, C.	406
Pompey, *Onondaga*, N. Y.	482
Port Elizabeth, *Cumberland*, N. J.	206
Portland, *Cumberland*, Ma.	603
Portroyal, *Caroline*, Vir.	84
Portroyal, *Montgomery*, T.	777
Portfmouth, *Rockingham*, N. H.	545
Portfmouth, *Norfolk*, Vir.	233
Port Tobacco, *Charles*, Md.	34
Pottfgrove, *Montgomery*, P.	165
Poughkeepfie, *Dutchefs*, N. Y.	327
Poultney, *Rutland*, Vt.	468
Powhatan c. h. *Powhatan*, Vir.	164
Powell's Valley, *Anderfon*, T.	550
Praires du Rochers, *Randolph*, I. T.	933
Prefque Ifle, *Erie*, P.	386
Pridefvil'e, *Amelia*, Vir.	187
Prince Edward c. h. *Prince Edward*, Vir.	212
Princefs Ann, *Somerfet*, Md.	153
Princeton, *Middlefex*, N. J.	188
Princeton, *Northampton*, N. C.	241
Profpect, *Hancock*, Ma.	736
Profpect Hill or Wileyfburg, *Fairfax*, Vir.	14
Providence, *Providence*, R. I.	439
Provinceton, *Barnftable*, Ms.	563
Pulafki c. h. *Pulafki*, K.	663
Putney, *Windham*, Vt.	463
Quakertown, *Bucks*, P.	184
Quarlefville, *Brunfwick*, Vir.	204
Queen Anns, *Prince George*, Md.	25
Queenftown, *Queen Anns*, Md.	65
Quincey, *Norfolk*, Ms.	491
Raleigh, *Wake*, N. C.	295
Randolph, *Orange*, Vt.	571
Randolph, *Norfolk*, Ms.	437
Randolph c. h. *Randolph*, N. C.	429
Rahway, *Middlefex*, N. J.	220
Raymondtown, *Cumberland*, Ma.	630
Readfield, *Kennebeck*, Ma.	671
Reading, *Berks*, P.	148
Readfboro' *Bennington*, Vt.	435
Reamftown, *Lancafter*, P.	132
Redhook, *Dutchefs*, N. Y.	353
Reedy River Shoal, *Greenfie'd*, S. C.	557
Rehoboth, *Briftol*, Ms.	453
Reifterftown, *Baltimore*, Md.	63
Rhinebeck, *Dutchefs*, N. Y.	345
Richardfon's Tavern, *Edgefield*, S. C.	588
Richardfonville, *Hancock*, G.	690
Richmond, *Henrico*, Vir.	134
Richmond, *Madifon*, K.	572
Richmond, *Chittenden*, Vt.	536
Richmond c. h. *Richmond*, Vir.	126
Richmond c. h. *Richmond*, N. C.	407
Riceboro' *Liberty*, G.	687
Ridge, *St. Mary's*, Md.	93
Ridgefield, *Fairfield*, C.	305
Ringo's, *Hunterdon*, N. J.	186
Rifing Sun, *Cecil*, Md.	112
Roadftown, *Cumberland*, N. J.	190
Rochefter, *Plymouth*, Ms.	477
Rockaway, *Morris*, N. J.	253
Rockford, *Surry*, N. C.	406
Rockingham, *Windham*, Vt.	482
Rockingham c. h. *Rockingham*, Vir.	152
Rockingham c. h. *Rockingham*, N. C.	352
Rocky Hill W. *Hartford*, C.	363
Rocky Mount, *Franklin*, Vir.	305
Rocky River, *Pendleton*, S. C.	625
Rome, *Oneida*, N. Y.	507
Romney, *Hampshire*, Vir.	132
Romulus, *Cayuga*, N. Y.	417
Rofsville, *Sullivan*, T.	449
Royalton, *Windfor*, Vt.	554
Ruffelville, *Logan*, K.	766
Ruffel c. h. *Ruffel*, Vir.	410
Rutherfordton, *Rutherford*, N. C.	511
Rutland, *Rutland*, Vt.	478
Rutland, *Worcefter*, Ms.	461
Rut'edge, *Granger*, T.	513
Rye, *Weft Chefter*, N. Y.	272
Ryegate, *Caledonia*, Vt.	588
Saccarappe, *Cumberland*, Ma.	609
Sag Harbour, *Suffolk*, N. Y.	352
Salem, *Effex*, Ms.	499
Salem, *Wafhington*, N. Y.	446
Salem, *Stokes*, N. C.	381
Salem, *Salem*, S. C.	504
Salem, *Salem*, N. J.	183
Salifbury, *Hillfboro'* N. H.	570
Salifbury, *Effex*, Vt.	527
Salifbury, *Addifon*, Vt.	503
Salifbury, *Litchfield*, C.	351
Salifbury, *Somerfet*, Md.	138
Salifbury, *Rowan*, N. C.	416
Sampfon c. h. *Sampfon*, N. C.	387
Sandwich, *Barnftable*, Ms.	497
Sandy Hill, *Wafhington*, N. Y.	454
Sanford, *York*, Ma.	571
Sangersfield, *Shenango*, N. Y.	479
Saratoga Springs, *Saratoga*, N. Y.	442
Satucket, *Suffolk*, N. Y.	306
Saundersville, *Wafhington*, G.	682

Savannah, *Chatham*, G.	653	Stamford, *Delaware*, N. Y.	447
Saybrook, *Middlesex*, C.	367	Stamford, *Lincoln*, K.	628
Scarboro', *Cumberland*, Ma.	600	Statesburg, *Claremont*, S. C.	493
Scaroon Lake, *Washington*, N. Y.	491	Statesville, *Iredell*, N. C.	441
Scipio, *Cayuga*, N. Y.	448	Staunton, *Augusta*, Vir.	177
Scituate, *Plymouth*, Ms.	509	Staunton, O.	598
Schenectady, *Schenectady*, N. Y.	416	Sterlingville, *Granville*, N. C.	267
Scodic or Brewers, *Washington*, Ma.	893	Stevensburg, *Frederick*, Vir.	90
Scotland Neck, *Halifax*, N. C.	250	Stevensburg, *Culpeper*, Vir.	83
Scottsburg, *Halifax*, Vir.	256	Steubenville, *Jefferson*, O.	312
Scull Camp, *Surry*, N. C.	410	Stillwater, *Saratoga*, N. Y.	421
Scuppernong, *Tyrrel*, N. C.	349	Stockbridge, *Berkshire*, Ms.	376
Sempronius, *Cayuga*, N. Y.	457	Stonington, *New-London*, C.	395
Sevier, c. h. *Sevier*, T.	555	Strasburg, *Franklin*, P.	114
Shackleford, *King William*, Vir.	143	Strasburg, *Lancaster*, P.	125
Shaftsbury, *Bennington*, Vt.	428	Strasburg, *Shenandoah*, Vir.	100
Shapleigh, *York*, Ma.	579	Stratford, *Fairfield*, C.	318
Sharon, *Litchfield*, C.	344	Stroudsburgh, *Northampton*, P.	222
Sharpsburg, *Washington*, Md.	75	St. Alban's, *Franklin*, Vt.	567
Shawangunk, *Ulster*, N. Y.	300	St. Clairsville, *Jefferson*, O.	320
Sheffield, *Berkshire*, Ms.	362	St. Georges, *New Castle*, D.	123
Sheldon, *Franklin*, Vt.	579	St. Georges Parish, *Colleton*, S. C.	584
Shelbyville, *Shelby*, K.	581	St. Innigoes, *St. Mary's*, Md.	93
Shepherdstown, *Jefferson*, Vir.	73	St. Johnsburg, *Caledonia*, Vt.	605
Shepherdsville, *Bullett*, K.	640	St. Leonards, *Calvert*, Md.	58
Sherburn, *Shenango*, N. Y.	452	St. Michaels, *Talbert*, Md.	69
Sheshequin, *Luzerne*, P.	342	St. Mary's, *Camden*, G.	774
Shippensburg, *Cumberland*, P.	103	St. Tammanys, *Mecklenburg*, Vir.	226
Shrewsbury, *Monmouth*, N. J.	223	Suffield, *Hartford*, C.	388
Simsbury, *Hartford*, C.	386	Suffolk, *Nansemond*, Vir.	240
Smithfield, *Johnston*, N. C.	322	Suffolk c. h. *Suffolk*, N. Y.	334
Smithfield, *Isle of Wight*, Vir.	218	Sullivan, *Hancock* Ma.	796
Smithland, *Livingston*, K.	851	Sullivan c. h. *Sullivan*, T.	432
Smithtown, *Suffolk*, N. Y.	298	Sullivan, *Chenango*, N. Y.	499
Sneedsboro', *Richmond*, N. C.	418	Sumpterfville, *Claremont*, S. C.	519
Snowhill, *Worcester*, Md.	158	Sunbury, *Northumberland*, P.	197
Somerset, *Bristol*, Ms.	459	Sunbury, *Liberty*, G.	690
Somerset, *Somerset*, P.	189	Surrey, c. h. *Surrey*, Vir.	285
Somerset c. h. *Somerset*, N. J.	218	Sussex c. h. *Sussex*, Vir.	185
Southampton, *Suffolk*, N. Y.	342	Swanton, *Franklin* Vt.	575
Southampton, *Genessee*, N. Y.	486	Swanzey, *Bristol*, Ms.	456
South East, *Duchess*, N. Y.	300	Sweedsboro', *Gloucester*, N. J.	166
Southfield, *Orange*, N. Y.	280	Sweet Springs, *Botetourt*, Vir.	300
South Hadley, *Hampshire*, Ms.	412	Taneyton, *Frederick*, Md.	71
Southold, *Suffolk*, N. Y.	352	Tappahannock, *Essex*, Vir.	117
South West Point, *Roane*, T.	587	Tarborough, *Edgecomb*, N. C.	273
Sparta, *Sussex*, N. J.	253	Taunton, *Bristol*, Ms.	460
Sparta, *Hancock*, G.	721	Tazewell, *Claibourne*, T.	517
Spartanburg, *Spartanburg*, S. C.	542	Tazewell c. h. *Tazewell*, Vir.	370
Speed and Wilson's store, *Halifax*, Vir.	260	Templeton, *Worcester*, Ms.	472
Springfield, *Hampshire*, Ms.	398	Thomafton, *Lincoln*, Ma.	702
Springfield, *Essex*, N. J.	243	Thornsburg, *Spotsylvania*, Vir.	74
Springfield, *Hampshire*, Vir.	140	Thurman, *Washington*, N. Y.	472
Springfield, *Washington*, K.	629	Tinmouth, *Rutland*, Vt.	466
Springfield, *Robertson*, T.	765	Tolland, *Tolland*, C.	387
Spottsylvania c. h. *Spotsylvania*, Vir.	78	Topsfield, *Essex* Ms.	509
Statesburg, *Dutches*, N. Y.	342	Tower Hill, *Washington*, R. I.	426
Standish, *Cumberland*, Ma.	616	Traceys Landing, *Annarundel*, Md.	60
Stamford, *Fairfield*, C.	288	Trap, *Worcester*, Md.	186

Trenton, *Hancock*, Ma.	784	Wafhington c. h. *Washington*, N. C.	323
Trenton, *Onedia*, N. Y.	508	Waterboro' *York*, Ma.	580
Trenton, *Hunterdon*, N. J.	176	Waterbury, *Chittenden*, Vt.	558
Trenton, *Jones*, N. C.	382	Waterbury, *New Haven*, C.	351
Troy, *Renfellear*, N. Y.	405	Waterford, *York*, Ma.	651
Trumbull, *Fairfield*, C.	309	Waterford, *Saratoga*, N. Y.	411
Truro, *Barnftable*, Ms.	556	Waterford or Le Beuf, *Erie*, P.	372
Tuckerton, *Burlington*, N. J.	201	Waterford, *Loudon*, Vir.	55
Tunckhannock, *Luzerne*, P.	290	Watertown, *Middlefex*, Ms.	474
Tully, *Onondaga*, N. Y.	486	Watertown, *Litchfield*, C.	356
Turin, *Oneida*, N. Y.	536	Waterville, *Kennebeck*, Ma.	686
Turner, *Cumberland*, Ma.	650	Waynefborough, *Green*, P.	299
Unadilla, *Otfego*, N. Y.	438	Waynefborough, *Augufta*, Vir.	166
Unicorn, *Lancafter*, P.	124	Waynefborough, *Wayne*, N. C.	346
Union, *Tioga*, N. Y.	390	Waynefborough, *Burke*, G.	633
Union, *Fayette*, P.	232	Wayne c. h. *Wayne*, K.	693
Union c. h. *Union*, S. C.	602	Wellfleet, *Barnftable*, Ms.	547
Union Mills, *Frederick*, Md.	70	Wells, *York*, Ma.	575
Upper Marlboro' *Prince George*, Md.	18	Weft Bridgewater, *Plymouth*, Ms.	474
Urbanna, *Middlefex*, Vir.	145	Weft Chefter, *Chefter*, P.	138
Urquhart's Store, *Southampton*, Vir.	217	Weftern Port or George's Creek, *Allegany*, Md.	152
Utica, *Oneida*, N. Y.	495	Wefterly, *Washington*, R. I.	400
Uxbridge, *Worcefter*, Ms.	430	Weftfield, *Hampshire*, Ms.	400
Vaffalboro' *Kennebeck*, Ma.	682	Weftfield, *Saratoga*, N. Y.	460
Vergennes, *Addifon*, Vt.	519	Weftford, *Middlefex*, Ms.	508
Verfailles, *Woodford*, K.	560	Wefthampton, *Suffolk*, N. Y.	327
Vernon, *Oneida*, N. Y.	510	Wett Liberty, *Ohio*, Vir.	299
Vienna, *Dorchefter*, Md.	120	Weft Middletown, *Washington*, P.	288
Vienna, *Abbeville*, S. C.	651	Weftminfter, *Windham*, Vt.	473
Vincennes, *Knox*, I. T.	743	Weftminfter, *Frederick*, Md.	75
Wadefboro' *Anfon*, N. C.	407	Weftmoreland, *Oneida*, N. Y.	506
Walden's Store, *Halifax*, Vir.	250	Weftmoreland c. h. *Weftmoreland*, Vir.	133
Waldoboro' *Lincoln*, Ma.	683	Weft Simfbury, *Hartford*, C.	388
Walkerton, *King & Queen*, Vir.	120	Weft Springfield, *Hampshire*, Ms.	399
Wallingford, *New Haven*, C.	344	Wethersfield, *Hartford*, C.	365
Wallkill, *Orange*, N. Y.	289	Wheeling, *Ohio*, Vir.	312
Walpole, *Cheshire*, N. H.	475	White Chimneys, *Caroline*, Vir.	100
Walton, *Delaware*, N. Y.	447	White Hall, *Wafhington*, N. Y.	471
Wardfbridge, *Orange*, N. Y.	295	White Marfh, *Montgomery*, P.	157
Wareham, *Plymouth*, Ms.	484	White Plains, *Weft Chefter*, N. Y.	170
Warminfter, *Amherft*, Vir.	188	Whitelyfburg, *Kent*, D.	117
Warm Springs, *Buncombe*, N. C.	554	Whiteftown, *Oneida*, N. Y.	499
Warren, *Lincoln*, Ma.	695	Whickford, *Wafhington*, R. I.	436
Warren, *Briftol*, R. I.	450	Wilkes, *Wilkes*, N. C.	439
Warren, *Albemarle*, Vir.	178	Wilkefbarre, *Luzerne*, P.	260
Warren, *Trumbull*, O.	341	Williefburg, *Charlottee*, Vir.	243
Warrenton, *Warren*, N. C.	240	Williamfboro' *Greenville*, N. C.	257
Warrenton, *Warren*, G.	633	Williamfburg, *James City*, Vir.	175
Warwick, *Orange*, N. Y.	274	Williamfburg, *Clermont*, O.	483
Warwick, *Cecil*, Md.	113	Williamfport, *Lycoming*, P.	247
Wafhington, *Cheshire*, N. H.	513	Williamfport, *Washington*, Md.	76
Wafhington, *Wafhington*, P.	274	Williamfton, *Orange*, Vt.	576
Wafhington City, *Washington*, Col.	—	Williamftown, *Birkfhire*, Ms.	405
Wafhington, *Culpeper*, Vir.	99	Williamfton, *Martin*, N. C.	292
Wafhington, *Mafon*, K.	488	Willifton, *Chittenden*, Vt.	541
Wafhington, *Beaufort*, N. C.	321	Williftown, *Chefter*, P.	163
Wafhington, *Wilkes*, G.	646	Wil'fboro' *Effex*, N. Y.	530
Wafhington, *Adams*, M. T.	1240	Willtown, *Georgetown*, S. C.	455
Wafhington, *Morris*, N. J.	207	Wilmington, *Windham*, Vt.	441

Wilmington, *New Caftle*, D.	117	Woodbury, *Gloucefter*, N. J.	155
Wilmington, *New Hanover*, N. C.	433	Woodftock, *Windfor*, Vt.	537
Winchendon, *Worcefter*, Ms.	492	Woodftock, *Shenandoah*, Vir.	112
Winchefter, *Litchfield*, C.	380	Woodftock, *Hyde*, N. C.	354
Winchefter, *Frederick*, Vir.	82	Woodfboro' *Frederick*, Md.	57
Winchefter, *Clark*, K.	546	Woodftown, *Salem*, N. J.	172
Windham, *Cumberland*, Ma.	614	Woodville, *Culpeper*, Vir.	94
Windham, *Rockingham*, N. H.	530	Worcefter, *Worcefter*, Ms.	447
Windham, *Windham*, C.	402	Worthington, *Hampfhire*, Ms.	408
Windham, *Green*, N. Y.	404	Wrentham, *Norfolk*, Ms.	456
Windfor, *Windfor*, Vt.	523	Wyalufing, *Luzerne*, P.	317
Windfor, *Hartford*, C.	377	Wythe c. h. *Wythe*, Vir.	351
Windfor, *Bertie*, N. C.	290	Yanceyville, *Louifa*, Vir.	118
Winnfield, *Marlboro'* S. C.	414	Yarmouth, *Barnftable*, Ma.	513
Winnfboro' *Fairfield*, S. C.	541	Yonkers, *Weft Chefter*, N. Y.	258
Winflow, *Kennebeck*, Ma.	686	York, *York*, Ma.	555
Winton, *Hertford*, N. C.	250	York, *York*, P.	95
Winthrop, *Kennebeck*, Ma.	657	York c. h. *York*, S. C.	490
Wifcaffet, *Lincoln*, Ma.	659	Yorktown, *York*, Vir.	192
Woburn, *Middlefex*, Ms.	491	Youngftown, *Trumbull*, O.	329
Woodbridge, *Middlefex*, N. J.	216	Young Glades, *Allegany*, Md.	173
Woodbury, *Litchfield*, C.	360	Zanefville, *Wafhington*, O.	389

Tunnage of the United States.

In 1790 Domeftic - - - - - - 492,100
Foreign - - - - - - - 269,610

Total 761,710.

1801 Regiftered - - - - - - 632,906
Enrolled - - - - - - 278,271
Coafters - - - - - - 28,296
Codfifhery - - - - - 8,101

Total 947,574

Amount of Duties received and Drawbacks paid by the United States in 1799, 1800 and 1801.

Duties in 1799 - - - - - - 13,610,814
Drawbacks in do. - - - - - - 4,905,345

Duties in 1800 - - - - - 15,261,279
Drawbacks in do. - - - - - - 5,249,282

Duties in 1801 - - - - - - 20,064,059
Drawbacks in do. - - - - - - 7,819,093

EXPORTS FROM THE SEVERAL STATES.

	1791.	1792.	1793.	1794.	1795.	1796.	1797.
N. Hampshire	0,142,858	0,181,412	0,198,204	0,153,860	0,229,426	0,378,161	0,275,840
Massachusetts	2,519,650	2,888,104	3,755,346	5,292,441	7,117,907	9,949,345	7,502,047
Rhode Island	0,470,131	0,698,109	0,616,432	0,954,599	1,222,916	1,589,872	0,975,530
Connecticut	0,710,352	0,879,752	0,770,254	0,812,764	0,819,465	1,452,713	0,814,506
New York	2,505,465	2,535,790	2,932,370	5,442,183	10,304,580	12,208,027	13,308,064
New Jersey	0,026,987	0,027,405	0,054,178	0,058,154	0,130,814	0,059,227	0,018,161
Pennsylvania	3,436,092	3,820,662	6,958,836	6,643,092	11,538,260	17,513,866	11,446,291
Delaware	0,119,878	0,133,972	0,093,559	0,207,985	0,158,041	0,201,142	0,098,929
Maryland	2,239,690	2,623,808	3,665,055	5,686,190	5,811,379	9,201,315	9,811,799
Virginia	3,131,865	3,552,824	2,987,097	3,321,635	3,490,140	5,268,615	4,908,713
N. Carolina	0,524,548	0,527,899	0,365,414	0,321,587	0,492,161	0,671,487	0,540,901
S. Carolina.	2,693,267	2,428,249	3,191,867	3,867,908	5,998,492	7,620,049	*0,949,622
Georgia	0,490,250	0,459,105	0,520,955	0,263,381	0,695,985	0,950,158	0,644,307
Total.	19,012,040	20,753,097	26,109,572	33,026,233	47,989,472	67,064,097	51,294,710

* Three quarterly returns in South Carolina wanting—estimated at 3 millions—total of 1797, about 54 millions.

EXPORTS FROM THE SEVERAL STATES.

	1798.	1799.	1800.	1801.	1802.	1803.	1804.
N. Hampshire	0,361,453	0,361,789	0,431,856	0,555,055	0,565,394	0,494,620	716,091
Massachusetts	8,639,252	11,421,591	11,326,876	14,870,565	13,492,632	8,768,566	16,894,379
Rhode Island	0,947,827	1,055,273	1,322,945	1,832,773	2,433,363	1,275,596	1,735,671
Connecticut	0,763,128	1,143,818	1,114,743	1,446,216	1,606,809	1,248,571	1,516,110
New York	14,300,892	18,719,727	14,045,079	19,851,136	13,792,276	10,818,387	16,081,281
New Jersey	0, 61,877	0, 9,722	0, 2,289	2,406	26,227	21,311	24,829
Pennsylvania	8,915,463	12,431,967	11,949,679	17,438,193	12,677,475	7,525,710	11,030,157
Delaware	0,183,729	0,297,065	0,418,695	662,042	440,504	428,153	697,396
Maryland	12,746,190	16,299,609	12,264,331	12,834,543	8,006,290	5,209,418	9,151,939
Virginia	6,113,451	6,292,968	4,431,689	6,483,028	4,660,361	7,414,346	5,790,001
N. Carolina	0,338,124	0,485,921	0,769,799	874,884	659,390	952,614	928,687
S. Carolina	6,994,176	8,729,015	10,668,510	14,304,045	10,639,365	7,811,108	7,451,616
Georgia	0,961,848	1,396,759	2,174,268	1,755,939	1,854,951	2,370,875	2, 77,572
Vermont			57,041	0, 57,267	31,479	117,450	191,725
U.S.Territory*				29,430	1,070,628	1,343,308	3,411,621
Total	61,327,411	78,665,522	70,971,780	93,020,513	71,957,144	55,800,033	77,699,074

* including Columbia District in 1804. 1,451,198

1803—Domestic Productions exported, 42,205,961——1804 Domestic, 41,467,477.
               Foreign 13,594,072   Foreign 36,231,537.

A

CHRONOLOGICAL TABLE

Of remarkable Events on the Eastern Continent,

From the Creation to 1805.

	Before Christ.
THE creation of the world, and Adam and Eve	4004
The birth of Cain	4003
Enoch tranflated to heaven	3013
The general deluge	2348
Babel built, languages confounded	2247
Noah migrated eaftward, and founded the Chinefe monarchy, about	2237
Celeftial obfervations begun at Babylon	2234
Egypt fettled by Mifraim, fon of Ham	2188
Affyria fettled by Ninus, fon of Belus	2059
Abraham migrated from Haran to Canaan	1921
Sodom and Gomorrah deftroyed by fire	1897
The ogygian flood in Attica	1796
Jacob went to refide in Egypt	1705
Jofeph died in Egypt	1635
Aaron born in Egypt	1574
Mofes born	1571
Cecrops with a colony from Egypt fettled in Attica	1556
Athens built	1537
The deluge of Deucalion in Greece	1503
The council of Amphictyons eftablifhed	1496
The ten plagues of Egypt, and exodus of the Ifraelites	1491
Sparta built by Lacedemon	1490
Troy built by Dardanus	1480
The Greeks fettled in Italy under Oenotrus	1470
The Pentateuch written, and death of Mofes	1452
The Ifraelites entered the promifed land	1451
The Ifthian games inftituted at Corinth	1326
The Olympic games inftituted by Pelops	1307
The city of Tyre built	1294
Carthage founded by the Tyrians	1233
The Argonautic expedition	1225
Gideon judged Ifrael	1223
The deftruction of Troy for the rape of Helen	1184
Sampfon judged Ifrael	1137
Thebes built by the Beotians	1124
Samuel a prophet and judge in Ifrael	1096
Saul anointed firft king of Ifrael	1095
David takes Jerufalem & is fole king of Ifrael	1048
The temple dedicated by Solomon	1004
The kingdom of Ifrael divided	979

	Before Christ.
Jerufalem taken by Shifhak	974
Elijah the prophet tranflated	896
Cadiz, Malaga, &c. built by Phenicians, about this time.	
Carthage founded or enlarged by Dido	864
Nineveh taken by Arbaces	821
The kingdom of Macedon begins	814
The city of Capua built	801
The kingdom of Lydia begins	799
The era of the Olympiads begins	776
The era of the building of Rome	753
The era of Nabonaffar, Feb. 26.	747
Samaria taken by Salmanazer, the kingdom of Ifrael ends, the ten tribes carried captives	720
The firft eclipfe of the moon on record	ib.
Byzantium [now Conftantinople] built	670
Pharaoh Necho attempts to unite the Nile and the red fea by a canal without fuccefs	610
By the order of Necho, fome Phenicians fail round Africa	607
Nineveh taken by Nebuchadnezzar and Affyrian Empire ends	601
Jehoiakim carried captive by Nebuchadnezzar	598
Solon made Archon at Athens	594
The Pythian games inftituted in Greece	591
Firft irruption of the Gauls into Italy	588
Jerufalem taken after a fiege of 18 months	586
The laft captivity of the Jews by Nebuchadnezzar	582
Tyre taken by Nebuchadnezzar	571
Cyrus the firft king of Perfia	559
Babylon taken by Cyrus	538
Edict of Cyrus for the return of the Jews	536
Foundation of the 2d. temple laid	534
The 2d. edict to rebuild Jerufalem	520
The 2d. temple finifhed under Darius	515
Tarquin expelled and monarchy abolifhed at Rome	509
Sardis burnt by the Athenians, the occafion of the Perfian invafion	504
The battle of Marathon, Sept. 28th.	490
Xerxes invades Greece	481

K k

Event	B.C.
Defence of Thermopylæ, battle of Salamin	480
Ezra sent from Babylon to Jerusalem	458
The Romans send to Greece for Solon's laws	454
The decemvirs created and the laws of the 12 tables compiled and ratified at Rome	451
Military tribunes created	445
Censors created at Rome	443
The Peloponesian war of 27 years began	431
Malachi, the last of the prophets, and end of the Old Testament history about	430
Athens taken by the Lacedemoneans	405
Socrates put to death by the Athenians, for his sublime doctrines	400
Rome burnt by the Gauls under Brennus	390
The Lacedemonians defeated by Epaminondas at Leuctra	371
Pretors established at Rome	367
Battle of Mantinea, Epaminondas killed	363
The social war began	358
The sacred war in Greece began	356
Birth of Alexander the great	ib.
Philip of Macedon gains the battle of Cheronea, and the sovereignty of Greece	338
Thebes taken and razed by Alexander	335
Alexander defeated the Persians at Granicus	334
Alexander took Tyre	332
Alexandria in Egypt built by Alexander	331
Alexander took Babylon	330
———invaded India	328
———defeated Porus	327
———died at Babylon	323
Antioch, Seleucia, &c. founded by Seleucus	307
Era of Dionysius, who first discovered the exact solar year, begins	285
The Pharos or Watch-tower of Alexandria built	285
The Septuagint translation of the Old Testament made by order of Ptolemy Philadelphus	285
Pyrrhus invaded Italy	280
First Punic war, which lasted 23 years	264
Chronology of Aurundelian marbles composed	ib.
Romans first engaged in naval war and defeated the Carthaginians	260
The records of China destroyed	246
The Tartars expelled from China	236
Rome in peace, the temple of Janus shut	235
Corsica and Sardinia subdued by the Romans	231
The second Punic war which lasted 17 years	218
Hannibal passed the Alps	ib.
Battle of Cannæ, Romans defeated	216
Syracuse besieged by Marcellus	214
Asdrubal invaded Italy, defeated	208
Hannibal defeated by Scipio at Zama	202
Sparta and Spain subdued by the Romans	194
Antiochus defeated by the Romans at Thermopylæ	191
A Roman army first entered Asia	190

Event	B.C.
The Jewish temple plundered by Antiochus	170
Macedon reduced to a Roman province	168
Government of the Maccabees begins	163
Philofophers and Rhetoricians banished from Rome	161
The third Punic war begun	150
Carthage razed to the ground by the Romans	146
Corinth destroyed by Mummius the consul	ib.
The Numantine war began	141
The city of Florence built	140
The history of the Apocrapha ends	135
Numantia destroyed by Scipio	133
The Cimbri and Teutones defeated by the Romans	105
The Teutones defeated by Marius	102
Rome besieged by the Marian faction	88
Sylla created perpetual dictator	82
Cataline's conspiracy	66
Julius Cesar invaded Britain	55
Crassus defeated by the Parthians	ib.
Gaul reduced to a Roman province	51
The battle of Pharsalia, in which Cesar triumphed over Pompey, and put an end to the commonwealth	48
The Alexandrian library of 400,000 volumes burnt by accident	ib.
War in Africa in which Cato killed himself	45
Cesar assassinated in the senate by Brutus	44
Battle of Phillippi	42
Battle of Actium in which Antony was defeated by Octavius	31
Alexandria taken by Octavius, Antony and Cleopatra killed themselves, Egypt reduced to a Roman province	30
Octavius become emperor	27
The temple rebuilt by Herod	19
The temple of Janus shut, universal peace and birth of JESUS CHRIST, Dec. 25	5

Event	A.D.
The vulgar era commences Jan. 1	1
Pilate made governor of Judea	27
Jesus baptized in Jordan by John	29
Crucifixion of Christ at Jerusalem	33
St. Paul converted	35
St. Matthew wrote his gospel	39
Pontius Pilate killed himself	ib.
The followers of Christ called christians	40
Claudius invaded Britain	43
St. Mark wrote his gospel	44
London founded by the Romans	50
Caractacus a British king, carried in chains to Rome	51
The council of Apostles at Jerusalem	52
St. Luke wrote his gospel	55
Rotterdam built	56
Christianity introduced into Britain	60
Boadicea a British queen, defeated by Suetonius	61
St. Paul sent in bonds to Rome	62

The Acts of the Apostles written	63
Rome burnt under Nero	64
First persecution of the christians	ib.
St. Peter and St. Paul put to death	66
Jerusalem taken and destroyed by Titus	70
Great earthquake and first recorded eruption of Vesuvius, by which perished the elder Pliny. Herculaneum and Pompeii overwhelmed	79
The Capitol and Pantheon burnt	80
Agricola built forts between Forth and Clyde, defeated Galgacus and failed round Britain	85
The empire of the Huns in Tartary destroyed by the Chinese	93
The evangelist John banished to Patmos	ib.
The second persecution under Domitian	94
Revelation of St. John written	96
Gospel of St. John written	97
Dacia reduced to a Roman province	103
The third persecution under Trajan	107
Armenia reduced to a Roman province	114
The Caledonians drove the Romans from Scotland. Adrian built a wall between New-Castle and Carlisle	121
Jerusalem rebuilt by Adrian	130
The second Jewish war began	132
The second Jewish war ends, all Jews banished	135
Antoninus restrained the persecution of the christians	152
The 4th persecution under M. A. Antoninus	163
Roman embassadors sent to China	166
A great part of Rome destroyed by fire	191
Byzantium taken and burnt by Severus	196
The 5th persecution under Severus	203
Wall of Severus built in Britain	209
The Barbarians begin their irruptions into the Roman empire	222
The 6th persecution under Maximin	236
The Franks first mentioned in history	241
The 7th persecution under Decius	250
The 8th persecution under Gallus	252
Europe ravaged by the Scythians and Goths	253
The 9th persecution under Valerian	258
Valerian taken prisoner by Sapor king of Persia and flead alive	260
The temple of Diana at Ephesus burnt	ib.
Palmyra taken by the Romans and Longinus the critic slain	273
The Franks settled in Gaul	277
The 10th persecution under Dioclesian	303
Constantine the great began his reign	306
Cardinals first began	308
Persecution restrained by Constantine	313
Crucifixion abolished	315
First council of Nice. 318 fathers attended against Arius. Nicene creed composed	325
Constantine removed the government from	

Rome to Byzantium, thence called Constantinople	328
Constantine ordered heathen temples to be destroyed	331
The gospel published in Ethiopia by Foumentius	341
The heathens first called pagans	351
Paris first mentioned in history, then a mere castle	357
The first monastery founded near Poictiers in France by Martin	360
Julian attempting to rebuild Jerusalem is defeated by eruptions of fire	363
Roman empire divided	364
The Bible translated into the Gothic	373
The Goths settled in Thrace	376
The Longobards first quit the north of Germany and migrated southward, forced by famin	384
Europe ravaged by the Goths under Alaric	401
Another irruption of the Goths	404
A third irruption of Goths and the Vandals, Alans and Suevi invaded France and Spain	406
The christian religion propagated in Persia	408
Rome taken and plundered by the Goths under Alaric, August 24	410
The Vandals began their kingdom in Spain	412
The kingdom of Burgundy begun in Alsace	413
The kingdom of Toulouse founded by the Visigoths	414
The Alans extirpated by the Goths	417
The kingdom of France said by some to have been begun upon the lower Rhine under Pharamond [see 486]	420
The Roman troops withdrawn from Britain	426
The gospel preached in Ireland by St. Patrick	432
Genseric and the Vandals settled in Africa	439
All Europe ravaged by the Huns	444
The Britons applied in vain to the Romans to defend them from the Scots	446
Attila and his Huns ravaged Italy	447
Meroveus founder of the first or Merovingian race of kings in France began his reign,	448
The city of Venice founded about	452
Genseric with the Vandals plundered Rome	455
The Saxons under Hengist established in Kent	455
Clovis and the Franks crossed the Rhine, defeated the Gauls and gave law and name to France—this is the true era of the kingdom	486
The Goths under Theodoric conquered Italy	493
Clovis king of France embraced christianity	496
Prince Arthur began his reign in Britain	508
Paris made the capital of France	510
Constantinople besieged by Vitelianus whose fleet was burnt by a speculum of brass made by Proclus	515
The kingdom of the Vandals in Africa ceased	534

Belifarius took Rome from the Goths	537
Antioch deftroyed by the Perfians	540
Bafilius the laft conful elected at Rome	541
The kingdom of Poland founded	550
Narfes deftroyed the empire of the Goths in Italy	553
The Lombards founded a kingdom in Italy	568
The Turks firft mentioned in hiftory	569
John of Conftantinople took the title of Univerfal Bifhop	596
The Slavi fettled in Dalmatia, Iftria, &c.	602
St. Pauls Church in London founded	604
Firft church and monaftery founded in Weftminfter by Mellitus, bifhop of London	614
The Romans expelled from Spain by the Goths	621
Era of the Hegira or flight of Mahomet	622
Jerufalem taken by the Saracens	637
Lent firft obferved in England	640
Alexandria taken by the Saracens under Omar, and the Library burnt	640
The Britons driven into Wales by the Saxons	685
The Saracens took Carthage and expelled the Romans from Africa	698
Cracow built, and Cracus its founder elected the firft prince of Poland	700
The firft Doge of Venice elected	703
The firft province given to the Pope	704
Spain conquered by the Saracens	713
Charles Martel founder of the Carlovingian or 2d. race of French kings reigned	717
The kingdom of Afturias in Spain founded by Pelagio	718
Chriftianity promulgated in Germany	719
The controverfy about images began	726
Ina firft paid the tax peter-pence to the Pope	727
The computation of time from the birth of Chrift began to be ufed in hiftory	748
The exarchate of Ravenna abolifhed	752
The temporal dominion of the Pope began	755
Burials which had been in the high ways permitted in towns	762
The Danes invaded England	787
The Huns extirpated by Charles the great	794
Charles the great began the empire of Germany	800
Bifhoprics founded by Charles the great	801
Harold of Denmark depofed by his fubjects for profeffing chriftianity	ib.
Egbert unites the Heptarchy of England	828
The Danes burnt London about	839
Decifive battle of the Picts and Scots	840
Germany feparated from the empire of the Franks	842
Rurie, firft prince of Ruffia began to reign	861
Alfred the great began to reign	872
Iceland peopled by Norwegians	874
Scotland invaded by the Danes	ib.
Alfred compofed laws, divided England in-	
to counties, hundreds and tythings	876
The Hungarians fettled near the Danube	88
The fifth land tax in England	89
The Normans took Rouen	90
The Danes become mafters of England	913
The low countries firft called Holland about	913
The Saracen empire divided into feven kingdoms	937
Denmark entirely become chriftian	966
Antioch recovered from the Saracens	967
The laft king of Italy Adelbert, vanquifhed by Otho, the title ended	968
Pope Bonaface VII. depofed for his crimes	975
The Bohemians fubdued by Otho	ib.
The Coronation oath firft ufed in England	979
Juries eftablifhed in England	ib.
The Danes invaded England and Scotland under Sweno	985
The Carlovingian race in France ended, and that of Capet began	987
England invaded by Danes and Norwegians	995
Otho made the empire of Germany elective	996
Otho erected Poland into a kingdom and made Boleflaus the firft king	999
The emperor Henry took the title of king of the Romans	1002
Sweno became mafter of England	1014
Parents in England forbid to fell their children	1015
Canute completed the conqueft of England	1017
Boleflaus made Ruffia tributary to Poland	1021
Sweno invaded Scotland, and was defeated	1030
The Danes driven from Scotland	1040
The Saxon line reftored in Edward the confeffor	1041
The Southern part of Hungary given by the Emp. Henry III. to Albert of Bavaria, with the new name Auftria	1042
The Turks poffed themfelves of Perfia	1043
Edward banifhed thofe who took intereft for money	1045
Pope Leo IX firft kept up an army	1054
The Turks took Bagdad and overturned the empire of the Saracens	1055
Malcolm III killed Macbeth	1057
Surnames appointed by the parliament of Scotland	1061
The Turks took Jerufalem from the Saracens	1065
Battle of Haftings, England conquered by William, the Norman; Harold flain	1066
The emperor, Henry IV. walked barefooted to the Pope	1075
Juftices of the peace firft appointed	1076
The tower of England built by William	1080
Domefday Book begun in 1080 finifhed	1086
The firft crufade to recover the holy land from infidels	1096
Jerufalem taken by the Crufaders	1099

Records of public acts first regularly kept in England by order of Henry I.	1101
Edgar Atheling, the last of the Saxon princes, died	1110
Bohemia erected into a kingdom	1119
The kingdom of Portugal began	1132
The factions called Guelphs, and Gibellines first known	1140
Philip banished the Jews from France	1143
Christianity introduced into Finland	1154
Moscow in Russia founded	1156
Rise of the Waldenses or Albigenses	1160
Henry II. took possession of Ireland	1172
The ceremony of wedding the sea began at Venice	1173
England divided into circuits by Henry II.	1176
Pope Alexander III. compelled the kings of England and France to hold his stirrups	1182
Seven thousand Albigenses massacreed	1183
A conjunction of all the planets Sept. 16	1186
Paris not paved till this year	
Jerusalem taken by Saladin	1187
The troops called Mamelukes established by Saladin about this time	
Richard of Eng. defeats Saladin at Ascalon whose army consisted of 300,000 men	1192
Dieu et mon Droit first used by Richard	1194
Constantinople taken by the French and Venetians	1204
The Inquisition established	ib.
London incorporated by king John	1208
The Pope excommunicated by king John	ib.
The works of Aristotle condemned to be burnt at Paris	1210
Otho excommunicated by the Pope	ib.
London bridge burnt, the ends taking fire, during a fire in Southwark, the passengers, to the number of 3000 burnt or drowned	1212
Magna Charter signed	1215
Courts of common pleas established in Eng.	ib.
The Council of Lateran established Transsubstantiation, auricular confession, and the supremacy of the Pope	ib.
Sterling money first coined by king John	
All Scotland excommunicated by the Pope	1216
A league in France against the Albigenses	1226
The Tartars under Gingis Kahn overrun the Saracen empire	1227
Liverpool incorporate , charter	1229
The kingdoms of Leon and Castile united	1230
Prussia subdued by the Teutonic knights	ib.
Coals dug in New castle, first mentioned	1234
London obtained a grant of certain springs in Tyburn, to convey water in leaden pipes to the city	1237
A writing on paper made of rags of the date of 1239 still extant.	
Hanseatic league formed by Lubeck and Hamburg	1241

The Mamelukes seized the sovereignty of Egypt	1242
Copenhagen burnt by the Lubeckers	1248
Koningsberg founded abount	1254
Stockholm built about	1255
The Tartars took Bagdad which ended the empire of the Saracens	1258
Marco Polo began his travels to Asia	1260
Commons of England first summoned to Parliament	1265
The Tartars invaded China	1268
Merchant usurers banished by Edward I.	1272
The empire of the Austrian family began by the election of Rodolph to the throne of Germany	1273
The Dollert sea in the Netherlands formed by an inundation, 33 villages destroyed	1277
Edward renounced his right to Normandy	1279
Lewellyn, prince of Wales slain, Wales united to England	1282
Edward II. born in Caernarvon, where his mother was sent for the purpose, first called Prince of Wales	1284
Alexander of Scotland died, the claims of 12 competitors for the throne submitted to Edward of England	1285
Ptolemais taken by the Turks, end of the Crusades	1291
Edward decided the claims to the crown of Scotland in favor of J. Baliol	1292
Hamburg became a free independent city	ib.
The Ottoman empire began	1298
The Scots defeated by the Eng. at Falkirk	ib.
First meeting of the states General in France under Philip the fair	1301
General Charter of protection granted by Edward I. to foreign merchants	1302
Helvetic union, origin of Switzerland as a nation 1303 or	1307
Coal began to be used as fuel in London	1305
The clergy & nobility remonstrated against the use of fossil coal, by reason of the annoyance of stench and danger of contagion	1306
The battle of Baanockburn—The English under Edward II. defeated—R. Bruce established on the Scots throne	1314
The Cardinals quarrelled about the choice of a Pope—set fire to the Conclave and separated—2 years vacancy in the papal chair	ib.
The estates of the Lombards in Eng seized for their usury and extortions	1337
Herald's office instituted in England	1340
Edward III. took the title of king of France	ib.
Titles by patent first granted by Edw. III.	1344
The most general and fatal plague ever known, began in the north of China, in Egypt and Syria 1346, in Italy in 1347, in	

France and England in 1348, in Ireland and Holland in 1349, in Germany in 1350, in many places one third of the people perished; *in fome cities, fcarcely a tenth furvived*—it raged many years, invading different countries and towns at different times.

The battle of Durham—David of Scotland taken prifoner 1347

The colony of chriftians at Greenland became extinct, whether by the peftilence or fevere feafons, uncertain 1348

The Turks firft entered Europe 1352

The battle of Poictiers---John of France taken prifoner by Edward the black prince 1356

Terrible plague in Italy, England, Ireland, France, &c.---Scotland loft nearly a third of its people 1361

The Janizaries eftablifhed in Turkey 1362

Peter pence forbid to be paid in England 1365

John Wickliffe oppofed the popifh religion 1369

The office of Grand Vizer eftablifhed 1370

Hanfeatic confederacy at its zenith, confifting of 64 cities, befides 44 in alliance ib.

Great peftilence, depopulating many cities in Italy, Greece, France, Germany, &c. Lubec loft 90,000 people 1382

Windfor Caftle built by Edward III. 1386

The firft lord high Admiral appointed in Eng. 1387

Battle of Otterburn between Hotfpur and Douglafs 1388

An act againft taking intereft in England 1391

The Jews banifhed from Germany 1392

The Jews maffacreed in Spain 1394

Madeira faid to be difcovered by Macham an Englifh man who was fhipwrecked 1395

All the Irifh ordered by proclamation to leave England ib.

Ireland conquered by Richard II. ib.

Weftminfter Abbey rebuilt and enlarged 1399

Order of Knights of the Bath inftituted at the coronation of Henry IV. ib.

Tamerlane defeated and took Bajazet 1402

Guild hall in London built 1410

Ordinary revenue of Henry V. £ 56,960 1415

Battle of Agincourt gained by Henry V. ib.

The Canaries conquered by Bentencourt 1417

Madeira difcovered by the Portuguefe 1419

Madeira planted with the fugar cane from Sicily and with vines from Candia 1420

The Zuyder Sea in Holland formed by an inundation 1421

Freemafons meetings forbid by act of parliament 1424

France renounced allegiance to Henry VI. of England 1436

Henry VI. granted licenfe to J. Cobb to tranfmute imperfect metals into gold and filver 1444

Conftantinople taken by the Turks, which ended the eaftern empire which had exifted 1123 years, May 29 1453

Paris contained 84,000 men able to bear arms 1468

The Grifons confederate and renounce the power of Auftria 1471

The Genoefe expelled by the Turks from the Euxine 1474

Certain perfons obtained from Edward IV. licenfe to make gold and filver from mercury 1476

Amfterdam furrounded with a brick wall 1482

The coaft of Guinea difcovered and fettled by the Portuguefe 1483

Richard III. defeated and flain at Bofworth, which puts an end to the civil war of 30 years between the houfes of York and Lancafter 1485

Englifh fhips firft failed to Italy, firft apointment of a conful for commercial purpofes 1485

Henry VII. eftablifhed a guard of 50 Yeomen, the firft body of ftanding troops in England 1486

The Jews to the number of a million banifhed from Spain 1492

Vafco de Gama firft doubled the Cape of Good Hope and failed to India 1497

Maximilian divided Germany into 6 circles 1500

St. Helena difcovered by the Portuguefe 1501

The Portuguefe eftablifhed a colony in Ceylon 1505

Madagafcar difcovered by the Portuguefe 1507

League of Cambray againft Venice diffolved 1508

Goa taken by the Portuguefe 1510

Battle of Flowden, James IV. of Scotland killed and the flower of his nobility 1513

Cannon bullets of ftone ftill in ufe 1514

Cats fwept away by a peftilence ib.

Selim I. fubdued the Mamelukes in Egypt 1516

The reformation from Popery begun by Luther 1517

Henry VIII. for his writings in favor of popery received the title of *Defender of the Faith* 1521

Rhodes taken by the Turks 1522

Firft voyage round the world by Magellan ib.

The inquifition eftablifhed in Portugal 1526

Lutheranifm eftablifhed in Germany 1527

Rome taken by the Imperialifts ib.

Popery abolifhed in Sweden 1528

The name, Proteftants, given to the Reformed from their protefting againft the church of Rome at the diet of Spires 1529

Malta affigned to the Knights of St. John by Charles V. 1530

Office of fecretary of ftate eftablifhed in Eng. ib.

The court of feffion inftituted in Scotland 1532

The reformation took place in England 1534

The reformation introduced into Ireland	1535
The fociety of Jefuits firft formed	ib.
Wales incorporated with England by act of parliament	1536
The leffer monafteries fuppreffed by Henry VIII.	ib.
Firft Englifh ftatute refpecting the poor in	ib.
Parith regifters firft directed to be kept	1538
All monafteries [645 in number] fuppreffed in England	1539
Society of the Jefuits eftablifhed	1540
Firft ftatute in Eng. refpecting bankrupts	1543
Firft ftatute for the prefervation of wood	1544
Lands in Eng. let for one fhilling an	ib.
The famous council of Trent of 18 years continuance	1545
A ftatute in Eng. eftablifhing the intereft of money at 10 per cent—37 Hen. VIII.	1546
Lord lieutenants of counties inftituted	1549
The houfes in Paris 10,000 by enumeration	ib.
The controller of the king's houfehold hired a houfe in Lon. for 30 fhillings a year	ib.
Horfe guards inftituted in England	1550
The book of common prayer eftablifhed	1552
Sir Hugh Willoughby with 3 fhips attempting a N. E. paffage to China, perifhed by cold at Lapland; but R. Chancellor in one of the fhips arrived in the White fea, and firft opened a trade to Archangel	1553
The wearing of filk by common people in England forbid	1554
Reformation in Scot. completed by J. Knox	1560
Hawkins the firft Englifhman who began the flave trade, the firft voyage in	1562 & 3
The firft ftatute compelling parifhes to fupport the poor in England 5 Eliz.	1563
Revolt of the low countries from Spain	1565
The 39 articles of the church of England eftablifhed	1566
Queen Mary imprifoned in England	1568
Toleration of proteftantifm in the low countries	ib.
Intolerance in Spain excites the Moors to rebel	ib.
The royal exchange firft built	1569
The great maffacre of Proteftants in France	1572
The toleration of the proteftant religion in France followed by a civil war	1576
Voyage of Sir F. Drake round the world began	1577
In 1577 there were employed in the codfifhery at Newfoundland 100 fhips from Spain, 50 from Port. 150 from France, and 15 from England; alfo 20 or 30 fhips from Bifcay for whales	
The Dutch fhake off the Yoke of Spain	1579
Company of merchants incorporated for an exclufive trade to the Baltic, called "Fellowfhip of Eaft-Land merchants"	ib.
The Englifh firft fent an envoy to Turkey and make peace with the Barbary powers	1582
Jefuits and popifh priefts banifhed by act of Parliament	1584
Horfe guards firft eftablifhed in Scotland	ib.
Mary, queen of Scots beheaded	1587
Interefteftablifhed in Scot. at 10 per cent	ib.
Spanifh Armada deftroyed by the Englifh under Sir F. Drake	1588
A fund for wounded feamen firft formed in England by voluntary contribution of mariners called the cheft at Chatham	ib.
The Jefuits expelled from France	1594
Cadiz facked by the earl of Effex, the forts deftroyed, fhips taken; the plunder amounted to 20 millions of ducats	1596
Englifh company of merchants driven from Germany by the emperor, inftigated by the Hanfeatics; in return the fteelyard merchants of the Hanf-towns banifhed from England	1597
Edict of Nantz by Henry IV. of France gave free toleration of the proteftant religion	1598
Eaft-India company incorporated for 15 years Dec. 31	1600
St. Helena fettled and fortified by the Eaft-India company	ib.
Commiffions to decide cafes on policies of infurance inftituted	1601
Edict of Henry IV. of France reducing intereft to 6 1-2 per cent	ib.
The Dutch traders to E. Indies united and incorporated by the States General	1602
The rebels in Ireland fubmitted to Elizabeth	1603
Queen Elizabeth died, James VI. of Scotland fucceeded her which united the kingdoms	ib.
The Jefuits banifhed from England	ib.
Oftend taken by the archduke of Auftria after a fiege of 3 years and the lofs of 120,000 men	1604
The gunpowder plot difcovered	1605
Oaths of allegiance firft adminiftered in Eng.	1606
Firft Englifh minfter appointed to refide in Turkey	ib.
The independence of the United States of Holland acknowledged by Spain	1609
Henry IV. of France murdered by Ravaillac	1610
Baronets firft created in England	1611
The Dutch eftablifh a trade with Japan	ib.
Ireland divided into counties—circuits of Judges and laws of England—markets and fairs eftablifhed	1612
Englifh merchants of the E. India company now firft unite their feparate ftocks into a joint ftock	ib.
Logarithms invented by Lord Napier of Scotland	1614
Laft meeting of the States General of France before the late revolution	ib.

Coffee firſt introduced into Holland from Mocha   1616

Jacatra now Batavia in Java firſt taken and fortified by the Dutch   1618

The circulation of the blood confirmed and illuſtrated by Harvey   1619

The broad ſilk manufacture introduced into England   1620

Navarre united to France   ib.

Copper coin firſt introduced into England   ib.

Profeſſorſhips of aſtronomy and geometry eſtabliſhed at Oxford   ib.

James renews his reſtrictions on the importation of tobacco   ib.

The parties called Whigs and Tories known in England   1621

Maſſacre of the Engliſh at Amboyna by the Dutch   1623

Intereſt of money in Eng. reduced by act of parliament to 8 per cent 21 James in which act the word *intereſt* as diſtinct from *uſury* is firſt uſed   1624

Tobacco, except from Engliſh colonies, prohibited to be imported and the planting of it in England forbid   ib.

Plague in London kills 35,000   1625

Hackney coaches firſt ply in London, 20 in number   ib.

The plague in Wittemburg and in Lyons where died 60,000   1626

New-Holland diſcovered by the Dutch----A new iſland among the Azores emerged   1628

A lottery authorized by royal grant   1630

A poſt maſter appointed by Charles I, before whoſe time a poſt office was erected by James, the year not named   1631

Battle of Lutzen, Guſt. Adolphus killed   1632

Gallileo condemned by the inquiſition at Rome   1633

Intereſt in Scotland reduced by parliament from 10 to 8 per cent   ib.

China conquered by the Tartars, who ſtill retain their dominion   1635

Firſt impoſition of ſhip money by Charles I.   ib.

An officer appointed to ſuperintend the game of wreſtling in Eng. ſo late as   1639

The Duke of Braganza recovers the independence of Portugal   1640

Triennial Parliaments eſtabliſhed   ib.

The maſſacre of 40,000 Engliſh Proteſtants in Ireland Oct. 23   1641

King Charles impeached 5 refractory members of parliament which began the civil war   1642

New Zealand diſcovered by the Dutch   ib.

The Exciſe firſt introduced in England   1643

Feudal tenures aboliſhed by the Lords and Commons, whoſe act was confirmed under the protectorate in 1656, and by an

act of parliament 12. Charles II. 1660

A joint ſtock tar company eſtabliſhed in Sweden   1647

The treaty of Weſtphalia which ends the wars of Auſtria with France and Sweden   1648

Charles I. beheaded Jany. 30th aged 49   1649

The ſect of Friends or quakers appeared   1651

Legal intereſt reduced in Eng. to 6 per cent   ib.

Engliſh navigation act paſſed   ib.

The Dutch ſettle at the Cape of Good Hope   1651 or 1653

Great naval action between the Eng. fleet and the Dutch under Van Tromp   ib.

Dutch ſhips firſt obliged by treaty to ſtrike their flags to the Engliſh   1654

The Dutch expelled from Braſil by the Portuguese   ib.

The ſtadt-houſe in Amſterdam erected   1655

The Dutch reduce the intereſt of their public debt from 5 to 4 per cent   ib.

The Jews permitted to reſide in England   ib.

The Engliſh admiral Penn took Jamaica   1656

Reſtoration of Charles II.   1660

Navigation act paſſed by parliament   ib.

Tea, coffee and chocolate firſt mentioned in Eng. Statutes   ib.

Revolution in Denmark---Frederic III. made abſolute   ib.

Pruſſia declared independent of Poland   1663

Great plague in London, carries off 68,000 inhabitants   1665

Great fire in Lond. conſumes 13,000 houſes   1666

Lewis XIV. overrun Holland   1672

The Habeas corpus act paſſed   1678

Vienna beſieged by the Turks---relieved by Sobieſki   1683

The edict of Nantz, tolerating the proteſtant religion in France, revoked by Lewis XIV. in conſequence of which 300,000 proteſtants left France   1685

A revolution in Eng. James abdicated the throne Nov. 5, 1688---William and Mary proclaimed Feb. 16.   1689

The Engliſh eſtabliſhed at Calcutta   ib.

Epiſcopacy aboliſhed in Scotland   ib.

Battle of Boyne---James defeated   1690

Naval battle of La Hogue---French defeated by Admiral Ruſſel   1692

Stamp duties laid in England   1694

A new company incorporated for trade to the E. Indies, three years before the charter of the old company expired   1698

Treaty of peace at Ryſwick   1697

Charles XII. of Sweden began his reign   1700

Pruſſia erected into a kingdom   1701

Society for propagating the goſpel in foreign parts eſtabliſhed   ib.

The old and new Eaſt India companies united July 22   ib.

Gibralter taken from the Spaniards by Admiral Rooke 1704

The battle of Blenheim, August 13th won by the Duke of Marlborough ib.

Battle of Ramilies won by the Allies 1706

Union of Eng. and Scot. signed July 22 ib.

The Allies defeated at Almanza 1707

Minorca taken from Spain by general Stanhope 1708

Battle of Oudenarde won by the Allies ib.

Peter, czar of Ruffia, defeated Charles XII. at Pultowa 1709

Battle of Malplaquet won by the Allies ib.

The French king granted an exclufive right to the trade of Louifiana to Crozat for 15 years 1712

Treaty of Utrecht April 11 1713

St. Petersburg made the feat of commerce ib.

Premium offered by Parliament for difcovery of the longitude 1714

Legal intereft in Eng. reduced to 5 per Cent ib.

Lewis xiv. died, fucceeded by his grandfon Lewis XV. 1715

Rebellion in Scotland in favor of the pretender fuppreffed ib.

Septennial parliaments eftablifhed 1716

Crozat refigned his grant of Louifiana trade and the " Company of the Weft" erected in France 1717

Sardinia erected into a kingdom 1718

The French Eaft India company and Miffifippi company united 1719

John Law, director general of the French bank, paid off public creditors in India ftock, which rofe to 13 hundred per cent ib.

The bank of France united to the India company ; a royal arret reduced the value of India ftock ; the bubble burft—Univerfal difirefs fucceeded 1720

The manufacture of iron in American colonies forbid by parliament 1719

South fea bubble in England, ftock rofe to 1000 pr cent ; the fcheme failed and great diftrefs enfued 1720

Death of George I. and of Sir Ifaac Newton 1727

Ruffia became an empire. ib.

Kouli Khan ufurped the throne of Perfia, conquered the Mogul, returned with 230 millions fterling 1732

The Jefuits expelled from Paraguay 1733

War begun between England and Spain 1739

Anfon failed on his voyage round the world 1740

The battle of Dettingen won by the allies 1743

War declared againft France, Anfon returns 1744

The allies loft the battle of Fontenoy 1745

Rebellion in Scot. crufhed by the D. of Cumberland ib.

Kouli Khan murdered 1747

Peace of Aix la Chapelle 1748

Intereft on the British funds reduced to 3 per cent 1749

123 Englifhmen perifh in the black-hole at Calcutta 1756

War declared by Eng. againft France May 18th. ib.

Minorca taken by the French June 29 ib.

Damien attempted to affaffinate the French king 1757

An attempt to affaffinate the king of Portugal 1758

The art of engraving prints begun in England by the patronage of W. Boydell 1760

Pondicherry taken by Col. Coote Jan. 15 1761

Bellifle taken by the Englifh June 7th ib.

War declared by England againft Spain 1762

Peter III. Emperor of Ruffia depofed ib.

Preliminaries of peace figned Nov. 3d. ib.

Definitive treaty of peace Feb. 10th. Jefuits expelled from France 1763

The fociety of artifts in Eng. incorporated 1765

The Jefuits expelled from Denmark and Bohemia 1766

Jefuits expelled from Spain, Venice and Genoa 1767

Proteftants tolerated in Poland Nov. 2d. ib.

The Turks imprifoned the Ruffian Embaffador and declared war againft Ruffia 1768

Jefuits expelled from Naples and Parma ib.

Corfica conquered by the French, Paoli fled 1769

The fhips of capt. Cook returned from circumnavigating the globe 1771

The conftitution of Sweden changed from ariftocracy to a limited monarchy 1772

Partition of Poland by Ruffia, Auftria and Pruffia ib.

The fociety of Jefuits fuppreffed by the pope Auguft 25th. 1773

Peace between the Ruffians and Turks 1774

The Spaniards defeated at Algiers July 8th 1775

Naval action between Admiral Keppel and d'Orvilliers off Breft, June 27 1778

Spain joined France in the war againft Great Britain 1779

Capt. Cook killed at Owyhee by the Natives February 14 ib.

Siege of Gibralter begun by the Spaniards July 8th. ib.

The Spanifh fleet defeated by admiral Rodney January 16th. 1780

Dreadful infurrection in London on account of the act for relieving the Papifts ib.

Armed neutrality, confifting of Ruffia, Sweden and Denmark figned in July ib.

The ftates general accede to the armed neutrality November 20th. ib.

Great Britain declared war againft the ftates of Holland December 20 ib.

Hyder ally made war on the Eng. in India ib.

King of Pruffia acceded to the armed neutrality   1781

The Emp. acceded to the armed neutrality

The Spaniards attacked Gibralter in vain   ib.

Severe engagements between the Britifh and Dutch fleets near the dogger bank Auguft 5th   ib.

Minorca furrendered to the Spaniards Feb. 4th.   1782

The Spanifh floating batteries before Gibralter deftroyed September 12th.   ib.

Change of miniftry in Eng'and March 27th   ib.

Trincomaleé in Ceylon taken by Sir E. Hughes from the Dutch, January   ib.

Revolution in Geneva effected by France, Sardinia and the Swifs cantons   ib.

Balloons difcovered by S and J Montgolfier in France

Preliminaries of a general peace figned January 20th. at Verfailles   1783

Treaty between the Eng. and the Mahrattas 24th. February   ib.

Definitive treaties of peace between Great Britain and the French, between Great Britain and Spain, and between Great Britain and the United States of America, September 3d.   ib.

Firft experiment of afcending in a balloon by Rozier, October 15th.   ib.

Definitive treaty of peace between Great Britain and the ftates general, May 20th.   1784

Mr. Lunardi afcends in a balloon, firft attempt in England, September 15th.   ib.

Treaty of commerce and navigation between G. Britain and France, Sept. 16th.   1786

Treaty of alliance between Great Britain and the ftates general April 15th.   1788

Treaty of alliance between Great Britain and Pruffia, Auguft 13th.   ib.

States general met at Verfailles May 5th.   1789

Baftil demolifhed by the populace July 14th.   ib.

The feudal fyftem abolifhed Auguft 4th.   ib.

National or conftituent affembly met at Paris October 19th.   ib.

Nobility abolifhed June 19th.   1790

Confederation in the Champ de Mars July 14th.   ib.

Treaty of Plinitz between the emperor and king of Pruffia for fupporting monarchy in France Auguft 27th.   1791

Decree of national affembly declaring people of color free citizens May 15th.   ib.

King and queen of France fled, June 21, but taken at Varennes by Drouet a poftmafter   ib.

Partition Treaty at Pavia figned in July   ib.

New conftitution of France accepted by the king September 13th   ib.

Conftituent affembly diffolved Sept. 30th.   ib.

Legiflative affembly met October 7th.   ib.

Great Riots at Birmingham July 14th.   ib.

Emperor Leopold died March 1ft.   1792

The king of Sweden affaffinated by Ankerftrom, March 16th.   ib.

France declared war againft the king of Hungary and Bohemia, April 20th.   ib.

Swifs guards maffacreed at the palace Auguft 10th.   ib.

Royal authority fufpended, a convention decreed   ib.

Maffacre of the clergy and other Prifoners September 2d. and 3d.   ib.

The French made war on Sardinia and took Savoy September 20th.   ib.

National convention affembled, September   ib.

Eternal abolition of Royal authority decreed and France declared a republic, Sept. 21ft   ib.

Decree of death ag'ft. all emigrants, Oct. 9th.

Decree of fraternity, promifing to aid all people who wifh to procure liberty Nov. 19th.

Decree for opening the navigation of the Scheldt, November 16th.

Battle of Gemappe Nov. 5th.

Geneva acknowledged the French republic, December 19th.

King of France arraigned before the convention, December 11th. condemned January 16th 1793, beheaded Jan. 21ft.

King of Poland compelled by Ruffia to reftore the old conftitution, July 23d.

French declare war againft England and the Stadtholder of Holland Feb. 1ft

Reprifals ordered by the Britifh Feb. 11th.

The French declare war againft Spain March 7th.

Declaration of war by Spain againft France, March 23d.

The French under Dumourier entered Holland, took Breda Feb. 24th. but driven back in March, commiffioners fent to arreft Dumourier, the army abandoned Dumourier and he abandoned his country, April 3d.

Infurrection of royalifts on the Loire, March

Congrefs of the combined powers at Antwerp April 8th.

Battle at Famars May 28th

The revolutionary tribunal eftablifhed, March

The Girondifts, to the number of 90, arrefted June

Marat affaffinated in July by Charlotte Cordé

A new conftitution formed by the Mountain or Jacobins

Duke of York defeated in attempting Dunkirk Auguft 24th.

The fecond conftitution for France, formed by the Jacobins

Lyons taken by the troops of the convention Oct. 8, dreadful massacres followed

Marseilles taken by the conventional troops in August—Toulon which had submitted to Lord Hood, besieged and taken December 19

Pondicherry surrendered to the English, August 28

Barrere procured a decree to raise the *Nation in Mass*. August 23

Gen. Cuitine tried and executed, July

The Queen arraigned tried and condemned, Oct. 15 and executed Oct. 16

Brissot and 20 other Girondists executed October 30

The Duke of Orleans afterwards executed

New table of weights and measures establish and a new calendar formed—The telegraph invented by Chappe about the end of 1793

Charleroi taken June 25, the Austrians defeated by Jourdan in a great battle at Fleurus June 26, and Flanders conquered by the French | 1794

Splendid victory of Lord Howe over the French fleet, June 1

Mad Elizabeth, sister to the late king of France executed May 10

Robespierre arrested and executed with the leaders of his faction, July 28

French attacked the whole Austrian lines, Sept. 15, 16, 17 and 18, and drove the Maese and Koer, Oct. 1

French overrun Holland—more than 2000 emigrants taken and put to death

The telegraph first used to notify the surrender of Quesnoy

Treaty of amity and commerce between Great Britain and the U. States of America, November 19

Severe frost rendered the Rhine, Waal, &c. passable on ice, January | 1795

The French took Amsterdam Jan. 16

The Polish patriots defeated—Kosciusko taken prisoner by the Russians, Oct. 10

Convention between Sweden and Denmark for the defense of commerce, March 27, | 1794

The convention decreed that no quarter should be given to the English or Hanoverian troops, May 26. That decree was repealed Dec. 29

Revolution in Geneva in favor of democracy under the influence of Soulavie and Merle, French commissioners, July 19

Plan of a Revolution in Sweden by Baron D Armfeldt detected early in 1794

Treaty of peace between France and Prussia, April 5 | 1795

Treaty of alliance between France and Holland, May 15

Luxemburg taken by the French, June 7

The third constitution of France, June 29

Treaty between France and Spain, July 22

Great Britain declared war against Holland Sept. 15

Cape of Good Hope surrendered to the English, Sept. 16

National convention dissolved and a directory of five appointed, Oct. 26

The king of G. B. assaulted in his coach, Oct. 29 and Feb. 1 following

First telegraph in Eng. erected. Jan. 28 | 1796

Piedmont conquered by the French, Ap. 23

Dutch fleet at the Cape taken by the English, Aug. 17

Bloody battles in Italy—Mantua blockaded, Wurmser took refuge in Mantua, Aug.

Jourdan defeated in Germany, Sept. 3—Moreau retreated Sept. 11

French expedition to Bantry Bay, Dec. 24

Spain declared war against G. B. Oct. 18

Empress Catherine of Russia died, Nov. 17

Lord Malmsbury failed of effecting a peace with France and returned Dec 29

Action of Rivoli, Jan. 14—Mantua surrendered to the French, Feb. 2 | 1797

Victory of Sir John Jervis over the Spanish fleet off Cape St Vincents, Feb. 13

The French landed a body of galley slaves in Wales, Feb. 22

Armistice between the French and Austrians in Italy, April 7

Preliminaries of peace signed at Leoben, April 18

Mutiny in the Eng. fleets, Ap. 15 & May 12

Lord Malmsbury's second negotiation for peace failed and he returned Sept. 18

Dutch fleet defeated by Ad. Duncan Oct. 11

Treaty of peace between France and Austria, signed at Campo Formio, Oct. 17

Gen. Duphot killed by the mob in Rome, Dec 28

Congress of Rastadt, for settling general peace, Jan. 1 | 1798

Bonaparte sailed for Egypt, May 20—took Malta, June 9—arrived at Alexandria, June 30

Alexandria taken July 3, and Cairo 23

Battle of the Nile—French fleet taken or destroyed by Admiral Nelson, Aug. 1

French under Gen. Humbert landed in Ireland, Aug. 22

King of Naples took possession of Rome, Nov. 29

Abdication of the king of Sardinia, Dec. 9

The Neapolitans defeated by the French and Rome again taken, Dec. 15

Treaty between G. B. and Russia for carrying on the war against France, Dec. 18

Jaffa taken by affault, March 6

Siege of Acre began March 20—raifed May 20

Suwarrow arrived at Verona—defeated the French in feveral battles and recovered moft of Italy from April to July

French deputies, Bonnier and Roberjot, affafinated near Raftadt by the Szecklar Huffars, April, 28

Seringapatam, capital of the Myfore, in India, taken by the Eng. by affault, Ap. 28

Change in the directory of Paris, June 19

Convention between G. B. and Ruffia for invading Holland, June 22

Mantua retaken by the Allies, July. 28

Bonaparte failed for Europe, Auguft 24

Englifh and Rufhans landed in Holland, Auguft 27

Dutch fleet furrendered to the Englifh, Auguft 30

Eng. and Ruffians defeated in Holland, compelled to retire—treaty for the purpofe, Oct. 18

A revolution in Paris—the directory diffolved—a new conftitution of government, with an executive of three confuls ; Bonaparte made Firft Conful for ten years, Nov. 9 and 10

Bonaparte croffed the St. Bernard with an army, May 14   **1800**

Severe and decifive battle at Maringo—the French victorious, Gen. Deffaix flain—the Auftrians loft 10,000 men flain, and the French nearly the fame number, June 14

Gen. Kleber affaffinated in Egypt, June 14

Preliminaries of peace figned at Paris, June 28

Malta furrendered to the Englifh, Sept. 5

Preliminaries of peace not being ratified by the Emperor, the war continued—the French fieze on Tufcany, Oct. 15

Severe battle of Hohenlinden, in which the French under Moreau took 80 pieces of cannon and 10,000 prifoners, Dec. 3

The French advance to within 17 leagues of Vienna—Armiftice figned Dec. 25

Convention of Ruffia, Sweden, Pruffia and Denmark to protect neutral rights, Dec. 16

Convention of Luneville figned Jan. 26   **1801**

Definitive treaty between France and Auftria, figned Feb. 9

Union of Ireland with Great Britain

Englifh expedition againft Egypt, arrived at Aboukir, March 7

Battle of Aboukir, Fr. defeated, March 21

The Emperor Paul of Ruffia found dead in his bed, March 22

Battle of Copenhagen, April 2

Convention between the Englifh Turks and French army at Cairo for the evacuation

of Egypt by the French figned June 27

Treaty between the French and the Pope, recognizing the catholic religion in France, Sept. 10

Treaty of Madrid between France and Portugal, Sept. 29

Preliminaries of peace between France and Great Britain. Oct. 1

Treaty of Amiens between France and G. Britain, March 27   **1802**

A French army under Le Clerc arrived at Cape Francois, February 2

Cape Francois burnt by the blacks

Bonaparte conftituted by the confervative fenate firft Concul for a fecond period of ten years to commence from the expiration of the firft period, May 2. But on a propofition of the tribunate, a decree for conftituting him firft Conful for *life* was offered to the people for fignature &being figned by 3,568,885 citizens, Bonaparte folemnly declared firft Conful for life, Auguft, 2

New conftitution of France declaring all the Confuls for life, Auguft. 5

Egypt evacuated by the Britifh, Feb. 10   **1803**

Bonaparte propofed to the heir of the French throne to renounce his pretenfions to the throne, Feb. 26

The propofition rejected Feb. 28—The rejection approved by the princes April 23

French expedition intended for Louifiana fufpended April

Great Britain declared war againft France, May 16

French entered Hanover, June 3

Bonaparte notified the commencement of war with Great Britain, June 7. Great preparations for the invafion of England

Pichegrue, Moreau, &c. arrefted in Paris, February 17,   **1804**

Bonaparte declared emperor of the French, May 3

War between France, Auftria and Ruffia commenced in September   **1805**

Battle of Wertingen Oct. 8, Auftrians defeated.—Battle of Guntburg Oct. 9, Auftrians defeated.—37,000 Auftrians under general Mack furrendered to Bonaparte at Ulm, Oct. 17. In the whole more than 60,000 prifoners were taken in two weeks

Greateft naval action on record between the combined fleets of France and Spain of 33 fail under Villeneuve and Gravina, and the Englifh fleet of 27 fail under Lord Nelfon. Lord Nelfon killed, but the Englifh obtained a fplendid victory by taking or deftroying 19 fail, Oct. 21

TABLE II.

A Chronological Table of the Invention and introduction of Arts and Improvements.

Before Chrift.

LETTERS invented by Memnon 1822
 Cadmus carried the Phenician letters into Greece 1492
Iron difcovered in Greece from the burning of woods 1406
Money firft made of gold and filver at Argos 894
Sculpture in marble difcovered 873
Scales and meafures invented by Phidon 869
Firft calculation of eclipfes on record, made by Thales, of Miletus 600
Money firft coined at Rome 580
Comedy firft acted at Atheus on a moveable fcaffold 562
Tragedy firft acted at Athens by Thefpis 534
A public library firft founded at Athens 526
The battering ram invented by Artemones 441
Wrought filk introduced into Egypt 323
Sun dials began to be ufed in Rome about 310
Barbers firft came from Sicily to Rome 299
Painting begun in Rome by Fabius Pictor 291
The Septuagint tranflation of the Old Teftament made by order of Ptolemy Philadelphus 285
The college and library at Alex. founded 283
Silver firft coined in Rome 296
Comedy firft acted at Rome 240
Surgery introduced at Rome 219
Gold firft coined at Rome 206
Paper invented in China 170
The firft library erected at Rome 168
Hipparchus began his aftron. obfervation 162
——————began his new cycle of the moon 143
Cherries, apricots, &c. introduced into Italy by Lucullus from Cerafus and other parts of Afia Minor about 114
The folar year introduced by J. Cefar 45
The vulgar era commenced in the 5th year of Chrift by miftake   A. D. 1
Mathematicians allowed to teach at Rome 225
Silk brought from India in the reign of Tiberius, or about 274
Vines began to be cultivated in Ger. & Eng. 276
Cycle of indiction began 312
Bells invented by Paulinus of Campania 400
The ufe of the chriftian era introduced by Dionyfius, the Monk 516
The Codex of Juftinian publifhed 529
The Digeft of Juftinian publifhed 533
The chriftian era ufed by Juftinian ib.
Manufacture of filk introduced into Europe by two monks from India 536
Water mills invented or introduced into ufe by Belifarius about 555

Anno Dom.

Bells introduced into churches 605
An Academy founded at Canterbury, Eng. 628
Organs firft ufed in Churches 660
Glafs-makers introduced into England by a Benedictine Monk 663 or 674
Plate firft ufed in England by Wilfred, bifhop of Northumberland 709
Computation of time by the chriftian era began to be ufed in hiftory 748
An academy founded at Paris 792
Charles the great of Germany introduced the prefent names of the months, the cardinal points, &c. 800
Bells and clocks firft ufed in Conftantinople 872
The chriftian era added to dates of public acts by Charles the fat 880
Bricks firft ufed in England 884
Octher, a Norwigean, failed round North Cape in Lapland about 886
A fchool at Oxford founded by Alfred 896
A fchool at Cambridge founded 915
The bible tranflated into Saxon 939
Arithmetic brought into Europe 941
The Arabian figures began to be ufed inftead of letters 991
Paper made of cotton rags in ufe 1000
Notes of mufic invented 1070
The Pandect of Juftinian found at Amalfi in Italy, which revived the ftudy of civil law about 1137
The bank of Venice, the firft in Europe, eftablifhed 1157 or 1176
The univerfity of Padua founded 1179
Glafs windows began to be ufed in private houfes in England 1180
Bills of Exchange ufed at Hamburg 1189
Legal intereft firft mentioned in England 10 per cent 1199
Chimneys not yet known in England 1200
Univerfity of Salamanca, in Spain founded ib.
The word *parliament* began to be ufed in England 1205
Ariftotle's works brought from Conftantinople into England 1209
Silk began to be manufactured at Venice ib.
London bridge built of ftone 1212
The ftudy of Aftronomy and Geography introduced into Europe by the Moors 1220
The univerfity of Thouloufe founded 1228
The univerfity of Naples founded 1230
The houfes in London, France and Germany ftill thatched with ftraw 1233
The univerfity of Vienna founded 1238

Ll

Tin mines discovered in Germany 1241
An order for covering houses in London with
 tiles or slate 1246
Astronomical tables composed by Alonso 1253
The christian era began to be used in Spain 1258
The academy of Florence founded 1272
Academy de la Crusca founded 1282
The university of Lisbon founded 1290
Lectures on theology begun at Cambridge 1293
Tallow candles insted of splinters of wood,
 spoons and cups began to be used in Eng.
 but considered luxuries.—Wine sold yet
 as a cordial by apothecaries 1298
Spectacles invented by a monk of Pisa 1299
Windmills invented about this time
The mariners compass invented or improv-
 ed by Giovia of Naples 1302
The university of Avignon founded
The weight of English coins fixed by statute
Bills of exchange used in England 1307
The university of Dublin founded 1319
Gold first coined in Christendom about 1320
Gunpowder invented by Swartz of Cologne 1330
Edward III. granted a protection to two
 weavers from Brabant to settle at York 1337
Exportation of Wool from England forbid
 and the manufacture encouraged
Copper money first used in Scotland and Ire-
 land 1340
Blankets first used in England
Gold first coined in England 1344
Cannon first used by Edward at Cressy 1346
Shaving the beard began in England 1357
The university of Cologne founded 1358
Law pleas which had been in French from
 the conquest, ordered to be in English 1362
The university of Geneva founded 1365
Side-saddles began to be used, before which
 women rode astride 1382
A company of linen weavers from the Neth-
 erlands established in London 1386
Bombs invented at Venloo 1388
Cards invented in France for the king's
 amusement 1391
Leaden seals first fixed to Eng. woollens 1403
Bank of St. George at Genoa which had its
 origin in the funds for paying the debts
 of the republic in 1345, established 1407
The Portuguese began their discoveries
 southward on the African coast 1410
Painting in oil colors invented by Vaneyck
 or D'Eyck at Bruges
The university of St. Andrews Scot. founded 1411
The christian era began to be used in Port. 1415
Standard of weights ordered by parliament 1429
The art of printing invented by L. Koster
 of Haerlem in Holland, who used wooden
 moveable types, about 1430 or 1440, or
 this art was invented at Mentz by J. Faust

about this time —Guttemburg improv-
 ed the art by making types of metal.—
 Scheffer invented the casting of them in
 matrixes.—The first printers carried their
 types about in bags and printed small
 pamphlets, letters, &c. in noblemen's houses
The Vatican library at Rome founded 1446
The university of Glasgow founded 1454
Engraving and etching in copper invented 1460
W. Caxton introduced printing into Eng. 1471
The study of Greek began in France 1473
The university of Aberdeen founded 1477
Measures of casks fixed by parliament 1483
Cape of Good Hope discovered by Diaz 1486
W. Grocyn first taught Greek at Oxford 1490
Weights and measures fixed as they now are
 and standards ordered to be kept in eve-
 ry town in England 1492
Algebra began to be known in Europe 1494
Spinning with a distaff first taught in Eng.
 by Bonvise, an Italian 1505
Shillings first coined in England
Gardening and many plants introduced in-
 to Eng. from the Netherlands 1509
The use and manufacture of felt hats in lieu
 of cloth hoods and knit caps began
Gardening introduced into Denmark 1515
First Polyglot bible printed at Alcala in Spain
Hops, carp and turkies introduced into Eng. 1523
Currants introduced into Eng. from Zante 1533
The Bible translated into English and published by W. Tindal & Miles Coverdale 1532
Tindal being burnt for herefy, his bible was
 revised by Coverdale, afterwards bishop
 of Exeter and archbishop Cranmer, and
 published by authority 1540
The Geneva translation was printed at Ge-
 neva in 1560
Archbishop Parker's translation or the bish-
 op's bible, was printed in 1565, and these
 translations revised and amended by 47
 men appointed by king James, were first
 published in 1613.—This is our present
 copy
Brass cannon first cast in England 1535
First newspaper in Europe printed at Venice 1536
Cannon began to be used in Ships 1539
Pins used by ladies insted of skewers 1543
Iron cannon first made in England 1547
Iron bullets for cannon began to be used in-
 sted of stones 1550
The manufacture of glass begun in England 1557
Silk stockings first worn by Henry II. of
 France at his sister's wedding 1559
Insurance against losses at sea mentioned 1560
The art of knitting stockings with needles
 introduced into Eng. from Spain 1561
Queen Elizabeth first wore silk stockings ib.
Before this time princes wore cloth hose

The ufe of cambric and lawn introduced the art of ftarching 1562
Knives firft made in England 1563
The making of bays or baize began in Eng.
Starching taught by Mrs. Dinghen a Flemifh lady, at the price of 4 pounds for the art 1564
Decimal arithmetic invented by Simon Steven of Bruges 1569
Book keeping by double entry began in Eng.
Turkies a great rarity at the nuptials of Charles IX. of France 1571
Watches brought into England from Germany about 1577
Tulips bro't into Eng. from Conftantinople 1578
Hackluyt fent a man to Perfia to learn the art of making and dying carpets 1579
Coaches introduced into Eng. by the earl of Arundel 1580
Copper firft ufed for money in France 1581
Pope Gregory introduced the New Style, the 5th of October being called the 15th 1582
Lectures on furgery firft read in London
Pippins introduced into England 1583
Tobacco introduced into England 1586
Duelling with the fmall fword introduced into England 1588
The ftocking loom invented by Wm. Lee of St. John's college, Cambridge
The telefcope invented by Janfen a maker of fpectacles in Germany about 1590
The manufacture of fail-cloth introduced into England
Trinity college Dublin, founded 1591
Firft patent for the exclufive right of printing a book, granted to R. Wright of Oxford
Firft voyage of the Englifh to the E. Indies
Firft whaling voyages of the Englifh to the bay of St. Laurence 1593
Firft voyage of the Dutch to E. Indies 1595
Firft Englifh fhip fo large as 800 tuns, built
Weekly bills of mortality in London kept and ftill extant 1603
In Eng. were 4 merchant fhips only, above 400 tons
Manufacture of alum began in England 1608
The mulbery tree introduced into England 1609
Bank of Amfterdam inftituted
Galileo difcovered the Satellites of Saturn 1610
The thermometer invented by Diebel a Dutchman, or Santorio
Firft fhip of 64 guns built in England
The Danes began to trade to E. Indies
The firft regular weekly newfpaper in England began 1622
The milling of coin firft practiced in Eng. 1631
Tranfit of mercury over the fun's difk firft obferved by Gaffendi
Firft fawmill in Eng. erected by a Dutchman 1633

Lacquer varnifh firft ufed in England
Regular pofts from London to Scotland and Ireland firft eftablifhed 1635
The bank of Rotterdam eftablifhed
Bows and arrows, and ftones for fhot as well as Iron, ftill ufed 1640
The fugar cane brought to Barbadoes from Brafil, where it had been introduced from the Canaries 1641
The barometer invented by Torricelli 1643
The pendulum firft ufed to regulate clocks, by Huygens in 1649 or 1657
Coffee introduced into England 1652
The air pump invented by Guericke of Magdeburg 1654
Spring pocket watches invented by Huygens or Dr. Hooke about 1658
Afparagus, artichokes, cauliflowers, oranges, lemons, introduced into England about this time
The Royal Society eftablifhed April 15 1662
Firft wire mill erected in England at Richmond by a Dutchman 1663
French academy of fciences inftituted 1666
Manufactory of tapeftry fet up in France 1667
India muflins began to be ufed in England 1670
The African company introduced gold into Eng. of which were made the coins called from the country, guineas 1672
Calicoes began to be printed in England 1676
The micrometer invented by Kircher 1677
The firft Eng. fhip went to China 1680
The Newtonian philofophy publifhed 1686
Fine writing paper firft made in England 1690
The glazing of ftone-ware by fait caft into the kiln, introduced into England by two Germans about this time
Bayonets firft ufed by the French againft the confederates at the battle of Turin 1693
Firft public lottery drawn in England
Bank of England incorporated July 27 1694
Greenwich Hofpital for difabled feamen founded
Bank of Scotland eftablifhed 1695
Exchequer bills invented, during the recoinage of filver
Society for propagating the gofpel in foreign parts inftituted 1701
A curious machine for throwing filk, erected at Derby, England 1719
Two infurance companies incorporated in England 1720
The imperial academy of arts and fciences in Ruffia founded 1724
Inoculation in Eng. firft tried on criminals 1727
The quadrant, called improperly Hadley's, invented by T. Godfrey of Phil. 1730
The Gentleman's Magazine the firft in England, began 1731

Weftminfter bridge begun 1738, finifhed 1750, at the expenfe of 389,000 £. Sterl.

The manufacture of tin plates by rolling-mills begun in England about this time—

The Monthly Review, the firft permanent publication of the kind in Europe began 1749

Antiquarian fociety at London founded 1751

New ftyle introduced in England by ftatute, May 22, 1751—directing the firft day of Jan. to be the firft day of the year in-fted of March 25; and the 3d of Sept. 1752 to be accounted the 14th.

The Britifh mufeum founded 1753

The fociety of arts, manufactures and com-merce inftituted at London 1754

Black-friars bridge begun 1760, finifhed 1770, at the expenfe of 152,840 £ Sterl.

The art of engraving prints begun in Eng. by the patronage of W. Boydell 1760

Queen's ware, fo called from the Queen who was pleafed with it, firft made by Wedgewood 1763

Mr. Harrifon received 10,000 £. Sterling for his accurate time piece by which lon-

gitude may be difcovered 1764

The jenny for fpinning cotton invented by James Hargrave 1767

The academy of painting eftablifhed in Lon. 1768

Manufacture of calicoes introduced in Eng. 1772

Manufacture of caft plateglafs eftablifhed in Lancafhire 1773

Oxygene gas difcovered by Dr. Prieftley, and called dephlogifticated air Auguft 1 1774

Water difcovered to be a compound fub-ftance by Henry Cavendifh 1781

Muflins began to be manufactured in Eng. 1781

Logographic printing invented by H. John-fon 1783

The Afiatic fociety in Calcutta inftituted 1784

Machine for bending and cutting wire for card teeth invented in Maff. 1787

New chemical nomenclature of Lavoifier and his affociates firft publifhed in 1789

Machine for bending, cutting and fticking card teeth, invented by Mr. Whittemore of Cambridge, Maff. 1797

Vaccination or inocculation of the cow-pocks, introduced by Dr. Jenner 1798

TABLE III.

A Chronological Table of the moft remarkable Events, in or refpecting America, intended as the outline of American Hiftory.

Anno Dom.

THE king of Spain granted a commiffion to Chriftopher Columbus, a Genoefe, for making dicoveries,* April 30 1492

Columbus failed from Palos in Spain Aug. 3, firft obferved the variation of the nee-dle Sept 14, difcovered Guanahana now Cat-Ifland, one of the Bahamas, Octo-ber 12th O. S. 23d. N. S.

Columbus difcovered Cuba Oct. 27, O. S. and Hayti, which he call'd Hifpaniola or Little Spain, December 6, O. S.

Columbus built a fort at Navidad in Hayti, where he left 3 officers and 38 men, and failed to Spain 1493

Pope Alexander granted to Spain all the lands weft of a line 100 leagues weft of the Azores, May 4.

Second voyage of Columbus, Sept. 25

Columbus built Ifabella on the north fide of Hayti, December 1493

Columbus difcovered Porto Rico in the fec-ond voyage, and Jamaica May 4, 1494

John Cabot, a Venetian by birth, but refi-

His real name was Chriftoval Colon, which was latinized into Chriftopher Columbus.

Anno Dom.

ding at Briftol in Eng. failed under a com-miffion from Henry VII. and difcovered Prima Vifta or Newfoundland 1494 or 5

Bartholomew Columbus, governor of Ifa-bella, built New Ifabella on the fouth fide of Hayti and on the eaft bank of the riv-er Ozama, to which he removed the col-ony 1496

Ch. Columbus returned to Spain, March 1496

Henry VII. granted a commiffion to John Cabot and his three fons, Lewis, Sebaft-ian and Sanctius, to make difcoveries of unknown countries, and to erect the king's banners on lands which they had already difcovered, March 5 1496

King Henry gave a licenfe to John Cabot to take fix veffels from any port, for ma-king difcoveries, Feb. 3 1498

Sebaftian Cabot failed to America, difcov-ered the land afterwards named Labra-dor, June 11, O. S. [22d.] and ranged along the coaft to Florida.—He was the firft difcoverer of the American continent 1497 or 1498

Ch. Columbus failed from Spain on his third

voyage May 30, difcovered Trinidad July 31, and the continent now Terra Firma, Auguft 1, — 1498

Ojeda who was with Columbus in his firft voyage, accompained by Amerigo Vefpucci, a Florentine, failed from Spain May 20th, and in June difcovered the continent of S. America, and Amerigo had the addrefs to give the continent his name — 1499

Vincent Y. Pinzon failed fouthward, difcovered the great river Maranon which he called Amazon — 1500

Pedro A. Cabral, a Portuguefe, difcovered the coaft now called Brafil

Bovadilla appointed governer of America, fent Columbus to Spain in chains, Aug. 23

Cortereal, a Portuguefe, failed to Newfoundland and gave name to Labrador

The town of New Ifabella being deftroyed by a hurricane, was rebuilt on the weft fide of Ozama. The name was afterward changed to St. Domingo, and this is the oldeft town in America — 1502

Columbus being acquitted, failed on his 4th voyage June 3, arrived at Hayti June 29, failed to the continent, difcovered the bay of Honduras, alfo named Porto Bello, Aug. to Nov.

Columbus fhipwrecked on Jamaica — 1503

Columbus relieved after being almoft a year on Jamaica, arrived at Hayti, and failed for Spain Sept. 2, arrived at St. Lucar in December — 1504

Adventurers from Bifcay and the north of France began a fihery on the banks of Newfoundland

Columbus died at Valladolid aged 58, May 20 — 1506

The fugar cane introduced into Hayti from the Canary iflands about this time

J. D. de Solis, and V. Y. Pinzon difcovered the great river Paraguay, called alfo river of plate or filver — 1508

Africans firft introduced into Hayti for flaves

Ojeda and Nicueffa began a fettlement at the gulf of Darien. Ovando fettled Porto Rico, and Efquivel began a fettlement on Jamaica — 1510

John Ponce de Leon difcovered and named Florida, from its being difcovered Eafter Day or feaft of flowers — 1512

Vafco Nunez de Balboa difcovered the South fea or Pacific Ocean — 1513

J. de Grijalva difcovered Mexico and named it New Spain — 1518

Hernando Cortez failed to Mexico, March 1519, after fevere contefts fubdued Mexico Auguft 21, — 1521

Ferdinand Magellan, a Portuguefe, in the

fervice of Spain, entered the ftrait now called by his name, Nov. 11, 1520, proceeded to the Phillippines where he was killed; but one of his fhips arrived in Spain in 1522---this being the firft voyage round the globe

Pizarro, with Almagro and Luque invaded Peru — 1531

Pizarro founded St. Michael, the firft Spanifh colony in Peru — 1532

Pizarro took Cuzco, the capital of Peru, after having taken Atahualpa, the Inca, and put him to death — 1533

P. Mendoza failed to the Paraguay with 2000 men, built Buenos Ayres, and firft introduced horfes, which have multiplied beyond calculation

Ferdinand de Soto landed in Florida with 900 men, 1539, penetrated to the Chickafaw country, croffed the Miffifippi where he died May 21, 1542, the remains of his men arrived in Mexico in 1543

Orellana entered the river Maranon and defcended to its mouth — 1541

Chili conquered by the Spaniards

The mines of Potofi difcovered — 1545

Peftilence in Peru, in Mexico 800,000 perfons perifhed — 1546

Ribaud with French proteftants, began a fettlement on the Edifto; but the people abandoned the place, and on their return, fome perifhed by famin — 1562

John Hawkins began the flave trade of the Englifh — 1563

Laudoniere failed with 3 fhips to relieve Ribaud; but ftopped at May river, now St. John's, built a fort called Caroline — 1564

Ribaud failed to Florida, took a part of the men from fort Caroline to oppofe a Spanifh fleet; Melandez, a Spanifh officer, arrived, maffacred moft of the French, and garrifoned the place with Spaniards — 1565

Gourge, a Gafcon, failed to Florida and maffacred the Spaniards, and Florida was abandoned — 1568

M. Frobifher attempted to find a N. Weft paffage, difcovered the ftrait of his name — 1576

Peftilence in Mexico, by which died, as appeared by regifters, 2 millions of perfons

Sir Walter Raleigh obtained a patent for making difcoveries, March 25 — 1584

Amidas and Barlow, by order of fir W. Raleigh, landed on Wecokon and Roanoke, July. On their return, the Queen gave to the country, the name Virginia; tho the places where they landed are now in N. Carolina

Sir W. Raleigh fent Sir R. Greenville with 7 veffels to fettle Virginia—a fmall colony

left at Roanoke under Gov. Lane, Aug. 1585
J. Davis failed to the ftrait of his name
Gov. Lane and the colony return to Eng.
with Sir F. Drake, who had been on an ex-
pedition againſt the Spaniſh fettlements
in America   1586
Gov. Lane carried tobacco to England
J. Davis, in his third voyage, difcovered and
named Cumberland iſlands   1587
Sir R. Grenville left a fecond colony at Ro-
anoke in 1586, which was deſtroyed by
the natives
A third colony under Gov. White left at
Roanoke.---Gov. White returned to Eng.
for fupplies   1587
Sir W. Raleigh aſſigned his patent to Gov.
White, Thos. Smith and others, March 7 1589
Gov. White returned to Roanoke, but not
finding the fettlers, went to the W. In-
dies, and finally to England   1590
Whale fiſhery begun by the Engliſh   1593
Sir W. Raleigh made a voyage to Guiana,
burnt St. Jofeph in Trinidad---failed into
the Oronoke   1595
Barthol. Gofnold came to America, named
Cape Cod, landed on Cuttahunk, and be-
gan to build, but returned   1602
Samuel Champlain, failed up the St. Lawr.
The Sieur de Mont, with Champlain for a
pilot, explored the coaſt of Acadia, entered the Bay of Fundy, named the river
Wegondy, St. John, built a fort and paffed the winter on St. Croix, an iſland in
the Scoodue   1604---5
De Mont fettled Port Royal, now Annapolis, the firſt fettlement in NovaScotia   1605
Virginia divided and by letters patent, the
fouthern part was granted to Sir Thomas
Gates and others, called the London company, the northern part to the Plymouth
company, April 10   1606
Capt. Newport, arrived in Virginia and be-
gan the firſt effectual fettlement on the
river Powhatan [James] called James-
town, April 26   1607
Capt. Smith firſt explored the Chefopeak   1608
Quebec founded by Samuel Champlain
Mr. Robinſon's church migrate to Holland
Second charter of Virginia to the earl of Sa-
lifbury and others, May 23   1609
Mr. Robinſon's church removed to Leyden
Capt. Hudfon difcovered the River Manhat-
tan, now called by his name
Newfoundland fettled under J. Gray, Gov. 1610
Capt. Hudfon difcovered the bay which bears
his name, his crew mutined and fet him
afloat in an open boat, and he periſhed 1610-11
Champlain difcovered and named Lake-
Champlain   1611

Third charter of Virg. extended to include
Bermuda, 300 leagues to fea, March 12   1612
Bermuda fettled under gov. Moor
J. Rolfe married Pocahontas, daughter of
Powhatan, April   1613
Capt. Smith made a fiſhing voyage to the
northern part of America, made a chart
of the coaſt, which he prefented to Prince
Charles who gave the country the name
of New England   1614
A fort or trading houſe, built on the Hudfon
near Albany by the Dutch between   1610-14
The Dutch lay claim to the difcoveries of
Hudfon and fettle Manhattan, now N. Y. 1614
W. Baffin difcovered the bay of his name 1616
Great peſtilence or yellow fever deſtroyed
moſt of the Indians from Naraganfett to
Penobfcot   1618
Capt. Dermer the firſt Engliſhman who fail-
ed thro Long-Iſland found and Hellgate 1619
Firſt colonial aſſembly in Virg. June 19
Mr. Robinfon's people left Holland in July
and England in Sept. for America, arri-
ved in Nov. landed at Plymouth Dec.
11. O.S. 22 N.S.   1620
Charter of New Eng. granted to the D. of
Lenox and others, or council of Ply-
mouth, Nov. 23
The Indians maſſacreed 349 of the Virgin-
ians, March 22   1622
Firſt fettlement of New Hampſhire at Little
Harbor on the Pafcataway and at Dover   1623
St. Chriſtopher's difcovered by Columbus
and cal'ed by his name, 1493, was fettled
by T. Warner, Jan.
The hrſt cattle brought into New England 1624
Barbadoes granted to Sir William Courteen,
and fett'ed
Cape Ann fettled
The Virg. company diſſolved and their char-
ter refumed by the crown
The king granted Barbadoes to the earl of
Carliſle   1627
Grant of Maff. from the council of Plym.
March 19   1628
Nevis fettled by the Engliſh   1628
Salem fettled by Gov. Endicott
Charter from the crown confirming the
Plymouth grant and erecting the Maffa-
chufetts company into a corporation Ma. 4 1629
Carolina granted to Sir Robert Heath Oct. 30 1629
Charleſtown, Boſton, Watertown and Dor-
cheſter fettled by Gov. Winthrop and
others   1630
Patent to Plymouth colony from the coun-
cil of Plymouth Jan. 13
The council of Plymouth granted lands to
fettlers on Pemaquid Feb. 29   1631
Patent of Connecticut from the earl of War-

wick March 19
Firft veffel built in Maffachufetts, called the
　Blſſing of the Bay, lanched July 4
Grant of Maryland to lord Baltimore June 20　1632
Montferrat and Antigua fettled by the Eng.
　and St. Euftatia by the Dutch
The Dutch built a fort on the weft bank of
　the Connecticut, in the prefent town of
　Hartford　　　　　　　　　　　　　　1633
The Plymouth people, after the Dutch, erect-
　ed a trading houfe on the weft bank of the
　Con. in the prefent town of Windfor Oct
Firft fettlement in Maryland at St Mary's
The council of Plymouth furrendered their
　Charter to the crown June 11
Firft Affembly in Maryland convened in
　Feb. 1635 divided into two branches 1639
Wethersfield the oldeft town in Con. fettled
　by people from Watertown, Maff.　　1634-5
Windfor fettled by people from Dorchefter　1635
Saybrook fettled by J Winthrop's men Nov.
Martinico and Guadaloupe fettled by the
　French, alfo Cayenne
Hartford fettled by Mr. Hooker and his con-
　gregation from Newtown, Cambridge,
　Maff.　　　　　　　　　　　　　　　1635-6
Roger Williams fettled and named Prov.　1636
The Pequots deftroyed by Connecticut,
　May 26　　　　　　　　　　　　　　1637
Rhode Ifland fettled by Mr. Coddington,
　March 24; Great earthquake June 1　1638
New-Haven fettled by Mr Davenport &c. Ap.
St. Lucia firft fettled by the Englifh, difpof-
　feffed by the natives　　　　　　　　1641
Newport fettled　　　　　　　　　　　1639
Maine granted to Sir F. Gorges, April 3.
Firft printing prefs eftablifhed at Cam. Maff.
Original conftitution of Connecticut eftab-
　lifhed, Jan. 14
Surinam fettled by the French 1640; who
　abandoned it for its infalubrity, 1641, the
　Englifh then took poffeffion
A code of laws firft eftablifhed in Maff.
New Hamp. united with Maff. April 14　1641
Confederation of Maffachufetts, Plymouth,
　Connecticut and New-Haven for defenfe　1643
The French fettled St Bartholomews
The earl of Warwick incorporated the fet-
　tlers of Prov. Newport &c. March 14　1644
Firft affembly of Rhode-Ifland agreed upon
　a body of laws, May 19　　　　　　　1647
Marigalante, fettled by the French
Firft influenza mentioned in Amer. annals
Peftilential yellow fever fwept away feveral
　thoufand of the inhabitants of Barbadoes
　and St. Kitts　　　　　　　　　　　1647-8
St. Bartholomew fettled by the French　1648
Maffachufetts laws firft publifhed
Cambridge platform compofed and adopted

Anguilla fettled by the Englifh　　　　1650
Grenada fettled by the French　　　　1652
The Englifh took and fettled Dominico　1661
Tranflation of the N. Teftament into Indian
　by Mr. Eliot finifhed and printed
Charles II granted a charter to Connecticut
　incorporating New-Haven with it. April 23 1662
Charles II. confirmed the charter of Maf-
　fachufetts by letter, June 28
Charter granted to Rhode-Ifland and Prov-
　idence Plantations, July 8
A great earthquake in Canada and New-
　England, Jan. 26　　　　　　　　　1663
Grant of Carolina to the Earl of Clarendon
　and 7 others, March 24
This grant enlarged by a new charter, June 1665
Firft fettlement in N. Carolina on Chowan,
　about the middle of this century
New-Haven confented to a union with con-
　necticut, December　　　　　　　　1664
Mr. Eliot's Indian bible completed & printed
New Netherlands taken from the Dutch
　and granted to the Duke of York by pat-
　ent, March 12, and called New-York. ---
　Fort Orange taken and called Albany
The Duke of York releafed to Lord Berkley
　and Sir G. Carteret, the territory now
　New-Jerfey, June 24
Sir J. Yeamans fettled on the fourthern
　banks of Cape Fear river with a colony
　from Barbadoes　　　　　　　　　　1665
Antigua, which had been abandoned by the
　firft fettlers, granted to Lord Willoughby
　in 1663 and fettled　　　　　　　　　1666
New-Providence, which had been difpeo-
　pled by the Spaniards in 1641, again fet-
　tled in 1666, again deferted till 1690,
　fettled and again depopulated by the
　Spaniards in 1705, repeopled in 1718
Firft colonial affembly of the fettlers at
　Chowan, now North Carolina, mention-
　ed on record　　　　　　　　　　　1666
Maffachufetts refumed the gov. of Maine　1668
Capt. Sayle with a colony began a planta-
　tion at Port Royal in Carolina, he died　1670
This colony removed and began a fettle-
　ment on the bank of Afhley river under
　Sir J. Yeamans which was called old
　Charleftown　　　　　　　　　　　1671
The inhabitants removed and began the
　town now called Charleftown　　　　1680
Fort Frontenac built, Marquette and Joliet
　fail down the Miffifippi　　　　　　1673
N. York taken by the Dutch 1673, reftored
　and confirmed to the Englifh by treaty　1674
Connecticut laws revifed in 1672, and firft
　printed by Mr. Green at Cambridge　1675
Indian war in N. England under Phillip
War ceafed by the death of Phillip, Aug. 12 1676

Bacon's infurrection in Virginia, Jameftown burnt by the infurgents, death of Bacon to 1677   1676

N. Hampfhire erected into a royal gov.   1679

Charter of Penn. to Wm. Penn, March 4   1681

Firft form of gov. for Penn. April 25   1682

The Duke of York's deed of Pennfylvania to Penn, Aug. 21

The Duke's deed of a tract of 12 miles from New-Caftle to the Hoarkills, Aug. 24

Firft affembly in the province at Chefter, December 4

Act of union annexing the Delaware counties to Penn. Act of fettlement Dec. 6

Firft fettlement of Philadelphia, Oct.

Charters of Maff. and Rhode Ifland vacated   1684

Albany incorporated, Port Royal in Carolina broke up by the Spaniards   1686

The firft epifc. church in Bofton formed

A charter given to New-York, by Gov. Dongan, Ap. 22, 1686; enlarged and confirmed Jan. 15, 1730; again Oct. 14, 1732

Procefs iffued againft Connecticut charter in 1685, but the charter was hid from Andros in a hollow oak and faved   1687

Andros feized, depofed and fent to England   1689

Expedition to Quebec failed Oct. and Nov.   1690

Firft bills of credit iffued by Maffachufetts

Schenectady burnt and the inhabitants flain or fcattered, Feb. 8   1690

Maffachufetts obtained a new charter, by which Plymouth was annexed to that colony   1691

Mild winter, veffels went to Alb. in Feb.   1692-3

Severe winter, loaded fleds paffed on the ice from Bofton to Nantafket, and on the Delaware   1697

Fatal yellow fever in Philadelphia   1699

Charlefton S. C. depopulated by a tempeft and inundation, followed by fmall pox and yellow fever, a great part of the town burnt

A library eftablifhed in Charlefton S. C.   1700

Charter of Philadelphia Oct. 25, charter of privileges for Penn. Oct. 28

The culture of filk and cotton introduced into Carolina about this time

Peftilential yellow fever in New-York   1702

Rice introduced into Car. from Madagafcar

Deerfield burnt and the inhabitants flain, taken captives or difperfed, Feb. 28   1704

Expedition by the New Eng. people againft Port Royal failed   1707

A projected invafion of Canada failed, no naval force arrived, and Nicholfon's troops, at Wood Creek, becoming fickly, returned   1709

Port Royal taken by Gen. Nickelfon and its

name changed to Annapolis, Oct. 2   1710

Poft offices in America firft eftablifhed

Congrefs of governors at New-London to confult on an expedition to Cana. May 1   1711

An expedition againft Quebec failed by the fhipwreck of tranfports in St. Lawrence, Auguft

The Tufcororas attacked N. Carolina, defeated by Col. Barnwell, migrated to the five nations, and formed a fixth tribe   1712

Iron began to be manufactured in Virginia

Spanifh invafion of S. Carolina defeated

Treaty of peace at Utrecht, April 11.---Nova Scotia ceded to France   1713

Confpiracy and invafion of the Yamafles defeated by Gov. Craven and Carolinians

The greateft fnow ftorm ever known, fnow feveral feet deep, Feb.   1717

Combination againft the proprietary govt. in Carolina and a revolution   1719

Northern lights which had difappeared for almoft a century appeared in N. England Dec. 11

Epidemic fmall pox in Bofton---inoculation firft introduced by Dr. Boylfton, at the recommendation of Dr. C. Mather   1721

Firft news paper printed in New-York by Wm. Bradford   1725

Printing introduced into Virginia by Wm. Parks   1726

Dry fummer followed by a violent earthquake, Oct. 29 O. S.   1727

A tempeft in Carolina inundated the low lands, drove the people into their upper rooms---the peftilential fever raged in Charleftown   1728

The proprietors of Carolina, except one, fold their property to the crown: the country was divided into S. and N. Carolina, and both became royal govern.

The firft news paper in S. Carolina printed   1730

Gen. Wafhington born in Weftmoreland county, Virginia, Feb. 22   1732

Georgia fettled by Gen. Oglethorpe   1733

Origin of Free Mafonry in America, July

Infurrection of the flaves in S. Carolina   1737

Very fevere winter   1741---2

Spanifh invafion of Georgia, failed   1742

The library company of Phil. incorporated

This company was formed in 1731, and in 1776 received the Loganian library

A large comet appeared in Dec.   1743

Lewifburg furrendered to the N. England troops, aided by an Englifh Squadron, June 17   1745

Indigo plant difcovered in S. Carolina

French expedition under D. Anville, which menaced N. Eng. failed by means of a ftorm, contagious fever in the fleet &c.   1746

Expedition againſt Nova Scotia failed, 1746-7	capitulated. Sept.
Riots in Boſton in oppoſition to an impreſſment of ſeamen 1747	Montreal capitulated to the Engliſh, Sept. 8
A library at Newport founded by A. Redwood 1747	Battle of Etchoe with the Cherokees 1760
Treaty of peace at Aix La Chapelle by which cape Breton and Lewiſburg were reſtored to France Oct. 18 1748	The Cherokees defeated by Col. Grant and compelled to make peace, June 1761
Pennſylvania hoſpital eſtabliſhed by act of aſſembly, Feb. 7 1751	Hava...a taken by the Britiſh and provincials 1762
A tempeſt laid Charleſton under water in Sept. 1752	Definitive treaty of peace ſigned at Paris, Feb. 10 1763
The proprietaries of Georgia ſurrendered their charter, and the colony became a royal government	The ſevereſt drouth known in America, no rain from May to Sept. 1762
Plan of a union of the Colonies agreed upon at Albany by commiſſioners---not ſanctioned by the crown 1754	An eruption of fire in Michuacan, began in 1760, continued ſeveral years and formed three mountains 6 miles in circuit, 1762 to 1766
Remarkably mild winters 1754-5 & 1755-6	Peſtilential difeaſe in Mexico ſo general as to prevent the gathering of the wheat 1762
Great earthquake, Nov. 18 1755	Bennington the oldeſt town in Vermont ſettled 1764
The French began to erect forts on the waters of Lake Erie and the Ohio 1752 & 1753	Medical lectures firſt read in Philadelphia
Major Waſhington ſent by Gov. Dinwiddee of Vir. to require the French to withdraw, Oct. and Nov.	Firſt ſettlement in Tenneſſee 1765
	Kentucky firſt ſettled by Col. Boon
The French erect fort Du Queſne, where Pittſburg now ſtands 1754	Stamp act received the Royal aſſent Ma. 22 1765
The French ſurprized and defeated by Col. Waſhington at the great meadows	Delegates from moſt of the colonies met at N. York in October, to remonſtrate againſt the ſtamp act and petition for its repeal
Col. Waſhington and his troops in fort Neceſſity ſurrendered to the French, July 4	Stamp act repealed. March 18 1766
Col. Waſhington appointed aiddecamp to Gen. Baddock, March 1755	An act impoſing a duty on tea, glaſs and painters colors imported into the colonies paſſed June 1767
Gen. Winſlow with Maſſachuſett's troops took poſſeſſion of Nova Scotia, June 1755, and the French inhabitants called Neutrals, were tranſplanted and their houſes deſtroyed	Two Brit. regiments arrived at Boſton Sept. 1768
	Non-importation agreements entered into by the inhabitants of Boſton, Virg. &c. 1768-9
Gen. Braddock defeated and killed at Monongahela, July 9	Riot in Boſton, the Britiſh troops fired upon the inhabitants and killed four, March 5 1770
French under Dielkau repulſed by Gen. Johnſon at Lake George	Inſurrection in N. Carolina to oppoſe courts of Juſtice, ſuppreſſed by Gov. Tryon.
War declared againſt France, May 18 1756	Guatimala overthrown by an earthquake and 30,000 people buried in the ruins July 29 1773
Oſwego capitulated to Montcalm	An Engliſh armed ſchooner, ſtationed in the Narraganſet, to enforce the collection of duties, burnt by a party of Americans 1773
Fort William Henry capitulated to the French 1757	The tea belonging to the E. India company thrown overboard at Boſton Dec. 16
Lewiſburg taken by the Britiſh. June 1758	An act to ſhut the port of Boſton, March 1774
Gen. Abercrombie defeated at Ticonderoga with great loſs, lord Howe killed, July	Gen. Gage and more troops arrived at Boſton
Fort frontenac taken by Col. Bradſtreet, Aug.	Firſt congreſs convened at Phil. Sept. 4
Fort du Queſne abandoned by the French and taken by the Engliſh, Nov.	All trade with the colonies forbid Dec. 23
Ticonderoga and Crown Point taken by Gen. Amherſt, July 27 and Aug. 4 1759	Battle at Lexington began the war April 19 1775
The French repulſed before Oſwego by Col. Haldiman, July 25	Ticonderoga ſiezed by Col. Allen, May
Niagara taken by the Engliſh, Gen. Prideaux killed, July 25	George Waſhington appointed commander in chief of the army, June 15, took command of the troops inveſting Boſton July 2
Battle of Quebec, Gen. Wolfe and Montcalm killed, French defeated, Quebec	Battle on Breed's hill---Gen. Warren killed, June 17
	Falmouth burnt by the Britiſh. Oct. 17
	Gen. Montgomery penetrated into Canada took fort Chamblee, St John's and Montreal, Nov.

Col. Arnold, with 3000 infantry, entered Canada by the Kenebec

Affault upon Quebec, Gen. Montgomery killed; Americans defeated, Dec. 31

Quebec blockaded by Gen. Thomas   1776

A body of Americans at the Cedars, furrendered in May

The Americans expelled from Canada

Norfolk in Vir. burnt by the Britifh, Jan. 1   1776

A party of Royalifts in N. Carolina defeated, February

Bofton evacuated by the Britifh, March 17

South Carolina invaded by Gen. Clinton who was repulfed June 28, and failed for N. York July 15

Gen. Wafhington arrived at N. York Ap. 14

The Britifh fleet and army arrived at Sandy Hook in June, landed on Staten Ifland July 2

DECLARATION OF INDEPENDENCE July 6

Battle on Long-Ifland, Americans defeated, July 27

The troops withdrawn from Long-Ifland July 28

N. York evacuated by the American army September 14

Gen. Arnold defeated on Lake Champlain, Oct. 12

Battle at the White Plains, Oct. 28

Fort Wafhington taken, with 2000 prifoners, Nov. 16

American army retreated thro' N. Jerfey and crofs the Delaware, Nov. and Dec.

Gen. Lee made prifoner Dec. 12

A body of Heffians attacked and made prifoners at Trenton, Dec. 26

Battle at Princeton, Gen. Mercer killed, Jan. 3   1777

A convention declared Vermont to be an independent ftate, Jan. 16

Danbury deftroyed, Gen. Woofter killed, April 27 and 28

Expedition of Col. Meig's to Sag-harbor, May 23

Gen. Prefcot taken prifoner by Col. Barton

Battle of Brandywine, Sept. 11

Britifh army entered Philadelphia Sept. 26

Ticonderoga evacuated by the American army July 5

Col. Baum defeated and made prifoner near Bennington, Auguft 16

Battle of Stillwater, Burg. checked Sept. 19

Battle of Saratoga, Burg. defeated, Oct. 7

Burgoyne furrendered to Gen. Gates Oct. 17

Battle of Germantown Gen. Nafh killed, October 5

Attack at Red Bank, Col. Donop killed, October 22

Forts Independence and Clinton trken by the Britifh, Oct.

Kingfton burnt by the Britifh, Oct. 16

Ticonderoga evacuated by the Britifh

Britifh Commiffioners arrived at Phil. with terms of conciliation   1778

Philadel. evacuated by the Britifh, June 18

Battle of Monmouth, June 28,

Gen. Lee arrefted June 30, tried and fufpended for one year

Wyoming deftroyed and the inhabitants butchered by Col. Butler and Indians July 1

French fleet under D. Eftaing arrived in July

Confederation of the ftates formed July 9

French fleet put to fea to encounter Lord Howe, Aug. 10

Both fleets difperfed by a tempeft Aug. 12

Gen. Sullivan laid feige to the Britifh army in Newport, Aug. 15

The French fleet returned, failed for Bofton, and the feige of Newport raifed, Aug. 28

Action on Rhode Ifland, Aug. 29

Col. Baylor's regiment furprized and cut to pieces, Sept. 28

Savannah taken by the Britifh under Col. Campbell, Dec.

Very mild winter, farmers in Connecticut plowed in February, and the peach bloffomed in Penn. in the fame month   1779

Infurrection of Royalifts in S. Carolina crufhed by Col. Pickens

Gen. Afh defeated by Col. Prevoft at Briar Creek

Gen. Matthews deftroyed the ftores at Norfork, &c. May

Gen. Tryon invaded New-Haven, deftroyed the ftores, July 5, then burnt Fairfield July 9, and Norwalk July 12

Stony Point taken by affault by General Wayne, July 15

Expedition againft a Britifh port at Penobfcot, failed, Aug.

Gen. Sullivan defeated the Indians and deftroyed all the villages &c. of the fix nations, Aug. and Sept.

Affault upon Savannah unfuccefsful, Pulafki killed, Oct. 9

The winter the moft rigorous ever known in America, Long-Ifland found was covered with ice, and the Chefapeak was paffed with loaded carriages at Annapolis 1779-80

Britifh army under Sir H. Clinton invefted Charlefton, March

The Spaniards took Penfacola and all Weft Florida from the Englifh, May

Gen. Lincoln capitulated and Charlefton furrendered May 12

Americans defeated at Camden, Aug. 16

A French fleet and army under Rochambeau arrived at Newport July 10

Gen. Arnold's treafon difcovered, he efcaped Sept. 25

Major Andre taken, executed October 2

Great hurricanes in the W. Indies Oct. 2 and 11, in Barbadoes alone perifhed 5 or 6000 perfons

Battle of the Cowpens, Britifh defeated, Jan. 17,   1781

St. Euftatia taken by Adm. Rodney, Feb. 3

Arnold burnt the ftores at Richmond, Jan. 5

Mutiny of the Pennfylvania troops, Jan. 1

Impoft of 5 per cent recommended by congrefs, Feb. 3

Confederation completed by the ratification of Maryland, Feb.

Battle of Guilford, Am. repulfed, March 15

Naval action and fplendid victory of Adm. Rodney over the French in the W. Indies April 12

The combined armies under Gen. Wafhington decamp from the Hudfon and march for Virginia, Auguft 19

N. London burnt, Fort Grifwold ftormed and the garrifon put to the fword by Arnold, Sept. 6

Battle at Eutaw Springs; victory of Gen. Green, Sept. 8

Lord Cornwallis and the army befieged in Yorktown. Sept. 25

The Britifh army furrendered to Gen. Wafhington, which decided the Revolutionary conteft, Oct. 19   1781

The Bible firft printed in America by Robert Aiken, Philadelphia   1782

Great ftorm in which the Ville de Paris of 110 guns and others of Rodney's prizes founded, Sept.

Circular addrefs of Gen. Wafhington to the governors of the feveral ftates, June

Mutiny of the Penfylvania troops for want of pay, June 21

Great difcontents in Con. on account of half-pay, a convention at Middletown, Sept. 3,   1783

The army difbanded Oct. 18, farewell addrefs of Gen. Wafhington to the army, November 2

N. York evacuated by the Britifh army, November 25

Gen. Wafhington refigned his commiffion December 23

Society of Cincinnati inftituted at the contonment of the army on the Hudfon, May 13 1783, altered and amended at a general meeting in Phil. May 3   1784

Severe winter 1783-4, great floods in the rivers in March

Hurricane at Jamaica deftroyed all the fhip-

ping, &c. July 30

A moft deftructive hurricane in the Windward iflands Aug. 25, in the Leward iflands Aug. 27

Mr. J. Madifon firft moved the houfe of delegates in Virginia to appoint commiffioners to meet commiffioners of the other ftates to form commercial regulations, which gave rife to the convention which formed the prefent conftitution, Dec.   1785

Infurrection in Maffachufetts began Aug.   1786

Commiffioners met at Annap. Sept. 14, 1786 but adjourned to May 25 1787, when delegates, with more ample powers, affembled and agreed upon the prefent conftitution, September 17   1787

Firft meeting of congrefs under the prefent conftitution at New-York, Gen. Wafhington inaugurated firft Prefident, April 30   1789

Philadelphia incorporated by the legiflature

Tenneffee ceded to the U. S. by N. Carolina

Dr. Franklin died in his 85th year, April 17   1790

Kentucky erected into an Independent ftate, December 6

Vermont admitted into the union Feb. 18   1791

Refolve of congrefs eftab. a mint Mar. 3   1791

Kentucky admitted into the union June 1   1792

Proclamation of neutrality by the Prefident of the United States, April 22   1793

Cape Francois burnt, and the white inhabitants maffacred by the blacks, June 20

A remarkable froft May 17   1794

An infurrection in the W. Counties, Penn.

Tenneffee admitted into the union, June 1   1796

Gen. Wafhington's addrefs to the people of the United States on his retiring from the Prefidency Sept 17   1796

A great earthquake at Quito, S. America, deftroyed towns and 40,000 inhabitants, February   1797

A law paffed for raifing a provifional army, and another authorizing the capture of French armed veffels, May 28   1798

Gen. Wafhington appointed Commander in Chief of the troops of the U. S. July

Congrefs paffed an act declaring the treaty with France null and void, July 7

Capt. Truxton in the Conftellation took the French frigate Infurgent Feb. 10   1799

An Infurrection in Northampton, Penn. Mar.

Great fnow in Carolina and Georgia Jan. 7   1800

Remarkable flood in the Connecticut, Mar. 20-25

Gen Wafhington died Dec. 14 aged 68

Mild winters, 1800-1, 1801-2, 1802-3, vegetation frefh in Dec. and Jan.

Great fnow ftorm Feb. 22. the firft confiderable fnow during the winter   1802

The college at Princeton burnt Mar. 7

The ftate of Ohio admitted into the union

A remarkable froft, and fnow of feveral inches, May 8,
Unexampled tempeft, began in W. Indies Sept. 1 and raged three days, on the 7, 8 and 9, it inundated Carolina and Georgia, with immenfe deftruction 1804
Severeft winter fince 1780 from Dec. 20 to the laft week in Feb. 1804-5
Treaties of the United States,
With France Feb. 6, 1778; Holland Oct. 8, 1782; Sweden April 3, 1783; of peace with Great Britain, prelim. Nov. 30, 1782; Definitive Sept. 3, 1783; Pruffia Sept. 10, 1785; of amity and commerce with Great Britain Nov. 19, 1794; with France for Louifiana April 30, 1803
Colleges and Univerfities founded.
Harvard, Maff. 1638; William and Mary, Vir. 1693; Yale College, Con. 1701; College in Phil. 1753; Univer. of Penn. 1791; Naffau Hall, N. Jerfey, 1746; N. York, 1754; Dartmouth, N. Hampfhire, 1769; Brown College, Providence 1764; Hampden Sidney, Vir. 1774; Wafhington, Ma. 1782; Dickinfon College, Carlifle, Penn. 1783; St. John's at Annapolis, Ma. 1784; Cokefbury, in Abingdon, Ma. 1785; Univerfity in Georgia, 1785; Franklin, at Lancafter, Penn 1787; Univerfity in N. Carolina, 1789; Georgetown, Ma. 1789; Williams College, Maff. 1790; Univer. of Burlington, Ver. 1791 Greenville, Ten. 1794; Union at Schenectady, 1794; Bowdoin, in Maine, 1794; at Winnefbury and Beaufort, S. Carolina, 1795; Tranfylvania, at Lex. Ken. 1798; at Middlebury Ver. 1800

Literary Societies inftituted.
American Philofophical, Phil, 1769; American Academy, Maff. 1780; N. York Agricultural incorp. 1793; Con. Academy, 1801; Maff. Hiftorical, 1791, incorp. 1794

Influenza in North America.
1647, 1655, 1697-8, 1732, 1737, 1747, 1756-7, 1761, 1772, 1781, 1789 and 90. 1802
Unufual darknefs, which rendered candles neceffary in the day time, Oct. 21, 1716; Aug. 9, 1732; Oct. 19, 1762 at Detroit; May 19, 1780; Oct. 9th, 15th and 16th, 1785 in Canada; Oct. 29th, 1789 in Kentucky
Great Fires, burnt, in Bofton 45 houfes, Nov. 27, 1676; 80 houfes, 70 ftores, &c. Aug. 8, 1679; Oct. 23, 1683; beft part of the town; 1711, 174 houfes, 175 ftores, March 20, 1760 one part of Charlefton 1740. In New-York 1776. In Bofton, 100 buildings Ap. 24, 1787, and 96 buildings July 30, 1794. Great in Charlefton, June 20, 1796—moft of Savannah Dec. 26, 1796. A fquare in New-York Dec. 9, 1796—in Richmond Nov. 22, 1798—moft of Wlmington, N. C. Oct. 31, 1798—moft of Norfolk Virg. Feb 22, 1804.

Firft News paper printed, In Bofton, the news letter Ap. 24, 1704—In Philadelphia, the American Weekly Mercury, Dec. 22, 1719—In New-York, the New-York Gazette, Oct. 16, 1725— In R. Ifland, the Rhode Ifland Gazette, Oct. 1732. In Con. New-Haven, the Connecticut Gazette, 1755—In New Hampfhire, 1756—In Providence, 1762—In Kentucky, 1787—In Tennefee, 1790.

Note.—Page 395, line 16 from the end, the year 1798 is omitted by miftake, as is the year 1799 in the firft line of page 396.

THE END.